# Timeline of Criminological Theories (continued)

**Andenaes** — *General Preventive Effects of Punishment* (1966)
**Martinson** — *What Works* (1974)
**Cohen & Felson** — *Routine Activities* (1979)
**Clarke** — *Situational Crime Prevention* (1992)
**Lott** — *More Guns, Less Crime* (2000) (2002)
**Felson** — *Crime and Everyday Life*
**Steffensmeier & Ulmer** — *Confessions of a Dying Thief: Understanding Criminal Careers and Illegal Enterprise* (2005)
**Simon** — *Governing Through Crime* (2010)
**Petrossian & Clarke** — *"The CRAVED Theft Model"* (2014)

**Packer** — *The Limits of Criminal Sanction* (1968)
**Newman** — *Defensible Space* (1973)
**J. Q. Wilson** — *Thinking About Crime* (1975)
**Katz** — *Seductions of Crime* (1988)
**Levitt** — *Understanding Why Crime Fell in the 1990s* (2004)

**Montagu** — *Man and Aggression* (1968)
**Jeffery** — *Crime Prevention* (1971)
**E. O. Wilson** — *Sociobiology* (1975)
**Mednick & Volavka** — *Biology and Crime* (1980)
**Rowe** — *The Limits of Family Influence* (1995)
**Harris** — *The Nurture Assumption* (1998)
**Ellis & Hoskin** — *"Criminality and the 2D:4D Ratio: Testing the Prenatal Androgen Hypothesis"* (2015)

**Sheldon** — *Varieties of Delinquent Youth* (1949)
**Dalton** — *The Premenstrual Syndrome* (1971)
**Ellis** — *Evolutionary Sociobiology* (1989)
**Schoenthaler** — *Intelligence, Academic Performance, and Brain Function* (2000)
**Friedman** — *"Violence and Mental Illness"* (2006)
**Beaver** — *Biosocial Criminology* (2009)
**Wright & Cullen** — *"The Future of Biosocial Criminology"* (2012)
**Barnes & Jacobs** — *"Genetic Risk for Violent Behavior"* (2013)

**Friedlander** — *Psychoanalytic Approach to Delinquency* (1947)
**Eysenck** — *Crime and Personality* (1964)
**Bandura** — *Aggression* (1973)
**Hirschi & Hindelang** — *Intelligence and Delinquency* (1977)
**Henggeler** — *Delinquency in Adolescence* (1989)
**Moffitt** — *Neuropsychology of Crime* (1992)
**Wilson & Daly** — *Evolutionary Psychology* (1997)

**Murray & Herrnstein** — *The Bell Curve* (1994)
**Bushman & Anderson** — *Media Violence* (2001)
**Dorn, Volavka & Johnson** — *"Mental Disorder and Violence"* (2012)

**Vold** — *Theoretical Criminology* (1958)
**Chambliss & Seidman** — *Law, Order and Power* (1971)
**Lea & Young** — *Left Realism* (1984)
**Hagan** — *Structural Criminology* (1989)
**Braithwaite** — *Crime, Shame, and Reintegration* (1989)
**Zehr & Mika** — *Fundamental Concepts of Restorative Justice* (1998)
**Sullivan & Tifft** — *Restorative Justice* (2001)
**Western** — *Punishment and Inequality in America* (2010)

**Dahrendorf** — *Class and Class Conflict in Industrial Society* (1959)
**Taylor, Walton, & Young** — *The New Criminology* (1973)
**Daly & Chesney-Lind** — *Feminist Theory* (1988)
**Quinney & Pepinsky** — *Criminology as Peacemaking* (1991)
**Barak & Henry** — *An Integrative-Constitutive Theory of Crime* (1999)
**Hagan and Wymond-Richmond** — *Darfur and the Crime of Genocide* (2009)
**Chesney-Lind & Morash** — *"Transformative Feminist Criminology"* (2013)

**Cloward & Ohlin** — *Delinquency and Opportunity* (1960)
**Kornhauser** — *Social Sources of Delinquency* (1978)
**Wilson** — *The Truly Disadvantaged* (1987)
**Agnew** — *General Strain Theory* (1992)
**Courtwright** — *Violent Land* (1996)
**Anderson** — *Code of the Street* (1999)

**Lewis** — *The Culture of Poverty* (1966)
**Blau & Blau** — *The Cost of Inequality* (1982)
**Messner & Rosenfeld** — *Crime and the American Dream* (1994)
**LaFree** — *Losing Legitimacy* (1998)
**Sampson & Raudenbush** — *Disorder in Urban Neighborhoods—Does It Lead to Crime?* (2001)
**LeBlanc** — *Random Family: Love, Drugs, Trouble, and Coming of Age in the Bronx* (2003)
**Wilson & Taub** — *There Goes the Neighborhood: Racial, Ethnic, and Class Tensions in Four Chicago Neighborhoods and Their Meaning for America* (2006)
**Wilson** — *More Than Just Race* (2009)

**Lemert** — *Social Pathology* (1951)
**Hirschi** — *Causes of Delinquency* (1969)
**Schur** — *Labeling Deviant Behavior* (1972)
**Akers** — *Deviant Behavior* (1977)
**Kaplan** — *General Theory of Deviance* (1992)
**Akers** — *Social Learning and Social Structure* (1998)
**Topalli** — *"When Being Good Is Bad: An Expansion of Neutralization Theory"* (2005)
**Conger** — *"Family Functioning and Crime"* (2014)

**Becker** — *Outsiders* (1963)
**Heimer & Matsueda** — *Differential Social Control* (1994)
**Maruna** — *Making Good: How Ex-convicts Reform and Rebuild Their Lives* (2001)

**Glueck & Glueck** — *Unraveling Juvenile Delinquency* (1950)
**West & Farrington** — *Delinquent Way of Life* (1977)
**Thornberry** — *Interactional Theory* (1987)
**Sampson & Laub** — *Crime in the Making* (1993)
**Loeber** — *Pathways to Delinquency* (1998)
**Conger** — *Long-term Consequences of Economic Hardship on Romantic Relationships* (2015)

**Weis** — *Social Development Theory* (1981)
**Moffitt** — *Adolescence-Limited and Life-Course Persistent Antisocial Behavior* (1995)
**Laub & Sampson** — *Shared Beginnings, Divergent Lives* (2003)
**Agnew** — *Why Do Criminals Offend?* (2005)
**Larson & Sweeten** — *"Breaking Up Is Hard to Do"* (2012)
**Bersani & Doherty** — *"When the Ties That Bind Unwind"* (2013)

**Hathaway & Monachesi** — *Analyzing and Predicting Juvenile Delinquency with the MMPI* (1953)
**Wolfgang, Figlio, & Sellin** — *Delinquency in Birth Cohorts* (1972)
**Wilson & Herrnstein** — *Crime and Human Nature* (1985)
**Tittle** — *Control Balance: Toward a General Theory of Deviance* (1995)
**Colvin** — *Crime and Coercion* (2000)
**Farrington** — *"Developmental and Life-Course Criminology"* (2003)
**Zimmerman, Botchkovar, Antonaccio, & Hughes** — *"Low Self-Control in 'Bad' Neighborhoods"* (2015)

**Eysenck** — *Crime and Personality* (1964)
**Gottfredson & Hirschi** — *General Theory of Crime* (1990)
**Piquero, Farrington, Nagin, & Moffitt** — *Trajectories of Offending* (2010)
**Boutwell, Barnes, Deaton, & Beaver** — *"On the Evolutionary Origins of Life-course Persistent Offending"* (2013)

1947  1969  1975  1980  1991  1995  1997  1998  2000  2001  2002  2003  2004  2005  2010  2016

# CRIMINOLOGY
## THE CORE

# CRIMINOLOGY

## THE CORE

## Larry J. Siegel
University of Massachusetts, Lowell

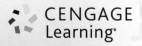

CENGAGE
Learning®

Australia • Brazil • Mexico • Singapore • United Kingdom • United States

# CENGAGE Learning

*Criminology: The Core*, **Sixth Edition**
Larry J. Siegel

Product Director: Marta Lee-Perriard

Senior Product Manager: Carolyn Henderson Meier

Senior Content Developer: Shelley Murphy

Product Assistant: Valerie Kraus

Senior Marketing Manager: Jennifer Levanduski

Senior Content Project Manager: Christy Frame

Managing Art Director: Andrei Pasternak

Senior Manufacturing Planner: Judy Inouye

Production Service: Linda Jupiter Productions

Photo Development Editor: Kim Adams Fox

Photo Researcher: Abdurrawoof Anwarali, Lumina Datamatics

Text Researcher: Kanchana Vijayarangan, Lumina Datamatics

Copy Editor: Lunaea Weatherstone

Proofreader: Mary Kanable

Indexer: Do Mi Stauber

Text and Cover Designer: Diane Beasley

Cover Image: Roy Scott/Ikon Images/ Getty Images

Composition: MPS Limited

For product information and technology assistance, contact us at **Cengage Learning Customer & Sales Support, 1-800-354-9706**

For permission to use material from this text or product, submit all requests online at **www.cengage.com/permissions**
Further permissions questions can be e-mailed to **permissionrequest@cengage.com**

Library of Congress Control Number: 2015948463

Student Edition:
ISBN: 978-1-305-64283-6

Looseleaf Edition:
ISBN: 978-1-305-66502-6

**Cengage Learning**
20 Channel Center Street
Boston, MA 02210
USA

Cengage Learning is a leading provider of customized learning solutions with employees residing in nearly 40 different countries and sales in more than 125 countries around the world. Find your local representative at **www.cengage.com**

Cengage Learning products are represented in Canada by Nelson Education, Ltd.

To learn more about Cengage Learning Solutions, visit **www.cengage.com**

Purchase any of our products at your local college store or at our preferred online store **www.cengagebrain.com**

Printed in the United States of America
Print Number: 01     Print Year: 2016

*This book is dedicated to*

*my children,* **Eric, Julie, Rachel, and Andrew;**

*my grandchildren,* **Jack, Brooke, and Kayla Jean;**

*and my wife, partner, and best friend,* **Therese J. Libby.**

# About the Author

**LARRY J. SIEGEL** was born in the Bronx, New York. While living on Jerome Avenue and attending City College (CCNY) in the 1960s, he was swept up in the social and political currents of the time. He became intrigued with the influence contemporary culture had on individual behavior: did people shape society or did society shape people? He applied his interest in social forces and human behavior to the study of crime and justice. After graduating from CCNY, he attended the newly opened program in criminal justice at the State University of New York at Albany, where he earned both his M.A. and Ph.D. degrees. After completing his graduate work, Dr. Siegel began his teaching career at Northeastern University, where he was a faculty member for nine years.

After leaving Northeastern, he held teaching positions at the University of Nebraska–Omaha and Saint Anselm College in New Hampshire, and the School of Criminology and Justice Studies at the University of Massachusetts–Lowell, where he taught for 27 years; he is now a professor emeritus, still teaching online courses in criminology and criminal justice. Dr. Siegel has written extensively in the area of crime and justice, including books on juvenile law, delinquency, criminology, criminal justice, and criminal procedure. He is a court-certified expert on police conduct and has testified in numerous legal cases. The father of four and grandfather of three, Larry Siegel now resides in Naples, Florida, with his wife, Terry, and their two dogs, Watson and Cody.

# Brief Contents

# Contents

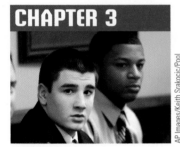

AP Images/Keith Srakocic/Pool

AP Images/David Coates

**CHAPTER 5**

Kateleen Foy/Getty Images News/ Getty Images

# Trait Theory   124

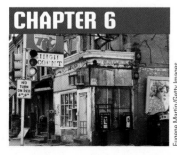

**CHAPTER 6**

Eugene Martin/Getty Images

# Social Structure Theory   158

**CHAPTER 7**

Luoman/E+/Getty Images

# Social Process Theory   194

## CHAPTER 8

# Social Conflict, Critical Criminology, and Restorative Justice  230

## CHAPTER 9

# Developmental Theories: Life Course, Propensity, and Trajectory  264

# PART 3
# Crime Typologies

**CHAPTER 12**

# Economic Crimes: Blue-Collar, White-Collar, and Green-Collar   378

**CHAPTER 13**

# Public Order Crimes   412

Stephen Voss/Redux

# Crimes of the New Millennium: Cybercrime and Transnational Organized Crime   452

# Preface

Reuters/via Myspace account of Chris Harper-Mercer

On October 1, 2015, the normally tranquil campus of Umpqua Community College in Roseburg, Oregon, was shaken when 26-year-old Chris Harper-Mercer went on a shooting spree that left nine people dead and nine wounded. Harper-Mercer brought six weapons to campus, entered a classroom, and methodically began a killing spree. After being wounded in an exchange of fire with police officers who rushed to the campus in response to 911 calls, he returned to the classroom and killed himself.

Experts soon tried to find a motive for what at first appeared to be a totally senseless crime. Early reports claimed that Harper-Mercer asked people their religion and singled out Christians for death—could this have been a hate crime? But other witnesses told authorities that he shot people who were not Christians. Some of his Internet posts indicated that he was an attention seeker. He wrote about other killers: "A man who was known by no one, is now known by everyone, his face splashed across every screen, his name across the lips of every person on the planet, all in the course of one day. Seems the more people you kill, the more you're in the limelight." Could his outburst have been prompted by a quest for notoriety?

Others who knew Harper-Mercer painted a picture of an angry young man who was filled with hate, who openly despised religion, and who posted violent screeds on the Internet. Investigators discovered an online photo of Harper-Mercer holding a rifle and expressing a deep interest in the exploits of the Irish Republican Army and its soldiers.

Other reports indicated that rather than being motivated by hate, Harper-Mercer was emotionally disturbed and socially isolated. He was extremely close to his mother but withdrawn from others. He did not have a girlfriend, a fact that deeply bothered him and which he wrote about online just before the killings. He wore the same outfit every day—combat boots, green army pants, and a white T-shirt. People viewed him as strange.

Descriptions of Harper-Mercer as an angry, mentally disturbed, loner were eerily similar to the terms used to describe other mass killers, such as Adam Lanza, who killed 26 people—including 20 children 6 and 7 years old—at Sandy Hook Elementary School in Newtown, Connecticut, and James Holmes, who killed 12 in a movie theater in Aurora, Colorado. With his death, we will probably never know Harper-Mercer's precise motives.

The Oregon shooting prompted gun control advocates to once again demand action from Congress. "Somehow this has become routine," said President Obama, visibly upset by this latest school shooting. "I'd ask the American people to think about how they can get our government to change these laws and to save these lives and let these people grow up."

These awful mass murders have shaken the American public. It is not surprising that many Americans are concerned about crime and worried about becoming victims of violent crime themselves. We alter our behavior to limit the risk of victimization and question whether legal punishment alone can control criminal offenders. We watch movies and TV shows about law firms and their clients, fugitives, and stone-cold killers. We are shocked when the news media offers graphic accounts of school shootings, police brutality, and sexual assaults.

I, too, have had a lifelong interest in crime, law, and justice. Why do people behave the way they do? What causes someone like Chris Harper-Mercer to kill? Was his behavior the result of a diseased mind and personality? Or was he a hate-filled person who knew exactly what he was doing? Could his murderous rampage have been predicted and prevented? And what should be done with people who commit such horrendous crimes? While Harper-Mercer and Lanza committed suicide, James Holmes was tried and sentenced to life in prison without the possibility of parole. Did he deserve to be executed for his crimes? Should Harper-Mercer and Lanza have been executed had they lived? Is it moral to execute a mentally disturbed killer no matter how horrendous his or her crimes? While the jury in the Holmes case rejected his insanity defense and found him guilty as charged, jury members still considered him mentally ill and therefore not eligible for a death sentence. Do you agree?

## Goals of This Book

For more than 40 years, I have channeled my fascination with issues related to crime and justice into a career as a student and teacher of criminology. My goal in writing this text is to help students share the same enthusiasm for criminology that has sustained me during my teaching career. What could be more important or fascinating than a field of study that deals with such wide-ranging topics as the motivation for mass murder, the effects of violent media on young people, drug abuse, and organized crime? Criminology is a dynamic field, changing constantly with the release of major research studies, Supreme Court rulings, and governmental policy. Its dynamism and diversity make it an important and engrossing area of study.

One reason why the study of criminology is so important is that debates continue over the nature and extent of crime and the causes and prevention of criminality. Some view criminals as society's victims who are forced to violate the law because of poverty and lack of opportunity. Others view aggressive, antisocial behavior such as the Umpqua Community College massacre as a product of mental and physical abnormalities, present at birth or soon after, that are stable over the life course. Still another view is that crime is a function of the rational choice of greedy, selfish people who can be deterred from engaging in criminal behavior only by the threat of harsh punishments. If the Umpqua Community College shooting was actually a hate crime, what could have been done to prevent its occurrence? It all comes down to this: Why do people do the things they do? How can we explain the intricacies and diversity of human behavior?

Because interest in crime and justice is so great and so timely, this text is designed to review these ongoing issues and cover the field of criminology in an organized and comprehensive manner. It is meant as a broad overview of the field, an introduction to whet the reader's appetite and encourage further and more in-depth exploration. I try to present how the academic study of criminology intersects with real-world issues. For example, diversity is a key issue in criminology and a topic that has important real-world consequences. Therefore the text attempts to integrate issues of racial, ethnic, gender, and cultural diversity throughout. The book opens with coverage of the killing of Michael Brown in Ferguson, Missouri, and then goes on to cover contemporary issues ranging from the Black Lives Matter movement to the most recent research on sexual assaults on campus.

My primary goals in writing this text were as follows:

1.  To separate the facts from the fiction about crime and criminality
2.  To provide students with a thorough knowledge of criminology and show its diversity and intellectual content
3.  To be as thorough and up-to-date as possible
4.  To be objective and unbiased
5.  To describe current theories, crime types, and methods of social control, and to analyze their strengths and weaknesses
6.  To show how criminological thought has influenced social policy

## Features

**FACT OR FICTION?** A main goal of this edition is to expose some of the myths that cloud people's thinking about crime and criminals. The media often paints a distorted picture of the crime problem in America and focuses only on the most sensational cases. Is the crime rate really out of control? Are unemployed people inclined to commit crime? Are immigrants more crime prone than the native-born, as some politicians suggest? Are married people less crime prone than singles? Distinguishing what is true from what is merely legend is one of the greatest challenges for instructors in criminology courses. Therefore a goal of this text is disabuse students of incorrect notions, perceptions, and biases. Each chapter opens with a set of statements highlighting common perceptions about crime that are related to the material discussed in the chapter. In the text, these statements are revisited so the student will become skilled at distinguishing the myths from the reality of crime and criminality.

**CONCEPT SUMMARY** There are ongoing debates about the nature and extent of crime and the causes and prevention of criminality. I try to present the various viewpoints on each topic and then draw a conclusion based on the weight of the existing evidence. Students become familiar with this kind of analysis by examining Concept Summary boxes that compare different viewpoints, reviewing both their main points and their strengths.

**THINKING LIKE A CRIMINOLOGIST**  It is important for students to think critically about law and justice and to develop a critical perspective toward the social institutions and legal institutions entrusted with crime control. Throughout the book, students are asked to critique research highlighted in boxed material and to think "outside the box," as it were. To aid in this task, each chapter ends with a brief section called Thinking Like a Criminologist, which presents a scenario that can be analyzed with the help of material found in the chapter. This section also includes critical thinking questions to guide classroom interaction.

**POLICIES AND ISSUES IN CRIMINOLOGY**  Throughout the book, every attempt is made to access the most current research and scholarship available. Most people who use the book have told me that this is one of its strongest features. I have attempted to present current research in a balanced fashion, even though this approach can be frustrating to students. It is comforting to reach an unequivocal conclusion about an important topic, but sometimes that simply is not possible. In an effort to be objective and fair, I have presented each side of important criminological debates in full. Throughout the text, boxed features titled Policies and Issues in Criminology review critically important research topics. In Chapter 10, for example, this feature looks as honor killing and honor crime, which involve violence directed against women and girls who are believed to have violated the customs of traditional societies in the Middle East, Southwest Asia, India, China, and Latin America.

**PROFILES IN CRIME** These features are designed to present to students actual crimes that help illustrate the position or views within the chapter. In Chapter 14, this feature focuses on the Lost Boys case, which involved the investigation into a transnational online bulletin board that provided a forum for men who had a sexual interest in young boys to trade child pornography.

**CONNECTIONS** are short inserts that help link the material to other areas covered in the book. A Connections insert in Chapter 14 points out how cyberspace is being used to facilitate public order crimes (covered in Chapter 13) by being a conduit to illegally distribute prescription drugs, advertise prostitution, and disseminate pornography.

**CHAPTER OUTLINES** provide a roadmap to coverage and serve as a useful review tool.

**LEARNING OBJECTIVES** spell out what students should learn in each chapter and are reinforced via a direct link to the end-of-chapter summary as well as all of the text's ancillary materials.

**A RUNNING GLOSSARY** in the margins ensures that students understand words and concepts as they are introduced.

In sum, the text has been carefully structured to cover relevant material in a comprehensive, balanced, and objective fashion. Every attempt has been made to make the presentation of material interesting and contemporary. No single political or theoretical position dominates the text; instead, the many diverse views that are contained within criminology and characterize its interdisciplinary nature are presented. While the text includes analysis of the most important scholarly works and scientific research reports, it also includes a great deal of topical information on recent cases and events, such as the death of Eric Garner at the hands of the police (known as the "I can't breathe" incident), the case of Dr. Farid Fata, a respected oncologist, who committed a multimillion-dollar health care fraud, and the story of Owen Labrie and the St. Paul's School rape case.

## Topic Areas

*Criminology: The Core* is a thorough introduction to this fascinating field and is intended for students in introductory courses in criminology. It is divided into three main sections or topic areas.

**PART 1** provides a framework for studying criminology. The first chapter defines the field and discusses its most basic concepts: the definition of crime, the component areas of criminology, the history of criminology, the concept of criminal law, and the ethical issues that arise in this field. Chapter 2 covers criminological research methods, as well as the nature, extent, and patterns of crime. Chapter 3 is devoted to the concept of victimization, including the nature of victims, theories of victimization, and programs designed to help crime victims.

**PART 2** contains six chapters that cover criminological theory: Why do people behave the way they do? Why do they commit crimes? These views focus on choice (Chapter 4), biological and psychological traits (Chapter 5), social structure and culture (Chapter 6), social process and socialization (Chapter 7), social conflict (Chapter 8), and human development (Chapter 9).

**PART 3** is devoted to the major forms of criminal behavior. The chapters in this section cover violent crime (Chapter 10), political crime and terrorism (Chapter 11), blue-collar, white-collar, and green-collar crimes (Chapter 12), public order crimes, including sex offenses and substance abuse (Chapter 13), and cybercrime and transnational organized crime (Chapter 14).

# Chapter-by-Chapter Changes

**CHAPTER 1,** *Crime and Criminology*, now begins with a detailed account of the death of Michael Brown and the Ferguson shooting. There is also a Profiles in Crime feature concerning the death of Trayvon Martin and the concept of "stand your ground" and legal self-defense.

**CHAPTER 2,** *The Nature and Extent of Crime*, begins with a vignette detailing the murder of Hanna Graham, a young University of Virginia student killed by a sexual predator. Self-report, victim, and official crime data have all been updated and the newest trends and patterns in the crime rate analyzed. There is a new section on co-offending and crime. Special attention has been paid to the issue of race and crime, including new data on the racial threat hypothesis.

**CHAPTER 3,** *Victims and Victimization*, begins with a vignette on the Steubenville High School football team sexual assault case. There is a new section on the costs of victimization and a boxed feature on the impact of wrongful convictions on crime victims. For some victims, the impact of the wrongful conviction may be comparable to—or even worse than—that of their original victimization. Another Policies and Issues feature looks at elder victims and finds that elder abuse and neglect are serious yet understudied problems in the United States. There is a new section on state victim compensation programs.

**CHAPTER 4,** *Rational Choice Theory*, opens with the story of Dr. Farid Fata, a Detroit-area hematologist and oncologist who pleaded guilty to a series of health care fraud charges, kickback conspiracy, and money laundering crimes. Two new sections cover the issues "Is Hate Crime Rational?" and "Is Sex Crime Rational?" The CRAVED model of crime choice is covered. A new section looks at marginal and restrictive deterrence, deterrence strategies that can lead to less than perfect results. In a Policies and Issues feature we look at how car thieves are rational decision makers and how their behavior is effected by the deterrent effect of the law—not enough to dissuade them from committing crime but enough to alter their behavior. A section on toughening punishment explores the issues of whether a specific deterrent effect can be achieved if the severity of punishment is increased and type of punishment is amplified.

**CHAPTER 5,** *Trait Theory*, begins with the Sandy Hook Elementary School shooting in Newtown, Connecticut. A new section compares the individual vulnerability model with the differential susceptibility model: the former assumes there is a direct link between traits and crime; the latter assumes there is an indirect association between traits and crime. There is new research on thrill seeking and a new section on mental illness and crime. Research is shown on how environmental contaminants can be harmful to the brains of babies and children, producing neurological deficits that may lead to delinquency and adult criminality.

**CHAPTER 6,** *Social Structure Theory*, begins with the case of Kaboni Savage, a small-time Philadelphia drug dealer who escalated his offending career by buying cocaine in bulk and building a criminal organization. While in jail, Savage ordered a firebomb attack against the family of a witness who had agreed to testify for the prosecution, an attack that resulted in the death of six people. New data on child poverty and minority group poverty are presented. A Policies and Issues in Criminology feature is devoted to the G.R.E.A.T. (Gang Resistance, Education, and Training) program, a school-based, law enforcement officer–instructed classroom curriculum.

**CHAPTER 7,** *Social Process Theory*, opens with the rise and fall of confidence man Vernon Matthews, who operated a company called First Capital Group (FCG) that targeted military personnel for fraudulent investment schemes. Rand and Katherine Conger's Family Stress Model is now covered, which shows that economic hardship increases parents' sadness, pessimism about the future, anger, despair, and withdrawal from other family members, factors that are critical given the family's key influence on crime and delinquency. There are new data on the association between having antisocial peers and engaging in antisocial behavior. A Policies and Issues in Criminology feature looks at research by Ray Paternoster, Jean Marie McGloin, Holly Nguyen, and Kyle Thomas, who conducted an interesting and informative experiment to measure whether peers influence behavior choices.

**CHAPTER 8, *Social Conflict, Critical Criminology, and Restorative Justice*,** begins by covering the attack by Saïd and Chérif Kouachi on the offices of the French satirical newspaper *Charlie Hebdo*. A new section on justice system inequality covers the issue of whether racial and ethnic minorities are the target of racist police officers and unfair prosecutorial practices. A new Profiles in Crime feature entitled "I Can't Breathe" covers the death of Eric Garner at the hands of police officers because he was believed to be selling "loosies" (single cigarettes) from packs without a tax stamp, prohibited by NYC law. A new section called "Being Victimized" discusses how critical feminists find that the sexual victimization of girls is a function of male socialization because so many young males learn to be aggressive and to exploit women. Another section on gender and the justice system shows that when the exploited girl finds herself in the arms of the justice system, her problems may just be beginning. Girls who get in trouble are seen as a threat to acceptable images of femininity; their behavior is considered even more unusual and dangerous than male delinquency. A Policies and Issues in Criminology feature on the Center for Restorative Justice (CRJ) focuses on a program that for over 30 years has provided a variety of restorative justice programming and services helping both young people and adults.

**CHAPTER 9, *Developmental Theories: Life Course, Propensity, and Trajectory*,** opens with a vignette on Daniel Dvorkin, a commercial real estate professional who tried to hire a hit man to settle a business deal. There is a new section called "Breaking Up" that asks, if marriage helps reduce criminality, what happens when things don't always work out as planned? There is a new section on social schematic theory (SST), a life-course learning approach that suggests that social schemas—cognitive frameworks that help people quickly process and sort through information—are the key theoretical mechanisms that account for the development of criminal behavior patterns. There is also a new section on first offenders.

**CHAPTER 10, *Violent Crime*,** begins with a vignette on Dylann Roof and the terrible hate-motivated shooting in a Charleston, South Carolina, church. Recent research is covered on testing the linkage between violence and mental process through the use of a magnetic resonance imaging device (MRI) to assess brain function. There is a section on rape on campus, including a recent national study that shows that more than 20 percent of all college women are victims of rape or attempted rape. Another new section looks at "rape by deception," a crime that occurs when the rapist uses fraud or trickery to convince the victim to engage in sex or impersonates someone with whom the victim has been intimate. The gender conflict view is reviewed, which holds that women are more likely to be targeted when they begin to make progress toward social, political, and economic equality; men fear them as a threat to their long-held dominance. The Campus Sexual Violence Elimination (SaVE) Act is now covered. There is a new section on carjackers, who attack occupied vehicles for the purpose of theft.

**CHAPTER 11, *Political Crime and Terrorism*,** opens with the case of Edward Snowden and his release of government documents. There is coverage of a recent report by the Senate Intelligence Committee that disparages the use of torture and disputes claims that it can be a valuable source of information. A number of terror incidents are covered, including the April 2, 2015, attack by gunmen belonging to the Somalia-based al-Shabaab terror group on the Garissa University campus in Kenya, which resulted in the killing of 148 students. There is increased and significant coverage of the Islamic State of Iraq and the Levant (ISIL) and Boko Haram, a fundamentalist Islamic group that has caused havoc in Nigeria.

**CHAPTER 12,** *Economic Crimes: Blue-Collar, White-Collar, and Green-Collar*, opens with the tale of Georgia native Aubrey Lee Price, formerly a devout Christian minister and trusted financial adviser, who was sentenced to 30 years in prison for bank fraud, embezzlement, and other crimes. The latest data from the National White Collar Crime Center, which conducts national surveys that tap into individual experiences with business crimes, are included. There are new data on health care fraud, which now costs the nation $80 billion per year. The harms perspective of environmental crime is presented.

**CHAPTER 13,** *Public Order Crimes*, begins with the case of Alfred Beckman, who sexually abused young children and streamed the abuse over the Internet to a child pornography network. There is a new section called "Are Victimless Crimes Victimless?" which addresses the harm caused by public order crimes. The chapter presents the theory of social harm and updates the effects of the same-sex marriage crusade. There is a Policies and Issues in Criminology feature on the sex trade in contemporary society that presents the findings of Meredith Dank and her colleagues at the Urban Institute, who conducted a study of prostitution in some of the nation's largest cities. A new section covers the costs of substance abuse, and a Policies and Issues in Criminology feature on substance abuse and psychosis finds that people diagnosed with mood or anxiety disorders are about twice as likely as the general population to also suffer from a substance use disorder.

**CHAPTER 14,** *Crimes of the New Millennium: Cybercrime and Transnational Organized Crime*, opens with a vignette on Julian Assange and the WikiLeaks scandal, which involved the publication of classified government documents. Also included is the story of how the distributor of SpyEye designed software to facilitate online theft from financial institutions and enable users to transfer money out of victims' bank accounts and into accounts controlled by criminals. Current distribution methods for online pornography are covered, including "porn-napping" and "typosquatted" websites. A Profiles in Crime feature addresses the Lost Boy case, about an online forum where men with a sexual interest in young boys traded child pornography. The significant problem of online drug sales is covered—for example, a single Internet pharmacy illegally sold more than 14 million doses of drugs over a four-year period. A new section covers Internet extortion schemes, such as uploading malware that freezes a computer system or encrypts its files, essentially holding the system hostage until a ransom is paid. There is a new section on the National Cyber Investigative Joint Task Force (NCIJTF), which consists of nearly two dozen federal intelligence, military, and law enforcement agencies.

## Supplements

An extensive package of supplemental aids is available for instructor and student use with this edition of *Criminology: The Core*. Supplements are available to qualified adopters. Please consult your local sales representative for details.

### For the Instructor

**ONLINE INSTRUCTOR'S MANUAL** The manual includes learning objectives, key terms, a detailed chapter outline, student activities, and media tools. The learning objectives are correlated with the discussion topics, student activities, and media tools. The manual is available for download on the password-protected website and can also be obtained by e-mailing your local Cengage Learning representative.

**ONLINE TEST BANK** Each chapter of the test bank contains questions in multiple-choice, true/false, completion, and essay formats, with a full answer key. The test bank is coded to the learning objectives that appear in the main text, references to the section in the main text where the answers can be found, and Bloom's taxonomy. Finally, each question in the test bank has been carefully reviewed by experienced criminal justice instructors for quality, accuracy, and content coverage. The Test Bank is available for download on the password-protected website and can also be obtained by e-mailing your local Cengage Learning representative.

**CENGAGE LEARNING TESTING, POWERED BY COGNERO** This assessment software is a flexible, online system that allows you to import, edit, and manipulate test bank content from the *Criminology: The Core* test bank or elsewhere, including your own favorite test questions; create multiple test versions in an instant; and deliver tests from your LMS, your classroom, or wherever you want.

**ONLINE POWERPOINT® LECTURES** Helping you make your lectures more engaging while effectively reaching your visually oriented students, these handy Microsoft PowerPoint slides outline the chapters of the main text in a classroom-ready presentation. The PowerPoint slides are updated to reflect the content and organization of the new edition of the text and feature some additional examples and real-world cases for application and discussion. Available for download on the password-protected instructor companion website, the presentations can also be obtained by e-mailing your local Cengage Learning representative.

## For the Student

**MINDTAP FOR CRIMINOLOGY** With MindTap™ Criminal Justice for *Criminology: The Core*, you have the tools you need to better manage your limited time, with the ability to complete assignments whenever and wherever you are ready to learn. Course material that is specially customized for you by your instructor in a proven, easy-to-use interface keeps you engaged and active in the course. MindTap helps you achieve better grades today by cultivating a true understanding of course concepts, and with a mobile app to keep you on track. With a wide array of course-specific tools and apps—from note taking to flashcards—you can feel confident that MindTap is a worthwhile and valuable investment in your education.

You will stay engaged with MindTap's video cases and career scenarios and remain motivated by information that shows where you stand at all times—both individually and compared to the highest performers in class. MindTap eliminates the guesswork, focusing on what's most important with a learning path designed specifically by your instructor and for your criminology course. Master the most important information with built-in study tools such as visual chapter summaries and integrated learning objectives that will help you stay organized and use your time efficiently.

# Acknowledgments

The preparation of this book would not have been possible without the aid of my colleagues who helped by reviewing the previous editions and gave me important suggestions for improvement.

## Reviewers of *Criminology: The Core* include

John Broderick, Stonehill College
Stephen J. Brodt, Ball State University
Doris Chu, Arkansas State University
Dana C. De Witt, Chadron State College
Dorinda L. Dowis, Columbus State University
Yvonne Downs, Hilbert College

Sandra Emory, University of New Mexico
Dorothy M. Goldsborough, Chaminade University
Michael Hallett, University of North Florida
Robert G. Hewitt, Edison Community College
Monica Jayroe, Faulkner University
Catherine F. Lavery, Sacred Heart University
Danielle Liautaud-Watkins, William Paterson University
Larry A. Long, Pioneer Pacific College
Heather Melton, University of Utah
Charles Ochie, Albany State University
Kay Kei-Ho Pih, California State University Northridge
Adam Rafalovich, Texas Technology University
Ronald Sopenhoff, Brookdale Community College
Mark A. Stelter, Montgomery College
Tom Tomlinson, Western Illinois University
Matt Vetter, Saint Mary's University
Scott Wagner, Columbus State Community College
Jay R. Williams, Duke University

My colleagues at Cengage Learning have done their typically outstanding job of aiding me in the preparation of this text and putting up with my yearly angst. Carolyn Henderson Meier, my wonderful editor, helped guide this project from start to finish. Shelley Murphy is an honorary co-author, product developer, and dear friend. Kim Adams Fox and Lumina Datamatics did an outstanding job on photo research. Linda Jupiter, the book's production editor, is another confidant and friend. I really appreciate the help of Lunaea Weatherstone, copy editor extraordinaire and my personal life coach. The sensational Christy Frame is an extraordinary production supervisor and Jennifer Levanduski, the marketing manager, is fantastic.

# CRIMINOLOGY
## THE CORE

# 1 Crime and Criminology

## Learning Objectives

**LO1**   Explain the various elements of criminology.

**LO2**   Differentiate between crime and deviance.

**LO3**   Discuss the three different views of the definition of crime.

**LO4**   Discuss the different purposes of the criminal law.

**LO5**   Describe the criminal justice process.

**LO6**   Identify the ethical issues in criminology.

# Chapter Outline

## FACT OR FICTION?

▶ Sex offender registration lists help deter potential offenders and reduce the incidence of child molestation.

▶ Criminals and victims are two totally different types of people.

On August 9, 2014, in Ferguson, Missouri, a suburb of St. Louis, Michael Brown, an 18-year-old unarmed African American youth, was fatally shot by Darren Wilson, a white police officer. According to most accounts, shortly before the shooting Brown and a friend, Dorian Johnson, had stolen some cigars from a local convenience store. Officer Wilson, who at the time was not aware of the theft, encountered the two young men as they were walking down the middle of the street. From his police car, Wilson ordered them to move to the sidewalk. According to Wilson, the two refused to obey the order, a scuffle broke out during which Michael Brown punched Wilson through the window of the police car. The fight went on until Wilson's gun was fired, and Brown and Johnson fled down the street. Wilson pursued Brown, eventually firing a total of twelve rounds at him from a distance ranging from 30 to under 10 feet. In all Michael Brown was hit eight times, the last shot causing his death.

A grand jury called to review the evidence in the case failed to find sufficient cause to indict Darren Wilson for the death of Michael Brown, prompting nationwide protests condemning racial bias in the justice system. The incident reminded people of the central role crime, law, and justice play in their daily lives and how a random encounter can escalate into the death of a young man.

Many questioned the grand jury's refusal to indict Officer Wilson, not being able to understand how the shooting of an unarmed suspect was not a crime. Legally, the grand jury's decision rested on what happened during the pursuit of Michael Brown: did he, as some witnesses asserted, have ▶

his hands raised in surrender as he moved towards Officer Wilson or was Michael Brown madly charging at the officer in an attempt to attack him further as Wilson claimed? If the latter, then the officer's behavior might be excused since he acted in self-defense if he actually felt threatened; if the former, Wilson's actions amounted to felony murder. Members of the jury obviously believed Wilson's story when they failed to indict.

The case also shows that crime is socially constructed: Wilson could have been indicted, tried, and convicted for his act and be considered a callous, violent criminal. Instead, the jury decided not to indict, meaning that Wilson is not a criminal in the eyes of the law. The fact that a jury of his peers failed to indict Wilson reinforces the fact that what is a crime and who is considered a criminal are not objective facts but open to interpretation.

The death of Michael Brown certainly raised issues about the role race plays in the construction and creation of crime and criminality. Would Michael Brown have been stopped by a police officer if he was a Caucasian college student? The law should and must be color and gender blind. Did this incident occur because of racial profiling? Many people believed that the incident showed that racism still exists in the justice system.

**criminology**
The scientific study of the nature, extent, cause, and control of criminal behavior.

The Ferguson shooting and similar incidents have captured headlines around the globe, raised fascinating questions about crime and its control, and spurred interest in **criminology**, an academic discipline that uses the scientific method to study the nature, extent, cause, and control of criminal behavior. Unlike political figures and media commentators, whose opinions about crime may be colored by personal experiences, biases, and election concerns, criminologists remain objective as they study crime and its consequences.[1] The field itself is far reaching, and subject matter ranges from street level drug dealing to international organized crime, from lone wolf terrorism to control of kiddie porn. It is an interdisciplinary field: while many have attended academic programs that award degrees in criminology or criminal justice, many criminologists have a background in other academic disciplines, including sociology, psychology, and legal studies.

In this chapter, we review the components of this diverse field of study, how this field developed, and how criminologists view crime and justice.

**L01** Explain the various elements of criminology.

# Criminology in Action

Several subareas exist within the broader arena of criminology. Some criminologists specialize in one area while ignoring others, and some are generalists whose research interests are wide ranging. What then are the most important subareas in the field?

## Criminal Statistics/Crime Measurement

The subarea of criminal statistics/crime measurement involves creating methodologies that are able to accurately measure activities, trends, and patterns in crime and then using these tools to calculate amounts and developments in criminal activity: How much crime occurs annually? Who commits it? When and where does it occur? Which crimes are the most serious?

Criminologists interested in computing criminal statistics focus on creating **valid** and **reliable measures** of criminal behavior:

- Criminologists help formulate techniques for collecting and analyzing official measures of criminal activities, such as crimes reported to the police.
- To measure unreported criminal activity criminologists develop survey instruments designed to have victims report loss and injury that may not have been reported to the police.
- Criminologists design methods that make it possible to investigate the cause of crime. They may create a self-administered survey instrument that contains questions measuring an adolescent's delinquent behaviors as well as social characteristics, education and occupation of parents, friendship patterns, and school activities in order to determine the association between a wide variety of social factors and criminal activities, such as whether school failure is related to drug abuse.

**valid measure**
A measure that actually measures what it purports to measure; a measure that is factual.

**reliable measure**
A measure that produces consistent results from one measurement to another.

## Sociology of Law/Law and Society/Sociolegal Studies

Sociology of law/law and society/sociolegal studies is a subarea of criminology concerned with the role that social forces play in shaping criminal law and the role of criminal law in shaping society. Criminologists interested in sociolegal studies might investigate the history of legal thought in an effort to understand how criminal acts (such as theft, rape, and murder) evolved into their present form. They may also play an active role in suggesting legal changes that benefit society.

Criminological research is also used extensively by the Supreme Court in shaping their decision making and creating legal precedence.[2] In the case of *Miller v. Alabama*, the Supreme Court relied on social research that had found juveniles not fully capable of anticipating the consequences of their actions. This finding led the justices to conclude that it would be inappropriate and unconstitutional for juveniles to receive mandatory life sentences without the possibility of parole. Since this research found that juveniles had a different mental capacity than adults, it seemed illogical that they should receive the same punishment; this would amount to cruel and unusual punishment.[3]

In the accompanying Policies and Issues in Criminology feature, criminological research on another policy issue—sex offender registration—is discussed in some detail.

**FACT OR FICTION?**

Sex offender registration lists help deter potential offenders and reduce the incidence of child molestation.

**FICTION** Research indicates that registration has little effect on either offenders or rates of child molesting.

## Developing Theories of Crime Causation

Criminologists also explore the causes of crime. How do the mechanisms of past experience influence an individual's propensity to offend? Is past behavior the best predictor of future behavior? Are the seeds of a criminal career planted early in life or do life events upend a person's normal life course?

Some criminologists focus on the individual and look for an association between decision making, psychological and biological traits, and antisocial behaviors. Those who have a psychological orientation view crime as a function of personality, development, social learning, or cognition. Others investigate the biological correlates of antisocial behavior and study the biochemical, genetic, and neurological linkages to crime.

Those with a sociological orientation look at the social forces producing criminal behavior, including

Monica Almeida/New York Times/Redux

Criminologists interested in the sociology of law conduct research on the effects of legal change on society. Take for example the Supreme Court's ruling in *Miller v. Alabama*, barring mandatory life sentences for juveniles convicted of murder. Criminologists may be called upon to test public opinion on whether violent young felons have the potential for rehabilitation. They may also try to measure the factors that may have influenced judicial decision making. In this case, they may try to determine whether scientific research on adolescent brain development influenced the ruling.

# Policies and Issues in Criminology

## SHOULD SEX OFFENDERS BE REGISTERED?

Criminologists evaluate the impact that new laws have had on society after they have been in effect for a while. Take the practice of sex offender registration, which requires convicted sex offenders to register with local law enforcement agencies whenever they move into a community. These provisions are often called Megan's Laws, in memory of 7-year-old Megan Kanka. Megan was killed in 1994 by sex offender Jesse Timmendequas, who had moved unannounced into her New Jersey neighborhood. Megan's Laws require law enforcement authorities to make information available to the public about registered sex offenders, including the offender's name, picture, address, incarceration date, and nature of crime. The information can be published in newspapers or put on a sex offender website.

In *Connecticut Dept. of Public Safety v. Doe* (2003), the U.S. Supreme Court upheld the legality of sex offender registration when it ruled that persons convicted of sexual offenses may be required to register with a state's Department of Public Safety and may then be listed on a sex offender registry that contains registrants' names, addresses, photographs, and descriptions and can be accessed on the Internet. In a 9–0 opinion upholding the plan, the Court reasoned that, because these defendants had been convicted of a sex offense, disclosing their names on the registry without a hearing did not violate their right to due process.

Thus sex offender registration laws have been ruled constitutional, are pervasive (they are used in all 50 states), and appeal to politicians who may be swayed by media crusades against child molesters (such as "To Catch a Predator" on *Dateline NBC*), and appease the public's desire to "do something" about child predators. But do they actually work? Does registration deter offenders from committing further sex offenses and reduce the incidence of predatory acts against children?

To answer this question, criminologists Kristen Zgoba and Karen Bachar conducted an in-depth study of the effectiveness of the New Jersey registration law and found that, although it was maintained at great cost to the state, the system did not produce effective results. Sex offense rates in New Jersey were in steep decline before the system was installed, and the rate of decline actually slowed down after 1995 when the law took effect. The study showed that the greatest rate of decline in sex offending occurred prior to the passage and implementation of Megan's Law. Zgoba and Bachar also found that the passage and implementation of Megan's Law did not reduce the number of rearrests for sex offenses, nor did it have any demonstrable effect on the time between when sex offenders were released from prison and the time they were rearrested for any new offense, such as a drug offense, theft, or another sex offense.

Zgoba and Bachar's results can be used to rethink legal changes such as sex offender registration. Rather than deterring crime, such laws may merely cause sex offenders to be more cautious, while giving parents a false sense of security. Sex offenders may target victims in other states or in communities where they do not live and parents are less cautious.

### Critical Thinking

1. Considering the findings of Zgoba and Bachar, would you advocate abandoning sex offender registration laws because they are ineffective? Or might there be other reasons to keep them active?

2. What other laws do you think should be the topic of careful scientific inquiry to see whether they actually work as advertised?

**Sources:** *Connecticut Dept. of Public Safety v. Doe*, 538 U.S. 1 (2003); Kristen Zgoba and Karen Bachar, "Sex Offender Registration and Notification: Limited Effects in New Jersey," National Institute of Justice, April 2009, www.ncjrs.gov/pdffiles1/nij/225402.pdf (accessed June 2015).

neighborhood conditions, poverty, socialization, and group interaction. Their belief is that people are a "product of their environment" and anyone living in substandard conditions could be at risk to crime. Kids are deeply affected by what goes on in their family, school, and neighborhood, and these are the keys to understanding the development of antisocial behavior.

Pinning down "one true cause" of crime remains a difficult problem because most people, even those living in the poorest disorganized neighborhood, or who suffered abuse and neglect as children, do not become criminals. If they did, there would be a lot more crimes committed each year than now occur. Since most of us are law abiding, despite enduring many social and psychological problems, it's tough to pinpoint the conditions that inevitably lead to a criminal way of life. Criminologists are still unsure why, given similar conditions, some people choose criminal solutions to their problems, whereas others conform to accepted social rules of behavior.

## Understanding and Describing Criminal Behavior

Another subarea of criminology involves research on specific criminal types and patterns: violent crime, theft crime, public order crime, organized crime, and so on. Numerous attempts have been made to describe and understand particular crime types. Marvin Wolfgang's 1958 study *Patterns in Criminal Homicide* is a landmark analysis of the nature of homicide and the relationship between victim and offender. Wolfgang discovered that in many instances victims caused or precipitated the violent confrontation that led to their death, spawning the term **victim precipitated homicide**.[4] Edwin Sutherland's pioneering analysis of business-related offenses also helped coin a new phrase, **white-collar crime**, to describe economic crime activities of the affluent.[5]

AP Photo/Christophe Ena

The study of terrorism and political crime has become a major focus of criminology. On November 13, 2015, 130 people were killed and another 350 injured in a series of terror attacks across Paris, including at the Stade de France (the French national stadium), at cafés and restaurants, and at the Bataclan Theater, where a concert was taking place. The attacks began when bombs were set off outside the Stade de France during a soccer match between France and Germany. Hundreds of people ran from the stadium in panic. The Islamic State of Iraq and the Levant (ISIL) claimed responsibility for the attacks that involved groups of jihadists who simultaneously attacked numerous sites in the city. Soon after, French President François Hollande closed the nation's borders and declared a state of emergency. The Paris attacks prompted massive retaliation on ISIL installations by France, the United States, and Russia. Criminologists conduct research on discovering what prompts people to join terror groups and what can be done to dissuade them from joining.

Criminologists are constantly broadening the scope of their inquiry because new crimes and crime patterns are constantly emerging. Whereas 50 years ago they might have focused their attention on rape, murder, and burglary, they now may be looking at stalking, environmental crimes, cybercrime, terrorism, and hate crimes. A number of criminologists are now doing research on terrorism and the terrorist personality in order to discover why some young people are motivated to join terror groups. Among the findings:

- Mental illness is not a critical factor in explaining terrorist behavior. Also, most terrorists are not "psychopaths."
- There is no "terrorist personality," nor is there any accurate profile—psychological or otherwise—of the terrorist.
- Rather than mental illness, perceived injustice, need for identity, and need for belonging are common among potential terrorists.[6]

## Penology: Punishment, Sanctions, and Corrections

The study of **penology** involves efforts to control crime through the correction of criminal offenders. Some criminologists advocate a therapeutic approach to crime prevention that relies on the application of **rehabilitation** services; they direct their efforts at identifying effective treatment strategies for individuals convicted of law violations, such as relying on community sentencing rather than prison. Others argue that crime can be prevented only through the application of formal social control, through such measures as **mandatory sentences** for serious crimes and even the use of **capital punishment** as a deterrent to murder.

Criminologists interested in penology direct their research efforts at evaluating the effectiveness of crime control programs and searching for effective treatments that

**victim precipitated homicide**
Refers to those killings in which the victim is a direct, positive precipitator of the incident.

**white-collar crime**
Illegal acts that capitalize on a person's status in the marketplace. White-collar crimes may include theft, embezzlement, fraud, market manipulation, restraint of trade, and false advertising.

**penology**
Subarea of criminology that focuses on the correction and control of criminal offenders.

**rehabilitation**
Treatment of criminal offenders that is aimed at preventing future criminal behavior.

**mandatory sentences**
A statutory requirement that a certain penalty shall be carried out in all cases of conviction for a specified offense or series of offenses.

**capital punishment**
The execution of criminal offenders; the death penalty.

AP Images

The motivation for crime is often baffling. The body of Danvers High School teacher Colleen Ritzer was found behind the school on October 22, 2013, in Danvers, Massachusetts. Philip Chism, 14, was charged with sexually assaulting and killing Ritzer.

can significantly lower **recidivism** rates. An evaluation of the Risk-Need-Responsivity (RNR) program, which classifies people on probation and orders the placement of some in anger management and cognitive behavioral therapy programs, has been found to cut the recidivism of high-risk offenders by as much as 20 percent.[7]

Not all penological measures work as expected. One might assume that inmates placed in the most punitive high-security prisons will "learn their lesson" and not dare to repeat their criminal offense. However, research shows that being sent to a high-security prison exposes inmates to the most violent peers who have a higher propensity to crime, and this exposure may actually increase criminal behavior, reinforce antisocial attitudes, and ultimately increase recidivism, a finding that supports the need for careful penological research.[8]

## Victimology

Criminologists recognize that the victim plays a critical role in the criminal process and that the victim's behavior is often a key determinant of crime.[9] **Victimology** includes the following areas of interest:

- Using victim surveys to measure the nature and extent of criminal behavior and to calculate the actual costs of crime to victims
- Calculating probabilities of victimization risk
- Studying victim culpability in the precipitation of crime
- Designing services for crime victims, such as counseling and compensation programs

Criminologists who study victimization have uncovered some startling results. For one thing, criminals have been found to be at greater risk of victimization than noncriminals.[10] This finding indicates that rather than being passive targets who are "in the wrong place at the

**recidivism**
Relapse into criminal behavior after apprehension, conviction, and correction for a previous crime.

**victimology**
The study of the victim's role in criminal events.

## Concept Summary 1.1    Criminology in Action

The following subareas constitute the discipline of criminology.

| | |
|---|---|
| **Criminal statistics** | *Gathering valid crime data.* Devising new research methods; measuring crime patterns and trends. |
| **Sociology of law/law and society/sociolegal studies** | *Determining the origin of law.* Measuring the forces that can change laws and society. |
| **Theory construction** | *Predicting individual behavior.* Understanding the cause of crime rates and trends. |
| **Criminal behavior systems** | *Determining the nature and cause of specific crime patterns.* Studying violence, theft, organized crime, white-collar crime, and public order crimes. |
| **Penology: punishment, sanctions, and corrections** | *Studying the correction and control of criminal behavior.* Using the scientific method to assess the effectiveness of criminal sanctions designed to control crime through the application of criminal punishments. |
| **Victimology** | *Studying the nature and cause of victimization.* Aiding crime victims; understanding the nature and extent of victimization; developing theories of victimization risk. |

wrong time," victims may themselves be engaging in a high-risk behavior, such as crime, that increases their victimization risk and renders them vulnerable to crime.

The various elements of criminology in action are summarized in Concept Summary 1.1.

# A Brief History of Criminology

How did this field of study develop? What are the origins of criminology? The scientific study of crime and criminality is a relatively recent development. During the Middle Ages (1200–1600), people who violated social norms or religious practices were believed to be witches or possessed by demons.[11] The use of cruel torture to extract confessions was common. Those convicted of violent or theft crimes suffered extremely harsh penalties, including whipping, branding, maiming, and execution.

## Classical Criminology

By the mid-eighteenth century, social philosophers began to argue for a more rational approach to punishment. Reformers stressed that the relationship between crime and punishment should be balanced and fair. This more moderate view of criminal sanctions can be traced to the writings of an Italian scholar, Cesare Beccaria (1738–1794), who was one of the first scholars to develop a systematic understanding of why people commit crime.

Beccaria believed that in choosing their behavior people act in their own self-interest: they want to achieve pleasure and avoid pain. People will commit crime when the potential pleasure and reward they believe they can achieve from illegal acts outweigh the threat of future punishment. To deter crime, punishment must be sufficient—no more, no less—to counterbalance the lure of criminal gain. If it were too lenient, people would risk committing crimes; too severe a punishment would be unfair and encourage crimes. If rape were punished by death, rapists might be encouraged to kill their victims to prevent identification; after all, they would have nothing to lose if both rape and murder were punished equally. Beccaria's famous theorem was that in order for punishment to be effective it must be public, prompt, necessary, the least possible in the given circumstances, proportionate, and dictated by law.[12]

The writings of Beccaria and his followers form the core of what today is referred to as **classical criminology**. As originally conceived in the eighteenth century, classical criminology theory had several basic elements:

- People have free will to choose criminal or lawful solutions to meet their needs or settle their problems.
- Crime is attractive when it promises great benefits with little effort.
- Crime may be controlled by the fear of punishment.
- Punishment that is (or is perceived to be) severe, certain, and swift will deter criminal behavior.

This classical perspective influenced judicial philosophy, and sentences were geared to be proportionate to the seriousness of the crime. Executions were still widely used but gradually came to be employed for only the most serious crimes. The catchphrase was "Let the punishment fit the crime."

## Positivist Criminology

During the nineteenth century, a new vision of the world challenged the validity of classical theory and presented an innovative way of looking at the causes of crime. The scientific method was beginning to take hold in Europe and North America.

Auguste Comte (1798–1857), considered the founder of sociology, argued that societies pass through stages that can be grouped on the basis of how people try to understand the world in which they live. People in primitive societies believe that inanimate objects have life (for example, the sun is a god); in later social stages, people

## CHECKPOINTS

▷ Criminologists engage in a variety of professional tasks.

▷ Those who work in criminal statistics create accurate measures of crime trends and patterns.

▷ Some criminologists study the origins and sociology of law.

▷ Theorists interested in criminal development seek insight into the causes of crime.

▷ Some criminologists try to understand and describe patterns and trends in particular criminal behaviors, such as serial murder or rape.

▷ Penologists evaluate the criminal justice system.

▷ Victimologists try to understand why some people become crime victims.

**classical criminology**
Theoretical perspective suggesting that people choose to commit crime and that crime can be controlled if potential criminals fear punishment.

Positivists use the scientific method to explain criminal behavior. Some look at social factors while others focus on physical and biological traits. Here, Dr. Michael Nicholas, a clinical psychologist from Paducah, Kentucky, displays a small red and white cube and a model of a human brain as he testifies in the Kevin Wayne Dunlap murder trial. Nicholas was using the props to show the approximate size of an abnormality detected in Dunlap's brain on MRI and PET scans. Nicholas was a defense witness testifying as to how the abnormality may have affected Dunlap, who confessed to the killing of three children and the assault of their mother in October 2008. Dunlap stabbed and killed a 5-year-old boy and his 14- and 17-year-old sisters in their home. He then raped and attempted to murder their mother by stabbing her with a knife. When he thought that the mother was dead, he set fire to the home and left. Despite evidence that Dunlap's abnormal brain structure may have controlled his behavior, he was convicted of murder and sentenced to death.

**positivism**
The branch of social science that uses the scientific method of the natural sciences and suggests that human behavior is a product of social, biological, psychological, or economic forces that can be empirically measured.

**scientific method**
The use of verifiable principles and procedures for the systematic acquisition of knowledge. Typically involves formulating a problem, creating hypotheses, and collecting data, through observation and experiment, to verify the hypotheses.

**FACT OR FICTION?**

Criminals and victims are two totally different types of people.

**FICTION** Criminals themselves actually have a very high rate of victimization.

embrace a rational, scientific view of the world. Comte called this the positive stage, and those who followed his writings became known as positivists.

**Positivism** has a number of elements:

- Use of the **scientific method** to conduct research. The scientific method is objective, universal, and culture-free.
- Predicting and explaining social phenomena in a logical manner. This means identifying necessary and sufficient conditions under which a phenomenon may or may not occur. Both human behavior and natural phenomenon operate according to laws that can be measured and observed.
- Empirical verification. All beliefs or statements must be proved through empirical investigation guided by the scientific method. Such concepts as "God" and "the soul" cannot be measured empirically and therefore are not the subject of scientific inquiry; they remain a matter of faith.
- Science must be value-free and should not be influenced by the observer/scientist's biases or political point of view.

**EARLY CRIMINOLOGICAL POSITIVISM** The earliest "scientific" studies examining human behavior now seem quaint and primitive. Physiognomists, such as J. K. Lavater (1741–1801), studied the facial features of criminals and found that the shape of the ears, nose, and eyes and the distances between them were associated with antisocial behavior. Phrenologists, such as Franz Joseph Gall (1758–1828) and Johann K. Spurzheim (1776–1832), studied the shape of the skull and bumps on the head and concluded that these physical attributes were linked to criminal behavior.[13]

By the early nineteenth century, abnormality in the human mind was being linked to criminal behavior patterns. Philippe Pinel, one of the founders of French psychiatry, coined the phrase *manie sans delire* to denote what eventually was referred to as a psychopathic personality.

In Italy, Cesare Lombroso (1835–1909), known as the "father of criminology," began to study the cadavers of executed criminals in an effort to determine scientifically how criminals differed from noncriminals. Lombroso was soon convinced that serious and violent offenders had inherited criminal traits. These "born criminals" suffered from "atavistic anomalies"; physically, they were throwbacks to more primitive times when people were savages and were believed to have the enormous jaws and strong canine teeth common to carnivores that devour raw flesh. Lombroso's version of criminal anthropology was brought to the United States via articles and textbooks that adopted his ideas.[14] By the beginning of the twentieth century, American authors were discussing "the science of penology" and "the science of criminology."[15]

## Sociological Criminology

At the same time that biological views were dominating criminology, another group of positivists were developing the field of sociology to study scientifically the major social changes taking place in nineteenth-century society. The foundations of **sociological criminology** can be traced to the work of Émile Durkheim (1858–1917).[16]

According to Durkheim's vision of social positivism, crime is normal because it is virtually impossible to imagine a society in which criminal behavior is totally absent.[17] Durkheim believed that crime is inevitable because people are so different from one another and use such a wide variety of methods and types of behavior to meet their needs. Even if "real" crimes were eliminated, human weaknesses and petty vices would be elevated to the status of crimes. Durkheim suggested that crime can be useful—and occasionally even healthful—for society in that it paves the way for social change. To illustrate this concept, Durkheim offered the example of the Greek philosopher Socrates, who was considered a criminal and was put to death for corrupting the morals of youth simply because he expressed ideas that were different from what people believed at that time.

In *The Division of Labor in Society*, Durkheim wrote about the consequences of the shift from a small, rural society, which he labeled "mechanical," to the more modern "organic" society with a large urban population, division of labor, and personal isolation.[18] From the resulting structural changes flowed **anomie**, or norm and role confusion. An anomic society is in chaos, experiencing moral uncertainty and an accompanying loss of traditional values. People who suffer anomie may become confused and rebellious. Is it possible that the loss of privacy created by widespread social media, a technology that can cause a private moment to go "viral," has helped create a sense of anomie in our own culture?

**THE CHICAGO SCHOOL** The primacy of sociological positivism was secured by research begun in the early twentieth century by Robert Ezra Park (1864–1944), Ernest W. Burgess (1886–1966), Louis Wirth (1897–1952), and their colleagues in the Sociology Department at the University of Chicago. The scholars who taught at this program created what is still referred to as the **Chicago School** in honor of their unique style of doing research.

These urban sociologists examined how neighborhood conditions, such as poverty levels, influenced crime rates. They found that social forces operating in urban areas created a crime-promoting environment; some neighborhoods were "natural areas" for crime.[19] In urban neighborhoods with high levels of poverty, the fabric of critical social institutions, such as the school and the family, came undone. Their traditional ability to control behavior was undermined, and the outcome was a high crime rate.

**SOCIALIZATION VIEWS** During the 1930s and 1940s, another group of sociologists began conducting research that linked criminal behavior to the quality of an individual's **socialization**—the relationship they have to important social processes, such as education, family life, and peer relations. They found that children who grew up in homes wracked by conflict, attended inadequate schools, or associated with deviant peers became exposed to forces that engendered crime. One position, championed by the preeminent American criminologist Edwin Sutherland, was that people learn criminal attitudes from older, more experienced law violators.

## Conflict Criminology

In his *Communist Manifesto* and other writings, Karl Marx (1818–1883) described the oppressive labor conditions prevalent during the rise of industrial capitalism. Marx was convinced that the character of every civilization is determined by its mode of production—the way its people develop and produce material goods. The most important relationship in industrial culture is between the owners of the means of production (the capitalist bourgeoisie) and the people who perform the labor (the

**CONNECTIONS**

Many of us have grown up with movies showing criminals as "homicidal maniacs." Some may laugh, but *Freddy vs. Jason*, *The Last House on the Left*, *American Psycho*, *Hannibal*, and similar films are usually box office hits. See Chapter 5 for more on psychosis as a cause of crime.

**sociological criminology**
Approach to criminology, based on the work of Émile Durkheim, that focuses on the relationship between social factors and crime.

**anomie**
A lack of norms or clear social standards. Because of rapidly shifting moral values, the individual has few guides to what is socially acceptable.

**Chicago School**
Group of urban sociologists who studied the relationship between environmental conditions and crime.

**socialization**
Process of human development and enculturation. Socialization is influenced by key social processes and institutions.

**CONNECTIONS**

Did your mother ever warn you about staying away from "bad neighborhoods" in the city? If she did, how valid were her concerns? To find out, go to Chapter 6 for a discussion of the structural conditions that cause crime.

**conflict theory**
The view that human behavior is shaped by interpersonal conflict and that those who maintain social power will use it to further their own ends.

**critical criminology**
The view that crime is a product of the capitalist system.

**rational choice theory**
The view that crime is a function of a decision-making process in which the would-be offender weighs the potential costs and benefits of an illegal act.

**trait theory**
The view that criminality is a product of abnormal biological or psychological traits.

proletariat). The economic system controls all facets of human life; consequently, people's lives revolve around the means of production. The exploitation of the working class, Marx believed, would eventually lead to class conflict and the end of the capitalist system.[20]

These writings laid the foundation for **conflict theory**, the view that human behavior is shaped by interpersonal conflict and that crime is a product of human conflict. However, it was not until the social and political upheaval of the 1960s—fueled by the Vietnam War, the development of an antiestablishment counterculture movement, the civil rights movement, and the women's movement—that criminologists began to analyze the social conditions in the United States that promoted class conflict and crime. What emerged from this intellectual ferment was a **critical criminology** that indicted the economic system as producing the conditions that support a high crime rate. Critical criminologists have played a significant role in the field ever since.

## Developmental Criminology

In the 1940s and 1950s, Sheldon and Eleanor Glueck, a husband-and-wife team of criminologists and researchers at Harvard Law School, conducted numerous studies of delinquent and criminal behavior that profoundly influenced criminological theory. Their work integrated sociological, psychological, and economic elements into a complex developmental view of crime causation. Their most important research efforts followed the careers of known delinquents to determine what factors predicted persistent offending; they also made extensive use of interviews and records in their elaborate comparisons of delinquents and nondelinquents.[21]

The Gluecks' vision integrated biological, social, and psychological elements. It suggested that the initiation and continuity of a criminal career was a developmental process influenced by both internal and external situations, conditions, and circumstances.

## Contemporary Criminology

These various schools of criminology, developed over 200 years, have been constantly evolving.

- Classical theory has evolved into modern **rational choice theory**, which argues that criminals are rational decision makers: before choosing to commit crime, criminals evaluate the benefits and costs of the contemplated criminal act; their choice is structured by the fear of punishment.

- Lombrosian biological positivism has evolved into contemporary biosocial and psychological **trait theory** views. Criminologists who consider themselves trait theorists no longer believe that a single trait or inherited characteristic can explain crime, but that biological and psychological traits interact with environmental factors to influence

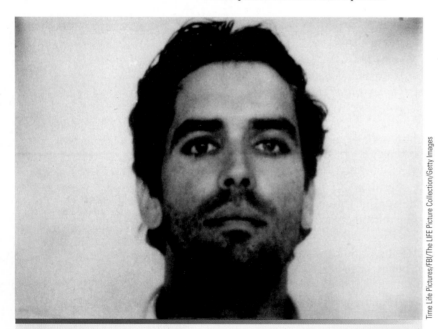

In 1980, Glen Stewart Godwin, along with his partner, Frank Soto, robbed a drug dealer and stabbed him 26 times with a butcher knife, then blew up the body to hide the evidence. Godwin was sentenced to 26 years to life in prison, but in 1987, he made a daring escape by digging a tunnel. Godwin fled to Mexico, where he got involved in the drug trade. Sent to a Mexican prison, he killed a member of a drug cartel and escaped once again. He is currently on the loose somewhere in Latin America, assumed to be dealing drugs, and on the FBI's 10 most wanted list. Developmental criminologists would view Godwin's criminal career as a product of sociological, psychological, and economic factors. His initiation into a criminal career is a developmental process, influenced by both internal and external situations, conditions, and circumstances.

Time Life Pictures/FBI/The LIFE Picture Collection/Getty Images

criminality. Contemporary trait theories suggest that there is a causal link between criminal behavior and such individual level factors as diet, hormonal makeup, personality, and intelligence.

- The original Chicago School sociological vision has transformed into a **social structure theory**, which maintains that a person's place in the social structure controls their behavior; people are a product of their environment. Those at the bottom of the social hierarchy, who find it impossible to achieve monetary and social success through conventional means, experience anomie, strain, failure, and frustration. Social pressures, and the personal turmoil they produce, lead people down a path to crime.
- **Social process theorists** focus their attention on socialization. They believe that children learn to commit crime by interacting with, and modeling their behavior after, others whom they admire. Some criminal offenders are people whose life experiences have shattered their social bonds to society.
- Many criminologists still view social and political conflict as the root cause of crime. These **critical criminologists** believe that crime is related to the inherently unfair economic structure of the United States and other advanced capitalist countries.
- The Gluecks' pioneering research has influenced a new generation of developmental theorists. Their focus today is identifying the personal traits and social conditions that lead to the creation and maintenance of criminal careers over the life course.

Each of the major perspectives is summarized in Concept Summary 1.2.

**social structure theory**
The view that disadvantaged economic class position is a primary cause of crime.

**social process theory**
The view that criminality is a function of people's interactions with various organizations, institutions, and processes in society.

**critical criminologists**
Critical criminologists examine how those who hold political and economic power shape the law to uphold their self-interests.

## Concept Summary 1.2  Criminological Perspectives

The major perspectives of criminology focus on individual factors (biological, psychological, and choice theories), social factors (structural and process theories), political and economic factors (conflict theory), and multiple factors (developmental theory).

| | |
|---|---|
| **Classical/choice perspective** | *Situational forces.* Crime is a function of free will and personal choice. Punishment is a deterrent to crime. |
| **Biological/psychological perspective** | *Internal forces.* Crime is a function of chemical, neurological, genetic, personality, intelligence, or mental traits. |
| **Structural perspective** | *Ecological forces.* Crime rates are a function of neighborhood conditions, cultural forces, and norm conflict. |
| **Process perspective** | *Socialization forces.* Crime is a function of upbringing, learning, and control. Peers, parents, and teachers influence behavior. |
| **Conflict perspective** | *Economic and political forces.* Crime is a function of competition for limited resources and power. Class conflict produces crime. |
| **Developmental perspective** | *Multiple forces.* Biological, social-psychological, economic, and political forces may combine to produce crime. |

## CHECKPOINTS

▶ Criminology has a long and rich history.

▶ The first criminologists believed that crime was a matter of free will. This outlook is referred to as classical criminology.

▶ In the nineteenth century, positivist criminologists began to use the scientific method to study crime. They were convinced that the cause of crime could be found in the individual offender.

▶ During the early twentieth century, sociological criminology was developed to explain the effect of the social environment on individual behavior.

▶ Critical criminologists attempted to explain how economic forces create crime.

▶ Developmental criminologists trace criminal careers over the life course.

▶ Contemporary criminology carries on and refines these traditions.

**L02** Differentiate between crime and deviance.

**deviant behavior**
Actions that depart from the social norm. Some are considered criminal, others merely harmless aberrations.

**crime**
An act, deemed socially harmful or dangerous, that is specifically defined, prohibited, and punished under the criminal law.

**decriminalized**
Having criminal penalties reduced rather than eliminated.

# Deviant or Criminal? How Criminologists Define Crime

Criminologists devote themselves to measuring, understanding, and controlling crime and deviance. How are these behaviors defined, and how do we distinguish between them?

Criminologists view **deviant behavior** as any action that departs from the social norms of society.[22] Deviance thus includes a broad spectrum of behaviors, ranging from the most socially harmful, such as rape and murder, to the relatively inoffensive, such as joining a religious cult or cross-dressing. A deviant act becomes a **crime** when it is deemed socially harmful or dangerous; it then will be specifically defined, prohibited, and punished under the criminal law.

Crime and deviance are often confused because not all crimes are deviant and not all deviant acts are illegal or criminal. For example, recreational drug use such as smoking marijuana may be a crime, but is it deviant? A significant percentage of the population has used recreational drugs (including some well-known politicians—even presidents!). If an illegal act, such as viewing Internet pornography, becomes a norm, should society reevaluate its criminal status and let it become merely an unusual or deviant act?

To argue that all crimes are behaviors that depart from the norms of society is probably erroneous. The shifting definition of deviant behavior is closely associated with our concepts of crime. Where should society draw the line between behavior that is considered merely deviant and unusual and behavior that is considered dangerous and criminal? Many deviant acts are not criminal, even though they may be shocking or depraved. A passerby who observes a person drowning is not legally required to jump in and render aid. Although the general public would probably condemn the person's behavior as callous, immoral, and deviant, no legal action could be taken because citizens are not required by law to effect rescues. In sum, many criminal acts, but not all, fall within the concept of deviance. Similarly, some deviant acts, but not all, are considered crimes.

## Becoming Deviant

To understand the nature and purpose of criminal law, criminologists study both the process by which deviant acts are criminalized (become crimes) and, conversely, how criminal acts are **decriminalized** (that is, the penalties attached to them are reduced) and/or legalized.

In some instances, individuals, institutions, or government agencies mount a campaign aimed at convincing both the public and lawmakers that what was considered merely deviant behavior is actually dangerous and must be outlawed. During the 1930s, Harry Anslinger, then head of the Federal Bureau of Narcotics, used magazine articles, public appearances, and public testimony to sway public opinion about the dangers of marijuana, which up until that time had been legal to use and possess.[23] In testimony before the House Ways and Means Committee considering passage of the Marijuana Tax Act of 1938, Anslinger stated,

Everett Collection

What is considered deviant behavior today can be socially acceptable tomorrow. This poster is for the 1936 film *Reefer Madness*, a movie depicting the dangers of smoking marijuana. Eighty years later, pot smoking is routine behavior and legal in several states.

In Florida a 21-year-old boy under the influence of this drug killed his parents and his brothers and sisters. The evidence showed that he had smoked marihuana. In Chicago recently two boys murdered a policeman while under the influence of marihuana. Not long ago we found a 15-year-old boy going insane because, the doctor told the enforcement officers, he thought the boy was smoking marihuana cigarettes. They traced the sale to some man who had been growing marihuana and selling it to these boys all under 15 years of age, on a playground there.[24]

As a result of Anslinger's efforts, a deviant behavior, marijuana use, became a criminal behavior, and previously law-abiding citizens were defined as criminal offenders. Today some national organizations, such as the Drug Policy Alliance, are committed to repealing draconian drug laws and undoing Anslinger's "moral crusade." They call for an end to the "war against drugs," which they believe has become overzealous in its effort to punish drug traffickers. In fact, they maintain, many of the problems the drug war purports to resolve are actually caused by the drug war itself. So-called "drug-related" crime is a direct result of drug prohibition's distortion of immutable laws of supply and demand. Public health problems such as HIV and hepatitis C are all exacerbated by zero-tolerance laws that restrict access to clean needles. The drug war is not the promoter of family values that some would have us believe. Children of inmates are at risk of educational failure, joblessness, addiction, and delinquency. Drug abuse is bad, but the drug war is worse.[25] Their efforts have borne some fruit: a number of states, including Colorado and Washington, have decriminalized the possession and sale of marijuana.

In sum, criminologists are concerned with the concept of deviance and its relationship to criminality. The shifting definition of deviant behavior is closely associated with our concept of crime.

## The Concept of Crime

Professional criminologists usually align themselves with one of several schools of thought, or perspectives. Each of these perspectives maintains its own view of what constitutes criminal behavior and what causes people to engage in criminality. A criminologist's choice of orientation or perspective depends, in part, on his or her definition of crime. The three most common concepts of crime used by criminologists are the consensus view, the conflict view, and the interactionist view.

**CONSENSUS VIEW OF CRIME** According to the **consensus view**, crimes are behaviors that all elements of society consider repugnant. The rich and powerful as well as the poor and indigent are believed to agree on which behaviors are so repugnant that they should be outlawed and criminalized. Therefore, the **criminal law**—the written code that defines crimes and their punishments—reflects the values, beliefs, and opinions of society's mainstream. The term *consensus* implies general agreement among a majority of citizens on what behaviors should be prohibited by criminal law and hence be viewed as crimes.[26]

This approach to crime implies that it is a function of the beliefs, morality, and rules inherent in Western civilization. Ideally, the laws apply equally to all members of society, and their effects are not restricted to any single element of society.

**CONFLICT VIEW OF CRIME** Although most practicing criminologists accept the consensus model of crime, others take a more political orientation toward its content. The **conflict view** depicts society as a collection of diverse groups—such as owners, workers, professionals, and students—who are in constant and continuing conflict. Groups able to assert their political power use the law and the criminal justice system to advance their economic and social position. Criminal laws, therefore, are viewed as created to protect the haves from the have-nots. Conflict criminologists often contrast the harsh penalties inflicted on the poor for their "street crimes" (burglary, robbery, and larceny) with the minor penalties the wealthy receive for their white-collar crimes (securities violations and other illegal business practices). Whereas the poor go

**LO3** Discuss the three different views of the definition of crime.

**consensus view**
The belief that the majority of citizens in a society share common values and agree on what behaviors should be defined as criminal.

**criminal law**
The written code that defines crimes and their punishments.

**conflict view**
The belief that criminal behavior is defined by those in power in such a way as to protect and advance their own self-interest.

# PROFILES IN CRIME

## TRAYVON MARTIN AND GEORGE ZIMMERMAN

In 2012, the shooting of Trayvon Martin, an African American youth, by George Zimmerman, an armed neighborhood watch member, rocked the nation. It all began on the night of February 26, when Zimmerman, 28, was driving his SUV though his Sanford, Florida, neighborhood when he called 911 to report "a real suspicious guy," a "black male" walking around. That was Trayvon Martin, a teen who was heading back to the house where he was staying after a 7-Eleven run. Martin was wearing a hooded sweatshirt and carrying a can of iced tea, a bag of Skittles, and his cell phone. Zimmerman followed Martin, and the two eventually got involved in an argument. Things escalated into a fight and the altercation culminated in Zimmerman firing a fatal shot into Martin's chest. Zimmerman was brought to the police station, claimed he acted in self-defense after being attacked by Martin, and was released without charges being filed. In the aftermath of the incident, Trayvon Martin's parents, Tracy Martin and Sybrina Fulton, went public, calling for Zimmerman to be prosecuted. Under public pressure, police in Sanford eventually released the 911 calls made by Zimmerman in which a police operator can be heard telling him not to chase after Martin. On April 12, 2012, after a great deal of media attention and public debate, including a famous statement by President Barack Obama saying that if he had a son he "would look like Trayvon Martin," George Zimmerman was charged with second-degree murder.

A key element of the case was Florida's "stand your ground" law, which allows the use of deadly force when a person reasonably believes it necessary to prevent the commission of a "forcible felony," including carjacking, robbery, and assault. Traditional self-defense laws allow people to use deadly force only when they reasonably believe their lives are in danger. The Florida law allows average citizens to use deadly force when they reasonably believe that their homes or vehicles have been illegally invaded. The Florida law authorizes the use of defensive force by anyone "who is not engaged in an unlawful activity and who is attacked in any other place where he or she has a right to be." Furthermore, under the law, such a person has no duty to retreat and can stand his or her ground and meet force with force. The statute also grants civil and criminal immunity to anyone found to have had such a reasonable belief. Was Zimmerman justified in using deadly force against an unarmed teen? If so, the death of Martin could not be considered murder. If, on the other hand, his actions were excessive under the circumstances and a reasonable person should not believe that his life was in danger from an unarmed youth, then Zimmerman's reaction would not fall under the "stand your ground" statute.

In the end, the jury believed Zimmerman and found him not guilty as charged. While many considered his acts murderous, the jury disagreed. Here we can see how the definition of crime and the labeling of a criminal is a highly subjective process; crime is a socially constructed event. ■

**Sources:** CNN Library, "Trayvon Martin Shooting Fast Facts," February 22, 2014, www.cnn.com/2013/06/05/us/trayvon-martin-shooting-fast-facts/; ABCNews, "Trayvon Martin News," abcnews.go.com/topics/news/trayvon-martin.htm (accessed June 2015).

(left) Trayvon Martin (right) George Zimmerman is seen with a bloody, swollen nose in this February 26, 2012, police photo taken on the night he shot and killed unarmed black teenager Trayvon Martin. Zimmerman's injuries helped convince a jury that he was not guilty of murder and acted in self-defense.

AP Images/Mark St George/Rex Features

Handout/Reuters/Landov

to prison for minor law violations, the wealthy are given lenient sentences for even serious breaches of law.

**INTERACTIONIST VIEW OF CRIME**  According to the **interactionist view**, there is no objective reality. People, institutions, and events are viewed subjectively and labeled either good or evil according to the interpretation of the evaluator. The content of the criminal law and consequently the definition of crime is subjective and can change at any moment. Marijuana is now legal in some jurisdictions (Colorado for one) and illegal in others. It could easily be the other way around, depending on the voting public's views, perceptions, and beliefs.

Whether a particular act fits the definition of a crime is also a function of interaction and perception: If a death occurs in the wake of an argument, a jury may be asked to decide whether the act was murder, self-defense, or merely an accidental fatality. Each person on the jury may have his or her own interpretation of what took place. Whether the act is labeled a crime and the actor a criminal depends on the juror's interpretation of events. The accompanying Profiles in Crime feature examines one of the most infamous cases in which the nation was split on whether an act was truly a crime.

Interactionists see criminal law as conforming to the beliefs of "moral crusaders," or moral entrepreneurs, who use their influence to shape the legal process as they see fit.[27] Laws against pornography, prostitution, and drugs are believed to be motivated more by moral crusades than by capitalist sensibilities. Consequently, interactionists are concerned with shifting moral and legal standards.

> **interactionist view**
> The belief that those with social power are able to impose their values on society as a whole, and these values then define criminal behavior.

## A Definition of Crime

Because of their diverse perspectives, criminologists have taken a variety of approaches in explaining crime's causes and suggesting methods for its control (see Concept Summary 1.3). Considering these differences, we can take elements from each school of thought to formulate an integrated definition of crime:

> Crime is a violation of societal rules of behavior as interpreted and expressed by the criminal law, which reflects public opinion, traditional values, and the viewpoint of people currently holding social and political power. Individuals who violate these rules are subject to sanctions by state authority, social stigma, and loss of status.

### Concept Summary 1.3   The Definition of Crime

The definition of crime affects how criminologists view the cause and control of illegal behavior and shapes their research orientation.

| | |
|---|---|
| **Consensus view** | • The law defines crime.<br>• Agreement exists on outlawed behavior.<br>• Laws apply to all citizens equally. |
| **Conflict view** | • The law is a tool of the ruling class.<br>• Crime is a politically defined concept.<br>• "Real crimes" such as racism, sexism, and classism are not outlawed.<br>• The law is used to control the underclass. |
| **Interactionist view** | • Moral entrepreneurs define crime.<br>• Acts become crimes because society defines them that way.<br>• Criminal labels are life-transforming events. |

This definition combines the consensus view that the criminal law defines crimes, the conflict perspective's emphasis on political power and control, and the interactionist concept of stigma. Thus crime as defined here is a political, social, and economic function of modern life.

**LO4** Discuss the different purposes of the criminal law.

# Criminology and the Criminal Law

No matter which definition of crime we embrace, criminal behavior is tied to the criminal law. It is therefore important for all criminologists to have some understanding of the development of criminal law, its objectives, its elements, and how it evolved over time.

The concept of criminal law has been recognized for more than 3,000 years. Hammurabi (1792–1750 BCE), the king of Babylon, created the most famous set of written laws of the ancient world, known today as the **Code of Hammurabi**. Preserved on basalt rock columns, the code established a system of crime and punishment based on physical retaliation (*lex talionis* or "an eye for an eye").

More familiar is the **Mosaic Code** of the Israelites (1200 BCE), including the Ten Commandments. The Mosaic Code is not only the foundation of Judeo-Christian moral teachings but also a basis for the U.S. legal system. Prohibitions against murder, theft, perjury, and adultery preceded, by several thousand years, the same laws found in the modern United States.

## Common Law

The present system of law can be traced back to the reign of Henry II (1154–1189), when royal judges began to publish their decisions in local cases and their legal reasoning began **precedent**, to be applied in similar cases around the land—hence the term **common law**. Crimes such as murder, burglary, arson, and rape are common-law crimes whose elements were initially defined by judges. They are referred to as *mala in se*, or inherently evil and depraved. When the situation required, the English Parliament enacted legislation to supplement the common law shaped by judges. Crimes defined by Parliament, which reflected existing social conditions, were referred to as *mala prohibitum*, or **statutory crimes**.

Before the American Revolution, the colonies, then under British rule, were subject to the common law. After the colonies acquired their independence, state legislatures standardized common-law crimes such as murder, burglary, arson, and rape by putting them into statutory form in criminal codes. As in England, whenever common law proved inadequate to deal with changing social and moral issues, the states and Congress supplemented it with legislative statutes, creating new elements in the various state and federal legal codes.

## Contemporary Criminal Law

Criminal laws are now divided into felonies and misdemeanors. The distinction is based on seriousness: a **felony** is a serious offense, a **misdemeanor** a minor or petty crime. Crimes such as murder, rape, and burglary are felonies; they are punished with long prison sentences or even death. Crimes such as unarmed assault and battery, petty larceny, and disturbing the peace are misdemeanors; they are punished with a fine or a period of incarceration in a county jail.

Regardless of their classification, acts prohibited by the criminal law constitute behaviors considered unacceptable and impermissible by those in power. People who engage in these acts are eligible for severe sanctions. By outlawing these behaviors, the government expects to achieve a number of social goals:

- *Enforces social control.* Those who hold political power rely on criminal law to formally prohibit behaviors believed to threaten societal well-being or to challenge their authority.

**Code of Hammurabi**
The first written criminal code, developed in Babylonia about 1750 BCE.

**Mosaic Code**
The laws of the ancient Israelites, found in the Old Testament of the Judeo-Christian Bible.

**precedent**
A rule derived from previous judicial decisions and applied to future cases; the basis of common law.

**common law**
Early English law, developed by judges, which became the standardized law of the land in England and eventually formed the basis of the criminal law in the United States.

**statutory crimes**
Crimes defined by legislative bodies in response to changing social conditions, public opinion, and custom.

**felony**
A serious offense that carries a penalty of imprisonment, usually for one year or more, and may entail loss of political rights.

**misdemeanor**
A minor crime usually punished by a short jail term and/or a fine.

- *Discourages revenge.* By punishing people who infringe on the rights, property, and freedom of others, the law shifts the burden of revenge from the individual to the state. Although the application of state retaliation may offend the sensibilities of some people, as Oliver Wendell Holmes stated, it prevents "the greater evil of private retribution."[28]

- *Expresses public opinion.* Criminal law reflects constantly changing public opinion on such controversial acts as using recreational drugs, selling obscene material, or performing abortions. Criminal law is used to codify these changes.

- *Teaches moral values.* By observing how the law is applied, people, especially children, learn to distinguish between appropriate and prohibited behavior. Application of the criminal law provides a moral lesson.

- *Deters criminal behavior.* Criminal law has a social control function. Because it applies criminal punishments such as fines, prison sentences and even death, it is designed to control, restrain, and direct human behavior and prevent crimes before they occur.

- *Applies "just desert."* Those who violate criminal law are subject to criminal sanctions because they have maltreated others and harmed society. It is only fair then that they should be punished for their misdeeds; offenders *deserve* their punishments.

- *Creates equity.* Criminals benefit from their misdeeds. People who violate security laws can make huge profits from their illegal transactions. Through fines, forfeiture, and other economic sanctions, the criminal law redistributes illegal gains back to society, thereby negating the criminal's unfair advantage.

- *Maintains the social order.* The legal system is designed to support and maintain the boundaries of the social system they serve. Our economic and social system is also supported and sustained by criminal law.

## The Evolution of Criminal Law

The criminal law is constantly evolving in an effort to reflect social and economic conditions. Sometimes legal changes are prompted by highly publicized cases that generate fear and concern. A number of cases of celebrity stalking, including Robert John Bardo's fatal shooting of actress Rebecca Schaeffer on July 18, 1989, prompted more than 25 states to enact stalking statutes. Such laws prohibit "the willful, malicious, and repeated following and harassing of another person."[29] California's sexual predator law, which took effect on January 1, 1996, allows people convicted of sexually violent crimes against two or more victims to be committed to a mental institution after their prison terms have been served.[30]

The criminal law may also change because of shifts in culture and social conventions and thus may reflect a newfound tolerance for behavior condemned only a few years before or conversely, condemnation of behavior that was heretofore considered normative and legal. An example of the former can be found in changes to the law of rape. In several states, including California and Maryland, the law has evolved so that it is now considered rape if a woman consents to sex, the sex act begins, she changes her mind during the act and tells her partner to stop, and he refuses and continues. Before this legal change, such a circumstance was not considered rape but merely aggressive yet consensual sex.[31] Another example of how changing morals may be reflected in the law can be found in the case of *Lawrence v. Texas*, where the Supreme Court declared that state laws criminalizing sexual relations between consenting adults, heretofore classified as sodomy, were unconstitutional because they violated the due process rights of citizens because of their sexual orientation.[32] Because consensual sex between same-sex adults was now legal, the *Lawrence* decision paved the way for the eventual legalization of same-sex marriage by the Supreme Court in 2015.[33]

A. C. Cooper Ltd. by permission of The Inner Temple, London

Common law was created by English judges during the Middle Ages. It unified local legal practices into a national system of laws and punishments. Common law serves as the basis for the American legal system.

# Criminology and Criminal Justice

**criminal justice**
System made up of the agencies of social control, such as police departments, courts, and correctional institutions that handle criminal offenders.

**criminal justice system**
The agencies of government—police, courts, and corrections—that are responsible for apprehending, adjudicating, sanctioning, and treating criminal offenders.

Not only is the study of criminology bound up in the criminal law, it is also closely linked to the workings of the criminal justice system. Although the terms *criminology* and *criminal justice* may seem similar, and people often confuse the two or lump them together, there are major differences between these fields of study. Criminology explains the etiology (origin), extent, and nature of crime in society, whereas **criminal justice** refers to the study of the agencies of social control—police, courts, and corrections. While criminologists are mainly concerned with identifying the suspected cause of *crime*, criminal justice scholars spend their time identifying effective methods of *crime control*.

Since both fields are crime-related, they do overlap. Some criminologists devote their research to justice and social control and are concerned with how the agencies of justice operate, how they influence crime and criminals, and how justice policies shape crime rates and trends. Conversely, criminal justice experts often want to design effective programs of crime prevention or rehabilitation and to do so must develop an understanding of the nature of crime and its causation. It is common, therefore, for criminal justice programs to feature courses on criminology and for criminology courses to evaluate the agencies of justice. What is the criminal justice system, how big is it, and how does it operate?

## The Criminal Justice System

The **criminal justice system** consists of the agencies of government charged with enforcing law, adjudicating crime, and correcting criminal conduct. It is essentially an instrument of social control: Society considers some behaviors so dangerous and destructive that it either strictly controls their occurrence or outlaws them outright. The agencies of justice are designed to prevent social harm by apprehending, trying, convicting, and punishing those who have already violated the law, as well as deterring those who may be contemplating future wrongdoing. Society maintains other types of informal social control, such as parental and school discipline, but these are designed to deal with moral, not legal, misbehavior. Only the criminal justice system maintains the power to control crime and punish those who violate the law.

The contemporary criminal justice system can be divided into three main components:

- Police and law enforcement, which consists of federal, state, and municipal agencies charged with such tasks as maintaining the peace, rendering emergency assistance, investigating crimes, and apprehending suspects
- The court system, which houses the prosecution and the judiciary, and is responsible for charging criminal suspects, carrying out trials, and sentencing those convicted of crime
- The correctional system, which incapacitates convicted offenders and attempts to aid in their treatment and rehabilitation

Because of its varied and complex mission, the contemporary criminal justice system in the United States is monumental in size. It now costs federal, state, and local governments more than $200 billion per year to administer civil and criminal justice, up more than 300 percent since 1982. There are now almost 18,000 U.S. law enforcement agencies employing more than 1 million people; of these, more than 800,000 are full-time sworn law enforcement officers, and the remainder are part-time officers and civilian employees. There are nearly 17,000 courts, more than 8,000 prosecutorial agencies, about 6,000 correctional institutions, and more than 3,500 probation and parole departments.

The system is massive because it must process, treat, and care for millions of people. Although the crime rate has declined substantially, more than 11 million people are still being arrested each year, including more than 2 million for serious felony offenses. In addition, about 1.5 million juveniles are handled by the juvenile courts. Today, state and federal courts convict almost 1 million adults a year on felony charges.

Considering the massive proportions of this system, it does not seem surprising that almost 7 million people are under some form of correctional supervision, including 2.3 million men and women in the nation's jails and prisons and almost 5 million adult men and women being supervised in the community while on probation or parole.[34] After many years of rapid increase, the correctional population has finally begun to stabilize and/or decline.

## The Process of Justice

In addition to viewing the criminal justice system as a collection of agencies, it is possible to see it as a series of decision points through which offenders flow. This process begins with initial contact with police and ends with the offender reentering society. At any point in the process, a decision may be made to drop further proceedings and allow the accused back into society without further penalty.[35] The justice process is transformative: at first a person is a suspect, then a convicted criminal, and finally an ex-offender. He is transformed from the accused to a thief, rapist, or killer. Stigma and labeling make reform efforts difficult to achieve.

Although each jurisdiction is somewhat different, a comprehensive view of the processing of a felony offender would probably contain the following decision points:

1. *Initial contact.* The initial contact an offender has with the justice system occurs when police officers observe a criminal act during patrol of city streets, parks, or highways. They may also find out about a crime through a citizen or victim complaint. Similarly, an informer may alert them about criminal activity in return for financial or other consideration. Sometimes political officials, such as the mayor or city council, ask police to look into ongoing criminal activity, such as gambling, and during their subsequent investigations police officers encounter an illegal *act*.

2. *Investigation.* An investigation may take a few minutes, as when patrol officers see a burglary in progress and apprehend the burglar at the scene of the crime. Other investigations may take years to complete and involve numerous investigators. When federal agents tracked and captured Theodore Kaczynski (known as the Unabomber) in 1996, his arrest completed an investigation that had lasted more than a decade.

3. *Arrest.* An **arrest** is legal when all of the following conditions exist: (a) the officer believes there is sufficient evidence (**probable cause**) that a crime is being or has been committed and that the suspect committed the crime; (b) the officer deprives the individual of freedom; and (c) the suspect believes that he or she is in the custody of a police officer and cannot voluntarily leave. The police officer is not required to use the word "arrest" or any similar word to initiate an arrest, nor does the officer first have to bring the suspect to the police station. For all practical purposes, a person who has been deprived of liberty is under arrest. Arrests can be made at the scene of a crime or after a warrant is issued by a magistrate.

4. *Custody.* After arrest, the suspect remains in police custody. The person may be taken to the police station to be fingerprinted and photographed and to have personal information recorded—a procedure popularly referred to as **booking**. Witnesses may be brought in to view the suspect in a lineup, and further evidence may be gathered on the case. Suspects may be interrogated by police officers to get their side of the story, they may be asked to sign a confession of guilt, or they may be asked to identify others involved in the crime. The law allows suspects to have their lawyer present whenever police conduct an in-custody **interrogation**.

5. *Complaint/charging.* After police turn the evidence in a case over to the prosecutor, the prosecution weighs the evidence to determine whether there are sufficient facts to support the accusation. If, in its discretion, the prosecutor's

**arrest**
The taking into police custody of an individual suspected of a crime.

**probable cause**
A set of facts, information, circumstances, or conditions that would lead a reasonable person to believe that an offense was committed and that the accused committed that offense. It is the level of proof needed to make a legal arrest.

**booking**
Fingerprinting, photographing, and recording personal information of a suspect in police custody.

**interrogation**
The questioning of a suspect in police custody.

**nolle prosequi**
A declaration that expresses the prosecutor's decision to drop a case from further prosecution.

**indictment**
A written accusation returned by a grand jury charging an individual with a specified crime, based on the prosecutor's demonstration of probable cause.

**grand jury**
A group of citizens chosen to hear testimony in secret and to issue formal criminal accusations (indictments).

**information**
A filing before an impartial lower-court judge who decides whether the case should go forward (this filing is an alternative to the use of a grand jury).

**preliminary hearing**
Alternative to a grand jury, in which an impartial lower-court judge decides whether there is probable cause sufficient for a trial.

**arraignment**
The step in the criminal justice process in which the accused is brought before the trial judge, formal charges are read, defendants are informed of their rights, a plea is entered, bail is considered, and a trial date is set.

**bail**
A money bond intended to ensure that the accused will return for trial.

**recognizance**
Pledge by the accused to return for trial, which may be accepted in lieu of bail.

**plea bargain**
Agreement between prosecution and defense in which the accused pleads guilty in return for a reduction of charges, a more lenient sentence, or some other consideration.

**hung jury**
A jury that is unable to agree on a decision, thus leaving the case unresolved and open for a possible retrial.

**appeal**
Taking a criminal case to a higher court on the grounds that the defendant was found guilty because of legal error or violation of his or her constitutional rights.

office believes there is insufficient evidence to move the case forward, it issues a *nolle prosequi* declaration, which signifies its decision to drop the case from further prosecution. If there is sufficient evidence, the case will be brought forth to a grand jury or preliminary hearing.

6. *Preliminary hearing/grand jury.* Because it is a tremendous personal and financial burden to stand trial for a serious felony crime, such as murder or rape, the U.S. Constitution provides that before a person can be charged, the state must first prove to an impartial decision-making authority that there exists probable cause that the accused committed the crime and that there is sufficient evidence to try the person as charged. In about half the states and in the federal system, the decision is made via an **indictment** issued by a **grand jury**, which considers the case in a closed hearing during which only the prosecutor is permitted to present evidence. If sufficient facts are presented, the grand jury will issue a *true bill of indictment*; insufficient evidence will result in a *no bill*. In the remaining states, a criminal **information** is filed before an impartial lower-court judge, who decides whether the case should go forward and be heard in a felony court. At this **preliminary hearing** (sometimes called a probable cause hearing), the defendant is permitted to appear and dispute the prosecutor's charges. In both procedures, if the prosecution's evidence is found to be factual and sufficient, the suspect will be summoned to stand trial for his or her crime. (In misdemeanor cases, the term typically used in charging is *criminal complaint*, an allegation made to a court in writing by either a victim or a police officer.)

7. *Arraignment.* At an **arraignment** the accused is brought before the court that will actually try the case. At this hearing, the formal charges are read, and defendants are informed of their constitutional rights (such as the right to legal counsel). Bail is considered, and a trial date is set.

8. *Bail or detention.* **Bail** is a money bond, the amount of which is set by judicial authority; it is intended to ensure the presence of suspects at trial, while allowing them their freedom until that time. Suspects who do not show up for trial forfeit their bail. Suspects who cannot afford bail or are considered too dangerous or too great a flight risk may be required to remain in detention until trial. Many jurisdictions now allow defendants awaiting trial to be released on their own **recognizance**, without bail, if they are stable members of the community.

9. *Plea bargaining.* After arraignment, it is common for the prosecutor to meet with the defendant and his or her attorney to discuss a possible **plea bargain**. If a bargain can be struck, the accused pleads guilty as charged, thus ending the criminal trial process. In return for the plea, the prosecutor may reduce charges, request a lenient sentence, or grant the defendant some other consideration.

10. *Adjudication/trial process.* If a plea bargain cannot be arranged, a criminal trial takes place. This involves a full-scale inquiry into the facts of the case before a judge, a jury, or both. The defendant can be found guilty or not guilty, or the jury can fail to reach a decision (**hung jury**), thereby leaving the case unresolved and open for a possible retrial.

11. *Disposition/sentencing.* If found guilty by trial or plea, a defendant is sentenced by the presiding judge. Disposition usually involves a fine, a term of community supervision (probation), a period of incarceration in a penal institution, or some combination of these penalties. About two-thirds of all defendants convicted of felonies receive incarceration sentences. Of course, this means that many people convicted of serious criminal offenses, including murder and rape, are granted a community sentence—that is, probation.

12. *Appeal.* After conviction, if the defendant believes he or she was not treated fairly by the justice system, the individual may **appeal** the conviction. An appellate court reviews trial procedures to determine whether an error was made. Such issues as whether evidence was used properly, whether the judge conducted the trial in an approved fashion, whether the jury was representative, and whether the attorneys in the case acted appropriately may be the basis for

an appeal. In most instances, if the appellate court rules in favor of the defendant, she or he is granted a new trial.

13. *Correctional treatment.* Offenders who are found guilty and are formally sentenced come under the jurisdiction of correctional authorities. They may serve a term of community supervision under control of the county probation department, they may spend time in a community correctional center, or they may be incarcerated in a large penal institution.

14. *Release.* At the end of the correctional sentence, the offender is released into the community. Most incarcerated offenders are granted parole before the expiration of the maximum term given them by the court, and therefore they finish their prison sentences in the community under supervision of the parole department.

15. *Postrelease/aftercare.* After termination of correctional treatment, the offender must successfully return to the community and be supervised by corrections department staff members, typically parole officers. Successful completion of the postrelease period marks the end of the criminal justice process.

## Ethical Issues in Criminology

A critical issue facing criminology students involves recognizing the field's political and social consequences. All too often criminologists forget the social responsibility they bear as experts in the area of crime and justice. When government agencies request their views on issues, their pronouncements and opinions may become the basis for sweeping changes in social policy.

The lives of millions of people can be influenced by criminological research data. Debates over gun control, capital punishment, and mandatory sentences are ongoing and contentious. Some criminologists have argued successfully for social service, treatment, and rehabilitation programs to reduce the crime rate; others consider these a waste of time, suggesting instead that a massive prison construction program coupled with tough criminal sentences can bring the crime rate down. By accepting their roles as experts on law-violating behavior, criminologists place themselves in a position of power. The potential consequences of their actions are enormous. Therefore, they must be both aware of the ethics of their profession and prepared to defend their work in the light of public scrutiny. Major ethical issues include what to study, whom to study, and how to conduct those studies.

- *What to study.* Criminologists must be concerned about the topics they study. Their research must not be directed by the sources of funding on which research projects rely. The objectivity of research may be questioned if studies are funded by organizations that have a vested interest in the outcome of the research. For example, a study on the effectiveness of the defensive use of handguns to stop crime may be tainted if the funding for the project comes from a gun manufacturer whose sales may be affected by the research findings. It has been shown over the past decades that criminological research has been influenced by government funding linked to the topics the government wants research on and those it wishes to avoid. Recently, funding by political agencies has increased the likelihood that criminologists will address drug issues, while spending less time on topics such as incapacitation and white-collar crime.[36] Should the nature and extent of scientific research be shaped by the hand of government, or should research remain independent of outside interference?

- *Whom to study.* Another ethical issue in criminology concerns selection of research subjects. Too often, criminologists focus their attention on the poor and minorities, while ignoring middle-class white-collar crime, organized crime, and government crime. For example, a few social scientists have suggested that criminals have lower intelligence quotients than the average citizen and that because the average IQ score is lower among some minority groups, their crime rates are high.[37] This was the conclusion reached in *The Bell Curve*, a popular but

## CHECKPOINTS

▶ There are a number of views of what crime entails. The three major views are the consensus, conflict, and interactionist perspectives.

▶ The American legal system is a direct descendant of the British common law.

▶ The criminal law has a number of different goals, including social control, punishment, retribution, deterrence, equity, and the representation of morality.

▶ The criminal law is constantly changing in an effort to reflect social values and contemporary issues and problems.

▶ The criminal justice system is designed to identify, apprehend, try, and treat criminal offenders.

▶ The system can be viewed as both a group of organizations and also as a process that begins with initial contact and ends with post-incarceration care.

**LO6** Identify the ethical issues in criminology.

highly controversial book written by Richard Herrnstein and Charles Murray.[38] Although such research is often methodologically unsound, it brings to light the tendency of criminologists to focus on one element of the community while ignoring others.

- *How to study.* A third area of concern involves the methods used in conducting research. One issue is whether subjects are fully informed about the purpose of research. For example, when European American and African American youngsters are asked to participate in a survey of their behavior or to take an IQ test, are they told in advance that the data they provide may later be used to demonstrate racial differences in their self-reported crime rates? Criminologists must also be careful to keep records and information confidential in order to maintain the privacy of research participants. But ethical questions still linger: Should a criminologist who is told in confidence by a research subject about a future crime report her knowledge to the police? How far should a criminologist go to protect her sources of information? Should stated intentions to commit offenses be disclosed?[39]

In studies that involve experimentation and treatment, care must be taken to protect those subjects who have been chosen for experimental and control groups. For example, is it ethical to provide a special program for one group while depriving others of the same opportunity just so the groups can later be compared? Conversely, criminologists must be careful to protect subjects from experiments that may actually cause harm. An examination of the highly publicized "Scared Straight" program, which brings youngsters into contact with hard-core felons in a prison setting, found that participants may have been harmed by their experience. Rather than being frightened into conformity, subjects actually increased their criminal behavior.[40] Finally, criminologists must take extreme care to ensure that research subjects are selected in a random and unbiased manner.[41]

Of course, it is critical that criminological research do no harm to subjects, but this may not be enough: criminological research can, and should, be empowering and directly useful to research participants. To be truly ethical, criminological research must have social value to research participants rather than simply doing no harm.[42]

# Thinking Like a Criminologist

**Testing Violent Brains**   You have been experimenting with various techniques in order to identify a surefire method for predicting violent behavior in delinquents. Your procedure involves brain scans, DNA testing, and blood analysis. Used with samples of incarcerated adolescents, your procedure has been able to distinguish with 75 percent accuracy between youths with a history of violence and those who are exclusively property offenders. Your research indicates that if all youths were tested with your techniques, potentially violence-prone career criminals could be easily identified for special treatment. For example, children in the local school system could be tested, and those identified as violence prone could be carefully monitored by teachers. Those at risk for future violence could be put into special programs as a precaution.

Some of your colleagues argue that this type of testing is unconstitutional because it violates the subjects' Fifth Amendment right against self-incrimination. There is also the problem of error: some children may be falsely labeled as violence prone.

## Writing Assignment

Write an essay addressing the issue of predicting antisocial behavior. Address such issues as the following: Is it fair or ethical to label people as potentially criminal and violent, even though they have not yet exhibited any antisocial behavior? Do the risks of such a procedure outweigh its benefits?

# SUMMARY

**LO1 Explain the various elements of criminology.**

The various subareas included within the scholarly discipline of criminology, taken as a whole, define the field of study. The subarea of criminal statistics/ crime measurement involves calculating the amount of, and trends in, criminal activity. Sociology of law/law and society/sociolegal studies is a subarea of criminology concerned with the role that social forces play in shaping criminal law and the role of criminal law in shaping society. Criminologists also explore the causes of crime. Another subarea of criminology involves research on specific criminal types and patterns: violent crime, theft crime, public order crime, organized crime, and so on. The study of penology, correction, and sentencing involves the treatment of known criminal offenders. Criminologists recognize that the victim plays a critical role in the criminal process and that the victim's behavior is often a key determinant of crime.

**LO2 Differentiate between crime and deviance.**

Criminologists devote themselves to measuring, understanding, and controlling crime and deviance. Deviance includes a broad spectrum of behaviors that differ from the norm, ranging from the most socially harmful to the relatively inoffensive. Criminologists are often concerned with the concept of deviance and its relationship to criminality.

**LO3 Discuss the three different views of the definition of crime.**

According to the consensus view, crimes are behaviors that all elements of society consider repugnant. It is the belief that the majority of citizens in a society share common values and agree on what behaviors should be defined as criminal. The conflict view depicts criminal behavior as being defined by those in power to protect and advance their own self-interest. According to the interactionist view, those with social power are able to impose their values on society as a whole, and these values then define criminal behavior.

**LO4 Discuss the different purposes of the criminal law.**

The criminal law serves several important purposes. It represents public opinion and moral values. It enforces social controls. It deters criminal behavior and wrongdoing. It punishes transgressors. It creates equity. And it abrogates the need for private retribution.

**LO5 Describe the criminal justice process.**

The criminal justice process involves 15 stages, beginning with initial contact and ending with postrelease aftercare. At each stage of the process, the offender can either be released or moved on to a higher level. At the end, they are transformed from a suspect to a convicted criminal who bears a label such as rapist or thief.

**LO6 Identify the ethical issues in criminology.**

Ethical issues arise when information-gathering methods appear biased or exclusionary. These issues may cause serious consequences because research findings can significantly affect individuals and groups. Criminologists must be concerned about the topics they study. Another ethical issue in criminology revolves around the selection of research subjects. A third area of concern involves the methods used in conducting research.

# Key Terms

| | | | |
|---|---|---|---|
| criminology 4 | victim precipitated | penology 7 | capital punishment 7 |
| valid measure 5 | homicide 7 | rehabilitation 7 | recidivism 8 |
| reliable measure 5 | white-collar crime 7 | mandatory sentences 7 | victimology 8 |

# Critical Thinking Questions

1. What are the specific aims and purposes of the criminal law? To what extent does the criminal law control behavior? Do you believe that the law is too restrictive? Not restrictive enough?

2. If you ran the world, which acts that are now legal would you make criminal? Which criminal acts would you legalize? What would be the probable consequences of your actions?

3. Beccaria argued that the threat of punishment controls crime. Are there other forms of social control? Aside from the threat of legal punishment, what else controls your own behavior?

4. Would it be ethical for a criminologist to observe a teenage gang by hanging with them, drinking, and watching as they steal cars? Should the criminologist report that behavior to the police?

# Notes

*All URLS accessed in 2015.*

1. John Hagan and Alberto Palloni, "Sociological Criminology and the Mythology of Hispanic Immigration and Crime," *Social Problems* 46 (1999): 617–632.

2. Christina Mancini and Daniel P. Mears, "U.S. Supreme Court Decisions and Sex Offender Legislation: Evidence of Evidence-Based Policy?" *Journal of Criminal Law and Criminology* 103 (2013): 1115–1156.

3. Ibid.; see also, "Brief for the American Psychological Association et al. as Amici Curiae in Support of Petitioners," at 3–4, *Miller v. Alabama*, 132 S. Ct. 2455 (2012) (Nos. 10-9646 and 10-9647).

4. Marvin Wolfgang, *Patterns in Criminal Homicide* (Philadelphia: University of Pennsylvania Press, 1958).

5. Edwin Sutherland, *White-Collar Crime: The Uncut Version* (New Haven, CT: Yale University Press, 1983).

6. Randy Borum, *Psychology of Terrorism* (Tampa: University of South Florida, 2004), www.ncjrs.gov/pdffiles1/nij/grants/208552.pdf.

7. Joan Petersilia, "Beyond the Prison Bubble," *NIJ Journal* 268 (2011), www.nij.gov/nij/journals/268/prison-bubble.htm.

8. M. Keith Chen and Jesse Shapiro, "Do Harsher Prison Conditions Reduce Recidivism? A Discontinuity-Based Approach," *American Law and Economics Review* 9 (2007): 1–29.

9. Hans von Hentig, *The Criminal and His Victim* (New Haven, CT: Yale University Press, 1948); Stephen Schafer, *The Victim and His Criminal* (New York: Random House, 1968).

10. Linda Teplin, Gary McClelland, Karen Abram, and Darinka Mileusnic, "Early Violent Death Among Delinquent Youth: A Prospective Longitudinal Study," *Pediatrics* 115 (2005): 1586–1593.

11. Eugene Weber, *A Modern History of Europe* (New York: W. W. Norton, 1971), p. 398.

12. Wolfgang, *Patterns in Criminal Homicide.*

13. Nicole Rafter, "The Murderous Dutch Fiddler: Criminology, History, and the Problem of Phrenology," *Theoretical Criminology* 9 (2005): 65–97.

14. Nicole Hahn Rafter, "Criminal Anthropology in the United States," *Criminology* 30 (1992): 525–547.

15. Ibid., p. 535.

16. See, generally, Robert Nisbet, *The Sociology of Emile Durkheim* (New York: Oxford University Press, 1974).

17. Emile Durkheim, *Rules of the Sociological Method*, reprint ed., trans. W. D. Halls (New York: Free Press, 1982).

18. Emile Durkheim, *The Division of Labor in Society*, reprint ed. (New York: Free Press, 1997).

19. Robert Park and Ernest Burgess, *The City* (Chicago: University of Chicago Press, 1925).

20. Karl Marx and Friedrich Engels, *Capital: A Critique of Political Economy*, trans. E. Aveling (Chicago: Charles Kern, 1906); Karl Marx, *Selected Writings in Sociology and Social Philosophy*, trans. P. B. Bottomore (New York: McGraw-Hill, 1956). For a general discussion of Marxist thought, see Michael Lynch and W. Byron Groves, *A Primer in Radical Criminology* (New York: Harrow and Heston, 1986), pp. 6–26.

21. Sheldon Glueck and Eleanor Glueck, *Unraveling Juvenile Delinquency* (Cambridge, MA: Harvard University Press, 1950).

22. Charles McCaghy, *Deviant Behavior* (New York: Macmillan, 1976), pp. 2–3.

23. Edward Brecher, *Licit and Illicit Drugs* (Boston: Little, Brown, 1972), pp. 413–416.

24. Hearings on H.R. 6385, April 27, 28, 29, 30, and May 4, 1937, www.druglibrary.org/schaffer/hemp/taxact/anslng1.htm.

25. See, generally, the Drug Policy Alliance, www.drugpolicy.org.

26. Edwin Sutherland and Donald Cressey, *Criminology*, 8th ed. (Philadelphia: J. B. Lippincott, 1960), p. 8.

27. Ibid.

28. Oliver Wendell Holmes, *The Common Law*, ed. Mark De Wolf (Boston: Little, Brown, 1881), p. 36.

29. National Institute of Justice, *Project to Develop a Model Anti-Stalking Statute* (Washington, DC: National Institute of Justice, 1994).

30. Associated Press, "Judge Upholds State's Sexual Predator Law," *Bakersfield Californian*, October 2, 1996.

31. Matthew Lyon, "No Means No? Withdrawal of Consent During Intercourse and the Continuing Evolution of the Definition of Rape," *Journal of Criminal Law and Criminology* 95 (2004): 277–314.

32. *Lawrence et al. v. Texas*, No. 02-102, June 26, 2003.

33. *Obergefell v. Hodges*, No. 14-556, June 26, 2015.

34. Lauren E. Glaze and Danielle Kaeble, *Correctional Populations in the United States, 2013* (Washington, DC: Bureau of Justice Statistics, 2014), www.bjs.gov/content/pub/pdf/cpus13.pdf.

35. Herbert L. Packer, *The Limits of the Criminal Sanction* (Stanford, CA: Stanford University Press, 1968), p. 159.

36. Joachim Savelsberg, Ryan King, and Lara Cleveland, "Politicized Scholarship? Science on Crime and the State," *Social Problems* 49 (2002): 327–349.

37. See, for example, Michael Hindelang and Travis Hirschi, "Intelligence and Delinquency: A Revisionist Review," *American Sociological Review* 42 (1977): 471–486.

38. Richard Herrnstein and Charles Murray, *The Bell Curve* (New York: Free Press, 1994).

39. Dermot Feenan, "Legal Issues in Acquiring Information About Illegal Behaviour Through Criminological Research," *British Journal of Criminology* 42 (2002): 762–781.

40. Anthony Petrosino, Carolyn Turpin-Petrosino, and James Finckenauer, "Well-Meaning Programs Can Have Harmful Effects! Lessons from Experiments on Programs Such as Scared Straight," *Crime and Delinquency* 46 (2000): 354–379.

41. Victor Boruch, Timothy Victor, and Joe Cecil, "Resolving Ethical and Legal Problems in Randomized Experiments," *Crime and Delinquency* 46 (2000): 330–353.

42. Ida Dupont, "Beyond Doing No Harm: A Call for Participatory Action Research with Marginalized Populations in Criminological Research," *Critical Criminology* 16 (2008): 197–207.

# 2 The Nature and Extent of Crime

## Learning Objectives

**L01**   Discuss the various forms of crime data.

**L02**   Analyze recent trends in the crime rate.

**L03**   List the factors that influence crime rates.

**L04**   Identify the gender and racial patterns in crime.

**L05**   Clarify what is meant by the term *aging-out process*.

**L06**   Define the concept of chronic offending and know its causes.

# Chapter Outline

## FACT OR FICTION?

▶ Crime is out of control and is more dangerous now in the United States than at any time in history.

▶ Immigrants who are in the United States illegally commit a lot of crime, a fact that justifies limiting immigration and closing down the borders.

On September 13, 2014, 18-year-old University of Virginia student Hannah Graham went missing. The night before, Graham had met friends at a restaurant for dinner before stopping by two off-campus parties. She left the second party alone and eventually texted a friend saying she was lost. After a search involving thousands of volunteers, Graham's remains were found on October 18 near Charlottesville, in a spot roughly six miles from where the body of another murder victim, 20-year-old Virginia Tech student Morgan Harrington, was found after she vanished in 2009.

A lead in the case developed when police examined surveillance videos taken the night Hannah disappeared. In the video, she seems disoriented and can be seen walking unsteadily past a bar and a service station and then on to a seven-block strip of bars, restaurants, and shops. Also caught on the tape was 32-year-old Jesse Leroy Matthew Jr., who had a long history of violent behavior with women. Matthew became a prime suspect in the case and was eventually arrested in Galveston, Texas, as he planned to leave the country; he was charged with abduction with intent to defile Graham. Forensic evidence linked Matthew to both murders as well as other sexual assaults.

**Uniform Crime Report (UCR)**
Large database, compiled by the FBI, of crimes reported and arrests made each year throughout the United States.

**Part I crimes**
The eight most serious offenses included in the UCR: murder, rape, assault, robbery, burglary, arson, larceny, and motor vehicle theft.

**murder and nonnegligent manslaughter**
The willful (nonnegligent) killing of one human being by another.

**LO1**  Discuss the various forms of crime data.

**forcible rape**
Under common law, the carnal knowledge of a female forcibly and against her will. In 2012, a new broader definition of rape was implemented: "The penetration, no matter how slight, of the vagina or anus with any body part or object, or oral penetration by a sex organ of another person, without the consent of the victim."

**robbery**
The taking or attempting to take anything of value from the care, custody, or control of a person or persons by force or threat of force or violence and/or by putting the victim in fear.

**aggravated assault**
An unlawful attack by one person upon another, accompanied by the use of a weapon, for the purpose of inflicting severe or aggravated bodily injury.

**burglary**
The unlawful entry of a structure to commit a felony or a theft.

**larceny**
The unlawful taking, carrying, leading, or riding away of property from the possession or constructive possession of another.

When splashed across the media and rehashed on nightly talk shows, cases such as the murder of Hannah Graham help convince most Americans that we live in a violent society. If an innocent student at an elite college can be brutally murdered, who among us is truly safe? Are Americans justified in their fear of violent crime? Should they barricade themselves behind armed guards? Are crime rates actually rising or falling? Where do most crimes occur and who commits them? To answer these and similar questions, criminologists have devised elaborate methods of crime data collection and analysis. Without accurate data on the nature and extent of crime, it would not be possible to formulate theories that explain the onset of crime or to devise social policies that facilitate its control or elimination. Accurate data collection is also critical in assessing the nature and extent of crime, tracking changes in the crime rate, and measuring the individual and social factors that may influence criminality.

In this chapter, we review how data are collected on criminal offenders and offenses and what this information tells us about crime patterns and trends. We also examine the concept of criminal careers and discover what available crime data can tell us about the onset, continuation, and termination of criminality. We begin with a discussion of the most important sources of crime data that criminologists use to measure the nature and extent of crime.

# Primary Sources of Crime Data

The primary sources of crime data are surveys and official records. Criminologists use these techniques to measure the nature and extent of criminal behavior and the personality, attitudes, and background of criminal offenders. Understanding how such data are collected provides insight into how professional criminologists approach various problems and questions in their field.

## Official Records: The Uniform Crime Report

In order to understand more about the nature and extent of crime, criminologists use the records of government agencies such as police departments, prisons, and courts. The Federal Bureau of Investigation collects the most important crime record data from local law enforcement agencies and publishes it yearly in their **Uniform Crime Report (UCR)**. The UCR includes crimes reported to local law enforcement departments and the number of arrests made by police agencies.[1] The FBI receives and compiles records from about 17,000 police departments serving a majority of the U.S. population. The FBI tallies and annually publishes the number of reported offenses by city, county, standard metropolitan statistical area, and geographical divisions of the United States for the most serious crimes. These **Part I crimes** are **murder and nonnegligent manslaughter, forcible rape, robbery, aggravated assault, burglary, larceny, motor vehicle theft**, and **arson**.

In addition to recording crimes reported to the police, the UCR also collects data on the number and characteristics (age, race, and gender) of individuals who have been arrested for committing a crime. Included in the arrest data are both people who have committed Part I crimes and people who have been arrested for all other crimes, known collectively as **Part II crimes**. This latter group includes such criminal acts as sex crimes, drug trafficking, and vandalism.

**COMPILING THE UNIFORM CRIME REPORT**  The methods used to compile the UCR are quite complex. Each month, law enforcement agencies report the number of Part I crimes reported by victims, by officers who discovered the infractions, or by other sources.

Whenever criminal complaints are found through investigation to be unfounded or false, they are eliminated from the actual count. However, the number of actual offenses known is reported to the FBI whether or not anyone is arrested for the crime, the stolen property is recovered, or prosecution ensues.

In addition, each month, law enforcement agencies also report how many crimes were cleared. Crimes are cleared in two ways: (1) when at least one person is arrested, charged, and turned over to the court for prosecution; or (2) by exceptional means, when some element beyond police control precludes the physical arrest of an offender (for example, the offender leaves the country). Data on the number of clearances involving the arrest of only juvenile offenders, data on the value of property stolen and recovered in connection with Part I offenses, and detailed information pertaining to criminal homicide are also reported. Nationwide slightly less than 50 percent of violent crimes and 20 percent of property crimes are cleared.

Violent crimes are more likely to be solved than property crimes because police devote more resources to these more serious acts, witnesses (including the victim) are frequently available to identify offenders, and in many instances the victim and offender were previously acquainted.

The UCR uses three methods to express crime data. First, the number of crimes reported to the police and arrests made are expressed as raw figures. Second, year over year percentage changes in the number of crimes are computed. Finally, the crime rate per 100,000 people is calculated. The equation used:

$$\frac{\text{Number of Repeated Crimes}}{\text{Total US Population}} \times 100,000$$

$$= \text{Rate per } 100,000$$

So, in 2013, there were 14,196 murders, a 4.4 percent decrease from 2012, and a 7.8 percent decrease from 2009; the murder rate was 4.5 per 100,000 people. Preliminary 2014 data indicate that the crime drop has continued.

## Charleston Police Department
180 Lockwood Blvd., Charleston, SC 29403
June 18, 2015

### Need To Identify

On June 17, 2015 at approximately 8:00PM, the below pictured white male suspect entered the Emanuel AME church located at 110 Calhoun Street and began shooting church members. The suspect was seen leaving the church in the below pictured black four door sedan.

Law Enforcement needs help to identify this individual as part of the ongoing homicide investigation. The suspect is considered armed and dangerous. Anyone with information regarding the suspect's identity or whereabouts is asked to call 1-800-CALLFBI (1-800-225-5324).

Suspect is described as a younger white male. He stands approximately 5'09" in height and has a slender build.

Handout/Reuters/Landov

Official crime data are made up of crimes reported to police. Acts are included even if the crime is never solved or a suspect identified. This is the "wanted" poster released by the Charleston (South Carolina) Police Department when they were searching for the perpetrator of the shooting at the Emanuel African Methodist Episcopal Church on June 18, 2015. At the time the gunman, now identified as Dylann Roof, was still at large. This horrific crime would have been reported to the FBI and become part of the Uniform Crime Report data regardless of whether the shooter had ever been identified.

**VALIDITY OF THE UCR** The UCR's accuracy has long been suspect. Many serious crimes are not reported to police and therefore are not counted by the UCR. The reasons for not reporting vary:

- Victims may consider the crime trivial or unimportant and therefore choose not to call police.
- Some victims fail to report because they do not trust the police or have little confidence in the ability of the police to solve crime. Cities in which people believe the police can help them are more likely to report crime.[2]
- People without property insurance believe it is useless to report theft.
- Victims may fear reprisals from an offender's friends or family.
- Some victims have "dirty hands" and are involved in illegal activities themselves. They do not want to get involved with police.

Because of these and other factors, less than half of all criminal incidents are reported to the police.

**motor vehicle theft**
The theft of a motor vehicle.

**arson**
The willful or malicious burning of a dwelling house, public building, motor vehicle, aircraft, personal property of another, or the like.

**Part II crimes**
All other crimes, aside from the eight Part I crimes, included in the UCR arrest data. Part II crimes include drug offenses, sex crimes, and vandalism, among others.

The way police departments record and report criminal activity also affects the validity of UCR statistics. Some departments may define crimes loosely—reporting a trespass as a burglary or an assault on a woman as an attempted rape—whereas others pay strict attention to FBI guidelines. Some make systematic errors in UCR reporting—for example, counting an arrest only after a formal booking procedure, even though the UCR requires arrests to be counted if the suspect is released without a formal charge. These reporting practices may help explain inter-jurisdictional differences in crime. Differences in the way crimes are defined may also influence reporting practices. Because many jurisdictions have broadened their classification of rape to include all forms of sexual assault, the FBI has followed suit, in 2012 changing the definition used in the UCR to, *"The penetration, no matter how slight, of the vagina or anus with any body part or object, or oral penetration by a sex organ of another person, without the consent of the victim."*

Some critics take issue with the way the FBI records data and counts crimes. According to the "Hierarchy Rule," in a multiple-offense incident, only the most serious crime is counted. Thus, if an armed bank robber commits a robbery, assaults a patron as he flees, steals a car to get away, and damages property during a police chase, only the robbery is reported because it is the most serious offense.

Although these issues are troubling, the UCR continues to be one of the most widely used sources of criminal statistics. Because data for the UCR are collected in a careful and systematic way, it is considered a highly reliable indicator of crime patterns and trends. That is, even if reporting problems impede a precise count of total crimes committed in a single year, measurement of year-to-year percentage change should be accurate because measurement problems are stable over time. If the UCR reports that the murder rate decreased about 5 percent between 2012 and 2013, that assessment is probably accurate because the reporting and counting problems that influenced data collection in 2012 had the same effect in 2013.

## NIBRS: The Future of the Uniform Crime Report

Clearly there must be a more reliable source for crime statistics than the UCR as it stands today. Beginning in 1982, a five-year redesign effort was undertaken to provide more comprehensive and detailed crime statistics. The effort resulted in the **National Incident-Based Reporting System (NIBRS)**, a program that collects data on each reported crime incident. Instead of submitting statements of the kinds of crime that individual citizens report to the police and summary statements of resulting arrests, NIBRS requires local police agencies to provide at least a brief account of each incident and arrest, including the incident, victim, and offender information.

**National Incident-Based Reporting System (NIBRS)** Program that requires local police agencies to provide a brief account of each incident and arrest within 22 crime patterns, including incident, victim, and offender information.

Under NIBRS, law enforcement authorities provide information to the FBI on each criminal incident involving 46 specific offenses, including the 8 Part I crimes, that occur in their jurisdiction; arrest information on the 46 offenses plus 11 lesser offenses is also provided in NIBRS. In addition to common-law crimes such as rape and murder, NIBRS reporting provides information on most of the criminal justice issues facing law enforcement today—terrorism, white-collar crime, information about assaults on law enforcement officers, offenses in which weapons were involved, drug/narcotic offenses, hate crimes, domestic and familial abuse including elder abuse, juvenile crime, gang-related crime, parental abduction, organized crime, and pornography, as well as arrest data related to driving under the influence. In addition, NIBRS reporting captures whether the offender was suspected of using drugs/narcotics or alcohol during or shortly before the incident and whether the offender used computer equipment to perpetrate the crime; this makes it possible to develop a national database on the nature of crime, victims, and criminals.

To date, the FBI has certified 33 state programs for NIBRS participation that together hold about one-third of the population (about 93 million people). Other state programs are in various stages of testing NIBRS.[3]

## Survey Research

Another important method of collecting crime data is through surveys in which people are asked about their attitudes, beliefs, values, and characteristics, as well as their experiences with crime and victimization. Surveys typically involve **sampling**, the process of selecting for study a limited number of subjects who are representative of an entire group that has similar characteristics, called the **population**. To understand the social forces that produce crime, a criminologist might interview a sample of 3,000 prison inmates drawn from the population of more than 2 million inmates in the United States; in this case, the sample represents the entire population of U.S. inmates. It is assumed that the characteristics of people or events in a carefully selected sample will be similar to those of the population at large. If the sampling is done correctly, the responses of the 3,000 inmates should represent those of the entire population of inmates.

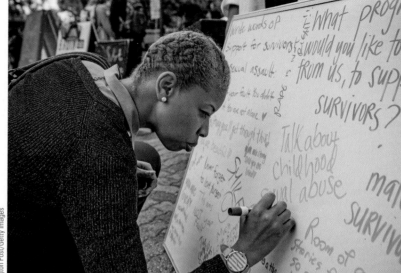

Washington Post/Getty Images

A passerby writes a message related to sexual assault during an event on UCLA's campus to pay respect to students who have experienced sexual violence. While campus sexual assault is a significant problem, many victims fail to report the crime to police or other authorities, so the true extent of this vicious crime remains unknown.

## The National Crime Victimization Survey (NCVS)

Because many victims do not report their experiences to the police, the UCR cannot measure all the annual criminal activity. To address the nonreporting issue, the federal government sponsors the **National Crime Victimization Survey (NCVS)**, a comprehensive, nationwide survey of victimization in the United States conducted annually by the U.S. Census Bureau for the Bureau of Justice Statistics (BJS).

In the most recent survey, 90,380 households and 158,090 persons age 12 or older were interviewed for the NCVS.[4] People are surveyed twice a year, so each interview covers a six-month period. Households stay in the sample for three years, and new households are rotated into the sample on an ongoing basis. The NCVS collects information on crimes suffered by individuals and households, whether or not those crimes were reported to law enforcement. It estimates the proportion of each crime type reported to law enforcement, and it summarizes the reasons that victims give for reporting or not reporting. In 1993, the survey was redesigned to provide detailed information on the frequency and nature of the crimes of rape, sexual assault, personal robbery, aggravated and simple assault, household burglary, theft, and motor vehicle theft. In 2006, significant changes were also made to the way the NCVS is collected. The methodological changes included a new sampling method, a change in the method of handling first-time interviews with households, and a change in the method of interviewing. Computer-assisted personal interviewing (CAPI) replaced paper and pencil interviewing (PAPI).

Through this massive and complex survey, the NCVS provides information about victims (age, sex, race, ethnicity, marital status, income, and educational level), offenders (sex, race, approximate age, and victim–offender relationship), and crimes (time and place of occurrence, use of weapons, nature of injury, and economic consequences). Questions also cover the experiences of victims with the criminal justice system, self-protective measures used by victims, and possible substance abuse by offenders.

The greatest advantage of the NCVS over official data sources such as the UCR is that it can estimate the total amount of annual crimes, not just those that are reported to police. As a result, the NCVS provides a more nearly complete picture of the nation's crime problem. Recently, the Bureau of Justice statistics surveyed trends

**sampling**
Selecting a limited number of people for study as representative of a larger group.

**population**
All people who share a particular characteristic, such as all high school students or all police officers.

**National Crime Victimization Survey (NCVS)**
The ongoing victimization study conducted jointly by the Justice Department and the U.S. Census Bureau that surveys victims about their experiences with law violation.

in reporting practices and calculated the percentage of serious violent crime—rape or sexual assault, robbery, or aggravated assault—that was not reported to police declined from 50 to 42 percent, a finding that indicates that people are more willing to report crime today than in the past. Only 17 percent of motor vehicle theft victimizations now go unreported, presumably because most cars are insured for theft. However, many crimes still remain significantly unreported, including theft (71 percent) and rape or sexual assault (65 percent) victimization.[5]

**VALIDITY OF THE NCVS** Although its utility and importance are unquestioned, the NCVS may also suffer from some methodological problems. As a result, its findings must be interpreted with caution. Among the potential problems are the following:

- Overreporting due to victims' misinterpretation of events. A lost wallet may be reported as stolen or an open door may be viewed as a burglary attempt.
- Underreporting due to the embarrassment of reporting crime to interviewers, fear of getting in trouble, or simply forgetting an incident.
- Inability to record the personal criminal activity of those interviewed, such as drug use or gambling; murder is also not included, for obvious reasons.
- Sampling errors, which produce a group of respondents who do not represent the nation as a whole.
- Inadequate question format that invalidates responses. Some groups, such as adolescents, may be particularly susceptible to error because of question format.

While these issues are critical, there is no substitute available that provides national information on crime and victimization with extensive detail on victims and the social context of the criminal event.

## Self-Report Surveys

Another tool commonly used by criminologists to measure crime is the **self-report survey** that asks people to describe, in detail, their recent and lifetime participation in criminal activity. Self-reports are given in groups, and the respondents are promised anonymity in order to ensure the validity and honesty of their responses. Most self-report studies have focused on juvenile delinquency and youth crime.[6] However, self-reports can also be used to examine the offense histories of prison inmates, drug users, and other segments of the criminal population.[7]

Most self-report surveys also contain questions related to the subjects' background and history: family makeup, upbringing, income, school performance, and personal beliefs. Using this information, criminologists can search for links between personal history and characteristics and criminal behaviors. For example, they can explore whether people who report being abused as children are also more likely to use drugs as adults or whether failure in school leads to delinquency.[8]

**VALIDITY OF SELF-REPORTS** Critics of self-report studies frequently suggest that expecting people to candidly admit illegal acts is unreasonable. This is especially true of those with official records—the very people who may be engaging in the most criminality. At the same time, some people may exaggerate their criminal acts, forget some of them, or be confused about what is being asked. Some surveys contain an overabundance of trivial offenses, such as shoplifting small items or using false identification to obtain alcohol, often lumped together with serious crimes to form a total crime index. Consequently, comparisons between groups can be highly misleading.

The "missing cases" phenomenon is also a concern. Even if 90 percent of a school population voluntarily participates in a self-report study, researchers can never be sure whether the few who refuse to participate or are absent that day constitute a significant portion of the school's population of persistent high-rate offenders. Research indicates that offenders with the most extensive prior criminality are also the most likely "to be poor historians of their own crime commission rates."[9] It is also unlikely that the most serious chronic offenders in the teenage population are willing to

**CONNECTIONS**
Criminologists suspect that a few high-rate offenders are responsible for a disproportionate share of all serious crime. Results would be badly skewed if even a few of these chronic offenders were absent or refused to participate in schoolwide self-report surveys. For more on chronic offenders, see "Chronic Offenders/Criminal Careers," later in this chapter.

cooperate with criminologists administering self-report tests.[10] Institutionalized youths, who are not generally represented in the self-report surveys, not only are more delinquent than the general youth population but also are considerably more misbehaving than the most delinquent youths identified in the typical self-report survey.[11] Consequently, self-reports may measure only nonserious, occasional delinquents, while ignoring hard-core chronic offenders who may be institutionalized and unavailable for self-reports.

To address these criticisms, various techniques have been used to verify self-report data. The "known group" method compares people known to be offenders with those who are not, to see whether the former report more crime, which they should. Research shows that when people are asked whether they have ever been arrested or sent to court, their responses accurately reflect their true-life experiences.[12]

**MONITORING THE FUTURE** One way to improve the reliability of self-reports is to use them in a consistent fashion with different groups of subjects over time. That makes it possible to measure trends in self-reported crime and drug abuse to see whether changes have occurred. One important source of longitudinal self-report data is the Monitoring the Future (MTF) study that researchers at the University of Michigan Institute for Social Research (ISR) have been conducting annually since 1978. This national survey, which typically involves more than 50,000 high school students, is one of the most important sources of self-report data on drug abuse.[13] A subsample of respondents is also asked about their self-reported delinquency.

Table 2.1 contains data from the most recent MTF survey. A surprising number of teenagers report involvement in serious criminal behavior. About 8 percent reported hurting someone badly enough that the victim needed medical care (4 percent said they did it more than once); about 20 percent reported stealing something worth less than $50, and another 7 percent stole something worth more than $50; 23 percent reported shoplifting one or more times; 7 percent damaged school property, 4 percent more than once.

If the MTF data are accurate, the crime problem is much greater than official statistics would lead us to believe. There are approximately 40 million youths between

| TABLE 2.1 Monitoring the Future Survey of Criminal Activity of High School Seniors | | |
| --- | --- | --- |
| Type of Delinquency | Committed at Least Once | Committed More than Once |
| Set fire on purpose | 1% | 1% |
| Damaged school property | 3% | 4% |
| Damaged work property | 1% | 2% |
| Auto theft | 2% | 2% |
| Auto part theft | 1% | 1% |
| Break and enter | 10% | 13% |
| Theft, less than $50 | 9% | 11% |
| Theft, more than $50 | 3% | 4% |
| Shoplift | 9% | 14% |
| Gang or group fight | 7% | 6% |
| Hurt someone badly enough to require medical care | 4% | 4% |
| Used force or a weapon to steal | 1% | 2% |
| Hit teacher or supervisor | 2% | 2% |
| Participated in serious fight | 6% | 4% |

**Source:** Data provided by *Monitoring the Future, 2014* (Ann Arbor, MI: Institute for Social Research, 2015).

the ages of 10 and 18. Extrapolating from the MTF findings, this group accounts for more than 100 percent of all the theft offenses reported in the UCR. About 3 percent of high school students said they had used force to steal (which is the legal definition of a robbery). Two-thirds of them said they committed this crime more than once in a year. At this rate, high school students alone commit more than 1.56 million robberies per year. In comparison, the UCR now tallies about 360,000 robberies for all age groups yearly. Like the official crime data, the MTF finds that self-reported participation in theft, violence, and damage-related crimes has also declined over the past few years.

Concept Summary 2.1 reviews the primary data collection methods used by criminologists today.

## Evaluating Crime Data

Each source of crime data has strengths and weaknesses. The FBI survey contains data on the number and characteristics of people arrested, information that the other data sources lack. For the most serious crimes, such as drug trafficking, arrest data can provide a meaningful measure of the level of criminal activity in a particular neighborhood environment, which other data sources cannot provide. It is also the source of information on particular crimes, such as murder, that cannot be measured by survey data.[14] The UCR remains the standard unit of analysis on which most criminological research is based. However, this survey omits the many crimes that victims choose not to report to police, and it is subject to the reporting caprices of individual police departments.

The NCVS includes unreported crime and important information on the personal characteristics of victims. However, the data consist of estimates made from relatively limited samples of the total U.S. population, so even narrow fluctuations in the rates

### Concept Summary 2.1    Data Collection Methods

| | |
|---|---|
| **Uniform Crime Report** | • Data are collected from records from police departments across the nation, crimes reported to police, and arrests.<br>• Strengths of the UCR are that it measures homicides and arrests and that it is a consistent, national sample.<br>• Weaknesses of the UCR are that it omits crimes not reported to police, omits most drug usage, and contains reporting errors. |
| **National Crime Victimization Survey** | • Data are collected from a large national survey.<br>• Strengths of the NCVS are that it includes crimes not reported to the police, uses careful sampling techniques, and is a yearly survey.<br>• Weaknesses of the NCVS are that it relies on victims' memory and honesty and that it omits substance abuse. |
| **Self-report surveys** | • Data are collected from local surveys.<br>• Strengths of self-report surveys are that they include nonreported crimes, substance abuse, and offenders' personal information.<br>• Weaknesses of self-report surveys are that they rely on the honesty of offenders and omit offenders who refuse or are unable, as a consequence of incarceration, to participate (and who therefore may be the most delinquent and/or criminal). |

of some crimes can have a major impact on findings. It also relies on personal recollections that may be inaccurate. The NCVS does not include data on important crime patterns, including murder and drug abuse.

Self-report surveys can provide information on the personal characteristics of offenders (such as their attitudes, values, beliefs, and psychological profiles) that is unavailable from any other source. Yet, at their core, self-reports rely on the honesty of criminal offenders and drug abusers, a population not generally known for accuracy and integrity.

Although their numerical tallies of crimes are certainly not in synch, the findings on crime patterns, rates, and trends are similar.[15] They all generally agree about the personal characteristics of serious criminals (such as age and gender) and where and when crime occurs (such as urban areas, nighttime, and summer months). The problems inherent in each source are consistent over time. Even if the data sources are incapable of providing a precise and valid count of crime at any given time, they are reliable indicators of changes and fluctuations in yearly crime rates.

In addition to these primary sources of crime data, criminologists use other data in their studies. These are discussed in Exhibit 2.1.

## Exhibit 2.1  Alternative Crime Measures

In addition to the primary sources of crime data—UCR, NCVS, and self-report surveys—criminologists use several other methods to acquire data. Although this list is not exhaustive, the methods described here are routinely used in criminological research and data collection.

### Cohort Research Data

Collecting cohort data involves observing over time a group of people who share certain characteristics. Researchers might select all girls born in Boston in 1990 and then follow their behavior patterns for 20 years. The research data might include their school experiences, arrests, and hospitalizations, along with information about their family life (marriages, divorces, parental relations). If the cohort is carefully drawn, it may be possible to accumulate a complex array of data that can be used to determine which life experiences are associated with criminal careers.

### Experimental Data

Sometimes criminologists conduct controlled experiments to collect data on the cause of crime. To conduct experimental research, criminologists manipulate, or intervene in, the lives of their subjects to see the outcome or the effect of the intervention. True experiments usually have three elements: (1) random selection of subjects, (2) a control or comparison group, and (3) an experimental condition.

### Observational and Interview Research

Sometimes criminologists focus their research on relatively few subjects, interviewing them in depth or observing them as they go about their activities. This research often results in the kind of in-depth data that large-scale surveys do not yield.

### Meta-analysis and Systematic Review

Meta-analysis involves gathering data from a number of previous studies. Compatible information and data are extracted and pooled together. When analyzed, the grouped data from several different studies provide a more powerful and valid indicator of relationships than the results provided by a single study. A systematic review involves collecting the findings from previously conducted scientific studies that address a particular problem, appraising and synthesizing the evidence, and using the collective evidence to address a particular scientific question.

### Data Mining

A relatively new criminological technique, data mining uses multiple advanced computational methods, including artificial intelligence (the use of computers to perform logical functions), to analyze large data sets that usually involve one or more data sources. The goal is to identify significant and recognizable patterns, trends, and relationships that are not easily detected through traditional analytical techniques.

### Crime Mapping

Criminologists now use crime mapping to create graphical representations of the spatial geography of crime. Computerized crime maps enable criminologists to analyze and correlate a wide array of data to create immediate, detailed visuals of crime patterns.

**Source:** © Cengage Learning

**L02** Analyze recent trends in the crime rate.

**FIGURE 2.1**
**Crime Rate Trends**

**Source:** FBI, *Crime in the United States, 2013*, www.fbi.gov/about-us/cjis/ucr /crime-in-the-u.s/2013/crime-in-the -u.s.-2013 (accessed 2015).

1960
Total crimes: 3.4 million
Violent crimes: 288,000
Property crimes: 3.1 million

1991
Total crimes: 14.8 million
Violent crimes: 1.9 million
Property crimes: 12.9 million

2008
Total crimes: 10.7 million
Violent crimes: 1.3 million
Property crimes: 9.4 million

2013
Total crimes: 9.8 million
Violent crimes: 1.2 million
Property crimes: 8.6 million

# Crime Trends

Crime is not new to this century. Studies have indicated that a gradual increase in the crime rate, especially in violent crime, occurred from 1830 to 1860. Following the Civil War, this rate increased significantly for about 15 years. Then, from 1880 up to the time of World War I, with the possible exception of the years immediately preceding and following the war, the number of reported crimes decreased. After a period of readjustment, the crime rate steadily declined until the Depression (about 1930), when another crime wave was recorded. As measured by the UCR, crime rates increased gradually following the 1930s until the 1960s, when the growth rate became much greater. The homicide rate, which had actually declined from the 1930s to the 1960s, also began a sharp increase that continued through the 1980s. During the following decade, there were sharp increases in rates of robbery, motor vehicle theft, and overall homicide and a disturbing increase in youth firearm homicide rates.[16]

## Contemporary Trends

After a decade of increases, crime rates peaked in 1991, when the UCR recorded almost 15 million crimes in a single year. Since then the number of crimes has been in decline; about 9.8 million crimes were reported in 2013, a drop of more than 5 million reported crimes since the 1991 peak, despite a boost of more than 50 million people in the general population. Figure 2.1 illustrates the changes in numbers of crimes reported between 1960 and 2013.

Especially welcome has been a significant drop in UCR violent crimes—murder, rape, robbery, and assault. About 1.16 million violent crimes are now being reported to the police each year, a rate of 368 per 100,000 Americans. Of course, people are still disturbed by media reports of violent incidents, but in reality there are 800,000 fewer violent crimes being reported today than in 1991, when almost 2 million incidents occurred yearly, a violence rate of 758 per 100,000. This means that the violence rate has dropped almost 50 percent from its peak because the number of violent crimes is far lower and the general population continues to increase.

Police departments are now using high-level data analysis tools prepared by crime analysts to identify crime trends and patterns and use their resources in a more effective manner. Here, a Command Operation Briefings to Revitalize Atlanta (COBRA) meeting is taking place at the Atlanta Police Department on January 15, 2015. The meetings are an opportunity for the Crime Analysis Unit to provide commanders with updates on citywide crime trends and evaluate responses.

Not only has violent crime been in decline, so too have theft offenses. The property crimes reported in the UCR include larceny, motor vehicle theft, and arson. Property crime rates have also declined in recent years, dropping more than 10 percent during the past decade. At its peak in 1991, about 13 million property crimes were reported, a rate of almost 5,000 per 100,000 citizens. Currently, about 8.6 million property crimes are reported annually to police, a rate of about 2,730 per 100,000 population. Property crimes remain a serious national problem, and losses totaling an estimated $17 billion now result from property crimes each year.

How has the rest of the world fared while the United States has undergone a significant crime drop? To find out, read the Policies and Issues in Criminology feature on international crime trends.

## Trends in Victimization

According to the latest NCVS survey, U.S. residents aged 12 or older experienced about 20.7 million violent and property victimizations.[17] Like the UCR data, NCVS data show that criminal victimizations have declined significantly during the past 30 years (see Figure 2.2). In 1973, an estimated 44 million victimizations were recorded, far higher than today; since 1993, the rate of violent victimization has declined about 80 percent. Especially striking has been the decline in the rate of serious violent crime against youth ages 12 to 17, which has declined more than 70 percent since 1994, falling from 62 victimizations per 1,000 youth to around 14 victimizations per 1,000. During this period, among serious violent crimes against youth, the rate of rape and sexual assault declined 68 percent, robbery declined 77 percent, and aggravated assault declined 80 percent.[18]

While there have been year-to-year fluctuations, there is little question that the NCVS data support the findings of the UCR: the United States has experienced a significant crime drop for more than two decades.

Nic Bothma/EPA/Landov

While crime rates have been declining in the United States, they are rising abroad. Here, on May 19, 2015, co-accused in the George "Geweld" Thomas trial sit prior to sentencing procedures at the High Court in Cape Town, South Africa. "Geweld," meaning violence, is the nickname of George Thomas, head of one of South Africa's most violent and notorious gangs, the 28s. Thomas, along with sixteen others, was found guilty of crimes ranging from murder to racketeering. The trial lasted over five years and resulted in Thomas being found guilty of seven murders—two for the murder of state witnesses while he was in prison.

**LO3** List the factors that influence crime rates.

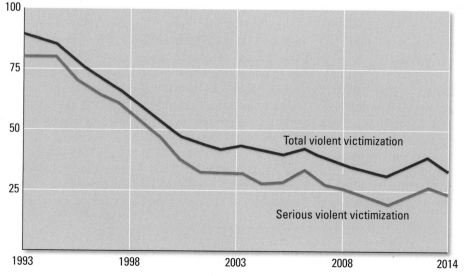

## FIGURE 2.2
### Violent and Property Victimization

**Source:** Lynn Langton and Jennifer L. Truman, *Criminal Victimization, 2014* (Washington, DC: Bureau of Justice Statistics, 2015).

# Policies and Issues in Criminology

## INTERNATIONAL CRIME TRENDS

There has been a marked decline in overall U.S. crime rates, which are now below those of other industrial nations, including England and Wales, Denmark, and Finland. Making international comparisons is often difficult because the legal definitions of crime vary from country to country. There are also differences in the way crime is measured. In the United States, crime may be measured by counting criminal acts reported to the police or by using victim surveys, whereas in many European countries, the number of cases solved by the police is used as the measure of crime. Despite these problems, valid comparisons can still be made about crime across different countries using a number of reliable data sources.

Countries with the highest crime and victimization rate are Ireland, England and Wales, New Zealand, and Iceland. Lowest overall victimization rates are found in Spain, Japan, Hungary, and Portugal. Just as in the United States, there has been a distinct downward trend in the level of crime and victimization during the past decade. Also similarly, some cities have much higher crime rates than others. The cities in developed countries with the lowest victimization rates are Hong Kong, Lisbon, Budapest, Athens, and Madrid; highest victimization rates are found in London and Tallinn, Estonia. Similar to the United States, most of the countries show a distinct downward trend in the level of victimization since 1995. The drops are most pronounced in property crimes such as vehicle-related crimes (bicycle theft, thefts from cars, and joyriding) and burglary. One reason is that people around the world are taking precautions to prevent crime. Improved security may well have been one of the main forces behind the universal drop in crimes such as joyriding and household burglary.

### Homicide

The global average homicide rate is about 6 per 100,000 population, but South Africa and Central America have rates over four times higher than that (above 24 victims per 100,000 population), making them the subregions with the highest homicide rates on record, followed by South America, Central Africa, and the Caribbean (between 16 and 23 homicides per 100,000 population). Subregions with very low homicide rates include Eastern Asia, Southern Europe, and Western Europe. Homicide levels in some countries, such as Brazil, are now stabilizing, and those in South Africa, Russia, and Central Asia are actually decreasing.

### Rape

Southern Africa, Oceania, and North America have the highest recorded rape rates, Asia the lowest. Violence against women is related to economic hardship and the social status of women. Rates are high in poor nations in which women are oppressed. Where women are more emancipated, the rates of violence against women are lower.

For many women, sexual violence starts in childhood and adolescence and may occur in the home, school, and community. Studies conducted in a wide variety of nations ranging from Cameroon to New Zealand found high rates of reported forced sexual initiation. In some nations, as many as half of adolescent women and 20 percent of adolescent men report sexual coercion at the hands of family members, teachers, boyfriends, or strangers.

Sexual violence has significant health consequences, including suicide, stress, mental illnesses, unwanted pregnancies, sexually transmitted diseases, HIV/AIDS, self-inflicted injuries, and (in the case of child sexual abuse) adoption of high-risk behaviors such as multiple sexual partners and drug use.

### Human Trafficking

The crime of trafficking in persons affects virtually every country in every region of the world. Data show that during the two-year period 2010–2012, victims with 152 different citizenships were identified in 124 countries across the globe. Most trafficking is intraregional, meaning that the origin and the destination of the trafficked victim are within the same region of the world. However, in the rich countries of the Middle East, Western Europe, and North America, trafficking victims may be imported from East and South Asia and sub-Saharan Africa. Richer countries attract victims from a variety of origins, including from other continents, whereas less affluent countries are mainly affected by domestic or subregional trafficking.

The most common form of human trafficking is sexual exploitation. The victims of sexual exploitation are predominantly women and girls. The second most common form of human trafficking is forced labor, although this may be a misrepresentation because forced labor is less frequently detected and reported than trafficking for sexual exploitation. Trafficking for exploitation that is neither sexual nor forced labor, including trafficking of children for armed combat or for petty crime or forced begging, is also increasing.

Worldwide, almost 20 percent of all trafficking victims are children. However, in some parts of Africa and Asia, children are the majority (up to 100 percent in parts of West Africa). Although trafficking seems to imply people moving across continents, most exploitation takes place close to home. Data show intraregional and domestic trafficking are the major forms of trafficking in persons.

## Child Abuse

According to the World Health Organization, up to 53,000 children are murdered worldwide each year. Between 80 and 93 percent of children suffer some form of physical punishment in their homes; a third are punished using implements. International studies reveal that approximately 20 percent of women and 5 to 10 percent of men report being sexually abused as children, while 25 to 50 percent of all children report being physically abused. Additionally, many children are subject to emotional abuse (sometimes referred to as psychological abuse) and to neglect.

Every year there are an estimated 31,000 homicide deaths in children under 15. This number underestimates the true extent of the problem, as a significant proportion of deaths due to child maltreatment are incorrectly attributed to falls, burns, drowning, and other causes.

In armed conflict and refugee settings, girls are particularly vulnerable to sexual violence, exploitation, and abuse by combatants, security forces, members of their communities, aid workers, and others.

## Drug Crimes

Drug use continues to exact a significant toll around the world on both human lives and economic productivity. An estimated 183,000 drug-related deaths now occur each year; a mortality rate of 40 deaths per million among the population aged 15 to 64. Globally, it is estimated that between 162 million and 324 million people, corresponding to between 3.5 and 7 percent of the world population aged 15 to 64, used an illicit drug—typically marijuana, opium, cocaine, or amphetamine-type stimulants group—at least once in the previous year. About 40 million people can be considered drug dependent.

Today there is an annual flow of about 450 tons of heroin into the global heroin market. Of that total, opium from Myanmar and the Lao People's Democratic Republic yields some 50 tons, while the rest, some 380 tons of heroin and morphine, is produced in Afghanistan. While approximately 5 tons are consumed and seized in Afghanistan, the remaining bulk of 375 tons is trafficked worldwide. The most common route is through Iran via Pakistan, Turkey, Greece, and Bulgaria, then across southeastern Europe to the Western European market, with an annual market value of some $20 billion. The northern route runs mainly through Tajikistan and Kyrgyzstan (or Uzbekistan or Turkmenistan) to Kazakhstan and the Russian Federation. The size of that market is estimated to total $13 billion per year.

## Critical Thinking

1. Although risk factors at all levels of social and personal life contribute to youth violence, young people in all nations who experience change in societal-level factors—such as economic inequalities, rapid social change, and the availability of firearms, alcohol, and drugs—seem the most likely to get involved in violence. Can anything be done to help alleviate these social problems?

2. The United States is notorious for employing much tougher penal measures than European nations. Do you believe that our tougher measures would work abroad and should be adopted there as well? Is there a downside to putting lots of people in prison?

**Sources:** United Nations Office on Drugs and Crime, *Drug Trafficking, 2014*, www.unodc.org/documents/wdr2014/World _Drug_Report_2014_web.pdf; United Nations Office on Drugs and Crime, *Global Report on Trafficking in Persons, 2014*, www .unodc.org/documents/data-and-analysis/glotip/GLOTIP_2014 _full_report.pdf; United Nations, *Global Studies on Homicide, 2013*, www.unodc.org/gsh/; Stefan Harrendorf, Markku Heiskanen, and Steven Malby, eds., *International Statistics on Crime and Justice*, European Institute for Crime Prevention and Control, Affiliated with the United Nations, www.heuni.fi/Oikeapalsta /Search/1266333832841; UN World Health Organization, *Child Maltreatment, 2014*, www.who.int/mediacentre/factsheets /fs150/en/ (all URLs accessed in 2015).

# Policies and Issues in Criminology

## EXPLAINING TRENDS IN CRIME RATES

Criminologists consider the explanation of crime trends one of their most important goals. Yet when they are asked, "Why have crime rates declined?" or "Why are rates increasing?" they tend to fumble around, mumble, and become lost in thought, because articulating a single explanation for crime rate change has proved elusive. And despite the fact that policy makers and politicians like simple solutions to complex problems, such as getting kids to watch less violence on TV, many different factors contribute to the ebb and flow of crime rates. The interplay of these social, economic, and demographic changes determines the crime rate. Let's look at a few of the most important influences.

### Age Structure

The age composition of the population has a significant influence on crime trends: Teenagers have extremely high crime rates, whereas seniors rarely commit crime. The greater the proportion of teens in the population, the higher the crime rate and the greater the number of persistent offenders. When the baby boomers hit their teen years in the mid-1960s, the crime rate began to increase. Because of better health care, the number of senior citizens is expanding, and the overall population is aging. Since older folks commit less crime, rates should be in decline for quite some time.

### Immigration

Immigration has become one of the most controversial issues in American society, and some people believe that immigrants should be prevented from entering the country because they have a disruptive effect on society. Research suggests the opposite: immigrants as a whole engage in criminal activities less than the general population; the more immigrants in the local population, the lower the crime rate. Violent crime rates, especially those for robbery, tend to *decrease* as metropolitan areas experience gains in their concentration of immigrants. Second-generation immigrants commit more crime, but if anything are merely catching up to their native born contemporaries. If immigration continues, expect it to have a short-term suppressor effect on crime rates, at least until the second generation begins to "catch up."

### Economy/Jobs

Although it seems logical that high unemployment should increase crime rates and that a good economy should reduce criminal activity, especially theft-related crimes, there is actually little evidence linking crime rates and the economy. The official crime rates have declined during periods of high unemployment and a poor economy (2000–2011), while increasing in others (the Depression era). They have also increased during periods of relative economic prosperity (the 1960s). Some crime experts believe that a poor economy actually helps lower crime rates because unemployed parents are at home to supervise children and guard their possessions. Since there is less to spend, a poor economy reduces the number of valuables worth stealing. And it is unlikely that law-abiding, middle-aged workers will suddenly turn to a life of crime if they are laid off during an economic downturn. Of course, a poor economy hurts some people more than others and if there is a long period of economic downturn, crime rates may eventually be impacted.

### Abortion

There is evidence that the recent drop in the crime rate can be attributed to the availability of legalized abortion. In 1973, *Roe v. Wade* legalized abortion nationwide, and the drop in crime rate began approximately 18 years later, in 1991. Crime rates began to decline when the first groups of potential offenders affected by the abortion decision began reaching the peak age of criminal activity. It is possible that the link between crime rates and abortion is the result of two mechanisms: (1) selective abortion on the part of women most at risk to have children who would engage in criminal activity, and (2) improved child rearing or environmental circumstances caused by better maternal, familial, or fetal care because women are having fewer children. If abortion is made illegal once again, crime rates may eventually rise.

### Gun Availability

As the number of guns in the population increases, so too do violent crime rates. As the number of gun-toting people increases, so does the seriousness of violent crime, because a fight between gun-toting people can easily turn into murder. Tighter gun control laws would reduce murder rates.

### Gang Membership

According to government sources, there are now about 850,000 gang members in the United States. Criminal gangs commit as much as 80 percent of the crime in many communities, including armed robbery, assault, auto theft, drug trafficking, extortion, fraud, home invasions, identity theft, murder, and weapons trafficking. Gang members are far more likely to possess guns than those not affiliated with gangs; criminal activity increases when kids join gangs. If gangs continue to grow, so too may crime rates.

## Drug Use

As drug use increases, crime rates increase. The surge in violent crime in the 1980s has been tied directly to the crack cocaine epidemic that swept the nation's largest cities. When crack use declined in urban areas after 1991, so too did crime rates. A sudden increase in drug use may be a harbinger of future increases in the crime rate, especially if guns are easily obtained and the economy is weak. But so far drug use rates have remained relatively stable.

## Media

The jury is still out, but some experts believe that violent media can influence the direction of crime rates. As the availability of media with a violent theme skyrocketed with the introduction of home video players, DVDs, cable TV, and computer and video games, teen violence rates increased as well. However, crime rates have been in decline though the media thrives on providing violent programming.

## Medical Technology

Some crime experts believe that the presence and quality of health care can have a significant impact on murder rates. The big breakthrough occurred in the 1970s, when technology that was developed to treat injured soldiers in Vietnam was applied to trauma care in the nation's hospitals. Ever since then, fluctuations in the murder rate have been linked to the level and availability of emergency medical services.

## Aggressive Law Enforcement

Reductions in crime rates may be attributed to adding large numbers of police officers and using them in aggressive police practices that target "quality of life" crimes, such as panhandling, graffiti, petty drug dealing, and loitering. By showing that even the smallest infractions will be dealt with seriously, aggressive police departments may be able to discourage potential criminals from committing more serious crimes. Cities that encourage aggressive, focused police work may be able to lower homicide rates in the area. Not all experts believe that aggressive policing can work, and others caution against the collateral damage to community relations produced by hardline police tactics that require patrol officers to stop, search, and question community residents on a routine basis.

## Incarceration

It is also possible that tough laws imposing lengthy prison terms on drug dealers and repeat offenders can affect crime rates. The fear of punishment may inhibit some would-be criminals, and placing a significant number of potentially high-rate offenders behind bars seems to help lower crime rates. As the nation's prison population has expanded, the crime rate has fallen. Even though putting people in prison may have a short-term positive effect on crime rates, in the long run, increasing punishments may backfire. The recidivism rate of paroled inmates is quite high, and about two-thirds of those released from state custody will eventually return to prison.

## Cultural Change

In contemporary society, cultural change, such as increases in the number of single-parent families, in high school dropout rates, in racial conflict, and in teen pregnancies, can affect crime rates.

## Internet

The number of cybercrimes seems to be expanding yearly. It is possible that official crime rates will drop even further as former thieves and burglars turn to Internet fraud schemes that are not counted in the official statistics. Prostitution arrests have been in sharp decline as Internet hookup sites are now being used to arrange "dates," a method safer from police interference than streetwalking.

### Critical Thinking

1. If crime rates are influenced by economic conditions, does it mean that criminals are rational decision makers who will choose to commit crime if the need arises?

2. Gang membership is linked to crime rates. Would effective crime control involve convincing perspective gang bangers that crime does not pay and offering them alternative methods for economic gain, such as job training and vocational education?

**Sources:** Bianca Bersani, "A Game of Catch-Up? The Offending Experience of Second-Generation Immigrants," *Crime and Delinquency* 60 (2014): 60–84; David Weisburd, Cody Telep, and Brian Lawton, "Could Innovations in Policing Have Contributed to the New York City Crime Drop Even in a Period of Declining Police Strength? The Case of Stop, Question and Frisk as a Hot Spots Policing Strategy," *Justice Quarterly* 31 (2014): 129–153; Richard Rosenfeld and Robert Fornango, "The Impact of Police Stops on Precinct Robbery and Burglary Rates in New York City, 2003–2010," *Justice Quarterly* 31 (2014): 96–122; Patricia L. McCall, Kenneth Land, Cindy Brooks Dollar, and Karen F. Parker, "The Age Structure–Crime Rate Relationship: Solving a Long-Standing Puzzle," *Journal of Quantitative Criminology* 29 (2013): 167–190; Tim Wadsworth, "Is Immigration Responsible for the Crime Drop? An Assessment of the Influence of Immigration on Changes in Violent Crime Between 1990 and 2000," *Social Science Quarterly* 91 (2010): 531–553; Jeremy Staff, D. Wayne Osgood, John Schulenberg, Jerald Bachman, and Emily Messersmith, "Explaining the Relationship Between Employment and Juvenile Delinquency," *Criminology* 48 (2010): 1101–1131; Jacob Stowell, Steven Messner, Kelly McGeever, and Lawrence Raffalovich, "Immigration and the Recent Violent Crime Drop in the United States: A Pooled Cross-Sectional Time-Series Analysis of Metropolitan Areas," *Criminology* 47 (2009): 889–928; John J. Donohue and Steven D. Levitt, "The Impact of Legalized Abortion on Crime," *Quarterly Journal of Economics* 116 (2001): 379–420.

## Predicting Future Crime Trends

Speculating about the future of crime trends is risky because current conditions can change rapidly, but some criminologists have tried to predict future patterns. There are approximately 50 million school-age children in the United States (ages 6–17), and about half are ages 6–11; this is a greater number than we have had for decades. Many come from stable homes, but some lack stable families and adequate supervision. These children will soon enter their prime crime years, and as a result, crime rates may increase in the future. However, whereas kids increase crime rates, the rising number of senior citizens helps bring rates down. Even if teens commit more crime in the future, their contribution may be offset by the aging of the population, which will produce a large number of senior citizens and elderly, a group with a relatively low crime rate.

Predicting the future is always fun, but there is, of course, no telling what changes are in store that may influence crime rates either up or down. Technological developments such as e-commerce on the Internet have created new classes of crime. Social conflict such as the recent highly publicized spate of police shootings on Staten Island, New York (Eric Garner), Ferguson, Missouri (Michael Brown), and Baltimore, Maryland (Freddy Gray) and the ongoing tension between police and the public may eventually impact on crime rates. Some commentators and pundits have suggested that the murder rate may be headed upward.[19] So it is too early to predict that the downward trend in the crime rate will continue unabated into the foreseeable future. The Policies and Issues in Criminology feature on page 42 discusses the factors that shape crime trends.

## Crime Patterns

Criminologists look for stable crime-rate patterns to gain insight into the nature of crime. The cause of crime may be better understood by examining the rate. If criminal statistics consistently show that crime rates are higher in poor

**L04**  Identify the gender and racial patterns in crime.

Gang crime plays a significant role in determining the direction of national crime rates. This composite image shows scores of men and women arrested and charged with crimes stemming from a large shootout and fight between biker gangs outside the Twin Peaks bar and restaurant at the Central Texas Marketplace in Waco, Texas, on May 17, 2015. Nine bikers were shot and killed and 18 others wounded. In the aftermath of the bloodbath, almost 200 people were facing charges of engaging in organized crime.

Mclennan County Sheriff/EPA/Landov

neighborhoods in large urban areas, the cause of crime may be related to poverty and neighborhood decline. If, in contrast, crime rates are spread evenly across society, and rates are equal in poor and affluent neighborhoods, this would provide little evidence that crime has an economic basis. Instead, crime might be linked to socialization, personality, intelligence, or some other trait unrelated to class position or income. In this section, we examine traits and patterns that may influence the crime rate.

## Co-Offending and Crime

It is generally accepted that crime tends to be a group activity and that adolescents, in particular, are overwhelmingly likely to commit crime in groups. Peer support encourages offending in adolescence.[20] Rather than being shunned by their peers, antisocial adolescents enjoy increased social status among peers who admire their risk-taking behaviors.[21]

Not all offenders enjoy being part of a group or gang; many are lone wolves who shun peer involvement.[22] Because co-offending requires offenders to cooperate with one another in a risky endeavor, it is more likely to occur in communities that contain a supply of appropriate criminal associates who can keep their mouth shut and never cooperate with police. Co-offending is more prevalent in neighborhoods that are less disadvantaged, more stable, and contain more people who can be trusted. Ironically, this means that efforts to improve neighborhood stability and cohesiveness may also help produce an environment that encourages group offending.[23]

## Gender and Crime

Male crime rates are much higher than those of females. The most recent Uniform Crime Report arrest statistics indicate that males account for about 80 percent of all arrests for serious violent crimes and more than 60 percent of the arrests for serious property crimes. Murder arrests are 8 males to 1 female. Even though gender differences in the crime rate have persisted over time, there seems little question that females are now involved in many serious criminal activities and that there are more similarities than differences between male and female offenders.[24] UCR arrest data show that over the past decade, while male arrest rates have declined by 18 percent, female arrest rates have been more stable, declining by 5 percent. Female arrest rates have actually increased for the crimes of robbery, burglary, and larceny during the past decade, while male rates have undergone a decline. Nonetheless, as measured by the arrest data, gender differences in the crime rate still persist. How can these persistent differences be explained?

**TRAIT DIFFERENCES** Early criminologists pointed to emotional, physical, and psychological differences between males and females to explain the differences in crime rates. They maintained that because females were weaker and more passive, they were less likely to commit crimes. Cesare Lombroso argued that a small group of female criminals lacked "typical" female traits of "piety, maternity, undeveloped

A great deal of crime, especially juvenile delinquency, occurs in groups, a phenomenon known as co-offending. On June 2, 2015, vandals inside Chesapeake High School in Pasadena, Maryland, caused thousands of dollars in property damage. Would a lone offender vandalize a school or is this a group experience produced and supported by peer pressure?

intelligence, and weakness."[25] Lombroso's theory became known as the **masculinity hypothesis**; in essence, a few "masculine" females were responsible for the handful of crimes that women committed.[26]

Although these early writings are no longer taken seriously, some criminologists still consider trait differences a key determinant of crime rate differences. They link antisocial behavior to hormonal influences by arguing that male sex hormones (androgens) account for the more aggressive male behavior; thus, gender-related hormonal differences can explain the gender gap in the crime rate.[27]

**masculinity hypothesis**
The view that women who commit crimes have biological and psychological traits similar to those of men.

**liberal feminist theory**
A view of crime that suggests that the social and economic role of women in society controls their crime rates.

**SOCIALIZATION DIFFERENCES** Although there are few gender-based differences in aggression during the first few years of life, girls are socialized to be less aggressive than boys and are supervised more closely by parents. Males are taught to be more aggressive and assertive and are less likely to form attachments to others. They may seek approval by knocking down or running through peers on the playing field, while females literally cheer them on.[28] Male perceptions of power, their relative freedom, and their ability to hang with their friends help explain the gender differences in crime and delinquency.

**COGNITIVE DIFFERENCES** Psychologists note significant cognitive differences between boys and girls that may affect their antisocial behaviors. Girls have been found to be superior to boys in verbal ability, whereas boys test higher in visual-spatial performance. Girls acquire language faster, learning to speak earlier and with better pronunciation. Their superior verbal skills may enable girls to talk rather than fight. When faced with conflict, women might be more likely to attempt to negotiate, rather than responding passively or resisting physically, especially when they perceive increased threat of harm or death.[29]

**SOCIAL/POLITICAL DIFFERENCES** In the 1970s, **liberal feminist theory** focused attention on the social and economic role of women in society and its relationship to female crime rates.[30] This view suggested that the traditionally lower crime rate for women could be explained by their "second-class" economic and social position. It was assumed that as women's social roles changed and their lifestyles became more like men's, their crime rates would converge.

Criminologists, responding to this research, began to refer to the "new female criminal." The rapid increase in the female crime rate, especially in what had traditionally been male-oriented crimes (such as burglary and larceny), supports the feminist view. In addition, self-report studies seem to indicate that (1) the pattern of female criminality, if not its frequency, is similar to that of male criminality, and (2) the factors that predispose male criminals to crime have an equal impact on female criminals.[31]

Recent trends seem to support the feminist view of crime rate differences. Although male arrest rates are

While women still commit less crime per capita than men, the gap is closing. Here, Katlyn Marin appears via video arraignment on January 5, 2015, in the District Courtroom in Nashua, New Hampshire. Marin was charged with second-degree murder in the beating death of her 3-year-old daughter.

AP Images/Don Himsel

still considerably higher than female rates, the gap is narrowing because male rates are declining at a much faster pace than female rates; it is possible that they may eventually converge. Of course, arrest trends may reflect changing attitudes by police who may be abandoning their traditional deference toward women, resulting in higher female arrest rates.[32] But whatever the reason, the gender gap in crime may be narrowing.

## Race and Crime

There is no more complex and controversial issue than that of race and crime. That is because UCR arrest data indicate that minority group members are involved in a disproportionate share of criminal activity. African Americans make up about 13 percent of the general population, yet they account for about 40 percent of arrests for Part I violent crime and for about 30 percent of property crime arrests. They also are responsible for a disproportionate number of Part II arrests (except for alcohol-related arrests, which involve primarily white offenders).

Self-report studies using large samples also show that about 30 percent of black males have experienced at least one arrest by age 18 (versus about 22 percent for white males), and by age 23 almost half of all black males have been arrested (versus about 38 percent for white males).[33]

Similarly, while data collected by the Monitoring the Future study generally show similarity in offending patterns between African American and European American youths for most crimes, there are some significant differences in reports for some serious offenses, such as stealing more than $50 and robbery, where African American youth do in fact admit more participation in the most serious crimes, a finding that is reflective of the UCR arrest data.[34] How can these differences be explained?

**INSTITUTIONAL BIAS** Racial differences in the arrest rate may be an artifact of institutional bias found in the justice system and not actual differences in criminal activity: police are more likely to stop, search, and arrest racial minorities than they are members of the white majority. Institutional bias creates a vicious cycle: because they are targeted more frequently, young black men are more likely to possess a criminal record; having a criminal record is associated with repeat stops and searches.[35]

The fact that police unfairly target African Americans is so widely accepted that the term **racial profiling** has been used to describe the practice of stopping and searching African Americans without probable cause or reasonable suspicion. Does such racial profiling truly exist? Numerous studies find that minority citizens are more likely to be stopped and searched than a member of the white majority especially if they seem "out of place" (i.e., driving in a white neighborhood).[36] Tammy Rinehart Kochel and her associates recently found significant evidence that minority suspects are more likely to be arrested than white suspects when stopped by police for the same behaviors.[37] Racial profiling may be more common in communities where there are relatively few racial minorities (i.e., "white neighborhoods"). In racially segregated neighborhoods and communities, police may be suspicious of people based on their race if it is inconsistent with the neighborhood racial composition.[38]

Racial profiling creates a cycle of hostility: young black men see their experience with police as unfair or degrading; they approach future encounters with preexisting hostility; police take this as a sign that young black men pose a special danger; they respond with harsh treatment; a never-ending cycle of mutual mistrust is created.[39]

Race-based differences are not confined to the arrest process. A significant body of research shows that bias can be found across the entire justice process.[40] Black and Latino adults are less likely than whites to receive bail in cases of violent crime.[41] African Americans, especially those who are indigent or unemployed, receive longer prison sentences than whites with the same employment status. Recent research conducted in New York City found that when compared to whites, black and Latino defendants were more likely than white defendants to be detained, to be incarcerated,

CONNECTIONS

Critical criminologists view gender inequality as stemming from the unequal power of men and women in a capitalist society and the exploitation of females by fathers and husbands. This perspective is considered more fully in Chapter 8.

**racial profiling**
Police-initiated action directed at a suspect or group of suspects based solely on race.

and if sent to prison to receive especially punitive outcomes, especially if they were convicted of violent crimes. In contrast, Asians received the most lenient treatment in the justice process.[42]

**racial threat hypothesis**
As the size of the black population increases, the perceived threat to the white population increases, resulting in a greater amount of social control imposed on blacks.

**THE RACIAL THREAT HYPOTHESIS** According to the **racial threat hypothesis** as the percentage of African Americans in the population increases, so does the amount of social control imposed on black citizens at every stage of the justice system, from arrest to final release.[43] The source of racial threat begins when white residents overestimate the proportion of minorities living in their neighborhood, a circumstance that leads to false perceptions of disorder.[44] When fear grips an area, police are more likely to aggressively patrol minority areas; suspect, search, and arrest minority group members; and make arrests for minor infractions, helping to raise the minority crime rate. As perceptions of racial threat increases, so too does the demand for greater law enforcement protection: the greater the perception of racial threat, the larger the community's police department.[45] The result is a stepped-up effort to control and punish minority citizens, which segregates minorities from the economic mainstream and reinforces the physical and social isolation of the minority community.

**STRUCTURAL RACISM** Another assumed source of racial differences in the crime rate is the racial discrimination that has pervaded American society for hundreds of years and has resulted in economic and social disparity. Racial and ethnic minorities face a greater degree of social isolation and economic deprivation than the white majority.[46] Many black youths are forced to attend essentially segregated schools that are underfunded and run-down, a condition that elevates the likelihood of their being incarcerated in adulthood.[47]

In the minority community, family dissolution may be tied to low employment rates among African American males, which places a strain on marriages.[48] When families are weakened or disrupted, social control over their children is compromised.[49]

In sum, racial differences in the crime rate have been linked to institutional and structural differences in society.[50] If racial and ethnic disparity in the application of justice and the distribution of social and economic resources were to end, crime rate differences between the races would evaporate.[51]

Spencer Platt/Getty Images News/Getty Images

Critics of the New York City Police Department (NYPD) stop-and-frisk policy celebrate after City Council members voted to establish an inspector general for the New York Police Department (NYPD) weeks after a federal judge ruled that the NYPD violated the civil rights of minorities with their stop-and-frisk policy. U.S. District Court Judge Shira Scheindlin ordered a monitor to focus on stop-and-frisk, a policy she declared that the department has used in a manner that violated the rights of hundreds of thousands of black and Hispanic men. After numerous appeals and years of court process, on October 31, 2014, a three-judge panel on the Second Circuit unanimously allowed the city to proceed with its overhaul of the police department policies.

## The Ecology of Crime

Patterns in the crime rate seem to be linked to temporal and ecological factors. Some of the most important of these are discussed here.

**DAY, SEASON, AND CLIMATE** Most reported crimes occur during the warm summer months of July and August. During the summer, teenagers, who usually have the highest crime levels, are out of school and have greater opportunity to commit crime. People spend more time outdoors during warm weather, making themselves easier targets. Similarly, homes are left vacant more often during the summer, making them more vulnerable to property crimes. Two exceptions to this trend are murders and robberies, which occur frequently in December and January (although rates are also high during the summer). One reason: robberies are more likely to take place when it gets dark out, something that occurs earlier in winter months (in the United States and Europe, at least).[52]

Crime rates also may be higher on the first day of the month than at any other time. Government welfare and Social Security checks arrive at this time, and with them come increases in such activities as breaking into mailboxes and accosting recipients on the streets. Also, people may have more disposable income at this time, and the availability of extra money may encourage behaviors associated with crime, such as drinking, partying, and gambling.[53]

**TEMPERATURE**  Weather effects (such as temperature swings) may have an impact on violent crime rates. Traditionally, the association between temperature and crime was thought to resemble an inverted U-shaped curve: crime rates increase with rising temperatures and then begin to decline at some point (85 degrees) when it may be too hot for any physical exertion.[54] However, criminologists continue to debate this issue:

- Some believe that crime rates rise with temperature (the hotter the day, the higher the crime rate).[55]
- Others have found evidence that the curvilinear model is correct.[56]
- Some research shows that a rising temperature causes some crimes (such as domestic assault) to continually increase, whereas other crimes (such as rape) decline after temperatures rise to an extremely high level.[57]

If, in fact, there is an association between temperature and crime, can it be explained? The relationship may be due to the stress and tension caused by extreme temperature. The human body generates stress hormones (adrenaline and testosterone) in response to excessive heat, and such hormonal activity has been linked to aggression.[58] Or as Shakespeare put it, "For now, these hot days, is the mad blood stirring."[59]

**REGIONAL DIFFERENCES**  Large urban areas have by far the highest violence rates; rural areas have the lowest per capita crime rates. Exceptions to this trend are low-population resort areas with large transient or seasonal populations that typically have higher crime rates than the norm; this phenomenon has been observed in the United States and abroad.[60]

Typically, the western and southern states have had consistently higher crime rates than the Midwest and Northeast. This pattern has convinced some criminologists that regional cultural values influence crime rates. At one time criminologists believed there was a "southern subculture of violence" that linked high violence rates among Southerners to their keen sense of honor that compelled them to use force to defend their name, family, and property. However, recent research suggests that the southern subculture hypothesis is merely myth and Southerners are no more likely to fight for their honor than people in any other area.[61] It's more likely that regional differences can be explained by economic and demographic disparities and not macho cultural values.

## Use of Firearms

Firearms play a dominant role in criminal activity. According to the NCVS, firearms are typically involved in about 20 percent of robberies, 10 percent of assaults, and more than 5 percent of rapes. According to the UCR, about 70 percent of all murders involve firearms; most of these weapons are handguns. Criminals of all races and ethnic backgrounds are equally likely to use guns in violent attacks, and the presence of a weapon increases the likelihood that a violent incident will result in serious injury and/or death.[62]

**FACT OR FICTION?**

Immigrants who are in the United States illegally commit a lot of crime, a fact that justifies limiting immigration and closing down the borders.

**FICTION** Immigrants, whether they are in this country legally or illegally, have very low crime rates. Immigration helps reduce crime rates.

**CONNECTIONS**

Using guns to fight back against victimization is discussed in more detail in Chapter 3. Would you carry a concealed weapon if research showed that armed people are less likely to become crime victims?

**resource deprivation**
The consequence of a lack of income and other resources, which cumulatively, leads to poverty.

**instrumental crimes**
Offenses designed to improve the financial or social position of the criminal.

**expressive crimes**
Offenses committed not for profit or gain but to vent rage, anger, or frustration.

Because of these findings, there is an ongoing debate over gun control. Some criminologists staunchly favor gun control. Franklin Zimring and Gordon Hawkins believe that the proliferation of handguns and the high rate of lethal violence they cause is the single most significant factor separating the crime problem in the United States from that in the rest of the developed world.[63] Differences between the United States and Europe in nonlethal crimes are modest at best and are getting smaller over time.[64]

In contrast, some criminologists, particularly Gary Kleck, believe that personal gun use can actually be a deterrent to crime and that guns "almost certainly" save lives. While guns are involved in murders, suicides, and accidents, Kleck believes the benefit of guns as a crime prevention device should not be overlooked and that at least 18 national surveys have consistently confirmed that defensive gun usage by potential victims is very common, probably more common than criminal uses of guns.[65] Needless to say, this remains a very controversial issue.

## Social Class and Crime

Crime is often considered a lower-class phenomenon: people living in inner-city, high-poverty areas are generally more likely to join gangs, sell drugs, and commit crimes than those residing in wealthy suburban areas. Neighborhoods experiencing income inequality, lack of informal social controls, and **resource deprivation** have crime rates significantly higher than those that can provide economic opportunities for their residents.[66] When these conditions exist, youth gangs flourish, resulting in high rates of the most serious violent crimes, including homicide and assault.[67]

It makes logical sense that crime is a lower-class phenomenon. After all, indigent people at the lowest rungs of the social structure, who are unable to obtain desired goods and services through conventional means, have the greatest incentive to commit crime. Their motivation comes from a lack of real opportunity in lower-class communities. As manufacturing moves overseas, less educated, untrained young males are frozen out of the legitimate job market and instead turn to gain through participation in illegal markets: selling drugs is generally more profitable than washing cars or working in a fast-food restaurant. However, when the economy turns around, drug dealers do not suddenly quit the trade and get a job with GE or IBM. As criminologist Shawn Bushway points out, lack of entry into legitimate labor markets creates incentives for teens and adolescents to participate in illegal activities.[68]

Some of them commit **instrumental crimes**, illegal acts whose goal is to provide desired goods and services that cannot be obtained through legitimate economic means; others get involved in **expressive crimes**, such as rape and assault, that express their rage, frustration, and anger against society; and some commit both kinds of crime. In contrast, when middle- and upper-class people commit crime, it's typically nonviolent, business-related, white-collar crimes that do not threaten the public or produce fear and anxiety.

Not all criminologists accept the class–crime association at face value. An alternative explanation is that the relationship between crime and social class is a function of law enforcement practices, not actual criminal behavior patterns. Police may devote more resources to poor areas, and consequently apprehension and arrest rates may be higher in these communities, giving a false picture of the true class–crime association. Prosecutors may be more likely to file charges against the poor, while handling cases involving the middle class informally, a practice which accounts for the overrepresentation of the lower class in the prison population.[69] And people in the middle and upper classes may commit white-collar crimes that are rarely detected or enforced.

## Unemployment and Crime

It stands to reason that crime rates should correlate with unemployment rates, peaking during tough economic times when people are out of work and money is tight. Unemployed people may feel frustrated and discouraged, leading not only to an increase in property crimes but to angry aggression and violence. Research has linked unemployment rates to higher crime rates, especially when the government does not provide sufficient economic support such as welfare and unemployment benefits.[70]

While this association seems logical, there is a great deal of conflicting research, some of which shows that the two factors are only weakly related: crime rates sometimes rise during periods of high employment and fall during periods when people are out of work.

How can the weak association be explained? One reason is that during times of full employment more people are being hired, including teens, and young people with after-school jobs, unsupervised by parents, who earn wages that they can spend on themselves, are more likely to engage in antisocial activities such as drinking and drug usage.[71] In contrast, when unemployment rates are high, jobless parents are at home to supervise teenagers reducing their opportunity to commit crimes. Also when people are unemployed, they have less money on hand and purchase fewer things worth stealing; they are also home to guard their meager possessions. They may even sell their valuables to raise cash to pay off debts, reducing suitable targets for burglars and thieves.

**L05** Clarify what is meant by the term *aging-out process.*

## Age and Crime

There is general agreement that age is inversely related to criminality. Criminologists Travis Hirschi and Michael Gottfredson state that "Age is everywhere correlated with crime. Its effects on crime do not depend on other demographic correlates of crime."[72]

Regardless of economic status, marital status, race, sex, and other factors, younger people commit crime more often than older people, and this relationship has been stable across time.[73] Official statistics tell us that young people are arrested at a rate disproportionate to their numbers in the population; victim surveys generate similar findings for crimes in which assailant age can be determined. As a general rule, the peak age for property crime is believed to be 16, and for violence, 18. The 10-to-24 age group make up about 21 percent of the population but commit 39 percent of serious violent crimes and 45 percent of all property crimes. In contrast, the elderly are particularly resistant to the temptations of crime. Elderly males 65 and over are predominantly arrested for alcohol-related matters (such as public drunkenness and drunk driving) and elderly females for larceny (such as shoplifting).

**AGING OUT OF CRIME** Criminologists agree that people commit less crime as they age.[74] Crime peaks in adolescence and then declines rapidly thereafter.

Most illegal acts are committed by teens who eventually age out of crime and become responsible adults. Kayla Hassall, 16 (center), one of five teenagers accused of beating fellow teen Victoria N. Lindsay, tries to contain her emotions as she sits in court prior to a plea hearing in Bartow, Florida. On the left is her father, Jeff Hassall, and to the right is her mother, Kari Hassall. Kayla Hassall and April Cooper were among the teens accused of attacking a 16-year-old girl. The attack was recorded on video and seen around the world via the Internet and TV. She received one year of juvenile probation for her crime.

AP Images/Michael Wilson/Pool

**LO6** Define the concept of chronic offending and know its causes.

**aging out**
Phrase used to express the fact that people commit less crime as they mature.

**chronic offenders (career criminals)**
The small group of persistent offenders who account for a majority of all criminal offenses.

In modern, industrial societies adolescents are given most of the privileges and responsibilities of adults but also experience less supervision and fewer responsibilities, which can result in a reduced ability to cope in a legitimate manner and increased incentive to solve problems in a criminal manner.[75] Young people tend to discount the future.[76] They are impatient, and because their future is uncertain, they are unwilling or unable to delay gratification. As they mature, troubled youths are able to develop a long-term life view and resist the need for immediate gratification.[77]

**Aging out** of crime may also be a function of the natural history of the human life cycle.[78] Deviance in adolescence is fueled by the need for money and sex and is reinforced by close relationships with peers who defy conventional morality. At the same time, teenagers are becoming independent from parents and other adults who enforce conventional standards of morality and behavior. They have a new sense of energy and strength and are involved with peers who are similarly vigorous and frustrated. Adults, on the other hand, develop the ability to delay gratification and forgo the immediate gains that law violations bring. They also start wanting to take responsibility for their behavior and to adhere to conventional mores, such as establishing long-term relationships and starting a family.[79] Some criminologists now believe that the key to desistance and aging out is linked to human biology. Levels of hormones and brain chemicals ebb and flow over the life course. During adolescence, dopamine increases while serotonin is reduced; in adulthood, dopamine levels recede while serotonin levels become elevated. It is possible that these biological changes influence behavioral choices.[80]

While the age–crime association is a key element of criminology, the association may soon have to be rethought. Though teens are still very active in crime, according to the most recent UCR data the arrest rate for teens dropped 37 percent since 2003, while adult arrests dropped only 3 percent, evening out the gap between adult and teen official crime rates. If these trends continue, the rates will eventually converge, calling into question the age–crime association.

## Chronic Offenders/Criminal Careers

Crime data show that most offenders commit a single criminal act and, upon arrest, discontinue their antisocial activity. Others commit a few less serious crimes. A small group of criminal offenders, however, account for a majority of all criminal offenses. These persistent offenders are referred to as **career criminals** or **chronic offenders**. The concept of the chronic, or career, offender is most closely associated with the research efforts of Marvin Wolfgang, Robert Figlio, and Thorsten Sellin.[81] In their landmark 1972 study *Delinquency in a Birth Cohort*, they used official records to follow the criminal careers of 9,945 boys born in Philadelphia in 1945 from the time of their birth until they reached 18 years of age in 1963. Official police records were used to identify delinquents. About one-third of the boys (3,475) had some police contact. The remaining two-thirds (6,470) had none. Each delinquent was given a seriousness weight score for every delinquent act.[82] The weighting of delinquent acts enabled the researchers to differentiate between a simple assault requiring no medical attention for the victim and serious battery in which the victim needed hospitalization. The best-known discovery of Wolfgang and his associates was that of the so-called chronic offender. The cohort data indicated that 54 percent (1,862) of the sample's delinquent youths were repeat offenders, whereas the remaining 46 percent (1,613) were one-time offenders. The repeaters could be further categorized as nonchronic recidivists and chronic recidivists. The former consisted of 1,235 youths who had been arrested more than once but fewer than five times and who made up 35.6 percent of all delinquents. The latter were a group of 627 boys arrested five times or more, who accounted for 18 percent of the delinquents and 6 percent of the total sample of 9,945.

The chronic offenders (known today as "the chronic 6 percent") were involved in the most dramatic amounts of delinquent behavior. They were responsible for 5,305 offenses, or 52 percent of all the offenses committed by the cohort. Even more strik-ing was the involvement of chronic offenders in serious criminal acts. The chronic 6 percent committed 71 percent of the homicides, 73 percent of the rapes, 82 percent of the robberies, and 69 percent of the aggravated assaults.

Wolfgang and his associates found that arrests and court experience did little to de-ter the chronic offender. In fact, punishment was inversely related to chronic offending: the more stringent the sanction chronic offenders received, the more likely they were to engage in repeated criminal behavior.

In a second cohort study, Wolfgang and his associates selected a new, larger birth cohort born in Philadelphia in 1958, which contained both male and female subjects.[83] Although the proportion of delinquent youths was about the same as that in the 1945 cohort, the researchers again found a similar pattern of chronic of-fending. Chronic female delinquency was relatively rare—only 1 percent of the fe-males in the survey were chronic offenders. Wolfgang's pioneering effort to identify the chronic career offender has been replicated by a number of other researchers in a variety of locations in the United States.[84] The chronic offender has also been found abroad.[85]

## What Causes Chronicity?

Criminologists believe that chronic offenders tend to be at-risk youth who are ex-posed to a variety of personal and social problems and who begin their law breaking at a very early age—a phenomenon referred to as **early onset**.[86] Research studies have also linked chronicity to relatively low intellectual development and to parental involvement in drugs.[87]

## Implications of the Chronic Offender Concept

The findings of the cohort studies and the discovery of the chronic offender revi-talized criminological theory. If relatively few offenders become chronic criminals, perhaps chronic offenders possess some individual trait that is responsible for their behavior. Most people exposed to troublesome social conditions, such as poverty, do not become chronic offenders, so it is unlikely that social conditions alone can cause chronic offending. Traditional theories of criminal behavior have failed to distinguish between chronic and occasional offenders. They concentrate more on explaining why people begin to commit crime and pay scant attention to why people stop offending. The discovery of the chronic offender 40 years ago forced criminologists to consider such issues as persistence and desistance in their explanations of crime; more recent theories account not only for the onset of criminality but also for its termination.

The chronic offender has become a central focus of crime control policy. Ap-prehension and punishment seem to have little effect on the offending behavior of chronic offenders, and most repeat their criminal acts after their release from cor-rections.[88] Because chronic offenders rarely learn from their mistakes, sentencing policies designed to incapacitate chronic offenders for long periods without hope of probation or parole have been established. Incapacitation rather than rehabilitation is the goal. Among the policies spurred by the chronic offender concept are man-datory sentences for violent or drug-related crimes; **three-strikes policies**, which require people convicted of a third felony offense to serve a mandatory life sen-tence; and truth-in-sentencing policies, which require that convicted felons spend a significant portion of their sentence behind bars. It remains to be seen whether such policies can reduce crime rates or are merely get-tough measures designed to placate conservative voters.

**early onset**
The view that repeat offenders begin their criminal careers at a very young age.

**three-strikes policies**
Laws that require offenders to serve life in prison after they are convicted of a third felony.

# Thinking Like a Criminologist

**Rough Justice**    The planning director for the State Department of Juvenile Justice has asked for your advice on how to reduce the threat of chronic offenders. Some of the more conservative members of her staff seem to believe that these kids need a strict dose of rough justice if they are to be turned away from a life of crime. They believe juvenile delinquents who are punished harshly are less likely to recidivate than youths who receive lesser punishments, such as community corrections or probation. In addition, they believe that hard-core, violent offenders deserve to be punished; excessive concern for offenders, and not enough concern for their acts, ignores the rights of victims and of society in general.

The planning director is unsure whether such an approach can reduce the threat of chronic offending. She is concerned that a strategy stressing punishment will have relatively little impact on chronic offenders and, if anything, may cause escalation in their serious criminal behaviors. She has asked you for your professional advice.

## Writing Assignment

Write an essay explaining both sides of the issue, comparing the potential effects of stigma and labeling with the need for control and security. Explain how you would handle chronic offenders, and tie your answer to the aging-out process.

# SUMMARY

**L01**    **Discuss the various forms of crime data.**

The Federal Bureau of Investigation collects data from local law enforcement agencies and publishes that information yearly in its Uniform Crime Report (UCR). The National Incident-Based Reporting System (NIBRS) is a program that collects data on each reported crime incident. The National Crime Victimization Survey (NCVS) is a nationwide survey of victimization in the United States. Self-report surveys ask people to describe, in detail, their recent and lifetime participation in criminal activity.

**L02**    **Analyze recent trends in the crime rate.**

Crime rates peaked in 1991, when police recorded almost 15 million crimes. Since then the number of crimes tallied by the FBI has been in a steep decline. In addition, NCVS data show that criminal victimizations have declined significantly during the past 40 years: in 1973, an estimated 44 million victimizations were recorded, compared to about 20 million today, a drop of nearly 50 percent.

**L03**    **List the factors that influence crime rates.**

The age composition of the population, the number of immigrants, the availability of legalized abortion, the number of guns, drug use, availability of emergency medical services, numbers of police officers, the state of the economy, cultural change, and criminal opportunities all influence crime rates.

**L04**    **Identify the gender and racial patterns in crime.**

Male crime rates are much higher than those of females. Gender differences in the crime rate have persisted over time, but there is little question that females are now involved in more crime than ever before and that there are more similarities than differences between male and female offenders. Official crime data indicate that minority group members are involved in a disproportionate share of criminal activity. Racial and ethnic differentials in crime rates may be tied to economic and social disparity and institutional racism.

**L05  Clarify what is meant by the term *aging-out process*.**

Regardless of economic status, marital status, race, sex, and other factors, younger people commit crime more often than older people, and this relationship has been stable across time. Most criminologists agree that people commit less crime as they age.

**L06  Define the concept of chronic offending and know its causes.**

The concept of the chronic, or career, offender is most closely associated with the research efforts of Marvin Wolfgang, Robert Figlio, and Thorsten Sellin. Chronic offenders are involved in significant amounts of delinquent behavior and tend later to become adult criminals. Unlike most offenders, they do not age out of crime. The cause of chronic offending has been linked to a variety of personal and social problems, and those who begin their lawbreaking at an early age are the most at risk to repeat offending. Chronic offenders often have problems in the home and at school, relatively low intellectual development, and parental drug involvement.

# Key Terms

Uniform Crime Report (UCR) 30
Part I crimes 30
murder and nonnegligent manslaughter 30
forcible rape 30
robbery 30
aggravated assault 30
burglary 30

larceny 30
motor vehicle theft 31
arson 31
Part II crimes 31
National Incident-Based Reporting System (NIBRS) 32
sampling 33
population 33

National Crime Victimization Survey (NCVS) 33
self-report survey 34
masculinity hypothesis 46
liberal feminist theory 46
racial profiling 47
racial threat hypothesis 48

resource deprivation 50
instrumental crimes 50
expressive crimes 50
aging out 52
chronic offenders (career criminals) 52
early onset 53
three-strikes policies 53

# Critical Thinking Questions

1. Would you answer honestly if a national crime survey asked you about your criminal behavior, including drinking and drug use? If not, why not? If you would not answer honestly, do you question the accuracy of self-report surveys?

2. How would you explain gender differences in the crime rate? Why do you think males are more violent than females?

3. Assuming that males are more violent than females, does that mean crime has a biological rather than a social basis (because males and females share a similar environment)?

4. The UCR reports that crime rates are higher in large cities than in small towns. What does that tell us about the effects of TV, films, and music on teenage behavior?

5. What social and environmental factors do you believe influence the crime rate?

6. Do you think a national emergency would increase or decrease crime rates?

# Notes

*All URLs accessed in 2015.*

1. Data in this chapter are from Federal Bureau of Investigation, *Crime in the United States, 2013* (Washington, DC: U.S. Government Printing Office, 2014), www.fbi.gov/about-us/cjis/ucr/crime-in-the-u.s/2013/crime-in-the-u.s.-2013.

2. Min Xie, "Area Differences and Time Trends in Crime Reporting: Comparing New York with Other Metropolitan Areas" *Justice Quarterly* 31 (2014): 43–73.

3. National Incident-Based Reporting System (NIBRS), General Information, www.fbi.gov/about-us/cjis/ucr/nibrs/2013.

4. Data in this section are from Lynn Langton and Jennifer L. Truman, *Criminal Victimization, 2014* (Washington, DC: Bureau of Justice Statistics, 2015).

5. Marcus Berzofsky, Chris Krebs, Lynn Langton, and Hope Smiley-McDonald, "Victimizations Not Reported to the Police, 2006–2010," Bureau of Justice Statistics, August 9, 2012, bjs.ojp.usdoj.gov/index.cfm?ty=pbdetail&iid=4393.

6. A pioneering effort in self-report research is A. L. Porterfield, *Youth in Trouble* (Fort Worth, TX: Leo Potishman Foundation, 1946).

7. See John Paul Wright and Francis Cullen, "Juvenile Involvement in Occupational Delinquency," *Criminology* 38 (2000): 863–896.

8. Christiane Brems, Mark Johnson, David Neal, and Melinda Freemon, "Childhood Abuse History and Substance Use Among Men and Women Receiving Detoxification Services," *American Journal of Drug and Alcohol Abuse* 30 (2004): 799–821.

9. Leonore Simon, "Validity and Reliability of Violent Juveniles: A Comparison of Juvenile Self-Reports with Adult Self-Reports Incarcerated in Adult Prisons," paper presented at the annual meeting of the American Society of Criminology, Boston, November 1995, p. 26.

10. Stephen Cernkovich, Peggy Giordano, and Meredith Pugh, "Chronic Offenders: The Missing Cases in Self-Report Delinquency Research," *Journal of Criminal Law and Criminology* 76 (1985): 705–732.

11. Terence Thornberry, Beth Bjerregaard, and William Miles, "The Consequences of Respondent Attrition in Panel Studies: A Simulation Based on the Rochester Youth Development Study," *Journal of Quantitative Criminology* 9 (1993): 127–158.

12. Alex R. Piquero, Carol A. Schubert, and Robert Brame, "Comparing Official and Self-Report Records of Offending Across Gender and Race/Ethnicity in a Longitudinal Study of Serious Youthful Offenders," *Journal of Research in Crime and Delinquency* 51 (2014): 526–556.

13. Richard Miech, Lloyd Johnston, Patrick O'Malley, Jerald Bachman, and John Schulenberg, *Monitoring the Future* (Ann Arbor, MI: Institute for Social Research, 2015), www.monitoringthefuture.org.

14. Sami Ansari and Ne He, "Convergence Revisited: A Multi-Definition, Multi-Method Analysis of the UCR and the NCVS Crime Series (1973–2008)," *Justice Quarterly* 32 (2015): 1–31.

15. Alfred Blumstein, Jacqueline Cohen, and Richard Rosenfeld, "Trend and Deviation in Crime Rates: A Comparison of UCR and NCVS Data for Burglary and Robbery," *Criminology* 29 (1991): 237–248. See also Michael Hindelang, Travis Hirschi, and Joseph Weiss, *Measuring Delinquency* (Beverly Hills, CA: Sage, 1981).

16. Clarence Schrag, *Crime and Justice: American Style* (Washington, DC: U.S. Government Printing Office, 1971), p. 17.

17. Data in this section are from Langton and Truman, *Criminal Victimization, 2014*.

18. Nicole White, Ph.D., and Janet L. Lauritsen, *Violent Crime Against Youth from 1994 to 2010* (Washington, DC: Bureau of Justice Statistics, 2012), bjs.ojp.usdoj.gov/content/pub/pdf/vcay9410.pdf.

19. Maggie Ybarra, "Violence Spikes in Major Cities as Cops Walk Tenuous Line Between Fighting Crime and Civil Rights," *Washington Times*, June 16, 2015, www.washingtontimes.com/news/2015/jun/16/murder-and-shooting-rates-spike-as-police-try-to-b/.

20. Franklin Zimring and Hannah Laqueur, "Kids, Groups, and Crime: In Defense of Conventional Wisdom," *Journal of Research in Crime and Delinquency*, first published online November 4, 2014.

21. Derek Kreager, "When It's Good to Be 'Bad': Violence and Adolescent Peer Acceptance," *Criminology* 45 (2007): 893–923.

22. Lisa Stolzenberg and Stewart D'Alessio, "Co-offending and the Age-Crime Curve," *Journal of Research in Crime and Delinquency* 45 (2008): 65–86.

23. David R. Schaefer, Nancy Rodriguez, and Scott H. Decker, "The Role of Neighborhood Context in Youth Co-offending," *Criminology* 52 (2014): 117–139.

24. Paul Tracy, Kimberly Kempf-Leonard, and Stephanie Abramoske-James, "Gender Differences in Delinquency and Juvenile Justice Processing: Evidence from National Data," *Crime and Delinquency* 55 (2009): 171–215.

25. Cesare Lombroso, *The Female Offender* (New York: Appleton, 1920), p. 122.

26. Ibid.

27. Alan Booth and D. Wayne Osgood, "The Influence of Testosterone on Deviance in Adulthood: Assessing and Explaining the Relationship," *Criminology* 31 (1993): 93–118.

28. Jean Bottcher, "Social Practices of Gender: How Gender Relates to Delinquency in the Everyday Lives of High-Risk Youths," *Criminology* 39 (2001): 893–932.

29. Debra Kaysen, Miranda Morris, Shireen Rizvi, and Patricia Resick, "Peritraumatic Responses and Their Relationship to Perceptions of Threat in Female Crime Victims," *Violence Against Women* 11 (2005): 1515–1535.

30. Freda Adler, *Sisters in Crime* (New York: McGraw-Hill, 1975); Rita James Simon, *The Contemporary Woman and Crime* (Washington, DC: U.S. Government Printing Office, 1975).

31. David Rowe, Alexander Vazsonyi, and Daniel Flannery, "Sex Differences in Crime: Do Mean and Within-Sex Variation Have Similar Causes?" *Journal of Research in Crime and Delinquency* 32 (1995): 84–100; Michael Hindelang, "Age, Sex, and the Versatility of Delinquency Involvements," *Social Forces* 14 (1971): 525–534; Martin Gold, *Delinquent Behavior in an American City* (Belmont, CA: Brooks/Cole, 1970); Gary

Jensen and Raymond Eve, "Sex Differences in Delinquency: An Examination of Popular Sociological Explanations," *Criminology* 13 (1976): 427–448.

32. Darrell Steffensmeier, Jennifer Schwartz, Hua Zhong, and Jeff Ackerman, "An Assessment of Recent Trends in Girls' Violence Using Diverse Longitudinal Sources: Is the Gender Gap Closing?" *Criminology* 43 (2005): 355–406.

33. Robert Brame, Shawn Bushway, Ray Paternoster, and Michael G. Turner, "Demographic Patterns of Cumulative Arrest Prevalence by Ages 18 and 23," *Crime and Delinquency* 60 (2014): 471–486.

34. Johnston, O'Malley, and Bachman, *Monitoring the Future,* pp. 102–104.

35. Rob Tillyer, "Opening the Black Box of Officer Decision-Making: An Examination of Race, Criminal History, and Discretionary Searches," *Justice Quarterly* 31 (2014): 961–986.

36. Leo Carroll and M. Lilliana Gonzalez. "Out of Place: Racial Stereotypes and the Ecology of Frisks and Searches Following Traffic Stops," *Journal of Research in Crime and Delinquency* 51 (2014): 559–584.

37. Tammy Rinehart Kochel, David Wilson, and Stephen Mastrofski, "Effect of Suspect Race on Officers' Arrest Decisions," *Criminology* 49 (2011): 473–512.

38. Kenneth Novak and Mitchell Chamlin, "Racial Threat, Suspicion, and Police Behavior: The Impact of Race and Place in Traffic Enforcement," *Crime and Delinquency* 58 (2012): 275–300.

39. Richard Rosenfeld, Jeff Rojek, and Scott Decker, "Age Matters: Race Differences in Police Searches of Young and Older Male Drivers" *Journal of Research in Crime and Delinquency* 49 (2011): 31–55.

40. Karen Parker, Brian Stults, and Stephen Rice, "Racial Threat, Concentrated Disadvantage and Social Control: Considering the Macro-Level Sources of Variation in Arrests," *Criminology* 43 (2005): 1111–1134; Lisa Stolzenberg, J. Stewart D'Alessio, and David Eitle, "A Multilevel Test of Racial Threat Theory," *Criminology* 42 (2004): 673–698.

41. Traci Schlesinger, "Racial and Ethnic Disparity in Pretrial Criminal Processing," *Justice Quarterly* 22 (2005): 170–192.

42. Besiki Kutateladze, Nancy Andiloro, Brian Johnson, and Cassia Spohn, "Cumulative Disadvantage: Examining Racial and Ethnic Disparity in Prosecution and Sentencing," *Criminology* 52 (2014): 514–551.

43. Andres F. Rengifo and Don Stemen, "The Unintended Effects of Penal Reform: African American Presence, Incarceration, and the Abolition of Discretionary Parole in the United States," *Crime and Delinquency*, first published May 25, 2012; *David Eitle and Susanne Monahan,* "Revisiting the Racial Threat Thesis: The Role of Police Organizational Characteristics in Predicting Race-Specific Drug Arrest Rates," *Justice Quarterly* 26 (2009): 528–561.

44. Rebecca Wickes, John R. Hipp, Renee Zahnow, and Lorraine Mazerolle, "'Seeing' Minorities and Perceptions of Disorder: Explicating the Mediating and Moderating Mechanisms of Social Cohesion," *Criminology* 51 (2013): 519–560.

45. David Jacobs, "Minority Threat and Police Strength from 1980 to 2000: A Fixed-Effects Analysis of Nonlinear and Interactive Effects in Large U.S. Cities," *Criminology* 52 (2014): 140–142.

46. Karen Parker and Patricia McCall, "Structural Conditions and Racial Homicide Patterns: A Look at the Multiple Disadvantages in Urban Areas," *Criminology* 37 (1999): 447–469.

47. Gary LaFree and Richard Arum, "The Impact of Racially Inclusive Schooling on Adult Incarceration Rates Among U.S. Cohorts of African Americans and Whites Since 1930," *Criminology* 44 (2006): 73–103.

48. R. Kelly Raley, "A Shortage of Marriageable Men? A Note on the Role of Cohabitation in Black–White Differences in Marriage Rates," *American Sociological Review* 61 (1996): 973–983.

49. Julie Phillips, "Variation in African-American Homicide Rates: An Assessment of Potential Explanations," *Criminology* 35 (1997): 527–559; James Comer, "Black Violence and Public Policy," in *American Violence and Public Policy,* ed. Lynn Curtis (New Haven, CT: Yale University Press, 1985), pp. 63–86.

50. Robert Sampson, Jeffrey Morenoff, and Stephen Raudenbush, "Social Anatomy of Racial and Ethnic Disparities in Violence," *American Journal of Public Health* 95 (2005): 224–233; Joanne Kaufman, "Explaining the Race/Ethnicity–Violence Relationship: Neighborhood Context and Social Psychological Processes," *Justice Quarterly* 22 (2005): 224–251.

51. LaFree and Arum, "The Impact of Racially Inclusive Schooling"; Sampson, Morenoff, and Raudenbush, "Social Anatomy of Racial and Ethnic Disparities in Violence."

52. Lisa Tompson and Kate Bowers, "A Stab in the Dark? A Research Note on Temporal Patterns of Street Robbery," *Journal of Research in Crime and Delinquency* 50 (2013): 616–631.

53. Ellen Cohn, "The Effect of Weather and Temporal Variations on Calls for Police Service," *American Journal of Police* 15 (1996): 23–43.

54. R. A. Baron, "Aggression as a Function of Ambient Temperature and Prior Anger Arousal," *Journal of Personality and Social Psychology* 21 (1972): 183–189.

55. Brad Bushman, Morgan Wang, and Craig Anderson, "Is the Curve Relating Temperature to Aggression Linear or Curvilinear? Assaults and Temperature in Minneapolis Reexamined," *Journal of Personality and Social Psychology* 89 (2005): 62–66.

56. Paul Bell, "Reanalysis and Perspective in the Heat–Aggression Debate," *Journal of Personality and Social Psychology* 89 (2005): 71–73.

57. Ellen Cohn, "The Prediction of Police Calls for Service: The Influence of Weather and Temporal Variables on Rape and Domestic Violence," *Journal of Environmental Psychology* 13 (1993): 71–83.

58. John Simister and Cary Cooper, "Thermal Stress in the U.S.A.: Effects on Violence and on Employee Behaviour," *Stress and Health* 21 (2005): 3–15.

59. William Shakespeare, *Romeo and Juliet*, Act 3, Scene 1.

60. Daniel Montolio and Simón Planells-Struse, "Does Tourism Boost Criminal Activity? Evidence from a Top Touristic Country," *Crime and Delinquency*, first published online October 28, 2013.

61. Heith Copes, Tomislav V. Kovandzic, J. Mitchell Miller, and Luke Williamson, "The Lost Cause? Examining the Southern Culture of Honor Through Defensive Gun Use," *Crime and Delinquency* 60 (2014): 356–378.

62. Amie Nielsen, Ramiro Martinez, and Richard Rosenfeld, "Firearm Use, Injury, and Lethality in Assaultive Violence: An Examination of Ethnic Differences," *Homicide Studies* 9 (2005): 83–108.

63. See, generally, Franklin Zimring and Gordon Hawkins, *Crime Is Not the Problem: Lethal Violence in America* (New York: Oxford University Press, 1997).

64. Ibid., p. 36.

65. Gary Kleck, "Defensive Gun Use Is Not a Myth," *Politico*, February 17, 2015, www.politico.com/magazine /story/2015/02/defensive-gun-ownership-gary-kleck -response-115082.html; see also the classic article, Gary Kleck and Marc Gertz, "Armed Resistance to Crime: The Prevalence and Nature of Self-Defense with a Gun," *Journal of Criminal Law and Criminology* 86 (1995): 219–249.

66. John R. Hipp and Adam Boessen, "Egohoods as Waves Washing Across the City: A New Measure of 'Neighborhoods'," *Criminology* 51 (2013): 287–327; Ramiro Martinez, Jacob Stowell, and Jeffrey Cancino, "A Tale of Two Border Cities: Community Context, Ethnicity, and Homicide," *Social Science Quarterly* 89 (2008): 1–16.

67. Robert J. Sampson, "Disparity and Diversity in the Contemporary City: Social (Dis)order Revisited," *British Journal of Sociology* 60 (2009): 1–31.

68. Shawn Bushway, "Economy and Crime," *The Criminologist* 35 (2010): 1–5.

69. Nancy Rodriguez, "Concentrated Disadvantage and the Incarceration of Youth: Examining How Context Affects Juvenile Justice," *Journal of Research in Crime and Delinquency*, first published December 13, 2011.

70. Mikko Aaltonen, John M. Macdonald, Pekka Martikainen, and Janne Kivivuor, "Examining the Generality of the Unemployment–Crime Association," *Criminology* 51 (2013): 561–594.

71. R. Ramchand, M. Elliott, S. Mrug, J. Grunbaum, M. Windle, A. Chandra, M. Peskin, S. Cooper, and M. Schuster, "Substance Use and Delinquency Among Fifth Graders Who Have Jobs," *American Journal of Preventive Medicine* 36 (2007): 297–303; Jeremy Staff and Christopher Uggen, "The Fruits of Good Work: Early Work Experiences and Adolescent Deviance," *Journal of Research in Crime and Delinquency* 40 (2003): 263–290.

72. Travis Hirschi and Michael Gottfredson, "Age and the Explanation of Crime," *American Journal of Sociology* 89 (1983): 552–584, at 581.

73. Darrell Steffensmeier and Cathy Streifel, "Age, Gender, and Crime Across Three Historical Periods: 1935, 1960 and 1985," *Social Forces* 69 (1991): 869–894.

74. Hirschi and Gottfredson, "Age and the Explanation of Crime."

75. Robert Agnew, "An Integrated Theory of the Adolescent Peak in Offending," *Youth and Society* 34 (2003): 263–302.

76. Margo Wilson and Martin Daly, "Life Expectancy, Economic Inequality, Homicide, and Reproductive Timing in Chicago Neighbourhoods," *British Journal of Medicine* 314 (1997): 1271–1274.

77. Edward Mulvey and John LaRosa, "Delinquency Cessation and Adolescent Development: Preliminary Data," *American Journal of Orthopsychiatry* 56 (1986): 212–224.

78. James Q. Wilson and Richard Herrnstein, *Crime and Human Nature* (New York: Simon & Schuster, 1985), pp. 126–147.

79. Ibid., p. 219.

80. Kevin Beaver, John Paul Wright, Matt DeLisi, and Michael Vaughn, "Desistance from Delinquency: The Marriage Effect Revisited and Extended," *Social Science Research* 37 (2008): 736–752.

81. Marvin Wolfgang, Robert Figlio, and Thorsten Sellin, *Delinquency in a Birth Cohort* (Chicago: University of Chicago Press, 1972).

82. See Thorsten Sellin and Marvin Wolfgang, *The Measurement of Delinquency* (New York: Wiley, 1964), p. 120.

83. Paul Tracy, Marvin Wolfgang, and Robert Figlio, *Delinquency Careers in Two Birth Cohorts* (New York: Plenum Press, 1990); Marvin Wolfgang, "Delinquency in Two Birth Cohorts," in *Perspective Studies of Crime and Delinquency*, ed. Katherine Teilmann Van Dusen and Sarnoff Mednick (Boston: Kluwer-Nijhoff, 1983), pp. 7–17. The following sections rely heavily on these sources.

84. Lyle Shannon, *Criminal Career Opportunity* (New York: Human Sciences Press, 1988).

85. D. J. West and David P. Farrington, *The Delinquent Way of Life* (London: Heinemann, 1977).

86. Michael Schumacher and Gwen Kurz, *The 8% Solution: Preventing Serious Repeat Juvenile Crime* (Thousand Oaks, CA: Sage, 1999).

87. Peter Jones, Philip Harris, James Fader, and Lori Grubstein, "Identifying Chronic Juvenile Offenders," *Justice Quarterly* 18 (2001): 478–507.

88. Michael Ezell and Amy D'Unger, "Offense Specialization Among Serious Youthful Offenders: A Longitudinal Analysis of a California Youth Authority Sample," (Durham, NC: Duke University, 1998, unpublished report).

# 3 Victims and Victimization

## Learning Objectives

LO1   Analyze the victim's role in the crime process.

LO2   Discuss the greatest problems faced by crime victims.

LO3   Clarify the term *cycle of violence*.

LO4   Assess the ecology of victimization risk.

LO5   Categorize the most dominant victim characteristics.

LO6   Compare and contrast the most important theories of victimization.

# Chapter Outline

## FACT OR FICTION?

▶ Men are more likely to be victimized by strangers, women by someone they know.

▶ Most crime victims are people who are simply in the wrong place at the wrong time.

In a case that made national headlines, two members of the champion Steubenville High School football team, Trent Mays, 17, and Ma'lik Richmond, 16, were found to be juvenile delinquents for an incident of sexual assault of a 16-year-old girl who was "substantially impaired" after a night of partying and drinking. The victim later told police she remembered holding Mays's hand as she left a party with him, Richmond, and others. The next thing she remembers was waking up in the morning naked on a couch in an unfamiliar house. At trial, the defense claimed the sex was consensual, and they employed expert witnesses who testified that even when drunk, people can engage in consensual sex.[1] In the end, the prosecution proved their case by showing videos, posted online, of the unconscious young woman being mocked by kids who were at the party. They produced emails from people who knew what was going on but did nothing to stop the attack. The prosecution was also aided by captured screenshots, including one showing Mays and Richmond carrying the naked victim. Other evidence—including scores of text messages, pictures, and videos—indicated the girl was barely conscious during much of the time the attacks occurred. Texts also showed that Mays had attempted to cover up his actions after police became aware of the attack.

On March 17, 2013, Judge Thomas Lipps found Mays and Richmond delinquent and ordered their detention in a juvenile facility. But the convictions did not end the case. A grand jury later indicted a number of school officials on obstruction of justice and evidence tampering charges for obstructing official business and ▶

falsification.[2] A volunteer football coach whose house was the scene of the drinking party pleaded no contest to two charges and served 10 days in jail, one year of supervision, and 40 hours of community service; the school superintendent agreed to resign in order to avoid criminal charges.

### CONNECTIONS

Sexual assault on campus will be revisited in Chapter 10 when the crime of rape is discussed in some detail. How is it possible to protect women from such abuse? Should viewing a recording of a sexual assault taken by the perpetrators be criminalized? Are the viewers equally guilty?

The Steubenville rape case is one of a slew of recent incidents during which an inebriated minor female is sexually assaulted; in some, photos are taken and then put on the Internet.[3] Some of these cases resulted in the young victim later taking her own life. In 2013, Rehtaeh Parsons, a 17-year-old Canadian girl, committed suicide 18 months after she was sexually assaulted by four boys while she was unconscious and photos taken of the assault were posted on the Internet. Audrie Pott, a student at Saratoga High School in Silicon Valley, hanged herself on September 10, 2012, after passing out drunk at a party where boys she had known for years took off her clothes, sexually assaulted her, and took pictures of the attack on their phones.[4] There are numerous cases of college-aged women who have been sexually assaulted by fellow students; the issue of sexual assault on campus has become a major national concern.

Why do some people become targets of predatory criminals? Is it because of their lifestyle and environment? Did these young women put themselves at risk by socializing and drinking with teenage boys? Should they have done more to protect themselves or is it unfair to expect women to always be on their guard, especially when their attackers were trusted friends and schoolmates? Is this unfairly "blaming the victim" for risky behavior? Can someone deflect or avoid criminal behavior, or is it a matter of fate and chance? And what of the bystanders who did nothing to stop the attack even though they knew it was about to happen? Should they be criminally liable?

**L01** Analyze the victim's role in the crime process.

## The Victim's Role

For many years, crime victims were viewed by criminologists as merely the passive targets of a criminal's anger, greed, or frustration; they were considered to have been "in the wrong place at the wrong time." More than 50 years ago, a number of criminologists, including Hans Von Hentig and Stephen Schafer, conducted pioneering studies that found that, contrary to popular belief, the victim's own behavior is important in the crime process.[5] Victims influence criminal behavior by playing an active role in a criminal incident—for example, by provoking the assault that ended in their death. Victims were also found to sometimes play an indirect role in a criminal incident, such as when they travel through a dangerous, high-crime neighborhood at night without companionship or protection.

The discovery that victims play an important role in the crime process has prompted the scientific study of victims, or **victimology**. Criminologists who focus their attention on crime victims refer to themselves as **victimologists**.

In this chapter, we examine victims and their relationship to the criminal process. First, using available victim data, we analyze the nature and extent of victimization. We then discuss the relationship between victims and criminal offenders. In this context, we look at various theories of victimization that attempt to explain the victim's role in the crime problem. Finally, we examine how society has responded to the needs of victims and consider what special problems they still face.

**victimology**
The study of the victim's role in criminal events.

**victimologists**
Criminologists who focus on the victims of crime.

## The Costs of Victimization

Criminal victimization exacts a heavy toll on all whom it touches, both the general society and its direct target, individual victims. The cost of victimization takes many forms, ranging from financial loss—property losses, productivity losses, and medical bills—and individual losses—stress, fear, emotional trauma, pain. We examine the social and individual costs of victimization in the following sections.

## Economic Costs of Victimization

Victimization brings with it a bevy of costs to society, including billions in economic losses (see Exhibit 3.1). When the costs of goods taken during property crimes is added to productivity losses caused by injury, pain, and emotional trauma, the cost of victimization is estimated to be in the hundreds of billions of dollars.

A number of different methods have been developed to measure the cost of victimization. Kathryn McCollister and her associates employed complex statistical analysis to determine how much an individual crime might cost society, looking at issues such as the cost to the criminal justice system, health care, and other costs. The crimes they could put a figure on included:

- Murder: $8,982,907 (range = $4,144,677 to $11,350,687)
- Rape/sexual assault: $240,776 (range = $80,403 to $369,739)
- Robbery: $42,310 (range = $18,591 to $280,237)
- Household burglary: $6,462 (range = $1,974 to $30,197)
- Stolen property: $7,974 (range = $151 to $22,739)

According to McCollister, the cost to society of an average murder is almost $9 million. Considering that about 14,000 Americans are the victims of murder each year, this crime alone costs the nation about $130 billion in losses each year.[6]

**WHY ARE THE COSTS SO HIGH?** Victimization takes such a significant toll because there are many types of expenses associated with each crime. Some of the direct, tangible costs of crime include the cost of damaged and lost property, pain and suffering, costs of medical care, lost wages, reduced quality of life imposed by debilitating injuries and/or fear of being victimized again, and the cost of psychological counseling. Some victims are physically disabled, including victims who suffer paralyzing spinal cord injuries and need long-term medical care. And if victims have no insurance, the long-term effects of the crime may have devastating financial as well as emotional and physical consequences.[7] The multimillion-dollar cost of homicide is calculated in the same manner: an insurance company values the life of someone killed in an accident when paying out benefits to survivors, and therefore the cost can be significant.

## Exhibit 3.1  Costs Associated with Victimization

### Victim Costs

Personal economic losses, including medical care costs, lost earnings, and property loss/damage.

### Criminal Justice System Costs

Local, state, and federal government funds spent on police protection and investigations, legal and adjudication services, such as prosecution, public defenders, and trial costs, and the cost of both community and secure corrections programs, including counseling and other programs.

### Crime Career Costs

Opportunity costs associated with the criminal's choice to engage in illegal rather than legal and productive activities, including funds spent on supporting their families.

### Intangible Costs

Indirect losses suffered by crime victims, including pain and suffering, decreased quality of life, and psychological distress.

**Source:** Kathryn McCollister, Michael T. French, and Hai Fang, "The Cost of Crime to Society: New Crime-Specific Estimates for Policy and Program Evaluation," *Drug and Alcohol Dependence* 108 (2010): 98–109.

**LO2** Discuss the greatest problems faced by crime victims.

**CONNECTIONS**

Chapter 10 will discuss the nature and extent of intimate partner violence in greater detail. The NCVS data show that this is far more traumatic than an attack by a stranger. Why do you suppose this is true?

**posttraumatic stress disorder (PTSD)**
Psychological reaction to a highly stressful event; symptoms may include depression, anxiety, flashbacks, and recurring nightmares.

Indirect or intangible costs include money spent on police and the justice system, legal defense costs, treatment costs, health care costs borne by society, and security costs. When the tangible and intangible costs are added together, the total loss due to crime can be in the hundreds of billions of dollars.

## Personal Costs of Victimization

There are also immense personal costs connected to crime victimization. Using NCVS data collected over a three-year period (2009–2012), Lynn Langton and Jennifer Truman found that more than two-thirds (68 percent) of serious violent-crime victims experienced socio-emotional problems as a result of the victimization.[8] Victims experienced moderate to severe emotional distress, increased relationship problems, and disruptions at school or work. They reported being worried, anxious, sad, and depressed and suffered from lack of sleep, headaches, fatigue, and high blood pressure, among other problems. Victims of intimate partner violence were more than five times as likely to experience socio-emotional problems than victims of violence by strangers.

The most troubling victim experiences? As might be expected, about three-quarters of victims of rape or sexual assault (75 percent), robbery (74 percent), violence involving a firearm (74 percent), and violence resulting in medical treatment for injuries (77 percent) experienced socio-emotional problems.

Victims may suffer stress and anxiety long after the incident is over and the justice process has run its course. Langton and Truman found that most violent crime victims with socio-emotional problems suffered from symptoms such as feeling anxious, depressed, or angry, or having trouble sleeping, for at least a month or more after the incident. Many victims suffer from long-term **posttraumatic stress disorder (PTSD)**—the symptoms of which include depression, anxiety, and self-destructive behavior—especially when the victim does not receive adequate support from family and friends.[9] Rape victims are particularly susceptible to PTSD, and its effects are felt whether the victim acknowledges the attack or remains in denial about what happened. In other words, there is no escaping the long-term effects of sexual assault, even if the victim refuses to acknowledge having been raped.[10]

Children who are victimized by parents or other adults, who have either witnessed or experienced child abuse or have been the victim of traumatic sexual experiences, also have been found to suffer a long list of negative psychological deficits. These include but are not limited to acute stress disorders, depression, eating disorders, nightmares, anxiety, suicidal ideation, and other psychological problems.[11] Many run away to escape their environment, which puts them at risk for juvenile arrest and involvement with the justice system.[12]

The stress accrued in childhood follows victims over the life course. Young victims are at greater risk of being abused as adults than those who escaped childhood victimization.[13] They may also suffer a wide range of personal deficits as they mature. Research shows that children repeatedly victimized before the age of 12 are the ones most susceptible to a number of physical and mental health issues, smoking, and homelessness.[14]

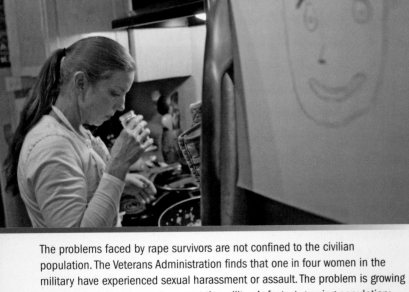

Washington Post/Getty Images

The problems faced by rape survivors are not confined to the civilian population. The Veterans Administration finds that one in four women in the military have experienced sexual harassment or assault. The problem is growing because female veterans represent the military's fastest-growing population: an estimated 2.2 million, or 10 percent, of the country's veterans are women. Army veteran Kate Weber, shown here, a survivor of military sexual trauma (MST), now spends most of her time doing MST advocacy with other victims.

**VICTIM FEAR** People who live in crime-ridden neighborhoods develop an overwhelming sense of fear.[15] Those who have actually experienced crime are the most fearful, dreading the fact that they may be victimized again.[16] Fear can become generalized: people who have been assaulted may develop fears that their house will be burglarized.[17]

There are gender differences in the fear of crime, and women are more fearful than men, especially those living in crime-ridden communities.[18] In a moving book called *Aftermath: Violence and the Remaking of a Self*, rape victim Susan Brison recounts the difficult time she had recovering from her ordeal. The trauma of rape disrupted her memory, cut off events that happened before the rape from those that occurred afterward, and undermined her ability to conceive of a happy or productive future. Although sympathizers encouraged her to forget the past, she found that confronting it can have healing power.[19]

Those who experience victimization directly are the most likely to be fearful and change their behaviors; some choose to move out of their neighborhood to a safer area.[20] But even those who have escaped attack themselves may develop fears and become timid after hearing about another's victimization.[21] Not only are people likely to move out of their neighborhood if they become crime victims, but they are also likely to relocate if a friend or neighbor has suffered a break-in or burglary.[22] Their fear is exacerbated by lurid news accounts of crime and violence.[23] News stories about serial killers on a rampage or mass killers shooting people in a movie theater can cause a chill felt throughout the city. Fear of these violent crimes prompts people to protect themselves and their family by implementing some sort of protective measure, such as carrying mace or pepper spray or installing a security device in their home.[24] Some may go overboard, carry weapons for protection, and react aggressively to provocations, no matter how slight; this group is the one most likely to engage in violence themselves.[25]

**VICTIM BLAME** The suffering endured by crime victims does not end when their attacker leaves the scene of the crime. They may suffer innuendos or insinuations from friends and family members who suggest that they are to blame for what happened or that the crime was somehow their fault.

Being blamed for what others perceive to be a result of risky behavior is especially painful for rape victims who may be made to feel they were somehow responsible for the attack because they used poor judgment or took risks.[26] Rape survivors are often the target of negative reactions from people who are supposed to give them support, including family friends and professionals. Some rape victims report that police seem suspicious of their involvement and question them about whether they may have helped precipitate the crime; the treatment they received from legal, medical, and mental health services was so destructive that they couldn't help feeling "re-raped."[27] In some instances these negative reactions cause survivors to blame themselves for the attack and even question whether the incident was really rape.[28]

Victims are especially prone to stress, blame, and fear if it turns out they may have made a false identification and the person they thought responsible for their attack was actually not guilty of the crime. The effect of exoneration on victims is discussed in the Policies and Issues in Criminology feature.

## Legal Costs of Victimization

People who are crime victims may be more likely to commit crime themselves. The process may begin early in life, because being abused or neglected as a child increases the odds of being arrested, both as a juvenile and as an adult.[29] People who were physically or sexually abused, especially young males, are much more likely to smoke, drink, and take drugs than nonabused youth. Incarcerated offenders report significant amounts of posttraumatic stress disorder as a result of prior victimization, which may in part explain their violent and criminal behaviors.[30] Some may run

# Policies and Issues in Criminology

## THE IMPACT OF WRONGFUL CONVICTIONS ON CRIME VICTIMS

When a wrongfully convicted individual is exonerated, the original crime victim may experience feelings of guilt, fear, helplessness, devastation, and depression. To find out more about the effect a wrongful conviction has on victims, researchers from ICF International conducted in-depth studies in six states to identify the shared experiences of victims in 11 cases of wrongful conviction for crimes ranging from rape and homicide to burglary and sex offenses.

### How Wrongful Convictions May Affect Victims

The researchers discovered that a number of factors including eyewitness misidentification, invalidated or improper forensic evidence and analysis, false testimony by informants, false confessions, and ineffective legal counsel contributed to the wrongful convictions. Regardless of cause, wrongful convictions have a significant impact on the original crime victims. As one victim told researchers, "For [several] years, I had been quite comfortable with my role as the victim. When the exoneration happened, that exoneree became the victim, and I, the rape victim, became the offender. The roles switch, and it's a role you don't know what to do with."

More than half of the victims in the study described the impact of the wrongful conviction as being comparable to—or worse than—that of their original victimization. Many said they were in shock when they first heard about the exoneration. The majority of the victims also reported intense feelings of guilt. This was especially true for the two-thirds of victims in the study who provided eyewitness identification. One victim recounted, "It was harder going through the revictimization than it was through the rape. . . . Now you have the same feelings of that pain. You have the same scariness. You have the same fear. You have the same panic, but now you have this flood of guilt on top of it."

As with many cases of wrongful conviction, most received media attention, generating notoriety for both the wrongfully convicted individuals and the crime victims. Some of the victims felt that the media insinuated that they had intentionally misidentified the wrongfully convicted individuals. Many found the anger directed toward them in blogs and comments that followed news articles particularly painful. One victim stated, "This is the thing—your name's not out there, but you are out there. This is your case. This is something that happened to your body. This is what happened to your mind, to your life. . . . I didn't give anybody permission to put this out in the newspaper."

The crime victims reported being afraid of the wrongfully convicted individual following the exoneration. One victim said, "My initial thought was [the wrongfully convicted individual] is going to kill me. [They] will hurt me, and if [they] can't get to me, [they] will get to my children. So I was hyper alert. The children could not leave my side. I went to school and told the teachers, 'They are to stay with you every second.' That went on for almost two years." The crime victims also reported being afraid of the actual offenders.

### Improving Support for Victims

When asked for recommendations, victims and stakeholders spoke of the need to improve notification, information, and services for the original crime victims in cases of wrongful conviction. In all of the case studies, those interviewed agreed that the criminal justice system should provide initial notification. Victims and other stakeholders recommended that, when appropriate and possible, officials involved in the original case should notify the crime victim. When this is not possible, many stakeholders suggested having a victim service provider present. Others stressed that law enforcement or prosecutors should be present, especially in cases that may involve additional litigation.

Victims and stakeholders stressed that the crime victims are often unfamiliar with the criminal justice system and need information explaining the exoneration process. Several victims in the study who provided eyewitness identification said that learning how misidentifications may occur helped them process their reactions and understand the wrongful conviction. Some officials, however, pointed out that providing such information might not be appropriate or legally advisable for law enforcement. Victims also said that information on how memories are formed helped them understand why they continued to envision the wrongfully convicted individual when they thought about the crime. Interviewees also highlighted the importance of counseling services in helping crime victims come to terms with the wrongful conviction. Victims recommended that counseling services be provided by someone with formal training and experience working with victims of trauma.

## Critical Thinking

Can anything be done to ease the pain of victims who wrongfully identify an innocent person? Should the state provide counseling services at taxpayer cost?

**Source:** Seri Irazola, Erin Williamson, Julie Stricker, and Emily Niedzwiecki, "Addressing the Impact of Wrongful Convictions on Crime Victims," *NIJ Journal* 274 (2014): 35–38.

## Exhibit 3.2   The Link Between Victimization and Crime

Given the evidence pointing to a link between victimization and crime, how can the association be explained?

- *Victimization causes social problems.* People who are crime victims experience long-term negative consequences, including problems with unemployment and developing personal relationships, factors related to criminality. Some young victims may run away from home, taking to the streets and increasing their risk of becoming a crime victim again.

- *Victimization causes stress and anger.* Victimization may produce anger, stress, and strain. Known offenders report significant amounts of posttraumatic stress disorder as a result of prior victimization, which may in part explain their violent and criminal behaviors. Victims, especially those who lack self-control, may try to cope with this stress by self-medicating, drinking, or taking drugs, a form of behavior highly correlated with future criminality.

- *Victimization prompts revenge.* Victims may seek revenge against the people who harmed them or whom they believe are at fault for their problems. In some cases, these feelings become generalized to others who share the same characteristics of their attackers (e.g., men, Hispanics). As a result, their reactions become displaced, and they may lash out at people who are not their attackers. They may take drastic measures, fearing revictimization, and arm themselves for self-protection. In some cultures, retaliation is an expected and accepted response to victimization.

- *Crime and victimization have a common cause.* Social and personal factors predictive of crime also produce victimization—substance abuse, experiencing violence, psychological deficits. When Marie Skubak Tillyer and Emily Wright studied the victims and perpetrators of intimate partner violence they found a great deal of overlap. Perpetrators and victim-perpetrators were more likely to live with a non-spouse partner, feel isolated, display negative temperaments, and report substance use problems.

- *Spurious association.* It is also possible that the association between victimization and crime is spurious and that victims and criminals are actually two separate groups. The personal traits that produce violent criminals, such as impulsive personality, may not be the same ones that produce victims. There may appear to be a connection because both criminals and victims tend to have the same lifestyle and live in the same neighborhoods, making it seem they are one and the same.

**Sources:** Marie Skubak Tillyer and Emily M. Wright, "Intimate Partner Violence and the Victim-Offender Overlap," *Journal of Research in Crime and Delinquency* 51 (2014): 29–55; Jillian J. Turanovic and Travis C. Pratt, "The Consequences of Maladaptive Coping: Integrating General Strain and Self-Control Theories to Specify a Causal Pathway Between Victimization and Offending," *Journal of Quantitative Criminology* 29 (2013): 321–345; Ulrich Orth, Leo Montada, and Andreas Maercker, "Feelings of Revenge, Retaliation Motive, and Posttraumatic Stress Reactions in Crime Victims," *Journal of Interpersonal Violence* 21 (2006): 229–243; Chris Melde, Finn-Aage Esbensen, and Terrance Taylor, "'May Piece Be with You': A Typological Examination of the Fear and Victimization Hypothesis of Adolescent Weapon Carrying," *Justice Quarterly* 26 (2009): 348–376.

away, increasing their risk of becoming a crime victim.[31] Others may seek revenge against the people who harmed them, and sometimes these feelings are generalized to others who exhibit the same characteristics as their attackers.[32] The abuse–crime phenomenon is referred to as the **cycle of violence**.[33]

As adults, there is evidence that crime victims themselves are more likely than nonvictims to commit crimes.[34] Fearing revictimization, they may take drastic measures and arm themselves for self-protection.[35] Such measures may amplify victimization risk.

The factors that link crime and victimization are set out more fully in Exhibit 3.2.

**cycle of violence**
Victims of crime, especially victims of childhood abuse, are more likely to commit crimes themselves.

**LO3** Clarify the term *cycle of violence.*

## The Nature of Victimization

How many crime victims are there in the United States, and what are the trends and patterns in victimization? Patterns in the victimization survey findings are stable and repetitive, suggesting that victimization is not random but is a function of personal and ecological factors. The stability of these patterns allows judgments to be made about the nature of victimization; policies can then be created in an effort to reduce the victimization rate. Who are victims? Where does victimization take place? What is the relationship between victims and criminals? The following sections discuss some of the most important victimization patterns and trends.

**L04** Assess the ecology of victimization risk.

## The Social Ecology of Victimization

Victim surveys show that violent crimes are slightly more likely to take place in an open, public area (such as a street, a park, or a field) or at a commercial establishment such as a tavern, and in daytime or early evening hours than in a private home during the morning or late evening hours.

The more serious violent crimes, such as rape and aggravated assault, typically take place after 6 P.M. Approximately two-thirds of rapes and sexual assaults occur at night—6 P.M. to 6 A.M. Less serious forms of violence, such as unarmed robberies and personal larcenies such as purse snatching, are more likely to occur during the daytime.

There are also seasonal variations in victimization. Household property crimes, such as burglaries, have higher rates in the summer and lower rates during other seasons of the year. Motor vehicle thefts do not exhibit the same seasonal patterns. Serious violent victimization rates—which include rape and sexual assault, robbery, and aggravated assault—are significantly higher during the summer than during the winter, spring, and fall. When all violent crimes are counted, including simple assault, rates of violence are highest in the fall.[36] One reason: many simple assaults occur in school, and victimization rate patterns correspond to the start of the school year.

Neighborhood characteristics affect the chances of victimization. Those living in the central city experience significantly higher rates of theft and violence than suburbanites; people living in rural areas have a victimization rate less than half that of city dwellers. The risk of murder for both men and women is significantly higher in disorganized inner-city areas where gangs flourish and drug trafficking is commonplace. Even if people are not personally victimized, city dwellers, especially those living in areas with large disadvantaged populations, are more likely to observe or be exposed to violence than those living in more advantaged neighborhoods. And observing violence can contribute to stress, fear, and flight.[37]

**CRIME IN SCHOOLS** Schools, unfortunately, are the scene of a great deal of victimization because they are populated by one of the most dangerous segments of society, teenage males. The latest data available (2013) from the National Center for Educational Statistics found that among students ages 12 to 18, there were about 1,421,000 nonfatal victimizations at school, which included 454,900 theft victimizations and 966,000 violent victimizations (simple assault and serious violent victimizations).[38] Twenty students died in schools, 15 from homicide, 5 from suicide.

One reason is that adult supervision is minimal before, during, and after school activities. School hallways and locker rooms are typically left unattended. Kids who participate in school sports may leave their valuables in locker rooms; others congregate in unguarded places, making them attractive targets for predators who come on school grounds.[39] So ironically, while for most people and most crimes summer is the most dangerous season, for adolescents victimization actually peaks in the fall when the school year begins and declines in the summer after the school year ends.[40]

## The Victim's Household

The NCVS tells us that within the United States, homes located in urban areas in the South and West are the ones most vulnerable to crime, especially those occupied by African American families. In contrast, European American homes in rural areas in

**CONNECTIONS**

As we saw in Chapter 2, the NCVS is currently the leading source of information on the nature and extent of victimization. It uses a sophisticated sampling methodology to collect data; statistical techniques are then applied to estimate victimization rates, trends, and patterns for the entire U.S. population.

the Northeast and Midwest are the least likely to become the target of crimes such as burglary and larceny. People who own their homes are less vulnerable than renters.

Population movement and changes may account for recent decreases in crime victimization. U.S. residents have become extremely mobile, moving from urban areas to suburban and rural areas. In addition, family size has been reduced; more people than ever before are living in single-person homes (which now account for about 27 percent of households). The fact that smaller households in less populated areas have a lower victimization risk is a possible explanation for the decline in household victimization rates during the past 25 years.[41]

## Victim Characteristics

Social and demographic characteristics also distinguish victims and nonvictims. The most important of these factors are gender, age, social status, and race.

**GENDER** Gender affects victimization risk. Except for the crimes of rape and sexual assault, males are somewhat more likely than females to be the victims of violent crime. Men are almost twice as likely as women to experience robbery. Women, however, are 10 times more likely than men to be victims of rape or sexual assault. Although males are more likely to be victimized than females, the gender difference in victimization has narrowed considerably during the past decade and is now approaching equality.[42]

Another significant gender difference is that women are much more likely to be victimized by someone they know or with whom they live. Of those offenders victimizing females, about two-thirds were described as someone the victim knew or was related to. In contrast, less than half of male victims were attacked by a friend, relative, or acquaintance.[43]

There are also gender differences in the aftermath of victimization. When men are the aggressors, injuries are more severe and victims are more likely to suffer injury. Female aggressors tend to engage in verbal rather than physical abuse.[44]

**AGE** Although violent crime rates declined in recent years for most age groups, victim data reveal that young people face a much greater victimization risk than older persons. Teens and young adults experience the highest rates of violent crime, but even the youngest kids are not immune. David Finkelhor and his colleagues found that compared to older siblings, younger children were just as likely to be hit with an object that could cause injury, were just as likely to be victimized on multiple occasions, and suffered similar injuries.[45]

Although the elderly are less likely to become crime victims than the young, they are most often the victims of a narrow band of criminal activities from which the young are more immune. Frauds and scams, purse snatching, pocket picking, stealing checks from the mail, and crimes committed in long-term care settings claim more older than younger victims. The elderly are especially susceptible to fraud because they have insurance, pension plans, proceeds from the sale of homes, and money from Social Security and savings that make them attractive financial targets. Because many elderly live by themselves and are lonely, they remain more susceptible to telephone and mail fraud. Unfortunately, once victimized, the elderly have more limited opportunities either to recover their lost money or to

L05 Categorize the most dominant victim characteristics.

**FACT OR FICTION?**

Men are more likely to be victimized by strangers, women by someone they know.

**FACT** Women are much more likely than men to be victimized by someone they know or someone with whom they live

The elderly are at particular risk for Internet fraud. Here, Ruth Wilson sits with her father while she displays some of the scam mail he has received in various attempts to defraud the elderly man. A Jamaica–U.S. task force launched to stop a network of aggressive gangs who run fake lottery scams has failed to stop the con artists, who are now stealing an estimated $1 billion a year, largely from elderly Americans.

AP Images/Elaine Thompson

# Policies and Issues in Criminology

## ELDER VICTIMS

Elder abuse and neglect are serious yet understudied problems in the United States. One reason is that the elderly, over age 65, have far lower rates of victimization (3.6 victimizations per 1,000 persons) than persons ages 12 to 24 (49.9 per 1,000), ages 25 to 49 (27.6 per 1,000), and ages 50 to 64 (15.2 per 1,000). Each year, the elderly account for approximately 2 percent of violence and 2 percent of serious violence. Many of these incidents occur at the hands of family members.

Because elder abuse was historically viewed as a social rather than a criminal problem, most states did not establish adult protective services units to address elderly victims until the mid-1980s. Elder abuse is frequently perpetrated by a spouse, relative, or acquaintance, which increases the likelihood that crimes are underreported. Low household income, unemployment or retirement, poor health, prior traumatic events, and low levels of social support all can indicate both a higher likelihood that older people may experience mistreatment and that the crime will be underreported.

Ron Aciemo and his colleagues surveyed more than 5,000 people 60 or older via telephone. Interviewers asked participants about their experiences in the previous year, as well as their lifetime overall. Though almost 2 percent of the respondents reported physical mistreatment, only 31 percent of those respondents had reported the problem to police. One reason is that strangers accounted for only 3 percent of these assaults as compared to family members, who were the perpetrators in 76 percent of the cases. Of those surveyed, slightly less than 1 percent reported being sexually abused in the previous year. About 16 percent of those people reported the assault to the police. Family members were responsible for about half of the assaults.

Other types of abuse include financial exploitation, 5 percent; neglect, 5 percent; and emotional mistreatment, 5 percent. Overall, 11 percent of those surveyed reported some form of mistreatment in the previous year; 1.2 percent reported two forms of mistreatment, and 0.2 percent reported three forms.

Adding to this undercount of older victims is the rising number of elderly living in long-term care facilities who are the target of physical abuse. There is much that is unknown about the abuse and criminal victimization of adults living in residential care facilities, but what is known is troubling. Available data suggest that adults are victimized at an alarming rate, and often have much more difficulty participating in the criminal justice system and receiving the help they need.

While widespread already, elder abuse will continue to be an important issue because of shifts in the U.S. population. Currently there are about 40 million people in the United States over age 65 and the Bureau of the Census predicts that by 2030 that population will reach 70 million people; the elderly will then make up more than 20 percent of the population (up from 12 percent in 1990).

---

## CONNECTIONS

The association between age and victimization is undoubtedly tied to lifestyle: adolescents often stay out late at night, go to public places, and hang out with other young people who have a high risk of criminal involvement. Go back to Chapter 2 and review the association between age and crime.

earn enough to replace what they have lost.[46] In addition, the elderly are also subject to physical and sexual abuse, most often from family members. This topic is explored in the accompanying Policies and Issues in Criminology feature.

**SOCIAL STATUS** The poorest Americans are the most likely to be victims of violent and property crime. This association occurs across all gender, age, and racial groups. The homeless, who are among the poorest individuals in America, suffer very high rates of assault.[47] Similarly, gang boys who are both lower class and live a high-risk lifestyle are more likely to become crime victims than the non–gang affiliated.[48]

In contrast, the wealthy are more likely to be targets of personal theft crimes such as pocket picking and purse snatching. Perhaps the affluent, who sport more expensive attire and drive better cars, attract the attention of thieves.

**RACE AND ETHNICITY** African Americans are significantly more likely than European Americans to be victims of violent crime. While interracial theft victimization rates are more similar, African Americans are still more likely to suffer violent victimizations than whites. While African Americans make up about 13 percent of

## What Causes Elder Abuse?

There are a number of possible causes of elder abuse. The most important are set out below:

- *The caregiver stress view* asserts that maltreatment occurs when family members caring for an impaired older adult are unable to adequately manage their caregiving responsibilities. The elderly victim is typically described as highly dependent on the caregiver, who becomes overwhelmed, frustrated, and abusive because of the continuous caretaking demands posed by the elderly person.

- *The social learning view* holds that elder abuse results from the abusive individual learning to use violence (perhaps from their elderly parent or relative) to either resolve conflicts or obtain a desired outcome.

- *The social exchange view* holds that people who abuse the elderly perceive themselves as not receiving their fair share from their relationship with the elderly person or other family members, and their resort to violence is an effort to restore or obtain what they feel they deserve.

- *The background-situational view* asserts that long-term discord results from a combination of factors, such as a history of family violence and/or a lack of relationship satisfaction, which primes a person's acceptance of violence as a conflict resolution strategy.

- *The power and control view* highlights an abusive individual's use of an ongoing pattern of coercive tactics to gain and maintain power and control during the course of a relationship with another person. A husband who abuses his elderly wife probably abused her when she was young.

- *The ecological view* explains elder abuse by including the impact of individual, relationship, community, and societal influences.

- *The biopsychosocial view* holds that elder maltreatment can be attributed to the characteristics of both the elderly person and the abusive individual and the influence of their environment.

### Critical Thinking

1. Can you think of anything that could be done to help identify elderly victims?

2. What could be done to aid in the prosecution of their attackers? Do we need elderly protective services similar to child protective services?

**Sources:** Rachel E. Morgan and Britney J. Mason, *Crimes Against the Elderly, 2003–2013*, Bureau of Justice Statistics, 2014, www.bjs.gov/content/pub/pdf/cae0313.pdf; Ron Acierno, Melba Hernandez-Tejada, Wendy Muzzy, and Kenneth Steve, "National Elder Mistreatment Study," National Institute of Justice, 2009, www.ncjrs.gov/pdffiles1/nij/grants/226456.pdf; Office of Justice Programs, *OJP Fact Sheet, Elder Abuse and Mistreatment, 2011*, ojp.gov/newsroom/factsheets/ojpfs_elderabuse.html; Philip Bulman, "Elder Abuse Emerges from the Shadows of Public Consciousness," *NIJ Journal* 26 (2010), www.nij.gov/journals/265/pages/elder-abuse.aspx; Shelley Jackson and Thomas Hafemeister, *Understanding Elder Abuse*, National Institute of Justice, 2013, www.ncjrs.gov/pdffiles1/nij/241731.pdf; data from the National Center for Elder Abuse, 2014, www.ncea.aoa.gov/Library/Data/index.aspx#population (all URLs accessed 2015).

the population they are the victims of more than half of all murders; black males, who are about 6 percent of the population, account for 47 percent of homicide victims.[49]

Why do these discrepancies exist? Because of income inequality, racial and minority group members are often forced to live in lower-income communities, a status that places them in the most at-risk population group.

**MARITAL STATUS** Victimization risk is also influenced by marital status. Never-married males and females are victimized more often than married people. Widows and widowers have the lowest victimization risk. This association between marital status and victimization is probably influenced by age, gender, and lifestyle:

- Many young people, who have the highest victim risk, are actually too young to have been married.

- Young, single people also go out in public more often and sometimes interact with high-risk peers, increasing their exposure to victimization.

- Widows and widowers suffer much lower victimization rates because they are generally older, interact with older people, and are more likely to stay home at night and to avoid public places.

People who suffer relationship stress may become crime victims. Dot, 61, displays the last of her teeth that have been recently pulled. She used meth for a period of time and says that meth caused her to lose her teeth. Her husband, Dutch, also used meth as a way to enhance his sex life. The two have a history of domestic violence.

Victimization may also influence the decision to marry: violent crime victims are the ones most likely to marry at an early age.[50] Why victimization spurs marriage is hard to determine. It is possible that those scarred by street violence seek stable relationships to provide a sense of security and tranquility. Unfortunately, getting married at an early age is associated with divorce, so while early victimization may cause people to seek the stability of marriage their decision may not bring long-term marital bliss.

**REPEAT VICTIMIZATION** Does prior victimization enhance or reduce the chances of future victimization? Individuals who have been crime victims have a significantly higher chance of future victimization than people who have remained nonvictims.[51]

The chances of repeat victimization may relate to lifestyle. When Marie Skubak Tillyer and her associates studied repeat sexual assault victimization among a high school sample they found that repeat victimization was normative, and that impulsive kids who hang out with antisocial peers and are involved in unsupervised social activities are the ones most at risk for repeat victimization.[52] Repeat victimization also applies to locations: households that have experienced victimization in the past are the ones most likely to experience it again in the future.[53]

What factors predict chronic victimization? Most repeat victimizations occur soon after the previous crime, suggesting that repeat victims share some personal characteristic that makes them a magnet for predators.[54] Children who are shy, physically weak, or socially isolated may share a set of characteristics making them prone to being repeatedly bullied in the schoolyard.[55] David Finkelhor and Nancy Asigian have found that three specific types of characteristics increase the potential for victimization:

- *Target vulnerability.* The victims' physical weakness or psychological distress renders them incapable of resisting or deterring crime and makes them easy targets.
- *Target gratifiability.* Some victims have some quality, possession, skill, or attribute that an offender wants to obtain, use, have access to, or manipulate. Having attractive possessions, such as a leather coat, may make one vulnerable to predatory crime.
- *Target antagonism.* Some characteristics increase risk because they arouse anger, jealousy, or destructive impulses in potential offenders. Gay men risk attacks by homophobes; being argumentative and alcoholic may provoke barroom assaults.[56]

Of course, not all victims are repeaters. Some take defensive measures to lessen their chance of future victimizations. Some may change their lifestyle, take fewer risks, and cut back on associating with dangerous people; once burned, twice shy.[57]

Repeat victimization may occur when the victim does not take defensive action. If an abusive husband finds out that his battered wife will not call police, he repeatedly victimizes her. If a hate crime is committed and the police do not respond to reported offenses, the perpetrators learn they have little to fear from the law.[58]

## Victims and Their Criminals

The victim data also tell us something about the relationship between victims and criminals. Males are more likely to be violently victimized by a stranger, and females

**CHECKPOINTS**

▶ Males are more often the victims of crime than females; women are more likely than men to be attacked by a relative.

▶ The indigent are much more likely than the affluent to be victims of violent crime; the wealthy are more likely to be targets of personal theft.

▶ Younger, single people are more often targets than older, married people.

▶ Crime victimization tends to be intraracial.

▶ Some people and places are targets and venues of repeat victimization.

are more likely to be victimized by a friend, an acquaintance, or an intimate.

Victims report that most crimes were committed by a single offender over age 20. Crime tends to be intraracial: African American offenders victimize blacks, and European Americans victimize whites.

Although many violent crimes are committed by strangers, a surprising number are committed by relatives or acquaintances. When Yale sociologist Andrew Papachristos studied 191 murder incidents that took place between 2005 and 2010 in two low-income Chicago neighborhoods, he found that while some killings were random, more often than not the victims knew their killers or at least someone linked to the offender. Papachristos found that 70 percent of the killings occurred within a social network of just 1,600 people out of a total neighborhood population of 80,000. His data showed that the risk of people in the network being murdered was approximately 30 in 1,000, compared to less than 1 in 1,000 for the others in the study neighborhoods. His conclusion was that murder victims are part of a relatively small network of people involved in some form of interpersonal conflict and who live in close proximity to one another.[59]

Frank Polich/Getty Image news/Getty Images

A great many victims knew or were acquainted with their attacker. Here, Chicago police remove a body from a home where 57-year-old Darnell Hudson Donerson, the mother of Oscar winner Jennifer Hudson, was found shot to death on the living room floor. Hudson's brother was also found dead in a bedroom of the home. In 2012, William Balfour, the former husband of Hudson's sister Julia, was convicted of the murders.

## Theories of Victimization

For many years, criminological theory focused on the actions of the criminal offender; the role of the victim was virtually ignored. More than 60 years ago, scholars began to realize that the victim was not simply a passive target in crime but someone whose behavior can influence his or her own fate, who "shapes and molds the criminal."[60] These early works helped focus attention on the role of the victim in the crime problem and led to further research efforts that have sharpened the image of the crime victim. Today a number of different theories attempt to explain the causes of victimization.

**LO6** Compare and contrast the most important theories of victimization.

### Victim Precipitation Theory

According to **victim precipitation theory**, some people actually initiate the confrontation that eventually leads to their injury or death. Victim precipitation can be either active or passive.

**Active precipitation** occurs when victims act provocatively, use threats or fighting words, or even attack first.[61] In 1971, Menachem Amir suggested that female rape victims often contribute to their attack by dressing provocatively or pursuing a relationship with the rapist.[62] Although Amir's findings are considered highly controversial and there has been a great deal of change in the way rape victims are treated and the laws have been written, rape myths still exist (for example, that women make false reports of rape when they later regret consensual sexual activity) and it is still not unusual for courts to exonerate defendants in rape cases unless there is overwhelming proof that the victim did not consent to sexual intimacy.[63]

In contrast, **passive precipitation** occurs when the victim was the first to act in the sequence of interactions that lead up to the criminal event; the victim encouraged the commission of the crime. Victim precipitation is a component in several different types of crime, most notably homicide, assault, rape, and robbery.[64] Passive precipitation may also be triggered when the victim exhibits some personal characteristic that unknowingly either threatens or encourages the attacker, such as their race or

**victim precipitation theory**
The view that victims may initiate, either actively or passively, the confrontation that leads to their victimization.

**active precipitation**
Aggressive or provocative behavior of victims that results in their victimization.

**passive precipitation**
Personal or social characteristics of victims that make them attractive targets for criminals; such victims may unknowingly either threaten or encourage their attackers.

Victim precipitation theory suggests that criminal violence may be encouraged by the active or passive behavior of its target. Consider the famous case of victimization known as the Jena 6 incident. It began when Justin Barker, 18, shown here, was beaten on December 4, 2006, by six black students at Jena High School in Jena, Louisiana. There had been an undercurrent of racial tension in the town, which had led to outbreaks of violence between white and black students. The tension escalated when a black student attempted to sit under a tree where white students congregated. The next day, three nooses were found hanging from the branches of this tree. Subsequent to the incident, six black students attacked Barker, who was not involved in the incident in any way and whose attack may have been a function of passive precipitation. At trial, where five of the defendants received probation and were asked to pay restitution, their lawyer read a statement apologizing to the Barker family and to the town. This statement also addressed the rumors that the attack had been provoked by Barker's using a racial epithet: "To be clear, not one of us heard Justin use any slur or say anything that justified Mychal Bell attacking Justin, nor did any of us see Justin do anything that would cause Mychal to react." The Barker case is a good example of passive victim precipitation: Justin was victimized because of ongoing racial tension and hostility that were simply not his doing.

Brent Stirton/Getty Images News/Getty Images

ethnicity. Gender may play a role in the decision-making process: criminals may target female victims because they perceive them to be easier, less threatening targets.[65] Thus, it is possible that a fearful or anxious demeanor may make a woman more vulnerable to attack.

Many victims knew their attacker, who might be an acquaintance, relative, or former intimate partner. Here, Johnny Brickman Wall appears before Judge James Blanch at the Matheson Courthouse in Salt Lake City on April 13, 2015. Wall was convicted of killing his ex-wife, Uta von Schwedler, over a bitter custody dispute. Wall was convicted of attacking the 49-year-old woman with a knife, dosing her with the anti-anxiety drug Xanax, and drowning her in her bathtub.

AP Images/Francisco Kjolseth/Salt Lake Tribune/Newspaper Member

## Personality Theories

Perhaps there is something about victims that provokes an attack. A number of research efforts have found that victims have an impulsive personality. They lack self-control, are less likely to have a high tolerance for frustration, tend to have a physical rather than a mental orientation, and are less likely to practice risk avoidance. These personality traits render them abrasive and obnoxious, characteristics that might incite victimization. It is possible that impulsive people are not only antagonistic and more likely to become targets, but they are also risk takers who get involved in dangerous situations and fail to take precautions.[66]

## Lifestyle Theories

Some criminologists believe that people may become crime victims because their lifestyle increases their exposure to criminal offenders. Victimization risk is increased by such behaviors as associating with young men, going out in public places late at night, and living in an urban area. Conversely, one's chances of victimization can be reduced by staying home at night, moving to a rural area, staying out of public places, earning more money, and getting married. The basis of such **lifestyle theories** is that crime is not a random occurrence; rather, it is a function of the victim's lifestyle.

**HIGH-RISK LIFESTYLES** People who have high-risk lifestyles—drinking, taking drugs, going out at night, being away from home, living on the streets—have a much greater chance of victimization.[67] One reason is that offenders have similar lifestyles, and being in close proximity to dangerous people increases chances of victimization.[68]

Teenage males have an extremely high victimization risk because their lifestyle places them at risk both at school and once they leave the school grounds.[69] They spend a great deal of time hanging out with their friends and pursuing recreational fun.[70] Their friends may give them a false ID so they can drink in the neighborhood bar. They may hang out in taverns at night, which places them at risk because many fights and assaults occur in places that serve liquor. Research conducted in a variety of nations shows boys who have an active nightlife (any time after 6 P.M.), who frequent public places, and who consume alcohol significantly increase their victimization risk.[71]

Exposure to violence and associating with violent peers enmeshes young men in a violent lifestyle that increases their own risk of violent offending. One way for young males to avoid victimization is to limit their male friends and hang out with girls! The greater the number of girls in their peer group, the lower their chances of victimization.[72]

Those who have a history of engaging in serious delinquency, getting involved in gangs, carrying guns, and selling drugs have an increased chance of being shot and killed. Kids who have done time and have a history of family violence are the ones most at risk for becoming homicide victims.[73] Lifestyle risks continue into young adulthood. As adults, those who commit crimes increase their chances of becoming the victims of homicide.[74]

The association between victimization and criminal lifestyle is probably one of risk rather than of propensity: people who are involved simply get close to violent, dangerous people and are therefore exposed to victimization themselves.

**COLLEGE LIFESTYLE** Some college students maintain a lifestyle—partying, taking recreational drugs—that makes them vulnerable to victimization. Of particular importance is the disturbing number of sexual assaults that now occur on college campuses. Recent research by the Bureau of Justice Statistics (2014) finds that the rate of rape and sexual assault for the 18 to 24 age group is somewhat higher for nonstudents (7.6 per 1,000) than for students (6.1 per 1,000) and that most victims in both groups (80 percent) were acquainted with their attacker.[75] However, there were some important differences between the two groups. Most student rape and sexual assault victimizations (51 percent) occurred while the victim was pursuing leisure activities away from home, compared to nonstudents who were engaged in activities at home (50 percent) when the victimization occurred. Rape and sexual assault victimizations of students were more likely (80 percent) than nonstudent victimizations (67 percent) to go unreported to police.

**lifestyle theories**
Views on how people become crime victims because of lifestyles that increase their exposure to criminal offenders.

**FACT OR FICTION?**

Most crime victims are people who are simply in the wrong place at the wrong time.

**FICTION** Criminologists believe that victims often engage in behaviors that increase the likelihood of their being targeted for crime. Victims are more likely to engage in risky behavior than nonvictims.

*Alex Gallardo/Reuters/Landov*

Some people are particularly vulnerable to crime because of their lifestyle, none more than the homeless. These posters show the images of four homeless men killed by Itzcoatl Ocampo, a former Marine. Before he could be tried for the crimes, Ocampo killed himself in jail by eating cleaning powder.

On March 1, 2013, University of North Carolina-Chapel Hill sophomore Landen Gambill (center) speaks with supporters during a rally on the steps of the South Building on campus. After Gambill publicly claimed that she was a rape victim, the school accused her of creating an intimidating environment for a fellow student, the one she accused of sexual assault. The university eventually dropped the charge and acknowledged that bringing the intimidation case before UNC's "honor court" may have violated Gambill's right to free speech.

It is a sad fact of modern life that victimization can occur anywhere, even while socializing on a college campus with acquaintances and fellow students. Why did the college victims fail to report a rape or sexual assault victimization to police? Many felt the victimization was not important enough to report: about a quarter of the students who did not report to police believed the incident was a personal matter; one in five stated a fear of reprisal.

**CRIMINAL LIFESTYLE** One element of lifestyle that may place some people at risk for victimization is an ongoing involvement in a criminal career. People who get involved in a criminal lifestyle, join a gang, deal drugs, and so on, are much more likely to be victimized than noncriminals.[76] There are groups of criminal offenders who specialize in preying upon other miscreants, such as drug dealers. After all, they have a ready supply of cash and are unlikely to call the cops. One way for dealers and other criminals to avoid victimization: use highly aggressive tactics and be prepared to do violence.[77]

What happens when a criminal experiences victimization? Does it encourage further criminal activities? Conversely, might the experience help convince a career criminal to choose another career?

While becoming a criminal may increase chances of victimization, it is also possible that becoming victims themselves may convince some criminals that crime does not pay and they might be better off going straight. Scott Jacques and Richard Wright found that for at least one set of criminal offenders—drug dealers—becoming a crime victim sets the stage for their breaking away from crime. According to these investigators, serious victimizations that drug dealers define as being caused by their own lawbreaking increase the probability of their transitioning out of crime. Terminating their drug dealing is an adaptation that enables them to gain control over their lives and to reduce the probability of future victimization.[78]

Considering these contradictory findings, there is a need for further research on the personality traits of victims.

## Deviant Place Theory

**deviant place theory**
The view that victimization is primarily a function of where people live.

According to **deviant place theory**, the greater their exposure to dangerous places, the more likely people are to become victims of crime and violence.[79] Some communities encourage both crime and victimization. If criminals and victims are one and the same, it's because of where they live and not who they are. Victims are vulnerable because they reside in socially disorganized, high-crime areas where they have the greatest risk of coming into contact with criminal offenders.[80] Neighborhood crime levels may be more significant than individual characteristics or lifestyle for determining the chances of victimization.[81]

So-called deviant places are poor, densely populated, highly transient neighborhoods in which commercial and residential properties exist side by side.[82] The commercial establishments provide criminals with easy targets for theft crimes, such as shoplifting and larceny. Successful people stay out of these stigmatized areas. They are home to "demoralized people" who are easy targets for crime: the homeless, the addicted, the mentally ill, and the elderly poor.[83]

**HONOR CODES** Deviant places also may house informal "honor codes" that promote victimization. According to the code, people who become crime victims are honor bound to retaliate against their attacker. Failure to do so may damage their reputation and make them vulnerable to future attacks. Honor codes are often bound up in gang cultures, so if violence occurs against one member, there is a significant likelihood that retaliation of some sort will occur.[84] This call to honor helps promote a climate where crime leads to victimization and vice versa.

In "less deviant" neighborhoods without a street honor culture, there is more of an emphasis on nonviolent methods of conflict resolution, a condition that minimizes the possibility of retaliation. In these communities, victims are less likely to strike back, more likely to repress their anger, and more likely to call the police to satisfy their need for justice. Victims within these settings may find it *unnecessary* to engage in a counterattack against their adversaries because it will have little bearing on their street rep and on their likelihood of future victimization.[85]

## Routine Activities Theory

A series of papers by Lawrence Cohen and Marcus Felson first articulated **routine activities theory**.[86] Cohen and Felson assume that both the motivation to commit crime and the supply of offenders are constant.[87] Every society will always have some people willing to break the law for revenge, greed, or some other motive. Therefore, the volume and distribution of predatory crime (violent crimes against a person and crimes in which an offender attempts to steal an object directly) are closely related to the interaction of three variables that reflect the routine activities of the typical American lifestyle:

- The availability of **suitable targets**, such as homes containing goods that are easily sold.
- The absence of **capable guardians**, such as police, homeowners, neighbors, friends, and relatives.
- The presence of **motivated offenders**, such as a large number of teenagers.

These components increase the likelihood that a predatory crime will take place and increases the likelihood of victimization. Targets are more likely to be victimized if they are poorly guarded and exposed to a large group of motivated offenders, such as teenage boys.[88] Increasing the number of motivated offenders and placing them in close proximity to valuable goods will increase property victimizations. Even after-school programs, which are designed to reduce criminal activity, may produce higher crime rates because they lump together motivated offenders, such as teenage boys, with vulnerable victims, such as teenage boys.[89] Figure 3.1 illustrates the interacting components of routine activities theory.

**CRIME AND EVERYDAY LIFE** Routine activities theory helps explain why U.S. citizens suffer such high rates of victimization. According to Felson, crime began to increase in the United States as the country changed from a nation of small villages and towns to one of large urban environments. Because metropolitan areas provide a critical population mass, predatory criminals are better able to hide and evade apprehension. After committing crime, criminals can blend into the crowd, disperse their loot, and make a quick escape using the public transportation system.[90]

As the population became more urban, the middle class, fearing criminal victimization, fled to the suburbs. Rather than being safe from crime, the suburbs produced a unique set of routine activities that promotes victimization risk. Both parents are likely to commute to work, leaving teens unsupervised. Affluent kids own or drive cars, date, and socialize with peers in unsupervised settings—all behaviors that are related to

**routine activities theory**
The view that victimization results from the interaction of three everyday factors: the availability of suitable targets, the absence of capable guardians, and the presence of motivated offenders.

**suitable targets**
Objects of crime (persons or property) that are attractive and readily available.

**capable guardians**
Effective deterrents to crime, such as police or watchful neighbors.

**motivated offenders**
People willing and able to commit crimes.

**FIGURE 3.1**
**Routine Activities Theory**
**Source:** © Cengage Learning

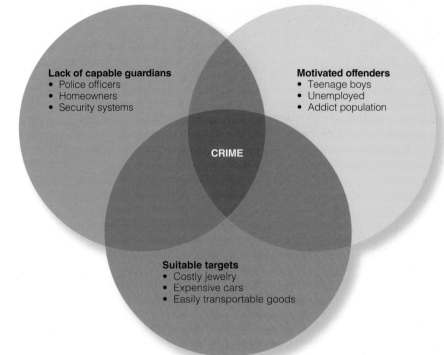

**Lack of capable guardians**
• Police officers
• Homeowners
• Security systems

**Motivated offenders**
• Teenage boys
• Unemployed
• Addict population

**CRIME**

**Suitable targets**
• Costly jewelry
• Expensive cars
• Easily transportable goods

both crime and victimization.[91] The downtown shopping district was replaced by the suburban shopping mall. Here strangers converge in large numbers, and youths hang out. The interior is filled with people, so drug deals can be concealed in the pedestrian flow. Stores have attractively displayed goods, encouraging shoplifting and employee pilferage. Substantial numbers of cars are parked in areas that make larceny and car theft virtually undetectable. Cars that carry away stolen merchandise have an undistinguished appearance: who notices people placing items in a car in a shopping mall parking lot? Also, shoppers can be attacked in parking lots as they walk in isolation to and from their cars. As car ownership increases, teens have greater access to transportation outside parental control. Thus, even though victimization rates in urban areas are still higher, the routine activities in the suburbs may also produce the risk of victimization.

A surveillance video of a robbery and beating at a jewelry store in Clifton, New Jersey. While most victims were acquainted with their attackers, strangers often become victims when they get caught up in the commission of a felony offense, such as this robbery.

Marko Georgiev/North Jersey/Landov

**RESEARCH SUPPORT** Research supports many facets of routine activities theory. Cohen and Felson themselves found that crime rates increased between 1960 and 1980 because the number of adult caretakers at home during the day (guardians) decreased as a result of increased female participation in the workforce. While mothers are at work and children in day care, homes are left unguarded. Similarly, with the growth of suburbia and the decline of the traditional neighborhood, the number of such familiar guardians as family, neighbors, and friends diminished.[92] Steven Messner and his associates found that as adult unemployment rates *increase*, juvenile homicide arrest rates *decrease*. One possible reason for this phenomenon: it is possible that juvenile arrests decreased because unemployed adults were at home to supervise their children and make sure they did not get into trouble or join gangs.[93] The availability and cost of easily

## Concept Summary 3.1    Victimization Theories

| Victimization Theory | Major Premise |
| --- | --- |
| Victim precipitation | Victims provoke criminals. |
| Lifestyle | Victims put themselves in danger by engaging in high-risk activities, such as going out late at night, living in a high-crime area, and associating with high-risk peers. |
| Deviant place | Victimization risk is related to neighborhood crime rates. |
| Routine activities | A pool of motivated offenders exists, and these offenders will take advantage of unguarded, suitable targets. |

transportable goods have also been shown to influence victimization rates: as the cost of goods such as smartphones and iPads declines, so too will burglary rates.[94]

**ROUTINE ACTIVITIES AND LIFESTYLE**   Routine activities theory and the lifestyle approach have a number of similarities. They both assume that a person's living arrangements can affect victim risk and that people who live in unguarded areas are at the mercy of motivated offenders. These two theories both rely on four basic concepts: (1) proximity to criminals, (2) time of exposure to criminals, (3) target attractiveness, and (4) guardianship.[95]

These theories also share five predictions: people increase their victimization risk if they (1) live in high-crime areas, (2) go out late at night, (3) carry valuables such as an expensive watch, (4) engage in risky behavior such as drinking alcohol, and (5) are without friends or family to watch or help them.[96] Young women who drink to excess in bars and fraternity houses may elevate their risk of date rape, because (1) they are easy targets, and (2) their attackers can rationalize raping them because they are intoxicated. ("She's loose and immoral, so I didn't think she'd care.") Intoxication is sometimes seen as making the victim culpable for the crime.[97] Conversely, people can reduce their chances of repeat victimization if they change their lifestyle and adopt crime-suppressing routines such as getting married, having children, or moving to a small town.[98]

The various theories of victimization are summarized in Concept Summary 3.1.

## Caring for the Victim

National victim surveys indicate that almost every American age 12 and over will one day become the victim of a common-law crime, such as larceny or burglary, and in the aftermath will suffer financial problems, mental stress, and physical hardship.[99] Surveys show that upward of 75 percent of the general public have been victimized by crime at least once in their lives. As many as 25 percent of the victims develop posttraumatic stress disorder, with symptoms that last for more than a decade after the crime occurred.[100]

Helping the victim to cope is the responsibility of all of society. Law enforcement agencies, courts, and correctional and human service systems have come to realize that due process and human rights exist not only for the criminal defendant but also for the victim of criminal behavior.

Because of public concern over violent personal crime, President Ronald Reagan created a Task Force on Victims of Crime in 1982.[101] This group suggested that a

### CHECKPOINTS

▶ Victim precipitation theory suggests that crime victims may trigger attacks by acting provocatively.

▶ Some experts link victimization to high-risk lifestyles.

▶ Some people live in places that are magnets for criminals.

▶ The routine activities approach suggests that the risk of victimization may be an interaction among suitable targets, effective guardians, and motivated criminals. Victims who have insufficient protection present motivated criminals with attractive targets.

## Exhibit 3.3    Crime Victims' Rights Act

18 U.S.C. § 3771. Crime victims' rights

(a)  RIGHTS OF CRIME VICTIMS.—A crime victim has the following rights:

  (1)  The right to be reasonably protected from the accused.

  (2)  The right to reasonable, accurate, and timely notice of any public court proceeding, or any parole proceeding, involving the crime or of any release or escape of the accused.

  (3)  The right not to be excluded from any such public court proceeding, unless the court, after receiving clear and convincing evidence, determines that testimony by the victim would be materially altered if the victim heard other testimony at that proceeding.

  (4)  The right to be reasonably heard at any public proceeding in the district court involving release, plea, sentencing, or any parole proceeding.

  (5)  The reasonable right to confer with the attorney for the Government in the case.

  (6)  The right to full and timely restitution as provided in law.

  (7)  The right to proceedings free from unreasonable delay.

  (8)  The right to be treated with fairness and with respect for the victim's dignity and privacy.

(b)  RIGHTS AFFORDED.—In any court proceeding involving an offense against a crime victim, the court shall ensure that the crime victim is afforded the rights described in subsection (a). Before making a determination described in subsection (a) (3), the court shall make every effort to permit the fullest attendance possible by the victim and shall consider reasonable alternatives to the exclusion of the victim from the criminal proceeding. The reasons for any decision denying relief under this chapter shall be clearly stated on the record.

**Source:** United States Department of Justice, Crime Victims' Rights Act, www.justice.gov/usao/resources/crime-victims -rights-ombudsman/victims-rights-act (accessed 2015).

---

balance be achieved between recognizing the victim's rights and providing the defendant with due process. Recommendations included providing witnesses and victims with protection from intimidation, requiring restitution in criminal cases, developing guidelines for fair treatment of crime victims and witnesses, and expanding programs of victim compensation.[102]

As a result, Congress passed the Omnibus Victim and Witness Protection Act, requiring the use of victim impact statements at sentencing in federal criminal cases, greater protection for witnesses, more stringent bail laws, and the use of restitution in criminal cases. In 1984, the Comprehensive Crime Control Act and the Victims of Crime Act authorized federal funding for state victim compensation and assistance projects.[103] Another important milestone was the Crime Victims' Rights Act of 2004 that extended crime victims the right to participate in the justice system and be informed and consulted on tactics and decisions being employed by the Justice Department "and other departments and agencies of the United States engaged in the detection, investigation, or prosecution of crime." The courts were required under the Act to "ensure that the crime victim is afforded the rights given by the law."[104] The most important elements of the CVRA are set out in Exhibit 3.3.

With these acts, the federal government recognized the plight of the victim and made victim assistance an even greater concern of the public and the justice system.

## Victim Service Programs

Thousands of **victim–witness assistance programs** have been developed throughout the United States. These programs are organized on a variety of government levels and serve a variety of clients.

**VICTIM COMPENSATION**  A primary goal of victim advocates has been to lobby for legislation creating crime **victim compensation programs**.[105] As a result of such legislation, the victim ordinarily receives compensation from the state to pay for damages associated with the crime. Exhibit 3.4 describes a few of these programs. Rarely are two compensation

**victim–witness assistance programs**
Government programs that help crime victims and witnesses; may include compensation, court services, and/or crisis intervention.

**victim compensation programs**
Financial aid awarded to crime victims to repay them for their loss and injuries; may cover medical bills, loss of wages, loss of future earnings, and/or counseling.

## Exhibit 3.4  State Victim Compensation Programs

- **The Idaho Crime Victims Compensation Program (ICVC)**, which has collected restitution since 1998, regularly serves as a mentor to other states interested in building their capacity in this area. ICVC collects payments through its website; in 2012, the program implemented a monthly billing system. Offenders with outstanding payments due are notified and ordered to make a payment. The program is reporting success, particularly in collecting large sums from offenders who were not aware they owed restitution.

- **The New Jersey Victims of Crime Compensation Office** is helping protect the rights of victims by providing funding for legal representation in court, which ensures that victims' rights are respected in situations where the victim might be overwhelmed by unfamiliar legal requirements and procedures. Many states permit victims to hire an attorney to help them file claims, but the New Jersey compensation program provides for assistance in any legal matter related to the victimization associated with the claim. There is a $1,000 cap for these services; payment is deducted from the maximum claim benefit.

- **The 17th Judicial District Crime Victim Compensation Program** in Brighton, Colorado, is almost entirely paperless—increasing efficiency while going green. Files are scanned, queued until they are assigned to victim files, and managed from a central storage drive. Staff members send board members case summaries and relevant documents through an encrypted online document management system. In turn, board members use their district-issued tablets to access the software, review claims, and prepare for monthly board meetings.

**Source:** Office for the Victims of Crime, "2013 OVC Report to the Nation," www.ovc.gov/pubs/reporttonation2013/voca_cn.html (accessed 2015).

schemes alike, however, and many state programs suffer from a lack of both adequate funding and proper organization within the criminal justice system. Compensation may be provided for medical bills, loss of wages, loss of future earnings, and counseling. In the case of death, the victim's survivors may receive burial expenses and aid for loss of support.[106] Awards typically range from $100 to $15,000. Occasionally, programs provide emergency assistance to indigent victims until compensation is available. Emergency assistance may come in the form of food vouchers or replacement of prescription medicines.

**VICTIM ADVOCATES** Some programs assign counselors to victims to serve as advocates, help them understand the operations of the justice system, and guide them through the process. Victims of sexual assault may be assigned the assistance of a rape victim advocate to stand by their side as they negotiate the legal and medical systems that must process their case. Research shows that rape survivors who had the assistance of an advocate were significantly more likely to have police reports taken, were less likely to be treated negatively by police officers, and reported less distress from their medical contact experiences.[107] Police departments are now instituting training designed to prepare officers to work more effectively with victim advocates.[108]

Court advocates prepare victims and witnesses by explaining court procedures: how to be a witness, how bail works, and what to do if the defendant makes a threat. Lack of such knowledge can cause confusion and fear, making some victims reluctant to testify in court proceedings. Many victim programs also provide transportation to and from court, as well as counselors who remain in the courtroom during hearings to explain procedures and provide support. Court escorts are particularly important for elderly and disabled victims, victims of child abuse and assault, and victims who have been intimidated by friends or relatives of the defendant.

**VICTIM IMPACT STATEMENTS** Every state jurisdiction allows victims to make an impact statement before the sentencing judge. Victim impact information is part of the Federal Crime Act of 1994, in which Congress gave federal victims of violent crime or sexual assault the right to speak at sentencing. Through the Child Protection Act of

AP Images/Sacramento Bee/Renee C. Byer/Newspaper Member

Don Hatfield reads a victim impact statement and addresses Todd Winkler who, on December 8, 2014, was sentenced to 26 years to life in El Dorado County Superior Court in Placerville, California. At right is prosecutor Lisette Suder. Winkler murdered Hatfield's daughter, Rachel Winkler, in their Cameron Park home during a painful marital breakup. Hatfield condemned Winkler for the "vile act" that will force the couple's three young children to have to ask: "Why did Daddy kill Mommy?"

1990, child victims of federal crimes are allowed to submit victim impact statements that are "commensurate with their age and cognitive development," which can include drawings, models, etc.[109] This gives the victim an opportunity to tell of his or her experiences and describe the ordeal; in the case of a murder trial, the surviving family can recount the effect the crime has had on their lives and well-being.[110]

Those who favor the use of impact statements argue that because the victim is harmed by the crime, she or he has a right to influence the outcome of the case. After all, the public prosecutor is allowed to make sentencing recommendations because the public has been harmed by the crime. Logically, the harm suffered by the victim legitimizes her or his right to make sentencing recommendations.[111]

The effect of victim/witness statements on sentencing has been the topic of some debate. Some research finds that victim statements result in a higher rate of incarceration.[112] There is also evidence that victim/witness statements are significant in deciding between community and incarceration sentences.[113] Yet, not all research efforts support the value of witness statements.[114]

**PUBLIC EDUCATION**  More than half of all victim programs include public education to help familiarize the general public with their services and with other agencies that help crime victims. In some instances, these are primary prevention programs, which teach methods of dealing with conflict without resorting to violence. School-based programs present information on spousal and dating abuse, followed by discussions of how to reduce violent incidents.[115]

**CRISIS INTERVENTION**  Most victim programs refer victims to specific services to help them recover from their ordeal. Clients are commonly referred to the local network of public and private social service agencies that provide emergency and long-term assistance with transportation, medical care, shelter, food, and clothing. In addition, more than half of all victim programs provide **crisis intervention** for victims who feel isolated, vulnerable, and in need of immediate services. Some programs counsel at their offices; others visit victims in their homes, at the crime scene, or in the hospital. The Good Samaritan program in Mobile County, Alabama, unites law enforcement with faith-based and community organizations to train and mobilize volunteers who can help crime victims. Good Samaritan volunteers provide services such as:

**crisis intervention**
Emergency counseling for crime victims.

**victim–offender reconciliation programs (VORPs)**
Mediated face-to-face encounters between victims and their attackers, designed to produce restitution agreements and, if possible, reconciliation.

- Making repairs to a home after a break-in
- Conducting home safety inspections to prevent revictimization
- Accompanying victims to court
- Supplying "victim care kits" or other support[116]

**VICTIM–OFFENDER RECONCILIATION PROGRAMS**  Mediators facilitate face-to-face encounters between victims and their attackers in **victim–offender reconciliation programs (VORPs)**. The aim is to engage in direct negotiations that lead to restitution agreements and, possibly, reconciliation between the parties involved.[117] Originally designed to handle routine misdemeanors such as petty theft and vandalism, such programs now commonly hammer out restitution agreements in more serious incidents, such as residential burglary and even attempted murder.

**VICTIM NOTIFICATION** There have been a number of efforts to notify victims (or potential victims) of offenders' locations. Every state has sex offender registration to keep potential victims aware of the location of convicted sex offenders in their community. In addition, most states have adopted the VINE (Victim Information and Notification Everyday) service through which victims of crime can use the telephone or Internet to search for information regarding their offender's custody status and register to receive telephone and email notification when their offender's status changes. The federal system has its own program, the Department of Justice's Victim Notification System (VNS). This is a cooperative effort among the Federal Bureau of Investigation, the U.S. Postal Inspection Service, the U.S. Attorney's Offices, the Federal Bureau of Prisons, and the Criminal Division. This computer-based system provides federal crime victims with information on scheduled court events, as well as the outcome of those court events. It also provides victims with information on the offender's custody status and release.[118]

**LEGAL PROTECTION FOR VICTIMS** Another way that victims have been served is the more rigorous enforcement of laws designed specially to protect certain classes of victims. For many years victim advocates complained that states did not offer adequate protection for victims of domestic violence, sometimes treating these crimes as a "private matter." Due to the impact of victim advocacy, state courts are now more likely to issue orders of protection, which require accused abusers to immediately stop stalking or harassing a victim and to stay away from the victim's home.

Typically, there are two types of these protective orders. The first, an *ex parte* order, is a temporary measure quickly issued by the court that grants immediate relief while an investigation can be conducted. For example, Massachusetts General Laws (M.G.L.) Chapter 209A Section 1 defines the conditions under which a restraining order may be issued:

> The occurrence of one or more of the following acts between family or household members:
>
> **1.** attempting to cause or causing physical harm;
>
> **2.** placing another in fear of imminent serious physical harm;
>
> **3.** causing another to engage involuntarily in sexual relations by force, threat or duress

Note that the order may be issued when the complaining party is put in fear—no actual abuse needs to have occurred. The accused abuser does not have to be present at the hearing.

When the court issues an *ex parte* order, it sets up another hearing with notice to the defendant; this is usually called a "return" day. If evidence is presented before the court that authenticates the original complaint, a full order may be issued. This is in effect for a longer period than the *ex parte* order and may become permanent.

Have these legal changes helped protect domestic violence victims? While it is always difficult to show a direct causal relationship between legal change and criminal behavior, there has in fact been a significant decline in domestic violence cases during the past decade.[119]

While providing legal redress may be responsible in part for the significant decade-long decline in domestic violence cases, it is also likely that victim advocacy programs and the availability of such services as emergency shelters and transitional housing also play a role. While these trends are encouraging, about 1 million people are still victims of intimate partner attacks each year.

**CONNECTIONS**

Chapter 1 has a feature on the effectiveness of offender registration systems. As you may recall, they do not seem to work as intended. Considering their ineffectiveness, would you advocate their elimination in order to save the taxpayers money?

## Victims' Rights

Because of the influence of victims' rights advocates, every state now has a set of legal rights for crime victims in its code of laws, often called a Victims' Bill of Rights.[120] These generally include the right

- To be notified of proceedings and the status of the defendant
- To be present at criminal justice proceedings
- To make a statement at sentencing and to receive restitution from a convicted offender
- To be consulted before a case is dismissed or a plea agreement entered
- To a speedy trial
- To keep the victim's contact information confidential

A controversial element of the victims' rights movement is the development of offender registration laws that require law enforcement agencies to post the name, and sometimes the address, of known sex offenders. Today, almost every state has adopted sex offender laws, and the federal government runs a National Sex Offender Public Registry with links to every state.[121]

## Victim Advocates

Ensuring victims' rights may involve an eclectic mix of advocacy groups—some independent, others government-sponsored, and some self-help. Advocates can be especially helpful when victims need to interact with the agencies of justice. Advocates can lobby police departments to keep investigations open and can request the return of recovered stolen property. They can demand that prosecutors and judges provide protection from harassment and reprisals by making "no contact" a condition of bail (research shows that victims who hire lawyers have a better chance of getting these orders enforced).[122] They can help victims make statements during sentencing hearings and during probation and parole revocation procedures. Victim advocates can also interact with news media, making sure that reporting is accurate and that victims' privacy is not violated. Victim advocates can be part of an independent agency similar to a legal aid society. Top-notch victim advocates sometimes open private offices, similar to attorneys, private investigators, or jury consultants.

## Self-Protection

Not all actual or potential victims are content with relying on victim services to provide after-the-fact comfort. As the Trayvon Martin case aptly illustrated, concerns about community safety have prompted some people to become their own "police force," taking an active role in community protection through creation of citizen watch and crime control groups.[123] The more crime in an area, the greater the amount of fear and the more likely residents will be to engage in self-protective measures.[124]

Another method of self-protection involves target hardening, or making one's home and business crime-proof through locks, bars, alarms, and other devices.[125] Some commonly used crime prevention techniques include a fence or barricade at the entrance; a doorkeeper, guard, or receptionist in an apartment building; an intercom or phone to gain access to the building; surveillance cameras; window bars; warning signs; and dogs chosen for their ability to guard the house. The use of these measures is inversely proportional to perception of neighborhood safety: people who fear crime are more likely to use crime prevention techniques. Although the true relationship is still unclear, there is mounting evidence that people who protect their homes are less likely to be victimized by property crimes.[126]

**FIGHTING BACK**  Some people take self-protection to its ultimate end by preparing to fight back when criminals attack them. How successful are victims when they resist? Research indicates that victims who fight back often frustrate their attackers but also face increased odds of being physically harmed during the attack.[127] In some cases, fighting back decreases the odds of a crime being completed but increases the victim's chances of injury.[128] Resistance may draw the attention of bystanders and make a violent crime physically difficult to complete, but it can also cause offenders to escalate their violence.[129] One reason for the association: victims may be ready to fight back when they sense that their attacker intends to use violence no matter what they do; why hold back if they have nothing to lose? Essentially, if the offender begins the assault using physical aggression, the victim is more likely to react with physical resistance.[130]

**USING FIREARMS** Not surprisingly, an offender who utilizes a weapon is more likely to become violent; carrying a weapon also increases the chances of offense completion. Take sexual assault: although male perpetrators are often more physically capable than their victims, who are most often women or children, the victim has a better chance to escape or to make the offender doubt his chances of success if the offender does not have a weapon.[131]

What about the use of firearms for self-protection? Each year, millions of victims use guns for defensive purposes (a number that is not surprising considering that about one-third of U.S. households contain guns).[132] Gary Kleck

AP Images/Seth Wenig

Does fighting back help? Jennifer Hilchey-Reyell believes so. She is shown here carrying a .22 rifle at her mother's house near Dannemora, New York. Hilchey-Reyell has been keeping a gun close at hand since the escape of two prisoners from the maximum-security Clinton Correctional Facility near her home. David Sweat, one of the two convicted killers, was captured after being shot during a firefight with law enforcement officers; the other escapee, Richard Matt, was killed in a shootout.

has estimated that armed victims kill more attackers than police and the risk of collateral injury is relatively rare. Fighting back significantly reduces the likelihood of property loss and injury, and the most forceful tactics, including resistance with a gun, appear to have the strongest effects in reducing the risk of injury. The conclusion: it is better to fight than flee.[133]

# Thinking Like a Criminologist

## Spare the Rod, Eliminate the Needle

The director of your state's Department of Human Services has asked you to evaluate a self-report survey of adolescents aged 12 to 18. She has provided you with the following information on physical abuse.

Adolescents experiencing abuse or violence are at high risk of immediate and lasting negative effects on their health and well-being. Of the middle school students surveyed, an alarming 1 in 5 (21 percent) said they had been physically abused. Of the older students, aged 15 to 18, 29 percent said they had been physically abused. Younger students, ages 10 and 11, also reported significant rates of abuse: 17 percent responded "yes" when asked whether they had been physically abused. Although girls were far less likely to report abuse than boys, 12 percent said they had been physically abused. Most abuse occurs at home, it occurs more than once, and the abuser is usually a family member. More than half of those physically abused had tried alcohol and drugs, and 60 percent had admitted to committing a violent act. Nonabused children were significantly less likely to abuse substances, and only 30 percent indicated that they had committed a violent act.

### Writing Assignment

Write an essay describing why being abused as a child leads to substance abuse and violence as an adult. In your essay, interpret these findings from environmental, socialization, psychological, and biological points of view, and provide evidence supporting each perspective.

# SUMMARY

**LO1  Analyze the victim's role in the crime process.**

Victims may influence criminal behavior by playing an active role in a criminal incident. Rather than being merely at the wrong place at the wrong time, a victim's lifestyle and activities may increase their risk of being crime targets. In some instances, victims may actually trigger or precipitate an aggressive act. The discovery that victims play an important role in the crime process has prompted the scientific study of victims, or victimology. Criminologists who focus their attention on crime victims refer to themselves as victimologists.

**LO2  Discuss the greatest problems faced by crime victims.**

The costs of victimization can include such things as damaged property, pain and suffering to victims, and the involvement of the police and other agencies of the justice system. The pain and suffering inflicted on an individual can result in the need for long-term medical care and counseling, the loss of wages from not being able to go to work, and reduced quality of life from debilitating injuries and/or fear of being victimized again.

**LO3  Clarify the term *cycle of violence*.**

People who were abused as children may be more likely to commit crimes themselves. Adult victims may seek revenge against their attackers. The abuse–crime phenomenon is referred to as the cycle of violence.

**LO4  Assess the ecology of victimization risk.**

Violent crimes are slightly more likely to take place in an open, public area, such as a street, a park, or a field. The more serious violent crimes, such as rape and aggravated assault, typically take place after 6 P.M. Those living in the central city have significantly higher rates of theft and violence than suburbanites; people living in rural areas have a victimization rate almost half that of city dwellers. Schools are the site of a great deal of victimization because they are populated by one of the most dangerous segments of society, teenage males.

**LO5  Categorize the most dominant victim characteristics.**

Except for the crimes of rape and sexual assault, males are more likely than females to be the victims of violent crime. Victim data reveal that young people face a much greater victimization risk than older persons. The poorest Americans are the most likely to be victims of violent and property crime. This association occurs across all gender, age, and racial groups. African Americans are about twice as likely as European Americans to be victims of violent crime. Never-married males and females are victimized more often than married people.

**LO6  Compare and contrast the most important theories of victimization.**

According to victim precipitation theory, some people may actually initiate the confrontation that eventually leads to their injury or death. Victim precipitation can be either active or passive. Some criminologists believe that people may become crime victims because their lifestyle increases their exposure to criminal offenders. People who have high-risk lifestyles—drinking, taking drugs, getting involved in crime—have a much greater chance of victimization. According to deviant place theory, the greater their exposure to dangerous places, the more likely people are to become victims of crime and violence. So-called deviant places are poor, densely populated, highly transient neighborhoods in which commercial and residential properties exist side by side. Routine activities theory links victimization to the availability of suitable targets, the absence of capable guardians, and the presence of motivated offenders.

# Key Terms

victimology 62
victimologists 62
posttraumatic stress
    disorder (PTSD) 64
cycle of violence 67
victim precipitation
    theory 73

active precipitation 73
passive precipitation 73
lifestyle theories 75
deviant place theory 76
routine activities theory 77
suitable targets 77

capable guardians 77
motivated offenders 77
victim–witness assistance
    programs 80
victim compensation
    programs 80

crisis intervention 82
victim–offender recon-
    ciliation programs
    (VORPs) 82

# Critical Thinking Questions

1. Considering what you have learned in this chapter about crime victimization, what measures can you take to better protect yourself from crime?

2. Do you agree with the assessment that a school is one of the most dangerous locations in the community? Did you find your high school to be a dangerous environment?

3. Do people bear some of the responsibility for their victimization if they maintain a lifestyle that contributes to the chances of becoming a crime victim? That is, should we "blame the victim"?

4. Have you ever observed someone habitually "precipitating" crime? If so, did you do anything to improve the situation?

5. What would you advise freshman women to do to lower their risk of being sexually assaulted?

# Notes

*All URLs accessed in 2015.*

1. Plain Dealer Staff, "Steubenville Rape Case: Defense Expert Says Teen Girl Could Have Made Decisions Even After Heavy Drinking," *Cleveland Plain Dealer*, March 16, 2013, www.cleveland.com/steubenville-rape-case/index.ssf/2013/03/steubenville_rape_case_defense.html.

2. Michael Muskal, "School Superintendent, 3 Others Charged in Steubenville Rape Case," *Los Angeles Times*, November 25, 2013, www.latimes.com/nation/nationnow/la-na-nn-steubenville-rape-indictiments-20131125,0,5866038.story#axzz2rR0OwNDl.

3. Sasha Goldstein, "Georgia Teens Charged in Connection with After-Prom Rape at Remote Cabin Party: Police," *New York Daily News*, May 28, 2014, www.nydailynews.com/news/crime/georgia-teens-charged-after-prom-rape-cabin-party-police-article-1.1808856.

4. Beth Stebner, "Audrie Pott Suicide: Details of Online Chats Emerge a Year After Teen Killed Herself Following Alleged Assault and Cyberbullying," *New York Daily News*, September 18, 2013, www.nydailynews.com/news/national/new-details-revealed-audrie-pott-cyber-bullying-suicide-article-1.1459904; CTV News, "Police Warn Against Vigilantism in Rehtaeh Parsons Case," atlantic.ctvnews.ca/police-warn-against-vigilantism-in-rehtaeh-parsons-case-1.1234199.

5. Hans Von Hentig, *The Criminal and His Victim: Studies in the Sociobiology of Crime* (New Haven, CT: Yale University Press, 1948); Stephen Schafer, *The Victim and His Criminal* (New York: Random House, 1968).

6. Kathryn McCollister, Michael T. French, and Hai Fang, "The Cost of Crime to Society: New Crime-Specific Estimates for Policy and Program Evaluation," *Drug and Alcohol Dependence* 108 (2010): 98–109.

7. James Anderson, Terry Grandison, and Laronistine Dyson, "Victims of Random Violence and the Public Health Implication: A Health Care of Criminal Justice Issue," *Journal of Criminal Justice* 24 (1996): 379–393.

8. Lynn Langton and Jennifer Truman, *Socio-Emotional Impact of Violent Crime*, Bureau of Justice Statistics, 2014, www.bjs.gov/content/pub/pdf/sivc.pdf.

9. Angela Scarpa, Sara Chiara Haden, and Jimmy Hurley, "Community Violence Victimization and Symptoms of Posttraumatic Stress Disorder: The Moderating Effects of Coping and Social Support," *Journal of Interpersonal Violence* 21 (2006): 446–469.

10. Heather Littleton and Craig Henderson, "If She Is Not a Victim, Does That Mean She Was Not Traumatized? Evaluation of Predictors of PTSD Symptomatology Among College Rape Victims," *Violence Against Women* 15 (2009): 148–167.

11. Noora Ilonen, Minna Piispa, Kirsi Peltonen, and Mikko Oranen, "Exposure to Parental Violence and Outcomes of Child Psychosocial Adjustment," *Violence and Victims* 28 (2013): 3–15; N. N. Sarkar and Rina Sarkar, "Sexual Assault on Woman: Its Impact on

Her Life and Living in Society," *Sexual and Relationship Therapy* 20 (2005): 407.

12. Jeanne Kaufman and Cathy Spatz Widom, "Childhood Victimization, Running Away, and Delinquency," *Journal of Research in Crime and Delinquency* 36 (1999): 347–370.

13. David Finkelhor, *Childhood Victimization: Violence, Crime, and Abuse in the Lives of Young People* (London: Oxford University Press, 2008).

14. Leana Bouffard and Maria Koeppel, "Understanding the Potential Long-Term Physical and Mental Health Consequences of Early Experiences of Victimization," *Justice Quarterly* 31 (2014): 568–587.

15. Jihong Solomon Zhao, Brian Lawton, and Dennis Longmire, "An Examination of the Micro-Level Crime–Fear of Crime Link," *Crime and Delinquency* 61 (2015): 19–44.

16. Ron Acierno, Alyssa Rheingold, Heidi Resnick, and Dean Kilpatrick, "Predictors of Fear of Crime in Older Adults," *Journal of Anxiety Disorders* 18 (2004): 385–396.

17. Ibid.

18. Karen A. Snedker, "Neighborhood Conditions and Fear of Crime: A Reconsideration of Sex Differences," *Crime and Delinquency* 61 (2015): 45–70.

19. Susan Brison, *Aftermath: Violence and the Remaking of a Self* (Princeton, NJ: Princeton University Press, 2001).

20. Min Xie and David McDowall, "Impact of Victimization on Residential Mobility: Explaining Racial and Ethnic Patterns Using the National Crime Victimization Survey," *Criminology* 52 (2014): 553–587.

21. Fawn T. Ngo and Raymond Paternoster, "Toward an Understanding of the Emotional and Behavioral Reactions to Stalking: A Partial Test of General Strain Theory," *Crime and Delinquency*, first published online November 7, 2013.

22. Min Xie and David McDowall, "Escaping Crime: The Effects of Direct and Indirect Victimization on Moving," *Criminology* 46 (2008): 809–840.

23. Mirka Smolej and Janne Kivivuori, "The Relation Between Crime News and Fear of Violence," *Journal of Scandinavian Studies in Criminology and Crime Prevention* 7 (2006): 211–227.

24. Matthew Lee and Erica DeHart, "The Influence of a Serial Killer on Changes in Fear of Crime and the Use of Protective Measures: A Survey-Based Case Study of Baton Rouge," *Deviant Behavior* 28 (2007): 1–28.

25. Tyler Frederick, Bill McCarthy, and John Hagan, "Perceived Danger and Offending: Exploring the Links Between Violent Victimization and Street Crime," *Violence and Victims* 28 (2013): 16–35.

26. Amy Rose Grubb and Julie Harrower, "Understanding Attribution of Blame in Cases of Rape: An Analysis of Participant Gender, Type of Rape and Perceived Similarity to the Victim," *Journal of Sexual Aggression* 15 (2009): 63–81.

27. Rebecca Campbell and Sheela Raja, "Secondary Victimization of Rape Victims: Insights from Mental Health Professionals Who Treat Survivors of Violence," *Violence and Victims* 14 (1999): 261–274.

28. Courtney Ahrens, "Being Silenced: The Impact of Negative Social Reactions on the Disclosure of Rape," *American Journal of Community Psychology* 38 (2006): 263–274.

29. Timothy Ireland and Cathy Spatz Widom, *Childhood Victimization and Risk for Alcohol and Drug Arrests* (Washington, DC: National Institute of Justice, 1995).

30. Brigette Erwin, Elana Newman, Robert McCracken, Carlo Morrissey, and Danny Kaloupek, "PTSD, Malevolent Environment, and Criminality Among Criminally Involved Male Adolescents," *Criminal Justice and Behavior* 27 (2000): 196–215.

31. Min Jung Kim, Emiko Tajima, Todd Herrenkohl, and Bu Huang, "Early Child Maltreatment, Runaway Youths, and Risk of Delinquency and Victimization in Adolescence: A Mediational Model," *Social Work Research* 33 (2009): 19–28.

32. Ulrich Orth, Leo Montada, and Andreas Maercker, "Feelings of Revenge, Retaliation Motive, and Posttraumatic Stress Reactions in Crime Victims," *Journal of Interpersonal Violence* 21 (2006): 229–243.

33. Cathy Spatz Widom, *The Cycle of Violence* (Washington, DC: National Institute of Justice, 1992), p. 1.

34. Amy Reckdenwald, Christina Mancini, and Eric Beauregard, "The Cycle of Violence: Examining the Impact of Maltreatment Early in Life on Adult Offending," *Violence and Victims* 28 (2013): 466–82; Marie Skubak Tillyer and Emily M. Wright, "Intimate Partner Violence and the Victim-Offender Overlap," *Journal of Research in Crime and Delinquency*, first published online April 29, 2013.

35. Chris Melde, Finn-Aage Esbensen, and Terrance Taylor, "'May Piece Be with You': A Typological Examination of the Fear and Victimization Hypothesis of Adolescent Weapon Carrying," *Justice Quarterly* 26 (2009): 348–376.

36. Janet Lauritsen and Nicole White, *Seasonal Patterns in Criminal Victimization Trends*, Bureau of Justice Statistics, 2014, www.bjs.gov/content/pub/pdf/spcvt.pdf.

37. Chris Gibson, Zara Morris, and Kevin Beaver, "Secondary Exposure to Violence During Childhood and Adolescence: Does Neighborhood Context Matter?" *Justice Quarterly* 26 (2009): 30–57.

38. Simone Robers, Anlan Zhang, Rachel Morgan, and Lauren Musu-Gillette, *Indicators of School Crime and Safety: 2014*, National Center for Education Statistics, U.S. Department of Education, and Bureau of Justice Statistics, Office of Justice Programs, U.S. Department of Justice, 2015, www.bjs.gov/content/pub/pdf/iscs14.pdf.

39. Pamela Wilcox, Marie Skubak Tillyer, and Bonnie S. Fisher, "Gendered Opportunity? School-Based Adolescent Victimization," *Journal of Research in Crime and Delinquency* 46 (2009): 245–269.

40. Kristin Carbone-Lopez and Janet Lauritsen, "Seasonal Variation in Violent Victimization: Opportunity and the Annual Rhythm of the School Calendar," *Journal of Quantitative Criminology* 29 (2013): 399–422.

41. Jonathan Vespa, Jamie Lewis, and Rose Kreider, *America's Families and Living Arrangements: 2012*, U.S. Census Bureau, 2013, www.census.gov /prod/2013pubs/p20-570.pdf.

42. Nicole White and Janet L. Lauritsen, *Violent Crime Against Youth from 1994 to 2010*, Bureau of Justice Statistics, 2012, bjs.ojp.usdoj.gov/content/pub/pdf /vcay9410.pdf.

43. Victoria Titterington, "A Retrospective Investigation of Gender Inequality and Female Homicide Victimization," *Sociological Spectrum* 26 (2006): 205–231.

44. Sherry Hamby, David Finkelhor, and Heather Turner, "Perpetrator and Victim Gender Patterns for 21 Forms of Youth Victimization in the National Survey of Children's Exposure to Violence," *Violence and Victims* 28 (2013): 915–939.

45. David Finkelhor, Heather Turner, and Richard Ormrod, "Kid's Stuff: The Nature and Impact of Peer and Sibling Violence on Younger and Older Children," *Child Abuse and Neglect* 30 (2006): 1401–1421.

46. Lamar Jordan, "Law Enforcement and the Elderly: A Concern for the 21st Century," *FBI Law Enforcement Bulletin* 71 (2002): 20–24.

47. Tracy Dietz and James Wright, "Age and Gender Differences and Predictors of Victimization of the Older Homeless," *Journal of Elder Abuse and Neglect* 17 (2005): 37–59.

48. David C. Pyrooz, Richard K. Moule, Jr., and Scott H. Decker, "The Contribution of Gang Membership to the Victim–Offender Overlap," *Journal of Research in Crime and Delinquency* 51 (2014): 315–348.

49. FBI, *Uniform Crime Reports, 2013*, Expanded Homicide Data Table 1, www.fbi.gov/about-us/cjis/ucr/crime -in-the-u.s/2013/crime-in-the-u.s.-2013/offenses -known-to-law-enforcement/expanded-homicide /expanded_homicide_data_table_1_murder_victims _by_race_and_sex_2013.xl.

50. Danielle Kuhl, David Warner, and Andrew Wilczak, "Adolescent Violent Victimization and Precocious Union Formation," *Criminology* 50 (2012): 1089–1127.

51. Daniel Birks, Michael Townsley, and Anna Stewart, "Emergent Regularities of Interpersonal Victimization: An Agent-Based Investigation," *Journal of Research in Crime and Delinquency* 51 (2014): 119–140.

52. Marie Skubak Tillyer, Brooke Miller Gialopsos, and Pamela Wilcox, "The Short-Term Repeat Sexual Victimization of Adolescents in School," *Crime and Delinquency*, first published online September 9, 2013.

53. Denise Osborn, Dan Ellingworth, Tim Hope, and Alan Trickett, "Are Repeatedly Victimized Households Different?" *Journal of Quantitative Criminology* 12 (1996): 223–245.

54. Graham Farrell, "Predicting and Preventing Revictimization," in *Crime and Justice: An Annual Review of Research*, ed. Michael Tonry and David Farrington, vol. 20 (Chicago: University of Chicago Press, 1995), pp. 61–126.

55. Ibid., p. 61.

56. David Finkelhor and Nancy Asigian, "Risk Factors for Youth Victimization: Beyond a Lifestyles/Routine Activities Theory Approach," *Violence and Victimization* 11 (1996): 3–19.

57. Graham C. Ousey, Pamela Wilcox, and Bonnie S. Fisher, "Something Old, Something New: Revisiting Competing Hypotheses of the Victimization–Offending Relationship Among Adolescents," *Journal of Quantitative Criminology*, published online July 2010.

58. Graham Farrell, Coretta Phillips, and Ken Pease, "Like Taking Candy: Why Does Repeat Victimization Occur?" *British Journal of Criminology* 35 (1995): 384–399.

59. Andrew Papachristos, "The Coming of a Networked Criminology?" *Advances in Criminological Theory* 17 (2011): 101–140.

60. Von Hentig, *The Criminal and His Victim*, p. 384.

61. Marvin Wolfgang, *Patterns of Criminal Homicide* (Philadelphia: University of Pennsylvania Press, 1958).

62. Menachem Amir, *Patterns in Forcible Rape* (Chicago: University of Chicago Press, 1971).

63. Rose Corrigan, *Up Against a Wall: Rape Reform and the Failure of Success* (New York: New York University Press, 2013); Sokratis Dinos, Nina Burrowes, Karen Hammond, and Christina Cunliffe, "A Systematic Review of Juries' Assessment of Rape Victims: Do Rape Myths Impact on Juror Decision-Making?" *International Journal of Law, Crime and Justice* 43 (2015): 36–49.

64. Molly Smith and Leana Bouffard, "Victim Precipitation," in *The Encyclopedia of Criminology and Criminal Justice*, ed. Jay S. Albanese (London: Blackwell, 2014).

65. Wilcox, Tillyer, and Fisher, "Gendered Opportunity? School-Based Adolescent Victimization."

66. M. Kunst and J. Van Wilsem, "Trait Impulsivity and Change in Mental Health Problems After Violent Crime Victimization: A Prospective Analysis of the Dutch Longitudinal Internet Studies for the Social Sciences Database," *Journal of Interpersonal Violence* 28 (2013): 1642–1656.

67. Margit Averdijk and Wim Bernasco, "Testing the Situational Explanation of Victimization Among Adolescents," *Journal of Research in Crime and Delinquency*, first published September 24, 2014; Lening Zhang, John W. Welte, and William F. Wieczorek, "Deviant Lifestyle and Crime Victimization," *Journal of Criminal Justice* 29 (2001): 133–143.

68. Joel Miller, "Individual Offending, Routine Activities, and Activity Settings: Revisiting the Routine Activity Theory of General Deviance," *Journal of Research in Crime and Delinquency*, first published online April 2, 2012.

69. See, generally, Gary Gottfredson and Denise Gottfredson, *Victimization in Schools* (New York: Plenum Press, 1985).

70. Gary Jensen and David Brownfield, "Gender, Lifestyles, and Victimization: Beyond Routine Activity Theory," *Violence and Victims* 1 (1986): 85–99.

71. Richard B. Felson, Jukka Savolainen, Mark T. Berg, and Noora Ellonen, "Does Spending Time in Public Settings Contribute to the Adolescent Risk of Violent Victimization?" *Journal of Quantitative Criminology*, first published online July 11, 2012.

72. Dana Haynie and Alex Piquero, "Pubertal Development and Physical Victimization in Adolescence," *Journal of Research in Crime and Delinquency* 43 (2006): 3–35.

73. Michael Ezell and Emily Tanner-Smith, "Examining the Role of Lifestyle and Criminal History Variables on the Risk of Homicide Victimization," *Homicide Studies* 13 (2009): 144–173; Rolf Loeber, Mary DeLamatre, George Tita, Jacqueline Cohen, Magda Stouthamer-Loeber, and David Farrington, "Gun Injury and Mortality: The Delinquent Backgrounds of Juvenile Offenders," *Violence and Victim* 14 (1999): 339–351.

74. Adam Dobrin, "The Risk of Offending on Homicide Victimization: A Case Control Study," *Journal of Research in Crime and Delinquency* 38 (2001): 154–173.

75. Sofi Sinozich and Lynn Langton, *Rape and Sexual Assault Among College-Age Females, 1995–2013*, Bureau of Justice Statistics, 2014, www.bjs.gov/content/pub/pdf/rsavcaf9513.pdf.

76. Rolf Loeber, Larry Kalb, and David Huizinga, *Juvenile Delinquency and Serious Injury Victimization* (Washington, DC: Office of Juvenile Justice and Delinquency Prevention, 2001).

77. Mark Berg and Rolf Loeber, "Violent Conduct and Victimization Risk in the Urban Illicit Drug Economy: A Prospective Examination," *Justice Quarterly* 32 (2015): 32–55.

78. Scott Jacques and Richard Wright, "The Victimization–Termination Link," *Criminology* 46 (2008): 47–91.

79. Maryse Richards, Reed Larson, and Bobbi-Viegas Miller, "Risky and Protective Contexts and Exposure to Violence in Urban African American Young Adolescents," *Journal of Clinical Child and Adolescent Psychology* 33 (2004): 138–148.

80. James Garofalo, "Reassessing the Lifestyle Model of Criminal Victimization," in *Positive Criminology*, ed. Michael Gottfredson and Travis Hirschi (Newbury Park, CA: Sage, 1987), pp. 23–42.

81. Terance Miethe and David McDowall, "Contextual Effects in Models of Criminal Victimization," *Social Forces* 71 (1993): 741–759.

82. Rodney Stark, "Deviant Places: A Theory of the Ecology of Crime," *Criminology* 25 (1987): 893–911.

83. Ibid., p. 902.

84. William Wells, Ling Wu, and Xinyue Ye, "Patterns of Near-Repeat Gun Assaults in Houston," *Journal of Research in Crime and Delinquency*, first published online May 12, 2011.

85. Mark Berg, Eric Stewart, Christopher Schreck, and Ronald Simons, "The Victim–Offender Overlap in Context: Examining the Role of Neighborhood Street Culture," *Criminology* 50 (2012): 359–390.

86. Lawrence Cohen and Marcus Felson, "Social Change and Crime Rate Trends: A Routine Activities Approach," *American Sociological Review* 44 (1979): 588–608.

87. For a review, see James LeBeau and Thomas Castellano, "The Routine Activities Approach: An Inventory and Critique," unpublished paper, Center for the Studies of Crime, Delinquency, and Corrections, Southern Illinois University, Carbondale, 1987.

88. Teresa LaGrange, "The Impact of Neighborhoods, Schools, and Malls on the Spatial Distribution of Property Damage," *Journal of Research in Crime and Delinquency* 36 (1999): 393–422.

89. Denise Gottfredson and David Soulé, "The Timing of Property Crime, Violent Crime, and Substance Use Among Juveniles," *Journal of Research in Crime and Delinquency* 42 (2005): 110–120.

90. Marcus Felson, *Crime and Everyday Life: Insights and Implications for Society*, 3rd ed. (Thousand Oaks, CA: Sage, 2002).

91. Amy Anderson and Lorine Hughes, "Exposure to Situations Conducive to Delinquent Behavior: The Effects of Time Use, Income, and Transportation," *Journal of Research in Crime and Delinquency* 46 (2009): 5–34.

92. Lawrence Cohen, Marcus Felson, and Kenneth Land, "Property Crime Rates in the United States: A Macrodynamic Analysis, 1947–1977, with Ex-ante Forecasts for the Mid-1980s," *American Journal of Sociology* 86 (1980): 90–118.

93. Steven Messner, Lawrence Raffalovich, and Richard McMillan, "Economic Deprivation and Changes in Homicide Arrest Rates for White and Black Youths, 1967–1998: A National Time Series Analysis," *Criminology* 39 (2001): 591–614.

94. Melanie Wellsmith and Amy Burrell, "The Influence of Purchase Price and Ownership Levels on Theft Targets: The Example of Domestic Burglary," *British Journal of Criminology* 45 (2005): 741–764.

95. Terance Miethe and Robert Meier, *Crime and Its Social Context: Toward an Integrated Theory of Offenders, Victims, and Situations* (Albany: State University of New York Press, 1994).

96. Richard Felson, "Routine Activities and Involvement in Violence as Actor, Witness, or Target," *Violence and Victimization* 12 (1997): 209–223.

97. Georgina Hammock and Deborah Richardson, "Perceptions of Rape: The Influence of Closeness of Relationship, Intoxication, and Sex of Participant," *Violence and Victimization* 12 (1997): 237–247.

98. Karin Wittebrood and Paul Nieuwbeerta, "Criminal Victimization During One's Life Course: The Effects of Previous Victimization and Patterns of Routine Activities," *Journal of Research in Crime and Delinquency* 37 (2000): 112–113.

99. Patricia Resick, "Psychological Effects of Victimization: Implications for the Criminal Justice System," *Crime and Delinquency* 33 (1987): 468–478.

100. Dean Kilpatrick, Benjamin Saunders, Lois Veronen, Connie Best, and Judith Von, "Criminal Victimization: Lifetime Prevalence, Reporting to Police, and Psychological Impact," *Crime and Delinquency* 33 (1987): 479–489.

101. U.S. Department of Justice, *Report of the President's Task Force on Victims of Crime* (Washington, DC: U.S. Government Printing Office, 1983).

102. Ibid., pp. 2–10; "Review on Victims: Witnesses of Crime," *Massachusetts Lawyers Weekly*, April 25, 1983, p. 26.

103. Robert Davis, *Crime Victims: Learning How to Help Them* (Washington, DC: National Institute of Justice, 1987).

104. Crime Victims' Rights Act 18 U.S.C. § 3771 (2004).

105. Randall Schmidt, "Crime Victim Compensation Legislation: A Comparative Study," *Victimology* 5 (1980): 428–437.

106. Ibid.

107. Rebecca Campbell, "Rape Survivors' Experiences with the Legal and Medical Systems: Do Rape Victim Advocates Make a Difference?" *Violence Against Women* 12 (2006): 30–45.

108. Karen Rich and Patrick Seffrin, "Police Officers' Collaboration with Rape Victim Advocates: Barriers and Facilitators," *Violence and Victims* 28 (2013): 681–696.

109. Information provided by the National Center for Victims of Crime, www.victimsofcrime.org.

110. *Payne v. Tennessee*, 111 S.Ct. 2597, 115 L.Ed.2d 720 (1991).

111. Douglas E. Beloof, "Constitutional Implications of Crime Victims as Participants," *Cornell Law Review* 88 (2003): 282–305.

112. Stacy Hoskins Haynes, "The Effects of Victim-Related Contextual Factors on the Criminal Justice System," *Crime and Delinquency* 57 (2011): 298–328.

113. Edna Erez and Pamela Tontodonato, "The Effect of Victim Participation in Sentencing on Sentence Outcome," *Criminology* 28 (1990): 451–474.

114. Robert Davis and Barbara Smith, "The Effects of Victim Impact Statements on Sentencing Decisions: A Test in an Urban Setting," *Justice Quarterly* 11 (1994): 453–469.

115. Pater Jaffe, Marlies Sudermann, Deborah Reitzel, and Steve Killip, "An Evaluation of a Secondary School Primary Prevention Program on Violence in Intimate Relationships," *Violence and Victims* 7 (1992): 129–145.

116. Good Samaritans Program, www.ojp.usdoj.gov/ovc /publications/infores/Good_Samaritans/welcome.html.

117. Andrew Karmen, "Victim–Offender Reconciliation Programs: Pro and Con," *Perspectives of the American Probation and Parole Association* 20 (1996): 11–14.

118. Department of Justice's Automated Victim Notification System (AVNS), www.justice.gov/criminal/vns /about/doj-avns.html.

119. Shannan M. Catalano, *Intimate Partner Violence, 1993–2010* (Washington, DC: Bureau of Justice Statistics, 2012), bjs.ojp.usdoj.gov/content/pub/pdf/ipv9310.pdf.

120. National Center for Victims of Crime, www .victimsofcrime.org.

121. Dru Sjodin National Sex Offender Public Website, www.nsopw.gov.

122. Alesha Durfee, "Victim Narratives, Legal Representation, and Domestic Violence Civil Protection Orders," *Feminist Criminology* 4 (2009): 7–31.

123. Sara Flaherty and Austin Flaherty, *Victims and Victims' Risk* (New York: Chelsea House, 1998).

124. Pamela Wilcox Rountree and Kenneth Land, "Burglary Victimization, Perceptions of Crime Risk, and Routine Activities: A Multilevel Analysis Across Seattle Neighborhoods and Census Tracts," *Journal of Research in Crime and Delinquency* 33 (1996): 1147–1180.

125. Ronald Clarke, "Situational Crime Prevention: Its Theoretical Basis and Practical Scope," in *Annual Review of Criminal Justice Research*, ed. Michael Tonry and Norval Morris (Chicago: University of Chicago Press, 1983).

126. See, generally, Dennis P. Rosenbaum, Arthur J. Lurigio, and Robert C. Davis, *The Prevention of Crime: Social and Situational Strategies* (Belmont, CA: Wadsworth, 1998).

127. Alan Lizotte, "Determinants of Completing Rape and Assault," *Journal of Quantitative Criminology* 2 (1986): 213–217.

128. Polly Marchbanks, Kung-Jong Lui, and James Mercy, "Risk of Injury from Resisting Rape," *American Journal of Epidemiology* 132 (1990): 540–549.

129. Caroline Wolf Harlow, *Robbery Victims* (Washington, DC: Bureau of Justice Statistics, 1987).

130. Samantha Balemba, Eric Beauregard, and Tom Mieczkowski, "To Resist or Not to Resist? The Effect of Context and Crime Characteristics on Sex Offenders' Reaction to Victim Resistance," *Crime and Delinquency* 58 (2012): 588–611.

131. Ibid.

132. Gary Kleck, "Defensive Gun Use Is Not a Myth," *Politico*, February 17, 2015, www.politico.com/magazine /story/2015/02/defensive-gun-ownership-gary -kleck-response-115082.html; Gary Kleck, *Targeting Guns: Firearms and Their Control* (Hawthorne, NY: Aldine de Gruyter, 1997); Gary Kleck and Marc Gertz, "Armed Resistance to Crime: The Prevalence and Nature of Self-Defense with a Gun," *Journal of Criminal Law and Criminology* 86 (1995): 150–187; Gary Kleck, *Point Blank: Guns and Violence in America* (Hawthorne, NY: Aldine de Gruyter, 1991).

133. Jongyeon Tark and Gary Kleck, "Resisting Rape: The Effects of Victim Self-Protection on Rape Completion and Injury," *Violence Against Women* 20 (2014): 270–292; Jongyeon Tark and Gary Kleck, "Resisting Crime: The Effects of Victim Action on the Outcomes of Crimes," *Criminology* 42 (2004): 861–909.

# 4 Rational Choice Theory

AP Images/David Coates

Dr. Farah Fata

www.ibcnews.com

# Chapter Outline

## FACT OR FICTION?

▶ Neighborhood watch programs are a waste of time.

▶ Living in a gated community decreases the risk of burglary.

In 2014, Dr. Farid Fata, a Detroit-area hematologist and oncologist, pleaded guilty to a series of health care fraud charges, kickback conspiracy, and money laundering crimes based on his:

- Administering unnecessary chemotherapy infusions
- Administering unnecessary iron infusions
- Administering unnecessary human growth factors
- Ordering unnecessary cancer tests
- Accepting kickbacks to refer patients for home health care services
- Promoting his cancer test fraud scheme with money laundered from his infusion fraud scheme[1]

Fata's complex criminal conspiracy was managed out of his cancer treatment clinic—Michigan Hematology Oncology, PC—which had multiple locations throughout Michigan. He also owned a diagnostic testing facility—United Diagnostics, PLLC—in Rochester Hills, Michigan. Using these facilities, he routinely diagnosed his patients with cancer, having them go through chemotherapy and/or other intensive treatments, all the while knowing that they never actually had the disease! Fata fraudulently billed Medicare and private insurance companies for hundreds of millions of dollars in unnecessary treatment costs. And it was not only cancer diagnoses. Some patients were told, wrongly, that they had other conditions that required expensive intravenous therapies, medications, and diagnostic tests—all of which jeopardized their health and well-being. After Fata's arrest, federal authorities had the delicate task of informing victims that they ▶

did not have a disease for which they had undergone painful and nerve-wracking treatments. In all, some 553 patients received medically unnecessary infusions or injections. On July 10, 2015, Fata received a 45-year prison terms. At his sentencing, he told the court, "I have violated the Hippocratic oath and violated the trust of my patients. I do not know how I can heal the wound. I do not know how to express the sorrow and the shame."

Fata's criminal plot displays both planning and expertise. He purposively used his status and occupation to dupe patients into believing they had a serious illness and then used his position as a physician to fraudulently bill the government, making millions of dollars in illegal gains. Did he know he was doing wrong? He must have, since he acknowledged violating the most sacred oath of his profession. ▪

The schemes of calculating criminals such as Dr. Fata suggest that the decision to commit crime involves rational decision making, designed to maximize personal gain and avoid capture and punishment. Some criminologists go as far as suggesting that the source of all criminal violations—even those involving drug abuse, vandalism, and violence—are a function of rational decision making. The decision to violate the law is made only after the potential offender carefully weighs the potential benefits and consequences of the planned action and decides that the benefits of crime are greater than its consequences. Criminals such as Fata may be motivated by a variety of human traits and emotions: greed, revenge, need, anger, lust, jealousy, thrill-seeking, or vanity. Regardless of the motive, criminal offenders are people who make the decision to put their own needs ahead of the rest of us, even though there may be serious consequences for their actions. Why? Because after reviewing all available information they believe that the rewards of crime outweigh its risks. This view of crime causation is referred to here as **rational choice theory (choice theory)**.

In this chapter, we review the philosophical underpinnings of rational choice theory—the view that criminals rationally choose crime. We then turn to theories of crime prevention and control that flow from the concept of choice: situational crime prevention, general deterrence theory, specific deterrence theory, and incapacitation. Finally, we take a brief look at how choice theory has influenced criminal justice policy.

## Development of Rational Choice Theory

Rational choice theory has its roots in the **classical criminology** developed by the Italian social thinker Cesare Beccaria, whose utilitarian approach powerfully influenced the criminal justice system and was widely accepted throughout Europe and the United States (see Chapter 1). Although the classical approach was influential for more than 100 years, by the end of the nineteenth century its popularity among criminologists declined, being replaced by positivist views that focused on social and personal factors rather than personal choice and decision making. The prevailing view was that crime was not a matter of choice but the by-product of destructive personal and social conditions and influences. Rather than controlling their behavior, people were at the mercy of their upbringing and environment.

Beginning in the late 1960s, criminologists once again began to embrace classical ideas, producing books and monographs expounding on the theme that criminals are rational actors who plan their crimes, who can be controlled by the fear of punishment,

**rational choice theory (choice theory)**
The view that crime is a function of a decision-making process in which the potential offender weighs the potential costs and benefits of an illegal act.

**classical criminology**
A theory of crime suggesting that criminal behavior is a matter of personal choice, made after the individual considers its costs and benefits, and that the criminal behavior reflects the needs of the offender.

**LO1** Describe the development of rational choice theory.

and who deserve to be penalized for their misdeeds. In the 1960s, Nobel Prize–winning economist Gary Becker applied his views on rational behavior and human capital (that is, human competence and the consequences of investments in human competence) to criminal activity. Becker argued that except for a few mentally ill people, criminals behave in a predictable or rational way when deciding to commit crime. Engaging in a cost-benefit analysis of crime, they weigh what they expect to gain against the risks they must undergo and the costs they may incur, such as going to prison.[2] Instead of regarding criminal activity as irrational behavior, Becker viewed criminality as rational behavior that might be controlled by increasing the costs of crime and reducing the potential for gain.

In *Thinking About Crime*, political scientist James Q. Wilson observed that people who are likely to commit crime are unafraid of breaking the law because they value the excitement and thrills of crime, have a low stake in conformity, and are willing to take greater chances than the average person. If they could be convinced that their actions would bring severe punishment, only the totally irrational would be willing to engage in crime.[3]

From these roots has evolved a more contemporary version of classical theory based on intelligent thought processes and criminal decision making; today this is referred to as the rational choice approach to crime causation.[4]

**L02** Explore the concepts of rational choice.

## Concepts of Rational Choice

According to contemporary rational choice theory, law-violating behavior is the product of careful thought and planning. It assumes that people are self-interested and will be willing to violate the law after considering both personal factors (such as money, revenge, thrills, and entertainment) and situational factors (such as target availability, security measures, and police presence). Anyone is a potential criminal if they calculate that the profits are great and the risks are small. Below, some of the decisions made by potential criminals are set out and discussed.

### Evaluating the Risks of Crime

Before deciding to commit a crime, the reasoning criminal evaluates the risk of apprehension, the seriousness of expected punishment, the potential value or benefit of the criminal enterprise, her ability to succeed, and the need for criminal gain. People who believe that the risks of crime outweigh the rewards may decide to "go straight."[5] Those who find the risks acceptable are more willing to take a gamble on crime.

Burglars seem to choose targets on the basis of their value, novelty, and resale potential. A piece of electronic gear that has not yet saturated the market and still retains high value, such as a new generation iPhone or Google Glass, may be a prime target.[6] The decision to commit crime is enhanced by the promise of easy gain with low risk.

David Maxwell/EPA/Landov

According to rational choice theory, criminals consider the risks they face before they commit criminal acts. Here, members of the Amish community leave a Cleveland, Ohio, federal courthouse where 16 members of a radical Amish group, led by Samuel Mullet Sr., were being tried for committing hate crimes, conspiracy, kidnapping, and destroying evidence in a series of beard- and hair-cutting attacks. Mullett, along with nine other men and six women members of his group, carried out the attacks as retaliation against more conventional Amish who had defied or denounced Mullet's authoritarian style. The Amish believe the Bible instructs women to let their hair grow long and men to grow beards once they marry; cutting either would be offensive to the Amish. Mullet received a 15-year sentence for leading the attacks. Why such a long sentence for cutting beards? Prosecutors successfully argued that they amounted to federal hate crimes, since the victims were chosen because of their "actual or perceived religion." Since the attacks were rational and planned, prosecutors argued they deserved to be punished harshly, and the jury agreed.

In contrast, the decision to forgo crime is reached when the potential criminal believes that the risks outweigh the rewards:

- They stand a good chance of getting caught and being punished.
- They fear the consequences of punishment.
- They risk losing the respect of their peers, damaged reputations, and feelings of guilt or shame.[7]
- The risk of apprehension outweighs the profit and/or pleasure of crime.

Risk evaluations may cover a wide range of topics: What's the chance of getting caught? How difficult will it be to commit the crime? Is the profit worth the effort? How familiar am I with the target?[8]

People who decide to get involved in crime compare the chances of arrest (based on their past experiences) with the subjective psychic rewards of crime (including the excitement and social status it brings and perceived opportunities for easy gains).[9] If the rewards are great, the perceived risk small, and the excitement high, the likelihood of their committing additional crimes increases.[10]

## Offense-Specific/Offender-Specific

**offense-specific crime**
The view that an offender reacts selectively to the characteristics of a particular criminal act.

**offender-specific crime**
The view that offenders evaluate their skills, motives, needs, and fears before deciding to commit the criminal act.

Rational choice theorists view crime as both **offense-specific** and **offender-specific**.[11] Crime is said to be offense-specific because offenders react selectively to the immediate characteristics of a specific criminal act. Take, for instance, the decision to commit a burglary. Potential offenders might consider:

- Their evaluation of the target yield
- The probability of security devices
- Police patrol effectiveness
- Likelihood of apprehension
- Ease of selling stolen merchandise
- Presence of occupants
- Neighbors who might notice a break-in
- Presence of guard dogs
- Escape routes
- Entry points and exits

**OFFENDER-SPECIFIC** Crime is also said to be offender-specific because criminals are not simply robots or automatons who engage in unthinking and unplanned acts of

According to rational choice theory, crime can be viewed as offender- and offense-specific. On June 10, 2015, New York Governor Andrew Cuomo and Vermont Governor Peter Shumlin appear during a news conference in front of the Clinton Correctional Facility in Dannemora, New York, after two convicted killers, David Sweat (photo on left) and Richard Matt (right), made a daring escape. The men had convinced prison employee Joyce Mitchell, who worked as an instructor in the facility's tailoring shop, to help them break out. She is accused of providing them with tools and blades; she also planned to serve as their getaway driver but backed out at the last minute. Why would a married prison employee choose to help criminals escape, thereby putting herself in jeopardy of becoming a felon herself?

AP Images/Seth Wenig

antisocial behavior. Before deciding to commit crime, individuals must decide whether they have the personal needs, skills, and prerequisites to commit a successful criminal act. These assessments might include evaluation of:

- Necessary skills to commit the crime
- Immediate need for money or other valuables
- Availability of legitimate financial alternatives to crime
- Available resources to commit the crime
- Fear of expected apprehension and punishment
- Availability of alternative criminal acts, such as selling drugs
- Physical ability, including health, strength, and dexterity

Note the distinction made here between "crime" and "criminality."[12] A crime is an event; criminality is a personal trait. Criminals do not commit crime all the time; conversely, even the most honest citizens may, on occasion, violate the law. Some high-risk people lacking opportunity may never commit crime. Given enough provocation or opportunity, a low-risk, law-abiding person may commit crime. What are the factors that (a) structure criminality and (b) structure crime?

## Structuring Criminality

Because crime is offender-specific, a number of personal factors and conditions must be evaluated before someone decides to choose criminality.

**PEERS AND GUARDIANSHIP** Though young people are believed to be more crime prone than adults, effective monitoring by parents reduces the likelihood kids will commit crime; in contrast, unsupervised activities increase the risk.[13] Kids are more likely to choose crime when they are out at night without adult supervision, partying and drinking with their buddies.[14]

Gender differences in crime may be explained by levels of guardianship and peer influence. Because adolescent girls are more likely to experience parental supervision than their brothers, they are more likely to socialize at home or at a friend's home with parents present. Adolescent boys are given more freedom to socialize away from home as they wish, thereby increasing the opportunity to engage in antisocial behaviors.[15] When girls do go out, they tend to gather in places like shopping malls, where there are security guards and cameras that monitor behavior and limit criminal choice.

**NEED FOR EXCITEMENT AND THRILLS** People may engage in illegal behavior because they love the excitement and the buzz that crime can provide. For some, crimes such as vandalism and shoplifting are alluring simply because they are stimulating and allow people to get what sociologist Jack Katz calls "sneaky thrills"; profit is not the primary motive.[16] The need for excitement may counter fear of apprehension: the riskier the act, the more attractive it becomes.[17]

**ECONOMIC NEED/OPPORTUNITY** Clearly, one important decision that people make before they embark on a life of crime is whether they need the money! Drug users, for instance, may turn to

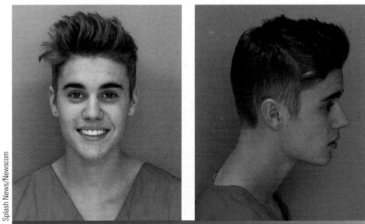

Miami Beach Police Department/Miami Beach PD/Photoshot/Newscom; Splash News/Newscom

Some people choose crime and deviance because it provides excitement and thrills. That might be the motive for celebrity crimes such as when, on January 2, 2014, pop singer Justin Bieber was arrested after drag racing in his yellow Lamborghini while under the influence of alcohol, marijuana, and prescription drugs and failing to cooperate when pulled over. Bieber's arrest came a week after his home in Los Angeles was searched by police following allegations he had thrown eggs at his neighbor's house. Prosecutors dropped the drunken driving charge in an agreement that required Bieber to get 12 hours of anger management counseling, attend a program that teaches about the impact on victims of drunken driving, and donate $50,000 to the Our Kids program.

crime to support their lifestyle, especially when entry into the legitimate job market closes. Heroin users may turn to petty crime in order to earn enough to support their habit.[18]

While the average take from crime is not that much, it's a lot quicker and more efficient to steal a car or flat screen TV than to get a job, save money, and purchase one legitimately. The FBI reports that the average take from a burglary is now a little more than $2,000 per crime; robberies average about $1,200 and bank robberies $3,500.[19] Despite the risk, earning $2,000 from a burglary that takes an hour is alluring to someone whose alternative is making minimum wage in a fast-food restaurant.

Adding to the allure of crime is the fact that many potential criminals may be misled about the potential of financial reward of crime. They may know people who brag about the "big scores" of $50,000 or more they have made: if their friend or brother-in-law can do well, they assume they will succeed also.[20]

There is also the potential for future riches no matter the current risks. When Steven Levitt and Sudhir Alladi Venkatesh interviewed drug gang members, they found that despite enormous risks to health, life, and freedom, average gang members earned just about minimum wage.[21] Why, then, did they continue to take risks? They believed there was a strong potential for future riches if they stayed in the drug business and earned a "management" position (gang leaders earned a lot more than street-level dealers). Like the college grad entering the executive training program at a Fortune 500 company, gang kids are willing to take risks and work hard today for the promise of a high-paid position tomorrow.[22] Of course, neither the corporate trainee nor the gang boy stand much chance of getting to the top rung of the organization; there are a lot more openings at the bottom of the pyramid than there are at the top.

**PERSONAL TRAITS AND EXPERIENCE** Personal experience and expertise may be an important element in structuring criminality.[23] Female crack dealers, for example, learn how to camouflage their activities to avoid police: they sell crack while hanging out in a park; they meet their customers in a lounge and try to act normal, as though they are having a casual, lighthearted good time—anything not to draw attention to themselves and their business; they use props to disguise drug deals.[24]

While criminals may learn when to commit crimes, they also become aware when to quit. No matter how successful, a criminal's physical strength and emotional toughness eventually begin to wane, and some get the message that it may be time to turn from a risky criminal way of life to a lower paying albeit safer conventional lifestyle.[25]

## Structuring Crime

According to the rational choice approach, the decision to commit crime, regardless of its substance, is structured by (a) where it occurs and (b) the characteristics of the target.

**CHOOSING THE PLACE OF CRIME** Criminals seem to carefully choose where they will commit their crime. Crack cocaine street dealers evaluate the desirability of their sales area before setting up shop.[26] Dealers consider the middle of a long block the best choice because they can see everything in both directions; police raids can be spotted before they occur.[27] Another tactic is to entice new buyers into spaces between apartment buildings or into back lots. Although the dealers may lose the tactical edge of being on a public street, they gain a measure of protection because their colleagues can watch over the operation and come to the rescue if the buyer tries to "pull something."[28]

**CHOOSING TARGETS** Evidence of rational choice may also be found in the way criminals locate their targets. Market forces can shape decision making. Targets that decline in value due to oversupply or obsolescence are avoided; materials such as metal parts and wire may become coveted when undersupply causes their value to skyrocket.[29]

Auto thieves are known to be very selective in their choice of targets, often making their selection based on cash value and ease of sale. German cars are selected for stripping because they usually have high-quality audio equipment that has good value on the secondhand market.[30]

**CONNECTIONS**

Rational choice theory dovetails with routine activities theory, which was discussed in Chapter 3. Though not identical, these approaches both claim that crime rates are a product of criminal opportunity. They suggest that increasing the number of guardians, decreasing the suitability of targets, or reducing the offender population should lower crime rates. Conversely, increased opportunity and reduced guardianship should increase crime rates.

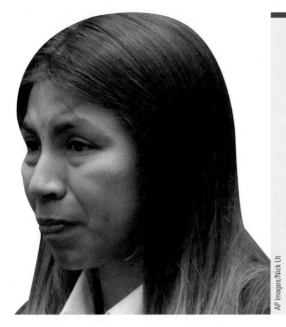

Criminals show rationality when they carefully plan and structure their illegal acts. One case that shows this type of rationality involved a criminal group called the Bling Ring, of which Diana Tamayo, shown in court, was a member. In 2012, she pleaded no contest to a burglary charge for stealing items from the home of actress Lindsay Lohan and was sentenced to three years of probation. Tamayo was one of six people charged in thefts of more than $3 million in clothes, jewelry, and art from the homes of celebrities such as Lohan, Paris Hilton, Orlando Bloom, and Megan Fox. The Bling Ring targeted victims who were considered fashion icons. If the members liked a celebrity's style, they became determined to steal the celebrity's clothes. They found their targets by using Google maps and information from a website showing where famous people live. They planned their crimes to coincide with the celebrities' schedules, such as appearances at events, through social media such as Facebook and Twitter.

AP Images/Nick Ut

Burglars also seem particularly rational when choosing targets. Interviews with active burglars indicate that they check to make sure no one is home before they enter a residence. Some call ahead; others ring the doorbell, preparing to claim they had the wrong address if someone answers. Some find out which families include star athletes, because those that do are sure to be at the weekend football game, leaving their houses unguarded.[31] Others read bridal announcements in the local newspaper, hoping to locate empty homes with expensive gifts left unguarded while the occupants are at the wedding.

Burglars seek unlocked doors and avoid the ones with deadbolts; houses with dogs are usually considered off-limits.[32] Being sensitive to the activities of their victims, burglars make note of the fact that homemakers often develop predictable behavior patterns.[33] Burglars also seem to prefer "working" between 9 A.M. and 11 A.M. and in mid-afternoon, when parents are either working or dropping off or picking up children at school. Some report monitoring car and pedestrian traffic; others avoid selecting targets on heavily traveled streets.[34] It does not seem surprising that well-organized communities that restrict traffic and limit neighborhood entrance and exit routes have experienced significant declines in property crime.[35]

**CREATING SCRIPTS** With experience, criminals create behavior scripts that guide their interactions with victims. If they follow the script, they can commit their crimes and avoid detection.

Pederasts rely on scripts when they target a child for sexual abuse. Before committing their crimes, offenders will go through a series of steps, from first encounter to sexual contact. After meeting their victims, they work on gaining their trust by giving them love and attention. Once trust is secured, some offenders will adopt strategies to proceed to the location for sexual contact. For that purpose, offenders will usually promise rewards or give inducements such as money to the victim or even threaten or use violence to get their way.[36]

In sum, rational choice involves both shaping and structuring criminality and crime. Personality, age, status, risk, and opportunity seem to influence the decision to become a criminal; place, target, and techniques help to structure crime.[37]

## Is Crime Truly Rational?

It is relatively easy to show that some crimes are the product of rational, objective thought, especially when they involve an ongoing criminal conspiracy centered on economic gain (such as the scheme discussed in the Profiles in Crime feature entitled "Planning to Steal").

**CHECKPOINTS**

▶ Choice theory can be traced to Beccaria's view that crime is rational and can be prevented by punishment that is swift, severe, and certain.

▶ Crime is said to be offense-specific because criminals evaluate the characteristics of targets to determine their suitability.

▶ Crime is offender-specific because criminals evaluate their own skills, motivations, and needs before committing a specific crime.

▶ Criminal choice involves such actions as choosing the place of crime, selecting targets, and learning criminal techniques.

**L03** Interpret the evidence showing that crime is rational.

# PROFILES IN CRIME

## PLANNING TO STEAL

In 2015, a Toledo, Ohio, man named Michael Wymer was sentenced to 27 years in prison after being convicted of charges relating to setting up a criminal enterprise designed to steal trucks, disassemble them in his chop shop, and sell them as scrap metal. Nine of his 13 co-conspirators—among them his son, two brothers, and two nephews—were convicted along with him.

Wymer's scheme was quite complex. He and his fellow conspirators traveled outside of the Toledo area—including to Michigan and Indiana—to steal trucks so they could avoid detection by one single jurisdiction. They would "shop" for semi-trucks and trailers at truck stops and other locations close to interstate highways. If they were traveling in Wymer's own semi-truck (minus a trailer), they would back the truck up to the trailer they wanted and tow it away. If traveling by car, one or two of the thieves would break into an empty semi-truck that had an attached trailer, manipulate the ignition to get it started, and drive the entire vehicle away.

The Wymer team preferred items that could be chopped into scrap metal, so they stole things like motorcycles, all-terrain vehicles, copper wire, spools of metal, even actual loads of scrap metal. Back in Toledo with the stolen property, Wymer would take the truck to one of his two chop shop locations, where he had everything he needed, from heavy moving equipment and floor jacks to blow torches and chain saws. He would remove saleable parts from the truck and then chop the rest of the truck, the trailer, and the trailer's contents into scrap metal, a process taking only a couple of hours. He would then load the material into one of his trucks and transport it to recycling companies or other businesses interested in buying scrap metal. Wymer used security cameras to keep an eye on his chop shops, and video footage from these cameras was used as evidence to convict the thieves.

The Wymer case did not make national headlines, but it clearly illustrates what choice theorists believe: crime involves rational and planned decision making, designed to maximize profits and avoid detection. Rather than being unthinking and spontaneous, most crimes involve thought and planning. In Wymer's case, his elaborate scheme ultimately failed but not for want of trying.

**Sources:** United States Attorney's Office, Northern District of Ohio, "Toledo Man Sentenced to 27 Years in Prison for Operating Chop Shop," www.justice.gov/usao-ndoh/pr/toledo-man-sentenced-27-years-prison-operating-chop-shop-0; FBI, "Multi-State Chop Shop Operation Disrupted: Criminal Enterprise Leader Among Those Convicted," June 23, 2015, www.fbi.gov/news/stories/2015/june/multi-state-chop-shop-operation-disrupted/ (URLs accessed 2015).

When prominent bankers and financial analysts such as Bernie Madoff were indicted for criminal fraud, their elaborate financial schemes not only showed signs of rationality but also exhibited brilliant, though flawed, financial expertise.[38] Dr. Fata's scheme to defraud Medicare and insurance companies by false cancer diagnoses seems highly rational albeit diabolical and depraved.

Similarly, the activities of organized drug-dealing street gangs demonstrate a reasoned analysis of market conditions, interests, and risks. Based on fieldwork and interviews with gang members in London, criminologist James Densley found an evolutionary cycle of street gangs, beginning as nonviolent, noncriminal adolescent peer groups and evolving into criminal enterprises.[39] Nothing is by happenstance, as one gang member, street name "Wolverine," explained:

> We was committing crimes so we sat down together, it was like a meeting, I suppose, and we just gave each other names and it started like that. Because it was not like socializing, it was actually going out to commit crime and do stuff. We was premeditating what we was doing before it happened. Planning it up.

Wolverine certainly seems like a rational decision maker. Densley found that gang boys learn special skills—how to seize territory, how to use violence, how to maintain secrecy, how to obtain intelligence—that enable them to successfully regulate and control the production and distribution of one or more given commodities or services unlawfully. With each step, Densley finds, gangs move further away from "crime that is organized" and closer to "organized crime."

But what about crimes that are immediate rather than ongoing? Do they too show signs of rationality?

## Is Drug Use Rational?

Did Oscar-winning actor Philip Seymour Hoffman make an objective, rational choice to overdose on heroin? Did rising young star Heath Ledger make a rational choice when he abused prescription drugs to the point that it killed him? And what about British singer Amy Winehouse—did she choose to drink herself to death? Or the King of Pop, Michael Jackson, who died of acute propofol and benzodiazepine intoxication? Is it possible that these and other drug users, a group not usually associated with clear thinking, make rational choices?

Philip Seymour Hoffman poses on the red carpet during a screening for the movie *The Master* at the Venice Film Festival in Italy. Hoffman died on February 2, 2014, of a drug overdose. Can his drug-use behavior ever be considered rational?

Research does in fact show that at its onset, drug use is controlled by rational decision making. Users report that they begin taking drugs when they believe the benefits of substance abuse outweigh its costs. That is, they believe drugs will provide a fun, exciting, thrilling experience. They choose what they consider safe sites to buy and sell drugs.[40] Their entry into substance abuse is facilitated by their perception that valued friends and family members endorse and encourage drug use and that these individuals abuse substances themselves.[41]

Drug dealers approach their profession in a businesslike fashion. Traffickers and dealers face many of the same problems as legitimate retailers. If they are too successful in one location, rivals will be attracted to the area, and stiff competition may drive down prices and undermine profits. The dealer can fight back against competitors by discounting the price of drugs or increasing quality, as long as this doesn't reduce profit margins.[42] If these "business tactics" are not working, dealers can always turn to violence. They may start drug wars on their rivals' turf and then convince customers to stay away from such a dangerous area; in retaliation, rivals may cut prices to lure customers back. Thus, drug dealers face many of the same problems as law-abiding businesspeople; they differ in the tactics they use to help settle disputes.[43]

## Is Violence Rational?

Is it possible that violent acts are the product of reasoned decision making? Evidence confirms that violent criminals, even serial killers, select suitable targets by picking people who are vulnerable and lack adequate defenses.[44] Street robbers use a considerable amount of rational thought before choosing a robbery, which may involve violence, over a burglary, which involves stealth and cunning.[45] Robbers generally choose targets close to their homes or in areas to which they routinely travel. Familiarity with the area gives them ready knowledge of escape routes; this is referred to as their "awareness space."[46] Robbers may be wary of people who are watching the community for signs of trouble; robbery levels are relatively low in neighborhoods where residents keep a watchful eye out for trouble and are quick to take notice of a stranger in their midst.[47]

Can violence be rational? Cop killer Christopher Jordan Dorner killed three LAPD officers and was the subject of an intense 2013 manhunt that resulted in his death. Dorner was a former Los Angeles police officer who believed he was unfairly dismissed from the force; the shootings were revenge for his dismissal. Would you consider killing people for revenge against an institution an example of rational behavior?

Robbers report that they avoid freestanding buildings because these can more easily be surrounded by police; others select targets that are known to do a primarily cash business, such as bars, convenience stores, and gas stations. Robbers also tend to shy away from victims who are perceived to be armed and potentially dangerous.[48]

In some instances, however, targets are chosen in order to send a message rather than to generate capital. Bruce Jacobs and Richard Wright conducted in-depth interviews with street robbers who target drug dealers and found that their crimes are a response to one of three types of provocations:

- *Market-related* robberies emerge from disputes involving partners in trade, rivals, or generalized predators.
- *Status-based* violations involve encounters in which the robber's essential character or values have been challenged.
- *Personalistic* violations flow from incidents in which the robber's autonomy or sense of values has been jeopardized.

Robbery in this instance is an instrument used to settle scores, display dominance, and stifle potential rivals. And as Jacobs and Wright conclude, retaliation certainly is rational in the sense that actors who lack legitimate access to the law and who prize respect above everything else will often choose to resolve their grievances through a rough and ready brand of self-help.[49]

**johns**
Men who solicit sex workers.

## Is Hate Crime Rational?

Can hate crimes possibly be rational? Hard to believe, but when Ryan King and Gretchen Sutto examined the characteristics of an outbreak of hate crimes they found that three factors seem to trigger these events: an incident that leaves one group with a grievance against another, a definable target group held responsible for the deed, and publicity sufficient to make the event known to a broad public. All these are signs of rationality.[50] Hate crimes, then, are not merely the product of a disturbed mind, but rather a calculated response to a concrete event whose impact is often fanned and inflamed by the media.

## Is Sex Crime Rational?

Are men who solicit sex workers (**johns**) rational decision makers? Recent research by Thomas Holt and his colleagues found that not only did johns make careful and rational decisions when engaging prostitutes, they shared their knowledge and expertise in Internet chat rooms and web forums. Topics ranged from what kind of car to drive and how to avoid police stops to how to spot undercover policewomen posing as street workers, with some johns suggesting that policewomen look more attractive and healthier than the average sex worker. In addition to avoiding law enforcement, johns shared information on how to protect themselves from becoming crime victims, such as finding spots for their sexual encounters that minimized the likelihood of detection or violence. After hearing horror stories like "I was robbed by a pimp," they learned to avoid motels recommended by prostitutes, as the risk of robbery or assault was too high. Homes were off limits because johns feared having their property taken; the

Are sex offenses rational? Here, Heather Keith shows her tattoo that says King Koby, the street name of her pimp, Vincent George Jr., as she testifies inside a Manhattan court. George and his father, Vincent George Sr., were each sentenced to three to nine years in prison for their crimes. During the trial Keith and others testified for the defense, saying they considered themselves to be one big family. They claimed they were treated to nice cars, vacations in Florida, and affection from their pimps. Keith testified she had been a drug-addicted 19-year-old stripper from upstate New York when King Koby moved her to Allentown, Pennsylvania, and helped her beat a cocaine habit. "I would say that I make my own choices," said the 26-year-old Keith.

New York Daily News/Getty Images

preferred rendezvous points were alleyways, empty parking lots, and trusted hourly motels.[51] Here we can see that johns are rational decision makers who learn to take precautions before engaging in an outlawed public order crime.

### Selfish or Concerned?

So, according to the rational choice approach, crime is not a random event but the product of calculation and planning, designed to provide the perpetrator with an overall benefit, whether it be monetary profit or an emotional thrill. To accept this rational choice view, you must believe that criminals are selfish, self-absorbed individuals who care nothing about others. If they believe they can get away with illegal and/or immoral behavior, they will try. What holds them back: fear of apprehension and punishment.

Not everyone accepts this version of events. Criminologist Robert Agnew argues that the average person is just as likely to give consideration to others as they are to satisfy their own self-interests. Most people feel distress at the suffering of others and are inclined to pitch in and help in an emergency, even if it means taking a risk or inconveniencing themselves. Agnew suggests that though many individuals are self-interested, most of us are also socially concerned, a state of mind that provides a natural restraint against crime. Social concern and self-interest can exist side by side.[52]

If Agnew's view is accurate, then the vision of the self-centered criminal who cares for no one but himself is incorrect. Rational choice theorists would disagree, of course, putting more stock into convincing would-be criminals that crime does not pay, rather than hoping such people will empathize with their victims. Given that conclusion, rational choice advocates have formulated a number of potential strategies for controlling crime. Among the most important of these are situational crime prevention strategies, general deterrence strategies, specific deterrence strategies, and incapacitation strategies, all of which are discussed in detail in the following sections.

## Situational Crime Prevention

According to the concept of **situational crime prevention**, because crime is rational and criminals calculating, effective crime prevention strategies must be aimed at reducing immediate and particular criminal opportunities, making it more difficult to engage in successful criminal enterprise. Such strategies as target hardening and improving surveillance are designed to convince would-be criminals that, even if they believe crime pays, it does not pay to commit it here and it pays more to go elsewhere.[53] Criminal acts can be prevented if (a) potential targets are carefully guarded, (b) the means to commit crime are controlled, and (c) potential offenders are carefully monitored. Desperate people may contemplate crime, but only the truly irrational will attack a well-defended, inaccessible target and risk strict punishment.

One way of preventing crime, then, is to reduce the opportunities people have to commit particular crimes. This approach was popularized in the United States in the early 1970s by Oscar Newman, who coined the term **defensible space**. The idea is that crime can be prevented or displaced through the use of residential designs that reduce criminal opportunity, such as well-lit housing projects that maximize surveillance.[54]

Another approach, suggested by Ron Clarke, is the CRAVED model, which identifies the factors that make theft-related crimes attractive to potential thieves so that steps can be taken to thwart their criminal ambitions. The CRAVED model is set out in Exhibit 4.1.

Recently Clarke along with colleague Brian Smith tested the CRAVED model in a rather unique way. They hypothesized that over-the-counter drugs, sold in supermarkets and other stores, can produce a "high" similar to illegal drugs. According

**L04** Discuss the elements of situational crime prevention.

**situational crime prevention**
A method of crime prevention that seeks to eliminate or reduce particular crimes in specific settings.

**defensible space**
The principle that crime can be prevented or displaced by modifying the physical environment to reduce the opportunity that individuals have to commit crime.

# Exhibit 4.1　The CRAVED Model

The CRAVED model of theft suggests that the appropriation of property is most likely to occur when the target is:

- *Concealable.* Merchandise that is easily hidden is more vulnerable to shoplifters than bulkier items. Things that are difficult to identify after being stolen are desirable. While it might be possible to identify a diamond ring, commodities such as copper tubing are easily concealable.
- *Removable.* Mobile items such as cars or bikes are desirable. A laptop makes a more appealing target than a desktop. Jewelry, cash, drugs, and the like are easy to carry and quite valuable on resale. Refrigerators may cost more, but you would need three people and a truck to remove them from a home.
- *Available.* Desirable objects that are widely available and easy to find are at high risk for theft. Cars actually become at greater risk as they get older, because similar models need parts and car thieves can bring them to chop shops to be

stripped. Older cars are also owned by people living in disorganized neighborhoods with motivated offenders and limited security.

- *Valuable.* Thieves will generally choose more expensive, in-demand goods that are easily sold. Some may want to keep valuable goods for themselves and target goods that will confer status, such as a Rolex.
- *Enjoyable.* Hot products tend to be enjoyable things to own or consume, such as the newest electronic gadget or flashy bling.
- *Disposable.* Thieves tend to target items that are easy to sell. Cartons of cigarettes can be resold at a discount to a convenience store. While more valuable, it's tougher to sell a Picasso print.

**Sources:** Gohar Petrossian and Ronald Clarke, "Explaining and Controlling Illegal Commercial Fishing, An Application of the CRAVED Theft Model," *British Journal of Criminology* 54 (2014): 73–90; Stephen Pires and Ronald Clarke, "Are Parrots CRAVED? An Analysis of Parrot Poaching in Mexico," *Journal of Research in Crime and Delinquency* 49 (2012): 122–146.

## CONNECTIONS

Shoplifting and retail theft will be discussed further in Chapter 11. While there have been ongoing efforts to prevent shoplifting, it is still a multibillion-dollar-a-year crime. It has proven difficult to deter professionals who know how to counter security measures. Do you have any new ideas?

## FACT OR FICTION?

Living in a gated community decreases the risk of burglary.

**FACT** Research does show that the gates really help reduce the risk of burglary. Locked gates may increase the effort needed to commit crime, convincing burglars to seek out easier targets elsewhere.

to the CRAVED model these items should be shoplifted at higher rates than other products because they are readily available, enjoyable to use, easily removed, and so on. Using data from more than 200 supermarkets Smith and Clarke found that products with an appeal to drug users were in fact stolen at significantly higher theft rates than products that were not drug related.[55]

## Crime Prevention Strategies

Situational crime prevention strategies involve developing tactics to reduce or eliminate a specific crime problem (such as shoplifting in an urban mall or street-level drug dealing). These efforts may be divided into the six strategies described in the following paragraphs.[56]

**INCREASE THE EFFORT NEEDED TO COMMIT CRIME** Tactics to increase effort include target-hardening techniques such as putting unbreakable glass on storefronts, locking gates, and fencing yards. Does it work? Removing signs from store windows to increase interior visibility, installing brighter lights, and instituting a pay-first policy have helped reduce thefts from gas stations and convenience stores.[57] Research by Lynn Addington and Callie Marie Rennison shows that living in a gated community reduces the risk of being targeted by burglars.[58]

**INCREASE THE RISK OF COMMITTING CRIME** If the risk of getting caught can be increased, rational offenders are less likely to commit crime. Marcus Felson argues that the risk of crime may be increased by improving the effectiveness of **crime discouragers**: people who serve as guardians of property or people and who can help control would-be criminals.[59] Discouragers can be grouped into three categories: "guardians," who monitor potential targets (such as police and store security guards), "handlers," who monitor potential offenders (such as parole officers and parents), and "managers," who monitor places (such as homeowners and garage attendants). If the discouragers do their jobs correctly, the potential criminal will be convinced that the risk of crime outweighs any potential gains.[60] Even if discouragers cannot prevent crime, their presence may convince offenders to limit the severity of offending since they know a guardian will intervene if they injure victims.[61]

Some crime discouragers are mechanical rather than human—closed-circuit TV cameras used to monitor locations may discourage crime while reducing the need for higher-cost security personnel. Some cities in the United States have large numbers of security cameras: New York City has more than 4,000 cameras in Manhattan alone; Chicago's linked public and private security cameras number around 10,000. In Great Britain, there are an estimated 4.2 million CCTV cameras, or 1 for every 14 citizens. Research shows that CCTV interventions (a) have a small but significant desirable effect on crime, (b) are most effective in reducing crime in car parks (parking lots), (c) are most effective in reducing vehicle crimes, and (d) are more effective in reducing crime in the United Kingdom than in other countries.[62]

**crime discouragers**
People who serve as guardians of property or people.

**REDUCE THE REWARDS OF CRIME** Target reduction strategies are designed to reduce the value of crime to the potential criminal. Jewelry stores display expensive rings with fake diamonds (cubic zirconia), while keeping the real stones under lock and key. Retail establishments put small but valuable items in tamper-proof hard plastic cases that emit electronic signals to trigger alarms if they are taken from the store; they can only be opened by store employees. Bike owners can put an indelible identification mark on their bicycle such as a serial number; thieves are less likely to steal a bicycle that can be positively identified.

**INDUCE GUILT: INCREASE SHAME** Crime may be reduced or prevented if we can communicate to people the wrongfulness of their behavior and how harmful it is to society. We may tell them to "say no to drugs" or that "users are losers." By making people aware of the shamefulness of their actions, we hope to prevent their criminal activities, even if the chances that they will be detected and punished are slight.

Sometimes punishment is designed to make people ashamed and embarrass them so that they will not repeat their criminal acts. In one incident a judge in Hudson, Kansas, ordered a man who admitted molesting an 11-year-old boy to post signs reading "A Sex Offender Lives Here" on all four sides of his home and to display the warning "Sex Offender in This Car" in bold yellow lettering on both sides of his automobile.[63]

Inducing guilt or shame might include such techniques as setting strict rules to embarrass offenders. Publishing "john lists" in the newspaper punishes those arrested for soliciting prostitutes. Facilitating compliance by providing trash bins might shame chronic litterers into using them. In a classic study, Ronald Clarke found that the introduction of caller ID systems created significant reductions in the number of obscene phone calls, presumably because of the shame presented by the threat of exposure.[64]

**REDUCE PROVOCATION** Some crimes are the result of extreme provocation—for example, road rage. It might be possible to reduce provocation by creating programs that reduce conflict. As Philip Cook and Jens Ludwig point out, alcohol is a significant factor in various kinds of crime, including rape and assaults. One way to reduce this sort of crime is to raise the price of beer, wine, and hard liquor. They suggest that raising the tax by 55 cents would reduce beer consumption by around 6 percent. And there would be significant fringe benefits, including fewer auto accidents and more money for state treasuries.[65] Another approach: mandating an early closing time in local bars and pubs might limit assaults that result from late-night drinking and conflicts at closing time.

**REMOVE EXCUSES** Crime may be reduced by making it difficult for people to excuse their criminal behavior by saying things like "I didn't know that was illegal" or "I had no choice." Municipalities have set up roadside displays that electronically flash a car's speed as it passes, eliminating the driver's excuse that she did not know how fast she was going when stopped by police. Trash containers, brightly displayed, can eliminate the claim that "I just didn't know where to throw my trash." Reducing or eliminating excuses in this way also makes it physically easy for people to comply with laws and regulations, thereby reducing the likelihood that they will choose crime.

## Evaluating Situational Crime Prevention

Situational crime prevention efforts bring with them certain hidden costs and benefits that can either undermine their success or increase their effectiveness. What are these costs and benefits, and what do they tell us about the effectiveness and efficiency of situational crime prevention?

**HIDDEN BENEFITS**  When efforts to prevent one crime unintentionally prevent another, it is known as **diffusion**.[66] Video cameras set up in a mall to reduce shoplifting can also reduce property damage, because would-be vandals fear they are being caught on camera. Police surveillance set up to reduce drug trafficking may unintentionally reduce the incidence of prostitution and other public order crimes by scaring off would-be clients.[67] Intensive police patrols designed to target specifically high-crime areas (hot spots) reduce crime in neighboring areas as well.[68]

Discouragement occurs when crime control efforts targeting a particular locale help reduce crime in surrounding areas and populations. Programs designed to control drug dealing in a particular area of the city have been found to decrease drug sales not only in targeted areas but also in adjacent areas. The message that drug dealing would not be tolerated in a particular neighborhood had a spillover effect, decreasing the total number of people involved in drug activity, even though they did not operate in the targeted areas.[69]

**HIDDEN COSTS**  Situational crime prevention efforts may also contain hidden costs that may limit their effectiveness.

- Displacement occurs when crime control efforts in one location simply move, or redirect, offenders to less heavily guarded alternative targets.[70] Beefed-up police patrols may appear to reduce crime but in reality merely shift it to a more vulnerable neighborhood.[71]
- Extinction occurs when crime reduction programs produce a short-term positive effect, but benefits dissipate as criminals adjust to new conditions; for example, burglars learn to dismantle alarms or avoid patrols. A Philadelphia police program that made use of foot patrols to lower violent crime rates found that while the program worked at first, the effects began to quickly fade. It is possible that at first publicity about the program scared would-be criminals, but as time went on their fear dissipated and they soon resumed illegal activities.[72]
- Replacement occurs when criminals try new offenses to replace those neutralized by crime prevention efforts. Foiled by burglar and car alarms, motivated offenders may turn to armed robbery, a riskier and more violent crime.

Before the effectiveness of situational crime prevention can be accepted, these hidden costs and benefits must be weighed and balanced.

## General Deterrence

According to the rational choice view, because human beings are self-interested, rational, and reasoning they will violate the law if they do not fear the consequences of their crimes. After all, crime left unchecked can bring profit and pleasure. It stands to reason, then, that crime can be controlled by increasing the real or perceived threat of criminal punishment; this is the concept of **general deterrence**. Based on Beccaria's famous equation, the greater the severity, certainty, and speed of legal sanctions, the less inclined people will be to commit crime and, consequently, the lower the crime rate.

**diffusion**
An effect that occurs when efforts to prevent one crime unintentionally prevent another.

**discouragement**
An effect that occurs when crime control efforts targeting a particular locale help reduce crime in surrounding areas and populations.

**displacement**
An effect that occurs when crime control efforts simply move, or redirect, offenders to less heavily guarded alternative targets.

**extinction**
An effect that occurs when crime reduction programs produce a short-term positive effect, but benefits dissipate as criminals adjust to new conditions.

**replacement**
An effect that occurs when criminals try new offenses they had previously avoided because situational crime prevention programs neutralized their crime of choice.

**general deterrence**
A crime control policy that depends on the fear of criminal penalties convincing the potential law violator that the pains associated with crime outweigh its benefits.

**LO5**  Analyze the elements of general deterrence.

## Perception and Deterrence

According to deterrence theory, not only the actual chance of punishment, but also the *perception that punishment will be forthcoming*, influence criminality.[73] A central theme of deterrence theory is that people who believe or imagine that they will be punished for crimes in the present will avoid doing those crimes in the future.[74] Even the most committed offenders (e.g., gang members, terrorists) will forego criminal activities if they fear legal punishments.[75] Conversely, the likelihood of being arrested or imprisoned will have little effect on crime rates if criminals believe that they have only a small chance of suffering apprehension and punishment in the future.[76] Because criminals are rational decision makers, if they can be convinced that crime will lead to punishment, then they will be deterred.

While logical, the association between perception and deterrence is not a simple one nor does it appear to be linear—that is, the greater the perception of punishment, the less people are willing to commit crime. Perception of punishment appears to change and evolve over time, shaped by a potential offender's experience and personality. There also may be different classes and types of offenders, some being more *deterrable* than others. The most significant deterrent effects can be achieved on minor petty criminals, whereas more serious offenders such as murderers are harder to discourage.[77] High-rate serious offenders may perceive less risk and more reward from crime, while others who commit less serious crime less frequently may view illegal acts as less rewarding; they tend to overestimate the risk of apprehension and punishment.[78] More experienced offenders who may have gotten away with crime in the past are less likely to fear punishment in the future.

## Marginal and Restrictive Deterrence

In some instances deterrence strategies can lead to less than perfect results. Rather than entirely eliminating crime, they may reduce its frequency, duration, and severity. **Marginal deterrence** refers to the relative effectiveness of punishments. Let's say when police are called to the scene of a domestic violence disturbance they choose to arrest some offenders and let others go with a warning. If getting arrested reduces the chance of repeat offending when compared to a warning, arrest is said to produce a higher marginal deterrent effect. Arresting someone for domestic violence may not eliminate future offending completely, but it provides a better outcome than merely warning the abuser.

**Restrictive deterrence** (sometimes called **partial deterrence**) refers to situations in which the threat of punishment can reduce but not eliminate the frequency, severity, and duration of a crime. Restrictive deterrence would be achieved if creating a steep fine for going 20 miles per hour or more over the posted speed limit resulted in the average motorist exceeding the speed limit by only 10 miles per hour. People still speed, but not by as much.

Criminologist Bruce Jacobs suggests that restrictive deterrence contains four separate but interrelated concepts:

- The offender reduces the number of crimes she or he commits over a particular period of time.
- The offender commits crimes of lesser seriousness than the contemplated act, believing that punishment won't be as severe for a more minor infraction.
- The offender engages in situational measures to enhance the probability that the contemplated offense will be undertaken without risk of detection.
- The offender recognizes a risky situational context, which causes him or her to commit the same crime at a different place or time.[79]

Recently Jacobs along with Michael Cherbonneau interviewed active auto thieves to determine whether their behavior was altered by their fear of apprehension and punishment. Their findings, discussed in the Policies and Issues in Criminology feature, show that thieves do perceive a restrictive deterrent effect of the law and use rational judgment to help them avoid detection and arrest.

**marginal deterrence**
Occurs when a relatively more severe penalty will produce *some* reduction in crime.

**restrictive (partial) deterrence**
Refers to situations in which the threat of punishment can reduce but not eliminate crime.

# Policies and Issues in Criminology

## DETERRING CAR THIEVES

Bruce Jacobs and Michael Cherbonneau interviewed 35 active auto thieves to find out whether they were in any way deterred by the threat of apprehension and punishment. They found that car thieves were indeed rational in their decision making, wary of the dangers they face and taking precautions to avoid detection, apprehension, and punishment. While the threat of legal sanction did not dissuade them from stealing cars, it did have a restrictive deterrent effect, shaping and limiting their activities.

The car thieves told Jacobs and Cherbonneau that the threat of getting caught shapes their target selection methodology. Some vehicles are avoided because they are certain to attract greater police attention. Some cars are just too flashy and don't match what a cop might believe is an appropriate ride for the driver. Car thieves want to take something nice but not too nice. Young African American men claimed they avoid new cars, as they did not want a patrol officer spying them on the road to instantly think "Where did that young black man get the money for that new ride?" So taking only age- and budget-appropriate cars was a must. One thief claimed stealing a car that was too new was unwise because the victim likely had insurance on it and would report it: "Old models are less hot because nobody really cares."

Sensitivity to the risk of crime also determined where the theft would occur. Several offenders underscored the importance of trolling in areas geographically removed from where they live. One reason: if you take cars from outside the city, it takes much longer for the theft to get reported outside the jurisdiction, giving the thieves a two or three day grace period to ride around without worrying about police.

Fear of apprehension also produces what Jacobs and Cherbonneau refer to as "normalcy illusions," a patchwork of tactics designed to prevent authorities from becoming wise to the fact that the thieves were driving a stolen vehicle. One instant precaution is affixing a fresh license plate to the stolen vehicle as quickly as possible after it is taken. Where to get a new plate? Some of the thieves go to a local junkyard and take plates off an abandoned car. Wary of police presence, they avoided areas where there were more cops on the street.

Attention-grabbing conduct that made police suspicious also had to be avoided at all costs. That meant driving sensibly; running lights, speeding, and so on brought grief rather than rewards. The more normal they were, the less likely they would incur police scrutiny. If they were being tailed by a patrol car they would immediately stop and knock on someone's door, as if they were out on a social call (rather than out stealing cars). Another ploy: find an innocent-looking driver to shield them from police attention. A number of male offenders asked females to drive stolen vehicles because police did not suspect females of being auto thieves. Female accomplices felt comfortable helping out because they too believe police are not out looking for female auto thieves.

Just in case they were caught, car thieves planned flight strategies in advance. They were ready for high-speed chases triggered by being asked to pull over. Some reported knowledge that for safety's sake police in the jurisdiction were forbidden to pursue speeding cars, making high-speed getaways that much more effective. Some waited until the officer exited the patrol car and approached their vehicle before taking off, giving them a head start. Some headed for jurisdictional boundaries knowing that it would effectively bring any chase to a halt. Others headed for concealment: an open garage offers shelter and a look of normalcy. Some stashed other cars around the city and, during a pursuit, would simply drive to one of these vehicles or "stash spots," ditch the vehicle being pursued, and escape in the stashed vehicle.

The Jacobs and Cherbonneau research shows that car thieves are rational decision makers and that their behavior is affected by the deterrent effect of the law—not enough to dissuade them from committing crime, but enough to alter their behavior. The research aptly illustrates the concept of partial or restrictive deterrent effect.

## Critical Thinking

Would car theft be eliminated if every car was equipped with a kill switch that enabled police and law enforcement agents to disengage the engine and lock the doors? Would a rational car thief be deterred by such a deterrence measure?

**Source:** Bruce Jacobs and Michael Cherbonneau, "Auto Theft and Restrictive Deterrence," *Justice Quarterly* 31 (2014): 344–367.

## Punishment and Deterrence

According to general deterrence theory, if the certainty, severity, and celerity or speed of arrest, conviction, and sanctioning increase, crime rates should decline. Crime will persist, however, if people believe they will get away with crime and even if they are caught, they will have a good chance of escaping punishment.[80] If people believe that their criminal transgressions will almost certainly result in punishment, then only the truly irrational will commit crime.[81] The sections below examine each of these associations in some detail.

**CERTAINTY OF PUNISHMENT** A number of research efforts do show a direct relationship between crime rates and the certainty of punishment. And although the issue is far from settled, people who believe that they will get caught if they commit crime are the ones most likely to be deterred from committing criminal acts.[82]

Certainty increases when local police officers are active, aggressive crime fighters, convincing would-be criminals that the risk of apprehension outweighs any benefits they can gain from crime.[83] Proactive, aggressive law enforcement seems more effective than routine patrol. Would-be criminals are deterred when police concentrate their forces and focus on so-called "hot spots" of crime, convincing them that these areas are now unsafe and off limits to criminal activity.[84] Improving response time and increasing the number of patrol cars that respond per crime may increase police efficiency and deter people from committing crime.[85]

There is still debate whether increasing the size of the local police force can actually reduce crime rates. When Steven Durlauf and Daniel Nagin carefully reviewed the existing scientific literature, they found that jurisdictions that increased the visibility of the police, hired more officers, and used patrol officers in ways that increased the perceived risk of apprehension did enjoy deterrent effects and lower crime rates.[86]

AP Images/Michael Graczyk

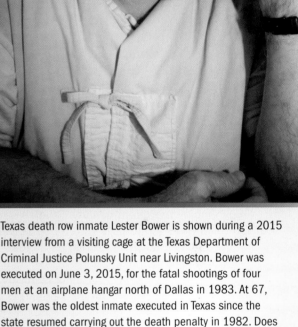

Texas death row inmate Lester Bower is shown during a 2015 interview from a visiting cage at the Texas Department of Criminal Justice Polunsky Unit near Livingston. Bower was executed on June 3, 2015, for the fatal shootings of four men at an airplane hangar north of Dallas in 1983. At 67, Bower was the oldest inmate executed in Texas since the state resumed carrying out the death penalty in 1982. Does Bower's execution help deter crime?

**SEVERITY OF PUNISHMENT** According to deterrence theory, people who believe they will be punished severely for a crime will forgo committing criminal acts.[87] Nonetheless, there is little consensus that strict punishments alone can reduce criminal activities, and most criminologists believe that the certainty of punishment, rather than its severity, is the key to deterring criminal behaviors.[88]

One reason for this skepticism is the alleged failure of the death penalty to deter murder. Because this topic is so important, it is discussed in the accompanying Policies and Issues in Criminology feature.

**SWIFTNESS OF PUNISHMENT** The third leg of Beccaria's equation involves the celerity, or speed, of punishment: the more rapidly punishment is applied and the more closely it is linked to the crime, the more likely it is to serve as a deterrent.[89] The deterrent effect of the law may be neutralized if there is a significant lag between apprehension and punishment. In the American justice system, court delays brought by numerous evidentiary hearings and requests for additional trial preparation time are common trial tactics. As a result, the criminal process can be delayed to a point where

# Policies and Issues
## in Criminology

## DOES THE DEATH PENALTY DISCOURAGE MURDER?

According to deterrence theory, the death penalty—the ultimate deterrent—should deter criminals from committing murder—the ultimate crime. A majority of Americans, even convicted criminals who are currently behind bars, approve of the death penalty. But is the public's approval warranted? Does the death penalty actually discourage murder?

Empirical research on the association between capital punishment and murder can be divided into three types: immediate impact studies, comparative research, and time-series analysis.

- *Immediate impact.* If capital punishment is a deterrent, the reasoning goes, then its impact should be greatest after a well-publicized execution. However, most research has failed to find evidence that an execution produces an immediate decline in the murder rate; even highly publicized executions had little impact on the murder rate.
- *Comparative research.* It is also possible to compare murder rates in jurisdictions that have abolished the death penalty with the rates in jurisdictions that routinely employ the death penalty. Studies using this approach have found little difference between the murder rates of adjacent states, regardless of their use of the death penalty; capital punishment did not appear to affect the reported rate of homicide.
- *Time-series studies.* If capital punishment is a deterrent, then periods that have an upswing in executions should also experience a downturn in violent crime and murder. Most research efforts have failed to show such a relationship. Economic conditions, population density, and incarceration rates have a much greater impact on the murder rate than does the death penalty.

### Rethinking the Deterrent Effect of Capital Punishment

Some recent studies have concluded that executing criminals may, in fact, bring the murder rate down. These newer studies, using sophisticated data analysis, have been able to uncover a more significant association—when a state routinely uses executions, the deterrent effect becomes significant.

These recent pro–death penalty studies are not without their detractors. Jeffrey Fagan, a highly regarded criminologist, finds fault with the methodology now being used, arguing that "this work fails the tests of rigorous replication and robustness analysis that are the hallmarks of good science." Fagan and his colleagues compared homicide rates in two Asian cities with vastly different execution risks. Singapore had at one time a surge in execution rate that made it the highest in the world, before significantly reducing the number of executions. Hong Kong, by contrast, has had no executions all. Nonetheless, homicide levels and trends are remarkably similar in these two cities, with neither the surge in Singapore executions nor the more recent steep drop producing any differential impact. By comparing two closely matched places with huge contrasts in actual execution but no differences in homicide trends, Fagan disputes the relative effectiveness of capital punishment as a crime deterrent.

Similarly, John Donohue and Justin Wolfers examined recent statistical studies that claimed to show a deterrent effect from the death penalty and found that they "are simply not credible." In fact, they reach an opposite conclusion: applying the death penalty actually *increases* the number of murders.

### Rethinking the Death Penalty

The death penalty debate continues. Advocates argue that even if marginally effective, capital punishment ensures that convicted criminals never again get the opportunity to

the connection between crime and punishment is broken. Take for instance how the death penalty is employed. Typically, more than 10 years elapse between the time a criminal is convicted and sentenced to death for murder and that person's execution. Delay in application of the death penalty may mitigate or neutralize the potential deterrent effect of capital punishment.

## Evaluating General Deterrence

Some experts believe that the purpose of the law and justice system is to create a "threat system."[90] The threat of legal punishment should, on the face of it, deter lawbreakers through fear. Nonetheless, crime rates and deterrent measures are much less

kill again: about 9 percent of all inmates on death row have had prior convictions for homicide. They note that the murder rate has been in dramatic decline since capital punishment has been reinstated, and the general public approves of its use as a deterrent to murder. Further, as Meredith Martin Rountree's research shows, more than 10 percent of inmates who have been executed hastened their executions by abandoning their appeals, many because they believed their execution was actually fair and justified. If so many death row inmates approve of the death penalty, how can its abolition be justified? Writing in the *Stanford Law Review*, Cass Sunstein and Adrian Vermeule conclude that "a government that settles upon a package of crime-control policies that does *not* include capital punishment might well seem, at least prima facie, to be both violating the rights and reducing the welfare of its citizens—just as would a state that failed to enact simple environmental measures promising to save a great many lives."

Far from being persuaded, abolitionists note that capital punishment has significant drawbacks. Since 1976, more than 100 people have been wrongfully convicted and sentenced to death in the United States only to be exonerated when new scientific evidence has proven their innocence; the possibility that an innocent person can be executed is real and frightening. In addition, as legal scholar David Baldus and his associates have found, racial bias may influence death penalty decisions in both civilian and military courts. People are more likely to be sentenced to death when a victim is white or in cases involving black criminals and white victims—a race-based outcome that tarnishes the validity of capital punishment.

## Critical Thinking

Even if it is effective, the death penalty is not without serious problems. When Geoffrey Rapp studied the effect of the death penalty on the safety of police officers, he found that the introduction of capital punishment actually created an extremely dangerous environment for law enforcement officers. Because the death penalty does not have a deterrent effect, criminals are more likely to kill police officers when the death penalty is in place. Tragically, the death penalty may lull officers into a false sense of security, causing them to let down their guard—killing fewer criminals but getting killed more often themselves. Given Rapp's findings, should we still maintain the death penalty?

**Sources:** Jeffrey A. Fagan, "Capital Punishment: Deterrent Effects and Capital Costs," Columbia University School of Law, www.law.columbia.edu/law_school/communications/reports/summer06/capitalpunish; Franklin Zimring, Jeffrey Fagan, and David Johnson, "Executions, Deterrence and Homicide: A Tale of Two Cities," papers.ssrn.com/sol3/papers.cfm?abstract_id=1436993; Meredith Martin Rountree, "'I'll Make Them Shoot Me': Accounts of Death Row Prisoners Advocating for Execution," *Law and Society Review* 46 (2012): 589–622; David Baldus, Catherine Grosso, George Woodworth, and Richard Newell, "Racial Discrimination in the Administration of the Death Penalty: The Experience of the United States Armed Forces (1984–2005)," *Journal of Criminal Law and Criminology* 101 (2011): 1227–1335; Cass R. Sunstein and Adrian Vermeule, "Is Capital Punishment Morally Required? Acts, Omissions, and Lifetime Tradeoffs," *Stanford Law Review* 58 (2006): 703–750, at 749; Tomislav Kovandzic, Lynne Vieraitis, and Denise Paquette Boots, "Does the Death Penalty Save Lives? New Evidence from State Panel Data, 1977 to 2006," *Criminology and Public Policy* 8 (2009): 803–843; Jeffrey Fagan, "Death and Deterrence Redux: Science, Law and Causal Reasoning on Capital Punishment," *Ohio State Journal of Criminal Law* 4 (2006): 255–320; Joanna Shepherd, "Deterrence versus Brutalization: Capital Punishment's Differing Impacts Among States," *Michigan Law Review* 104 (2005): 203–253; John Donohue and Justin Wolfers, "Uses and Abuses of Empirical Evidence in the Death Penalty Debate," *Stanford Law Review* 58 (2005): 791–845; Geoffrey Rapp, "The Economics of Shootouts: Does the Passage of Capital Punishment Laws Protect or Endanger Police Officers?" *Albany Law Review* 65 (2002): 1051–1084 (URLs accessed 2015).

closely related than choice theorists might expect. Despite efforts to punish criminals and make them fear crime, there is little evidence that the fear of apprehension and punishment alone can reduce crime rates. How can this discrepancy be explained?

**RATIONALITY** Deterrence theory assumes a rational offender who weighs the costs and benefits of a criminal act before deciding on a course of action. Criminals may be desperate people who choose crime because they believe there is no reasonable alternative. Some may suffer from personality disorders that impair their judgment and render them incapable of making truly rational decisions. Psychologists believe that chronic offenders suffer from an emotional state that renders them both incapable of fearing punishment and less likely to appreciate the consequences of crime.[91] Research on repeat sex offenders finds that they suffer from an elevated emotional state that negates the deterrent effect of the law.[92] There is also evidence that drinking alcohol impedes a person's ability to reasonably assess the costs and benefits of crime.[93] If the benefits of crime are exaggerated, the law's deterrent effect may be deflated.

**SYSTEM EFFECTIVENESS**  As Beccaria's famous equation tells us, the threat of punishment involves not only its severity but also its certainty and speed. The American legal system is not very effective. About half of all crimes are reported to police, and police make arrests in only about 20 percent of reported crimes. Even when offenders are detected, police officers may choose to warn rather than arrest.[94] The odds of receiving a prison term are less than 20 per 1,000 crimes committed. As a result, some offenders believe they will not be severely punished for their acts, and they consequently have little regard for the law's deterrent power. Even those accused of murder are often convicted of lesser offenses and spend relatively short amounts of time behind bars.[95] In making their "rational choice," offenders may be aware that the deterrent effect of the law is minimal.

**CRIMINALS DISCOUNT PUNISHMENTS**  Would-be criminals are not well informed about the actual risks of sanctions. They may know somebody who made a big score and that shapes their perceptions: according to their thinking, crime may actually pay.[96] Criminals who have already been punished may believe that the likelihood of getting caught twice for the same type of crime is remote: "Lightning never strikes twice in the same spot," they may reason; no one is that unlucky.[97]

**SOME OFFENDERS—AND SOME CRIMES—ARE MORE "DETERRABLE" THAN OTHERS**  Not every crime can be discouraged nor is every criminal deterrable.[98] Some people may be suffering from personality disorders and mental infirmity that make them immune to the deterrent power of the law.[99] Others live in economically depressed neighborhoods, where the threat of formal sanctions is irrelevant because people living in these areas have little to lose if arrested; their opportunities are few, and they have little attachment to social institutions such as school and family. Even if they truly fear the consequences of the law, they must commit crime to survive in a hostile environment.

It also appears that it is easier to deter offenders from some crimes than from others.[100] The most significant deterrent effects appear to be achieved in minor crimes and offenses, such as recreational drug use, whereas more serious crimes such as homicide are harder to discourage.[101]

**L06**  Discuss the basic concepts of specific deterrence.

# Specific Deterrence

**specific deterrence**
The view that criminal sanctions should be so powerful that offenders will never repeat their criminal acts.

The theory of **specific deterrence** (also called special or particular deterrence) holds that criminal sanctions should be so powerful that known criminals will never repeat their criminal acts. According to this view, the drunk driver whose sentence is a substantial fine and a week in the county jail should be convinced that the price to be paid for drinking and driving is too great to consider future violations. Similarly, burglars who spend five years in a tough, maximum-security prison should find their enthusiasm for theft dampened.[102] In principle, punishment works when a connection can be established between the planned action and memories of its consequence; if these recollections are adequately intense, the action is unlikely to occur again.[103] The theory supposes that people can "learn from their mistakes" and that those who are caught and punished will perceive greater risk than those who have escaped detection.[104] As the perceived benefits of crime decline, so too should criminal acts.[105]

The evidence on specific deterrence is decidedly mixed: the association between experiencing punishment and desistance from crime is not always perfect. For example, while some initial research found that domestic violence offenders who received severe punishments were less likely to offend, follow-up studies failed to replicate a significant specific deterrent effect.[106] Many offenders recidivate, even after suffering a prison sentence; the effect of incarceration on rearrest sometimes appears to be minimal.[107]

## Toughen Punishment?

It's possible that a specific deterrent can be achieved if the severity of punishment is increased and type of punishment is amplified. Research by Benjamin Meade and his associates found that inmates serving long sentences (five years or more) are less likely to recidivate once released than those serving shorter sentences.[108]

Some states are now employing high-security "supermax" prisons that apply a bare minimum of treatment and impose lockdown 23 hours a day. Certainly, such a harsh regimen should discourage future criminality. However, studies that compare supermax prisoners with inmates from more traditional prisons on a one-to-one basis show that upon release supermax prisoners had significantly higher felony **recidivism** rates than controls from less restrictive prisons. Those released directly into the community from a supermax prison commit new offenses sooner than supermax prisoners who were first sent to traditional institutions three months or more before their release.[109] Creating tougher prisons, then, may not produce the desired deterrent effect.

**WHY IS THE EVIDENCE MIXED?** How is it possible that even the harshest treatment fails to produce the desired specific deterrent effect on future crime?

- Punishment may breed defiance rather than deterrence. People who are harshly treated may want to show that they cannot be broken by the system.
- The stigma of harsh treatment labels people and helps lock offenders into a criminal career instead of convincing them to avoid one.
- Experiencing the harshest punishments, such as a stay in a supermax prison, may cause severe psychological problems because these prisons isolate convicts, offer little sensory stimulation, and provide minimal opportunities for interaction with other people.[110]
- The effect of punishment is negligible in neighborhoods where almost everyone has a criminal record.[111]

Thus, although the concept of specific deterrence should work on paper, the reality can be far different.

## Incapacitation

Even if severe punishments cannot effectively turn criminals away from crime, it stands to reason that if more criminals are sent to prison, the crime rate should go down. Because most people age out of crime, the duration of a criminal career is limited. Placing offenders behind bars during their prime crime years should reduce their lifetime opportunity to commit crime. The shorter the span of opportunity, the fewer offenses they can commit during their lives; hence, crime is reduced. This theory, which is known as the **incapacitation effect**, seems logical, but does it work?

Today, more than one in every hundred adults is behind bars (about 2.3 million people.[112] Advocates of incapacitation suggest that this growth in the prison/jail population is directly responsible for the decade-long decline in the crime rate. Putting

**recidivism**
Repetition of criminal behavior.

**incapacitation effect**
The idea that keeping offenders in confinement will eliminate the risk of their committing further offenses.

Kevork Djansezian/Getty Images News/Getty Images

Using an incapacitation strategy to control crime may work, but it also brings unpleasant side effects such as prison overcrowding. Here, an inmate at Chino State Prison in California, which houses 5,500 inmates, relaxes on a bunk bed in a gymnasium that was modified to house 213 prisoners. In 2009, the US Supreme Court ordered the state to release 40,000 prisoners in order to cope with overcrowding so severe that it violated their human rights.

dangerous felons under lock and key for longer periods of time significantly reduces the opportunity they have to commit crime, so the crime rate declines as well.

Although it is difficult to measure precisely, there is at least some evidence that crime rates and incarceration rates are related.[113] Economist Steven Levitt, author of the widely read book *Freakonomics*, concludes that each person put behind bars results in a decrease of 15 serious crimes per year.[114] He argues that the social benefits associated with crime reduction equal or exceed the social and financial costs of incarceration.[115]

Even though Levitt's argument is persuasive, not all criminologists buy into the incapacitation effect:

- There is little evidence that incapacitating criminals will deter them from future criminality, and there *is* reason to believe they may be more inclined to commit even more crimes upon release. There is a significant correlation between incarceration and recidivism. In other words, the more prior incarceration experiences people have, the more likely they are to recidivate within 12 months of their release; incapacitation does not produce a specific deterrent effect.[116]
- Former inmates often suffer postrelease personal and financial problems that cause them to commit more crimes than they might have had they not been sentenced to prison. The crimes that are "saved" while they serve time are more than made up for by the extra ones they commit because they are now ex-cons.[117]
- By its nature, the prison experience exposes young, first-time offenders to higher-risk, more experienced inmates who can influence their lifestyle and help shape their attitudes; prisons are "schools for crime."
- Imprisoning established offenders may open new opportunities for competitors. Incarcerating gang members or organized crime figures may open illegal markets to new groups that are even hungrier and more aggressive than the gangs they replaced.

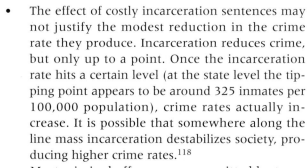

- The effect of costly incarceration sentences may not justify the modest reduction in the crime rate they produce. Incarceration reduces crime, but only up to a point. Once the incarceration rate hits a certain level (at the state level the tipping point appears to be around 325 inmates per 100,000 population), crime rates actually increase. It is possible that somewhere along the line mass incarceration destabilizes society, producing higher crime rates.[118]
- Most criminal offenses are committed by teens and very young adult offenders who are unlikely to be sent to prison for a single felony conviction. Older criminals are already past the age when they are likely to commit crime. As a result, a strict incarceration policy may keep people in prison beyond the time when they cease being a threat to society, while a new cohort of high-risk adolescents is on the street.[119] A strict incarceration policy would result in a growing number of elderly inmates whose maintenance costs are much higher than those of younger inmates.

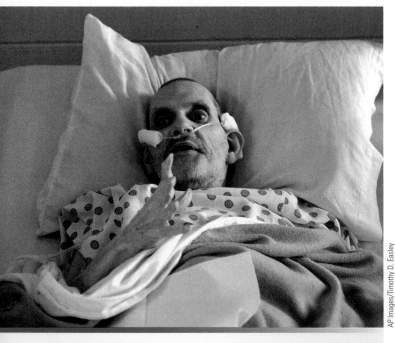

AP Images/Timothy D. Easley

On April 17, 2014, Patrick O'Hara, a patient in the medical unit, speaks with staff members of the Kentucky State Reformatory in LaGrange. It costs Kentucky $3.3 million a year to care for 50 elderly inmates who can't take care of themselves, a burden the state is preparing to shift to the federal government. Do you agree that there is no real purpose in keeping inmates like O'Hara behind bars?

It is also possible that any incarceration–crime rate relationship is not linear or predictable. There are times when a surge in incarceration coincided with a significant decline in crime rates (1991–2000); however, during other time periods, crime rate increases coincided with increasing incarceration rates

## Concept Summary 4.1    Choice Theories

| Theory | Major Premise | Strengths | Research Focus |
|---|---|---|---|
| **Rational choice** | Law-violating behavior occurs after offenders weigh information on their personal needs and the situational factors involved in the difficulty and risk of committing a crime. | Explains why high-risk people do not constantly engage in crime. Relates theory to crime control policy. It is not limited by class or other social variables. | Offense patterns—where, when, and how crime takes place. |
| **General deterrence** | People will commit crime if they perceive that the benefits outweigh the risks. Crime is a function of the severity, certainty, and speed of punishment. | Shows the relationship between crime and punishment. Suggests a real solution to crime. | Perception of punishment, effect of legal sanctions, probability of punishment, and crime rates. |
| **Specific deterrence** | If punishment is severe enough, criminals will not repeat their illegal acts. | Provides a strategy to reduce crime. | Recidivism, repeat offending, punishment type, and crime. |
| **Incapacitation** | Keeping known criminals out of circulation will reduce crime rates. | Recognizes the role that opportunity plays in criminal behavior. Provides a solution to chronic offending. | Prison population and crime rates, sentence length, and crime. |

(1984–1991).[120] Such findings weaken the argument that the key to lower crime rates is locking people up for long periods of time.

Concept Summary 4.1 summarizes the main features of choice theories.

## Policy Implications of Choice Theory

In some instances, research showing a deterrent effect has shaped public policy. In a famous study conducted in Minneapolis, Lawrence Sherman and Richard Berk evaluated the effect of police action on repeat domestic violence and found clear evidence that when police take formal action (arrest), offenders are less likely to recidivate than when less severe methods are used (a warning or a cooling-off period).[121] Subsequent to this study, a number of states adopted legislation mandating that police either take formal action in domestic abuse cases or explain in writing their failure to act. However, when the Minneapolis experiment was repeated in other locales, evaluations failed to duplicate the original results.[122] In these locales, formal arrest was not a greater specific deterrent to domestic abuse than warning or advising the assailant.

Sherman and his associates later found that the effect of arrest quickly decays and that in the long run, arrest may actually escalate the frequency of repeat domestic violence.[123] A possible explanation is that offenders who are arrested fear punishment initially, but when their cases do not result in severe punishment their fear is eventually replaced with anger and violent intent toward their mates. This result implies that even if punishment can produce a short-term specific deterrent effect, it fails to produce longer-term behavior change.[124]

Another example of policy based on choice theory is the "three strikes and you're out" laws that require state courts to hand down mandatory periods of incarceration for up to life in prison to persons who have been convicted of a serious criminal offense on three or more separate occasions. The rationale for its use relies on both general deterrence (scaring off would-be criminals) and incapacitation (keeping repeat offenders off the streets).

Can such hard-line policies work? The results are mixed. Some criminologists, using highly sophisticated research techniques, have found a significant association between the increased use of incarceration and reductions in the crime rate.[125] A strict incarceration policy may also have residual benefits. Ilyana Kuziemko and Steven Levitt found that as the number of prisoners incarcerated on drug-related offenses rose dramatically (1,500 percent) between 1980 and 2000, crime rates dropped. One reason was that the incarceration policy had an unforeseen impact on drug markets: putting dealers in prison increased the cost of cocaine by 10 to 15 percent, and the higher prices spelled a drop of as much as 20 percent in the use of cocaine.[126]

Although this type of get-tough policy appeals to the public, it may be premature to embrace a three-strikes policy:

- Most three-time losers are on the verge of aging out of crime anyway.
- Current sentences for violent crimes are already quite severe. Chronic offending is already punished severely.
- An expanding prison population will drive up already high prison costs.
- The police would be in danger because two-time offenders would violently resist a third arrest, knowing that conviction would mean a life sentence.[127]

So whether crime control policy that rests on a strict choice theory orientation can work remains to be seen.

# Thinking Like a Criminologist

**Just Punishment** The governor has asked you, a death penalty expert, to give your advice on abolishing the death penalty in the state. He has recently read an article by philosopher Bradley Wilson that sets out the argument against the death penalty using this train of thought:

1. Capital punishment is not morally required in any case.
2. Mercy is a morally valuable trait; all things being equal, actions that demonstrate mercy have more moral worth than those that do not. Thus, a moral viewpoint that incorporates mercy is preferable to one that does not.
3. Not executing those who have committed capital crimes demonstrates mercy.
4. Just punishment of capital crimes is compatible with showing mercy.
5. Thus, not executing those who have committed capital crimes is morally preferable to executing them.[128]

## Writing Assignment

Write a critical essay commenting on this reasoning. Address the issue of whether executing people is an effective crime control policy—or might it have hidden costs that undermine its effectiveness? Address the moral issue for abolition.

# SUMMARY

**L01 Describe the development of rational choice theory.**

Rational choice theory has its roots in the classical school of criminology developed by the eighteenth-century Italian social thinker Cesare Beccaria. In the 1960s, Nobel Prize–winning economist Gary Becker applied his views on rational behavior and human capital to criminal activity. James Q. Wilson observed that people who are likely to commit crime are unafraid of breaking the law because they value the excitement and thrills of crime, have a low stake in conformity, and are willing to take greater chances than the average person.

**L02 Explore the concepts of rational choice.**

Law-violating behavior is the product of careful thought and planning. People who commit crime believe that the rewards of crime outweigh the risks. If they think they are likely to get arrested and punished, people will not risk engaging in criminal activities. Before choosing to commit a crime, reasoning criminals carefully select targets, and their behavior is systematic and selective. Rational choice theorists view crime as both offense-specific and offender-specific.

**L03 Interpret the evidence showing that crime is rational.**

There is a great deal of anecdotal evidence showing that crime is rational. Even drug use is controlled by rational decision making. Users report that they began taking drugs when they believed the benefits of substance abuse outweighed its costs. Drug dealers approach their profession in a businesslike fashion. Violent criminals who are seemingly irrational, even serial killers, select suitable targets by picking people who are vulnerable and lack adequate defenses. Even johns make careful and rational decisions when engaging prostitutes and then share their knowledge and expertise in Internet chat rooms and web forums.

**L04 Discuss the elements of situational crime prevention.**

Situational crime prevention involves developing tactics to reduce or elimi-nate a specific crime problem. Such tactics include increased efforts to discourage crime, such as putting unbreakable glass on storefronts, locking gates, and fencing yards. Another approach is to increase the risks of crime through better security efforts. Reducing the rewards of crime is designed to lessen the value of crime to the potential criminal. Crime may be re-duced or prevented if we can communicate to people the wrongfulness of their behavior and how harmful it is to society. Crime may be reduced by making it difficult for people to excuse their criminal behavior by saying things like "I didn't know that was illegal" or "I had no choice."

**L05 Analyze the elements of general deterrence.**

Crime can be controlled by increasing the real or perceived threat of crimi-nal punishment. According to deterrence theory, criminality is affected not only by the actual chance of punishment but also by the *perception* that one is likely to be punished. A central theme of deterrence theory is that people who believe they will be punished for crimes will avoid committing those crimes. According to general deterrence theory, if the certainty of ar-rest, conviction, and sanctioning increases, crime rates should decline. The threat of severe punishment should also bring the crime rate down. The more rapidly punishment is applied and the more closely it is linked to the crime, the more likely it will serve as a deterrent. The factors of severity, certainty, and speed of punishment may also influence one another.

**LO6    Discuss the basic concepts of specific deterrence.**

The theory of specific deterrence holds that criminal sanctions should be so powerful that convicted criminals will never repeat their criminal acts. However, research on specific deterrence does not provide any clear-cut evidence that punishing criminals is an effective means of stopping them from committing future crimes. Punishment may bring defiance rather than deterrence. People who are harshly treated may want to show that they cannot be broken by the system. The stigma of harsh treatment labels people and helps lock offenders into a criminal career instead of convincing them to avoid one.

## Key Terms

rational choice theory
    (choice theory) 94
classical criminology 94
offense-specific crime 96
offender-specific
    crime 96

johns 102
situational crime
    prevention 103
defensible
    space 103
crime discouragers 104

diffusion 106
discouragement 106
displacement 106
extinction 106
replacement 106
general deterrence 106

marginal deterrence 107
restrictive (partial)
    deterrence 107
specific deterrence 112
recidivism 113
incapacitation effect 113

## Critical Thinking Questions

1.  Are criminals rational decision makers, or are most of them motivated by uncontrollable psychological and emotional drives or social forces such as poverty and despair?

2.  Would you want to live in a society where crime rates were quite low because they were controlled by extremely harsh punishments, such as flogging for vandalism?

3.  Which would you be more afraid of if you were caught by the police while shoplifting: receiving criminal punishment or having to face the contempt of your friends or relatives?

4.  Is it possible to create a method of capital punishment that would actually deter people from committing murder? Would televising executions work? What might be some of the negative consequences of such a policy?

## Notes

*All URLs accessed in 2015.*

1.  FBI, "Egregious Case of Health Care Fraud: Cancer Doctor Admits Prescribing Unnecessary Chemotherapy," www.fbi.gov/news/stories/2014/november /egregious-case-of-health-care-fraud/.

2.  Gary Becker, "Crime and Punishment: An Economic Approach," *Journal of Political Economy* 76 (1968): 169–217.

3.  James Q. Wilson, *Thinking About Crime*, rev. ed. (New York: Vintage Books, 1983), p. 260.

4.  See, generally, Derek Cornish and Ronald Clarke, eds., *The Reasoning Criminal: Rational Choice Perspectives on Offending* (New York: Springer Verlag, 1986); Philip Cook, "The Demand and Supply of Criminal Opportunities," in *Crime and Justice*, vol. 7, ed. Michael Tonry and Norval Morris (Chicago: University of Chicago

Press, 1986), pp. 1–28; Ronald Clarke and Derek Cornish, "Modeling Offenders' Decisions: A Framework for Research and Policy," in *Crime and Justice*, vol. 6, ed. Michael Tonry and Norval Morris (Chicago: University of Chicago Press, 1985), pp. 147–187; Morgan Reynolds, *Crime by Choice: An Economic Analysis* (Dallas: Fisher Institute, 1985).

5.  Hung-en Sung and Linda Richter, "Rational Choice and Environmental Deterrence in the Retention of Mandated Drug Abuse Treatment Clients," *International Journal of Offender Therapy and Comparative Criminology* 51 (2007): 686–702.

6.  Melanie Wellsmith and Amy Burrell, "The Influence of Purchase Price and Ownership Levels on Theft Targets: The Example of Domestic Burglary," *British Journal of Criminology* 45 (2005): 741–764.

7. Jeffrey Bouffard, "Predicting Differences in the Perceived Relevance of Crime's Costs and Benefits in a Test of Rational Choice Theory," *International Journal of Offender Therapy and Comparative Criminology* 51 (2007): 461–485.

8. Carlo Morselli and Marie-Noële Royer, "Criminal Mobility and Criminal Achievement," *Journal of Research in Crime and Delinquency* 45 (2008): 4–21.

9. Bouffard, "Predicting Differences."

10. Ross Matsueda, Derek Kreager, and David Huizinga, "Deterring Delinquents: A Rational Choice Model of Theft and Violence," *American Sociological Review* 71 (2006): 95–122.

11. Derek Cornish and Ronald Clarke, "Understanding Crime Displacement: An Application of Rational Choice Theory," *Criminology* 25 (1987): 933–947.

12. Michael Gottfredson and Travis Hirschi, *A General Theory of Crime* (Stanford, CA: Stanford University Press, 1990).

13. D. Wayne Osgood and Amy Anderson, "Unstructured Socializing and Rates of Delinquency," *Criminology* 42 (2004): 519–550.

14. Wim Bernasco, Stijn Ruiter, Gerben Bruinsma, Lieven Pauwels, and Frank Weerman, "Situational Causes of Offending: A Fixed-Effects Analysis of Space–Time Budget Data," *Criminology* 51 (2013): 895–926.

15. Megan Bears Augustyn and Jean Marie McGloin, "The Risk of Informal Socializing with Peers: Considering Gender Differences Across Predatory Delinquency and Substance Use," *Justice Quarterly* 30 (2013): 117–143.

16. Jack Katz, *The Seductions of Crime* (New York: Basic Books, 1988).

17. Holly Nguyen and Jean Marie McGloin, "Does Economic Adversity Breed Criminal Cooperation? Considering the Motivation Behind Group Crime," *Criminology* 51 (2013): 833–870.

18. Melissa Thompson and Christopher Uggen, "Dealers, Thieves, and the Common Determinants of Drug and Nondrug Illegal Earnings," *Criminology* 59 (2012): 1057–1087; Uggen and Thompson, "The Socioeconomic Determinants of Ill-Gotten Gains: Within-Person Changes in Drug Use and Illegal Earnings," *American Journal of Sociology* 109 (2003): 146–185.

19. FBI, *Crime in the United States, 2013*, www.fbi.gov/about-us/cjis/ucr/crime-in-the-u.s/2013/crime-in-the-u.s.-2013/property-crime/burglary-topic-page.

20. Pierre Tremblay and Carlo Morselli, "Patterns in Criminal Achievement: Wilson and Abrahamse Revisited," *Criminology* 38 (2000): 633–660.

21. Steven Levitt and Sudhir Alladi Venkatesh, "An Economic Analysis of a Drug-Selling Gang's Finances," NBER Working Papers 6592 (Cambridge, MA: National Bureau of Economic Research, 1998).

22. Bill McCarthy, "New Economics of Sociological Criminology," *Annual Review of Sociology* (2002): 417–442.

23. Ronald Akers, "Rational Choice, Deterrence and Social Learning Theory in Criminology: The Path Not Taken," *Journal of Criminal Law and Criminology* 81 (1990): 653–676.

24. Bruce Jacobs and Jody Miller, "Crack Dealing, Gender, and Arrest Avoidance," *Social Problems* 45 (1998): 550–566.

25. Neal Shover, *Aging Criminals* (Beverly Hills, CA: Sage, 1985).

26. Bruce Jacobs, "Crack Dealers' Apprehension Avoidance Techniques: A Case of Restrictive Deterrence," *Justice Quarterly* 13 (1996): 359–381.

27. Ibid., p. 367.

28. Ibid., p. 372.

29. Aiden Sidebottom, Matt Ashby, and Shane D. Johnson, "Copper Cable Theft: Revisiting the Price–Theft Hypothesis," *Journal of Research in Crime and Delinquency* 51 (2014): 684–700.

30. Ronald Clarke and Patricia Harris, "Auto Theft and Its Prevention," in *Crime and Justice: An Annual Edition*, ed. Michael Tonry and Norval Morris (Chicago: University of Chicago Press, 1992), pp. 1–54, at pp. 20–21.

31. Paul Cromwell, James Olson, and D'Aunn Wester Avary, *Breaking and Entering: An Ethnographic Analysis of Burglary* (Newbury Park, CA: Sage, 1989), p. 24.

32. Ibid., pp. 30–32.

33. George Rengert and John Wasilchick, *Space, Time, and Crime: Ethnographic Insights into Residential Burglary* (Washington, DC: National Institute of Justice, 1989); see also Rengert and Wasilchick, *Suburban Burglar: A Tale of 2 Suburbs* (Springfield, IL: Charles C Thomas, 2000).

34. Matthew Robinson, "Lifestyles, Routine Activities, and Residential Burglary Victimization," *Journal of Criminal Justice* 22 (1999): 27–52.

35. Patrick Donnelly and Charles Kimble, "Community Organizing, Environmental Change, and Neighborhood Crime," *Crime and Delinquency* 43 (1997): 493–511.

36. Benoit Leclerc, Richard Wortley, and Stephen Smallbone, "Getting into the Script of Adult Child Sex Offenders and Mapping Out Situational Prevention Measures," *Journal of Research in Crime and Delinquency* 48 (2011): 209–237.

37. Ronald Clarke and Marcus Felson, "Introduction: Criminology, Routine Activity and Rational Choice," in *Routine Activity and Rational Choice* (New Brunswick, NJ: Transaction, 1993), pp. 1–14.

38. Associated Press, "Thrift Hearings Resume Today in Senate," *Boston Globe*, January 2, 1991, p. 10.

39. James A. Densley, "It's Gang Life, but Not As We Know It: The Evolution of Gang Business," *Crime and Delinquency*, first published April 4, 2012.

40. Gordon Knowles, "Deception, Detection, and Evasion: A Trade Craft Analysis of Honolulu, Hawaii's Street

Crack Cocaine Traffickers," *Journal of Criminal Justice* 27 (1999): 443–455.

**41.** John Petraitis, Brian Flay, and Todd Miller, "Reviewing Theories of Adolescent Substance Use: Organizing Pieces in the Puzzle," *Psychological Bulletin* 117 (1995): 67–86.

**42.** George Rengert, *The Geography of Illegal Drugs* (Boulder, CO: Westview Press, 1996).

**43.** Levitt and Venkatesh, "An Economic Analysis of a Drug-Selling Gang's Finances."

**44.** Richard Felson and Steven Messner, "To Kill or Not to Kill? Lethal Outcomes in Injurious Attacks," *Criminology* 34 (1996): 519–545, at 541.

**45.** Richard Wright and Scott Decker, *Armed Robbers in Action: Stickups and Street Culture* (Boston: Northeastern University Press, 1997).

**46.** William Smith, Sharon Glave Frazee, and Elizabeth Davison, "Furthering the Integration of Routine Activity and Social Disorganization Theories: Small Units of Analysis and the Study of Street Robbery as a Diffusion Process," *Criminology* 38 (2000): 489–521.

**47.** Paul Bellair, "Informal Surveillance and Street Crime: A Complex Relationship," *Criminology* 38 (2000): 137–167.

**48.** Gary Kleck and Don Kates, *Armed: New Perspectives on Guns* (Amherst, NY: Prometheus Books, 2001).

**49.** Bruce A. Jacobs and Richard Wright, "Moralistic Street Robbery," *Crime and Delinquency* 54 (2008): 511–531.

**50.** Ryan King and Gretchen Sutto, "High Times for Hate Crimes: Explaining the Temporal Clustering of Hate-Motivated Offending," *Criminology* 51 (2013): 871–894.

**51.** Thomas Holt, Kristie Blevins, and Joseph Kuhns, "Examining Diffusion and Arrest Avoidance Practices Among Johns," *Crime and Delinquency* 60 (2014): 261–283.

**52.** Robert Agnew, "Social Concern and Crime: Moving Beyond the Assumption of Simple Self-Interest," *Criminology* 52 (2014): 1–32.

**53.** Patricia Brantingham, Paul Brantingham, and Wendy Taylor, "Situational Crime Prevention as a Key Component in Embedded Crime Prevention," *Canadian Journal of Criminology and Criminal Justice* 47 (2005): 271–292.

**54.** Ronald Clarke, *Situational Crime Prevention: Successful Case Studies* (Albany, NY: Harrow and Heston, 1992).

**55.** Brian Smith and Ronald Clarke, "Shoplifting of Everyday Products that Serve Illicit Drug Uses," *Journal of Research in Crime and Delinquency*, first published online September 11, 2014.

**56.** Derek Cornish and Ronald Clarke, "Opportunities, Precipitators and Criminal Decisions: A Reply to Wortley's Critique of Situational Crime Prevention," *Crime Prevention Studies* 16 (2003): 41–96; Ronald Clarke and Ross Homel, "A Revised Classification of Situational Prevention Techniques," in *Crime Prevention at a Crossroads*, ed. Steven P. Lab (Cincinnati: Anderson Publishing, 1997).

**57.** Nancy LaVigne, "Gasoline Drive-Offs: Designing a Less Convenient Environment," in *Crime Prevention Studies*, vol. 2, ed. Ronald Clarke (Monsey, NY: Criminal Justice Press, 1994), pp. 91–114.

**58.** Lynn A. Addington and Callie Marie Rennison, "Keeping the Barbarians Outside the Gate? Comparing Burglary Victimization in Gated and Non-Gated Communities," *Justice Quarterly* 32 (2015): 168–192.

**59.** Marcus Felson, "Those Who Discourage Crime," in *Crime and Place, Crime Prevention Studies*, vol. 4, ed. John Eck and David Weisburd (New York: Criminal Justice Press, 1995), pp. 53–66.

**60.** John Eck, "Drug Markets and Drug Places," in *Problem-Oriented Policing: Crime-Specific Problems, Critical Issues and Making POP Work*, vol. II, ed. Corina Solé Brito and Tracy Allan (Washington, DC: Police Executive Research Forum, 1999), p. 29.

**61.** Marie Tillyer, Holly Miller, and Rob Tillyer, "The Environmental and Situational Correlates of Victim Injury in Nonfatal Violent Incidents," *Criminal Justice and Behavior* 38 (2010): 433–452.

**62.** Keith Proctor, "The Great Surveillance Boom," CNN News, April 26, 2013, fortune.com/2013/04/26/the-great-surveillance-boom/; Brandon C. Welsh and David P. Farrington, *Making Public Places Safer: Surveillance and Crime Prevention* (New York: Oxford University Press, 2008).

**63.** "Pervert's Tough Sign-tence," *The Sun*, March 26, 2008, www.thesun.co.uk/sol/homepage/news/960199/Perverts-tough-sign-tence-Ordered-to-put-signs-on-car-and-home.html.

**64.** Ronald Clarke, "Deterring Obscene Phone Callers: The New Jersey Experience," in *Situational Crime Prevention*, ed. Ronald Clarke (Albany, NY: Harrow and Heston, 1992), pp. 124–132.

**65.** Philip Cook and Jens Ludwig, "The Economist's Guide to Crime Busting," *NIJ Journal* 270 (2012), nij.gov/nij/journals/270/economists-guide.htm.

**66.** Ronald Clarke and David Weisburd, "Diffusion of Crime Control Benefits: Observations of the Reverse of Displacement," in *Crime Prevention Studies*, vol. 2, ed. Ronald Clarke (New York: Criminal Justice Press, 1994).

**67.** David Weisburd and Lorraine Green, "Policing Drug Hot Spots: The Jersey City Drug Market Analysis Experiment," *Justice Quarterly* 12 (1995): 711–734.

**68.** Anthony A. Braga, Andrew V. Papachristos, and David M. Hureau, "The Effects of Hot Spots Policing on Crime: An Updated Systematic Review and Meta-Analysis," *Justice Quarterly*, first published online May 16, 2012.

69. Lorraine Green, "Cleaning Up Drug Hot Spots in Oakland, California: The Displacement and Diffusion Effects," *Justice Quarterly* 12 (1995): 737–754.

70. Robert Barr and Ken Pease, "Crime Placement, Displacement, and Deflection," in *Crime and Justice, A Review of Research*, vol. 12, ed. Michael Tonry and Norval Morris (Chicago: University of Chicago Press, 1990), pp. 277–319.

71. Clarke, *Situational Crime Prevention*, p. 27.

72. Evan Sorg, Cory Haberman, Jerry Ratcliffe, and Elizabeth Groff, "Foot Patrol in Violent Crime Hot Spots: The Longitudinal Impact of Deterrence and Posttreatment Effects of Displacement," *Criminology* 51 (2013): 65–101.

73. Robert Apel, Greg Pogarsky, and Leigh Bates, "The Sanctions–Perceptions Link in a Model of School-Based Deterrence," *Journal of Quantitative Criminology* 25 (2009): 201–226.

74. Daniel Nagin and Greg Pogarsky, "Integrating Celerity, Impulsivity, and Extralegal Sanction Threats into a Model of General Deterrence: Theory and Evidence," *Criminology* 39 (2001): 865–892.

75. Jennifer Varriale Carson, "Counterterrorism and Radical Eco-Groups: A Context for Exploring the Series Hazard Model," *Journal of Quantitative Criminology*, first published online October 2013; Cheryl L. Maxson, Kristy N. Matsuda, and Karen Hennigan, "Deterrability Among Gang and Nongang Juvenile Offenders: Are Gang Members More (or Less) Deterrable than Other Juvenile Offenders?" *Crime and Delinquency* 57 (2011): 516–543.

76. Robert Bursik, Harold Grasmick, and Mitchell Chamlin, "The Effect of Longitudinal Arrest Patterns on the Development of Robbery Trends at the Neighborhood Level," *Criminology* 28 (1990): 431–450; Theodore Chiricos and Gordon Waldo, "Punishment and Crime: An Examination of Some Empirical Evidence," *Social Problems* 18 (1970): 200–217.

77. Dieter Dolling, Horst Entorf, Dieter Hermann, and Thomas Rupp, "Deterrence Effective? Results of a Meta-Analysis of Punishment," *European Journal on Criminal Policy and Research* 15 (2009): 201–224.

78. Thomas Loughran, Alex Piquero, Jeffrey Fagan, and Edward Mulvey, "Differential Deterrence: Studying Heterogeneity and Changes in Perceptual Deterrence Among Serious Youthful Offenders," *Crime and Delinquency* 58 (2012): 3–27.

79. Bruce Jacobs, "Deterrence and Deterrability," *Criminology* 48 (2010): 417–441.

80. R. Steven Daniels, Lorin Baumhover, William Formby, and Carolyn Clark-Daniels, "Police Discretion and Elder Mistreatment: A Nested Model of Observation, Reporting, and Satisfaction," *Journal of Criminal Justice* 27 (1999): 209–225.

81. Nagin and Pogarsky, "Integrating Celerity, Impulsivity, and Extralegal Sanction Threats."

82. Daniel Nagin, "Criminal Deterrence Theory at the Outset of the Twenty-First Century," in *Crime and Justice: An Annual Review of Research*, vol. 23, ed. Michael Tonry (Chicago: University of Chicago Press, 1998), pp. 51–92; for an opposing view, see Bursik, Grasmick, and Chamlin, "The Effect of Longitudinal Arrest Patterns on the Development of Robbery Trends at the Neighborhood Level."

83. Michael White, James Fyfe, Suzanne Campbell, and John Goldkamp, "The Police Role in Preventing Homicide: Considering the Impact of Problem-Oriented Policing on the Prevalence of Murder," *Journal of Research in Crime and Delinquency* 40 (2003): 194–226.

84. Braga, Papachristos, and Hureau, "The Effects of Hot Spots Policing on Crime."

85. Richard Timothy Coupe and Laurence Blake, "The Effects of Patrol Workloads and Response Strength on Arrests at Burglary Emergencies," *Journal of Criminal Justice* 33 (2005): 239–255.

86. Steven Durlauf and Daniel Nagin, "Imprisonment and Crime: Can Both Be Reduced?" *Criminology and Public Policy* 10 (2011): 13–54.

87. Antonio Tavares, Silvia Mendes, and Claudia Costa, "The Impact of Deterrence Policies on Reckless Driving: The Case of Portugal," *European Journal on Criminal Policy and Research* 14 (2008): 417–429; Greg Pogarsky, "Identifying 'Deterrable' Offenders: Implications for Research on Deterrence," *Justice Quarterly* 19 (2002): 431–453.

88. Ed Stevens and Brian Payne, "Applying Deterrence Theory in the Context of Corporate Wrongdoing: Limitations on Punitive Damages," *Journal of Criminal Justice* 27 (1999): 195–209; Jeffrey Roth, *Firearms and Violence* (Washington, DC: National Institute of Justice, 1994); Thomas Marvell and Carlisle Moody, "The Impact of Enhanced Prison Terms for Felonies Committed with Guns," *Criminology* 33 (1995): 247–281; Gary Green, "General Deterrence and Television Cable Crime: A Field Experiment in Social Crime," *Criminology* 23 (1986): 629–645.

89. Richard D. Clark, "Celerity and Specific Deterrence: A Look at the Evidence," *Canadian Journal of Criminology* 30 (1988): 109–122.

90. Ernest Van Den Haag, "The Criminal Law as a Threat System," *Journal of Criminal Law and Criminology* 73 (1982): 709–785.

91. David Lykken, "Psychopathy, Sociopathy, and Crime," *Society* 34 (1996): 30–38.

92. George Lowenstein, Daniel Nagin, and Raymond Paternoster, "The Effect of Sexual Arousal on Expectations of Sexual Forcefulness," *Journal of Research in Crime and Delinquency* 34 (1997): 443–473.

93. Lyn Exum, "The Application and Robustness of the Rational Choice Perspective in the Study of

Intoxicated and Angry Intentions to Aggress," *Criminology* 40 (2002): 933–967.

94. David Klinger, "Policing Spousal Assault," *Journal of Research in Crime and Delinquency* 32 (1995): 308–324.

95. James Williams and Daniel Rodeheaver, "Processing of Criminal Homicide Cases in a Large Southern City," *Sociology and Social Research* 75 (1991): 80–88.

96. Raymond Paternoster, "How Much Do We Really Know About Criminal Deterrence?" *Journal of Criminal Law and Criminology* 100 (2010): 765–823.

97. Greg Pogarsky and Alex R. Piquero, "Can Punishment Encourage Offending? Investigating the 'Resetting' Effect," *Journal of Research in Crime and Delinquency* 40 (2003): 92–117.

98. Pogarsky, "Identifying 'Deterrable' Offenders: Implications for Deterrence Research."

99. Nagin and Pogarsky, "Integrating Celerity, Impulsivity, and Extralegal Sanction Threats."

100. Michael Tonry, "Learning from the Limitations of Deterrence Research," *Crime and Justice: A Review of Research* 37 (2008): 279–311.

101. Owen Gallupe and Stephen Baron, "Morality, Self-Control, Deterrence, and Drug Use: Street Youths and Situational Action Theory," *Crime and Delinquency* 60 (2014): 284–305.

102. James Q. Wilson, *Thinking About Crime* (New York: Basic Books, 1975).

103. James Q. Wilson and Richard Herrnstein, *Crime and Human Nature* (New York: Simon & Schuster, 1985), p. 494.

104. Shamena Anwar and Thomas Loughran, "Testing a Bayesian Learning Theory of Deterrence Among Serious Juvenile Offenders," *Criminology* 49 (2011): 667–698.

105. Ibid.; Rudy Haapanen, Lee Britton, and Tim Croisdale, "Persistent Criminality and Career Length," *Crime and Delinquency* 53 (2007): 133–155.

106. Frank Sloan, Alyssa Platt, Lindsey Chepke, and Claire Blevins, "Deterring Domestic Violence: Do Criminal Sanctions Reduce Repeat Offenses?" *Journal of Risk and Uncertainty* 46 (2013): 51–80.

107. Daniel Nagin and G. Matthew Snodgrass, "The Effect of Incarceration on Re-Offending: Evidence from a Natural Experiment in Pennsylvania," *Journal of Quantitative Criminology* 29 (2013): 601–642.

108. Benjamin Meade, Benjamin Steiner, Matthew Makarios, and Lawrence Travis, "Estimating a Dose–Response Relationship Between Time Served in Prison and Recidivism," *Journal of Research in Crime and Delinquency* 50 (2013): 525–550.

109. David Lovell, L. Clark Johnson, and Kevin Cain, "Recidivism of Supermax Prisoners in Washington State," *Crime and Delinquency* 53 (2007): 633–656.

110. Bruce Arrigo and Jennifer Bullock, "The Psychological Effects of Solitary Confinement on Prisoners in Supermax Units: Reviewing What We Know and Recommending What Should Change," *International Journal of Offender Therapy and Comparative Criminology* 52 (2008): 622–640.

111. Jeffrey Fagan and Tracey Meares, "Deterrence and Social Control: The Paradox of Punishment in Minority Communities," *Ohio State Journal of Criminal Law* 6 (2008): 173–229.

112. Bureau of Justice Statistics, "U.S. Correctional Population Declined by Less than 1 Percent for the Second Consecutive Year," December 19, 2014, www.bjs.gov/content/pub/press/cpus13pr.cfm; see also Pew Charitable Trust, *One in 100: Behind Bars in America 2008* (Washington, DC: Pew Charitable Trusts, 2008), www.pewtrusts.org/en/research-and-analysis/reports/2008/02/28/one-in-100-behind-bars-in-america-2008.

113. William Spelman, "Specifying the Relationship Between Crime and Prisons," *Journal of Quantitative Criminology* 24 (2008): 149–178.

114. Steven D. Levitt and Stephen J. Dubner, *Freakonomics: A Rogue Economist Explores the Hidden Side of Everything* (New York: William Morrow, 2006).

115. Steven Levitt, "Why Do Increased Arrest Rates Appear to Reduce Crime: Deterrence, Incapacitation, or Measurement Error?" *Economic Inquiry* 36 (1998): 353–372; see also Thomas Marvell and Carlisle Moody, "The Impact of Prison Growth on Homicide," *Homicide Studies* 1 (1997): 205–233.

116. John Wallerstedt, *Returning to Prison, Bureau of Justice Statistics Special Report* (Washington, DC: U.S. Department of Justice, 1984).

117. Michael Ostermann and Joel Caplan, "How Much Do the Crimes Committed by Released Inmates Cost?" *Crime and Delinquency*, first published November 5, 2013.

118. James Byrne and Karin Tusinski Miofsky, "From Preentry to Reentry: An Examination of the Effectiveness of Institutional and Community-Based Sanctions," *Victims and Offenders* 4 (2009): 348–356.

119. Jose Canela-Cacho, Alfred Blumstein, and Jacqueline Cohen, "Relationship Between the Offending Frequency of Imprisoned and Free Offenders," *Criminology* 35 (1997): 133–171.

120. Cook and Ludwig, "The Economist's Guide to Crime Busting."

121. Lawrence Sherman and Richard Berk, "The Specific Deterrent Effects of Arrest for Domestic Assault," *American Sociological Review* 49 (1984): 261–272.

122. J. David Hirschel, Ira Hutchison, and Charles Dean, "The Failure of Arrest to Deter Spouse Abuse," *Journal of Research in Crime and Delinquency* 29 (1992): 7–33; Franklyn Dunford, David Huizinga, and Delbert Elliott, "The Role of Arrest in Domestic Assault: The Omaha Experiment," *Criminology* 28 (1990): 183–206.

123. Lawrence Sherman, Janell Schmidt, Dennis Rogan, Patrick Gartin, Ellen Cohn, Dean Collins, and Anthony Bacich, "From Initial Deterrence to Long-Term Escalation: Short-Custody Arrest for Domestic Violence," *Criminology* 29 (1991): 821.

124. Andrew Klein and Terri Tobin, "A Longitudinal Study of Arrested Batterers, 1995–2005: Career Criminals," *Violence Against Women* 14 (2008): 136–157.

125. Thomas Marvell and Carlisle Moody, "The Impact of Out-of-State Prison Population on State Homicide Rates: Displacement and Free-Rider Effects," *Criminology* 36 (1998): 513–538; Thomas Marvell and Carlisle Moody, "The Impact of Prison Growth on Homicide," *Homicide Studies* 1 (1997): 205–233.

126. Ilyana Kuziemko and Steven D. Levitt, "An Empirical Analysis of Imprisoning Drug Offenders," NBER Working Papers 8489 (Cambridge, MA: National Bureau of Economic Research, 2001).

127. Marc Mauer, testimony before the U.S. Congress, House Judiciary Committee, on "Three Strikes and You're Out," March 1, 1994.

128. Bradley Wilson, "Justice with Mercy: An Argument Against Capital Punishment," *International Journal of Applied Philosophy* 26 (2012): 119–135.

# 5 Trait Theory

## Learning Objectives

LO1   Discuss the development of trait theory.

LO2   Differentiate between the biochemical conditions that produce crime.

LO3   Describe the link between genetics and crime, according to trait theory.

LO4   Discuss the elements of the psychodynamic perspective.

LO5   Correlate behavior theory to crime.

LO6   Discuss the controversy surrounding the link between intelligence and crime.

## FACT OR FICTION?

▶ You are what you eat! "Eating healthy" can reduce antisocial behaviors.

▶ The acorn does not fall far from the tree; that is, the children of deviant parents are more likely than other kids to be antisocial themselves.

On December 14, 2012, a young man named Adam Lanza walked into the Sandy Hook Elementary School in Newtown, Connecticut, and, using high-powered weapons, methodically took the lives of 20 children and 6 adults. Before he went on his murderous rampage, he shot his own mother in the home they shared. Former classmates and acquaintances of Lanza (pictured here in 2005) described him as an awkward loner who was deeply uncomfortable in social situations. He was described as someone who lived in their world but was not really part of it, a youth who would go through crises where he totally withdrew from whatever he was supposed to be doing and simply stared into space. When people approached Lanza in the hallways, he would press himself against the wall or walk in a different direction. Few seemed to know him well and those who did described him as someone who may have had serious psychological problems.[1]

Tragically, Lanza's violent act is not unique but just one of a spate of recent mass shootings involving disturbed young men using high-powered weapons. Consider the following:

- On April 20, 1999, at Columbine High School in Littleton, Colorado, two heavily armed students, Eric Harris, 18, and Dylan Klebold, 17, went on a shooting spree which claimed the lives of 12 students and 1 teacher and wounded 24 others, many seriously. When police entered the school, the two boys committed suicide.
- On April 16, 2007, 23-year-old Seung-Hui Cho methodically took the lives of 32 people—27 students and 5 professors—at Virginia Tech before taking his own life. In the aftermath of ▶

the tragedy, Cho was described as a loner unable to make social connections. He had been involuntarily institutionalized in a mental health facility.

- On February 14, 2008, Steven Kazmierczak, a former student at Northern Illinois University, entered a large auditorium-style lecture hall with a shotgun and three handguns. Standing on the stage, he began shooting into the crowded classroom, killing 5 and wounding 16 others before taking his own life.[2]
- On January 8, 2011, Jared Lee Loughner opened fire in a supermarket parking lot in Tucson, Arizona, in an attempt to kill Congresswoman Gabrielle Giffords. Before the shooting stopped, 19 people were hit, 6 of them fatally, including Gabe Zimmerman, an aide to Giffords; John Roll, a federal judge; and Christina-Taylor Green, a 9-year-old girl interested in politics, who had been brought to the meeting by a neighbor.
- On July 20, 2012, James Holmes walked into the Century movie theater in Aurora, Colorado, during a midnight screening of the film *The Dark Knight Rises*, set off tear gas grenades, and shot into the audience with a 12-gauge Remington 870 Express Tactical shotgun, a Smith & Wesson M&P15 with a 100-round drum magazine, and a Glock 22 handgun. When he was done, 12 people were dead and 58 more wounded. Holmes had a history of mental illness.[3]

These senseless tragedies remind us that, at least in some instances, it is hard to conclude that crime is a matter of rational choice—rather than being rational, crime is anything but. Take Jared Lee Loughner, a deeply disturbed person who as a college student had numerous run-ins with campus security and bizarre outbursts in class. Pima Community College school officials sent a letter to his parents stating that if he wished to return to the school, he would have to "obtain a mental health clearance indicating, in the opinion of a mental health professional, his presence at the college does not present a danger to himself or others." Rather than get help, Loughner decided to drop out.

After his murderous frenzy Loughner was ruled incompetent to stand trial, having been diagnosed with schizophrenia. Court proceedings were suspended while Loughner underwent treatment at the psychiatric wing of the U.S. Medical Center for Federal Prisoners in Springfield, Missouri. Finally, in August 2012, Loughner was deemed fit to stand trial and allowed to plead guilty to 19 counts of murder and attempted murder, sparing him the death penalty. Loughner is currently serving a mandatory sentence of life imprisonment without the possibility of parole. He was also ordered to pay restitution of $19 million, $1 million for each of the victims, and forfeit any money earned from efforts to sell his story. ∎

Why would these killers, most of whom at one time had attended college, gone out on dates, and had friendships, engage in mass murder unless they were suffering from some form of mental instability or collapse? People who knew them claimed they seemed to have gone through a significant personality change just before the murders took place.

The image of a disturbed, mentally ill offender seems plausible because a whole generation of Americans has grown up on films and TV shows that portray violent criminals as mentally deranged and physically abnormal. Beginning with Alfred Hitchcock's film *Psycho*, producers have made millions depicting the ghoulish acts of people who at first seem normal and even friendly but turn out to be demented and dangerous. As children they are possessed (*Paranormal Activity*, *The Omen*), maybe because they play with demonic dolls (*Chucky*, *Annabelle*). As they grow older, they turn into deranged female (*Obsession*) and male (*Fear*) teens who have lunatic high school friends (*Scream*), who evolve into even crazier college classmates (*Scream II*) and then grow up to become deranged young adults (*Scream III*). Some of these psychos do not act alone but are part of extended demented families (*Texas Chainsaw Massacre*, *The Hills Have Eyes*). No one is safe when doctors, psychologists, and psychiatrists turn out to be demonic murderers themselves (*The Human Centipede*, *Silence of the Lambs*, *Hannibal*, *Red Dragon*). And even after they are dead, they can turn into zombies (*28 Days Later*, *Zombieland*, *World War Z*). Is it any wonder that we respond to a particularly horrible crime by saying of the perpetrator, "That guy must be crazy" or "She is a monster"?

This chapter reviews the theories that suggest that criminality is an outgrowth of abnormal human traits. These **trait theories** can be subdivided into two major categories: those that stress biological makeup and those that stress psychological functioning. Although these views often overlap (that is, brain function may have a biological basis), each branch has its unique characteristics and will be discussed separately.

**trait theory**
The view that criminality is a product of abnormal biological or psychological traits.

**sociobiology**
The view that human behavior is motivated by inborn biological urges to survive and preserve the species.

## Development of Trait Theory

**L01** Discuss the development of trait theory.

As you may recall (Chapter 1), the view that criminals have physical or mental traits that make them different and abnormal is not restricted to movie plots but began with the Italian physician and criminologist Cesare Lombroso and his contemporaries, who conducted the first "scientific" studies of crime. Today their efforts are regarded as historical curiosities, not scientific fact, mainly because the research methodology used was slipshod and invalid, not employing control groups and the scientific method. What they assumed was a biological cause could just as easily have resulted from environment or upbringing.

As criticism of biological explanations mounted, the view that human traits were responsible for antisocial behaviors fell out of favor and were abandoned in the early twentieth century.[4] Then, spurred by the publication of Edmund O. Wilson's *Sociobiology: The New Synthesis* in 1975, explanations of crime based on human traits received renewed interest from criminologists.[5]

**Sociobiology** stresses the following principles:

- Behavioral traits are shaped by both inherited traits and the environment.
- Biological and genetic conditions affect how social behaviors are learned and perceived.
- Behavior is determined by the need to ensure survival of offspring and replenishment of the gene pool.
- Biology, environment, and learning are mutually interdependent factors.

Simply put, sociobiology assumes that while social behavior is genetically transmitted, it adapts to and is shaped by existing environmental conditions. This view revived interest in finding a biological or psychological basis for crime and delinquency. It prompted some criminologists to conclude that personal traits must be what separates the deviant members of society from the nondeviant. Possessing these traits may help explain why, when faced with the same life situation, one person commits crime whereas another obeys the law. Living in a disadvantaged neighborhood will not cause a well-adjusted person to commit crime, and living in an affluent area will not stop a maladapted person from offending.[6] All people may be aware of and even fear the sanctioning power of the law, but their behavior is controlled by traits that are present at birth or developed soon afterwards. Possession of these traits do not guarantee that their bearer will commit crime, but given equivalent environmental conditions those who possess the suspect traits will be more likely to employ deviant or outlawed behaviors to attain their life goals and desires.

## Contemporary Trait Theory

For years many criminologists ignored any linkage made between traits and crime. To suggest so would mean that personal differences and not social factors such as poverty and racism were responsible for antisocial behavior. Today that view is softening, and trait theory has entered the criminological mainstream. As criminologists John Paul Wright and Francis Cullen put it:

> . . . the ideological dam preventing the development of biosocial perspectives is weakening and has sprung some leaks. The reality that humans are biological creatures who vary in biological traits is becoming too obvious to ignore.[7]

As a result of this newfound acceptance, more criminologists are conducting research on the individual traits related to crime and their findings are being published in mainstream journals.

Unlike their forebears, these contemporary trait theorists do not suggest that a single biological or psychological attribute adequately explains all criminality. Rather, each offender is considered physically and mentally unique, so there must be different explanations for each person's behavior. Some may have inherited criminal tendencies; others may be suffering from neurological problems; still others may have blood chemistry disorders that heighten their antisocial activity. What often appears as an effect of environment and socialization may actually be linked to genetically determined physical and/or mental traits. Personal traits and biological conditions, not parenting or social environment, best explain behavioral choices.[8]

### Individual Vulnerability vs. Differential Susceptibility

Trait theorists today recognize that crime-producing interactions involve both personal traits (such as defective intelligence, impulsive personality, and abnormal brain chemistry) and environmental factors (such as family life, educational attainment, socioeconomic status, and neighborhood conditions). People living in a disadvantaged community may be especially at risk to crime, but that risk is significantly increased if they also bear a genetic makeup that makes them vulnerable to the crime-producing influences in their environment.[9]

There are actually two views on how this interaction unfolds. The **individual vulnerability model** supposes a direct link between traits and crime: some people

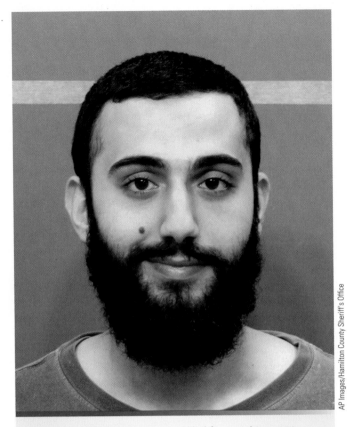

Muhammad Youssef Abdulazeez killed four servicemen at two Chattanooga military facilities before taking his own life. Was he a terrorist or someone suffering from a mental disease or defect? People who knew him said he was a quiet kid but well-liked. One told the press, "He was friendly, funny, kind. I never would have thought it would be him." She added that his whole family seemed normal: "They were your average Chattanooga family." On the other hand, Abdulazeez sent the *Times Free Press* photos of what appears to be his high school senior picture and senior quote in the school's yearbook. "My name causes national security alerts," the quote reads. "What does yours do?"

**individual vulnerability model**
Assumes there is a direct link between traits and crime; some people are vulnerable to crime from birth.

develop physical or mental conditions at birth, or soon thereafter, that affect their social functioning no matter where they live or how they are raised.[10]

In contrast, the **differential susceptibility model** suggests that there is an indirect association between traits and crime: some people possess physical or mental traits that make them vulnerable to adverse environmental influences. While a positive environment provides benefits, those people whose genetic makeup makes them predisposed to violence manifest more aggression when their surroundings become troubled. Someone like this may benefit from a supportive, therapeutic environment, but a more adverse one may trigger a violent response.

## Biological Trait Theories

One branch of contemporary trait theory focuses on the biological conditions that control human behavior (see Figure 5.1). Criminologists who work in this area typically refer to themselves as biocriminologists, biosocial criminologists, or biologically oriented criminologists; the terms are used here interchangeably.

The following sections examine some important subareas within biological criminology. First we review the biochemical factors that are believed to affect how proper behavior patterns are learned. Then we consider the relationship between brain function and crime. Next we analyze current ideas about the association between genetic factors and crime. Finally, we evaluate evolutionary views of crime causation.

### Biochemical Conditions and Crime

In 1978, the biology of crime began to receive national attention when Dan White, the confessed killer of San Francisco Mayor George Moscone and city councilman Harvey Milk, claimed that his behavior was precipitated by an addiction to sugar-laden junk foods.[11] White's successful "Twinkie defense" prompted a California jury

**differential susceptibility model**
The belief that there is an indirect association between traits and crime.

**CONNECTIONS**
Although it may seem reasonable to believe there is a biological basis for aggression and violence, it is more difficult to explain how insider trading and fraud are biologically related. The causes of white-collar crime are discussed in Chapter 12.

**L02** Differentiate between the biochemical conditions that produce crime.

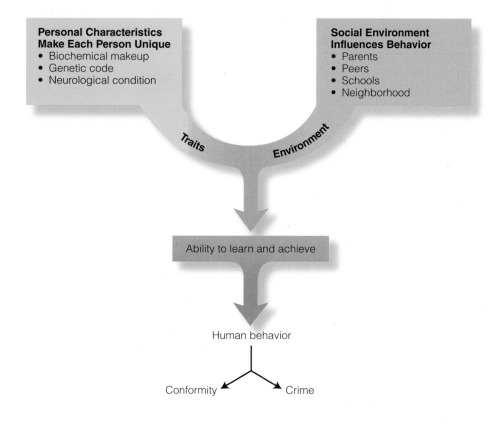

**FIGURE 5.1**
Biosocial Perspectives on Criminality
**Source:** © Cengage Learning

On March 17, 2014, Ebony Wilkerson enters the courtroom with attorney Craig Dyer for a bail hearing at the Justice Center in Daytona Beach, Florida. Wilkerson was charged with attempted murder for driving her three children into the ocean. At the time of the incident, Wilkerson's blood showed a glucose level of 44. A normal reading would be between 70 and 80; her heart was racing at 146 beats per minute. Could her action have been caused by hypoglycemia that affected her thought process?

to find him guilty of the lesser offense of diminished-capacity manslaughter rather than first-degree murder. (In 1985, White committed suicide after serving his prison sentence; 24 years later he was played by Josh Brolin in the film *Milk*, for which Sean Penn won an Oscar for his portrayal of Harvey Milk.)

Today, trait theorists believe that biochemical conditions, including both those that are genetically predetermined and those that are acquired through diet and environment, influence antisocial behavior. In some cases, the influence of chemicals and minerals is direct. Adolescent drinking may have a direct and long-term influence on antisocial behavior.[12] The association between biochemical factors may also be indirect: chemical imbalance can lead to intellectual deficits that produce school underachievement; educational failure has been linked to antisocial behaviors.[13] Similarly, blood mercury levels of children diagnosed with attention deficit hyperactivity disorder (ADHD) are significantly higher than the levels found in the general population, indicating a clear association between an environmental pollutant and a behavior disorder linked to antisocial behavior.[14]

Some of the biochemical factors that have been linked to criminality are discussed in detail here.

**DIET**  Biocriminologists maintain that a healthful diet can provide minimal levels of minerals and chemicals needed for normal brain functioning and growth, especially in the early years of life. An improper diet can cause chemical and mineral imbalance and can lead to cognitive and learning deficits and problems, and these factors in turn are associated with antisocial behaviors.[15]

Research conducted over the past decade shows that an oversupply or undersupply of certain chemicals and minerals (including caffeine, sodium, mercury, potassium, calcium, amino acids, and iron) can lead to depression, hyperactivity, cognitive problems, memory loss, or abnormal sexual activity.[16] Either eliminating harmful substances or introducing beneficial ones into the diet can reduce the threat of antisocial behaviors.[17]

People whose diets lack sufficient polyunsaturated fats, minerals, and vitamins, and/or contain too much saturated fat (or other elements, including sugar and a range of food and agricultural chemicals), seem to be at higher risk of developing psychological disturbances, such as schizophrenia, that are directly related to antisocial acts.[18]

**hypoglycemia**
A condition that occurs when glucose (sugar) in the blood falls below levels necessary for normal and efficient brain functioning.

**androgens**
Male sex hormones.

**HYPOGLYCEMIA**  When blood glucose (sugar) falls below levels necessary for normal and efficient brain functioning, a condition called **hypoglycemia** occurs. Symptoms of hypoglycemia include irritability, anxiety, depression, crying spells, headaches, and confusion. Research studies have linked hypoglycemia to outbursts of antisocial behavior and violence.[19] High levels of reactive hypoglycemia have been found in groups of habitually violent and impulsive offenders.[20]

**HORMONAL INFLUENCES**  Biosocial research has found that abnormal levels of male sex hormones (**androgens**) can produce aggressive behavior.[21] Other androgen-related male traits include sensation seeking, impulsivity, dominance, and reduced verbal skills; all of these traits are related to antisocial behavior.[22] A growing body of evidence suggests that hormonal changes are also related to mood and behavior. Adolescents experience more intense mood swings, anxiety, and restlessness than their elders, explaining in part the high violence rates found among teenage males.[23]

**Testosterone**, the most abundant androgen, which controls secondary sex characteristics such as facial hair and voice timbre, has been linked to criminality and violence.[24] Research conducted on both human and animal subjects has found that prenatal exposure to unnaturally high levels of testosterone permanently alters behavior. Girls who were unintentionally exposed to elevated amounts of testosterone during their fetal development display a marked, long-term tendency toward aggression.[25]

Conversely, boys who were prenatally exposed to steroids that decrease testosterone levels display decreased aggressiveness.[26] Gender differences in the crime rate, therefore, may be explained by the relative difference in testosterone and other androgens between the two sexes. Females may be biologically protected from deviant behavior in the same way that they enjoy immunity from some diseases that strike males.[27] Hormone levels also help explain the aging-out process: levels of testosterone decline during the life cycle, and so do violence rates.[28]

**PREMENSTRUAL SYNDROME** The suspicion has long existed that the onset of the menstrual cycle triggers excessive amounts of the female sex hormones, which stimulate antisocial, aggressive behavior. This condition is commonly referred to as **premenstrual syndrome (PMS)**.[29] The link between PMS and delinquency was first popularized more than 40 years ago by Katharina Dalton, whose studies of English women indicated that females are more likely to commit suicide and to be aggressive and otherwise antisocial just before or during menstruation.[30]

Diana Fishbein, a noted expert on biosocial theory, also concludes that there is in fact an association between menstruation and elevated levels of female aggression. Research efforts, she argues, show that (a) a significant number of incarcerated females committed their crimes during the premenstrual phase, and (b) at least a small percentage of women appear vulnerable to cyclical hormonal changes that make them more prone to anxiety and hostility.[31]

**LEAD EXPOSURE** Exposure to lead has been linked to emotional and behavioral disorders.[32] This association is especially important because so many children suffer harmful levels of lead exposure. According to the Centers for Disease Control and Prevention, even low levels of lead in the blood have been shown to affect IQ, ability to pay attention, and academic achievement. And effects of lead exposure cannot be corrected. Experts now use a reference level of 5 micrograms per deciliter (of blood) to identify children with blood lead levels that are much higher than most children's levels. That means that about 2 million kids 18 and under have dangerously high lead levels according to CDC standards.[33]

Delinquents have been found to have much higher bone lead levels than children in the general population.[34] There is also evidence linking lead exposure to mental illnesses, such as schizophrenia.[35] Locales with the highest concentrations of lead also report the highest levels of homicide.[36] Long-term worldwide trends in crime levels correlate significantly with changes in environmental levels of lead.[37]

Some experts, such as economist Rick Nevin, have gone as far as linking the decrease in the use of leaded gasoline, which began to be phased out in the mid-1970s, to a drop in violent crimes in the United States and abroad. Nevin's research shows a significant fit between the rise and fall of gas lead and the rise and fall of the violent crime rate with a time lag of 23 years. As the presence of lead in the bloodstream of school children declined, so eventually did the crime rate.[38]

**ENVIRONMENTAL CONTAMINANTS** Research has linked prenatal exposure to PCBs (polychlorinated biphenyls) to lower IQs and attention problems, both considered risk factors for serious behavioral and learning problems.[39] Similarly, exposure to

**FACT OR FICTION?**

You are what you eat! "Eating healthy" can reduce antisocial behaviors.

**FACT** Biocriminologists link antisocial behavior to diet and chemical intake. You may in fact be what you eat.

**testosterone**
The principal male hormone.

**premenstrual syndrome (PMS)**
Condition, postulated by some theorists, wherein several days before and during menstruation excessive amounts of female sex hormones stimulate antisocial, aggressive behavior.

severe air pollution has been found to cause cognitive deficits and changes in the brain structure of otherwise healthy children. These destructive changes affect intelligence, influence cognitive control, and produce other neurological deficits that have been associated with school failure; educational underachievement is a condition that has long been associated with delinquency and adult criminality.[40] In addition, PCBs, polybrominated diphenyl ethers (PBDEs), polycyclic aromatic hydrocarbons (PAHs), and inorganic gases such as chlorine and nitrogen dioxide can cause severe illness or death. These environmental contaminants can be especially harmful to the brains of babies and small children because they may affect their developing nervous systems; they can be exposed to harmful chemicals even before they are born.[41]

## Neurophysiological Conditions and Crime

**neurophysiology**
The study of brain activity.

**conduct disorder (CD)**
A pattern of repetitive behavior in which the rights of others or social norms are violated.

Some researchers focus their attention on **neurophysiology**, the study of brain activity. Using brain-scanning techniques such as magnetic resonance imaging (MRI), positron emission tomography (PET), brain electrical activity mapping (BEAM), and the superconducting quantum interference device (SQUID), they assess areas of the brain that are directly linked to antisocial behavior.[42]

Studies carried out in the United States and elsewhere have shown that both violent criminals and substance abusers have impairment in the prefrontal lobes, thalamus, medial temporal lobe, and superior parietal and left angular gyrus areas of the brain.[43] Such damage may be associated with a reduction in executive functioning (EF) a condition that refers to impairment of the cognitive processes that facilitate the planning and regulation of goal-oriented behavior (such as abstract reasoning, problem solving, and motor skills). Impairments in EF have been implicated in a range of developmental disorders, including attention deficit hyperactivity disorder (ADHD), conduct disorder (CD), autism, and Tourette syndrome. EF impairments also have been implicated in a range of neuropsychiatric and medical disorders, including schizophrenia, major depression, alcoholism, structural brain disease, diabetes mellitus, and normal aging.[44]

Neurological impairment may also lead to the development of personality traits linked to antisocial behaviors. There is now evidence that low self-control may in fact be regulated and controlled by the prefrontal cortex of the brain.[45] Under this scenario, neurological impairment reduces impulse management and self-control, a condition that often results in antisocial behaviors.

There is a suspected link between brain dysfunction and **conduct disorder (CD)**, which is considered a precursor of long-term chronic offending. Children with CD lie, steal, bully other children, get into fights frequently, and break schools' and parents' rules; many are callous and lack empathy and/or guilt.[46] Adolescent boys with antisocial substance disorder (ASD) repeatedly engage in risky antisocial and drug-using behaviors. Research has linked this behavior with misfiring in particular areas of the brain and suppressed neural activity.[47]

**BRAIN STRUCTURE** Research psychiatrist Guido Frank finds that aggressive teen behavior may be linked to the amygdala, an area of the brain that processes information regarding threats and fear, and to a lessening of activity in the frontal lobe, a brain region linked to decision making and impulse control. Frank investigated why some teenagers are more prone than others to "reactive" aggression—that is, unpremeditated aggression in response to a trigger (for instance, an accidental bump from a passerby). He found that reactively aggressive adolescents—most commonly boys—frequently misinterpret their surroundings, feel threatened, and act inappropriately aggressive. They tend to strike back when being teased, blame others when getting into a fight, and overreact to accidents. Their behavior is emotionally "hot," defensive, and impulsive; teens with this behavior are at high risk for lifelong social, career, or legal problems.

Frank's research helps explain what goes on in the brains of some teenage boys who respond with inappropriate anger and aggression to perceived threats. It is possible that such behavior is associated with brain functioning and not environment, socialization, personality, or other social and psychological functions.[48]

**ATTENTION DEFICIT HYPERACTIVITY DISORDER**  Many parents have noticed that their children do not pay attention to them—they run around and do things in their own way. Sometimes this inattention is a function of age; in other instances it is a symptom of **attention deficit hyperactivity disorder (ADHD)**, in which a child shows a developmentally inappropriate lack of attention, along with impulsivity and hyperactivity. Some of the various symptoms of ADHD include easy distraction, acting without thinking, and inability to sit still. About 3 percent of U.S. children, most often boys, are believed to suffer from this disorder, and it is the most common reason why children are referred to mental health clinics. The condition has been associated with poor school performance, retention for another year in the same grade, placement in classes for those with special needs, bullying, stubbornness, and lack of response to discipline.[49]

Although the origin of ADHD is still unknown, suspected causes include neurological damage, prenatal stress, and even reactions to food additives and chemical allergies; some research suggests a genetic link.[50] There are also links to family turmoil: mothers of children with ADHD are more likely to be divorced or separated, and they are much more likely than others to move to new locales.[51] It may be possible that emotional turmoil either produces symptoms of ADHD or, if they already exist, causes them to intensify.

Many children with ADHD also suffer from conduct disorder (CD) and continually engage in aggressive and antisocial behavior in early childhood.[52] Children diagnosed with ADHD are more likely to be suspended from school and to engage in criminal behavior as adults.[53] A series of research studies now links ADHD to the onset and sustenance of a criminal career. Children with ADHD are more likely than non-ADHD youths to use illicit drugs, alcohol, and cigarettes, be physically aggressive, and engage in sex offenses in adolescence. In addition to adolescent misbehavior, hyperactive or ADHD children are at greater risk for antisocial activity and drug use/abuse that persists into adulthood. They are more likely to be arrested, to be charged with a felony, and to have multiple arrests.[54]

**BRAIN CHEMISTRY**  Chemical compounds called **neurotransmitters** influence or activate brain functions. Those studied in relation to aggression and other antisocial behaviors include dopamine, norepinephrine, serotonin, monoamine oxidase (MAO), and gamma-aminobutyric acid (GABA).[55] Evidence exists that abnormal levels of these chemicals are associated with aggression.[56]

Research efforts have linked low levels of MAO to high levels of violence and property crime, as well as defiance of punishment, impulsivity, hyperactivity, poor academic performance, sensation seeking and risk taking, and recreational drug use.[57] Abnormal MAO levels may explain both individual and group differences in the crime rate. Females naturally have higher MAO levels than males, which may contribute to gender differences in the crime rate.[58] The effect of MAO on crime persists throughout the life span: delinquent youth with low levels of MAO have been found to have a greater likelihood of engaging in physical aggression later in adulthood than those with normal or higher levels.[59]

What is the link between brain chemistry and crime? One view is that prenatal exposure

**attention deficit hyperactivity disorder (ADHD)**
A developmentally inappropriate lack of attention, along with impulsivity and hyperactivity.

**neurotransmitters**
Chemical compounds that influence or activate brain functions.

Dr. Alan Zamitkin, "Clinical Brain Imaging." Courtesy of the Office of Scientific Information, NIHM.

This scan compares a normal brain (left) and the brain of an individual with ADHD (right). Areas of orange and white demonstrate a higher rate of metabolism, whereas areas of blue and green represent an abnormally low metabolic rate. Why is ADHD so prevalent in the United States today? Some experts believe that our immigrant forebears, risk takers who impulsively left their homelands for life in a new world, may have brought with them a genetic predisposition to ADHD.

of the brain to high levels of androgens can result in a brain structure that is less sensitive to environmental inputs and more prone to criminal behavior choices.[60] Affected individuals seek more intense and varied stimulation and are willing to tolerate more adverse consequences than individuals not so affected.[61] Because this link has been found, it is not uncommon for violence-prone people to be treated with antipsychotic drugs such as Haldol, Stelazine, Prolixin, and Risperdal. These drugs, which help control levels of neurotransmitters (such as serotonin or dopamine), are sometimes referred to as chemical restraints or chemical straitjackets.

**AROUSAL THEORY** According to **arousal theory**, for a variety of genetic and environmental reasons, people's brains function differently in response to environmental stimuli. All of us seek to maintain a preferred or optimal level of arousal: too much stimulation leaves us anxious and stressed, whereas too little makes us feel bored and weary. However, people vary in the way their brains process sensory input. Some nearly always feel comfortable with little stimulation, whereas others require a high degree of environmental input to feel comfortable. The latter group of "sensation seekers" looks for stimulating activities, which may include aggressive, violent behavior patterns.[62]

Although the factors that determine a person's level of arousal are not fully understood, suspected sources include brain chemistry (such as serotonin levels) and brain structure. Some brains have many more nerve cells, with receptor sites for neurotransmitters, than other brains have. Another view is that people with low heart rates are more likely to commit crime because they seek stimulation to increase their arousal to normal levels.[63]

**arousal theory**
The view that people seek to maintain a preferred level of arousal but vary in how they process sensory input. A need for high levels of environmental stimulation may lead to aggressive, violent behavior patterns.

**LO3** Describe the link between genetics and crime, according to trait theory.

Jeremy Jarvis, 13 (left), and his brother Denver Colorado Jarvis, 15, appear in juvenile court, October 13, 2009, in Fort Lauderdale, Florida, at the Broward County Courthouse. The boys were charged with aggravated battery for participating in setting Michael Brewer, 15, on fire. Brewer suffered severe burns over 65 percent of his body. The boys are the product of a troubled family: both parents have had alcohol-related arrests; their father, Denver Sr., was accused in 1984 of tossing a Molotov cocktail into a neighbor's yard. Denver Jarvis was sentenced to eight years in prison and 22 years of probation after pleading no contest to attempted second-degree murder, while Jeremy escaped prosecution due to his age. Could their violent and destructive behavior be a function of their genes? Or are other forces involved?

## Genetics and Crime

Another biosocial theme is that the human traits associated with criminality have a genetic basis.[64] The genes–crime association may be direct: (1) antisocial behavior is inherited, (2) the genetic makeup of parents is passed on to children, and (3) genetic abnormality is directly linked to a variety of antisocial behaviors.[65]

It is also possible that the association is indirect: genes are related to some personality or physical trait linked to antisocial behavior.[66] Genetic makeup may shape friendship patterns and orient people toward deviant peer associations, which cause them to become crime prone.[67] Adolescent attachment to parents may be controlled by their genetic makeup; attachment that is weak and attenuated has been linked to criminality.[68]

Whether it be direct or indirect, the genes–crime relationship has been explored by a number of different methods, described below:

**PARENTAL DEVIANCE** If criminal tendencies are inherited, children of criminal parents should be more likely to become law violators than the offspring of conventional parents. A number of studies have found that growing up in a family with criminal or otherwise troubled parents has a powerful influence on criminal behavior.[69] The Cambridge Youth Survey, a longitudinal cohort study conducted in England, indicates that a significant number of delinquent youths have criminal fathers.[70] David Farrington found that one type of parental deviance—schoolyard aggression, or bullying—may be both inter- and intragenerational. Bullies have children who bully others, and these second-generation bullies grow up to father children who are also bullies, in a never-ending cycle.[71]

**ADOPTION STUDIES** Several studies indicate that some relationship exists between biological parents' behavior and the behavior of their children, even when they have been adopted at birth and had no contact.[72] Studies of adopted youths have found that the biological father's criminality strongly predicted the child's criminal behavior even if the adopting parent was noncriminal.[73] When the biological father and the adoptive father were both criminal, the probability that the youth would engage in criminal behavior greatly increased.

**TWIN BEHAVIOR** If, in fact, inherited traits cause criminal behavior, we might expect that twins would be quite similar in their antisocial activities. And as predicted, research efforts confirm a significant correspondence of twin behavior in activities ranging from frequency of sexual activity to crime.[74] However, because twins are usually brought up in the same household and exposed to the same social conditions, determining whether their similar behavior is a result of similar biological, sociological, or psychological conditions is difficult. To control for environmental factors, criminologists have compared identical, **monozygotic (MZ) twins** with fraternal, **dizygotic (DZ) twins**.[75] MZ twins are genetically identical, whereas DZ twins have only half their genes in common. Studies of MZ twins reared apart, who have never met, show that their behavior is nearly identical.

Studies conducted on twin behavior have detected a significant relationship between the criminal activities of MZ twins and a much lower association between those of DZ twins; these genetic effects can be seen in children as young as 3 years old.[76] MZ twins are closer than DZ twins in such crime-relevant measures as level of aggression and verbal skills.[77]

**IS CRIME INHERITED?** Those who support a gene–crime relationship maintain that antisocial behavior is roughly 50 percent heritable; some calculate that the influence of genes on deviant behaviors may be as high as 85 percent. Genetic influences appear strongest for chronic offenders whose behavior is persistent, severe, and involves callous unemotional symptoms, such as a lack of remorse.

The theoretical association between crime and genes is by no means certain. There has been and continues to be serious debate over the heritability of human behavior. Some critics, such as Callie Burt and Ronald Simons, believe the social environment plays a more critical role in shaping behavior than genes and heredity, especially during the critical periods of childhood and adolescence. The environment, they argue, shapes biological processes and enables people to function and survive in existing social conditions; human biological makeup helps people respond to the everyday situations and events they face in their social world. As environmental conditions change, so do the brain and nervous system. Adverse, dangerous, and negative environments sculpt or change an individual's brain functioning, causing them to respond to

**monozygotic (MZ) twins** Identical twins.

**dizygotic (DZ) twins** Fraternal (nonidentical) twins.

AP Images/U.S. Marshals Service

Research using twin subjects indicates that there might be a genetic basis for crime. On January 27, 2015, Pedro Flores (left) and his twin brother, Margarito Flores, were sentenced to 14 years in prison each for running a nearly $2 billion North American drug ring. Their sentence was reduced for agreeing with prosecutors to testify against Joaquin "El Chapo" Guzman and other Mexican cartel leaders.

environmental events with aggression, violence, and coercion.[78] However, when Burt and Simons called for an end to gene-based research they were challenged by groups of criminologists who found fault with their assumptions and who believe that a great deal of human behavior is shaped by inherited rather than learned traits.[79] Needless to say, the debate over the heritability of crime remains an open issue among criminologists.

## Evolutionary Views of Crime

Some criminologists believe that the human traits that produce violence and aggression have been advanced by the long process of human evolution.[80] According to this evolutionary view, the competition for scarce resources has influenced and shaped the human species.[81] Over the course of human existence, people whose personal characteristics enabled them to accumulate more than others were the most likely to breed successfully, have more offspring, and (genetically speaking) dominate the species. People have been shaped to engage in actions that promote their well-being and ensure the survival and reproduction of their genetic line. Males who are impulsive risk takers may be able to father more children because they are reckless in their social relationships and have sexual encounters with numerous partners. If, according to evolutionary theories, such behavior patterns are inherited, impulsive behavior becomes intergenerational, passed down from parents to children. It is therefore not surprising that human history has been marked by war, violence, and aggression.

**THE EVOLUTION OF GENDER AND CRIME** Evolutionary concepts that have been linked to gender differences in violence rates are based loosely on mammalian mating patterns. To ensure survival of the gene pool (and the species), it is beneficial for a male of any species to mate with as many suitable females as possible because each can bear his offspring. Those males that maximize an aggressive mating effort strategy also possess traits such as a strong sexual drive, a reduced ability to form strong emotional bonds, a lack of conscience, and aggressive and violent tendencies. Not surprisingly, those individuals who possess the traits associated with a high-mating-effort strategy (i.e., sexual promiscuity) are also more likely to engage in antisocial conduct.[82] They are also likely to produce offspring who are also prone to criminal behaviors. Therefore, over the long history of the human species, aggressive males have had the greatest impact on the gene pool. The descendants of these aggressive males now account for the disproportionate amount of male aggression and violence.[83] In contrast, because of the long period of gestation, females require a secure home and a single, stable, nurturing partner to ensure their survival.

Crime rate differences between the genders, then, may be less a matter of socialization than of inherent differences in mating patterns that have developed over time.[84] The various biosocial views of crime are set out in Concept Summary 5.1.

# Psychological Trait View

The second branch of trait theory focuses on the psychological aspects of crime, including the associations among intelligence, personality, learning, and criminal behavior. This view has a long history, and psychologists, psychiatrists, and other mental health professionals have long played an active role in formulating criminological theory.

Among nineteenth-century pioneers in this area were Charles Goring (1870–1919) and Gabriel Tarde (1843–1904). Goring studied 3,000 English convicts and found little difference in the physical characteristics of criminals and noncriminals. However, he uncovered a significant relationship between crime and a condition he referred to as "defective intelligence," which involved such traits as feeblemindedness, epilepsy, insanity, and defective social instinct.[85] Tarde was the forerunner of modern learning theorists, who hold that people learn from one another through imitation.[86]

**CHECKPOINTS**

▶ Brain chemistry and hormonal differences are related to aggression and violence.

▶ The male hormone testosterone is linked to criminality.

▶ Neurological impairments have been linked to crime.

▶ Genetic theory holds that violence-producing traits are passed from generation to generation.

▶ According to evolutionary theory, instinctual drives control behavior. The urge to procreate influences male violence.

## Concept Summary 5.1    Biosocial Theories of Crime

| | |
|---|---|
| **Biochemical** | • The major premise of the theory is that crime, especially violence, is a function of diet, vitamin intake, hormonal imbalance, or food allergies.<br>• The strengths of the theory are that it explains irrational violence and shows how the environment interacts with personal traits to influence behavior.<br>• The research focuses of the theory are diet, hormones, enzymes, environmental contaminants, and lead intake. |
| **Neurological** | • The major premise of the theory is that criminals and delinquents often suffer brain impairment. Attention deficit hyperactivity disorder and minimal brain dysfunction are related to antisocial behavior.<br>• The strengths of the theory are that it explains irrational violence and shows how the environment interacts with personal traits to influence behavior.<br>• The research focuses of the theory are CD, ADHD, learning disabilities, brain injuries, and brain chemistry. |
| **Genetic** | • The major premise of the theory is that criminal traits and predispositions are inherited. The criminality of parents can predict the delinquency of children.<br>• The strengths of the theory include the fact that it explains why only a small percentage of youths in high-crime areas become chronic offenders.<br>• The research focuses of the theory are twin behavior, sibling behavior, and parent–child similarities. |
| **Evolutionary** | • The major premise of the theory is that as the human race evolved, traits and characteristics became ingrained. Some of these traits make people aggressive and predisposed to commit crime.<br>• The strengths of the theory include its explanation of high violence rates and aggregate gender differences in the crime rate.<br>• The research focuses of the theory are gender differences and understanding human aggression. |

In their quest to understand and treat all varieties of abnormal mental conditions, psychologists have encountered clients whose behavior falls within the categories that society has labeled criminal, deviant, violent, and antisocial. A number of different psychological views have various implications for the causation of criminal behavior. The most important of these theoretical perspectives and their association with criminal conduct are discussed in the following sections.

## The Psychodynamic Perspective

**Psychodynamic** (or **psychoanalytic**) **psychology** was originated by Viennese psychiatrist Sigmund Freud (1856–1939) and has remained a prominent segment of psychological theory ever since.[87] Freud believed that we all carry with us the residue of the most significant emotional attachments of our childhood, which then guides our future interpersonal relationships.

According to psychodynamic theory, the human personality has a three-part structure. The **id** is the primitive part of people's mental makeup, is present at birth,

**psychodynamic (psychoanalytic) psychology**
Theory, originated by Freud, that the human personality is controlled by unconscious mental processes that develop early in childhood and involve the interaction of id, ego, and superego.

**id**
The primitive part of people's mental makeup, present at birth, that represents unconscious biological drives for food, sex, and other life-sustaining necessities. The id seeks instant gratification without concern for the rights of others.

**L04** Discuss the elements of the psychodynamic perspective.

**ego**
The part of the personality developed in early childhood that helps control the id and keep people's actions within the boundaries of social convention.

**superego**
The part of the personality representing the conscience, formed in early life by internalization of the standards of parents and other models of behavior.

**attachment theory**
Bowlby's theory that being able to form an emotional bond to another person is an important aspect of mental health throughout the life span.

**behavior theory**
The view that all human behavior is learned through a process of social reinforcement (rewards and punishment).

**social learning theory**
The view that human behavior is modeled through observation of human social interactions, either directly from observing those who are close and from intimate contact, or indirectly through the media. Interactions that are rewarded are copied, while those that are punished are avoided.

**CONNECTIONS**

Chapter 1 discussed how some of the early founders of psychiatry tried to understand the criminal mind. Early theories suggested that mental illness and insanity were inherited and that deviants were inherently mentally damaged by their inferior genetic makeup.

**L05** Correlate behavior theory to crime.

and represents unconscious biological drives for food, sex, and other life-sustaining necessities. The id seeks instant gratification without concern for the rights of others. The ego develops early in life, when a child begins to learn that his or her wishes cannot be instantly gratified. The **ego** is the part of the personality that compensates for the demands of the id by helping the individual keep his or her actions within the boundaries of social convention. The **superego** develops as a result of incorporating within the personality the moral standards and values of parents, community, and significant others. It is the moral aspect of people's personalities; it judges their own behavior.

The psychodynamic model of the criminal offender depicts an aggressive, frustrated person dominated by events that occurred early in childhood. Because they had unhappy experiences in childhood or had families that could not provide proper love and care, criminals suffer from weak or damaged egos that make them unable to cope with conventional society. Weak egos are associated with immaturity, poor social skills, and excessive dependence on others. People with weak egos may be easily led into crime by antisocial peers and drug abuse. Some have underdeveloped superegos and consequently lack internalized representations of those behaviors that are punished in conventional society. They commit crimes because they have difficulty understanding the consequences of their actions.[88]

In sum, the psychodynamic tradition links crime to a manifestation of feelings of oppression and the inability to develop the proper psychological defenses and rationales to keep these feelings under control. Criminality enables troubled people to survive by producing positive psychic results: it helps them to feel free and independent, and it offers them the possibility of excitement and the chance to use their skills and imagination.

**ATTACHMENT THEORY** According to psychologist John Bowlby's **attachment theory**, the ability to form an emotional bond to another person has important psychological implications that follow people across the life span.[89] Attachments are formed soon after birth, when infants bond with their mothers. Babies will become frantic, crying and clinging, to prevent separation or to reestablish contact with a missing parent. Attachment figures, especially the mother, must provide support and care, and without attachment an infant would be helpless and could not survive.

Failure to develop proper attachment may cause people to fall prey to a number of psychological disorders, some of which resemble attention deficit hyperactivity disorder (ADHD). Such individuals may be impulsive and have difficulty concentrating—and consequently experience difficulty in school. As adults, they often have difficulty initiating and sustaining relationships with others and find it difficult to sustain romantic relationships. Criminologists have linked people who have detachment problems with a variety of antisocial behaviors, including sexual assault and child abuse.[90] It has been suggested that boys disproportionately experience disrupted attachment and that these disruptions are causally related to disproportionate rates of male offending.[91]

## The Behavioral Perspective: Social Learning Theory

**Behavior theory** maintains that human actions are developed through learning experiences. The major premise of behavior theory is that people alter their behavior in accordance with the response it elicits from others. In other words, behavior is supported by rewards and extinguished by negative reactions, or punishments. The behaviorist views crimes—especially violent acts—as learned responses to life situations, which do not necessarily represent abnormality or moral immaturity.

The branch of behavior theory most relevant to criminology is **social learning theory**.[92] Social learning theorists argue that people are not born with the ability to act violently; rather, they learn to be aggressive through their life experiences. These experiences include personally observing others acting aggressively to achieve some goal or watching people being rewarded for violent acts on television or in movies (see the Policies and Issues in Criminology feature entitled "Violent Media/Violent

Behavior?"). People learn to act aggressively when, as children, they model their behavior after the violent acts of adults. Later in life, these violent behavior patterns persist in social relationships. The boy who sees his father repeatedly strike his mother with impunity is likely to become a battering parent and husband.

Although social learning theorists agree that mental or physical traits may predispose a person toward violence, they believe a person's violent tendencies are activated by factors in the environment. The specific form of aggressive behavior, the frequency with which it is expressed, the situations in which it is displayed, and the specific targets selected for attack are largely determined by social learning. However, people are also self-aware and engage in purposeful learning. Their interpretations of behavior outcomes and situations influence the way they learn from experiences. One adolescent who spends a weekend in jail for drunk driving may find it the most awful experience of her life—an ordeal that convinces her never to drink and drive again. Another person, however, may find it an exciting experience about which he can brag to his friends.

**SOCIAL LEARNING AND VIOLENCE** Social learning theorists view violence as something learned through a process called **behavior modeling**. In modern society, aggressive acts are usually modeled after three principal sources:

- *Family interactions.* Studies of family life show that aggressive children have parents who use aggressive tactics when dealing with others. The children of wife batterers are more likely to use aggressive tactics themselves than children in the general population, especially if the victims (their mothers) suffer psychological distress from the abuse.[93]
- *Environmental experiences.* People who reside in areas where violence occurs daily are more likely to act violently than those who dwell in low-crime areas whose norms stress conventional behavior.
- *Mass media.* Films, video games, and television shows commonly depict violence graphically. Violence is often portrayed as acceptable, especially for heroes who never have to face legal consequences for their actions.[94] As the Policies and Issues in Criminology feature suggests, viewing violence is believed to influence behavior in a number of ways.

Social learning theorists have tried to determine what triggers violent acts. One position is that a direct, pain-producing, physical assault will usually set off a violent response. Yet the relationship between painful attacks and aggressive responses has been found to be inconsistent. Whether people counterattack depends, in part, on their fighting skill and their perception of the strength of their attackers. Verbal taunts and insults have also been linked to aggressive responses. People who are predisposed to aggression by their learning experiences are likely to view insults from others as a challenge to their social status and to react violently.

In summary, social learning theorists suggest that the following factors may contribute to violent or aggressive behavior:

- *An event that heightens arousal.* For example, a person may frustrate or provoke another through physical assault or verbal abuse.
- *Aggressive skills.* Learned aggressive responses picked up from observing others, either personally or through the media.
- *Expected outcomes.* The belief that aggression will somehow be rewarded. Rewards can come in the form of reducing tension or anger, gaining some financial reward, building self-esteem, or receiving praise from others.
- *Consistency of behavior with values.* The belief, gained from observing others, that aggression is justified and appropriate, given the circumstances of the current situation.

## Cognitive Theory

One area of psychology that has received increasing recognition in recent years is **cognitive theory**. Psychologists with a cognitive perspective focus on mental

**behavior modeling**
The process of learning behavior (notably, aggression) by observing others. Aggressive models may be parents, criminals in the neighborhood, or characters on television or in movies.

**cognitive theory**
Psychological perspective that focuses on the mental processes by which people perceive and represent the world around them and solve problems.

# Policies and Issues in Criminology

## VIOLENT MEDIA/VIOLENT BEHAVIOR?

Does the media influence behavior? Does broadcast violence cause aggressive behavior in viewers? This has become a hot topic because of the persistent theme of violence in video games, television, and films. Critics have called for drastic measures, ranging from banning TV violence to limiting access to video games.

If there is in fact a media–violence link, the problem is indeed alarming. Systematic viewing of TV begins at 2.5 years of age and continues at a high level during the preschool and early school years. Children 6 and under spend an average of two hours a day using screen media (TV and computer games)—about the same amount of time they spend playing outside and significantly more time than they spend reading or being read to (about 39 minutes per day). Marketing research indicates that adolescents ages 11 to 14 view violent horror movies at a higher rate than any other age group. Children this age use older peers and siblings and apathetic parents to gain access to R-rated films. In all, the average child views 8,000 TV murders before finishing elementary school.

Not all experts believe that media violence is a direct *cause* of violent behavior (if it were, there would be millions of daily incidents in which viewers imitated the aggression they watched on games, on TV, or in movies), but many do agree that media violence *contributes* to aggression. Developmental psychologists have concluded that viewing media violence is related to both short- and long-term increases in aggressive attitudes, values, and behaviors; the effects of media violence are both real and strong.

One source of influence is violent video games. In 2015, a research team sponsored by the American Psychological Association investigated the effects of violent video games on the onset of aggressive behavior. Team members conducted a review of the research literature published between 2005 and 2013 that involved analysis of more than 170 research reports. They found clear evidence that playing violent video games increases aggressive behavior, aggressive cognitions, and aggressive affect, and decreases prosocial behavior, empathy, and sensitivity to aggression. No single risk factor consistently leads a person to act aggressively or violently, the report states. It is the accumulation of risk factors that tends to lead to aggressive or violent behavior. The research reviewed here demonstrates that playing violent video games is one such risk factor.

There is also evidence that kids who watch violent media are more likely to persist in aggressive behavior as adults. Kids who watch more than an hour of violent media each day show an increase in assaults, fights, robberies, and other acts of aggression later in life and into adulthood. One reason may be that violent media viewing in childhood creates changes in personality and cognition that produce long-term behavioral changes.

There are several explanations for the effects of games, television, and film violence on behavior:

- Media violence can provide aggressive "scripts" that children store in memory. Repeated exposure to these scripts can increase their retention and lead to changes in attitudes.
- Children learn from what they observe. In the same way that they learn cognitive and social skills from their parents and friends, children learn to be violent from violent media.
- Media violence increases the arousal levels of viewers and makes them more prone to act aggressively. Studies measuring the galvanic skin response of subjects—a physical indication of arousal based on the amount of electricity conducted across the palm of the hand—show that viewing violent media led to increased arousal levels in young children.
- Watching media violence promotes such negative attitudes as suspiciousness and the expectation that the viewer will become involved in violence. Those who watch violent media frequently come to view aggression and violence as common and socially acceptable behavior.
- Media violence enables aggressive youths to justify their behavior. It is possible that, instead of causing violence, media violence helps violent youths

processes—how people perceive and mentally represent the world around them and solve problems. The pioneers of this school were Wilhelm Wundt (1832–1920), Edward Titchener (1867–1927), and William James (1842–1920). Today the cognitive area includes several subdisciplines. The moral development branch is concerned with how people morally represent and reason about the world. Humanistic psychology stresses

rationalize their behavior as a socially acceptable and common activity.

- Media violence may disinhibit aggressive behavior, which is normally controlled by other learning processes. Disinhibition takes place when adults are viewed as being rewarded for violence and when violence is seen as socially acceptable. This contradicts previous learning experiences in which violent behavior was viewed as wrong.

### Debating the Link Between Media Violence and Violent Behavior

Even though this research is quite persuasive, not all criminologists are convinced that watching violent incidents on TV and in the movies or playing violent video games predisposes young people to violent behavior. Even the APA report linking video games to aggressive attitudes did not find sufficient evidence to extend the link to actual criminal violence or delinquency.

There is little evidence that areas that experience the highest levels of violent media viewing also have rates of violent crime that are above the norm. Millions of children watch violence every day but do not become violent criminals. If violent media did, indeed, cause interpersonal violence, then there should be few ecological and regional patterns in the crime rate, but in fact there are many. To put it another way, how can regional differences in the violence rate be explained, considering the fact that people all across the nation watch the same TV shows and films? Nor can the link between media violence and violent behavior explain recent crime trends. Despite a rampant increase in violent TV shows, films, and video games, the violence rate among teens has been in significant decline.

One possibility is that media violence may affect one subset of the population but have relatively little effect on other groups. Sociologist George Comstock has identified the attributes that make some people especially prone to the effects of media violence:

- Predisposition to aggressive or antisocial behavior
- Rigid or indifferent parenting
- Unsatisfactory social relationships
- Low psychological well-being

- Having been diagnosed as suffering from DBD—disruptive behavior disorder

Thus, if the impact of media on behavior is not in fact universal, it may have the greatest effect on those who are the most socially and psychologically vulnerable.

## Critical Thinking

1. Should the government control the content of TV shows and limit the amount of weekly violence? How could the national and world news be shown if violence were omitted? What about boxing matches and hockey games?

2. How can we explain the fact that millions of kids watch violent TV shows and remain nonviolent? If there is a link between violence in the media and violent behavior, how can we explain the fact that violence rates were higher before media was invented?

**Sources:** Mark Appelbaum, Sandra Calvert, Kenneth Dodge, Sandra Graham, Gordon N. Hall, Sherry Hamby, and Larry Hedges, "The American Psychological Association Task Force on Violent Media: Technical Report on the Review of Violent Video Game Literature," www.apa.org/news/press/releases/2015/08/technical-violent-games.pdf; Sukkyung You, Euikyung Kim, and Unkyung No, "Impact of Violent Video Games on the Social Behaviors of Adolescents: The Mediating Role of Emotional Competence," *School Psychology International* 36 (2015): 94–111; Morgan Tear and Mark Nielsen, "Video Games and Prosocial Behavior: A Study of the Effects of Non-violent, Violent and Ultra-violent Gameplay," *Computers in Human Behavior* 41 (2014): 8; Seth Gitter, Patrick Ewell, Rosanna Guadagno, Tyler Stillman, and Roy Baumeister, "Virtually Justifiable Homicide: The Effects of Prosocial Contexts on the Link Between Violent Video Games, Aggression, and Prosocial and Hostile Cognition," *Aggressive Behavior* 39 (2013): 346; Ingrid Möller, Barbara Krahé, Robert Busching, and Christina Krause, "Efficacy of an Intervention to Reduce the Use of Media Violence and Aggression: An Experimental Evaluation with Adolescents in Germany," *Journal of Youth and Adolescence* 41 (2012): 105–120; George Comstock, "A Sociological Perspective on Television Violence and Aggression," *American Behavioral Scientist* 51 (2008): 1184–1211; John Murray, "Media Violence: The Effects Are Both Real and Strong," *American Behavioral Scientist* 51 (2008): 1212–1230; Victoria Rideout, Elizabeth Vandewater, and Ellen Wartella, *Zero to Six: Electronic Media in the Lives of Infants, Toddlers and Preschoolers* (Menlo Park, CA: Kaiser Foundation, 2003); Craig Anderson and Brad J. Bushman, "The Effects of Media Violence on Society," *Science* 295 (2002): 2377–2379; Brad Bushman and Craig Anderson, "Media Violence and the American Public," *American Psychologist* 56 (2001): 477–489.

self-awareness and getting in touch with feelings. **Information-processing theory** focuses on how people process, store, encode, retrieve, and manipulate information to make decisions and solve problems.

Cognitive theorists explain antisocial behavior in terms of mental perception and how people use information to understand their environment. When people

**information-processing theory**
Theory that focuses on how people process, store, encode, retrieve, and manipulate information to make decisions and solve problems.

make decisions, they engage in a sequence of cognitive thought processes. First, they encode information so that it can be interpreted; next, they search for a proper response and decide on the most appropriate action; and finally, they act on their decision.[95]

According to this cognitive approach, people who use information properly, who are better conditioned to make reasoned judgments, and who can make quick and reasoned decisions when facing emotion-laden events are best able to avoid antisocial behavior choices. In contrast, crime-prone people may have cognitive deficits and use information incorrectly when they make decisions. They view crime as an appropriate means to satisfy their immediate personal needs, which take precedence over more distant social needs such as obedience to the law.[96] They are not deterred by the threat of legal punishments because when they try to calculate the costs and consequences of an action—that is, when they are deciding whether to commit a crime—they make mistakes because they are imperfect processors of information. As a result of their faulty calculations, they pursue behaviors that they perceive as beneficial and satisfying but that turn out to be harmful and detrimental.[97]

Law violators may be sensation seekers who are constantly looking for novel experiences, whereas others lack deliberation and rarely think through problems.[98] Others maintain inappropriate attitudes and beliefs; they are thrill-seeking, manipulative, callous, deceptive, and hold rule-breaking attitudes. Some may give up easily, whereas others act without thinking when they get upset.[99]

People with inadequate cognitive processing perceive the world as stacked against them; they believe they have little control over the negative events in their life. They find it difficult to understand or sympathize with other people's feelings and emotions, which leads them to blame their victims for their problems. Thus, the sexual offender believes his target either led him on or secretly wanted the forcible sex to occur: "She was asking for it."

**MENTAL SCRIPTS**  One reason for this faulty reasoning is that people may be relying on mental scripts learned in childhood that tell them how to interpret events, what to expect, how they should react, and what should be the outcome of the interaction.[100] Some may have learned improper scripts because as children they had early, prolonged exposure to violence (such as child abuse), which increased their sensitivity to slights and maltreatment.[101] Violence becomes a stable behavior because the scripts that emphasize aggressive responses are repeatedly rehearsed as the child matures. These errors in cognition and information processing have been used to explain the behavior of pedophiles. They may perceive children as being able to and wanting to engage in sexual activity with adults and also as not harmed by such sexual contact.[102]

The various psychological theories of crime are set out in Concept Summary 5.2.

# Personality and Crime

**personality**
The reasonably stable patterns of behavior, including thoughts and emotions, that distinguish one person from another.

**Personality** can be defined as the reasonably stable patterns of behavior, including thoughts and emotions, that distinguish one person from another.[103] One's personality reflects a characteristic way of adapting to life's demands and problems. The way we behave is a function of how our personality enables us to interpret life events and make appropriate behavioral choices. Can the cause of crime be linked to personality?

Several research efforts have attempted to identify criminal personality traits. Surveys show that traits such as impulsivity, hostility, narcissism, hedonism, and aggression are highly correlated with criminal and antisocial behaviors.[104] Personality defects have been linked not only to aggressive antisocial behaviors such as assault and rape, but also to white-collar and business crimes.[105] Hans Eysenck's PEN model contains three elements: psychoticism (P), extraversion (E), and neuroticism (N). He associates two personality traits, extroversion and introversion, with antisocial behavior:

## Concept Summary 5.2   Psychological Theories

| Theory | Major Premise | Strengths | Research Focus |
|---|---|---|---|
| **Psychodynamic** | The development of the unconscious personality early in childhood influences behavior for the rest of a person's life. Criminals have weak egos and damaged personalities. | Explains the onset of crime and why crime and drug abuse cut across class lines. | Mental illness and crime. |
| **Behavioral** | People commit crime when they model their behavior after others they see being rewarded for the same acts. Behavior is reinforced by rewards and extinguished by punishment. | Explains the role of significant others in the crime process. Shows how media can influence crime and violence. | Media and violence; effects of child abuse. |
| **Cognitive** | Individual reasoning processes influence behavior. Reasoning is influenced by the way people perceive their environment. | Shows why criminal behavior patterns change over time as people mature and develop their reasoning powers. May explain the aging-out process. | Perception; environmental influences. |

- Extroverts are energetic, enthusiastic, action-oriented, chatty, glib, and self-confident.
- Introverts tend to be quiet, low-key, deliberate, and detached from others.

People who fall at the far ends of either trait, either extremely extroverted or extremely introverted, are at risk for antisocial behaviors. Extroverts who are also unstable, a condition that Eysenck calls neuroticism, are anxious, tense, and emotionally volatile.[106] They may act self-destructively by abusing drugs and repeating their criminal activity over and over.[107]

## Psychopathic/Antisocial Personality

Some people lack affect, cannot empathize with others, and are shortsighted and hedonistic. These traits make them prone to problems ranging from psychopathology to drug abuse, sexual promiscuity, and violence.[108] As a group, people who share these traits are believed to have a character defect referred to as sociopathic, psychopathic, or **antisocial personality**. Although these terms are often used interchangeably, some psychologists distinguish between sociopaths and psychopaths by suggesting that the former are a product of a destructive home environment, whereas the latter are a

**antisocial personality** Combination of traits, such as hyperactivity, impulsivity, hedonism, and inability to empathize with others, that make a person prone to deviant behavior and violence; also referred to as sociopathic or psychopathic personality.

Lee Celano/Reuters/Landov

Some criminologists link the onset of violence to serious psychological disturbance, including mental illness. Not surprisingly, some notorious criminals manifest severe problems. Take for instance Robert Durst, shown here on March 17, 2015, in a police vehicle in New Orleans. Durst, scion of one of New York's largest real estate empires, was arrested in New Orleans on a first-degree murder warrant issued by Los Angeles County. Once diagnosed as having "personality decomposition and possibly even schizophrenia," Durst has been linked to multiple crimes, including killing a neighbor and cutting up his body. In the 2015 HBO documentary *The Jinx: The Life and Deaths of Robert Durst,* he was recorded muttering to himself: "What the hell did I do? Killed them all, of course."

product of a defect or aberration within themselves.[109] Today antisocial personality is the more accepted term.

Studies of the antisocial personality have been conducted worldwide.[110] There is evidence that offenders with an antisocial personality are crime prone, respond to frustrating events with strong negative emotions, feel stressed and harassed, and are adversarial in their interpersonal relationships. They maintain "negative emotionality"—a tendency to experience aversive affective states such as anger, anxiety, and irritability. They also tend to have weak personal constraints and have difficulty controlling impulsive behavior urges. Because they are both impulsive and aggressive, crime-prone people are quick to act against perceived threats.

A large number of factors are believed to contribute to the development of a criminal personality.[111] Some factors are related to improper socialization, such as having a psychopathic parent, experiencing parental rejection and lack of love during childhood, maternal cigarette smoking, and receiving inconsistent discipline.[112] Some psychologists believe the cause is related to neurological or brain dysfunction.[113] They suspect that psychopaths suffer from a low level of arousal as measured by the activity of their autonomic nervous system. It is possible, therefore, that psychopaths are thrill seekers who engage in high-risk antisocial activities to raise their general neurological arousal level. Psychopaths may have brain-related physical anomalies that cause them to process emotional input differently from nonpsychopaths.

Considering these personality traits, it is not surprising that research studies show that people evaluated as psychopaths are significantly more prone to criminal and violent behavior than the members of nonpsychopathic control groups. Psychopaths tend to continue their criminal careers long after other offenders burn out or age out of crime. They are continually in trouble with the law and therefore are likely to wind up in penal institutions. After reviewing available data, forensic psychologist James Blair and his colleagues conclude that approximately 15 to 25 percent of U.S. prison inmates meet diagnostic criteria for psychopathy. Once they are released, former inmates who suffer from psychopathy are three times as likely as other prisoners to reoffend within a year—and four times as likely to reoffend violently.[114]

The Profiles in Crime feature details the life of the Iceman, one of the most feared sociopaths of all time.

**LO6** Discuss the controversy surrounding the link between intelligence and crime.

## IQ and Criminality

**nature theory**
The view that intelligence is largely determined genetically and that low intelligence is linked to criminal behavior.

**nurture theory**
The view that intelligence is not inherited but is largely a product of environment. Low IQ scores do not cause crime but may result from the same environmental factors.

Early criminologists maintained that many delinquents and criminals have below-average intelligence and that low IQ causes their criminality. However, there was disagreement over the development of intellectual ability. Some believed that law violators had inherently substandard intelligence and thus were naturally inclined to commit crimes. These proponents of **nature theory** argued that intelligence is largely determined genetically, that ancestry determines IQ, and that low intelligence, as demonstrated by low IQ, is linked to criminal behavior. In contrast, proponents of **nurture theory** argued that environmental stimulation from parents, relatives, social contacts, schools, peer groups, and innumerable others accounts for a child's IQ level and that low IQs may result from an environment that also encourages delinquent and criminal behavior. Thus, if low IQ scores are recorded among criminals, these

# PROFILES IN CRIME

## THE ICEMAN

Richard Kuklinski was known as the Iceman. There are few people who fit the description of sociopath better than Kuklinski, who enjoyed killing and made a career out of his special talent for mayhem and death by becoming a Mafia hitman. During his career, he killed somewhere between 100 and 200 people. He earned his nickname because he sometimes froze corpses to disguise the time of death and confound authorities. Never shy or remorseful, Kuklinski submitted to many interviews and appeared in two HBO documentaries before he died in prison in 2006 at age 70.

At 6-foot-5, 300 pounds, Kuklinski was pretty scary. And for good reason. His early life was punctuated by savage abuse from his father, who beat his wife and children so badly that one son, Florian, died at his hands. Fearing for their lives, the family covered up the crime. Richard, an eighth-grade dropout, worked out his hatred of his father by killing his neighbors' pets. He soon progressed to people. His first victim, whom he killed when he was just 14, was a young boy who had bullied him at school. Kuklinski dumped his victim's body off a bridge in South Jersey after removing his teeth and chopping off his fingertips in an effort to prevent identification of the body.

Kuklinski routinely made trips to New York looking for victims to beat and kill. His violence became known to organized crime families in New Jersey and his career took off; he soon became one of the top enforcers for the Gambino family. He killed with guns, ice picks, crossbows, and chain saws, but his favorite weapon was cyanide solution administered with a nasal-spray bottle in the victim's face. Finally, through the efforts of undercover agents, the Iceman was convicted of five murders and given consecutive life sentences. But he added to his sentence by admitting to other murders while in prison. In 2003, he confessed to killing Peter Calabro, a New York City police detective, and got another 30 years tacked on to his life sentence.

When he was not working, the Iceman had a surprisingly normal home life. He married his wife, Barbara, in 1961, lived a suburban, relatively affluent lifestyle, and had three kids. His wife called them "the all-American family." And while he occasionally struck his wife, the Iceman would never harm a child, including his own. Despite this soft side, Kuklinski was a true psychopath who thought nothing of killing strangers for practice and to test out his weapons.

**Sources:** Douglas Martin, "Richard Kuklinski, 70, a Killer of Many People and Many Ways, Dies," *New York Times*, March 9, 2006, www.nytimes.com/2006/03/09/nyregion/09kuklinski.html (accessed 2015); Philip Carlo, *The Ice Man: Confessions of a Mafia Contract Killer* (New York: Macmillan, 2009).

Everett Collection

scores may reflect the criminals' cultural background, not their inherited mental ability.[115] These ideas led to the "nature versus nurture" controversy that continues to rage today.

The IQ–crime link controversy was reignited nearly 40 years ago, when the influential criminologists Travis Hirschi and Michael Hindelang suggested a link existed between intelligence and crime. Youths with low IQs, they found, do poorly in school, and school failure and academic incompetence are highly related to delinquency and later to adult criminality.[116] Their findings were supported by James Q. Wilson and Richard Herrnstein in their influential book *Crime and Human Nature*, which also concluded that low intelligence leads to poor school performance, which enhances the chances of criminality.[117] In another widely read book, *The Bell Curve*, Herrnstein with Charles Murray confirmed that adolescents with low IQs are more likely to commit crime, get caught, and be sent to prison. Conversely, at-risk kids with higher IQs seem

In 2012, Pedro Hernandez (shown here in Manhattan criminal court in New York) confessed to killing a long-missing New York City boy, Etan Patz. When the case went to trial in 2015, the prosecution had little evidence to back up his confession, since Patz's body has never been found. Hernandez's defense claimed his confessions were the false imaginings of a man who has an IQ in the lowest 2 percent of the population, and doctors testified that he had trouble telling reality from illusion. "Pedro Hernandez is the only witness against himself," defense lawyer Harvey Fishbein said during his closing argument. "The stories he told over the years . . . are the only evidence. Yet he is inconsistent and unreliable." During 18 days of deliberations, the jury emerged three times with a deadlock before the judge declared a mistrial. Since 11 members voted to convict, the prosecution plans to retry the case.

**mood disorder**
A condition in which the prevailing emotional mood is distorted or inappropriate to the circumstances.

**oppositional defiant disorder (ODD)**
A pattern of negativistic, hostile, and defiant behavior, during which a child often loses her or his temper, often argues with adults, and often actively defies or refuses to comply with adults' requests or rules.

**schizophrenia**
A severe disorder marked by hearing nonexistent voices, seeing hallucinations, and exhibiting inappropriate responses.

**bipolar disorder**
An emotional disturbance in which moods alternate between periods of wild elation and deep depression.

to be protected from becoming criminals by their superior ability to succeed in school and in social relationships.[118]

In addition to these individual-level studies, others using macro-level national state and county data have found that IQ and crime rates are associated.[119] A number of research projects have found evidence that residents living in geographic areas—nations, states, and counties—whose residents have higher than average IQs experience lower crime rates than those whose citizens have lower than average IQ scores.[120]

The IQ–criminality debate is unlikely to be settled soon. Measurement is beset by many methodological problems and charges that IQ tests are biased against members of racial minority groups. Even if it can be shown that known offenders have lower IQs than the general population, it is difficult to reconcile the effect of intelligence with some important correlates of crime: Why do crime rates vary by time of year and even weather patterns? Why does aging out occur? IQs do not rise with age or fall with temperature and season, so why should these factors affect crime rates?

## Mental Disorders and Crime

Psychologists and psychiatrists have long debated the origin of mental disorders and mental illness, linking it to a variety of sources such as genetic predisposition, traumatic family and upbringing, brain trauma, and substance abuse. Cognitive theories link learning to development of mental disorders. Children growing up in an abusive home may be "rewarded" by not getting beaten if they learn to be quiet, introverted, and withdrawn, a condition that often leads to clinical depression in adulthood.[121]

Regardless of its source, criminologists have connected antisocial behavior to mental instability and turmoil. Offenders may suffer from a wide variety of mood and/or behavior disorders rendering them histrionic, depressed, antisocial, or narcissistic.[122]

Some have been diagnosed with some form of **mood disorder** characterized by disturbance in expressed emotions. Children with **oppositional defiant disorder (ODD)**, for example, experience an ongoing pattern of uncooperative, defiant, and hostile behavior toward authority figures that seriously interferes with day-to-day functioning. Symptoms of ODD may include frequent loss of temper, constant arguing with adults, defying adults or refusing adult requests or rules, deliberately annoying others, blaming others for mistakes or misbehavior, being angry and resentful, being spiteful or vindictive, swearing or using obscene language, or having a low opinion of oneself.[123] ODD has been linked to a great many social problems, including delinquency and bullying.[124]

Adolescent boys with antisocial substance disorder (ASD) repeatedly engage in risky antisocial and drug-using behaviors. Research has linked this disorder with misfiring in particular areas of the brain and suppressed neural activity.[125] Children who are diagnosed with conduct disorder (CD) have great difficulty following rules and behaving in a socially acceptable way.[126] They are often viewed by other children, adults, and social agencies as severely antisocial. Research shows that they are frequently involved in such activities as bullying, fighting, committing sexual assaults, and behaving cruelly toward animals.

### Crime and Mental Illness

The most serious forms of mental illness are psychotic disorders, such as **schizophrenia** and **bipolar disorder** (manic-depression), which affect the mind and alter a person's ability to understand reality, think clearly, respond emotionally, communicate effectively, and behave appropriately. People with psychotic disorders may hear nonexistent voices, hallucinate, and make inappropriate behavioral responses. Others exhibit illogical and incoherent thought processes and a lack of insight into their own behavior. They may see themselves as agents of the devil, avenging angels, or the recipients of messages from animals and plants.

There is evidence that law violators, especially those involved in violent crime, suffer from a disproportionate amount of severe mental health problems. Recently, Richard Dorn and his associates, using a longitudinal sample of about 35,000 subjects, examined the association between mental disorder and violence. They found that when compared to the mentally sound, people suffering mental illness were significantly more likely to engage in violent episodes, especially if they abused drugs and alcohol.[127] The diagnosed mentally ill also appear in arrest and court statistics at a rate disproportionate to their presence in the population and if sentenced to prison are more likely to recidivate upon release.[128]

Mental illness dogs offenders across the life course. Delinquent adolescents have higher rates of clinical mental disorders than adolescents in the general population.[129]

Here, movie theater shooter James Holmes makes his first court appearance at the Arapahoe County Courthouse with his public defender Tamara Brady on July 23, 2012, in Centennial, Colorado. Holmes committed one of the worst mass shootings in American history, killing 12 people and injuring 58 when he opened fire in a movie theater showing the premiere of *The Dark Knight Rises*. In 2015, he was sentenced to life in prison without the possibility of parole. Is it possible that mass killers like Holmes are mentally sound?

As adult criminals, people who have been arrested for multiple crimes are more likely to suffer from a psychiatric disorder, particularly a psychotic disorder, than nonchronic offenders.[130] Even if apprehended, the mentally ill are much more likely to experience repeated incarcerations if they continue to suffer from major psychiatric disorders (such as depressive disorder, bipolar disorder, schizophrenia, and nonschizophrenic psychotic disorders).[131] In sum, there is a body of research showing that people who suffer from severe mental illness and distress seem to be more antisocial than members of the general population and that punishment may do little to reduce their criminal offending.[132]

Although these findings are persuasive, the association between crime and mental illness must be interpreted with some caution. It is possible that the link between mental illness and crime is spurious and that, in fact, both mental illness and criminal behavior are caused by some other, independent factor:

- People who suffer from prior social problems (for example, child abuse) may be more likely to commit criminal acts, use drugs and alcohol to cope, and to suffer mental illness.[133]
- Mentally ill people may also be more likely than the mentally sound to lack financial resources. They are thus forced to reside in deteriorated high-crime neighborhoods, a social factor that may increase criminal behavior.[134] Living in a stress-filled urban environment may produce symptoms of both mental illness and crime.[135]
- The police may be more likely to arrest the mentally ill, which fosters the impression that they are crime prone.[136]
- People with severe mental illness are more at risk to violent victimization than the mentally healthy. Violent victimization has been linked to increased crime rates.[137]
- Those suffering mental illness may self-medicate by using illegal substances, a practice linked to criminal behavior.[138]

## Evaluation of Trait Theory

Trait theories have raised some challenging questions. Critics find some of these theories racist and faulty in other ways as well. If there are biological and/or psychological explanations for street crimes such as assault, murder, or rape (the argument goes),

**CHECKPOINTS**

- According to psychodynamic theory, unconscious motivations developed early in childhood propel some people into destructive or illegal behavior.

- Behaviorists view aggression as a learned behavior.

- Learning may be either direct and experiential or observational, such as watching TV and movies.

- Cognitive theory stresses knowing and perception. Some people have a warped view of the world.

- Some evidence suggests that people with abnormal or antisocial personalities are more likely than others to commit crime.

- Although some criminologists find a link between intelligence and crime, others dispute any link between IQ level and law-violating behaviors.

- Mental illness has been linked to crime, but the association is still actively debated.

**primary prevention programs**
Programs, such as substance abuse clinics and mental health associations, that seek to treat personal problems before they manifest themselves as crime.

**secondary prevention programs**
Programs that provide treatment, such as psychological counseling, to youths and adults after they have violated the law.

and if, as official crime statistics suggest, the poor and minority-group members commit a disproportionate number of such acts, then by implication, trait theory is suggestive of the fact that members of these groups are different, flawed, or inferior.

Trait-based explanations for the geographic, social, and temporal patterns in the crime rate are also problematic. Is it possible that more people are genetically predisposed to crime in the South and the West than in New England and the Midwest? Or that people in large cities are psychologically impaired compared to people in small towns and villages? Furthermore, trait theory seems to divide people into criminals and noncriminals on the basis of their makeup, ignoring self-reports that indicate that almost everyone has engaged in some type of illegal activity.

Trait theorists counter that their views should not be confused with the early deterministic views of Lombroso and his contemporaries, which suggest that people are born either criminals or noncriminals, and nothing can alter their life course. Contemporary trait theories instead maintain that some people carry the potential to be violent or antisocial, and antisocial behavior occurs when these preexisting tendencies are triggered by environmental conditions.[139]

AP Images/Mike DeVries/Capital Times

Treatment programs based on trait theory can take many forms. Here, Wensdae Rauls and Linda Miles participate in a meditation class held in the gym at the Dane County Jail in Madison, Wisconsin. The stress management and relaxation class, which incorporates basic yoga poses, is offered to female inmates at the jail.

## Social Policy and Trait Theory

For quite some time, biological and psychological views of criminality have influenced crime control and prevention policy. The result has been **primary prevention programs** that seek to treat personal problems before they manifest themselves as crime. To this end, thousands of family therapy organizations, substance abuse clinics, and mental health associations operate throughout the United States. Teachers, employers, courts, welfare agencies, and others make referrals to these facilities.

These services are based on the premise that if a person's problems can be treated before they become overwhelming, some future crimes will be prevented. **Secondary prevention programs** provide treatment such as psychological counseling to youths and adults *after* they have violated the law. Attendance at such programs may be a requirement of a probation order, part of a diversionary sentence, or aftercare at the end of a prison sentence.

Biologically oriented therapy is also being used in the criminal justice system. Programs have altered diets, changed lighting, compensated for learning disabilities, treated allergies, and so on.[140] More controversial has been the use of mood-altering chemicals, such as lithium, pemoline, imipramine, phenytoin, and benzodiazepines, to control behavior. Another practice that has elicited concern is the use of psychosurgery (brain surgery) to control antisocial behavior. Surgical procedures have been used to alter the brain structure of convicted sex offenders in an effort to eliminate or control their sex drives. Results are still preliminary, but some critics argue that these procedures are without scientific merit.[141]

The numerous psychologically based treatments that are available range from individual counseling to behavior modification. Treatment based on how people process information takes into account that people are more likely to respond aggressively to provocation if their thoughts intensify the insult or otherwise stir feelings of anger. Cognitive therapists attempt to teach explosive people to control aggressive impulses by viewing social provocations as problems demanding a solution rather than retaliation. Programs are aimed at teaching problem-solving skills such as self-disclosure, role playing, listening, following instructions, joining in, and using self-control.[142] Therapeutic interventions designed to make people better problem solvers may involve measures that enhance:

- Coping and problem-solving skills
- Relationships with peers, parents, and other adults
- Conflict resolution and communication skills, and methods for resisting peer pressure related to drug use and violence
- Decision-making abilities and thinking about consequences
- Prosocial behaviors, including cooperation with others, self-responsibility, respecting others, and efficacy in public speaking
- Empathy[143]

# Thinking Like a Criminologist

**Girl Interrupted** Fourteen-year-old Daphne is a product of Boston's best private schools; she lives with her wealthy family on Beacon Hill. Her father is an executive at a local financial services conglomerate and makes close to $1 million per year. Daphne, however, has a hidden, darker side. She is always in trouble at school, and teachers report that she is impulsive and has poor self-control. At times she can be kind and warm, but on other occasions she is obnoxious, unpredictable, insecure, and hungry for attention. She is overly self-conscious about her body and has a drinking problem. Daphne attends AA meetings and is on the waiting list at High Cliff Village, a residential substance abuse treatment program. Her parents seem intimidated by her and confused by her complexities; her father even filed a harassment complaint against her once, saying she had slapped him.

Despite repeated promises to get her life together, Daphne likes to hang out most nights in the Public Gardens and drink with neighborhood kids. On more than one occasion she went to the park with her friend and confidant Chris, a quiet boy who had his own set of personal problems. His parents had separated, and subsequently he began to suffer severe anxiety attacks. He stayed home from school and was diagnosed with depression for which he took two drugs—Zoloft, an antidepressant, and Lorazepam, a sedative.

One night, Daphne and Chris met up with Michael, a 44-year-old man with a long history of alcohol problems. After a night of drinking, a fight broke out and Michael was stabbed, his throat cut, and his body dumped in the pond. Daphne was quickly arrested when soon after the attack she placed a 911 call to police, telling them that a friend had "jumped in the lake and didn't come out." Police searched the area and found Michael's slashed and stabbed body in the water; he had been disemboweled by Chris and Daphne in an attempt to sink the body.

At a waiver hearing, Daphne admits that she participated in the killing but cannot articulate what caused her to get involved. She had been drinking and remembers little of the events. She says that she was flirting with Michael and that Chris stabbed him in a jealous rage. She speaks in a flat, hollow voice and shows little remorse for her actions. It was a spur-of-the-moment thing, she claims, and after all it was Chris, not she herself, who had the knife. Later Chris testifies, claiming that Daphne instigated the fight and egged him on, taunting him that he was too scared to kill someone. Chris says that when she was drunk, Daphne often talked of killing an adult because she hated older people, especially her parents.

Daphne's parents claim that although she has been a burden with her mood swings and volatile behavior, she is still a child and can be helped with proper treatment. They are willing to supplement any state intervention with privately funded psychiatrists. Given that this is her first real offense and because of her age (14), her parents believe that home confinement with intense treatment is the best course.

The district attorney, however, wants Daphne treated as an adult and waived to adult court where, if she is found guilty, she can receive a 25-year sentence for second-degree murder; there is little question of her legal culpability.

## Writing Assignment

Take the role of a defense lawyer in the juvenile court. Write a brief to the juvenile court judge that could be used at the waiver hearing. Use your essay to persuade the judge to keep Daphne in the juvenile court, where she could be treated rather than punished. How would you convince the court that Daphne's crime was a function of some abnormal trait or condition that is amenable to treatment? Be sure to refute the notion that she is a calculating criminal who understood the seriousness of her actions. If you want to read about the actual case, search online for "Daphne Abdela," or go to this website: topics.nytimes.com/top/reference/timestopics/people/a/daphne _abdela/. But do that after you write your essay—no cheating.

# SUMMARY

Key Terms

**LO1  Discuss the development of trait theory.**

The view that criminals have physical or mental traits that make them different originated with the Italian physician and criminologist Cesare Lombroso. In the early 1970s, spurred by the publication of *Sociobiology: The New Synthesis*, by Edmund O. Wilson, biological explanations of crime once again emerged. Trait theorists today recognize crime-producing interactions that involve both personal traits and environmental factors. If only a few offenders become persistent repeaters, what sets them apart from the rest of the criminal population may be some crime-producing trait.

**LO2  Differentiate between the biochemical conditions that produce crime.**

Biochemical conditions influence antisocial behavior. Biocriminologists maintain that an improper diet can cause chemical and mineral imbalance and lead to cognitive and learning deficits and problems, and these factors in turn are associated with antisocial behaviors. Abnormal levels of male sex hormones (androgens) can incline individuals to aggressive behavior. Exposure to lead has been linked to emotional and behavioral disorders.

**LO3  Describe the link between genetics and crime, according to trait theory.**

Another biosocial theme is that the human traits associated with criminality have a genetic basis. According to this view, (1) antisocial behavior is inherited, (2) the genetic makeup of parents is passed on to children, and (3) genetic abnormality is linked to a variety of antisocial behaviors.

**LO4  Discuss the elements of the psychodynamic perspective.**

The id is the primitive part of people's mental makeup. The ego is shaped by learning and experience, and the superego reflects the morals and values of parents and significant others. Criminals are id-driven people who suffer from weak or damaged egos. Crime is a manifestation of feelings of oppression and the inability to develop the proper psychological defenses and rationales to keep these feelings under control.

**L05    Correlate behavior theory to crime.**

People are not born with the tendency to act violently; rather, they learn to be aggressive through their life experiences. These experiences include personally observing others acting aggressively to achieve some goal or observing people being rewarded for violent acts.

**L06    Discuss the controversy surrounding the link between intelligence and crime.**

Proponents of nature theory argue that intelligence is largely determined genetically, that ancestry determines IQ, and that low intelligence is linked to criminal behavior. Proponents of nurture theory argue that intelligence is not inherited and that low-IQ parents do not necessarily produce low-IQ children. The debate about any link between IQ and criminality is unlikely to be settled soon. Measurement is beset by many methodological problems.

## Key Terms

trait theory  127
sociobiology  127
individual vulnerability
    model  128
differential susceptibility
    model  129
hypoglycemia  130
androgens  130
testosterone  131
premenstrual syndrome
    (PMS)  131
neurophysiology  132
conduct disorder (CD)  132

attention deficit
    hyperactivity
    disorder
    (ADHD)  133
neurotransmitters  133
arousal theory  134
monozygotic (MZ)
    twins  135
dizygotic (DZ) twins  135
psychodynamic
    (psychoanalytic)
    psychology  137

id  137
ego  138
superego  138
attachment theory  138
behavior theory  138
social learning theory  138
behavior modeling  139
cognitive theory  139
information-processing
    theory  141
personality  142
antisocial personality  143

nature theory  144
nurture theory  144
mood disorder  146
oppositional defiant
    disorder (ODD)  146
schizophrenia  146
bipolar disorder  146
primary prevention
    programs  148
secondary prevention
    programs  148

## Critical Thinking Questions

1. If research could show that the tendency to commit crime is inherited, what should be done with the young children of violence-prone criminals? Would it be fair to monitor their behavior from an early age?

2. Considering the evidence on the association between media and crime, would you recommend that young children be forbidden to view films with violent content?

3. Knowing what you do about trends and patterns in the crime rate and where and when crime takes place, how would you counteract the assertion that people who commit crime are physically or mentally abnormal?

4. Aside from becoming a criminal, what other career paths are open to psychopaths?

5. Should sugar be banned from school lunches?

6. Can gender differences in the crime rate be explained by evolutionary factors? Do you agree that male aggression is linked to mating patterns developed millions of years ago?

## Notes

*All URLs accessed in 2015.*

1. David M. Halbfinger, "A Gunman, Recalled as Intelligent and Shy, Who Left Few Footprints in Life," *New York Times*, December 14, 2012, www.nytimes .com/2012/12/15/nyregion/adam-lanza-an-enigma -who-is-now-identified-as-a-mass-killer.html.

2. Abbie Boudreau and Scott Zamost, "Girlfriend: Shooter Was Taking Cocktail of 3 Drugs," CNN, February 20, 2008, www.cnn.com/2008/CRIME /02/20/shooter.girlfriend/.

3. BBC, "Profile: Aurora Cinema Shooting Suspect James Holmes," July 21, 2012, www.bbc.co.uk /news/world-us-canada-18937513.

4. Lee Ellis, "A Discipline in Peril: Sociology's Future Hinges on Curing Biophobia," *American Sociologist* 27 (1996): 21–41.

5. Edmund O. Wilson, *Sociobiology: The New Synthesis* (Cambridge, MA: Harvard University Press, 1975).

6. Per-Olof Wikstrom and Rolf Loeber, "Do Disadvantaged Neighborhoods Cause Well-Adjusted Children to Become Adolescent Delinquents?" *Criminology* 38 (2000): 1109–1142.

7. John Paul Wright and Francis T. Cullen, "The Future of Biosocial Criminology: Beyond Scholars' Professional Ideology," *Journal of Contemporary Criminal Justice* 28 (2012): 237–253, at 244.

8. Bernard Rimland, *Dyslogic Syndrome: Why Today's Children Are "Hyper," Attention Disordered, Learning Disabled, Depressed, Aggressive, Defiant, or Violent—and What We Can Do About It* (London: Jessica Kingsley Publishers, 2008).

9. J. C. Barnes and Bruce Jacobs, "Genetic Risk for Violent Behavior and Environmental Exposure to Disadvantage and Violent Crime: The Case for Gene-Environment Interaction," *Journal of Interpersonal Violence* 28 (2013): 92–120.

10. Rimland, *Dyslogic Syndrome*.

11. John Cloud, "Harvey Milk: People Told Him No Openly Gay Man Could Win Political Office. Fortunately, He Ignored Them," *Time*, June 14, 1999, www .time.com/time/time100/heroes/profile/milk01.html.

12. F. T. Crews, A. Mdzinarishvili, D. Kim, J. He, and K. Nixon, "Neurogenesis in Adolescent Brain Is Potently Inhibited by Ethanol," *Neuroscience* 137 (2006): 437–445.

13. G. B. Ramirez, O. Pagulayan, H. Akagi, A. Francisco Rivera, L. V. Lee, A. Berroya, M. C. Vince Cruz, and D. Casintahan, "Tagum Study II: Follow-Up Study at Two Years of Age After Prenatal Exposure to Mercury," *Pediatrics* 111 (2003): 289–295.

14. D. K. L. Cheuk and Virginia Wong, "Attention Deficit Hyperactivity Disorder and Blood Mercury Level: A Case-Control Study in Chinese Children," *Neuropediatrics* 37 (2006): 234–240.

15. Ramirez et al., "Tagum Study II."

16. A. L. Kristjansson, I. D. Sigfusdottir, S. S. Frost, and J. E. James, "Adolescent Caffeine Consumption and Self-Reported Violence and Conduct Disorder," *Journal of Youth and Adolescence* 43 (2013): 1053–1062; Eric Konofal, Samuele Cortese, Michel Lecendreux, Isabelle Arnulf, and Marie Christine Mouren, "Effectiveness of Iron Supplementation in a Young Child with Attention-Deficit/Hyperactivity Disorder," *Pediatrics* 116 (2005): 732–734.

17. Alexandra Richardson and Paul Montgomery, "The Oxford-Durham Study: A Randomized Controlled Trial of Dietary Supplementation with Fatty Acids in Children with Developmental Coordination Disorder," *Pediatrics* 115 (2005): 1360–1366.

18. Crystal Haskell, Andrew Scholey, Philippa Jackson, Jade Elliott, Margaret Defeyter, Joanna Greer, Bernadette Robertson, Tom Buchanan, Brian Tiplady, and David Kennedy, "Cognitive and Mood Effects in Healthy Children During 12 Weeks' Supplementation with Multi-Vitamin/Minerals," *British Journal of Nutrition* 100 (2008): 1086–1096.

19. Diana Fishbein, "Neuropsychological Function, Drug Abuse, and Violence: A Conceptual Framework," *Criminal Justice and Behavior* 27 (2000): 139–159.

20. Matti Virkkunen, "Reactive Hypoglycemic Tendency Among Habitually Violent Offenders," *Nutrition Reviews Supplement* 44 (1986): 94–103.

21. Stephanie H. M. van Goozen, Walter Matthys, Peggy Cohen-Kettenis, Jos Thijssen, and Herman van Engeland, "Adrenal Androgens and Aggression in Conduct Disorder Prepubertal Boys and Normal Controls," *Biological Psychiatry* 43 (1998): 156–158.

22. Paul Bernhardt, "Influences of Serotonin and Testosterone in Aggression and Dominance: Convergence with Social Psychology," *Current Directions in Psychological Science* 6 (1997): 44–48.

23. Christy Miller Buchanan, Jacquelynne Eccles, and Jill Becker, "Are Adolescents the Victims of Raging Hormones? Evidence for Activational Effects of Hormones on Moods and Behavior at Adolescence," *Psychological Bulletin* 111 (1992): 62–107.

24. Angel Romero-Martínez, Marisol Lila, Patricia Sariñana-González, Esperanza González-Bono, and Luis Moya-Albiol, "High Testosterone Levels and Sensitivity to Acute Stress in Perpetrators of Domestic Violence with Low Cognitive Flexibility and Impairments in Their Emotional Decoding Process: A Preliminary Study," *Aggressive Behavior* 39 (2013): 355–369.

25. Celina Cohen-Bendahan, Jan Buitelaar, Stephanie van Goozen, Jacob Orlebeke, and Peggy Cohen-Kettenis, "Is There an Effect of Prenatal Testosterone on Aggression and Other Behavioral Traits? A Study Comparing Same-Sex and Opposite-Sex Twin Girls," *Hormones and Behavior* 47 (2005): 230–237.

26. Albert Reiss and Jeffrey Roth, eds., *Understanding and Preventing Violence* (Washington, DC: National Academy Press, 1993), p. 118.

27. Anthony Walsh, "Genetic and Cytogenetic Intersex Anomalies: Can They Help Us to Understand Gender Differences in Deviant Behavior?" *International Journal of Offender Therapy and Comparative Criminology* 39 (1995): 151–166.

28. Walter Gove, "The Effect of Age and Gender on Deviant Behavior: A Biopsychosocial Perspective," in *Gender and the Life Course*, ed. A. S. Rossi (New York: Aldine, 1985), pp. 115–144.

29. For a review of this concept, see Anne E. Figert, "The Three Faces of PMS: The Professional, Gendered, and Scientific Structuring of a Psychiatric Disorder," *Social Problems* 42 (1995): 56–72.

30. Katharina Dalton, *The Premenstrual Syndrome* (Springfield, IL: Charles C Thomas, 1971).

31. Diana Fishbein, "Selected Studies on the Biology of Antisocial Behavior," in *New Perspectives in Criminology*, ed. John Conklin (Needham Heights, MA: Allyn & Bacon, 1996), pp. 26–38.

32. David C. Bellinger, "Lead," *Pediatrics* 113 (2004): 1016–1022.

33. Centers for Disease Control and Prevention, "What Do Parents Need to Know to Protect Their Children?" www.cdc.gov/nceh/lead/ACCLPP/blood_lead_levels.htm.

34. Jeff Evans, "Asymptomatic, High Lead Levels Tied to Delinquency," *PediatricNews* 37 (2003): 13.

35. Mark Opler, Alan Brown, Joseph Graziano, Manisha Desai, Wei Zheng, Catherine Schaefer, Pamela Factor-Litvak, and Ezra S. Susser, "Prenatal Lead Exposure, [Delta]-Aminolevulinic Acid, and Schizophrenia," *Environmental Health Perspectives* 112 (2004): 548–553.

36. Paul Stretesky and Michael Lynch, "The Relationship Between Lead Exposure and Homicide," *Archives of Pediatric Adolescent Medicine* 155 (2001): 579–582.

37. Rick Nevin, "Understanding International Crime Trends: The Legacy of Preschool Lead Exposure," *Environmental Research* 104 (2007): 315–336.

38. Rick Nevin, "Understanding International Crime Trends: The Legacy of Preschool Lead Exposure," *Environmental Research* 104 (2007): 315–336.

39. Paul Stewart, Edward Lonky, Jacqueline Reihman, James Pagano, Brooks Gump, and Thomas Darvill, "The Relationship Between Prenatal PCB Exposure and Intelligence (IQ) in 9-Year-Old Children," *Environmental Health Perspectives* 116 (2008): 1416–1422.

40. Lilian Calderón-Garcidueñas et al., "Air Pollution, Cognitive Deficits and Brain Abnormalities: A Pilot Study with Children and Dogs," *Brain and Cognition* 68 (2008): 117–127.

41. Centers for Disease Control and Prevention, *Exposure and Risk, 2014,* ephtracking.cdc.gov/showDevelopmental DisabilitiesExposureRisk.action.

42. Nathaniel Pallone and James Hennessy, "Brain Dysfunction and Criminal Violence," *Society* 35 (1998): 21–27.

43. Adrian Raine, Monte Buchsbaum, and Lori LaCasse, "Brain Abnormalities in Murderers Indicated by Positron Emission Tomography," *Biological Psychiatry* 42 (1997): 495–508.

44. James Ogilvie, Anna Stewart, Raymond Chan, and David Shum, "Neuropsychological Measures of Executive Function and Antisocial Behavior: A Meta-Analysis," *Criminology* 49 (2011): 1063–1107.

45. Kevin Beaver, John Paul Wright, and Matt DeLisi, "Self-Control as an Executive Function: Reformulating Gottfredson and Hirschi's Parental Socialization Thesis," *Criminal Justice and Behavior* 34 (2007): 1345–1361.

46. Alice Jones, Kristin Laurens, Catherine Herba, Gareth Barker, and Essi Viding, "Amygdala Hypoactivity to Fearful Faces in Boys with Conduct Problems and Callous-Unemotional Traits," *American Journal of Psychiatry* 166 (2009): 95–102.

47. Thomas Crowley, Manish S. Dalwani, Susan K. Mikulich-Gilbertson, Yiping P. Du, Carl W. Lejuez, Kristen M. Raymond, and Marie T. Banich, "Risky Decisions and Their Consequences: Neural Processing by Boys with Antisocial Substance Disorder," *PLoS One* 5 (2010), published online, www.ncbi.nlm.nih.gov/pmc/articles/PMC2943904/.

48. Society for Neuroscience News Release, "Studies Identify Brain Areas and Chemicals Involved in Aggression; May Speed Development of Better Treatment," www.sfn.org/Press-Room/News-Release-Archives/2007/STUDIES-IDENTIFY-BRAIN.

49. Stephen Faraone et al., "Intellectual Performance and School Failure in Children with Attention Deficit Hyperactivity Disorder and in Their Siblings," *Journal of Abnormal Psychology* 102 (1993): 616–623.

50. Leonore M. J. Simon, "Does Criminal Offender Treatment Work?" *Applied and Preventive Psychology* 7 (1998): 137–159.

51. Ibid.

52. Molina Pelham, Jr., "Childhood Predictors of Adolescent Substance Use in a Longitudinal Study of Children with ADHD," *Journal of Abnormal Psychology* 112 (2003): 497–507; Peter Muris and Cor Meesters, "The Validity of Attention Deficit Hyperactivity and Hyperkinetic Disorder Symptom Domains in Nonclinical Dutch Children," *Journal of Clinical Child and Adolescent Psychology* 32 (2003): 460–466.

53. Elizabeth Hart et al., "Criterion Validity of Informants in the Diagnosis of Disruptive Behavior Disorders in Children: A Preliminary Study," *Journal of Consulting and Clinical Psychology* 62 (1994): 410–414.

54. W. R. Lindsay, D. Carson, A. J. Holland, J. L. Taylor, G. O'Brien, and J. R. Wheeler, "The Impact of Known Criminogenic Factors on Offenders with Intellectual Disability: Previous Findings and New Results on

ADHD," *Journal of Applied Research in Intellectual Disabilities* 26 (2013): 71–80.

55. Ronald Simons, Man Kit Lei, Steven Beach, Gene Brody, Robert Philibert, and Frederick Gibbons, "Social Environmental Variation, Plasticity Genes, and Aggression: Evidence for the Differential Susceptibility Hypothesis," *American Sociological Review* 76 (2011): 833–912.

56. Susan Young, Andrew Smolen, Robin Corley, Kenneth Krauter, John DeFries, Thomas Crowley, and John Hewitt, "Dopamine Transporter Polymorphism Associated with Externalizing Behavior Problems in Children," *American Journal of Medical Genetics* 114 (2002): 144–149.

57. M. Skondras, M. Markianos, A. Botsis, E. Bistolaki, and G. Christodoulou, "Platelet Monoamine Oxidase Activity and Psychometric Correlates in Male Violent Offenders Imprisoned for Homicide or Other Violent Acts," *European Archives of Psychiatry and Clinical Neuroscience* 254 (2004): 380–386.

58. Lee Ellis, "Monoamine Oxidase and Criminality: Identifying an Apparent Biological Marker for Antisocial Behavior," *Journal of Research in Crime and Delinquency* 28 (1991): 227–251.

59. Rose McDermott, Chris Dawes, Elizabeth Prom-Wormley, Lindon Eaves, and Peter Hatemi, "MAOA and Aggression: A Gene–Environment Interaction in Two Populations," *Journal of Conflict Resolution* 57 (2013): 1043–1064.

60. Lee Ellis and Anthony Hoskin, "Criminality and the 2D:4D Ratio: Testing the Prenatal Androgen Hypothesis," *International Journal of Offender Therapy and Comparative Criminology* 59 (2015): 295–312.

61. Lee Ellis, "Left and Mixed-Handedness and Criminality: Explanations for a Probable Relationship," in *Left-Handedness: Behavioral Implications and Anomalies*, ed. S. Coren (Amsterdam: Elsevier, 1990), pp. 485–507.

62. Lee Ellis, "Arousal Theory and the Religiosity–Criminality Relationship," in *Contemporary Criminological Theory*, ed. Peter Cordella and Larry Siegel (Boston: Northeastern University, 1996), pp. 65–84.

63. Adrian Raine, Peter Venables, and Sarnoff Mednick, "Low Resting Heart Rate at Age 3 Years Predisposes to Aggression at Age 11 Years: Evidence from the Mauritius Child Health Project," *Journal of the American Academy of Adolescent Psychiatry* 36 (1997): 1457–1464.

64. Thomas Frisell, Yudi Pawitan, Niklas Långström, and Paul Lichtenstein, "Heritability, Assortative Mating and Gender Differences in Violent Crime: Results from a Total Population Sample Using Twin, Adoption, and Sibling Models," *Behavior Genetics* 42 (2012): 3–18.

65. Ronald L. Simons, Man Kit Lei, Eric A. Stewart, Steven R. H. Beach, Gene H. Brody, Robert A. Philibert, and Frederick X. Gibbons, "Social Adversity, Genetic Variation, Street Code, and Aggression: A Genetically Informed Model of Violent Behavior," *Youth Violence and Juvenile Justice* 10 (2012): 3–24; Anita Thapar, Kate Langley, Tom Fowler, Frances Rice, Darko Turic, Naureen Whittinger, John Aggleton, Marianne Van den Bree, Michael Owen, and Michael O'Donovan, "Catechol O-methyltransferase Gene Variant and Birth Weight Predict Early-Onset Antisocial Behavior in Children with Attention-Deficit/Hyperactivity Disorder," *Archives of General Psychiatry* 62 (2005): 1275–1278.

66. Kevin Beaver, John Paul Wright, and Matt DeLisi, "Delinquent Peer Group Formation: Evidence of a Gene X Environment Correlation," *Journal of Genetic Psychology* 169 (2008): 227–244.

67. Kevin Beaver, Chris Gibson, Michael Turner, Matt DeLisi, Michael Vaughn, and Ashleigh Holand, "Stability of Delinquent Peer Associations: A Biosocial Test of Warr's Sticky-Friends Hypothesis," *Crime and Delinquency* 57 (2011): 907–927.

68. Kevin M. Beaver, "The Effects of Genetics, the Environment, and Low Self-Control on Perceived Maternal and Paternal Socialization: Results from a Longitudinal Sample of Twins," *Journal of Quantitative Criminology* 27 (2011): 85–105.

69. K. Dean, P. B. Mortensen, H. Stevens, R. M. Murray, E. Walsh, and E. Agerbo, "Criminal Conviction Among Offspring with Parental History of Mental Disorder," *Psychological Medicine* 42 (2012): 571–581.

70. D. J. West and D. P. Farrington, "Who Becomes Delinquent?" in *The Delinquent Way of Life*, ed. D. J. West and D. P. Farrington (London: Heinemann, 1977), pp. 1–28; D. J. West, *Delinquency: Its Roots, Careers, and Prospects* (Cambridge, MA: Harvard University Press, 1982).

71. David Farrington, "Understanding and Preventing Bullying," in *Crime and Justice*, vol. 17, ed. Michael Tonry (Chicago: University of Chicago Press, 1993), pp. 381–457.

72. R. J. Cadoret, C. Cain, and R. R. Crowe, "Evidence for a Gene–Environment Interaction in the Development of Adolescent Antisocial Behavior," *Behavior Genetics* 13 (1983): 301–310.

73. Barry Hutchings and Sarnoff A. Mednick, "Criminality in Adoptees and Their Adoptive and Biological Parents: A Pilot Study," in *Biological Bases in Criminal Behavior*, ed. S. A. Mednick and K. O. Christiansen (New York: Gardner Press, 1977).

74. Michael Lyons, Karestan Koenen, Francisco Buchting, Joanne Meyer, Lindon Eaves, Rosemary Toomey, Seth Eisen, et al., "A Twin Study of Sexual Behavior in Men," *Archives of Sexual Behavior* 33 (2004): 129–136.

75. Sarnoff Mednick and Jan Volavka, "Biology and Crime," in *Crime and Justice*, ed. Norval Morris and Michael Tonry (Chicago: University of Chicago Press, 1980), pp. 85–159, at p. 94.

76. Edwin J. C. G. van den Oord, Frank Verhulst, and Dorret Boomsma, "A Genetic Study of Maternal and

Paternal Ratings of Problem Behaviors in 3-Year-Old Twins," *Journal of Abnormal Psychology* 105 (1996): 349–357.

77. Ginette Dionne, Richard Tremblay, Michel Boivin, David Laplante, and Daniel Perusse, "Physical Aggression and Expressive Vocabulary in 19-Month-Old Twins," *Developmental Psychology* 39 (2003): 261–273.

78. Callie Burt and Ronald Simons, "Pulling Back the Curtain on Heritability Studies: Biosocial Criminology in the Postgenomic Era," *Criminology* 52 (2014): 223–262.

79. J. C. Barnes, John Paul Wright, Brian B. Boutwell, Joseph A. Schwartz, Eric J. Connolly, Joseph L. Nedelec, and Kevin M. Beaver," Demonstrating the Validity of Twin Research in Criminology," *Criminology* 52 (2014): 588–626.

80. Lawrence Cohen and Richard Machalek, "A General Theory of Expropriative Crime: An Evolutionary Ecological Approach," *American Journal of Sociology* 94 (1988): 465–501.

81. For a general review, see Martin Daly and Margo Wilson, "Crime and Conflict: Homicide in Evolutionary Psychological Theory," in *Crime and Justice: An Annual Edition*, ed. Michael Tonry (Chicago: University of Chicago Press, 1997), pp. 51–100.

82. Joseph Nedelec and Kevin Beaver, "The Association Between Sexual Behavior and Antisocial Behavior: Insights from an Evolutionary Informed Analysis," *Journal of Contemporary Criminal Justice* 28 (2012): 329–345.

83. Ibid.

84. David Rowe, Alexander Vazsonyi, and Aurelio Jose Figuerdo, "Mating-Effort in Adolescence: A Conditional Alternative Strategy," *Personal Individual Differences* 23 (1997): 105–115.

85. Edwin Driver, "Charles Buckman Goring," in *Pioneers in Criminology*, ed. Hermann Mannheim (Montclair, NJ: Patterson Smith, 1970), p. 440.

86. Gabriel Tarde, *Penal Philosophy*, trans. R. Howell (Boston: Little, Brown, 1912).

87. See, generally, Donn Byrne and Kathryn Kelly, *An Introduction to Personality* (Englewood Cliffs, NJ: Prentice Hall, 1981).

88. See, generally, D. A. Andrews and James Bonta, *The Psychology of Criminal Conduct* (Cincinnati: Anderson, 1994), pp. 72–75.

89. John Bowlby, *Maternal Care and Mental Health*, World Health Organization Monograph, WHO Monographs Series No. 2 (Geneva: World Health Organization, 1951).

90. Eric Wood and Shelley Riggs, "Predictors of Child Molestation: Adult Attachment, Cognitive Distortions, and Empathy," *Journal of Interpersonal Violence* 23 (2008): 259–275.

91. Karen L. Hayslett-McCall and Thomas J. Bernard, "Attachment, Masculinity, and Self-Control: A Theory of Male Crime Rates," *Theoretical Criminology* 6 (2002): 5–33.

92. This discussion is based on three works by Albert Bandura: *Aggression: A Social Learning Analysis* (Englewood Cliffs, NJ: Prentice Hall, 1973); *Social Learning Theory* (Englewood Cliffs, NJ: Prentice Hall, 1977); and "The Social Learning Perspective: Mechanisms of Aggression," in *Psychology of Crime and Criminal Justice*, ed. Hans Toch (New York: Holt, Rinehart & Winston, 1979), pp. 198–236.

93. Amy Street, Lynda King, Daniel King, and David Riges, "The Associations Among Male-Perpetrated Partner Violence, Wives' Psychological Distress and Children's Behavior Problems: A Structural Equation Modeling Analysis," *Journal of Comparative Family Studies* 34 (2003): 23–46.

94. David Phillips, "The Impact of Mass Media Violence on U.S. Homicides," *American Sociological Review* 48 (1983): 560–568.

95. Kenneth Dodge, "A Social Information Processing Model of Social Competence in Children," in *Minnesota Symposium in Child Psychology*, vol. 18, ed. M. Perlmutter (Hillsdale, NJ: Erlbaum, 1986), pp. 77–125.

96. Tony Ward and Claire Stewart, "The Relationship Between Human Needs and Criminogenic Needs," *Psychology, Crime and Law* 9 (2003): 219–225.

97. David Ward, Mark Stafford, and Louis Gray, "Rational Choice, Deterrence, and Theoretical Integration," *Journal of Applied Social Psychology* 36 (2006): 571–585.

98. Glenn Walters and Matt DeLisi, "Antisocial Cognition and Crime Continuity: Cognitive Mediation of the Past Crime–Future Crime Relationship," *Journal of Criminal Justice* 41 (2013): 135–140.

99. Donald Lynam and Joshua Miller, "Personality Pathways to Impulsive Behavior and Their Relations to Deviance: Results from Three Samples," *Journal of Quantitative Criminology* 20 (2004): 319–341.

100. L. Huesman and L. Eron, "Individual Differences and the Trait of Aggression," *European Journal of Personality* 3 (1989): 95–106.

101. Rolf Loeber and Dale Hay, "Key Issues in the Development of Aggression and Violence from Childhood to Early Adulthood," *Annual Review of Psychology* 48 (1997): 371–410.

102. Vincent Marziano, Tony Ward, Anthony Beech, and Philippa Pattison, "Identification of Five Fundamental Implicit Theories Underlying Cognitive Distortions in Child Abusers: A Preliminary Study," *Psychology, Crime and Law* 12 (2006): 97–105.

103. See, generally, Walter Mischel, *Introduction to Personality*, 4th ed. (New York: Holt, Rinehart & Winston, 1986).

104. Edelyn Verona and Joyce Carbonell, "Female Violence and Personality," *Criminal Justice and Behavior* 27 (2000): 176–195.

105. Gerhard Blickle, Alexander Schlegel, Pantaleon Fassbender, and Uwe Klein, "Some Personality Correlates of Business White-Collar Crime," *Applied Psychology: An International Review* 55 (2006): 220–233.

106. Hans Eysenck and M. W. Eysenck, *Personality and Individual Differences* (New York: Plenum, 1985).

107. Catrien Bijleveld and Jan Hendriks, "Juvenile Sex Offenders: Differences Between Group and Solo Offenders," *Psychology, Crime and Law* 9 (2003): 237–246.

108. Laurie Frost, Terrie Moffitt, and Rob McGee, "Neuropsychological Correlates of Psychopathology in an Unselected Cohort of Young Adolescents," *Journal of Abnormal Psychology* 98 (1989): 307–313.

109. David Lykken, "Psychopathy, Sociopathy, and Crime," *Society* 34 (1996): 30–38.

110. Avshalom Caspi, Terrie Moffitt, Phil Silva, Magda Stouthamer-Loeber, Robert Krueger, and Pamela Schmutte, "Are Some People Crime-Prone? Replications of the Personality–Crime Relationship Across Countries, Genders, Races and Methods," *Criminology* 32 (1994): 163–195.

111. Lykken, "Psychopathy, Sociopathy, and Crime."

112. Kevin Beaver, Michael G. Vaughn, Matt DeLisi, J. C. Barnes, and Brian B. Boutwell, "The Neuropsychological Underpinnings to Psychopathic Personality Traits in a Nationally Representative and Longitudinal Sample," *Psychiatric Quarterly* 81 (2010): 325–334.

113. Kent Kiehl, Andra Smith, Adrianna Mendrek, Bruce Forster, Robert Hare, and Peter F. Liddle, "Temporal Lobe Abnormalities in Semantic Processing by Criminal Psychopaths as Revealed by Functional Magnetic Resonance Imaging," *Psychiatry Research: Neuroimaging* 130 (2004): 27–42.

114. James Blair, Derek Mitchell, and Karina Blair, *The Psychopath: Emotion and the Brain* (London: Wiley Blackwell, 2005).

115. Joseph Lee Rogers, H. Harrington Cleveland, Edwin van den Oord, and David Rowe, "Resolving the Debate over Birth Order, Family Size and Intelligence," *American Psychologist* 55 (2000): 599–612.

116. Travis Hirschi and Michael Hindelang, "Intelligence and Delinquency: A Revisionist Review," *American Sociological Review* 42 (1977): 471–586.

117. James Q. Wilson and Richard Herrnstein, *Crime and Human Nature* (New York: Simon & Schuster, 1985), p. 148.

118. Richard Herrnstein and Charles Murray, *The Bell Curve: Intelligence and Class Structure in American Life* (New York: Free Press, 1994).

119. Kevin M. Beaver, Joseph A. Schwartz, Joseph L. Nedelec, Eric J. Connolly, Brian B. Boutwell, and J. C. Barnes, "Intelligence Is Associated with Criminal Justice Processing: Arrest Through Incarceration," *Intelligence* 41 (2013): 277–288.

120. Kevin Beaver and John Paul Wright, "The Association Between County-Level IQ and County-Level Crime Rates," *Intelligence* 39 (2011): 22–26; Jared Bartels, Joseph Ryan, Lynn Urban, and Laura Glass, "Correlations Between Estimates of State IQ and FBI Crime Statistics," *Personality and Individual Differences* 48 (2010): 579–583; Philippe Rushton and Donald Templer, "National Differences in Intelligence, Crime, Income, and Skin Color," *Intelligence* 37 (2009): 341–346.

121. Aaron Beck, Neil Rector, Neal Stolar, and Paul Grant, *Schizophrenia: Cognitive Theory, Research, and Therapy* (New York, Guilford Press, 2008).

122. Paige Crosby Ouimette, "Psychopathology and Sexual Aggression in Nonincarcerated Men," *Violence and Victimization* 12 (1997): 389–397.

123. Ellen Kjelsberg, "Gender and Disorder-Specific Criminal Career Profiles in Former Adolescent Psychiatric In-Patients," *Journal of Youth and Adolescence* 33 (2004): 261–270.

124. Paula Fite, Spencer Evans, John Cooley, and Sonia Rubens, "Further Evaluation of Associations Between Attention-Deficit/Hyperactivity and Oppositional Defiant Disorder Symptoms and Bullying-Victimization in Adolescence," *Child Psychiatry and Human Development* 45 (2014): 32–41.

125. Thomas Crowley, Manish S. Dalwani, Susan K. Mikulich-Gilbertson, Yiping P. Du, Carl W. Lejuez, Kristen M. Raymond, and Marie T. Banich, "Risky Decisions and Their Consequences: Neural Processing by Boys with Antisocial Substance Disorder," *PLoS One* 5 (2010), published online, www.ncbi.nlm.nih.gov/pmc/articles/PMC2943904/.

126. Barbara Maughan, Richard Rowe, Julie Messer, Robert Goodman, and Howard Meltzer, "Conduct Disorder and Oppositional Defiant Disorder in a National Sample: Developmental Epidemiology," *Journal of Child Psychology and Psychiatry and Allied Disciplines* 45 (2004): 609–621.

127. Richard Dorn, Jan Volavka, and Norman Johnson, "Mental Disorder and Violence: Is There a Relationship Beyond Substance Use?" *Social Psychiatry and Psychiatric Epidemiology* 47 (2012): 487–503.

128. Michael Ostermann and Jason Matejkowski. "Estimating the Impact of Mental Illness on Costs of Crimes," *Criminal Justice and Behavior* 41 (2014): 20–40.

129. Robert Vermeiren, "Psychopathology and Delinquency in Adolescents: A Descriptive and Developmental Perspective," *Clinical Psychology Review* 23 (2003): 277–318.

130. David Vinkers, Edwin de Beurs, and Marko Barendregt, "Psychiatric Disorders and Repeat Offending," *American Journal of Psychiatry* 166 (2009): 489.

131. Jacques Baillargeon, Ingrid Binswanger, Joseph Penn, Brie Williams, and Owen Murray, "Psychiatric Disorders and Repeat Incarcerations: The Revolving Prison Door," *American Journal of Psychiatry* 166 (2009): 103–109.

132. John Monahan, *Mental Illness and Violent Crime* (Washington, DC: National Institute of Justice, 1996).

133. Thomas O'Hare, Ce Shen, and Margaret Sherrer, "High-Risk Behaviors and Drinking-to-Cope as

Mediators of Lifetime Abuse and PTSD Symptoms in Clients with Severe Mental Illness," *Journal of Traumatic Stress* 23 (2010): 255–263; Eric Silver, "Mental Disorder and Violent Victimization: The Mediating Role of Involvement in Conflicted Social Relationships," *Criminology* 40 (2002): 191–212.

134. Eric Silver, "Extending Social Disorganization Theory: A Multilevel Approach to the Study of Violence Among Persons with Mental Illness," *Criminology* 38 (2000): 1043–1074.

135. B. Lögdberg, L-L. Nilsson, M. T. Levander, and S. Levander, "Schizophrenia, Neighbourhood, and Crime," *Acta Psychiatrica Scandinavica* 110 (2004): 92–97; Stacy DeCoster and Karen Heimer, "The Relationship Between Law Violation and Depression: An Interactionist Analysis," *Criminology* 39 (2001): 799–837.

136. Courtenay Sellers, Christopher Sullivan, Bonita Veysey, and Jon Shane, "Responding to Persons with Mental Illnesses: Police Perspectives on Specialized and Traditional Practices," *Behavioral Sciences and the Law* 23 (2005): 647–657.

137. Tamsin B. R. Short, Stuart Thomas, Stefan Luebbers, Paul Mullen, and James Ogloff, "A Case-Linkage Study of Crime Victimisation in Schizophrenia-Spectrum Disorders over a Period of Deinstitutionalization," *BMC Psychiatry* 13 (2013): 1–9.

138. Tamar Mendelson, Alexandria Turner, and Darius Tandon, "Violence Exposure and Depressive Symptoms Among Adolescents and Young Adults Disconnected from School and Work," *Journal of Community Psychology* 38 (2010): 607–621.

139. Beaver, Wright, and DeLisi, "Delinquent Peer Group Formation."

140. Susan Pease and Craig T. Love, "Optimal Methods and Issues in Nutrition Research in the Correctional Setting," *Nutrition Reviews Supplement* 44 (1986): 122–131.

141. Mark O'Callaghan and Douglas Carroll, "The Role of Psychosurgical Studies in the Control of Antisocial Behavior," in *The Causes of Crime: New Biological Approaches*, ed. Sarnoff Mednick, Terrie Moffitt, and Susan Stack (Cambridge: Cambridge University Press, 1987), pp. 312–328.

142. Reiss and Roth, *Understanding and Preventing Violence*, p. 389.

143. Kathleen Cirillo, B. E. Pruitt, Brian Colwell, Paul M. Kingery, Robert S. Hurley, and Danny Ballard, "School Violence: Prevalence and Intervention Strategies for At-Risk Adolescents," *Adolescence* 33 (1998): 319–331.

# 6 Social Structure Theory

## Learning Objectives

**LO1** Describe the association between social structure and crime.

**LO2** Identify the elements of social disorganization theory.

**LO3** Explain the views of Shaw and McKay.

**LO4** Differentiate between the various elements of ecological theory.

**LO5** Discuss the concept of strain.

**LO6** List and compare the elements of cultural deviance theory.

# Chapter Outline

## FACT OR FICTION?

▶ Political, social, and economic programs such as affirmative action have erased the economic gulf between whites and minorities.

▶ Crime rates go down in a healthy economy and rise along with unemployment.

Twenty years ago, Kaboni Savage—then a small-time Philadelphia drug dealer—began buying cocaine in bulk and building his criminal organization. His often-brutal methods of operation—which included murders, beatings, kidnappings, and threats against anyone who crossed him (customers, rival gang members, his own underlings, even law enforcement)—helped make a name for him as someone to be feared and respected. His reputation was not lost on law enforcement agents, who began to investigate Savage, resulting an indictment in May 2004 for conspiring to distribute cocaine, money laundering, firearms offenses, and later on, witness intimidation.

Savage and his gang were arrested and held for trial; one of the gang members, Eugene Coleman, agreed to cooperate with the prosecution in the case. Hearing of this, Savage orchestrated an arson attack on Coleman's family, meant to send a clear warning of what happens to those who "rat." From his jail cell, Savage solicited the help of his sister Kidada and two other gang members—Lamont Lewis and Robert Merritt—to carry out his plan. On October 9, 2004, Lewis and Merritt drove to Coleman's mother's house, fired warning shots into the residence, and threw two full gasoline cans with lit cloth fuses into the home. Prosecutors later told the jury the people inside never had a chance; within seconds, temperatures from the firebomb exceeded 1,000 degrees. Six people died in the inferno: Coleman's mother Marcella Coleman (54); his cousins Tameka Nash (34), Sean Rodriguez (15), and Tajh Porchea (12); his niece Khadijah (10); and his 15-month-old son Damir. ▶

Kidada Savage and four other gang members were convicted and received long prison sentences. Kaboni Savage was eventually convicted for the Coleman murders and a slew of others:

- Kenneth Lassiter, killed on March 19, 1998
- Mansur "Shafiq" Abdullah, killed on September 6, 2000
- Carlton "Mohammed" Brown, killed on September 13, 2001
- Barry Parker, killed on February 26, 2003
- Tyrone Toliver, killed on March 14, 2003
- Tybius Flowers, killed on March 1, 2004

For his crimes, Kaboni Savage received 13 death sentences.[1]

To criminologists it comes as no surprise that drug-dealing gangs develop in poor, deteriorated urban neighborhoods and that gang-related homicides are highest in these crowded, inner-city communities.[2] Many kids in these areas grow up hopeless and alienated, believing that they have little chance of being part of the American Dream.[3]

Noting the universal association between poverty, neighborhood conditions, and criminal behavior, social structure theorists suggest that antisocial behavior is a direct result of destructive social forces on human behavior.[4] According to this view, it is *social forces*—not individual traits—that cause crime. Inner-city residents are indigent and desperate, not abnormal, calculating, or evil. Raised in deteriorated parts of town, they lack the social support and economic resources available to more affluent members of society. Dealing drugs or joining a gang holds the promise of economic rewards and status enhancements that the conventional world simply cannot provide.

# Economic Structure

**stratified society**
People grouped according to economic or social class; characterized by the unequal distribution of wealth, power, and prestige.

**social class**
Segment of the population whose members are at a relatively similar economic level and who share attitudes, values, norms, and an identifiable lifestyle.

**culture of poverty**
A separate lower-class culture, characterized by apathy, cynicism, helplessness, and mistrust of social institutions such as schools, government agencies, and the police, that is passed from one generation to the next.

People in the United States live in a **stratified society**. Social strata are created by the unequal distribution of wealth, power, and prestige. **Social classes** are segments of the population whose members have a relatively similar portion of desirable things and who share attitudes, values, norms, and an identifiable lifestyle. In U.S. society, it is common to identify people as belonging to the upper, middle, or lower socioeconomic class, although a broad range of economic variations exist within each group. The upper-upper class is reserved for a small number of exceptionally well-to-do families who control enormous financial and social resources. In contrast, there are now about 46 million Americans living in poverty, defined as a family of four earning about $24,000 per year, who have scant, if any, resources, and suffer socially and economically as a result; this number has been increasing during the past decade.[5] Income inequality has become a national concern. The top 1 percent of households have an annual income of about $394,000 and/or about $1.5 million in liquid assets. The top 1/10th of the 1 percent have an income of almost $2 million a year; the top 1/100th of the top 1 percent have an annual income of at least $10.2 million with a net worth of about $20 million. The 16,000 wealthiest families in the United States have $6 trillion in total assets.[6] Clearly the wealth gap creates two Americas, one that can afford the finest luxuries the world can offer and the other just scraping by, often with government assistance to supplement meager earnings.

## Problems of the Lower Class

In 1966, sociologist Oscar Lewis argued that the crushing lifestyle of lower-class areas produces a **culture of poverty** that is passed from one generation to the next.[7] Apathy, cynicism, helplessness, and mistrust of social institutions, such as schools, government agencies, and the police, mark the culture of poverty. This mistrust prevents the inner-city poor from taking advantage of the meager opportunities available to them. Lewis's work was the first of a number of studies that described the plight of at-risk children and adults. In 1970, Swedish economist Gunnar Myrdal described a worldwide **underclass** that was cut off from society, its members lacking the education and skills needed to function successfully in modern society.[8]

Lower-class areas are scenes of inadequate housing and health care, disrupted family lives, underemployment, and despair. Members of the lower class also suffer in other ways. They are more prone to depression, less likely to have achievement motivation, and less likely to put off immediate gratification for the sake of future gain or security. Members of the lower classes may be less willing to stay in school because the rewards for educational achievement are in the distant future.

Poverty is not always an urban problem. Here, a Montgomery County sheriff's deputy walks away from an old school bus where two children were found living on their own in Spendora, Texas. Their parents, Mark and Sherrie Shorten, were in prison when the children, then 11 and 5, were found living alone. The Shortens had left the children in the care of an aunt, but she became overwhelmed and left them to fend for themselves.

## Child Poverty

Economic disadvantage and poverty can be especially devastating to younger children.[9] About 15 million youths under 18 in the United States—nearly 22 percent of all youth—live in families with incomes below the poverty line. Another 22 percent escape poverty but live in families considered "poor."[10] Many kids living in poverty have working parents, but low wages and unstable employment leave their families struggling to make ends meet.[11] Being a child in a low-income or poor family does not happen by chance and is a function of parental education and employment, race/ethnicity, and other factors associated with economic insecurity.

Not only are they poor, but the number of homeless children in the U.S. has surged in recent years to an all-time high, amounting to one child in every 30. The National Center on Family Homelessness calculates that nearly 2.5 million American children were homeless at some point in the past year. The number is based on the Department of Education's latest count of 1.3 million homeless children in public schools, supplemented by estimates of homeless preschool children not counted by the DOE.[12] The problem is particularly severe in California, which has one-eighth of the U.S. population but accounts for more than one-fifth of the homeless children with a tally of nearly 527,000.

Being poor and homeless hits adolescents hard. Children who grow up in low-income homes are less likely to achieve in school and less likely to complete their schooling than children with more affluent parents.[13] Poor kids are also more likely to suffer from health problems and to receive inadequate health care.

## Minority Group Poverty

The burdens of underclass life are often felt most acutely by minority group members. Whereas many urban European Americans use their economic, social, and political advantages to live in sheltered gated communities patrolled by security guards and police, most minorities do not have access to similar protections and privileges.[14]

The median family income of Latinos and African Americans is two-thirds that of whites, and the percentage of racial and ethnic minorities living in poverty is double that of European Americans.[15] According to the U.S. Census Bureau, the African American household median income was $33,762, compared to $56,565 for

**underclass**
The lowest social stratum in any country, whose members lack the education and skills needed to function successfully in modern society.

**CONNECTIONS**

Concern about the ecological distribution of crime, the effect of social change, and the interactive nature of crime itself has made sociology the foundation of modern criminology. This chapter reviews sociological theories that emphasize the relationship between social status and criminal behavior. In Chapter 7, the focus shifts to theories that emphasize socialization and its influence on crime and deviance; Chapter 8 covers theories based on the concept of social conflict.

Income inequality and poverty have become major social issues in the United States. While the top 1 percent can live comfortable lives, those living below the poverty line suffer inadequate health care, housing, and education. Poverty hits the African American community the hardest. These men in Detroit are queuing up at a local soup kitchen to receive free food to ward off their hunger. Do you believe that poverty is a direct cause of crime?

**LO1** Describe the association between social structure and crime.

**social structure theory**
The view that disadvantaged economic class position is a primary cause of crime.

non-Hispanic white households. About 28 percent of African Americans were living at the poverty level, compared to 11 percent of non-Hispanic whites. The unemployment rate for blacks is twice that for non-Hispanic whites (10 percent versus about 5 percent), a finding consistent for both men and women.[16] There are also race-based differences in high school completion; white rates are higher than those of minorities.[17]

These economic and social disparities continually haunt members of the minority underclass and their children. Even if they value education and other middle-class norms, their desperate life circumstances, such as high unemployment and nontraditional family structures, may prevent them from developing the skills and habits that lead first to educational success and later to success in the workplace; these deficits have been linked to crime and drug abuse.[18]

The issue of minority poverty is explored further in the accompanying Policies and Issues in Criminology feature entitled "The Truly Disadvantaged."

## Social Structure and Crime

According to **social structure theory**, the root cause of crime can be traced directly to the socioeconomic disadvantages that have become embedded in American society. The social problems found in lower-class areas have been described as an "epidemic" that spreads through a community, destroying the inner workings that enable neighborhoods to survive; they become "hollowed out."[19] As neighborhood quality decreases, the probability that residents will develop problems sharply increases. Because they lack ties to the mainstream culture, some lower-class people are driven to desperate measures, such as crime and substance abuse, to cope with their economic plight.[20] Crime and violence may also take the form of a "slow epidemic," with a course consisting of stages: onset, peak, and decline. Violence and crime have been found to spread and then contract in a pattern similar to a contagious disease.[21]

Because lower-class kids are exposed to a continual stream of violence, they are more likely to engage in violent acts themselves.[22] Their involvement with conventional social institutions, such as schools and after-school programs, is either absent or blocked, which puts them at risk for recruitment into gangs.[23] When informal and formal avenues of social control have become frayed, kids are given a free hand to mix with deviant peers.[24] As a result, poor kids are more likely to engage in drug use and violence than the affluent.[25]

Aggravating this dynamic is the constant media bombardment linking material possessions to self-worth. Because they are unable to obtain desired goods and services through conventional means, members of the lower class may turn to illegal solutions to their economic plight. They may deal drugs for profit, steal cars and sell them to "chop shops," or commit armed robberies for desperately needed funds. They may become so depressed that they take alcohol and drugs as a form of self-tranquilization,

# Policies and Issues in Criminology

## THE TRULY DISADVANTAGED

William Julius Wilson, one of the nation's most prominent sociologists, has produced an impressive body of work that details racial problems and racial politics in American society. He has coined the phrase "the truly disadvantaged" to describe the socially isolated racial minorities who dwell in urban inner cities, occupy the bottom rung of the social ladder, and are the victims of discrimination. They live in areas in which the basic institutions of society—family, school, housing—have long since declined. Neighborhood decline triggers breakdowns in community cohesion and loss of the ability of people living in the area to control the flow of drugs and criminal activity. In a more affluent area, neighbors might complain to parents that their children were being disruptive. In distressed areas, this element of informal social control may be absent, because parents are under stress or (all too often) absent. These effects magnify the isolation of the underclass from mainstream society and promote a ghetto culture characterized by hopelessness and lawless behavior.

Because the truly disadvantaged rarely come into contact with the actual source of their oppression, they direct their anger and aggression at those with whom they are in close contact, such as neighbors, businesspeople, and landlords. Plagued by under- or unemployment, they begin to lose self-confidence, a feeling exacerbated by the plight of kin and friendship groups who also experience extreme economic marginality. Self-doubt is a neighborhood norm that threatens to overwhelm those forced to live in areas of concentrated poverty.

In his book *When Work Disappears*, Wilson assesses the effect of joblessness and underemployment on residents in poor neighborhoods on Chicago's south side. Wilson focuses on the plight of the African American community, which had enjoyed periods of relative prosperity in the 1950s and 1960s. He suggests that as difficult as life was for African Americans in the 1940s and 1950s, they at least had a reasonable hope of steady work. Now, because of the globalization of the economy, those opportunities have evaporated. In the past, growth in the manufacturing sector fueled upward mobility and lay the foundation of today's African American middle class. Those opportunities no longer exist, because manufacturing plants have been moved to inaccessible rural and overseas locations where the cost of doing business is lower. With manufacturing opportunities all but absent in the United States, service and retail establishments that depended on blue-collar spending have similarly disappeared, leaving behind an economy based on welfare and government supports. In less than 20 years, formerly active African American neighborhoods have become crime-infested inner-city ghettos.

The hardships faced by residents on Chicago's south side are not unique to that community. In addition to perpetuating inner-city poverty, the absence of employment opportunities has torn at the social fabric of the nation's inner-city neighborhoods. Couples are less likely to marry because minority women no longer see men as breadwinners. Epidemic unemployment among minority males also undermines the community. Work helps socialize young people into the wider society, instilling in them such values as hard work, caring, and respect for others. When work becomes scarce, the discipline and structure it provides are absent. Community-wide underemployment destroys social cohesion, increasing the presence of neighborhood social problems ranging from drug use to educational failure. Schools in these areas are unable to teach basic skills, and because desirable employment is lacking, there are few adults to serve as role models. In contrast to more affluent suburban households where daily life is organized around job and career demands, children in inner-city areas are not socialized in the workings of the mainstream economy.

In *More than Just Race: Being Black and Poor in the Inner City*, Wilson concludes that a law-and-order political philosophy and fear of racial conflict have led to high incarceration rates among African American males. Although black women can get jobs in service industries, employers are less likely to hire black men, especially those with a criminal record. As a result, there has been a decline in the ability of black men to be providers, which has tended to undermine the stability of the African American family: why get married to someone who cannot support the family? Here we can see how structure and culture intertwine to produce stress in the African American community.

### Critical Thinking

1. Can you describe the linkage between the African American experience, relations with law enforcement, and the Black Lives Matter movement?

2. Is income inequality the key to understanding the racial divide in the crime rate? And how can this problem be fixed?

3. Can government programs help?

**Sources:** William Julius Wilson, *More than Just Race: Being Black and Poor in the Inner City* (New York: Norton, 2009); Wilson and Richard Taub, *There Goes the Neighborhood: Racial, Ethnic, and Class Tensions in Four Chicago Neighborhoods and Their Meaning for America* (New York: Knopf, 2006); Wilson, *The Truly Disadvantaged* (Chicago: University of Chicago Press, 1987); Wilson, *When Work Disappears: The World of the Urban Poor* (New York: Knopf, 1996).

and because of their poverty, they may acquire the drugs and alcohol through illegal channels.

Because of income inequality, minority group members are the citizens most likely to be hit hard economically and forced to live in the most deteriorated neighborhoods in the city. Interracial differences in the crime rate could be significantly reduced by improving levels of education, lowering levels of poverty, ending racial segregation in housing and neighborhood makeup, and reducing the extent of male unemployment among minority populations.[26]

**LO2** Identify the elements of social disorganization theory.

**social disorganization theory**
Branch of social structure theory that focuses on the breakdown in inner-city neighborhoods of institutions such as the family, school, and employment.

**strain theory**
Branch of social structure theory that sees crime as a function of the conflict between people's goals and the means available to obtain them.

**strain**
The anger, frustration, and resentment experienced by people who believe they cannot achieve their goals through legitimate means.

**cultural deviance theory**
Branch of social structure theory that sees strain and social disorganization together resulting in a unique lower-class culture that conflicts with conventional social norms.

**subculture**
A set of values, beliefs, and traditions unique to a particular social class or group within a larger society.

**FACT OR FICTION?**
Political, social, and economic programs such as affirmative action have erased the economic gulf between whites and minorities.

**FICTION** Despite governmental efforts and programs, the income differential between European Americans and minority group members persists.

# Social Structure Theories

Social structure theories view the cause of crime through the lens of poverty, income inequality, hopelessness and despair. Social and economic forces operating in deteriorated lower-class areas push many of their residents into criminal behavior patterns. It seems logical that if crime rates are higher in lower-class urban centers than in middle-class suburbs, social forces must influence or control behavior.

The social structure perspective encompasses three independent yet overlapping branches:

- According to **social disorganization theory**, crime flourishes in a disorganized area in which institutions of social control, such as the family, commercial establishments, and schools, have broken down and can no longer perform their expected or stated functions. There are high unemployment and school dropout rates, deteriorated housing, low income levels, and large numbers of single-parent households. Young people living in these areas experience conflict and despair, are more likely to join gangs, and as a result, cannot avoid the lure of antisocial behaviors.
- **Strain theory** holds that crime occurs when members of the lower class experience anger and frustration over their inability to achieve success. Because they fail to achieve success through conventional means, lower-class people feel **strain**, pushing some to find alternative means of achieving their life goals. Striving for success may involve engaging in criminal activities.
- **Cultural deviance theory** combines elements of both strain and social disorganization: in disorganized neighborhoods, the presence of strain locks people into an independent **subculture** with unique values and beliefs. Criminal behavior is an expression of conformity to lower-class subcultural values and traditions that often are at odds with conventional society.

Although these views differ in critical aspects, each approach has at its core the view that socially isolated people, living in disorganized neighborhoods, are likely to experience crime-producing social forces.

# Social Disorganization Theory

Social disorganization theory links crime rates to neighborhood ecological characteristics. Crime rates are highest in transient, mixed-use (where residential and commercial property exist side by side), and changing neighborhoods in which the fabric of social life has become frayed. These localities are unable to provide essential services, such as education, health care, and proper housing, and as a result, they experience significant levels of unemployment, single-parent families, and families on welfare.

Residents in crime-ridden neighborhoods flee at the earliest opportunity. Those planning to leave take little interest in community matters, so the common sources of control—the family, school, business community, and social service agencies—are weak and disorganized. Personal relationships are strained because neighbors are constantly moving. Continuous resident turnover weakens communications and blocks attempts at solving neighborhood problems or establishing common goals.[27]

Because social institutions are frayed or absent, law-violating youth groups and gangs form and are free to recruit neighborhood youth. Both boys and girls who feel detached and alienated from their social world are at risk to become gang members.[28]

Not surprisingly, then, there are now more than 30,000 law-violating gangs in the United States, containing about 850,000 members.[29] This represents a 15 percent increase from 2006 and is the highest annual estimate since 1996.

## The Work of Shaw and McKay

Social disorganization theory was popularized by the work of two Chicago sociologists, Clifford R. Shaw and Henry McKay, who linked life in transitional slum areas to the inclination to commit crime. Shaw and McKay began their pioneering work on Chicago crime during the early 1920s, while working as researchers for a state-supported social service agency.[30]

Shaw and McKay explained crime and delinquency within the context of the changing urban environment and ecological development of the city. They saw that Chicago had developed into distinct neighborhoods (natural areas), some affluent and others wracked by extreme poverty. These poverty-ridden **transitional neighborhoods** suffered high rates of population turnover and were incapable of inducing residents to remain and defend the neighborhoods against criminal groups.

In transitional areas, successive changes in population composition, disintegration of traditional cultures, diffusion of divergent cultural standards, and gradual industrialization dissolve neighborhood culture and organization. The continuity of conventional neighborhood traditions and institutions is broken, leaving people feeling displaced and without a strong or definitive set of values.

**CONCENTRIC ZONES** Shaw and McKay identified the areas in Chicago that had excessive crime rates. They noted that distinct ecological areas had developed in the city, forming a series of nine concentric circles, or zones, and that there were stable and significant interzone differences in crime rates (see Figure 6.1). The areas beset by the most crime appeared to be the transitional inner-city zones, where large numbers of the city's poorest citizens had settled.[31] The zones farthest from the city's center had correspondingly lower crime rates.

Analysis of these data indicated a surprisingly stable pattern of criminal activity in the nine ecological zones over a period of 65 years. Shaw and McKay concluded that multiple cultures and diverse values, both conventional and deviant, coexist in the transitional neighborhoods. People growing up in the street culture often find residents who have adopted a deviant lifestyle (gamblers, pimps, drug dealers) are the most financially successful people in the neighborhood. Forced to choose between conventional and deviant lifestyles, many slum kids opt for the latter. They join other like-minded youths and form law-violating gangs and cliques. The development of teenage law-violating groups is an essential element of misbehavior in slum areas. The values that slum youths adopt often conflict with existing middle-class norms, which demand strict obedience to the legal code. Consequently, a value conflict further separates the delinquent youth and his or her peer group from conventional society; the result is a more solid embrace of deviant goals and behavior. To further justify their choice of goals, these youths seek support for their choice by recruiting new members and passing on the delinquent tradition.

Kirsten Luce/New York Times/Redux

Disorganized neighborhoods lack the ability to apply social control. Institutions of social control are weak and attenuated. In the absence of formal (police) and informal (families, neighbors) social control mechanisms, gangs and law-violating youth groups are free to rule the streets. Under such conditions, crime flourishes and people seek to relocate if they have sufficient financial resources.

**CHECKPOINTS**

▶ Because crime rates are higher in lower-class areas, many criminologists believe that the causes of crime are rooted in socioeconomic factors.

▶ Despite economic headway, there are still more than 30 million indigent Americans. Minority groups are more likely than the white majority to be poor.

▶ Some criminologists believe that destructive social forces in poverty-stricken areas are responsible for high crime rates.

▶ The strain and frustration inflicted by poverty are a suspected cause of crime.

▶ Indigents may become involved in a deviant subculture that sustains and supports criminality.

**L03** Explain the views of Shaw and McKay.

**transitional neighborhood**
An area undergoing a shift in population and structure, usually from middle-class residential to lower-class mixed-use.

**FIGURE 6.1**

**Shaw and McKay's Concentric Zones Map of Chicago**

**Note:** Arabic numbers represent the rate of male delinquency. Numbers indicate the crime rate in various zones; the crime rates decline in zones farthest from inner-city Chicago.

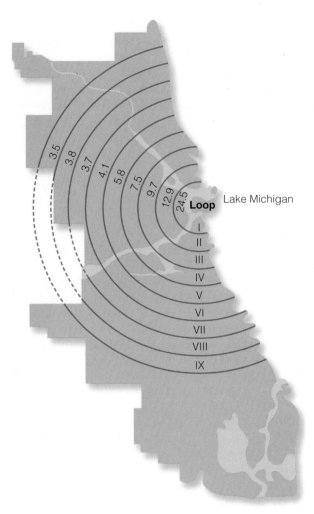

**CONNECTIONS**

If social disorganization causes crime, why are most low-income people law abiding? To explain this anomaly, some sociologists have devised theoretical models suggesting that individual socialization experiences mediate environmental influences. These theories will be discussed in Chapter 7.

**L04** Differentiate between the various elements of ecological theory.

Shaw and McKay's statistical analysis confirmed that even though crime rates changed, the highest rates were always in Zones I and II (the central city and a transitional area, respectively). The areas with the highest crime rates retained high rates even when their ethnic composition changed (the areas that Shaw and McKay examined shifted from German and Irish to Italian and Polish).[32]

**THE LEGACY OF SHAW AND MCKAY** The social disorganization concepts articulated by Shaw and McKay have remained prominent within criminology for more than 75 years. Although cultural and social conditions have changed over time, and today we live in a much more heterogeneous, mobile society, the most important of Shaw and McKay's findings—crime rates correspond to neighborhood structure—still holds up.[33]

Their research supported the fact that crime is a constant fixture in areas of poverty, regardless of residents' racial or ethnic identity. Because the basis of their theory was that neighborhood disintegration is the primary cause of criminal behavior, Shaw and McKay paved the way for many of the community action and development programs that have been developed in the last half-century.

## The Social Ecology School

Contemporary social disorganization theory seeks to identify the ecological conditions—poverty, disorganization, instability, incivility, economy—that produce high crime rates and while so doing formulate strategies to bring these community-level crime rates down.[34] Referred to as the **social ecology school**, what has been developed is a purer form of structural theory that emphasizes the association of community deterioration and economic decline with criminality but places less emphasis on value conflict. The following sections discuss some of the more recent social-ecological research.

**social ecology school**
An interdisciplinary approach to the study of interdependent social and environmental problems that cause crime.

**COMMUNITY DISORDER**  Contemporary social ecologists believe that crime rates are associated with community deterioration: disorder, poverty, alienation, disassociation, and fear of crime.[35] Even in rural areas, which normally have low crime rates, increased levels of crime and violence are associated with indicators of social disorganization such as residential instability (a large number of people moving in and out), family disruption, and changing ethnic composition.[36]

In larger cities, neighborhoods with a high percentage of deserted houses and apartments experience high crime rates; abandoned buildings serve as a "magnet for crime."[37] Areas in which houses are in poor repair, boarded up, and burned out, whose owners are best described as slumlords, are also the location of the highest violence rates and gun crime.[38] These neighborhoods, in which retail establishments often go bankrupt, are abandoned and deteriorate physically.[39]

**COMMUNITY FEAR**  In neighborhoods where people help each other, residents are less likely to fear crime or to be afraid of becoming a crime victim.[40] In disorganized neighborhoods that suffer social and physical incivilities, residents experience unruly youths, trash and litter, graffiti, abandoned storefronts, burned-out buildings, littered lots, strangers, drunks, vagabonds, loiterers, prostitutes, noise, congestion, angry words, dirt, and stench. Having parks and playgrounds where teens hang out and loiter may contribute to fear.[41] And as fear increases, quality of life deteriorates.[42]

Fear is often based on experience: people living in areas with especially high crime rates are the ones most likely to experience fear.[43] People who live in public housing projects, who come into daily contact with civil disorder, are not surprisingly the ones most likely to see their community as disorderly and dangerous.[44] Residents who have already been victimized or know someone else who has are more fearful of the future than those who have escaped crime.[45] People become afraid when they are approached by someone in the neighborhood selling drugs. They may fear that their children will also be approached and will be seduced into the drug life.[46] The presence of such incivilities, especially when accompanied by relatively high crime rates, convinces residents that their neighborhood is dangerous; becoming a crime victim seems inevitable.[47]

Fear can be contagious. People tell others when they have been victimized, thus spreading the word that the neighborhood is getting dangerous and that the chance of future victimization is high.[48] As a result, people dread leaving their homes at night and withdraw from community life.

**SIEGE MENTALITY**  People who live in neighborhoods that experience high levels of crime and civil disorder become suspicious and mistrusting.[49] Minority group members may experience greater levels of fear than whites, perhaps because they may have fewer resources to address ongoing social problems.[50] They develop a sense of powerlessness, which increases levels of mistrust. Some residents become so suspicious of authority that they

Jim Young/Reuters/Landov

On July 3, 2015, people gather for a candlelight vigil against gun violence in the Englewood neighborhood of Chicago. Extra police patrols were not enough to prevent 9 deaths and about 50 injuries from gun violence in Chicago over the Fourth of July weekend, when homicides increase almost every year. Chicago is currently experiencing an upswing in violence, with poverty, street gangs, and a pervasive gun culture all contributing to the problem.

AP Photo/David Goldman

Living in segregated neighborhoods may cause minority group members to develop a sense of powerlessness that in turn creates a "siege mentality," characterized by mistrust of social institutions, including law enforcement, business, government, and schools. Local police are believed to ignore crime in minority communities and, when they do take action, they use excessive force against young black men. When an arrest or use of force seems unjust, such as when Michael Brown was killed in Ferguson, Missouri, people take to the streets in angry protests, as seen here.

develop a "siege mentality," in which the outside world is considered the enemy bent on destroying the neighborhood.

Siege mentality often results in an expanding mistrust of social institutions, including law enforcement, business, government, and schools. Government officials seem arrogant and haughty. The police are believed to ignore crime in minority communities and, when they do take action, they use excessive force against young black men.[51] When a seemingly unjust shooting occurs, such as the case when on August 9, 2014, Michael Brown was killed in Ferguson, Missouri, people in the community lose respect for the police: they are forced to protest that "Black Lives Matter."[52]

The Michael Brown case is not unique: research does show that police are more likely to use higher levels of force when suspects are encountered in disadvantaged neighborhoods, regardless of the suspects' behaviors or reactions.[53] When police ignore crime in poor areas, or, conversely, when they are violent and corrupt, anger flares, and people take to the streets and react in violent ways.

**COMMUNITY CHANGE** Change, not stability, is the hallmark of inner-city areas. A neighborhood's residents, wealth, density, and purpose are constantly evolving. Even disorganized neighborhoods acquire new identifying features. Some may become multiracial and others racially homogeneous. Some areas become stable and family-oriented, whereas in others, mobile, never-married people predominate.[54] Urban areas undergoing rapid structural changes in racial and economic composition also seem to experience the greatest change in crime rates.[55] In contrast, stable neighborhoods, even those with a high rate of poverty, experience relatively low crime rates and have the strength to restrict substance abuse and criminal activity.[56]

As areas decline, residents flee to safer, more stable localities. Those who can move to more affluent neighborhoods find that their lifestyles and life chances improve immediately and continue to do so over their life span.[57] Those who cannot leave because they cannot afford to live in more affluent communities face an increased risk of victimization. Because of racial differences in economic well-being, those who remain are all too often minority citizens.[58] Whites may feel threatened as the percentage of minorities in the population increases and there is more competition for jobs and political power.[59] As racial prejudice increases, the call for "law and order" aimed at controlling the minority population grows louder.[60]

Those who cannot move find themselves surrounded by a constant influx of new residents. In response to this turnover, a culture may develop that dictates to neighborhood youths standards of dress, language, and behavior that are in opposition to those of conventional society. All these factors are likely to produce increased crime rates.

As communities change, neighborhood deterioration precedes increasing rates of crime and delinquency.[61] Neighborhoods most at risk for increased crime contain large numbers of single-parent families and unrelated people living together, have changed from owner-occupied to renter-occupied units, and have lost semiskilled and unskilled jobs (hence the growing number of discouraged workers who are no longer seeking employment).[62] These ecological disruptions strain existing social control mechanisms and undermine their ability to control crime and delinquency.

**POVERTY CONCENTRATION**  One aspect of community change may be the concentration of poverty in deteriorated urban neighborhoods.[63] William Julius Wilson describes how working- and middle-class families flee inner-city areas where poverty is pervasive, resulting in a poverty **concentration effect** in which the most disadvantaged population is consolidated in the most disorganized urban neighborhoods. Poverty concentration has been associated with income and wealth disparities, nonexistent employment opportunities, inferior housing patterns, and unequal access to health care.[64] Urban areas marked by concentrated poverty become isolated and insulated from the social mainstream and more prone to criminal activity, violence, and homicide.[65]

How does neighborhood poverty concentration produce high crime rates? White families are more likely to leave an area when they perceive that the surrounding neighborhoods have become predominantly minority.[66] As the working and middle classes move out to the suburbs, they take with them their financial and institutional resources and support.[67] The people left behind have an even tougher time coping with urban decay and conflict and controlling youth gangs and groups; after all, the most successful people in the community have left for "greener pastures." Businesses are disinclined to locate in poverty-stricken areas; banks become reluctant to lend money for new housing or businesses.[68] Unemployment rates skyrocket, destabilizing households, and unstable families are likely to produce children who use violence and aggression to deal with limited opportunity. Large groups or cohorts of people of the same age are forced to compete for relatively scarce resources.[69]

Limited employment opportunities reduce the stabilizing influence of parents and other adults, who might once have counteracted the allure of youth gangs. In a classic study, sociologist Elijah Anderson's analysis of Philadelphia neighborhood life found that "old heads" (respected neighborhood residents), who at one time played an important role in socializing youths, were displaced by younger street hustlers and drug dealers. Although the old heads may complain that these newcomers have not earned or worked for their fortunes in the old-fashioned way, they nevertheless envy these young people whose grills and luxury cars advertise their wealth amid poverty.[70] So the old heads admire the fruits of crime, even as they disdain the violent manner in which they are acquired.

## Collective Efficacy

Cohesive communities with high levels of social control and social integration, where people know one another and develop interpersonal ties, develop **collective efficacy**: a sense of mutual trust, a willingness to intervene in the supervision of children, and the maintenance of public order.[71] Cohesion among neighborhood residents, combined with shared expectations for informal social control of public space, promotes collective efficacy.[72] Residents in these areas enjoy a better life because the fruits of cohesiveness can be better education, health care, and housing opportunities.[73]

In contrast, socially disorganized neighborhoods, where the population is transient, and interpersonal relationships remain superficial and nonsupportive, efforts at social control are weak and attenuated.[74] In these unstable neighborhoods, residents find that the social support they need to live a conventional life is absent or lacking. The resulting lack of social cohesion produces an atmosphere where antisocial behavior becomes normative.[75] As the number of people who have a stake in the community (i.e., they are homeowners) increases, crime rates drop.[76] These more cohesive neighborhoods report less disorder than less-unified communities.[77]

People living in economically disadvantaged areas are significantly more likely to perceive their immediate surroundings in more negative terms (with higher levels of incivilities) than those living in areas that maintain collective efficacy.[78] When community social control efforts are blunted, crime rates increase, further weakening neighborhood cohesiveness.[79] This suggests that there are spillover effects that extend beyond the geographic boundaries of a single neighborhood.

**concentration effect**
As working-class and middle-class families flee inner-city poverty-ridden areas, the most disadvantaged population is consolidated in urban ghettos.

**collective efficacy**
Social control exerted by cohesive communities and based on mutual trust, including intervention in the supervision of children and maintenance of public order.

There are many forms of collective efficacy. Here, community police officers spend time with kids at a block party at the Ed Rice Community Center in Memphis, Tennessee. In a proactive effort to fight crime at its roots, police build relationships with children who live in their community. Police hold camps, attend local festivals, and have activities throughout the year that children can enjoy. Building trust within a neighborhood helps officers improve community collective efficacy.

Karen Pulfer Focht/Commercial Appeal/Landov

## CHECKPOINTS

▶ Social disorganization theory holds that destructive social forces present in inner-city areas cause the breakdown of institutions of social control and promote crime.

▶ Shaw and McKay first identified the concepts central to social disorganization. They found stable patterns of crime in the central city.

▶ The social ecology school associates community deterioration and economic decline with crime rates.

▶ Ecological factors such as community deterioration, changing neighborhoods, fear, lack of employment opportunities, incivility, poverty, and deterioration produce high crime rates.

▶ Collective efficacy can reduce neighborhood crime rates by creating greater cohesiveness.

There are three forms of collective efficacy—informal social control, institutional social control, and public social control—and all three contribute to community stability.

**INFORMAL SOCIAL CONTROL**  Some elements of collective efficacy operate on the primary, or private, level and involve peers, families, and relatives. These sources exert informal control by either awarding or withholding approval, respect, and admiration. Informal control mechanisms include direct criticism, ridicule, ostracism, desertion, and physical punishment.[80]

The most important wielder of informal social control is the family, which may keep at-risk kids in check through such mechanisms as effective parenting, withholding privileges, or ridiculing lazy or disrespectful behavior. The informal social control provided by the family takes on greater importance in neighborhoods with few social ties among adults and limited collective efficacy. In these areas, parents cannot call upon neighborhood resources to take up the burden of controlling children; family members face the burden of providing adequate supervision.[81] In neighborhoods with high levels of collective efficacy, parents are better able to function and effectively supervise their children. Confident and authoritative parents who live in areas that have developed collective efficacy are able to effectively deter their children from affiliating with deviant peers and getting involved in delinquent behavior.[82]

In some neighborhoods, even high-risk areas, people are willing to participate in anticrime programs.[83] Neighbors may get involved in informal social control through surveillance practices—for example, by keeping an "eye out" for intruders when their neighbors go out of town. Informal surveillance has been found to reduce the levels of some crimes such as street robberies; however, if robbery rates remain high, surveillance may be terminated because people become fearful for their safety.[84]

**INSTITUTIONAL SOCIAL CONTROL**  Social institutions such as schools and churches cannot work effectively in a climate of alienation and mistrust. Unsupervised peer groups and gangs, which flourish in disorganized areas, disrupt the influence of those neighborhood control agents that do exist.[85] Children who reside in these neighborhoods find that involvement with conventional social institutions, such as schools and afternoon programs, is blocked; they are instead at risk for recruitment into gangs and law-violating groups.[86] As crime flourishes, neighborhood fear increases, which in turn decreases a community's cohesion and thwarts the ability of its institutions to exert social control over its residents.[87]

To combat these influences, communities that have collective efficacy attempt to use their local institutions to control crime. Sources of institutional social control include businesses, stores, schools, churches, and social service and volunteer organizations. When these institutions are effective, rates for some crimes (such as burglary) decline.[88] Some institutions, such as recreation centers for teens, have been found to lower crime rates because they exert a positive effect; others, such as taverns and bars, tend to destabilize neighborhoods and increase the rate of violent crimes such as rape and robbery.[89]

**PUBLIC SOCIAL CONTROL** Stable neighborhoods are also able to arrange for external sources of social control. If they can draw on outside help and secure external resources—a process referred to as public social control—they are better able to reduce the effects of disorganization and maintain lower levels of crime and victimization.[90]

One primary source of public social control is the police. Neighborhoods that are sufficiently organized to demand and get additional police resources are likely to have lower crime rates than neighborhoods that lack such political clout.[91] The presence of police sends a message that the area will not tolerate deviant behavior. Because they can respond vigorously to crime, police prevent criminal groups from gaining a toehold in the neighborhood.[92] Criminals and drug dealers avoid such areas and relocate to easier and more appealing "targets."[93]

In disorganized areas, the absence of political power brokers limits access to external funding and protection. Without money from the outside, the neighborhood lacks the ability to "get back on its feet."[94] In these areas there are fewer police, and those that do patrol the area are less motivated and their resources are stretched thinner.[95]

Spencer Platt/Getty Images/Getty Images North America/Getty Images

Public social control promotes a sense of collective efficacy. On June 3, 2015, teens attend a meeting in East New York, a neighborhood that in recent years has been plagued by gun violence. Organized by the city Department of Probation and the Mayor's Office of Criminal Justice, the "One Message Many Voices: Anti-Gun Violence Town Hall" meeting featured a number of speakers and an inspirational dance performance. Following news of a more than 20 percent increase in murders and a 9 percent increase in shootings in the first half of 2015, the NYPD started its Summer All Out program a month early. This anticrime program trains and puts 330 administrative officers on the streets to help deter shootings and gun crimes.

**THE EFFECTS OF COLLECTIVE EFFICACY** In areas where collective efficacy remains high, crime rates remain low. Young people are less likely to become involved with deviant peers and engage in problem behaviors.[96] In these more stable areas, kids are better able to avoid violent confrontations and to feel safe in their own neighborhood, a concept referred to as **street efficacy**.[97]

In contrast, people who live in neighborhoods with concentrated disadvantage and low collective efficacy begin to lose confidence in their ability to avoid violence. They perceive that the community cannot provide the level of social control needed to neutralize or make up for what they lack in personal self-control.[98] The lack of community controls may convince them to take matters into their own hands—for example, joining a gang or carrying a weapon for self-protection. In these disorganized areas, interpersonal relationships remain superficial and nonsupportive. People who are forced to live in these areas either because of limited finances or legal restrictions, such as sex offenders, may find that the social support they need to live a conventional life is absent or lacking.[99] And even when an attempt is made in these areas to revitalize a disorganized neighborhood by creating institutional support programs such as community centers and better schools, the effort may be neutralized by the ongoing drain of deep-rooted economic and social deprivation.[100]

Concept Summary 6.1 lists some of the basic concepts and theories of the social disorganization view.

**street efficacy**
A concept in which more cohesive communities with high levels of social control and social integration foster the ability for kids to use their wits to avoid violent confrontations and to feel safe in their own neighborhood. Adolescents with high levels of street efficacy are less likely to resort to violence themselves or to associate with delinquent peers.

## Concept Summary 6.1  Social Disorganization Theories

| Theory | Major Premise | Strengths | Research Focus |
|---|---|---|---|
| **Shaw and McKay's concentric zones theory** | Crime is a product of transitional neighborhoods that manifest social disorganization and value conflict. | Identifies why crime rates are highest in slum areas. Points out the factors that produce crime. Suggests programs to help reduce crime. | Poverty; disorganization. |
| **Social ecology theory** | The conflicts and problems of urban social life and communities (including fear, unemployment, deterioration, and siege mentality) influence crime rates. | Accounts for urban crime rates and trends. | Social control; fear; collective efficacy; unemployment. |

**L05** Discuss the concept of strain.

# Strain Theories

Inhabitants of a disorganized inner-city area feel isolated, frustrated, ostracized from the economic mainstream, hopeless, and eventually angry. How do these feelings affect criminal activities?

Strain theorists view crime as a direct result of frustration and anger among the lower socioeconomic classes. Although most people share similar values and goals, the ability to achieve personal goals is stratified by socioeconomic class. Strain is limited in affluent areas because educational and vocational opportunities are available. In disorganized areas, strain proliferates because legitimate avenues for success are all but closed. To relieve strain, indigent people may achieve their goals through deviant methods, such as theft or drug trafficking, or they may reject socially accepted goals and substitute more deviant goals, such as being tough and aggressive

### Theory of Anomie

Sociologist Robert Merton applied the sociological concepts first identified by Durkheim to criminology in his theory of anomie.[101] He found that two elements of culture interact to produce potentially anomic conditions: culturally defined goals and socially approved means for obtaining them. U.S. society stresses the goals of acquiring wealth, success, and power. Socially permissible means include hard work, education, and thrift.

Merton argues that, in the United States, legitimate means to acquire wealth are stratified across class and status lines. Those with little formal education and few economic resources soon find that they are denied the ability to legally acquire wealth—the preeminent success symbol. When socially mandated goals are uniform throughout society and access to legitimate means is bound by class and status, the resulting strain produces anomie among those who are locked out of the legitimate opportunity structure. Consequently, they may develop criminal or delinquent solutions to the problem of attaining goals.

**SOCIAL ADAPTATIONS** Merton argues that each person has his or her own concept of society's goals and his or her own degree of access to the means to attain them. Some people have inadequate means of attaining success; others, who have the means, reject societal goals. The result is a variety of social adaptations:

- *Conformity.* When individuals embrace conventional social goals and also have the means to attain them, they can choose to conform. They remain law abiding.
- *Innovation.* When individuals accept the goals of society but are unable or unwilling to attain them through legitimate means, the resulting conflict forces them to adopt innovative solutions to their dilemma: they steal, sell drugs, or extort money. Of the five adaptations, innovation is most closely associated with criminal behavior.
- *Ritualism.* Ritualists gain pleasure from practicing traditional ceremonies, regardless of whether they have a real purpose or goal. The strict customs in religious orders, feudal societies, clubs, and college fraternities encourage and appeal to ritualists.
- *Retreatism.* Retreatists reject both the goals and the means of society. They attempt to escape their lack of success by withdrawing, either mentally or physically, through taking drugs or becoming drifters.
- *Rebellion.* Some individuals substitute an alternative set of goals and means for conventional ones. Revolutionaries who wish to promote radical change in the existing social structure and who call for alternative lifestyles, goals, and beliefs are engaging in rebellion. Rebellion may be a reaction against a corrupt, hated government or an effort to create alternative opportunities and lifestyles within the existing system.

**EVALUATION OF ANOMIE THEORY** According to **anomie theory**, social inequality leads to perceptions of anomie. To resolve the goals–means conflict and relieve their sense of strain, some people innovate by stealing or extorting money; others retreat into drugs and alcohol; some rebel by joining revolutionary groups; and still others get involved in ritualistic behavior by joining a religious cult.

Merton's view of anomie has been one of the most enduring and influential sociological theories of criminality. By linking deviant behavior to the success goals that control social behavior, anomie theory attempts to pinpoint the cause of the conflict that engenders personal frustration and consequent criminality. By acknowledging

**anomie theory**
The view that anomie results when socially defined goals (such as wealth and power) are universally mandated but access to legitimate means (such as education and job opportunities) is stratified by class and status.

Native Americans are particularly vulnerable to social strain. Here, a 16-year-old Lakota girl is holding an M1 assault rifle. It is easy to get guns in the Pine Ridge Reservation in South Dakota, as gang activity and violence are rampant. On the reservation, Native American Sioux are the majority and most live in poverty due to nearly nonexistent job opportunities—the unemployment rate is around 80 percent. A person's life span on the reservation used to be 80 years but is now 57 years for men and 63 for women. In addition to rampant health problems—diabetes, heart attacks, cancer—from limited and unhealthy dietary options, the reservation also faces rising youth violence and contaminated water from uranium mines. All these problems continue to be ignored not only by the federal and state governments but even by the local tribal governments. Is it any wonder that residents perceive strain and anomie?

Q. Sakamaki/Redux

that society unfairly distributes the legitimate means to achieving success, anomie theory helps explain the existence of high-crime areas and the apparent predominance of delinquent and criminal behavior in the lower class. By suggesting that social conditions, not individual personalities, produce crime, Merton greatly influenced the directions taken to reduce and control criminality during the latter half of the twentieth century.

Even so, anomie theory leaves a number of questions unanswered.[102] Merton does not explain why people choose to commit certain types of crime. For example, why does one anomic person become a mugger whereas another deals drugs? Anomie may explain differences in crime rates, but it cannot explain why most young criminals desist from crime as adults. Does this mean that perceptions of anomie dwindle with age? Is anomie short-lived?

## Institutional Anomie Theory

**institutional anomie theory**
The view that anomie pervades U.S. culture because the drive for material wealth dominates and undermines social and community values.

**American Dream**
The goal of accumulating material goods and wealth through individual competition; the process of being socialized to pursue material success and to believe it is achievable.

Steven Messner and Richard Rosenfeld's **institutional anomie theory (IAT)** is an updating of Merton's work.[103] For them, the **American Dream** refers to both a goal and a process. As a goal, the American Dream involves accumulating material goods and wealth via open individual competition. As a process, it involves both being socialized to pursue material success and believing that prosperity is achievable in American culture. Anomic conditions arise because the desire to succeed at any cost drives people apart, weakens the collective sense of community, fosters ambition, and restricts the desire to achieve anything other than material wealth. Achieving respect is not sufficient.

Why does anomie pervade American culture? According to Messner and Rosenfeld, it is because institutions that might otherwise control the exaggerated emphasis on financial success, such as religious or charitable institutions, have been rendered powerless or obsolete. These social institutions have been undermined in three ways:

- Noneconomic functions and roles have been devalued. Performance in other institutional settings—the family, school, or community—is assigned a lower priority than the goal of financial success.
- When conflicts emerge, noneconomic roles become subordinate to and must accommodate economic roles. The schedules, routines, and demands of the workplace take priority over those of the home, the school, the community, and other aspects of social life. People think nothing of leaving their neighborhood, city, or state for a better job, disrupting family relationships, and undermining informal social control.
- Economic language, standards, and norms penetrate noneconomic realms. Economic terms become part of the common vernacular: People want to get to the "bottom line." Spouses view themselves as "partners" who "manage" the household. Retired people say they want to "downsize" their household. We "outsource" home repairs instead of doing them ourselves. Corporate leaders run for public office promising to "run the country like a business."

According to Messner and Rosenfeld, the relatively high American crime rates can be explained by the interrelationship of culture and institutions. At the cultural level, the dominance of the American Dream mythology ensures that many people will develop desires for material goods that cannot be satisfied by legitimate means. Anomie becomes a norm, and extralegal means become a strategy for attaining material wealth. At the institutional level, the dominance of economic concerns weakens the informal social control exerted by family, church, and school. These institutions have lost their ability to regulate behavior and have instead become a conduit for promoting material success. Schools are evaluated not in terms of their effectively imparting knowledge but in terms of their ability to train students to get high-paying jobs. Social conditions reinforce each other: culture determines institutions, and institutional change influences culture.[104] Crime rates may rise in a healthy economy because national prosperity heightens the attractiveness of monetary rewards, encouraging people to gain financial success by any means necessary, including illegal means. In this culture of competition, self-interest prevails and generates amorality, acceptance of inequality, and disdain for the less fortunate.[105]

A number of research efforts have found support for the principles set out in the IAT. On a macro level, research shows that there is an association between national homicide rates and cultural stress on individual achievement and the fetishism of money.[106] On an individual or micro level, commitment to economic success is positively related to criminality. The more people say that making money is what's important to them, the more likely they are to get involved in crime.[107] And while there is general support for the IAT, a number of issues remain, such as developing an understanding of gender differences in the crime rate.[108] Assuming that women desire money, success, and the American Dream as much as men, why is their crime rate lower?

## Relative Deprivation Theory

There is ample evidence that neighborhood-level income inequality is a significant predictor of neighborhood crime rates.[109] Sharp divisions between the rich and the poor create an atmosphere of envy and mistrust. Criminal motivation is fueled both by perceived humiliation and by the perceived right to humiliate a victim in return.[110] Psychologists warn that under these circumstances young males will begin to fear and envy "winners" who are doing very well at their expense. If they fail to use risky aggressive tactics, they are surely going to lose out in social competition and have little chance of future success.[111] These generalized feelings of **relative deprivation** are precursors to high crime rates.[112]

The concept of relative deprivation was proposed by sociologists Judith Blau and Peter Blau, who combined concepts from anomie theory with those derived from social disorganization models.[113] According to the Blaus, lower-class people may feel both deprived and embittered when they compare their life circumstances to those of the more affluent. People who feel deprived because of their race or economic class eventually develop a sense of injustice and discontent. The less fortunate begin to distrust the society that has nurtured social inequality and reduced their chances of progressing by legitimate means. The constant frustration that results from these feelings of inadequacy produces pent-up aggression and hostility, eventually leading to violence and crime. The effect of inequality may be greatest when the impoverished believe that they are becoming less able to compete in a society whose balance of economic and social power is shifting further toward the already affluent. Under these conditions, the relatively poor are increasingly likely to choose illegitimate life-enhancing activities.[114] Research studies using national data sets do show a strong positive association between income inequality and violent crime, a finding that supports the relative deprivation concept. [115]

Relative deprivation is felt most acutely by African American youths because they consistently suffer racial discrimination and economic deprivation that inflict on them a lower status than that of other urban residents.[116] Wage inequality may motivate young African American males to enter the drug trade, an enterprise that increases the likelihood that they will become involved in violent crimes.[117]

In sum, according to the relative deprivation concept, people who perceive themselves as economically deprived relative to people they know, as well as to society in general, may begin to form negative self-feelings and hostility, which motivate them to engage in deviant and criminal behaviors.[118]

## General Strain Theory (GST)

Sociologist Robert Agnew's **general strain theory (GST)** helps identify the micro-level, or individual-level, influences of strain. Whereas Merton and Messner and Rosenfeld try to explain social class differences in the crime rate, Agnew tries to explain why individuals who feel stress and strain are likely to commit crimes. Agnew also offers a more general explanation of criminal activity among all elements of society, rather than restricting his views to crime among the lower socioeconomic classes.[119]

**relative deprivation**
Envy, mistrust, and aggression resulting from perceptions of economic and social inequality.

**general strain theory (GST)**
The view that multiple sources of strain interact with an individual's emotional traits and responses to produce criminality.

**FIGURE 6.2**
Elements of General Strain Theory (GST)
**Source:** © Cengage Learning

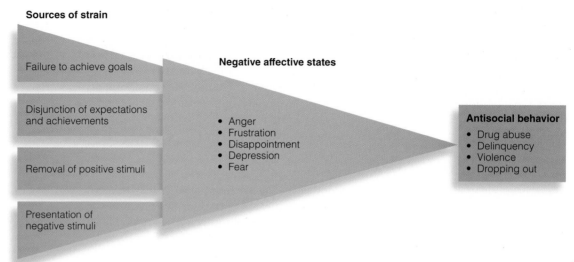

**Sources of strain**

- Failure to achieve goals
- Disjunction of expectations and achievements
- Removal of positive stimuli
- Presentation of negative stimuli

**Negative affective states**

- Anger
- Frustration
- Disappointment
- Depression
- Fear

**Antisocial behavior**

- Drug abuse
- Delinquency
- Violence
- Dropping out

**negative affective states**
Anger, frustration, and adverse emotions produced by a variety of sources of strain.

**MULTIPLE SOURCES OF STRAIN**  Agnew suggests that criminality is the direct result of **negative affective states**—the anger and frustration that emerge in the wake of destructive social relationships. He finds that negative affective states are produced by a variety of sources of strain. These are described below and summarized in Figure 6.2.

- *Failure to achieve positively valued goals.* This cause of strain, similar to what Merton speaks of in his theory of anomie, is a result of the disjunction between aspirations and expectations. This type of strain occurs when someone aspires to wealth and fame but, lacking financial and educational resources, assumes that such goals are impossible to achieve; he or she then turns to crime and drug dealing.
- *Disjunction of expectations and achievements.* Strain can also be produced by a disjunction between expectations and achievements. When people compare themselves to peers who seem to be doing a lot better financially or socially (making more money, for example, or getting better grades), even those doing relatively well feel strain. When a high school senior is accepted at a good college but not at a prestigious school, like some of her friends, she will feel strain. Perhaps she is not being treated fairly because the playing field is tilted against her: "Other kids have connections," she may say. Perceptions of inequity may result in many adverse reactions, ranging from running away from its source to lowering others' benefits through physical attacks or property vandalism.
- *Removal of positively valued stimuli.* Strain may occur because of the actual or anticipated loss of positively valued stimuli.[120] For example, the loss of a girlfriend or boyfriend can produce strain, as can the death of a loved one, or moving to a new neighborhood or school, or the divorce or separation of parents. The loss of positive stimuli may lead to delinquency as the adolescent tries to prevent the loss, retrieve what has been lost, obtain substitutes, or seek revenge against those responsible for the loss. For example, recent research by Matthew Larson and Gary Sweeten shows that both males and females increase their involvement in antisocial activities after they suffer a romantic breakup.[121]
- *Presentation of negative stimuli.* Strain may also be caused by negative or noxious stimuli, such as child abuse or neglect, crime victimization, physical punishment, family or peer conflict, school failure, or stressful life events ranging from verbal threats to air pollution.[122] The onset of delinquency has been linked to maltreatment through the rage and anger it generates. Children who are abused at home may take out their rage on younger children at school or become involved in violent delinquency.[123] Nor is the effect of negative stimuli a one-shot deal: victims who continually interact with the source of negative stimuli

(the school yard bully, the abusive parent, the demanding boss) may find that the cumulative effects of strain are overwhelming. Negative affective states experienced in childhood can follow a person to the grave.[124]

Although these sources of strain are independent of one another, they may overlap. For example, if a teacher insults a student, it may be viewed as an unfair application of negative stimuli that interferes with a student's academic aspirations. The greater the intensity and frequency of strain experiences, the greater their impact and the more likely they are to cause delinquency.

**CONSEQUENCES OF STRAIN** According to Agnew, each type of strain increases the likelihood of experiencing negative emotions such as disappointment, depression, fear, and (most important) anger. Anger increases perceptions of injury and of being wronged. It produces a desire for revenge, energizes individuals to take action, and lowers inhibitions. Violence and aggression seem justified if you have been wronged and are righteously angry. Because it produces these emotions, chronic, repetitive strain can be considered a predisposing factor for delinquency when it creates a hostile, suspicious, aggressive attitude. Individual strain episodes may trigger delinquency, such as when a particularly stressful event ignites a violent reaction.

Kids who report feelings of stress and anger are more likely to interact with delinquent peers and to engage in criminal behaviors.[125] They may join deviant groups and gangs whose law-violating activities produce even more strain and pressure to commit even more crime. For example, the angry youngster who gets involved with substance-abusing peers may feel forced to go on unwanted shoplifting sprees to pay for drugs.[126]

**COPING WITH STRAIN** Not all people who experience strain eventually resort to criminality. Some marshal their emotional, mental, and behavioral resources to cope with the anger and frustration produced by strain. Some defenses are cognitive; individuals may be able to rationalize frustrating circumstances. Not getting the career they desire is "just not that important"; they may be poor, but the "next guy is worse off"; and if things didn't work out, then they "got what they deserved." Others seek behavioral solutions: they run away from adverse conditions or seek revenge against those who caused the strain. Others will try to regain emotional equilibrium with techniques ranging from physical exercise to drug abuse. Some may change their daily routine in order to avoid the negative influences that are causing emotional duress.[127] Some people, especially those who are overly sensitive or emotional and who have an explosive temperament, low tolerance for adversity, and poor problem-solving skills, are less likely to cope well with strain.[128] As their perception of strain increases, so does their involvement in antisocial behaviors.[129]

Although these traits, which are linked to aggressive, antisocial behavior, seem to be stable over the life cycle, they may peak during adolescence.[130] This is a period of social stress caused by weakening parental supervision and the development of relationships with a diverse peer group. Many adolescents going through the trauma of family breakup and frequent changes in family structure feel a great deal of strain. They may react by becoming involved in precocious sexuality or by turning to substance abuse to mask the strain.[131]

As children mature, their expectations increase. Some are unable to meet academic and social demands. Adolescents are very concerned about their standing with peers. Teenagers who are deficient in these areas may find they are social outcasts, another source of strain. In adulthood, crime rates may drop because these sources of strain are reduced. New sources of self-esteem emerge, and adults seem more likely to align their goals with reality.

**EVALUATING GST** Agnew's important work both clarifies the concept of strain and directs future research agendas. The model has been shown to predict crime and deviance within a number of subject, racial, gender, and age groups and in different cultures and nations.[132] It also adds to the body of literature describing how social and life history events influence patterns of offending. Because sources of strain vary over the life course, so too do crime rates.

There is also empirical support for GST:[133]

- Indicators of strain—family breakup, unemployment, moving, feelings of dissatisfaction with friends and school, dropping out of school—are associated with criminality.[134]
- As predicted by GST, kids who report feelings of stress and anger are more likely to interact with delinquent peers and to engage in criminal behaviors.[135]
- Minority group members are forced to live in difficult and unique social conditions that produce strain, and they may cope with strain and negative emotions through crime.[136]
- People who perceive strain because their success goals are blocked are more likely to engage in criminal activities.[137]
- The interactions predicted by GST have cross-cultural validity. Recent research conducted in South Korea found support for an association between strain factors and involvement in criminal acts. However, some culture-based differences were found, indicating that the factors that cause damaging strain may vary by time and place.[138]

Concept Summary 6.2 reviews major concepts and theories of the strain perspective.

## Concept Summary 6.2  Strain Theories

| Theory | Major Premise | Strengths | Research Focus |
|---|---|---|---|
| **Anomie theory** | People who adopt the goals of society but lack the means to attain them seek alternatives, such as crime. | Points out how competition for success creates conflict and crime. Suggests that social conditions, and not personality, can account for crime. Explains high lower-class crime rates. | Frustration; anomie; effects of failure to achieve goals. |
| **Institutional anomie theory** | Material goods pervade all aspects of American life. | Explains why crime rates are so high in American culture. | Frustration; effects of materialism. |
| **Relative deprivation theory** | Crime occurs when the wealthy and the poor live close to one another. | Explains high crime rates in deteriorated inner-city areas located near more affluent neighborhoods. | Relative deprivation. |
| **General strain theory** | Strain has a variety of sources. Strain causes crime in the absence of adequate coping mechanisms. | Identifies the complexities of strain in modern society. Expands on anomie theory. Shows the influence of social events on behavior over the life course. Explains middle-class crimes. | Strain; inequality; negative affective states; influence of negative and positive stimuli. |

# Cultural Deviance Theory

The third branch of social structure theory combines the effects of social disorganization and strain to explain how people living in deteriorated neighborhoods react to social isolation and economic deprivation. Because their lifestyle is draining, frustrating, and dispiriting, members of the lower socioeconomic class create an independent subculture with its own set of rules and values. Whereas middle-class culture stresses hard work, delayed gratification, formal education, and being cautious, the lower-class subculture stresses excitement, toughness, taking risks, fearlessness, immediate gratification, and street smarts.

The subculture of the lower socioeconomic class is an attractive alternative because the urban poor find it impossible to meet the behavioral demands of middle-class society. However, subcultural norms often clash with conventional values. Urban dwellers must violate the law in order to obey the rules of the deviant culture with which they are in immediate contact.

**L06** List and compare the elements of cultural deviance theory.

## Focal Concerns

More than 50 years ago, sociologist Walter Miller identified the unique conduct norms that help define lower-class culture.[139] Miller referred to these norms as **focal concerns**, values that have evolved specifically to fit conditions in lower-class environments. The major lower-class focal concerns are set out in Exhibit 6.1.[140]

According to Miller, clinging to lower-class focal concerns promotes illegal or violent behavior. Toughness may mean displaying fighting prowess; street smarts may lead to drug deals; excitement may result in drinking, gambling, or drug abuse. In lower-class culture, violence helps young men such as Kaboni Savage (whose crimes are discussed in the opening vignette) acquire social power, while insulating them from becoming victims. Violence is also seen as a means to acquire the trappings of wealth (such as nice clothes, flashy cars, and access to clubs), control or humiliate another person, defy authority, settle drug-related disputes, attain retribution, satisfy the need for thrills or risk taking, and respond to challenges to one's manhood.[141] These subcultural values are handed down from one generation to the next in a process called **cultural transmission**.

**focal concerns**
Values, such as toughness and street smarts, that have evolved specifically to fit conditions in lower-class environments.

**cultural transmission**
Process whereby values, beliefs, and traditions are handed down from one generation to the next.

## Exhibit 6.1   Focal Concerns

- *Trouble.* In lower-class communities, people are evaluated by their actual or potential involvement in making trouble. Getting into trouble includes such behaviors as fighting, drinking, and sexual misconduct. Dealing with trouble can confer prestige—for example, when a man establishes a reputation for being able to handle himself well in a fight. Not being able to handle trouble, and having to pay the consequences, can make a person look foolish and incompetent.
- *Toughness.* Lower-class males want local recognition of their physical and spiritual toughness. They refuse to be sentimental or soft and instead value physical strength, fighting ability, and athletic skill. Those who cannot meet these standards risk getting a reputation for being weak, inept, and effeminate.
- *Smartness.* Members of the lower-class culture want to maintain an image of being streetwise and savvy, using their street smarts, and having the ability to outfox and out-con the opponent. Although

formal education is not admired, knowing essential survival techniques (such as gambling, conning, and outsmarting the law) is a requirement.
- *Excitement.* Members of the lower class search for fun and excitement to enliven an otherwise drab existence. The search for excitement may lead to gambling, fighting, getting drunk, and sexual adventures. In between, the lower-class citizen may simply "hang out" and "be cool."
- *Fate.* Lower-class citizens believe their lives are in the hands of strong spiritual forces that guide their destinies. Getting lucky, finding good fortune, and hitting the jackpot are the daily dreams of most slum dwellers.
- *Autonomy.* Being independent of authority figures, such as the police, teachers, and parents, is required; losing control is an unacceptable weakness, incompatible with toughness.

**Source:** Walter Miller, "Lower-Class Culture as a Generating Milieu of Gang Delinquency," *Journal of Social Issues* 14 (1958): 5–19.

# Policies and Issues in Criminology

## THE CODE OF THE STREETS

A widely cited view of the interrelationship of culture and behavior is Elijah Anderson's concept of the "code of the streets." He sees that life circumstances are tough for the "ghetto poor"—lack of jobs that pay a living wage, stigma of race, fallout from rampant drug use and drug trafficking, and alienation and lack of hope for the future. Living in such an environment places young people at special risk of crime and deviant behavior.

There are two cultural forces running through the neighborhood that shape these young people's reactions. "Decent values" are taught by families who are committed to middle-class values and to mainstream goals and standards of behavior. Although they may be better off financially than some of their street-oriented neighbors, they are generally "working poor." They value hard work and self-reliance and are willing to sacrifice for their children; they harbor hopes that their sons and daughters will achieve a better future. Most go to church and take a strong interest in education. Some see their difficult situation as a test from God and derive great support from their faith and from the church community.

"Street values," by contrast, are born in the despair of inner-city life and are in opposition to those of mainstream society. The street culture has developed what Anderson calls a code of the streets, a set of informal rules setting down both proper attitudes and ways to respond if challenged. If the rules are violated, there are penalties and sometimes violent retribution.

At the heart of the code is the issue of respect—loosely defined as being treated "right." The code demands that disrespect be punished or else hard-won respect be lost. With the right amount of respect, a person can avoid "being bothered" in public. If he is bothered, not only may he be in physical danger, but he has been disgraced or "dissed" (disrespected). Some forms of dissing, such as maintaining eye contact for too long, may seem pretty mild. But to street kids who live by the code, these actions become serious indications of the other person's intentions and a warning of imminent physical confrontation.

These two orientations—decent values and street values—socially organize the community. Their coexistence means that kids who are brought up in "decent" homes must be able to successfully navigate the demands of the "street" culture. Even in decent families, parents recognize that the code must be obeyed or, at the very least, "negotiated"; it cannot simply be ignored.

### The Respect Game

Young men in poor inner-city neighborhoods build their self-image on the foundation of respect. It is understood

---

To some criminologists, the influence of lower-class focal concerns and culture seems as relevant today as when it was first identified by Miller more than half a century ago. One of the most important statements of this culture is Elijah Anderson's "code of the streets," which is discussed in the accompanying Policies and Issues in Criminology feature.

**GANG CULTURE** The cultural deviance model assumes that kids will be drawn to the culture of the gang. Adolescents who feel alienated from the normative culture can find a home in the gang. In a disorganized area, gangs are a stable community feature rather than a force of disruption. Gang membership has appeal to adolescents who are alienated from their families as well as the mainstream of society. It is not surprising that kids who have had problems with the law and suffer juvenile justice processing are more likely to join gangs than nonstigmatized kids.[142]

Joining a gang is a type of turning point that changes the direction of people's lives. Gang membership portends a substantial change in emotions, attitudes, and social controls conducive to criminality.[143] The more embedded a boy becomes in the gang and its processes, the less likely he is to leave. When David Pyrooz and his research team interviewed gang members, they found that most of the less involved gang boys leave within six months of their first gang contact, while more involved

that those who have "juice" (as respect is sometimes called on the street) can take care of themselves, even if it means resorting to violence. For street youths, losing respect on the street can be damaging and dangerous. Once they have demonstrated that they can be insulted, beaten up, or stolen from, they become an easy target. Kids from decent families may be able to keep their self-respect by getting good grades or a scholarship. Street kids do not have that luxury. With nothing to fall back on, they cannot walk away from an insult. They must retaliate with violence.

The code of the street concept has been verified by a number of research efforts. Eric Stewart and Ronald Simons have conducted empirical research that supports Anderson's observations. They find that there is a link between living in a deteriorated neighborhood, family values, and adopting the code of the street, and those who adopt the code are more likely to engage in violent behaviors. Moreover, the code is so powerful that adolescents who live in areas where the code of the street is widely accepted are more likely to conform to the code even if it violates their own personal values and attitudes.

In one recent study (2012), Kristy Matsuda and her associates found that kids who join a gang also increase their street code–related attitudes and emotions. Those whose loyalty to the code of the streets is the greatest also experience the greatest frequency of violent offending.

## Critical Thinking

According to the code, one method of preventing attacks is to go on the offensive. Aggressive, violence-prone people are not seen as "easy prey." Robbers do not get robbed, and street fighters are not the favorite targets of bullies. A youth who communicates an image of not being afraid to die and not being afraid to kill has given himself a sense of power on the street. Did a similar code exist in your neighborhood or high school? Did going on the offensive prevent someone from being bullied?

**Sources:** Elijah Anderson, *Code of the Street: Decency, Violence, and the Moral Life of the Inner City* (New York: Norton, 2000); Eric Stewart and Ronald Simons, "Race, Code of the Street, and Violent Delinquency: A Multilevel Investigation of Neighborhood Street Culture and Individual Norms of Violence," *Criminology* 482 (2010): 569–606; Eric Stewart and Ronald Simons, "Structure and Culture in African American Adolescent Violence: A Partial Test of the 'Code of the Street' Thesis," *Justice Quarterly* 23 (2006): 1–33; Kristy N. Matsuda, Chris Melde, Terrance J. Taylor, Adrienne Freng, and Finn-Aage Esbensen, "Gang Membership and Adherence to the "Code of the Street," *Justice Quarterly*, first published online May 8, 2012; Timothy Brezina, Robert Agnew, Francis T. Cullen, and John Paul Wright, "The Code of the Street: A Quantitative Assessment of Elijah Anderson's Subculture of Violence Thesis and Its Contribution to Youth Violence Research," *Youth Violence and Juvenile Justice* 2 (2004): 303–328.

kids stay at least two more years.[144] Similarly, Pyrooz found that gang membership can have a significant effect on critical life domains: youth who join gangs are 30 percent less likely to graduate from high school and 58 percent less likely to earn a four-year degree than a matched sample of non-gang peers. The effects of gang membership on educational attainment begin within one year of joining; gang membership's influence is both quick and long lasting.[145]

## Theory of Delinquent Subculture

Albert Cohen first articulated the theory of **delinquent subculture** in his classic 1955 book *Delinquent Boys*.[146] Cohen's central argument was that delinquent behavior of lower-class youths is actually a protest against the norms and values of middle-class U.S. culture. Because social conditions prevent them from achieving success legitimately, lower-class youths experience a form of culture conflict that Cohen labels **status frustration**.[147] As a result, many of them join gangs and engage in behavior that is "non-utilitarian, malicious, and negativistic."[148]

Cohen viewed the delinquent gang as a separate subculture possessing a value system directly opposed to that of the larger society. He described the subculture as one that "takes its norms from the larger culture, but turns them upside down.

**delinquent subculture**
A value system adopted by lower-class youths that is directly opposed to that of the larger society.

**status frustration**
A form of culture conflict experienced by lower-class youths because social conditions prevent them from achieving success as defined by the larger society.

AP Images/Charles Dharapak

Community programs have been aimed at improving neighborhood climate in order to counteract negative subcultural forces. Here, children get off a bus in front of the headquarters for the DC Promise Neighborhood Initiative (DCPNI), which provides afterschool programs in the Kenilworth-Parkside neighborhood of Washington. Backed by a multiyear $28 million Education Department grant, DCPNI vows to tackle generational poverty with a fresh approach: if a parent's level of education improves, so do a child's prospects. In Kenilworth-Parkside, helping the children get a good education is a primary focus, but it's the adults they must first engage.

**middle-class measuring rods** The standards by which authority figures, such as teachers and employers, evaluate lower-class youngsters and often prejudge them negatively.

The delinquent's conduct is right by the standards of his subculture precisely because it is wrong by the norms of the larger culture."[149]

According to Cohen, the development of the delinquent subculture is a consequence of socialization practices in lower-class environments. Here children lack the basic skills necessary to achieve social and economic success, including a proper education, which renders them incapable of developing the skills they need to succeed in society. Lower-class parents are incapable of teaching children the necessary techniques for entering the dominant middle-class culture. The consequences of this deprivation include developmental handicaps, poor speech and communication skills, and inability to delay gratification.

**MIDDLE-CLASS MEASURING RODS** One significant handicap that lower-class children face is the inability to positively impress authority figures, such as teachers, employers, or supervisors. In U.S. society, these positions tend to be held by members of the middle class, who have difficulty relating to the lower-class youngster. Cohen calls the standards set by these authority figures **middle-class measuring rods**.

The conflict and frustration that lower-class youths experience when they fail to meet these standards is a primary cause of delinquency. They may find themselves prejudged by others and not measuring up in the final analysis. Negative evaluations become part of a permanent "file" that follows an individual for the rest of his or her life. When the individual wants to improve, evidence of prior failures is used to discourage advancement.

**FORMATION OF DEVIANT SUBCULTURES** Cohen believes that lower-class boys rejected by middle-class decision makers usually join one of three existing subcultures: the corner boy, the college boy, or the delinquent boy.

The "corner boy" role is the most common response to middle-class rejection. The corner boy is not a chronic delinquent but may be a truant who engages in petty or status offenses, such as precocious sex and recreational drug abuse. His main loyalty is to his peer group, on which he depends for support, motivation, and interest. His values, therefore, are those of the group with which he is in close contact. The corner boy, well aware of his failure to achieve the standards of the American Dream, retreats into the comforting world of his lower-class peers and eventually becomes a stable member of his neighborhood, holding a menial job, marrying, and remaining in the community.

The "college boy" embraces the cultural and social values of the middle class. Rather than scorning middle-class measuring rods, he actively strives to succeed by those standards. Cohen views this type of youth as one who is embarking on an almost hopeless path because he is ill-equipped academically, socially, and linguistically to achieve the rewards of middle-class life.

The "delinquent boy" adopts a set of norms and principles that directly oppose middle-class values. He engages in short-run hedonism, living for today and letting "tomorrow take care of itself."[150] Delinquent boys strive for group autonomy. They resist efforts by family, school, or other sources of authority to control their behavior. Frustrated by their inability to succeed, these boys resort to a process to which Cohen attaches the psychoanalytic term **reaction formation**. This process includes overly intense responses that seem disproportionate to the stimuli that trigger them. For the delinquent boy, this takes the form of irrational, malicious, and unaccountable hostility to the enemy, which in this case is "the norms of respectable middle-class society."[151]

Cohen's approach skillfully integrates strain and social disorganization theories and has become an enduring element of criminological literature.

## Theory of Differential Opportunity

In their classic 1960 work *Delinquency and Opportunity*, Richard Cloward and Lloyd Ohlin combined strain and social disorganization principles to portray a gang-sustaining criminal subculture.[152] The centerpiece of Cloward and Ohlin's theory is **differential opportunity**. According to this concept, people in all strata of society share the same success goals; however, those in the lower socioeconomic class have limited means of achieving them. People who perceive themselves as failures within conventional society will seek alternative or innovative ways to succeed. People who conclude that there is little hope for legitimate advancement may join like-minded peers to form a gang, which can provide them with emotional support. The youth who is considered a failure at school and is qualified for only a menial job at the minimum wage can earn thousands of dollars, plus the respect of his or her peers, by joining a gang and taking part in drug deals or armed robberies.

Cloward and Ohlin recognize that the opportunity for success in both conventional and criminal careers is limited. In stable areas, adolescents may be recruited by professional criminals, drug traffickers, or organized crime groups. Unstable areas, however, cannot support flourishing criminal opportunities. In these socially disorganized neighborhoods, adult role models are absent, and young criminals have few opportunities to join established gangs or learn the fine points of professional crime. Their most important finding, then, is that all opportunities for success, both illegal and conventional, are closed for the most disadvantaged youths. Because of differential opportunity, young people are likely to join one of three types of gangs:

- *Criminal gangs*. These gangs exist in stable neighborhoods where close connections among adolescent, young adult, and adult offenders create an environment for successful criminal enterprise.[153] Youths are recruited into established criminal gangs that provide training for a successful criminal career. Gang membership is a learning experience in which the knowledge and skills needed for success in crime are acquired. During this apprenticeship, older, more experienced members of the criminal subculture hold youthful trainees on tight reins, limiting activities that might jeopardize the gang's profits (for example, engaging in nonfunctional, irrational violence).
- *Conflict gangs*. These gangs develop in communities unable to provide either legitimate or illegitimate opportunities.[154] They attract tough adolescents who fight with weapons to win respect from rivals and engage in unpredictable and destructive assaults on people and property. Conflict gang members must be ready to fight to protect their own and their gang's integrity and honor. By doing so, they acquire a "rep," which gains them admiration from their peers and consequently helps them buttress their self-image.
- *Retreatist gangs*. Retreatists are double failures, unable to gain success through legitimate means and unwilling to do so through illegal ones. Members of the retreatist subculture constantly search for ways of getting high—alcohol, pot, heroin, unusual sexual experiences, music. To feed their habits, retreatists develop a "hustle"—pimping, conning, selling drugs, or committing petty crimes. Personal status in the retreatist subculture is derived from peer approval.

**reaction formation**
Irrational hostility evidenced by young delinquents, who adopt norms directly opposed to middle-class goals and standards that seem impossible to achieve.

**differential opportunity**
The view that lower-class youths, whose legitimate opportunities are limited, join gangs and pursue criminal careers as alternative means to achieve universal success goals.

## Concept Summary 6.3   Cultural Deviance Theories

| Theory | Major Premise | Strengths | Research Focus |
|---|---|---|---|
| **Miller's focal concern theory** | Citizens who obey the street rules of lower-class life (focal concerns) find themselves in conflict with the dominant culture. | Identifies the core values of lower-class culture and shows their association to crime. | Cultural norms; focal concerns. |
| **Cohen's theory of delinquent subculture** | Status frustration of lower-class boys, created by their failure to achieve middle-class success, causes them to join gangs. | Shows how the conditions of lower-class life produce crime. Explains violence and destructive acts. Identifies conflict of lower class with middle class. | Gangs; culture conflict; middle-class measuring rods; reaction formation. |
| **Cloward and Ohlin's theory of opportunity** | Blockage of conventional opportunities causes lower-class youths to join criminal, conflict, or retreatist gangs. | Shows that even illegal opportunities are structured in society. Indicates why people become involved in a particular type of criminal activity. Presents a way of preventing crime. | Gangs; cultural norms; culture conflict; effects of blocked opportunity. |

Cloward and Ohlin's theory integrates cultural deviance and social disorganization variables and recognizes different modes of criminal adaptation. The fact that criminal cultures can be supportive, rational, and profitable seems to reflect the actual world of the delinquent more realistically than Cohen's original view of purely negativistic, destructive delinquent youths who reject all social values. Concept Summary 6.3 reviews the major concepts of cultural deviance theory.

## Social Structure Theory and Public Policy

Social structure theory has significantly influenced public policy. If the cause of criminality is viewed as a schism between lower-class individuals and conventional goals, norms, and rules, it seems logical that alternatives to criminal behavior can be provided by giving inner-city youth opportunities to share in the rewards of conventional society.

One approach is to give indigent people direct financial aid through public assistance or welfare. Although welfare has been curtailed under the Federal Welfare Reform Act of 1996, research shows that crime rates decrease when families receive supplemental income through public assistance payments.[155]

Efforts have also been made to reduce crime by improving the community structure in inner-city high-crime areas. Crime prevention efforts based on social structure

# Policies and Issues in Criminology

## G.R.E.A.T. (GANG RESISTANCE, EDUCATION, AND TRAINING)

The G.R.E.A.T. (Gang Resistance, Education, and Training) program is a school-based, law enforcement officer–instructed classroom curriculum. The program is aimed at preventing delinquency, youth violence, and gang membership by partnering police and schools.

G.R.E.A.T. was first developed among a number of Arizona police departments in an effort to reduce adolescent involvement in criminal behavior. Today the program can be found in all 50 states and the District of Columbia. The program has three stated goals: (1) to reduce gang membership, (2) to reduce delinquency, especially violent offending, and (3) to improve students' attitudes toward the police.

Trained police officers administer the program in school classrooms about once a week. The program consists of four components: a 13-week middle school curriculum, a 6-week elementary school curriculum, a summer program, and family training. The course is designed to

- Provide children with the skills necessary to combat the stresses that set the stage for gang involvement.
- Provide children with accurate knowledge about gang involvement.
- Provide children with the skills necessary to resolve conflicts peacefully.
- Help children understand the need to set realistic goals.

Early evaluations of G.R.E.A.T. show that students who completed the curriculum developed more prosocial attitudes and had lower rates of gang membership and delinquency than those in a comparison group who were not exposed to G.R.E.A.T.; however, the reduction in gang activity was less than expected or desired.

As a result of these mixed reviews, in 2006 the program was revamped. More recent evaluations found that G.R.E.A.T. students self-reported more positive attitudes to police, less positive attitudes about gangs, more use of refusal skills, more resistance to peer pressure, lower rates of gang membership, and lower rates of delinquency. Most importantly, analyses of one-year post-treatment data indicate that students receiving the program had lower odds of gang membership compared to a control group made up of students who did not participate in the program.

### Critical Thinking

Is it possible that a course taught in school by police officers can really convince kids not to join gangs? Are you comfortable with the results showing the program really does work?

**Sources:** Finn-Aage Esbensen, Dana Peterson, Terrance Taylor, and D. Wayne Osgood, "Results from a Multi-Site Evaluation of the G.R.E.A.T. Program," *Justice Quarterly* 29 (2012): 125–151. Finn-Aage Esbensen, Dana Peterson, Terrance Taylor, Adrienne Freng, D. Wayne Osgood, Dena Carson, and Kristy Matsuda. "Evaluation and Evolution of the Gang Resistance Education and Training (G.R.E.A.T.) Program," *Journal of School Violence* 10 (2011): 53–70; Finn-Aage Esbensen, Kristy Matsuda, Terrance J. Taylor, and Dana Peterson, "Multi-method Strategy for Assessing Program Fidelity: The National Evaluation of the Revised G.R.E.A.T. Program," *Evaluation Review* 35 (2011): 14–39; National Institute of Justice, *Preliminary Short-Term Results from the Evaluation of the G.R.E.A.T. Program* (Washington, DC: U.S. Department of Justice, National Institute of Justice, 2009).

precepts can be traced back to the Chicago Area Project supervised by Clifford Shaw. This program attempted to organize existing community structures to develop social stability in otherwise disorganized slums. The project sponsored recreation programs for neighborhood children, including summer camping. It campaigned for community improvements in education, sanitation, traffic safety, resource conservation, and law enforcement. Project members also worked with police and court agencies to supervise and treat gang youth and adult offenders.

Social structure concepts, especially Cloward and Ohlin's views, were a critical ingredient in the Kennedy and Johnson administrations' War on Poverty, begun in the early 1960s. War on Poverty programs—Head Start, Neighborhood Legal Services, and the Community Action Program—have continued to help people. Another similar program, called Weed and Seed, involved a two-pronged approach: law enforcement agencies and prosecutors cooperated in "weeding out" violent criminals and drug abusers, and public agencies and community-based private organizations collaborated to "seed" much-needed human services, including prevention, intervention, treatment, and neighborhood restoration programs.[156] However, most funding for this program ended in 2012.

Another approach is the Communities That Care (CTC) model, a national program that emphasizes the reduction of risk factors and the enhancement of protective factors against crime and delinquency. One example of the CTC approach is Project COPE, which serves the Lynn, Massachusetts, area. Established in 2004, COPE works collaboratively with multiple local agencies, including Girls Incorporated of Lynn, the city's health department, police department, public schools, and other agencies whose goals include reducing risk factors for youth and promoting healthy family and neighborhood development. The coalition includes a large and active youth subcommittee. Originally focused on substance abuse prevention in youth, the coalition expanded its initiatives to include the prevention of fatal and nonfatal opiate overdoses, teen suicide, teen pregnancy, bullying and violence, and obesity. Project COPE cares for individuals of all ages. As an advocate for individuals needing specialized services, COPE assumes the responsibility for leadership in developing new and creative programs and addressing the needs of the many populations it serves.[157] In 2014, COPE merged with Bridgewell, a larger service organization that provides residential services, day habilitation, behavioral health services, employment training, transitional homeless services, affordable housing, and substance abuse and addiction services.

Some programs based on a social structure motif engage existing community institutions such as schools, police, and religious institutions in an effort to help kids see and access legitimate growth opportunities. One such program is examined in the Polices and Issues in Criminology feature.

# Thinking Like a Criminologist

**Mean Streets**  You have accepted a position in Washington as an assistant to the undersecretary of urban affairs. The undersecretary informs you that he wants to initiate a demonstration project in a major city to show that government can reduce poverty, crime, and drug abuse.

The area he has chosen is a large inner-city neighborhood in a midwestern city of more than 3 million people. It suffers disorganized community structure, poverty, and hopelessness. Predatory delinquent gangs run free, terrorizing local merchants and citizens. The school system has failed to provide opportunities and educational experiences sufficient to dampen enthusiasm for gang recruitment. Stores, homes, and public buildings are deteriorated and decayed. Commercial enterprise has fled the area, and civil servants are reluctant to enter the neighborhood. There is an uneasy truce among the varied ethnic and racial groups that populate the area. Residents feel that little can be done to bring the neighborhood back to life. Merchants are afraid to open stores, and there is little outside development from major retailers or manufacturers. People who want to start their own businesses find that banks will not lend them money.

One of the biggest problems has been the large housing projects built in the 1960s. These are now overcrowded and deteriorated. Police are actually afraid to enter the buildings unless they arrive with a SWAT team. Each building is controlled by a gang whose members demand tribute from the residents.

## Writing Assignment

Write a proposal outlining a redevelopment program to revitalize the area and eventually bring down the crime rate. In your essay, describe how the public or private sector can help with this overwhelming problem. Discuss how private industry can help in the struggle. What programs would you recommend to break the cycle of urban poverty?

# SUMMARY

**LO1  Describe the association between social structure and crime.**

According to social structure theory, the root cause of crime is the socioeconomic disadvantages that have become embedded in American society. People in the lower class are driven to desperate measures, such as crime and substance abuse, to cope with their economic plight. Aggravating this dynamic is the constant media bombardment linking material possessions to self-worth.

**LO2  Identify the elements of social disorganization theory.**

This theory focuses on the urban conditions that affect crime rates. Crime occurs in disorganized areas where institutions of social control, such as the family, commercial establishments, and schools, have broken down and can no longer perform their expected or stated functions. Indicators of social disorganization include high unemployment and school dropout rates, deteriorated housing, low income levels, and large numbers of single-parent households. Residents in these areas experience conflict and despair, and as a result, antisocial behavior flourishes.

**LO3  Explain the views of Shaw and McKay.**

Shaw and McKay explained crime and delinquency within the context of the changing urban environment and ecological development of the city. Poverty-ridden transitional neighborhoods suffer high rates of population turnover and often cannot induce residents to remain and defend the neighborhoods against criminal groups. The values that slum youths adopt often conflict with existing middle-class norms, which demand strict obedience to the legal code. Consequently, a value conflict further separates the delinquent youth and his or her peer group from conventional society; the result is a more solid embrace of deviant goals and behavior.

**LO4  Differentiate between the various elements of ecological theory.**

Crime rates and the need for police services are associated with community deterioration: disorder, poverty, alienation, disassociation, and fear of crime. In larger cities, neighborhoods with a high percentage of deserted houses and apartments experience high crime rates. As fear increases, quality of life deteriorates. People who live in neighborhoods that experience high levels of crime and civil disorder become suspicious, distrust authorities, and may develop a "siege mentality." As areas decline, residents flee to safer, more stable localities.

**LO5  Discuss the concept of strain.**

Strain theorists argue that although people in all economic strata share similar social and economic goals, the ability to obtain these goals is class dependent. Most people in the United States desire wealth, material possessions, power, prestige, and other life comforts. Members of the lower class are unable to obtain these symbols of success through conventional means. Consequently, they feel anger, frustration, and resentment, referred to collectively as strain. To resolve the goals–means conflict and relieve their sense of strain, some people innovate by stealing or extorting money; others retreat into drugs and alcohol; some rebel by joining revolutionary groups; and still others get involved in ritualistic behavior by joining a religious cult.

**LO6  List and compare the elements of cultural deviance theory.**

Cultural deviance theory combines elements of both strain theory and social disorganization theory. A unique lower-class culture has developed in disorganized neighborhoods. These independent subcultures maintain unique values and beliefs that conflict with conventional social norms. Criminal behavior is an expression of conformity to lower-class subcultural values and traditions, not a rebellion from conventional society. Subcultural values are handed down from one generation to the next in a process called cultural transmission.

## Key Terms

stratified society 160
social classes 160
culture of poverty 160
underclass 161
social structure
     theory 162
social disorganization
     theory 164
strain theory 164
strain 164

cultural deviance
     theory 164
subculture 164
transitional
     neighborhood 165
social ecology
     school 166
concentration effect 169
collective efficacy 169
street efficacy 171

anomie theory 173
institutional anomie
     theory (IAT) 174
American Dream 174
relative deprivation 175
general strain theory
     (GST) 175
negative affective
     states 176
focal concerns 179

cultural
     transmission 179
delinquent
     subculture 181
status frustration 181
middle-class
     measuring rods 182
reaction formation 183
differential
     opportunity 183

## Critical Thinking Questions

1. Is there a "transitional" area in your town or city? Does the crime rate remain constant there, regardless of who moves in or out?

2. Is it possible that a distinct lower-class culture exists? Do you know anyone who has the focal concerns Miller talks about? Were there "focal concerns" in your high school or college experience?

3. Have you ever perceived anomie in your own life? How did you cope with these feelings

4. How would Merton explain middle-class crime? How would Agnew?

5. Could "relative deprivation" produce crime among college-educated white-collar workers?

## Notes

*All URLs accessed in 2015.*

1. Federal Bureau of Investigation, "Extreme Case of Witness Intimidation Justice for Six Slain Victims in Philadelphia," January 15, 2015, www.fbi.gov/news /stories/2015/january/extreme-case-of-witness -intimidation/extreme-case-of-witness-intimidation; George Anastasia, "As Witness Intimidation Case Drags On, Haunting Memories Remain," *Philadelphia Citypaper*, September 19, 2013, citypaper.net/News /As-witness-intimidation-case-drags-on-haunting -memories-remain/.

2. David Pyrooz, "Structural Covariates of Gang Homicide in Large U.S. Cities," *Journal of Research in Crime and Delinquency*, first published online on August 17, 2011.

3. Steven Messner and Richard Rosenfeld, *Crime and the American Dream* (Belmont, CA: Wadsworth, 1994), p. 11.

4. Sara Thompson and Rosemary Gartner, "The Spatial Distribution and Social Context of Homicide in Toronto's Neighborhoods," *Journal of Research in Crime and Delinquency* 51 (2014): 88–118.

5. U.S. Census Bureau, "Poverty," www.census.gov /hhes/www/poverty/about/overview/.

6. Phil DeMuth, "Are You Rich Enough? The Terrible Tragedy of Income Inequality Among the 1%," *Forbes Magazine*, November 25, 2013, www.forbes.com/sites /phildemuth/2013/11/25/are-you-rich-enough-the -terrible-tragedy-of-income-inequality-among-the-1/.

7. Oscar Lewis, "The Culture of Poverty," *Scientific American* 215 (1966): 19–25.

8. Gunnar Myrdal, *The Challenge of World Poverty* (New York: Vintage Books, 1970).

9. Jeanne Brooks-Gunn and Greg J. Duncan, "The Effects of Poverty on Children," *Future of Children* 7 (1997): 34–39.

10. National Center for Children in Poverty (NCCP), *Child Poverty, 2015*, www.nccp.org/publications/pub_1100 .html.

11. Ibid.

12. National Center on Family Homelessness, "America's Youngest Outcasts," www.homelesschildrenamerica .org.

13. Greg Duncan, W. Jean Yeung, Jeanne Brooks-Gunn, and Judith Smith, "How Much Does Childhood Poverty Affect the Life Chances of Children?" *American Sociological Review* 63 (1998): 406–423.

14. Maria Velez, Lauren Krivo, and Ruth Peterson, "Structural Inequality and Homicide: An Assessment of the Black-White Gap in Killings," *Criminology* 41 (2003): 645–672.

15. U.S. Department of Census Data, "Poverty Main," www.census.gov/hhes/www/poverty/.

16. U.S. Department of Health and Human Services, "African Americans," minorityhealth.hhs.gov/omh/browse.aspx?lvl=3&lvlid=61.

17. National Center for Education Statistics, *The Condition of Education 2014* (NCES 2014-083), Status Dropout Rates, nces.ed.gov/fastfacts/display.asp?id=16.

18. James Ainsworth-Darnell and Douglas Downey, "Assessing the Oppositional Culture Explanation for Racial/Ethnic Differences in School Performances," *American Sociological Review* 63 (1998): 536–553.

19. Jonathan Crane, "The Epidemic Theory of Ghettos and Neighborhood Effects on Dropping Out and Teenage Childbearing," *American Journal of Sociology* 96 (1991): 1226–1259; see also Rodrick Wallace, "Expanding Coupled Shock Fronts of Urban Decay and Criminal Behavior: How U.S. Cities Are Becoming 'Hollowed Out,'" *Journal of Quantitative Criminology* 7 (1991): 333–355.

20. Barbara Warner, "The Role of Attenuated Culture in Social Disorganization Theory," *Criminology* 41 (2003): 73–97.

21. April Zeoli, Jesenia Pizarro, Sue Grady, and Christopher Melde, "Homicide as Infectious Disease: Using Public Health Methods to Investigate the Diffusion of Homicide," *Justice Quarterly* 31 (2014): 609–632; Jeffrey Fagan and Garth Davies, "The Natural History of Neighborhood Violence," *Journal of Contemporary Criminal Justice* 20 (2004): 127–147.

22. Justin Patchin, Beth Huebner, John McCluskey, Sean Varano, and Timothy Bynum, "Exposure to Community Violence and Childhood Delinquency," *Crime and Delinquency* 52 (2006): 307–332.

23. For a classic look, see Frederick Thrasher, *The Gang* (Chicago: University of Chicago Press, 1927).

24. Dana Haynie, Eric Silver, and Brent Teasdale, "Neighborhood Characteristics, Peer Networks, and Adolescent Violence," *Journal of Quantitative Criminology* 22 (2006): 147–169.

25. Office of National Drug Control Policy, "Teens, Drugs and Violence," June 2007, www.hsdl.org/?view&did=477440.

26. John Hipp, "Spreading the Wealth: The Effect of the Distribution of Income and Race/Ethnicity Across Households and Neighborhoods on City Crime Trajectories," *Criminology* 49 (2011): 631–665; Julie A. Phillips, "White, Black, and Latino Homicide Rates: Why the Difference?" *Social Problems* 49 (2002): 349–374.

27. See Ruth Kornhauser, *Social Sources of Delinquency* (Chicago: University of Chicago Press, 1978), p. 75.

28. Kerryn E. Bell, "Gender and Gangs: A Quantitative Comparison," *Crime and Delinquency* 55 (2009): 363–387.

29. National Gang Center (NGC), "Measuring the Extent of Gang Problems," National Youth Gang Survey Analysis, www.nationalgangcenter.gov/Survey-Analysis/Measuring-the-Extent-of-Gang-Problems#estimatednumbergangs

30. Clifford R. Shaw and Henry D. McKay, *Juvenile Delinquency and Urban Areas,* rev. ed. (Chicago: University of Chicago Press, 1972).

31. Ibid., p. 52.

32. Ibid., p. 171.

33. Claire Valier, "Foreigners, Crime and Changing Mobilities," *British Journal of Criminology* 43 (2003): 1–21.

34. For a general review, see James Byrne and Robert Sampson, eds., *The Social Ecology of Crime* (New York: Springer Verlag, 1985).

35. See, generally, Robert Bursik, "Social Disorganization and Theories of Crime and Delinquency: Problems and Prospects," *Criminology* 26 (1988): 521–539.

36. D. Wayne Osgood and Jeff Chambers, "Social Disorganization Outside the Metropolis: An Analysis of Rural Youth Violence," *Criminology* 38 (2000): 81–117.

37. William Spelman, "Abandoned Buildings: Magnets for Crime?" *Journal of Criminal Justice* 21 (1993): 481–493.

38. Keith Harries and Andrea Powell, "Juvenile Gun Crime and Social Stress: Baltimore, 1980–1990," *Urban Geography* 15 (1994): 45–63.

39. Ellen Kurtz, Barbara Koons, and Ralph Taylor, "Land Use, Physical Deterioration, Resident-Based Control, and Calls for Service on Urban Streetblocks," *Justice Quarterly* 15 (1998): 121–149.

40. Marc Swatt, Sean Varano, Craig Uchida, and Shellie Solomon, "Fear of Crime, Incivilities, and Collective Efficacy in Four Miami Neighborhoods," *Journal of Criminal Justice* 41 (2013): 1–11; Matthew Lee and Terri Earnest, "Perceived Community Cohesion and Perceived Risk of Victimization: A Cross-National Analysis," *Justice Quarterly* 20 (2003): 131–158.

41. Pamela Wilcox, Neil Quisenberry, and Shayne Jones, "The Built Environment and Community Crime Risk Interpretation," *Journal of Research in Crime and Delinquency* 40 (2003): 322–345.

42. Yili Xu, Mora Fiedler, and Karl Flaming, "Discovering the Impact of Community Policing: The Broken Windows Thesis, Collective Efficacy, and Citizens' Judgment," *Journal of Research in Crime and Delinquency* 42 (2005): 147–186.

43. Michael Hanslmaier, "Crime, Fear and Subjective Well-Being: How Victimization and Street Crime Affect Fear and Life Satisfaction," *European Journal of Criminology* 10 (2013): 515–533.

44. Wendy Kilewer, "The Role of Neighborhood Collective Efficacy and Fear of Crime in Socialization of Coping with Violence in Low-Income Communities," *Journal of Community Psychology* 41 (2013): 920–930; Danielle Wallace, "A Test of the Routine Activities and Neighborhood Attachment Explanations for Bias in Disorder Perceptions," *Crime and Delinquency,* first published online December 7, 2011.

45. Michele Roccato, Silvia Russo, and Alessio Vieno, "Perceived Community Disorder Moderates the

Relation Between Victimization and Fear of Crime," *Journal of Community Psychology* 39 (2011): 884–888.

46. C. L. Storr, C. Y. Chen, and J. C. Anthony, "'Unequal Opportunity': Neighborhood Disadvantage and the Chance to Buy Illegal Drugs," *Journal of Epidemiology and Community Health* 58 (2004): 231–238.

47. Pamela Wilcox Rountree and Kenneth Land, "Burglary Victimization, Perceptions of Crime Risk, and Routine Activities: A Multilevel Analysis Across Seattle Neighborhoods and Census Tracts," *Journal of Research in Crime and Delinquency* 33 (1996): 147–180.

48. Ted Chiricos, Ranee McEntire, and Marc Gertz, "Social Problems, Perceived Racial and Ethnic Composition of Neighborhood and Perceived Risk of Crime," *Social Problems* 48 (2001): 322–341; Wesley Skogan, "Fear of Crime and Neighborhood Change," in *Communities and Crime*, ed. Albert Reiss and Michael Tonry (Chicago: University of Chicago Press, 1986), pp. 191–232.

49. Catherine E. Ross, John Mirowsky, and Shana Pribesh, "Powerlessness and the Amplification of Threat: Neighborhood Disadvantage, Disorder, and Mistrust," *American Sociological Review* 66 (2001): 568–580.

50. Jodi Lane and James Meeker, "*Social Disorganization* Perceptions, Fear of Gang Crime, and Behavioral Precautions Among Whites, Latinos, and Vietnamese," *Journal of Criminal Justice* 32 (2004): 49–62.

51. John Hagan, Carla Shedd, and Monique Payne, "Race, Ethnicity, and Youth Perceptions of Criminal Injustice," *American Sociological Review* 70 (2005): 381–407.

52. Jane Sprott and Anthony Doob, "The Effect of Urban Neighborhood Disorder on Evaluations of the Police and Courts," *Crime and Delinquency* 55 (2009): 339–362.

53. Bradley Smith, "Structural and Organizational Predictors of Homicide by Police," *Policing: An International Journal of Police Strategies and Management* 27 (2004): 539–557; William Terrill and Michael Reisig, "Neighborhood Context and Police Use of Force," *Journal of Research in Crime and Delinquency* 40 (2003): 291–321.

54. Finn-Aage Esbensen and David Huizinga, "Community Structure and Drug Use: From a Social Disorganization Perspective," *Justice Quarterly* 7 (1990): 691–709.

55. Karen Parker, Brian Stults, and Stephen Rice, "Racial Threat, Concentrated Disadvantage, and Social Control: Considering the Macro-Level Sources of Variation in Arrests," *Criminology* 43 (2005): 1111–1134.

56. Bridget Freisthler, Elizabeth Lascala, Paul Gruenewald, and Andrew Treno, "An Examination of Drug Activity: Effects of Neighborhood Social Organization on the Development of Drug Distribution Systems," *Substance Use and Misuse* 40 (2005): 671–686.

57. Micere Keels, Greg Duncan, Stefanie Deluca, Ruby Mendenhall, and James Rosenbaum, "Fifteen Years Later: Can Residential Mobility Programs Provide a Long-Term Escape from Neighborhood Segregation, Crime, and Poverty?" *Demography* 42 (2005): 51–72.

58. Allen Liska and Paul Bellair, "Violent-Crime Rates and Racial Composition: Convergence over Time," *American Journal of Sociology* 101 (1995): 578–610.

59. Patricia McCall and Karen Parker, "A Dynamic Model of Racial Competition, Racial Inequality, and Interracial Violence," *Sociological Inquiry* 75 (2005): 273–294.

60. Steven Barkan and Steven Cohn, "Why Whites Favor Spending More Money to Fight Crime: The Role of Racial Prejudice," *Social Problems* 52 (2005): 300–314.

61. Leo Scheurman and Solomon Kobrin, "Community Careers in Crime," in *Communities and Crime*, ed. Reiss and Tonry, pp. 67–100.

62. Ibid.

63. Paul Stretesky, Amie Schuck, and Michael Hogan, "Space Matters: An Analysis of Poverty, Poverty Clustering, and Violent Crime," *Justice Quarterly* 21 (2004): 817–841.

64. Gregory Squires and Charis Kubrin, "Privileged Places: Race, Uneven Development and the Geography of Opportunity in Urban America," *Urban Studies* 42 (2005): 47–68; Matthew Lee, Michael Maume, and Graham Ousey, "Social Isolation and Lethal Violence Across the Metro/Nonmetro Divide: The Effects of Socioeconomic Disadvantage and Poverty Concentration on Homicide," *Rural Sociology* 68 (2003): 107–131.

65. Lee, Maume, and Ousey, "Social Isolation and Lethal Violence Across the Metro/Nonmetro Divide"; Charis E. Kubrin, "Structural Covariates of Homicide Rates: Does Type of Homicide Matter?" *Journal of Research in Crime and Delinquency* 40 (2003): 139–170; Darrell Steffensmeier and Dana Haynie, "Gender, Structural Disadvantage, and Urban Crime: Do Macrosocial Variables Also Explain Female Offending Rates?" *Criminology* 38 (2000): 403–438.

66. Kyle Crowder and Scott South, "Spatial Dynamics of White Flight: The Effects of Local and Extralocal Racial Conditions on Neighborhood Out-Migration," *American Sociological Review* 73 (2008): 792–812.

67. Paul Jargowsky and Yoonhwan Park, "Cause or Consequence? Suburbanization and Crime in U.S. Metropolitan Areas," *Crime and Delinquency* 55 (2009): 28–50.

68. Jeffrey Morenoff, Robert Sampson, and Stephen Raudenbush, "Neighborhood Inequality, Collective Efficacy, and the Spatial Dynamics of Urban Violence," *Criminology* 39 (2001): 517–560.

69. Scott Menard and Delbert Elliott, "Self-Reported Offending, Maturational Reform, and the Easterlin Hypothesis," *Journal of Quantitative Criminology* 6 (1990): 237–268.

70. Elijah Anderson, *Streetwise: Race, Class and Change in an Urban Community* (Chicago: University of Chicago Press, 1990), pp. 243–244.

71. Jeffrey Michael Cancino, "The Utility of Social Capital and Collective Efficacy: Social Control Policy in Nonmetropolitan Settings," *Criminal Justice Policy Review*

16 (2005): 287–318; Chris Gibson, Jihong Zhao, Nicholas Lovrich, and Michael Gaffney, "Social Integration, Individual Perceptions of Collective Efficacy, and Fear of Crime in Three Cities," *Justice Quarterly* 19 (2002): 537–564; Felton Earls, *Linking Community Factors and Individual Development* (Washington, DC: National Institute of Justice, 1998).

72. Robert J. Sampson and Stephen W. Raudenbush, *Disorder in Urban Neighborhoods: Does It Lead to Crime?* (Washington, DC: National Institute of Justice, 2001).

73. Andrea Altschuler, Carol Somkin, and Nancy Adler, "Local Services and Amenities, Neighborhood Social Capital, and Health," *Social Science and Medicine* 59 (2004): 1219–1230.

74. Kelly Socia and Janet Stamatel, "Neighborhood Characteristics and the Social Control of Registered Sex Offenders," *Crime and Delinquency* 58 (2012): 565–587.

75. Todd A. Armstrong, Charles M. Katz, and Stephen M. Schnebly, "The Relationship Between Citizen Perceptions of Collective Efficacy and Neighborhood Violent Crime" *Crime and Delinquency* 61 (2015): 121–142.

76. M. R. Lindblad, K. R. Manturuk, and R. G. Quercia, "Sense of Community and Informal Social Control Among Lower Income Households: The Role of Homeownership and Collective Efficacy in Reducing Subjective Neighborhood Crime and Disorder," *American Journal of Community Psychology* 51 (2013): 123–139.

77. Rebecca Wickes, John Hipp, Renee Zahnow, and Lorraine Mazerolle, "'Seeing' Minorities and Perceptions of Disorder: Explicating the Mediating and Moderating Mechanisms of Social Cohesion," *Criminology* 51 (2013): 519–560.

78. Michael Reisig and Jeffrey Michael Cancino, "Incivilities in Nonmetropolitan Communities: The Effects of Structural Constraints, Social Conditions, and Crime," *Journal of Criminal Justice* 32 (2004): 15–29.

79. Robert Sampson, Jeffrey Morenoff, and Felton Earls, "Beyond Social Capital: Spatial Dynamics of Collective Efficacy for Children," *American Sociological Review* 64 (1999): 633–660.

80. Donald Black, "Social Control as a Dependent Variable," in *Toward a General Theory of Social Control,* ed. D. Black (Orlando, FL: Academic Press, 1990).

81. Jennifer Beyers, John Bates, Gregory Pettit, and Kenneth Dodge, "Neighborhood Structure, Parenting Processes, and the Development of Youths' Externalizing Behaviors: A Multilevel Analysis," *American Journal of Community Psychology* 31 (2003): 35–53.

82. Ronald Simons, Leslie Gordon Simons, Callie Harbin Burt, Gene Brody, and Carolyn Cutrona, "Collective Efficacy, Authoritative Parenting and Delinquency: A Longitudinal Test of a Model Integrating Community and Family-Level Processes," *Criminology* 43 (2005): 989–1029.

83. April Pattavina, James Byrne, and Luis Garcia, "An Examination of Citizen Involvement in Crime Prevention in High-Risk versus Low to Moderate-Risk Neighborhoods," *Crime and Delinquency* 52 (2006): 203–231.

84. Paul Bellair, "Informal Surveillance and Street Crime: A Complex Relationship," *Criminology* 38 (2000): 137–170.

85. Wesley G. Skogan, *Disorder and Decline: Crime and the Spiral of Decay in American Neighborhoods* (New York: Free Press, 1990), pp. 15–35.

86. Robert Sampson and W. Byron Groves, "Community Structure and Crime: Testing Social Disorganization Theory," *American Journal of Sociology* 94 (1989): 774–802; Denise Gottfredson, Richard McNeill, and Gary Gottfredson, "Social Area Influences on Delinquency: A Multilevel Analysis," *Journal of Research in Crime and Delinquency* 28 (1991): 197–206.

87. Fred Markowitz, Paul Bellair, Allen Liska, and Jianhong Liu, "Extending Social Disorganization Theory: Modeling the Relationships Between Cohesion, Disorder, and Fear," *Criminology* 39 (2001): 293–320.

88. George Capowich, "The Conditioning Effects of Neighborhood Ecology on Burglary Victimization," *Criminal Justice and Behavior* 30 (2003): 39–62.

89. Ruth Peterson, Lauren Krivo, and Mark Harris, "Disadvantage and Neighborhood Violent Crime: Do Local Institutions Matter?" *Journal of Research in Crime and Delinquency* 37 (2000): 31–63.

90. Lee Ann Slocum, Andres Rengifo, Tiffany Choi, and Christopher Herrmann, "The Elusive Relationship Between Community Organizations and Crime: An Assessment Across Disadvantaged Areas of the South Bronx," *Criminology* 51 (2013): 167–216; Maria Velez, "The Role of Public Social Control in Urban Neighborhoods: A Multi-Level Analysis of Victimization Risk," *Criminology* 39 (2001): 837–864.

91. Tammy Rinehart Kochel, "Robustness of Collective Efficacy on Crime in a Developing Nation: Association with Crime Reduction Compared to Police Services," *Journal of Crime and Justice* 36 (2013): 334–352.

92. David Klinger, "Negotiating Order in Patrol Work: An Ecological Theory of Police Response to Deviance," *Criminology* 35 (1997): 277–306.

93. Rodney Stark, "Deviant Places: A Theory of the Ecology of Crime," *Criminology* 25 (1987): 893–911.

94. Robert Bursik and Harold Grasmick, "Economic Deprivation and Neighborhood Crime Rates, 1960–1980," *Law and Society Review* 27 (1993): 263–278.

95. Robert Kane, "Compromised Police Legitimacy as a Predictor of Violent Crime in Structurally Disadvantaged Communities," *Criminology* 43 (2005): 469–498.

96. Keri Burchfield and Eric Silver, "Collective Efficacy and Crime in Los Angeles Neighborhoods: Implications for the Latino Paradox," *Sociological Inquiry* 83 (2013): 154–176.

97. Patrick Sharkey, "Navigating Dangerous Streets: The Sources and Consequences of Street Efficacy," *American Sociological Review* 71 (2006): 826–846.

98. Per-Olof H. Wikström and Kyle Treiber, "The Role of Self-Control in Crime Causation," *European Journal of Criminology* 4 (2007): 237–264.

99. Socia and Stamatel, "Neighborhood Characteristics and the Social Control of Registered Sex Offenders."

100. Peterson, Krivo, and Harris, "Disadvantage and Neighborhood Violent Crime: Do Local Institutions Matter?"

101. Robert Merton, *Social Theory and Social Structure*, enlarged ed. (New York: Free Press, 1968).

102. Albert Cohen, "The Sociology of the Deviant Act: Anomie Theory and Beyond," *American Sociological Review* 30 (1965): 5–14.

103. Messner and Rosenfeld, *Crime and the American Dream*.

104. Jon Gunnar Bernburg, "Anomie, Social Change and Crime: A Theoretical Examination of Institutional-Anomie Theory," *British Journal of Criminology* 42 (2002): 729–743.

105. John Hagan, Gerd Hefler, Gabriele Classen, Klaus Boehnke, and Hans Merkens, "Subterranean Sources of Subcultural Delinquency Beyond the American Dream," *Criminology* 36 (1998): 309–340.

106. Lorine Hughes, Lonnie Schaible, and Benjamin Gibbs, "Economic Dominance, the 'American Dream,' and Homicide: A Cross-National Test of Institutional Anomie Theory," *Sociological Inquiry* 85 (2015): 100–128.

107. Brian Stults and Christi Falco, "Unbalanced Institutional Commitments and Delinquent Behavior: An Individual-Level Assessment of Institutional Anomie Theory," *Youth Violence and Juvenile Justice* 12 (2014): 77–100.

108. Steven Messner and Samantha Applin, "Her American Dream: Bringing Gender into Institutional-Anomie Theory," *Feminist Criminology* 10 (2015): 36–59.

109. Morenoff, Sampson, and Raudenbush, "Neighborhood Inequality, Collective Efficacy, and the Spatial Dynamics of Urban Violence."

110. John Braithwaite, "Poverty, Power, White-Collar Crime and the Paradoxes of Criminological Theory," *Australian and New Zealand Journal of Criminology* 24 (1991): 40–58.

111. Margo Wilson and Martin Daly, "Life Expectancy, Economic Inequality, Homicide, and Reproductive Timing in Chicago Neighbourhoods," *British Journal of Medicine* 314 (1997): 1271–1274.

112. Judith Blau and Peter Blau, "The Cost of Inequality: Metropolitan Structure and Violent Crime," *American Sociological Review* 147 (1982): 114–129.

113. Ibid.

114. Tomislav Kovandzic, Lynne Vieraitis, and Mark Yeisley, "The Structural Covariates of Urban Homicide: Reassessing the Impact of Income Inequality and Poverty in the Post-Reagan Era," *Criminology* 36 (1998): 569–600.

115. Aki Roberts and Dale Willits, "Income Inequality and Homicide in the United States: Consistency Across Different Income Inequality Measures and Disaggregated Homicide Types," *Homicide Studies* 19 (2015): 28–57.

116. Scott South and Steven Messner, "Structural Determinants of Intergroup Association," *American Journal of Sociology* 91 (1986): 1409–1430; Steven Messner and Scott South, "Economic Deprivation, Opportunity Structure, and Robbery Victimization," *Social Forces* 64 (1986): 975–991.

117. Richard Fowles and Mary Merva, "Wage Inequality and Criminal Activity: An Extreme Bounds Analysis for the United States 1975–1990," *Criminology* 34 (1996): 163–182.

118. Beverly Stiles, Xiaoru Liu, and Howard Kaplan, "Relative Deprivation and Deviant Adaptations: The Mediating Effects of Negative Self Feelings," *Journal of Research in Crime and Delinquency* 37 (2000): 64–90.

119. Robert Agnew, "Foundation for a General Strain Theory of Crime and Delinquency," *Criminology* 30 (1992): 47–87.

120. Ibid., p. 57.

121. Matthew Larson and Gary Sweeten, "Breaking Up Is Hard to Do: Romantic Dissolution, Offending, and Substance Use During the Transition to Adulthood," *Criminology* 50 (2012): 605–636.

122. Stephen Watts and Thomas McNulty, "Childhood Abuse and Criminal Behavior: Testing a General Strain Theory Model," *Journal of Interpersonal Violence* 28 (2013): 3023–3040.

123. Timothy Brezina, "Adolescent Maltreatment and Delinquency: The Question of Intervening Processes," *Journal of Research in Crime and Delinquency* 35 (1998): 71–99.

124. Susan Sharp, Mitchell Peck, and Jennifer Hartsfield, "Childhood Adversity and Substance Use of Women Prisoners: A General Strain Theory Approach," *Journal of Criminal Justice* 40 (2012): 202–211.

125. Paul Mazerolle, Velmer Burton, Francis Cullen, T. David Evans, and Gary Payne, "Strain, Anger, and Delinquent Adaptations Specifying General Strain Theory," *Journal of Criminal Justice* 28 (2000): 89–101; Paul Mazerolle and Alex Piquero, "Violent Responses to Strain: An Examination of Conditioning Influences," *Violence and Victimization* 12 (1997): 323–345.

126. George E. Capowich, Paul Mazerolle, and Alex Piquero, "General Strain Theory, Situational Anger, and Social Networks: An Assessment of Conditioning Influences," *Journal of Criminal Justice* 29 (2001): 445–461.

127. Fawn Ngo and Raymond Paternoster, "Toward an Understanding of the Emotional and Behavioral Reactions to Stalking: A Partial Test of General Strain Theory," *Crime and Delinquency*, first published on November 7, 2013.

128. Robert Agnew, Timothy Brezina, John Paul Wright, and Francis T. Cullen, "Strain, Personality Traits, and Delinquency: Extending General Strain Theory," *Criminology* 40 (2002): 43–71.

129. Robert Agnew, "When Criminal Coping Is Likely: An Extension of General Strain Theory," *Deviant Behavior* 34 (2013): 653–670; Lee Ann Slocum, Sally Simpson, and Douglas Smith, "Strained Lives and Crime: Examining Intra-Individual Variation in Strain and Offending in a Sample of Incarcerated Women," *Criminology* 43 (2005): 1067–1110.

130. Robert Agnew, "Stability and Change in Crime over the Life Course: A Strain Theory Explanation," in *Advances in Criminological Theory: Vol. 7, Developmental Theories of Crime and Delinquency,* ed. Terence Thornberry (New Brunswick, NJ: Transaction Books, 1995), pp. 113–137.

131. Lawrence Wu, "Effects of Family Instability, Income, and Income Instability on the Risk of Premarital Birth," *American Sociological Review* 61 (1996): 386–406.

132. Ekaterina Botchkovar and Lisa Broidy, "Accumulated Strain, Negative Emotions, and Crime: A Test of General Strain Theory in Russia," *Crime and Delinquency* 59 (2013): 837–860.

133. Robert Agnew and Helene Raskin White, "An Empirical Test of General Strain Theory," *Criminology* 30 (1992): 475–499.

134. John Hoffman and Alan Miller, "A Latent Variable Analysis of General Strain Theory," *Journal of Quantitative Criminology* 13 (1997): 111–113; Raymond Paternoster and Paul Mazerolle, "General Strain Theory and Delinquency: A Replication and Extension," *Journal of Research in Crime and Delinquency* 31 (1994): 235–263; G. Roger Jarjoura, "The Conditional Effect of Social Class on the Dropout–Delinquency Relationship," *Journal of Research in Crime and Delinquency* 33 (1996): 232–255.

135. Mazerolle, Burton, Cullen, Evans, and Payne, "Strain, Anger, and Delinquent Adaptations: Specifying General Strain Theory."

136. Joanne Kaufman, Cesar Rebellon, Sherod Thaxton, and Robert Agnew, "A General Strain Theory of Racial Differences in Criminal Offending," *Australian and New Zealand Journal of Criminology* 41 (2008): 421–437.

137. Stephen Cernkovich, Peggy Giordano, and Jennifer Rudolph, "Race, Crime and the American Dream," *Journal of Research in Crime and Delinquency* 37 (2000): 131–170.

138. Byongook Moon, Merry Morash, Cynthia Perez McCluskey, and Hye-Won Hwang, "A Comprehensive Test of General Strain Theory: Key Strains, Situational- and Trait-Based Negative Emotions, Conditioning Factors, and Delinquency," *Journal of Research in Crime and Delinquency* 46 (2009): 182–212.

139. Walter Miller, "Lower-Class Culture as a Generating Milieu of Gang Delinquency," *Journal of Social Issues* 14 (1958): 5–19.

140. Ibid., pp. 14–17.

141. Jeffrey Fagan, *Adolescent Violence: A View from the Street,* NIJ Research Preview (Washington, DC: National Institute of Justice, 1998).

142. Jon Gunnar Bernburg, Marvin Krohn, and Craig Rivera, "Official Labeling, Criminal Embeddedness, and Subsequent Delinquency: A Longitudinal Test of Labeling Theory," *Journal of Research in Crime and Delinquency* 43 (2006): 67–88.

143. Chris Melde and Finn-Aage Esbensen, "Gang Membership as a Turning Point in the Life Course," *Criminology* 49 (2011): 513–552.

144. David C. Pyrooz, Gary Sweeten, and Alex R. Piquero, "Continuity and Change in Gang Membership and Gang Embeddedness," *Journal of Research in Crime and Delinquency*, online publication February 7, 2012.

145. David C. Pyrooz, "From Colors and Guns to Caps and Gowns? The Effects of Gang Membership on Educational Attainment," *Journal of Research in Crime and Delinquency* 51 (2014): 56–87.

146. Albert Cohen, *Delinquent Boys* (New York: Free Press, 1955).

147. Ibid., p. 25.

148. Ibid., p. 28.

149. Ibid.

150. Ibid., p. 30.

151. Ibid., p. 133.

152. Richard Cloward and Lloyd Ohlin, *Delinquency and Opportunity* (New York: Free Press, 1960).

153. Ibid., p. 171.

154. Ibid., p. 73.

155. James DeFronzo, "Welfare and Burglary," *Crime and Delinquency* 42 (1996): 223–230.

156. Weed and Seed, www.justice.gov/usao-edny/what-weed-seed.

157. Project COPE, www.bridgewell.org/projectcope/.

# 7 Social Process Theory

## Learning Objectives

**LO1** Explain the concepts of social process and socialization.

**LO2** Discuss the effect of family relationships on crime.

**LO3** Describe how the educational setting influences crime.

**LO4** Discuss the link between peers and delinquency.

**LO5** Contrast social learning, social control, and social reaction (labeling) theories.

**LO6** Link social process theory to crime prevention efforts.

Luoman/E+/Getty Images

Tim Pannell/Corbis

# Chapter Outline

## FACT OR FICTION?

▶ Parents today are too lenient. If they toughened up discipline, they could straighten out rebellious teens.

▶ "Idle hands are the devil's workshop" is not merely an old saying. Getting involved in sports and other activities helps prevent crime and delinquency.

Vernon Matthews operated a company called First Capital Group (FCG), located in Virginia Beach. He had a license to sell insurance, not to give anyone investment advice or transact securities—but that didn't stop him from soliciting members of the military and their families to make investments with FCG. He set up booths at establishments known to be frequented by the military—like restaurants located near military bases—and offered promotions, such as a free night at a hotel, for those who would listen to his spiel. When potential victims came to his office to claim the prizes, Matthews would pitch them on an investment. Among his misrepresentations:

- He received compensation from the U.S. government for his investment advice and services (he did not).
- He would invest his clients' funds in certificates of deposit, mutual funds, or similar safe investments. (Matthews misappropriated all the funds for his own personal or business use.)
- FCG was affiliated with several reputable investment companies and funds (it was not).
- The investment provided a good return—anywhere from 4 to 300 percent—and was low-risk or no-risk (it did not and was not).

In one particular instance, a U.S. Naval Academy graduate who invested $20,000 with FCG tried withdrawing funds. Matthews mailed a check that bounced. After being notified about it, he mailed another one and instructed the victim not to deposit the check until he could put the funds into his account. That, of course, never happened. ▶

Matthews received more than $235,600 from victim investors. Only a few of his victims were able to recover any money, so at his sentencing, the judge ordered Matthews to repay the outstanding balance of $204,465 in restitution to his victims, in addition to serving to a four-year prison term.[1]

**socialized**
The process of acquiring social norms, values, behavior, and skills through interaction with significant others such as parents, peers, and teachers.

**social process theory**
The view that criminality is a function of people's interactions with various organizations, institutions, and processes in society.

**social learning theory**
The view that people learn the techniques and attitudes of crime from close relationships with criminal peers: crime is a learned behavior.

**social control theory**
The view that everyone has the potential to become a criminal, but most people are controlled by their bonds to society. Crime occurs when the forces that bind people to society are weakened or broken.

**social reaction (labeling) theory**
The view that people become criminals when significant members of society label them as such and they accept those labels as a personal identity.

While fraud schemes such as the one committed by Vernon Matthews are certainly not unusual, what makes this somewhat unique is the target of the crime: military personnel. It takes a special kind of person to target members of the armed forces for fraud at a time when the rest of the nation considers them heroes who are willing to undergo personal sacrifice to protect the nation. Someone like Matthews must have not only learned how to carry out fraud but also to neutralize any guilt he might feel for targeting a highly respected group of people. Matthew's bond to society must be pretty weak if he was able to target such people for his criminal schemes. He did not seem to care what others thought of his predatory behavior.

Rather than focus on the criminal behaviors of the alienated poor who live in disorganized neighborhoods, some criminologists focus their attention on the social processes and interactions that occur in all segments of society. They believe that human behavior is shaped by interactions with social institutions such as schools, and social groups, such as family, peers, and neighbors. As people are **socialized** over the life course, relationships can be either positive and supportive or dysfunctional and destructive. If the latter is the norm, then conventional success may be impossible for that individual to achieve. Criminal solutions may become the only feasible alternative. This view of crime is referred to as **social process theory**.

The social process approach has several independent branches: **social learning theory**, **social control theory**, and **social reaction (labeling) theory**, discussed in detail later in this chapter.

Social learning theories assume that people are born good and learn to be bad; social control theory assumes that people are born bad and must be controlled in order to be good; and social reaction theory assumes that whether good or bad, people are shaped, directed, and influenced by the evaluations of others.

All three forms of social process theories share some basic concepts:

- Socialization is the key to understanding criminal behavior choices.
- Socialization occurs through contact with significant others.
- Anyone can turn to antisocial behavior if their socialization is damaging and/or destructive; crime is not solely a lower-class phenomenon.
- Because criminal behavior is a function of socialization, it can be reversed and criminals turned around by proper re-socialization and prosocial interactions.

**L01** Explain the concepts of social process and socialization.

# Institutions of Socialization

Social process theorists have long studied the critical elements of socialization to determine how they contribute to a burgeoning criminal career. Their view relies on the fact that interaction with key social institutions helps control human behavior. Prominent among these elements are the individual's family, peer group, school, and church.

**L02** Discuss the effect of family relationships on crime.

## Family Relations

Family relationships are considered a major determinant of behavior.[2] Parenting factors, such as the ability to communicate and to provide proper discipline, may play a critical role in determining whether people misbehave as children and even later as adults. The family–crime relationship is significant across racial, ethnic, and gender lines, and this is one of the most replicated findings in the criminological literature.[3]

Many factors impact on the parent–child relationship. Rand and Katherine Conger's Family Stress Model finds that economic hardship, such factors as low income and income loss, increase parents' sadness, pessimism about the future, anger, despair, and withdrawal from other family members. As parents become more emotionally distressed, they tend to interact with each other and their children in a more irritable and less supportive fashion. These patterns of behavior increase instability in the marriage and also disrupt effective parenting practices, such as monitoring children's activities and using consistent and appropriate disciplinary strategies. Marital instability and disrupted parenting, in turn, increase children's risk of suffering developmental problems, such as depressed mood, substance abuse, and engaging in delinquent behaviors. These economic stress processes also decrease children's ability to function in a competent manner in school and with peers.[4]

Adolescents who do not receive affection from their parents during childhood are more likely to use illicit drugs and to be more aggressive as they mature.[5] In contrast, those growing up in a home where parents are supportive and effectively control their children in a noncoercive way are more likely to refrain from delinquency; this phenomenon is referred to as **parental efficacy**.[6] Delinquency is reduced when parents provide the type of structure that integrates children into families, while giving them the ability to assert their individuality and regulate their own behavior.[7] Children who have warm and affectionate ties to their parents report greater levels of self-esteem beginning in adolescence and extending into their adulthood; high self-esteem is inversely related to criminal behavior.[8]

Family functioning is often compromised by disruption and separation. Divorce forces many kids to live in single-parent households that are more likely to suffer economic and other social problems than intact families. These factors have been linked to delinquency and antisocial activities.[9]

**VIOLENCE AND ABUSE** Children who grow up in homes where parents use overly strict discipline become prone to antisocial behavior.[10] A significant amount of literature suggests that being the target of abuse is associated with subsequent episodes of delinquency and violence.[11] The more often a child is physically disciplined and the harsher the discipline, the more likely they will engage in antisocial behaviors.[12] The effects of abuse appear to be long term: exposure to abuse in early life provides a foundation for violent and antisocial behavior in late adolescence and adulthood.[13] Kids who were abused are less likely to graduate from high school, hold a job, and be happily married; they are more likely to encounter juvenile and adult arrests.[14] They are also more likely to grow up to be abusers themselves.[15]

Bonnie Jo Mount/Washington Post/Getty Images

According to social process theories, socialization at home, in school, and in the community is the key element in determining adolescent behavior. A strong, positive relationship with significant others insulates youth from delinquency promoting forces in the environment. Here, Reginald Wilson II, age 9, learns a math trick from his father, Reginald Wilson, at their home in Rockville, Maryland. Parental attachment and guidance are important elements of socialization.

**parental efficacy**
The ability of parents to be supportive of their children and effectively control them in noncoercive ways.

Lucy Nicholson/Reuters/Landov

Economic stress can undermine families and block proper socialization. Here, Tracy and Elizabeth Burger prepare food in their 8-year-old son Dylan's room, in a converted garage in Los Angeles, California. The Burgers lost their apartment after both losing their jobs with combined earnings of $100,000 a year. They were forced to sell most of their possessions and live in a motel before moving into Elizabeth's mother's garage. An estimated 2.5 million children are now living on the streets of the United States or in shelters, motels, or doubled-up with other families.

**LO3** Describe how the educational setting influences crime.

Abused kids also suffer more from other social problems, such as depression, suicide attempts, and self-injurious behaviors.[16] Mental health and delinquency experts have found that abused kids experience mental and social problems across their life span, problems ranging from substance abuse to damaged personality.[17] In one recent study, family expert Lynette Renner found that children who experienced any form of family violence were more likely to act out and engage in antisocial behaviors. Renner also found that children who experienced indirect types of family violence, such as exposure to the physical abuse of a sibling, were more likely to act out than children who had personally experienced maltreatment and physical abuse.[18]

The effects of family dysfunction are felt well beyond childhood. Kids who experience high levels of family conflict grow up to lead stressful adult lives, punctuated by periods of depression.[19] Children whose parents are harsh, angry, and irritable are likely to behave in the same way toward their own children, putting their own offspring at risk.[20] Thus, the seeds of adult dysfunction are planted early in childhood.

## Educational Experience

The educational process and adolescent school achievement have been linked to criminality. Children who fail at school soon feel frustrated and rejected. Believing they will never achieve success through conventional means, they seek like-minded companions and together engage in antisocial behaviors. Educational failure evokes negative responses from important people in the child's life, including teachers, parents, and prospective employers. These reactions solidify feelings of inadequacy and low-self esteem, in some cases, lead to a pattern of chronic delinquency. Studies using a variety of measures of academic competence and self-esteem demonstrate that good students have a better attitude about themselves than poor students; low self-esteem has been found to contribute to delinquent behavior.[21]

All too often educational problems lead students to leave school early and become dropouts. Even though national dropout rates are in decline, more than 10 percent of Americans aged 16 to 24 have left school permanently without a diploma; of these, more than 1 million withdrew before completing 10th grade. Most kids who drop out show danger signs as early as the 4th grade and serious problems begin to manifest in their first year of high school.[22]

Why do kids drop out? Reasons include a lack of interest in the educational curriculum, a development that leads to course failure and low grade point average.[23] Some kids are pushed out of school because they lack attention, have poor attendance records, and are labeled troublemakers.

**RACE AND EDUCATIONAL PROBLEMS** African American children are much more likely than their European American peers to suffer problems at school.[24] As a result, minority students are more likely to disengage from schools at a younger age than Caucasian students.[25] One reason may be their being the focus of school disciplinary practices. According to the U.S. Department of Education, minority students, especially boys, face much harsher discipline in public schools than other students. One in five African American boys and more than one in ten African American girls received an out-of-school suspension, and were three and a half times more likely to be suspended or expelled than white students. Many of the nation's largest districts had very different disciplinary rates for students of different races. In Los Angeles, for example, black students made up 9 percent of those enrolled, but 26 percent of those suspended; in Chicago, they made up 45 percent of the students, but 76 percent of the suspensions.[26]

**GETTING BULLIED** Students are also subject to violence and intimidation on school grounds. National data indicate that in a single year about one quarter of all public schools report that bullying occurred among students on a daily or weekly basis, and 9 percent reported widespread disorder in classrooms on a daily or weekly basis.[27] Six percent of students ages 12 to 18 report being cyberbullied, and about 3 percent reported being subject to harassing text messages; girls are twice as likely to be subject to harassing text messages than boys. It may come as no surprise that about one-third of lesbian, gay, bisexual, and transgender young people, a group not known for violent retaliation, experience harassment each year in an educational setting. However, recent national surveys indicate that there has been a slight decline in targeting LGBT students; nonetheless, more than 40 percent of LGBT students still report being harassed.[28]

## Peer Relations

Criminologists have long recognized that peer group relations have a powerful effect on human conduct and can dramatically influence decision making and behavior choices.[29] The more antisocial the peer group, the more likely its members will engage in delinquency; nondelinquent friends will help moderate delinquency.[30]

Friendship helps reduce antisocial behaviors: kids who have lots of friends and a variety of peer group networks tend to be less delinquent than their less popular mates.[31] However, some of the most popular kids get to hang out with their friends without parental supervision.[32] If their peer group includes kids who take risks, drink, and take drugs, the lack of parental supervision gives them the opportunity to get into trouble.[33] In contrast, conventional friendship networks help to moderate antisocial behavior.[34] Having prosocial friends who are committed to conventional success may help shield people from crime-producing inducements in their environment.[35]

Bullying has become a major national issue, and a number of students have taken their own lives when they felt nothing could be done to end the torment. Others have fought back. Isabella "Belle" Hankey, 18, shown walking with her mother, filed a $2 million lawsuit against the Concord-Carlisle school system in Massachusetts for repeated bullying by other students, including death threats. Hankey believes her complaints were ignored by school officials.

John Tlumacki/Boston Globe/Getty Images

Even kids who are not usually at risk to crime (young girls, immigrants, college students) may find themselves outside the law if their peers engage in or support antisocial activities.[36] Conversely, children born into high-risk families—such as those with single teen mothers—can avoid delinquency if their friends refrain from drug use and criminality.[37]

In disorganized neighborhoods, deviant peers may help kids become independent and socially accepted.[38] Joining a gang or deviant group may help members increase their social standing and popularity within their age cohort. By ninth grade kids, who belong to a group that engages in underage drinking gain social capital. Participation in the "party" subculture has some short-term costs (e.g., lower grades, detachment from school), but in the long term provides gains in the form of social capital and popularity.[39]

Not all kids join law-violating groups out of choice. Some find it tough to make friends and therefore choose antisocial peers out of necessity rather than desire.[40] Being a social outcast causes them to choose friends who are dangerous and get them into further trouble.[41] Because group involvement helps them neutralize their fear of punishment, loyalty to deviant peers can help sustain or amplify antisocial behavior and reinforce criminal careers.[42] Antisocial friends tend to be, as criminologist Mark Warr puts it, "sticky": once acquired, they are not easily lost; peer influence therefore may continue through the life span.[43]

While the association between having antisocial peers and engaging in antisocial behavior seems solid, the causal direction of these associations is still open to debate. A number of possible scenarios have been suggested, including:

- Impressionable adolescents are led astray by antisocial peers.
- Troubled youth seek out like-minded peers; "birds of a feather flock together."

**L04** Discuss the link between peers and delinquency.

## CONNECTIONS

One aspect of the peer effect on crime and delinquency is the development of gangs. Chapter 6 showed how law-violating peer groups exist in all levels of the social strata, from rural counties to metropolitan areas. The number of gangs and gang members has been increasing in recent years.

**FIGURE 7.1**
The Complex Web of Social
Processes that Controls
Human Behavior

**Source:** © Cengage Learning

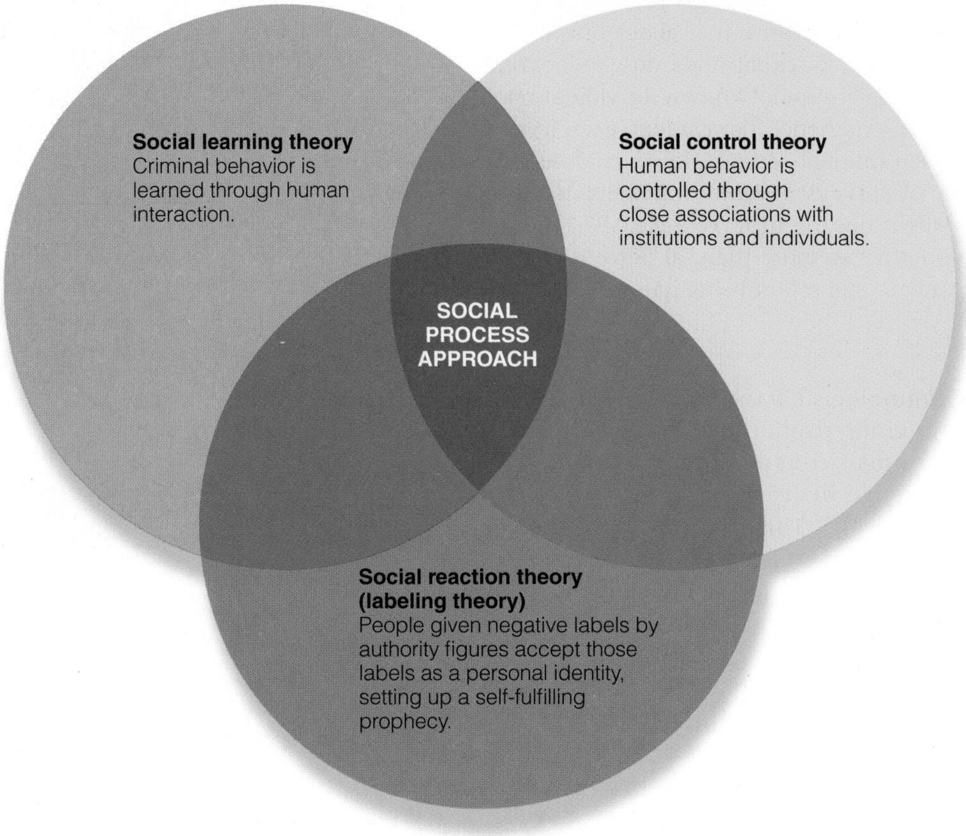

- Criminal tendencies are reinforced and expanded by like-minded peers.
- Members of friendship groups created in disorganized neighborhoods are all exposed to destructive, crime-producing social forces. What appears to be a peer effect on crime is in reality an ecological one.[44]

### Religion and Belief

Logic would dictate that people who hold high moral values and beliefs, who have learned to distinguish right from wrong, and who regularly attend religious services should also eschew crime and other antisocial behaviors. Religion binds people together and forces them to confront the consequences of their behavior. Having high moral beliefs may enhance the deterrent effect of punishment by convincing even motivated offenders not to risk apprehension and punishment. Committing crimes would violate the principles of all organized religions.[45]

Recent research findings suggest that attending religious services does in fact have a significant negative impact on crime.[46] Kids living in disorganized, high-crime areas who attend religious services are better able to resist illegal drug use than nonreligious youths.[47] Interestingly, participation seems to be a more significant inhibitor of crime than merely having religious beliefs and values. That is, actually attending religious services has a more dramatic effect on behavior than merely holding religious beliefs.[48] Figure 7.1 summarizes the various views of how socialization influences behavioral choices.

**L05** Contrast social learning, social control, and social reaction (labeling) theories.

## Social Learning Theories

Social learning theorists believe that crime is a product of learning the norms, values, and behaviors associated with criminal activity. Social learning can involve the actual techniques of crime (how to steal a car, sell drugs, or engage in identity theft) as well as the psychological aspects of criminality (how to deal with the guilt or shame associated with illegal activities).

Learning negative attitudes and beliefs can start early in life. Some kids become jaundiced, pessimistic, and cynical early in their adolescence. They learn to trust no one, take a dim view of their future, and figure out that the only way to get ahead in life is to break social rules. Their life experience teaches them a contemptuous view of accepted social rules. Learning to disparage conventional norms increases the probability of their engaging in criminal behavior. Criminologists Ronald Simons and Callie Burt find that persistent exposure to antagonistic social circumstances and lack of exposure to positive conditions increase the chances of someone developing social schemas involving a hostile view of relationships. Embracing these schemas fosters situational definitions that lead to actions that are aggressive, opportunistic, and criminal. According to Simons and Burt, learning to distrust the world and the people in it, to embrace a here-and-now orientation, and to discount prohibitions against deviance is what drives people into a criminal way of life.[49]

This section briefly reviews two of the most prominent forms of social learning theory: differential association theory and neutralization theory.

## Differential Association Theory

One of the most prominent social learning theories is Edwin H. Sutherland's **differential association theory**. Often considered the preeminent U.S. criminologist, Sutherland first put forth his theory in 1939 in *Principles of Criminology*.[50] The final version of the theory appeared in 1947. When Sutherland died in 1950, his longtime associate Donald Cressey continued his work until his own death in 1987.

Sutherland believed crime was a function of a learning process that could affect any individual in any culture. Acquiring a behavior is a socialization process, not a political or legal process. Skills and motives conducive to crime are learned as a result of contact with procrime values, attitudes, and definitions and other patterns of criminal behavior.

> **differential association theory**
> The view that people commit crime when their social learning leads them to perceive more definitions favoring crime than favoring conventional behavior.

**PRINCIPLES OF DIFFERENTIAL ASSOCIATION** Sutherland and Cressey explain the basic principles of differential association as follows:[51]

- *Criminal behavior is learned.* This statement differentiates Sutherland's theory from prior attempts to classify criminal behavior as an inherent characteristic of criminals. Sutherland implies that criminality is learned in the same manner as any other learned behavior, such as writing, painting, or reading.
- *Criminal behavior is learned as a by-product of interacting with others.* An individual does not start violating the law simply by living in a criminogenic environment or by manifesting personal characteristics associated with criminality, such as low IQ or family problems. People actively learn as they are socialized and interact with other individuals who serve as teachers and guides to crime. Some kids may meet and associate with criminal "mentors" who teach them how to be successful criminals and to reap the greatest benefits from their criminal activities.[52] Criminality cannot occur without the aid of others.
- *Learning criminal behavior occurs within intimate personal groups.* People's contacts with their most intimate social companions—family, friends, and peers—have the greatest influence on their development of deviant behavior and an antisocial attitude. Relationships with these influential individuals color and control the way individuals interpret everyday events.
- *Learning criminal behavior involves assimilating the techniques of committing crime, including motives, drives, rationalizations, and attitudes.* Novice criminals learn from their associates the proper way to

Do kids learn delinquent attitudes and values from their parents? According to differential association, they do, and that may be why Bernard Peters and his son Scott have shared a cell for the last 18 years at the Elmira Correctional Facility in New York. In the summer of 1995, they embarked on a brief but violent string of robberies that netted them $2,900 in cash. Among their victims was Mary Halloran, 61, the manager of a Salvation Army thrift shop. The Peterses shot and robbed Halloran in the parking lot of the store as she carried a bag filled with $726 to her car.

Fred R. Conrad/New York Times/Redux Pictures

pick a lock, shoplift, and obtain and use narcotics. They must learn the proper terminology for their acts and acquire approved reactions to law violations. Criminals must learn how to react properly to their illegal acts, such as when to defend them, when to rationalize them, and when to show remorse for them.

- *The specific direction of motives and drives is learned from perceptions of various aspects of the legal code as favorable or unfavorable.* Because the reaction to social rules and laws is not uniform across society, people constantly meet others who hold different views on the utility of obeying the legal code. Some people admire others who may openly disdain or flout the law or ignore its substance. People experience what Sutherland calls **culture conflict** when they are exposed to opposing attitudes toward right and wrong or moral and immoral. The conflict of social attitudes and cultural norms is the basis for the concept of differential association.

- *A person becomes a criminal when he or she perceives more favorable than unfavorable consequences to violating the law.* According to Sutherland's theory, individuals become law violators when they are in contact with persons, groups, or events that produce an excess of definitions favorable toward criminality and are isolated from counteracting forces. A definition favorable toward criminality occurs, for example, when a person hears friends talking about the virtues of getting high on drugs. A definition unfavorable toward crime occurs when friends or parents demonstrate their disapproval of crime.

- *Differential associations may vary in frequency, duration, priority, and intensity.* Whether a person learns to obey the law or to disregard it is influenced by the quality of that person's social interactions. Those of lasting duration have greater influence than those that are brief. Similarly, frequent contacts have greater effect than rare, haphazard contacts. "Priority" means the age of children when they first encounter definitions of criminality. Contacts made early in life probably have more influence than those developed later. Finally, "intensity" is generally interpreted to mean the importance and prestige attached to the individuals or groups from whom the definitions are learned. The influence of a father, mother, or trusted friend far outweighs that of more socially distant figures.

- *The process of learning criminal behavior by association with criminal and anticriminal patterns involves all of the mechanisms that are involved in any other learning process.* Learning criminal behavior patterns is similar to learning nearly all other patterns and is not a matter of mere imitation.

- *Although criminal behavior expresses general needs and values, it is not excused by those general needs and values, because noncriminal behavior expresses the same needs and values.* This principle suggests that the motives for criminal behavior cannot logically be the same as those for conventional behavior. Sutherland rules out such motives as desire to accumulate money or social status, personal frustration, and low self-concept as causes of crime because they are just as likely to produce noncriminal behavior, such as getting a better education or working harder on a job. Only the learning of deviant norms through contact with an excess of definitions favorable toward criminality produces illegal behavior.

In sum, differential association theory holds that people learn criminal attitudes and behavior during their adolescence from close, trusted friends or relatives. A criminal career develops if learned antisocial values and behaviors are not matched or exceeded by the conventional attitudes and behaviors the individual learns. Criminal behavior, then, is learned in a process that is similar to learning any other human behavior.

**TESTING DIFFERENTIAL ASSOCIATION THEORY**   Studies testing differential association theory have found it predicts a variety of criminal behavior patterns, ranging from school yard bullying to domestic violence.[53]

Learning from parents is related to criminal behaviors in children. We know that crime is intergenerational; a number of studies have found that parental deviance has a powerful influence on delinquent behavior.[54] Kids whose parents are deviant and

---

**culture conflict**
Result of exposure to opposing norms, attitudes, and definitions of right and wrong, moral and immoral.

criminal are more likely to become criminals themselves and eventually to produce criminal children.[55] In sum, the more that kids are involved with criminal parents, the more likely they are to commit crime, suggesting a pattern of learning rather than inheritance.[56]

The effect of peer influence also supports differential association. Learning from deviant friends is highly supportive of delinquency, regardless of race and/or class.[57] In stable friendships, the more accepted popular partner exerts greater influence over the less accepted partner. If the more popular friend engages in antisocial behaviors, the less popular "follower" will soon learn and emulate similar attitudes and behaviors.[58] Kids who associate with and presumably learn from popular, assertive, and aggressive peers are more likely to behave aggressively themselves.[59] Deviant peers interfere with the natural process of aging out of crime by helping provide the support that keeps kids in criminal careers.[60] The Policies and Issues in Criminology feature entitled "Measuring the Effect of Deviant Peers" looks at a research study designed to test the impact of peer influence on behavior.

Romantic partners who engage in antisocial activities may influence their partner's behavior, which suggests that partners learn from one another.[61] Adolescents with deviant romantic partners are more delinquent than those youths with more prosocial partners, regardless of friends' and parents' behavior.[62]

**ANALYSIS OF DIFFERENTIAL ASSOCIATION THEORY** Differential association theory is important because it does not specify that criminals come from a disorganized area or are members of the lower class. Outwardly law-abiding, middle-class parents can encourage delinquent behavior by their own drinking, drug use, or family violence. The influence of differential associations is not dependent on social class; deviant learning experiences can affect youths in all classes.[63]

There are, however, a number of valid criticisms of Sutherland's work. It fails to account for the origin of criminal definitions. How did the first "teacher" learn criminal attitudes and definitions in order to pass them on? Another criticism of differential association theory is that it assumes criminal and delinquent acts to be rational and systematic. This ignores spontaneous, wanton acts of violence and damage that appear to have little utility or purpose, such as the isolated psychopathic killing that is virtually unsolvable because of the killer's anonymity and lack of delinquent associations.

Some critics suggest that the reasoning behind the theory is circular: How can we know when a person has experienced an excess of definitions favorable toward criminality? When he or she commits a crime! Why do people commit crime? When they are exposed to an excess of criminal definitions!

## Differential Reinforcement Theory

First proposed by Ronald Akers in collaboration with Robert Burgess in 1966, differential reinforcement theory is a version of the social learning view that employs both differential association concepts and elements of psychological learning theory.[64]

According to Akers, the same process is involved in learning both deviant and conventional behavior. People learn to be neither "all deviant" nor "all conforming," but rather strike a balance between the two opposing poles of behavior. This balance is usually stable, but it can undergo revision over time.

A number of learning processes shape behavior. Direct conditioning, also called **differential reinforcement**, occurs when behavior is reinforced by being either rewarded or punished while interacting with others. **Negative reinforcement** occurs when the rate of a behavior increases because an aversive event or stimulus is removed or prevented from happening. If a person discovers that drinking heavily results in a severe and painful hangover, he or she can switch to coffee and soft drinks in order to avoid the pains associated with binge drinking; the negative stimulus is removed. Positive reinforcement occurs when a pleasurable result is linked to a particular behavior: studying hard results in getting an A on a test, encouraging a student to continue to study in order to receive more As.

**differential reinforcement**
Behavior is reinforced by being either rewarded or punished while interacting with others; also called direct conditioning.

**negative reinforcement**
Using either negative stimuli (punishment) or loss of reward (negative punishment) to curtail unwanted behaviors.

# Policies and Issues in Criminology

## MEASURING THE EFFECT OF DEVIANT PEERS

Recently, criminologists Ray Paternoster, Jean Marie McGloin, Holly Nguyen, and Kyle J. Thomas conducted an interesting and informative experiment to measure whether peers influence behavior choices. They set up an experiment at a local university that was allegedly designed to measure short-term memory. The experimenter would read a list of 20 words, which the subjects would be asked to recall at the end of the experiment; they were told they would receive $1 for each word they recalled correctly, for a maximum possible payment of $20. The participants were also asked to complete a short online survey about their background (demographic information), self-perceived memory ability, and other factors. Participants were told they had eight minutes to answer the survey questions on the computer and that if they finished before then, they should simply sit quietly and wait so that every person waited the same amount of time before recalling the words. The experimenter left the room, and when he returned he told the subjects how to enter the words online. The experimenter then appeared to be shocked as he noticed four "junk web links" located at the bottom of the recall page.

The experimenter clicked on the links and then announced that they opened up lists of the words to be recalled (i.e., each of the four links opened a page of five words, giving participants access to all 20 words).

The experimenter said the presence of the links was a software error and the participants should ignore the links when recalling the words. He then told the participants that he was going to leave the room to speak with a technician about removing the links. All subjects were well aware that there was an opportunity to cheat on this task.

Unknown to the participants, a hired actor was also in the room who looked and acted like the other students (he was a student at another university). In some cases, the peer confederate completed the memory task without cheating and said nothing. In the experimental condition, once the experimenter left the room to talk to the technician, the peer confederate addressed the other subjects in the room using the following script:

> That guy was right—you can totally see the words if you click the links. Screw it. I'm using the lists. I thought we were guaranteed the 20 dollars—now we have to remember all the words? That's ridiculous. I am doing it.

The confederate then openly and clearly cheated on the task by clicking on all four links and using them to fill in the word recall list.

When the experimenter came back, he told the group that because of the need to fix the software glitch, there was no time to count the number of correct words for each subject in order to determine payment, so everyone would receive the $20 compensation.

Despite the fact the peer deviance was committed by a stranger offering a verbal intention and justification for cheating that lasted less than 15 seconds, his behavior significantly increased the probability of subjects engaging in deviance. While none of the control subjects cheated, 38 percent of the participants exposed to the cheating peer chose to do so!

This experiment lends significant support to both the influence of peers and the theory of differential association: people exposed to positive attitudes toward deviant behavior are more likely to adapt similar behaviors themselves. And remember, the actor was merely a peer and not a close friend. Had a best friend approved cheating, for a longer duration than 15 seconds, we can only imagine what the outcome would have been.

### Critical Thinking

Would you be influenced by someone loudly proclaiming it is okay to cheat on a test if an instructor left the room? Be honest now: would another student whom you hardly knew influence your behavior? What if everyone around you started to cheat?

**Source:** Ray Paternoster, Jean Marie McGloin, Holly Nguyen, and Kyle J. Thomas, "The Causal Impact of Exposure to Deviant Peers: An Experimental Investigation," *Journal of Research in Crime and Delinquency* 50 (2013): 476–503.

According to Akers, people learn to evaluate their own behavior through their interactions with significant others and groups in their lives. These groups control sources and patterns of reinforcement, define behavior as right or wrong, and provide behaviors that can be modeled through observational learning. The more individuals learn to define their behavior as good or at least as justified, rather than as undesirable, the more likely they are to engage in that behavior. Adolescents who join a peer group whose members value drugs and alcohol, encourage their use, and provide opportunities to observe people abusing substances will be encouraged, through this social learning experience, to use drugs themselves.[65]

Akers's theory suggests that the principal influence on behavior comes from "those groups that control individuals' major sources of reinforcement and punishment and expose them to behavioral models and normative definitions." The important groups are the ones with which a person is in differential association—peer and friendship groups, schools, churches, and similar institutions. Within the context of these critical groups, according to Akers, "deviant behavior can be expected to the extent that it has been differentially reinforced over alternative behavior . . . and is defined as desirable or justified." Once people are indoctrinated into crime, their behavior can be reinforced by being exposed to deviant behavior models—associating with deviant peers—without being subject to negative reinforcements for their antisocial acts. The deviant behavior, originally executed by imitating someone else's behavior, is sustained by social support. Kids who engage in computer crime and computer hacking may find their behavior reinforced by peers who are playing the same game.[66] Similarly, adolescents whose deviant behavior (recreational drug use) is reinforced by significant others (parents and/or peers) are more likely to accelerate their rates of deviance than those who do not receive reinforcements.[67]

## Neutralization Theory

**Neutralization theory** is identified with the writings of Gresham Sykes and his associate David Matza.[68] These criminologists also view the process of becoming a criminal as a learning experience. They theorize that law violators must learn and master techniques that enable them to neutralize conventional values and attitudes, which enables them to drift back and forth between illegitimate and conventional behavior.

Neutralization theory points out that even the most committed criminals and delinquents are not involved in criminality all the time; they also attend schools, family functions, and religious services. Thus, their behavior falls along a continuum between total freedom and total restraint. This process of **drift**, or movement from one extreme to another, produces behavior that is sometimes unconventional or deviant and at other times constrained and sober.[69] Learning **neutralization techniques** equips a person to temporarily drift away from conventional behavior and become involved in antisocial behaviors, including crime and drug abuse.[70]

**neutralization theory**
The view that law violators learn to neutralize conventional values and attitudes, enabling them to drift back and forth between criminal and conventional behavior.

**drift**
Movement in and out of delinquency, shifting between conventional and deviant values.

**neutralization techniques**
Methods of rationalizing deviant behavior, such as denying responsibility or blaming the victim.

**NEUTRALIZATION TECHNIQUES** Sykes and Matza suggest that people develop a distinct set of justifications for their law-violating behavior. Several observations form the basis of their theoretical model:[71]

- *Criminals sometimes voice guilt over their illegal acts.* If they truly embraced criminal or antisocial values, criminals would probably not exhibit remorse for their acts, apart from regret at being apprehended.
- *Offenders frequently respect and admire honest, law-abiding persons.* Those admired may include entertainers, sports figures, priests and other members of the clergy, parents, teachers, and neighbors.
- *Criminals define whom they can victimize.* Members of similar ethnic groups, churches, or neighborhoods are often off-limits. This practice implies that criminals are aware of the wrongfulness of their acts.
- *Criminals are not immune to the demands of conformity.* Most criminals participate in the same social functions as law-abiding people, such as school, church, and family activities. Few engage in illegal activity all the time.

Sykes and Matza conclude that criminals must first neutralize accepted social values before they are free to commit crimes; they do so by learning a set of techniques that allow them to counteract the moral dilemmas posed by illegal behavior.[72]

Through their research, Sykes and Matza have identified the following techniques of neutralization:

- *Denial of responsibility.* Young offenders sometimes claim that their unlawful acts are not their fault—that such acts result from forces beyond their control or are accidents.
- *Denial of injury.* By denying the injury their acts cause, criminals neutralize illegal behavior. For example, stealing is viewed as borrowing; vandalism is considered mischief that has gotten out of hand. Offenders may find that their parents and friends support their denial of injury. In fact, parents and friends may claim that the behavior was merely a prank, which helps affirm the offender's perception that crime can be socially acceptable.
- *Denial of the victim.* Criminals sometimes neutralize wrongdoing by maintaining that the crime victim "had it coming." Vandalism may be directed against a disliked teacher or neighbor, or a gang may engage in gay bashing.
- *Condemnation of the condemners.* An offender views the world as a corrupt place with a dog-eat-dog code. Because police and judges are on the take, teachers show favoritism, and parents take out their frustrations on their children, offenders claim it is ironic and unfair for these authorities to condemn criminal misconduct. By shifting the blame to others, criminals repress their awareness that their own acts are wrong.
- *Appeal to higher loyalties.* Novice criminals often argue that they are caught in the dilemma of being loyal to their peer group while attempting to abide by the rules of society. The needs of the group take precedence because group demands are immediate and localized.

In sum, neutralization theory states that people neutralize conventional norms and values by using excuses that enable them to drift into crime (see Figure 7.2).

**FIGURE 7.2**
**Techniques of Neutralization**
**Source:** © Cengage Learning

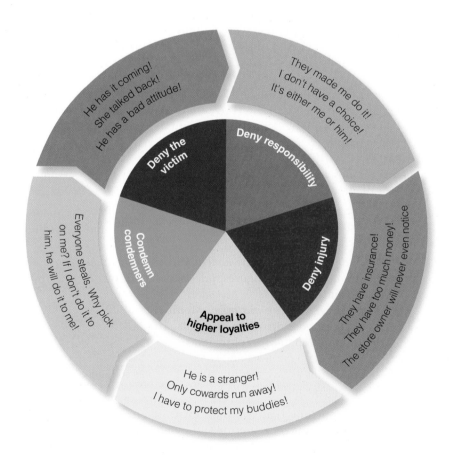

**TESTING NEUTRALIZATION THEORY** Attempts have been made to verify neutralization theory empirically, but the results have been inconclusive.[73] One area of research has been directed at determining whether law violators really need to neutralize moral constraints. The thinking behind this research is that if criminals hold values in opposition to accepted social norms, there is really no need to neutralize. So far, the evidence is mixed. Some studies show that law violators approve of criminal behavior such as theft and violence, whereas other studies yield evidence that even though they may be active participants themselves, criminals voice disapproval of illegal behavior.[74] Some studies indicate that law violators approve of social values such as honesty and fairness; other studies support the opposite conclusion.[75]

Although the existing research findings are ambiguous, the weight of the evidence suggests that most adolescents generally disapprove of deviant behaviors such as violence, and that neutralizations do in fact enable youths to engage in socially disapproved behavior.[76] And, as Matza predicted, people seem to drift into and out of antisocial behavior, rather than being committed solely to a criminal way of life.[77]

**DO CRIMINALS REALLY NEUTRALIZE?** Not all criminologists accept Matza's vision. Volkan Topalli conducted in-depth interviews with active criminals in St. Louis, Missouri, and found that street criminals living in disorganized, gang-ridden neighborhoods "disrespect authority, lionize honor and violence, and place individual needs above those of all others." Rather than having to neutralize conventional values in order to engage in deviant ones, these offenders do not experience guilt that requires neutralizations; they are "guilt free." There is no need for them to "drift" into criminality, Topalli finds, because their allegiance to nonconventional values and their lack of guilt perpetually leave them in a state of openness to crime. Rather than being embarrassed, they take great pride in their criminal activities and abilities. In fact, rather than neutralizing conventional values, these street kids embrace criminal values: they are expected to be bad and have to explain good behavior! Street criminals are expected to seek vengeance if they themselves are the target of theft or violence. If they don't, their self-image is damaged and they look weak and ineffective. If they decide against vengeance, they must neutralize their decision by convincing themselves that they are being merciful out of respect for their enemies' friends and family.[78]

## Evaluating Learning Theories

Learning theories contribute significantly to our understanding of the onset of criminal behavior. Nonetheless, the general learning model has been criticized. One complaint is that learning theorists fail to account for the origin of criminal definitions. How did the first criminal learn the necessary techniques and definitions? Who came up with the original neutralization technique?

Learning theories imply that people systematically learn techniques that enable them to be active, successful criminals. However, as Topalli's research indicates, street criminals may be proud of their felonious exploits and have little need to neutralize their guilt. Learning theory also fails to adequately explain spontaneous, wanton acts of violence, damage, and other expressive crimes that appear to have little utility or purpose. Although principles of differential association can easily explain shoplifting, is it possible that a random shooting is caused by excessive deviant definitions? It is estimated that about 70 percent of all arrestees were under the influence of drugs and alcohol when they committed their crimes. Do "crackheads" pause to neutralize their moral inhibitions before mugging a victim? Do drug-involved kids stop to consider what they have learned about moral values? Little evidence exists that people learn the techniques that enable them to become criminals before they actually commit criminal acts. It is equally plausible that people who are already deviant seek others with similar lifestyles to learn from. Early onset of deviant behavior is now considered a key determinant of criminal careers. It is difficult to see how very young children have had the opportunity to learn criminal behavior and attitudes within a peer group setting.

Despite these criticisms, learning theories have an important place in the study of delinquent and criminal behavior. They help explain the role that peers, family, and education play in shaping criminal and conventional behaviors. If crime were a matter of personal traits alone, these elements of socialization would not play such an important part in determining human behavior. And unlike social structure theories, learning theories are not limited to explaining a single facet of antisocial activity; they explain criminality across all class structures. Even corporate executives may be exposed to procrime definitions and learn to neutralize moral constraints. Learning theories can thus be applied to a wide variety of criminal activity.

## Social Control Theory

Social control theorists maintain that all people have the potential to violate the law and that modern society presents many opportunities for illegal activity. Criminal activities, such as drug abuse and car theft, are often exciting pastimes that hold the promise of immediate reward and gratification.

Considering the attractions of crime, social control theorists question why people obey the rules of society. They argue that people obey the law because behavior and passions are controlled by internal and external forces. Some individuals have **self-control**—a strong moral sense that renders them incapable of hurting others and violating social norms.

Other people have been socialized to have a **commitment to conformity**. They have developed a real, present, and logical reason to obey the rules of society, and they instinctively avoid behavior that will jeopardize their reputation and achievements.[79] The stronger people's commitment to conventional institutions, individuals, and processes, the less likely they are to commit crime. If that commitment is absent, there is little to lose, and people are free to violate the law.[80]

**self-control**
A strong moral sense that renders a person incapable of hurting others or violating social norms.

**commitment to conformity**
Obedience to the rules of society and the avoidance of nonconforming behavior that may jeopardize an individual's reputation and achievement.

According to Hirschi's version of social control theory, having a strong bond to society helps neutralize the lure of delinquency. Here, Normandy High School senior Eboni Boykin talks with her mother, Lekista Flurry, about her day at school before heading to her job at Johnny Rockets in St. Louis. Boykin spent a lot of time in homeless shelters, and her family moved so often she could barely keep track of the schools she's attended. But that didn't stop the teenager from pursuing her dream of attending an Ivy League school. Despite a childhood with enough hardship to last several lifetimes, Boykin's hard work and perseverance paid off, and she was given a full scholarship to attend Columbia University in New York.

AP Images/St. Louis Post-Dispatch, J.B. Forbes

### Hirschi's Social Control Theory

The version of control theory articulated by Travis Hirschi in his influential 1969 book *Causes of Delinquency* is today the dominant version of control theory.[81] Hirschi links the onset of criminality to weakening of the ties that bind people to society. He assumes that all individuals are potential law violators, but most are kept under control because they fear that illegal behavior will damage their relationships with friends, family, neighbors, teachers, and employers. Without these social bonds, or ties, a person is free to commit criminal acts. Across all ethnic, religious, racial, and social groups, people whose bond to society is weak may fall prey to criminogenic behavior patterns. People who care little for others are the ones most likely to prey upon them.

Hirschi argues that the social bond a person maintains with society is divided into four main elements: attachment, commitment, belief, and involvement (see Figure 7.3).

- Attachment consists of a person's sensitivity to and interest in others.[82] Hirschi views parents, peers, and schools as the important social institutions with which a person should maintain ties. Attachment to parents is the most important. Even if a family is shattered

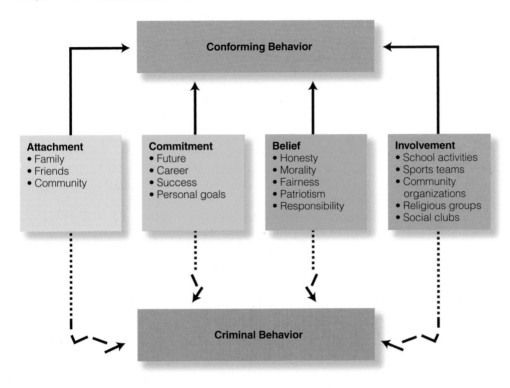

**FIGURE 7.3**
**Elements of the Social Bond**
**Source:** © Cengage Learning

by divorce or separation, a child must retain a strong attachment to one or both parents. Without this attachment, it is unlikely that respect for other authorities will develop.

- Commitment involves the time, energy, and effort expended in conventional actions such as getting an education and saving money for the future. If people build a strong commitment to conventional society, they will be less likely to engage in acts that jeopardize their hard-won position. Conversely, the lack of commitment to conventional values may foreshadow a condition in which risk-taking behavior, such as crime, becomes a reasonable behavior alternative.

- People who live in the same social setting often share common moral beliefs; they may adhere to such values as sharing, sensitivity to the rights of others, and admiration for the legal code. If these beliefs are absent or weakened, individuals are more likely to participate in antisocial or illegal acts.

- Involvement in conventional activities such as sports, clubs, and school leaves little time for illegal behavior. Hirschi believes that involvement in school, recreation, and family insulates people from the lure of criminal behavior. Idleness, on the other hand, enhances that lure.

Hirschi further suggests that the interrelationship among the elements of the social bond controls subsequent behavior. People who feel kinship and sensitivity to parents and friends should be more likely to adopt and work toward legitimate goals. A person who rejects such social relationships is more likely to lack commitment to conventional goals. Similarly, people who are highly committed to conventional acts and beliefs are more likely to be involved in conventional activities.

## Testing Social Control Theory: Supportive Research

One of Hirschi's most significant contributions to criminology was his attempt to test the principal hypotheses of social control theory. He administered a detailed self-report survey to a sample of more than 4,000 junior and senior high school students in Contra Costa County, California.[83] In a detailed analysis of the data, Hirschi found considerable evidence to support the control theory model society.

Even when the statistical significance of Hirschi's findings was less than he expected, the direction of his research data was notably consistent. Only rarely did his

**FACT OR FICTION?**

"Idle hands are the devil's workshop" is not merely an old saying. Getting involved in sports and other activities helps prevent crime and delinquency.

**FACT** Old sayings are sometimes accurate. Kids who are involved in conventional leisure activities, such as supervised social activities and noncompetitive sports, are less likely to engage in delinquency.

findings contradict the theory's most critical assumptions. Hirschi's version of social control theory has been corroborated by numerous research studies showing that delinquent youths often feel detached from society.[84] What are some of the most important findings?

**ATTACHMENT** Kids who are attached to their families, friends, and school are less likely to get involved in a deviant peer group and consequently are less likely to engage in criminal activities.[85] Kids who feel attached to their parents, especially if they are authoritative and respected, are the ones less likely to engage in antisocial behaviors.[86] In contrast, unattached kids are more likely to get involved in a deviant peer group and consequently prone to engage in criminal activities.[87] Attachment is significant regardless of gender or family structure.[88]

Attachment to education is equally important. Youths who are detached from the educational experience are at risk of criminality; those who are committed to school are less likely to engage in delinquent acts.[89] Detachment and alienation from school may be even more predictive of delinquency than school failure and/or educational underachievement.[90]

**BELIEF** Research efforts have shown that holding positive beliefs is inversely related to criminality. Children who are involved in religious activities and hold conventional religious beliefs are less likely to become involved in substance abuse.[91] Kids who live in areas marked by strong religious values and who hold strong religious beliefs themselves are less likely to engage in delinquent activities than adolescents who do not hold such beliefs or who live in less devout communities.[92]

**COMMITMENT** As predicted by Hirschi, kids who are committed to school and educational achievement are less likely to become involved in delinquent behaviors than those who lack such commitment.[93] The association may be reciprocal: kids who drink and engage in deviant behavior are more likely to fail in school; kids who fail in school are more likely to later drink and engage in deviant behavior.[94]

**INVOLVEMENT** Research shows that youths who are involved in conventional leisure activities, such as supervised social activities and noncompetitive sports, are less likely to engage in delinquency than those who are involved in unconventional leisure activities and unsupervised, peer-oriented social pursuits.[95] Although there are gender differences in involvement, members of both sexes are less likely to commit crime if they are engaged in conventional activities.[96]

## Critiquing Social Control Theory

Few theoretical models in criminology have garnered as much attention as Hirschi's social control theory. And although there is a great deal of supportive research, a number of questions have been raised about the validity of his work.

**THE INFLUENCE OF FRIENDSHIP** One significant concern is Hirschi's contention that delinquents are detached loners whose bond to friends has been broken. A number of researchers have argued that delinquents seem not to be "lone wolves" whose only personal relationships are exploitive; rather, their friendship patterns seem quite close to those of conventional youths.[97] Some types of offenders, such as drug abusers, have been found to maintain even more intimate relations with their peers than nonabusers do.[98] Hirschi would counter that what appears to be a close friendship is really a relationship of convenience and that "birds of a feather flock together" only when it suits their criminal activities. His view is supported by a number of research studies that question the influence of peers and suggest that deviant youth do not accurately perceive their friends' behavior and that their perceptions of peer deviance influence their own behavior.[99] It comes as no surprise then that most juvenile offenses are committed by individuals acting alone and that group offending, when it does occur, is incidental and of little importance to explaining the onset of delinquency. Committed delinquents, as Hirschi suggests, may truly be "lone wolves."[100]

**FAILURE TO ACHIEVE** Hirschi argues that commitment to career and economic advancement reduces criminal involvement. But he does not deal with the issue of failure: what about kids who are committed to the future but fail in school and perceive few avenues for advancement? Some research indicates that people who are committed to success but fail to achieve it may be crime prone.[101]

**DEVIANT INVOLVEMENT** Adolescents who report high levels of involvement, which Hirschi suggests should reduce delinquency, actually engage in high levels of criminal behavior. Typically, these are teenagers who are involved in activities outside the home without parental supervision.[102] Teens who spend a lot of time hanging out with their friends, unsupervised by parents and/or other authority figures, and who own cars that give them the mobility to get into even more trouble, are the ones most likely to get involved in antisocial acts such as drinking and taking drugs.[103] This is especially true of dating relationships: teens who date, especially if they have multiple partners, are the ones who are likely to get into trouble and engage in delinquent acts.[104] It is possible that although involvement is important, it depends on the behavior in which a person is involved!

**DEVIANT PEERS AND PARENTS** Perhaps the most controversial of Hirschi's conclusions is that any form of social attachment is beneficial, even attachment to deviant peers and parents. Despite Hirschi's claims, there is evidence that rather than deterring youths from delinquency, attachment to deviant peers and parents may support and nurture antisocial behavior.[105] A number of research efforts have found that youths attached to drug-abusing parents are more likely to use drugs themselves.[106] Attachment to deviant family members, peers, and associates may help motivate youths to commit crime and facilitate their antisocial acts.[107]

**MISTAKEN CAUSAL ORDER** Hirschi's theory proposes that a weakened bond leads to delinquency, but there is evidence that the chain of events may flow in the opposite direction: youngsters who break the law find that their bonds to parents, schools, and society are weakened.[108] *Increases* in adolescent behavior problems, such as substance abuse, may result in *decreases* in parental control and support, and not vice versa. Recent research by Martha Gault-Sherman shows that attachment to parents weakens *after* kids get involved in delinquency.[109]

While antisocial behavior may fray parents' nerves, even the most distraught may not totally abandon their delinquent kids. Sonja Siennick found that young adult offenders receive more parental financial assistance than do their nonoffending peers (and siblings). Parents are not adverse to helping troubled teens even after they have engaged in criminal activity.[110]

These criticisms are important, but Hirschi's views still constitute one of the preeminent theories in criminology.[111] Many criminologists consider social control theory the primary way of understanding the onset of youthful misbehavior.

# Social Reaction (Labeling) Theory

The third type of social process theory, social reaction theory, also called labeling theory (the two terms are used interchangeably), explains criminal careers in terms of stigma-producing encounters. Social reaction theory has a number of key points:

- *Behaviors that are considered criminal are highly subjective.* Even such crimes as murder, rape, and assault are bad or evil only because people label them as such. The difference between a forcible rape and a consensual sexual encounter often rests on whom the members of a jury believe and how they interpret the events that took place. The difference between an excusable act and a criminal one is often

**CHECKPOINTS**

▶ Social control theories maintain that behavior is a function of the attachment that people feel toward society.

▶ People who have a weak commitment to conformity are "free" to commit crime.

▶ A strong self-image may insulate people from crime.

▶ According to Travis Hirschi, social control is measured by a person's attachment, commitment, involvement, and belief.

▶ Significant research supports Hirschi's theory, but a number of criminologists question its validity.

▶ One important issue is whether delinquents are influenced by their peers or are lone wolves alienated from others.

subject to change and modification. Acts such as performing an abortion, using marijuana, possessing a handgun, and gambling have been legal at some times and places and illegal at others.

- *Crime is defined by those in power*. The content and shape of criminal law is defined by the values of those who rule and is not an objective standard of moral conduct. Howard Becker refers to people who create rules as **moral entrepreneurs**. An example of a moral entrepreneur is someone who campaigns against violence in the media and wants laws passed to restrict the content of television shows.

- *Not only acts are labeled, but also people*. Labels define not just an act but also the actor. Valued labels, such as "smart," "honest," and "hardworking," suggest overall competence. Sometimes labels are highly symbolic, such as being named "most likely to succeed" or class valedictorian. People who hold these titles are automatically assumed to be leaders who are well on their way to success. Without meeting them, we know that they are hardworking, industrious, and bright. These positive labels can improve self-image and social standing. Research shows that people who are labeled with one positive trait, such as being physically attractive, are assumed to have other positive traits, such as being intelligent and competent.[112] In contrast, people who run afoul of the law or other authorities, such as school officials, are given negative labels, including "troublemaker," "mentally ill," and "stupid," that **stigmatize** them and reduce their self-image. Negative labels also define the whole person. People labeled "insane" are also assumed to be dangerous, dishonest, unstable, violent, strange, and otherwise unsound. Such labels can have long-term consequences, as the Policies and Issues in Criminology feature shows.

- *Both positive and negative labels involve subjective interpretation of behavior*. A "troublemaker" is merely someone whom people label as "troublesome."

In a famous statement, Howard Becker sums up the importance of the audience's reaction:

> Social groups create deviance by making rules whose infractions constitute deviance, and by applying those rules to particular people and labeling them as outsiders. From this point of view, deviance is not a quality of the act a person commits, but rather a consequence of the application by others of rules and sanctions to an "offender." The deviant is one to whom the label has successfully been applied; deviant behavior is behavior that people so label.[113]

Even if some acts are labeled as bad or evil, those who participate in them can be spared a negative label. It is possible to take another person's life but not be considered a murderer, because the killing was considered self-defense or even an accident. Acts have negative consequences only when they are labeled by others as being wrong or evil.

## Consequences of Labeling

Although a label may be a function of rumor, innuendo, or unfounded suspicion, its adverse impact can be immense. If a devalued status is conferred by a significant other—a teacher, police officer, parent, or valued peer—the negative label may permanently harm the target. The degree to which a person is perceived as a social deviant may affect his or her treatment at home, at work, at school, and in other social situations. Children may find that their parents consider them a bad influence on younger

---

**moral entrepreneur**
A person who creates moral rules that reflect the values of those in power rather than any objective, universal standards of right and wrong.

**stigmatize**
To apply negative labeling with enduring effects on a person's self-image and social interactions.

AP Images/Jeff Chiu

Once labeled deviant, a person's identity becomes damaged. Here, Kenneth Barillas is interviewed under a sign he attached to his home, which is near the residence of sex offender Donald Robinson, in East Palo Alto, California. After being locked away for 25 years for sex crimes, Robinson, now 57 years old, moved to a little block of unassuming homes. The timing was particularly bad. The day before, Philip Garrido's arrest for kidnapping 11-year-old Jaycee Lee Dugard and keeping her for 18 years made headlines around the world. The spotlight was on sex offenders. And Robinson, who had spent 12 years after his release from prison in a state mental hospital for recidivist sex offenders, remained under state-sponsored treatment as an outpatient. His release caused a significant neighborhood reaction despite assurances he was no longer a danger to the community.

# Policies and Issues in Criminology

## THE LONG-TERM CONSEQUENCES OF BEING LABELED

*I am writing this letter . . . out of desperation and to tell you a little about the struggles of re-entering society as a convicted felon. I have worked hard to turn my life around. I have remained clean for nearly eight years, I am succeeding in college, and I continue to share my story in schools, treatment facilities, and correctional institutions, yet I have nothing to show for it. . . . I have had numerous interviews and sent out more than 200 résumés for jobs for which I am more than qualified. I have had denial after denial because of my felony. I do understand that you are not responsible for the choices that have brought me to this point. Furthermore, I recognize that if I was not abiding by the law, if I was not clean, and if I was not focusing my efforts toward a successful future, I would have no claim to make.*

So writes Jay, a man convicted of involuntary vehicular manslaughter and sentenced to 38 months in state prison nine years before. He is not alone: a criminal label can haunt people for the rest of their life, well beyond their offending years and despite the fact that they have stayed "clean" for quite some time.

Many people with records suffer stigma that prevents them from getting jobs. A recent study shows that nearly one-third of American adults have been arrested by age 23. This record will keep many people from obtaining employment, even if they have paid their dues, are qualified for the job, and are unlikely to reoffend.

Criminal records run the gamut from one-time arrests where charges are dropped to lengthy, serious, and violent criminal histories. Many people who have been arrested—and, therefore, technically have a criminal record that shows up on a background check—were never convicted of a crime. This is true not only among those charged with minor crimes, but also for many individuals arrested for serious offenses.

The impact of having a criminal record is most often felt among African Americans, who may already experience racial discrimination in the labor market and are more likely than whites to have a criminal record. Research shows that a criminal record reduces the likelihood of a job callback or offer by approximately 50 percent. This criminal record "penalty" is substantially greater for African Americans than for white applicants. Latinos suffer similar penalties in the employment market.

In addition to these significant and often overlapping challenges, an extra set of punishments, or "collateral consequences," is imposed on individuals as a direct result of their criminal convictions. These legal restrictions create barriers to jobs, housing, benefits, and voting. More than 80 percent of the statutes that place restrictions on people convicted of crime operate as denial of employment opportunities. Although some of these consequences serve important public safety purposes, others may be antiquated and create unnecessary barriers to legitimate work opportunities. A commonly cited example is that in some states formerly incarcerated people who were trained as barbers cannot hold those jobs after release because state laws prohibit felons from practicing the trade, presumably because their access to sharp objects makes them a threat to the public. Regardless of the legal restrictions, the majority of employers indicate they would "probably" or "definitely" not be willing to hire an applicant with a criminal record. A recent report by the National Employment Law Project found frequent use of blanket "no-hire" policies among major corporations. Employers do not want to hire individuals who might commit future crimes and who may be a risk to their employees' and customers' safety. The assumption, of course, is that a prior record signals higher odds that the individual will commit more crimes in the future.

### Critical Thinking

What can be done to reduce the effect of labels and stigma placed on people who have paid their debt? Should records be expunged within a certain time frame if a person does not reoffend? Or should knowledge of a prior criminal record be available since an employer has a right to know about the background of people they are considering hiring?

**Source:** Amy Solomon, "In Search of a Job: Criminal Records as Barriers to Employment," *NIJ Journal* 270 (2012), www.nij.gov/nij/journals/270/criminal-records.htm (accessed 2015).

brothers and sisters. School officials may limit them to classes reserved for people with behavioral problems. Likewise, when adults are labeled as "criminal," "ex-con," or "drug addict," they may find their eligibility for employment severely restricted. If the label is bestowed as the result of conviction for a criminal offense, the labeled person may also be subjected to official sanctions ranging from a mild reprimand to incarceration. The simultaneous effects of labels and sanctions reinforce feelings of isolation and detachment.

Public denunciation plays an important part in the labeling process. Condemnation is often carried out in "ceremonies" in which the individual's identity is officially transformed. One example of such a reidentification ceremony is a competency hearing in which a person is declared "mentally ill"; another is a public trial in which a person is found to be a "rapist" or "child molester." During the process, a permanent record is produced, such as an arrest or conviction record, so that the denounced person is ritually separated from a place in the legitimate order and set outside the world occupied by citizens of good standing. Harold Garfinkle has called transactions that produce irreversible, permanent labels **successful degradation ceremonies**.[114]

**successful degradation ceremony**
A course of action or ritual in which someone's identity is publicly redefined and destroyed and he or she is thereafter viewed as socially unacceptable.

**retrospective reading**
The reassessment of a person's past to fit a current generalized label.

**SELF-LABELING** According to labeling theory, depending on the visibility of the label and the manner and severity with which it is applied, negatively labeled individuals will become increasingly committed to a deviant career. Labeled persons may find themselves turning for support and companionship to others who have been similarly stigmatized.

Isolated from conventional society, labeled people may identify themselves as members of an outcast group and become locked into deviance. Kids who view themselves as delinquents after being labeled as such are giving an inner voice to their perceptions of how parents, teachers, peers, and neighbors view them. When they believe that others view them as antisocial or as troublemakers, they take on attitudes and roles that reflect this assumption; they expect to become suspects and then to be rejected.[115]

**JOINING DEVIANT CLIQUES** People labeled as deviant may join with similarly outcast peers who facilitate their behavior. Eventually, antisocial behavior becomes habitual and automatic.[116] The desire to join deviant cliques and groups may stem from self-rejecting attitudes ("At times, I think I am no good at all") that eventually weaken commitment to conventional values and behaviors. In turn, stigmatized individuals may acquire motives to deviate from social norms because they now share a common bond with similarly labeled social outcasts.[117]

**RETROSPECTIVE READING** Beyond any immediate results, labels tend to redefine the whole person. The label "ex-con" may evoke in people's imaginations a whole series of behavior descriptions—tough, mean, dangerous, aggressive, dishonest, sneaky—that may or may not apply to a particular person who has been in prison. People react to the label and its connotations instead of reacting to the actual behavior of the person who bears it. The labeled person's past is reviewed and reevaluated to fit his or her current status—a process known as **retrospective reading**. Boyhood friends of an assassin or serial killer, interviewed by the media, may report that the suspect was withdrawn, suspicious, and negativistic as a youth; they were always suspicious but never thought to report their concerns to the authorities. According to this retrospective reading, we can now understand what prompted his current behavior; therefore, the label must be accurate.[118]

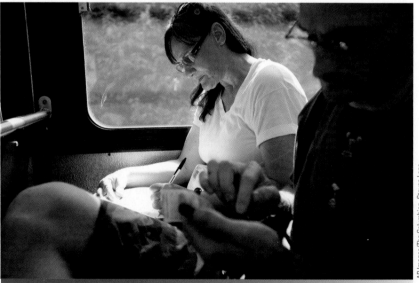

One problem faced by those bearing a criminal label is that it sends a negative message to potential employers. Here, Debra Lepak, who is serving the last 6 months of a 17-month prison sentence, fills out a job application. When the economy is bad and unemployment high, it becomes difficult for those with the ex-con label to find jobs, especially when experienced workers without criminal records are applying for jobs they traditionally wouldn't pursue in a better economy.

Labels, then, become the basis of personal identity. As the negative feedback of law enforcement agencies, parents, friends, teachers, and other figures amplifies the force of the original label, stigmatized offenders may begin to reevaluate their own identities (see Figure 7.4). If they are not really evil or bad, they may ask themselves, "Why is everyone making such a fuss?" This process has been referred to as the "dramatization of evil."[119]

## Primary and Secondary Deviance

One of the better-known views of the labeling process is Edwin Lemert's concept of primary deviance and secondary deviance.[120] According to Lemert, **primary deviance** involves norm violations or crimes that have little influence on the actor and can be quickly forgotten. For example, a college student successfully steals a textbook at the campus bookstore, gets an A in the course, graduates, is admitted to law school, and later becomes a famous judge. Because his shoplifting goes unnoticed, it is a relatively unimportant event that has little bearing on his future life.

In contrast, **secondary deviance** occurs when a deviant event comes to the attention of significant others or social control agents, who apply a negative label. The newly labeled offender then reorganizes his or her behavior and personality around the consequences of the deviant act. The shoplifting student is caught by a security guard and expelled from college. With his law school dreams dashed and his future cloudy, his options are limited; people say he lacks character, and he begins to share their opinion. He eventually becomes a drug dealer and winds up in prison (see Figure 7.5).

Secondary deviance involves resocialization into a deviant role. The labeled person is transformed into one who, according to Lemert, "employs his behavior or a role based upon it as a means of defense, attack, or adjustment to the overt and covert problems created by the consequent social reaction to him."[121] Secondary deviance produces a **deviance amplification** effect: offenders feel isolated from the mainstream of society and become locked within their deviant role. They may seek others similarly labeled to form deviant groups. Ever more firmly enmeshed in their deviant role, they are trapped in an escalating cycle of deviance, apprehension, more powerful labels, and identity transformation. Lemert's concept of secondary deviance expresses the core of social reaction theory: deviance is a process in which one's identity is transformed. Efforts to control offenders, whether by treatment or punishment, simply help to lock them in their deviant role.

## Crime and Labeling

Because the process of becoming stigmatized is essentially interactive, labeling theorists blame the establishment of criminal careers on the social agencies originally

**FIGURE 7.4**
**The Labeling Process**
Source: © Cengage Learning

**Initial criminal act** People commit crimes for a number of reasons.

**Detection by the justice system** Arrest is influenced by racial, economic, and power relations.

**Decision to label** Some are labeled "official" criminals by police and court authorities.

**Creation of a new identity** Those labeled are known as troublemakers, criminals, and so on, and are shunned by conventional society.

**Acceptance of labels** Labeled people begin to see themselves as outsiders (secondary deviance, self-labeling).

**Deviance amplification** Stigmatized offenders are now locked into criminal careers.

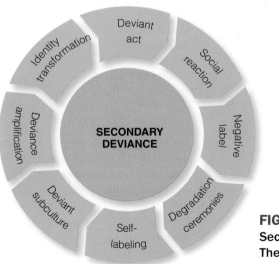

**FIGURE 7.5**
**Secondary Deviance: The Labeling Process**
Source: © Cengage Learning

**primary deviance** A norm violation or crime that has little or no long-term influence on the violator.

**secondary deviance** A norm violation or crime that comes to the attention of significant others or social control agents, who apply a negative label that has long-term consequences for the violator's self-identity and social interactions.

**deviance amplification** Process whereby secondary deviance pushes offenders out of mainstream society and locks them into an escalating cycle of deviance, apprehension, labeling, and criminal self-identity.

designed for crime control, such as police, courts, and correctional agencies. These institutions, labeling theorists claim, are inflicting the very stigma that harms the people they are trying to treat or correct. As a result, they actually help to maintain and amplify criminal behavior.

Because crime and deviance are defined by the social audience's reaction to people and their behavior and by the subsequent effects of that reaction, these institutions form the audience that helps define behavior as evil or wrong, locking people into deviant identities.

## Differential Enforcement

An important principle of social reaction theory is that the law is differentially applied, benefiting those who hold economic and social power and penalizing the powerless. The probability of being brought under the control of legal authority is a function of a person's race, wealth, gender, and social standing. A core concept of social reaction theory is that police officers are more likely to formally arrest males, minority group members, and those in the lower socioeconomic class, and to use their discretionary powers to give beneficial treatment to more favored groups.[122]

Minorities and the poor are more likely to be prosecuted for criminal offenses and to receive harsher punishments when convicted.[123] Judges may sympathize with white defendants and help them avoid criminal labels, especially if they seem to come from "good families," whereas minority youths are not afforded that luxury.[124] This helps to explain the significant racial and economic differences in the crime rate.

In sum, a major premise of social reaction theory is that the law is differentially constructed and applied, depending on the offender. It favors powerful members of society, who direct its content, and penalizes the powerless, such as minority group members and the poor, who demand equal rights.[125]

## Research on Social Reaction Theory

Research on social reaction theory can be divided into two distinct categories. The first focuses on the characteristics of those offenders who are chosen for labeling. The theory predicts that they will be relatively powerless people who are unable to defend themselves against the negative labeling. The second type of research attempts to discover the effects of being labeled. Labeling theorists predict that people who are negatively labeled will view themselves as deviant and will commit increasing amounts of crime.

**TARGETS OF LABELING** There is evidence that, just as predicted by labeling theory, poor and powerless people are victimized by the law and justice system. Labels are not equally distributed across class and racial lines. From the police officer's decision on whom to arrest, to the prosecutor's decision on whom to charge and how many and what kinds of charges to bring, to the court's decision on whom to release or free on bail or personal recognizance, to the grand jury's decision on indictment, to the judge's decision on sentence length—at every step, discretion works to the detriment of minorities.[126] The fact that labels are unfairly applied has focused attention on such practices as **racial profiling**, the practice of singling out minority group members for

**racial profiling**
The use of racial and ethnic characteristics by police in their determining whether a person is likely to commit a crime or engage in deviant and/or antisocial activities.

According to the labeling perspective, minority group members are unfairly targeted for official labels. Racial profiling has also resulted in a slew of high-profile police shootings involving young African American men. Here, on January 21, 2015, a protester representing the Black Lives Matter movement, marches to the Capitol to call on Congress to take action on racial justice.

AP Images/Tom Williams/CQ Roll Call

investigation, arrest, and prosecution simply on the basis of their racial characteristics. In 2011, the team of Tammy Rinehart Kochel, David Wilson, and Stephen Mastrofski thoroughly reviewed the existing literature on police arrest practices, screening more than 4,500 published and unpublished research studies. Their meta-analysis found that minority suspects stopped by police are significantly more likely to be arrested than are white suspects.[127] This research suggests that labels are not applied in a fair and evenhanded manner.

**EFFECTS OF LABELING**   Empirical evidence shows that negative labels may dramatically influence the self-image of offenders. Considerable evidence indicates that social sanctions lead to self-labeling and deviance amplification.[128] Children negatively labeled by their parents routinely suffer a variety of problems, including antisocial behavior and school failure.[129] In contrast, when parents stick by kids, the effect of negative labels bestowed by others can be neutralized.[130] This process has been observed in the United States and abroad, indicating that the labeling process is universal, especially in nations in which a brush with the law brings personal dishonor, such as China and Japan.[131]

This labeling process is important because once they are stigmatized as troublemakers, adolescents begin to reassess their self-image. Parents who label their children as troublemakers promote deviance amplification. Labeling alienates parents from their children, and negative labels reduce children's self-image and increase delinquency; this process is referred to as **reflected appraisals**.[132] Labeling, however, is rarely a one-way street; what some parents are quick to condemn, others are quite willing to defend. When they learn that their child has been in trouble at school or in the community, some parents are willing to join in and condemn their kids as a "troublemaker," thereby helping to add to the label's impact and further damage their child's self-image. In contrast, when parents stick by kids, the effect of negative labels bestowed by others can be neutralized, helping to ward off the damaging effects of labeling.[133]

The effects of stigma may be both long-term and cumulative. As they mature, children are in danger of undergoing repeated, intensive, official labeling, which has been shown to produce self-labeling and to damage identities.[134] Kids who perceive that they have been negatively labeled by significant others, such as peers and teachers, are also more likely to self-report delinquent behavior and to adopt a deviant self-concept.[135] They are likely to make deviant friends and join gangs, associations that escalate their involvement in criminal activities.[136] Youngsters labeled as troublemakers in school are the most likely to drop out, and dropping out has been linked to delinquent behavior.[137] These effects can plague people over the life course. Children who get involved with the police in adolescence suffer long-term effects of this negative labeling experience well into their 30s: early police intervention is indirectly related to adult social problems such as substance abuse, unemployment, and welfare receipt.[138] Using data collected from middle-school students in seven cities to examine the deviance amplification process, Stephanie Ann Wiley and her associates compared for youth with no police contact, those who were stopped by police, and those who were arrested; the latter group reported higher levels of future delinquency.[139] Those with weak social bonds and delinquent peers are the ones most likely to be effected by the negative consequences of police contact. Arrest may amplify a person's "cumulative disadvantage" and trigger exclusionary processes that limit conventional opportunities, such as educational attainment and employment.

Even as adults, the labeling process can take its toll. Male drug users labeled as addicts by social control agencies eventually become self-labeled and increase their drug use.[140] People arrested in domestic violence cases, especially those with a low stake in conformity (for example, those who are jobless and unmarried), increase their offending after being given official labels.[141] And once in prison, inmates labeled high-risk are more likely to have disciplinary problems than those who are spared such negative labels.[142]

Empirical evidence supports the view that labeling plays a significant role in persistent offending.[143] Although labels may not cause adolescents to initiate criminal

**reflected appraisal**
When parents are alienated from their children, their negative labeling reduces their children's self-image and increases delinquency.

behaviors, experienced delinquents are significantly more likely to continue offending if they believe their parents and peers view them in a negative light.[144] Labeling, then, may help sustain criminality over time.

### Is Labeling Theory Valid?

Labeling theory has been the subject of much debate among criminologists. Those who criticize it point to its inability to specify the conditions that must exist before an act or individual is labeled deviant—that is, why some people are labeled and others remain "secret deviants." There are also questions about whether stigma produces crime. Labeling often comes after, rather than before, chronic offending. Getting labeled by the justice system and having an enduring criminal record may have little effect on people who have been burdened with social and emotional problems since birth.[145]

While these criticisms are telling, there has been significant research showing that, as the theory predicts, people who suffer official labels are prone to a delinquent and criminal way of life. Recent research by Emily Restivo and Mark Lanier found that official labeling may lead to an increased delinquent self-identity, decreased prosocial expectations, and an increased association with delinquent peers, which then lead to an increased likelihood of engaging in subsequent delinquency. Restivo and Lanier conclude that the labeling process creates a new damaged identity for the individual that places them in the company of other damaged people. The result is they are expected to fail and their association with delinquent peers helps make sure that happens.[146]

Criminologists Raymond Paternoster and Leeann Iovanni have identified features of the labeling perspective that are important contributions to the study of criminality:[147]

- The labeling perspective identifies the role played by social control agents in crime causation. Criminal behavior cannot be fully understood if the agencies and individuals empowered to control and treat it are neglected.
- Labeling theory recognizes that criminality is not a disease or pathological behavior. It focuses attention on the social interactions and reactions that shape individuals and their behavior.
- Labeling theory distinguishes between criminal acts (primary deviance) and criminal careers (secondary deviance) and shows that these concepts must be interpreted and treated differently.

Labeling theory also contributes to understanding crime by focusing on interaction as well as the situation surrounding the crime. Rather than viewing the criminal as a robot-like creature whose actions are predetermined, it recognizes that crime often results from complex interactions and processes. The decision to commit crime involves actions of a variety of people, including peers, victim, police, and other key characters. Labels may foster crime by dictating the actions of all parties involved in these criminal interactions. Actions deemed innocent when performed by one person are considered provocative when performed by someone who has been labeled deviant. Similarly, labeled people may become quick to judge, take offense, or misinterpret others' behavior because of past experience.

**L06** Link social process theory to crime prevention efforts.

## Social Process Theory and Public Policy

Social process theories have had a major influence on public policy since the 1950s. Learning theories have greatly influenced the way criminal offenders are treated. The effect of these theories has been felt mainly by young offenders, who are viewed as being more salvageable than hardened criminals. Advocates of the social learning approach argue that if people become criminal by learning definitions and attitudes favoring criminality, they can unlearn these attitudes by being exposed to definitions favoring conventional behavior.

This philosophy has been applied in numerous treatment facilities modeled in part on two pioneering efforts: the Highfields Project in New Jersey and the Silverlake Program in Los Angeles. These residential treatment programs, geared toward young male offenders, used group interaction sessions to attack criminal behavior orientations while promoting conventional modes of behavior. It is common today for residential and nonresidential programs to offer similar treatment, teaching children and adolescents to refuse drugs, to forgo delinquent behavior, and to stay in school. It is even common for celebrities to return to their old neighborhoods to urge young people to stay in school or stay off drugs. If learning did not affect behavior, such exercises would be futile.

Control theories have also influenced criminal justice and other social policies. Programs have been developed to increase people's commitment to conventional lines of action. Some focus on trying to create and strengthen bonds early in life before the onset of criminality. The educational system has hosted numerous programs designed to improve students' basic skills and create an atmosphere in which youths will develop a bond to their schools.

Control theory's focus on the family has played a key role in programs designed to strengthen the bond between parent and child. Other programs attempt to repair bonds that have been broken and frayed. Examples of this approach are the career, work furlough, and educational opportunity programs being developed in the nation's prisons. These programs are designed to help inmates maintain a stake in society so they will be less willing to resort to criminal activity after their release.

Although labeling theorists caution that too much intervention can be harmful, programs aimed at reconfiguring an offender's self-image may help him or her develop revamped identities and desist from crime. With proper treatment, labeled offenders can cast off their damaged identities and develop new ones. As a result, they develop an improved self-concept that reflects the positive reinforcement they receive while in treatment.[148]

AP Images/John Spaulding/JetBlue's Soar with Reading Program

It is common for community programs to be based on social process principles. Here, on July 8, 2015, Robert Griffin III (aka RGIII) helps kick off the JetBlue airline summer reading initiative Soar with Reading. RGIII helped launch the pilot program that will put three customized, one-of-a-kind book vending machines at select locations throughout Washington, D.C., to provide free books to kids in the area. The program is designed to help kids and families that have little or no ability to purchase age-appropriate books. Since 2011, JetBlue's Soar with Reading has donated over $1,250,000 worth of books to kids and communities in need. Can such a reading program help socialize kids and insulate them from crime?

Joel Bissell/MLive.com/Landov

Restitution sentences can be used to keep offenders in the community while having to pay back society for their crimes. On April 7, 2015, Jordann Nicole Lockhart, the former treasurer of Mona Shores Campbell Elementary School Parent Teacher Organization, pleaded guilty to embezzling nearly $50,000 from the organization. Lockhart was sentenced to 90 days in jail with work release, two years probation, and $42,378 in restitution.

**diversion programs**
Programs of rehabilitation that remove offenders from the normal channels of the criminal justice process, thus enabling them to avoid the stigma of a criminal label.

**restitution**
Permitting an offender to repay the victim or do useful work in the community rather than facing the stigma of a formal trial and a court-ordered sentence.

The influence of labeling theory can also be seen in diversion and restitution programs. **Diversion programs** remove both juvenile and adult offenders from the normal channels of the criminal justice process by placing them in rehabilitation programs. A college student whose drunken driving hurts a pedestrian may, before trial, be placed for six months in an alcohol treatment program. If he successfully completes the program, charges against him will be dismissed; thus he avoids the stigma of a criminal label. Such programs are common throughout the United States. They frequently offer counseling, medical advice, and vocational, educational, and family services.

Another popular label-avoiding program is **restitution**. Rather than face the stigma of a formal trial, an offender is asked either to pay back the victim of the crime for any loss incurred or to do some useful work in the community in lieu of receiving a court-ordered sentence.

Despite their good intentions, stigma-reducing programs have not met with great success. Critics charge that they substitute one kind of stigma for another—for instance, attending a mental health program in lieu of undergoing a criminal trial. In addition, diversion and restitution programs usually screen out violent and repeat offenders. Finally, there is little hard evidence that these alternative programs improve recidivism rates.

Concept Summary 7.1 outlines the major concepts of social process theories.

## Concept Summary 7.1  Social Process Theories

| Theory | Major Premise | Strengths | Research Focus |
|---|---|---|---|
| **Social Learning Theories** | | | |
| Differential association theory | People learn to commit crime from exposure to antisocial definitions. | Explains onset of criminality. Explains the presence of crime in all elements of social structure. Explains why some people in high-crime areas refrain from criminality. Can apply to adults and juveniles. | Measures definitions toward crime; influence of deviant peers and parents. |
| Neutralization theory | Youths learn ways of neutralizing moral restraints and periodically drift in and out of criminal behavior patterns. | Explains why many delinquents do not become adult criminals. Explains why youthful law violators can participate in conventional behavior. | Whether people who use neutralizations commit more crimes; beliefs, values, and crime. |
| **Social Control Theory** | | | |
| Hirschi's control theory | A person's bond to society prevents him or her from violating social rules. If the bond weakens, the person is free to commit crime. | Explains the onset of crime. Can apply to both middle- and lower-class crime. Explains its theoretical constructs adequately so they can be measured. Has been empirically tested. | The association among commitment, attachment, involvement, belief, and crime. |
| **Social Reaction Theory** | | | |
| Labeling theory | People enter into law-violating careers when they are labeled and organize their personalities around the labels. | Explains society's role in creating deviance. Explains why some juvenile offenders do not become adult criminals. Develops concepts of criminal careers. | Measures the association between self-concept and crime; differential application of labels; the effect of stigma. |

# Thinking Like a Criminologist

**Shaming the Rogues** The state legislature is considering a bill that requires posting the names of people convicted of certain offenses (such as vandalism, soliciting a prostitute, and nonpayment of child support) in local newspapers under the heading "The Rogues Gallery." Those who favor the bill cite similar practices elsewhere: In Boston, men arrested for soliciting prostitutes are forced to clean streets. In Dallas, shoplifters are made to stand outside stores with signs stating their misdeeds.

Members of the state Civil Liberties Union have opposed the bill, stating, "It's simply needless humiliation of the individual." They argue that public shaming is inhumane and further alienates criminals who already have little stake in society, further ostracizing them from the mainstream. According to civil liberties attorneys, applying stigma helps criminals acquire a damaged reputation, which locks them more rigidly into criminal behavior patterns.

This "liberal" position is challenged by those who believe that convicted lawbreakers have no right to conceal their crimes from the public. Shaming penalties seem attractive as cost-effective alternatives to imprisonment. These critics ask what could be wrong with requiring a teenage vandal to personally apologize at the school he or she defaced and to wear a shirt with a big "V" on it while cleaning up the mess. If you do something wrong, they argue, you should have to face the consequences.

## Writing Assignment

You have been asked to submit a position paper to the legislative committee on the issue of whether shaming could deter crime. What will you say? What are the advantages? What are the possible negative consequences?

# SUMMARY

**LO1  Explain the concepts of social process and socialization.**
Social process theories view criminality as a function of people's interaction with various organizations, institutions, and processes in society. People in all walks of life have the potential to become criminals if they maintain destructive social relationships. Improper socialization is a key component of crime.

**LO2  Discuss the effect of family relationships on crime.**
Family dysfunction can lead children to have long-term social problems. Interactions between parents and children provide opportunities for children to acquire or inhibit antisocial behavior patterns. Good parenting, known as parental efficacy, lowers the risk of delinquency for children living in high-crime areas. Parents who closely supervise their children and have close ties with them help reduce the likelihood of adolescent delinquent behavior. Kids who suffer abuse are likely to be deeply affected and externalize problem behavior.

**LO3  Describe how the educational setting influences crime.**
School failure is linked to delinquency. Kids who are alienated are more likely to drop out, a decision that can later influence criminality. Minority kids are often the target of school discipline and are more likely to suffer alienation and drop out. School violence and conflict are also a problem. School bullying has become a significant social problem.

**LO4  Discuss the link between peers and delinquency.**
Delinquent peers sustain individual offending patterns. Delinquent friends may help kids neutralize the fear of punishment. Both popular kids and loners can have problems.

**LO5** **Contrast social learning, social control, and social reaction (labeling) theories.**

Social learning theory suggests that criminal behavior is learned. The most significant model, known as differential association theory, was formulated by Edwin Sutherland. It holds that criminality is a result of a person's perceiving an excess of definitions in favor of crime. Gresham Sykes and David Matza formulated the theory of neutralization, which stresses that youths learn mental techniques that enable them to overcome societal values and hence break the law. In contrast, social control theory maintains that all people have the potential to become criminals, but their bonds to conventional society prevent them from violating the law. Travis Hirschi's social control theory describes the social bond as containing elements of attachment, commitment, involvement, and belief. Weakened bonds allow youths to behave antisocially. Social reaction or labeling theory holds that criminality is promoted by becoming negatively labeled by significant others. Such labels as "criminal," "ex-con," and "junkie" isolate people from society and lock them into lives of crime. Edwin Lemert suggests that people who accept labels are involved in secondary deviance, while primary deviants are able to maintain an undamaged identity.

**LO6** **Link social process theory to crime prevention efforts.**

Social process theories have greatly influenced social policy. They have been applied in treatment orientations as well as community action policies. Some programs teach kids conventional attitudes and behaviors. Others are designed to improve the social bond. Those based on social reaction theory attempt to shield people from criminal labels by diverting them from the system in order to avoid stigma.

## Key Terms

socialized 196
social process theory 196
social learning theory 196
social control theory 196
social reaction (labeling)
    theory 196
parental efficacy 197
differential association
    theory 201

culture conflict 202
differential
    reinforcement 203
negative
    reinforcement 203
neutralization theory 205
drift 205
neutralization
    techniques 205

self-control 208
commitment to
    conformity 208
moral entrepreneur 212
stigmatize 212
successful degradation
    ceremony 214
retrospective
    reading 214

primary deviance 215
secondary deviance 215
deviance
    amplification 215
racial profiling 216
reflected appraisal 217
diversion
    programs 220
restitution 220

## Critical Thinking Questions

1. If criminal behavior is learned, who taught the first criminal? Have you ever been exposed to procrime definitions? How did you handle them? Did they affect your behavior?

2. Children who do well in school are less likely to commit criminal acts than those who are school failures. Which element of Hirschi's theory is supported by the school failure–delinquency link?

3. Have you ever been given a negative label, and, if so, did it cause you social harm? How did you lose the label, or did it become a permanent marker that still troubles you today?

4. If negative labels are damaging, do positive ones help insulate children from crime-producing forces in their environment? Has a positive label ever changed your life?

5. How would a social process theorist explain the fact that many children begin offending at an early age and then desist from crime as they mature? Are you involved in fewer antisocial acts in college than you were in high school? If so, how do you explain your behavioral changes?

# Notes

*All URLs accessed in 2015.*

1. U.S. Attorney's Office, Eastern Virginia, "Chesterfield Man Sentenced to 48 Months for Defrauding Military Personnel and Their Dependents," January 31, 2014, www.justice.gov/usao/vae/news/2014/01/20140131matthewsnr.html; FBI, "Investment Fraud Scheme Uncovered: Members of Military and Dependents Victimized," April 25, 2014, www.fbi.gov/news/stories/2014/april/investment-fraud-scheme-uncovered/investment-fraud-scheme-uncovered.

2. Sheldon Glueck and Eleanor Glueck, *Unraveling Juvenile Delinquency* (Cambridge, MA: Harvard University Press, 1950); Ashley Weeks, "Predicting Juvenile Delinquency," *American Sociological Review* 8 (1943): 40–46.

3. Alexander Vazsonyi and Lloyd Pickering, "The Importance of Family and School Domains in Adolescent Deviance: African American and Caucasian Youth," *Journal of Youth and Adolescence* 32 (2003): 115–129; Denise Kandel, "The Parental and Peer Contexts of Adolescent Deviance: An Algebra of Interpersonal Influences," *Journal of Drug Issues* 26 (1996): 289–315; Ann Goetting, "The Parenting–Crime Connection," *Journal of Primary Prevention* 14 (1994): 167–184.

4. Rand Conger and Katherine Conger, "Understanding the Processes Through Which Economic Hardship Influences Families and Children," in *Handbook of Families and Poverty*, ed. D. Russell Crane and Tim B. Heaton (Thousand Oaks, CA: Sage Publications, 2008), pp. 64–81.

5. Tiffany Field, "Violence and Touch Deprivation in Adolescents," *Adolescence* 37 (2002): 735–749.

6. John Paul Wright and Francis Cullen, "Parental Efficacy and Delinquent Behavior: Do Control and Support Matter?" *Criminology* 39 (2001): 677–706.

7. Carter Hay, "Parenting, Self-Control, and Delinquency: A Test of Self-Control Theory," *Criminology* 39 (2001): 707–736.

8. Robert Roberts and Vern Bengston, "Affective Ties to Parents in Early Adulthood and Self-Esteem Across 20 Years," *Social Psychology Quarterly* 59 (1996): 96–106.

9. Cesar Rebellon, "Reconsidering the Broken Homes/Delinquency Relationship and Exploring Its Mediating Mechanism(s)," *Criminology* 40 (2002): 103–135.

10. Eric Slade and Lawrence Wissow, "Spanking in Early Childhood and Later Behavior Problems: A Prospective Study of Infants and Young Toddlers," *Pediatrics* 113 (2004): 1321–1330; Ronald Simons, Chyi-In Wu, Kuei-Hsiu Lin, Leslie Gordon, and Rand Conger, "A Cross-Cultural Examination of the Link Between Corporal Punishment and Adolescent Antisocial Behavior," *Criminology* 38 (2000): 47–79.

11. Joshua Mersky, James Topitzes, and Arthur J. Reynolds, "Unsafe at Any Age: Linking Childhood and Adolescent Maltreatment to Delinquency and Crime," *Journal of Research in Crime and Delinquency*, first published August 1, 2011; Cesar Rebellon and Karen Van Gundy, "Can Control Theory Explain the Link Between Parental Physical Abuse and Delinquency? A Longitudinal Analysis," *Journal of Research in Crime and Delinquency* 42 (2005): 247–274.

12. Jennifer Lansford, Laura Wager, John Bates, Gregory Pettit, and Kenneth Dodge, "Forms of Spanking and Children's Externalizing Behaviors," *Family Relations* 6 (2012): 224–236.

13. Sara Culhane and Heather Taussig, "The Structure of Problem Behavior in a Sample of Maltreated Youths," *Social Work Research* 33 (2009): 70–78.

14. Maureen A. Allwood and Cathy Spatz Widom, "Child Abuse and Neglect, Developmental Role Attainment, and Adult Arrests," *Journal of Research in Crime and Delinquency* 50 (2013): 551–578.

15. Egbert Zavala, "Testing the Link Between Child Maltreatment and Family Violence Among Police Officers," *Crime and Delinquency*, first published online November 22, 2010.

16. Kristi Holsinger and Alexander Holsinger, "Differential Pathways to Violence and Self-Injurious Behavior: African American and White Girls in the Juvenile Justice System," *Journal of Research in Crime and Delinquency* 42 (2005): 211–242; Carolyn Smith and Terence Thornberry, "The Relationship Between Childhood Maltreatment and Adolescent Involvement in Delinquency," *Criminology* 33 (1995): 451–479.

17. Fred Rogosch and Dante Cicchetti, "Child Maltreatment and Emergent Personality Organization: Perspectives from the Five-Factor Model," *Journal of Abnormal Child Psychology* 32 (2004): 123–145.

18. Lynette M. Renner, "Single Types of Family Violence Victimization and Externalizing Behaviors Among Children and Adolescents" *Journal of Family Violence* 27 (2012): 177–186.

19. Todd Herrenkohl, Rick Kosterman, David Hawkins, and Alex Mason, "Effects of Growth in Family Conflict in Adolescence on Adult Depressive Symptoms: Mediating and Moderating Effects of Stress and School Bonding," *Journal of Adolescent Health* 44 (2009): 146–152.

20. Rand Conger, Center for Poverty Research, University of California, Davis, poverty.ucdavis.edu/profile/rand-conger.

21. Brent Donnellan, Kali H. Trzesniewski, Richard W. Robins, Terrie E. Moffitt, and Avshalom Caspi, "Low Self-Esteem Is Related to Aggression, Antisocial Behavior, and Delinquency," *Psychological Research* 16 (2005): 328–335; Martin Gold, "School Experiences, Self-Esteem, and Delinquent Behavior: A Theory for Alternative Schools," *Crime and Delinquency* 24 (1978): 294–295.

22. Jessica B. Heppen and Susan Bowles Therriault, "Developing Early Warning Systems to Identify Potential High School Dropouts," National High School Center, www.betterhighschools.org/pubs/ews_guide.asp.

23. Kimberly Henry, Kelly Knight, and Terence Thornberry, "School Disengagement as a Predictor of Dropout, Delinquency, and Problem Substance Use During Adolescence and Early Adulthood," *Journal of Youth and Adolescence* 41 (2012): 156–166.

24. Allison Ann Payne and Kelly Welch, "Modeling the Effects of Racial Threat on Punitive and Restorative School Discipline Practices," *Criminology* 48 (2010): 1019–1062.

25. Michael Rocques and Raymond Paternoster, "Understanding the Antecedents of the 'School-to-Jail' Link: The Relationship Between Race and School Discipline," *Journal of Criminal Law and Criminology* 101 (2011): 633–665.

26. Department of Education, "New Data from U.S. Department of Education Highlights Educational Inequities Around Teacher Experience, Discipline and High School Rigor," March 6, 2012, www.ed.gov/news/press-releases/new-data-us-department-education-highlights-educational-inequities-around-teacher-experience-discipline-and-high-school-rigor.

27. National Center for Educational Statistics, *Indicators of School Crime and Safety: 2011*, nces.ed.gov/programs/crimeindicators/crimeindicators2011/.

28. Reuters, "Harassment of Gay Students Declining: Survey," September 5, 2012, www.reuters.com/article/2012/09/05/us-usa-schools-gay-idUSBRE8841H220120905.

29. Jean Marie McGloin and Wendy Povitsky Stickle, "Influence or Convenience? Disentangling Peer Influence and Co-offending for Chronic Offenders," *Journal of Research in Crime and Delinquency* 48 (2011): 419–447.

30. Callie H. Burt and Carter Rees, "Behavioral Heterogeneity in Adolescent Friendship Networks," *Justice Quarterly*, first published online January 3, 2014.

31. Caterina Gouvis Roman, Meagan Cahill, Pamela Lachman, Samantha Lowry, Carlena Orosco, and Christopher McCarty, with Megan Denver and Juan Pedroza, *Social Networks, Delinquency, and Gang Membership: Using a Neighborhood Framework to Examine the Influence of Network Composition and Structure in a Latino Community* (Washington, DC: Urban Institute, 2012), www.urban.org/UploadedPDF/412519-Social-Networks-Delinquency-and-Gang-Membership.pdf.

32. Jean Marie McGloin, "Delinquency Balance and Time Use: A Research Note," *Journal of Research in Crime and Delinquency* 49 (2012): 109–121.

33. Wesley Younts, "Status, Endorsement and the Legitimacy of Deviance," *Social Forces* 87 (2008): 561–590; Amy Anderson and Lorine Hughes, "Exposure to Situations Conducive to Delinquent Behavior: The Effects of Time Use, Income, and Transportation," *Journal of Research in Crime and Delinquency* 46 (2009): 5–34.

34. Sara Battin, Karl Hill, Robert Abbott, Richard Catalano, and J. David Hawkins, "The Contribution of Gang Membership to Delinquency Beyond Delinquent Friends," *Criminology* 36 (1998): 93–116.

35. John Paul Wright and Francis Cullen, "Employment, Peers, and Life-Course Transitions," *Justice Quarterly* 21 (2004): 183–205.

36. Stephanie Dipietro and Jean Marie McGloin, "Differential Susceptibility? Immigrant Youth and Peer Influence," *Criminology* 50 (2012): 711–742; Raymond Paternoster, Jean Marie McGloin, Holly Nguyen, and Kyle Thomas, "The Causal Impact of Exposure to Deviant Peers: An Experimental Investigation," *Journal of Research in Crime and Delinquency*, first published online July 20, 2012.

37. J. C. Barnes and Robert Morris, "Young Mothers, Delinquent Children: Assessing Mediating Factors Among American Youth," *Youth Violence and Juvenile Justice* 10 (2012): 172–189.

38. Gregory Zimmerman and Bob Edward Vásquez, "Decomposing the Peer Effect on Adolescent Substance Use: Mediation, Nonlinearity, and Differential Nonlinearity," *Criminology* 49 (2011): 1235–1272.

39. Frank Weerman, "Delinquent Peers in Context: A Longitudinal Network Analysis of Selection and Influence Effects," *Criminology* 49 (2011): 253–286.

40. Paul Friday, Xin Ren, Elmar Weitekamp, Hans-Jürgen Kerner, and Terrance Taylor, "A Chinese Birth Cohort: Theoretical Implications," *Journal of Research in Crime and Delinquency* 42 (2005): 123–146.

41. Daneen Deptula and Robert Cohen, "Aggressive, Rejected, and Delinquent Children and Adolescents: A Comparison of Their Friendships," *Aggression and Violent Behavior* 9 (2004): 75–104; Stephen W. Baron, "Self-Control, Social Consequences, and Criminal Behavior: Street Youth and the General Theory of Crime," *Journal of Research in Crime and Delinquency* 40 (2003): 403–425.

42. Shelley Keith Matthews and Robert Agnew, "Extending Deterrence Theory: Do Delinquent Peers Condition the Relationship Between Perceptions of Getting Caught and Offending?" *Journal of Research in Crime and Delinquency* 45 (2008): 91–118; Sylvie Mrug, Betsy Hoza, and William Bukowski, "Choosing or Being Chosen by Aggressive-Disruptive Peers: Do They Contribute to Children's Externalizing and Internalizing Problems?" *Journal of Abnormal Child Psychology* 32 (2004): 53–66.

43. Mark Warr, "Age, Peers, and Delinquency," *Criminology* 31 (1993): 17–40; David Fergusson, L. John Horwood, and Daniel Nagin, "Offending Trajectories in a New Zealand Birth Cohort," *Criminology* 38 (2000): 525–551.

44. Jacob Young, Cesar Rebellon, J. C. Barnes, and Frank Weerman, "Unpacking the Black Box of Peer Similarity in Deviance: Understanding the Mechanisms Linking Personal Behavior, Peer Behavior, and Perceptions," *Criminology* 52 (2014): 60–86.

45. Alex R. Piquero, Jeffrey A. Bouffard, Nicole Leeper Piquero, and Jessica M. Craig, "Does Morality Condition

the Deterrent Effect of Perceived Certainty Among Incarcerated Felons?" *Crime and Delinquency*, first published online October 20, 2013.

46. Colin Baier and Bradley Wright, "'If You Love Me, Keep My Commandments': A Meta-Analysis of the Effect of Religion on Crime," *Journal of Research in Crime and Delinquency* 38 (2001): 3–21; Byron Johnson, Sung Joon Jang, David Larson, and Spencer De Li, "Does Adolescent Religious Commitment Matter? A Reexamination of the Effects of Religiosity on Delinquency," *Journal of Research in Crime and Delinquency* 38 (2001): 22–44.

47. Sung Joon Jang and Byron Johnson, "Neighborhood Disorder, Individual Religiosity, and Adolescent Use of Illicit Drugs: A Test of Multilevel Hypothesis," *Criminology* 39 (2001): 109–144.

48. T. David Evans, Francis Cullen, R. Gregory Dunaway, and Velmer Burton, Jr., "Religion and Crime Reexamined: The Impact of Religion, Secular Controls, and Social Ecology on Adult Criminality," *Criminology* 33 (1995): 195–224.

49. Ronald L. Simons and Callie Harbin Burt, "Learning to Be Bad: Adverse Social Conditions, Social Schemas, and Crime," *Criminology* 49 (2011): 553–598.

50. Edwin H. Sutherland, *Principles of Criminology* (Philadelphia: Lippincott, 1939).

51. See Edwin Sutherland and Donald Cressey, *Criminology*, 8th ed. (Philadelphia: Lippincott, 1970), pp. 77–79.

52. Carlo Morselli, Pierre Tremblay, and Bill McCarthy, "Mentors and Criminal Achievement," *Criminology* 44 (2006): 17–43.

53. Byongook Moon, Hye-Won Hwang, and John McCluskey, "Causes of School Bullying: Empirical Test of a General Theory of Crime, Differential Association Theory, and General Strain Theory," *Crime and Delinquency* 57 (2011): 849–877; John Cochran, Christine Sellers, Valerie Wiesbrock, and Wilson Palacios, "Repetitive Partner Victimization: An Exploratory Application of Social Learning," *Deviant Behavior* 32 (2011): 790–817.

54. For an early review, see Barbara Wooton, *Social Science and Social Pathology* (London: Allen and Unwin, 1959).

55. Joseph Murray, Rolf Loeber, and Dustin Pardini, "Parental Involvement in the Criminal Justice System and the Development of Youth Theft, Marijuana Use, Depression, and Poor Academic Performance," *Criminology* 50 (2012): 255–312; Michael Roettger and Raymond Swisher, "Associations of Fathers' History of Incarceration with Sons' Delinquency and Arrest Among Black, White, and Hispanic Males in the United States," *Criminology* 49 (2011): 1109–1148; Marieke van de Rakt, Joseph Murray, and Paul Nieuwbeerta, "The Long-Term Effects of Paternal Imprisonment on Criminal Trajectories of Children," *Journal of Research in Crime and Delinquency* 49 (2012): 81–108. Daniel Shaw, "Advancing Our Understanding of

Intergenerational Continuity in Antisocial Behavior," *Journal of Abnormal Child Psychology* 31 (2003): 193–199.

56. Terence P. Thornberry, "The Apple Doesn't Fall Far from the Tree (or Does It?): Intergenerational Patterns of Antisocial Behavior—The American Society of Criminology 2008 Sutherland Address," *Criminology* 47 (2009): 297–325; Terence Thornberry, Adrienne Freeman-Gallant, Alan Lizotte, Marvin Krohn, and Carolyn Smith, "Linked Lives: The Intergenerational Transmission of Antisocial Behavior," *Journal of Abnormal Child Psychology* 31 (2003): 171–184.

57. Wesley Church II, Tracy Wharton, and Julie Taylor, "An Examination of Differential Association and Social Control Theory: Family Systems and Delinquency," *Youth Violence and Juvenile Justice* 7 (2009): 3–15.

58. Brett Laursen, Christopher Hafen, Margaret Kerr, and Hakin Stattin, "Friend Influence over Adolescent Problem Behaviors as a Function of Relative Peer Acceptance: To Be Liked Is to Be Emulated," *Journal of Abnormal Psychology* 121 (2012): 88–94.

59. Joel Hektner, Gerald August, and George Realmuto, "Effects of Pairing Aggressive and Nonaggressive Children in Strategic Peer Affiliation," *Journal of Abnormal Child Psychology* 31 (2003): 399–412; Matthew Ploeger, "Youth Employment and Delinquency: Reconsidering a Problematic Relationship," *Criminology* 35 (1997): 659–675; William Skinner and Anne Fream, "A Social Learning Theory Analysis of Computer Crime Among College Students," *Journal of Research in Crime and Delinquency* 34 (1997): 495–518; Denise Kandel and Mark Davies, "Friendship Networks, Intimacy, and Illicit Drug Use in Young Adulthood: A Comparison of Two Competing Theories," *Criminology* 29 (1991): 441–467.

60. Warr, "Age, Peers, and Delinquency."

61. Dana Haynie, Peggy Giordano, Wendy Manning, and Monica Longmore, "Adolescent Romantic Relationships and Delinquency Involvement," *Criminology* 43 (2005): 177–210.

62. Robert Lonardo, Peggy Giordano, Monica Longmore, and Wendy Manning, "Parents, Friends, and Romantic Partners: Enmeshment in Deviant Networks and Adolescent Delinquency Involvement," *Journal of Youth and Adolescence* 38 (2009): 367–383.

63. Craig Reinerman and Jeffrey Fagan, "Social Organization and Differential Association: A Research Note from a Longitudinal Study of Violent Juvenile Offenders," *Crime and Delinquency* 34 (1988): 307–327.

64. Ronald Akers, *Deviant Behavior: A Social Learning Approach*, 2nd ed. (Belmont, CA: Wadsworth, 1977).

65. Ronald Akers, Marvin Krohn, Lonn Lanza-Kaduce, and Marcia Radosevich, "Social Learning and Deviant Behavior: A Specific Test of a General Theory," *American Sociological Review* 44 (1979): 638.

66. Robert G. Morris and Ashley G. Blackburn, "Cracking the Code: An Empirical Exploration of Social Learning

Theory and Computer Crime," *Journal of Crime and Justice* 32 (2009): 1–34.

67. Jonathan Brauer, "Testing Social Learning Theory Using Reinforcement's Residue: A Multilevel Analysis of Self-Reported Theft and Marijuana Use in the National Youth Survey," *Criminology* 47 (2009): 929–970.

68. Gresham Sykes and David Matza, "Techniques of Neutralization: A Theory of Delinquency," *American Sociological Review* 22 (1957): 664–670; David Matza, *Delinquency and Drift* (New York: John Wiley, 1964).

69. Matza, *Delinquency and Drift*, p. 51.

70. Sykes and Matza, "Techniques of Neutralization"; see also David Matza, "Subterranean Traditions of Youths," *Annals of the American Academy of Political and Social Science* 378 (1961): 116.

71. Sykes and Matza, "Techniques of Neutralization."

72. Ibid.

73. Ian Shields and George Whitehall, "Neutralization and Delinquency Among Teenagers," *Criminal Justice and Behavior* 21 (1994): 223–235; Robert A. Ball, "An Empirical Exploration of Neutralization Theory," *Criminologica* 4 (1966): 22–32. See also M. William Minor, "The Neutralization of Criminal Offense," *Criminology* 18 (1980): 103–120; Robert Gordon, James Short, Desmond Cartwright, and Fred Strodtbeck, "Values and Gang Delinquency: A Study of Street Corner Groups," *American Journal of Sociology* 69 (1963): 109–128.

74. Michael Hindelang, "The Commitment of Delinquents to Their Misdeeds: Do Delinquents Drift?" *Social Problems* 17 (1970): 500–509; Robert Regoli and Eric Poole, "The Commitment of Delinquents to Their Misdeeds: A Reexamination," *Journal of Criminal Justice* 6 (1978): 261–269.

75. Larry Siegel, Spencer Rathus, and Carol Ruppert, "Values and Delinquent Youth: An Empirical Reexamination of Theories of Delinquency," *British Journal of Criminology* 13 (1973): 237–244.

76. Robert Agnew, "The Techniques of Neutralization and Violence," *Criminology* 32 (1994): 555–580.

77. Jeffrey Fagan, *Adolescent Violence: A View from the Street*, NIJ Research Preview (Washington, DC: National Institute of Justice, 1998).

78. Volkan Topalli, "When Being Good Is Bad: An Expansion of Neutralization Theory," *Criminology* 43 (2005): 797–836.

79. Scott Briar and Irving Piliavin, "Delinquency: Situational Inducements and Commitment to Conformity," *Social Problems* 13 (1965–1966): 35–45.

80. Lawrence Sherman and Douglas Smith, with Janell Schmidt and Dennis Rogan, "Crime, Punishment, and Stake in Conformity: Legal and Informal Control of Domestic Violence," *American Sociological Review* 57 (1992): 680–690.

81. Travis Hirschi, *Causes of Delinquency* (Berkeley: University of California Press, 1969).

82. Ibid., p. 231.

83. Ibid., pp. 66–74.

84. Michael Wiatroski, David Griswold, and Mary K. Roberts, "Social Control Theory and Delinquency," *American Sociological Review* 46 (1981): 525–541.

85. Abigail A. Fagan, M. Lee Van Horn, J. David Hawkins, and Thomas Jaki, "Differential Effects of Parental Controls on Adolescent Substance Use: For Whom Is the Family Most Important?" *Journal of Quantitative Criminology* 29 (2013): 347–368.

86. Rick Trinkner, Ellen S. Cohn, Cesar J. Rebellon, and Karen Van Gundy, "Don't Trust Anyone over 30: Parental Legitimacy as a Mediator Between Parenting Style and Changes in Delinquent Behavior over Time," *Journal of Adolescence* 35 (2012): 119–132.

87. Jennifer Kerpelman and Sondra Smith-Adcock, "Female Adolescents' Delinquent Activity: The Intersection of Bonds to Parents and Reputation Enhancement," *Youth and Society* 37 (2005): 176–200.

88. Tiffiney Barfield-Cottledge, "The Triangulation Effects of Family Structure and Attachment on Adolescent Substance Use," *Crime and Delinquency*, published online November 8, 2011; Sonia Cota-Robles and Wendy Gamble, "Parent–Adolescent Processes and Reduced Risk for Delinquency: The Effect of Gender for Mexican American Adolescents," *Youth and Society* 37 (2006): 375–392.

89. Allison Ann Payne, "A Multilevel Analysis of the Relationships Among Communal School Organization, Student Bonding, and Delinquency," *Journal of Research in Crime and Delinquency* 45 (2008): 429–455.

90. Norman White and Rolf Loeber, "Bullying and Special Education as Predictors of Serious Delinquency," *Journal of Research in Crime and Delinquency* 45 (2008): 380–397.

91. John Cochran and Ronald Akers, "An Exploration of the Variable Effects of Religiosity on Adolescent Marijuana and Alcohol Use," *Journal of Research in Crime and Delinquency* 26 (1989): 198–225.

92. Mark Regnerus and Glen Elder, "Religion and Vulnerability Among Low-Risk Adolescents," *Social Science Research* 32 (2003): 633–658; Mark Regnerus, "Moral Communities and Adolescent Delinquency: Religious Contexts and Community Social Control," *Sociological Quarterly* 44 (2003): 523–554.

93. Eugene Maguin and Rolf Loeber, "Academic Performance and Delinquency," *Justice Review* 28 (2003): 254–277.

94. Robert Crosnoe, "The Connection Between Academic Failure and Adolescent Drinking in Secondary School," *Sociology of Education* 79 (2006): 44–60.

95. Jonathan Zaff, Kristin Moore, Angela Romano Papillo, and Stephanie Williams, "Implications of Extracurricular Activity Participation During Adolescence on Positive Outcomes," *Journal of Adolescent Research* 18 (2003): 599–631; Robert Agnew and David Peterson,

"Leisure and Delinquency," *Social Problems* 36 (1989): 332–348.

96. Jeb Booth, Amy Farrell, and Sean Varano, "Social Control, Serious Delinquency, and Risky Behavior: A Gendered Analysis," *Crime and Delinquency* 54 (2008): 423–456.

97. Peggy Giordano, Stephen Cernkovich, and M. D. Pugh, "Friendships and Delinquency," *American Journal of Sociology* 91 (1986): 1170–1202.

98. Denise Kandel and Mark Davies, "Friendship Networks, Intimacy, and Illicit Drug Use in Young Adulthood: A Comparison of Two Competing Theories," *Criminology* 29 (1991): 441–467.

99. Young, Rebellon, Barnes, and Weerman, "Unpacking the Black Box of Peer Similarity in Deviance."

100. Lisa Stolzenberg and Stewart D'Alessio, "Co-offending and the Age–Crime Curve," *Journal of Research in Crime and Delinquency* 45 (2008): 65–86.

101. Stephen Cernkovich, Peggy Giordano, and Jennifer Rudolph, "Race, Crime and the American Dream," *Journal of Research in Crime and Delinquency* 37 (2000): 131–170.

102. Velmer Burton, Francis Cullen, T. David Evans, R. Gregory Dunaway, Sesha Kethineni, and Gary Payne, "The Impact of Parental Controls on Delinquency," *Journal of Criminal Justice* 23 (1995): 111–126.

103. Amy Anderson and Lorine Hughes, "Exposure to Situations Conducive to Delinquent Behavior: The Effects of Time Use, Income, and Transportation," *Journal of Research in Crime and Delinquency* 46 (2009): 5–34.

104. Patrick Seffrin, Peggy Giordano, Wendy Manning, and Monica Longmore, "The Influence of Dating Relationships on Friendship Networks, Identity Development, and Delinquency," *Justice Quarterly* 26 (2009): 238–267.

105. Michael Hindelang, "Causes of Delinquency: A Partial Replication and Extension," *Social Problems* 21 (1973): 471–487.

106. Gary Jensen and David Brownfield, "Parents and Drugs," *Criminology* 21 (1983): 543–554. See also M. Wiatrowski, D. Griswold, and M. Roberts, "Social Control Theory and Delinquency," *American Sociological Review* 46 (1981): 525–541.

107. Leslie Samuelson, Timothy Hartnagel, and Harvey Krahn, "Crime and Social Control Among High School Dropouts," *Journal of Crime and Justice* 18 (1990): 129–161.

108. David Huh, Jennifer Tristan, Emily Wade, and Eric Stice, "Does Problem Behavior Elicit Poor Parenting? A Prospective Study of Adolescent Girls," *Journal of Adolescent Research* 21 (2006): 185–204.

109. Martha Gault-Sherman, "It's a Two-Way Street: The Bidirectional Relationship Between Parenting and Delinquency," *Journal of Youth and Adolescence* 41 (2012): 121–145.

110. Sonja Siennick, "Tough Love? Crime and Parental Assistance in Young Adulthood," *Criminology* 49 (2011): 163–196.

111. Wiatrowski, Griswold, and Roberts, "Social Control Theory and Delinquency."

112. Linda Jackson, John Hunter, and Carole Hodge, "Physical Attractiveness and Intellectual Competence: A Meta-Analytic Review," *Social Psychology Quarterly* 58 (1995): 108–122.

113. Howard Becker, *Outsiders: Studies in the Sociology of Deviance* (New York: Macmillan, 1963), p. 9.

114. Harold Garfinkle, "Conditions of Successful Degradation Ceremonies," *American Journal of Sociology* 61 (1956): 420–424.

115. Stacy DeCoster and Karen Heimer, "The Relationship Between Law Violation and Depression: An Interactionist Analysis," *Criminology* 39 (2001): 799–837.

116. Karen Heimer and Ross Matsueda, "Role-Taking, Role-Commitment and Delinquency: A Theory of Differential Social Control," *American Sociological Review* 59 (1994): 365–390.

117. See, for example, Howard Kaplan and Hiroshi Fukurai, "Negative Social Sanctions, Self-Rejection, and Drug Use," *Youth and Society* 23 (1992): 275–298; Howard Kaplan and Robert Johnson, "Negative Social Sanctions and Juvenile Delinquency: Effects of Labeling in a Model of Deviant Behavior," *Social Science Quarterly* 72 (1991): 98–122; Howard Kaplan, Robert Johnson, and Carol Bailey, "Deviant Peers and Deviant Behavior: Further Elaboration of a Model," *Social Psychology Quarterly* 30 (1987): 277–284.

118. John Lofland, *Deviance and Identity* (Englewood Cliffs, NJ: Prentice Hall, 1969).

119. Frank Tannenbaum, *Crime and the Community* (New York: Columbia University Press, 1938), pp. 19–20.

120. Edwin Lemert, *Social Pathology* (New York: McGraw-Hill, 1951).

121. Ibid., p. 75.

122. Christy Visher, "Gender, Police Arrest Decision, and Notions of Chivalry," *Criminology* 21 (1983): 5–28.

123. Marjorie Zatz, "Race, Ethnicity and Determinate Sentencing," *Criminology* 22 (1984): 147–171.

124. Christina DeJong and Kenneth Jackson, "Putting Race into Context: Race, Juvenile Justice Processing, and Urbanization," *Justice Quarterly* 15 (1998): 487–504.

125. Joan Petersilia, "Racial Disparities in the Criminal Justice System: A Summary," *Crime and Delinquency* 31 (1985): 15–34.

126. Carl Pope and William Feyerherm, "Minority Status and Juvenile Justice Processing," *Criminal Justice Abstracts* 22 (1990): 327–336. See also Carl Pope, "Race and Crime Revisited," *Crime and Delinquency* 25 (1979): 347–357; National Minority Council on Criminal Justice, *The Inequality of Justice* (Washington, DC: National Minority Advisory Council on Criminal Justice, 1981), p. 200.

127. Tammy Rinehart Kochel, David Wilson, and Stephen Mastrofski, "Effect of Suspect Race on Officers' Arrest Decisions," *Criminology* 49 (2011): 473–512.

128. Howard Kaplan and Robert Johnson, "Negative Social Sanctions and Juvenile Delinquency: Effects of Labeling in a Model of Deviant Behavior," *Social Science Quarterly* 72 (1991): 98–122.

129. Ruth Triplett, "The Conflict Perspective, Symbolic Interactionism, and the Status Characteristics Hypothesis," *Justice Quarterly* 10 (1993): 540–558.

130. Dylan B. Jackson and Carter Hay, "The Conditional Impact of Official Labeling on Subsequent Delinquency: Considering the Attenuating Role of Family Attachment," *Journal of Research in Crime and Delinquency*, first published online July 20, 2012.

131. Lening Zhang, "Official Offense Status and Self-Esteem Among Chinese Youths," *Journal of Criminal Justice* 31 (2003): 99–105.

132. Ross Matsueda, "Reflected Appraisals, Parental Labeling, and Delinquency: Specifying a Symbolic Interactionist Theory," *American Journal of Sociology* 97 (1992): 1577–1611.

133. Dylan Jackson and Carter Hay, "The Conditional Impact of Official Labeling on Subsequent Delinquency: Considering the Attenuating Role of Family Attachment," *Journal of Research in Crime and Delinquency* 50 (2013): 300–322.

134. Suzanne Ageton and Delbert Elliott, *The Effect of Legal Processing on Self-Concept* (Boulder, CO: Institute of Behavioral Science, 1973).

135. Mike Adams, Craig Robertson, Phyllis Gray-Ray, and Melvin Ray, "Labeling and Delinquency," *Adolescence* 38 (2003): 171–186.

136. Jón Gunnar Bernburg, Marvin Krohn, and Craig Rivera, "Official Labeling, Criminal Embeddedness, and Subsequent Delinquency: A Longitudinal Test of Labeling Theory," *Journal of Research in Crime and Delinquency* 43 (2006): 67–88.

137. Christine Bowditch, "Getting Rid of Troublemakers: High School Disciplinary Procedures and the Production of Dropouts," *Social Problems* 40 (1993): 493–507.

138. Robert Morris and Alex Piquero, "For Whom Do Sanctions Deter and Label?" *Justice Quarterly* 30 (2013): 837–868; Giza Lopes, Marvin Krohn, Alan Lizotte, Nicole Schmidt, Bob Edward Vásquez, and Jón Gunnar Bernburg, "Labeling and Cumulative Disadvantage: The Impact of Formal Police Intervention on Life Chances and Crime During Emerging Adulthood," *Crime and Delinquency* 58 (2012): 456–488.

139. Stephanie Ann Wiley, Lee Ann Slocum, and Finn-Aage Esbensen, "The Unintended Consequences of Being Stopped or Arrested: An Exploration of the Labeling Mechanisms Through Which Police Contact Leads to Subsequent Delinquency," *Criminology* 51 (2013): 927–966.

140. Melvin Ray and William Downs, "An Empirical Test of Labeling Theory Using Longitudinal Data," *Journal of Research in Crime and Delinquency* 23 (1986): 169–194.

141. Sherman and Smith, with Schmidt and Rogan, "Crime, Punishment, and Stake in Conformity."

142. Lawrence Bench and Terry Allen, "Investigating the Stigma of Prison Classification: An Experimental Design," *Prison Journal* 83 (2003): 367–382.

143. Charles Tittle, "Two Empirical Regularities (Maybe) in Search of an Explanation: Commentary on the Age/Crime Debate," *Criminology* 26 (1988): 75–85.

144. Robert Sampson and John Laub, "A Life-Course Theory of Cumulative Disadvantage and the Stability of Delinquency," in *Developmental Theories of Crime and Delinquency,* ed. Terence Thornberry (New Brunswick, NJ: Transaction Press, 1997), pp. 133–161; Douglas Smith and Robert Brame, "On the Initiation and Continuation of Delinquency," *Criminology* 4 (1994): 607–630.

145. Megan Kurlychek, Robert Brame, and Shawn Bushway, "Enduring Risk? Old Criminal Records and Predictions of Future Criminal Involvement," *Crime and Delinquency* 53 (2007): 64–83.

146. Emily Restivo and Mark M. Lanier, "Measuring the Contextual Effects and Mitigating Factors of Labeling Theory," *Justice Quarterly* 32 (2015): 116–141.

147. Raymond Paternoster and Leeann Iovanni, "The Labeling Perspective and Delinquency: An Elaboration of the Theory and an Assessment of the Evidence," *Justice Quarterly* 6 (1989): 358–394.

148. Shadd Maruna, Thomas Lebel, Nick Mitchell, and Michelle Maples, "Pygmalion in the Reintegration Process: Desistance from Crime Through the Looking Glass," *Psychology, Crime and Law* 10 (2004): 271–281.

# 8 Social Conflict, Critical Criminology, and Restorative Justice

Vincent Boisot/Riva Press/Redux

Prefecture de Police/Corbis News/Corbis

Prefecture de Police/Corbis News/Corbis

# Chapter Outline

## FACT OR FICTION?

▶ It is illegal for the police to monitor people in public places with cameras and secretly record their activities.

▶ The CIA has sent terror suspects to foreign prisons where they can be subjected to harsh interrogation tactics.

On January 7, 2015, Saïd and Chérif Kouachi, two brothers with long ties to Jihadist groups and causes, forced their way into the offices of the French satirical newspaper *Charlie Hebdo* in Paris. Armed with assault rifles and other weapons, they killed 11 people and wounded 12 others. Afterwards, they killed a French National Police officer stationed outside the building. After a massive manhunt by French security forces, the suspects were cornered and shot dead as they attempted to flee their hiding place.

Why was *Charlie Hebdo* chosen to be a target? In videos, Al-Qaeda leaders in Yemen claimed responsibility and said the attacks were not spontaneous but years in the planning, prompted by images of the prophet Muhammad that routinely appeared in the newspaper. France was also targeted because it had supported U.S. activities in the Middle East and conducted military raids against Muslims in North and Central Africa. The *Charlie Hebdo* massacre prompted millions of people to rally in Paris and other cities around the world in support of free speech and in protest against terrorism.

**social conflict**
The struggle for power in society. Human behavior in social contexts results from conflicts between competing groups.

**critical criminologists**
Criminologists who believe that the cause of crime can be linked to economic, social, and political disparity.

The *Charlie Hebdo* murders are an extreme example of the **social conflict** that dominates and shapes contemporary society. We live in a world rife with political, social, and economic turmoil in nearly every corner of the globe. Conflict comes in many forms, occurs at many levels of society, and involves a whole slew of adversaries: workers and bosses, the United States and its overseas enemies, religious zealots and apostates, citizens and police. It occurs within cities, in neighborhoods, and even within the family.

Social conflict can be destructive when it leads to war, violence, and death; it can be functional when it results in positive social change. Conflict promotes crime by creating a social atmosphere in which the law is a mechanism for controlling dissatisfied, have-not members of society while the wealthy maintain their power. This is why crimes that are the province of the wealthy, such as illegal corporate activities, are sanctioned much more leniently than those, such as burglary, that are considered lower-class activities.

Criminologists who view crime as a function of social conflict are most commonly referred to as **critical criminologists** and their field of study as critical criminology. As their title hints, critical criminologists view themselves as social critics who dig beneath the surface of society to uncover its inequities. They reject the notion that law is designed to maintain a tranquil, fair society and that criminals are malevolent people who wish to trample the rights of others. They believe that the law is an instrument of power, wielded by those who control society in order to maintain their wealth, social position, and class advantage.

Critical criminologists consider acts of racism, sexism, imperialism, unsafe working conditions, inadequate child care, substandard housing, pollution of the environment, and war-making used as tools of foreign policy to be the "true crimes." The crimes of the helpless—burglary, robbery, and assault—are more often expressions of rage over unjust economic conditions more than actual crimes.[1] Some groups in society, particularly the working class and ethnic minorities, are seen as the most likely to suffer oppressive social relations based on class conflict and racism and hence to be more prone to criminal behavior.

Contemporary critical criminologists try to explain crime within economic and social contexts and to express the connection between social class, crime, and social control.[2] They are concerned with issues such as these:

- The role government plays in creating a criminogenic environment
- The relationship between personal or group power and the shaping of criminal law
- The prevalence of bias in justice system operations
- The relationship between a capitalist, free enterprise economy and crime rates

Critical criminologists reject strictly legal definitions of crime, viewing racism, ageism, sexism, and classism as causing greater social harm than burglary, robbery, and rape.[3]

This chapter briefly reviews the development of critical criminology. It covers its principal ideas, and then looks at policies that have been embraced by critical thinkers that focus on peace and restoration rather than punishment and exclusion. Figure 8.1 illustrates the various independent branches of critical theory.

**LO1** List the core ideas of critical criminology.

# Origins of Critical Criminology

The roots of critical criminology can be traced to the political-economic vision created by philosopher Karl Marx who believed that modern capitalism had turned workers into a dehumanized mass who lived an existence that was at the mercy of their employers. Young children were being sent to work in mines and factories from dawn to dusk. Workers were being beaten down by a system that demanded obedience and cooperation and offered little in return. These oppressive conditions led Marx to conclude that the character of every civilization is determined by its mode of production—the way its people develop and produce material goods.

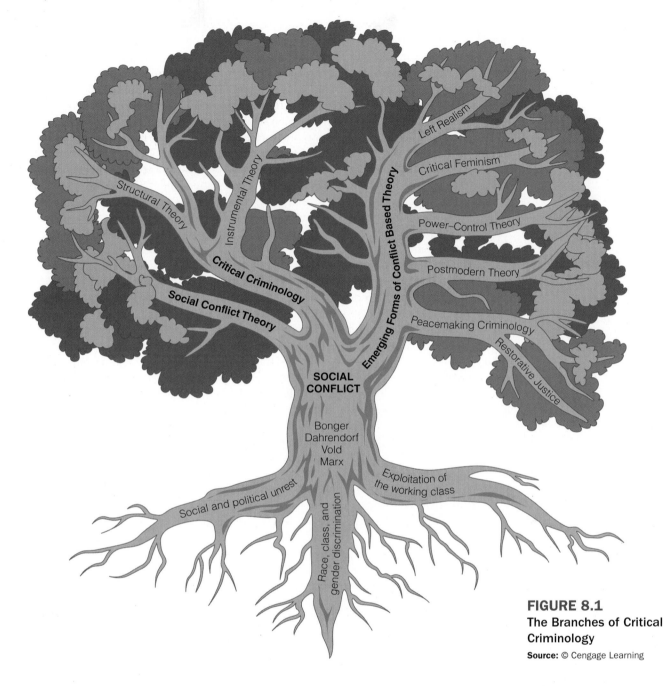

**FIGURE 8.1**
**The Branches of Critical Criminology**
**Source:** © Cengage Learning

Marx's vision of economic inequality, and the resulting social conflict it produced, had a profound influence on twentieth-century thought. Willem Bonger, Ralf Dahrendorf, and George Vold employed a Marxist perspective to identify the crime-producing social and economic forces in capitalist society.[4] The Dutch scholar Bonger proclaimed in his 1916 work *Criminality and Economic Conditions* that in every society that is divided into a ruling class and an inferior class, penal law serves the will of the ruling class. Even though criminal laws may appear to protect members of both classes, hardly any act is punished that does not injure the interests of the dominant ruling class. Crimes, then, are considered to be antisocial acts because they are harmful to those who have the power at their command to control society. Under capitalism, the legal system discriminates against the poor by defending the actions of the wealthy. Because the proletariat are deprived of the materials that are monopolized by the bourgeoisie, they are more likely to violate the law.[5]

However, it was the social ferment of the 1960s that gave birth to critical criminology and placed it within the criminological mainstream. In 1968, a group of British

**CONNECTIONS**

As you may recall from Chapter 1, the philosophical and economic analysis of Karl Marx forms the historical roots of the conflict perspective of criminology.

sociologists formed the National Deviancy Conference (NDC). With about 300 members, this organization sponsored several national symposiums and dialogues. Members came from all walks of life, but at its core was a group of academics who were critical of the positivist criminology being taught in British and American universities. More specifically, they rejected the conservative stance of criminologists and their close association with the government that funded many of their research projects. The NDC called attention to ways in which social control might actually *cause* deviance rather than just being a response to antisocial behavior. Many conference members became concerned about the political nature of social control.

In 1973, critical theory was given a powerful academic boost when British scholars Ian Taylor, Paul Walton, and Jock Young published *The New Criminology*.[6] This brilliant, thorough, and well-constructed critique of existing concepts in criminology called for the development of new methods of criminological analysis and critique. *The New Criminology* became the standard resource for scholars critical of both the field of criminology and the existing legal process. Since its publication, critical criminologists have established a tradition of focusing on the field itself and questioning the role criminology plays in supporting the status quo and collaborating in the oppression of the poor and powerless.[7]

U.S. scholars were also influenced, during the late 1960s and early 1970s, by the widespread unrest and social change that shook the world. The war in Vietnam, prison struggles, and the civil rights and feminist movements produced a climate in which criticism of the ruling class seemed a natural by-product. Mainstream, positivist criminology was criticized as being overtly conservative, pro-government, and antihuman. Critical criminologists scoffed when their fellow scholars used statistical analysis of computerized data to describe criminal and delinquent behavior. Several influential scholars embraced the idea that the social conflict produced by the unequal distribution of **power** and wealth was the root cause of crime. William Chambliss and Robert Seidman wrote the well-respected treatise *Law, Order, and Power*, which documented how the justice system protects the rich and powerful.[8] Chambliss and Seidman's work showed how control of the political and economic system affects the way criminal justice is administered and demonstrated that the definitions of crime used in contemporary society favor those who control the justice system.

In *The Social Reality of Crime*, sociologist Richard Quinney also proclaimed that in contemporary society, criminal law represents the interests of those who hold power in society.[9] Where there is conflict between social groups—the wealthy and the poor—those who hold power will create laws that benefit themselves and keep rivals in check. Criminals are not simply social misfits but people who have come up short in the struggle for success and are seeking alternative means of achieving wealth, status, or even survival.

In his numerous works, including *Disobedience and Democracy*, historian and social commentator Howard Zinn forcibly argued that the American criminal justice system was far from just. He lambasted unjust laws and a judicial tyranny that created cruel punishments that treated convicted criminals as less than human. The application of due process, Zinn argued, was counterbalanced by the unchecked discretion and arbitrary judgments of those given state-sanctioned authority over the lives of others. And of course, greedy white-collar criminals who engage in million-dollar frauds are treated far more leniently than indigent and desperate common-law criminals who commit burglaries and larcenies, even if the social harm they cause is significantly greater.[10]

## Contemporary Critical Criminology

Today, critical criminologists devote their attention to a number of important themes and concepts. One is to show how, in our postindustrial, capitalist society, the economic system invariably produces haves and have-nots, shapes social life, and controls behavior. Economic competitiveness increases interpersonal conflict and eventually destabilizes both social institutions and social groups.[11]

**power**
The ability of persons and groups to control the behavior of others, to shape public opinion, and to define deviance.

Another concern is the widening gap between rich and poor. While spending is being cut on social programs for the indigent, corporations are now more powerful than ever and corporate execs more highly paid. According to the prestigious Pew Foundation, the wealth gap between America's high-income group and everyone else has now reached record high levels. Economic predictions show a clear pattern of increasing wealth for the upper-income families and no wealth growth for the middle- and lower-income families. In 2013, the median wealth of the nation's upper-income families ($639,400) was nearly seven times that of middle-income families ($96,500), the widest gap seen in more than 30 years.[12] And while the rich are getting richer, conservatives renew their calls for dismantling welfare and health programs (i.e., Obamacare), resisting any increase in the minimum wage, increasing tax cuts that favor the wealthy, ending affirmative action, and reducing environmental control and regulation.[13] The result is a growing income inequality that has created both public outrage and political movements such as Occupy Wall Street and Black Lives Matter.

**JUSTICE SYSTEM INEQUALITY** Trends in the criminal justice system are equally disturbing to critical thinkers. They believe the racial and ethnic minorities are now the target of racist police officers and unfair prosecutorial practices. The shooting of Michael Brown in Ferguson (see Chapter 1) was one incident that illustrates the tragic result caused by racial profiling of minorities; the Eric Garner case in New York City (see the Profiles in Crime feature) was another.

The rapid buildup of the prison system is also seen as the result of draconian criminal laws that threaten civil rights and liberties—the death penalty, three-strikes laws, and especially the decades long "war on drugs" that has resulted in hundreds of thousands of people being incarcerated, most of whom are poor and powerless minority group members.[14] Critical thinkers criticize the use of mass incarceration as a crime control device, fearing that it has racial overtones. In her provocative book *The New Jim Crow: Mass Incarceration in the Age of Colorblindness* (2010), legal scholar Michelle Alexander notes that the number of people in prison has skyrocketed in the past 30 years; there are now more African Americans behind bars than there were slaves at the time of the Civil War. This system of mass incarceration now works as a "tightly networked system of laws, policies, customs, and institutions that operate collectively to ensure the subordinate status of a group defined largely by race."[15] In a sense, the Jim Crow laws, which worked to segregate minorities and prevented them from voting, have been replaced by the war on drugs, which has placed millions behind bars and restricted their civil rights upon release. Existing laws prevent convicted felons from gaining employment, education, or housing, obtaining loans, and voting.

**DEMYSTIFYING DOMINATION** Another central theme of critical criminology is the concept of domination: how one class or group works to dominate another and retain power. By controlling the justice system, the elites can preserve political-economic, racial, and ethnic domination. Domination is demonstrated in the racism and sexism that still pervade the American system and is manifested in a wide variety of social practices, ranging from discriminatory practices in the administration of criminal justice to a racially skewed teaching force.[16]

One way those in power exercise domination is to use the fear of crime as a tool to maintain their control over society: the middle class is diverted from caring about the crimes of the powerful by media stories focusing on the crimes of the powerless.[17] Ironically, the middle class may have more to lose from the economic crimes committed by the rich than the common-law crimes of the poor. When on occasion a stock market or business fraud is prosecuted it is merely a symbolic gesture made to show the general public that the justice system is fair. More often than not, the victims of these high-profile frauds are wealthy stockholders who demand justice. When it's only the poor who are victimized, punishments are more lenient.

**CHECKPOINTS**

▶ Critical criminologists view themselves as social critics who dig beneath the surface of society to uncover its inequities.

▶ They consider acts of racism, sexism, imperialism, and unsafe working conditions as tools of foreign policy to be the "true crimes."

▶ Contemporary critical criminologists try to explain crime within economic and social contexts and to express the connection between social class, crime, and social control.

▶ One of the roots of criminological theory is the political-economic vision created by philosopher Karl Marx.

▶ Even though criminal laws may appear to protect members of both classes, the crimes committed by the dominant ruling class receive more lenient treatment.

▶ Racial and ethnic discrimination causes social conflict and unrest.

# PROFILES IN CRIME

## "I CAN'T BREATHE"

On July 17, 2014, on Staten Island, Eric Garner was confronted by police officers because he was believed to be selling "loosies" (single cigarettes) from packs without a tax stamp, prohibited by New York City law. During the confrontation, which was recorded, Garner raised both hands in the air and told the officers to leave him alone. A few seconds later, the police officers tackled Garner and one applied what appeared to be a chokehold as the officers pulled him to the sidewalk and rolled Garner onto his stomach; the New York City Police Department prohibits chokeholds. Garner repeatedly cried out, "I can't breathe! I can't breathe!" as he was held down on the pavement. Though the incident lasted only a few seconds, he lost consciousness. An ambulance was called and Garner was taken to a hospital, where he was pronounced dead. Daniel Pantaleo, the police officer who applied what appeared to be a chokehold, later claimed he actually used a takedown technique he was taught in the academy. He claimed he never exerted any pressure on the windpipe, never intended to injure Eric Garner, and was deeply sorry for his death. He was merely trying to arrest someone who was noncompliant. Despite public outrage, a grand jury made up of 14 white and 9 nonwhite members created to investigate the case believed the officers' story and found no "reasonable cause" to indict the officers who applied the hold. Ironically, there was little evidence that Garner was actually selling the illegal cigarettes, and even if he had been, the penalty was at most a fine.

Unfortunately, that was not the end of the incident. Six months later, on December 20, 2014, two police officers, Wenjian Liu and Rafael Ramos, were killed while sitting in their patrol car in Brooklyn. The killer, Ismaaiyl Brinsley, had earlier told people that he wanted to kill cops in revenge for the Garner killing. Brinsley shot himself as police closed in to make an arrest.

Critical criminologists maintain that class and racial conflict control outcomes in the criminal justice system. The Garner case and its aftermath is an unfortunate reminder of the toll conflict takes on society. Should Garner have been gang-tackled for an act that was punishable by a fine? Would it not have been better to find some other solution that did not involve a violent takedown? In July 2015, Eric Garner's family was awarded a $5.9 million settlement from New York City. Eric Garner's death sparked the "Black Lives Matter" movement.

Eric Garner being arrested by police.

New York Daily News/Getty Images

**Source:** CBS news, "The Eric Garner Case," www.cbsnews.com /eric-garner-case/ (accessed 2015).

## Defining Crime and Justice

According to critical theorists, crime is a political concept designed to protect the power and position of the upper classes at the expense of the poor. Some, but not all, would include in a list of "real" crimes such acts as violations of human rights due to racism, sexism, and imperialism and other violations of human dignity and physical needs and necessities. Take for instance what Alette Smeulers and Roelof Haveman call **supranational crimes**: war crimes, crimes against humanity, genocide, and other human rights violations. Smeulers and Haveman believe that these types of crimes should merit more attention by criminologists, and therefore they call for a separate specialization.[18]

In our advanced technological society, those with economic and political power control the definition of crime and the manner in which the criminal justice system enforces the law.[19] The only crimes available to the poor are the severely sanctioned "street crimes": rape, murder, theft, and mugging. Members of the middle class cheat on their taxes and engage in petty corporate crime (employee theft), acts that generate social disapproval but are rarely punished severely. The wealthy are involved in business-related crimes that should be controlled and criminalized by regulatory laws, but those that exist are rarely enforced, and most violations are lightly punished.

One reason for the laws ignoring white-collar crimes is that an essential feature of capitalism is the need to expand business and create new markets. If American businesspeople were tightly controlled they would be placed at a disadvantage to foreign capitalists, threatening U.S. business interests and its global economic position. While ignoring illegal business practices or punishing them with an economic fine may enrage those who are concerned about labor practices, environmental protection, and similar social needs, in our postindustrial society, the need for capitalist expansion usually triumphs. Corporate spokespeople and their political allies will brand environmentalists as "tree huggers" who stand in the way of jobs and prosperity.[20] When construction of the Keystone Pipeline was being debated union officials and spokespeople for the fossil fuel industry lambasted environmentalists as "extremist job killers."[21] One union president went so far as to describe those who opposed the climate-destroying pipeline as being "under the skirts of delusional environmental groups which stand in the way of creating good, much needed American jobs."[22]

## Instrumental vs. Structural Theory

Not all critical thinkers share a similar view of how crime is defined and how society works to control criminal behavior. **Instrumental theorists** view criminal law and the criminal justice system solely as instruments for controlling the poor, have-not members of society. They view the state as the tool of capitalists. In contrast, **structural theorists** believe that the law is not the exclusive domain of the rich; rather, it is used to maintain the long-term interests of the capitalist system and to control members of any class who threaten its existence.

**INSTRUMENTAL THEORY** According to the instrumental view, the law and justice system serve the powerful and rich and enable them to impose their morality and standards of behavior on the entire society. Those who wield economic power are able to extend their self-serving definition of illegal or criminal behavior to encompass those who might threaten the status quo or interfere with their quest for ever-increasing

**supranational criminology**
Comprising the study of war crimes, crimes against humanity, and the penal system in which such crimes are prosecuted and tried.

**instrumental theorists**
Critical criminologists who view the law and justice system as serving the interests of the upper classes.

**structural theorists**
Critical criminologists who believe the law is designed to keep the capitalist system operating in an efficient manner.

Structuralists believe that capitalism is self-preserving. To survive, it moderates the worst aspects of capitalist inequalities, while preserving the overall capitalist system. Here, demonstrators march on McDonald's corporate headquarters in Oak Brook, Illinois, demanding a wage increase to $15 per hour. The protest coincided with McDonald's annual shareholder's meeting and with the decision of the Los Angeles City Council to raise its minimum wage from the current $9 per hour to $15 per hour by the year 2020. Increasing the minimum wage maintains a pool of compliant workers while maintaining the power of the ownership classes.

**surplus value**
The excess profits that are produced by the laboring classes and accrued by business owners.

**marginalization**
Displacement of workers, pushing them outside the economic and social mainstream.

profits.[23] The concentration of economic assets in the nation's largest industrial firms translates into the political power needed to control tax laws to limit the firms' tax liabilities and control elections to make sure the government reflects their capitalistic views.[24] Some have the economic clout to hire top attorneys to defend them against antitrust actions, making them almost immune to regulation.

The poor, according to this branch of critical theory, may or may not commit more crimes than the rich, but they certainly are arrested and punished more often. Under the capitalist system, the poor are driven to crime because a natural frustration exists in a society in which affluence is well publicized but unattainable. Because of class conflict, a deep-rooted hostility is generated among members of the lower class toward a social order they are not allowed to shape and whose benefits are unobtainable.[25]

**STRUCTURAL THEORY** Structural theorists disagree with the view that the relationship between law and capitalism is unidirectional, always working for the rich and against the poor.[26] If law and justice were purely instruments of the wealthy, why would laws controlling corporate crimes, such as price-fixing, false advertising, and illegal restraint of trade, have been created and enforced?

To a structuralist, the law is designed to keep the system operating efficiently, and anyone, worker or owner, who rocks the boat is targeted for sanction. For example, antitrust legislation is designed to prevent any single capitalist from dominating the system. If the free enterprise system is to function, no single person can become too powerful at the expense of the economic system as a whole. Structuralists would regard the efforts of the U.S. government to break up a monopoly or prevent one from being created, such as when ATT and T-Mobile were prevented from merging, as an example of the state using its clout to keep the system on an even keel.

## The Cause of Crime

Critical thinkers believe that the key crime-producing element of modern corporate capitalism is the effort to create **surplus value**—the profits produced by the laboring classes that are accrued by business owners. Once accumulated, surplus value can be either reinvested or used to enrich the owners. To increase the rate of surplus value, workers can be made to toil harder for less pay, be made more efficient, or be replaced by machines or technology. Therefore, economic growth does not benefit all elements of the population, and in the long run it may produce the same effect as a depression or recession.

As the rate of surplus value increases, more people are displaced from productive relationships and the size of the marginal population swells. As corporations downsize to increase profits, high-paying labor and managerial jobs are lost to computer-driven machinery. Displaced workers are forced into service jobs at minimum wage. Many become temporary employees without benefits or a secure position.

As more people are thrust outside the economic mainstream, a condition referred to as **marginalization**, a larger portion of the population is forced to live in areas conducive to crime. Once people are marginalized, commitment to the system declines, producing another criminogenic force: a weakened bond to society.

The government may be quick to respond during periods of economic decline because those in power assume that poor economic conditions breed crime and social disorder. When unemployment is increasing, public officials assume the worst and devote greater attention to the criminal justice system, perhaps building new prisons to prepare for the coming "crime wave."[27] Empirical research confirms that economic downturns are indeed linked to both crime rate increases and government activities such as passing anticrime legislation.[28] As the level of surplus value increases, so too do police expenditures, most likely because of the perceived or real need for the state to control those on the economic margin.[29]

## Globalization

The new global economy is a particularly vexing development for critical theorists and their use of the concept of surplus value. **Globalization**, which usually refers to the process of creating transnational markets and political and legal systems, has shifted the focus of critical inquiry to a world perspective.

Globalization began when large companies decided to establish themselves in foreign markets by adapting their products or services to the local culture. The process took off with the fall of the Soviet Union, which opened new European markets. The development of China into a super industrial power encouraged foreign investors to take advantage of China's huge supply of workers. As the cyber revolution unfolded, companies were able to establish instant communications with their far-flung corporate empires, a technological breakthrough that further aided trade and foreign investments. A series of transnational corporate mergers and takeovers, such as when Ford bought Swedish car maker Volvo in 1999 and then in 2010 sold Volvo to the Chinese car company Geely, produced ever-larger transnational corporations.

Some experts believe globalization can improve the standard of living in third-world nations by providing jobs and training, but critical theorists question the altruism of multinational corporations. They believe that modern global capitalism helps destroy the lives of workers in less developed countries. Capitalists hailed China's entry into the World Trade Organization in 2001 as a significant economic event. However, critical thinkers point out that the economic boom has significant costs: the average wage in China is less than $5,000 per year; pollution created by rapid industrialization has caused the deaths of thousands of workers each year and rendered millions more disabled.[30]

Companies have gone global because of the unrestrained opportunity for exploiting natural resources and avoiding regulation. When these giant corporations set up a factory in a developing nation, it is not to help the local population but to get around U.S. environmental laws and take advantage of needy workers who may be forced to labor in substandard conditions. In some instances, transnational companies exploit national unrest and calamity in order to engage in profiteering. Take the case of illegal mineral expropriation in the Democratic Republic of Congo (DRC), a crime that could only take place because of the existing disorder and violence in the area, allowing profiteers to make huge sums in the theft of Congolese gold. Although these companies did not directly encourage the conflict or the massive human rights violations and crimes against humanity committed in the region, they used the opportunity social conflict presented for profit.[31]

Globalization has replaced imperialism and colonization as a new form of economic domination and oppression and now presents, according to critical thinkers, a threat to the world economy:

- Growing global dominance and the reach of the free market capitalist system, which disproportionately benefits wealthy and powerful organizations and individuals
- Increasing vulnerability of indigenous people with a traditional way of life to the forces of globalized capitalism
- Growing influence and impact of international financial institutions (such as the World Bank) and the related relative decline of power of local or state-based institutions
- Nondemocratic operation of international financial institutions[32]

Globalization has created a fertile ground for contemporary enterprise crimes. By expanding the reach of both criminal and noncriminal organizations, globalization also increases the vulnerability of indigenous people with a traditional way of life.[33] With money and power to spare, criminal enterprise groups can recruit new members, bribe government officials, and even fund private armies. International organized crime has globalized its activities for the same reasons legitimate multinational

**LO2** Link globalization to crime and criminality.

**globalization**
The creation and maintenance of transnational markets.

**CONNECTIONS**

The enforcement of laws against illegal business activities such as price fixing, restraint of trade, environmental crimes, and false advertising will be discussed in Chapter 12. Because of recent scandals such as the savings and loan scandal and subprime mortgage frauds, white-collar criminals are being punished more severely than in the past, a fact that supports the structural view.

corporations have expanded around the world: new markets bring new sources of profits. As international crime expert Louise Shelley puts it:

> Just as multinational corporations establish branches around the world to take advantage of attractive labor or raw material markets, so do illicit businesses. Furthermore, international businesses, both legitimate and illicit, also establish facilities worldwide for production, marketing, and distribution needs. Illicit enterprises are able to expand geographically to take advantage of these new economic circumstances thanks to the communications and international transportation revolution.[34]

Shelley argues that two elements of globalization encourage criminality: one technological, the other cultural. Technological advances such as efficient and widespread commercial airline traffic, improvements in telecommunications (ranging from global cell phone connectivity to the Internet), and the growth of international trade have all aided the growth in illicit transnational activities. These changes have facilitated the cross-border movement of goods and people, conditions exploited by criminals who now use Internet chat rooms to plan their activities. On a cultural level, globalization brings with it an ideology of free markets and free trade. The cultural shift means less intervention and regulation, conditions exploited by crime groups to cross unpatrolled borders and to expand their activities to new regions of the world. Transnational crime groups freely exploit this new freedom to travel to regions where they cannot be extradited, base their operations in countries with ineffective or corrupt law enforcement, and launder their money in countries with bank secrecy or few effective controls. Globalization has allowed both individual offenders and criminal gangs to gain tremendous operational benefits while reducing the risks of apprehension and punishment.

Globalization may have a profound influence on the concept of surplus value. Workers in the United States may be replaced in high-paying manufacturing jobs not by machines but by foreign workers. Instant communication via the Internet and global communications, a development that Marx could not have foreseen, will speed the effect immeasurably.

## State (Organized) Crime

**LO3** Define the concept of state (organized) crime.

**state (organized) crime** Criminal acts committed by government officials.

While mainstream criminologists focus on the crimes of the poor and powerless, critical criminologists focus their attention on the law violations of the powerful. One area of concern is referred to as **state (organized) crime**—acts defined by law as criminal and committed by state officials, both elected or appointed, in the pursuit of their jobs as government representatives. Their actions, or in some cases failure to act, amount to a violation of the criminal law they are bound by oath or duty to uphold.

Those who study state crime argue that these antisocial behaviors arise from efforts to either maintain governmental power or to uphold the race, class, and gender advantages of those who support the government. In an industrial society, the state will do everything to protect the property rights of the wealthy while opposing the real interests of the poor. They might even go to war to support the capitalist classes who need the wealth and resources of other nations. The desire for natural resources such as rubber, oil, and metals was one of the primary reasons for Japan's invasion of China and other Eastern nations that sparked their entry into World War II. Sixty years later, the United States was accused by many media commentators and political pundits of invading Iraq in order to secure its oil for American use.[35]

There are a number of categories of state crime, and these are set out in some detail below.[36]

**ILLEGAL DOMESTIC SURVEILLANCE** In 2013, a leak of documents stolen from the National Security Agency (NSA) by contract employee Edward Snowden set off an international firestorm. Among other things, Snowden's documents revealed that the NSA had programs that gave it access to a vast quantity of emails, chat logs, and other data directly from Internet companies, including Google, Facebook, and Apple. Snowden revealed that the NSA was collecting millions of email and instant messaging contact lists, searching email content, and tracking and mapping the location of cell phones. The NSA was shown to be "secretly" tapping into Yahoo and Google data centers to collect information from "hundreds of millions" of account holders worldwide by monitoring undersea cables.[37]

Before fleeing to Russia, Edward Snowden's illegal copying and dissemination of NSA documents showed that the U.S. government was engaging in a wide range of domestic and foreign surveillance activities. Among other things, without a warrant the agency was collecting and analyzing the content of communications of foreigners talking to persons inside the United States. They were able to collect data and information off of fiber-optic cables used by the communications industry. Was this a crime? The government was quick to point out that the programs were designed to combat terrorism and protect the United States. While the NSA programs disturbed many people in the U.S. and abroad, their actions would only be considered criminal if government agents listened in on tele-phone conversations or intercepted emails without proper approval in order to stifle dissent and monitor political opponents.

AP Images/Mel Evans

State (organized) crimes are criminal acts committed by state officials, both elected and appointed, in pursuit of their jobs as government officials. Here, Hamilton Township Mayor John Bencivengo (center), 58, walks from federal court with his attorney Jerome A. Ballarotto (right), in Trenton, New Jersey, after surrendering to the FBI to face an extortion charge. Federal prosecutors charged Bencivengo with taking $12,400 in bribes in exchange for using his influence over a health insurance contact with the township's school district. Bencivengo served 18 months in federal prison.

Snowden's acts were prompted by his fear of government surveillance. The dangers of illegal surveillance have become magnified because closed-circuit TV cameras are now routinely used by metropolitan police agencies. Many cities, including Washington, New York, Chicago, and Los Angeles, have installed significant numbers of police-operated cameras trained on public spaces. While ostensibly used to deter crime, once these surveillance facilities are put in place, police departments can use them to record the faces of political demonstrators, to record what people are reading, and to store photographs of people on computer databases without their knowledge or permission. This capability worries both civil libertarians and critical criminologists.[38]

**HUMAN RIGHTS VIOLATIONS** Some governments, such as Iran, routinely deny their citizens basic civil rights, holding them without trial and using "disappearances" and summary executions to rid themselves of political dissidents. In July 1999, after students rioted against governmental controls, more than 70 simply disappeared, another 1,200 to 1,400 were detained, and dozens were killed when security forces broke up demonstrations.[39] Similar violent actions to break up demonstrations took place in the wake of the disputed election in 2009 that returned President Mahmoud Ahmadinejad to power.

Can this kind of government suppression and misrepresentation happen in the United States? In his book *Mass Deception*, criminologist Scott Bonn argues that the George W. Bush administration manufactured public support for war with Iraq by

Can terror groups commit state (organized) crime? Malala Yousafzai, a 16-year-old girl from Pakistan, was shot in the head by the Taliban in Afghanistan for advocating education for girls. She survived and became an international activist for women's and children's rights; in 2014, she received the Nobel Peace Prize for her work. Can terror groups such as the Taliban and ISIL be considered "states"?

**extraordinary rendition**
The practice of sending suspected terrorists to foreign prisons that permit torture in the interrogation of suspects.

falsely claiming that its leader, Saddam Hussein, was involved in the terrorist attacks of 9/11 and that Iraq possessed weapons of mass destruction. Bonn explains that the war was a function of a "moral panic" engineered by the Bush administration even though there may be little actual evidence to support his views. Bonn believes that despite overwhelming evidence that the attacks had been solely orchestrated by Osama bin Laden and al-Qaeda, the Bush administration initiated a campaign to link 9/11 to Iraq so the United States would have an excuse to topple Saddam Hussein and his Ba'ath Party. The Bush administration's propaganda campaign was so successful that 70 percent of the U.S. public believed Iraq was directly involved in the attacks of 9/11 when the U.S.-led invasion of Iraq began. As a result, Bonn believes that the war in Iraq amounts to state organized crime.[40]

**EXTRAORDINARY RENDITION** Another state crime involves the operation of the correctional systems in nations that are notorious for depriving detainees of basic necessities and routinely using hard labor and torture to punish political dissidents. During the Bush presidency, the Central Intelligence Agency (CIA) used a practice known as **extraordinary rendition**, in which suspected terrorists were sent to secret prisons abroad, without trial or indictment. There they were subject to harsh interrogation tactics forbidden in the United States; it is unknown whether the practice still continues.[41]

**STATE-CORPORATE CRIME** This type of state crime is committed by individuals who abuse their state authority or who fail to exercise it when working with people and organizations in the private sector. For example, a state environmental agency may fail to enforce laws, resulting in the pollution of public waterways. State-corporate crime is particularly alarming, considering that regulatory law aimed at controlling private corporations is being scaled back while globalization has made corporations worldwide entities both in production and in advancing the consumption of their products.[42]

**STATE VIOLENCE** Sometimes nations engage in violence to maintain their power over dissident groups. Army or police officers form death squads—armed vigilante groups that kill suspected political opponents or other undesirables. These groups commit assassinations and kidnappings using extremely violent methods to intimidate the population and deter political activity against the government.[43] Death squads were widely used in Russia's two wars against breakaway province Chechnya, which went on from the mid-1990s until 2009, when with massive firepower they crushed the separatist rebel groups; hundreds of thousands died during the conflict. As the war raged, Chechen fighters launched suicide attacks against civilians in the Moscow metro and at a rock festival. In 2002, a gang that included 18 female suicide bombers seized more than 800 hostages in a Moscow theater, 129 of whom died when the Russians pumped poisonous gas into the building on day three of the siege. In 2004, rebels took hundreds of schoolchildren and their relatives hostage in Beslan. After a three-day siege, Russian security forces stormed the school; 334 hostages died, more than half of them children.

Enraged by the Chechen actions, the Russians created death squads made up of elite Russian special forces, commandos who would stop at nothing to find, torture, and kill enemy combatants. The bodies were either buried in unmarked pits or pulverized. The scenes would occasionally be filmed and circulated among enemy combatants as a form of psychological warfare.[44]

## Crime and Social Institutions

Critical thinkers often focus on contemporary social institutions to show how they operate as instruments of class and racial oppression. Critical scholars find that class bias and racial oppression exist from the cradle to the grave. There are significant race-based achievement differences in education, ranging from scores on standardized tests to dropout and high school completion rates. There are a few high schools, mostly in poverty-stricken inner-city neighborhoods, where the high school completion rate is 40 percent or less; these are referred to as **dropout factories**. There are more than 1,700 of these failing schools in the United States. Although they represent only a small fraction of all public high schools in America, they account for about half of all high school dropouts each year.[45]

**RACE AND RACISM** One reason for these persistent problems may be linked to differences in discipline meted out in poor and wealthy districts. As you may recall, African American children receive more disciplinary infractions than children from other racial categories, despite the fact that their behavior is quite similar. Having a higher percentage of black students in a school translates into a greater use of disciplinary tactics, a factor that may explain why minority students fare less well and are more likely to disengage from schools at a younger age than whites.[46] Critical thinkers might suggest that these class- and race-based burdens make crime inevitable.

The problems faced by racial minorities do not stop at the schoolhouse door. According to the racial threat hypothesis (see Chapter 2), as the number of minority group members in the community increases, law enforcement agents become more punitive. Research now shows that racial threat is a universal phenomenon, occurring in the United States and abroad.[47]

Highly publicized cases ranging from Trayvon Martin to Eric Garner have alerted the public to the practice of racial profiling. Police are more likely to use racial profiling to stop black motorists as they travel further into the boundaries of predominantly white neighborhoods. Black motorists driving in an all-white neighborhood send up a red flag because they are "out of place."[48] All too often these unwarranted stops lead to equally unfair arrests.[49] Considering this unfair treatment, it is not surprising that police brutality complaints are highest in minority neighborhoods, especially those that experience relative deprivation (African American residents earn significantly less money than the European American majority).[50]

Critical research also shows that racial and economic bias is present in prosecution and punishment. Surveys show that as the numbers of racial and ethnic minorities in the population increase, so too do calls for harsher punishments. Unwarranted fear drives people to believe that a defendant's race and ethnicity should be considered during sentencing.[51] These attitudes then find traction in the justice system: African American defendants are more likely to be prosecuted

**LO4** Explain the goals and findings of critical research.

**dropout factories**
High schools in which the completion rate is consistently 40 percent or less.

Protesters call for justice following yet another widely publicized case of police misconduct toward African Americans. Freddie Gray died while in police custody in Baltimore on April 19, 2015, after being arrested for possession of a knife thought to be an illegal switchblade. A medical examiner declared Gray's death to be a homicide, and six local police officers were brought up on charges of murder and manslaughter.

under habitual offender statutes if they commit crimes where there is a greater like-lihood of a white victim—for example, larceny and burglary—than if they commit violent crimes that are largely intraracial; where there is a perceived "racial threat," punishment is enhanced.[52] After conviction, criminal courts also are more likely to dole out harsh punishments to members of powerless, disenfranchised groups.[53] Both white and black offenders have been found to receive stricter sentences if their per-sonal characteristics (single, young, urban, male) show them to be members of the "dangerous classes."[54] Unemployed racial minorities may be perceived as "social dy-namite" who present a real threat to society and must be controlled and incapaci-tated.[55] Critical analysis also shows that despite legal controls the use of the death penalty seems to be skewed against racial minorities.[56]

The rush to punish must be observed through the lens of race: as the percentage of minority group members increases in a population, the imprisonment rate does likewise.[57] States with a substantial minority population have a much higher impris-onment rate than those with predominantly white populations.[58]

# Forms of Critical Criminology

Critical criminologists are exploring new avenues of inquiry that fall outside the tra-ditional models of conflict and critical theories. The following sections discuss in de-tail some recent developments in the conflict approach to crime.

## Left Realism

Some critical scholars are now addressing the need for the left wing to respond to the increasing power of right-wing conservatives. They are troubled by the emergence of a strict "law and order" philosophy, which has as its centerpiece such policies as ag-gressive police patrol, severe sentences for drug offenders, capital punishment, and punishing juveniles in adult court. At the same time, they find the focus of most critical scholarship—the abuse of power by the ruling elite—too narrow. It is wrong, they argue, to ignore inner-city gang crime and violence, which often target indigent people, while focusing solely on the depravations of the rich and powerful.[59]

**left realism**
An approach that is left-leaning but realistic in its appraisal of crime and its causes. Crime is seen as class conflict in an advanced industrial society.

This branch of critical theory, referred to as **left realism**, is most often connected to the writings of British scholars John Lea and Jock Young. In their well-respected 1984 work *What Is to Be Done About Law and Order?* they reject the utopian views of ide-alists who portray street criminals as revolutionaries.[60] They take the more "realistic" approach that street criminals prey on the poor and disenfranchised, thus making the poor doubly abused, first by the capitalist system and then by members of their own class.

Lea and Young's view of crime causation borrows from conventional sociological theory and closely resembles the relative deprivation approach, which posits that ex-periencing poverty in the midst of plenty creates discontent and breeds crime. As they put it, "The equation is simple: relative deprivation equals discontent; discontent plus lack of political solution equals crime."[61]

In *Crime in Context: A Critical Criminology of Market Societies*, Ian Taylor recognizes that anyone who expects an instant socialist revolution to take place is simply engag-ing in wishful thinking.[62] He uses data from both Europe and North America to show that the world is currently in the midst of multiple crises that are shaping all human interaction, including criminality. These crises include lack of job creation, social in-equality, social fear, political incompetence and failure, gender conflict, and family and parenting issues. These crises have led to a society in which the government seems incapable of creating positive social change: people have become more fearful and iso-lated from one another and some are excluded from the mainstream because of racism and discrimination; manufacturing jobs have been exported overseas to nations that pay extremely low wages; and fiscal constraints inhibit the possibility of reform. These problems often fall squarely on the shoulders of young black men, who suffer from ex-clusion and poverty and who now feel the economic burden created by the erosion of manufacturing jobs due to the globalization of the economy. In response, they engage in a form of hypermasculinity, which helps increase their crime rates.[63]

**LEFT REALISM AND CRIME** Left realists view the cause of serious violent crime as a function of economic inequality, community deprivation, and lack of supportive institutions that characterize today's postmodern society. The economic disparity that puts some citizens at risk of crime and protects others from harm can be directly laid at the feet of crony capitalism. Rewarding CEOs with multimillion-dollar bonuses for firing workers and sending jobs overseas increases corporate profits at the expense of workers' pay. As economic disparity increases, so too do drug abuse and crime. Here left realism can be distinguished from traditional liberal criminology, which views criminals as people who have trouble making it in society and sees crime as a result of their failures. People commit crime, liberals claim, because their opportunities are blocked. Left realists counter that legitimate opportunities are not blocked because in reality they never actually existed. As legal scholar Elliott Currie claims, our present capitalist socioeconomic system is such that it generates "inequality, injustice, social fragmentation and a 'hard' and unsupportive culture." This view separates left realists from liberal criminologists.[64]

Although implementing a socialist economy might help eliminate the crime problem, left realists recognize that something must be done to control crime under the existing system rather than waiting for the development of an ideal society. They argue that crime victims in all classes need and deserve protection; crime control reflects community needs. They do not view police and the courts as inherently evil tools of capitalism whose tough tactics alienate the lower classes. In fact, they recognize that these institutions offer life-saving public services. The left realists wish, however, that police would reduce their use of force and increase their sensitivity to the public.[65] They want the police to be more responsive to community needs, end racial profiling, and improve efforts at self-regulation and enforcement through citizen review boards and other control mechanisms. Left realists call for an end to aggressive policing, arguing that the use of force and formal arrest with minor crimes convinces many people to withhold support and information that the police need to solve much more serious crimes.[66]

In contrast to these harsh measures, left realists believe that community-based efforts hold the greatest promise of crime control. According to left realists, it is possible for community organization efforts to eliminate or reduce crime before police involvement becomes necessary, a process they call **preemptive deterrence**. The reasoning behind this approach is that if the number of marginalized youths (those who feel they are not part of society and have nothing to lose by committing crime) could be reduced, then delinquency rates would decline.[67]

**preemptive deterrence**
Efforts to prevent crime through community organization and youth involvement.

Surprisingly, this left realist perspective may be gaining traction even in the nation's most conservative states (including Texas), which have begun to reduce their prison expenditures while funding treatment, reentry, and alternative to incarceration programs. In part this policy shift corresponds to a change in public opinion: as crime rates have declined and state budgets are in crisis, the public demands low-cost alternatives to the "lock 'em up" policies that have been predominant for the past few decades. It's possible that a more realistic vision of punishment may be on the horizon.[68]

**LEFT REALISM AND TERRORISM** Left realists have focused their attention on street crime and how it affects its targets: lower-class citizens are forced to live in dangerous neighborhoods and communities. Recently, left realist Jennifer Gibbs applied the basic concepts to explain the motivation for terrorist activity. She finds four key elements of left realism that should, if valid, underpin terrorist involvement:

- People are recruited into terrorist organizations because of relative deprivation.
- Terrorist organizations are subcultures that provide peer support.
- Victims/targets are selected based on opportunity/routine activities.
- Get-tough policies that create a police state may backfire.

Gibbs finds evidence to support the first proposition: terrorists are drawn not from extremely poor populations but from those who realize they have fallen behind other groups. Absolute deprivation (e.g., the inability to provide basic necessities) is not the cause of terrorism; relative deprivation (e.g., being less well off than one's peers) seems to carry more weight, an association predicted by left realism. Feelings of deprivation are exacerbated by the new technology. Advancements like the Internet make communication easier, and people can see how much better off others are, increasing the perception of relative deprivation.

Second, left realist theory argues that men who experience stress as a result of relative deprivation and do not have socially appropriate coping mechanisms turn to similarly situated peers, who provide support; they often form subcultures. Likewise, terrorist group members seek peer support with like-minded people, forming subcultures supportive of these values or ideology. In today's postmodern world, technology has created the opportunity for virtual peer groups and subcultures. Peer support does not necessarily need to be face to face within groups but can exist in blogs and chat rooms. Those adhering to a particular ideology may find peer support in written communications such as online forums, Twitter, and other social media.

Gibbs finds weaker support for the role of opportunity in terrorist activities because they tend to be planned rather than spontaneous events. However, there is some evidence that opportunity plays a role in choosing victims: targeting businesses and citizens is easier than targeting government entities or military installations or personnel. Other reasons may include having the "biggest bang for the buck" by targeting businesses—symbolic of capitalism—or civilians, whose deaths generate widespread attention.

The final proposition of left realist theory addressed by Gibbs is that get-tough policies will not reduce crime. She notes that left realism focuses on individualized or community-focused responses to crime. Get-tough policies alienate people and legitimate terrorist organizations. The "war on terror" legitimized groups like al-Qaeda, attracting more terrorism instead of decreasing it. Also, the military response to terrorism is not a deterrent. Military "solutions," in particular, lead to retaliation, generating a cycle of violence because they tend to be reactive rather than proactive. They provide short-term solutions that fail to address the underlying causes that lead to terrorism in the first place. Instead, left realism theory directs policy toward minimal official response and maximizing informal social control. With terrorism, attempting to address the underlying grievances may be helpful.[69]

**L05** Articulate the basic ideas of critical feminism.

## Critical Feminist Theory

Like so many theories in criminology, most of the efforts of critical theorists have been devoted to explaining male criminality.[70] To remedy this theoretical lapse, a number of feminist writers have attempted to explain the cause of crime, gender differences in crime rates, and the exploitation of female victims from a critical perspective.

**Critical feminism** views gender inequality as stemming from the unequal power of men and women in a capitalist society, which leads to the exploitation of women by fathers, boyfriends, and husbands.

The origin of gender differences can be traced to the development of private property and male domination of the laws of inheritance, which led to male control over property and power.[71] Women were considered a commodity worth possessing, like land or money.[72] A **patriarchal** system eventually developed in which men's work was valued and women's work was devalued. As capitalism prevailed, the division of labor by gender made women responsible for the unpaid maintenance and reproduction of the current and future labor force, which was derisively called "domestic work." Although this unpaid work done by women is crucial and profitable for capitalists, who reap these free benefits, such labor is exploitative and oppressive for women.[73] Even when women gained the right to work for pay, they were exploited as cheap labor. The dual exploitation of women within the household and in the labor market means that women produce far greater surplus value for capitalists than men.

**critical feminism**
The view that gender inequality is a result of the exploitation of women in a male-dominated society.

**patriarchal**
A social structure in which males hold primary power and enjoy social, political, economic, and social privilege.

**PATRIARCHY AND CRIME** Patriarchy, or male supremacy, has been and continues to be supported by those who hold political, social, and economic power. This system sustains female oppression at home and in the workplace.[74] Although the number of traditional patriarchal families is in steep decline, in those that still exist a wife's economic dependence ties men more securely to wage-earning jobs, further serving the interests of capitalists by undermining potential rebellion against the system.

Critical feminists link criminal behavior patterns to the gender conflict shaped by both patriarchy and class conflict. Capitalists control the labor of workers, and men control women both economically and biologically.[75] This "double marginality" explains why females in a capitalist society commit fewer crimes than males. Because they are isolated in the family, they have fewer opportunities to engage in elite deviance (white-collar and economic crimes). Although powerful females as well as males will commit white-collar crimes, the female crime rate is restricted because of the patriarchal nature of the modern economic system.[76]

The male-centered economic system still maintains the privilege of white men and renders minority and lower-class women powerless. It even shapes their opportunity to commit crimes, forcing them into less serious, nonviolent, self-destructive crimes, such as abusing drugs and sex work. Recent efforts of the capitalist classes to undermine the social support of the poor has hit women particularly hard. The end of welfare, concentration on welfare fraud, and cutbacks to social services all have directly and uniquely affected women.[77]

Pat Carlen claims that underclass women have two sets of social compromises that shape their lives and power. The first is the *class deal*, which stipulates that women's ability to cope is shaped by the opportunity available for them to earn their own wages and achieve financial success, a status that is beyond the means and capabilities of most lower-class women. Then there is the *gender deal*, motivated by the promise that a woman can find happiness and a fulfilling family life if she is able to find a man who is the primary breadwinner. The gender deal does not always work as expected and breaks down when the woman finds that her mate is actually abusive and she becomes socially isolated. According to Carlen, women turn to crime when the class deal is impossible to achieve and the gender deal falls apart.[78]

**MASCULINITY AND CRIME** According to the concept of **hegemonic masculinity**, each culture creates an ideal vision of male behavior. In U.S. culture, there is a hierarchy of masculine behavior that glorifies competitiveness and reflects a tendency for males to seek to dominate other males, to be homophobic, and to subordinate females.[79]

In every culture males try to emulate "ideal" masculine behaviors. In Western culture, this means being authoritative, in charge, combative, and controlling.[80] Failure to adopt these roles leaves men feeling effeminate and unmanly. Their struggle to dominate women in order to prove their manliness is called "doing gender." Crime is a vehicle for men to "do gender" because it separates them from the weak and allows them to demonstrate physical bravery. Violence directed toward women is an especially economical way to demonstrate manhood. Would a weak, effeminate male ever attack a woman?

In contemporary society men must convince others that in no way are they feminine or have female qualities. Popular movies and TV shows may give the impression that left to their own devices men are sloppy and refuse to cook or do housework because these are "female" activities. More ominously, men may work at excluding, hurting, denigrating, exploiting, or otherwise abusing women. Even in all-male groups, men often prove their manhood by treating the weakest member of the group as "woman-like" and abusing him accordingly. Men need to defend themselves at all costs from being contaminated with femininity, and these efforts begin in children's playgroups and continue into adulthood and marriage.[81]

This attitude has produced numerous incidents of sexual assault against young women, in which gender-centered humiliation, such as taking nude photos and videos of unsuspecting victims and posting them online, plays a major role. College fraternities have become notorious for this type of behavior, prompting closings or suspensions at

**hegemonic masculinity**
The belief in the existence of a culturally normative ideal of male behavior.

AP Images/Matt Rourke

Critical feminists identify ways in which women are objectified and victimized. One concern is that incidents of sexual assaults and Internet attacks on women occur regularly on college campuses. Here, on March 20, 2015, students and others demonstrate on the Penn State campus in support of women who were depicted on the Kappa Delta Rho fraternity's Facebook pages. Kappa Delta Rho fraternity members used two secret Facebook pages to post photos of nude females, some of whom appeared to be sleeping or passed out, as well as posts relating to hazing or drug deals.

major schools such as Penn State.[82] This attitude also helps explain the sexual assault culture that dominates the club scene in which men feel free to victimize women because that is just what men do. According to Philip Kavanaugh, various types of unwanted sexual contact become expected in bars, clubs, and lounges because sexually aggressive or coercive behavior is considered a normal part of gendered interactions in public places devoted to urban nightlife.[83]

**BEING VICTIMIZED** Critical feminists also show how sexual and other victimization of girls is a function of male socialization because so many young males learn to be aggressive and to exploit women. Males seek out same-sex peer groups for social support; these groups encourage members to exploit and sexually abuse women. On college campuses, peers encourage sexual violence against women who are considered "sluts." Such derogatory labels allow the males to justify their actions. Slut-shaming, the practice of embarrassing, humiliating, or attacking a woman for being sexual or acting on sexual feelings, has now become common on college campuses.

According to the critical feminist view, when female victims run away and abuse substances, they may be reacting to abuse they have suffered at home or at school.[84] Those who are on the street, who are homeless, are more likely to have experienced significant social problems, including childhood molestation, adult sexual assault, and arrests for prostitution and to have been in treatment for substance misuse.[85]

Powerlessness increases the likelihood that women will become targets of violent acts.[86] When lower-class males are shut out of the economic opportunity structure, they try to build their self-image through acts of machismo; such acts may involve violent abuse of women. This type of reaction accounts for a significant percentage of female victims who are attacked by a spouse or intimate partner. It is not surprising to find that incarcerated female offenders report higher rates of interpersonal violence and mental health problems than incarcerated men and that there is a strong association between suffering intimate partner violence, mental health issues, and involvement with the justice system.[87]

Female victimization should decline as women's place in society is elevated and they are able to obtain more power at home, in the workplace, and in government. Empirical research seems to support this view. In nations where the status of women is generally high, sexual violence rates are significantly lower than in nations where women do not enjoy similar educational and occupational opportunities.[88] Women's victimization rates decline as they are empowered socially, economically, and legally.[89]

**GENDER AND THE JUSTICE SYSTEM** When the exploited girl finds herself in the arms of the justice system, her problems may just be beginning. Boys who get in trouble may be considered "overzealous" youth or kids who just went too far. Girls who get in trouble are seen as a threat to acceptable images of femininity; their behavior is considered even more unusual and dangerous than male delinquency.[90]

Critical feminists such as Meda Chesney-Lind have found gender differences not only in criminality but also in the way girls and women are treated in both the juvenile and criminal justice system.[91] While it is true males are sanctioned more heavily than females, and they are overrepresented in the correctional system, it is also true that they commit more serious violent crimes.

These outcomes may be misleading. As Chesney-Lind has repeatedly found, women and girls receive more punitive treatment than men and boys, especially in cases involving sexual matters or offenses. Nor is this a recent phenomenon. Through-out history females have been more likely to be punished for their immoral behavior than for their criminal activities. Chesney-Lind's now classic research first identified the fact that police are more likely to arrest female adolescents for sexual activity while ignoring similar behaviors when engaged in by males. Girls are more likely than boys to be picked up by police for status offenses such as being truant, run-aways, or disobedient, and are more likely to be kept in detention for such offenses.[92]

The sexual stigmatization of girls is not a thing of the past. Critical feminists note that girls are still disadvantaged if their behavior is viewed as morally incorrect by government officials or if they are considered beyond parental control.[93] Girls may still be subject to harsh punishments if they are considered dangerously immoral or fail to measure up to stereotypes of proper female behavior.[94] Research by Tia Stevens and her associates found that over the past decades, regardless of racial/ethnic group, young girls who are involved in behavior considered inappropriate for females are more likely to be formally charged and involved in the juvenile justice system. Tolerance for misbehavior significantly de-creases when girls violate gender norms.[95] Lisa Pasko's research confirms that the focus of the juvenile justice system continues to be on girls' sexual behavior. While girls are not directly arrested and adjudicated for sexual immorality, they are still told to take responsi-bility for their "bad choices." In the contemporary era, the correctional focus remains on the control and micromanagement of girls' bodies and sexuality.[96]

The justice system also seems biased against people who identify as lesbian, gay, bisexual, or transgender (LGBT), who are disproportionately incarcerated. Though they make up approximately 6 percent of the youth population, it is now estimated that LGBT youth comprise 13 percent to 15 percent of youth involved in the juvenile justice system.[97]

As they mature, women may become more adept at navigating the justice sys-tem and use their street smarts and savvy to control their experience. When Corey S. Shdaimah and Chrysanthi Leon interviewed female sex-workers who were placed within justice system programs they found that rather than acting passively, they demonstrated skills and moral reasoning that included the ability to make choices, work the systems that dominate their lives, and assert power and control. Rather than being passive they were creative, resilient, and rational in their efforts to deal with the life circumstances in which they were placed.[98]

## Power–Control Theory

John Hagan and his associates have created a critical feminist model, **power–control theory**, that uses gender differences to explain the onset of criminality.[99] Hagan's view is that crime and delinquency rates are a function of two factors: class position (power) and family functions (control).[100] The link between these two variables is that, within the family, parents reproduce the power relationships they hold in the workplace; a po-sition of dominance at work is equated with control in the household. As a result, par-ents' work experiences and class position influence the criminality of their children.[101]

In **paternalistic families**, fathers assume the traditional role of breadwinners, while mothers tend to have menial jobs or remain at home to supervise domestic mat-ters. Within the paternalistic home, mothers are expected to control the behavior of their daughters while granting greater freedom to sons. In such a home, the parent–daughter relationship can be viewed as a preparation for the "cult of domesticity," which makes girls' involvement in delinquency unlikely, whereas boys are freer to de-viate because they are not subject to maternal control. Girls growing up in patriarchal families are socialized to fear legal sanctions more than are males; consequently, boys in these families exhibit more delinquent behavior than their sisters. The result is that

**power–control theory**
A criminological theory that maintains that the structure of gender relations within the family explains gender differences in the crime rate.

**paternalistic families**
Families in which fathers assume the traditional role of breadwinners, while mothers tend to have menial jobs or remain at home to supervise domestic matters.

boys not only engage in more antisocial behaviors but have greater access to legitimate adult behaviors, such as working at part-time jobs or possessing their own transportation. In contrast, without these legitimate behavioral outlets, girls who are unhappy or dissatisfied with their status are forced to seek out risky **role exit behaviors**, including such desperate measures as running away and contemplating suicide.

In **egalitarian families**—those in which couples share similar positions of power at home and in the workplace—daughters gain a kind of freedom that reflects reduced parental control. These families produce daughters whose law-violating behavior mirrors their brothers'. In an egalitarian family, girls may have greater opportunity to engage in legitimate adult status behaviors and less need to enact deviant role exits.[102]

Ironically, Hagan believes that these relationships also occur in female-headed households with absent fathers. Hagan and his associates found that when fathers and mothers hold equally valued managerial positions, the similarity between the rates of their daughters' and sons' delinquency is greatest. By implication, middle-class girls are the most likely to violate the law because they are less closely controlled than their lower-class counterparts. In homes in which both parents hold positions of power, girls are more likely to have the same expectations of career success as their brothers. Consequently, siblings of both sexes will be socialized to take risks and engage in other behavior related to delinquency.

Though empirical analysis of the premises of power–control theory has generally been supportive, some critics have questioned its core assumption that power and control variables can explain crime.[103] More specifically, critics fail to replicate the finding that upper-class girls are more likely to deviate than their lower-class peers or that class and power interact to produce delinquency.[104] Some researchers have found few gender-based supervision and behavior differences in worker-, manager-, or owner-dominated households.[105] Research indicates that single-mother families may be different than two-parent egalitarian families, though Hagan's theory equates the two.[106]

Finally, power and control may interact with other personal traits, such as personality and self-control, to shape behavior.[107] Further research is needed to determine whether power–control can have an independent influence on behavior and can explain gender differences in the crime rate.

## Peacemaking Criminology

To members of the **peacemaking** movement, the main purpose of criminology is to promote a peaceful, just society. Rather than standing on empirical analysis of data, peacemaking draws its inspiration from religious and philosophical teachings ranging from Quakerism to Zen.[108] For example, rather than seeing socioeconomic status as a "variable" that is correlated with crime, as do mainstream criminologists, peacemakers view poverty as a source of suffering—almost a crime in and of itself. Poverty enervates people and becomes a master status that subjects them to lives filled with suffering. From a peacemaking perspective, a key avenue for preventing crime is, in the short run, diminishing the suffering poverty causes and, in the long run, embracing social policies that reduce the prevalence of economic suffering in contemporary society.[109]

Peacemakers view the efforts of the state to punish and control as crime-encouraging rather than crime-discouraging. These views were first articulated in a series of books with an anarchist theme written by criminologists Larry Tifft and Dennis Sullivan in 1980.[110] Tifft argues, "The violent punishing acts of the state and its controlling professions are of the same genre as the violent acts of individuals. In each instance these acts reflect an attempt to monopolize human interaction."[111]

Sullivan stresses the futility of correcting and punishing criminals in the context of our conflict-ridden society: "The reality we must grasp is that we live in a culture of severed relationships, where every available institution provides a form of banishment but no place or means for people to become connected, to be responsible to and for each other."[112] Sullivan suggests that mutual aid rather than coercive punishment is the key to a harmonious society. In *Restorative Justice*, Sullivan

**role exit behaviors**
The process of disengagement from a role that is central to one's self-identity in order to establish a new identity.

**egalitarian families**
Families in which couples share similar positions of power at home and in the workplace.

**peacemaking**
An approach that considers punitive crime control strategies to be counterproductive and favors the use of humanistic conflict resolution to prevent and control crime.

## Concept Summary 8.1 Emerging Forms of Critical Criminology

| Theory | Major Premise | Strengths | Research Focus |
|---|---|---|---|
| Left realism | Crime is a function of relative deprivation; criminals prey on the poor. | Represents a compromise between conflict and traditional criminology. | Deterrence; protection. |
| Critical feminist theory | The capitalist system creates patriarchy, which oppresses women. | Explains gender bias, violence against women, and repression. | Gender inequality; oppression; patriarchy. |
| Power–control theory | Girls are controlled more closely than boys in traditional male-dominated households; there is gender equity in contemporary egalitarian homes. | Explains gender differences in the crime rate as a function of class and gender conflict. | Power and control; gender differences; domesticity. |
| Peacemaking criminology | Peace and humanism can reduce crime; conflict resolution strategies can work. | Offers a new approach to crime control through mediation. | Punishment; nonviolence; mediation. |

and Tifft reaffirm their belief that society must seek humanitarian forms of justice without resorting to brutal punishments:

> By allowing feelings of vengeance or retribution to narrow our focus on the harmful event and the person responsible for it—as others might focus solely on a sin committed and the sinner—we tell ourselves we are taking steps to free ourselves from the effects of the harm or the sin in question. But, in fact, we are putting ourselves in a servile position with respect to life, human growth, and the further enjoyment of relationships with others.[113]

Today, advocates of the peacemaking movement, such as Harold Pepinsky and Richard Quinney, try to find humanist solutions to crime and other social problems.[114] Rather than punishment and prison, they advocate such policies as mediation and conflict resolution.[115]

Concept Summary 8.1 summarizes the various forms of critical criminology.

## Critical Theory and Restorative Justice

Some critical theorists believe that crime will only vanish when there is a reordering of society so that capitalism is destroyed and a socialist state is created. Others call for a more "practical" approach to crime control, making use of inclusionary, nonpunitive strategies for crime prevention and control, an approach known as **restorative justice**.[116] The next sections discuss the foundation and principles of restorative justice.

### The Concept of Restorative Justice

The term *restorative justice* is often hard to define because it encompasses a variety of programs and practices. According to a leading restorative justice scholar,

**L06** Discuss how restorative justice is related to peacemaking criminology.

**restorative justice**
A view of justice that focuses on the needs of victims, the community, and offenders, and focuses on nonpunitive strategies to heal the wounds caused by crime.

Restorative justice takes many forms. Here, the program coordinator, a policewoman, and volunteers on the board of the Neighborhood Restoration Justice Program in Apoka, Florida, meet for an accountability conference. This pretrial diversion program for first-time juvenile offenders is an alternative to juvenile court. At this meeting, youths were given sanctions for the crimes they committed.

Howard Zehr, restorative justice requires that society address victims' harms and needs, hold offenders accountable to put right those harms, and involve victims, offenders, and communities in the process of healing. Zehr maintains that the core value of the restoration process can be translated into respect for all, even those who are different from us, even those who seem to be our enemies. At its core, Zehr argues, restorative justice is a set of principles, a philosophy, an alternate set of guiding questions that provide an alternative framework for thinking about wrongdoing.[117] Restorative justice would reject concepts such as "punishment," "deterrence," and "incarceration" and embrace "apology," "rehabilitation," "reparation," "healing," "restoration," and "reintegration."

Restorative justice has grown out of a belief that the traditional justice system has done little to involve the community in the process of dealing with crime and wrongdoing. What has developed is a system of coercive punishments, administered by bureaucrats, that are inherently harmful to offenders and reduce the likelihood that offenders will ever become productive members of society. This system relies on punishment, stigma, and disgrace. Advocates of restorative justice argue that rather than today's lockdown mentality, what is needed is a justice policy that repairs the harm caused by crime and that includes all parties who have suffered from that harm: the victim, the community, and the offender. They have made an ongoing effort to reduce the conflict created by the criminal justice system when it hands out harsh punishments to offenders, many of whom are powerless social outcasts. Based on the principle of reducing social harm, restorative justice argues that the old methods of punishment are a failure: after all, upwards of two-thirds of all prison inmates recidivate soon after their release. And tragically, not all inmates are released. Some are given life sentences for relatively minor crimes under three-strikes laws, which mandate such a sentence for a third conviction; some are given sentences of life with no parole, which are in essence death sentences.[118]

## Reintegrative Shaming

One of the key foundations of the restoration movement is contained in John Braithwaite's influential book *Crime, Shame, and Reintegration*.[119] Braithwaite's vision rests on the concept of shame: the feeling we get when we don't meet the standards we have set for ourselves or that significant others have set for us. Shame can lead people to believe that they are defective, that there is something wrong with them. Braithwaite notes that countries such as Japan, in which conviction for crimes brings an inordinate amount of shame, have extremely low crime rates. In Japan, criminal prosecution proceeds only when the normal process of public apology, compensation, and the victim's forgiveness breaks down.

Shame is a powerful tool of informal social control. Citizens in cultures in which crime is not shameful, such as the United States, do not internalize an abhorrence for crime because when they are punished they view themselves as mere victims of the justice system. Their punishment comes at the hands of neutral strangers, such as police and judges, who are being paid to act. In contrast, shaming relies on the victim's participation.[120]

Braithwaite divides the concept of shame into two distinct types. The most common form of shaming typically involves stigmatization, an ongoing process of degradation in which the offender is branded as an evil person and cast out of society. Shaming can occur at a school disciplinary hearing or at a criminal court trial. Bestowing stigma and degradation may have a general deterrent effect: it makes people afraid of social rejection and public humiliation. As a specific deterrent, stigma is doomed to failure; people who suffer humiliation at the hands of the justice system "reject their rejectors" by joining a deviant subculture of like-minded people who collectively resist social control. Despite these dangers, there has been an ongoing effort to brand offenders and make their shame both public and permanent. All states have passed sex offender registry and notification laws that make public the names of those convicted of sex offenses and warn neighbors of their presence in the community.

But the fear of shame can backfire or be neutralized. When shame is managed well, people acknowledge they made mistakes and suffered disappointments, and try to work out what can be done to make things right; this is referred to as shame management. However, in some cases, to avoid the pain of shaming, people engage in improper shame management, a psychological process in which they deny shame by shifting the blame of their actions to their target or to others.[121] They may get angry and take out their frustrations on those whom they can dominate. Improper shame management of this sort has been linked to antisocial acts ranging from school yard bullying to tax evasion.[122]

Massive levels of improper shame management may occur on a societal scale during periods of social upheaval. Because of this, some nations that previously have had low crime rates may experience a surge of antisocial behavior during periods of war and revolution. Rape, an act which may have been unthinkable to most men, suddenly becomes commonplace because of the emergence of narcissistic pride, feeling dominant and arrogant, and developing a sense of superiority over others, in this case the enemy. This sense of hubris fosters aggressive actions and allows combatants to rape women whom they perceive as belonging to an enemy group.[123]

Braithwaite argues that crime control can be better achieved through a policy of **reintegrative shaming**. Here disapproval is extended to the offenders' evil deeds, while at the same time they are cast as respected people who can be reaccepted by society. A critical element of reintegrative shaming occurs when the offenders begin to understand and recognize their wrongdoing and shame themselves. To be reintegrative, shaming must be brief and controlled and then followed by ceremonies of forgiveness, apology, and repentance.

To prevent crime, Braithwaite charges, society must encourage reintegrative shaming. For example, the women's movement can reduce domestic violence by mounting a crusade to shame spouse abusers. Similarly, parents who use reintegrative shaming techniques in their childrearing practices may improve parent–child relationships and ultimately reduce the delinquent involvement of their children.[124] Because informal social controls may have a greater impact than legal or formal ones, it may not be surprising that the fear of personal shame can have a greater deterrent effect than the fear of legal sanctions. It may also be applied to produce specific deterrence. Offenders can meet with victims so that the offenders can experience shame. Family members and peers can be present to help the offender reintegrate. Such efforts can humanize a system of justice that today relies on repression rather than forgiveness as the basis of specific deterrence.

**reintegrative shaming**
The concept that people can be reformed if they understand the harm they have caused and are brought back into the social mainstream.

## The Process of Restoration

The restoration process begins by redefining crime in terms of a conflict among the offender, the victim, and affected constituencies (families, schools, workplaces, and so forth). Therefore, it is vitally important that the resolution take place within the context in which the conflict originally occurred rather than being transferred to a specialized institution that has no social connection to the community or group from which the conflict originated. In other words, most conflicts are better settled in the community than in a court.

By maintaining "ownership" or jurisdiction over the conflict, the community is able to express its shared outrage about the offense. Shared community outrage is directly communicated to the offender. The victim is also given a chance to voice his or her story, and the offender can directly communicate his or her need for social re-integration and treatment. All restoration programs involve an understanding among all the parties involved in a criminal act: the victim, the offender, and the community. Although processes differ in structure and style, they generally include these elements:

- The offender is asked to recognize that he or she caused injury to personal and social relations along with a determination and acceptance of responsibility (ideally accompanied by a statement of remorse). Only then can the offender be restored as a productive member of the community.
- Restoration involves turning the justice system into a "healing" process rather than being a distributor of retribution and revenge.
- Reconciliation is a big part of the restorative approach. Most people involved in offender–victim relationships actually know one another or were related in some way before the criminal incident took place. Instead of treating one of the involved parties as a victim deserving of sympathy and the other as a criminal deserving of punishment, it is more productive to address the issues that produced conflict between these people.[125]
- The effectiveness of justice ultimately depends on the stake a person has in the community (or in a particular social group). If a person does not value his or her membership in the group, the person will be unlikely to accept responsibility, show remorse, or repair the injuries caused by his or her actions. In contrast, people who have a stake in the community and its principal institutions, such as work, home, and school, find that their involvement enhances their personal and familial well-being.[126]
- The offender must make a commitment to both material (monetary) restitution and symbolic reparation (an apology). A determination must also be made of community support and assistance for both victim and offender.

The intended result of this process is to repair injuries suffered by the victim and the community while ensuring reintegration of the offender.

**RESTORATION PROGRAMS**  Negotiation, mediation, consensus-building, and peace-making have been part of the dispute resolution process in European and Asian communities for centuries.[127] Native American and First Nations (Canadian aboriginal) people have long used the type of community participation in the adjudication process (for example, sentencing circles, sentencing panels, elders panels) that restorative justice advocates are now embracing.[128]

In some Native American communities, people accused of breaking the law meet with community members, victims (if any), village elders, and agents of the justice system in a **sentencing circle**. Each member of the circle expresses his or her feelings about the act that was committed and raises questions or concerns. The accused can express regret about his or her actions and a desire to change the harmful behavior. People may suggest ways the offender can make things up to the community and those he or she harmed. A treatment program, such as Alcoholics Anonymous, can be suggested, if appropriate.

**FAMILY GROUP CONFERENCE**  A popular restorative justice method is the family group conference, made up of the person who has committed the offense (usually a young first-time offender), members of his or her family and whomever the family invites, the victim(s) or their representative, a support person for the victim(s), a representative of the police, and the mediator or manager of the process. Sometimes a social worker and/or a lawyer is present. The main goal of a conference is to formulate a plan about how best to deal with the offending. There are three principal components to this process:

- Ascertaining whether or not the young person admits the offense. Conferences only proceed if the young person does so or if the offense has been proved in the Youth Court.

**sentencing circle**
A method of dispensing justice involving discussion between offenders, victims, and members of the community.

- Sharing information among all the parties at the conference about the nature of the offense, the effects of the offense on the victims, the reasons for the offending, any prior offending by the young person, and so on.
- Deciding the outcome or recommendation.

The family group conference is a meeting between those entitled to attend, in a relatively informal setting. The room is usually arranged with comfortable chairs in a circle. When all are present, the meeting may open with a prayer or a blessing, depending on the customs of those involved. The coordinator then welcomes the participants, introduces each of them, and describes the purposes of the meeting. What happens next can vary, but usually the police representative reads out the summary of the offense. The young person is asked if he or she agrees that this is what happened and any variation is noted. If he or she does not agree, the meeting progresses no further and the police may consider referring the case to the Youth Court for a hearing. Assuming the young person agrees, the victim, or a spokesperson for the victim, is then usually asked to describe what the events meant for them. Next, a general discussion of the offense and the circumstances underlying it occurs. There can be a lot of emotion expressed at this point. It is at this point too that the young person and his or her family may express their remorse for what has happened and make an apology to the victim, although more often this occurs later on. Once everybody has discussed what the offending has meant and options for making good the damage, the professionals and the victim leave the family and the young person to meet privately to discuss what plans and recommendation they wish to make to repair the damage and to prevent reoffending. The private family time can take as little as half an hour or much longer. When the family is ready, the others return and the meeting is reconvened. This is the point at which the young person and the family apologize to the victim. A spokesperson for the family outlines what they propose and all discuss the proposal. Once there is agreement among all present, the details are formally recorded and the conference concludes with the sharing of food.[129]

**RECONCILIATION** Restoration has also been used as a national policy to heal internal rifts. For example, after 50 years of oppressive white rule in South Africa, the race-dividing apartheid policy was abolished in the early 1990s, and in 1994 Nelson Mandela, leader of the African National Congress (ANC), was elected president.[130] Some black leaders wanted revenge for the political murders carried out during the apartheid era, but Mandela established the Truth and Reconciliation Commission. Rather than seeking vengeance for the crimes, this government agency investigated the atrocities with the mandate of granting amnesty to those individuals who confessed their roles in the violence and could prove that their actions served some political motive rather than being based on personal factors such as greed or jealousy.

Supporters of the commission believed that this approach would help heal the nation's wounds and prevent years of racial and ethnic strife. Mandela, who had been unjustly jailed for 27 years by the regime, had reason to desire vengeance. Yet he wanted to move the country forward after the truth of what happened in the past had been established. Though many South Africans, including some ANC members, believe that the commission is too lenient, Mandela's attempts at reconciliation have prevailed. The commission is a model of restoration over revenge.

In sum, restoration can be or has been used at the following stages of justice:

- As a form of final warning to young offenders
- As a tool for school officials
- As a method of handling complaints to police
- As a diversion from prosecution
- As a presentencing, postconviction add-on to the sentencing process
- As a supplement to a community sentence (probation)
- As a preparation for release from long-term imprisonment[131]

The Policies and Issues in Criminology feature discusses the programming provided by one prominent restorative justice effort.

# Policy and Practice
# in Criminology

## THE CENTER FOR RESTORATIVE JUSTICE (CRJ)

There are numerous restorative justice initiatives now in operation around the United States and overseas. One prominent example is the Center for Restorative Justice (CRJ) in Vermont, a nonprofit community justice agency that for more than 30 years has provided a variety of restorative justice programming and services helping both young people and adults. Originally incorporated in 1982 as the Bennington County Court Diversion Program, the agency now known as CRJ provides programming that begins with prevention and intervention work in the schools through reentry work helping people returning to the community from incarceration. The services discussed below provide an example of the various forms that restorative justice now take in the community

### Pre-Charge and KAOS Programs

These programs are designed to provide early intervention and support to prevent young people from entering the juvenile justice system. Students identified as having broken school rules or who have committed chargeable offenses on school grounds may be offered this program as an alternative to school punitive sanctions. Using restorative justice principles, the Pre-Charge Program at Mount Anthony Union High School and the Kids Are Our Strength (KAOS) Program at Mount Anthony Union Middle School help first-time offenders make amends to those affected by their actions as well as the school community.

### Truancy Project

The program is designed to work with students whose chronic truancy issues have not responded to school interventions. The Truancy Project is offered as a final option to the student and his/her parents as a way to address and correct the truancy problems before the case is filed with family court. Through identifying barriers, case management, community resources, and integrating contract conditions students are supported to successfully attend school on a daily basis.

### Court Diversion

Court diversion is a community-based alternative to the formal court process and gives the offender a chance to make amends to the victim and community. Restorative justice panels hold offenders accountable to victims and the community. Court diversion is a confidential and voluntary program that results in the offender's record being sealed upon successful completion of the program.

### Youth Substance Abuse Safety Program (YSASP)

The focus of YSASP is to help young people (ages 16–20) who have been civilly cited for underage drinking or possession of marijuana get proper screening, education, and treatment for identified substance abuse problems. Once a young person successfully completes the program their civil ticket is voided. This is a voluntary program; individuals who choose not to participate in the program face a $300 fine from the State of Vermont, 90-day driver's license suspension with a $71 reinstatement fee, dramatically increased insurance rates, and civil conviction on their driving record.

### Civil DLS Diversion Program

This diversion program is designed to help people regain their driver's license while they pay off their fines and fees. Participants work with a case manager to develop a contract and payment plan that is presented to the Vermont Judicial Bureau for review and approval. Some people may be eligible for a reduction in their debt, and some may provide community service and/or participate in an educational program in exchange for a reduction in fines and fees owed. Upon successful completion of their contract, an individual's prior suspensions are removed from their record.

### Juvenile Restorative Programs

The Juvenile Restorative Probation Program (JRPP) provides restorative justice panels and restitution case management to youth on probation. Restorative justice panels hold youth accountable to victims and their community. Case managers provide follow-up services to ensure that restorative conditions of probation are completed. In addition, the program provides young offenders with an opportunity to increase their skills and participate in a variety of community activities.

The Juvenile Direct Court Referral Program is offered to youth as an alternative sentence set by the Family Court judge. Youth may be adjudicated in Family Court, but not placed on probation. The youth participate in a restorative justice panel, learn new skills, and repair harm caused to their victims.

## Community Support and Supervision (Street Checker Program)

This program provides progressive levels of community support and supervision for at-risk youth or for youth who are on probation. Community case managers provide home-based support such as curfew checks and ensuring youth's activities are consistent with probation conditions. This program offers youth opportunities to build their skills and successfully reintegrate into their own communities.

## Life Skills Development

CRJ offers a wide array of skill-building opportunities. Groups vary throughout the year and cover topics such as anger management, conflict resolution, impact on victims, self-esteem, peer pressure, and substance abuse. Individualized life skills instruction is available year-round.

## Adult Restorative Programs

The Reparative Probation Program is offered to adults through the criminal court as a condition of their probation. Restorative justice panels run by trained volunteers provide an offender the opportunity to take responsibility for his/her actions and repair the harm caused to victims and communities. Offenders who participate in this program must accept responsibility for their role in the crime that was committed.

The Direct Referral Reparative Program is offered to offenders convicted in criminal court but not placed on probation. Participants meet with a restorative justice panel to discuss the impact of their crime and develop a contract that helps make amends to their victim and community. Only those offenders who take responsibility for their crime qualify for the program.

The Suspended Fine Program provides an alternative sentencing option with a fine reduction upon successful program completion.

## Community Reentry Program

The Reentry Program provides intensive case management services to help individuals who are returning to the community from incarceration. Providing support to individuals who are struggling to reintegrate into the community is the key to their success. Area case managers' focuses include housing, employment, prosocial leisure activities, transportation, connection to community resources, and mentoring.

## Circle of Support and Accountability (COSA)

A team of trained community volunteers helps individuals returning to the community from incarceration meet the challenges of everyday living and learn ways to become productive, contributing members of the community. In addition to supporting the individual to successfully reintegrate into the community, volunteers help guide the offender to make amends to those impacted by her/his past behavior.

### Critical Thinking

What do you think about restorative justice? Is it better to help a person reintegrate into the community than to cast them out and stigmatize them as "criminals" and "convicts"? Or is the restorative justice movement simply wishful thinking?

**Source:** Information provided by the Center for Restorative Justice, Bennington, Vermont, 2015, www.bcrj.org/programs/ (accessed 2015).

# Thinking Like a Criminologist

**Is It a Bribe?**  A student wants to discuss a personal matter. A few weeks ago she was at a party when she was sexually assaulted by a fellow student. The attack was quite traumatic and she suffered both physical and emotional injury. The police were called and the young man charged with rape. Now she has been contacted by a local program that bills itself as a restorative treatment program. It seems that her attacker is now a client and wants to engage in some form of reconciliation. At an arranged meeting, he professes his regret for the attack and wishes to make amends. He and the program director have worked out a schedule in which the victim will be compensated for her pain and suffering in the amount of $5,000 in exchange for her agreeing to a recommendation to the prosecutor that the case be treated informally rather than going to trial. She doesn't know what to do: she needs the money, having missed work after the attack, but at the same time is concerned that people will think she has accepted a bribe to withdraw the charges.

## Writing Assignment

Write a paper describing the advice you would give to the student in this situation. How would you suggest that she respond to the program director? Do you consider the payment a bribe or restitution for an evil deed? Can restorative justice be used in a crime such as rape?

# SUMMARY

**LO1**  **List the core ideas of critical criminology.**

Critical criminology is based on the view that crime is a function of the conflict that exists in society. Critical theorists suggest that crime in any society is caused by economic and class conflict. Laws are created by those in power to protect their own rights and to serve their own interests. Criminal law is designed to protect the wealthy and powerful and to control the poor, have-not members of society. The poor commit crimes because of their frustration, anger, and need. The wealthy engage in illegal acts because they are used to competition and because they must do so to maintain their position in society. Crime would disappear if equality rather than discrimination was the norm.

**LO2**  **Link globalization to crime and criminality.**

Globalization disproportionately benefits wealthy and powerful organizations and individuals and impoverishes indigenous people. As the influence and impact of international financial institutions increase, there is a related relative decline in power of local or state-based institutions, resulting in the recent unrest in world financial systems. With money and power to spare, global criminal enterprise groups can recruit new members, bribe government officials, and even fund private armies.

**LO3**  **Define the concept of state (organized) crime.**

State crimes involve a violation of citizen trust. They are acts defined by law as criminal and committed by state officials in pursuit of their jobs as government representatives. Some state crimes are committed by individuals who abuse their state authority, or fail to exercise it, when working with people and organizations in the private sector. State–corporate crime involves the deviant activities by which the privileged classes strive to maintain or increase their power.

## L04   Explain the goals and findings of critical research.

Research on critical theory focuses on how the justice system was designed and how it operates to further class interests. It sometimes employs historical analysis to show how the capitalist classes have exerted control over the police, the courts, and correctional agencies. Contemporary research exposes how race and class influence decision making in the criminal justice system.

## L05   Articulate the basic ideas of critical feminism.

Critical feminist writers draw attention to the influence of patriarchal society on crime. According to power–control theory, gender differences in the crime rate can be explained by the structure of the family in a capitalist society.

## L06   Discuss how restorative justice is related to peacemaking criminology.

Peacemaking criminology brings a call for humanism to criminology. The restorative justice model holds that reconciliation rather than retribution should be applied to prevent and control crime. Restoration programs are now being used around the United States in schools, justice agencies, and community forums. They employ mediation, sentencing circles, and other techniques.

## Key Terms

social conflict 232
critical criminologists 232
power 234
supranational
    criminology 237
instrumental
    theorists 237
structural theorists 237
surplus value 238

marginalization 238
globalization 239
state (organized)
    crime 240
extraordinary
    rendition 242
dropout factories 243
left realism 244
preemptive deterrence 245

critical feminism 246
patriarchal 246
hegemonic
    masculinity 247
power–control
    theory 249
paternalistic
    families 249
role exit behaviors 250

egalitarian
    families 250
peacemaking 250
restorative
    justice 251
reintegrative
    shaming 253
sentencing circle 254

## Critical Thinking Questions

1. How would a conservative reply to a call for more restorative justice? How would a restorative justice advocate respond to a conservative call for more prisons?

2. Considering recent changes in American culture, how would a power–control theorist explain recent drops in the U.S. crime rate? Can it be linked to changes in the structure of the American family?

3. Is conflict inevitable in all cultures? If not, what can be done to reduce the level of conflict in our own society?

4. If Marx were alive today, what would he think about the prosperity enjoyed by the working class in industrial societies? Might he alter his vision of the capitalist system?

5. Has religious conflict replaced class conflict as the most important issue facing modern society? Can anything be done to heal the rifts between people of different faiths?

# Notes

*All URLs accessed in 2015.*

1. Michael Lynch and W. Byron Groves, *A Primer in Radical Criminology*, 2nd ed. (Albany, NY: Harrow & Heston, 1989), pp. 32–33.

2. Michael Lynch, "Rediscovering Criminology: Lessons from the Marxist Tradition," in *Marxist Sociology: Surveys of Contemporary Theory and Research*, ed. Donald McQuarie and Patrick McGuire (New York: General Hall, 1994).

3. Andrew Woolford, "Making Genocide Unthinkable: Three Guidelines for a Critical Criminology of Genocide," *Critical Criminology* 14 (2006): 87–106.

4. Willem Bonger, *Criminality and Economic Conditions*, abridged ed. (Bloomington: Indiana University Press, 1969, first published 1916); Ralf Dahrendorf, *Class and Class Conflict in Industrial Society* (Palo Alto, CA: Stanford University Press, 1959); George Vold, *Theoretical Criminology* (New York: Oxford University Press, 1958).

5. Bonger, *Criminality and Economic Conditions*.

6. Ian Taylor, Paul Walton, and Jock Young, *The New Criminology: For a Social Theory of Deviance* (London: Routledge & Kegan Paul, 1973).

7. Biko Agozino, "Imperialism, Crime and Criminology: Towards the Decolonisation of Criminology," *Crime, Law, and Social Change* 41 (2004): 343–358.

8. William Chambliss and Robert Seidman, *Law, Order, and Power* (Reading, MA: Addison-Wesley, 1971), p. 503.

9. Richard Quinney, *The Social Reality of Crime* (Boston: Little, Brown, 1970).

10. Howard Zinn, *Disobedience and Democracy: Nine Fallacies on Law and Order* (New York: Random House, 1968); Zinn, *Passionate Declarations: Essays on War and Justice* (New York: HarperCollins, 2003).

11. Barbara Sims, "Crime, Punishment, and the American Dream: Toward a Marxist Integration," *Journal of Research in Crime and Delinquency* 34 (1997): 5–24.

12. Richard Fry and Rakesh Kochhar, "America's Wealth Gap Between Middle-Income and Upper-Income Families Is Widest on Record," December 17, 2014, Pew Research Center, www.pewresearch.org/fact-tank/2014/12/17/wealth-gap-upper-middle-income/.

13. Kitty Kelley Epstein, "The Whitening of the American Teaching Force: A Problem of Recruitment or a Problem of Racism?" *Social Justice* 32 (2005): 89–102.

14. Tony Platt and Cecilia O'Leary, "Patriot Acts," *Social Justice* 30 (2003): 5–21.

15. Michelle Alexander, *The New Jim Crow: Mass Incarceration in the Age of Colorblindness* (New York: New Press, 2010), p. 2.

16. Epstein, "The Whitening of the American Teaching Force."

17. Sims, "Crime, Punishment, and the American Dream."

18. Alette Smeulers and Roelof Haveman, eds., *Supranational Criminology: Towards a Criminology of International Crimes* (Belgium: Intersentia, 2008).

19. Jeffery Reiman, *The Rich Get Richer and the Poor Get Prison* (New York: Wiley, 1984), pp. 43–44.

20. Rob White, "Environmental Harm and the Political Economy of Consumption," *Social Justice* 29 (2002): 82–102.

21. Jane McAlevey, "Unions and Environmentalists: Get It Together!" *The Nation*, May 7, 2012, www.thenation.com/article/167460/unions-and-environmentalists-get-it-together.

22. Ibid.

23. Gresham Sykes, "The Rise of Critical Criminology," *Journal of Criminal Law and Criminology* 65 (1974): 211–229.

24. David Jacobs, "Corporate Economic Power and the State: A Longitudinal Assessment of Two Explanations," *American Journal of Sociology* 93 (1988): 852–881.

25. Richard Quinney, "Crime Control in Capitalist Society," in *Critical Criminology*, ed. Ian Taylor, Paul Walton, and Jock Young (London: Routledge & Kegan Paul, 1975), p. 199.

26. John Hagan, *Structural Criminology* (New Brunswick, NJ: Rutgers University Press, 1989), pp. 110–119.

27. Steven Box, *Recession, Crime, and Unemployment* (London: Macmillan, 1987).

28. David Barlow, Melissa Hickman-Barlow, and W. Wesley Johnson, "The Political Economy of Criminal Justice Policy: A Time-Series Analysis of Economic Conditions, Crime, and Federal Criminal Justice Legislation, 1948–1987," *Justice Quarterly* 13 (1996): 223–241.

29. Mahesh Nalla, Michael Lynch, and Michael Leiber, "Determinants of Police Growth in Phoenix, 1950–1988," *Justice Quarterly* 14 (1997): 144–163.

30. Lily Quo, "The Average Chinese Private-Sector Worker Earns About the Same as a Cleaner in Thailand," *Quartz*, January 24, 2014, qz.com/170363/the-average-chinese-private-sector-worker-earns-about-the-same-as-a-cleaner-in-thailand/.

31. Dawn L. Rothe, Jeffrey Ian Ross, Christopher W. Mullins, David Friedrichs, Raymond Michalowski, Gregg Barak, David Kauzlarich, and Ronald C. Kramer, "That Was Then, This Is Now, What About Tomorrow? Future Directions in State Crime Studies," *Critical Criminology* 17 (2009): 3–13.

32. David Friedrichs and Jessica Friedrichs, "The World Bank and Crimes of Globalization: A Case Study," *Social Justice* 29 (2002): 13–36.

33. Ibid.

34. Louise Shelley, "The Globalization of Crime and Terrorism," State Department's Bureau of International Information Programs (IIP), 2006.

35. Greg Palast, "Secret US Plan for Iraqi Oil, BBC News," March 17, 2005, news.bbc.co.uk/1/hi/programmes /newsnight/4354269.stm.

36. Jeffrey Ian Ross, *The Dynamics of Political Crime* (Thousand Oaks, CA: Sage, 2003).

37. Charlie Savage and Mark Mazzetti, "Cryptic Overtures and a Clandestine Meeting Gave Birth to a Blockbuster Story," *New York Times*, June 10, 2013, www .nytimes.com/2013/06/11/us/how-edward-j-snowden -orchestrated-a-blockbuster-story.html.

38. American Civil Liberties Union, "What's Wrong with Public Video Surveillance?" www.aclu .org/technology-and-liberty/whats-wrong -public-video-surveillance.

39. BBC News, "Six Days That Shook Iran," July 11, 2000, news.bbc.co.uk/2/hi/middle_east/828696.stm.

40. Scott A. Bonn, *Mass Deception: Moral Panic and the U.S. War on Iraq* (New Brunswick, NJ: Rutgers University Press, 2010).

41. MSNBC News, "Bush Acknowledges Secret CIA Prisons," September 6, 2006, www.msnbc.msn.com /id/14689359/; American Civil Liberties Union, "FBI Inquiry Details Abuses Reported by Agents at Guantanamo," January 3, 2007, www.aclu.org/news/fbi -inquiry-details-abuses-reported-agents-guantanamo.

42. Ross, *The Dynamics of Political Crime*.

43. Human Rights Watch, "Chechnya: Research Shows Widespread and Systematic Use of Torture," www .hrw.org/news/2006/11/12/chechnya-research-shows -widespread-and-systematic-use-torture.

44. *London Times*, April 26, 2009, "Russian Death Squads 'Pulverise' Chechens," www.thesundaytimes.co.uk /sto/news/world_news/article165191.ece.

45. America's Promise Alliance, "Building a Grad Nation: Progress and Challenge in Ending the High School Dropout Epidemic," November 30, 2010, www .americaspromise.org/building-grad-nation-report.

46. Michael Rocques and Raymond Paternoster, "Understanding the Antecedents of the 'School-to-Jail' Link: The Relationship Between Race and School Discipline," *Journal of Criminal Law and Criminology* 101 (2011): 633–665.

47. Graham Ousey and James Unnever, "Racial-Ethnic Threat, Out-Group Intolerance, and Support for Punishing Criminals: A Cross-National Study," *Criminology* 50 (2012): 565–603.

48. Albert Meehan and Michael Ponder, "Race and Place: The Ecology of Racial Profiling African American Motorists," *Justice Quarterly* 29 (2002): 399–431.

49. Tammy Rinehart Kochel, David Wilson, and Stephen Mastrofski, "Effect of Suspect Race on Officers' Arrest Decisions," *Criminology* 49 (2011): 473–512.

50. Malcolm Homes, "Minority Threat and Police Brutality: Determinants of Civil Rights Criminal Complaints in U.S. Municipalities," *Criminology* 38 (2000): 343–368.

51. Brian Johnson, Eric Stewart, Justin Pickett, and Marc Gertz, "Ethnic Threat and Social Control: Examining Public Support for Judicial Use of Ethnicity in Punishment," *Criminology* 49 (2011): 401–441.

52. Charles Crawford, Ted Chiricos, and Gary Kleck, "Race, Racial Threat, and Sentencing of Habitual Offenders," *Criminology* 36 (1998): 481–511.

53. Darrell Steffensmeier and Stephen Demuth, "Ethnicity and Judges' Sentencing Decisions: Hispanic-Black-White Comparisons," *Criminology* 39 (2001): 145–178; Alan Lizotte, "Extra-Legal Factors in Chicago's Criminal Courts: Testing the Conflict Model of Criminal Justice," *Social Problems* 25 (1978): 564–580.

54. Terance Miethe and Charles Moore, "Racial Differences in Criminal Processing: The Consequences of Model Selection on Conclusions about Differential Treatment," *Sociological Quarterly* 27 (1987): 217–237.

55. Tracy Nobiling, Cassia Spohn, and Miriam DeLone, "A Tale of Two Counties: Unemployment and Sentence Severity," *Justice Quarterly* 15 (1998): 459–485.

56. Michael Lenza, David Keys, and Teresa Guess, "The Prevailing Injustices in the Application of the Missouri Death Penalty (1978 to 1996)," *Social Justice* 32 (2005): 151–166.

57. Thomas Arvanites, "Increasing Imprisonment: A Function of Crime or Socioeconomic Factors?" *American Journal of Criminal Justice* 17 (1992): 19–38.

58. David Greenberg and Valerie West, "State Prison Populations and Their Growth, 1971–1991," *Criminology* 39 (2001): 615–654.

59. Anthony Platt, "Criminology in the 1980s: Progressive Alternatives to 'Law and Order,'" *Crime and Social Justice* 21–22 (1985): 191–199.

60. John Lea and Jock Young, *What Is to Be Done About Law and Order?* (Harmondsworth, England: Penguin, 1984).

61. Ibid., p. 88.

62. Ian Taylor, *Crime in Context: A Critical Criminology of Market Societies* (Boulder, CO: Westview Press, 1999).

63. Ibid., pp. 30–31.

64. Elliott Currie, "Plain Left Realism: An Appreciation, and Some Thoughts for the Future," *Crime, Law and Social Change* 54 (2010): 111–124.

65. Richard Kinsey, John Lea, and Jock Young, *Losing the Fight Against Crime* (London: Blackwell, 1986).

66. Martin Schwartz and Walter DeKeseredy, "The Current Health of Left Realist Theory," *Crime, Law and Social Change* 54 (2010): 107–110.

67. Martin Schwartz and Walter DeKeseredy, *Contemporary Criminology* (Belmont, CA: Wadsworth, 1993), p. 249.

68. Michael Jacobson and Lynn Chancer, "From Left Realism to Mass Incarceration: The Need for Pragmatic

Vision in Criminal Justice Policy," *Crime, Law and Social Change* 55 (2011): 187–196.

69. Jennifer Gibbs, "Looking at Terrorism Through Left Realist Lenses." *Crime, Law and Social Change* 54 (2010): 171–185.

70. For a general review of this issue, see Kathleen Daly and Meda Chesney-Lind, "Feminism and Criminology," *Justice Quarterly* 5 (1988): 497–538; Douglas Smith and Raymond Paternoster, "The Gender Gap in Theories of Deviance: Issues and Evidence," *Journal of Research in Crime and Delinquency* 24 (1987): 140–172; and Pat Carlen, "Women, Crime, Feminism, and Realism," *Social Justice* 17 (1990): 106–123.

71. Daly and Chesney-Lind, "Feminism and Criminology."

72. Herman Schwendinger and Julia Schwendinger, *Rape and Inequality* (Newbury Park, CA: Sage, 1983).

73. Janet Saltzman Chafetz, "Feminist Theory and Sociology: Underutilized Contributions for Mainstream Theory," *Annual Review of Sociology* 23 (1997): 97–121.

74. Ibid.

75. James Messerschmidt, *Capitalism, Patriarchy, and Crime* (Totowa, NJ: Rowman & Littlefield, 1986); for a critique of this work, see Herman Schwendinger and Julia Schwendinger, "The World According to James Messerschmidt," *Social Justice* 15 (1988): 123–145.

76. Kathleen Daly, "Gender and Varieties of White-Collar Crime," *Criminology* 27 (1989): 769–793.

77. Gillian Balfour, "Re-imagining a Feminist Criminology," *Canadian Journal of Criminology and Criminal Justice* 48 (2006): 735–752.

78. Pat Carlen, *Women, Crime and Poverty* (London: Open University Press, 1988).

79. R. W. Connell and James W. Messerschmidt, "Hegemonic Masculinity: Rethinking the Concept," *Gender Society* 19 (2005): 829–858.

80. James Messerschmidt, *Masculinities and Crime: Critique and Reconceptualization of Theory* (Lanham, MD: Rowman & Littlefield, 1993).

81. Angela P. Harris, "Gender, Violence, Race, and Criminal Justice," *Stanford Law Review* 52 (2000): 777–810.

82. Fox News, "Penn State Frat Suspended for Year over Nude Facebook Pics," March 17, 2015, www.foxnews.com/us/2015/03/17/penn-state-frat-suspended-for-year-over-nude-facebook-pics/.

83. Philip Kavanaugh, "The Continuum of Sexual Violence: Women's Accounts of Victimization in Urban Nightlife," *Feminist Criminology* 8 (2013): 20–39.

84. Daly and Chesney-Lind, "Feminism and Criminology." See also Drew Humphries and Susan Caringella-MacDonald, "Murdered Mothers, Missing Wives: Reconsidering Female Victimization," *Social Justice* 17 (1990): 71–78.

85. Kia Asberg and Kimberly Renk, "Safer in Jail? A Comparison of Victimization History and Psychological Adjustment Between Previously Homeless and Non-Homeless Incarcerated Women," *Feminist Criminology* 10 (2015): 165–187.

86. Jane Roberts Chapman, "Violence Against Women as a Violation of Human Rights," *Social Justice* 17 (1990): 54–71.

87. Shannon Lynch, April Fritch, and Nicole Heath, "Looking Beneath the Surface: The Nature of Incarcerated Women's Experiences of Interpersonal Violence, Treatment Needs, and Mental Health," *Feminist Criminology* 7 (2012): 381–400.

88. Carrie Yodanis, "Gender Inequality, Violence Against Women, and Fear," *Journal of Interpersonal Violence* 19 (2004): 655–675.

89. Victoria Titterington, "A Retrospective Investigation of Gender Inequality and Female Homicide Victimization," *Sociological Spectrum* 26 (2006): 205–236.

90. Kjersti Ericsson and Nina Jon, "Gendered Social Control: 'A Virtuous Girl' and 'a Proper Boy'," *Journal of Scandinavian Studies in Criminology and Crime Prevention* 9 (2006): 126–141.

91. Meda Chesney-Lind and Vickie Paramore, "Are Girls Getting More Violent? Exploring Juvenile Robbery Trends," *Journal of Contemporary Criminal Justice* 17 (2001): 142–166; Joanne Belknap, Kristi Holsinger, and Melissa Dunn, "Understanding Incarcerated Girls," *Prison Journal* 77 (1997): 381–404.

92. Thomas J. Gamble, Sherrie Sonnenberg, John Haltigan, and Amy Cuzzola-Kern, "Detention Screening: Prospects for Population-Management and the Examination of Disproportionality by Race, Age, and Gender," *Criminal Justice Policy Review* 13 (2002): 380–395; Kimberly Kempf-Leonard and Lisa Sample, "Disparity Based on Sex: Is Gender-Specific Treatment Warranted?" *Justice Quarterly* 17 (2000): 89–128.

93. Holly Hartwig and Jane Myers, "A Different Approach: Applying a Wellness Paradigm to Adolescent Female Delinquents and Offenders," *Journal of Mental Health Counseling* 25 (2003): 57–75; Meda Chesney-Lind and Randall Shelden, *Girls, Delinquency, and Juvenile Justice* (Belmont, CA: West/Wadsworth, 1998).

94. Hartwig and Myers, "A Different Approach: Applying a Wellness Paradigm to Adolescent Female Delinquents and Offenders."

95. Tia Stevens, Merry Morash, and Meda Chesney-Lind, "Are Girls Getting Tougher, or Are We Tougher on Girls? Probability of Arrest and Juvenile Court Oversight in 1980 and 2000," *Justice Quarterly* 28 (2011): 719–744.

96. Lisa Pasko, "Damaged Daughters: The History of Girls' Sexuality and the Juvenile Justice System," *Journal of Criminal Law and Criminology* 100 (2010): 1099–1130.

97. Kristi Holsinger and Jessica P. Hodge, "The Experiences of Lesbian, Gay, Bisexual, and Transgender Girls in Juvenile Justice Systems," *Feminist Criminology*, first published online February 2014.

98. Corey S. Shdaimah and Chrysanthi Leon, "First and Foremost They're Survivors: Selective Manipulation,

Resilience, and Assertion Among Prostitute Women," *Feminist Criminology* 1–22, first published online 2014.

99. Hagan, *Structural Criminology*.

100. John Hagan, A. R. Gillis, and John Simpson, "The Class Structure and Delinquency: Toward a Power–Control Theory of Common Delinquent Behavior," *American Journal of Sociology* 90 (1985): 1151–1178; John Hagan, John Simpson, and A. R. Gillis, "Class in the Household: A Power–Control Theory of Gender and Delinquency," *American Journal of Sociology* 92 (1987): 788–816.

101. John Hagan, Bill McCarthy, and Holly Foster, "A Gendered Theory of Delinquency and Despair in the Life Course," *Acta Sociologica* 45 (2002): 37–47.

102. Brenda Sims Blackwell, Christine Sellers, and Sheila Schlaupitz, "A Power–Control Theory of Vulnerability to Crime and Adolescent Role Exits—Revisited," *Canadian Review of Sociology and Anthropology* 39 (2002): 199–219.

103. Christopher Uggen, "Class, Gender, and Arrest: An Intergenerational Analysis of Workplace Power and Control," *Criminology* 38 (2001): 835–862.

104. Gary Jensen and Kevin Thompson, "What's Class Got to Do with It? A Further Examination of Power–Control Theory," *American Journal of Sociology* 95 (1990): 1009–1023. For some critical research, see Simon Singer and Murray Levine, "Power–Control Theory, Gender and Delinquency: A Partial Replication with Additional Evidence on the Effects of Peers," *Criminology* 26 (1988): 627–648.

105. Kevin Thompson, "Gender and Adolescent Drinking Problems: The Effects of Occupational Structure," *Social Problems* 36 (1989): 30–38.

106. Kristin Mack and Michael Leiber, "Race, Gender, Single-Mother Households, and Delinquency: A Further Test of Power–Control Theory," *Youth and Society* 37 (2005): 115–144.

107. Brenda Sims Blackwell and Alex Piquero, "On the Relationships Between Gender, Power Control, Self-Control, and Crime," *Journal of Criminal Justice* 33 (2005): 1–17.

108. Liz Walz, "One Blood," *Contemporary Justice Review* 6 (2003): 25–36.

109. John F. Wozniak, "Poverty and Peacemaking Criminology: Beyond Mainstream Criminology," *Critical Criminology* 16 (2008): 209–223.

110. See, for example, Dennis Sullivan and Larry Tifft, *Restorative Justice: Healing the Foundations of Our Everyday Lives* (Monsey, NY: Willow Tree Press, 2005); Dennis Sullivan, *The Mask of Love: Corrections in America, Toward a Mutual Aid Alternative* (Port Washington, NY: Kennikat Press, 1980).

111. Larry Tifft, "Foreword," in Sullivan, *The Mask of Love*, p. 6.

112. Sullivan, *The Mask of Love*, p. 141.

113. Sullivan and Tifft, *Restorative Justice*.

114. Richard Quinney, "The Way of Peace: On Crime, Suffering, and Service," in *Criminology as Peacemaking*, ed. Harold Pepinsky and Richard Quinney (Bloomington: Indiana University Press, 1991), pp. 8–9.

115. For a review of Quinney's ideas, see Kevin B. Anderson, "Richard Quinney's Journey: The Marxist Dimension," *Crime and Delinquency* 48 (2002): 232–242.

116. Kathleen Daly and Russ Immarigeon, "The Past, Present and Future of Restorative Justice: Some Critical Reflections," *Contemporary Justice Review* 1 (1998): 21–45.

117. Howard Zehr, *The Little Book of Restorative Justice* (Intercourse, PA: Good Books, 2002): 1–10.

118. Alfred Villaume, "'Life Without Parole' and 'Virtual Life Sentences': Death Sentences by Any Other Name," *Contemporary Justice Review* 8 (2005): 265–277.

119. John Braithwaite, *Crime, Shame, and Reintegration* (Melbourne, Australia: Cambridge University Press, 1989).

120. Ibid., p. 81.

121. Eliza Ahmed, Nathan Harris, John Braithwaite, and Valerie Braithwaite, *Shame Management Through Reintegration* (Cambridge, England: Cambridge University Press, 2001).

122. Eliza Ahmed, "'What, Me Ashamed?' Shame Management and School Bullying," *Journal of Research in Crime and Delinquency* 41 (2004): 269–294.

123. John Braithwaite, "Rape, Shame and Pride," *Journal of Scandinavian Studies in Criminology and Crime Prevention* 7 (2006): 2–16.

124. Carter Hay, "An Exploratory Test of Braithwaite's Reintegrative Shaming Theory," *Journal of Research in Crime and Delinquency* 38 (2001): 132–153.

125. Gene Stephens, "The Future of Policing: From a War Model to a Peace Model," in *The Past, Present and Future of American Criminal Justice*, ed. Brendan Maguire and Polly Radosh (Dix Hills, NY: General Hall, 1996), pp. 77–93.

126. Rick Shifley, "The Organization of Work as a Factor in Social Well-Being," *Contemporary Justice Review* 6 (2003): 105–126.

127. Kay Pranis, "Peacemaking Circles: Restorative Justice in Practice Allows Victims and Offenders to Begin Repairing the Harm," *Corrections Today* 59 (1997): 74–78.

128. Carol LaPrairie, "The 'New' Justice: Some Implications for Aboriginal Communities," *Canadian Journal of Criminology* 40 (1998): 61–79.

129. Natalie Kroovand Hipple, Jeff Gruenewald, and Edmund F. McGarrell, "Restorativeness, Procedural Justice, and Defiance as Predictors of Reoffending of Participants in Family Group Conferences," *Crime and Delinquency*, first published online December 7, 2011.

130. John W. De Gruchy, *Reconciliation: Restoring Justice* (Minneapolis: Fortress, 2002).

131. Lawrence W. Sherman and Heather Strang, *Restorative Justice: The Evidence* (London: Smith Institute, 2007).

# 9 Developmental Theories: Life Course, Propensity, and Trajectory

Phil Velasquez/Chicago Tribune/Tns/Landov

## Learning Objectives

**LO1** Discuss the history of and influences on developmental theory.

**LO2** List the principles of the life course approach to developmental theory.

**LO3** Explain the term *problem behavior syndrome*.

**LO4** Outline the basic principles of Sampson and Laub's age-graded life course theory.

**LO5** Explain the concept of the latent trait and the basic principles of the general theory of crime (GTC).

**LO6** Articulate the basic principles of trajectory theory.

Daniel Dvorkin

# Chapter Outline

## FACT OR FICTION?

▶ Getting married helps people stay out of trouble.

▶ Criminals are impulsive risk takers.

D aniel Dvorkin, a commercial real estate professional, had taken out business loans to keep his company afloat, but when the economy took a downturn in 2008 he was unable to make payments to the lending bank. His loans were bought out by a Texas businessman, and after legal proceedings Dvorkin was ordered to pay him about $8 million, which he did not have. After negotiations broke down in April 2012, Dvorkin called an acquaintance and asked for help with finding a hit man. Dvorkin said he wanted his target, the Texas financier, to "stop breathing." He offered to pay $50,000 for the deed, providing he could be out of the country when the hit went down. However, rather than go to the hit man, Dvorkin's friend went to law enforcement and offered to record any related future conversations with Dvorkin. The acquaintance-turned-cooperating-witness called and met with Dvorkin several times, making him believe that the plot was moving along. Then Dvorkin mentioned that he had hired another hit man—one who only charged somewhere in the $20,000 range and only needed a 10 percent down payment—in other words, a discount hit man. The FBI, concerned by this turn of events, immediately contacted the intended victim in Texas and arranged for protection for him and his family. Dvorkin was arrested and after a five-day trial, a jury found him guilty. At the sentencing hearing, Dvorkin's attorney asked the judge to "show leniency," noting his client's history of charitable giving and his "caring, compassion, and generosity."[1] The judge was not impressed, sentencing Dvorkin to eight years in federal prison for attempted murder. ■

**criminal career**
Engaging in antisocial acts early in adolescence and continuing illegal behaviors into adulthood. A pattern of persistent offending across the life course.

**developmental theories**
The view that criminality is a dynamic process, influenced by social experiences as well as individual characteristics.

**L01** Discuss the history of and influences on developmental theory.

**CONNECTIONS**

Chapter 2 discussed how Wolfgang found that although many offenders commit a single criminal act and thereafter desist from crime, a small group of chronic offenders engage in frequent and repeated criminal activity and continue to do so across their life span.

Daniel Dvorkin's strange behavior shows why crime is such a puzzling phenomenon and **criminal careers** so difficult to explain with a simple theorem. One reason is that there are many paths into crime. Some people become enmeshed in a criminal career early in life, engaging in antisocial acts as adolescents and continuing their misbehaviors into adulthood. Others such as Dvorkin begin their foray into crime as adults, previously living a conventional and uneventful life. Some are vicious, merciless killers, while others are described by friends as being caring, generous, and compassionate.

Developmental criminologists try to understand why some people begin their involvement in illegal activity as children, while others are late starters like Daniel Dvorkin. Some offenders may engage in petty crimes; others continually increase the severity and frequency of their offending. Some may be deeply affected by criminal penalties, while others are career criminals who persist in their illegal activities over their life course despite being caught and punished many times. Efforts to understand the onset, continuity, and termination of crime and criminality have resulted in the construction of a variety of **developmental theories** that focus not so much on a single criminal act but on the creation and persistence of a criminal career.

## Foundations of Developmental Theory

As you may recall (Chapter 1), the research efforts of Sheldon and Eleanor Glueck formed the basis of today's developmental approach. Soon after the publication of their work, the Gluecks' methodology and their integration of biological, psychological, and social factors were sharply criticized, and for many years their work was ignored in criminology texts and overlooked in the academic curriculum.

During the 1990s, the Glueck legacy was rediscovered in a series of papers by criminologists Robert Sampson and John Laub, who used modern statistical techniques to reanalyze the Gluecks' carefully drawn empirical measurements. Sampson and Laub's findings, published in a series of books and articles, fueled the popularity of the developmental approach.[2]

The Philadelphia cohort research by Marvin Wolfgang and his associates also sparked interest in explaining criminal career development. Wolfgang's research focused attention on criminal careers. His work prompted criminologists to ask this fundamental question: What prompts one person to engage in persistent criminal activity, while another, who on the surface suffers the same life circumstances, finds a way to steer clear of crime and travel a more conventional path?

A 1990 review paper by Rolf Loeber and Marc Le Blanc was another important event that spurred interest in a developmental criminology. In this landmark work, Loeber and Le Blanc proposed that criminologists should devote time and effort to understanding basic questions about the evolution of criminal careers. Rather than viewing criminality as static and constant—a person simply is either a criminal or a noncriminal—they viewed criminality as a dynamic process, with a beginning, middle, and end and changes all along the way. Loeber and Le Blanc challenged criminologists to answer these questions: Why do some people begin committing antisocial acts in adulthood, such as Dvorkin, while most begin offending at a very early age? Why do some stop, whereas others continue? Why do some escalate the severity of their criminality (that is, go from shoplifting to drug dealing to armed robbery), whereas others deescalate and commit less serious crimes as they mature? If some terminate their criminal activity, what (if anything) causes them to begin again? Why do some criminals specialize in certain types of crime, whereas others are generalists engaging in a variety of antisocial activities? Loeber and Le Blanc's developmental view suggests that criminologists must pay attention to how a criminal career unfolds—how it begins, why it is sustained, and how it comes to an end.[3]

From these and similar efforts, a view of crime has emerged that incorporates personal change and growth. The factors that produce crime and criminality at one point in the life cycle may not be relevant at another; as people mature, the social, physical, and environmental influences on their behavior are transformed.

People may show a propensity to offend early in their lives, but the nature and frequency of their activities are often affected by forces beyond their control, which elevate and sustain their criminal activity.[4]

## Three Views of Criminal Career Development

There are actually three independent yet interrelated developmental views. The first, referred to as **life course theory**, suggests that criminal behavior is a dynamic process, influenced by individual characteristics as well as social experiences, and that the factors that cause antisocial behaviors change dramatically over a person's life span.

A second view, referred to here as the **propensity theory**, suggests that human development is controlled by a master **latent trait** that remains stable and unchanging throughout a person's lifetime. As people travel through their life course, this propensity is always there, directing their behavior. Because this hidden trait is enduring, the ebb and flow of criminal behavior is shaped less by personal change and more by the impact of external forces such as opportunity. Criminality may increase upon joining a gang, a status that provides more opportunities to steal, take drugs, and attack others. In other words, the propensity to commit criminal acts is constant, but the opportunity to commit them is constantly fluctuating.

A third view, **trajectory theory**, suggests there are multiple trajectories or paths into a criminal career. According to this approach, there are subgroups within a population that follow distinctively different developmental routes toward and away from a criminal career. Some people may begin early in antisocial activities and demonstrate a propensity for crime, while others begin later and are influenced by life circumstances. Unlike the latent trait and life course views, trajectory theory suggests that there are different types and classes of offenders.[5]

The main points, similarities, and differences of these positions are set out in Concept Summary 9.1.

**life course theory**
Theory that focuses on changes in criminality over the life course brought about by shifts in experience and life events.

**propensity theory**
The view that a stable unchanging feature, characteristic, property, or condition, such as defective intelligence or impulsive personality, makes some people crime prone.

**latent trait**
A stable feature, characteristic, property, or condition, such as defective intelligence or impulsive personality, that makes some people crime prone over the life course.

**trajectory theory**
The view that there are multiple independent paths to a criminal career and that there are different types and classes of offenders.

## Concept Summary 9.1   Three Developmental Theories

| | |
|---|---|
| **Life course theory** | People have multiple traits: social, psychological, economic.<br>People change over the life course.<br>Family, job, peers influence behavior. |
| **Propensity theory/ Latent trait theory** | People do not change, criminal opportunities change; maturity brings fewer opportunities.<br>People have a master trait: personality, intelligence, genetic makeup.<br>Early social control and proper parenting can reduce criminal propensity. |
| **Trajectory theory** | There is more than one path to a criminal career.<br>There are different types of offenders and offending. |
| **Similarities** | Focus on criminal careers.<br>Criminality must be viewed as a path rather than an event.<br>Criminal careers are enduring, begin early in adolescence, and continue into adulthood.<br>Integration of multiple factors. |
| **Differences** | Life course: People are constantly evolving and so is their criminal behavior.<br>Propensity: An unchanging master trait controls antisocial behavior.<br>Trajectory: There is more than one path to crime and more than one crime-producing trait. |

## Population Heterogeneity vs. State Dependence

**population heterogeneity**
The propensity to commit crime is stable; those who have it continue to commit crime over their life course.

**state dependence**
The propensity to commit crime is constantly changing, affected by environmental influences and changing life events.

Are people truly different, or are we more or less all the same but shaped by our different experiences? This question is the core issue separating the various branches of developmental theory.

The concept of **population heterogeneity** assumes that the propensity of an individual to participate in antisocial and/or criminal behaviors is a relatively stable trait, unchanging over their life course. Within a given population people differ in their behavior choices: some are hotheaded, violent, and inclined to commit crime, while others remain reasonable, unruffled, and presumably law abiding. According to this view, individual differences remain stable and are not affected by the consequences of participation in crime or any other changing life circumstances.[6] Because people affect their environment and not vice versa, the best predictor of future behavior is past behavior: people who are criminally active in their childhood should remain so in their adulthood, no matter what happens to them in the meantime. The cause of misbehavior remains the same as people traverse the life course.

In contrast, the concept of **state dependence** suggests that people change and develop as they mature; life events have a significant influence on future behavior. Life course theorists embrace this concept because it can explain continuity and desistance from crime: while positive experiences can help the troubled person adjust and conform, damaging encounters and events have the potential to increase future criminal involvement. Adolescents who are at risk for crime can avoid a criminal way of life if they encounter people who help, nurture, and support them in their adolescence and adulthood. If past antisocial behavior influences future offending, it's not because they have a similar cause, but because offending disrupts prosocial bonds and informal mechanisms of social controls. Those people who have the propensity to commit crime find that life events disrupt socialization and thereafter increase the risk of prolonged antisocial behavior. In this view, early rule breaking increases the probability of future rule breaking because it weakens inhibitions to crime and/or strengthens criminal motivation. Some teens who get a taste of antisocial behavior like it and want to continue down a deviant path; others learn they have no choice.[7]

## Life Course Theory

According to the life course view, even as toddlers, people begin relationships and behaviors that will determine their entire life course. As children they must learn to conform to social rules and function effectively in society. Later they are expected to begin thinking about careers, complete their schooling, leave their parents' home, enter the workforce, find permanent relationships, and eventually marry and begin their own families.[8] These transitions are expected to take place in an orderly fashion. Disruptions in life's major transitions can be destructive and ultimately promote criminality. Those who are already at risk because of socioeconomic problems or family dysfunction are the most susceptible during these awkward transitions. The cumulative impact of these disruptions sustains criminality from childhood into adulthood.

In some cases, transitions can occur too early—an adolescent engages in precocious sex and becomes pregnant. In other cases, transitions may occur too late—a student fails to graduate on time because of bad grades. Sometimes disruption of one trajectory can harm another—becoming a teenage parent is likely to disrupt future educational and career development. These negative life experiences can become cumulative; as kids acquire more personal deficits, the chances of acquiring additional ones increase.[9]

People who get in trouble early in life, especially those who are arrested and given an official criminal label, may find it difficult to shake the criminal way of life as they mature.[10] Racial disparity in the criminal justice system helps put minority

**CHECKPOINTS**

▶ Pioneering criminologists Sheldon and Eleanor Glueck tracked the onset and termination of criminal careers.

▶ Their work led to the creation of developmental theories.

▶ Developmental theories attempt to provide a global vision of a criminal career that encompasses its onset, continuation, and termination.

▶ Developmental theories come in three different varieties: life course, propensity or latent trait, and trajectory.

▶ Life course theories look at such issues as the onset of crime, escalation of offenses, continuity of crime, and desistance from crime.

▶ Latent trait theories assume that a "master trait" exists that guides human development.

▶ Trajectory theories assume there is more than one type of criminal and more than one criminal path.

▶ The concept of population heterogeneity assumes that the propensity of an individual to participate in antisocial and/or criminal behaviors is a relatively stable trait, unchanging over their life course.

▶ The concept of state dependence suggests that life events have a significant influence on future behavior.

**LO2** List the principles of the life course approach to developmental theory.

group members at a disadvantage, increasing the likelihood that they will become embedded in criminal careers.[11]

While most kids age out of crime, the ability to change wilts with age as people become embedded in a criminal lifestyle. What may help a person resist a life of crime while they are still in their teens—for example, school achievement and positive family relations—may have little impact once they reach their 20s.[12]

One way of getting embedded in a criminal way of life is to join a youth gang, a choice that has both short- and long-term consequences. Those who join gangs are more likely to get involved in antisocial behavior after they leave the gang than before they joined.[13] Gang membership disrupts conventional life transitions and provides roadblocks to success long after membership has ceased.[14]

So the person who experiences significant amounts of anger in early adolescence, who joins a gang, gets in trouble with the law and drops out of school, is also the one who is more likely to become involved in antisocial

Emotions catch up with classmates Shaneecia Tyson, Erin Van Cleve, and Zakeera Ward at their Lincoln Challenge Academy graduation in Springfield, Illinois. The academy is a rigorous 22-week military-style residential program for high school dropouts on the former Chanute Air Force Base. Such programs can help people change their life trajectories and reduce the chance of becoming enmeshed in a criminal career.

behavior as a teen and to mature into a law-violating adult.[15] While most adolescents age out of crime and become responsible adults, those growing up in a criminogenic environment and engaging in antisocial behavior as adolescents are the ones who are most likely to engage in antisocial behavior as adults.[16]

But even those who have been in trouble throughout their adolescence may manage to find stable work and maintain intact marriages as adults; positive life events help them desist from crime. It is the less fortunate adolescents who develop arrest records and get involved with the wrong crowd who may find themselves at risk for delinquency and later adult criminal careers.

Life course theories also recognize that as people mature, the factors that influence their behavior change.[17] As people make important life transitions—from child to adolescent, from adolescent to adult, from unwed to married—the nature of social interactions also changes.[18] At first, family relations may be most influential; it comes as no shock to life course theorists when research shows that criminality runs in families and that having criminal relatives is a significant predictor of future misbehaviors.[19] In later adolescence, school and peer relations predominate; in adulthood, vocational achievement and marital relations may be the most critical influences. Some antisocial children who are in trouble throughout their adolescence manage to find stable work and maintain intact marriages as adults. These life events help them desist from crime. In contrast, less fortunate adolescents who develop arrest records and get involved with the wrong crowd may find themselves limited to menial jobs and at risk for criminal careers.

The following sections review and discuss some prominent life course concepts.

## Age of Onset

We know that most young criminals desist and do not become adult offenders.[20] But some do go on to have a long career as a chronic offender. The seeds of a criminal career are planted early in life (preschool); **early onset** of deviance strongly predicts more frequent, varied, and sustained criminality later in life.[21] What causes some kids to begin offending at an early age? Among the suspected root causes are inadequate emotional support, distant peer relationships, and psychological issues

**early onset**
The view that kids who begin engaging in antisocial behaviors at a very early age are the ones most at risk for a criminal career.

and problems.[22] Among the psychological conditions associated with early onset are attention deficit hyperactivity disorder (ADHD) and conduct disorder (CD).[23]

Poor parental discipline and monitoring seem to be keys to the early onset of criminality, and these influences may follow kids into their adulthood. Recent research by Kristin Carbone-Lopez and Jody Miller shows that for girls, early entry into adult roles—precocious sexuality, motherhood, independent living, romantic relationships—is a key ingredient in the entry into a substance-abusing lifestyle as an adult.[24] The psychic scars of childhood are hard to erase.[25]

Most of these early onset delinquents begin their careers with disruptive behavior, truancy, cruelty to animals, lying, and theft.[26] They also appear to be more violent than their less precocious peers.[27] The earlier the onset, the more likely an adolescent will engage in serious criminality and for a longer period of time. Studies of the juvenile justice system show that many incarcerated youths began their offending careers very early in life and that a significant number had engaged in heavy drinking and drug abuse by age 10 or younger.[28]

## Problem Behavior Syndrome

**L03** Explain the term *problem behavior syndrome*.

**problem behavior syndrome (PBS)**
Antisocial behaviors that cluster together, including family dysfunction, substance abuse, smoking, precocious sexuality and early pregnancy, educational underachievement, suicide attempts, sensation seeking, and unemployment, as well as criminality.

One life course view is that criminality is but one of many social and personal problems faced by people who live a risky lifestyle. Referred to collectively as **problem behavior syndrome (PBS)**, these behaviors include social, personal, and environmental dysfunction ranging from poor health to unemployment (see Exhibit 9.1).[29]

Those who exhibit PBS are prone to more difficulties than the general population. They find themselves experiencing personal dilemmas ranging from drug abuse to being accident prone, requiring more health care and hospitalization, becoming teenage parents, or having mental health problems.[30] PBS has been linked to individual-level personality problems (such as impulsiveness, rebelliousness, and low ego), family problems (such as intrafamily conflict and parental mental disorder), substance abuse, poor health, and educational failure.[31] Adolescents who get in trouble with the law are likely to exhibit a combination of externalizing behaviors, including conduct disorder, attention deficit hyperactivity disorder (ADHD), drug abuse, familial and interpersonal difficulties (such as conflict with parents), and low intelligence.[32] All varieties of antisocial behavior, including violence, theft, and drug offenses, may be part of a generalized PBS, indicating that all forms of criminal behavior have similar developmental patterns.[33]

Considering the types of problems that cluster together, it is not surprising that people who have a long and varied criminal career are more likely than others to die early and to have greater than average mortality rates.[34] Criminal conduct has been

## Exhibit 9.1  Problem Behaviors

**Social**
Family dysfunction
Unemployment
Educational underachievement
School misconduct

**Personal**
Substance abuse
Suicide attempts
Early sexuality
Premature death
Poor health
Sensation seeking

Early parenthood
Accident prone
Medical problems
Mental disease
Anxiety
Eating disorders (bulimia, anorexia)

**Environmental**
High-crime area
Disorganized area
Racism
Exposure to poverty

**Source:** © Cengage Learning

found to increase the chances of premature death due to both natural and unnatural causes, including deaths from accidents, homicide, and suicide. The more crime a person commits, the more likely he or she is to suffer premature death.[35]

In sum, problem behavior syndrome portrays crime as a type of social problem rather than as the product of other social problems.[36] People involved in crime may fall prey to other social problems, ranging from poverty to premature death.[37]

## Continuity of Crime

Another aspect of life course theory is continuity of crime: the best predictor of future criminality is past criminality. Children who are repeatedly in trouble during early adolescence will generally still be antisocial in their middle teens; people who display conduct problems in youth are the ones most likely to commit crime as adults.[38] As adults, people involved in the most serious crimes continue to misbehave even when they are behind bars.[39]

Life course theorists believe that the continuity of crime is state dependent: criminal activity is sustained because law violators and rule breakers seem to lack the social survival skills necessary to find work or to develop the interpersonal relationships they need to allow them to desist. As a result, antisocial behavior may be *contagious*: people at risk for criminality may infect those around them, thereby creating an ever-widening circle of peers and acquaintances who support deviant behavior.[40]

Research shows that as they emerge into adulthood, persisters are beset with additional social and personal problems (as was predicted by PBS): they report less emotional support, lower job satisfaction, distant peer relationships, and more psychiatric problems than those who desist.[41] But even if they manage to forgo criminal activity, they are still at risk for a large variety of social behavior problems.

A number of systematic life course theories have been formulated that account for such factors as early onset, the clustering of behavioral problems, and the continuance (and/or termination) of a criminal career.[42] As a group, these theories integrate *personal factors* such as personality and intelligence, *social factors* such as income and neighborhood, *socialization factors* such as marriage and military service, *cognitive factors* such as information processing and attention/perception, and *situational factors* such as criminal opportunity, effective guardianship, and apprehension risk into complex multifactor explanations of human behavior. They do not focus on the relatively simple question of why people commit crime but, rather, on more complex issues: Why do some offenders persist in criminal careers, whereas others desist from or alter their criminal activity as they mature?[43] Why do some people continually escalate their criminal involvement, whereas others slow down and turn their lives around? The most prominent life course theory is Robert Sampson and John Laub's **age-graded theory**, which is discussed below.

One of the key principles of life course theory is that the seeds of a criminal career are planted early in life and the early onset of antisocial behavior strongly predicts later and more serious criminality. The psychic scars of a crippling childhood are hard to erase. Here, attorney John Henry Browne places his hand on the shoulder of Colton Harris-Moore, after Browne concluded defense testimony that included details of Harris-Moore's troubled childhood. Harris-Moore, known as the "Barefoot Bandit," was sentenced to more than seven years in prison after pleading guilty to dozens of state charges stemming from a two-year crime spree.

**age-graded theory**
A state dependence theory formulated by Sampson and Laub that assumes that the causal association between early delinquent offending and later adult deviant behavior involves the quality of relationships encountered at different times in human development.

## Age-Graded Theory

In an important 1993 work, *Crime in the Making*, Robert Sampson and John Laub find that the course of a criminal career can be affected by events that occur later in life, even after a chronic criminal career has been undertaken.[44] While in some cases a career in crime begins early in life and continues over the life course, it is wrong to

**L04** Outline the basic principles of Sampson and Laub's age-graded life course theory.

**turning points**
According to Laub and Sampson, the life events that alter the development of a criminal career.

**social capital**
Positive, life-sustaining relations with individuals and institutions.

**cumulative disadvantage**
The tendency of prior social problems to produce future ones that accumulate and undermine success.

believe that once this course is set nothing can impede its progress. There are **turning points** in a criminal career that can alter its course and direction, changing a lifetime n'er-do-well into a productive citizen.

To conduct their research, Laub and Sampson reanalyzed the data originally collected by the Gluecks more than 50 years before. Using modern statistical analysis, Laub and Sampson found that discrete factors influence people at different stages of their development, and therefore the propensity to commit crimes is neither stable nor unyielding. Children who enter delinquent careers are those who have trouble at home and at school; their parents and family life are the greatest influence on their behavior. Supervision, parental styles of discipline, and parental attachment are the most important predictors of serious and persistent delinquency. Later as adolescents, peer relations become all important, and kids who maintain deviant friends are the ones most at risk of committing crime. In adulthood, behavior choices are influenced by elements of informal social control such as marriage, family, and work.

**SOCIAL CAPITAL** Social scientists have long recognized that people build **social capital**—positive relations with individuals and institutions that are life-sustaining. In the same manner that building financial capital improves the chances for personal success, building social capital supports conventional behavior and inhibits deviant behavior.[45]

In their age-graded theory, Laub and Sampson recognize the role of social capital and its ability to create turning points, allowing some at-risk people to *knife off* from a criminal career.[46] People who can make the right connections and gain advantage through family connections are the ones most likely to knife off from crime. Laub and Sampson found that criminal careers can be reversed if life conditions improve by such fortunate events as moving to a more attractive environment, doing well in school, finding a good job and a supportive mate. Social capital is also gained by joining the military, serving overseas, and receiving veterans' benefits. Gaining social capital may help erase some of the damage caused by its absence.

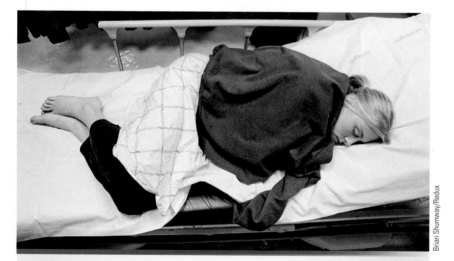

Social and personal disadvantages tend to accumulate. Here, homeless teenager Pamila sleeps in the emergency room of an Orange County hospital, waiting to find out if she is sick or pregnant again. At only 18, Pamila found herself homeless. She was living with her boyfriend Rob, 32, in a tent in a small wooded area beside a freeway off-ramp. Pamila had followed Rob west from Baltimore in an attempt to find his father. They had gotten heavily into drugs and Pamila became pregnant. The search for Rob's father, along with their relationship, failed. Rob was arrested on a warrant from the Midwest, and Pamila moved in with a mother and daughter she had befriended, who lived at a motel. She bounced around to different motel rooms, dating a new guy. Eventually, Pamila got out of Orange County, but she continues to struggle with life, a failed marriage, and pregnancy.

In contrast, some people not only fail to accumulate social capital, but instead experience social problems that weigh down their life chances. Nor do these social problems simply go away; they linger and vex people throughout their lives. Past miscues are highly correlated with future social problems—for example, people arrested in their teens are less likely to find jobs as adults. People who acquire this **cumulative disadvantage** are more likely to commit criminal acts and become victims of crime.[47] When faced with personal crisis, they lack the social supports that can help them reject criminal solutions and maintain a conventional behavior trajectory. Not surprisingly, research shows that adolescents whose parents were convicted of crime and suffered incarceration were also more likely to engage in theft offenses. Parental incarceration erases social capital and escalates cumulative disadvantage: it reduces family income, gives kids the opportunity to gain antisocial peers, and subjects them to negative labels and stigma.[48] Kids whose fathers were incarcerated are more likely to suffer an arrest by age 25 than

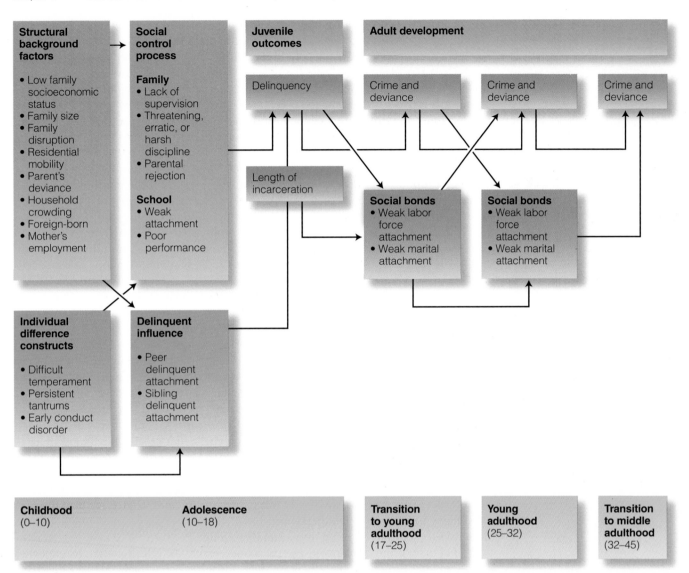

**FIGURE 9.1**

**Sampson and Laub's Age-Graded Theory**

**Source:** Robert Sampson and John Laub, *Crime in the Making: Pathways and Turning Points through Life* (Cambridge, MA: Harvard University Press, 1993), pp. 244–245.

the offspring of conventional, law-abiding parents.[49] Adolescents lacking capital may also suffer criminal victimization. Criminologist Joan Reid found that kids who were the victims of sex traffickers had limited social capital that led to them experiencing initial exploitation during young adulthood; those trafficked internationally lost even more capital because of their citizenship status and language or cultural barriers.[50]

**TURNING POINTS** One of Laub and Sampson's most important contributions is identifying the life events that enable adult offenders to desist from crime (Figure 9.1). Because criminal careers are a dynamic process, an important life event or turning point can change the direction of a person's life course trajectory. Two critical turning points are marriage and military service. Adolescents who are at risk for crime can live conventional lives if they can find a supportive mate and serve some time in the military.

**LOVE, MARRIAGE, AND CRIMINALITY** Age-graded theory places a lot of emphasis on the stability brought about by romantic relationships leading eventually to a good marriage. When they achieve adulthood, adolescents who had significant problems with the law are able to desist from crime if they become attached to a spouse who supports and sustains them even when the spouse knows they were in trouble when they were young. Happy marriages are life-sustaining, and marital quality improves over time (as people work less and have fewer parental responsibilities).[51] Spending time in marital and family activities also reduces exposure to deviant peers, which in

**FACT OR FICTION?**

Getting married helps people stay out of trouble.

**FACT** Marriage, according to Sampson and Laub, is one of those turning points that help people get out of a criminal career.

## CONNECTIONS

Discrete factors influence people at different stages of their development, so the propensity to commit crimes is neither stable nor unyielding. The likelihood of committing crime is linked to the accumulation (or absence) of social capital, social control, and human decision making. This conclusion seems to intersect with the rational choice theory discussed in Chapter 4. Is it possible that the reasons people choose to commit crime fluctuate according to their position in the life course?

turn reduces the opportunity to become involved in criminal activities.[52] People who cannot sustain secure marital relations are less likely than others to desist from crime.

The marriage effect is supported by research on both an individual and societal level. On an individual level, people headed toward a life of crime can knife off from that path if they meet the right mate, fall in love, and get married. On a social level, communities with high marriage rates have correspondingly low crime rates.[53] And it is marriage and not merely cohabiting that has a crime suppression effect.[54] Even unstable marriages appear to reduce conviction frequency, at least while they last.[55]

What is it about love that prevents criminality? Bill McCarthy and Teresa Casey examined the associations between love, sex, and criminality among a sample of teens and found that adolescent romantic love can help fill the emotional void that occurs between the time people break free of parental bonds and when they learn to accept adult responsibilities.[56] But only meaningful relationships seem to work: love, not sex, is the key to success. Kids who get involved in sexual activity without the promise of love actually increase their involvement in crime and criminality; only true love reduces the likelihood of offending. Loveless sexual relations produce feelings of strain, which are correlated with antisocial activity. It is possible that kids who engage in sex without love or romance are willing to partake in other risky and/or self-indulgent behaviors, including criminality and drug usage. In contrast, romantic love discourages offending by strengthening the social bond.

**BREAKING UP** Things don't always work out as planned and many relationships end in a breakup, a state of affairs that often brings about increases in criminal behavior and drug use. The breakup effect is critical because between 40 to 50 percent of first marriages, 67 percent of second marriages, and 74 percent of third marriages end in divorce.[57] And while a happy marriage can reduce crime, separation and divorce seem to have an opposite effect: both men and women have a greater likelihood of arrest when divorced (or legally separated) compared with when they were married.[58]

It is tough to stay married when life circumstances are chaotic, especially when people are in trouble with the law. And the roots of divorce may be traced back to adolescence: kids who get involved with police during adolescence are also the ones most likely to experience financial hardship during young adulthood, which, in turn, decreases the odds of entering into a stable marriage.[59]

Of course, not all marriages are the same. Research indicates that, as expected, people in long-term marriages increase their antisocial behavior when they divorce.[60] However, shorter marriages, those that dissolve prior to the first anniversary, have little effect on offending rates. It's possible that "bad marriages" that are doomed to quickly fail may produce so much tension and conflict that marriage does little to suppress antisocial behaviors even while the couple is still married.[61] Those who can find the right mate and stick with them for the duration are the most likely to live happier, crime-free lives.

**MARITAL SUCCESS** What prompts some people to engage in loving relationships, while others are doomed to fall in and out of love without finding lasting happiness? Sociologist Rand Conger and his colleagues have discovered that the seeds of marital success are planted early in childhood: kids who grow up with warm, nurturing parents are the ones most likely to have positive romantic relationships and later intact marriages. Well-nurtured kids develop into warm and supportive romantic partners who have relationships that are likely to endure.[62] It is the quality of parenting, not the observation of adult romantic relations, that socializes a young person to engage in behaviors likely to promote successful and lasting romantic unions as an adult.

Do love and other prosocial life experiences work to help kids avoid antisocial behavior over the long haul? To find out, Laub and Sampson conducted an important follow-up to their original research. They found and interviewed survivors from the original Glueck research, the oldest subject being 70 years old and the youngest 62. This study is the subject of the accompanying Policies and Issues in Criminology feature.

**HOW VALID IS AGE-GRADED THEORY?** There has been a great deal of effort to prove the validity of age-graded theory. Empirical research now shows that, just as Sampson and Laub predicted, people change over the life course, and the factors that predict criminal involvement change as an offender moves from adolescent misbehavior to adult criminality. Criminal careers appear to be dynamic and evolving, not static and constant. Cumulative disadvantage can indeed lock a person into a criminal way of life. Ex-offenders find that their career paths are blocked well into adulthood. If they accumulate deviant peers, criminal behavior may escalate. If they cannot find relevant work, the lure of crime may escalate: the unemployed or underemployed report higher criminal participation rates than those in the workforce.

Despite the support given to age-graded theory some important questions remain, including the theory's time order. Are people who desist from crime able to find a suitable mate, get married, and find a good job? Or are people who find an appropriate mate and a good job then able to desist from crime? In other words, does desistance result in the accumulation of social capital or does the accumulation of social capital produce desistance? Laub and Sampson believe the latter, but there is also evidence that people who desist from crime undergo a cognitive change, and only after they quit a criminal way of life are they able to acquire mates, jobs, and other benefits that support their life change.[63]

Another issue is the current relevance of the Glueck data used in the study. The data were collected at a time when there was no TV or Internet, when divorce was less common, and drug abuse relatively unknown.

## Social Schematic Theory (SST)

Age-graded theory is not the only life course view. In what they call a life course learning approach, social schematic theory (SST), criminologists Ronald Simons and Callie Burt propose that social **schemas**—cognitive frameworks that help people quickly process and sort through information—are the key theoretical mechanisms that account for the development of criminal behavior patterns.

The SST relies on how people develop these cognitive shortcuts to organize and interpret information. In some instances schemas can exclude pertinent information and instead focus only on things that confirm preexisting beliefs and ideas. If a member of some group commits a notorious crime, we think "those people are all criminals," forgetting that the vast majority in any grouping are law-abiding citizens. Or if someone is hassled by a police officer, the experience can shape the way they view all police officers and cause them to alter their behavior accordingly (i.e., avoid contact with cops, refuse to cooperate, call them names, and so on). Schemas can contribute to stereotypes and make it difficult to retain new information that does not conform to our established ideas about the world.

Simons and Burt argue that seemingly unrelated family, peer, and community conditions—harsh parenting, racial discrimination, and community disadvantage—lead to crime because the lessons communicated by these events are actually similar and promote social schemas involving (a) a hostile view of people and relationships, (b) a preference for immediate rewards, and (c) a cynical view of conventional norms.[64] Because these negative schemas are interconnected they combine to form a **criminogenic knowledge structure (CKS)**. When someone with a CKS forged by negative life events encounters a stressful situation, their past experiences compel them to respond with criminal and antisocial behavior. Prior negative life experiences allow them to legitimize their behavior: people abused me, so it's okay to abuse other people.

While developed at an early age, the CKS can improve when people experience positive life events, such as having a healthy romantic relationship, or worsen when experiencing some negative life event, such as racial discrimination. Negative social schemas combined with situational events that set them off produce antisocial behavior. Actions, including crime, result from the combination of individual characteristics and situational cues. Moreover, individuals are not randomly placed in various contexts, but they actively seek out settings consistent with their aims and

**schemas**
Cognitive frameworks that help people quickly process and sort through information.

**criminogenic knowledge structure (CKS)**
The view that negative life events are connected and produce a hostile view of people and relationships, preference for immediate rewards, and a cynical view of conventional norms.

## Policies and Issues in Criminology

### SHARED BEGINNINGS, DIVERGENT LIVES

Why are some people destined to become persistent criminals as adults? To find out, John Laub and Robert Sampson located the survivors of the sample first collected by Sheldon and Eleanor Glueck. At the time of the follow-up study, the oldest was 70 years old and the youngest was 62. The study involved three sources of new data collection—criminal record checks (both local and national), death record checks (local and national), and personal interviews with a sample of 52 of the original Glueck men, stratified to ensure variability in patterns of persistence and desistance in crime.

They found that explanations of desistance from crime and also for persistent offending in crime are two sides of the same coin. Desistance is a process rather than an event, and it must be continually renewed. The processes of desistance operate simultaneously at different levels (individual, situational, and community) and across different contextual environments (especially family, work, and military service). The process of desistance is more than mere aging and more than individual predisposition.

The interviews showed that criminality and other forms of antisocial conduct in childhood are strongly related to adult criminality and drug and alcohol abuse. Former delinquents also suffer consequences in other areas of social life, such as school, work, and family life. They are far less likely to finish high school than are nondelinquents and subsequently are more likely to be unemployed, receive welfare, and experience separation or divorce as adults.

Laub and Sampson also addressed a key question posed by life course theories: Is it possible for former delinquents to turn their lives around as adults? The researchers found that most antisocial children do not remain antisocial as adults. Of men in the study cohort who survived to 50 years of age, 24 percent had

no arrests for delinquent acts of violence and property (predatory criminality) after age 17 (6 percent had no arrests for total criminality); 48 percent had no arrests for predatory criminality after age 25 (19 percent for total criminality); 60 percent had no arrests for predatory criminality after age 31 (33 percent for total criminality); and 79 percent had no arrests for predatory criminality after age 40 (57 percent for total criminality). Laub and Sampson concluded that desistance from criminality is the norm and that most, if not all, serious delinquents desist from criminality.

### Why Do People Desist?

Laub and Sampson's earlier research indicated that building social capital through marriage and jobs was the key component of desistance from criminality. The follow-up showed a dramatic drop in criminal activity as the men aged. Between 17 and 24 years of age, 84 percent of the subjects had committed violent crimes; in their 30s and 40s, that number dropped to 14 percent; it fell to 3 percent as the men reached their 60s and 70s. Property crimes and alcohol- and drug-related crimes showed significant decreases. Former delinquents who desisted from crime were rooted in structural routines and had strong social ties to family and community. They found that one important element for going straight is the knifing off of individuals from their immediate environment, offering the men a new script for the future. Joining the military can provide this knifing-off effect, as can marriage or changing one's residence. One former criminal (age 69) told them:

> I'd say the turning point was, number one, the Army. You get into an outfit, you had a sense of belonging, you made your friends. I think I became a pretty good judge of character. In the Army, you met some good ones, you met some foul balls. Then I met the wife. I'd say probably that would be the turning point. Got married, then naturally, kids come. So now you got to get a better job, you got to make more money. And that's how I got to the Navy Yard and tried to improve myself.

preferences. Consequently, any preexisting thought patterns will be reinforced by surrounding influences in a never-ending loop.

While still being tested, early results have given strong support for the SST.[65]

## Latent Trait/Propensity Theory

In a popular 1985 book, *Crime and Human Nature*, two prominent social scientists, James Q. Wilson and Richard Herrnstein, argued that personal traits, such as genetic makeup, intelligence, and body build, operate in tandem with social variables

Former delinquents who went straight were able to put structure into their lives. Structure often led the men to disassociate from criminal peers, reducing the opportunity to get into trouble. Getting married, for example, may limit the number of nights available to "hang with the guys." As one wife of a former offender said, "It is not how many beers you have, it's who you drink with." Even multiple offenders who did time in prison were able to desist with the help of a stabilizing marriage. So love does in fact conquer all!

People who can turn their life around, who have acquired a degree of maturity by taking on family and work responsibilities, and who have forged new commitments are most likely to make a fresh start and find new direction and meaning in life. It seems that men who desisted changed their identity as well, and this, in turn, affected their outlook and sense of maturity and responsibility. The ability to change did not reflect any criminality "specialty": violent offenders followed the same path as property offenders.

Although many former delinquents desisted, others did not and continued a life of crime late into adulthood. These persisters experienced considerable residential instability, marital instability, job instability, failure in the school and the military, and relatively long periods of incarceration. Many were "social nomads," without permanent addresses, steady jobs, spouses, or children. As a consequence of chaotic and unstructured routines, the persisters had increased contact with those individuals who were similarly situated—in this case, similarly unattached and free from nurturing and informal social control. And they paid the price for their unstructured lives: they faced the risk of an early and untimely death. Thirteen percent (N = 62) of the criminal subjects as compared to 6 percent (N = 28) of the noncriminal subjects died unnatural deaths, such as by violence, cirrhosis of the liver caused by alcoholism, poor self-care, and suicide. By 65 years of age, 29 percent (N = 139) of the offenders and 21 percent (N = 95) of the non-offenders

had died from natural causes. Frequent involvement in criminality during adolescence and alcohol abuse were the strongest predictors of an early and untimely death. So, while many troubled youths are able to reform, their early excesses may haunt them across their life span.

These findings are important because they suggest that criminality and other social problems are cumulative. Consequently, early prevention efforts that reduce criminality in adolescence will probably also reduce alcohol abuse, drunk driving, drug abuse, sexual promiscuity, and family violence in adulthood. The best way to achieve these goals is through four significant life-changing events: marriage, joining the military, getting a job, and changing one's environment or neighborhood. What appears to be important about these processes is that they all involve, to varying degrees, the following items: a knifing off of the past from the present; new situations that provide both supervision and monitoring as well as new opportunities of social support and growth; and new situations that provide the opportunity for transforming identity.

## Critical Thinking

1. Do you believe that the factors that influenced the men in the original Glueck sample are still relevant for change—for example, a military career?

2. Would it be possible for men such as these to join the military today?

3. Do you believe that some sort of universal service program might be beneficial and help people turn their lives around?

**Sources:** John Laub and Robert Sampson, *Shared Beginnings, Divergent Lives: Delinquent Boys to Age 70* (Cambridge, MA: Harvard University Press, 2003); John Laub and Robert Sampson, "Understanding Desistance from Criminality," in *Criminality and Justice: An Annual Review of Research*, vol. 28, ed. Michael Tonry (Chicago: University of Chicago Press, 2001), pp. 1–71.

that include poverty and family function. Together these factors influence people to "choose criminality" over noncriminal behavioral alternatives.[66]

Following their lead, David Rowe, D. Wayne Osgood, and W. Alan Nicewander proposed the concept of latent traits, the idea that a number of people in the population have a personal attribute or propensity that controls their inclination to commit criminal acts.[67] This disposition, or latent trait, is either present at birth or established early in life, and it remains stable over time. Suspected latent traits include defective intelligence, impulsive personality, genetic abnormalities, the physical–chemical functioning of the brain, and environmental influences on brain function, such as drugs, chemicals, and injuries.[68] Those who carry one of these latent traits are in danger of becoming career criminals; those who lack the propensity to commit have a much lower risk.[69]

According to this view, the *propensity* to commit crime is stable, but the *opportunity* to commit crime fluctuates over time. People age out of crime because as they mature there are simply fewer opportunities to commit such acts and greater inducements to remain "straight." They may marry, have children, and obtain jobs. The former delinquents' newfound adult responsibilities leave them little time to hang with their friends, abuse substances, and get into scrapes with the law.

Assume, for example, that a stable latent trait such as low IQ causes some people to commit criminal acts. Teenagers have more opportunity to do so than adults, so at every level of intelligence, adolescent criminality rates will be higher. As they mature, however, teens with both high and low IQs will slowly age out of crime, not due to a change in makeup or propensity, but because adult responsibilities provide them with fewer opportunities to engage in antisocial acts.

## Crime and Human Nature

Wilson and Herrnstein's *Crime and Human Nature* was a milestone in the development of propensity theory. Quite controversial at the time, they speculated that individual levels factors played a significant role in shaping behavior choices.[70]

According to Wilson and Herrnstein, all human behavior, including criminality, is determined by its perceived consequences. A criminal incident occurs when an individual chooses criminal over conventional behavior (which Wilson and Herrnstein refer to as non-crime) after weighing the potential gains and losses associated with each: "The larger the ratio of net rewards of crime to the net rewards of non-crime, the greater the tendency to commit the crime."[71]

Wilson and Herrnstein's model assumes that both biological and psychological traits influence the choice between crime and non-crime. They see a close link between a person's decision to choose crime and such biosocial factors as low intelligence, mesomorphic body type, genetic influences (parental criminality), and possessing an autonomic nervous system that responds too quickly to stimuli. Psychological traits, such as an impulsive or extroverted personality or generalized hostility, also affect the potential to commit crime.

In their focus on the association between these constitutional and psychological factors and crime, Wilson and Herrnstein seem to be suggesting the existence of an elusive latent trait that predisposes people to commit crime.[72] Their vision helped inspire other criminologists to identify the elusive latent trait that causes criminal behavior. The most prominent latent trait/propensity theory is Gottfredson and Hirschi's general theory of crime (GTC).

## General Theory of Crime (GTC)

Michael Gottfredson and Travis Hirschi's **general theory of crime (GTC)** modifies and redefines some of the principles articulated in Hirschi's social control theory by integrating the concepts of control with those of biosocial, psychological, routine activities, and rational choice theories.[73]

Gottfredson and Hirschi attribute the tendency to commit crimes to a person's level of **self-control**. People with limited self-control tend to be **impulsive**; they are insensitive to other people's feelings, physical (rather than mental), risk takers, short-sighted, and nonverbal.[74] They have a here-and-now orientation and refuse to work for distant goals; they lack diligence, tenacity, and persistence. People lacking self-control tend to be adventuresome, active, and self-centered. As they mature, they often have unstable marriages, jobs, and friendships.[75] They are less likely to feel shame if they engage in deviant acts and are more likely to find them pleasurable.[76] They are also more likely to engage in dangerous behaviors such as drinking,

---

**general theory of crime (GTC)**
Gottfredson and Hirschi's developmental theory that links crime to impulsivity and a lack of self-control.

**self-control**
Refers to a person's ability to exercise restraint and control over his or her feelings, emotions, reactions, and behaviors.

**impulsive**
Lacking in thought or deliberation in decision making. An impulsive person lacks close attention to details, has organizational problems, and is distracted and forgetful. Criminals are impulsive risk takers.

---

**CONNECTIONS**

Hirschi's original theory was reviewed in Chapter 7. At first he linked crime to a lack of social control due to the weakening of social bonds. In this newer version, he shifts his focus to self-control.

---

**LO5** Explain the concept of the latent trait and the basic principles of the general theory of crime (GTC).

smoking, and reckless driving. All of these behaviors are associated with criminality.[77] The Profiles in Crime feature discusses a well-known case involving two people who fit Gottfredson and Hirschi's profile of impulsive criminals lacking in self-control who are not deterred by punishment.

Because those with low self-control enjoy risky, exciting, or thrilling behaviors with immediate gratification, they are more likely to enjoy criminal acts, which require stealth, agility, speed, and power, than conventional acts, which demand

# PROFILES IN CRIME

## STEVEN HAYES AND JOSHUA KOMISARJEVSKY

Few crimes are as horrific as the murder of Jennifer Hawke-Petit and her daughters Michaela and Hayley Petit during a home invasion in the leafy suburb of Cheshire, Connecticut. The crime began on July 23, 2007, when career criminals Steven Hayes and Joshua Komisarjevsky spotted the Petits at a grocery store and followed them home. Hayes and Komisarjevsky burst into the house, beat Dr. William Petit and tied him up in the basement, and locked Hawke-Petit and the two girls in their rooms. Finding the household haul inadequate, they forced Hawke-Petit to go to a local bank to withdraw funds. She was able to inform a bank employee of the situation, who called the police. Returning to the Petits' house, Hayes and Komisarjevsky raped Hawke-Petit and 11-year-old Michaela. William Petit managed to free himself, escape, and call to a neighbor for help. As police surrounded the house, Hayes and Komisarjevsky strangled Hawke-Petit and set the house on fire with the two girls tied to their beds; they died of smoke inhalation. The crime scene photos were so gruesome that some jurors had to be treated for posttraumatic stress disorder (PTSD).

During the trial, defense lawyers presented evidence in an effort to spare Hayes and Komisarjevsky the death penalty. Komisarjevsky was portrayed as a damaged person who was sexually abused as a child, suffered mood disorders and head injuries, abused drugs, and cut himself with glass, knives, and razors. The defense stated that his evangelical Christian adoptive parents denied him proper care, relying instead on religion. Dr. Eric Goldsmith, a psychiatrist who interviewed Hayes for about 37 hours on eight occasions, noted that Hayes had a troubled and abusive upbringing, was sexually abused by a teenage babysitter when he was 10 or 11, and had developed a sexual fetish that caused him to associate an object—a woman's old sneaker—with sexual arousal. Goldsmith said Hayes sought out women who shared his fetish. Hayes claimed that he had killed 17 women in the Northeast and also committed date rapes.

Despite defense efforts, both men were found guilty and sentenced to death. Komisarjevsky's family issued a statement: "From the very beginning, we have spoken out about the horror of the crime and taken the position that whatever verdict the jury reached was the right verdict. With today's jury decision, our view is the same. The crime was monstrous and beyond comprehension. There are no excuses." At the sentencing hearing, Komisarjevsky put the blame on Hayes, claiming the murders were unplanned and occurred because they snapped and things got out of control. He told the judge, "I was a condemned man long before this day. Millions have judged me guilty of capital offenses I did not commit. I did not intend for those women to die. They were never supposed to lose their lives. I don't need 12 people to tell me what I'm guilty or not guilty of. None of them were there that morning."

Connecticut ended capital punishment in August 2015, sparing the killers from the death penalty and reducing their sentences to life in prison. Would you have recommended the death penalty for these two impulsive criminals who lacked any sort of self-control? And if not them, who?

**Sources:** Stephanie Slifer, "Petit Family Murders: "I Just Snapped," Says Stephen Hayes, Convicted in Deadly Conn. Home Invasion," CBS News, September 9, 2013, www.cbsnews.com/news/petit-family-murders-i-just-snapped-says-stephen-hayes-convicted-in-deadly-conn-home-invasion/; David Gardner, "'Things Got Out of Control': Chilling Confession of Connecticut Massacre 'Killer,'" *Daily Mail*, September 23, 2010, www.dailymail.co.uk/news/article-1314418/Steven-Hayes-Chilling-confession-Connecticut-massacre-killer.html; Alaine Griffin, "Judge Sentences Komisarjevsky to Death," *Hartford Courant*, January 27, 2012, www.courant.com/community/cheshire/cheshire-home-invasion/hc-komisarjevsky-sentenced-0128-20120127,0,1199254.story (URLs accessed 2015).

long-term study and cognitive and verbal skills. As Gottfredson and Hirschi put it, they derive satisfaction from "money without work, sex without courtship, revenge without court delays."[78] Many of these individuals who have a propensity for committing crime also engage in other risky, impulsive behaviors such as smoking, drinking, gambling, and illicit sexuality.[79] Although these acts are not illegal, they too provide immediate, short-term gratification.

**WHAT CAUSES IMPULSIVITY/LOW SELF-CONTROL TO DEVELOP?** Gottfredson and Hirschi trace the root cause of poor self-control to inadequate child-rearing practices. Parents who refuse or are unable to monitor a child's behavior, to recognize deviant behavior when it occurs, and to punish that behavior will produce children who lack self-control. Children whose social bond is weak and frayed, who are not attached to their parents, who are poorly supervised, and whose parents are criminal or deviant themselves are the most likely to develop poor self-control.[80] Even in disadvantaged communities, children whose parents provide adequate and supportive discipline are the ones most likely to develop self-control.[81]

The association between poor parents and lack of self-control may be both reciprocal and intergenerational. Kids who have low self-control may strain parental attachments and the ability of parents to control children; parents who themselves have low self-control are the ones most likely to use damaging and inappropriate supervision and punishment mechanisms. Impulsive kids grow up to become poor parents who themselves use improper discipline, producing yet another generation of impulsive kids who lack self-control.[82]

**LEARNING OR BIOLOGY?** There may also be a genetic/biosocial component to the development of impulsivity. Children of impulsive parents are the ones most likely to exhibit a lack of self-control.[83] Research by David Farrington shows that antisocial behavior runs in families and that having criminal relatives is a significant predictor of future misbehaviors.[84] While these studies are not definitive, they raise the possibility that the intergenerational transfer of impulsivity has a biological basis.

Measures of neuropsychological deficits, birth complications, and low birth weight have all been found to have significant direct or indirect effects on levels of self-control.[85] Recent research shows that children who suffer anoxia (oxygen starvation) during the birthing process are the ones most likely to lack self-control later in life, which suggests that impulsivity may have a biological basis.[86] When Kevin Beaver and his associates examined impulsive personality and self-control in twin pairs, they discovered evidence that these traits may be inherited rather than developed. That might help explain the stability of these latent traits over the life course.[87]

Another biological basis for impulsivity may be low resting heart rate. People with low heart rates may seek out dangerous and arousing behaviors, such as criminality, to compensate for their biological condition; they become thrill seekers who engage in dangerous behaviors simply because it gives them the jolt they need to feel good, i.e., normal.[88]

**THE ACT AND THE OFFENDER** Not all impulsive people become criminals, nor does impulsivity mean that someone is consistently antisocial. In their general theory of crime (GTC), Gottfredson and Hirschi consider the criminal offender and the criminal act as separate concepts. On the one hand, criminal acts, such as robberies or burglaries, are illegal events or deeds that offenders engage in when they perceive them to be advantageous. For example, burglaries are typically committed by young males looking for cash, liquor, and entertainment; the crime provides "easy, short-term gratification."[89]

On the other hand, criminal offenders are people predisposed to commit crimes. However, they are not robots who commit crime without restraint; their days are also filled with conventional behaviors, such as going to school, parties, concerts, and church. But given the same set of criminal opportunities, such as having a lot of free time for mischief and living in a neighborhood with unguarded homes containing

## Exhibit 9.2   Elements of Impulsivity: Signs that a Person Has Low Self-Control

- Insensitive
- Physical (rather than mental)
- Shortsighted
- Nonverbal
- Here-and-now orientation
- Unstable social relations
- Enjoys deviant behaviors
- Risk taker
- Refuses to work for distant goals

- Lacks diligence
- Lacks tenacity
- Adventuresome
- Self-centered
- Shameless
- Imprudent
- Lacks cognitive and verbal skills
- Enjoys danger and excitement

**Source:** © Cengage Learning

valuable merchandise, crime-prone people have a much higher probability of violating the law than do noncriminals. It bears repeating: according to the GTC, the propensity to commit crimes remains stable throughout a person's life. Change in the frequency of criminal activity is purely a function of change in criminal opportunity.

Exhibit 9.2 lists the elements of impulsivity, or low self-control.

**TESTING THE GENERAL THEORY OF CRIME** Following the publication of *A General Theory of Crime*, dozens of research efforts tested the validity of Gottfredson and Hirschi's theoretical views. Not only has an association between impulsivity and crime been found, but levels of self-control may be used to explain the association between crime and other factors ranging from gender to religiosity: Because religious people are less likely to be impulsive than nonbelievers, people who attend services and believe in God tend to be noncriminal.[90] There is also research showing that patterns of antisocial behavior mimic those predicted by Gottfredson and Hirschi: persistent offenders who begin their criminal career at an early age are the ones who are most lacking in self-control.[91]

Another approach has been to identify indicators of impulsiveness and self-control and determine whether these factors correlate with measures of criminal activity: according to the GTC, the lower a person's self-control, the more likely they are to engage in future antisocial behaviors.[92] Kids with low self-control are the ones most likely to fall in with a bad crowd, and once they do so their impulsivity makes them vulnerable to antisocial peer influence.[93] It is not surprising that career criminals have been shown to have significantly lower levels of self-control than nonoffenders, and that the lower the level of a person's self-control, the greater his or her chance of becoming a career criminal. Some studies have found self-control to be the strongest predictor of career criminality, exceeding the impact of age, race, ethnicity, and gender.[94]

By integrating the concepts of socialization and criminality, Gottfredson and Hirschi help explain why some people who lack self-control can escape criminality, and conversely, why some people who have self-control might not escape criminality. People who are at risk because they have

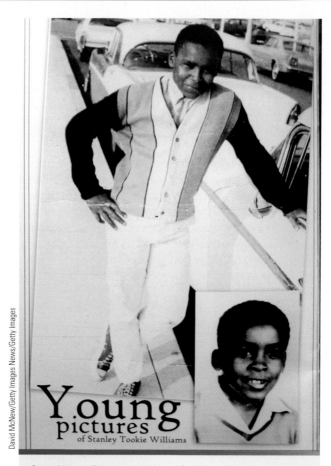

David McNew/Getty Images News/Getty Images

One criticism of the general theory of crime is that people actually do change over their lifetime. Here are early photos of Stanley "Tookie" Williams, executed cofounder of the Crips gang, as seen in a memorial service program. Sentenced to prison for the 1979 murders of four people, Williams spent several years involved with violent activities in prison, but around 1993 he changed his behavior and became an antigang activist. Williams coauthored such books as *Life in Prison*, which encouraged kids to stay out of gangs, and his memoir *Blue Rage, Black Redemption*. Williams was nominated for the Nobel Peace Prize for his efforts. Do you believe that a gang leader such as "Tookie" Williams really can change? Or did his changing life circumstances simply prevent him from committing violent criminal acts? Regardless of his change, Williams was executed in 2005.

impulsive personalities may forgo criminal careers because there are no opportunities to commit criminal acts; instead, they may find other outlets for their impulsive personalities. In contrast, if the opportunity is strong enough, even people with relatively strong self-control may be tempted to violate the law; the incentives to commit criminal acts may overwhelm their self-control.

**CRITICISMS AND QUESTIONS**  Although the GTC seems persuasive, several questions and criticisms remain to be answered. Among the most important are the following:

- *Impulsivity is only one of many personality traits correlated with crime.* Lack of self-control may in fact be a trait associated with crime, but so are many others. There is too much variety in personality traits, ranging from psychopathy to decision-making style, to say that a single element is responsible for all crimes.[95] People who score low on scales measuring an honesty-humility personality dimension (honesty-humility refers to individuals who are willing to use others for personal gain and includes greed, immodesty, and active violations of social norms through insincerity and unfairness) are more likely than high scorers to make criminal choices.[96] Other personality traits such as low self-direction (the tendency not to act in one's long-term benefit) may be a better predictor of criminality than impulsivity or lack of self-control.[97]

Pool/Reuters/Landov

Jodi Arias (center) talks to defense attorneys Jennifer Willmott and Kirk Nurmi during her trial at Maricopa County Superior Court in Phoenix, Arizona, April 3, 2013. Arias was on trial for the 2008 killing of her boyfriend, Travis Alexander, whom she claimed repeatedly abused her. Was hers an impulsive response to a violent environment or a calculated act of murder? The jury did not believe her claims: on May 8, 2013, Arias was found guilty of first-degree murder. In 2015, she was sentenced to life in prison without the possibility of parole.

- *The GTC does not explain racial and gender differences.* Although distinct gender differences in the crime rate exist, there is little evidence that males are more impulsive or lacking in self-control than females.[98] Differences in impulsivity and self-control alone may not be able to explain differences in male and female offending rates.[99] Similarly, Gottfredson and Hirschi explain racial differences in the criminality rate as a failure of childrearing practices in the African American community.[100] In so doing, they overlook issues of institutional racism, poverty, and relative deprivation, which have been shown to have a significant impact on crime rates.

- *People change and so does their level of self-control.* The general theory of crime assumes that criminal propensity does not change; opportunities change. This is a critical issue because it assumes that the human personality is stable from childhood into adulthood. However, social scientists recognize that behavior-shaping factors that are dominant in early adolescence, such as peer groups, may fade in adulthood and be replaced by others, such as the nuclear family.[101] Personality also undergoes change and so does its impact on antisocial behavior.[102]

  It is not surprising that research efforts show that the stability in self-control predicted by Gottfredson and Hirschi may be an illusion.[103] As kids mature, the focus of their lives likewise changes and they may be better able to control their impulsive behavior.[104] As Callie Burt and her associates recently found, adolescence is a period of dramatic biological, behavioral, and social changes; a young person's physical and neurological makeup is undergoing remodeling and restructuring. Environmental influences operate in concert with neurobiological changes to create a period of heightened change. During this period levels of impulsivity also change, a result that is not predicted by the GTC.[105]

- *Environmental influences.* Because their theory rests on the concept of population heterogeneity, Gottfredson and Hirschi discount the influence of environmental factors. This issue has become a center of some contention. Some research indicates that social factors do in fact mediate the influence of self-control on crime and that such factors as community solidarity and morality help moderate the effects of low self-control.[106]

  Recently, criminologist Gregory Zimmerman found that in disadvantaged neighborhoods, most people tend to possess a feeling of fatalism and adopt an "I have nothing to lose" attitude. These factors cause both non-impulsive and impulsive individuals to take advantage of criminal opportunities. In these disorganized neighborhoods, nearly everyone commits crime, so having self-control means relatively little.[107] In disadvantaged neighborhoods, then, people's behavior seems to be more closely influenced by environmental factors and conditions; individual-level factors, such as lack of self-control, remain in the background.[108] This observation contradicts the GTC.

Although questions remain, the strength of the general theory of crime lies in its scope and breadth. By integrating concepts of criminal choice, criminal opportunity, socialization, and personality, Gottfredson and Hirschi make a plausible argument that all deviant behaviors may originate from the same source. Continued efforts are needed to test the GTC and establish the validity of its core concepts. It remains one of the key developments of modern criminological theory.

# Trajectory Theory

Trajectory theory is a third developmental approach that combines elements of propensity and life course theories. The basic premise is that there is more than one path to crime and more than one class of offender; there are different trajectories or pathways in a criminal career.

Since all people are different, it is unlikely that one model can hope to describe every person's journey through life. According to this view, not all persistent offenders begin at an early age nor do they take the same journey into crime. Some are precocious, beginning their careers early and persisting into adulthood.[109] Others stay out of trouble in adolescence and do not violate the law until their teenage years; they are late bloomers. Some offenders may peak at an early age and quickly desist, whereas others persist into adulthood. Some are high-rate offenders, whereas others offend at relatively low rates.[110] Similarly, offenders who manifest unique behavioral problems, such as conduct disorder or oppositional defiant disorders, may have different career paths. Some offenders are quite social and have a large peer group, while others are loners who make decisions on their own.[111] Males and females may also have different offending trajectories. Factors that predict offending in males may have little influence on females; there are significant gender differences in offending careers.[112] As external influences shift and change so too do offending trajectories. For example, as parents change their parenting style, their children alter their antisocial behavior involvement.[113]

Recognizing that people take different paths into criminality sets trajectory theory apart from both life course and propensity theories. Take for instance the view on early onset.[114] Life course and propensity theories maintain that persistent offenders are early starters, beginning their criminal careers in their adolescence and persisting into adulthood. In contrast, trajectory theory recognizes that some people stay out of trouble until relatively late in adolescence. Though these late starters have trouble-free childhoods, they are actually the people most likely to get involved in serious adult offending![115] Because latent trait theories disregard social influences during the life span, and life course theories maintain that social events seem to affect all people equally, they both miss out on the fact that there are different classes and types of offenders, something that trajectory theory can help us understand.[116]

**L06** Articulate the basic principles of trajectory theory.

## Offending Trajectories

The reality is that there are different paths or trajectories to a criminal career. People offend at a different pace, commit different kinds of crimes, and are influenced by different external forces.[117] Those who begin offending at an early age may engage in more age-appropriate crimes as they mature: the violent adolescent school yard bully may mature into an abusive husband in adulthood, but he remains violent over the life course.[118]

There may even be different classes of chronic offenders. As you may recall, when Wolfgang first identified the concept of chronicity (see Chapter 2) he did not distinguish within that grouping. Now research shows that chronic offenders can be divided into subgroupings: some are very high-rate offenders, whereas other chronics offend relatively infrequently but are persistent in their criminal activities, never really stopping.[119] Alex Piquero and his associates examined data from the Cambridge Study in Delinquent Development (CSDD), a longitudinal survey of 411 South London males, most born in 1953, and found that the group could be further subdivided into five classes based on their offending histories:

- Non-offenders (62 percent)
- Low-adolescence peak offenders (19 percent)
- Very low-rate chronic offenders (11 percent)
- High adolescence peak offenders (5 percent)
- High-rate chronic offenders (3 percent)

Following them over time until they reached their 40s, Piquero found that boys in each of these offending trajectories faced a different degree of social and personal problems, such as poor housing, a troubled romantic life, mental illness, and drug involvement. Not surprisingly, those youth classified as high-rate chronic offenders were more likely to experience life failure than kids placed in the other groups. The research shows that people who fall into different offender trajectories have different outcomes reaching into midlife.[120] Each of these categories of offenders presents unique problems, and each presents serious social and economic cost differentials over the life course. Piquero, along with Wesley Jennings and David Farrington, found that the cost to society presented by each high-rate chronic offender can be up to 10 times greater than the cost of those in the other offending categories.[121]

## Pathways to Crime

Trajectory theorists recognize that career criminals may travel more than a single road. Some may specialize in violence and extortion; some may be involved in theft and fraud; others may engage in a variety of criminal acts.[122] For example, people who commit violent crimes may be different from nonviolent property and drug offenders.[123] But even among these violent offenders, there may be distinct career paths. Some start out as violent kids who eventually desist, while others are *escalators* whose severity of violence increases over time. Escalators are more likely to live in racially mixed communities, experience racism, and have less parental involvement than people who avoid or decrease their violent behaviors.[124] A study by Georgia Zara and David Farrington identified still another group of violent kids: late-onset escalators. These youths began their violent careers relatively late in their adolescence after suffering a variety of psychological and social disturbances earlier in childhood, including high levels of anxiety. Zara and Farrington conclude that childhood risk factors may predict this late-onset group of violent young adults.[125]

Some of the most important research on criminal career paths or trajectories has been conducted by Rolf Loeber and his associates. Using data from a longitudinal study of Pittsburgh youth, Loeber has identified three distinct paths to a criminal career (Figure 9.2):[126]

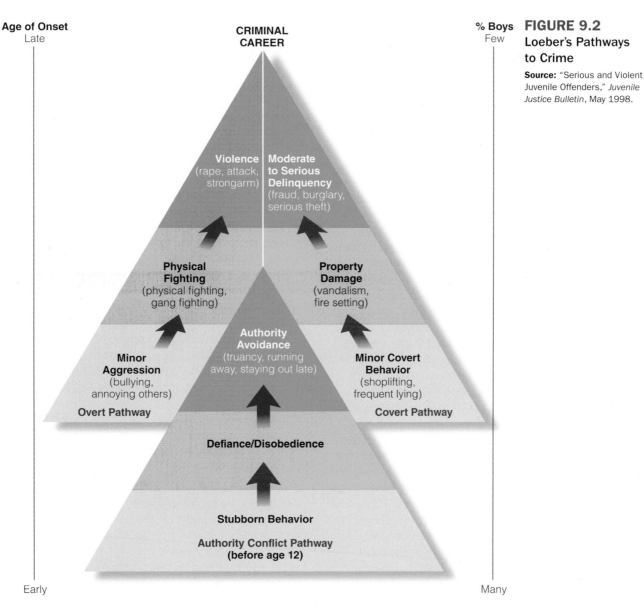

**Age of Onset**
Late

**CRIMINAL CAREER**

% Boys
Few

**FIGURE 9.2**
**Loeber's Pathways to Crime**

**Source:** "Serious and Violent Juvenile Offenders," *Juvenile Justice Bulletin*, May 1998.

Violence (rape, attack, strongarm) | Moderate to Serious Delinquency (fraud, burglary, serious theft)

Physical Fighting (physical fighting, gang fighting) | Property Damage (vandalism, fire setting)

Authority Avoidance (truancy, running away, staying out late)

Minor Aggression (bullying, annoying others)
Overt Pathway | Minor Covert Behavior (shoplifting, frequent lying)
Covert Pathway

Defiance/Disobedience

Stubborn Behavior

Authority Conflict Pathway (before age 12)

Early | Many

- The **authority conflict pathway** begins at an early age with stubborn behavior. This leads to defiance (doing things one's own way, disobedience) and then to authority avoidance (staying out late, truancy, running away).
- The **covert pathway** begins with minor, underhanded behavior (lying, shoplifting) that leads to property damage (setting nuisance fires, damaging property). This behavior eventually escalates to more serious forms of criminality, ranging from joyriding, pocket picking, larceny, and fencing to passing bad checks, using stolen credit cards, stealing cars, dealing drugs, and breaking and entering.
- The **overt pathway** escalates to aggressive acts beginning with aggression (annoying others, bullying), leading to physical (and gang) fighting, and then to violence (attacking someone, forced theft).

The Loeber research indicates that each of these paths may lead to a sustained deviant career. Some people enter two and even three paths simultaneously: They are stubborn, lie to teachers and parents, are bullies, and commit petty thefts. These adolescents are the most likely to become persistent offenders as they mature. The path to criminality is further discussed in the Policies and Issues in Criminology feature.

**authority conflict pathway**
Pathway to deviance that begins at an early age with stubborn behavior and leads to defiance and then to authority avoidance.

**covert pathway**
Pathway to a criminal career that begins with minor underhanded behavior, leads to property damage, and eventually escalates to more serious forms of theft and fraud.

**overt pathway**
Pathway to a criminal career that begins with minor aggression, leads to physical fighting, and eventually escalates to violent crime.

# Policies and Issues in Criminology

## THE PATH TO CRIMINALITY

One of the most important longitudinal studies tracking persistent offenders is the Cambridge Study in Delinquent Development, which has followed the offending careers of 411 London boys born in 1953. This cohort study, directed since 1982 by David Farrington, is one of the most serious attempts to isolate the factors that predict lifelong continuity of criminal behavior. The study uses self-report data as well as in-depth interviews and psychological testing. The boys have been interviewed eight times over 24 years, beginning at age 8 and continuing to age 32.

The results of the Cambridge study show that many of the same patterns found in the United States are repeated in a cross-national sample: the existence of chronic offenders, the continuity of offending, and early onset of criminal activity. Each of these patterns leads to persistent criminality.

Farrington found that the traits present in persistent offenders can be observed as early as age 8. The chronic criminal begins as a property offender, is born into a large low-income family headed by parents who have criminal records, and has criminal older siblings. The future criminal receives poor parental supervision, including the use of harsh or erratic punishment and childrearing techniques; the parents are likely to divorce or separate. The chronic offender tends to associate with friends who are also future criminals. By age 8, the child exhibits antisocial behavior, including dishonesty and aggressiveness; at school the chronic offender tends to have low educational achievement and is restless, troublesome, hyperactive, impulsive, and often truant. After leaving school at age 18, the persistent criminal tends to take a relatively well-paid but low-status job and is likely to have an erratic work history and periods of unemployment.

Farrington found that deviant behavior tends to be versatile rather than specialized. That is, the typical offender not only commits property offenses, such as theft and burglary, but also engages in violence, vandalism, drug use, excessive drinking, drunk driving, smoking, reckless driving, and sexual promiscuity—evidence of a generalized problem behavior syndrome. Chronic offenders are more likely to live away from home and have conflicts with their parents. They get tattoos, go out most evenings, and enjoy hanging out with groups of their friends. They are much more likely than non-offenders to get involved in fights, to carry weapons, and to use them in violent encounters. The frequency of offending reaches a peak in the teenage years (about 17 or 18) and then declines in the 20s, when offenders marry or live with a significant other.

By the 30s, the former criminal is likely to be separated or divorced and be an absent parent. His employment record remains spotty, and he moves often between rental units. His life is still characterized by evenings out, heavy drinking, substance abuse, and more violent behavior than his contemporaries.

Because the typical offender provides the same kind of deprived and disrupted family life for his own children that he experienced, the social experiences and conditions that produce criminality are carried on from one generation to the next. The following list summarizes the specific risk factors that Farrington associates with forming a criminal career:

- *Prenatal and perinatal.* Early childbearing increases the risk of such undesirable outcomes for children as low school attainment, antisocial behavior, substance use, and early sexual activity. An increased risk of offending among children of teenage mothers is associated with low income, poor housing, absent fathers, and poor childrearing methods.
- *Personality.* Impulsiveness, hyperactivity, restlessness, and limited ability to concentrate are associated with low attainment in school and a poor ability to foresee the consequences of offending.
- *Intelligence and attainment.* Low intelligence and poor performance in school, although important statistical predictors of offending, are difficult to disentangle from each other. One plausible explanation of the link between low intelligence and criminality is its association with a poor ability to manipulate abstract concepts and to appreciate the feelings of victims.
- *Parental supervision and discipline.* Harsh or erratic parental discipline and cold or rejecting parental

## Adolescent-Limited and Life Course Persistent Offenders

**adolescent-limited offenders**
Kids who get into minor scrapes as youth but whose misbehavior ends when they enter adulthood.

According to psychologist Terrie Moffitt, most young offenders follow one of two paths. **Adolescent-limited offenders** may be considered typical teenagers who get into minor scrapes and engage in what might be considered rebellious teenage behavior with their friends.[127] As they reach their mid-teens, adolescent-limited delinquents

attitudes have been linked to criminality and are associated with children's lack of internal inhibitions against offending. Physical abuse by parents has been associated with an increased risk of the children themselves becoming violent offenders in later life.

- *Parental conflict and separation.* Living in a home affected by separation or divorce is more strongly related to criminality than when the disruption has been caused by the death of one parent. However, it may not be a "broken home" that creates an increased risk of offending so much as the parental conflict that leads to the separation.

- *Socioeconomic status.* Social and economic deprivation are important predictors of antisocial behavior and crime, but low family income and poor housing are better measurements than the prestige of parents' occupations.

- *Criminal friends.* Delinquents tend to have criminal friends. But it is not certain whether membership in a delinquent peer group leads to offending or whether delinquents simply gravitate toward each other's company (or both). Breaking up with criminal friends often coincides with desisting from crime.

- *School influences.* The prevalence of offending by pupils varies widely between secondary schools. But it is not clear how far schools themselves have an effect on criminality (for example, by paying insufficient attention to bullying or providing too much punishment and too little praise), or whether it is simply that troublesome children tend to go to high-criminality-rate schools.

- *Community influences.* The risks of becoming criminally involved are higher for young people raised in disorganized inner-city areas, characterized by physical deterioration, overcrowded households, publicly subsidized renting, and high residential mobility. It is not clear, however, whether this is due to a direct influence on children, or whether environmental stress causes family adversities, which in turn cause criminality.

## What Caused Offenders to Desist?

Holding a relatively good job helped reduce criminal activity. Conversely, unemployment seemed to be related to the escalation of theft offenses; violence and substance abuse were unaffected by unemployment. In a similar vein, getting married also helped diminish criminal activity. However, finding a spouse who was also involved in criminal activity and had a criminal record increased criminal involvement.

Physical relocation also helped some offenders desist because they were forced to sever ties with co-offenders. For this reason, leaving the city for a rural or suburban area was linked to reduced criminal activity. Although employment, marriage, and relocation helped potential offenders desist, not all desisters found success. At-risk youths who managed to avoid criminal convictions were unlikely to avoid other social problems. Rather than becoming prosperous homeowners with flourishing careers, they tended to live in unkempt homes and have large debts and low-paying jobs. They were also more likely to remain single and live alone. Youths who experienced social isolation at age 8 were also found to experience it at age 32.

Farrington suggests that life experiences shape the direction and flow of behavior choices. He finds that while there may be continuity in offending, the factors that predict criminality at one point in the life course may not be the ones that predict criminality at another. Although most adult delinquents begin their careers in childhood, life events may help some children forgo criminality as they mature.

## Critical Thinking

Farrington finds that the traits present in persistent offenders can be observed as early as age 8. Should such young children be observed and monitored, even though they have not actually committed crimes? Would such monitoring create a self-fulfilling prophecy?

**Sources:** David Farrington, "Key Results from the First Forty Years of the Cambridge Study in Delinquent Development," in *Taking Stock of Criminality: An Overview of Findings from Contemporary Longitudinal Studies*, ed. Terence Thornberry and Marvin Krohn (New York: Kluwer, 2002), pp. 137–185; David Farrington, "The Development of Offending and Anti-Social Behavior from Childhood: Key Findings from the Cambridge Study of Delinquent Development," *Journal of Child Psychology and Psychiatry* 36 (1995): 2–36; David Farrington, *Understanding and Preventing Youth Crime* (London: Joseph Rowntree Foundation, 1996).

begin to mimic the antisocial behavior of more troubled teens, only to reduce the frequency of their offending as they mature to around age 18.[128]

The second path is the one taken by a small group of **life course persisters** who begin their offending career at a very early age and continue to offend well into adulthood.[129] Moffit finds that life course persisters combine family dysfunction with

**life course persisters**
Delinquents who begin their offending career at a very early age and continue to offend well into adulthood.

severe neurological problems that predispose them to antisocial behavior patterns. These afflictions can be the result of maternal drug abuse, poor nutrition, or exposure to toxic agents such as lead. Research using twin pairs indicates that there may be a genetic basis to life course persistence that may be linked through neurological deficiencies.[130] It is not surprising that life course persisters display social and personal dysfunctions, including lower than average verbal ability, reasoning skills, learning ability, and school achievement.

Research shows that the persistence patterns predicted by Moffitt are valid and accurate.[131] Life course persisters offend more frequently and engage in a greater variety of antisocial acts than other offenders; they also manifest significantly more mental health problems, including psychiatric pathologies, than adolescent-limited offenders.[132] Many have deviant friends who support their behavior choices.[133] Persisters are more likely to manifest traits such as low verbal ability and hyperactivity; they display a negative or impulsive personality and seem particularly impaired on spatial and memory functions.[134] Individual traits rather than environment seem to have the greatest influence on life course persistence.[135]

## Late Starters and Abstainers

There is also evidence that there may be other classes of offenders. For example, some people begin their offending career much later in adolescence than the typical offender but persist into adulthood.[136] These late starters are more likely to be involved in nonviolent crimes such as theft.[137]

**abstainers**
Adolescents who do not engage in any deviant behavior, a path that places them outside the norm for their age group.

**LATE STARTERS** The reason why some offenders start early, others late, and some not at all may be linked to psychological problems and disturbance. Mental disease and personality disorders progress differently, affecting some people in early adolescence and others later in life.[138] Research shows that offending trajectories do in fact differ among people with mental disorders, creating different classes of offenders. There are early starters (ES) who begin to engage in antisocial behavior at a young age before the onset of the psychiatric disorder, most likely because they maintain other psychological issues such as an antisocial personality. There are also late starters (LS) who begin to engage in antisocial behavior after the onset of the psychiatric disorder. Their criminal and deviant behavior is attributed to symptoms of the disorder. The final category, called first offenders (FO), are men in their late thirties with a schizophrenia disorder who suddenly commit a very serious, typically violent, offense. Though they are late starters, they differ from those people in the LS grouping because while the latter start a criminal career with a variety of less serious offenses, the FO men suddenly commit a very serious (often fatal) offense without prior identified psychological abnormality.[139]

Kids who have close parental monitoring and/or family relations are able to abstain from crime. Here, Regina Saiz, 15, a Mexican American from Goshen, California, and her grandmother share a moment in their Catholic church before her quinceañera mass. Although some girls' quinceañeras are focused around a big party, Regina's also included a strong religious component. A crown was placed on her head, signifying, as the deacon who officiated said, "the victory that she has won so far in her life" as a Christian. Regina saw the church service as "a way to show people that ever since baptism, I've been following God's path and living my life with God." Afterward, her family and all her friends, who served as a sort of homecoming court wearing fancy dresses and zoot suits, had a party at a local Elks Club.

Sylvia Plachy/Redux

**ABSTAINERS** Still another subgroup consists of kids who never break the law, **abstainers**, whose conventional behavior makes them deviant in the teenage world where offending is the norm! Why do these nonstarters refrain from criminality of any sort? According to social psychologist Terrie Moffitt, abstainers are social introverts, whose unpopularity shields them from group pressure to commit criminal acts.[140] David Farrington also finds that kids may be able to remain non-offenders if they also maintain a unique set of personal traits that shield them from antisocial activity: shy personality, having few friends, having nondeviant families, and being highly regarded by their mothers.[141] Shy children with few friends avoid damaging relationships with other adolescents (members of a high-risk group) and are therefore able to avoid criminality. Still another explanation may be biological: abstainers maintain a genetic code that insulates them from criminality-producing factors in the environment.[142]

Recent research by Xiaojin Chen and Michele Adams puts a different spin on the abstention phenomenon.[143] They found that rather than being shy loners, abstainers have prosocial friends who themselves are good students and less likely to participate in deviant activities. Abstention may be more the result of careful parental monitoring and strong moral beliefs and not social isolation. Not surprisingly, abstainers are more likely than other youth to become successful, well-adjusted adults.[144]

## Public Policy Implications of Developmental Theory

Policies based on the premises of developmental theory have inspired a number of initiatives. Since the aim is to set people on the right developmental track, these efforts typically feature multisystemic treatment efforts designed to provide at-risk youths with personal, social, educational, and family services. Interventions are aimed at promoting academic success, social competence, and educational enhancement during the elementary grades.[145] Many of the most successful programs are aimed at strengthening children's social-emotional competence and positive coping skills and suppressing the development of antisocial, aggressive behavior.[146]

The most promising multicomponent prevention programs are designed to improve developmental skills. They may include a school component, an after-school component, and a parent-involvement component. All of these components share the goal of increasing protective factors and decreasing risk factors in the areas of the family, the community, the school, and the individual.[147] One example is the Boys and Girls Clubs and School Collaborations' Substance Abuse Prevention Program, which includes a school component called SMART (Skills Mastery And Resistance Training), an after-school component called SMART Kids, and a parent-involvement component called SMART Parents. Each component is designed to reduce specific risk factors in the children's school, family, community, and personal environments.[148] Another effort, Guiding Good Choices (GGC, formerly known as "Preparing for the Drug Free Years"), is designed to aid parents on many fronts, including teaching them about the risk and protective factors for substance abuse. GGC is a multimedia substance abuse prevention program that gives parents of children in grades 4 through 8 (ages 9 to 14) the knowledge and skills needed to guide their children through early adolescence.[149]

AP Images/Steve Ruark

Programs based on developmental theory try to help kids knife off from a pathway to crime. Here, staff and volunteers huddle during the Triple Play Mobile Tour in Baltimore. With the support of partners Coca-Cola and the Anthem Foundation, the tour brings Boys and Girls Clubs' healthy lifestyles program to clubs around the country, providing a unique experience focused on mind, body, and soul.

# Thinking Like a Criminologist

## A Question of Life or Death

You are a state supreme court judge. Before you is the case of Gary L. Sampson, 41, a man addicted to alcohol and cocaine, a deadbeat dad, a two-bit thief, and a bank robber with a long history of violence. On August 1, 2001, he turned himself in to the Vermont State Police after fleeing from pursuit for a string of three murders he committed in Massachusetts and New Hampshire.

Those who knew Sampson speculated that his murders were a desperate finale to a troubled life. During his early life in New England, he once bound, gagged, and beat three elderly women in a candy store. He had hijacked cars at knifepoint and was medically diagnosed as schizophrenic. In 1977, he married a 17-year-old girl he had impregnated; two months later he was arrested and charged with rape for having "unnatural intercourse with a child under 16." Although he was acquitted of that charge, his wife noticed that Sampson had developed a hair-trigger temper and had become increasingly violent; their marriage soon ended. As the years passed, Sampson had at least four failed marriages, was an absentee father to two children, and became an alcoholic and a drug user. He spent nearly half of his adult life behind bars.

Jumping bail after being arrested for theft from an antique store, he headed south to North Carolina and took on a new identity: Gary Johnson, a construction worker. He took up with Ricki Carter, a transvestite, but their relationship was anything but stable. Sampson once put a gun to Carter's head, broke his ribs, and threatened to kill his family. After his breakup with Carter, Sampson moved in with a new girlfriend, Karen Anderson, and began robbing banks. When the police closed in, Sampson fled north. Needing transportation, he pulled three carjackings and killed the drivers, one a 19-year-old college freshman who had stopped to give Sampson a hand. In December 2003, Sampson received a sentence of death from a jury that was not swayed by his claim that he was mentally unfit.

## Writing Assignment

Write an opinion on whether Sampson should receive the death penalty or a sentence of life in prison. Do you believe that Sampson's crimes were a product of his impaired development, and if so, should his life be spared?

# SUMMARY

**LO1**  **Discuss the history of and influences on developmental theory.**

The developmental theory of criminality looks at the onset, continuity, and termination of a criminal career. The foundation of developmental theory can be traced to the pioneering work of Sheldon and Eleanor Glueck, who identified a number of personal and social factors related to persistent offending. A 1990 review paper by Rolf Loeber and Marc Le Blanc proposed that criminologists should devote time and effort to understanding basic questions about the evolution of criminal careers.

**LO2**  **List the principles of the life course approach to developmental theory.**

Life course theory suggests that the development of a criminal career is a dynamic process. Behavior is influenced by individual characteristics as well as social experiences, and the factors that cause antisocial behaviors change dramatically over a person's life span. Even as toddlers people begin relationships and behaviors that will determine their adult life course. Some individuals are incapable of maturing in a reasonable and timely fashion because of family, environmental, or personal problems. The propensity to commit crimes is neither stable nor constant, it is a developmental process. Disruptions in life's major transitions can be destructive and ultimately can promote criminality.

**LO3    Explain the term *problem behavior syndrome*.**

One element of life course theory is that criminality may best be understood as one of many social problems faced by people. This is referred to as problem behavior syndrome (PBS), which typically involves family dysfunction, sexual and physical abuse, substance abuse, smoking, precocious sexuality and early pregnancy, educational underachievement, suicide attempts, sensation seeking, and unemployment.

**LO4    Outline the basic principles of Sampson and Laub's age-graded life course theory.**

According to Sampson and Laub's age-graded theory, the course of a criminal career can be affected by events that occur across the life span. There are turning points in a criminal career that can alter its course and direction, changing a lifetime n'er do well into a productive citizen. Acquiring social capital helps some at-risk people to knife off from a criminal career. However, people who acquire cumulative disadvantage are more likely to commit criminal acts and become victims of crime. Because criminal careers are a dynamic process, an important life event or turning point can change the direction of a person's life course trajectory.

**LO5    Explain the concept of the latent trait and the basic principles of the General Theory of Crime (GTC).**

Propensity or latent trait theory suggests that a stable feature, characteristic, property, or condition, such as defective intelligence or impulsive personality, makes some people crime prone over the life course. Suspected latent traits include defective intelligence, damaged or impulsive personality, genetic abnormalities, the physical–chemical functioning of the brain, and environmental influences on brain function such as drugs, chemicals, and injuries. In *A General Theory of Crime*, Michael Gottfredson and Travis Hirschi argue that the propensity to commit antisocial acts is tied directly to a person's level of self-control. By integrating the concepts of socialization and criminality, Gottfredson and Hirschi help explain why some people who lack self-control can escape criminality, and, conversely, why some people who have self-control might live conventional lives.

**LO6    Articulate the basic principles of trajectory theory.**

Trajectory theorists recognize that career criminals may travel more than a single road. Some may specialize in violence and extortion; some may be involved in theft and fraud; others may engage in a variety of criminal acts. Some offenders begin their careers early in life, whereas others are late bloomers who begin committing crime when most people desist. Some are frequent offenders, while others travel a more moderate path or are even abstainers. Experiences in young adulthood and beyond can redirect criminal trajectories or paths. In some cases people can be turned in a positive direction, while in others negative life experiences can be harmful and injurious.

## Key Terms

criminal career 266
developmental theory 266
life course theory 267
propensity theory 267
latent trait 267
trajectory theory 267
population heterogeneity 268

state dependence 268
early onset 269
problem behavior syndrome (PBS) 270
age-graded theory 271
turning points 272
social capital 272
cumulative disadvantage 272

schemas 275
criminogenic knowledge structure (CKS) 275
general theory of crime (GTC) 278
self-control 278
impulsive 278
authority conflict pathway 285

covert pathway 285
overt pathway 285
adolescent-limited offenders 286
life course persisters 287
abstainers 288

# Critical Thinking Questions

1. Do you consider yourself a holder of "social capital"? If so, what form does it take?

2. A person gets a 1600 on the SAT. Without knowing this person, what personal, family, and social characteristics would you assume he or she has? Another person becomes a serial killer. Without knowing this person, what personal, family, and social characteristics would you assume he or she has? If "bad behavior" is explained by multiple problems, is "good behavior" explained by multiple strengths?

3. Do you believe there is a latent trait that makes a person criminality prone, or is criminality a function of environment and socialization?

4. Do you agree with Loeber's multiple pathways model? Do you know people who have traveled down those paths?

5. Do you think that marriage is different than merely being in love? The McCarthy and Casey research discussed earlier indicates that having a romantic relationship may help reduce crime; if so, what happens when the couple breaks up? Does that increase the likelihood of criminal involvement?

# Notes

*All URLs accessed in 2015.*

1. FBI, "Murder-for-Hire Plot Uncovered: Subject Wanted Out of $8 Million Debt," www.fbi.gov/news/stories/2014/september/murder-for-hire-plot-uncovered/murder-for-hire-plot-uncovered; Micah Maidenberg, "Ex-developer Daniel Dvorkin Gets 8 Years for Trying to Hire a Hit Man," *Chicago Real Estate Daily*, August 4, 2014.

2. See, generally, John Laub and Robert Sampson, "The Sutherland–Glueck Debate: On the Sociology of Criminological Knowledge," *American Journal of Sociology* 96 (1991): 1402–1440; John Laub and Robert Sampson, "Unraveling Families and Criminality: A Reanalysis of the Gluecks' Data," *Criminology* 26 (1988): 355–380.

3. Rolf Loeber and Marc Le Blanc, "Toward a Developmental Criminology," in *Crime and Justice*, vol. 12, ed. Norval Morris and Michael Tonry (Chicago: University of Chicago Press, 1990), pp. 375–473; Rolf Loeber and Marc Le Blanc, "Developmental Criminology Updated," in *Crime and Justice*, vol. 23, ed. Michael Tonry (Chicago: University of Chicago Press, 1998), pp. 115–198.

4. Raymond Paternoster, Charles Dean, Alex Piquero, Paul Mazerolle, and Robert Brame, "Generality, Continuity, and Change in Offending," *Journal of Quantitative Criminology* 13 (1997): 231–266.

5. Alex Piquero, "Taking Stock of Developmental Trajectories of Criminal Activity over the Life Course," in *The Long View of Crime: A Synthesis of Longitudinal Research*, ed. Akiva Liberman (New York: Springer, 2008), pp. 23–78.

6. Shawn Bushway, Robert Brame, and Raymond Paternoster, "Assessing Stability and Change in Criminal Offending: A Comparison of Random Effects, Semiparametric, and Fixed Effects Modeling Strategies," *Journal of Quantitative Criminology* 15 (1999): 23–61.

7. Sarah Bacon, Raymond Paternoster, and Robert Brame, "Understanding the Relationship Between Onset Age and Subsequent Offending During Adolescence," *Journal of Youth and Adolescence* 38 (2009): 301–311.

8. Marvin Krohn, Alan Lizotte, and Cynthia Perez, "The Interrelationship Between Substance Use and Precocious Transitions to Adult Sexuality," *Journal of Health and Social Behavior* 38 (1997): 88.

9. Peggy Giordano, Stephen Cernkovich, and Jennifer Rudolph, "Gender, Crime, and Desistance: Toward a Theory of Cognitive Transformation?" *American Journal of Sociology* 107 (2002): 990–1064.

10. Lara DePadilla, Molly Perkins, Kirk Elifson, and Claire Sterk, "Adult Criminal Involvement: A Cross-Sectional Inquiry into Correlates and Mechanisms over the Life Course," *Criminal Justice Review* 37 (2012): 110–126.

11. Besiki Kutateladze, Nancy Andiloro, Brian Johnson, and Cassia Spohn, "Cumulative Disadvantage: Examining Racial and Ethnic Disparity in Prosecution and Sentencing," *Criminology* 52 (2014): 514–551.

12. Shawn Bushway, Marvin Krohn, Alan Lizotte, Matthew Phillips, and Nicole Schmidt, "Are Risky Youth Less Protectable as They Age? The Dynamics of Protection During Adolescence and Young Adulthood," *Justice Quarterly* 30 (2013): 84–116.

13. Chris Melde and Finn-Aage Esbensen, "The Relative Impact of Gang Status Transitions: Identifying the Mechanisms of Change in Delinquency," *Journal of Research in Crime and Delinquency* 51 (2014): 349–376.

14. David C. Pyrooz, "From Colors and Guns to Caps and Gowns? The Effects of Gang Membership on Educational Attainment," *Journal of Research in Crime and Delinquency* 51 (2014): 56–87.

15. John Hagan and Holly Foster, "S/He's a Rebel: Toward a Sequential Stress Theory of Criminality and Gendered Pathways to Disadvantage in Emerging Adulthood," *Social Forces* 82 (2003): 53–86.

16. Patrick Lussier, David Farrington, and Terrie Moffitt, "Is the Antisocial Child Father of the Abusive Man? A 40-Year Prospective Longitudinal Study on the Development Antecedents of Intimate Partner Violence," *Criminology* 47 (2009): 741–780.

17. Gerald Patterson, Barbara DeBaryshe, and Elizabeth Ramsey, "A Developmental Perspective on Antisocial Behavior," *American Psychologist* 44 (1989): 329–335.

18. Robert Sampson and John Laub, "Crime and Deviance in the Life Course," *American Review of Sociology* 18 (1992): 63–84.

19. David Farrington, Darrick Jolliffe, Rolf Loeber, Magda Stouthamer-Loeber, and Larry Kalb, "The Concentration of Offenders in Families, and Family Criminality in the Prediction of Boys' Criminality," *Journal of Adolescence* 24 (2001): 579–596.

20. Lila Kazemian, David Farrington, and Marc Le Blanc, "Can We Make Accurate Long-Term Predictions About Patterns of De-escalation in Offending Behavior?" *Journal of Youth and Adolescence* 38 (2009): 384–400.

21. Alex R. Piquero and He Len Chung, "On the Relationships Between Gender, Early Onset, and the Seriousness of Offending," *Journal of Delinquent Justice* 29 (2001): 189–206.

22. Mary Campa, Catherine Bradshaw, John Eckenrode, and David Zielinski, "Patterns of Problem Behavior in Relation to Thriving and Precocious Behavior in Late Adolescence," *Journal of Youth and Adolescence* 37 (2008): 627–640; Alex Mason, Rick Kosterman, J. David Hawkins, Todd Herrenkohl, Liliana Lengua, and Elizabeth McCauley, "Predicting Depression, Social Phobia, and Violence in Early Adulthood from Childhood Behavior Problems," *Journal of the American Academy of Child and Adolescent Psychiatry* 43 (2004): 307–315; Rolf Loeber and David Farrington, "Young Children Who Commit Crime: Epidemiology, Developmental Origins, Risk Factors, Early Interventions, and Policy Implications," *Development and Psychopathology* 12 (2000): 737–762.

23. Matt DeLisi, Tricia K. Neppl, Brenda J. Lohman, Michael G. Vaughn, and Jeffrey J. Shook, "Early Starters: Which Type of Criminal Onset Matters Most for Delinquent Careers?" *Journal of Criminal Justice* 41 (2013): 12–17.

24. Kristin Carbone-Lopez and Jody Miller, "Precocious Role Entry as a Mediating Factor in Women's Methamphetamine Use: Implications for Life-Course and Pathways Research," *Criminology* 50 (2012): 187–220.

25. David Gadd and Stephen Farrall, "Criminal Careers, Desistance and Subjectivity: Interpreting Men's Narratives of Change," *Theoretical Criminology* 8 (2004): 123–156.

26. Rolf Loeber and David Farrington, "Young Children Who Commit Criminality: Epidemiology, Developmental Origins, Risk Factors, Early Interventions, and Policy Implications," *Development and Psychopathology* 12 (2000): 737–762.

27. Mason, Kosterman, Hawkins, Herrenkohl, Lengua, and McCauley, "Predicting Depression, Social Phobia, and Violence in Early Adulthood from Childhood Behavior Problems"; Loeber and Farrington, "Young Children Who Commit Crime"; Patrick Lussier, Jean Proulx, and Marc Le Blanc, "Criminal Propensity, Deviant Sexual Interests and Criminal Activity of Sexual Aggressors Against Women," *Criminology* 43 (2005): 249–282.

28. Ronald Prinz and Suzanne Kerns, "Early Substance Use by Juvenile Offenders," *Child Psychiatry and Human Development* 33 (2003): 263–268.

29. Magda Stouthamer-Loeber and Evelyn Wei, "The Precursors of Young Fatherhood and Its Effect on Criminality of Teenage Males," *Journal of Adolescent Health* 22 (1998): 56–65; Richard Jessor, John Donovan, and Francis Costa, *Beyond Adolescence: Problem Behavior and Young Adult Development* (New York: Cambridge University Press, 1991).

30. James Marquart, Victoria Brewer, Patricia Simon, and Edward Morse, "Lifestyle Factors Among Female Prisoners with Histories of Psychiatric Treatment," *Journal of Criminal Justice* 29 (2001): 319–328; Rolf Loeber, David Farrington, Magda Stouthamer-Loeber, Terrie Moffitt, Avshalom Caspi, and Don Lynam, "Male Mental Health Problems, Psychopathy, and Personality Traits: Key Findings from the First 14 Years of the Pittsburgh Youth Study," *Clinical Child and Family Psychology Review* 4 (2002): 273–297.

31. John Stogner, Chris Gibson, and J. Mitchell Miller, "Examining the Reciprocal Nature of the Health-Violence Relationship: Results from a Nationally Representative Sample," *Justice Quarterly* 31 (2014): 473–499.

32. J. Rayner, T. Kelly, and F. Graham, "Mental Health, Personality and Cognitive Problems in Persistent Adolescent Offenders Require Long-Term Solutions: Pilot Study," *Journal of Forensic Psychiatry and Psychology* 16 (2005): 248–262.

33. Deborah Capaldi and Gerald Patterson, "Can Violent Offenders Be Distinguished from Frequent Offenders? Prediction from Childhood to Adolescence," *Journal of Research in Crime and Criminality* 33 (1996): 206–231.

34. Alex Piquero, David Farrington, Jonathan Shepherd, and Katherine Auty, "Offending and Early Death in the Cambridge Study in Delinquent Development," *Justice Quarterly* 31 (2014): 445–472.

35. Paul Nieuwbeerta and Alex Piquero, "Mortality Rates and Causes of Death of Convicted Dutch Criminals 25 Years Later," *Journal of Research in Crime and Criminality* 45 (2008): 256–286.

36. David Fergusson, L. John Horwood, and Elizabeth Ridder, "Show Me the Child at Seven II: Childhood Intelligence and Later Outcomes in Adolescence and Young Adulthood," *Journal of Child Psychology and Psychiatry and Allied Disciplines* 46 (2005): 850–859.

37. Krysia Mossakowski, "Dissecting the Influence of Race, Ethnicity, and Socioeconomic Status on Mental

Health in Young Adulthood," *Research on Aging* 30 (2008): 649–671.

38. Nicole Leeper Piquero and Terrie Moffitt, "Can Childhood Factors Predict Workplace Deviance?" *Justice Quarterly* 31 (2014): 664–693; Margit Wiesner and Michael Windle, "Young Adult Substance Use and Depression as a Consequence of Criminality Trajectories During Middle Adolescence," *Journal of Research on Adolescence* 16 (2006): 239–264.

39. Alan Drury and Matt DeLisi, "Gangkill: An Exploratory Empirical Assessment of Gang Membership, Homicide Offending, and Prison Misconduct," *Crime and Criminality* 57 (2011): 130–146.

40. Marshall Jones and Donald Jones, "The Contagious Nature of Antisocial Behavior," *Criminology* 38 (2000): 25–46.

41. W. G. Clingempeel and S. W. Henggeler, "Aggressive Juvenile Offenders Transitioning into Emerging Adulthood," *American Journal of Orthopsychiatry* 73 (2003): 310–323.

42. Robert Agnew, *Why Do Criminals Offend? A General Theory of Crime and Criminality* (Los Angeles: Roxbury Publishing, 2005); Terence Thornberry, "Toward an Interactional Theory of Criminality," *Criminology* 25 (1987): 863–891; Richard Catalano and J. David Hawkins, "The Social Development Model: A Theory of Antisocial Behavior," in *Criminality and Crime: Current Theories*, ed. J. David Hawkins (New York: Cambridge University Press, 1996), pp. 149–197.

43. Stephen Farrall and Benjamin Bowling, "Structuration, Human Development, and Desistance from Crime," *British Journal of Criminology* 39 (1999): 253–268.

44. Robert Sampson and John Laub, *Crime in the Making: Pathways and Turning Points Through Life* (Cambridge, MA: Harvard University Press, 1993).

45. Matthew Moore and Nicholas Recker, "Social Capital, Type of Crime, and Social Control," *Crime and Delinquency*, first published online November 15, 2013.

46. John Laub and Robert Sampson, *Shared Beginnings, Divergent Lives: Delinquent Boys to Age 70* (Cambridge, MA: Harvard University Press, 2003), p. 149.

47. Daniel Nagin and Raymond Paternoster, "Personal Capital and Social Control: The Deterrence Implications of a Theory of Criminal Offending," *Criminology* 32 (1994): 581–606.

48. Joseph Murray, Rolf Loeber, and Dustin Pardini, "Parental Involvement in the Criminal Justice System and the Development of Youth Theft, Marijuana Use, Depression, and Poor Academic Performance," *Criminology* 50 (2012): 255–302.

49. Michael Roettger and Raymond Swisher, "Associations of Fathers' History of Incarceration with Sons' Criminality and Arrest Among Black, White, and Hispanic Males in the United States," *Criminology* 49 (2011): 1109–1148.

50. Joan Reid, "Exploratory Review of Route-Specific, Gendered, and Age-Graded Dynamics of Exploitation: Applying Life Course Theory to Victimization in Sex Trafficking in North America," *Aggression and Violent Behavior* 17 (2012): 257–271.

51. Terri Orbuch, James House, Richard Mero, and Pamela Webster, "Marital Quality over the Life Course," *Social Psychology Quarterly* 59 (1996): 162–171; Lee Lillard and Linda Waite, "'Til Death Do Us Part': Marital Disruption and Mortality," *American Journal of Sociology* 100 (1995): 1131–1156.

52. Mark Warr, "Life-Course Transitions and Desistance from Crime," *Criminology* 36 (1998): 183–216.

53. Michael Rocque, Chad Posick, Steven E. Barkan, and Ray Paternoster, "Marriage and County-Level Crime Rates: A Research Note," *Journal of Research in Crime and Delinquency* 52 (2015): 130–145; Ronald Simons and Ashley Barr, "Shifting Perspectives: Cognitive Changes Mediate the Impact of Romantic Relationships on Desistance from Crime," *Justice Quarterly*, first published online July 20, 2012.

54. Sonja Siennick, Jeremy Staff, D. Wayne Osgood, John Schulenberg, Jerald Bachman, and Matthew VanEseltine, "Partnership Transitions and Antisocial Behavior in Young Adulthood: A Within-Person, Multi-Cohort Analysis," *Journal of Research in Crime and Delinquency* 51 (2014): 735–758.

55. Marieke van Schellen, Robert Apel, and Paul Nieuwbeerta, "'Because You're Mine, I Walk the Line'? Marriage, Spousal Criminality, and Criminal Offending over the Life Course," *Journal of Quantitative Criminology*, first published online April 9, 2012.

56. Bill McCarthy and Teresa Casey, "Love, Sex, and Crime: Adolescent Romantic Relationships and Offending," *American Sociological Review* 73 (2008): 944–969.

57. Centers for Disease Control and Prevention, "Marriage and Divorce," www.cdc.gov/nchs/fastats/marriage-divorce.htm.

58. Matthew Larson and Gary Sweeten, "Breaking Up Is Hard to Do: Romantic Dissolution, Offending, and Substance Use During the Transition to Adulthood," *Criminology* 50 (2012): 605–636.

59. Nicole M. Schmidt, Giza Lopes, Marvin D. Krohn, and Alan J. Lizotte "Getting Caught and Getting Hitched: An Assessment of the Relationship Between Police Intervention, Life Chances, and Romantic Unions," *Justice Quarterly*, first published online January 3, 2014.

60. Torkild Hovde Lyngstad and Torbjørn Skardhamar, "Changes in Criminal Offending Around the Time of Marriage," *Journal of Research in Crime and Delinquency* 50 (2013): 608–615.

61. Bianca Bersani and Elaine Eggleston Doherty, "When the Ties that Bind Unwind: Examining the Enduring and Situational Processes of Change Behind the Marriage Effect," *Criminology* 51 (2013): 399–433.

62. Rand Conger, "Long-Term Consequences of Economic Hardship on Romantic Relationships," Center for Poverty Research, University of California, Davis, poverty.ucdavis.edu/research-paper/long-term-consequences-economic-hardship-romantic-relationships.

63. Torbjørn Skardhamar and Jukka Savolainen, "Changes in Criminal Offending Around the Time of Job Entry: A Study of Employment and Desistance," *Criminology* 52 (2014): 263–291.

64. Ronald L. Simons and Callie Harbin Burt, "Learning to Be Bad: Adverse Social Conditions, Social Schemas, and Crime," *Criminology* 49 (2011): 553–598.

65. Ronald L. Simons, Callie H. Burt, Ashley B. Barr, Man-Kit Lei, and Eric A. Stewart, "Incorporating Routine Activities, Activity Spaces, and Situational Definitions into the Social Schematic Theory of Crime," *Criminology* 52 (2014): 655–687.

66. James Q. Wilson and Richard Herrnstein, *Crime and Human Nature* (New York: Simon and Schuster, 1985).

67. David Rowe, D. Wayne Osgood, and W. Alan Nicewander, "A Latent Trait Approach to Unifying Criminal Careers," *Criminology* 28 (1990): 237–270.

68. Lee Ellis, "Neurohormonal Bases of Varying Tendencies to Learn Delinquent and Criminal Behavior," in *Behavioral Approaches to Crime and Criminality*, ed. E. Morris and C. Braukmann (New York: Plenum, 1988), pp. 499–518.

69. David Rowe, Alexander Vazsonyi, and Daniel Flannery, "Sex Differences in Crime: Do Means and Within-Sex Variation Have Similar Causes?" *Journal of Research in Crime and Criminality* 32 (1995): 84–100.

70. Wilson and Herrnstein, *Crime and Human Nature*.

71. Ibid., p. 44.

72. Ibid., p. 171.

73. Michael Gottfredson and Travis Hirschi, *A General Theory of Crime* (Stanford, CA: Stanford University Press, 1990).

74. Ibid., p. 90.

75. Ibid., p. 89.

76. Alex Piquero and Stephen Tibbetts, "Specifying the Direct and Indirect Effects of Low Self-Control and Situational Factors in Offenders' Decision Making: Toward a More Complete Model of Rational Offending," *Justice Quarterly* 13 (1996): 481–508.

77. David Forde and Leslie Kennedy, "Risky Lifestyles, Routine Activities, and the General Theory of Crime," *Justice Quarterly* 14 (1997): 265–294.

78. Gottfredson and Hirschi, *A General Theory of Crime*, p. 112.

79. Ibid.

80. Jeffrey Bouffard and Stephen Rice, "The Influence of the Social Bond on Self-Control at the Moment of Decision: Testing Hirschi's Redefinition of Self-Control," *American Journal of Criminal Justice* 36 (2011): 138–157.

81. Chris L. Gibson, Christopher J. Sullivan, Shayne Jones, and Alex R. Piquero, "Does It Take a Village? Assessing Neighborhood Influences on Children's Self-Control," *Journal of Research in Crime and Criminality* 47 (2010): 31–62.

82. Ryan Meldrum, Jacob Young, Carter Hay, and Jamie Flexon, "Does Self-Control Influence Maternal Attachment? A Reciprocal Effects Analysis from Early Childhood Through Middle Adolescence," *Journal of Quantitative Criminology*, first published online March 24, 2012; Stacey Nofziger, "The 'Cause' of Low Self-Control: The Influence of Maternal Self-Control," *Journal of Research in Crime and Criminality* 45 (2008): 191–224.

83. Brian Boutwell and Kevin Beaver, "The Intergenerational Transmission of Low Self-Control," *Journal of Research in Crime and Criminality* 47 (2010): 174–209.

84. Farrington, Jolliffe, Loeber, Stouthamer-Loeber, and Kalb, "The Concentration of Offenders in Families, and Family Criminality in the Prediction of Boys' Criminality."

85. Marie Ratchford and Kevin Beaver, "Neuropsychological Deficits, Low Self-Control, and Delinquent Involvement: Toward a Biosocial Explanation of Criminality," *Criminal Justice and Behavior* 36 (2009): 147–162.

86. Kevin Beaver and John Paul Wright, "Evaluating the Effects of Birth Complications on Low-Control in a Sample of Twins," *International Journal of Offender Therapy and Comparative Criminology* 49 (2005): 450–472.

87. Kevin M. Beaver, J. Eagle Shutt, Brian Boutwell, Marie Ratchford, Kathleen Roberts, and J. C. Barnes, "Genetic and Environmental Influences on Levels of Self-Control and Delinquent Peer Affiliation: Results from a Longitudinal Sample of Adolescent Twins," *Criminal Justice and Behavior* 36 (2009): 41–60.

88. Jill Portnoy, Adrian Raine, Frances R. Chen, Dustin Pardini, Rolf Loeber, and J. Richard Jennings, "Heart Rate and Antisocial Behavior: The Mediating Role of Impulsive Sensation Seeking," *Criminology* 52 (2014): 292–311.

89. Gottfredson and Hirschi, *A General Theory of Crime*, p. 27.

90. Michael Reisig, Scott Wolfe, and Travis Pratt, "Low Self-Control and the Religiosity-Crime Relationship," *Criminal Justice and Behavior* 39 (2012): 1172–1191; Michael Reisig, Scott Wolfe, and Kristy Holtfreter, "Legal Cynicism, Legitimacy, and Criminal Offending: The Non-Confounding Effect of Low Self-Control," *Criminal Justice and Behavior* 38 (2011): 1170–1184; Daniel Nagin and Greg Pogarsky, "Time and Punishment: Delayed Consequences and Criminal Behavior," *Journal of Quantitative Criminology* 20 (2004): 295–317.

91. Christopher Sullivan, Jean Marie McGloin, Travis Pratt, and Alex Piquero, "Rethinking the 'Norm' of Offender Generality: Investigating Specialization in the Short-Term," *Criminology* 44 (2006): 199–233; Annemaree

Carroll, Francene Hemingway, Julie Bower, Adrian Ashman, Stephen Houghton, and Kevin Durkin, "Impulsivity in Juvenile Criminality: Differences Among Early-Onset, Late-Onset, and Non-Offenders," *Journal of Youth and Adolescence* 35 (2006): 517–527.

92. Reisig, Wolfe, and Pratt, "Low Self-Control and the Religiosity-Crime Relationship."

93. Kyle Thomas and Jean Marie McGloin, "A Dual-Systems Approach for Understanding Differential Susceptibility to Processes of Peer Influence," *Criminology* 51 (2013): 435–474.

94. Matt DeLisi and Michael Vaughn, "The Gottfredson-Hirschi Critiques Revisited: Reconciling Self-Control Theory, Criminal Careers, and Career Criminals," *International Journal of Offender Therapy and Comparative Criminology* 52 (2008): 520–537.

95. Michael Courey and Paul-Philippe Pare, "A Closer Look at the Relationship Between Low Self-Control and Delinquency: The Effects of Identity Styles," *Crime and Delinquency*, first published online September 16, 2013.

96. Jean-Louis Van Gelder and Reinout E. De Vries, "Traits and States: Integrating Personality and Affect into a Model of Criminal Decision Making," *Criminology* 50 (2012): 637–371.

97. Richard Wiebe, "Reconciling Psychopathy and Low Self-Control," *Justice Quarterly* 20 (2003): 297–336.

98. Alan Feingold, "Gender Differences in Personality: A Meta-Analysis," *Psychological Bulletin* 116 (1994): 429–456.

99. Brent Benda, "Gender Differences in Life-Course Theory of Recidivism: A Survival Analysis," *International Journal of Offender Therapy and Comparative Criminology* 49 (2005): 325–342.

100. Gottfredson and Hirschi, *A General Theory of Crime*, p. 153.

101. Scott Menard, Delbert Elliott, and Sharon Wofford, "Social Control Theories in Developmental Perspective," *Studies on Crime and Criminality Prevention* 2 (1993): 69–87.

102. Dustin Pardini, Jelena Obradovic, and Rolf Loeber, "Interpersonal Callousness, Hyperactivity/Impulsivity, Inattention, and Conduct Problems as Precursors to Criminality Persistence in Boys: A Comparison of Three Grade-Based Cohorts," *Journal of Clinical Child and Adolescent Psychology* 35 (2006): 46–59.

103. Ojmarrh Mitchell and Doris Layton MacKenzie, "The Stability and Resiliency of Self-Control in a Sample of Incarcerated Offenders," *Crime and Criminality* 52 (2006): 432–449.

104. Charles R. Tittle and Harold G. Grasmick, "Delinquent Behavior and Age: A Test of Three Provocative Hypotheses," *Journal of Criminal Law and Criminology* 88 (1997): 309–342.

105. Callie Burt, Gary Sweeten, and Ronald Simons, "Self-Control Through Emerging Adulthood: Instability,

Multidimensionality, and Criminological Significance," *Criminology* 52 (2014): 450–487.

106. Gregory Zimmerman, Ekaterina Botchkovar, Olena Antonaccio, and Lorine Hughes, "Low Self-Control in 'Bad' Neighborhoods: Assessing the Role of Context on the Relationship Between Self-Control and Crime," *Justice Quarterly* 32 (2015): 56–84; Burt, Sweeten, and Simons, "Self-Control Through Emerging Adulthood: Instability, Multidimensionality, and Criminological Significance."

107. Gregory Zimmerman, "Impulsivity, Offending, and the Neighborhood: Investigating the Person–Context Nexus," *Journal of Quantitative Criminology* 26 (2010): 301–332.

108. Chris Gibson, "An Investigation of Neighborhood Disadvantage, Low Self-Control, and Violent Victimization Among Youth" *Youth Violence and Juvenile Justice* 10 (2012): 41–63.

109. Stacy Tzoumakis, Patrick Lussier, Marc Le Blanc, and Garth Davies, "Onset, Offending Trajectories, and Crime Specialization in Violence," *Youth Violence and Juvenile Justice* 11 (2013): 143–164.

110. Amy D'Unger, Kenneth Land, Patricia McCall, and Daniel Nagin, "How Many Latent Classes of Delinquent/Criminal Careers? Results from Mixed Poisson Regression Analyses," *American Journal of Sociology* 103 (1998): 1593–1630.

111. George E. Higgins, Melissa L. Ricketts, Catherine D. Marcum, and Margaret Mahoney, "Primary Socialization Theory: An Exploratory Study of Delinquent Trajectories," *Criminal Justice Studies* 23 (2010): 133–146.

112. Nicole Leeper Piquero and Terrie E. Moffitt, "Can Childhood Factors Predict Workplace Deviance?" *Justice Quarterly*, published online February 21, 2012; Yao Zheng and Harrington Cleveland, "Identifying Gender-Specific Developmental Trajectories of Nonviolent and Violent Delinquency from Adolescence to Young Adulthood," *Journal of Adolescence* 36 (2013): 371–381.

113. Ryan Schroeder and Thomas Mowen, "Parenting Style Transitions and Delinquency," *Youth and Society* 46 (2014): 228–254.

114. Stacy Tzoumakis, Patrick Lussier, Marc Le Blanc, and Garth Davies, "Onset, Offending Trajectories, and Crime Specialization in Violence," *Youth Violence and Juvenile Justice* 11 (2013): 143–164.

115. Bacon, Paternoster, and Brame, "Understanding the Relationship Between Onset Age and Subsequent Offending During Adolescence"; Victor van der Geest, Arjan Blokland, and Catrien Bijleveld, "Delinquent Development in a Sample of High-Risk Youth: Shape, Content, and Predictors of Delinquent Trajectories from Age 12 to 32," *Journal of Research in Crime and Criminality* 46 (2009): 111–143.

116. Wesley Jennings and Jennifer Reingle, "On the Number and Shape of Developmental/Life-Course Violence, Aggression, and Delinquency Trajectories:

A State-of-the-Art Review," *Journal of Criminal Justice* 40 (2012): 472–489.

117. Alex Piquero, Robert Brame, Paul Mazerolle, and Rudy Haapanen, "Crime in Emerging Adulthood," *Criminology* 40 (2002): 137–170.

118. Alex Piquero, Delphine Theobald, and David Farrington, "The Overlap Between Offending Trajectories, Criminal Violence, and Intimate Partner Violence," *International Journal of Offender Therapy and Comparative Criminology* 58 (2014): 286–302.

119. D'Unger, Land, McCall, and Nagin, "How Many Latent Classes of Delinquent/Criminal Careers? Results from Mixed Poisson Regression Analyses."

120. Alex R. Piquero, David P. Farrington, Daniel S. Nagin, and Terrie E. Moffitt, "Trajectories of Offending and Their Relation to Life Failure in Late Middle Age: Findings from the Cambridge Study in Delinquent Development," *Journal of Research in Crime and Criminality* 47 (2010): 151–173.

121. Alex Piquero, Wesley Jennings, and David Farrington, "The Monetary Costs of Crime to Middle Adulthood: Findings from the Cambridge Study in Delinquent Development," *Journal of Research in Crime and Delinquency* 50 (2013): 53–74.

122. Margit Wiesner and Ranier Silbereisen, "Trajectories of Delinquent Behaviour in Adolescence and Their Covariates: Relations with Initial and Time-Averaged Factors," *Journal of Adolescence* 26 (2003): 753–771.

123. Donald Lynam, Alex Piquero, and Terrie Moffitt, "Specialization and the Propensity to Violence: Support from Self-Reports but Not Official Records," *Journal of Contemporary Criminal Justice* 20 (2004): 215–228.

124. Jennifer Reingle, Wesley Jennings, and Mildred Maldonado-Molina, "Risk and Protective Factors for Trajectories of Violent Criminality Among a Nationally Representative Sample of Early Adolescents," *Youth Violence and Juvenile Justice*, published online February 16, 2012.

125. Georgia Zara and David Farrington, "Childhood and Adolescent Predictors of Late Onset Criminal Careers," *Journal of Youth and Adolescence* 38 (2009): 287–300.

126. Rolf Loeber, Phen Wung, Kate Keenan, Bruce Giroux, Magda Stouthamer-Loeber, Welmoet Van Kammen, and Barbara Maughan, "Developmental Pathways in Disruptive Behavior," *Development and Psychopathology* 23 (1993): 12–48.

127. Alex Piquero and Timothy Brezina, "Testing Moffitt's Account of Adolescent-Limited Criminality," *Criminology* 39 (2001): 353–370.

128. Terrie Moffitt, "Adolescence-Limited and Life-Course Persistent Antisocial Behavior: A Developmental Taxonomy," *Psychological Review* 100 (1993): 674–701.

129. Terrie Moffitt, "Natural Histories of Criminality," in *Cross-National Longitudinal Research on Human Development and Criminal Behavior*, ed. Elmar Weitekamp and Hans-Jurgen Kerner (Dordrecht, Netherlands: Kluwer, 1994), pp. 3–65.

130. J. C. Barnes, Kevin Beaver, and Brian Boutwell, "Examining the Genetic Underpinnings to Moffitt's Developmental Taxonomy: A Behavioral Genetic Analysis," *Criminology* 49 (2011): 923–954.

131. Andrea Donker, Wilma Smeenk, Peter van der Laan, and Frank Verhulst, "Individual Stability of Antisocial Behavior from Childhood to Adulthood: Testing the Stability Postulate of Moffitt's Developmental Theory," *Criminology* 41 (2003): 593–609.

132. Robert Vermeiren, "Psychopathology and Criminality in Adolescents: A Descriptive and Developmental Perspective," *Clinical Psychology Review* 23 (2003): 277–318; Paul Mazerolle, Robert Brame, Ray Paternoster, Alex Piquero, and Charles Dean, "Onset Age, Persistence, and Offending Versatility: Comparisons Across Sex," *Criminology* 38 (2000): 1143–1172.

133. Margit Wiesner, Deborah Capaldi, and Hyoun Kim, "General versus Specific Predictors of Male Arrest Trajectories: A Test of the Moffitt and Patterson Theories," *Journal of Youth and Adolescence* 42 (2012): 217–228.

134. Adrian Raine, Rolf Loeber, Magda Stouthamer-Loeber, Terrie Moffitt, Avshalom Caspi, and Don Lynam, "Neurocognitive Impairments in Boys on the Life-Course Persistent Antisocial Path," *Journal of Abnormal Psychology* 114 (2005): 38–49.

135. Per-Olof Wikstrom and Rolf Loeber, "Do Disadvantaged Neighborhoods Cause Well-Adjusted Children to Become Adolescent Delinquents? A Study of Male Juvenile Serious Offending, Individual Risk and Protective Factors, and Neighborhood Context," *Criminology* 38 (2000): 1109–1142.

136. Nicole Buck, Frank Verhulst, Hjalmar van Marle, and Jan van der Ende, "Childhood Psychopathology Predicts Adolescence-Onset Offending: A Longitudinal Study," *Crime and Criminality*, first published online July 22, 2009.

137. Dawn Jeglum Bartusch, Donald Lynam, Terrie Moffitt, and Phil Silva, "Is Age Important? Testing a General versus a Developmental Theory of Antisocial Behavior," *Criminology* 35 (1997): 13–48; Daniel Nagin and Richard Tremblay, "What Has Been Learned from Group-Based Trajectory Modeling? Examples from Physical Aggression and Other Problem Behaviors," *Annals of the American Academy of Political and Social Science* 602 (2005): 82–117.

138. Selma Salihovic, Metin Özdemir, and Margaret Kerr, "Trajectories of Adolescent Psychopathic Traits," *Journal of Psychopathology and Behavioral Assessment* 36 (2014): 47–59.

139. Josanne van Dongen, Nicole Buck, and Hjalmar van Marle, "First Offenders with Psychosis: Justification of a Third Type Within the Early/Late Start Offender Typology," *Crime and Delinquency* 60 (2014): 126–142.

140. Terrie Moffitt, "A Review of Research on the Taxonomy of Life-Course Persistent versus Adolescence-Limited Antisocial Behavior," in *Taking Stock: The Status*

*of Criminological Theory*, vol. 15, ed. F. T. Cullen, J. P. Wright, and K. R. Blevins (New Brunswick, NJ: Transaction Publications, 2006), pp. 277–311.

**141.** David Farrington, "Key Results from the First Forty Years of the Cambridge Study in Delinquent Development," in *Taking Stock of Criminality: An Overview of Findings from Contemporary Longitudinal Studies*, ed. Terence Thornberry and Marvin Krohn (New York: Kluwer, 2002), pp. 137–185.

**142.** Barnes, Beaver, and Boutwell, "Examining the Genetic Underpinnings to Moffitt's Developmental Taxonomy."

**143.** Xiaojin Chen and Michele Adams, "Are Teen Criminality Abstainers Social Introverts? A Test of Moffitt's Theory," *Journal of Research in Crime and Criminality* 47 (2010): 439–468.

**144.** Jennifer Gatewood Owens and Lee Ann Slocum, "Abstainers in Adolescence and Adulthood: Exploring the Correlates of Abstention Using Moffitt's Developmental Taxonomy" *Crime and Criminality*, published online February 7, 2012.

**145.** Heather Lonczk, Robert Abbott, J. David Hawkins, Rick Kosterman, and Richard Catalano, "Effects of the Seattle Social Development Project on Sexual Behavior, Pregnancy, Birth, and Sexually Transmitted Disease Outcomes by Age 21 Years," *Archive of Pediatrics and Adolescent Medicine* 156 (2002): 438–447.

**146.** Kathleen Bodisch Lynch, Susan Rose Geller, and Melinda G. Schmidt, "Multi-Year Evaluation of the Effectiveness of a Resilience-Based Prevention Program for Young Children," *Journal of Primary Prevention* 24 (2004): 335–353.

**147.** This section leans on Thomas Tatchell, Phillip Waite, Renny Tatchell, Lynne Durrant, and Dale Bond, "Substance Abuse Prevention in Sixth Grade: The Effect of a Prevention Program on Adolescents' Risk and Protective Factors," *American Journal of Health Studies* 19 (2004): 54–61.

**148.** Nancy Tobler and Howard Stratton, "Effectiveness of School Based Drug Prevention Programs: A Meta-Analysis of the Research," *Journal of Primary Prevention* 18 (1997): 71–128.

**149.** Alex Mason, Rick Kosterman, J. David Hawkins, Kevin P. Haggerty, and Richard L. Spoth, "Reducing Adolescents' Growth in Substance Use and Criminality: Randomized Trial Effects of a Parent-Training Prevention Intervention," *Prevention Science* 4 (2003): 203–212.

## Learning Objectives

**LO1** Differentiate among the various causes of violent crime.

**LO2** Define rape and be familiar with why men commit rape.

**LO3** Discuss the issues involving rape and the law.

**LO4** Analyze the different types of murder.

**LO5** Explain the nature and patterns of robbery.

**LO6** Discuss newly emerging forms of violence, such as stalking, hate crimes, and workplace violence.

Kevin Liles/UPI/Landov

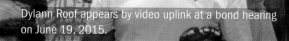

Attendees at a vigil for the nine people killed inside Emanuel A.M.E. Church sing "We Shall Overcome"

Dylann Roof appears by video uplink at a bond hearing on June 19, 2015.

# Chapter Outline

## FACT OR FICTION?

▶ Rape is essentially a sex crime.

▶ You can't be convicted of murder unless you personally and intentionally kill someone.

On the evening of June 17, 2015, 21-year-old Dylann Roof entered the Emanuel African Methodist Episcopal Church in downtown Charleston, South Carolina, spent an hour in Bible study with the parishioners, and then opened fire. Nine people were shot and killed, including the senior pastor, state senator Clementa C. Pinckney; a tenth person was shot and survived. Police arrested Roof in Shelby, North Carolina, the morning after the attack.

Roof's website gave hints as to why he chose the Emanuel Church for his rage-filled slaughter. In a long, hate-filled screed, the 21-year-old claimed that the shooting of Trayvon Martin had prompted him to research what he called "black on White crime. He wrote, "At this moment I realized that something was very wrong. How could the news be blowing up the Trayvon Martin case while hundreds of these black on White murders got ignored?" His online manifesto concluded:

> I have no choice. I am not in the position to, alone, go into the ghetto and fight. I chose Charleston because it is most historic city in my state, and at one time had the highest ratio of blacks to Whites in the country. We have no skinheads, no real KKK, no one doing anything but talking on the internet. Well someone has to have the bravery to take it to the real world, and I guess that has to be me.

His website, called "The Last Rhodesian," contains photos of him wearing a jacket with the flags of apartheid-era South Africa and Rhodesia. Other photos show a .45-caliber Glock pistol; Roof taking aim with the gun, and posing in front of a sign that says, "Sacred burial site. Our African ancestors" as well as outside South Carolina's ▶

Museum and Library of Confederate History; and Roof standing on a burning an American flag.[1] In the aftermath of his crime, South Carolina passed legislation ordering the removal of the Confederate battle flag from the state capitol building. Protesters argued that the flag was a symbol of racism and white supremacy that shouldn't remain on the capitol grounds after the Charleston massacre. ■

**expressive violence**
Violence that is designed not for profit or gain but to vent rage, anger, or frustration.

**instrumental violence**
Violence used in a rational, controlled, and purposeful fashion; for example, an attempt to improve the financial or social position of the criminal.

**LO1** Differentiate among the various causes of violent crime.

This terrible case reminds us that violence and violent acts are part of the human condition. Some violent acts, such as Roof's deadly outburst, are deemed **expressive violence**, acts that vent rage, anger, frustration, or in his case hate and racial animus. Some acts are called **instrumental violence**, designed to improve the financial or social position of the criminal—for example, through an armed robbery or murder for hire.

This chapter explores the concept of violence in some depth. It first reviews some of the possible causes of violent crime and the various types of interpersonal violence, such as rape, homicide, assault, and robbery. It then addresses some types of interpersonal violence, such as stalking and workplace violence, that have more recently developed in contemporary society.

# Causes of Violence

What sets off a violent person such as Dylann Roof? Criminologists have a variety of views on this subject. Some believe that violence is a function of human traits and makeup. Others point to improper socialization and upbringing. Violent behavior may be culturally determined and relate to destructive social values. This section explores a number of the suspected causes of individual and group violence.

## Personal Traits

Research has shown that a significant number of people involved in violent episodes may be suffering from mental abnormalities.[2] Young people convicted of murder have been shown to suffer signs of neurological impairment such as abnormal electroencephalograms (EEGs), multiple psychomotor impairments, and severe seizures; low intelligence as measured on standard IQ tests; psychotic close relatives; psychotic symptoms such as paranoia, illogical thinking, hallucinations; mental impairment and intellectual dysfunction; and animal cruelty.[3] Other elements of personality associated with violence include depression, impulsivity, aggression, dishonesty, pathological lying, lack of remorse, borderline personality syndrome, and psychopathology.[4] Aggressive men have been found to have a long history of torturing and killing animals.[5] Animal cruelty has been associated with a number of psychiatric disorders, including antisocial personality disorder.[6]

Is there is a connection between psychological instability and/or brain structure and violence? One recent effort to test the linkage between violence and mental process used a magnetic resonance imaging device (MRI) to assess brain function in male domestic batterers and compared the results with a matched sample of non-batterers. The brain scans indicated that men who engaged in domestic violence had distinctive brain structures that made them hypersensitive to threat stimuli in a variety of regions of the brain. Hypersensitive men are hard-wired to respond with violence to even mild provocations; they have a neurobiological predisposition that makes them prone to spouse abuse.[7]

## Child Abuse and Neglect

A number of research studies have found that children who were diagnosed as abused later engage in violent behaviors at a rate significantly greater than that of children who were not abused.[8] This view is most closely identified with criminologist Cathy Spatz Widom and her concept of the **cycle of violence**. In a series of research studies, Widom found that physical abuse by parents or caregivers is a direct cause of subsequent violent behavior among youth. Kids who were abused are then likely to grow up to be abusers themselves, creating a never-ending cycle of abuse and violence.[9]

The abuse–violence link can take different forms. Some violent offenders have long histories of abuse and neglect and this condition is a direct conduit to their personal involvement in violence. Others develop posttraumatic stress disorder (PTSD) in the aftermath of their abuse; their subsequent violence can be linked to the emotional upheaval brought on by their history of personal traumas. While these linkages are powerful predictors of violence, there are other groups of violent offenders who did not experience abuse or PTSD and still others who develop PTSD as a consequence of their violent acts. Yet, for the most part, the abuse–violence link is quite powerful.[10]

Widom's view is that people who suffer abuse in childhood and adolescence are more likely to get involved in violent behavior as teens and adults. They are significantly more likely to be arrested for violent crime sometime during their life course. Of course, not all abused children become violent criminals. Many do not, and many violent youths come from what appear to be model homes.[11] Widom herself finds that the majority of both abused and nonabused kids do not engage in antisocial behavior, so more research is needed to clarify this very important association.

## Human Instinct

Some anthropologists trace the roots of violence back to our prehistory, when our ancestors lived in social groups and fought for dominance. The earliest humans would not hesitate to retaliate violently against aggressors, and it was common for family, tribe, or clan members to protect one another if they were attacked.[12] According to Harvard psychologist Steven Pinker, violence declined during the period of human evolution when our hunter-gatherer ancestors began to settle into agricultural civilizations, which he calls the *pacification process*.[13]

The fact that our ancient ancestors were so violent seems to suggest that violence is instinctual and part of the human condition. Sigmund Freud believed that human aggression and violence are produced by instinctual drives.[14] Freud maintained that humans possess two opposing instinctual drives that interact to control behavior: **eros**, the life instinct, which drives people toward self-fulfillment and enjoyment; and **thanatos**, the death instinct, which impels toward self-destruction. Thanatos can be expressed externally (as violence and sadism) or internally (as suicide, alcoholism, or other self-destructive habits). Because aggression is instinctual, Freud saw little hope for its treatment.

A number of biologists and anthropologists have also speculated that instinctual violence-promoting traits may be common in the human species. One view is that aggression and violence are the result of instincts inborn in all animals, humans among them.[15] Unlike other animals, however, humans lack the inhibition against killing members of their own species, which protects animals from self-extinction, and are capable of killing their own kind in war or as a result of interpersonal conflicts.

## Exposure to Violence

Kids who are constantly exposed to violence at home, at school, or in the environment may adopt violent methods themselves.[16] Exposure to violence can also occur at the neighborhood level when people are forced to live in violent, dangerous neighborhoods.[17] Even a single exposure to firearm violence doubles the chance that a young person will later engage in violent behavior.[18] Children living in areas marked by extreme violence may in time become desensitized to the persistent neighborhood brutality and conflict they witness, eventually succumbing to violent behaviors themselves.[19] And not surprisingly, those children who are exposed to violence in

**cycle of violence**
The phenomenon in which abused children grow up to be abusers themselves.

**eros**
The life instinct, which drives people toward self-fulfillment and enjoyment.

**thanatos**
The death instinct, which impels people toward self-destruction.

the home and also live in neighborhoods with high violence rates are the ones most likely to engage in violent crime themselves.[20]

## Substance Abuse

On a micro level, substance abusers have higher rates of violence than nonabusers; on a macro level, neighborhoods with high levels of drug and alcohol usage have higher than average violence rates.[21]

Substance abuse influences violence in three ways:[22]

**psychopharmacological relationship**
In such a relationship, violence is the direct consequence of ingesting mood-altering substances.

**economic compulsive behavior**
Violence committed by drug users to support their habit.

**systemic link**
A link between drugs and violence that occurs when drug dealers turn violent in their competition with rival gangs.

**subculture of violence**
A segment of society in which violence has become legitimized by the custom and norms of that group.

- A **psychopharmacological relationship** may be the direct consequence of ingesting mood-altering substances. Binge drinking, for example, has been closely associated with violent crime rates.[23] Heavy drinking reduces cognitive ability, information-processing skills, and the ability to process and react to verbal and nonverbal behavior. As a result, miscommunication becomes more likely, and the capacity for rational dialogue is compromised.[24] It is not surprising that males involved in sexual assaults often claim that they were drinking and misunderstood their victim's intentions.[25]
- Drug ingestion may also cause **economic compulsive behavior**, in which drug users resort to violence to support their habit. Studies conducted in the United States and Europe show that addicts commit hundreds of crimes each year.[26]
- A **systemic link** occurs as violence escalates when drug-dealing gangs flex their muscle to dominate territory and drive out rivals. Studies of gangs that sell drugs show that their violent activities may result in a significant proportion of all urban homicides.[27] Drug dealers/traders also are more likely to carry and use firearms in their daily activities. When Richard Felson and Luke Bonkiewicz studied the drug–violence nexus, they found relatively high levels of gun possession among traffickers who handle stashes of moderately large market value, who have central roles in the trade, and who are members of drug organizations.[28]

## Firearm Availability

Although firearm availability alone does not cause violence, it may be a facilitating factor. A petty argument can escalate into a fatal encounter if one party has a handgun. The nation has also been rocked by the recent slew of well-publicized school shootings. Research indicates that a significant number of kids routinely carry guns to school; those who have been the victims of crime themselves and those who hang with peers who carry weapons are most likely to bring guns to school.[29]

The Uniform Crime Report (UCR) indicates that about 70 percent of all murders, 40 percent of all robberies, and 20 percent of aggravated assaults involve firearms.[30] Handguns kill two-thirds of all police who die in the line of duty.[31] The presence of firearms in the home also significantly increases the risk of suicide among adolescents, regardless of how carefully the guns are secured or stored.[32]

## Cultural Values

In urban areas, neighborhoods that experience violence seem to cluster together.[33] To explain this phenomenon, criminologists Marvin Wolfgang and Franco Ferracuti formulated the famous concept that some areas are characterized by an independent **subculture of violence**.[34]

The subculture's norms are separate from society's central, dominant value system. In this subculture, a potent theme of violence influences lifestyles, the socialization process, and interpersonal relationships. Even though the members of the subculture share some of the dominant culture's values, they expect that violence will be used to solve social conflicts and dilemmas.

In some cultural subgroups, then, violence has become legitimized by custom and norms. It is considered appropriate behavior within culturally defined conflict situations in which an individual who has been offended by a negative outcome in

# Policies and Issues in Criminology

## HONOR KILLING

In 2014, a young newlywed couple, Sajjad Ahmed, 26, and Muawia Bibi, 18, were killed by the bride's family in northeastern Pakistan because they did not approve of the marriage. The bride's father and uncles lured the couple back to the village of Satrah in the Punjab province, where the pair were tied up and decapitated. The family members turned themselves in to police, maintaining that their brutal attack was a matter of honor.

Honor killing and honor crime involve violence against women and girls, including such acts as beating, battering, or killing, by a family member or relative. They are most common in traditional societies in the Middle East, Southwest Asia, India, China, and Latin America but are now being exported to Europe and North America. The attacks are provoked by the belief or perception that an individual's or family's honor has been threatened because of the actual or perceived sexual misconduct of the female. The United Nations now estimates that 5,000 of these honor killings occur each year, more than 800 in Pakistan alone, and they are increasing rapidly in other areas such as Palestinian territories. Most of the women were killed by husbands or brothers. "Illicit relations" was cited as a reason most often, and demanding to marry a partner of their choice was noted in more than 200 cases.

The killings often seem illogical to an outsider. Even when a woman is raped she may be accused of being the sexual aggressor who must be punished. Honor killing/crime is based on the shame that a loss of control of the woman or girl brings to the family and to the male heads of the family.

According to criminologist Linda Williams, men consider honor killings culturally necessary because any suspicion of sexual activity or suspicion that a girl or a woman is unchaste is enough to raise questions about the family's honor. Strict control of women and girls within the home and outside the home is justified. Women are restricted in their activities in the community, religion, and politics. These institutions, in turn, support the control of females. Williams believes that honor killing is designed for maintaining male dominance. Submissiveness may be seen as a sign of sexual purity, and a woman's or girl's attempts to assert her rights is a violation of the family's honor that needs to be redressed. Rules of honor and threats against females who violate such rules reinforce the control of women and have a powerful impact on their lives. Honor killings/crimes serve to keep women and girls from "stepping out of line." The manner in which such behaviors silence women and kill their spirit has led some to label honor killings/crimes more broadly as "femicide."

### Critical Thinking

While we may scoff at the idea of honor killings, are there elements of American culture and life that you consider harmful to women yet are still tolerated? What can be done to change them?

**Sources:** Shelby Lin Erdman, "Pakistani Newlyweds Decapitated by Bride's Family in Honor Killing," CNN, June 29, 2014, www.cnn.com/2014/06/28/world/asia/pakistan-honor-murders/; Anne-Marie O'Connor, "Honor Killings Rise in Palestinian Territories, Sparking Backlash," *Washington Post*, March 3, 2014, www.washingtonpost.com/world/middle_east/honor-killings-rise-in-palestinian-territories-sparking-backlash/2014/03/02/1392d144-940c-11e3-9e13-770265cf4962_story.html; Julia Dahl, "'Honor Killing' Under Growing Scrutiny in the U.S.," CBS News, April 5, 2012, www.cbsnews.com/news/honor-killing-under-growing-scrutiny-in-the-us/; Linda M. Williams, "Honor Killings," in *Encyclopedia of Interpersonal Violence*, ed. Claire M. Renzetti and Jeffrey I. Edelson (Thousand Oaks, CA: Sage Publications, 2007). (All URLs accessed 2015.)

a dispute seeks reparations through violent means ("disputatiousness").[35] That is, in some neighborhoods residents resolve interpersonal conflicts informally—without calling the police—even if it means injuring or killing their opponent; neighbors understand and support violent methods of retaliation.[36] Because police and other agencies of formal social control are viewed as weak and devalued, understaffed, and/or corrupt, people are willing to take matters into their own hands and commit what is referred to as "cultural retaliatory homicide."[37]

**GANG VIOLENCE** Involvement with gangs is another precursor of increased violent activity, though it can be debated whether extremely violent youth join gangs or kids who join gangs become desensitized to violence. One indication can be found in

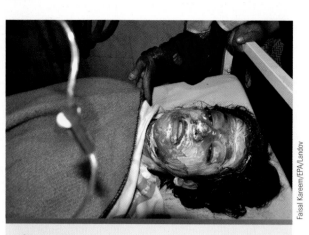

Some cultures may promote violence, especially if they brand certain behaviors as forbidden and immoral. Here, teenage gang-rape victim Amina is shown receiving medical treatment at a hospital in Multan, Pakistan, after setting herself on fire to protest the release of one of her alleged rapists from police custody. She died the next day. Violence against women is a very big issue in Pakistan, where 90 percent of women experience domestic abuse and thousands of women are killed in the name of honor each year—behaviors that reflect Pakistan's patriarchal culture.

research conducted by Chris Melde and Finn-Aage Esbensen, who found that active gang members experienced a significant increase in violent behavior, which declines significantly after leaving the gang, a finding that suggests that gang involvement is in fact a cause of violence.[38]

The association between gang membership and violence has a number of roots. It can result from drug trafficking activities and turf protection, but it may also stem from personal vendettas and a perceived need for self-protection.[39] Once a gang shooting occurs, there is a significant likelihood that violent retaliation of some sort will occur.[40]

## National Values

Some nations—including Colombia, Brazil, Sri Lanka, Angola, Uganda, and the Philippines—have relatively high violence rates, while others such as Japan are relatively nonviolent. There are two possible explanations for this discrepancy. One is that high-violence nations embrace value structures that support violence, while others that have a strong communitarian spirit and an emphasis on forgiveness and restorative justice have low violence rates.[41]

The other explanation is that nations with high violence rates also have negative structural factors such as a high level of poverty, income inequality, illiteracy, and alcohol consumption level, and it is the presence of these components, rather than a regional culture of violence, that produces high crime rates.[42]

The accompanying Policies and Issues in Criminology feature discusses one type of culturally based violent crime: the honor killing of women.

**LO2** Define rape and be familiar with why men commit rape.

**rape**
Under common law, the carnal knowledge of a female forcibly and against her will. Contemporary statues are gender neutral ("a person") and can include various acts of sexual penetration.

# Rape

The common-law definition of **rape** (from the Latin *rapere*, "to take by force") is "the carnal knowledge of a female forcibly and against her will."[43] It is one of the most loathed, misunderstood, and frightening crimes. Under traditional common-law definitions, rape involves nonconsensual sexual intercourse inflicted on a female by a male. There are, of course, other forms of sexual assault, including male-on-male and female-on-male sexual assaults (some studies estimate that up to 25 percent of males have been the target of unwanted sexual advances by women), but these are not considered here within the traditional concept of rape.[44] However, recognizing these other forms of sexual assault, states have now revised their rape statutes to make them gender neutral. As you may recall (Chapter 2), the FBI has revised its definition of rape to include crimes involving other forms of sexual assault, including oral and anal penetration. Regardless of what form it takes, rape can have devastating long-term effects on the victim's emotional and physical well-being.[45]

Rape was often viewed as a sexual offense in the traditional criminological literature. It was presented as a crime that involved overwhelming lust, driving a man to force his attentions on a woman. Criminologists now consider rape a violent, coercive act of aggression, not a forceful expression of sexuality. Take for instance the use of rape in war crimes, a practice that became routine during the civil war in the former Yugoslavia; human rights groups have estimated that more than 30,000 Bosnian women and young girls were sexually abused during the fighting.[46] Though shocking, the war crimes discovered in Bosnia have not deterred conquering armies from using rape as a weapon. Pro-government militias in the Darfur region of Sudan were accused of using rape and other forms of sexual violence "as a weapon of war" to humiliate African women and girls as well as the rebels fighting the Sudanese government in Khartoum.[47] More recently, the Boko Haram terror group in Nigeria has

Faisal Kareem/EPA/Landov

made kidnapping and sexual assaults of young women a centerpiece of its campaign to unseat the government and replace it with one based on their religious beliefs.[48] In May 2014, group members kidnapped 276 high school girls with the intent of selling them into sexual slavery, an act that prompted worldwide outrage.[49]

## Incidence of Rape

According to the most recent UCR data, about 80,000 rapes or attempted rapes are now being reported each year—a rate of about 25 per 100,000 females.[50] As is true of other violent crimes, the rape rate has been in a decade-long decline, and current totals are significantly below 1992 levels, when more than 100,000 rapes were reported to police; reported rape has declined about 16 percent in the past decade.

Rape is a warm-weather crime—most incidents occur during July and August, with the lowest rates occurring during December, January, and February. Population density also influences the rape rate. Metropolitan areas today have rape rates significantly higher than rural areas; nonetheless, urban areas have experienced a much greater drop in rape reports than rural areas. The police make arrests in about 40 percent of all reported rape offenses. The racial and age pattern of rape arrests has been fairly consistent for some time. Of the offenders arrested, about 45 percent were under 25 years of age, and about two-thirds were Caucasian.

These data must be interpreted with caution. According to the National Crime Victimization Survey (NCVS), approximately 300,000 rapes and sexual assaults take place annually.[51] There is little question, then, that rape may be significantly underreported to police and that there are significantly more rape victims than the official data suggest.[52] Some research efforts have found that less than 20 percent of all rapes are reported to police.[53]

Why the significant discrepancy between incidents and reporting? Many victims of rape and sexual assault fail to report the crime to the police because they are embarrassed, think it a personal matter, believe nothing can be done, or blame themselves. Some may even question whether they have really been raped; research indicates that victims may not label their experience as a "real" rape when the assault involved an acquaintance or boyfriend, if they were severely impaired by alcohol or drugs, or if the act involved oral or digital sex.[54] Some victims refuse to report rape because they have histories of excessive drinking and sexual promiscuity, convincing themselves that their intemperate and/or immoderate behavior contributed to their victimization. A Bureau of Justice Statistics national survey found that about a quarter of rape victims who did not report to police believed the incident was a personal matter, and one in five stated a fear of reprisal. Others felt the incident was just not important enough.[55] But whether or not victims acknowledge that their attack is a "real" rape, the experience can have shattering psychological effects that last long after the attack itself is over.[56]

## Types of Rapists

Some rapes are planned, whereas others are spontaneous; some focus on a particular victim, whereas others occur almost as an afterthought during the commission of another crime, such as a burglary. Some rapists commit a single crime, whereas others are multiple offenders; some attack alone, and others engage in group or gang rapes. Because there is no single type of rape or rapist, criminologists have attempted to define and categorize the vast variety of rape situations.

Criminologists now recognize that there are numerous motivations for rape—and, consequently, various types of rapists. One of the best-known attempts to classify the personalities of rapists was that of A. Nicholas Groth, an expert on classifying and treating sex offenders. According to Groth, every rape encounter contains at least one of three elements: anger, power, or sadism.[57] Consequently, rapists can be classified according to one of the three dimensions described in Exhibit 10.1. In treating rape offenders, Groth found that about 55 percent represented the power type, about 40 percent the anger type, and about 5 percent the sadistic type. Groth's major contribution has been his recognition that rape is generally a crime of violence, not

**FACT OR FICTION?**

Rape is essentially a sex crime.

**FICTION** Most criminologists consider rape an aggressive act in which sex is merely a means of inflicting violence and intimidation.

# Exhibit 10.1　Varieties of Forcible Rape

- *Anger rape* occurs when sexuality becomes a means of expressing and discharging pent-up anger and rage. The rapist uses far more brutality than would have been necessary if his real objective had been simply to have sex with his victim. His aim is to hurt his victim as much as possible; the sexual aspect of rape may be an afterthought. Often the anger rapist acts on the spur of the moment after an upsetting incident has caused him conflict, irritation, or aggravation. Surprisingly, anger rapes are less psychologically traumatic for the victim than might be expected. Because a woman is usually physically beaten during an anger rape, she is more likely to receive sympathy from her peers, relatives, and the justice system and consequently be immune from any suggestion that she complied with the attack.

- *Power rape* involves an attacker who does not want to harm his victim as much as he wants to possess her sexually. His goal is sexual conquest, and he uses only the amount of force necessary to achieve his objective. The power rapist wants to be in control, to be able to dominate women and have them at his mercy. Yet it is not sexual gratification that drives the power rapist; in fact, he

often has a consenting relationship with his wife or girlfriend. Rape is instead a way of putting personal insecurities to rest, asserting heterosexuality, and preserving a sense of manhood. The power rapist's victim is usually a woman equal in age to or younger than the rapist. The lack of physical violence may reduce the support given the victim by family and friends. Therefore, the victim's personal guilt over her rape experience is increased—perhaps, she thinks, she could have done something to get away.

- *Sadistic rape* involves both sexuality and aggression. The sadistic rapist is bound up in ritual—he may torment his victim, bind her, or torture her. In the rapist's view, victims are usually related to a personal characteristic that he wants to harm or destroy. The rape experience is intensely exciting to the sadist; he gets satisfaction from abusing, degrading, or humiliating his captive. This type of rape is particularly traumatic for the victim. Victims of such crimes need psychiatric care long after their physical wounds have healed.

**Source:** A. Nicholas Groth and Jean Birnbaum, *Men Who Rape* (New York: Plenum Press, 1979).

a sexual act. In all of these circumstances, rape involves a violent criminal offense in which a predatory criminal chooses to attack a victim.[58]

## Types of Rape

In addition to the variety of types of rapists, there are also different categories of rapes.

**date rape**
A rape that involves people who are in some form of courting relationship.

**DATE RAPE** One disturbing trend involves people who are in some form of courting relationship—this type of attack is known as **date rape**. Some date rapes occur on first dates, others after a relationship has begun developing, and still others after the couple has been involved for some time. In long-term or close relationships, the male partner may feel he has invested so much time and money in his partner that he is owed sexual relations or that sexual intimacy is an expression or acknowledgment that the involvement is progressing.[59]

Date rape was first identified as a significant social problem in the 1980s when Mary Koss conducted surveys and found that a significant number of college-age women had been sexually assaulted by a dating partner; about 27 percent of the respondents had been the victim of rape or attempted rape. However, only about a quarter of the women called what had happened to them "rape"; the majority either blamed themselves or denied they had really been raped.[60]

Koss's research helped identify a social problem that all too long had remained below the radar. Even though the problem has been identified, many victims still fail to report date rape. Some do not view their experience as a "real" rape, which, they believe, involves a strange man "jumping out of the bushes." Other victims are embarrassed and frightened. Many tell their friends about their rape while refusing to let authorities know what happened. Reporting is most common in the most serious cases, such as when a weapon is used; it is less common when drugs or alcohol is involved.[61] This leads to significant underreporting of rape, especially on college campuses, since many incidents involve the victim's voluntary involvement in drinking or substance abuse before the assault occurred.[62] Underreporting of these incidents is important because so many victims who abused substances before the rape suffer PTSD and other disorders and require help and counseling.[63]

The Profiles in Crime feature discusses a recent case of date rape on a high school campus.

**RAPE ON CAMPUS** A great deal of date and acquaintance rape is committed on college campuses. It is quite troubling that research studies indicate that by the start of the second year of school, more than 20 percent of college women had been raped while incapacitated and a similar number had experienced forcible rape sometime in their lives.[64]

The most extensive national survey of sexual assault on college campuses was conducted by the Westat research corporation for the Association of American Universities.[65] The survey involved 150,000 students at 27 universities and found that

> **CONNECTIONS**
>
> Chapter 3 introduced the concept of victim precipitation. The jury in the Labrie case may have concluded the victim precipitated the rape by agreeing to accompany the boy to a darkened room and removing her outer clothing. Is this an instance of blaming the victim?

# PROFILES IN CRIME

## THE ST. PAUL'S SCHOOL RAPE CASE

In 2015, in a case that made national news, 19-year-old Owen Labrie was tried for the rape of a fellow student at the exclusive St. Paul's School in Concord, New Hampshire. Labrie, who was 18 at the time the attack took place, used email to convince the 15-year-old freshman to meet him as part of the "senior salute" ritual in which graduating seniors seduce younger students. She claimed that she had intended merely to kiss or make out with Labrie but then as things got out of hand. She said no to his sexual advances and resisted him as best she could. In the end her resistance was futile and he forced himself on her and engaged in three unwanted sex acts.

Labrie, a popular scholarship student and athlete who was accepted at Harvard, testified that the young woman consented to his advances and that sexual intercourse had not actually taken place. They had exchanged pleasant emails after the assault, evidence of her consent.

The jury found Labrie not guilty of the most serious charge of forcible rape but convicted him of several lesser charges, including endangering the welfare of a child, and using a computer to "seduce, solicit, lure, or entice a child" in order to commit a sexual assault. He was also found guilty of three counts of misdemeanor sexual assault. Why was he found not guilty of the most serious charge even though the jury believed he did have sex with the young woman, who was still a minor? The reason is that under New Hampshire law, an individual can be found guilty of aggravated felonious sexual assault only if the victim clearly indicates that she doesn't "freely consent," or before she has "an adequate chance to flee and/or resist." The jury obviously concluded that Labrie did have sex with the girl, but there was no real proof that she resisted. Also, under New Hampshire law, if a person has penetrative consensual sex with a minor between the ages 13 and 16 but is within four years of that age, they are guilty of *misdemeanor* sexual assault. If the age difference is more than four years, they are guilty of *felony* sexual assault. Since Labrie was 18 and the young woman 15, he could only be convicted of a misdemeanor. On October 29, 2015, Labrie was sentenced to a year in jail and five years probation.

The St. Paul's case illustrates some of the problems associated with bringing rape cases to trial. The young woman testified under oath that she did not consent to sex, but the jury did not believe her story. Despite all we know about sexual assault, the victim is still on trial in rape cases. The unanswered question is: What would she gain by lying? What could possibly motivate someone to bring false charges in this case?

**Sources:** Jess Bidgood, "Owen Labrie of St. Paul's School Not Guilty of Main Rape Charge," *New York Times*, August 28, 2015, www.nytimes.com/2015/08/29/us/st-pauls-school-rape-trial-owen-labrie.html; Andy Rosen and Peter Schworm, "Labrie Acquitted of Felony Rape in St. Paul's School Trial," *Boston Globe*, August 28, 2015 (accessed 2015).

by 2015 campus rape has reached epidemic proportions: nearly a quarter of women reported nonconsensual sexual contact by physical force, threats of physical force, or incapacitation while enrolled at a university. About 12 percent of all students experienced misconduct: the majority were female students (23 percent); however, about 5 percent of male students reported being sexually assaulted. Students identifying themselves as transgender or gay faced an extremely high risk of being sexually assaulted. A significant portion of the incidents involved drugs and alcohol. While the risk of the most serious types of nonconsensual sexual contact, due to physical force or incapacitation, declines from freshman to senior year, the fact remains that about 1 in 10 female students say they have experienced sexual assault involving penetration, by force or incapacitation, sometime during their college experience.

Especially troubling is the underreporting of rape on college campuses, where relatively few victims (less than 20 percent) report the incident to police.[66] One reason may be that many incidents occur in fraternity houses and dorms, and involve the victims' drinking or abusing substances before the assaults occurred. Victims may hold themselves responsible for the attack; they may not believe the incident was a "real rape" because they were at fault.[67] The recent Westat/Association of American Universities survey found that a relatively small percentage (28 percent or less) of even the most serious incidents (e.g., forced penetration) are reported to an organization or agency. More than 50 percent of these victims say they did not report the event because they did not consider it "serious enough." A significant percentage of students say they did not report because they felt "embarrassed, ashamed, or that it would be too emotionally difficult" or ". . . did not think anything would be done about it."

Misplaced guilt may also explain why so many college women suffer PTSD and other disorders soon after they were attacked.[68] And when they do report rape and file a lawsuit against the frat house or university, the defense is to blame the victim: if she had not been drinking and taking risks, the attack would never have occurred.[69]

Another reason for the lack of reporting may be that colleges and universities are notorious for trying to sweep sexual assault incidents under the rug to protect the image of a safe environment for young women. Even such prestigious schools as The Johns Hopkins University have been accused of not disclosing an alleged rape at a fraternity house, leading a group of students to file a complaint with the U.S. Department of Education. Amid the pressure, university president Ronald J. Daniels said that the university would immediately begin an independent review of how the case was handled.[70]

In order to reduce campus rape, California became the first state to enact legislation requiring affirmative consent before a sexual encounter can take place. The law states, "Lack of protest or resistance does not mean consent, nor does silence mean consent. Affirmative consent must be ongoing throughout a sexual activity and can be revoked at any time." This bill removes the requirement that a rape victim prove she or he said "no" and instead requires that the accused prove that the alleged victim said "yes".[71] Lack of protest does not mean agreement; consent can't be given if someone is asleep or incapacitated by drugs or alcohol.

**MARITAL RAPE** Traditionally, a legally married husband could not be charged with raping his wife; this immunity was referred to as the **marital exemption**. However, research indicates that many women are raped each year by their husbands as part of an overall pattern of spousal abuse, and these women deserve the protection of the law. Many spousal rapes are accompanied by brutal, sadistic beatings and have little to do with normal sexual interests.[72] Not surprisingly, the marital exemption has undergone significant revision. In 1980, only three states had laws against marital rape; today every state recognizes marital rape as a crime.[73]

**STATUTORY RAPE** The term **statutory rape** refers to sexual relations between an underage minor female and an adult male. Although the sex is not forced or coerced, the law says that young girls are incapable of giving informed consent, so the act is

**marital exemption**
The formerly accepted tradition that a legally married husband could not be charged with raping his wife.

**statutory rape**
Sexual relations between an underage minor female and an adult male.

legally considered nonconsensual. In most instances, state law cites an age of consent above which there can be no criminal prosecution for consensual sexual relations. The crime typically applies only when the parties' ages are more than three years apart. Those accused of statutory rape can defend themselves by claiming the victim lied about their age or provided false documentation such as a fake driver's license. However, mistake is not an absolute defense and a defendant can still be convicted in some courts even if they were mistaken about the victim's age.

**RAPE BY DECEPTION** Rape by deception occurs when the rapist uses fraud or trickery to convince the victim to engage in sex or impersonates someone with whom the victim has been intimate.[74] In one Massachusetts case, a man was convicted of rape after he allegedly impersonated his brother in order to have sex with his brother's girlfriend in the middle of the night. The conviction was later overturned because Massachusetts law does not recognize that sex by deception can be considered rape.

A few jurisdictions recognize rape by deception. In Tennessee, the legal definition of rape includes "sexual penetration . . . accomplished by fraud"; in Idaho, sex with a woman is defined as rape when because of his "artifice, pretense or concealment," the victim believes him to be "someone other than" who he is.[75] Despite these exceptions, rape by deception is not universally recognized in American criminal law. However, a number of legal scholars believe that sex by deception ought to be defined as rape because "a consent procured through deception is no consent at all."[76] Consequently, some states are now considering adoption of rape-by-deception laws.

## Causes of Rape

What factors predispose some men to commit rape? Criminologists' responses to this question are almost as varied as the crime itself. However, most explanations can be grouped into a few consistent categories.

**EVOLUTIONARY FACTORS** According to the evolutionary psychology view, sexual violence may be instinctual, developed over the ages as a means of perpetuating the species.[77] The evolutionary view is that the sexual urge corresponds to the unconscious need to preserve the species by spreading one's genes as widely as possible. Males who were sexually aggressive had a reproductive edge over their more passive peers. These prehistoric drives remain active in some males who still have a natural sexual drive that encourages them to have intimate relations with as many women as possible. From the evolutionary perspective, it makes sense that women at the peak of their fertility would be preferential targets, and rape studies have documented that younger women are most often victimized by rapists.[78] However, in a civilized society such as ours sexual violence is subject to both social and legal disapproval and punishment so that rape as a reproductive strategy brings with it significant disadvantages.[79]

**MALE SOCIALIZATION** In contrast to the evolutionary biological view, some researchers argue that rape is a function of socialization. Some men have been socialized to be aggressive with women and believe that the use of violence or force is legitimate if their sexual advances are rebuffed ("Women like to play hard to get and expect to be forced to have sex"). Those who have been socialized to believe that "no means yes" are more likely to be sexually aggressive.[80] The use of sexual violence is aggravated if pro-force socialization is reinforced by peers who share similar values.[81]

Diana Russell describes the **virility mystique**—the belief that males must separate their sexual feelings from their need for love, respect, and affection. She believes men are socialized to be the aggressors and expect to be sexually active with many women; consequently, male virginity and sexual inexperience are shameful. Similarly, sexually aggressive women frighten some men and cause them to doubt their own masculinity. Sexual insecurity may lead some men to commit rape to bolster their self-image and masculine identity.[82]

**virility mystique**
The belief that males must separate their sexual feelings from their need for love, respect, and affection.

**CONNECTIONS**

The social learning view of rape will be explored further in Chapter 13 when the issue of pornography and violence is analyzed in greater detail.

**narcissistic personality disorder**
A pattern of traits and behaviors indicating infatuation and fixation with one's self to the exclusion of all others, along with the egotistic and ruthless pursuit of one's own gratification, dominance, and ambition.

**PSYCHOLOGICAL ABNORMALITY** Rapists may suffer from some type of personality disorder or mental illness. Research shows that a significant percentage of incarcerated rapists exhibit psychotic tendencies, and many others have hostile, sadistic feelings toward women.[83] A high proportion of serial rapists and repeat sexual offenders exhibit psychopathic personality structures.[84] There is evidence linking rape proclivity with **narcissistic personality disorder**, a pattern of traits and behaviors that indicate infatuation and fixation with one's self to the exclusion of all others and the egotistic and ruthless pursuit of one's own gratification, dominance, and ambition.[85]

**SOCIAL LEARNING** According to this perspective, men learn to commit rapes in much the same way they learn any other behavior. For example, sexual aggression may be learned through interaction with peers who articulate attitudes supportive of sexual violence.[86] Observing or experiencing sexual violence has also been linked to sexual aggression. Nicholas Groth found that 40 percent of the rapists he studied were sexually victimized as adolescents.[87] Experiencing sexual trauma has been linked with the desire to inflict sexual trauma on others.[88] Watching violent or pornographic films featuring women who are beaten, raped, or tortured has been linked to sexually aggressive behavior in men.[89]

**GENDER CONFLICT VIEW** According to the gender conflict view, as women make progress toward social, political, and economic equality, men fear them as a threat to their long-held dominance.[90] Men react through efforts of formal and informal controls over women. One informal method of social control is to dominate women sexually through the commission of rape. The male-dominated criminal justice system may exert less effort in handling rape cases in an effort to maintain male superiority. Research by Richard Johnson does in fact show that regions with higher levels of progress toward gender equality actually experience higher rates of rape and lower rates of rape case clearances.[91]

**SEXUAL MOTIVATION** Even though criminologists now consider rape a violent act without sexual motivation, there is evidence that at least some rapists have sexual feelings for their victim.[92] NCVS data reveal that rape victims tend to be young and that rapists prefer younger, presumably more attractive victims. Data show an association between the ages of rapists and those of their victims, indicating that men choose rape targets of approximately the same age as their consensual sex partners. And despite the fact that younger criminals are usually the most violent, older rapists tend to harm their victims more than younger rapists. This pattern indicates that older criminals may rape for motives of power and control, whereas younger offenders may be seeking sexual gratification. Victims may, therefore, suffer less harm from severe beatings and humiliation from younger attackers.

**LO3** Discuss the issues involving rape and the law.

## Rape and the Law

On May 14, 2011, Dominique Strauss-Kahn, the distinguished head of the International Monetary Fund and a leading French politician, was arrested in New York City for allegedly raping Nafissatou Diallo, a 32-year-old maid. He claimed the sex was consensual. After a thorough investigation, the case soon began to fall apart. It seems that Diallo had lied on her application for citizenship, and mysterious bank deposits were uncovered that may have been linked to criminal activity. She also admitted that she returned to Strauss-Kahn's room and cleaned it before calling the police![93]

Unlike other crime victims, women may find that their claim of sexual assault is greeted with some skepticism by police and court personnel.[94] They will soon discover that they have to prove they did not engage in consensual sex and then develop remorse afterwards. Research shows that people are more likely to "blame the victim" in a case of sexual assault than they are in other common-law crimes such as armed robbery. Victim blaming is exacerbated if a prior relationship existed or if the victim did not fight back because she was intoxicated—factors that have less impact in other crimes.[95]

However, police and courts are becoming more sensitive to the plight of rape victims and are now just as likely to investigate acquaintance rape as they are **aggravated rape** involving multiple offenders, weapons, and victim injuries. In some jurisdictions, the justice system takes all rape cases seriously and does not ignore those in which victim and attacker have had a prior relationship or those that did not involve serious injury.[96]

**PROVING RAPE** On March 13, 2006, after a performance by two strippers at a private residence, three members of Duke University's men's lacrosse team were accused of raping one of the women who had been hired to entertain the team. Media outlets had a field day with a case involving a young African American victim and her alleged attackers, who were wealthy and white. However, evidence soon emerged that the charges were false, the players falsely accused and wrongfully vilified.[97] In 2014, a *Rolling Stone* article claimed that a University of Virginia student identified only as "Jackie" was gang raped at a frat house. The article made headlines when it described a culture of binge-drinking and casual sex tolerated by a university administration that ignored protocol when students filed sexual assault complaints. A thorough investigation turned up no evidence of a sexual assault or any wrongdoing by the school, suggesting the entire incident was a made-up story.[98]

Stories such as these help make proving guilt in a rape case extremely challenging for prosecutors. Some judges fear that women may charge men with rape because of jealousy, withdrawn marriage proposals, revenge, or pregnancy. There is evidence that juries may consider the race of the victim and offender in their decision making; for example, they may believe victims and convict defendants more often in interracial rapes than when both parties are the same race.[99] Although the law does not recognize it, jurors are sometimes swayed by the insinuation that the rape was victim precipitated; thus, the blame is shifted from rapist to victim. To get a conviction, prosecutors must establish that the act was forced and violent and that no question of voluntary compliance exists. They may be reluctant to prosecute cases where they have questions about the victim's moral character or if they believe the victim's demeanor and attitude will turn off the jury and undermine the chance of conviction.[100]

**CONSENT** It is essential to prove that the attack was forced and that the victim did not give voluntary **consent** to her attacker. In a sense, the burden of proof is on the victim to show that her character is beyond question and that she in no way encouraged, enticed, or misled the accused rapist. A common defense tactic is to introduce suspicion into the minds of the jury that the woman may have consented to the sexual act and later regretted her decision or suspicion that her dubious moral character casts doubt on the veracity of her claims. Even the appearance of impropriety can undermine a case. Proving the victim had good character is not a requirement in any other crime.

**LEGAL REFORM** Because of the difficulty that rape victims have in obtaining justice, rape laws have been changing around the country. Reform efforts include changing the language of statutes, dropping the condition of victim resistance, and changing the requirement of *use* of force to include the *threat* of force or injury.[101] **Shield laws**, which protect women from being questioned about their

**aggravated rape**
Rape involving multiple offenders, weapons, and victim injuries.

**consent**
The victim of rape must prove that she in no way encouraged, enticed, or misled the accused rapist.

**shield laws**
Laws that protect women from being questioned about their sexual history unless such questioning directly bears on the case.

Brendan McDermid/Reuters/Landov; Barry Gutierrez/Reuters/Landov

Proving rape can be challenging because the prosecution must prove the victim did not consent. Actress Lili Bernard (center) and writer Sammie Mays (right), two alleged victims of Bill Cosby (on far right), speak at a press conference with lawyer Gloria Allred on May 1, 2015, in New York City. More than 40 women have accused Cosby of sexual assault. While the famed comedian denies the charges, he has admitted to acquiring Quaaludes and giving them to women with whom he wanted to have sex.

sexual history unless it directly bears on the case, have become universal. Although some are quite restrictive, others grant the trial judge considerable discretion to admit prior sexual conduct in evidence if it is deemed relevant for the defense. In an important case, *Michigan v. Lucas*, the Supreme Court upheld the validity of shield laws and ruled that excluding evidence of a prior sexual relationship between the parties did not violate the defendant's right to a fair trial.[102]

In addition to requiring evidence that consent was not given, the common law of rape required corroboration that the crime of rape actually took place. This involved the need for independent evidence from police officers, physicians, and witnesses that the accused was actually the person who committed the crime, that sexual penetration took place, and that force was present and consent absent. This requirement shielded rapists from prosecution in cases where the victim delayed reporting the crime or physical evidence had been compromised or lost. Corroboration is no longer required except under extraordinary circumstances, such as when the victim is too young to understand the crime, has had a previous sexual relationship with the defendant, or gives a version of events that is improbable and self-contradictory.[103]

The federal government may have given rape victims another source of redress when it passed the Violence Against Women Act in 1994. This statute allows rape victims to sue in federal court on the grounds that sexual violence violates their civil rights; so far, the provisions of this act have been upheld by appellate courts.[104] Despite these reform efforts, prosecutors may be influenced in their decision to bring charges by the circumstances of a crime.[105] Another important piece of legislation, the Campus Sexual Violence Elimination (SaVE) Act, increases transparency on campus about incidents of sexual violence, guarantees victims enhanced rights, sets standards for disciplinary proceedings, and requires campus-wide prevention education programs. The act broadens this requirement to mandate fuller reporting of sexual violence to include incidents of domestic violence, dating violence, and stalking. Signed into law on March 7, 2013, it also requires schools to protect victim confidentiality when reporting criminal threats to the campus community.[106]

**L04** Analyze the different types of murder.

# Murder and Homicide

The common-law definition of **murder** is "the unlawful killing of a human being with malice aforethought."[107] It is the most serious of all common-law crimes and the only one in the United States that can still be punished by death. Western society's abhorrence of murderers is illustrated by the fact that there is no statute of limitations in murder cases. Whereas state laws limit prosecution of other crimes to a fixed period (usually 7 to 10 years), accused killers can be brought to justice at any time after their crimes were committed. In 1991, the abused and decomposed body of 4-year-old Anjelica Castillo—known as "Baby Hope"—was found in an ice chest by the side of a New York roadway; in 2013, her killer, Conrado Juarez, was arrested in New York City, 22 years after that infamous crime took place.[108]

To legally prove that a murder has taken place, most state jurisdictions require prosecutors to show that the accused *maliciously* intended to kill the victim. "Express or actual malice" is the state of mind assumed to exist when someone kills another person in the absence of any apparent provocation. "Implied or constructive malice" is considered to exist when a death results from negligent or unthinking behavior. In these cases, even though the perpetrator did not wish to kill the victim, the killing resulted from an inherently dangerous act and therefore is considered murder.

## Degrees of Murder

There are different levels, or degrees, of homicide. **First-degree murder** occurs when a person kills another after premeditation and deliberation. **Premeditation** means that the killing was considered beforehand and suggests that it was motivated by more than a simple desire to engage in an act of violence. **Deliberation** means the killing was planned after careful thought rather than carried out on impulse: "To constitute a

**murder**
The unlawful killing of a human being with malice aforethought.

**first-degree murder**
Killing a person after premeditation and deliberation.

**premeditation**
Considering the criminal act beforehand, which suggests that it was motivated by more than a simple desire to engage in an act of violence.

**deliberation**
Planning a criminal act after careful thought, rather than carrying it out on impulse.

deliberate and premeditated killing, the slayer must weigh and consider the question of killing and the reasons for and against such a choice; having in mind the consequences, he decides to and does kill."[109] The planning implied by this definition need not be a long process; it may be an almost instantaneous decision to take another's life. Also, a killing that accompanies a felony, such as robbery or rape, usually constitutes first-degree murder (**felony murder**).

**Second-degree murder** requires the killer to have malice aforethought but not premeditation or deliberation. A second-degree murder occurs when a person's wanton disregard for the victim's life and his or her desire to inflict serious bodily harm on the victim result in the victim's death. Homicide without malice is called **manslaughter** and is usually punished by anywhere from 1 to 15 years in prison. **Voluntary or nonnegligent manslaughter** refers to a killing committed in the heat of passion or during a sudden quarrel that provoked violence. Although intent may be present, malice is not. **Involuntary or negligent manslaughter** refers to a killing that occurs when a person's acts are negligent and without regard for the harm they may cause others. Most involuntary manslaughter cases involve motor vehicle deaths—for example, when a drunk driver kills a pedestrian. The Profiles in Crimes feature describes a famous case deemed to be negligent homicide.

**DELIBERATE INDIFFERENCE MURDER** Murder is often considered an intentional act, but a person can also be held criminally liable for the death of another even if she or he did not intend to injure another person but exhibited *deliberate indifference* to the danger her or his actions might cause. The deliberate indifference standard is met

---

**felony murder**
A killing that accompanies a felony, such as robbery or rape.

**second-degree murder**
A person's wanton disregard for the victim's life and his or her desire to inflict serious bodily harm on the victim, which results in the victim's death.

**manslaughter**
Homicide without malice.

**voluntary or nonnegligent manslaughter**
A killing committed in the heat of passion or during a sudden quarrel that provoked violence.

**involuntary or negligent manslaughter**
A killing that occurs when a person's acts are negligent and without regard for the harm they may cause others.

---

# PROFILES IN CRIME

## OSCAR PISTORIUS

In 2014, the trial of South African athlete Oscar Pistorius made headlines around the world. Pistorius, a double amputee known as the "Blade Runner" for his scythe-like prosthetic legs, was a Paralympics champion who began competing in able-bodied events. At the 2011 World Championships in Athletics, Pistorius became the first amputee to win a track medal at an international competition. At the 2012 Summer Olympics, Pistorius became the first double leg amputee to participate in the Olympics, making him world famous. Then on February 14, 2013, he was charged with the murder of his beautiful model girlfriend, Reeva Steenkamp. Reeva was killed in the bathroom of his Pretoria home, when Pistorius shot four times through the closed door. But why the shooting occurred was the key and only issue in the case. According to Pistorius, he was awakened by a noise, heard the bathroom window open, believed an intruder had broken into the house, and shot to defend himself and Reeva before realizing he had made a terrible mistake. His story was disputed by prosecutors who argued that Pistorius fought with Steenkamp for some unknown reasons and then shot her in anger when she took refuge in the bathroom. Their case was supported by neighbors who testified they heard screams and then shots being fired. The defense rebutted that the neighbors who thought they heard a woman's screams were mistaken: the screams were actually Pistorius, who became frenzied when he realized his mistake. The prosecution also brought witnesses who said that Pistorius had a hot temper, routinely carried guns, and on more than one occasion shot them off in anger.

Pistorius was found guilty of culpable homicide and received a five-year prison sentence, the judge refusing to find Pistorius guilty of the more serious crime of premeditated murder. Culpable homicide, in the South African legal system, is the "unlawful or negligent killing" of a person. Steenkamp was found to have been killed by Pistorius without intent or premeditation but negligence, the U.S. equivalent of involuntary manslaughter. The judge obviously believed his claim that it was all a grievous mistake and he did not intend to kill.

Pistorius is scheduled to be released in August 2015. Prosecutors, appalled that the sentence was too lenient, appealed the verdict, and the case is now winding its way through the South African appeals process.

**Source:** Anita Powell, "Pistorius Trial Week 2 Features Blood, Tears," *Voice of America*, March 14, 2014, www.voanews.com /content/week-2-of-pistorius-trial-blood-tears-and-vomit/1871130 .html (accessed 2015).

when a person knows of and yet disregards or ignores an excessive risk to another's health or safety. One of the most famous cases illustrating deliberate indifference murder occurred on January 26, 2001, when Diane Whipple, a San Francisco woman, died after two large dogs attacked her in the hallway of her apartment building. One of the dogs' owners/keepers, Robert Noel, was found guilty of manslaughter, and his wife, Marjorie Knoller, was convicted on charges of second-degree murder, because they knew that the dogs were highly dangerous but did little or nothing to control the animals' behavior. Their deliberate indifference put their neighbor at risk, with tragic consequences. After a long series of appeals, on June 1, 2007, the California Supreme Court ruled that a dog owner who knows the animal is a potential killer and exposes other people to that danger may be guilty of murder even though he or she did not intend that particular victim to be injured or killed. In a unanimous decision, the appellate court ruled that Knoller could be convicted of murder because she acted with "conscious disregard of the danger to human life." On September 22, 2008, the court sentenced Marjorie Knoller to serve 15 years to life for the death of Diane Whipple.[110]

## Nature and Extent of Murder

It is possible to track the trends in U.S. murder rates from 1900 to the present with the aid of coroners' reports and UCR data. The murder rate peaked in 1933, a time of prolonged economic depression and lawlessness, and then fell until 1958. The homicide rate doubled from the mid-1960s to a peak in 1991 when almost 25,000 people were killed in a single year, a rate of about 10 per 100,000 people. The murder rate has since been in a decline. In 2014, there were about 14,000 murders, a rate of about 4.5 per 100,000 population. So today there are about 10,000 fewer people being killed every year than 25 years ago even though the population has become much larger!

What else do official crime statistics tell us about murder today? Murder tends to be an urban crime. More than half of all homicides occur in cities with a population of 100,000 or more; nearly one-quarter of homicides occur in cities with a population of more than 1 million. Why is homicide an urban phenomenon? Large cities experience the greatest rates of structural disadvantage—poverty, joblessness, racial heterogeneity, residential mobility, family disruption, and income inequality—that are linked to high murder rates.[111] Not surprisingly, large cities are much more commonly the site of drug-related killings and gang-related murders and are relatively less likely to be the location of family-related homicides, including murders of intimates.

Murder victims and offenders tend to be males; about 80 percent of homicide victims and nearly 90 percent of offenders are male. Murder, like rape, tends to be an intraracial crime; about 90 percent of victims are slain by members of their own race. About half of all murder victims are African Americans.

Approximately one-third of murder victims and almost half the offenders are under the age of 25. For both victims and offenders, the rate per 100,000 peaks in the 18- to 24-year-old age group. Some murders involve very young children, a crime referred to as **infanticide** (killing older children is called **filicide**), and others involve senior citizens, a crime referred to as **eldercide**.[112] The UCR indicates that about 400 children under 4 years of age are murdered each year. The younger the child, the greater the risk for infanticide. At the opposite end of the age spectrum, about 5 percent of all homicides involve people age 65 or older. Males age 65 or older are more likely than females of the same age to be homicide victims. Although most of the offenders who committed eldercide were age 50 or younger, elderly females were more likely than elderly males to be killed by an elderly offender.

Murderers typically have a long involvement in crime; few people begin a criminal career by killing someone. Research shows that people arrested for homicide are significantly more likely to have been in trouble with the law prior to their arrest than people arrested for other crimes.[113] A recent longitudinal study by David Farrington and his associates found that among the risk predictors for homicide, prior

**infanticide**
Murder of a very young child.

**filicide**
Murder of an older child.

**eldercide**
Murder of a senior citizen.

criminal offenses up to age 14 was the most important; 95 percent of offenders had records of violence.[114]

**"BORN AND ALIVE"** Can a murder victim be a fetus that has not yet been delivered; is **feticide** a crime? The answer is yes. Today about 38 states have some form of fetal homicide laws and more than two-thirds of the states have passed some form of legislation that criminalizes the killing of a fetus as murder even if it is not "born and alive."[115] In some states, there exists legislation creating a separate class of crime that increases criminal penalties when a person causes injury to a woman they know is pregnant, and the injury results in miscarriage or stillbirth.

At the federal level, the Unborn Victims of Violence Act of 2004 makes it a separate crime to harm a fetus during an assault on the mother. If the attack causes death or bodily injury to a child who is in utero at the time the conduct takes place, the penalty is the same as that for conduct had the injury or death occurred to the unborn child's mother.[116] There is still a great deal of state-to-state variation in feticide laws. Some make it a separate crime to kill a fetus or commit an act of violence against a pregnant woman. Others have a viability requirement: feticide can only occur if the unborn child could at the time have potentially lived outside the mother's body.[117]

Today, few would deny that some relationship exists between social and ecological factors and murder. The following section explores some of the more important issues related to these factors.

## Murderous Relations

Most murders are expressive—that is, motivated by rage or anger—and they typically involve friends, relatives, and acquaintances. Stranger homicides typically involve commission of another crime (such as a robbery, rape, or drug deal) where the perpetrator applied too much force in completing the crime.[118]

Murderous relations are also shaped by gender: males are more likely to kill others of similar social standing in more public contexts, whereas women kill family members and intimate partners in private locations.[119] What other forms do murderous relations take?

**INTIMATE PARTNER MURDER** Many murders involve husbands and wives, boyfriends and girlfriends, and others involved in romantic relationships. Intimate partner murder is a gendered phenomenon. When women commit homicide, the most likely victim is an intimate partner; about 40 percent of all female homicide incidents involve killing a male partner. However, while less than 10 percent of all murders committed by men involve a female partner, intimate partner homicides make up 40 to 50 percent of all murders of women in the United States.[120]

Men who kill romantic partners typically have a long history of violence, while for women killing their partner may be their first violent offense.[121] This may be the reason that there is a "chivalry effect" in domestic violence murders. In death penalty states such as California, the death-sentence rate for single-victim domestic violence murders is significantly lower than the overall death-sentence rate for other kinds of killings. Not surprisingly, when women in these states are found guilty of capital murder, they are far less likely than men to be sentenced to death.[122]

Research also shows most females who kill their mates do so after suffering repeated violent attacks.[123] Women who kill or seriously assault intimate partners are often battered women unable to flee a troubled relationship.[124] Perhaps the number of males killed by their partners has declined because alternatives to abusive relationships, such as shelters for battered women, are becoming more prevalent around the United

AP Images/Dave Kettering

Older people tend to be victimized by a family member. Isaiah Sweet, 18, pleaded guilty to two charges of first-degree murder for the May 2012 killings of his grandparents, 55-year-old Richard Sweet and 62-year-old Janet Sweet. The teenage Sweet told friends he hated his grandparents before shooting both in the head. He received a life sentence for the murders.

**feticide**
Intentional or negligent killing of a human fetus.

States. Regions that provide greater social support for battered women and that have passed legislation to protect abuse victims also have lower rates of female-perpetrated homicide.[125] This escape valve may help them avoid retaliation through lethal violence.

Some people kill their mates because they find themselves involved in a love triangle.[126] Interestingly, women who kill out of jealousy aim their aggression at their partners; in contrast, men are more likely to kill their rivals (their mates' suitors). Love triangles tend to become lethal when the offenders believe they have been lied to or betrayed. Lethal violence is more common when (1) the rival initiated the affair, (2) the killer knew the spouse was already in a steady relationship outside the marriage, and (3) the killer was repeatedly lied to or betrayed.[127]

**ACQUAINTANCE MURDERS**   Most murders occur among people who are acquainted. Although on the surface the killing might seem senseless, it is often the result of a long-simmering dispute motivated by revenge, dispute resolution, jealousy, drug deals, racial bias, or threats to identity or status.[128] For example, a prior act of violence, motivated by profit or greed, such as when a buyer robs his dealer during a drug transaction, may generate revenge killing.

How do these murderous relations develop between two people who may have had little prior conflict? In a now classic study, David Luckenbill examined murder transactions to determine whether particular patterns of behavior are common between the killer and the victim.[129] He found that many homicides follow a sequential pattern. First, the victim makes what the offender considers an offensive move. The offender typically retaliates verbally or physically. An agreement to end things violently is forged with the victim's provocative response. The battle ensues, leaving the victim dead or dying. The offender's escape is shaped by his or her relationship to the victim or by the reaction of the audience, if any.

**STRANGER MURDERS**   About 20 percent of all murders involve strangers. Stranger homicides occur most often as felony murders during rapes, robberies, and burglaries. Others are random acts of urban violence that fuel public fear: a homeowner tells a motorist to move his car because it is blocking the driveway, an argument ensues, and the owner gets a pistol and kills the motorist. Stranger homicides can result from random gang violence: someone is killed inadvertently in a drive-by shooting. They may also stem from hate crimes (covered later in this chapter) directed at victims merely because of their race, class, gender, and so on. The killing of homeless people by adolescent groups and gangs has become all too common.[130]

**SEXUALLY BASED MURDERS**   Some murders are sexually related. Research indicates that sexually related homicide can take a variety of forms:[131]

- Domestic disputes involving husbands and wives, men and women, boyfriends and girlfriends, same-sex couples, and even on occasion siblings. Sometimes these events are triggered by a partner's unwanted or unexpected pregnancy: homicidal injury is a leading cause of death among pregnant and postpartum women in the United States.[132]
- Love triangles involving former husbands and/or wives and jilted lovers.
- Rape and/or sodomy oriented assault in which a person intends to commit a rape or sexual assault but uses excessive force to overcome resistance, resulting in the victim's death.
- "Lust murders" that are motivated by obsessive sexual fantasies.
- Vengeance for sexual violence. In these cases someone exacts vengeance on a sexual violence perpetrator, either on his or her own behalf or on the behalf of a sexual violence victim.
- Self-defense during sexual violence. In these incidents, sexual violence was taking place and the victim defended herself or himself resulting in the death of the sexual violence perpetrator; or another person intervened to defend the sexual violence victim and this resulted in the death of the sexual violence perpetrator.

Although not much is known about sexually motivated killers, Paul Greenall and Michelle Wright recently found that they tend to be generalists and that sexual homicide was part of a long history of antisocial acts that included a variety of violent crimes in addition to murder.[133]

**SCHOOL MURDERS** Sadly, violence in schools has become commonplace. There have been a number of mass killings, such as the 1999 shootings at Columbine High School in Colorado that resulted in the deaths of 15 people, and the Newtown, Connecticut, massacre in 2012 in which Adam Lanza killed 20 children and 6 staff members. On average, about 25 students are killed each year at school, on the way to or returning from regular sessions at school, or while attending or traveling to or from an official school-sponsored event.[134] School massacres tend to be committed by white males but the presence of female perpetrators is not unknown, especially when the attack is not carried out with a firearm but with a knife or some other instrument.[135]

In many instances, these events are linked to bullying with the target turning the tables on their tormentors, such as what occurred in the Columbine High School massacre.[136] Bullying is a serious social problem: the latest data from the National Center for Education Statistics indicate that about 28 percent of students ages 12 to 18 reported being bullied at school during the school year, including being pushed, shoved, tripped, or spit on at school.[137]

T. J. Lane is escorted by sheriff's deputies after his court appearance for shooting and killing three students at Chardon High School in Chardon, Ohio, February 28, 2012. Two other students were seriously injured in the shooting, one of whom was permanently paralyzed. Lane was sentenced to three life sentences without the possibility of parole. After entering the courtroom, he took off his dress shirt to reveal a white T-shirt with the word "Killer" handwritten across the front.

## Serial Killers, Mass Murderers, and Spree Killers

For 31 years, citizens of Wichita, Kansas, lived in fear of the serial killer self-described as BTK (for Bind, Torture, Kill). During his murder spree, BTK sent taunting letters and packages to the police and the media. Suddenly, after committing gruesome killings in the 1970s, he went underground and disappeared from view. Then, after 25 years of silence, he renewed contact with a local news station. His last communication contained a computer disk, which was analyzed by the FBI and traced to 59-year-old Dennis Rader, who later confessed to 10 murders in an effort to escape the death penalty.

**SERIAL KILLERS** Criminologists consider a **serial killer**, such as Rader, to be a person who kills three or more persons in three or more separate events. In between the murders, a serial killer reverts to his or her normal lifestyle. Serial killers come from all walks of life, though the majority are white males.[138] Approximately 17 percent of all serial homicides in the United States are committed by women and 20 percent by African Americans.[139]

There are different types of serial killers.[140] Some are sadists who gain satisfaction from torturing and killing their victims. In contrast, others believe they are helping people by ending their suffering. Dr. Harold Frederick Shipman, Britain's most notorious serial killer, was convicted of 15 murders, though he may have killed more than 200 patients, most of them elderly, claiming his actions were motivated by compassion rather than psychosis.[141]

**serial killer**
A person who kills three or more persons in three or more separate events.

Some experts have attempted to classify serial killers on the basis of their motivations and offense patterns.[142] According to James A. Fox and Jack Levin, there are at least three different types of serial killers:[143]

- "Thrill killers" strive for either sexual sadism or dominance. They enjoy the thrill, the sexual gratification, and the dominance they achieve over the lives of their victims. Serial killers rarely use a gun because this method is too quick and would deprive them of their greatest pleasure—exulting in the victim's suffering. Extending the time it takes the victim to die increases the pleasure they experience from killing and prolongs their ability to ignore or enjoy their victims' suffering. They typically have a propensity for basking in the media limelight when apprehended for their crimes. Killing provides a way for them to feed their emotional hunger and reduce their anxiety levels.[144]
- "Mission killers" want to reform the world or have a vision that drives them to kill.
- "Expedience killers" are out for profit or want to protect themselves from a perceived threat.

**FEMALE SERIAL KILLERS** While rare, female serial killers have been around for quite some time. Locusta, a poisoner, was active in Rome during the first century CE. Lucretia Patricia Cannon, the first known female serial killer in the United States, was active between 1802 and 1829 in Delaware.[145]

An estimated 10 to 15 percent of serial killers are women, and there are striking differences between male and female killers.[146] Males are much more likely than females to use extreme violence and torture. Whereas males used a "hands-on" approach, including beating, bludgeoning, and strangling their victims, females are more likely to poison or smother their victims. Men track or stalk their victims, but women are much more likely to kill family members and acquaintances. Female serial killers kill those closest to them—husbands, lovers, children, and other relatives. They also target those who are weak or dependent on them, such as children and the elderly. Men choose victims whom they can render helpless, and women choose victims who are already helpless.[147]

There are also gender-based personality and behavior characteristics. Female killers, somewhat older than their male counterparts, abuse both alcohol and drugs; males are not likely to be substance abusers. Women were diagnosed as having histrionic, manic-depressive, borderline, dissociative, and antisocial personality disorders; men were more often diagnosed as having antisocial personalities. Aileen Wuornos, executed for killing seven men, was diagnosed with a severe psychopathic personality, which probably arose from her horrific childhood marked by beatings, alcoholism, rape, incest, and prostitution.[148]

Thus, the typical female serial killer is a person who smothers or poisons someone she knows. During childhood she suffered from an abusive relationship in a disrupted family. Female killers' education levels are below average, and if they hold jobs, they are in low-status positions. And because they use stealth and cunning rather than overt brutality, women are more likely to remain at large longer before arousing suspicion. They also avoid detection due to the fact that they tend to be older and more mature than their male counterparts and, quite possibly, due to the gender biases that underpin the misconception that women cannot be serial murderers.[149]

**mass murder**
The killing of four or more victims by one or a few assailants within a single event.

**MASS MURDERERS** In contrast to serial killings, **mass murder**, such as the mass shooting by James Holmes, who killed 12 people at a movie theater in Aurora, Colorado, on July 20, 2012, involves the killing of four or more victims by one or a few assailants within a single event.[150] The murderous incident can last but a few minutes or as long as several hours. In order to qualify as a mass murder, the incident must be carried out by one or a few offenders. Highly organized or institutionalized killings (such as war crimes and large-scale acts of political terrorism, as well as certain acts of highly organized crime rings), though atrocious, are not considered mass murder and are motivated by a totally different set of factors.

Fox and Levin define four types of mass murderers:

- "Revenge killers" want to get even with individuals or society at large. Their typical target is an estranged wife and "her" children or an employer and "his" employees.
- "Love killers" are motivated by a warped sense of devotion. They are often despondent people who commit suicide and take others, such as a wife and children, with them.
- "Profit killers" are usually trying to cover up a crime, eliminate witnesses, and carry out a criminal conspiracy.
- "Terrorist killers" are trying to send a message. Gang killings tell rivals to watch out; cult killers may actually leave a message behind to warn society about impending doom.

A recent study by Adam Lankford compared mass murderers who took their own life with those who survived their attack. Lankford found that while only 4 percent of murderers commit suicide, by contrast, 38 percent of mass shooters who attacked in the United States between 1966 and 2010 committed suicide by their own hand. Another 10 percent were shot after threatening police officers ("suicide by cop"), so overall, 48 percent of these offenders died as a result of their attacks. Those mass shooters who died armed themselves with more weapons, killed more victims, and often struck at different locations (commercial areas) than those who survived their attacks. The suicidal killers tended to engage in profound self-loathing, whereby they felt guilty and ashamed about their inadequacies and weaknesses, including their uncontrolled anger and violent tendencies. They had a vengeful desire to punish themselves and were propelled by more powerful perceptions of personal victimization, social injustice, and general hopelessness than other mass shooters.[151]

**spree killer**
A killer of multiple victims whose murders occur over a relatively short span of time and often follow no discernible pattern.

**battery**
Offensive touching, such as slapping, hitting, or punching a victim.

**SPREE KILLERS** Unlike mass murders, spree killing is not confined to a single outburst, and unlike serial killers, spree killers do not return to their normal identities in between killings. **Spree killers** engage in a rampage of violence over a period of days or weeks. The most notorious spree killing to date occurred in October 2002 in the Washington, D.C., area.[152] John Lee Malvo, 17, a Jamaican citizen, and his traveling companion John Allen Muhammad, 41, an Army veteran with an expert's rating in marksmanship, went on a rampage that left more than 10 people dead.

Some spree killers target a specific group or class. Joseph Paul Franklin targeted mixed-race couples (African Americans and Jews), committing over 20 murders in 12 states in an effort to instigate a race war. (Franklin also shot and paralyzed *Hustler* publisher Larry Flynt because he published pictures of interracial sex.)[153] Others, such as the D.C. snipers Malvo and Muhammad, kill randomly and do not seek a specific class of victim; their targets included the young and old, African Americans and whites, men and women.[154]

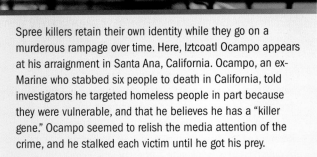

Spree killers retain their own identity while they go on a murderous rampage over time. Here, Iztcoatl Ocampo appears at his arraignment in Santa Ana, California. Ocampo, an ex-Marine who stabbed six people to death in California, told investigators he targeted homeless people in part because they were vulnerable, and that he believes he has a "killer gene." Ocampo seemed to relish the media attention of the crime, and he stalked each victim until he got his prey.

## Assault and Battery

Although many people mistakenly believe that the phrase "assault and battery" refers to a single act, they are actually two separate crimes. **Battery** requires offensive touching, such as slapping, hitting, or punching a victim.

**assault**
Either attempted battery or intentionally frightening the victim by word or deed (actual touching is not involved).

**road rage**
Violent assault by a motorist who loses control of his or her emotions while driving.

**child abuse**
Any physical or emotional trauma to a child for which no reasonable explanation, such as an accident or ordinary disciplinary practices, can be found.

**neglect**
Not providing a child with the care and shelter to which he or she is entitled.

victim. **Assault** requires no actual touching but involves either attempted battery or intentionally frightening the victim by word or deed. Although common law originally intended these twin crimes to be misdemeanors, most jurisdictions now upgrade them to felonies either when a weapon is used or when they occur during the commission of a felony (for example, when a person is assaulted during a robbery).[155]

Under common law, battery required bodily injury, such as broken limbs or wounds. However, under modern law, an assault and battery occurs if the victim suffers a temporarily painful blow, even if no injury results. Battery can also involve offensive touching, such as a man kissing a woman against her will or putting his hands on her body. In some legal jurisdictions, biting someone when one is infected with AIDS is considered an aggravated assault; some people with AIDS have been convicted of aggravated assault for spitting on their victims.[156]

## Nature and Extent of Assault

The pattern of criminal assault is quite similar to that of homicide and rape; one could say that the only difference is that the victim survives.[157] Assaults may be common in our society simply because of common life stresses. Motorists who assault each other have become such a familiar phenomenon that the term **road rage** has been coined. There have even been frequent incidents of violent assault among frustrated airline passengers who lose control while traveling.[158]

About 725,000 assaults are now being reported to police agencies annually—about 229 per 100,000 inhabitants. Just as for other violent crimes, the number of assaults has been in decline, down more than one-third from its peak in 1993, when 1.1 million assaults were reported to the police. People arrested for assault and those identified by victims are usually young, male (about 75 percent), and white (65 percent). Assault victims tend to be male, but females also face a significant danger. Assault rates are highest in urban areas, during summer, and in southern and western regions. The weapons most commonly used in assaults are blunt instruments and hands and feet.

The NCVS indicates that more than 5 million assaults take place each year; about 1 million are considered aggravated, and 4 million simple or weaponless assaults. Like other violent crimes, the number of assaults has been in steep decline—down more than 30 percent during the past decade.

## Acquaintance and Family Assaults

Violent attacks in the home are one of the most frightening types of assault. Criminologists recognize that assault among friends and intimates and within the family has become an enduring social problem in the United States and abroad. What forms do these attacks take?

**CHILD ABUSE** One area of intrafamily violence that has received a great deal of media attention is **child abuse**. This term describes any physical or emotional trauma inflicted on a child for which no reasonable explanation, such as an accident or ordinary disciplinary practice, can be found.[159] Child abuse can result from physical beatings administered to a child by hands, feet, weapons, belts, sticks, burning, and so on. Another form of abuse results from **neglect**—not providing a child with the care and shelter to which he or she is entitled.

Estimating the actual number of child abuse cases is difficult, because many incidents are never reported to the police.

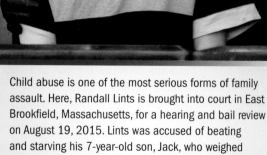

Child abuse is one of the most serious forms of family assault. Here, Randall Lints is brought into court in East Brookfield, Massachusetts, for a hearing and bail review on August 19, 2015. Lints was accused of beating and starving his 7-year-old son, Jack, who weighed 38 pounds and was taken to a hospital in a coma.

AP Images/Rick Cinclair

Child Protective Services (CPS) agencies throughout the United States receive almost 4 million complaints of child abuse and of these one-fifth or more than 675,000 children are found to be victims of abuse, about half males and half females.[160]

Although child abuse is still a serious social problem, child maltreatment rates are lower today than they were a decade ago. It is difficult to pinpoint the reason for the reduction in reported abuse, but it may be the result of better treatment strategies, lower substance abuse rates, reduced reliance on physical punishment, and the availability of abortion (which reduces the number of unwanted children).

**Child sexual abuse** is the exploitation of children through rape, incest, and molestation by parents or other adults. The CPS data indicate that about 65,000 children are the victims of sexual abuse each year. Many of these are subjected to some form of sexual exploitation, which often begins with sexual assaults by relatives and acquaintances, such as a teacher, a coach, or a neighbor. Sexual abuse is of particular concern because children who have been abused experience a long list of symptoms, including fear, posttraumatic stress disorder, behavior problems, sexualized behavior, and poor self-esteem.[161] As they mature, abused girls are more likely than other girls to drop out of high school, become teen parents, be obese, and experience psychiatric problems, substance dependence, and domestic violence.[162] Women who were abused as children are also at greater risk of being abused as adults than those who escaped childhood victimization.[163]

> **child sexual abuse**
> The exploitation of children through rape, incest, and molestation by parents or other adults.

**CAUSES OF CHILD ABUSE** Why do parents physically assault their children? Such maltreatment is a highly complex problem with neither a single cause nor a readily available solution. It cuts across ethnic, religious, and socioeconomic lines. Abusive parents cannot be categorized by sex, age, or educational level, and they come from all walks of life.[164]

A number of factors have been commonly linked to child abuse and neglect:

- Abusive parents may themselves have been abused, creating an intergenerational cycle of violence.
- Blended families, which include children living with an unrelated adult such as a stepparent or with another unrelated co-resident, have higher incidence of abuse.[165]
- Parents may become abusive if they are isolated from friends, neighbors, or relatives who can help in times of crisis.[166]
- Abusive parents may be suffering from depression and other forms of psychological distress.[167]

Regardless of its cause, child abuse can have devastating long-term effects, ranging from depression to loss of self-esteem.[168] Not surprisingly, a history of childhood sexual and physical abuse is observed at a disproportionately high rate among persons with severe mental illness.[169]

**PARENTAL ABUSE** Parents are sometimes the target of abuse from their own children. The following facts emerge from studies of child-to-parent violence (CPV):

- The younger the child, the higher the rate of CPV.
- At all ages, more children were violent to mothers than to fathers.
- Both boys and girls hit mothers more than they hit fathers.
- At all ages, slightly more boys than girls hit parents.
- Child-to-parent violence is associated with some form of earlier violence by parents: husband-to-wife, wife-to-husband, or child abuse.[170]

**SPOUSAL ABUSE** Spousal abuse has occurred throughout recorded history. By the mid-nineteenth century, severe wife beating fell into disfavor, and accused wife beaters were subject to public ridicule. Nonetheless, limited chastisement of wives was still the rule. These ideas form the foundation of men's traditional physical control of women and have led to severe cases of spousal assault. Spouse abuse is still a

# Exhibit 10.2 Factors that Predict Spousal Abuse

- *Presence of alcohol.* Excessive alcohol use may turn otherwise docile spouses into abusers.
- *Access to weapons.* The perpetrator's access to a gun and previous threat with a weapon may lead to abuse.
- *Blended family.* Having a child living in a blended family may provoke abuse because one parent may have a more limited bond to the child.
- *Estrangement.* Alienation or separation from a controlling partner and subsequent involvement with another partner are contributing factors in abuse.
- *Hostility toward dependency.* Some spouses who appear docile and passive may resent their dependence on their partners and react with rage and violence; this reaction has been linked to sexual inadequacy.
- *Excessive brooding.* Obsession with a spouse's behavior, however trivial, can result in violent assaults.
- *Social learning.* Some males believe society approves of spouse or mate abuse and may use these beliefs to justify their violent behavior. Peer support helps shape their attitudes and behaviors.
- *Socioeconomic factors.* Men who fail as providers and are under economic stress may take their frustrations out on their wives.
- *Flashes of anger.* Research shows that a significant amount of family violence results from a sudden burst of anger after a verbal dispute.
- *Military service.* Spousal abuse among men who have served in the military is extremely high. Similarly, those serving in the military are more likely to assault their wives than are civilian husbands. The reasons for this phenomenon may be the violence promoted by military training and the close proximity in which military families live to one another.
- *Having been battered as children.* Spouses who assault their partners were generally battered as children.
- *Unpredictability.* Batterers are unpredictable, unable to be influenced by their spouses, and impossible to prevent from battering once an argument has begun.

**Sources:** Christine Sellers, John Cochran, and Kathryn Branch, "Social Learning Theory and Partner Violence: A Research Note," *Deviant Behavior* 26 (2005): 379–395; Jacquelyn Campbell, Daniel Webster, Jane Koziol-McLain, Carolyn Block, Doris Campbell, Mary Ann Curry, Faye Gary, et al., "Risk Factors for Femicide in Abusive Relationships: Results from a Multisite Case Control Study," *American Journal of Public Health* 93 (2003): 1089–1097; Neil Jacobson and John Mordechai Gottman, *When Men Batter Women: New Insights into Ending Abusive Relationships* (New York: Simon and Schuster, 1998); Kenneth Leonard and Brian Quigley, "Drinking and Marital Aggression in Newlyweds: An Event-Based Analysis of Drinking and the Occurrence of Husband Marital Aggression," *Journal of Studies on Alcohol* 60 (1999): 537–541.

significant problem. In their classic study of family violence, Richard Gelles and Murray Straus found that 16 percent of surveyed families had experienced husband-to-wife assaults.[171] The consequences of abuse can be significant, ranging from physical injury to psychological trauma, to exposure to sexually transmitted disease.[172] Moreover, physical abuse is commonly accompanied by mental abuse and coercion that can have long-term damaging psychological effects.[173] Exhibit 10.2 examines some factors that predict the likelihood of spousal abuse.

## Dating Violence

Date rape is not the only form of violence aimed at a boyfriend or girlfriend.[174] A significant portion of all teens have been the target of dating violence, and it is estimated that one high school girl in five may suffer sexual or physical abuse from a boyfriend. Dating violence has been linked to substance abuse, unsafe sex, and eating disorders.[175]

    Physical dating violence can involve a wide spectrum of activities ranging from moderate to severe: scratching, slapping, pushing, slamming or holding someone against a wall, biting, choking, burning, beating someone up, and assault with a weapon. There is also emotional and psychological abuse that includes insulting, criticizing, threatening, humiliating, or berating. An emerging form of emotional abuse is referred to as **relational aggression** in which a partner tries to damage a person's relationship with friends by spreading smears and false rumors or by revealing information or images intended to be private.

**relational aggression**
Psychological and emotional abuse that involves the spreading of smears, rumors, and private information in order to harm his or her partner.

# Robbery

The common-law definition of **robbery** (and the one used by the FBI) is "the taking or attempting to take anything of value from the care, custody, or control of a person or persons by force or threat of force or violence and/or by putting the victim in fear."[176] A robbery is considered a violent crime because it involves the use of force to obtain money or goods. Robbery is punished severely because the victim's life is put in jeopardy. In fact, the severity of punishment is based on the amount of force used during the crime, not on the value of the items taken.

The FBI records about 345,000 robberies a year, a rate of about 109 per 100,000 population. As with most other violent crimes, there has been a significant reduction in the robbery rate during the past decade; the robbery rate is down 40 percent since 1991, when about 687,000 robberies were committed. According to the NCVS, about 550,000 robberies are committed or attempted each year, a discrepancy that illustrates that many of the most serious crimes go unreported to police agencies.

**LO5** Explain the nature and patterns of robbery.

**robbery**
Taking or attempting to take anything of value from the care, custody, or control of a person or persons by force or threat of force or violence and/or by putting the victim in fear.

## Robbers in Action

Even though most robbers may be opportunistic rather than professional, robberies still demonstrate rationality and planning. Marcus Felson describes robbers as foragers, predators who search for victims, preferably close to their homes, where numerous "nutritious" victims are abundant, where the robbers know the territory so that their prey cannot easily escape, and where their victims may be less vigilant because they are on their home turf.[177] Robbers, then, select targets that are *vulnerable, accessible*, and *profitable*. Their choice of victim dictates whether violence is used. If a victim looks tough—"street credible"—the robber may choose to use violence at the outset rather than wait for the victim to resist. During the robbery itself, victims who fight back are the ones most likely to be attacked and injured. Victim passivity may work best during a robbery.[178]

The ecological pattern for robbery is similar to that of other violent crimes, with one significant exception: northeastern states have the highest robbery rates by far. Whereas most crime rates are higher in the summer, robberies seem to peak during the winter months. One reason may be that the cold weather allows for greater disguise; another reason is that robbers may be attracted to the large amounts of cash people and merchants carry during the Christmas shopping season.[179] Robbers may also be more active in winter because days are shorter, affording them greater concealment in the dark.

## Choosing Targets

Some robbers target fellow criminals—for example, drug dealers.[180] Although these fellow criminals may be dangerous, robbers recognize that people with "dirty hands" are unlikely to call police and get entangled with the law. Ripping off a dealer kills three birds with one stone, providing both money and drugs at the same time, while targeting victims who are quite unlikely to call the police.[181]

When Bruce Jacobs interviewed armed robbers, he found that some specialize in targeting drug dealers because they believe that even though their work is hazardous, the rewards outweigh the risks: drug dealers are plentiful, visible, and accessible, and they carry plenty of cash. Their merchandise is valuable, is easily transported, and can be used by the robber or sold to another. Drug dealers are

Reuters/Landov

Randolph Bruce Adair, a retired Los Angeles Police Department detective, was arrested for a string of bank robberies attributed to the so-called "Snowbird Bandit" after several of his family members tipped off authorities. At the police station, the white-haired 70-year-old told officers, "I'm cooked, I think I should have a lawyer."

not particularly popular, so they cannot rely on bystanders to come to their aid. Of course, drug dealers may be able to "take care of business" themselves, but surprisingly, Jacobs found that many choose not to carry a pistol.[182] Drug dealers may be tough and bad, the robbers claim, but *they* are tougher and badder.

In their important book *Armed Robbers in Action: Stickups and Street Culture*, Scott Decker and Richard Wright interviewed active robbers in St. Louis, Missouri, and found that robbers are rational decision makers who look for easy prey. One ideal target is the married man who is looking for illicit sexual adventures and hires a prostitute, only to be robbed by her and her pimp. The robbers know that this victim will not be inclined to call the police and bring himself to their attention.

Because they realize that the risk of detection and punishment is the same whether the victim is carrying a load of cash or is penniless, experienced robbers use discretion in selecting targets. People whose clothing, jewelry, and demeanor mark them as carrying substantial amounts of cash make suitable targets; people who look like they can fight back are avoided. Some robbers station themselves at cash machines to spot targets who are flashing rolls of money.[183]

Wright and Decker are not the only researchers who found that most robbers seek out vulnerable victims. According to research by criminologist Jody Miller, female armed robbers are likely to choose female targets, reasoning that they will be more vulnerable and offer less resistance.[184] When robbing males, women "set them up" to catch them off guard; some feign sexual interest or prostitution to gain the upper hand.[185]

Wright and Decker found that most armed robberies are motivated by a pressing need for cash. Many robbers career from one financial crisis to the next, prompted by their endless quest for stimulation and thrills. Interviewees described how they partied, gambled, drank, and abused substances until they were broke. Their partying not only provided excitement but also helped generate a street reputation as someone who can "make things happen." Robbers had a "here and now" mentality and required a constant supply of cash to fuel their appetites.

## Acquaintance Robbery

**acquaintance robbery**
Robbery in which the victim or victims are people the robber knows.

Some robbers target people they know, a phenomenon referred to as **acquaintance robbery**. This seems puzzling, because victims can easily identify their attackers and report them to the police. However, despite this threat, acquaintance robbery may be attractive for a number of reasons:[186]

- Victims may be reluctant to report these crimes because they do not want to get involved with the police. They may be involved in crime themselves (drug dealers, for example), or they may fear retaliation if they report the crime. Some victims may be reluctant to gain the label of "rat" or "fink" if they go to the police.
- Some robberies are motivated by street justice. The robber has a grievance against the victim and settles the dispute by stealing the victim's property. In this instance, robbery may be considered a substitute for an assault—that is, the robber wants retribution and revenge rather than remuneration.[187]
- Because the robber knows the victim personally, the robber has inside information that there will be a "good take." Offenders may target people whom they know to be carrying a large amount of cash or who just purchased expensive jewelry.
- When a person in desperate need for immediate cash runs out of money, the individual may target people in close proximity simply because they are convenient targets.

When Richard Felson and his associates studied acquaintance robbery, they found that victims were more likely to be injured in acquaintance robberies than in stranger robberies, indicating that revenge rather than reward was the primary motive.[188] Similarly, robberies of family members were more likely to have a bigger payoff than stranger robberies, an indication that the offender was aware that the target had a large amount of cash on hand.

**CARJACKING** We can see this element of rationality and planning in the strategies of one type of robber: carjackers, who attack occupied vehicles for the purpose of theft. Carjacking is not a random event committed by amateurs but is carefully planned and carried out by experienced criminals. To be successful, carjackers must develop both perceptual (choosing the vehicle) and procedural (commandeering the vehicle) skills.[189] Carjackers must learn when their efforts are having a desired effect—scaring the victim. Developing these perceptual skills lets carjackers know exactly how effective their efforts are and helps them instantly adjust the application of those skills. They must constantly process information and make split-second decisions to react properly to a rapidly changing environment, not a task for amateurs.

When Heith Copes, Andy Hochstetler, and Michael Cherbonneau interviewed a sample of carjackers, they were told that, to get the upper hand, robbers avoid the likelihood of victims fighting back by devoting attention to selecting "proper victims" who are the least likely to resist.[190] Ironically, some steer clear of women drivers, fearing that their victims will panic and start to yell for help or act erratically, making them difficult to control.

Once a victim has been chosen, carjackers carefully form a line of attack designed to shock the victim into compliance. Some use a blitz method, attacking so rapidly that the target does not have time to respond. Others manipulate their appearance, posing as a street vendor, in order to approach potential victims without causing alarm. Some wait for an opportune moment, lurking in parking lots and approaching inattentive victims as they enter their cars, demanding that they surrender their keys. The research uncovered the fact that carjackers used and reused scripts when committing their crimes. Sticking to their scripts enabled carjackers to reduce danger and to use their skills and experience to prevent detection. Sticking to the script also prolongs a criminal career. It builds confidence and helps the carjacker act quickly and decisively, analyzing the situation and figuring out what must be done. No matter what the strategy, carjackers seem rational and calculating.

## Contemporary Forms of Interpersonal Violence

Assault, rape, robbery, and murder are traditional forms of interpersonal violence. As more data have become available, criminologists have recognized relatively new subcategories of these types of crimes, such as serial murder and date rape. Additional new categories of interpersonal violence are also receiving attention in criminological literature; the next sections describe three of these forms of violent crime.

### Hate Crimes

**Hate crimes**, or **bias crimes**, are violent acts directed toward a particular person or members of a group merely because the targets share a discernible racial, ethnic, religious, or gender characteristic. Such crimes range from desecration of a house of worship or cemetery to racially motivated murder.

Though normally associated with racially motivated attacks, hate crimes can involve convenient, vulnerable targets who are incapable of fighting back. There have been numerous reported incidents of teenagers attacking vagrants and the homeless in an effort to rid their town or neighborhood of people they consider undesirable.[191]

Another group targeted for hate crimes is gay men and women. The murder of Matthew Shepard, a gay college student who was kidnapped and beaten to death in Wyoming in 1998, was a grim reminder that gay bashing is all too common in America.[192] A national survey of gay, lesbian, and bisexual adults, conducted by psychologist Gregory Herek, found that approximately 20 percent of the sample reported having experienced a crime based on their sexual orientation; gay men were

---

**CHECKPOINTS**

▶ Forcible rape has been known throughout history and is often linked with war and violence.

▶ Types of rape include date rape, marital rape, and statutory rape; types of rapists include serial rapists and sadists.

▶ Suspected causes of rape include male socialization, hypermasculinity, and biological determinism.

▶ Murder can involve either strangers or acquaintances. Typically, stranger murder occurs during a felony; acquaintance murder involves an interaction or interpersonal transaction between people who may be related romantically, through business dealings, or in other ways.

▶ Mass murder is the killing of numerous victims in a single outburst; serial killing involves numerous victims over an extended period of time. Spree killers attack multiple victims over a short period of time.

▶ Patterns of assault are quite similar to those for homicide.

▶ Numerous cases of child abuse and spousal abuse occur each year. There are also numerous cases of parent abuse.

▶ Robbers use force to steal. Some are opportunists looking for ready cash; others are professionals who have a long-term commitment to crime. Both types pick their targets carefully, which suggests that their crimes are calculated rather than spontaneous.

---

**LO6** Discuss newly emerging forms of violence, such as stalking, hate crimes, and workplace violence.

---

**hate crimes (bias crimes)** Violent acts directed toward a particular person or members of a group merely because the targets share a discernible racial, ethnic, religious, or gender characteristic.

Hate crimes are most often based on race, religion, or sexual orientation. Here, Jonathan Whyte and his wife, Sol, holding a friend's child, talk about finding a cross and the letters "KKK" burned into their lawn in Medford, Oregon. Chief U.S. District Judge Ann Aiken sentenced two Medford men, Gary Moss, 37, and Devan Klausegger, 30, to federal prison for the burning incidents. The two, both white, pleaded guilty to conspiracy to deprive individuals of civil rights related to fair housing.

significantly more likely than lesbians or bisexuals to experience violence and property crimes.[193] Exhibit 10.3 lists the factors that predict hate crimes.

**ROOTS OF HATE**   Why do people commit bias crimes? What motivates someone like Dylann Roof to kill? In a series of research studies, Jack McDevitt, Jack Levin, and Susan Bennett identify four motivations for hate crimes:[194]

- *Thrill-seeking hate crimes.* In the same way some kids like to get together to shoot hoops, hatemongers join forces to have fun by bashing minorities or destroying property. Inflicting pain on others gives them a sadistic thrill.
- *Reactive (defensive) hate crimes.* Perpetrators of these crimes rationalize their behavior as a defensive stand taken against outsiders whom they believe threaten their community or way of life. A gang of teens that attacks a new family in the neighborhood because they are the "wrong" race is committing a reactive hate crime.
- *Mission hate crimes.* Some disturbed individuals see it as their duty to rid the world of evil. Those "on a mission," such as skinheads, the Ku Klux Klan (KKK), and white supremacist groups, may seek to eliminate people who threaten their religious beliefs because they are members of a different faith or threaten "racial purity" because they are of a different race.
- *Retaliatory hate crimes.* These offenses are committed in response to a hate crime either real or perceived; whether the original incident actually occurred is irrelevant. Sometimes a rumor of an incident may cause a group of offenders to exact vengeance, even if the original information was unfounded or inaccurate; the retaliatory crimes are perpetrated before anyone has had a chance to verify the accuracy of the original rumor. Attacks based on revenge tend to have the greatest potential for fueling and refueling additional hate offenses.

## Exhibit 10.3  Factors that Predict Hate Crimes

- Poor or uncertain economic conditions
- Racial stereotypes in films and on television
- Hate-filled discourse on talk shows or in political advertisements
- The use of racial code language, such as "welfare mothers" and "inner-city thugs"

- An individual's personal experiences with members of particular minority groups
- Scapegoating—blaming a minority group for the misfortunes of society as a whole

**Source:** "A Policymaker's Guide to Hate Crimes," *Bureau of Justice Assistance Monograph* (Washington, DC: Bureau of Justice Assistance, 1997).

The research by McDevitt and his colleagues indicates that most hate crimes can be classified as thrill-motivated (66 percent), followed by defensive (25 percent) and retaliatory hate crimes (8 percent); few if any cases had mission-oriented offenders.

**NATURE AND EXTENT OF HATE CRIMES** At last count, law enforcement agencies receive reports of about 6,000 hate crimes each year from about 7,000 victims.[195] Most such incidents are motivated by race; a lesser proportion by religion (most often anti-Semitism), sexual orientation, or ethnicity; and about 1 percent by victim disability. Vandalism and property crimes are the products of hate crimes motivated by religion. However, criminals are more likely to turn to violent acts when race, ethnicity, and sexual orientation are the motivation. Most targets of hate crimes, especially the violent variety, are young white men. Similarly, the majority of known hate crime offenders are young white men.

In crimes where victims could identify the culprits, most victims reported that they were acquainted with their attackers or that their attackers were actually friends, coworkers, neighbors, or relatives.[196] Younger victims were more likely to be victimized by persons known to them. Hate crimes can occur in many settings, but most are perpetrated in public settings.

**CONTROLLING HATE CRIMES** Hate crime laws actually originated after the Civil War and were designed to safeguard the rights of freed slaves.[197] Today, almost every state jurisdiction has enacted some form of legislation designed to combat hate crimes: 45 states have enacted laws against bias-motivated violence and intimidation; 27 states have statutes that specifically mandate the collection of hate crime data.[198]

Some critics argue that it is unfair to punish criminals motivated by hate any more severely than those who commit similar crimes and whose motivation is revenge, greed, or anger. There is also the danger that what appears to be a hate crime, because the target is a minority group member, may actually be motivated by some other factor such as vengeance or monetary gain. Aaron McKinney, who is serving a life sentence for killing Matthew Shepard, told ABC News correspondent Elizabeth Vargas that he was high on methamphetamine when he killed Shepard, and that his intent was robbery, not hate. His partner, Russell Henderson, also claims that the killing was simply a robbery gone bad: "It was not because me and Aaron had anything against gays."[199]

However, in his important book *Punishing Hate: Bias Crimes under American Law*, Frederick Lawrence argues that criminals motivated by bias deserve to be punished more severely than those who commit identical crimes for other motives.[200] He suggests that a society dedicated to the equality of all its people must treat bias crimes differently than other crimes for several reasons:[201]

- Bias crimes are more likely to be violent and to involve serious physical injury to the victim.
- Bias crimes will have significant emotional and psychological impact on the victim; they result in a "heightened sense of vulnerability," which causes depression, anxiety, and feelings of helplessness.
- Bias crimes harm not only the victim but also the "target community."
- Bias crimes violate the shared value of equality among citizens and racial and religious harmony in a heterogeneous society.

**FREE SPEECH?** Should symbolic acts of hate, such as drawing a swastika or burning a cross, be banned, or are they protected by the free speech clause of the First Amendment? The U.S. Supreme Court helped answer this question in the case of *Virginia v. Black* (2003) when it upheld a Virginia statute that makes it a felony "for any person . . . with the intent of intimidating any person or group . . . , to burn . . . a cross on the property of another, a highway or other public place," and specifies that "[a]ny such burning . . . shall be prima facie evidence of an intent to intimidate a person or group." In its decision, the Court upheld Virginia's law, which criminalized cross

AP Images/PA

One of the most disturbing cases of workplace violence occurred on August 26, 2015, when up-and-coming news reporter Alison Parker (left) and photojournalist Adam Ward, employees of CBS affiliate WDBJ in Roanoke, Virginia, were shot to death while conducting a live television interview with Vicki Gardner (right), executive director of the local chamber of commerce. Though wounded, Gardner survived the attack. The shooter was Vester Lee Flanagan, known professionally as Bryce Williams, a former reporter at WDBJ who was fired for disruptive conduct in 2013 and held a grudge against the station and Parker and Ward in particular. He committed suicide soon after the shooting.

burning. The Court ruled that cross burning was intertwined with the Ku Klux Klan and its reign of terror throughout the South. The Court has long held that statements in which the speaker communicates intent to commit an act of unlawful violence to a particular individual or group of individuals are not protected free speech and can be criminalized; the speaker need not actually intend to carry out the threat.[202]

## Workplace Violence

In a shocking case of workplace violence, two WDBJ (Roanoke, Virginia) television journalists, Alison Parker and Adam Ward, were killed on air while doing a live newsfeed. The two were gunned down by a former coworker named Vester Flanagan (professional name Bryce Williams), who had a grudge against the station and its employees.[203] The shooter later took his own life rather than surrendering to police.

**Workplace violence** is now considered the second leading cause of occupational injury or death.[204] Who engages in workplace violence? The typical offender is a middle-aged white male who faces termination in a worsening economy. The fear of economic ruin is especially strong in agencies such as the U.S. Postal Service, where long-term employees fear job loss because of automation and reorganization. In contrast, when younger workers kill, it is usually while committing a robbery or some other felony. A number of factors precipitate workplace violence. One suspected cause is a management style that appears cold and insensitive to workers. As corporations cut their staffs because of an economic downturn or workers are summarily replaced with cost-effective technology, long-term employees may become irate and irrational; their unexpected layoff can lead to violent reactions.

Not all workplace violence is triggered by management-induced injustice. In some incidents, coworkers have been killed because they refused romantic relationships with the assailants or reported them for sexual harassment. Others have been killed because they got a job the assailant coveted. Irate clients and customers have also killed because of poor service or perceived slights.[205] Hospital patients whose demands are not met may attack people who are there to be caregivers. In fact, health care and social services workers have the highest rate of nonfatal assault injuries. Nurses and nursing assistants are significantly more likely to experience workplace violence than any other professional group.[206]

**workplace violence**
Violence such as assault, rape, or murder committed at the workplace.

**stalking**
A course of conduct that is directed at a specific person and involves repeated physical or visual proximity, nonconsensual communication, or verbal, written, or implied threats sufficient to cause fear in a reasonable person.

## Stalking

In 2008, Frank Mendoza began a romantic relationship with a woman in Jacksonville, Florida. When he became emotionally and psychologically abusive toward the victim she broke it off and moved to Connecticut, telling him that she was moving to Rhode Island for a work-related training program. When Mendoza found out about the ruse, he began making harassing and threatening phone calls to her, her friends, and her work colleagues. He then traveled to Connecticut and placed bottles containing hydrochloric acid in her car, set to explode. When the victim noticed the bombs she ran from the car before the acid bottles blew up. In 2014, Mendoza was sentenced to 10 years in prison for what is now a recognized form of long-term and repeat victimization: **stalking**.[207]

A complex phenomenon, stalking can be defined as a course of conduct that is directed at a specific person and involves repeated physical or visual proximity, non-consensual communication, or verbal, written, or implied threats sufficient to cause fear in a reasonable person.[208] The most recent data indicate that stalkers victimize more than 3 million people each year.[209] If anything this figure undercounts the problem because stalkers may be juveniles who use text messages and emails, along with direct contact, to harass their victims.[210] Women are much more likely to be stalked than men. In nearly 75 percent of stalking cases, victims know their stalker in some way; in about 30 percent of cases, the stalker is a current or former intimate partner. Former partners have leverage over their victim; they can use the information they have about their former partner's friends and family members, where they work, shop, and go for entertainment.[211]

Although stalking usually stops within one or two years, victims experience its social and psychological consequences long afterward. About one-third seek psychological treatment, and about one-fifth lose time from work; indeed, some never return to work at all. Stalking can also be lethal. More than 75 percent of women who were murdered by their current or former intimate partners were stalked by their killers before the murder.[212]

Even though stalking is a serious problem, research indicates that many cases are dropped by the courts despite the fact that stalkers often have extensive criminal histories and are frequently the subject of protective orders. A lenient response may be misplaced, considering that stalkers very often repeat their criminal activity within a short time after a stalking charge is lodged with police authorities.[213]

## CHECKPOINTS

▶ Hate crimes are violent acts against targets selected because of their religion, race, ethnic background, gender, or sexual orientation.

▶ Some hate criminals are thrill seekers; others are motivated by hatred of outsiders; still others believe they are on a mission. More than 6,000 people are the targets of hate crimes each year in the United States.

▶ Workplace violence has become commonplace. It is believed to be related to a number of factors, including job stress and insensitive management style.

▶ About 3 million people are victims of stalking each year.

# Thinking Like a Criminologist

## Enforcing Statutory Rape Laws

The state legislature has asked you to prepare a report on statutory rape because of the growing number of underage girls who have been impregnated by adult men. Studies reveal that many teenage pregnancies result from affairs that underage girls have with older men, with age gaps ranging from 7 to 10 years. For example, the typical relationship prosecuted in California involves a 13-year-old girl and a 22-year-old male partner. Some outraged parents adamantly support a law that will provide state grants to counties to prosecute statutory rape. These grants would allow more vigorous enforcement of the law and could result in the conviction of more than 1,500 offenders each year.

However, some critics suggest that implementing statutory rape laws to punish males who have relationships with minor girls does not solve the problems of teenage pregnancies and out-of-wedlock births. Liberals dislike the idea of using criminal law to solve social problems, because doing so does not provide for the girls and their children and focuses only on punishing offenders. In contrast, conservatives fear that such laws give the state power to prosecute people for victimless crimes, thereby increasing the government's ability to control people's private lives. Not all cases involve much older men, and critics ask whether we should criminalize the behavior of 19-year-old boys and their 15-year-old girlfriends.

### Writing Assignment

Write an essay on statutory rape and how different states address sex with minors. Decide whether current laws should be changed to reflect current social behaviors.

# SUMMARY

**LO1     Differentiate among the various causes of violent crime.**

Research has shown that a significant number of people involved in violent episodes may be suffering from severe mental abnormalities. Absent or deviant parents, inconsistent discipline, physical abuse, and lack of supervision have all been linked to persistent violent offending. A number of criminologists have speculated that instinctual violence-promoting traits may be common in the human species. Kids who are constantly exposed to violence at home, at school, or in the environment may adopt violent methods themselves. Substance abuse has been associated with violence on both the individual and social levels. Although firearm availability alone does not cause violence, it may be a facilitating factor. Furthermore, some areas contain an independent subculture of violence in which a potent theme of violence influences lifestyles, the socialization process, and interpersonal relationships. Some nations have cultures that support relatively high violence rates.

**LO2     Define rape and be familiar with why men commit rape.**

The common-law definition of rape is "the carnal knowledge of a female forcibly and against her will." One explanation for rape focuses on the evolutionary, biological aspects of the male sexual drive. Some researchers argue that rape is a function of socialization. Rapists may suffer from some type of personality disorder or mental illness. Men may learn to commit rapes much as they learn any other behavior. Rape arises primarily from a desire to inflict pain and humiliation, but there is evidence that at least some rapists have sexual feelings for their victim.

**LO3     Discuss the issues involving rape and the law.**

Proving guilt in a rape case is extremely challenging for prosecutors. It is essential to prove that the attack was forced and that the victim did not give voluntary consent to her attacker. Shield laws that protect women from being questioned about their sexual history unless it directly bears on the case have become universal.

**LO4     Analyze the different types of murder.**

First-degree murder occurs when a person kills another after premeditation and deliberation. Second-degree murder is the charge when the killer had malice aforethought but not premeditation or deliberation. Voluntary or nonnegligent manslaughter is a killing committed in the heat of passion or during a sudden quarrel that provoked violence. Involuntary or negligent manslaughter is a killing that occurs when a person's acts are negligent and without regard for the harm they may cause others. Serial killers murder three or more persons in three or more separate events. Mass murder involves the killing of four or more victims by one or a few assailants within a single event. Spree killers engage in a rampage of violence over a period of days or weeks.

**LO5     Explain the nature and patterns of robbery.**

The common-law definition of robbery is "the taking or attempting to take anything of value from the care, custody, or control of a person or persons by force or threat of force or violence and/or by putting the victim in fear." Some robbers are opportunists looking for ready cash; others are professionals who have a long-term commitment to crime. The typical armed robber is a rational decision maker. Many robbers choose victims who themselves are involved in illegal behavior, most often drug dealers. Female armed robbers are likely to choose female targets, reasoning that women will be more vulnerable and offer less resistance.

**LO6** **Discuss newly emerging forms of violence, such as stalking, hate crimes, and workplace violence.**

Hate crimes, or bias crimes, are violent acts directed toward a particular person or members of a particular group merely because the targets share a discernible racial, ethnic, religious, or gender characteristic. Workplace violence is now considered the second leading cause of occupational injury or death. Stalking can be defined as conduct that is directed at a specific person and involves repeated physical or visual proximity, nonconsensual communication, and/or verbal, written, or implied threats sufficient to cause fear in a reasonable person.

## Key Terms

expressive violence 302
instrumental violence 302
cycle of violence 303
eros 303
thanatos 303
psychopharmacological
    relationship 304
economic compulsive
    behavior 304
systemic link 304
subculture of
    violence 304
rape 306
date rape 308
marital exemption 310

statutory rape 310
virility mystique 311
narcissistic personality
    disorder 312
aggravated rape 313
consent 313
shield laws 313
murder 314
first-degree
    murder 314
premeditation 314
deliberation 314
felony murder 315
second-degree
    murder 315

manslaughter 315
voluntary or nonnegligent
    manslaughter 315
involuntary or negligent
    manslaughter 315
infanticide 316
filicide 316
eldercide 316
feticide 317
serial killer 319
mass murder 320
spree killer 321
battery 321
assault 322
road rage 322

child abuse 322
neglect 322
child sexual
    abuse 323
relational
    aggression 324
robbery 325
acquaintance
    robbery 326
hate crimes
    (bias crimes) 327
workplace
    violence 330
stalking 330

## Critical Thinking Questions

1. Should the perpetrators of different types of rape receive different legal sanctions? For example, should someone who rapes a stranger be punished more severely than someone who is convicted of marital rape or date rape? If your answer is yes, do you think someone who kills a stranger should be punished more severely than someone who kills a spouse or a friend?

2. Is there a subculture of violence in your home city or town? If so, how would you describe the environment and values of that subculture?

3. There have been significant changes in rape law involving issues such as corroboration and shield laws. What other measures would you take to protect victims of rape when they have to testify in court?

4. Should hate crimes be punished more severely than crimes motivated by greed, anger, or revenge? Why should crimes be distinguished in terms of the motivations of the perpetrator? Is hate a more heinous motivation than revenge?

# Notes

*All URLs accessed in 2015.*

1. Ray Sanchez and Ed Payne, "Charleston Church Shooting: Who Is Dylann Roof?" CNN, June 23, 2015, www.cnn.com/2015/06/19/us/charleston-church-shooting-suspect/.

2. Rokeya Farrooque, Ronnie Stout, and Frederick Ernst, "Heterosexual Intimate Partner Homicide: Review of Ten Years of Clinical Experience," *Journal of Forensic Sciences* 50 (2005): 648–651; Miltos Livaditis, Gkaro Esagian, Christos Kakoulidis, Maria Samakouri, and Nikos Tzavaras, "Matricide by Person with Bipolar Disorder and Dependent Overcompliant Personality," *Journal of Forensic Sciences* 50 (2005): 658–661.

3. David P. Farrington, Rolf Loeber, and Mark T. Berg, "Young Men Who Kill: A Prospective Longitudinal Examination from Childhood," *Homicide Studies* 16 (2012): 99–128; Roman Gleyzer, Alan Felthous, and Charles Holzer, "Animal Cruelty and Psychiatric Disorders," *Journal of the American Academy of Psychiatry and the Law* 30 (2002): 257–265.

4. Richard Rogers, Randall Salekin, Kenneth Sewell, and Keith Cruise, "Prototypical Analysis of Antisocial Personality Disorder," *Criminal Justice and Behavior* 27 (2000): 234–255; Amy Holtzworth-Munroe and Gregory Stuart, "Typologies of Male Batterers: Three Subtypes and the Differences Among Them," *Psychological Bulletin* 116 (1994): 476–497.

5. Christopher Hensley and Suzanne Tallichet, "Childhood and Adolescent Animal Cruelty Methods and Their Possible Link to Adult Violent Crimes," *Journal of Interpersonal Violence* 24 (2009): 147–158.

6. Gleyzer, Felthous, and Holzer, "Animal Cruelty and Psychiatric Disorders."

7. Tatia M. C. Lee, Siu-Ching Chan, and Adrian Raine, "Hyperresponsivity to Threat Stimuli in Domestic Violence Offenders: A Functional Magnetic Resonance Imaging Study," *Journal of Clinical Psychiatry* 70 (2009): 36–45.

8. See, for example, Egbert Zavala, "Testing the Link Between Child Maltreatment and Family Violence Among Police Officers," *Crime and Delinquency*, first published online November 22, 2010; Cesar Rebellon and Karen Van Gundy, "Can Control Theory Explain the Link Between Parental Physical Abuse and Delinquency? A Longitudinal Analysis," *Journal of Research in Crime and Delinquency* 42 (2005): 247–274.

9. Cathy Spatz Widom, "The Cycle of Violence," *Science* 244 (1989): 160–166; Widom, "Understanding Child Maltreatment and Juvenile Delinquency: The Research," Child Welfare League of America, 2010, 66.227.70.18/programs/juvenilejustice/ucmjd03.pdf.

10. Cathy Spatz Widom, "Varieties of Violent Behavior," *Criminology* 52 (2014): 313–344.

11. Emily M. Wright and Abigail A. Fagan, "The Cycle of Violence in Context: Exploring the Moderating Roles of Neighborhood Disadvantage and Cultural Norms," *Criminology* 51 (2013): 217–249.

12. Christopher Boehm, "Retaliatory Violence in Human Prehistory," *British Journal of Criminology* 51 (2011): 518–534.

13. Steven Pinker, *The Better Angels of Our Nature: Why Violence Has Declined* (New York: Viking, 2011).

14. Sigmund Freud, *Beyond the Pleasure Principle* (London: Inter-Psychoanalytic Press, 1922).

15. Konrad Lorenz, *On Aggression* (New York: Harcourt Brace Jovanovich, 1966).

16. Wade Myers, *Sexual Homicide by Juveniles* (London: Academic Press, 2002).

17. Justin Patchin, Beth Huebner, John McCluskey, Sean Varano, and Timothy Bynum, "Exposure to Community Violence and Childhood Delinquency," *Crime and Delinquency* 52 (2006): 307–332.

18. Jeffrey B. Bingenheimer, Robert T. Brennan, and Felton J. Earls, "Firearm Violence Exposure and Serious Violent Behavior," *Science* 308 (2005): 1323–1326; "Witnessing Gun Violence Significantly Increases Likelihood that a Child Will Also Commit Violent Crime; Violence May Be Viewed as Infectious Disease," *A Scribe Health News Service*, May 26, 2005.

19. Eric Stewart, Ronald Simons, and Rand Conger, "Assessing Neighborhood and Social Psychological Influences on Childhood Violence in an African-American Sample," *Criminology* 40 (2002): 801–830.

20. David Farrington, Rolf Loeber, and Magda Stouthamer-Loeber, "How Can the Relationship Between Race and Violence Be Explained?" in *Violent Crimes: Assessing Race and Ethnic Differences*, ed. D. F. Hawkins (New York: Cambridge University Press, 2003), pp. 213–237.

21. William Alex Pridemore and Tony Grubesic, "Alcohol Outlets and Community Levels of Interpersonal Violence: Spatial Density, Outlet Type, and Seriousness of Assault," *Journal of Research in Crime and Delinquency*, first published May 17, 2011; Chris Allen, "The Links Between Heroin, Crack Cocaine and Crime: Where Does Street Crime Fit In?" *British Journal of Criminology* 45 (2005): 355–372.

22. Paul Goldstein, Henry Brownstein, and Patrick Ryan, "Drug-Related Homicide in New York: 1984–1988," *Crime and Delinquency* 38 (1992): 459–476.

23. Robert Brewer and Monica Swahn, "Binge Drinking and Violence," *JAMA: Journal of the American Medical Association* 294 (2005): 16–20.

24. Tomika Stevens, Kenneth Ruggiero, Dean Kilpatrick, Heidi Resnick, and Benjamin Saunders, "Variables Differentiating Singly and Multiply Victimized Youth:

Results from the National Survey of Adolescents and Implications for Secondary Prevention," *Child Maltreatment* 10 (2005): 211–223; James Collins and Pamela Messerschmidt, "Epidemiology of Alcohol-Related Violence," *Alcohol Health and Research World* 17 (1993): 93–100.

25. Antonia Abbey, Tina Zawacki, Philip Buck, Monique Clinton, and Pam McAuslan, "Sexual Assault and Alcohol Consumption: What Do We Know About Their Relationship and What Types of Research Are Still Needed?" *Aggression and Violent Behavior* 9 (2004): 271–303.

26. Martin Grann and Seena Fazel, "Substance Misuse and Violent Crime: Swedish Population Study," *British Medical Journal* 328 (2004): 1233–1234; Susanne Rogne Gjeruldsen, Bjørn Myrvang, and Stein Opjordsmoen, "Criminality in Drug Addicts: A Follow-Up Study over 25 Years," *European Addiction Research* 10 (2004): 49–56; Kenneth Tardiff, Peter Marzuk, Kira Lowell, Laura Portera, and Andrew Leon, "A Study of Drug Abuse and Other Causes of Homicide in New York," *Journal of Criminal Justice* 30 (2002): 317–325.

27. Paul Goldstein, Patricia Bellucci, Barry Spunt, and Thomas Miller, "Volume of Cocaine Use and Violence: A Comparison Between Men and Women," *Journal of Drug Issues* 21 (1991): 345–367.

28. Richard Felson and Luke Bonkiewicz, "Guns and Trafficking in Crack-Cocaine and Other Drug Markets," *Crime and Delinquency*, first published February 10, 2011.

29. Pamela Wilcox and Richard Clayton, "A Multilevel Analysis of School-Based Weapon Possession," *Justice Quarterly* 18 (2001): 509–542.

30. FBI, *Crime in the United States, 2013* (Washington, DC: U.S. Government Printing Office, 2014), www.fbi.gov /about-us/cjis/ucr/crime-in-the-u.s/2013/crime-in -the-u.s.-2013/violent-crime/violent-crime-topic-page /violentcrimemain_final.

31. FBI, *Law Enforcement Officers Killed and Assaulted, 2013,* www.fbi.gov/about-us/cjis/ucr/leoka/2013/officers -feloniously-killed/felonious_topic_page_-2013.

32. David Brent, Joshua Perper, Christopher Allman, Grace Moritz, Mary Wartella, and Janice Zelenak, "The Presence and Accessibility of Firearms in the Home and Adolescent Suicides," *Journal of the American Medical Association* 266 (1991): 2989–2995.

33. Robert Baller, Luc Anselin, Steven Messner, Glenn Deane, and Darnell Hawkins, "Structural Covariates of U.S. County Homicide Rates Incorporating Spatial Effects," *Criminology* 39 (2001): 561–590.

34. Marvin Wolfgang and Franco Ferracuti, *The Subculture of Violence* (London: Tavistock, 1967).

35. David Luckenbill and Daniel Doyle, "Structural Position and Violence: Developing a Cultural Explanation," *Criminology* 27 (1989): 419–436.

36. Charis Kubrin and Ronald Weitzer, "Retaliatory Homicide: Concentrated Disadvantage and Neighborhood Culture," *Social Problems* 50 (2003): 157–180.

37. Robert J. Kane, "Compromised Police Legitimacy as a Predictor of Violent Crime in Structurally Disadvantaged Communities," *Criminology* 43 (2005): 469–499.

38. Chris Melde and Finn-Aage Esbensen, "Gangs and Violence: Disentangling the Impact of Gang Membership on the Level and Nature of Offending," *Journal of Quantitative Criminology*, first published online January 24, 2012.

39. Daniel Neller, Robert Denney, Christina Pietz, and R. Paul Thomlinson, "Testing the Trauma Model of Violence," *Journal of Family Violence* 20 (2005): 151–159; James Howell, "Youth Gang Homicides: A Literature Review," *Crime and Delinquency* 45 (1999): 208–241.

40. William Wells, Ling Wu, and Xinyue Ye, "Patterns of Near-Repeat Gun Assaults in Houston," *Journal of Research in Crime and Delinquency*, first published May 12, 2011.

41. Lonnie Schaible and Lorine Hughes, "Crime, Shame, Reintegration, and Cross-national Homicide: A Partial Test of Reintegrative Shaming Theory," *Sociological Quarterly* 52 (2011): 104–131.

42. Marc Ouimet, "A World of Homicides: The Effect of Economic Development, Income Inequality, and Excess Infant Mortality on the Homicide Rate for 165 Countries in 2010," *Homicide Studies* 16 (2012): 238–258; Don Chon, "Contributing Factors for High Homicide Rate in Latin America: A Critical Test of Neapolitan's Regional Subculture of Violence Thesis," *Journal of Family Violence* 26 (2011): 299–307.

43. William Green, *Rape* (Lexington, MA: Lexington Books, 1988), p. 5.

44. Barbara Krahé, Renate Scheinberger-Olwig, and Steffen Bieneck, "Men's Reports of Nonconsensual Sexual Interactions with Women: Prevalence and Impact," *Archives of Sexual Behavior* 32 (2003): 165–176.

45. Heidi Zinzow, Heidi Resnick, Ananda Amstadter, Jenna McCauley, Kenneth Ruggiero, and Dean Kilpatrick, "Drug- or Alcohol-Facilitated, Incapacitated, and Forcible Rape in Relationship to Mental Health Among a National Sample of Women," *Journal of Interpersonal Violence* 25 (2010): 2217–2236.

46. Marlise Simons, "Bosnian Serb Pleads Guilty to Rape Charge Before War Crimes Tribunal," *New York Times*, March 10, 1998, p. 8.

47. Joshua Kaiser and John Hagan, "Gendered Genocide: The Socially Destructive Process of Genocidal Rape, Killing, and Displacement in Darfur," *Law and Society Review* 49 (2015): 69–107.

48. Jacob Zenn and Elizabeth Pearson, "Women, Gender and the Evolving Tactics of Boko Haram," *Journal of Terrorism Research* 5 (2014), ojs.st-andrews.ac.uk /index.php/jtr/article/view/828/707.

49. CNN, "Boko Haram Kidnapping of Nigerian Schoolgirls, a Year Later," April 14, 2015, www.cnn.com/2015/04/14/africa/nigeria-kidnapping-anniversary/.

50. FBI, *Uniform Crime Reports, Crime in the United States, 2013*, www.fbi.gov/about-us/cjis/ucr/crime-in-the-u.s/2013/crime-in-the-u.s.-2013/violent-crime/rape.

51. Lynn Langton and Jennifer Truman, *Criminal Victimization, 2013*, Bureau of Justice Statistics, 2014, www.bjs.gov/content/pub/pdf/cv13.pdf.

52. Sarah Cook, Christine Gidycz, Mary Koss, and Megan Murphy, "Emerging Issues in the Measurement of Rape Victimization," *Violence Against Women* 17 (2011): 201–218; Bonnie S. Fisher, "The Effects of Survey Question Wording on Rape Estimates: Evidence from a Quasi-Experimental Design," *Violence Against Women* 15 (2009): 133–147. Amy Buddie and Maria Testa, "Rates and Predictors of Sexual Aggression Among Students and Nonstudents," *Journal of Interpersonal Violence* 20 (2005): 713–725.

53. Dean Kilpatrick, Heidi Resnick, Kenneth Ruggiero, Lauren Conoscenti, and Jenna McCauley, "Drug-Facilitated, Incapacitated, and Forcible Rape: A National Study," U.S. Department of Justice, 2007, www.ncjrs.gov/pdffiles1/nij/grants/219181.pdf.

54. Carol Vanzile-Tamsen, Maria Testa, and Jennifer Livingston, "The Impact of Sexual Assault History and Relationship Context on Appraisal of and Responses to Acquaintance Sexual Assault Risk," *Journal of Interpersonal Violence* 20 (2005): 813–822.

55. Lynn Langton and Sofi Sinozich, "Rape and Sexual Assault Among College-Age Females, 1995–2013," Bureau of Justice Statistics, 2014, www.bjs.gov/content/pub/pdf/rsavcaf9513.pdf.

56. Heather Littleton and Craig Henderson, "If She Is Not a Victim, Does That Mean She Was Not Traumatized? Evaluation of Predictors of PTSD Symptomatology Among College Rape Victims," *Violence Against Women* 15 (2009): 148–167.

57. A. Nicholas Groth and Jean Birnbaum, *Men Who Rape* (New York: Plenum Press, 1979).

58. For another typology, see Raymond Knight, "Validation of a Typology of Rapists," in *Sex Offender Research and Treatment: State-of-the-Art in North America and Europe*, ed. W. L. Marshall and J. Frenken (Beverly Hills, CA: Sage, 1997), pp. 58–75.

59. R. Lance Shotland, "A Model of the Causes of Date Rape in Developing and Close Relationships," in *Close Relationships*, ed. C. Hendrick (Newbury Park, CA: Sage, 1989), pp. 247–270.

60. Mary Koss, "Hidden Rape: Sexual Aggression and Victimization in a National Sample of Students in Higher Education," in *Rape and Sexual Assault*, vol. 2, ed. Anne Wolbert Burgess (New York: Garland Publishing, 1988), p. 824.

61. Bonnie Fisher, Leah Daigle, Francis Cullen, and Michael Turner, "Reporting Sexual Victimization to the Police and Others: Results from a National-Level Study of College Women," *Criminal Justice and Behavior* 30 (2003): 6–39.

62. Steven Lawyer, Heidi Resnick, Von Bakanic, Tracy Burkett, and Dean Kilpatrick, "Forcible, Drug-Facilitated, and Incapacitated Rape and Sexual Assault Among Undergraduate Women," *Journal of American College Health* 58 (2010): 453–460.

63. Heidi M. Zinzow, Heidi S. Resnick, Jenna L. McCauley, Ananda B. Amstadter, Kenneth J. Ruggiero, and Dean G. Kilpatrick, "The Role of Rape Tactics in Risk for Posttraumatic Stress Disorder and Major Depression: Results from a National Sample of College Women," *Depression and Anxiety* 27 (2010): 708–715.

64. Kate Carey, Sarah Durney, Robyn Shepardson, and Michael Carey, "Incapacitated and Forcible Rape of College Women: Prevalence Across the First Year," *Journal of Adolescent Health* 56 (2015): 678–680.

65. David Cantor, Bonnie Fisher, Susan Chibnall, Reanne Townsend, Hyunshik Lee, Carol Bruce, and Gail Thomas, "Report on the AAU Campus Climate Survey on Sexual Assault and Sexual Misconduct," Westat, September 21, 2015, www.aau.edu/registration/public/PAdocs/Survey_Communication_9-18/Final_Report_9-18-15.pdf.

66. Kate Wolitzky-Taylor, Heidi Resnick, Ananda Amstadter, Jenna McCauley, Kenneth Ruggiero, and Dean Kilpatrick, "Reporting Rape in a National Sample of College Women," *Journal of American College Health* 59 (2011): 582–587.

67. Steven Lawyer, Heidi Resnick, Von Bakanic, Tracy Burkett, and Dean Kilpatrick, "Forcible, Drug-Facilitated, and Incapacitated Rape and Sexual Assault Among Undergraduate Women," *Journal of American College Health* 58 (2010): 453–460.

68. Zinzow, Resnick, McCauley, Amstadter, Ruggiero, and Kilpatrick, "The Role of Rape Tactics in Risk for Posttraumatic Stress Disorder and Major Depression."

69. Caitlin Flanagan, "The Dark Power of Fraternities," *Atlantic Monthly*, February 19, 2014, www.theatlantic.com/features/archive/2014/02/the-dark-power-of-fraternities/357580/.

70. Carrie Wells, Erica L. Green, and Justin Fenton, "Johns Hopkins University Under Fire Over Not Disclosing Alleged Rape," May 7, 2014, www.washingtonpost.com/local/johns-hopkins-university-under-fire-over-not-disclosing-alleged-rape/2014/05/03/c86582b4-d305-11e3-8a78-8fe50322a72c_story.html

71. California Senate Bill No. 967, Chapter 748, An Act to Add Section 67386 to the Education code, Relating to Student Safety, 2014. https://leginfo.legislature.ca.gov/faces/billNavClient.xhtml?bill_id=201320140SB967.

**337**

72. David Finkelhor and K. Yllo, *License to Rape: Sexual Abuse of Wives* (New York: Holt, Rinehart and Winston, 1985).

73. Raquel Kennedy Bergen, with contributions from Elizabeth Barnhill, "Marital Rape: New Research and Directions," National Online Resource Center for Violence Against Women, vawnet.org/assoc_files _vawnet/ar_maritalraperevised.pdf.

74. Jed Rubenfeld, "The Riddle of Rape-by-Deception and the Myth of Sexual Autonomy," *Yale Law Journal* 122 (2013): 1372–1443.

75. Tennessee Code Annotated § 39-i3-5O3(a)(4) (2010); Idaho Tennessee Code Annotated § 18-6101(8) (Supp. 2011).

76. Rubenfeld, "The Riddle of Rape-by-Deception and the Myth of Sexual Autonomy."

77. William McKibbin, Todd Shackelford, Aaron Goetz, and Valerie Starratt, "Why Do Men Rape? An Evolutionary Psychological Perspective," *Review of General Psychology* 12 (2008): 86–97.

78. Lawrence Miller "Rape: Sex Crime, Act of Violence, or Naturalistic Adaptation?" *Aggression and Violent Behavior* 19 (2014): 67–81.

79. Ibid.

80. Suzanne Osman, "Predicting Men's Rape Perceptions Based on the Belief that 'No' Really Means 'Yes,'" *Journal of Applied Social Psychology* 33 (2003): 683–692.

81. Martin Schwartz, Walter DeKeseredy, David Tait, and Shahid Alvi, "Male Peer Support and a Feminist Routine Activities Theory: Understanding Sexual Assault on the College Campus," *Justice Quarterly* 18 (2001): 623–650.

82. Diana Russell and Rebecca M. Bolen, *The Epidemic of Rape and Child Sexual Abuse in the United States* (Thousand Oaks, CA: Sage, 2000).

83. Paul Gebhard, John Gagnon, Wardell Pomeroy, and Cornelia Christenson, *Sex Offenders: An Analysis of Types* (New York: Harper & Row, 1965), pp. 198–205; Richard Rada, ed., *Clinical Aspects of the Rapist* (New York: Grune & Stratton, 1978), pp. 122–130.

84. Stephen Porter, David Fairweather, Jeff Drugge, Huues Herve, Angela Birt, and Douglas Boer, "Profiles of Psychopathy in Incarcerated Sexual Offenders," *Criminal Justice and Behavior* 27 (2000): 216–233.

85. Brad Bushman, Angelica Bonacci, Mirjam van Dijk, and Roy Baumeister, "Narcissism, Sexual Refusal, and Aggression: Testing a Narcissistic Reactance Model of Sexual Coercion," *Journal of Personality and Social Psychology* 84 (2003): 1027–1040.

86. Schwartz, DeKeseredy, Tait, and Alvi, "Male Peer Support and a Feminist Routine Activities Theory."

87. Groth and Birnbaum, *Men Who Rape*, p. 101.

88. See, generally, Edward Donnerstein, Daniel Linz, and Steven Penrod, *The Question of Pornography* (New York:

Free Press, 1987); Diana Russell, *Sexual Exploitation* (Beverly Hills, CA: Sage, 1985), pp. 115–116.

89. Neil Malamuth and John Briere, "Sexual Violence in the Media: Indirect Effects on Aggression Against Women," *Journal of Social Issues* 42 (1986): 75–92.

90. Richard Johnson, "Rape and Gender Conflict in a Patriarchal State," *Crime and Delinquency* 60 (2014): 1110–1128.

91. Ibid.

92. Richard Felson and Marvin Krohn, "Motives for Rape," *Journal of Research in Crime and Delinquency* 27 (1990): 222–242.

93. CBS News, "DA: Strauss-Kahn Accuser Cleaned After Encounter," July 1, 2011, www.cbsnews.com/news /da-strauss-kahn-accuser-cleaned-after-encounter/.

94. Laura Monroe, Linda Kinney, Mark Weist, Denise Spriggs Dafeamekpor, Joyce Dantzler, and Matthew Reynolds, "The Experience of Sexual Assault: Findings from a Statewide Victim Needs Assessment," *Journal of Interpersonal Violence* 20 (2005): 767–776.

95. Steffen Bieneck and Barbara Krahé, "Blaming the Victim and Exonerating the Perpetrator in Cases of Rape and Robbery: Is There a Double Standard?" *Journal of Interpersonal Violence* 26 (2011): 1785–1797.

96. Julie Horney and Cassia Spohn, "The Influence of Blame and Believability Factors on the Processing of Simple versus Aggravated Rape Cases," *Criminology* 34 (1996): 135–163.

97. "Duke Lacrosse 'Rape' Accuser Changes Story Again, Says Seligmann Didn't Touch Her," Associated Press, January 12, 2007, www.foxnews.com/story/0,2933, 243063,00.html; Sal Ruibal, "Rape Allegations Cast Pall at Duke," *USA Today*, March 29, 2006, usato-day30.usatoday.com/sports/college/lacrosse/2006-03-29-duke-fallout_x.htm.

98. Juliet Linderman, "Victim Advocates Worry About Discredited UVa Rape Account," Associated Press, March 24, 2015, koin.com/ap/police-report-on-virginia-gang-rape-not-the-final-word/.

99. Patricia Landwehr, Robert Bothwell, Matthew Jeanmard, Luis Luque, Roy Brown III, and Marie-Anne Breaux, "Racism in Rape Trials," *Journal of Social Psychology* 142 (2002): 667–670.

100. Cassia Spohn, Dawn Beichner, and Erika Davis-Frenzel, "Prosecutorial Justifications for Sexual Assault Case Rejection," *Social Problems* 48 (2001): 206–235.

101. Susan Estrich, *Real Rape* (Cambridge, MA: Harvard University Press, 1987), pp. 58–59.

102. *Michigan v. Lucas* 90-149 (1991); Comment, "The Rape Shield Paradox: Complainant Protection Amidst Oscillating Trends of State Judicial Interpretation," *Journal of Criminal Law and Criminology* 78 (1987): 644–698.

103. Andrew Karmen, *Crime Victims* (Pacific Grove, CA: Brooks/Cole, 1990), p. 252.

104. "Court Upholds Civil Rights Portion of Violence Against Women Act," *Criminal Justice Newsletter* 28 (1997): 3.

105. Cassia Spohn and David Holleran, "Prosecuting Sexual Assault: A Comparison of Charging Decisions in Sexual Assault Cases Involving Strangers, Acquaintances, and Intimate Partners," *Justice Quarterly* 18 (2001): 651–688.

106. Campus Sexual Violence Elimination Act, www.cleryact.info/campus-save-act.html.

107. Donald Lunde, *Murder and Madness* (San Francisco: San Francisco Book, 1977), p. 3.

108. "'Baby Hope' Case: Cousin Confesses to Sexually Assaulting, Killing Toddler Anjelica Castillo More than Two Decades Ago," *New York Daily News*, October 13, 2013, www.nydailynews.com/news/crime/relative-arrested-baby-hope-case-article-1.1483690.

109. Wayne LaFave and Austin Scott, *Criminal Law* (St. Paul: West, 1986; updated 1993).

110. Bob Egelko, "State's Top Court OKs Dog Maul Murder Charge, Judge Ordered to Reconsider Owner's Original Conviction," *San Francisco Chronicle*, June 1, 2007, www.sfgate.com/bayarea/article/SAN-FRANCISCO-State-s-top-court-OKs-dog-maul-2557910.php; Evelyn Nieves, "Woman Gets 4-Year Term in Fatal Dog Attack," *New York Times*, July 16, 2002, p. 1.

111. Dana Haynie and David Armstrong, "Race and Gender-Disaggregated Homicide Offending Rates: Differences and Similarities by Victim-Offender Relations Across Cities," *Homicide Studies* 10 (2006): 3–32.

112. Todd Shackelford, Viviana Weekes-Shackelford, and Shanna Beasley, "An Exploratory Analysis of the Contexts and Circumstances of Filicide-Suicide in Chicago, 1965–1994," *Aggressive Behavior* 31 (2005): 399–406.

113. Philip Cook, Jens Ludwig, and Anthony Braga, "Criminal Records of Homicide Offenders," *JAMA: Journal of the American Medical Association* 294 (2005): 598–601.

114. David P. Farrington, Rolf Loeber, and Mark T. Berg, "Young Men Who Kill: A Prospective Longitudinal Examination from Childhood," *Homicide Studies* 16 (2012): 99–128.

115. The National Conference of State Legislatures Fetal Homicide Laws, April 2012, www.ncsl.org/issues-research/health/fetal-homicide-state-laws.aspx.

116. Ibid.

117. Ibid.

118. C. Gabrielle Salfati and Paul Taylor, "Differentiating Sexual Violence: A Comparison of Sexual Homicide and Rape," *Psychology, Crime and Law* 12 (2006): 107–125.

119. Terance Miethe and Wendy Regoeczi with Kriss Drass, *Rethinking Homicide: Exploring the Structure and Process Underlying Deadly Situations* (Cambridge, England: Cambridge University Press, 2004).

120. National Institute of Justice, "How Widespread Is Intimate Partner Violence?" www.nij.gov/topics/crime/intimate-partner-violence/pages/extent.aspx.

121. Carol Jordan, James Clark, Adam Pritchard, and Richard Charnigo, "Lethal and Other Serious Assaults: Disentangling Gender and Context," *Crime and Delinquency* 58 (2012): 425–455.

122. Steven Shatz and Naomi Shatz, "Chivalry Is Not Dead: Murder, Gender, and the Death Penalty," *Berkeley Journal of Gender, Law and Justice* 27 (2012): 64–112.

123. Linda Saltzman and James Mercy, "Assaults Between Intimates: The Range of Relationships Involved," in *Homicide: The Victim/Offender Connection*, ed. Anna Victoria Wilson (Cincinnati: Anderson Publishing, 1993), pp. 65–74.

124. Jordan, Clark, Pritchard, and Charnigo, "Lethal and Other Serious Assaults: Disentangling Gender and Context."

125. Angela Browne and Kirk Williams, "Exploring the Effect of Resource Availability and the Likelihood of Female-Perpetrated Homicides," *Law and Society Review* 23 (1989): 75–94.

126. Richard Felson, "Anger, Aggression, and Violence in Love Triangles," *Violence and Victimization* 12 (1997): 345–363.

127. Ibid., p. 361.

128. Scott Decker, "Deviant Homicide: A New Look at the Role of Motives and Victim–Offender Relationships," *Journal of Research in Crime and Delinquency* 33 (1996): 427–449.

129. David Luckenbill, "Criminal Homicide as a Situational Transaction," *Social Problems* 25 (1977): 176–186.

130. Jeff Gruenewald, "A Comparative Examination of Homicides Perpetrated by Far-Right Extremists," *Homicide Studies* 15 (2011): 177–203.

131. Sharon Smith, Kathleen Basile, and Debra Karch, "Sexual Homicide and Sexual Violence–Associated Homicide: Findings from the National Violent Death Reporting System," *Homicide Studies* 15 (2011): 132–153; Vernon J. Geberth, "The Classification of Sex-Related Homicides," www.practicalhomicide.com/Research/sexrelatedhomicides.htm.

132. Peter Lin and James Gill, "Homicides of Pregnant Women," *American Journal of Forensic Medicine and Pathology* 32 (2011): 161–163.

133. Paul Greenall and Michelle Wright, "Exploring the Criminal Histories of Stranger Sexual Killers," *Journal of Forensic Psychiatry and Psychology* 26 (2015): 242–259.

134. National Center for Education Statistics, "Violent Deaths at School and Away from School, 2012," nces.ed.gov/programs/crimeindicators/crimeindicators2012/ind_01.asp.

135. Laura Agnich, "A Comparative Analysis of Attempted and Completed School-Based Mass Murder Attacks," *American Journal of Criminal Justice* 40 (2015): 1–22.

136. Ibid.

137. National Center for Education Statistics, "Bullying," nces.ed.gov/fastfacts/display.asp?id=719.

138. Anthony Walsh, "African Americans and Serial Killing in the Media: The Myth and the Reality," *Homicide Studies* 9 (2005): 271–291.

139. Scott Bonn, *Why We Love Serial Killers: The Curious Appeal of the World's Most Savage Murderers* (New York: Skyhorse Press, 2014).

140. Alasdair Goodwill and Laurence Alison, "Sequential Angulation, Spatial Dispersion and Consistency of Distance Attack Patterns from Home in Serial Murder, Rape and Burglary," *Journal of Psychology, Crime and Law* 11 (2005): 161–176.

141. Aneez Esmail, "Physician as Serial Killer—The Shipman Case," *New England Journal of Medicine* 352 (2005): 1843–1844.

142. Christopher Ferguson, Diana White, Stacey Cherry, Marta Lorenz, and Zhara Bhimani, "Defining and Classifying Serial Murder in the Context of Perpetrator Motivation," *Journal of Criminal Justice* 31 (2003): 287–293.

143. James Alan Fox and Jack Levin, "Multiple Homicide: Patterns of Serial and Mass Murder," in *Crime and Justice: An Annual Edition*, vol. 23, ed. Michael Tonry (Chicago: University of Chicago Press, 1998): 407–455. See also James Alan Fox and Jack Levin, *Overkill: Mass Murder and Serial Killing Exposed* (New York: Plenum, 1994); James Alan Fox and Jack Levin, "A Psycho-Social Analysis of Mass Murder," in *Serial and Mass Murder: Theory, Policy, and Research*, ed. Thomas O'Reilly-Fleming and Steven Egger (Toronto: University of Toronto Press, 1993); James Alan Fox and Jack Levin, "Serial Murder: A Survey," in *Serial and Mass Murder*; Jack Levin and James Alan Fox, *Mass Murder* (New York: Plenum Press, 1985).

144. Terry Whitman and Donald Akutagawa, "Riddles in Serial Murder: A Synthesis," *Aggression and Violent Behavior* 9 (2004): 693–703.

145. Amanda L. Farrell, Robert D. Keppel, and Victoria B. Titterington, "Lethal Ladies: Revisiting What We Know About Female Serial Murderers," *Homicide Studies* 15 (2011): 228–252.

146. Belea Keeney and Kathleen Heide, "Gender Differences in Serial Murderers: A Preliminary Analysis," *Journal of Interpersonal Violence* 9 (1994): 37–56.

147. Farrell, Keppel, and Titterington, "Lethal Ladies: Revisiting What We Know About Female Serial Murderers."

148. Wade Myers, Erik Gooch, and Reid Meloy, "The Role of Psychopathy and Sexuality in a Female Serial Killer," *Journal of Forensic Sciences* 50 (2005): 652–658.

149. Farrell, Keppel, and Titterington, "Lethal Ladies: Revisiting What We Know About Female Serial Murderers," p. 245.

150. Fox and Levin, "Multiple Homicide: Patterns of Serial and Mass Murder"; Fox and Levin, *Overkill: Mass Murder and Serial Killing Exposed*; James Alan Fox, Jack Levin, and Kenna Quinet, *The Will to Kill: Making Sense of Senseless Murder*, 2nd ed. (Boston: Allyn & Bacon, 2004); Fox and Levin, "A Psycho-Social Analysis of Mass Murder."

151. Adam Lankford, "Mass Shooters in the USA, 1966–2010: Differences Between Attackers Who Live and Die," *Justice Quarterly*, published online June 20, 2013.

152. Elissa Gootman, "The Hunt for a Sniper: The Victim; 10th Victim Is Recalled as Motivator on Mission," *New York Times*, October 14, 2002, p. A15; Sarah Kershaw, "The Hunt for a Sniper: The Investigation; Endless Frustration but Little Evidence in Search for Sniper," *New York Times*, October 14, 2002, p. A1.

153. "Serial Killers, Part 4: White Supremacist Joseph Paul Franklin," www.fbi.gov/news/stories/2014/january /serial-killers-part-4-joseph-paul-franklin.

154. Francis X. Clines with Christopher Drew, "Prosecutors to Discuss Charges as Rifle Is Tied to Sniper Killings," *New York Times*, October 25, 2002, p. A1.

155. FBI, *Crime in the United States, 2000* (Washington, DC: U.S. Government Printing Office, 2001), p. 34.

156. Associated Press, "Woman with HIV Gets 3 Years for Spitting in Face," www.11alive.com/news/watercooler /story.aspx?storyid=118948&catid=186.

157. Gabrielle Salfati and Paul Taylor, "Differentiating Sexual Violence: A Comparison of Sexual Homicide and Rape," *Psychology, Crime and Law* 12 (2006): 107–125; Keith Harries, "Homicide and Assault: A Comparative Analysis of Attributes in Dallas Neighborhoods, 1981–1985," *Professional Geographer* 41 (1989): 29–38.

158. Laurence Zuckerman, "The Air-Rage Rage: Taking a Cold Look at a Hot Topic," *New York Times*, October 4, 1998, p. A3.

159. See, generally, Ruth S. Kempe and C. Henry Kempe, *Child Abuse* (Cambridge, MA: Harvard University Press, 1978).

160. Administration for Children and Families, Children's Bureau, *Child Maltreatment, 2013* (Washington, DC: U.S. Department of Health and Human Services, 2014), www.acf.hhs.gov/sites/default/files/cb/cm2013 .pdf#page=10.

161. Eva Jonzon and Frank Lindblad, "Adult Female Victims of Child Sexual Abuse," *Journal of Interpersonal Violence* 20 (2005): 651–666.

162. Jennie Noll, Penelope Trickett, William Harris, and Frank Putnam, "The Cumulative Burden Borne by Offspring Whose Mothers Were Sexually Abused as Children: Descriptive Results from a Multigenerational Study," *Journal of Interpersonal Violence* 24 (2009): 424–449.

163. Jane Siegel and Linda Williams, "Risk Factors for Sexual Victimization of Women," *Violence Against Women* 9 (2003): 902–930.

164. Glenn Wolfner and Richard Gelles, "A Profile of Violence Toward Children: A National Study," *Child Abuse and Neglect* 17 (1993): 197–212.

165. Martin Daly and Margo Wilson, "Violence Against Stepchildren," *Current Directions in Psychological Science* 5 (1996): 77–81.

166. Ruth Inglis, *Sins of the Fathers: A Study of the Physical and Emotional Abuse of Children* (New York: St. Martin's Press, 1978), p. 53.

167. Cindy Schaeffer, Pamela Alexander, Kimberly Bethke, and Lisa Kretz, "Predictors of Child Abuse Potential Among Military Parents: Comparing Mothers and Fathers," *Journal of Family Violence* 20 (2005): 123–129.

168. April Chiung-Tao Shen, "Self-Esteem of Young Adults Experiencing Interparental Violence and Child Physical Maltreatment: Parental and Peer Relationships as Mediators," *Journal of Interpersonal Violence* 24 (2009): 770–794.

169. Christina Meade, Trace Kershaw, Nathan Hansen, and Kathleen Sikkema, "Long-Term Correlates of Childhood Abuse Among Adults with Severe Mental Illness: Adult Victimization, Substance Abuse, and HIV Sexual Risk Behavior," *AIDS and Behavior* 13 (2009): 207–216.

170. Arina Ulman and Murray Straus, "Violence by Children Against Mothers in Relation to Violence Between Parents and Corporal Punishment by Parents," *Journal of Comparative Family Studies* 34 (2003): 41–63.

171. Richard Gelles and Murray Straus, "Violence in the American Family," *Journal of Social Issues* 35 (1979): 15–39.

172. Lauren Josephs and Eileen Mazur Abel, "Investigating the Relationship Between Intimate Partner Violence and HIV Risk-Propensity in Black/African-American Women," *Journal of Family Violence* 24 (2009): 221–229.

173. Maureen Outlaw, "No One Type of Intimate Partner Abuse: Exploring Physical and Non-Physical Abuse Among Intimate Partners," *Journal of Family Violence* 24 (2009): 263–272.

174. This section leans heavily on Priscilla Offenhauer and Alice Buchalter, *Teen Dating Violence: A Literature Review and Annotated Bibliography, A Report Prepared by the Federal Research Division, Library of Congress Under an Interagency Agreement with the Violence and Victimization Research Division, National Institute of Justice*, April 2011, www.ncjrs.gov/pdffiles1/nij/grants/235368.pdf.

175. Jay Silverman, Anita Raj, Lorelei Mucci, and Jeanne Hathaway, "Dating Violence Against Adolescent Girls and Associated Substance Abuse, Unhealthy Weight Control, Sexual Risk Behavior, Pregnancy and Suicidality," *Journal of the American Medical Association* 286 (2001): 572–579.

176. FBI, *Crime in the United States, 2000*, p. 29.

177. Marcus Felson, *Crime and Nature* (Thousand Oaks, CA: Sage, 2006).

178. Marie Rosenkrantz Lindegaard, Wim Bernasco, and Scott Jacques, "Consequences of Expected and Observed Victim Resistance for Offender Violence during Robbery Events," *Journal of Research in Crime and Delinquency* 52 (2015): 32–61.

179. Peter Van Koppen and Robert Jansen, "The Time to Rob: Variations in Time of Number of Commercial Robberies," *Journal of Research in Crime and Delinquency* 36 (1999): 7–29.

180. Elizabeth Ehrhardt Mustaine and Richard Tewksbury, "Predicting Risks of Larceny Theft Victimization: A Routine Activity Analysis Using Refined Lifestyle Measures," *Criminology* 36 (1998): 829–858.

181. Volkan Topalli, Richard Wright, and Robert Fornango, "Drug Dealers, Robbery and Retaliation: Vulnerability, Deterrence and the Contagion of Violence," *British Journal of Criminology* 42 (2002): 337–351.

182. Bruce A. Jacobs, *Robbing Drug Dealers: Violence Beyond the Law* (Hawthorne, NY: Aldine de Gruyter, 2000).

183. Richard Wright and Scott Decker, *Armed Robbers in Action: Stickups and Street Culture* (Boston: Northeastern University Press, 1997).

184. Jody Miller, "Up It Up: Gender and the Accomplishment of Street Robbery," *Criminology* 36 (1998): 37–67.

185. Ibid., pp. 54–55.

186. Richard Felson, Eric Baumer, and Steven Messner, "Acquaintance Robbery," *Journal of Research in Crime and Delinquency* 37 (2000): 284–305.

187. Ibid., p. 287.

188. Ibid.

189. Volkan Topalli, Scott Jacques, and Richard Wright, "It Takes Skills to Take a Car: Perceptual and Procedural Expertise in Carjacking," *Aggression and Violent Behavior* (2014): 19–25.

190. Heith Copes, Andy Hochstetler, and Michael Cherbonneau, "Getting the Upper Hand: Scripts for Managing Victim Resistance in Carjackings," *Journal of Research in Crime and Delinquency*, published online May 3, 2011.

191. "Boy Gets 18 Years in Fatal Park Beating of Transient," *Los Angeles Times*, December 24, 1987, p. 9B.

192. James Brooke, "Gay Student Who Was Kidnapped and Beaten Dies," *New York Times*, October 13, 1998, p. A1.

193. Gregory Herek, "Hate Crimes and Stigma-Related Experiences Among Sexual Minority Adults in the United States: Prevalence Estimates from a National Probability Sample," *Journal of Interpersonal Violence* 24 (2009): 54–74.

194. Jack McDevitt, Jack Levin, and Susan Bennett, "Hate Crime Offenders: An Expanded Typology," *Journal of Social Issues* 58 (2002): 303–318; Jack Levin and Jack McDevitt, *Hate Crimes: The Rising Tide of Bigotry and Bloodshed* (New York: Plenum, 1993).

195. FBI, *Hate Crime Statistics, 2013*, www.fbi.gov/about-us/cjis/ucr/hate-crime/2013/topic-pages/incidents-and-offenses/incidentsandoffenses_final.

196. Gregory Herek, Jeanine Cogan, and Roy Gillis, "Victim Experiences in Hate Crimes Based on Sexual Orientation," *Journal of Social Issues* 58 (2002): 319–340.

197. Brian Levin, "From Slavery to Hate Crime Laws: The Emergence of Race- and Status-Based Protection in American Criminal Law," *Journal of Social Issues* 58 (2002): 227–246.

198. National LGBTQ Task Force, "Hate Crime Laws in the U.S., 2013," www.thetaskforce.org/static_html /downloads/reports/issue_maps/hate_crimes_06_13 _new.pdf.

199. Felicia Lee, "Gays Angry over TV Report on a Murder," *New York Times*, November 26, 2004, A3.

200. Frederick M. Lawrence, *Punishing Hate: Bias Crimes Under American Law* (Cambridge, MA: Harvard University Press, 1999).

201. Ibid., p. 3.

202. *Virginia v. Black et al.*, No. 01-1107, 2003.

203. Eliott McLaughlin and Catherine Shoichet, "Police: Bryce Williams fatally shoots self after killing journalists on air," CNN, August 27, 2015, www.cnn .com/2015/08/26/us/virginia-shooting-wdbj/.

204. Bureau of Labor Statistics, "Census of Fatal Occupational Injuries Summary, 2013," www.bls.gov/news .release/cfoi.nr0.htm.

205. Robert Simon, *Bad Men Do What Good Men Dream* (Washington, DC: American Psychiatric Press, 1999).

206. Bureau of Labor Statistics, "Census of Fatal Occupational Injuries Summary, 2013."

207. U.S. Attorney's Office, "Florida Man Sentenced to 10 Years for Stalking, Attempting to Injure Victim with Acid-Filled Bombs," October 13, 2014, www .fbi.gov/newhaven/press-releases/2014/florida-man -sentenced-to-10-years-for-stalking-attempting-to -injure-victim-with-acid-filled-bombs.

208. Patrick Kinkade, Ronald Burns, and Angel Ilarraza Fuentes, "Criminalizing Attractions: Perceptions of Stalking and the Stalker," *Crime and Delinquency* 51 (2005): 3–25.

209. Michelle Garcia, "Voices from the Field: Stalking," *NIJ Journal* 266 (2010), www.nij.gov/journals/266 /stalking.htm.

210. Rosemary Purcell, Bridget Moller, Teresea Flower, and Paul Mullen, "Stalking Among Juveniles," *British Journal of Psychiatry* 194 (2009): 451–455.

211. Garcia, "Voices from the Field: Stalking."

212. Ibid.

213. Carol Jordan, T. K. Logan, and Robert Walker, "Stalking: An Examination of the Criminal Justice Response," *Journal of Interpersonal Violence* 18 (2003): 148–165.

# 11 Political Crime and Terrorism

## Learning Objectives

**LO1** Define the term *political crime*.

**LO2** Assess the cause of political crime.

**LO3** Compare and contrast the terms *espionage* and *treason*.

**LO4** Distinguish among terrorists, insurgents, guerillas, and revolutionaries.

**LO5** Enumerate the various forms of terrorism.

**LO6** Explain what motivates the terrorist to commit violent acts.

AP Images

Edward Snowden, recipient of the Sam Adams Award, smiles during the presentation ceremony in Moscow, Russia.

# Chapter Outline

Edward Snowden, born in North Carolina in 1983, worked for Booz Allen Hamilton, a provider of management and technology consulting services to the U.S. government.[1] Booz Allen was hired to consult with the National Security Agency, and as a trusted employee Snowden was assigned to the NSA's Oahu, Hawaii, office. In May 2013, Snowden began collecting top-secret documents regarding NSA domestic surveillance practices, including spying on millions of American citizens. He found this invasion of privacy disturbing and left his employment, going to Hong Kong. Soon after, newspapers began printing excerpts from the purloined NSA documents. They detailed NSA spying practices against American citizens and foreign nationals. Snowden was charged under the Espionage Act but, before he could be apprehended, fled to Russia.

In a series of interviews given in Hong Kong and Russia, Snowden told the press, "I'm willing to sacrifice [my former life] because I can't in good conscience allow the U.S. government to destroy privacy, Internet freedom, and basic liberties for people around the world with this massive surveillance machine they're secretly building." He saw himself as a truth teller, informing the press that the American people have a right to know ▶

## FACT OR FICTION?

▶ Treason is the only crime mentioned in the United States Constitution.

▶ Terrorist attacks have been increasing every year; the world is becoming more dangerous.

about government abuses that were kept hidden: "The secret continuance of these programs represents a far greater danger than their disclosure . . . So long as there's broad support amongst a people, it can be argued there's a level of legitimacy even to the most invasive and morally wrong program, as it was an informed and willing decision. . . . However, programs that are implemented in secret, out of public oversight, lack that legitimacy, and that's a problem. It also represents a dangerous normalization of 'governing in the dark,' where decisions with enormous public impact occur without any public input."[2] Is Snowden a patriot or a political criminal? After fleeing the country, he took refuge somewhere in Russia where he remains to this day.

Political crimes have recently become a very important area of criminological inquiry, and many criminologists who previously paid scant attention to the interaction between political motivation and crime have now made it the focus of intense study. In this chapter, we will briefly discuss the concept of **political crime**—illegal acts that are designed to undermine an existing government and threaten its survival.[3] Some political acts are nonviolent, such as election fraud and espionage. Others are extremely violent and involve terrorism, which now occupies the center stage of both world opinion and government policy. It is important for students of criminology to develop a basic understanding of terrorism's definition, history, and structure, and review the steps being taken to limit or eliminate its occurrence.

**political crime**
Illegal acts that are designed to undermine an existing government and threaten its survival. Political crimes can include both violent and nonviolent acts and range in seriousness from dissent, treason, and espionage to violent acts such as terrorism or assassination.

L01 Define the term *political crime.*

## Political Crime

Political crimes can include both violent and nonviolent acts and range in seriousness from taking bribes to espionage to violent acts such as terrorism or assassination. When an act becomes a political crime and when an actor is considered a political criminal are often extremely subjective. In highly repressive nations, any form of unsanctioned political activity, including writing a newspaper article critical of the regime, may be considered a political crime, punishable by a prison term or even death. In contrast, people whom some label as terrorists and insurrectionists are viewed by others as freedom fighters and revolutionaries. What would have happened to George Washington and Benjamin Franklin had the British won the Revolutionary War? Would they have been hanged for their political crimes or considered heroes and freedom fighters?

One reason for this vagueness and subjectivity is that the political criminal and political crimes may stem from religious or ideological sources. Because their motivations shift between selfish personal needs and selfless, noble, or altruistic desires, political crimes often occupy a gray area between conventional and outlawed behavior. It is easy to condemn interpersonal violent crimes such as rape or murder because their goals are typically selfish and self-centered (e.g., revenge or profit). In contrast, political criminals may be motivated by principle, faith, or conviction. While it is true that some political crime involves profit (such as selling state secrets for money), many political criminals, including Edward Snowden, do not consider themselves antisocial but instead patriotic and altruistic. They are willing to sacrifice themselves for what they consider to be the greater good. While some concoct elaborate schemes to hide or mask their actions, others are quite brazen, hoping to provoke the government to overreact in their zeal to crack down on dissent. Because state authorities may engage in a range of retaliatory actions that result in human rights violations, even those who support the government may begin to question its activities—maybe the government is corrupt and authoritarian? On the other hand, if the government does nothing, it appears weak and corrupt and unable to protect citizens.

Even those political criminals who profit personally from their misdeeds, such as someone who spies for an enemy nation for financial payoffs, may believe that their acts are motivated by a higher calling than common theft. "My ultimate goal is to weaken or overthrow a corrupt government," they reason, "so selling secrets to the enemy is justified." Political criminals may believe that their acts are criminalized only because the group holding power fears them and wants to curtail their behavior. And while the general public has little objection to laws that control extreme behaviors such as plotting a bloody revolution, they may have questions when a law criminalizes ordinary political dissent or bans political meetings in order to control suspected political criminals.

## The Goals of Political Criminals

One survivor of a bombing attack in Iraq told reporters, "There may be a state, there may be a government. But what can that state do? What can they do with all the terrorists? Are they supposed to set up a checkpoint in every house?" In their attack, the bombers succeeded in their efforts to create an atmosphere of intimidation and fear designed to oust the government.[4] Unsettling the populace and reducing faith in the government may be one goal of political criminals; some of the others include:

- *Intimidation.* Some political criminals want to intimidate or threaten an opponent who does not share their political orientation or views.
- *Revolution.* Some political criminals plot to overthrow the existing government and replace it with one that holds views they find more acceptable.
- *Profit.* Another goal of political crime is profit: selling state secrets for personal enrichment or trafficking in stolen arms and munitions.
- *Conviction.* Some political criminals are motivated by altruism; they truly believe their crimes will benefit society and are willing to violate the law and risk punishment in order to achieve what they see as social improvement.
- *Pseudo-conviction.* These political criminals conceal conventional criminal motivations behind a mask of conviction and altruism. They may form a revolutionary movement out of a hidden desire to engage in violence rather than their stated goal of reforming society. The pseudo-convictional criminal is particularly dangerous because they convince followers to join them in their crimes without fully revealing their true motivations.[5]

## Becoming a Political Criminal

Why does someone become a political criminal? There is no set pattern or reason; motivations vary widely. Some use political crime as a stepping stone to public office, while others use it as a method to focus their frustrations. Others hope they can gain respect from their friends and family. Although the motivations for political crime are complex and varied, there does appear to be some regularity in the way ideas are formed. Political crime expert Randy Borum finds that this pattern takes the form of a series of cognitive stages:

**L02** Assess the cause of political crime.

- Stage 1: *"It's not right."* An unhappy, dissatisfied individual identifies some type of undesirable event or condition. It could be economic (e.g., poverty, unemployment, poor living conditions), social (e.g., government-imposed restrictions on individual freedoms, lack of order, or morality), or personal ("I am being cheated of what is due me"). While the conditions may vary, those involved perceive the experience as "things are not as they should be."
- Stage 2: *"It's not fair."* The prospective political criminal concludes that the undesirable condition is a product of "injustice"—that is, it does not apply to everyone.

A government worker may feel his or her low pay scale is "not fair" and that corporate workers with less skill are making more money and getting more benefits. At the same time, government workers are portrayed as lazy and corrupt. For those who are deprived, this facilitates feelings of resentment and injustice.

- Stage 3: *"It's your fault."* Someone or some group must be held accountable for the extremist's displeasure. It always helps to identify a potential target. A youth who joins a racist group may become convinced that minorities get all the good jobs while his family is suffering financially. Extremist groups spread this propaganda to attract recruits. Americans may be portrayed as rich and undeserving by overseas enemies looking to recruit disenfranchised young men and women to become terrorists.

- Stage 4: *"You're evil."* Because good people would not intentionally hurt others, targeted groups are appropriate choices for revenge and/or violence. The disaffected government worker concludes that since his country has let him down it is only fair to sell state secrets to foreign nations for profit or to join a terrorist group or both. Aggression becomes justifiable when aimed against bad people, particularly those who intentionally cause harm to others. Second, by casting the target as evil, it dehumanizes them and makes justifying aggression even easier. So it's not so bad to rig an election, because the opposing candidates are evil and do not deserve to hold office.[6]

## Types of Political Crimes

Considering this cognitive thought that produces political crime and terrorism, what are the specific crimes and what form do they take?

### Election Fraud

**election fraud**
Illegal interference with the process of an election. Acts of fraud tend to involve affecting vote counts to bring about a desired election outcome, whether by increasing the vote share of the favored candidate, depressing the vote share of the rival candidates, or both. Varieties of election fraud include intimidation, disruption of polling places, distribution of misinformation such as the wrong election date, registration fraud, and vote buying.

Some political criminals want to shape elections to meet their personal needs (even elections for student council president). In some instances their goal is altruistic: the election of candidates who reflect their personal political views. In others, their actions are motivated by profit: they are paid by a candidate to rig the election. Whatever the motive, **election fraud** is illegal interference with the political process. Acts of fraud tend to involve affecting vote counts to bring about a desired election outcome, whether by increasing the vote share of the favored candidate, depressing the vote share of the rival candidates, or both.

In some third-world dictatorships, election fraud is the norm, and it is common for the ruling party to announce, after party members counted the votes, that they were returned to office with an overwhelming majority. Election fraud, a feature of political life since Roman times, includes a variety of behaviors designed to give a candidate or his/her party an unfair advantage:

Kelli Jo Griffin wipes away tears as she is embraced by Sister Peggy from the Holy Family Catholic Church of Fort Madison, Iowa, following her not-guilty verdict on March 20, 2014. The former drug offender, who believed her voting rights had been restored when she cast a ballot last year, was acquitted of perjury in a voter fraud case. Some states have begun to crack down on alleged voter fraud, and in some cases, such as Griffin's, prosecutions may be overzealous.

- *Intimidation.* Voters can be scared away from the polls through threats or intimidation. Having armed guards posted at polling places may convince people it is dangerous to vote. Lists of registered voters can be obtained and people subjected to threatening calls before the election.

- *Disruption.* Bomb threats can be called into voting places in areas that are known to heavily favor the opposing party, with the goal of suppressing the vote. There can be outright sabotage of polling places, ballots, ballot boxes, and voting machines.

- *Misinformation.* Flyers are sent out to voters registered with the opposition party containing misleading information such as the wrong election date or saying that rules have been changed about who is eligible to vote.

- *Registration fraud.* Political operatives may try to shape the outcome of an election by busing in ineligible voters from other districts. Because many jurisdictions require minimal identification and proof of citizenship, political criminals find it easy to get around residency requirements. They may provide conspirators with "change of address" forms to allow them to vote in a particular election, when in fact no actual change of address has occurred.
- *Vote buying.* Securing votes by payment or other rewards or the selling of one's vote is an age-old problem that still exists. One popular method is to buy absentee ballots from people who are in need of cash. The fraudulent voter can then ensure that the vote goes their way, an outcome that cannot be guaranteed if the conspirator casts a secret ballot at a polling place.

Most states have created laws to control and punish vote fraud. The federal government has a number of statutes designed to control and/or restrict fraud, including 18 U.S.C. § 594, which provides:

> Whoever intimidates, threatens, coerces, or attempts to intimidate, threaten, or coerce, any other person for the purpose of interfering with the right of such other person to vote or to vote as he may choose, or of causing such other person to vote for, or not to vote for, any candidate for the office of President, Vice President, Presidential elector, Member of the Senate, Member of the House of Representatives, Delegate from the District of Columbia, or Resident Commissioner, at any election held solely or in part for the purpose of electing such candidate, shall be fined under this title or imprisoned not more than one year, or both.

## Abuse of Office/Public Corruption

In 2015, Senator Robert Menendez became the 12th senator to be indicted while in office. Menendez, the top Democrat on the Senate Foreign Relations Committee, was indicted on corruption charges alleging that he used his office to help Salomon Melgen, a Florida ophthalmologist and political donor, who was accused of overbilling Medicare.[7] Menendez is believed to have received personal favors from Melgen including plane tickets to vacation resorts; he denied all charges. He is by far not the only well-known politician accused of using their office for personal enrichment:

- On August 14, 2013, former Congressman Jesse L. Jackson Jr. was sentenced to 30 months in prison for conspiring to defraud his reelection campaigns by converting $750,000 in campaign funds to pay for personal items and expenses, including high-end appliances and electronics. Jackson, who filed misleading reports to conceal his illegal activities, was released in March 2015.[8]
- Illinois Governor Rod Blagojevich received a 14-year sentence in federal prison following conviction for corruption and the soliciting of bribes for political appointments, including an attempt to sell the U.S. Senate seat formerly occupied by Barack Obama.[9]
- Detroit Mayor Kwame Kilpatrick was incarcerated for corruption. His story is told in the Profiles in Crime feature.

Public corruption involves a breach of public trust and/or abuse of position by government officials and their private sector accomplices. Whether elected, appointed, or hired, they are committing a crime if while in office they demand, solicit, accept, or agree to receive anything of value in return for being manipulated in the performance of their official duties. They and their relatives and friends may be the recipients of illegal funds paid for by businesspeople willing to bribe to gain public contracts and other government actions. The victims of public corruption are the general public, who pay for corruption through inflated costs and sometimes higher taxes.

## Treason

"I have learned to hate all traitors, and there is no disease that I spit on more than treachery."[10] So said the Greek poet and playwright Aeschylus 2,500 years ago.

**CONNECTIONS**

Public corruption is also considered a white-collar crime. We will return to this issue in Chapter 12 when we cover bribery and extortion. Should public officials who accept bribes go to prison? After all, they are not really dangerous people. How about requiring that they really do public service: volunteering in the community after their illegal gains are confiscated?

**L03** Compare and contrast the terms *espionage* and *treason*.

# PROFILES IN CRIME

## KWAME KILPATRICK: BETRAYING THE PUBLIC'S TRUST

When Kwame Kilpatrick became mayor of Detroit in 2002, he promised to revitalize the city but instead used his position for personal gain. After being incarcerated on one corruption charge, he was re-indicted on others as soon as he was paroled. After a lengthy trial, Kilpatrick was sentenced in 2013 to a 28-year prison term for his role in a wide-ranging racketeering conspiracy that included extortion, bribery, and fraud. Thirty-two other associates were also convicted of crimes in connection with the case, including contractor Bobby Ferguson, a close friend of Kilpatrick, who received a 21-year prison term.

What did the conspirators do to earn such draconian punishment? Kilpatrick extorted money from people doing business with the city, rigged bids, and took bribes. He illegally appropriated funds from nonprofit civic organizations Kilpatrick and Ferguson obtained more than $500,000 from the state of Michigan and private donors for nonprofit organizations they controlled. The organizations were supposed to help the community. Instead, the mayor spent large sums on himself for luxury vacations, spa treatments, and golf clubs. In addition, Kilpatrick coerced contractors to include Ferguson in public contracts and to rig the awarding of the contracts to ensure that Ferguson got a portion of the revenue. Ferguson received at least $73 million in revenues from municipal contracts through this scheme, a portion of which he shared with his co-conspirators.

The government obtained text messages from Kilpatrick, given to them by his cell phone service provider, that discussed bid rigging, bribes, and other criminal activity. Kilpatrick had no idea the messages were being recorded and saved. Federal investigators also found that he was making large cash deposits—his bank account records revealed more than $840,000 in unexplained expenditures above and beyond his salary as mayor, and none of that money was disclosed on his tax returns. He actually would hand officers on his protective detail an envelope with cash and tell them to take it to the bank and pay his credit card bill. The amazing aspect of the case was that the mayor did little to cover his tracks. Believing he was above the law, he thought he could get away with repeated and prolonged betrayal of the public trust—but he didn't.

**Source:** U.S. Attorney's Office, Eastern District of Michigan, "Former Detroit Mayor Kwame Kilpatrick, Contractor Bobby Ferguson, and Bernard Kilpatrick Sentenced on Racketeering, Extortion, Bribery, Fraud, and Tax Charges," press release, October 17, 2013, www.fbi.gov/detroit/press-releases/2013/former-detroit-mayor-kwame-kilpatrick-contractor-bobby-ferguson-and-bernard-kilpatrick-sentenced-on-racketeering-extortion-bribery-fraud-and-tax-charges (accessed 2015).

**treason**
An act of disloyalty to one's nation or state.

Yet, while the crime of treason has been around since ancient times, and the word "traitor" is a generic term, there have actually been fewer than 40 prosecutions for **treason** in the entire history of the United States and most have resulted in acquittal. The most famous case: the 1807 trial of former Vice President Aaron Burr, who was accused of hatching a plot to separate the western states from the union. When that plot went awry, he conspired to seize Mexico and set up a puppet government with himself as king! Arrested on charges of treason, Burr was acquitted when the federal court, headed by John Marshall, ruled that to be guilty of treason an overt act must be committed; planning is not enough.[11]

Because treason is considered such a heinous crime, and to deter would-be traitors, many nations apply or have applied the death penalty to those convicted of attempting to overthrow the existing government. Treason was considered particularly loathsome under English common law, and until the nineteenth century it was punishable by being "drawn and quartered," a method of execution that involved hanging the offender, removing their intestines while still living, and finally cutting the offender into four pieces for public display. William Wallace, the Scottish patriot made famous in the film *Braveheart,* was so displayed after his execution.

Acts can be considered treasonous in order to stifle political dissent. In eighteenth-century England, it was considered treasonous to merely criticize the king or his behavior, and not surprisingly, the American colonists feared giving their own central government that much power. Therefore treason is the only crime mentioned in the United States Constitution, which defines treason as levying war against the United States or "in adhering to their Enemies, giving them Aid and Comfort," and requires the testimony of two witnesses or a confession in open court for conviction. The purpose of this was to limit the government's ability to bring charges of treason against opponents and to make it more difficult to prosecute those who are so charged.[12]

Today, the United States Criminal Code codifies treason as "whoever, owing allegiance to the United States, levies war against them or adheres to their enemies, giving them aid and comfort within the United States or elsewhere, is guilty of treason and shall suffer death, or shall be imprisoned not less than five years and fined under this title but not less than $10,000; and shall be incapable of holding any office under the United States."[13] Helping or cooperating with the enemy in a time of war would be considered treason; so too would be creating or recruiting a military force to help a foreign nation overthrow the government. After World War II, two women, Iva Ikuko Toguri D'Aquino, a Japanese American born in Los Angeles and known as Tokyo Rose, and Mildred Elizabeth Gillars, born in Portland, Maine, and known as Axis Sally, served prison terms for broadcasting for the Axis powers in an effort to demoralize American troops.

## Espionage

Robert Hanssen was a counterintelligence agent for the FBI assigned to detect and identify Russian spies. A former Chicago police officer, Hanssen's assignment required him to have access to sensitive top-secret information. In one of the most shocking cases in U.S. history, Hanssen volunteered to become a paid spy for the KGB during the Cold War and over a period of 15 years received at least $1.4 million in cash and diamonds. He was arrested on February 18, 2001, after leaving a package of classified documents for his Russian handlers under a footbridge in a park outside Washington. During his years as a double agent, Hanssen not only provided more than 6,000 pages of documents to the Soviet Union but also caused the death of two U.S. double agents whose identities were uncovered with the aid of his secret documents. The Hanssen case was the subject of the 2007 film *Breach*, which starred Chris Cooper as the corrupt agent.[14] Another infamous case of espionage involved Aldrich Hazen Ames, a 31-year veteran of the Central Intelligence Agency (CIA) who spied for the Russians, receiving $1.88 million in pay before being caught and sentenced to life without the possibility of parole.[15]

**Espionage** (more commonly called "spying") is the practice of obtaining information about a government, organization, or society that is considered secret or confidential without the permission of the holder of the information. Espionage involves obtaining the information illegally by covertly entering the area where the information is stored, secretly photographing forbidden areas, or subverting through threat or payoff people who know the information and will divulge it through subterfuge.[16]

Espionage is typically associated with spying on potential or actual enemies, by a foreign agent who is working for his or her nation's intelligence service. With the end of the Cold War, the threat of espionage seemed reduced until 2010, when a major Russian spy group was unraveled and 10 people arrested. These were sleeper agents who had spent decades fitting seamlessly in their new environment. Neighbors were shocked to find out that "Richard Murphy" and "Cynthia Murphy" were actually spies named Vladimir Guryev and Lydia Guryev, while "Michael Zottoli" and "Patricia Mills" were in reality Mikhail Kutsik and Natalia Pereverzeva, agents of the Russian Federation. The case was settled when the Russians were exchanged for four American spies being held in Russian prisons. The TV shows *The Americans* and *Allegiance* were roughly based on this Russian spy group.

**INDUSTRIAL ESPIONAGE** The concept of espionage has been extended to spying involving corporations, referred to as industrial espionage. This involves such unethical

---

**FACT OR FICTION?**

Treason is the only crime mentioned in the United States Constitution.

**FACT** Treason is considered so serious that it is the only crime set out in the Constitution. Article 3, Section 3 defines treason and its punishment:

*Treason against the United States, shall consist only in levying War against them, or in adhering to their Enemies, giving them Aid and Comfort. No Person shall be convicted of Treason unless on the Testimony of two Witnesses to the same overt Act, or on Confession in open Court. The Congress shall have Power to declare the Punishment of Treason, but no Attainder of Treason shall work Corruption of Blood, or Forfeiture except during the Life of the Person attainted.*

The phrase "Corruption of Blood" refers to the fact that the children of people convicted of treason would not be punished or attainted as they were in England.

---

**espionage**
The practice of obtaining information about a government, organization, or society that is considered secret or confidential without the permission of the holder of the information. Commonly called spying.

Industrial espionage is aimed at illegally appropriating information from rival networks or nations. A "Wanted by the FBI" document announces a criminal indictment against five Chinese military hackers for cyberespionage. Wen Xinyu, Wang Dong, Sun Kailiang, Huang Zhenyu, and Gu Chunhui are charged with targeting U.S. corporations and labor organizations for commercial advantage.

or illegal activities as bribing employees to reveal trade secrets such as computer codes or product formulas. The traditional methods of industrial espionage include recruiting agents and inserting them into the target company or breaking into an office to take equipment and information. It can also involve surveillance and spying on commercial organizations in order to determine the direction of their new product line or even what bid they intend to make on a government contract. Such knowledge can provide vast profits when it allows a competitor to save large sums on product development or to win an undeserved contract by underbidding.[17]

**FOREIGN INDUSTRIAL ESPIONAGE** In 2014, five Chinese men were indicted for stealing thousands of "sensitive, internal communications" from U.S. companies, including Alcoa, United States Steel Corporation, and Westinghouse.[18] This international hacking case shows that not all corporate espionage is home-grown, and some attacks have been carried out by foreign agents. A report of the National Counterintelligence Center lists biotechnology, aerospace, telecommunications, computer software, transportation, advanced materials, energy research, defense, and semiconductor companies as the top targets for foreign economic espionage.[19]

Industrial espionage by foreign agents' efforts has hurt the United States by eroding the U.S. military advantage. Foreign militaries have been able to acquire sophisticated capabilities that might otherwise have taken years to develop. Such efforts also undercut the U.S. economy by making it possible for foreign firms to gain a competitive economic edge over U.S. companies.

Many foreign agents did not come to the United States specifically to engage in espionage, but when an opportunity arose they jumped on the chance to satisfy their desire for profits, for academic or scientific acclaim, or out of a sense of patriotism to their home countries. A number of factors have combined to facilitate private-sector technology theft. Globalization, while generating major gains for the U.S. economy, has given foreigners unprecedented access to U.S. firms and to sensitive technologies. There has also been a proliferation of devices that have made it easy for private-sector experts to illegally retrieve, store, and transfer massive amounts of information, including trade secrets and proprietary data; such devices are increasingly common in the workplace.

In addition to private citizens conducting espionage, foreign government organizations also mount their own operations, including:

- Targeting U.S. firms for technology that would strengthen their foreign defense capabilities
- Posting personnel at U.S. military bases to collect classified information to bolster military modernization efforts
- Employing commercial firms in the United States in a covert effort to target and acquire U.S. technology
- Recruiting students, professors, scientists, and researchers to engage in technology collection
- Making direct requests for classified, sensitive, or export-controlled information via personal contacts, telephone, email, fax, and other forms of communication
- Forming ventures with U.S. firms in the hope of placing collectors in proximity to sensitive technologies or else establishing foreign research

Foreign companies seek entrée into U.S. firms and other targeted institutions by pursuing business relationships that provide access to sensitive or classified information, technologies, or projects:

- *Conferences, conventions, and trade shows.* These public venues offer opportunities for foreign adversaries to gain access to U.S. information and experts in dual-use and sensitive technologies.
- *Official foreign visitors and exploitation of joint research.* Foreign government organizations, including intelligence services, use official visits to U.S. government and cleared defense contractor facilities, as well as joint research projects between foreign and U.S. entities, to target and collect information.
- *Foreign targeting of U.S. visitors overseas.* Whether traveling for business or personal reasons, U.S. travelers overseas—businesspeople, government employees, and contractors—are routinely targeted by foreign collectors, especially if they are assessed as having access to some sensitive information. Some U.S. allies engage in this practice, as do less friendly powers such as Russia and China. Targeting takes many forms: exploitation of electronic media and devices, surreptitious entry into hotel rooms, aggressive surveillance, and attempts to set up sexual or romantic entanglements.
- *Open source information.* Foreign collectors are aware that much U.S. economic and technological information is available in professional journals, social networking and other public websites, and the media.[20]

**LEGAL CONTROLS** Before 1996, there was no federal statute that explicitly penalized industrial espionage. Recognizing the increasingly important role that intellectual property plays in the well-being of the American economy, Congress enacted the Economic Espionage Act (EEA) of 1996, which criminalizes the theft of trade secrets. The EEA actually contains two separate provisions, one that penalizes foreign agents from stealing American trade secrets and one directed at domestic spying.

Convictions of foreign agents under the Economic Espionage Act have been relatively rare. It was not until 2006 that the first conviction occurred, when two Chinese Nationals, Fei Ye and Ming Zhong, pleaded guilty to stealing secret information from Sun Microsystems and Transmeta Corporation.[21]

## State Political Crime

While some political crimes are committed by people who oppose the state, others are perpetrated by state authorities against the people they are supposed to serve; this is referred to as **state political crime**. Critical criminologists argue that rather than being committed by disaffected people, a great deal of political crime arises from the efforts of the state to either maintain governmental power or to uphold the race, class, and gender advantages of those who support the government. In an industrial society, the state will do everything to protect the property rights of the wealthy while opposing the real interests of the poor. They might even go to war to support the capitalist classes who need the wealth and resources of other nations. The desire for natural resources such as rubber, oil, and metals was one of the primary reasons for Japan's invasion of China and other Eastern nations that sparked their entry into World War II.

**USING TORTURE** Of all state political crimes, the use of **torture** to gain information from suspected political criminals is perhaps the most notorious. Government intelligence agencies claim that torturing suspected terrorists can produce important information needed to thwart plots against U.S. interests. However, a recent report by the Senate Intelligence Committee disparaged the use of torture and disputed claims that it can be a valuable source of information. The Senate report gives

**state political crime**
Political crime that arises from the efforts of the state to either maintain governmental power or to uphold the race, class, and gender advantages of those who support the government. It is possible to divide state political crimes into five varieties: (1) political corruption, (2) illegal domestic surveillance, (3) human rights violations, (4) state violence such as torture, illegal imprisonment, police violence and use of deadly force, and (5) state corporate crime committed by individuals who abuse their state authority or who fail to exercise it when working with people and organizations in the private sector.

**torture**
An act that causes severe pain or suffering, whether physical or mental, that is intentionally inflicted on a person for such purposes as obtaining a confession, punishing them for a crime they may have committed, or intimidating or coercing them into a desired action.

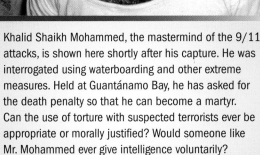

Khalid Shaikh Mohammed, the mastermind of the 9/11 attacks, is shown here shortly after his capture. He was interrogated using waterboarding and other extreme measures. Held at Guantánamo Bay, he has asked for the death penalty so that he can become a martyr. Can the use of torture with suspected terrorists ever be appropriate or morally justified? Would someone like Mr. Mohammed ever give intelligence voluntarily?

a detailed accounting of the most gruesome techniques that the CIA used to torture and imprison terrorism suspects. In some cases, suspected terrorists were deprived of sleep for a week and threatened with death. Some prisoners were subjected to medically unnecessary rectal feeding or rectal hydration, a technique used to gain total control over the detainee. The waterboarding of Khalid Shaikh Mohammed, the chief planner of the 9/11 attacks, was described as near drownings. The Senate committee found that more prisoners were subjected to waterboarding than the three the CIA had acknowledged in the past and found photographs of waterboarding paraphernalia in facilities where the CIA had claimed that waterboarding was never used. Some facilities were described as dungeon-like and prisoners described as dogs in a kennel. When Abu Zubaydah was interrogated in a facility in Thailand, the sessions became so extreme that some CIA officers were "to the point of tears and choking up" when Abu Zubaydah became "completely unresponsive with bubbles rising through his open, full mouth."[22]

**THE TICKING BOMB SCENARIO** Despite the damning findings of the Senate report, can the torture of a suspected terrorist determined to destroy the government and harm innocent civilians ever be permissible or is it always an example of state-sponsored political crime? While most people loathe the thought of torturing anyone, some experts argue that torture can sometimes be justified in what they call the ticking bomb scenario. Suppose the government found out that a captured terrorist knew the whereabouts of a dangerous explosive device that was set to go off and kill thousands of innocent people. Would it be permissible to engage in the use of torture on this single suspect if it would save the population of a city?

The ticking bomb scenario has appeal. Famed social commentator and legal scholar Alan Dershowitz argues that the "vast majority" of Americans would expect law enforcement agents to use any means necessary to obtain information needed to prevent a terror attack. To protect against abuse, Dershowitz proposes the creation of a "torture warrant" that can only be issued by a judge in cases where (a) there is an absolute need to obtain immediate information in order to save lives and (b) there is probable cause that the suspect has such information and is unwilling to reveal it to law enforcement agents. The suspect would be given immunity from prosecution based on information elicited by the torture; it would only be to save lives. The warrant would limit the torture to nonlethal means, such as sterile needles being inserted beneath the nails to cause excruciating pain without endangering life.[23]

Not everyone agrees with Dershowitz.[24] Opponents of torture believe that even imminent danger does not justify state violence. There is a danger that such state-sponsored violence would become calculated and premeditated; torturers would have to be trained, ready, and in place for the ticking bomb argument to work. We couldn't be running around looking for torturers with a bomb set to go off, could we? Because torturers would be part of the government bureaucracy, there is no way to ensure that they would only use their skills in certain morally justifiable cases.[25] What happens if a superior officer tells them to torture someone, but they believe the order is unjustified? Should they follow orders or risk a court martial for being disobedient? Furthermore, there is very little empirical evidence suggesting that torture provides any real benefits and much more that suggests it can create serious problems. It can damage civil rights and democratic institutions and cause the general public to have sympathy for the victims of torture no matter their evil intent.[26]

# Terrorism

On April 2, 2015, gunmen belonging to the Somalia-based al-Shabaab terror group attacked the Garissa University campus in neighboring Kenya, killing 148 students before being rooted out by security forces. Four of the gunmen were killed and five more later apprehended as they attempted to flee. In the aftermath of the attack al-Shabaab spokespersons pledged a "long, gruesome war" in retaliation for Kenya's security forces joining with other nations of the African Union to fight al-Shabaab.[27] What is unsettling about this deadly outrageous attack was while it made headlines for a day it was quickly forgotten. The world has become so used to large-scale terror attacks that incidents during which "only" 150 people are killed in a faraway land rarely get more than a day or maybe two of news coverage.

The Garissa University attack reminds us that the political crime people are most concerned with is terrorism. The remainder of this chapter focuses on the history, nature, and extent of terrorism and the methods being employed for its control.

## Defining Terrorism

Despite its long history, it is often difficult to precisely define terrorism (from the Latin *terrere*, which means to frighten) and to separate terrorist acts from interpersonal crimes of violence. If a group robs a bank to obtain funds for its revolutionary struggles, should the act be treated as terrorism or as a common bank robbery? In this instance, defining a crime as terrorism depends on the kind of legal response the act evokes from those in power. To be considered **terrorism**, an act must carry with it the intent to disrupt and change the government and must not be merely a common-law crime committed for greed or egotism.

Because of its complexity, an all-encompassing definition of terrorism is difficult to formulate, although most experts agree that it generally involves the illegal use of force against innocent people to achieve a political objective.

- According to the U.S. State Department, the term *terrorism* means premeditated, politically motivated violence perpetrated against noncombatant targets by subnational groups or clandestine agents, usually intended to influence an audience.[28]
- The U.S. Department of Defense defines terrorism as "the calculated use of unlawful violence or threat of unlawful violence to inculcate fear; intended to coerce or to intimidate governments or societies in the pursuit of goals that are generally political, religious, or ideological."[29]
- The Federal Bureau of Investigation (FBI) defines terrorism as "the unlawful use of force or violence against persons or property to intimidate or coerce a government, the civilian population, or any segment thereof, in furtherance of political or social objectives."[30]

Terrorism usually involves a type of political crime that emphasizes violence as a mechanism to promote change. Whereas some political criminals sell secrets, spy, and the like, terrorists systematically murder and destroy or threaten such violence to terrorize individuals, groups, communities, or governments into conceding to the terrorists' political demands. Because terrorists lack large armies and formidable weapons, their use of subterfuge, secrecy, and hit-and-run tactics is designed to give them a psychological advantage and the power to neutralize the physical superiority of their opponents.

However, it may be erroneous to assume that all terrorists have political goals. Some may try to bring about what they consider to be social reform—for example, by attacking women wearing fur coats or sabotaging property during a labor dispute. Terrorism must also be

**ticking bomb scenario**
A scenario that some experts argue in which torture can perhaps be justified if the government discovers that a captured terrorist knows the whereabouts of a dangerous explosive device that is set to go off and kill thousands of innocent people.

**terrorism**
The illegal use of force against innocent people to achieve a political objective.

Federal Bureau of Investigation/Redux Pictures

Tamerlan Tsarnaev and Dzhokhar Tsarnaev, the two brothers who carried out the Boston Marathon bombings, are shown here on a video capture as they prepare to plant their bombs. The marathon bombing shows that the threat of domestic terror is real and that a terrorist may be the young man sitting next to you in class (Dzhokhar Tsarnaev was a student at the University of Massachusetts at Dartmouth at the time of the bombing).

distinguished from conventional warfare, because it requires secrecy and clandestine operations to exert social control over large populations.[31] So terrorist activities may be aimed at promoting an ideology other than political change.

## Terrorist and Guerilla

**LO4** Distinguish among terrorists, insurgents, guerillas, and revolutionaries.

**guerilla**
Armed military bands, typically located in rural areas, that use hit-and-run terror tactics to destabilize the existing government.

**insurgent**
The typical goal of an insurgency is to confront the existing government for control of all or a portion of its territory, or force political concessions in sharing political power. While terrorists may operate in small bands with a narrow focus, insurgents represent a popular movement and may also seek external support from other nations to bring pressure on the government.

The word *terrorist* is often used interchangeably with the word *guerilla*, but the terms are quite different. **Guerilla** comes from the Spanish term meaning "little war," which developed out of the Spanish rebellion against French troops after Napoleon's 1808 invasion of the Iberian Peninsula.[32] Terrorists have an urban focus. Operating in small bands, or cadres, of three to five members, they target the property or persons of their enemy, such as members of the ruling class.[33] However, terrorists may not have political ambitions, and their actions may be aimed at stifling or intimidating other groups who oppose their political, social, or economic views. For example, terrorists who kill abortion providers in order to promote their "pro-life" agenda are not aiming for regime change. Guerillas, on the other hand, are armed military bands, typically located in rural areas, that attack military, police, and government officials in an effort to destabilize the existing government. Their organizations can grow quite large and eventually take the form of a conventional military force. Some guerilla bands infiltrate urban areas (urban guerillas). For the most part, guerillas are a type of insurgent band.

## Terrorist and Insurgent

An insurgency is a political movement that may use terror tactics to achieve its goals. Insurgents wish to confront the existing government for control of all or a portion of its territory, or force political concessions in sharing political power by competing with the opposition government for popular support.[34] What makes the **insurgent** unique is that they have the luxury of receiving aid from neighboring sympathizers, allowing them to base their insurgency outside the target nation, thereby protecting them from their enemies. For example, Taliban members took shelter in Pakistan when the United States military drove them out of Afghanistan. Insurgencies may attract recruits who do not actually live in the disputed area but are sympathetic to the cause.

ISIL (Islamic State of Iraq and the Levant) started out as an insurgency, raiding into Iraq from Syria and occupying major cities such as Mosul. ISIL has the goal of creating a caliphate, based on a very conservative Islamic religious code, that spans Sunni-dominated sections of Iraq and Syria. ISIL was able to launch their insurgency after organizing outside of Iraq and then filtering through the porous border with Syria where they achieved territorial gains. ISIL is discussed more fully in the Policies and Issues in Criminology feature.

Insurgents tend to live isolated and stressful lives and enjoy varying levels of public support.[35] Although insurgents may engage in violence, they also may use nonviolent methods or political tactics. For example, they may set up food distribution centers and schools in areas in which they gain control in order to provide the population with needed services while contrasting their benevolent rule with the government's incompetence and corruption.

Here, militants from the Islamic State of Iraq and the Levant (ISIL, also known as ISIS) lead away captured Iraqi soldiers. The militants boasted on Twitter that they had executed 1,700 Iraqi government soldiers. ISIL has beheaded and burned to death those who oppose their regime and destroyed ancient relics in their effort to create an independent and all-powerful caliphate in Syria and Iraq.

Handout/New York Times/Redux

# Policies and Issues in Criminology

## ISLAMIC STATE OF IRAQ AND THE LEVANT (ISIL)

The Islamic State of Iraq and the Levant (ISIL), also known as the Islamic State of Iraq and al-Sham (ISIS), startled the world in the summer of 2014 when it took control of cities in Syria and Iraq defended by large contingents of enemy soldiers, who threw down their weapons and abandoned their posts. Those who actually fought were captured and killed in extremely brutal ways, through burning or decapitation. In the aftermath of its success, the group declared itself a caliphate, governed by Sharia law. Nonbelievers and opponents were killed in public executions. When Iraqi and Syrian forces tried to recapture lost territory, they only made headway under cover of U.S. and other allies' air strikes. Despite this show of force, ISIL still held sway over significant territory.

Where did this deadly group come from? How did it get its start? ISIL origins can be traced back to 2002, when Abu Musab al-Zarqawi founded a jihadist organization called Tawhid wal-Jihad in the north of Iraq. Affiliated with al-Qaeda, Tawhid wal-Jihad focused its attention on elements of the Islamic world rather than the West. When the United States invaded Iraq, Zarqawi's organization morphed into al-Qaeda in Iraq (AQI), and began to recruit locally as a jihadist organization, while at the same time allowing al-Qaeda to gain a foothold in Iraq.

Al-Qaeda in Iraq was involved in internal conflicts until Zarqawi was killed in an airstrike in 2006 and the group joined with other hard-core Islamist groups to create the Islamic State of Iraq (ISI), whose goal was creating an ultra-religious caliphate, governed by Islamic law, to whom all Muslims owed allegiance. Drone attacks by the U.S. helped degrade ISI until Abu Bakr al-Baghdadi took over in 2010. This change in leadership, coupled with the withdrawal of U.S. forces from Iraq and the start of the Syrian civil war, helped revive the group's prospects. ISI, now renamed ISIL, gained significant amounts of territory in both Syria and Iraq, including the Syrian city of Raqqa. The major Iraqi cities of Tikrit and Fallujah fell in 2014, followed by Mosul, Iraq's second-largest city. In 2015, ISIL begun to be the target of attacks by Kurdish forces. Other Muslim nations, including Jordan and Turkey, have either heavily criticized or actually attacked ISIL. Russia began bombing targets in September 2015.

In addition to its terrorist activities, ISIL is a governing body that imposes a very strict version of Islamic law in the territory it holds. It guarantees protection in exchange for the payment of a tax and the acceptance of second-class citizenship for minorities, including Shia Muslims. ISIL has engaged in massacres, beheadings, burnings, and executions of foreign journalists and humanitarian aid workers who have fallen into their hands. Ironically, this brutality has helped them draw an estimated 30,000 recruits who applaud their ruthlessness and want to be part of an Islamic caliphate that will not abide any element of Western culture. Western leaders fear that some of the recruits will return to their homes after being trained in jihad, creating tremendous danger for their home nations since they can blend in and have families and friends for support. Some well-known groups such as Boko Haram in Nigeria have allied themselves with ISIL.

### Critical Thinking

Considering the refugee crisis caused by people desperately trying to flee violence, should Western states intervene militarily every time a group such as ISIL or the Taliban forms in the Middle East? Are there solutions other than military intervention?

**Sources:** Peter Welby, "What Is ISIS?" Tony Blair Faith Foundation, March 16, 2015, tonyblairfaithfoundation.org/religion-geopolitics/commentaries/backgrounder/what-isis; BBC News, "What Is 'Islamic State'?" June 29, 2015, www.bbc.com/news/world-middle-east-29052144; Tim Arango, Kareem Fahim, and Ben Hubbard, "Rebels' Fast Strike in Iraq Was Years in the Making," *New York Times*, June 15, 2014, www.nytimes.com/2014/06/15/world/middleeast/rebels-fast-strike-in-iraq-was-years-in-the-making.html; Andrew Silke, "Holy Warriors: Exploring the Psychological Processes of Jihadi Radicalization," *European Journal of Criminology* 5 (2008): 99–123; Farouk Chothia, "Who Are Nigeria's Boko Haram Islamists?" BBC News Africa, May 20, 2014, www.bbc.com/news/world-africa-13809501 (**URLs accessed 2015**).

## Terrorist and Revolutionary

A revolution (from the Latin *revolutio*, "a revolving," and *revolvere*, "turn, roll back") is generally seen as a civil war fought between nationalists and a sovereign power that holds control of the land, or between the existing government and local groups over issues of ideology and power. Historically, the American Revolution may be considered an example of a struggle between nationalistic groups and an imperialistic

## Concept Summary 11.1    Forms of Radical Political Groups

|  | Terrorist | Guerilla | Insurgent | Revolutionary |
|---|---|---|---|---|
| **Description** | Groups who engage in premeditated, politically motivated violence perpetrated against noncombatant targets. | Armed groups operating in rural areas who attack the military, the police, and other government officials. | Groups who engage in armed uprising, or revolt against an established civil or political authority. | Groups who engage in civil war against sovereign power that holds control of the land. |
| **Examples** | Al-Qaeda, Hamas | Mao's People's Liberation Army, Ho Chi Minh's Viet Cong | Iraqi insurgent groups; ISIS | American Revolution, French Revolution, Russian Revolution |
| **Goals** | Personal, criminal, or political gain or change. | Replace or overthrow existing government. | Win over population by showing government's incompetence. Force government into political concessions and/or power sharing. | Gain independence or oust existing government or monarchy. |
| **Methods** | Small, clandestine cells who use systematic violence for purpose of intimidation. | Use unconventional warfare and mobile tactics. May grow large and use tactics similar to conventional military force. | May use violent (bombings and kidnappings) or nonviolent means (food distribution centers and creating schools). | Can use violent armed conflict or nonviolent methods such as Gandhi used in India. |

overseas government. Classic examples of ideological rebellions are the French Revolution, which pitted the middle class and urban poor against the aristocracy, and the Russian Revolution of 1917, during which the Czarist government was toppled by the Bolsheviks. More recent ideological revolutions have occurred in China, Cuba, Nicaragua, and Chile, to name but a few.

While some revolutions (such as the American, French, and Russian) rely on armed force, terror activities, and violence, others can be nonviolent, depending on large urban protests and threats. Such was the case when the Shah Mohammad Reza Pahlavi was toppled in Iran in the 1979 revolution that transformed Iran into an Islamic republic under the rule of Ayatollah Ruhollah Khomeini. Similar events unfolded in Egypt in early 2011 in the effort to topple the government of Hosni Mubarak that had been in power for 30 years.

Concept Summary 11.1 describes the components of various types of radical political groups.

## A Brief History of Terrorism

**Reign of Terror**
The origin of the term *terrorism*, the French Revolution's Reign of Terror began in 1795 and was initiated by the revolutionary government during which agents of the Committee of Public Safety and the National Convention were referred to as terrorists.

While terrorist-like activities have been known since Roman times, the term *terrorist* first became popular during the French Revolution. Use of the word *terrorism* began in 1795 in reference to the **Reign of Terror** initiated by the revolutionary government during which agents of the Committee of Public Safety and the National Convention were referred to as terrorists. In response, royalists and opponents of the revolution employed terrorist tactics in resistance to the revolutionists. The widespread use of the guillotine is an infamous reminder of the revolutionary violence; urban mobs demanded blood, and many government officials and aristocrats were beheaded in gruesome public spectacles. From the fall of the Bastille on July 14, 1789, until July 1794, thousands suspected of counterrevolutionary activity were killed on the guillotine. Here again, the relative nature of political crime is documented: most victims of the French Reign of Terror were revolutionaries who had been denounced by rival factions, whereas thousands of the hated nobility lived in relative tranquility. The end of the terror was signaled by the death of its prime mover, Maximilien Robespierre, on July 28, 1794, as the result of a successful plot to end his rule. He was executed on the same guillotine to which he had sent almost 20,000 people.

In the hundred years following the French Revolution, terrorism continued to be a political tool around the world. Terrorist acts became the preferred method of political action for national groups in the early years of the twentieth century. In Eastern Europe, the Internal Macedonian Revolutionary Organization campaigned against the Turkish government, which controlled its homeland (Macedonia became part of the former Yugoslavia). Similarly, the protest of the Union of Death Society, or Black Hand, against the Austro-Hungarian Empire's control of Serbia led to the group's assassination of Archduke Franz Ferdinand, which started World War I. Russia was the scene of left-wing revolutionary activity, which killed the czar in 1917 and gave birth to the Marxist state.

After the war ended, the Treaty of Versailles restructured Europe and broke up the Austro-Hungarian Empire. The result was a hodgepodge of new nations controlled by majority ethnic groups. Self-determination was limited to European nations and ethnic groups and denied to others, especially the colonial possessions of the major European powers, creating bitterness and setting the stage for the long conflicts of the anticolonial period. The Irish Republican Army, established around 1916, steadily battled British forces from 1919 to 1923, culminating in the Republic of Ireland gaining independence.

Between the World Wars, right-wing terrorism existed in Germany, Spain, and Italy. One source of tension, according to author Michael Kellogg, was the virulently anti-Communist exiles (called White Russians) who fled Russia after the 1917 revolution and took up residence in Germany and other Western nations. According to Kellogg, between 1920 and 1923, Adolf Hitler was deeply influenced by the Aufbau (Reconstruction), the émigrés' organization. Members of the Aufbau allied with the Nazis to overthrow the legitimate German government and thwart German communists from seizing power. The White Russians' deep-seated anti-Semitism may have inspired Hitler to go public with his campaign to kill the European Jews, prompting both the Holocaust and the invasion of Russia, which spelled the eventual doom of Hitler and National Socialism.

During World War II, resistance to the occupying German troops was common throughout Europe. The Germans considered the resistors to be terrorists, but the rest of the world considered them heroes. Meanwhile, in Palestine, Jewish terrorist groups—the Haganah, Irgun, and Stern Gang, whose leaders included Menachem Begin, who later became Israel's prime minister—waged war against the British to force them to allow Jewish survivors of the Holocaust to settle in their traditional homeland. Today, of course, many of these alleged terrorists are considered freedom fighters who laid down their lives for a just cause.

After the war, Arab nationalists felt that they had been betrayed. Believing they were promised postwar independence, they were doubly disappointed—first when the French and British were given authority over their lands, and then especially when the British allowed Zionist immigration into Palestine in keeping with a promise contained in the Balfour Declaration. Hence, the creation of the PLO and Hamas.

Since the end of World War II, terrorism has accelerated its development into a major component of contemporary conflict. Primarily in use immediately after the war as a subordinate element of anticolonial insurgencies, it has expanded beyond that role. In the service of various ideologies and aspirations, terrorism sometimes supplanted other forms of conflict completely. It became a far-reaching weapon capable of effects no less global than the intercontinental bomber or missile. It has also proven to be a significant tool of diplomacy and international power for states inclined to use it.

**L05** Enumerate the various forms of terrorism.

# Contemporary Forms of Terrorism

Today the term *terrorism* encompasses many different behaviors and goals. Some of the more common forms are briefly described here.

## Revolutionary Terrorism

Revolutionary terrorists use violence to frighten those in power and their supporters in order to replace the existing government with a regime that holds political or religious views that the terror group finds acceptable. Terrorist actions such as kidnapping, assassination, and bombing are designed to draw repressive responses from governments trying to defend themselves. These responses help revolutionaries to expose, through the skilled use of media coverage, the government's inhumane nature. The original reason for the government's harsh response may be lost as the effect of counterterrorist activities is felt by uninvolved people.

Jemaah Islamiyah, an Indonesian terrorist organization aligned with al-Qaeda, is believed to be intent on driving away foreign tourists and ruining the nation's economy so they can usurp the government and set up a pan-Islamic nation in Indonesia and neighboring Malaysia. Another example is Boko Haram, a fundamentalist Islamic group that has caused havoc in Nigeria, Africa's most populous country, through bombings, assassinations, and abductions. Its aim is to overthrow the government and create an Islamic state based on the concept "Anyone who is not governed by what Allah has revealed is among the transgressors." Boko Haram promotes a version of Islam that makes it *haram* (forbidden) for Muslims to take part in any political or social activity associated with Western society. This includes voting in elections, wearing shirts and trousers, or receiving a secular education. Boko Haram regards the Nigerian state as being run by nonbelievers—even when the country had a Muslim president—and it has extended its military campaign by targeting neighboring African states. It made international news in 2014 when the group abducted nearly 300 girls attending a Western school, saying it would treat them as slaves and marry them off—a reference to an ancient Islamic belief that women captured in conflict are part of the "war booty."[36]

## Political Terrorism

Political terrorism is directed at people or groups who oppose the terrorists' political ideology or whom the terrorists define as "outsiders" who must be destroyed. Domestic terrorists in the United States can be found across the political spectrum. On the right, they tend to be heavily armed groups organized around such themes as white supremacy, militant tax resistance, and religious revisionism. Identified groups have included, at one time or another, the Aryan Republican Army, the Aryan Nation, the Posse Comitatus, and the Ku Klux Klan. These groups want to shape U.S. government policy over a range of matters, including ending abortion rights, extending the right to bear arms, and eliminating federal taxation. Anti-abortion groups have demonstrated at abortion clinics, attacked clients, bombed offices, and killed doctors who perform abortions. Although unlikely to topple the government, these individualistic acts of terror are difficult to predict or control. On April 19, 1995, 168 people were killed during the Oklahoma City bombing, the most severe example of political terrorism in the United States so far.

Research conducted at the University of Maryland's National Consortium for the Study of Terrorism and Responses to Terrorism found that between 1990 and 2013 there were 155 ideologically motivated homicide events committed by far-right extremists in the United States, of which 13 percent were anti-government in nature. During these incidents 50 federal, state, and local law enforcement officers were killed in the line of duty; more than two-thirds were killed during ideologically motivated attacks.[37]

Some political terrorists focus on saving the environment. Founded in 1992 in Brighton, England, by members of the Earth First! environmental movement, the Earth Liberation Front (ELF) conducted a series of actions intent on damaging individuals or corporations that they consider a threat to the environment. On October 19, 1998, ELF members claimed responsibility for fires that were set atop Vail Mountain, a luxurious ski resort in Colorado, designed to stop the resort from expanding into animal habitats. Fires have also been set in government labs conducting animal research, and spikes have been driven into trees to prevent logging in fragile areas.

Another group, the Animal Liberation Front (ALF), focuses their efforts on protecting animals from being used as food, in clothing, or as experimental subjects. Their philosophy is that animals are entitled to the moral right to possess their own lives and control their own bodies, while rejecting the view that animals are merely capital goods or property intended for the benefit of humans and can be bought, sold, or killed by humans.[38] ALF is still active and in 2015, members were responsible for "liberating" 5,740 mink from farms in Idaho, Iowa, Pennsylvania, Wisconsin, and Minnesota and also vandalizing property and destroying breeding records in an attempt to disrupt the fur breeding economy.[39]

Political terrorists may target groups whom they consider outsiders who must be eliminated. Here, Frazier Glenn Cross, also known as Frazier Glenn Miller, is escorted by police in Overland Park, Kansas. Cross, 73, a white supremacist and former Ku Klux Klan leader, was convicted of killing three people in attacks at a Jewish community center and Jewish retirement complex near Kansas City. At his 2015 trial he called the shootings "righteous" and "honorable"; none of his three victims was Jewish. Cross faces the death penalty.

The federal government began cracking down on environmental terrorists in the 1990s, and some environmental activists have received long prison sentences for their crimes, including Justin Solondz, a member of an eco-terrorist cell known as "The Family," who received a seven-year sentence for committing an estimated $48 million worth of arson and vandalism across the Pacific Northwest and western United States.[40]

While eco-terrorists have been relatively dormant in recent years, there have been many other examples of anti-government domestic terrorists who planned to use violence to push their political agenda. Recently, federal agents broke up an anarchist extremist cell that planned to blow up a bridge in Cleveland, Ohio, and arrested members of a militia in Georgia who were planning to acquire silencers and explosives to use against various U.S. government targets in Atlanta.[41]

## Nationalist Terrorism

Nationalist terrorism promotes the interests of a minority ethnic or religious group that believes it has been persecuted under majority rule. Terrorist acts are designed to force the government to cede land so that the minority group can have its own independent nation. While revolutionary terrorists are aiming for regime change in their home country, nationalists want to create a separate country of their own.

In the Middle East, terrorist activities have been linked to the Palestinians' desire to create an independent state. At first, the Palestinian Liberation Organization (PLO), led by Yasser Arafat, directed terrorist activities against Israel. Now the group Hamas is perpetuating the conflict with Israel and is behind terrorist attacks that have sent thousands of missiles into Israeli territory, designed to elicit a sharp response from the Israeli army and air force in order to demonstrate to the world the righteousness of their cause. In 2014, three Israeli youths were kidnapped and killed by Hamas members, prompting Israeli military retaliation. Hamas amped up the tension by sending thousands of missiles into Israel, prompting increased intervention. Worldwide outrage prompted both sides to eventually back down and honor a ceasefire.

Hezbollah (from the Arabic, meaning "party of God") is a Lebanese Shi'ite Islamist organization founded in 1982 in response to the presence of Israeli forces in southern Lebanon. At inception, its goals were to both drive Israeli troops out of Lebanon and to form a Shi'ite Islamic republic in Lebanon. Taking its inspiration from Iran, Hezbollah members follow a distinct version of Shia ideology developed in Iran and have also received arms and financial support from Iran. Hezbollah is anti-West and anti-Israel and has engaged in a series of terrorist actions, including kidnappings, car bombings, and airline hijackings.[42] Recently, Hezbollah has shifted its focus and has become increasingly embroiled in the Syrian civil war, fighting for the Assad regime. Ironically, this shift has alienated some of its Lebanese constituents and prompted deadly reprisals in Beirut from partisans of the predominantly Sunni Muslim Syrian rebels. The U.S. government and its European allies consider Hezbollah a global terrorist threat and a menace to Middle East stability.

The Middle East is not the only source of nationalistic fervor and terrorism. The Chinese government has been trying to suppress separatist groups fighting for an independent state in the northwestern province of Xinjiang. The rebels are drawn from the region's Uyghur people, most of whom practice Sufi Islam, speak a Turkic language, and wish to set up a Muslim state called Eastern Turkistan. During the past decade, the Uyghur separatists have organized demonstrations, bombings, and political assassinations. To control their rebellion, over the past decade, many prominent Uighurs have been imprisoned after being accused of terrorism. Mass immigration of Han Chinese to Xinjiang have made Uighurs a minority group in their own region.[43]

## Retributive Terrorism

**retributive terrorists**
Terror groups who refrain from tying specific acts to direct demands for change. They want to instead redirect the balance between what they believe is good and evil. They see their revolution as existing on a spiritual plane; their mission is to exact retribution against sinners.

Some terrorist groups are not nationalist, political, or revolutionary organizations. They do not wish to set up their own homeland or topple a government but rather want to punish people or governments for ideological, political, or religious reasons.[44] Al-Qaeda is the paradigm of the **retributive terrorist** organization. Rather than fighting for a homeland, its message is a call to take up a cause: there is a war of civilizations in which "Jews and Crusaders" want to destroy Islam and must therefore be defeated. Armed jihad is the individual obligation of every Muslim; terrorism and violence are appropriate methods for defeating even the strongest powers. The end product would be a unified Muslim world, the destruction of the West, and the end of decadent and depraved Western influence.

These themes are preached in schools, on the Internet, and disseminated in books and pamphlets. Videos are distributed in which al-Qaeda's leaders expound on political topics, going as far as calling Western leaders liars and drunkards. As a result of this media strategy, al-Qaeda's messages have penetrated deeply into Muslim communities around the world, finding a sympathetic response among many Muslims who have a sense of helplessness both in the Arab world and in the Western Muslim diaspora. Al-Qaeda offers a sense of empowerment to young men who feel lost in their adopted cultures, prompting many to travel to the East to receive terror training.[45]

Retributive terrorists have a number of characteristics that are unique and separate them from guerrillas, revolutionaries, and other terrorists:[46]

Adam Gadahn, also known as Azzam al-Amriki, is shown delivering a statement in English with Arabic subtitles, laying out al-Qaeda's justifications for conducting future attacks against the United States. Gadahn was an American originally from California. On January 19, 2015, he was killed in a CIA drone strike in Pakistan.

- Violence is used as a method of influence, persuasion, or intimidation. The true target of the terrorist act extends far beyond those directly affected by the attack and is designed to lead to some desired behavior on the part of the larger target population or government.

- Victims are usually selected for their maximum propaganda value, ensuring a high degree of media coverage. The message is that the target population had better comply with their demands because the terrorists are desperate enough to "do anything." Sometimes this may backfire if the attack results in the death of innocents, especially children, along with the symbolic targets.
- Unconventional military tactics are used, especially secrecy and surprise, as well as targeting civilians, including women and children. Because the goal is to inflict maximum horror, it makes sense to choose targets that contain the largest number of victims from all walks of life. The message: everyone is a target; no one is safe.

## State-Sponsored Terrorism

**State-sponsored terrorism** occurs when a repressive government regime forces its citizens into obedience, oppresses minorities, and stifles political dissent. Death squads and the use of government troops to destroy political opposition parties are often associated with political terrorism. Much of what we know about state-sponsored terrorism comes from the efforts of human rights groups such as London-based Amnesty International, whose research shows that tens of thousands of people continue to become victims of security operations that result in disappearances and executions. Political prisoners are now being tortured in about 100 countries, people have disappeared or are being held in secret detention in about 20 countries, and government-sponsored death squads have been operating in more than 35 countries. Countries known for encouraging violent control of dissidents include Brazil, Colombia, Guatemala, Honduras, Peru, Iraq, and Sudan.

State-sponsored terrorism became a world issue when South and Central American dictatorships in the 1970s and 1980s unleashed state violence against political dissidents through forced disappearance, political imprisonment, torture, blacklisting, and massive exile. The region-wide *state* repression in this period emerged in response to the rise of the 1960s radical movements, which demanded public reforms and programs to help the lower classes in urban areas and agricultural workers in the countryside. Local authoritarian governments, which used repression to take control of radical political groups, were given financial support by the economic elites who dominated Latin American politics and were fearful of a socialist revolution.[47]

As might be expected, governments claim that repressive measures are needed to control terror and revolutionary groups that routinely use violence. Thus the use of terror is sometimes a way of defending the nation against violence, a conundrum that supports the idea that a state is both protective and destructive.[48]

It is sometimes difficult to assess blame for state terror—is it a few rogue government agents who act on their own authority or the government itself? The issue of responsibility for improper acts hit home during the Abu Ghraib scandal in Iraq. Photos beamed around the world embarrassed the United States when they showed military personnel victimizing suspected insurgents. The U.S. government's response was to prosecute and imprison the perpetrators. However, some critics, such as criminologist Mark Hamm, suggest that these images constitute the photographic record of a state-sponsored crime.[49] He argues that rather than being the work of a few rogue officers, the sophisticated interrogation practices at Abu Ghraib were designed and executed by the U.S. Central Intelligence Agency and that the torturing of detainees at Abu Ghraib followed directly from decisions made by top government officials to get tough with prisoner interrogations. So while we condemn state-sponsored violence, it is not easy to identify who is truly responsible.

## Criminal Terrorism

Sometimes terrorist groups become involved in common-law crimes such as drug dealing, kidnapping, and piracy to support their cause. Illegal activities may on occasion become so profitable that they replace the group's original focus. In some instances, the line between being a terrorist organization with political support and

**state-sponsored terrorism** Terrorism that occurs when a repressive government regime forces its citizens into obedience, oppresses minorities, and stifles political dissent.

vast resources and an organized criminal group engaging in illicit activities for profit becomes blurred. What appears to be a politically motivated action, such as the kidnapping of a government official for ransom, may turn out to be merely a crime for profit.[50]

In some cases, there has been close cooperation between organized criminal groups and guerillas in which illegal activity is used to fund terror operations. The Revolutionary Armed Forces of Colombia (FARC) imposes a tax on Colombian drug producers, but evidence indicates that the group cooperates with Colombia's top drug barons in running the trade (currently the FARC and the Colombian government are in peace talks which hope to end their long-running guerilla war).

Al-Shabaab, the Somalia-based terror group infamous for their 2015 attack on Garissa University and the 2013 attack on Westgate Mall in Nairobi, Kenya, which resulted in hundreds of casualties and more than 60 deaths, has long been linked to criminal activity. They require a share of the payment of ransoms given to Somalian pirates who launch cross-ocean raids from the al-Shabaab–controlled territory; piracy would be impossible without cooperation from al-Shabaab. The group is also heavily involved in smuggling, slapping taxes on illegal charcoal exports to the Gulf, arms shipments from Yemen, and electronic goods destined for the region.[51]

## Lone-Actor Terrorism

On November 5, 2009, U.S. Army Major Nidal Malik Hasan attacked fellow soldiers at Fort Hood, leaving 12 dead and 31 wounded. On July 22, 2011, Anders Breivik killed 77 civilians in and around Oslo, Norway. Dzhokhar and Tamerlan Tsarnaev set off bombs at the finish line of the 2013 Boston Marathon, killing 3 and wounding more than 250. These mass killings have drawn attention to so-called lone-actor terrorists who plan and carry out an attack without assistance from others. They are not affiliated with terror organizations nor are they under orders to take violent action.[52]

Why would any individual take this kind of risk and choose to sacrifice himself or herself for a cause? Research by Clark McCauley and Sophia Moskalenko shows that lone actors may see themselves as representing some larger group or cause and may have had some experience in a group, organization, or social movement related to this cause.[53] However, it was difficult for them to stay or be part of a group because they tend to suffer from some form of psychological disturbance, are socially isolated, and tend to be loners with few friends.

Many have a military background and have recently suffered some form of serious personal disruption that triggered a violent attack, such as divorce or the death of a partner. For example, Major Hasan had no close relationships. He had turned to the Quran after the death of his parents and was about to be transferred to Afghanistan. He saw himself discriminated against as a Muslim and viewed the war on terrorism as a war on Islam, thereby developing both personal and political grievances.

Taken together, these results provide a portrait of the typical lone actor as a grievance-fueled individual, likely to have weapons experience, who suffers from depression or other mental disorders, and experiences temporary or chronic social isolation. McCauley and Moskalenko call this the *disconnected-disordered* profile.

However, not all lone-actor terrorists fit the disconnected-disordered profile: there are some who are neither loners nor suffer mental disorder, but who nonetheless undertake lone-actor terrorist violence. They may be motivated by some emotionally charged event that sets them off on a destructive path: the political becomes personal. They are radicalized by feelings of moral obligation to right a perceived wrong: a man bombs abortion clinics after a family member loses a child at birth; a woman burns down a factory farm after witnessing the suffering of animals. The Tsarnaev brothers, who planned and carried out the Boston Marathon bombing, were motivated by their sensitivity to what they perceived as the oppression of Muslims by the West. A note that Dzhokhar Tsarnaev wrote while hiding from authorities on a dry-docked boat said in part: "God has a plan for each person. Mine was to hide in this boat and shed some light on our actions. . . . Stop killing our innocent people

## Concept Summary 11.2  The Variety of Terror Groups

| | |
|---|---|
| **Revolutionary terrorists** | Use violence to frighten those in power and their supporters in order to replace the existing government with a regime that holds acceptable political or religious views. |
| **Political terrorists** | Political terrorism is directed at people or groups who oppose the terrorists' political ideology or whom the terrorists define as "outsiders" who must be destroyed. |
| **Eco-terrorists** | Political terror groups involved in violent actions to protect the environment. |
| **Nationalist terrorists** | Groups whose actions promote the interests of a minority ethnic or religious group that has been persecuted under majority rule and/or wishes to carve out its own independent homeland. |
| **Retributive terrorists** | Groups that use violence as a method of influence, persuasion, or intimidation in order to achieve a particular aim or objective. |
| **State-sponsored terrorists** | Carried out by a repressive government regime in order to force its citizens into obedience, oppress minorities, and stifle political dissent. |
| **Criminal terrorists** | Terrorist groups that become involved in common-law crimes such as drug dealing and kidnapping, even selling nuclear materials. |
| **Lone-actor terrorists** | Individuals who carry out terror acts without guidance from a group or organization. They are motivated by a variety of reasons and beliefs, including feelings of alienation, racial hatred, and religious oppression. |

and we will stop." On April 8, 2015, Dzhokhar (the surviving brother—Tamerlan was killed in a shootout with police) was found guilty on all 30 federal counts with which he was charged; on June 24, he was sentenced to death.[54]

What sets this type of lone terrorist apart is their unusual capacity to care about the suffering of others. Those who fit this *caring-compelled profile* have social relations and are not mentally ill. But they care too much and find that there is a dark side to caring greatly about others. Individuals can kill for love, including love of strangers seen as victimized.

In sum, McCauley and Moskalenko believe that lone-actor terrorists fit one of these two profiles: disconnected-disordered or caring-compelled. They suspect that the caring-compelled profile is less common than the disconnected-disordered profile—not least because self-sacrifice for others is less common than self-interest—but this hypothesis remains to be tested.

The various forms that terror groups take are summarized in Concept Summary 11.2.

## What Motivates the Terrorist?

In the aftermath of the September 11, 2001, destruction of the World Trade Center in New York City, many Americans asked themselves the same simple question: Why? What could motivate someone like Osama bin Laden to order the deaths of thousands of innocent people? How could someone who had never been to the United States or suffered personally at its hands develop such lethal hatred? Some experts believed the attacks had a political basis, claiming that bin Laden's anger was fueled

### CHECKPOINTS

▶ Revolutionary terrorists use violence to frighten those in power and their supporters in order to replace the existing government with a regime that holds acceptable political or religious views.

▶ Political terrorism is directed at people or groups who oppose the terrorists' political ideology or whom the terrorists define as "outsiders" who must be destroyed.

▶ Nationalist terrorism promotes the interests of a minority ethnic or religious group that believes it has been persecuted under majority rule and wishes to carve out its own independent homeland.

▶ Retributive terrorist groups want to impose their social and religious code on others.

▶ State-sponsored terrorism occurs when a repressive government regime forces its citizens into obedience, oppresses minorities, and stifles political dissent.

▶ Lone-actor terrorists do not belong to an organized group but act on their own, motivated by political, religious, or social beliefs.

**L06** Explain what motivates the terrorist to commit violent acts.

by the U.S.'s Middle East policies. Others saw a religious motivation and claimed that Osama was a radical Muslim at war with the liberal religions of the West. Another view was that Osama's rage was fueled by deep-rooted psychological problems.

As such, there have been a number of competing visions of why terrorists engage in criminal activities such as bombings, shootings, and kidnappings to achieve a political end. Several views stand out.

## Psychological View

One of the most controversial views of terrorists is that some if not all suffer from psychological deficits, and that the typical terrorist can be described as an emotionally disturbed individual who acts out his or her psychoses within the confines of violent groups. According to this view, terrorist violence is not so much a political instrument as an end in itself; it is the result of compulsion or psychopathology. Terrorists do what they do because of garden variety emotional problems, including but not limited to self-destructive urges and disturbed emotions combined with problems with authority.[55] As terrorism expert Jerrold M. Post puts it, "Political terrorists are driven to commit acts of violence as a consequence of psychological forces, and . . . their special psychology is constructed to rationalize acts they are psychologically compelled to commit."[56]

Some terror experts say that the majority of research on terrorists indicates that most are not psychologically abnormal.[57] Even suicide bombers, a group that should show signs of psychological abnormality, exhibit few signs of the mental problems such as depression that are typically found in people who choose to take their own life. Rather than acting disturbed and disoriented, those terrorists willing to die for their cause display a heightened sense of purpose, group allegiance, and task focus.[58] After carefully reviewing existing evidence on the psychological state of terrorists, mental health experts have concluded that terrorism is not linked to mental illness or personality defects, nor is there a "terrorist personality." Histories of childhood abuse and trauma and themes of perceived injustice and humiliation often are prominent in terrorist biographies, but do not really help to explain terrorism.[59]

## Alienation View

Another explanation for terrorist activity is that a lack of opportunity creates a sense of alienation that motivates men and women to embrace terrorism.[60] Regions such as South Asia breed terrorists because they house an incendiary mix of strong ethnic identities and diverse religious communities, many of which are concentrated within exclusionary ghettos. Young men and women residing in these areas are motivated to join terror groups when they feel left out of the social and economic mainstream because of their religious or ethnic status.[61] According to this view, terror recruits suffer alienation from friends, family, and society.[62] Many have been raised to hate the groups who are in power and believe that they have been victimized by state authorities whom they view as oppressors.

Terrorism expert Arie Kruglanski finds that the need for coherence in their lives is what drives young foreigners to travel to Iraq/Syria to join ISIL. The group's ideology, he finds, offers an invaluable psychological reward: by joining the fight against infidels, recruits earn the status of heroes and martyrs, thus gaining a larger-than-life significance and earning a spot in history. Groups like ISIL can provide a greater meaning and purpose to life, giving young people a chance to be noticed, to matter, and to be esteemed in a way that their home country can never provide. And the quest for significance is inflamed by claims that Muslims have been humiliated by the West in Iraq, Bosnia, and other areas. Frustrated youths, Kruglanski finds, without coherent purpose, with uncertain prospects, and on the receiving end of rejection are particularly prone to jihadism.[63]

Not all experts abide by the alienation view. When Marc Sageman studied members of extremist Islamist groups he found that most tend to be well educated; about 60 percent had some form of higher education. More than 75 percent came from upper- or middle-class backgrounds. When they joined a terror organization, the majority had professional occupations such as doctor or engineer, or semiskilled employment, such as civil service; fewer than 25 percent were unemployed or working in unskilled jobs. Surprisingly, Sageman found that almost three-quarters were married and that most had children.[64] These findings suggest that terrorists are not suffering from the social problems usually associated with alienation: poverty, lack of education, and ignorance.

**RELIGIOUS BELIEFS** Terrorism has also become an alternative for people whose religious beliefs alienate them from our postmodern, technological, global society in which foreign influences routinely clash with age-old traditions. They may believe that modern forms of communication, entertainment, and social interaction have brought foreign influences that are corrupting and disrespectful to their traditional way of life. Religious beliefs can become so powerful that the terrorist may even believe that a suicide mission will help cleanse them of the corruption of the modern world while at the same time scaring off outsiders.

How do terrorists justify using violence if they are truly religious, since most of the world's religions eschew violence? Islamic terrorists believe that their commitment to God justifies their extreme actions. They regard the actions of people they trust as a testimony to the righteousness of their acts. They trust significant others, and rely on their wisdom, experience, and testimony and accept their expressions of faith. To the terrorist, someone like Osama bin Laden demonstrated the strength of his faith by living in poverty and giving up a more luxurious and leisurely life in the name of God. When a charismatic leader calls them to jihad, they are likely to follow, even if it means killing those who deny their faith or beliefs. Perceived miracles, such as the defeat of a superpower through faith alone (e.g., the Soviet/Afghan war or the fight against the United States in Iraq), also increase confidence in the righteousness of the cause. Some have mystical experiences during prayers or dreams that demonstrate the existence of God and reinforce faith.[65] Tales of religious oppression by the West can incense individuals who may otherwise be seen as well-adjusted and with a promising future.[66]

## Family Conflict View

Terrorists report that they are products of dysfunctional families in which the father was absent or, even if present, was a distant and cold figure.[67] Because of this family estrangement, the budding terrorist may have been swayed to join a group or cult by a charismatic leader who serves as an alternative father figure. Some find it in religious schools run by strong leaders who demand strict loyalty from their followers while indoctrinating them in political causes.[68] In this sense, terror groups, similar to what happens in urban street gangs, provide a substitute family–like environment, which can nurture a heretofore emotionally underprivileged youth.

## Political View

When people are left out of the political process, having their votes restricted or even losing the right to vote, they may be inclined to join terror groups.[69] Research shows that most of the risk for political violence lies in those nations that are nearly democracies, which experience three times as many terror attacks as full democracies. Ironically, the most autocratic countries, governed by dictators and without free elections, generally had the lowest average number of attacks. In contrast, **failed states**—those where governments have lost physical control of their own territory, are unable to provide reasonable public services, and cannot interact properly with other states—have extremely high rates of terrorist activity. Terrorist attacks against failed states are much more lethal than attacks against other nations. Nations that provide access to the political process for people holding a wide range of diverse viewpoints create a culture that helps reduce the frustration that leads to terrorist violence. Those states that cannot maintain order or provide services to its citizens are fertile grounds for terrorists. And while iron-handed dictators may keep terrorism under control in the short term, their long-term prospects are sketchy at best, as recent events in Egypt, Libya, and Syria have shown.

**failed state**
A nation whose government has lost control of its own territory, is unable to provide public services and protection, and lacks the ability to interact with other states as a full member of the international community.

## Socialization/Friendship View

Many jihadist recruits are living in foreign countries where they were looking for economic opportunity when they get involved with terrorist organizations. Feeling homesick, they seek out people with similar backgrounds, whom they often find at mosques.[70] Though many appear to be motivated by religious fervor, their devotion is fueled by an effort to seek comrades while living in a foreign land. Some move in together to share the rent and also to eat together under Muslim dietary laws. Group relations and activities solidify beliefs and create a sense of solidarity. If one group member becomes committed to terrorism, others may follow rather than let him down.

## Ideological View

Another view is that terrorists hold extreme ideological beliefs that prompt their behavior. They may have developed heightened perceptions of oppressive conditions, believing they are being victimized by some group or government for their beliefs or way of life. Once they conclude that the government will not help people with their beliefs, they decide to resort to violence to encourage change.

Facilitating the use of violence is the ability to divide people into two categories based on religious, ethnic, racial, or other cultural criteria: those with common interests and beliefs who are avenged through terrorist activities ("us") and those against whom the terrorist activities are to be directed ("them"). Those associated with "us" are viewed as moral, right, good, and strong. Those associated with "them" are seen as immoral, wrong, bad, and weak.[71] Once this division is made, the terrorist can act with impunity to further their ideological beliefs because those harmed have beliefs that make them less than human.

## Explaining State-Sponsored Terrorism

How can state-sponsored terrorism be explained? After all, these violent acts are not directed at a foreign government or overseas adversaries but against natives of one's own country. In her book *Reigns of Terror*, Patricia Marchak finds that people willing to kill or maim their fellow countrymen are likely to be highly susceptible to unquestioning submission to authority. They are conformists who want to be part of the central group and who are quite willing to be part of a state regime. They are vulnerable to ideology that dehumanizes their targets and can utilize propaganda to distance themselves psychologically from those they are terrorizing.[72] So the Nazis had little trouble recruiting people to carry out horrific acts during the Holocaust because many Germans wanted to be part of the popular social/political movement and were easily indoctrinated by the Nazi propaganda that branded Jews as subhuman. Stalin was able to carry out his reign of terror in Russia because his victims were viewed as state enemies who were trying to undermine the Communist regime. How can these tendencies be neutralized? Marchak sees little benefit to international intervention that results in after-the-fact punishment of the perpetrators, a course of action that was attempted in the former Yugoslavia after death squads had performed "ethnic cleansing" of undesirables. Instead she argues for a prevention strategy that involves international aid and economic development by industrialized nations to those in the Third World that are on the verge of becoming collapsed states, the construction of social welfare systems, and the acceptance of international legal norms and standards of human rights.[73]

# Extent of the Terrorism Threat

The most recent and comprehensive data on terrorist attacks (2013) are generated by the National Consortium for the Study of Terrorism and Responses to Terrorism (START) based at the University of Maryland. START estimates that during that single year, 11,952 terrorist attacks occurred resulting in 22,178 fatalities across 91 countries.

This represents a sharp increase over the past few years. More than half of all attacks (54 percent), fatalities (61 percent), and injuries (69 percent) occurred in just three countries: Iraq, Pakistan, and Afghanistan, countries that have seen the majority of attacks for the past several years. While Asia and Africa remain the location of most attacks, there were some shifts within these regions: total attacks increased for Iraq, Pakistan, the Philippines, Syria, Egypt, Libya, and Lebanon; total attacks decreased for Nigeria and Turkey.[74]

Who were the most active groups? They included the Taliban in Afghanistan, Boko Haram in Nigeria, al-Qaeda in the Arabian Peninsula, ISIL and al-Qaida in Iraq, Tehrik-i-Taliban in Pakistan, al-Shabaab in Somalia, al-Nusra Front in Syria and Lebanon, the David Yau Yau militia in the Sudan, and the New People's Army (NPA) in the Philippines. Some of these groups are generally considered allied with the central al-Qaeda group, and its alliance with these groups means that it remains a central player in a network of highly lethal and active terrorist organizations.[75]

These data indicate that terrorism is rapidly evolving, with an increasing number of groups around the world—including both al-Qaeda affiliates and other terrorist organizations—still posing a significant threat. There has been a rise in increasingly aggressive and autonomous al-Qaeda affiliates who disregard the central command's order to avoid collateral damage to civilians. At the time of this writing, the area around Northern Iraq and Syria continues to be a major battleground for terrorism, and thousands of foreign fighters have traveled to Syria to join violent extremist groups. The Syrian conflict also empowered ISIL to expand its cross-border operations into Iraq.

## Response to Terrorism

After the 9/11 attacks, agencies of the criminal justice system began to focus their attention on combating the threat of terror. Even local police agencies created anti-terror programs designed to protect their communities from the threat of attack. How should the nation best prepare itself to thwart potential attacks? The National Commission on Terrorist Attacks Upon the United States (also known as the 9/11 Commission), an independent, bipartisan commission, was created in late 2002 and given the mission of preparing an in-depth report of the events leading up to the 9/11 attacks. Part of their goal was to create a comprehensive plan to ensure that no further attacks of that magnitude take place.

To monitor the more than 500 million people who annually cross in and out of the U.S., the commission recommended that a single agency should be created to screen border crossings. They also recommended creation of an investigative agency to monitor all aliens in the United States and to gather intelligence on the way terrorists travel across borders. The commission suggested that people who wanted passports be tagged with biometric measures to make them easily identifiable.

In response to the commission report, a **Director of National Intelligence (DNI)** was created and charged with coordinating data from the nation's primary intelligence-gathering agencies. The DNI serves as the principal intelligence adviser to the president and the statutory intelligence adviser to the National Security Council. On February 17, 2005, President George W. Bush named U.S. Ambassador to Iraq John Negroponte to be the first person to hold the post; he was confirmed on April 21, 2005; the current director is James R. Clapper, a former Air Force general and director of the Defense Intelligence Agency.

Among the agencies reporting to the DNI is the National Counterterrorism Center (NCTC), which is staffed by terrorism experts from the CIA, FBI, and the Pentagon; the Privacy and Civil Liberties Board; and the National Counterproliferation Center. The NCTC serves as the primary organization in the U.S. government for analyzing and integrating all intelligence possessed or acquired by the government pertaining to terrorism and counterterrorism, excepting purely domestic counterterrorism information.

**FACT OR FICTION?**

Terrorist attacks have been increasing every year; the world is becoming more dangerous.

**TRUE** The number of terror attacks has risen sharply in the past few years.

**Director of National Intelligence (DNI)** Government official charged with coordinating data from the nation's primary intelligence-gathering agencies.

While the 9/11 Commission report outlined what has already been done, what has not been done, and what needed to be done to protect the nation, agencies of the justice system rapidly began to respond to the challenge.

## Confronting Terrorism with Law Enforcement

Ending the threat of terror is not easy. One reason is the very nature of American society. Because we live in a free and open nation, it is extremely difficult to seal the borders and prevent the entry of terrorist groups. In his book *Nuclear Terrorism*, Graham Allison, an expert on nuclear weapons and national security, describes the almost superhuman effort it would take to seal the nation's borders from nuclear attack considering the thousands of trucks, rail cars, and ships that deliver goods every day. The potential for terrorists to obtain bombs is significant: there are more than 100 nuclear research reactors now in operation around the world, and many are contained in states hostile to the United States, such as Iran and North Korea. Even if terrorists lack the knowledge to build their own bomb, they may be able to purchase an intact device on the black market. Russia alone has thousands of nuclear warheads and material for many thousands of additional weapons; all of these are vulnerable to theft. Terrorists may also be able to buy the knowledge to construct bombs. In one well-known incident, Pakistan's leading nuclear scientist, A. Q. Khan, sold comprehensive "nuclear starter kits" that included advanced centrifuge components, blueprints for nuclear warheads, and uranium samples in quantities sufficient to make a small bomb, and even provided personal consulting services to assist in nuclear development.[76]

Recognizing this problem, law enforcement agencies around the country began to realign their resources to combat future terrorist attacks. In response to 9/11, law enforcement agencies undertook a number of steps: increasing the number of personnel engaged in emergency response planning; updating response plans for chemical, biological, or radiological attacks; and reallocating internal resources or increasing departmental spending to focus on terrorism preparedness.[77] Actions continue to be taken on the federal, state, and local levels.

AP Images/Elaine Thompson

Law enforcement agencies at every level are preparing for terror attacks. During a drill, SWAT team members step over a downed "terrorist" while clearing the Washington State ferry MV *Salish*, out of Bainbridge Island, Washington. In winds that kicked up whitecaps and drenched the small boarding boats, the Coast Guard and several police agencies drilled for a potential terrorist attack on a state ferry.

**FEDERAL BUREAU OF INVESTIGATION (FBI)** One of the most significant changes has been a realignment of the Federal Bureau of Investigation (FBI), the federal government's main law enforcement agency. The FBI has announced a reformulation of its priorities, making protecting the United States from terrorist attack its number one commitment. It is now charged with coordinating intelligence collection with the Border Patrol, Secret Service, and the CIA. The FBI must also work with and share intelligence with the National Counterterrorism Center (NCTC). Another initiative has been the creation of Joint Terrorism Task Forces (JTTFs), which are now located in 103 cities nationwide. The JTTFs include more than 4,400 members nationwide, hailing from over 600 state and local agencies and 50 federal agencies (the Department of Homeland Security, the U.S. military, Immigration and Customs Enforcement, and the Transportation Security Administration, to name a few). JTTFs enable a shared intelligence base across many agencies, among other benefits.[78]

**DEPARTMENT OF HOMELAND SECURITY (DHS)** Soon after the 9/11 attack, President George W. Bush proposed the creation of a new cabinet-level agency called the **Department of Homeland Security (DHS)**, which is engaged in:

- Preventing terrorist attacks within the United States
- Reducing America's vulnerability to terrorism
- Minimizing the damage and recovering from attacks that do occur

Rather than start from the ground up, the DHS combined a number of existing agencies into a superagency. Among its components are:

- *Border and transportation security.* The Department of Homeland Security is responsible for securing our nation's borders and transportation systems, which include 350 ports of entry. The department manages who and what enters the country, and works to prevent the entry of terrorists and the instruments of terrorism while simultaneously ensuring the speedy flow of legitimate traffic. The DHS also is in charge of securing territorial waters, including ports and waterways.
- *Emergency preparedness and response.* The department ensures the preparedness of emergency response professionals, provides the federal government's response, and aids America's recovery from terrorist attacks and natural disasters. The department is responsible for reducing the loss of life and property and protecting institutions from all types of hazards through an emergency management program of preparedness, mitigation, response, and recovery.
- *Chemical, biological, radiological, and nuclear countermeasures.* The department leads the federal government's efforts in preparing for and responding to the full range of terrorist threats involving weapons of mass destruction. To do this, the department sets national policy and establishes guidelines for state and local governments. It directs exercises and drills for federal, state, and local chemical, biological, radiological, and nuclear (CBRN) response teams and plans. The department is assigned to prevent the importation of nuclear weapons and material.
- *Information analysis and infrastructure protection.* The department analyzes information from multiple available sources, including the CIA and FBI, in order to assess the dangers facing the nation. It also analyzes law enforcement and intelligence information.[79]

The DHS has numerous and varied duties. It is responsible for port security and transportation systems and manages airport security with its Transportation Security Administration (TSA). It has its own intelligence section, and it covers special events in the United States, such as political conventions.

**STATE AND LOCAL LAW ENFORCEMENT** In the wake of the 9/11 attacks, a number of states have beefed up their intelligence-gathering capabilities and aimed them directly at homeland security. For example, Arizona maintains the Arizona Counter Terrorism Information Center (ACTIC), a statewide intelligence system designed to combat terrorism.[80] It consists of two divisions. One is unclassified and draws together personnel from various public safety agencies. The other operates in a secretive manner and cooperates with the FBI's Joint Terrorism Task Force. Its Fusion Center is responsible for sharing information about situations that might affect jurisdictions in the state and combs through diverse informational sources to provide early warning of incidents at the local, regional, and state levels.[81] ACTIC also has an outreach program known as the Community Liaison Program (CLP). Community partners, including religious groups, businesses, and community crime watches, provide intelligence information to ACTIC personnel as the need arises.

In addition to state systems, some local police agencies have established counterterrorism units, including New York City, one of the main targets of the 9/11 attacks.[82] After the 9/11 attacks, the NYPD augmented its anti-terrorism forces from 17 to 125 and assigned them to the operational control of the Counterterrorism Bureau.

**Department of Homeland Security (DHS)**
An agency of the federal government charged with preventing terrorist attacks within the United States, reducing America's vulnerability to terrorism, and minimizing the damage and aiding recovery from attacks that do occur.

Teams within the bureau have been trained to examine potential targets in the city and attempt to insulate them from possible attack. Viewed as prime targets are the city's bridges, and landmark sites such as the Empire State Building, Rockefeller Center, and the United Nations. Bureau detectives are assigned overseas to work with the police in several foreign cities, including cities in Canada and Israel. The department has backup command centers in different parts of the city in case a terror attack puts headquarters out of operation. In January 2015, the NYPD announced it was expanding the counterterrorism unit by creating a Strategic Response Group, whose officers will receive training on counterterrorism and be equipped with heavy protective gear, including long rifles and machine guns.[83]

## Confronting Terrorism with the Law

Soon after the September 11 terrorist attacks, the U.S. government enacted several laws focused on preventing further acts of violence against the United States and creating greater flexibility in the fight to control terror activity. Most importantly, Congress passed the **USA Patriot Act (USAPA)** on October 26, 2001. The bill is over 342 pages long, creates new laws, and makes changes to more than 15 existing statutes. Its aim is to give new powers to domestic law enforcement and international intelligence agencies in an effort to fight terrorism, to expand the definition of terrorist activities, and to alter sanctions for violent terrorism. While it is impossible to discuss every provision of this sweeping legislation here, a few of its more important elements will be examined.

**USA Patriot Act (USAPA)**
Legislation giving U.S. law enforcement agencies a freer hand to investigate and apprehend suspected terrorists.

**THE USA PATRIOT ACT** USAPA expands all four traditional tools of surveillance—wiretaps, search warrants, pen/trap orders (installing devices that record phone calls), and subpoenas. The Foreign Intelligence Surveillance Act (FISA), which allows domestic operations by intelligence agencies, is also expanded. USAPA gives greater power to the FBI to check and monitor phone, Internet, and computer records without first needing to demonstrate that they were being used by a suspect or target of a court order.

The government may now serve a single wiretap, or pen/trap order, on any person regardless of whether that person or entity is named in a court order. Prior to this act, telephone companies could be ordered to install pen/trap devices on their networks that would monitor calls coming to a surveillance target and to whom the surveillance target made calls; the USAPA extends this monitoring to the Internet. Law enforcement agencies may now also obtain the email addresses and websites visited by a target, and emails of the people with whom they communicate. It is possible to require that an Internet service provider install a device that records email and other electronic communications on its servers, looking for communications initiated or received by the target of an investigation. Under USAPA, the government does not need to show a court that the information or communication is relevant to a criminal investigation, nor does it have to report where it served the order or what information it received.

The act also allows enforcement agencies to monitor cable operators and obtain access to their records and systems. Before the act, a cable company had to give prior notice to the customer, even if that person was a target of an investigation. Information can now be obtained on people with whom the cable subscriber communicates, the content of the person's communications, and the person's subscription records; prior notice is still required if law enforcement agencies want to learn what television programming a subscriber purchases.

The act also expands the definition of "terrorism" and enables the government to monitor more closely those people suspected of "harboring" and giving "material support" to terrorists (Sections 803, 805). It increases the authority of the U.S. attorney general to detain and deport noncitizens with little or no judicial review. The attorney general may certify that she has "reasonable grounds to believe" that a noncitizen endangers national security and is therefore eligible for deportation.

The attorney general and secretary of state are also given the authority to designate domestic groups as terrorist organizations and deport any noncitizen who is a member.

**CIVIL RIGHTS AND THE USA PATRIOT ACT** Although law enforcement agencies may applaud these laws, civil libertarians are troubled because they view the act as eroding civil rights. Some complain that there are provisions that permit the government to share information from grand jury proceedings and from criminal wiretaps with intelligence agencies. First Amendment protections may be violated because the Patriot Act authority is not limited to true terrorism investigations but covers a much broader range of activity involving reasonable political dissent. Though many critics have called for its repeal, the act has been repeatedly revised and extended. There have been a slew of provisions ensuring that the act does not violate civil rights by limiting its surveillance and wiretap authorizations.[84] The PATRIOT Sunsets Extension Act of 2011 extended provisions of the act concerning roving electronic surveillance orders, requests for the production of business records and other tangible things until June 1, 2015, and amended and extended the Intelligence Reform and Terrorism Prevention Act of 2004, revising the definition of an "agent of a foreign power" to include any non-U.S. person who engages in international terrorism or preparatory activities (the "lone wolf" provision).[85] On June 2, 2015, the three sections of the Patriot Act anti-terrorism law set to expire were restored and extended through 2019. However, under a new law called the USA Freedom Act the National Security Agency (NSA) was prevented from continuing its mass phone data collection program. Instead, phone companies will retain the data and the NSA can obtain information about targeted individuals with permission from a federal court.[86]

## Combating Terrorism with Social Change

In the long run, it may simply be impossible to defeat terror groups and end terrorism using military, law enforcement, or legal solutions. Using force may play into terrorists' hands and convince them that they are freedom fighters valiantly struggling against a better armed and more ruthless foe. No matter how many terrorists are killed and/or captured, military/deterrence-based solutions may be doomed. Aggressive reprisals will cause terrorist ideology to spread and gain greater acceptance in the underdeveloped world. The resulting anger and alienation will produce more terrorists than can be killed off through violent responses. In contrast, if the terrorist ideology is countered and discredited, the appeal of terror groups such as al-Qaeda will wither and die.

One approach suggested by policy experts is to undermine support for terrorist groups by being benevolent nation-builders giving aid to the nations that house terror groups.[87] This is the approach the United States took after World War II to rebuild Germany and Japan (the Marshall Plan) all the while gaining support for its Cold War struggle against the Soviet Union. According to the Rand Corporation, a nonprofit research group, the following steps are required to defeat jihadist groups such as al-Qaeda:

- Attack the ideological underpinnings of global jihadism
- Sever ideological and other links between terrorist groups
- Strengthen the capabilities of front-line states to counter local jihadist threats

This approach may work because al-Qaeda's goal of toppling "apostate" regimes in Saudi Arabia, Egypt, and Pakistan and creating an ultraorthodox pan-Islamic government spanning the world does not sit well with large groups of Muslims; their monolithic vision has no room for other Muslim sects such as Shi'ites and Sunni moderates. Therefore, political and social appeals may help fracture local support for al-Qaeda. In addition, the United States should seek to deny sanctuaries to terrorist groups and strengthen the capabilities of foreign governments to deal with terrorist threats, but in an advisory capacity by providing intelligence. In his book *Unconquerable Nation*, Brian Michael Jenkins, a noted expert on the topic, identifies the strategic principles he believes are the key to combating terror in contemporary society. These beliefs are summarized in Exhibit 11.1.

## Exhibit 11.1   Countering Terror

- *Destroy the jihadist enterprise.* Jihadists have proven to be flexible and resistant and capable of continued action despite sustained military actions. They remain the primary threat to U.S. national security and will continue to be so for the foreseeable future. Therefore, they must be destroyed and their ability to operate damaged.
- *Conserve resources for a long war.* These include blood, treasure, the will of the American people, and the support of needed allies. This means picking future fights carefully, making security measures both effective *and* efficient, maintaining domestic support, avoiding extreme measures that alienate the people, and cultivating rather than bullying other countries.
- *Wage more-effective political warfare.* Political solutions must be pragmatic. We must be ready to compromise. Amnesty should be offered to terrorists who have become disillusioned. Local leaders should be accommodated and deals cut to co-opt enemies.
- *Break the cycle of jihadism.* Jihadism is a cycle beginning with recruitment and ending with death, arrest, or detention. Combating terror must involve neutralizing terror groups' ability to radicalize and indoctrinate potential recruits before the cycle begins and then, at the end of the cycle, deal effectively with terror suspects once they have been captured and detained.

- *Impede recruitment.* Recruitment sites must be identified and made dangerous and therefore unusable. Alternatives to terror must be offered. Former, now disillusioned terrorists can be used to denounce terror and counteract its appeal with potential recruits.
- *Encourage defections and facilitate exits.* Potential defectors must be identified and encouraged to quit through the promise of amnesty, cash, job training, and homes.
- *Persuade detainees to renounce terrorism.* Rehabilitation of known terror suspects may be more important than prosecution and imprisonment.
- *Maintain international cooperation.* International cooperation is a prerequisite to success, a precious commodity not to be squandered by bullying, unreciprocated demands, indifference to local realities, or actions that repel even America's closest friends.
- *Reserve the right to retaliate—a muscular deterrent.* Terror groups and their sponsors should know that any attack using weapons of mass destruction will be met with all-out warfare against any group or government known to be or even suspected of being responsible.

**Source:** Brian Michael Jenkins, *Unconquerable Nation: Knowing Our Enemy, Strengthening Ourselves* (Santa Monica, CA: RAND Corporation, 2006).

# Thinking Like a Criminologist

**Torture or Not?**    As a criminologist whose specialty is terrorism, it comes as no surprise that the director of the CIA asks you to draw up a protocol setting out the rules for the use of torture with suspected terrorists. The reason for his request is that a series of new articles has exposed the agency's practice of sending suspected terrorists to friendly nations that are less squeamish about using torture. Shocking photo evidence of torture from detention facilities at the Guantánamo base in Cuba support these charges. Legal scholars have argued that these tactics violate both international treaties and domestic statutes prohibiting torture. Some maintain that the U.S. Constitution limits the authority of an executive agency like the CIA to act against foreigners abroad and also limits physical coercion by the government under the Fifth Amendment due process and self-incrimination clauses and the Eighth Amendment prohibition against cruel and unusual punishments. Legally, it is impermissible for United States authorities to engage in indefinite detention or torture regardless of the end, the place, or the victim.

### Writing Assignment

Write a memo to the CIA director outlining the protocol you recommend for the use of torture with suspected terrorists. In your document, address when torture should be used, who it should be used on, and what tortures you recommend using. Of course, if you believe the use of torture is always unethical, you could let the director know why you have reached this conclusion.

# SUMMARY

**L01 Define the term *political crime*.**

The term *political crime* is used to signify illegal acts that are designed to undermine an existing government and threaten its survival. Political crimes can include both violent and nonviolent acts and range in seriousness from dissent, treason, and espionage to terrorism or assassination.

**L02 Assess the cause of political crime.**

The political criminal and political crimes may stem from religious or ideological sources. They often occupy a gray area between conventional and outlawed behavior. While common criminals may be motivated by greed, vengeance, or jealousy, political criminals have a somewhat different agenda. There is no set pattern or reason why someone becomes a political criminal. Some use political crime as a stepping stone to public office while others use it as a method to focus their frustrations.

**L03 Compare and contrast the terms *espionage* and *treason*.**

Helping or cooperating with the enemy in a time of war would be considered treason. Espionage is the practice of obtaining information about a government, organization, or society that is considered secret or confidential without the permission of the holder of the information. Industrial espionage involves unethical or illegal activities such as bribing employees to reveal trade secrets such as computer codes or product formulas.

**L04 Distinguish among terrorists, insurgents, guerillas, and revolutionaries.**

Terrorism is generally defined as the illegal use of force against innocent people to achieve a political objective. The term *guerilla* refers to antigovernment forces located in rural areas that attack the military, the police, and government officials. The typical goal of an insurgency is to confront the existing government for control of all or a portion of its territory, or force political concessions in sharing political power. A revolution is generally seen as a civil war fought between nationalists and a sovereign power that holds control of the land, or between the existing government and local groups over issues of ideology and power.

**L05 Enumerate the various forms of terrorism.**

Revolutionary terrorists use violence to frighten those in power and their supporters in order to replace the existing government with a regime that holds acceptable political or religious views. Political terrorism is directed at people or groups who oppose the terrorists' political ideology or whom the terrorists define as "outsiders" who must be destroyed. Nationalist terrorism promotes the interests of a minority ethnic or religious group that believes it has been persecuted under majority rule and wishes to carve out its own independent homeland. Retributive terrorists want to impose their social and religious code on others. State-sponsored terrorism occurs when a repressive government regime forces its citizens into obedience, oppresses minorities, and stifles political dissent. Sometimes terrorist groups become involved in common-law crimes such as drug dealing and kidnapping, even selling nuclear materials.

**L06 Explain what motivates the terrorist to commit violent acts.**

While not all terrorists suffer from psychological deficits, enough do so that the typical terrorist can be described as an emotionally disturbed individual who acts out his or her psychoses within the confines of violent groups. Another view is that because they are out of the political and social mainstream, young men and women are motivated to join terror groups because they suffer alienation and lack the tools to compete in a post-technological society. Yet another view is that terrorists hold extreme religious and/or ideological beliefs that prompt their behavior.

# Key Terms

political crime  344
election fraud  346
treason  348
espionage  349
state political crime  351
torture  351

ticking bomb
  scenario  352
terrorism  353
guerilla  354
insurgent  354
Reign of Terror  356

retributive terrorists  360
state-sponsored
  terrorism  361
failed states  365
Director of National
  Intelligence (DNI)  367

Department of Homeland
  Security (DHS)  369
USA Patriot Act
  (USAPA)  370

# Critical Thinking Questions

1. Would you be willing to give up some of your civil rights in order to aid the war on terror?

2. Should terror suspects arrested in a foreign land be given the same rights and privileges as an American citizen accused of crime?

3. What groups in America might be the breeding ground for terrorist activity in the United States?

4. In light of the 9/11 attack, should acts of terrorism be treated differently from other common-law violent crimes? Should terrorists be executed for their acts even if no one is killed during their attack?

5. Can the use of torture ever be justified? Is the "ticking bomb" scenario valid?

6. A spy gives plans for a new weapon to the enemy. They build the weapon and use it to kill American soldiers. Is the spy guilty of murder?

# Notes

*All URLs accessed in 2015.*

1. Charlie Savage and Mark Mazzetti, "Cryptic Overtures and a Clandestine Meeting Gave Birth to a Blockbuster Story," *New York Times*, June 10, 2013, www.nytimes.com/2013/06/11/us/how-edward-j-snowden-orchestrated-a-blockbuster-story.html.

2. James Risen, "Snowden Says He Took No Secret Files to Russia," *New York Times*, January 20, 2014, www.nytimes.com/2013/10/18/world/snowden-says-he-took-no-secret-files-to-russia.html.

3. Jeffrey Ian Ross, *The Dynamics of Political Crime* (Thousand Oaks, CA: Sage, 2003).

4. Anthony Shadid, "Coordinated Attacks Strike 13 Iraqi Cities," *New York Times*, August 25, 2010, www.nytimes.com/2010/08/26/world/middleeast/26iraq.html.

5. Stephen Schafer, *The Political Criminal, The Problem of Morality and Crime* (New York: Free Press, 1974), pp. 154–157.

6. Randy Borum, "Understanding the Terrorist Mind-Set," *FBI Law Enforcement Bulletin* 72 (2003): 7–10.

7. Evan Perez and Shimon Prokupecz, "Sen. Bob Menendez: 'I Am Not Going Anywhere,'" CNN, March 9, 2015, www.cnn.com/2015/03/06/politics/robert-menendez-criminal-corruption-charges-planned/.

8. Internal Revenue Service, "Examples of Public Corruption Investigations – Fiscal Year 2013," www.irs.gov/uac/Examples-of-Public-Corruption-Investigations-Fiscal-Year-2013.

9. *Chicago Tribune*, Rod Blagojevich, July 1, 2015, www.chicagotribune.com/topic/politics-government/government/rod-blagojevich-PEPLT007479-topic.html.

10. Aeschylus (525–456 BCE), *Prometheus Bound*.

11. Douglas Linder, University of Missouri–Kansas City School of Law, "The Treason Trial of Aaron Burr," www.law.umkc.edu/faculty/projects/ftrials/burr/burraccount.html.

12. John Ziff and Austin Sarat, *Espionage and Treason* (New York: Chelsea House, 1999).

13. United States Criminal Code at 18 U.S.C. § 2381.

14. Lawrence Schiller, *Into the Mirror: The Life of Master Spy Robert P. Hanssen* (Darby, PA: Diane Publications, 2004); CNN, "Accused FBI Spy Hanssen Pleads Not Guilty," May 31, 2001, edition.cnn.com/2001/LAW/05/31/hanssen.arraignment.02/.

15. FBI, "Famous Cases and Criminals: Aldrich Hazen Ames," www.fbi.gov/about-us/history/famous-cases/aldrich-hazen-ames/aldrich-hazen-ames/.

16. David Owen, *Hidden Secrets: The Complete History of Espionage and the Technology Used to Support It* (Ontario, Canada: Firefly Books, 2002).

17. Hedieh Nasheri, *Economic Espionage and Industrial Spying* (Cambridge, England: Cambridge University Press, 2004).

18. Tim Culpan, "China's Clock-Punching Hackers Show Spying as Routine Job," *Bloomberg News*, May 27, 2014, www.bloomberg.com/news/2014-05-27/china -s-clock-punching-hackers-show-spying-as-routine -job.html.

19. Office of the National Counterintelligence Executive, "Annual Report to Congress on Foreign Economic Collection and Industrial Espionage, 2005," www.fas .org/irp/ops/ci/docs/2005.pdf.

20. Office of the National Counterintelligence Executive, "Foreign Spies Stealing US Economic Secrets in Cyber-space," 2011, www.ncsc.gov/publications/reports /fecie_all/Foreign_Economic_Collection_2011.pdf.

21. Department of Justice news release, "Two Men Plead Guilty to Stealing Trade Secrets from Silicon Valley Companies to Benefit China," December 14, 2006, www.justice.gov/archive/criminal/cybercrime/press -releases/2006/yePlea.htm.

22. The Senate Intelligence Committee Report on Torture: Committee Study of the Central Intelligence Agency's Detention and Interrogation Program, 2014, www .washingtonpost.com/wp-srv/special/national/cia -interrogation-report/document/.

23. Alan M. Dershowitz, *Shouting Fire: Civil Liberties in a Turbulent Age* (New York: Little, Brown, 2002); Dershowitz, "Want to Torture? Get a Warrant," *San Francisco Chronicle*, January 22, 2002.

24. Human Rights Watch, "The Twisted Logic of Torture," January 2005, hrw.org/wr2k5/darfurandabughraib/6 .htm.

25. Jessica Wolfendale, "Training Torturers: A Critique of the 'Ticking Bomb' Argument," *Social Theory and Practice* 31 (2006): 269–287. Elizabeth Sepper, "The Ties That Bind: How the Constitution Limits the CIA's Actions in the War on Terror," *New York University Law Review* 81 (2006): 1805–1843.

26. Vittorio Bufacchi and Jean Maria Arrigo, "Torture, Terrorism and the State: A Refutation of the Ticking-Bomb Argument," *Journal of Applied Philosophy* 23 (2006): 355–373.

27. Josh Levs and Holly Yan, "147 Dead, Islamist Gunmen Killed after Attack at Kenya College, CNN, April 2, 2015, www.cnn.com/2015/04/02/africa/kenya -university-attack/.

28. Title 22 of the United States Code section 2656f (d) (1999).

29. United States Army, *Terrorism in the Twenty-First Century*, 2007, fas.org/irp/threat/terrorism/guide.pdf.

30. For this and other definitions, see National Institute of Justice, "Terrorism," www.nij.gov/topics/crime /terrorism/pages/welcome.aspx.

31. Jack Gibbs, "Conceptualization of Terrorism," *American Sociological Review* 54 (1989): 329–340, at 330.

32. Robert Friedlander, *Terrorism* (Dobbs Ferry, NY: Oceana Publishers, 1979), p. 14.

33. Daniel Georges-Abeyie, "Political Crime and Terror-ism," in *Crime and Deviance: A Comparative Perspective*, ed. Graeme Newman (Beverly Hills: Sage, 1980), pp. 313–333.

34. Terrorism Research, "Differences Between Terrorism and Insurgency," www.terrorism-research.com /insurgency/.

35. Andrew Silke, "Holy Warriors: Exploring the Psycho-logical Processes of Jihadi Radicalization," *European Journal of Criminology* 5 (2008): 99–123.

36. Farouk Chothia, "Who Are Nigeria's Boko Haram Is-lamists?" BBC News Africa, May 20, 2014, www.bbc .com/news/world-africa-13809501.

37. Joshua Freilich, Steven M. Chermak, Jeff Grue-newald, and William S. Parkin, "Far-Right Violence in the United States: 1990–2013," National Consortium for the Study of Terrorism and Responses to Terrorism, June 2014, www.start.umd.edu/pubs/START_ECDB _FarRightViolence_FactSheet_June2014.pdf.

38. Fiona Proffitt, "Costs of Animal Rights Terror," *Science* 304 (2004): 1731–1739.

39. "Animal Activists Face 'Domestic Terrorism' Charge in Freeing 5,740 Mink," *Guardian*, July 25, 2015, www.theguardian.com/us-news/2015/jul/25 /animal-activists-minks-domestic-terrorism-charges.

40. FBI, "Eco-Terrorist Sentenced," March 20, 2012, www.fbi.gov/news/stories/2012/march/eco -terrorist_032012.

41. Michael Clancy, Deputy Assistant Director, Counter-terrorism Division, Federal Bureau of Investigation, "Statement Before the Senate Judiciary Committee, Subcommittee on the Constitution, Civil Rights, and Human Rights," September 19, 2012, www.fbi.gov /news/testimony/the-domestic-terrorism-threat.

42. Council on Foreign Relations, "Hezbollah," www.cfr .org/lebanon/hezbollah-k-hizbollah-hizbullah/p9155.

43. BBC News, "Who Are the Uighurs?" April 30, 2014, www.bbc.com/news/world-asia-china-22278037.

44. Angel Rabasa, Peter Chalk, Kim Cragin, Sara A. Daly, Heather S. Gregg, Theodore W. Karasik, Kevin A. O'Brien, and William Rosenau, *Beyond al-Qaeda Part 1, The Global Jihadist Movement*, xviii, and *Part 2, The Outer Rings of the Terrorist Universe* (Santa Monica, CA: Rand Corporation, 2006).

45. Ibid.

46. Lawrence Miller, "The Terrorist Mind: A Psychological and Political Analysis, Part I," *International Journal of Offender Therapy and Comparative Criminology* 50 (2006): 121–138.

47. Gabriela Fried, "Piecing Memories Together After State Terror and Policies of Oblivion in Uruguay: The Female Political Prisoner's Testimonial Project (1997–2004)," *Social Identities* 12 (2006): 543–562.

48. Martin Miller, "Ordinary Terrorism in Historical Perspective." *Journal for the Study of Radicalism* 2 (2008): 125–154.

49. Mark Hamm, "'High Crimes and Misdemeanors': George W. Bush and the Sins of Abu Ghraib," *Crime, Media, Culture: An International Journal* 3 (2007): 259–284.

50. Chris Dishman, "Terrorism, Crime, and Transformation," *Studies in Conflict and Terrorism* 24 (2001): 43–56.

51. Richard Lough, "Piracy Ransom Cash Ends Up with Somali Militants," Reuters, July 6, 2011, www.reuters.com/article/2011/07/06/somalia-piracy-idUSLDE7650U320110706.

52. Jeff Gruenewald, Steven Chermak, and Joshua Freilich, "Distinguishing 'Loner' Attacks from Other Domestic Extremist Violence," *Criminology and Public Policy* 12 (2013): 65–91.

53. Clark McCauley and Sophia Moskalenko, "Two Possible Profiles of Lone-Actor Terrorists," National Consortium for the Study of Terrorism and Responses to Terrorism (START), 2013, www.start.umd.edu/publication/two-possible-profiles-lone-actor-terrorists.

54. *Boston Globe*, "Text from Dzhokhar Tsarnaev's Note Written in Watertown Boat," May 22, 2014, www.bostonglobe.com/metro/2014/05/22/text-from-dzhokhar-tsarnaev-note-left-watertown-boat/KnRIeqqr95rJQbAbfnj5EP/story.html.

55. Andrew Silke, "Courage in Dark Places: Reflections on Terrorist Psychology," *Social Research* 71 (2004): 177–198.

56. Arie Kruglanski and Shira Fishman, "Terrorism: Between 'Syndrome' and 'Tool,'" *Current Directions in Psychological Science* 15 (2006): 45–48.

57. Charles Ruby, "Are Terrorists Mentally Deranged?" *Analyses of Social Issues and Public Policy* 2 (2002): 15–26.

58. David Lester, Bijou Yang, and Mark Lindsay, "Suicide Bombers: Are Psychological Profiles Possible?" *Studies in Conflict and Terrorism* 27 (2004): 283–295.

59. Randy Borum, *Psychology of Terrorism*, www.ncjrs.gov/pdffiles1/nij/grants/208552.pdf.

60. Ethan Bueno de Mesquita, "The Quality of Terror," *American Journal of Political Science* 49 (2005): 515–530.

61. Saroj Kumar Rath, "Root Cause of Terrorism: A Brief Survey of South Asia," *Social Research Reports* 21 (2012): 23–36.

62. Jerrold Post, "When Hatred Is Bred in the Bone: Psychocultural Foundations of Contemporary Terrorism," *Political Psychology* 25 (2005): 615–637.

63. Arie W. Kruglanski, "Psychology Not Theology: Overcoming ISIS' Secret Appeal," *E-International Relations*, October 28, 2014, www.e-ir.info/2014/10/28/psychology-not-theology-overcoming-isis-secret-appeal/.

64. Marc Sageman, *Understanding Terror Networks* (Philadelphia: University of Pennsylvania Press, 2004), Ch. 4.

65. Ibid.

66. Kruglanski, "Psychology Not Theology."

67. This section leans heavily on Anthony Stahelski, "Terrorists Are Made, Not Born: Creating Terrorists Using Social Psychological Conditioning," *Journal of Homeland Security* (March 2004), docs.google.com/document/d/1PF1hNe_V0Jc3w3v-zyEctdq4NOypxWWWMSMu7nmHHXc/.

68. Sageman, *Understanding Terror Networks*, Chapter 4.

69. Seth Schwartz, Curtis Dunkel, and Alan Waterman, "Terrorism: An Identity Theory Perspective," *Studies in Conflict and Terrorism* 32 (2009): 537–559.

70. Ibid.

71. Schwartz, Dunkel, and Waterman, "Terrorism: An Identity Theory Perspective."

72. Patricia Marchak, *Reigns of Terror* (Montreal: McGill-Queen's University Press, 2003).

73. Ibid., pp. 153–155.

74. Jessica Rivinius, "Majority of 2013 Terrorist Attacks Occurred in Just a Few Countries: More than Half of All Attacks Carried Out in Iraq, Pakistan and Afghanistan," National Consortium for the Study of Terrorism and Responses to Terrorism (START), August 18, 2014, www.start.umd.edu/news/majority-2013-terrorist-attacks-occurred-just-few-countries.

75. William Braniff, "Discussion Point: The State of Al-Qaida, its Affiliates and Associated Groups," House Armed Services Committee Oral Testimony, February 4, 2014, www.start.umd.edu/news/discussion-point-state-al-qaida-its-affiliates-and-associated-groups.

76. Graham Allison, *Nuclear Terrorism: The Ultimate Preventable Catastrophe* (New York: Times Books, 2004).

77. Rand Corporation, "How Prepared Are State and Local Law Enforcement for Terrorism?" www.rand.org/publications/RB/RB9093/.

78. FBI, "Protecting America from Terrorist Attack: Our Joint Terrorism Task Forces," www.fbi.gov/about-us/investigate/terrorism/terrorism_jttfs.

79. Homeland Security, "Information Sharing," www.dhs.gov/topic/information-sharing. The section on homeland security relies heavily on "Homeland Security," www.whitehouse.gov/infocus/homeland/.

80. Arizona Department of Public Safety, "Arizona Fusion Center," www.azdps.gov/about/Task_Forces/Fusion/; Arizona Counter Terrorism Information Center, www.azactic.gov/.

81.  Arizona Department of Public Safety, "How Does the ACTIC Operate?" www.azactic.gov/About/Operation/.

82.  NYPD, Counterterrorism Units, www.nyc.gov/html /nypd/html/administration/counterterrorism_units .shtml.

83.  Pervaiz Shallwani, "New York City Police Department to Create New Counterterrorism Unit," *Wall Street Journal*, January 29, 2015, www.wsj.com/articles /new-york-city-police-department-to-create-new -counterterrorism-unit-1422570131.

84.  Statement of U.S. Senator Russ Feingold on the Anti-Terrorism Bill, from the Senate Floor, October 25, 2001, epic.org/privacy/terrorism/usapatriot/feingold .html.

85.  United States Department of Justice, "Uniting and Strengthening America by Providing Appropriate Tools Required to Intercept and Obstruct Terrorism (USA PATRIOT) Act of 2001," it.ojp.gov/PrivacyLiberty /authorities/statutes/1281.

86.  H.R.3361 – USA FREEDOM Act, www.congress.gov /bill/113th-congress/house-bill/3361.

87.  Rabasa et al., *Beyond al-Qaeda Part 1, The Global Jihadist Movement*.

# 12 Economic Crimes: Blue-Collar, White-Collar, and Green-Collar

Alan Youngblood/Ocala Star-Banner/Landov

Aubrey Lee Price before going on the run for a year (left) and after his arrest (right).

Reuters/Landov

# Chapter Outline

## FACT OR FICTION?

▶ Most theft offenses are committed by trained professionals who know what they are doing and escape detection.

▶ Most white-collar and green-collar criminals get a slap on the wrist if they are convicted of crime.

In 2014, Georgia native Aubrey Lee Price, formerly a devout Christian minister and trusted financial adviser, was sentenced to 30 years in prison for bank fraud, embezzlement, and other crimes. How did this pillar of the community fall so far? Price got involved in the investment business to help fund his overseas missionary efforts. He worked for two well-known investment firms and later started his own company, PFG. Many of his clients were personal friends who knew him from church—he gave seminars on how to be a wise Christian investor. Others had been on mission trips with him. Eventually, he consolidated PFG to about 100 significant investors. Then unbeknownst to his clients, Price began gambling with their money, making risky investments and falsified documents to hide the transactions. He had his clients invest in a local bank and used its resources to fund his schemes. Price eventually gained access to more than $21 million in investor money and lost more than $16 million through risky investments—all the while telling his victims that the money was being used to purchase very safe securities. In the end, Price's deception resulted in the bank's failure and losses of more than $70 million.

When he knew he was in serious trouble, Price faked his suicide on a boat in Key West, Florida, and fled first to Mexico and later returned to Florida, where he grew marijuana and sold it along with other drugs, sometimes working as a bodyguard for prostitutes. On New Year's Eve in 2013, a routine traffic stop in Georgia resulted in his arrest, nearly 18 months after his "death." Aubrey Lee Price was tried, convicted, and sentenced to serve at least 30 years behind bars.[1]

**economic crime**
An act committed in violation of the criminal law for the purpose of monetary gain and financial benefits.

**blue-collar crimes**
Traditional common-law theft crimes such as larceny, burglary, and arson.

**white-collar crimes**
Crimes of business enterprise such as embezzlement, price fixing, and bribery.

**green-collar crimes**
Crimes that affect the environment.

**theft**
The intentional taking, keeping, or using of another's property without authorization or permission.

**LO1** Discuss the history of theft offenses.

An eighteenth-century woodcut shows what happened when smugglers were discovered by authorities. One watches through the keyhole, another loads a pistol, and a third hides contraband. High customs duties meant that smuggling was common at that time.

HIP/Art Resource, NY

Price's fraudulent scheme is certainly not unique. Each year millions of people suffer billions in losses to some form of **economic crime**. As a group, these offenses can be defined as illegal acts designed to bring financial reward. They range in scope from simple theft involving a few dollars to swindles such as Price's that involve millions of dollars.

Economic crimes are here divided into three distinct categories:

- **Blue-collar crimes**—common-law theft crimes such as larceny, burglary, and arson
- **White-collar crimes**—crimes that involve business enterprise such as embezzlement, price fixing, and bribery
- **Green-collar crimes**—violations of laws designed to protect the environment

The development of these crime types and their nature and extent are discussed in some detail below.

# History of Economic Crimes

Economic crimes have been known throughout recorded history. Three thousand years ago, the Code of Hammurabi ordered the death penalty for such crimes as stealing from a palace or temple treasury, selling stolen goods, or making false claim to goods.[2] Theft was a problem in Roman bath houses, and slaves were assigned to watch bathers' property and clothes; of course, some slaves stole the clothes themselves and made a tidy profit.[3]

Under English common law, **theft** was defined as the taking of another person's property without their permission or consent. To be convicted of theft, the thief had to (a) deliberately deprive the owner of their lawful property (b) using stealth, trickery, or fraud and (c) with the intent of permanently keeping the item for themselves. Taking something by accident or mistake was not considered theft if there was no intent to deprive the victim of their property (for example, someone accidentally takes the wrong jacket from the restaurant's coat rack). However, taking something by accident becomes a theft if once the mistake is discovered no effort is made to return the item to its rightful owner.

While first committed by amateur thieves and pickpockets, as cities developed and a permanent class of urban poor came into being, theft became professional.[4] By the eighteenth century, three separate groups of property criminals were active:

- *Skilled thieves* typically worked in the larger cities, such as London and Paris. This group included pickpockets, forgers, and counterfeiters, who operated freely. They congregated in "flash houses"—public meeting places, often taverns, that served as headquarters for gangs. Here deals were made, crimes were plotted, and the sale of stolen goods was negotiated.[5]
- *Smugglers* moved freely in sparsely populated areas and transported goods, such as spirits, gems, gold, and spices, without paying tax or duty.
- *Poachers* typically lived in the country and supplemented their diet and income with game that belonged to a landlord.

By the eighteenth century, professional thieves in the larger cities had banded together into gangs to protect themselves, increase the scope of their activities, and help dispose of stolen goods.

## Development of White-Collar and Green-Collar Crime

While we sometimes think of these business-related crimes as a new phenomenon, they have actually been around for hundreds of years, ever since the Industrial Revolution began. The period between 1750 and 1850 witnessed the widespread and unprecedented emergence of financial offences—such as fraud and embezzlement—frequently perpetrated by respectable middle-class offenders as the banking and commercial systems developed.[6] In 1907, pioneering sociologist Edward Alsworth Ross recognized the phenomenon when he coined the phrase "the criminaloid" to describe the kind of person who hides behind his or her image as a pillar of the community and paragon of virtue to get personal gain through any means necessary.[7]

In the late 1930s, the distinguished criminologist Edwin Sutherland first used the phrase "white-collar crime" to describe the criminal activities of the rich and powerful. He defined white-collar crime as "a crime committed by a person of respectability and high social status in the course of his occupation."[8] As Sutherland saw it, white-collar crime involved conspiracies by members of the wealthy classes to use their position in commerce and industry for personal gain without regard to the law. Often, these actions were handled by civil courts because injured parties were more concerned with recovering their losses than with seeing the offenders punished criminally. Consequently, Sutherland believed that the great majority of white-collar criminals did not become the subject of criminological study. Yet the cost of white-collar crime is probably several times greater than all the crimes customarily regarded as the crime problem. And, in contrast to street crimes, white-collar offenses breed distrust in economic and social institutions, lower public morale, and undermine faith in business and government.[9]

Green-collar crime, a relatively new concept, can be viewed as a subdivision of white-collar crime. Green criminals are motivated by profit and are therefore not eco-terrorists or vandals. They want to make profits by avoiding the payment of governmental fees, logging in restricted areas, or poaching protected fish and animals. Each of these elements of economic crimes is discussed in the sections below.

# Blue-Collar Crimes

Of the millions of common-law property- and theft-related crimes that occur each year, such as larceny, burglary, and arson, most are committed by amateur **occasional criminals** who do not define or view themselves as committed career criminals. Their crimes are in the moment, spontaneous, unplanned, and often not very lucrative.

Occasional property crime often occurs when an unplanned opportunity to commit crime, known as a **situational inducement**, suddenly occurs: an unlocked car, a purse left out on a counter, an unobservant store manager. Situational inducements are short-term influences on a person's behavior that increase risk taking. When coupled with financial and social problems they help push people into theft.

Occasional criminals may deny their criminality and instead view their transgressions as out of character. They claim they were only "borrowing" the car when stopped by police; when confronted by the store security guard they contend they really were going to pay for the merchandise they had hidden under their coat. Because of their lack of commitment to a criminal lifestyle, occasional offenders may be the most likely to respond to the general deterrent effect of the law.

In contrast to these amateur offenders, **professional criminals** make a significant portion of their income from crime. Professionals do not delude themselves with the belief that their acts are impulsive, one-time efforts, nor do they use elaborate rationalizations to excuse the harmfulness of their actions. While the amateur may try to neutralize their guilt by claiming that their victim was insured, the professional's only regret is a slow market for stolen goods. Guiltless, professionals pursue their craft with vigor, attempting to learn from older, experienced criminals the techniques that will enable them to "earn" the most money with the least risk. Although they are relatively few in number, professionals engage in crimes that inflict the greater losses on society and perhaps cause the more significant social harm.

Professional theft consists of nonviolent forms of criminal behavior that are undertaken with a high degree of skill for monetary gain and that maximize financial opportunities and minimize the odds of apprehension. These include pocket picking, burglary, shoplifting, forgery, counterfeiting, extortion, sneak theft, and confidence swindling. Let's look at some of these blue-collar theft offense categories in some detail.

**occasional criminals** Offenders who do not define themselves by a criminal role or view themselves as committed career criminals.

**situational inducement** Short-term influence on a person's behavior, such as financial problems or peer pressure, which increases risk taking.

**professional criminals** Offenders who make a significant portion of their income from crime.

**LO2** Differentiate between professional and amateur thieves.

## CONNECTIONS

Situational crime prevention measures, discussed in Chapter 4, are designed to make it more difficult to commit crimes. Some stores are now using these methods—for example, placing the most valuable goods in the least vulnerable places, posting warning signs to deter potential thieves, and using closed-circuit cameras.

## FACT OR FICTION?

Most theft offenses are committed by trained professionals who know what they are doing and escape detection.

**FICTION** Most theft is the work of amateurs whose acts are spontaneous and unskilled.

## Larceny

**larceny**
Taking for one's own use the property of another, by means other than force or threats on the victim or forcibly breaking into a person's home or workplace; simple theft.

**constructive possession**
A legal fiction that applies to situations in which persons voluntarily give up physical custody of their property but still retain legal ownership.

**petit (petty) larceny**
Theft of a small amount of money or property, punished as a misdemeanor.

**grand larceny**
Theft of money or property of substantial value, punished as a felony.

**shoplifting**
The taking of goods from retail stores.

Theft, or **larceny** (from *latrocinium,* Latin for "theft," and *latio,* "robber"), was one of the earliest common-law crimes created by English judges to define acts in which one person took for his or her own use the property of another.[10] According to common law, larceny was defined as "the trespassory taking and carrying away of the personal property of another with intent to steal."[11]

As originally construed, larceny involved taking property that was in the possession of the rightful owner. It would have been considered larceny for someone to sneak into a farmer's field and steal a cow. Thus, the original common-law definition required a "trespass in the taking"; that is, for an act to be considered larceny, goods had to have been taken from the physical possession of the rightful owner. In creating this definition of larceny, English judges were more concerned with disturbance of the peace than with theft itself. They reasoned that if someone tried to steal property from another's possession, the act could eventually lead to a physical confrontation and—possibly—to the death of one party or the other. Consequently, the original definition of larceny did not include the misappropriation of goods by trickery or deceit.

The definition of larceny evolved with the growth of manufacturing and the development of the free enterprise system. Because commercial enterprise often requires that property be entrusted to a second party, larceny evolved to include the misappropriation of goods that had come into a person's possession through legitimate means. For example, the commercial system would grind to a halt if people who were given merchandise to sell or transport could not be held liable for keeping the merchandise for their own use.

To get around the element of "trespass in the taking," English judges created the concept of **constructive possession**. This legal fiction applies to situations in which persons voluntarily give up temporary custody of their property but still believe that the property is legally theirs. If a person gives a jeweler her watch for repair, she still believes she owns the watch, in spite of the fact that she has handed it over to the jeweler. If the jeweler kept the watch or sold it, he would be guilty of larceny even though he did not "take" the watch; rather, it was given to him on a temporary basis. Over the years, new forms of larceny have been created, including shoplifting, purse snatching, and auto theft.

The FBI records more than 6 million acts of larceny annually, a rate of about 1,900 per 100,000 persons. Larceny rates declined more than 20 percent between 1994 and 2013.[12] According to the NCVS, more than 12 million larceny thefts occur each year. And like the UCR, the victim survey indicates that a steep decline (more than 33 percent) has occurred in the number and rate of larcenies during the past decade.[13]

Most U.S. state criminal codes separate larceny into **petit (petty) larceny** and **grand larceny**. The former involves small amounts of money or property and is punished as a misdemeanor. Grand larceny, involving merchandise of greater value, is a felony punished by a sentence to serve time in the state prison. Each state sets its own boundary between grand larceny and petty larceny, but $100 to $500 is not unusual.

How larceny is categorized can have a significant influence on the level of punishment. Contemporary legal codes include a variety of theft offenses within the general category of larceny. The following sections cover the various forms of larceny that have been defined in law.

**L03**   Describe the various forms of shoplifting.

**SHOPLIFTING Shoplifting** is a very common form of larceny/theft involving the taking of goods from retail stores. Usually shoplifters try to snatch goods—such as jewelry, clothes, records, and appliances—when store personnel are otherwise occupied and to hide the goods on their bodies. The "five-finger discount" is an extremely common crime, and retailers lose billions annually to inventory shrinkage. A national survey of 23 large retailers with about 20,000 stores found that about 1 million shoplifters were apprehended in 2013 by store security personnel, who recovered over $144 million from these thieves. All this from just 23 retail chains![14]

Retail security measures add to the already high cost of this crime, all of which is passed on to the consumer. Shoplifting may be attractive to some thieves because discount stores, such as Lowes, Walmart, and Target, have minimal sales help and depend on highly visible merchandise displays to attract purchasers, all of which makes them particularly vulnerable to shoplifters.

In a classic study, Mary Owen Cameron found that the majority of shoplifters are amateur pilferers, called **snitches** in thieves' argot.[15] Snitches are "otherwise respectable people" according to Cameron, who do not conceive of themselves as thieves but systematically steal merchandise for their own use. Some snitches are simply overcome by an uncontrollable urge to snatch something that attracts them, whereas others arrive at the store intending to steal.[16]

Criminologists view amateur shoplifters as people who are most likely to reform if apprehended. Cameron reasoned that because snitches are not part of a criminal subculture and do not think of themselves as criminals, they are deterred by initial contact with the law. Because getting arrested traumatizes them, they will not risk a second offense.

Cameron also found that about 10 percent of all shoplifters were professionals, who derived the majority of their income from shoplifting. Called **boosters** or **heels**, professional shoplifters steal with the intention of reselling stolen merchandise to pawnshops or fences, or sell on the Internet.

These professionals can walk into a department store, fill up a cart with expensive medicines, electronics, and other high-cost items, and use deceptive techniques to slip past security guards.[17] Hitting several stores in a day and the same store once a month, a professional thief can make between $100,000 and $200,000 a year. Some enter a store carrying a "shopping list" provided by a fence who will pay them in cash or drugs. Fences later sell the merchandise in their own discount stores, at flea markets, or through online auctions. Some sell to higher-level fences who repackage—or "scrub"—the goods and pawn them off on retailers at prices that undercut legitimate distributors. Ironically, some stolen merchandise can actually make its way back onto the shelves of the chain store from which it was stolen.

Cameron may have overlooked another type of snitch: shoplifters whose goal is quick cash to feed a drug habit. Research shows that products that serve a role in illicit drug use are actually the ones most often stolen from retail stores.[18] Both male and female drug users report that shoplifting is a form of work which helps support their habits, preferable and less dangerous than robbery for men and sex work for women.[19]

Fewer than 10 percent of shoplifting incidents are detected by store employees. To encourage the arrest of shoplifters, a number of states have passed **merchant privilege laws** designed to offer retailers and their employees some protection from lawsuits stemming from improper or false arrests of suspected shoplifters. These laws require that arrests be made on reasonable grounds or probable cause, that detention be short, and that store employees or security guards conduct themselves reasonably. In addition, security systems now feature source tagging, a process by which manufacturers embed the tag in the packaging or in the product itself. Thieves have trouble removing or defeating such tags, and retailers save on the time and labor needed to attach the tags at the store.

**CREDIT CARD THEFT** Use of stolen credit cards and credit card numbers has become a major problem in the United States, costing consumers and merchants hundreds of billions each year.[20] Most credit card abuse is the work of amateurs who acquire stolen cards through theft or mugging and then use them for two or three days at local stores. However, professional credit card rings have gotten into the act.

To curtail individual losses from credit card theft, in 1971 Congress limited a cardholder's liability to $50 per stolen card. Similarly, some states, such as California, have passed laws making it a misdemeanor to obtain property or services by means of cards that have been stolen, forged, canceled, or revoked, or whose use is unauthorized for any reason.[21]

**snitch**
Amateur shoplifter who does not self-identify as a thief but who systematically steals merchandise for personal use.

**booster (heel)**
Professional shoplifter who steals with the intention of reselling stolen merchandise.

**merchant privilege laws**
Legislation that protects retailers and their employees from lawsuits if they arrest and detain a suspected shoplifter on reasonable grounds.

**AUTO THEFT** Motor vehicle theft is another common larceny offense. Because of its frequency and seriousness, it is treated as a separate category in the Uniform Crime Report (UCR). The FBI now records 700,000 auto thefts per year, which account for a total loss of about $4 billion. Just as for other crimes, there has been a significant reduction in motor vehicle theft rates over the past decade, and the number of car thefts has declined more than 40 percent. Almost every state requires owners to insure their vehicles, and auto theft is one of the most highly reported of all major crimes (75 percent of all auto thefts are reported to police).

Amateur thieves steal cars for a number of reasons that involve some form of temporary personal use.[22] Among the reasons why an amateur would steal a car:

- *Joyriding.* Many car thefts are motivated by teenagers' desire to acquire the power, prestige, sexual potency, and recognition associated with an automobile. Joyriders steal cars not for profit or gain but to experience, even briefly, the benefits associated with owning an automobile.
- *Short-term transportation.* Auto theft for short-term transportation is similar to joyriding. It involves the theft of a car simply to go from one place to another. In more serious cases, the thief may drive to another city or state and then steal another car to continue the journey.
- *Long-term transportation.* Thieves who steal cars for long-term transportation intend to keep the cars for their personal use. Usually older than joyriders and from a lower-class background, these auto thieves may repaint and otherwise disguise cars to avoid detection.
- *Profit.* Auto theft for profit is motivated by the hope of monetary gain. Some amateurs hope to sell the stolen car, but most are auto strippers who steal batteries, tires, and wheel covers to sell or to reequip their own cars.
- *Commission of another crime.* A few auto thieves steal cars to use in other crimes, such as robberies and thefts. This type of auto thief desires both mobility and anonymity.

At one time, most auto theft was the work of amateurs, and most cars were taken by relatively affluent, middle-class teenagers looking for excitement. But this pattern seems to have changed: fewer cars are being taken today, and fewer stolen cars are being recovered. Part of the reason is an increase in the numbers of highly organized professionals reselling expensive cars after altering their identification numbers and falsifying their registration papers. Some cars are stolen in order to be sold to chop shops for spare parts, including blue-white, high-intensity discharge headlights, air bags, and custom rims.[23]

**BAD CHECKS** Another form of larceny is cashing bad checks to obtain money or property. The checks are intentionally drawn on a nonexistent or underfunded bank account. In general, for a person to be guilty of passing a bad check, the bank the check is drawn on must refuse payment and the check casher must fail to make the check good within 10 days after finding out the check was not honored.

Edwin Lemert conducted the best-known study of check forgers 60 years ago.[24] Lemert found that the majority of check forgers—he called them **naive check forgers**—are amateurs who do not believe their actions will hurt anyone. Most naive check forgers come from middle-class backgrounds and have little identification with a criminal subculture. They cash bad checks because of a financial crisis that demands an immediate resolution—perhaps they have lost money at the racetrack and have some pressing bills to pay.

Lemert found that a few professionals, whom he called **systematic forgers**, make a substantial living passing bad checks. Estimating the number of such forgeries committed each year or the amounts involved is difficult. Stores and banks may choose not to press charges because it is not worth it to them to make the effort to collect the money due them. It is also difficult to separate the true check forger from the neglectful shopper.

**naive check forgers**
Amateurs who cash bad checks because of some financial crisis but have little identification with a criminal subculture.

**systematic forgers**
Professionals who make a living by passing bad checks.

**RECEIVING AND FENCING STOLEN PROPERTY** The crime of receiving stolen goods is a type of larceny/theft that involves the buying or acquiring possession of property by a person who knows (or should know) that the seller acquired it through theft or some other illegal means. For this to constitute a crime, the receiver must know the goods were stolen at the time he receives them and must have the intent to aid the thief. Depending on the value of the property received, *receiving* stolen property is either a misdemeanor or a felony. *Fencing* is a crime that involves an ongoing effort to be a middleman or distributor of illegally received goods.

Today, the professional **fence**, who earns his or her living solely by buying and reselling stolen merchandise, seems more like the "professional criminal" described by Sutherland earlier in the chapter than almost any other kind of criminal offender. Fences use stealth rather than violence, guile and knowledge rather than force or threat, as they buy and sell stolen merchandise ranging from diamonds to wheel rims.[25] The advent of the Internet, which allows for the international sale of goods, has changed the nature of fencing from a local to global crime, and created a new breed of fence whose customers and clients can be found anywhere in the world.

**fence**
A buyer and seller of stolen merchandise.

**burglary**
Entering a home by force, threat, or deception with intent to commit a crime.

## Burglary

Under common law, the crime of **burglary** was defined as "the breaking and entering of a dwelling house of another in the nighttime with the intent to commit a felony within." Burglary is considered a much more serious crime than larceny/theft because it involves entering another's home, which threatens occupants. Even though the home may be unoccupied at the time of the burglary, the potential for harm to the occupants is so significant that most state jurisdictions punish burglary as a felony.

The legal definition of burglary has undergone considerable change since its common-law origins. When first created by English judges during the late Middle Ages, laws against burglary were designed to protect people whose homes might be set upon by wandering criminals. Including the phrase "breaking and entering" in the definition protected people from unwarranted intrusions; if an invited guest stole something, it would not be considered a burglary. Similarly, the requirement that the crime be committed at nighttime was added because evening was considered the time when honest people might fall prey to criminals.[26]

More recent U.S. state laws have changed the requirements of burglary, and most have discarded the necessity of forced entry. Entry through deceit (for example, by posing as a deliveryman), through threat, or through conspiracy with others (such as guests or servants) is deemed legally equivalent to breaking and is called "constructive breaking." Many states now protect all structures, not just dwelling houses. A majority of states have also removed the nighttime element from their definitions of burglary. States commonly enact laws creating different degrees of burglary. The more serious, heavily punished crimes involve nighttime forced entry into the home; the least serious involve daytime entry into a nonresidential structure by an unarmed offender.

**NATURE AND EXTENT OF BURGLARY** The FBI's definition of burglary is not restricted to burglary from a person's home; it includes any unlawful entry of a structure to commit a theft or felony. Burglary is further categorized into three subclasses: forcible entry, unlawful entry where no force is used, and attempted forcible entry.

According to the UCR, slightly less than 2 million burglaries now occur each year. Like other crimes,

Splash/Maine State Police/Splash News/Corbis

Most burglars are not professionals. Christopher Knight, arrested by Maine police on suspicion of being involved in 1,000 burglaries since 1986, is pictured here on surveillance cameras at the Pine Tree Camp in Rome, Maine. Knight lived in a makeshift camp in the woods for 27 years and supported himself through burglary.

burglaries and burglary rates have declined for the past decade.[27] Burglars target homes more often than nonresidential structures such as factories and stores. Most residential burglaries occur during the day, from 6:00 A.M. to 6:00 P.M., when few people are home, whereas nonresidential structures are targeted in the evening, when businesses and shops are closed. The average dollar loss per burglary offense is more than $2,300; in all, burglaries cost victims more than $4.5 billion per year.

While the NCVS also recorded a decline in the number of annual burglaries reported by victims, it reports that about 3 million residential burglaries are either attempted or completed each year, more than a million more than the UCR. According to the NCVS, those most likely to be burglarized are relatively poor Hispanic and African American families. Owner-occupied and single-family residences had lower burglary rates than renter-occupied and multiple-family dwellings.

**RATIONAL BURGLARS** Burglars seem to embody rational decision making in their choice of targets. Even those who are occasional thieves follow a script when they decide where to burgle. Most adapt their behavior to the community in which they reside. They avoid difficult and well-guarded targets with security gates.[28] They travel farther to commit crimes when there are good roadways and getting around is easy. When they live in densely populated communities with plenty of targets they stay closer to home.[29] And while security guards may deter some burglars, alarms and other devices designed to protect homes may actually have an opposite effect on a savvy burglar: why have an alarm unless there was something worth taking inside?[30]

Some make burglary their career and continually develop new specialized skills. In a now classic study, Neal Shover uncovered the existence of a particularly successful type—the "good burglar."[31] Characteristics of the good burglar include technical competence, personal integrity, specialization in burglary, financial success, and the ability to avoid prison sentences. Shover found that to become good burglars, novices must develop four key requirements of the trade:

- The good burglar must master the many skills needed to commit lucrative burglaries. These skills may include gaining entry into homes and apartment houses, selecting targets with high potential payoffs, choosing items with a high resale value, opening safes properly without damaging their contents, and using the proper equipment, including cutting torches, electric saws, explosives, and metal bars.
- The good burglar must be able to team up to form a criminal gang. Choosing trustworthy companions is essential if the obstacles to completing a successful job—police, alarms, secure safes—are to be overcome.
- The good burglar must have inside information. Without knowledge of what awaits them inside, burglars can spend a tremendous amount of time and effort on empty safes and jewelry boxes.
- The good burglar must cultivate fences or buyers for stolen wares. Once the burglar gains access to people who buy and sell stolen goods, he or she must also learn how to successfully sell these goods for a reasonable profit.

According to Shover, an older burglar teaches the novice how to handle such requirements of the trade as dealing with defense attorneys, bail bond agents, and other agents of the justice system. Apprentices must be known to have the appropriate character before they are accepted for training. Usually the opportunity to learn burglary comes as a reward for being a highly respected juvenile gang member, from knowing someone in the neighborhood who has made a living at burglary, or, more often, from having built a reputation for being solid while serving time in prison. Consequently, the opportunity to become a good burglar is not open to everyone.

## Arson

**Arson** is the willful, malicious burning of a home, public building, vehicle, or commercial building. Although arson data can be sketchy since only a limited number of jurisdictions report arsons, the FBI reports that about 45,000 arsons are now recorded annually,

---

> **CONNECTIONS**
>
> According to the rational choice approach discussed in Chapter 4, burglars make rational and calculated decisions before committing crimes. If circumstances and culture dictate their activities, their decisions must be considered a matter of choice.

---

**arson**
The willful, malicious burning of a home, building, or vehicle.

with an average cost of about $14,000 each. Arson attacks are not unique to the United States.

There are several motives for arson. Adult arsonists may be motivated by severe emotional turmoil or a disturbed personality.[32] Research on the background characteristics of juvenile fire setters shows that their acts are often associated with antisocial behavior and psychopathology.[33] These findings support the claim that arson should be viewed as a mental health problem, not a criminal act, and should be treated with counseling and other therapeutic measures, rather than with severe punishments.[34]

Not all fires are the work of emotionally disturbed people; some are set by professionals who engage in arson for profit. People who want to collect insurance money but are afraid or unable to set the fires themselves hire professional arsonists who know how to set fires and make the cause seem accidental (such as an electrical short circuit). Another form is arson fraud, which involves a business owner burning his or her own property.

Some arsons cause millions in damages. On December 8, 2014, Los Angeles firefighters battled a fire in the seven-story Da Vinci apartment complex under construction in downtown Los Angeles. Investigators later determined that arson caused the massive fire, resulting in an estimated $100 million in damages. The intense heat also melted a freeway sign and cracked or shattered hundreds of windows in nearby office buildings. Fifty-six-year-old Dawud Abdulwali was arrested and charged in the case, but his motive remains unknown.

## White-Collar Crime

L04   Summarize the various forms of white-collar crime.

White-collar crime is defined as any business-related act that uses deceit, deception, or dishonesty to carry out criminal enterprise. Included within the scope of white-collar crime are such diverse acts as income tax evasion, employee theft, soliciting bribes, accepting kickbacks, and embezzlement. Nor do criminologists restrict the definition to the wealthy and powerful; members of all social classes may engage in white-collar crimes.

How much white-collar crime takes place each year? While it's difficult to calculate, the National White Collar Crime Center conducts periodic national surveys of thousands of people and taps into individual experiences with business crimes to give a picture of how widespread white-collar crime is and how many citizens are affected by these business enterprise crimes.[35] The most recent survey found that:

- 24 percent of households and 17 percent of individuals reported experiencing at least one form of white-collar crime within the previous year.
- White-collar crimes happened at both household and individual levels, most often as a result of credit card fraud, price misrepresentation, and unnecessary repairs.
- More than half (55 percent) of the households surveyed reported a white-collar crime to a credit card company, the business or person involved, law enforcement, consumer protection agency, or their personal attorney.
- Only about 12 percent of the crimes were reported to law enforcement or some other crime control agency.
- The general public views white-collar crimes as a serious problem, considering them more damaging than traditional crimes.[36]

It is not surprising, then, that some estimates of the annual cost of white-collar crime are as high as $660 billion.[37] These losses far outstrip the expense of any other type of crime. Nor is it likely that the full extent of white-collar crime will ever be known because many victims (70 percent) are reluctant to report their crime to police, believing that nothing can be done and that getting further involved is pointless.[38]

White-collar crime today represents a wide spectrum of behaviors involving individuals acting alone and within the context of a business structure. The victims of white-collar crime can be the general public, the organization that employs the offender, or a competing organization. Here we break down white-collar crime into a number of independent yet interrelated criminal activities, ranging from an individual using a business enterprise to commit theft-related crimes to a business enterprise engaging in activities that violate laws that regulate business and commerce.[39]

## Business Frauds and Swindles

Business frauds and swindles occur when someone uses their institutional or business position to trick others out of their money. One type is called contract fraud, in which a swindler lures a victim into signing a long-term agreement without informing them that the small print included on the sales contract obligates them to purchase some high-priced services they did not really want in the first place. Another ploy is to trick the victim into thinking the contract is from a legitimate vendor because it has a familiar look. A business office receives an invoice in the mail with a self-addressed envelope that without close examination looks like a legitimate bill from Verizon or AT&T. On the back, in small print, is written, "By returning this confirmation, you're signing a contract to be an advertiser in the upcoming, and all subsequent, issues of the 'People's Yellow Pages.'" If an employee returns the invoice, the business soon finds that it has agreed to a costly long-term contract to advertise in some private publication that is not widely distributed.

**LO5** Explain what is meant by the term *Ponzi scheme.*

**PONZI SCHEMES** A Ponzi scheme is a type of swindle that involves the payment of purported returns to existing investors from funds contributed by new investors. Someone sets up a mutual fund and promises a 20 percent interest guaranteed. The scheme organizers solicit new investors by promising these high returns with little or no risk. However, nothing is actually invested; the 20 percent interest is paid by returning part of the principle each year. At that rate the scheme can go on for at least five years. It can even go on longer if new investors are brought in and their capital is used to pay the original shareholders' interest payments. The swindlers take the bulk of the money and stash it away in hidden bank accounts. Ponzi schemes collapse when it becomes difficult to recruit new investors or when a large number of investors ask to cash out and find that the money has disappeared.

Why are they called "Ponzi schemes"? The term comes from one Charles Ponzi, who duped thousands of New England residents into investing in a postage stamp speculation scheme back in the 1920s. At a time when the annual interest rate for bank accounts was 5 percent, Ponzi promised investors that he could provide a 50 percent return in just 90 days. Ponzi used incoming funds to pay off earlier investors.[40]

**THE MADOFF CASE** The most famous and costly Ponzi scheme involved financier Bernard Madoff, who eventually pleaded guilty to an 11-count criminal complaint for violations of the antifraud provisions of the Securities Act of 1933, the Securities Exchange Act of 1934, and the Investment Advisers Act of 1940. At his hearing, Madoff admitted that he had swindled thousands of investors in one of the nation's most elaborate financial crimes. On June 29, 2009, Madoff was sentenced to 150 years in prison, a life sentence.

How did Madoff's swindle unfold? He founded the Wall Street firm Bernard L. Madoff Investment Securities LLC in 1960, and it soon became one of Wall Street's largest "specialist" firms, handling the money of celebrities such as Kevin Bacon and Steven Spielberg. Rather than being a Wall Street genius, Madoff was running a giant Ponzi scheme. Madoff had not actually invested any of the money but instead deposited it in various banks. He used money given to him to pay dividends and interest owed investors, and encouraged people to keep their money in the account and reinvest profit and dividends. Every month investors got a statement showing more and more paper profits. When the stock market melted down in 2007 and people wanted to cash in their stock, Madoff's house of cards fell apart: all the money was gone. Losses amounted to about $18 billion. In the end, Madoff was regarded as the symbol of the greed run amuck that almost destroyed the nation's financial system.

## Chiseling

Another type of business swindle, **chiseling** involves an ongoing conspiracy to use one's business position to cheat institutions or individuals by providing them with faulty or bogus goods and services or by providing services that violate legal controls on business practices. Chiselers may be individuals who want to make quick profits in their own business or employees of large organizations who deceive their superiors and violate company policy to make illegal gains.

Chiseling schemes sometimes involve overbilling or charging for goods and services that the customer never received, such as for bogus auto repairs that were not required and never performed. It can also involve substituting cheap off-brand merchandise for higher priced name brands, or short weighting (intentionally tampering with the accuracy of scales used to weigh products) in supermarkets. Typically chiseling is an ongoing criminal enterprise in which rules are bent and broken.[41]

**PROFESSIONAL CHISELING**  Some chiselers are highly educated professionals who are in a position to defraud clients. Pharmacists have been known to alter prescriptions or substitute low-cost generic drugs for more expensive name brands.[42] The most notorious case of professional chiseling involved Kansas City pharmacist Robert R. Courtney, who was charged with fraud when it was discovered that he had been selling diluted mixtures of the medications Taxol, Gemzar, Paraplatin, and Platinol, which are used to treat cancer.[43] After he pleaded guilty, Courtney told authorities that his criminal activities affected the patients of 400 doctors, involved 98,000 prescriptions, and harmed approximately 4,200 patients.[44]

**FINANCIAL CHISELING**  A great deal of professional chiseling takes place on the commodities and stock markets, where individuals engage in deceptive schemes to defraud clients. For example, dishonest investment counselors and insurance agents may use their positions to cheat individual clients by misleading them on the quality of their investments; financial organizations cheat their clients by promoting risky investments as being iron-clad safe.

Financial chiseling schemes can involve stockbrokers, mortgage brokers, bankers, and other fiduciary agents who violate accepted commercial practices. Their schemes include *churning*, in which a stockbroker manipulates a client's account by repeated, excessive, and unnecessary buying and selling of stock, and *front running*, where a broker places personal orders ahead of a customer's large order to profit from the market effects of the trade.[45]

Financial chiselers also engage in **insider trading**, which occurs when someone uses their position of trust to profit from information unavailable to the public in order to buy and sell securities for personal profit. The law prohibiting insider trading was originally conceived to make it illegal for corporate employees with direct knowledge of market-sensitive information to use that information for their own benefit or that of their friends and relatives. For example, it would be illegal for employees to buy stock, using their insider information, in a company that their employer was about to take over at a much higher price. In recent years, the definition of insider trading has been expanded by federal courts to include employees of financial institutions, such as law or banking firms, who have access to confidential information about corporate clients.[46] Federal laws and the rules of the Securities and Exchange Commission require that all profits from such trading be returned and provide for both fines and a prison sentence.

Recently, chiseling in the mortgage markets almost wrecked the U.S. economy. Schemes targeting distressed homeowners have emerged throughout the country, increasing 300 percent in the three years following the housing crash (2008) in cases

**chiseling**
Using illegal means to cheat an organization, its consumers, or both, on a regular basis.

**insider trading**
Illegal buying of stock in a company on the basis of information provided by someone who has a fiduciary interest in the company.

involving distressed homeowner fraud.[47] White-collar criminals were quick to feed off of the financial desperation of their victims.

## Exploitation

In 2009, an employee of the U.S. Army Corps of Engineers in Iraq and Afghanistan was charged with soliciting and receiving a $40,000 payment from a contractor, which was then awarded a $2.5 million project to build city parks in Kirkuk, Iraq. The engineer had responsibility for supervising various construction projects, including oil pipeline barriers, water projects, schools, and roads, so the contractor feared it would not get paid or would lose contracts if it failed to meet the engineer's demands for money.[48]

It is sad but true that some individuals exploit their position, even during times of war, in order to extort people to make an illegal profit. They use their power to take advantage of others who have an interest in how that power is used. A fire inspector who threatens a restaurant owner with a safety violation unless he is given a financial consideration is abusing his institutional position. In a recent case, an immigration officer demanded and received sexual favors from a woman after he threatened to withhold her green card.[49]

**exploitation**
Forcing victims to pay for services or contracts to which they have a clear right.

**influence peddling**
Using one's institutional position to grant favors and sell information to which one's co-conspirators are not entitled.

**Exploitation** occurs when the victim has a clear right to expect a service, and the offender threatens to withhold the service unless an additional payment or bribe is forthcoming. In the Iraq case, a contractor feared that it would be excluded from military contracts unless it paid an engineer a bribe; the woman involved with the immigration officer feared that she would be deported unless she complied with his demands.

Exploitation can also occur in private industry. For example, a company employee might refuse to award a contract to a supplier unless it gave him or her a "piece of the action." Purchasing agents in large companies often demand payment for awarding contracts to suppliers and distributors. Managing agents in some of New York City's most luxurious buildings have been convicted on charges that they routinely extorted millions of dollars from maintenance contractors and building suppliers before awarding them contracts that they deserved on the merits of their service.[50]

## Influence Peddling

In 2014, a scam was exposed in which corrupt state employees and their accomplices were selling California driver's licenses for cash. A man who owned a driving school let his students know that—for a price—he could guarantee them a license, even if they had already failed the driving test. Those willing to pay anywhere from $500 to $2,500 to corrupt DMV employees could get a license with no questions asked. As word got around, people actually flew in from other states just to take a California driving test. A number of DMV employees who participated in the scam went to prison for up to 18 months.[51]

Sometimes individuals holding important institutional positions sell power, influence, and information to outsiders who have an interest in influencing the activities of the institution or buying information on what the institution may do in the future. In addition to DMV employees selling licenses to people who do not deserve them, offenses within this category include government employees taking kickbacks from contractors in return for awarding them contracts they could not have won on merit, or outsiders bribing government officials.[52]

While exploiters are extortionists who force victims to pay for services to which they are legally entitled, influence peddlers take bribes in exchange for granting undeserved favorable treatment. The "victim" of **influence peddling** is the organization whose integrity is compromised by one of its employees for their own interests.

**INFLUENCE PEDDLING IN GOVERNMENT** It is unfortunately common for government workers and office holders to engage in official corruption, a circumstance that is particularly disturbing because society expects a higher standard of moral integrity from people empowered to uphold the law and judge their fellow citizens.

One of the worst and most notorious cases of influence peddling involved two judges who took bribes to put kids in detention. Pennsylvania judges Mark Ciavarella and Michael Conahan were convicted for accepting $2.6 million in payoffs to put juvenile offenders in lock-ups run by a privately managed youth detention corporation. Thousands of kids were put away for minor infractions so that the judges could earn millions in illegal payoffs, and the detention centers were kept filled at the expense of the state. Both judges eventually pleaded guilty and received long prison sentences.[53]

**INFLUENCE PEDDLING IN BUSINESS** Politicians and government officials are not the only ones accused of bribery; business has had its share of scandals. People who hold power in a business may force those wishing to work with the company to pay them some form of bribe or gratuity to gain a contract. In the building industry, a purchasing agent may demand a kickback from contractors hoping to gain a service contract. Other employees are willing to disclose confidential company information, giving competitors and suppliers a market advantage, in exchange for payments.[54]

Sandy Fonzo confronts former Luzerne County Judge Mark A. Ciavarella as he leaves the federal courthouse in Scranton, Pennsylvania. Fonzo's son, who was jailed when he was 17 by Ciavarella, committed suicide at the age of 23. Ciavarella is serving a 28-year sentence and fellow ex-judge Michael Conahan 17 years for taking $2.6 million from companies looking to build and fill a youth detention center for Luzerne County. The scam entangled thousands of innocent children in Pennsylvania's juvenile court system and sent many to the detention center who should never have been incarcerated.

Business-related bribery is not unique to the United States. In some foreign countries, soliciting bribes to do business is a common, even expected, practice. In some European countries, such as Italy and France, giving gifts to secure contracts is a routine practice.[55] It is common for foreign officials to solicit bribes to allow American firms to do business in their countries. In 2013, the International Business Machines Corporation (IBM) settled a case and agreed to pay some $10 million over improper gifts to government officials in South Korea and China. That did not end IBM's ordeal: the Department of Justice continues to investigate allegations of illegal activity by a former IBM employee in Poland, Argentina, Bangladesh, and Ukraine.[56] In response to these revelations, Congress passed the Foreign Corrupt Practices Act (FCPA), which makes it a criminal offense to bribe foreign officials or to make other questionable overseas payments. Violations of the FCPA draw strict penalties for both the defendant company and its officers.[57] Moreover, all fines imposed on corporate officers are paid by them, not absorbed by the company. If a domestic company violates the anti-bribery provisions of the FCPA, it can be fined up to $1 million. Company officers, employees, or stockholders who are convicted of bribery may have to serve a prison sentence of up to five years and pay a $10,000 fine.

## Embezzlement

**Embezzlement** occurs when someone who is trusted with someone else's personal property fraudulently converts it—that is, keeps it for his or her own use or for the use of others. Such acts include converting company assets for personal benefit, fraudulently receiving increases in compensation (such as raises or bonuses), fraudulently increasing personal holdings of company stock, retaining one's present position within the company by manipulating accounts, and concealing unacceptable performance from stockholders.[58]

The number of people arrested for embezzlement in the United States has increased in the past decade, indicating that (1) more employees are willing to steal from their employers, (2) more employers are willing to report instances of embezzlement, and/or (3) law enforcement officials are more willing to prosecute embezzlers. There has also been a rash of embezzlement-type crimes around the world, especially in third-world countries where poverty is all too common and the economy is poor

**embezzlement**
A type of larceny in which someone who is trusted with someone else's personal property fraudulently converts it to his or her own use or for the use of others.

and supported by foreign aid and loans. Government officials and businesspeople through whose hands this money passes may be tempted to convert it to their own use, a scenario that is sure to increase the likelihood of embezzlement.[59]

## Client Fraud

Client fraud involves cheating an organization (such as a government agency or insurance company) by filing false claims for reimbursement for services provided or, conversely, failing to pay what is owed. The victim is an organization that reimburses clients for their loss, such as an insurance company, or who should collect money for services rendered, such as the U.S. government. An example might be, an insurance policy holder reports the loss of a diamond ring even though the ring has not been lost or stolen.

**HEALTH CARE FRAUD** In 2014, Arrey Kingsly Etchi-Banyi was arrested by federal agents investigating health care fraud. He and four others were involved in a scheme that involved fraud, kickbacks, and false billings in the growing field of home care services for Medicaid patients, this time in Washington, D.C. Medicaid provides for personal care aides who help clients in performing activities of daily living, such as getting in and out of bed, bathing, dressing, keeping track of medication, and so forth. In order to be covered for such benefits, the beneficiaries must get a doctor's prescription. Etchi-Banyi and his associates are accused of recruiting and teaming up with Medicaid beneficiaries who faked or exaggerated symptoms so they could sign up for home health care. They then received cash payments of approximately $200 every two weeks to sign timesheets falsely stating that they received home care services. Bills were submitted on behalf of these individuals for services that never were provided, costing D.C. Medicaid millions of dollars.[60]

Crooked health care providers find it lucrative to engage in fraud in obtaining patients and administering their treatment and for patients to try to scam the system for their own benefit. The FBI estimates that health care fraud now costs the nation $80 billion per year.[61] There are numerous health care–related schemes, including:

- Billing for services that were never rendered by using genuine patient information to fabricate entire claims or by adding to claims with charges for procedures or services that did not take place.

- Billing for more expensive services or procedures than were actually provided or performed, commonly known as "upcoding." This practice requires "inflation" of the patient's diagnosis code to a more serious condition consistent with the false procedure code.

- Performing medically unnecessary services solely for the purpose of generating insurance payments. This scheme occurs most often in nerve-conduction and other diagnostic-testing schemes. Some Southern California clinics performed unnecessary, and sometimes harmful, surgeries on patients who had been recruited and paid to have these unnecessary surgeries performed.

Craig Ruttle/Redux

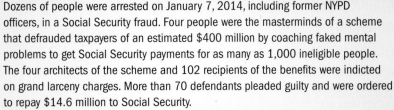

Dozens of people were arrested on January 7, 2014, including former NYPD officers, in a Social Security fraud. Four people were the masterminds of a scheme that defrauded taxpayers of an estimated $400 million by coaching faked mental problems to get Social Security payments for as many as 1,000 ineligible people. The four architects of the scheme and 102 recipients of the benefits were indicted on grand larceny charges. More than 70 defendants pleaded guilty and were ordered to repay $14.6 million to Social Security.

- Misrepresenting noncovered treatments as medically necessary covered treatments for purposes of obtaining insurance payments. This scheme occurs in cosmetic surgery in which noncovered procedures such as nose jobs, tummy tucks, liposuction, or breast augmentations are billed to patients' insurers as deviated-septum repairs, hernia repairs, or lumpectomies.[62]

The government has attempted to tighten control over the industry in order to restrict the opportunity for physicians to commit fraud. Health care companies providing services to federal health care programs are also regulated by federal laws that prohibit kickbacks and self-referrals. It is now a crime, punishable by up to five years in prison, to provide anything of value, money or otherwise, directly or indirectly, with the intent to induce the referral of a patient to a health care service. Liability attaches to both parties in the transaction—the entity or individual providing the kickbacks and the individual receiving payment for the referral.

Federal law also prohibits physicians and other health care providers from referring beneficiaries in federal health care programs to clinics or other facilities in which the physician or health care provider has a financial interest. It is illegal for a doctor to refer her patients to a blood-testing lab in which she has an ownership share. These practices—kickbacks and self-referrals—are prohibited under federal law because they would compromise a medical professional's independent judgment. Federal law prohibits arrangements that tend to corrupt medical judgment and tempt the prescriber to put the provider's bottom line ahead of the patient's well-being.[63]

**TAX EVASION**  Another important aspect of client fraud is tax evasion. Here, the victim is the government that is cheated by one of its clients, the errant taxpayer to whom it extended credit by allowing the taxpayer to delay paying taxes on money he or she had already earned. Underpaying or avoiding taxes is considered client fraud because the taxpayer has received a service, such as military protection or use of national parks, and is now avoiding payment. Tax fraud is a particularly challenging area for criminological study because so many U.S. citizens regularly underreport their income, and it is often difficult to separate honest error from deliberate tax evasion.

The basic law on tax evasion is contained in the U.S. Internal Revenue Code, section 7201, which states that

> Any person who willfully attempts in any manner to evade or defeat any tax imposed by this title or the payment thereof shall, in addition to other penalties provided by law, be guilty of a felony and, upon conviction thereof, shall be fined not more than $100,000 or imprisoned not more than five years, or both, together with the costs of prosecution.

To prove tax fraud, the government must find that the taxpayer either underreported his or her income or did not report taxable income. No minimum dollar amount is stated before fraud exists, but the government can take legal action when there is a "substantial underpayment of tax." A second element of tax fraud is "willfulness" on the part of the tax evader. In the major case on this issue, willfulness was defined as a "voluntary, intentional violation of a known legal duty and not the careless disregard for the truth."[64] Finally, to prove tax fraud, the government must show that the taxpayer has purposely attempted to evade or defeat a tax payment. If the offender is guilty of passive neglect, the offense is a misdemeanor. "Passive neglect" means simply not paying taxes, not reporting income, or not paying taxes when due. On the other hand, "affirmative tax evasion," such as keeping double books, making false entries, destroying books or records, concealing assets, or covering up sources of income, constitutes a felony.

## Corporate Crime

Yet another component of white-collar crime involves situations in which powerful institutions or their representatives willfully violate the laws that restrain these institutions from doing social harm or require them to do social good. This is also known as **corporate**, or **organizational**, **crime**.

**corporate (organizational) crime**
Powerful institutions or their representatives willfully violate the laws that restrain these institutions from doing social harm or require them to do social good.

Does the prohibition against illegal price-fixing, aimed at controlling large corporations, also apply to individuals? Sierra Poulson, shown here on October 16, 2015, in Omaha, Nebraska, has donated her eggs three times, and helped start an online forum for egg donors. On their websites, next to glossy pictures of babies, some fertility clinics and egg-donor agencies refer to eggs as "priceless gifts" from caring young women who want to help people with fertility problems. There is a price tag for eggs, though, that is now the subject of a legal battle. In a federal lawsuit, a group of women are challenging industry guidelines that say it is "inappropriate" to pay a woman more than $10,000 for her eggs. The women say the $10,000 limit amounts to illegal price-fixing, and point out that there is no price restriction on the sale of human sperm. Should the courts set a price limit on what a woman can charge for her eggs?

**Sherman Antitrust Act**
Federal law that subjects to criminal or civil sanctions any person "who shall make any contract or engage in any combination or conspiracy" in restraint of interstate commerce.

**price fixing**
The illegal control by agreement among producers or manufacturers of the price of a commodity to avoid price competition and deprive the consumer of reasonable prices.

Corporate crimes are socially injurious acts committed to further the business interests of people who control companies. The target of these crimes can be the general public, the environment, or even company workers. What makes these crimes unique is that the perpetrator is a legal fiction—a corporation—and not an individual. In reality, it is company employees or owners who commit corporate crimes and who ultimately benefit through career advancement or greater profits.

Some of the acts included within corporate crime are price fixing and illegal restraint of trade, false advertising, and the use of company practices that violate environmental protection statutes. The variety of crimes contained within this category is great, and they cause vast damage. The following subsections examine some of the most important offenses.

**ILLEGAL RESTRAINT OF TRADE** A restraint of trade involves a contract or conspiracy designed to stifle competition, create a monopoly, artificially maintain prices, or otherwise interfere with free market competition.[65] The control of restraint-of-trade violations has its legal basis in the **Sherman Antitrust Act**, which subjects to criminal or civil sanctions any person "who shall make any contract or engage in any combination or conspiracy" in restraint of interstate commerce.[66] For violations of its provisions, this federal law created criminal penalties of up to three years' imprisonment and $100,000 in fines for individuals and $10 million in fines for corporations.[67] The act outlaws conspiracies between corporations that are designed to control the marketplace.

In most instances, the act lets the presiding court judge decide whether corporations have conspired to "unreasonably restrain competition." However, through the Sherman Antitrust Act, four types of market conditions considered inherently anticompetitive have been defined by federal courts as illegal per se, without regard to the facts or circumstances of the case:

- *Division of markets.* Firms divide a region into territories, and each firm agrees not to compete in the others' territories.
- *Tying arrangement.* A corporation requires customers of one of its services to use other services it offers. It would be an illegal restraint of trade if a railroad required that companies doing business with it or supplying it with materials ship all goods they produce on trains owned by the rail line.[68]
- *Group boycott.* An organization or company boycotts retail stores that do not comply with its rules or desires.
- *Price fixing.* A conspiracy to set and control the price of a necessary commodity is considered an absolute violation of the act.

**PRICE FIXING** A violation of the Sherman Antitrust Act occurs when two or more business competitors conspire to sell the same or similar products or services at an agreed-on price. The purpose is to maximize prices, reduce the costs of competition, and sell the product at a price higher than would be possible with normal competition.

An example of **price fixing** occurred in 2013, when nine Japan-based companies pleaded guilty and were forced to pay a total of more than $740 million in criminal fines for their roles in conspiracies to fix the prices of more than 30 different products sold to U.S. car manufacturers, including Chrysler, Ford, and General Motors, as well as to the U.S. subsidiaries of Honda, Mazda, Mitsubishi, Nissan, Toyota, and Subaru. Executives in the companies attended meetings and communicated by telephone in the United States and Japan to set prices, to conspire to keep bids for merchandise higher than needed, and to control the supply of auto parts sold to the car manufacturers. They took measures to keep their conduct secret by using code names and meeting in remote locations. Afterwards they had further secret communications to monitor and enforce their illegal agreements.[69]

**DECEPTIVE PRICING**  Deceptive pricing occurs when contractors provide the government or other corporations with incomplete or misleading information on how much it will actually cost to fulfill the contracts on which they are bidding, or use mischarges once the contracts are signed.[70] For example, defense contractors have been prosecuted for charging the government for costs incurred on work they are doing for private firms or for shifting the costs on fixed-price contracts to ones in which the government reimburses the contractor for all expenses ("cost-plus" contracts).

**FALSE CLAIMS ADVERTISING**  Executives in even the largest corporations sometimes face stockholders' expectations of ever-increasing company profits that seem to demand that sales be increased at any cost. At times they respond to this challenge by making claims about their products that cannot be justified by actual performance. However, there is a fine line between clever, aggressive sales techniques and fraudulent claims. It is traditional to show a product in its best light, even if that involves resorting to fantasy. Showing a delivery service vehicle taking off into outer space or implying that taking one sip of beer will make people feel they have just jumped into a freezer are not fraudulent. But it is illegal to knowingly and purposely advertise a product as possessing qualities that the manufacturer realizes it does not have, such as the ability to cure the common cold, grow hair, or turn senior citizens into rock stars (though some rock stars are senior citizens these days).

# Green-Collar Crime

On April 20, 2010, an explosion occurred on the *Deepwater Horizon* oil rig, killing 11 platform workers and injuring 17 others.[71] The rig was built by Hyundai Heavy Industries of Korea, owned by the Transocean Drilling Corporation, and leased by BP (formerly British Petroleum) in order to drill a deepwater oil well in the Gulf of Mexico. The drilling was overseen by Halliburton. Following the explosion, the *Deepwater Horizon* burned for 36 hours before sinking to the ocean floor 5,000 feet below, where oil was gushing from the now-uncapped well. At first, estimates of the oil spill were 5,000 barrels a day, but they quickly rose to 60,000. For more than three months, company officials frantically tried to stem the flow with a variety of failed schemes, while millions of barrels of escaping oil created a slick that covered thousands of square miles, devastating wildlife and causing one of the greatest natural disasters in U.S. history.

On June 1, 2010, the Obama administration announced that it had launched a criminal probe in order to "prosecute to the fullest extent of the law" any persons or companies that broke the law in the time leading up to the spill.[72] Under federal environmental laws, a company may be charged with a misdemeanor for negligent conduct, or a felony if there is evidence that company personnel knowingly engaged in conduct risking injury. It would be a criminal act if, for example, employees of BP or its subcontractors, Transocean and Halliburton:

- Lied in the permit process for obtaining a drilling license
- Tried to cover up the severity of the spill
- Knowing of negligence in construction, chose to ignore the danger it imposed
- Engaged in or approved of unsafe, risky, or dangerous methods to remove the drill, knowing that such methods could injure those on board

To prove a felony, and potentially put BP executives in prison, the government must show that company officials knew in advance that its actions would lead to the explosion and oil spill but chose to ignore the danger; a misdemeanor requires only mere negligence. But even a misdemeanor conviction would amp up the loss to the company, because the Federal Alternative Fines Act allows the government to request monetary fines that are twice the loss associated with an offense.[73] This provision can also have a devastating effect on employees, because fines imposed on individuals under the act may *not* be paid by their employer.[74] On September 4, 2014,

U.S. District Judge Carl Barbier ruled BP was guilty of gross negligence and willful misconduct. He apportioned 67 percent of the blame for the spill to BP, 30 percent to Transocean, and 3 percent to Halliburton. Barbier ruled that BP had acted with "conscious disregard of known risks" and that "employees took risks that led to the largest environmental disaster in U.S. history." In the final tally, the company paid almost $54 billion in order to settle all claims: federal Clean Water Act fines, claims by states (Alabama, Florida, Louisiana, Mississippi, and Texas), and 400 local government entities.[75] In addition, a number of BP employees were indicted on criminal charges relating to their negligence in the spill and their efforts to cover up company involvement and responsibility.

While some may argue that it is overly harsh to put company executives in prison for what is essentially an accident, civil penalties do not seem to deter companies such as BP. Before the Gulf of Mexico oil spill, BP had already paid hundreds of millions in civil penalties for similar if lesser disasters. One fine of $87 million was paid to the Occupational Safety and Health Administration—the largest fine in OSHA's history—for a Texas refinery explosion; an additional $50 million was paid to the Department of Justice for the same explosion. BP also paid $3 million to OSHA for 42 safety violations at an Ohio refinery and was fined $20 million by the Department of Justice for another spill that violated the Clean Water Act.

Oil spills are just part of the green-collar crime problem. Environmental activists have long called attention to a variety of ecological threats that they feel should be deemed criminal. Green crimes involve a wide range of actions and outcomes that harm the environment and that stem from decisions about what is produced, where it is produced, and how it is produced.[76] Global warming, overdevelopment, population growth, and other changes will continue to bring these issues front and center.[77]

While crimes targeting the environment have received scant attention in the criminological literature, recent events have shifted attention to what is variously called green crime, green criminology, and green-collar crime. The Gulf Coast disaster in 2010 is a powerful and tragic example of how environmental destruction and green crimes may be linked to enterprise systems: the need for corporate profit may outweigh attention to safety, with subsequent catastrophic consequences.

## Defining Green-Collar Crime

There is no single vision to define the concept of green-collar crimes. Three independent views exist:

- *Legalist.* According to the legalist perspective, environmental crimes are violations of existing criminal laws designed to protect people, the environment, or both. This definition would include crimes against workers such as occupational health and safety crimes, as well as laws designed to protect nature and the environment (the Clean Air Act, Clean Water Act, and so on).
- *Environmental justice.* According to the environmental justice view, limiting environmental crimes to actual violations of the criminal law is too narrow. A great deal of environmental damage occurs in third-world nations desperate for funds and willing to give mining and oil companies a free hand to develop resources. These nations have meager regulatory laws and therefore allow businesses wide latitude in environmental contamination that would be forbidden in the United States. In addition, environmental justice advocates believe that corporations themselves have attempted to co-opt or manipulate environmental laws, thereby limiting their scope and reach. Executives fear that the environmental movement will force changes in their production practices and place limits on their growth and corporate power. Some have tried to co-opt green laws by public relations and advertising campaigns that suggest they are doing everything in their power to respect the environment, thereby reducing the need for government regulation. Criminologists must take a broader view of green crimes than the law allows.

- *Biocentric.* According to the biocentric approach, environmental harm is viewed as any human activity that disrupts a biosystem, destroying plant and animal life. This more radical approach would criminalize any intentional or negligent human activity or manipulation that impacts negatively on the earth's natural resources, resulting in trauma to those resources.[78] Environmental harm, according to this view, is much greater than what is defined by law as environmental crimes. As criminologist Rob White points out, this is because some of the most ecologically destructive activities, such as clear felling of old-growth forests, are quite legal. Environmental crimes are typically oriented toward protecting humans and their property and have a limited interest in the interests of animals and plants.[79] Environmental laws protect animal and fish processing plants that treat "nature" and "wildlife" simply and mainly as resources for human exploitation. Human beings are the cause of environmental harm and need to be controlled.

**THE HARMS PERSPECTIVE** Green criminologists typically use what is known as the *harms perspective* when they conceptualize crime and deviance.[80] Accordingly, crime is a social construction that can and should be expanded to include all serious *social harms*, activities that cause any discomfort, present or future, to individuals. Harms may include physical, financial/economic, emotional or psychological, and cultural safety harm. Using the harms perspective, it would be appropriate to sanction toxic waste dumping or air pollution severely because they cause residual harm that will last many years, poisoning the environment and producing diseases such as cancer. However, in many instances this action is punished civilly, not criminally. In the Policies and Issues in Criminology feature, one enterprise that may fit the harms test, chicken farming, is discussed in some detail.

## Forms of Green Crime

Green crime can take many different forms, ranging from deforestation and illegal logging to violations of worker safety. A few of the most damaging forms are set out below.

**WORKER SAFETY/ENVIRONMENTAL CRIMES** Some corporations have endangered the lives of their own workers by maintaining unsafe conditions in their plants and mines. It has been estimated that more than 20 million workers have been exposed to hazardous materials while on the job. Some industries have been hit particularly hard by complaints and allegations. The control of workers' safety in the United States has been the province of the Occupational Safety and Health Administration (OSHA), which sets industry standards for the proper use of such chemicals as benzene, arsenic, lead, and coke (from coal). Intentional violation of OSHA standards can result in criminal penalties.

**ILLEGAL LOGGING** Illegal logging involves harvesting, processing, and transporting timber or wood products in violation of existing laws and treaties.[81] It is a universal phenomenon in major timber-producing countries, especially in the third world where enforcement is lax. Logging violations include taking trees in protected areas such as national parks, going over legally prescribed logging quotas, processing logs without acquiring licenses, and exporting logs without paying export duties. By sidestepping the law, loggers can create greater profits than those generated through legal methods.

The situation is serious because illegal logging can have severe environmental and social impact:

- Illegal logging exhausts forests, destroys wildlife, and damages its habitats. Illegal logging in central Africa is destroying the habitats and threatening the survival of populations of the great apes, including gorillas and chimpanzees.
- It causes ruinous damage to the forests, including deforestation and forest degradation worldwide. The destruction of forest cover can cause flash floods and landslides that have killed thousands of people.

# Policies and Issues
# in Criminology

## THE HARM OF CHICKEN FARMING

Green criminologists who favor the harms perspective believe that business enterprise that damages people and hurts animals should be a crime. One good example is the chicken farming industry, whose practices, though currently legal, are actually destructive and harmful.

Green criminologists point out that the modern poultry industry began about 50 years ago with the use of artificial incubators and food additives added to chicken feed. These additives stimulated unnatural and rapid growth and also staved off potential diseases that were spread due to the cramped confinement of the indoor farms. Some chemicals made chickens produce more eggs, while different mixtures were used to make chickens grow larger and faster. With the discovery of genetic and chemical manipulation, chickens became a moldable product used to embody what humans need for their own consumption.

The results of these modifications have created a bird that no longer resembles the natural chicken. From 1935 to 1995, the average weight of a broiler chicken increased by 65 percent. The time they took to grow to this size decreased by 60 percent, while their food was decreased by 57 percent. The chicken industry created a product that drove down costs by producing more meat in a shorter amount of time while spending far less on food.

The chicken industry has grown tremendously within the last 50 years. Today, America raises over 9 billion chickens, China 7 billion, and Europe about 6 billion. Some estimate about 50 billion chickens are raised around the world each year.

Of course, there is a price to pay. On average the modern chicken farm houses 30,000 to 40,000 birds. Of these chickens, up to 4 percent will die from sudden death syndrome, a cardiovascular disorder that can be compared to having a heart attack. This syndrome is most often associated with an abnormally fast growth rate. Five percent will develop excess fluid in their body cavities that is caused from growth rates, cold temperatures, and excessive salt in their feed; three out of four will be unable to walk. Other problems include bacterial infections in the bones, internal bleeding, respiratory disease, and weakened immune systems.

Only seven weeks after they're born, chickens are crowded onto trucks that transport them to the slaughterhouse; millions have their wings and legs broken in the process. They are trucked through all weather extremes, sometimes over hundreds of miles, without any food or water.

When they arrive at the processing plant, they are strung up by their ankles and moved through a water bath that is electrified in order to stun them. The chicken is then brought to a throat-slitter machine; this cuts the throat to drain blood from the carcass. It is common for the major arteries to be missed and for these cases they have "kill men" whose job it is to slaughter those chickens left alive; they also sometimes miss the arteries, causing severe pain. The birds are then dumped into a scald tank containing water heated to 140 degrees Fahrenheit, which loosens the chicken's feathers so they are easily removed without burning off the chicken skin; scald water may be a source of salmonella. When the birds are beheaded, a high-speed machine cuts the bodies vertically, often nicking the intestines and contaminating the body with feces. After inspection the chickens are dunked in a tank of cold water. In this tank the feces that released from the bowels is mixed with and sits in the water.

Beyond the inhumane treatment of chickens during the factory process, the process can have a devastating effect on the human consumer. It is clear that many birds are sent into the market covered in feces and bacteria. Between 39 and 75 percent of chickens in grocery stores are infected with E. coli, 8 percent contain salmonella, and 70 to 90 percent contain campylobacter, which causes diarrhea, nausea, and vomiting.

Despite these cruel and dangerous practices, chicken farming is legal. Green criminologists believe that the practices constitute a crime according to the harms perspective, and if changes cannot be made the practice should be abandoned entirely.

## Critical Thinking

Is it realistic, considering how much chicken is produced and how critical it is for diets here and abroad, that chicken farming could be halted? Is this just the price that must be paid to feed 7 billion people around the world? Or would it be worth doubling or tripling the price of this food product to make it more humane?

**Sources:** Jonathan Safran Foer, *Eating Animals* (New York: Back Bay Books, 2010); PETA, "Top 10 Reasons Not to Eat Chicken," 2015, www.peta.org/living/other/top-10-reasons-eat-chickens/; Julie Siegel, "Capitalism and Green Crime: An Examination of Chicken Farming," University of South Florida, 2014; Humane Society of America, Cruel Confinement, 2014, www.humanesociety.org /issues/confinement_farm/ (URLs accessed 2015).

- By reducing forest cover, illegal logging impairs the ability of land to absorb carbon emissions.
- Illegal logging costs billions each year in government revenue, impairing the ability of third-world nations to provide needed social services.
- It creates unsustainable economic devastation in the poorest countries. Vietnam, for example, has lost a third of its forest cover, while in nearby Cambodia illegal logging is at least 10 times the size of the legal harvest. These rates of extraction are clearly unsustainable, destroying valuable sources of employment and export revenues for the future.
- The substantial revenues from illegal logging fund national and regional conflict. In Cambodia, for several years Khmer Rouge insurgents were sustained primarily by the revenue from logging areas under their control.[82]

While the scale of illegal logging is difficult to estimate, it is believed that more than half of all logging activities in the most vulnerable forest regions—southeast Asia, central Africa, South America, and Russia—may be conducted illegally. World-wide, estimates suggest that illegal activities may account for over a tenth of the total global timber trade, representing products worth at least $15 billion per year.

**ILLEGAL WILDLIFE EXPORTS** The smuggling of wildlife across national borders is a serious matter.[83] Exporters find a lucrative trade in the demand for such illicit wildlife commodities as tiger parts, caviar, elephant ivory, rhino horn, and exotic birds and reptiles. Wildlife contraband may include live pets, hunting trophies, fashion accessories, cultural artifacts, ingredients for traditional medicines, wild meat for human consumption (or bush meat), and other products. Illegal profits can be immense.

There are numerous problems presented by illegal wildlife exporting. Poachers imperil endangered species and threaten them with extinction. By evading government controls, they create the potential for introducing pests and diseases into formerly unaffected areas.[84] They import nonnative species, which could harm the receiving habitats. Florida's Everglades have been overrun with nonnative species such as pythons, imported as pets and abandoned in the wild. Illegal wildlife traders range from independent one-person operations that sell a single item to complex, multi-ton, commercial-sized consignments shipped all over the world. Adding all these sources together, the global trade in illegal wildlife is a growing phenomenon and is now estimated to be somewhere between $5 and $20 billion annually.[85]

The United States is estimated to purchase nearly 20 percent of all illegal wildlife and wildlife products on the market, costing as much as $3 billion annually. The trade is so lucrative because exotic animals and animal parts are enormously expensive. The U.S. Congress has passed numerous laws that regulate and restrict wildlife imports and exports, including the Endangered Species Act of 1973 and the Lacey Act, which protects both plants and wildlife by creating civil and criminal penalties for a wide array of violations. The original act was directed at preserving game and wild birds and prohibiting the introduction of nonnative birds and animals into native ecosystems. The act has been amended and in 1981 was changed to include illegal trade in plants, fish, and wildlife both domestically and abroad. The maximum penalty was increased to $10,000 with possible imprisonment for one year. Additionally, the mental state required for a criminal violation was increased to "knowingly and willfully;" civil penalties were expanded to apply to negligent violations.[86] There are also international laws restricting the wildlife trade. The United Nations Convention on International Trade in Endangered Species of Wild Fauna and Flora (CITES) serves as the primary vehicle for regulating wildlife trade.

**ILLEGAL FISHING** Unlicensed and illegal fishing practices are another billion-dollar green crime. They can take on many forms and involve highly different parties, ranging from huge factory ships operating on the high seas that catch thousands of tons of fish on each voyage, to smaller, locally operating ships that confine themselves to national waters. Illegal fishing occurs when these ships sign on to their home nation's rules but then

Rungroj Yongrit/EPA/Landov

A cook prepares shark fin soup at a restaurant in Bangkok, Thailand. Animal rights groups in Thailand have launched a campaign against the sale and consumption of shark fin soup, calling businesses to ban the dish and advising their customers against ordering the controversial Chinese delicacy. The global demand for shark fin soup has led to a catastrophic decline in shark populations. Some species have been reduced by 99 percent since the 1950s due to legal and illegal fishing. Environmentalists have called for controls on shark fishing to preserve some endangered species.

choose to ignore their scope and boundary, or operate in a country's waters without permission or on the high seas without a flag. When catches are not reported by the fishing vessels, their illegal fishing can have a detrimental effect on species because government regulators have no idea how many are being caught. Stocks become depleted and species endangered. In addition, illegal fishing techniques, including fishermen using the wrong sized nets or fishing in prohibited areas, can damage fragile marine ecosystems, threatening coral reefs, turtles, and seabirds. In underdeveloped nations, regulators may look the other way because the need for short-term economic, social, or political gains is given more weight than long-term sustainability. As a result, species of whales, abalone, lobsters, and Patagonian toothfish (known in the United States as Chilean sea bass) have become endangered.[87]

## ILLEGAL DUMPING AND POLLUTING

Some green-collar criminals want to skirt local, state, and federal restrictions on dumping dangerous substances in the environment. Rather than pay expensive processing fees, they may secretly dispose of hazardous wastes in illegal dump sites. Illegally dumped wastes can be hazardous or nonhazardous materials that are discarded in an effort to avoid disposal fees or the time and effort required for proper disposal. Materials dumped ranged from used motor oil to waste from construction sites.

**Criminal environmental pollution** is defined as the intentional or negligent discharge of a toxic or contaminating substance into the biosystem that is known to have an adverse effect on the natural

**criminal environmental pollution**
A crime involving the intentional or negligent discharge into the biosystem of a toxic waste that destroys plant or animal life.

environment or life. It may involve the ground release of toxic chemicals such as kepone, vinyl chloride, mercury, PCBs, and asbestos. Illegal and/or controlled air pollutants include hydrochlorofluorocarbons (HCFCs), aerosols, asbestos, carbon monoxide, chlorofluorocarbons (CFCs), criteria air pollutants, lead, mercury, methane, nitrogen oxides ($NO_x$), radon, refrigerants, and sulfur oxides ($SO_2$). Water pollution is defined as the dumping of a substance that degrades or alters the quality of the waters to an extent that is detrimental to their use by humans or by an animal or a plant that is useful to humans. This includes the disposal into rivers, lakes, and streams of:

- Excess fertilizers, herbicides, and insecticides from agricultural lands and residential areas
- Oil, grease, and toxic chemicals from urban runoff and energy production
- Sediment from improperly managed construction sites, crop and forest lands, and eroding stream banks
- Salt from irrigation practices and acid drainage from abandoned mines
- Bacteria and nutrients from livestock, pet wastes, and faulty septic systems

One of the largest and fastest growing problems is the disposal of 7 million tons of obsolete high-tech electronics, called e-waste, such as televisions, desktop computers and monitors, laptops, VCRs, and so on.[88] While most e-waste in the United States is disposed of in landfills or is incinerated, the toxic material contained in electronic gear (such as lead) encourages illegal dumping in order to avoid recycling costs. Consequently, a considerable amount of e-waste is sent abroad to developing nations for recycling, often in violation of international laws restricting such commerce. All too often, the material overwhelms recycling plants and is instead dumped in local villages near people and water sources. Illegal dump sites have been documented in Nigeria, Ghana, China, the Philippines, Indonesia, Pakistan, and India, and they pose severe threats to both human health and the natural environment.

Not all illegal dumping is intentional; some is caused by negligence. When the oil tanker *Exxon Valdez* hit a reef in Prince William Sound in 1989 and devastated Prudhoe Bay on the coast of Alaska, the ship was on autopilot; its captain, Joseph Hazelwood, was in his stateroom at the time of the accident. Exxon Mobil was fined $150 million and paid an additional $100 million as restitution for damage caused to fish, wildlife, and land, and also agreed to pay $900 million in 10 annual installments to civil claimants. In 1994, a jury found that Exxon acted recklessly, and awarded victims $5 billion in punitive damages. The U.S. Supreme Court cut the amount to $507.5 million in June 2008, hardly a day's pay for the largest company on earth. Hazelwood was convicted of a misdemeanor charge of negligent discharge of oil, fined $50,000, and sentenced to 1,000 hours of community service.[89]

# Theories of White-Collar and Green-Collar Crime

Why do people get involved in risky schemes to use their institutional positions to steal money? Why do people risk going to prison because they pollute the environment? Can the same factors that predict other types of criminal offenses also apply to crimes of criminal enterprise? After all, unlike other criminal offenses, white-collar and green-collar crimes are not committed by impoverished teenagers living in the inner city, but by otherwise respectable people, many of whom are educated and financially well off. By their very nature, business and environmental crimes require that offenders attain a position of power and trust before they can be committed. Therefore, can the theories that predict and explain common-law crime be applied to enterprise-type crime?

## Rational Choice: Greed

When Kansas City pharmacist Robert Courtney was asked after his arrest why he substituted improper doses of drugs instead of what doctors had prescribed, he told investigators he cut the drugs' strength "out of greed."[90] Courtney is not alone. One view is that white-collar and green-collar criminals are greedy people who rationally choose to take shortcuts to acquire wealth, believing that the potential profits far outweigh future punishments. Most believe they will not get caught; they are far too clever to be detected by mere civil servants who work for government agencies.

Greed was rampant in the 1980s. Ivan Boesky was a famous Wall Street trader who had amassed a fortune of about $200 million by betting on corporate takeovers, a practice called *arbitrage*. In 1986, he was investigated by the Securities and Exchange Commission for insider trading. To escape serious punishment, he informed on several associates. In exchange for cooperation, Boesky received a sentence of three and a half years in prison and a $100 million fine. Released after serving two years, Boesky was barred from working in the securities business for the remainder of his life. Caught in Boesky's web was billionaire junk bond trader Michael Milken. Indicted by a federal grand jury, Milken pleaded guilty to five securities and reporting violations and was sentenced to 10 years in prison; he served 22 months. He also paid a $200 million fine and another $400 to $800 million in settlements relating primarily to civil lawsuits.

**LURE** Greed unfortunately did not end in the 1980s, and the greed that begat the Wall Street scandals of 2008 to 2010 almost sank the world economy. Recently, criminologists Neal Shover and Peter Grabosky introduced the concept of "lure" to help explain why some people succumb to the illegal yet alluring benefits of crime.[91] Tempted individuals possess qualities or experiences that make them more likely than peers who lack these distinctions to weigh illicit exploitation of lure.[92] Lure is something that is alluring—something that is so attractive and covetable that it can turn the heads of those who are tempted or predisposed. When a would-be green-collar criminal sees the wide expanses of uninhabited countryside, he becomes tempted to dispose of trash quickly and cheaply. When states create loopholes in the law that provide opportunities that can be manipulated easily for criminal purposes—such as tax incentives, subsidies, low-interest loans, and other forms of access to public funds—these benefits may prove too much of a lure for businessmen to resist. The lure of crime expands in the absence of capable control systems. When financial oversight was absent in the United States economic markets, the crash of 2008 became inevitable.

## Rational Choice: Need

Greed is not the only motivation for white-collar and green-collar crime; need also plays an important role. Some people turn to crime to fulfill an overwhelming financial or psychological need. Executives may tamper with company books because they feel the need to keep or improve their jobs, satisfy their egos, or support their children. Even people in the upper echelons of the financial world, such as Boesky, may carry scars from an earlier needy period in their lives that can be healed only by accumulating ever-greater amounts of money. As one of Boesky's associates put it:

> I don't know what his devils were. Maybe he's greedy beyond the wildest imaginings of mere mortals like you and me. And maybe part of what drives the guy is an inherent insecurity that was operative here even after he had arrived. Maybe he never arrived.[93]

## Rationalization/Neutralization View

Rationalizing guilt is a common trait of white-collar and green-collar criminals.[94] What they did was not so bad; what some call crime is merely a "technicality." They didn't really break the law, just bent it slightly.

In his research on fraud, Donald Cressey found that the door to solving personal financial problems through criminal means is opened by the rationalizations people develop for white-collar crime: "Some of our most respectable citizens got their start in life by using other people's money temporarily." "In the real estate business, there is nothing wrong about using deposits before the deal is closed." "All people steal when they get in a tight spot."[95] Offenders use these and other rationalizations to resolve the conflict they experience over engaging in illegal behavior.

It is especially easy for corporate offenders to neutralize wrongdoing when the target is a fellow businessperson or government regulatory agency. Because the victim is knowledgeable and sophisticated, they should have known better. *Caveat emptor*, as they say: let the buyer beware. The line between smart business practice and corporate crime is typically blurry. When the victim can be denied, it is often difficult to accept blame.

## Cultural View

Business culture may also influence white-collar and green-collar crime. According to this view, some business organizations promote criminality in the same way that lower-class culture encourages the development of juvenile gangs and street crime. They may place excessive demands on employees while at the same time maintaining a business climate tolerant of employee deviance. New employees learn the attitudes and techniques needed to commit crime from their business peers. Under these circumstances, the attitudes of closest coworkers and the perceived attitudes of executives have a more powerful control over decision making.[96]

## Self-Control View

In their general theory of crime, Travis Hirschi and Michael Gottfredson suggest that the motives that produce white-collar and green-collar crimes—quick benefits with minimal effort—are the same as those that produce any other criminal behaviors.[97] Those who violate business or environmental laws have low self-control and are inclined to follow momentary impulses without considering the long-term costs of such behavior.[98] Hirschi and Gottfredson have collected data showing that the demographic distribution of white-collar crime is similar to other crimes. For example, gender, race, and age ratios are the same for crimes such as embezzlement and fraud as they are for street crimes such as burglary and robbery.

# Controlling White-Collar and Green-Collar Crime

**LO6** Discuss efforts to control white-collar and green-collar crime.

On the federal level, detection of these crimes is primarily in the hands of administrative departments and agencies.[99] The decision whether to pursue these activities as criminal or civil violations is usually based on the seriousness of the case and the perpetrator's intent, on any actions taken to conceal the violation, and on the individual's prior record. Any evidence of criminal activity is then sent to the Department of Justice or the FBI for investigation. Some other federal agencies, such as the Securities and Exchange Commission and the U.S. Postal Service, have their own investigative arms. Enforcement is generally reactive (generated by complaints) rather than proactive (involving ongoing investigations or the monitoring of activities). Investigations are carried out by the various federal agencies and the FBI. If criminal prosecution is called for, the case will be handled by attorneys from the criminal, tax, antitrust, and civil rights divisions of the Justice Department. If insufficient evidence is available to warrant a criminal prosecution, the case will be handled civilly or administratively by some other federal agency. For example, the Federal Trade Commission can issue a cease and desist order in antitrust or merchandising fraud cases.

The number of state-funded technical assistance offices to help local prosecutors has increased significantly; more than 40 states offer such services. On the state and local levels, law enforcement officials have made progress in a number of areas, such as controlling consumer fraud. For example, the Environmental Crimes Strike Force in Los Angeles County is considered a model for the control of illegal dumping and pollution. Some of the more common environmental offenses investigated and prosecuted by the task force are oil spills, fraudulent certification of automobile smog tests, and illegal transportation, treatment, storage, or disposal of hazardous waste.[100]

Nonetheless, although local agencies recognize the seriousness of enterprise-type crimes, they rarely have the funds necessary for effective enforcement.[101] Local prosecutors pursue white-collar criminals more vigorously if the prosecutors are part of a team effort involving a network of law enforcement agencies.[102] National surveys of local prosecutors find that many do not consider white-collar crimes particularly serious problems. They are more willing to prosecute cases if the offense causes substantial harm and if other agencies fail to act. Relatively few prosecutors participate in interagency task forces designed to investigate white-collar criminal activity.[103]

## Environmental Laws

The United States and most sovereign nations have passed laws making it a crime to pollute or damage the environment. For example, among environmental laws in the United States are the following:

- *Clean Water Act (1972).* Establishes and maintains goals and standards for U.S. water quality and purity. It was amended in 1987 to increase controls on toxic pollutants, and in 1990 to more effectively address the hazard of oil spills.
- *Emergency Planning and Community Right-to-Know Act (1986).* Requires companies to disclose information about toxic chemicals they release into the air and water and dispose of on land.

- *Endangered Species Act (1973)*. Designed to protect and recover endangered and threatened species of fish, wildlife, and plants in the United States and beyond. The law works in part by protecting species habitats.
- *Oil Pollution Act (1990)*. Enacted in the aftermath of the *Exxon Valdez* oil spill in Alaska's Prince William Sound, this law streamlines federal response to oil spills by requiring oil storage facilities and vessels to prepare spill-response plans and provide for their rapid implementation. The law also increases polluters' liability for cleanup costs and damage to natural resources.

## Enforcing the Law

A typical environmental crime—such as the knowing discharge of raw sewage into one of the nation's waterways or the killing of a bald eagle—is investigated by federal authorities such as special agents of the U.S. Fish and Wildlife Service. These agents are plainclothes criminal investigators who enforce federal wildlife laws throughout the United States. They target crimes that undermine U.S. efforts to conserve wildlife resources, such as wildlife trafficking and habitat destruction.[104] Service special agents protect threatened and endangered species, migratory birds, marine mammals, and imperiled animals and plants around the world. Their investigations document violations of federal wildlife laws as well as such crimes as smuggling, conspiracy, money laundering, mail and wire fraud, and making false statements.

Another agency empowered to investigate environmental crimes is the Environmental Protection Agency, which was given full law enforcement authority in 1988. The EPA has successfully prosecuted significant violations across all major environmental statutes, including data fraud cases (for instance, private laboratories submitting false environmental data to state and federal environmental agencies); indiscriminate hazardous waste dumping that resulted in serious injuries and death; industry-wide ocean dumping by cruise ships; oil spills that caused significant damage to waterways, wetlands, and beaches; international smuggling of CFC refrigerants that damage the ozone layer and increase skin cancer risk; and illegal handling of hazardous substances such as pesticides and asbestos that exposed children, the poor, and other especially vulnerable groups to potentially serious illness.[105] Its Criminal Investigation Division (EPA CID) investigates allegations of criminal wrongdoing prohibited by various environmental statutes. Such investigations involve but are not limited to:

- The illegal disposal of hazardous waste
- The export of hazardous waste without the permission of the receiving country
- The illegal discharge of pollutants to a water of the United States
- The removal and disposal of regulated asbestos-containing materials in a manner inconsistent with the law and regulations
- The illegal importation of certain restricted or regulated chemicals into the United States
- Tampering with a drinking water supply
- Mail fraud
- Wire fraud
- Conspiracy and money laundering relating to environmental criminal activities

If a culprit is identified by the EPA or other agency investigators, they are prosecuted by the Environmental Crime Section (ECS) of the U.S. Justice Department. The prosecutor often gets involved early in an investigation, such as when the investigator swears out a search warrant or when a grand jury's investigative power is needed. Once the necessary evidence is collected, the prosecutor presents the case to the grand jury for indictment. After indictment, the prosecutor guides the case through complex white-collar and environmental law issues and prepares it for trial. Although many cases settle through plea agreements, some do not. From October 1, 1998, through September 30, 2014, ECS prosecutors concluded criminal cases against more than 1,083 individuals and 404 corporate defendants, leading to 774 years of incarceration (903 years with incarceration, halfway house and home detentions) and $825 million in criminal fines and restitution.[106]

In many instances, the same criminal actions may be violations of federal, state, and local laws. In order to conserve resources and improve the efficiency of environmental enforcement efforts, ECS attorneys help assemble environmental crime task forces made up of federal, state, and local personnel. These task forces have successfully identified and handled many environmental crime cases.

## Deterrence vs. Compliance

The prevailing wisdom is that, unlike common-law criminals, white-collar and green-collar criminals are rarely prosecuted and, when convicted, receive relatively light sentences. There have also been charges that efforts to control white-collar and green-collar crime are biased against specific classes and races. Authorities seem to be less diligent when victims are poor or minority group members or when the crimes take place in areas populated largely by minority groups. When Michael Lynch and his associates studied whether petroleum refineries violating environmental laws in black, Latino, and low-income communities receive smaller fines than those refineries in white and affluent communities, they found that violations of the Clean Air Act, the Clean Water Act, and the Resource Conservation and Recovery Act in minority areas received much smaller fines than the same types of violations occurring in white areas ($108,563 compared to $341,590).[107]

What efforts have been made to bring violators of the public trust to justice? White-collar criminal enforcement typically involves two strategies designed to control organizational deviance: compliance and deterrence.[108]

**Compliance strategies** rely on the threat of economic sanctions or civil penalties to control potential violators. They attempt to create a marketplace incentive to obey the law. Under this system, the greater the violation, the larger the economic penalty. Compliance strategies also avoid stigmatizing and shaming businesspeople by focusing on the act, rather than the actor, in white-collar crime.[109] Compliance is regulated by administrative agencies set up to oversee business activity. For example, the Securities and Exchange Commission regulates Wall Street activities, and the Food and Drug Administration regulates drugs, cosmetics, medical devices, meats, and other foods. The legislation creating these agencies usually spells out the penalties for violating regulatory standards. This approach has been used to control environmental crimes by levying heavy fines based on the quantity and dangerousness of the pollution released into the environment.[110]

In contrast, **deterrence strategies** rely on the punishment of individual offenders to deter other would-be violators. Deterrence systems are oriented toward apprehending violators and punishing them, rather than creating conditions that induce conformity to the law. Law enforcement agencies and the courts have traditionally been reluctant to throw corporate executives in jail, but a number of well-publicized cases (such as that of Bernard Madoff) indicate that the gloves are off and the government is willing to punish high-profile white-collar criminals by seeking long prison sentences. Because Madoff and other billion-dollar swindlers have deprived so many people of their life savings and caused such disruptions in the financial markets, both justice system personnel and the general public now consider white-collar crimes as more serious than common-law theft offenses and believe they should be punished accordingly.[111]

Both fines and penalties have been increasing, and long prison sentences are being routinely handed out for white-collar crimes. In fact, deterrence strategies have become so routine—and punishments so severe—that some commentators now argue that the government may actually be going overboard in its efforts to punish white-collar and green-collar criminals, especially for crimes that are the result of negligent business practices rather than intentional criminal conspiracy.[112] Is this a welcome change or an instance of governmental overkill? It depends on one's perspective.

**compliance strategies**
Methods of controlling white-collar crime that rely on the threat of economic sanctions or civil penalties to control potential violators, creating a marketplace incentive to obey the law.

**deterrence strategies**
Methods of controlling white-collar crime that rely on the punishment of individual offenders to deter other would-be violators.

## FACT OR FICTION?

Most white-collar and green-collar criminals get a slap on the wrist if they are convicted of crime.

**FICTION** The recent trend has been to toughen sentences and send offenders to jail.

## CHECKPOINTS

▶ There are numerous explanations for white-collar crime.

▶ Some offenders are motivated by greed; others offend in response to personal problems.

▶ The rationalization view is that white-collar crime enables offenders to meet their financial needs without compromising their values.

▶ Corporate culture theory suggests that some businesses actually encourage employees to cheat or cut corners.

▶ The self-control view is that white-collar criminals are like any other law violators: impulsive people who lack self-control.

▶ Compliance strategies for controlling white-collar crime rely on the threat of civil penalties for violating the law.

▶ Deterrence systems seek to control white-collar crime by threatening to punish individuals with prison sentences.

# Thinking Like a Criminologist

## Who Are the Real Criminals?

You may recall that style guru Martha Stewart was imprisoned as a result of an investigation into an insider-trading scheme. The case caused quite a bit of controversy since Martha did not present a danger to society, and she was not convicted of insider trading but of the charge of lying to federal investigators. As trial attorney Kevin Mahoney put it:

> It is a shameful day. The federal government will imprison a woman for lying to its investigators. Not a lie that stampeded a country into an unnecessary war, that defrauded the country of millions of dollars, or endangered people's lives. The lie was no more than the denial of wrongdoing, a protestation of innocence. Shame on us for permitting our government to terrorize us.

Yet the people who were shocked when décor diva Stewart did time seem to have no problem with imprisoning a lower-class woman who is caught possessing drugs. Even though both crimes have no discernible victim, Martha's white-collar crime seemed like the more trivial offense—or was it?

### Writing Assignment

Write an essay that confronts this critical issue: Is it ethical to imprison nondangerous white-collar criminals to set an example, or should they merely suffer financial penalties? What is the purpose of putting someone like Martha Stewart in prison for a trivial white-collar offense? Is she a danger to society? Is multibillion-dollar swindler Bernard Madoff? Or would it be better, to quote Billy Ray Valentine (Eddie Murphy in the classic 1983 film *Trading Places*), "You know, it occurs to me that the best way you hurt rich people is by turning them into poor people"?

# SUMMARY

**LO1  Discuss the history of theft offenses.**

Common theft offenses include larceny, fraud, and embezzlement. These are common-law crimes, originally defined by English judges. Skilled thieves included pickpockets, forgers, and counterfeiters, who operated freely. Smugglers transported goods, such as spirits, gems, gold, and spices, without paying tax or duty. Poachers supplemented their diet and income with game that belonged to a landlord.

**LO2  Differentiate between professional and amateur thieves.**

Economic crimes are designed to reap financial rewards for the offender. Opportunistic amateurs commit the majority of economic crimes. Economic crime has also attracted professional criminals. Professionals earn most of their income from crime, view themselves as criminals, and possess skills that aid them in their law-breaking behavior. An example of the professional criminal is the fence who buys and sells stolen merchandise.

**LO3  Describe the various forms of shoplifting.**

Some shoplifters are amateurs who steal on the spur of the moment. These snitches are otherwise respectable persons who do not conceive of themselves as thieves but systematically steal merchandise for their own use. Some adolescents become shoplifters because they have been coerced by older kids. Called boosters or heels, professional shoplifters steal with the intention of reselling stolen merchandise to pawnshops or fences, usually at half the original price. Boosters know how to hit stores without being detected and have partners who can unload merchandise after it is stolen.

**LO4  Summarize the various forms of white-collar crime.**

White-collar fraud involves using a business enterprise as a front to swindle people. Chiseling involves professionals who cheat clients. Embezzlement and employee fraud occur when a person uses a position of trust to steal from an organization. Client fraud involves theft from an organization that advances credit, covers losses, or reimburses for services. Corporate, or organizational, crime involves various illegal business practices such as price fixing, restraint of trade, and false advertising.

**L05  Explain what is meant by the term *Ponzi scheme*.**

A Ponzi scheme is an investment fraud that involves the payment of purported returns to existing investors from funds contributed by new investors. In many Ponzi schemes, the fraudsters focus on attracting new money to make promised payments to earlier-stage investors and to use for personal expenses, instead of engaging in any legitimate investment activity. The term comes from one Charles Ponzi, who duped thousands of New England residents into investing in a postage stamp speculation scheme back in the 1920s.

**L06  Discuss efforts to control white-collar and green-collar crime.**

The government has used various law enforcement strategies to combat white-collar and green-collar crime. Some involve deterrence, which uses punishment to frighten potential abusers. Others involve economic or compliance strategies, which create economic incentives to obey the law. Most offenders do not view themselves as criminals and therefore do not seem to be deterred by criminal statutes. Although thousands of white-collar criminals are prosecuted each year, their numbers are insignificant compared with the magnitude of the problem. The Commerce Clause of the U.S. Constitution gives the federal government the authority to regulate business-related crime. Detection and enforcement are primarily in the hands of administrative departments and agencies, including the FBI, the Internal Revenue Service, the Secret Service, U.S. Customs, the Environmental Protection Agency, and the Securities and Exchange Commission. On the state and local levels, law enforcement officials have made progress in a number of areas, such as controlling consumer fraud and environmental pollution.

## Key Terms

economic crime  380
blue-collar crimes  380
white-collar crimes  380
green-collar crimes  380
theft  380
occasional criminals  381
situational
    inducement  381
professional
    criminals  381

larceny  382
constructive
    possession  382
petit (petty) larceny  382
grand larceny  382
shoplifting  382
snitch  383
booster (heel)  383
merchant privilege
    laws  383

naive check forgers  384
systematic forgers  384
fence  385
burglary  385
arson  386
chiseling  389
insider trading  389
exploitation  390
influence peddling  390
embezzlement  391

corporate (organiza-
    tional) crime  393
Sherman Antitrust
    Act  394
price fixing  394
criminal environmental
    pollution  400
compliance
    strategies  405
deterrence strategies  405

## Critical Thinking Questions

**1.** Differentiate between an occasional and a professional criminal. Which one would be more likely to resort to violence?

**2.** What crime occurs when a person who owns an antiques store sells a client an "original" Tiffany lamp that she knows is a fake? Would it still be a crime if the seller were not aware that the lamp was a copy?

Should antiques dealers have a duty to determine the authenticity of the products they sell?

**3.** What is the difference between a booster and a snitch? If caught, should they receive different punishments? What about naive and systematic check forgers?

**4.** What are the characteristics of the "good burglar"? Can you compare them to any other professionals?

# Notes

*All URLs accessed in 2015.*

1. FBI, "The Fraudster Who Faked His Own Death: Inside the Aubrey Lee Price Case," December 18, 2014, www.fbi.gov/news/stories/2014/december/the-fraudster-who-faked-his-own-death-inside-the-aubrey-lee-price-case/; Arielle Kass and J. Scott Trubey, "'Dead' Banker Aubrey Lee Price Sentenced to 70 Years," *Atlanta Journal-Constitution*, October 27, 2014, www.ajc.com/news/business/dead-banker-aubrey-lee-price-scheduled-for-sentenc/nhsXH/.

2. Code of Hammurabi, www.commonlaw.com/Hammurabi.html.

3. Garrett Fagan, *Bathing in Public in the Roman World* (Ann Arbor: University of Michigan Press, 1999).

4. J. J. Tobias, *Crime and Police in England, 1700–1900* (London: Gill and Macmillan, 1979).

5. Ibid., p. 9.

6. John Locker and Barry Godfrey, "Ontological Boundaries and Temporal Watersheds in the Development of White-Collar Crime," *British Journal of Criminology* 46 (2006): 976–999.

7. Edward Alsworth Ross, *Sin and Society: An Analysis of Latter-Day Iniquity* (Boston: Houghton Mifflin, 1907), pp. 45–71.

8. Edwin Sutherland, *White-Collar Crime: The Uncut Version* (New Haven, CT: Yale University Press, 1983).

9. Edwin Sutherland, "White-Collar Criminality," *American Sociological Review* 5 (1940): 2–10.

10. This section depends heavily on a classic book: Wayne LaFave and Austin Scott, *Handbook on Criminal Law* (St. Paul, MN: West, 1972).

11. Ibid., p. 622.

12. FBI, "Larceny-Theft," *Crime in the United States, 2013,* www.fbi.gov/about-us/cjis/ucr/crime-in-the-u.s/2013/crime-in-the-u.s.-2013/property-crime/larceny-theft-topic-page.

13. Jennifer Truman and Lynn Langton, "Criminal Victimization, 2013," Bureau of Justice Statistics, *2014,* bjs.ojp.usdoj.gov/content/pub/pdf/cv13.pdf.

14. Jack L. Hayes, "Annual Retail Theft Survey, 2014," hayesinternational.com/wp-content/uploads/2014/06/26th-Annual-Retail-Theft-Survey-Hayes-International-Thoughts-Behind-Numbers.pdf.

15. Mary Owen Cameron, *The Booster and the Snitch* (New York: Free Press, 1964).

16. Janne Kivivuori, "Crime by Proxy: Coercion and Altruism in Adolescent Shoplifting," *British Journal of Criminology* 47 (2007): 817–833.

17. FBI, "Organized Retail Theft: A $30 Billion-a-Year Industry," www.fbi.gov/news/stories/2011/january/retail_010311.

18. Brian T. Smith and Ronald V. Clarke, "Shoplifting of Everyday Products that Serve Illicit Drug Uses," *Journal of Research in Crime and Delinquency*, first published online September 11, 2014.

19. Gail A. Caputo and Anna King, "Shoplifting by Male and Female Drug Users: Gender, Agency, and Work," *Criminal Justice Review* 40 (2015): 47–66.

20. Jennifer Conlin, "Credit Card Fraud Keeps Growing on the Net," *New York Times*, May 11, 2007, www.nytimes.com/2007/05/11/your-money/11iht-mcredit.1.5664687.html.

21. LaFave and Scott, *Handbook on Criminal Law*, p. 672.

22. Charles McCaghy, Peggy Giordano, and Trudy Knicely Henson, "Auto Theft," *Criminology* 15 (1977): 367–381.

23. "Hot Cars: Parts Crooks Love Best," *BusinessWeek,* September 15, 2003, p. 104.

24. Edwin Lemert, "An Isolation and Closure Theory of Naive Check Forgery," *Journal of Criminal Law, Criminology and Police Science* 44 (1953): 297–298.

25. Carl Klockars, *The Professional Fence* (New York: Free Press, 1976); Darrell Steffensmeier, *The Fence: In the Shadow of Two Worlds* (Totowa, NJ: Rowman and Littlefield, 1986).

26. William Blackstone, *Commentaries on the Laws of England* (London: Clarendon Press, 1769), p. 224.

27. FBI, "Burglary," *Crime in the United States, 2013,* www.fbi.gov/about-us/cjis/ucr/crime-in-the-u.s/2013/crime-in-the-u.s.-2013/property-crime/burglary-topic-page.

28. Lynn A. Addington and Callie Marie Rennison, "Keeping the Barbarians Outside the Gate? Comparing Burglary Victimization in Gated and Non-Gated Communities" *Justice Quarterly* 32 (2015): 168–192.

29. Christophe Vandeviver, Stijn Van Daele, and Tom Vander Beken, "What Makes Long Crime Trips Worth Undertaking? Balancing Costs and Benefits in Burglars' Journey to Crime," *British Journal of Criminology* 55 (2014): 399–420.

30. Nick Tilley, Rebecca Thompson, Graham Farrell, Louise Grove, and Andromachi Tseloni, "Do Burglar Alarms Increase Burglary Risk? A Counter-Intuitive Finding and Possible Explanations," *Crime Prevention and Community Safety* 17 (2015): 1–19.

31. Neal Shover, "Structures and Careers in Burglary," *Journal of Criminal Law, Criminology and Police Science* 63 (1972): 540–549.

32. Nancy Webb, George Sakheim, Luz Towns-Miranda, and Charles Wagner, "Collaborative Treatment of Juvenile Firestarters: Assessment and Outreach," *American Journal of Orthopsychiatry* 60 (1990): 305–310.

33. Pekka Santtila, Helina Haikkanen, Laurence Alison, and Carrie Whyte, "Juvenile Firesetters: Crime Scene Actions and Offender Characteristics," *Legal and Criminological Psychology* 8 (2003): 1–20.

34. John Taylor, Ian Thorne, Alison Robertson, and Ginny Avery, "Evaluation of a Group Intervention for Convicted Arsonists with Mild and Borderline Intellectual Disabilities," *Criminal Behaviour and Mental Health* 12 (2002): 282–294.

35. Rodney Huff, Christian Desilets, and John Kane, "2010 National Public Survey on White Collar Crime," www.nw3c.org/docs/publications/2010-national-public-survey-on-white-collar-crime.pdf.

36. Ibid.

37. Ibid.

38. Natalie Taylor, "Under-Reporting of Crime Against Small Business: Attitudes Towards Police and Reporting Practices," *Policing and Society* 13 (2003): 79–90.

39. This structure is based on an analysis contained in Mark Moore, "Notes Toward a National Strategy to Deal with White-Collar Crime," in *A National Strategy for Containing White-Collar Crime*, ed. Herbert Edelhertz and Charles Rogovin (Lexington, MA: Lexington Books, 1980), pp. 32–44.

40. Securities and Exchange Commission, "Ponzi Schemes," www.sec.gov/answers/ponzi.htm#PonziCollapse.

41. Joel Grover and Matt Goldberg, "Jiffy Lube Reacts to Hidden Camera Report," NBC LA News, October 17, 2008, www.nbclosangeles.com/Jiffy_Lube_Reacts_to_Hidden_Camera_Report.html. See also Channel 6 News, "Buried Secret: Quick Lube Chain Cheats Customers: Customers Pay Premium for Low-Priced Oil," November 1, 2007, www.theindychannel.com/news/buried-secret-quick-lube-chain-cheats-customers.

42. Richard Quinney, "Occupational Structure and Criminal Behavior: Prescription Violation of Retail Pharmacists," *Social Problems* 11 (1963): 179–185. See also John Braithwaite, *Corporate Crime in the Pharmaceutical Industry* (London: Routledge and Kegan Paul, 1984).

43. Pam Belluck, "Prosecutors Say Greed Drove Pharmacist to Dilute Drugs," *New York Times*, August 18, 2001, p. 3.

44. FBI press release, April 22, 2002, Kansas City Division.

45. James Armstrong et al., "Securities Fraud," *American Criminal Law Review* 33 (1995): 973–1016.

46. *Carpenter v. United States* 484 U.S. 19 (1987). See also John Boland, "The SEC Trims the First Amendment," *Wall Street Journal*, December 4, 1986, p. 28.

47. FBI, "Distressed Homeowner Initiative: Don't Let Mortgage Fraud Happen to You," October 9, 2012, www.fbi.gov/news/stories/2012/october/dont-let-mortgage-fraud-happen-to-you/.

48. U.S. Department of Justice, "U.S. Charges Bolingbrook, Illinois Man with Bribery in Connection with Army Corps of Engineers Contract in Iraq," May 4, 2009, www.fbi.gov/chicago/press-releases/2009/cg050409.htm.

49. CNN, "Officer Charged with Demanding Sex for Green Card," March 21, 2008, www.cnn.com/2008/CRIME/03/21/immigration.officer/.

50. Charles V. Bagli, "Kickback Investigation Extends to Middle-Class Buildings in New York," *New York Times*, October 14, 1998, p. A19.

51. FBI, "A (Driver's) License to Steal: Corruption in a San Diego Motor Vehicle Office," February 25, 2014, www.fbi.gov/news/stories/2014/february/corruption-in-a-san-diego-motor-vehicle-office/corruption-in-a-san-diego-motor-vehicle-office.

52. FBI, "Cheating in Contracts: A $30 Million Case of Corruption," July 19, 2013, www.fbi.gov/news/stories/2013/july/a-30-million-case-of-corruption/a-30-million-case-of-corruption.

53. MSNBC, "Pa. Judges Accused of Jailing Kids for Cash: Judges Allegedly Took $2.6 Million in Payoffs to Put Juveniles in Lockups," February 11, 2009, www.nbcnews.com/id/29142654/ns/us_news-crime_and_courts/t/pa-judges-accused-jailing-kids-cash/.

54. Henry Blodget, "Apple Manager Paul Shin Devine Busted in $1 Million Kickback Scheme," *Business Insider*, August 15, 2010, www.businessinsider.com/apple-manager-paul-shin-devine-busted-in-1-million-kickback-scheme-2010-8.

55. Marshall Clinard and Peter Yeager, *Corporate Crime* (New York: Free Press, 1980), p. 67.

56. Alina Selyukh, "U.S. Judge Approves IBM's Foreign Bribery Case Settlement with SEC," Reuters, July 25, 2013, www.reuters.com/article/2013/07/25/us-ibm-sec-idUSBRE96O1FB20130725.

57. PL No. 95-213, 101-104, 91 Stat. 1494.

58. J. Sorenson, H. Grove, and T. Sorenson, "Detecting Management Fraud: The Role of the Independent Auditor," in *White-Collar Crime, Theory and Research*, ed. G. Geis and E. Stotland (Beverly Hills, CA: Sage, 1980), pp. 221–251.

59. To learn more about fraud in the United States and abroad, go to the StopFraud.gov website, www.stopfraud.gov.

60. U.S. Attorney's Office, District of Columbia, "More Than 20 People Arrested Following Investigations into Widespread Health Care Fraud in D.C. Medicaid Program," February 20, 2014, www.fbi.gov/washingtondc/press-releases/2014/more-than-20-people-arrested-following-investigations-into-widespread-health-care-fraud-in-d.c.-medicaid-program.

61. FBI, "Rooting Out Health Care Fraud Is Central to the Well-Being of Both Our Citizens and the Overall Economy," www.fbi.gov/about-us/investigate/white_collar/health-care-fraud.

62. National Health Care Anti-Fraud Association, "The Challenge of Health Care Fraud," 2014, www.nhcaa .org/resources/health-care-anti-fraud-resources /the-challenge-of-health-care-fraud.aspx.

63. 42 USC 1320a-7b(b); 42 USC 1320a-7b(b)(3); 42 CFR 1001.952 (regulatory safe harbors); 42 USC 1395nn (codifying "Stark I" and "Stark II" statutes).

64. *United States v. Bishop*, 412 U.S. 346 (1973).

65. Kylie Cooper and Adrienne Dedjinou, "Antitrust Violations," *American Criminal Law Review* 42 (2005): 179–221.

66. 15 U.S.C. section 1 (1994).

67. 15 U.S.C. 1–7 (1976).

68. *Northern Pacific Railways v. United States*, 356 U.S. 1 (1958).

69. U.S. Department of Justice, "Nine Automobile Parts Manufacturers and Two Executives Agree to Plead Guilty to Fixing Prices on Automobile Parts Sold to U.S. Car Manufacturers and Installed in U.S. Cars: Companies Agree to Pay Total of More than $740 Million in Criminal Fines," September 26, 2013, www.fbi.gov /news/pressrel/press-releases/nine-automobile-parts -manufacturers-and-two-executives-agree-to-plead -guilty-to-fixing-prices-on-automobile-parts-sold-to -u.s.-car-manufacturers-and-installed-in-u.s.-cars.

70. Tim Carrington, "Federal Probes of Contractors Rise for Year," *Wall Street Journal*, February 23, 1987, p. 50.

71. Thomas Catan and Guy Chazan, "Spill Draws Criminal Probe," *Wall Street Journal*, June 2, 2010, online.wsj .com/article/SB100014240527487048756045752809 83140254458.html; Environmental Protection Agency press release, "Exxon to Pay Record One Billion Dollars in Criminal Fines and Civil Damages in Connection with Alaskan Oil Spill," March 13, 1991, www2 .epa.gov/aboutepa/exxon-pay-record-one-billion -dollars-criminal-fines-and-civil-damages-connection -alaskan; Tyson Slocum, "BP: The Worst Safety and Environmental Record of All Oil Companies Operating in the United States," *Monthly Review*, mrzine.month- lyreview.org/2010/slocum060510.html.

72. Helene Cooper and Peter Baker, "U.S. Opens Criminal Inquiry into Oil Spill," *New York Times*, June 1, 2010, www.nytimes.com/2010/06/02/us/02spill.html.

73. Alternative Fines Act, 18 U.S.C. § 3571(d).

74. 15 U.S.C. §§ 78dd-2(g)(3), 78dd-3(e)(3), 78ff(c)(3).

75. Terry Wade and Kristen Hays, "BP Reaches $18.7 Billion Settlement over Deadly 2010 Spill," Reuters, July 2, 2015, www.reuters.com/article/2015/07/02/us-bp -gulfmexico-settlement-idUSKCN0PC1BW20150702.

76. Michael J. Lynch and Paul Stretesky, "Green Criminology in the United States," in *Issues in Green Criminology*, ed. Piers Beirne and Nigel South (Portland, OR: Willan, 2008), pp. 248–269, at 249.

77. Michael M. O'Hear, "Sentencing the Green-Collar Offender: Punishment, Culpability, and Environmental

Crime," *Journal of Criminal Law and Criminology* 95 (2004): 133–276.

78. F. J. W. Herbig and S. J. Joubert, "Criminological Semantics: Conservation Criminology—Vision or Vagary? *Acta Criminologica* 19 (2006): 88–103.

79. Rob White, "Researching Transnational Environmental Harm: Toward an Eco-Global Criminology," *International Journal of Comparative and Applied Criminal Justice* 33 (2009): 229–248.

80. Paddy Hillyard, Christina Pantazis, Dave Gordon, and Steve Tombs, *Beyond Criminology: Taking Harm Seriously* (London: Pluto Press, 2004).

81. This section relies on Duncan Brack, *Illegal Logging* (London: Chatham House, 2007), www.illegal-logging .info/uploads/1_Illegal_logging_bp_07_01.pdf.

82. Ibid.

83. This section leans heavily on Liana Sun Wyler and Pervaze A. Sheikh, *International Illegal Trade in Wildlife: Threats and U.S. Policy* (Washington, DC: Congressional Research Service, 2008), fpc.state.gov/documents /organization/110404.pdf.

84. White, "Researching Transnational Environmental Harm: Toward an Eco-Global Criminology."

85. For more information, go to the World Wildlife Fund, www.worldwildlife.org/.

86. The Lacey Act, 16 U.S.C. §§ 3371–3378.

87. National Oceanic and Atmospheric Administration, "Endangered and Threatened Marine Species Under NMFS' Jurisdiction," www.nmfs.noaa.gov/pr /species/esa/listed.htm#fish; U. R. Sumaila, J. Alder, and H. Keith, "Global Scope and Economics of Illegal Fishing," *Marine Policy* 30 (2006): 696–703.

88. Carole Gibbs, Edmund F. McGarrell, and Mark Axelrod, "Transnational White-Collar Crime and Risk: Lessons from the Global Trade in Electronic Waste," *Criminology and Public Policy* 9 (2010): 543–560.

89. Andrew Oliveira, Christopher Schenck, Christopher Cole, and Nicole Janes, "Environmental Crimes (Annual Survey of White-Collar Crime)," *American Criminal Law Review* 42 (2005): 347–380.

90. Belluck, "Prosecutors Say Greed Drove Pharmacist to Dilute Drugs," p. 3.

91. See also Neal Shover and Andrew Hochstetler, *Choosing White-Collar Crime* (Cambridge, England: Cambridge University Press, 2006).

92. Neal Shover and Peter Grabosky, "White-Collar Crime and the Great Recession," *Criminology and Public Policy* 9 (2010): 429–433.

93. Quoted in Tim Metz and Michael Miller, "Boesky's Rise and Fall Illustrate a Compulsion to Profit by Getting Inside Track on Market," *Wall Street Journal*, November 17, 1986, p. 28.

94. Mandeep Dhami, "White-Collar Prisoners' Perceptions of Audience Reaction," *Deviant Behavior* 28 (2007): 57–77.

95. Donald Cressey, *Other People's Money: A Study of the Social Psychology of Embezzlement* (Glencoe, IL: Free Press, 1973), p. 96.

96. Nicole Leeper Piquero, Stephen Tibbetts, and Michael Blankenship, "Examining the Role of Differential Association and Techniques of Neutralization in Explaining Corporate Crime," *Deviant Behavior* 26 (2005): 159–188.

97. Travis Hirschi and Michael Gottfredson, "Causes of White-Collar Crime," *Criminology* 25 (1987): 949–974.

98. Michael Gottfredson and Travis Hirschi, *A General Theory of Crime* (Stanford, CA: Stanford University Press, 1990), p. 191.

99. This section relies heavily on Daniel Skoler, "White-Collar Crime and the Criminal Justice System: Problems and Challenges," in *A National Strategy for Containing White-Collar Crime*, ed. Edelhertz and Rogovin, pp. 57–76.

100. *United States Attorneys' Bulletin, Environmental Crimes, 2011,* www.justice.gov/usao/eousa/foia_reading_room/usab5904.pdf.

101. Ronald Burns, Keith Whitworth, and Carol Thompson, "Assessing Law Enforcement Preparedness to Address Internet Fraud," *Journal of Criminal Justice* 32 (2004): 477–493.

102. Michael Benson, Francis Cullen, and William Maakestad, "Local Prosecutors and Corporate Crime," *Crime and Delinquency* 36 (1990): 356–372.

103. Ibid., pp. 369–370.

104. U.S. Fish & Wildlife Service, "About Service Special Agents," www.fws.gov/le/special-agents.html.

105. Environmental Protection Agency, Criminal Investigation Division, www.epa.gov/region9/enforcement/cid/.

106. U.S. Department of Justice, Environmental Crimes Section, www.justice.gov/enrd/environmental-crimes-section.

107. Michael Lynch, Paul Stretesky, and Ronald Burns, "Slippery Business," *Journal of Black Studies* 34 (2004): 421–440.

108. This section relies heavily on Albert Reiss Jr., "Selecting Strategies of Social Control over Organizational Life," in *Enforcing Regulation*, ed. Keith Hawkins and John M. Thomas (Boston: Kluwer, 1984), pp. 25–37.

109. Michael Benson, "Emotions and Adjudication: Stat Degradation Among White-Collar Criminals," *Justice Quarterly* 7 (1990): 515–528; John Braithwaite, *Crime, Shame, and Reintegration* (Sydney, Australia: Cambridge University Press, 1989).

110. John Braithwaite, "The Limits of Economism in Controlling Harmful Corporate Conduct," *Law and Society Review* 16 (1981–1982): 481–504.

111. Sean Rosenmerkel, "Wrongfulness and Harmfulness as Components of Seriousness of White-Collar Offenses," *Journal of Contemporary Criminal Justice* 17 (2001): 308–328.

112. Kris Dighe and Lana Pettus, "Environmental Justice in the Context of Environmental Crimes," *United States Attorneys' Bulletin, Environmental Crimes, 2011,* www.justice.gov/usao/eousa/foia_reading_room/usab5904.pdf.

# Public Order Crimes

AP Images/Cliff McBride

## Learning Objectives

**LO1** Interpret what is meant by the term *social harm*.

**LO2** Discuss the activities of moral crusaders.

**LO3** Describe the various forms of outlawed deviant sexuality.

**LO4** Distinguish among the different types of prostitutes.

**LO5** State the arguments for and against legalizing prostitution.

**LO6** Discuss the causes of substance abuse.

Sex traffickers have online access.
Don't let them access and recruit your kids

# Chapter Outline

## FACT OR FICTION?

▶ Prostitution should be legalized because it is a victimless crime and many prostitutes make a substantial amount of money.

▶ Fewer kids are drinking today than 20 years ago.

In 2012, a mother contacted the Michigan State Police and reported that James Alfred Beckman had sexually abused her young child. The youngster told his mother that during the abuse, a computer and webcam had been present.

After interviewing the child, Michigan State Police (MSP) investigators interviewed Beckman and performed forensic exams on his computer that turned up not only photos of child pornography but also evidence of a network of individuals trafficking in child pornography. Working with the FBI, since the conspiracy crossed state lines, the MSP obtained evidence of online chats that Beckman had with others in his child pornography network. During many of the chats, Beckman was soliciting individuals who were conducting sexual acts with children, usually encouraging conversations about these activities and exchanging pornographic images and videos. Beckman was arrested and charged with multiple counts of attempted sexual exploitation of a child, attempted coercion of a child, and receipt and distribution of child pornography.

Evidence presented at trial showed that Beckman sexually abused and exploited two young children, and that he streamed and attempted to stream live video of this abuse and exploitation to others. Because he streamed his child pornography via webcam, there were no actual images or videos to enter as evidence, but people Beckman streamed to testified against him in court. Beckman was convicted and sentenced to 30 years in prison; others have been indicted and sentenced in the case for receiving child pornography.[1] ■

Societies have long banned or limited behaviors believed to run contrary to social norms, customs, and values. These behaviors are often referred to as **public order crimes** and are sometimes called victimless crimes, although as the Beckman case aptly shows, the latter term can be misleading.[2] Public order crimes involve acts that interfere with the operations of society and the ability of people to function efficiently. Whereas common-law crimes such as rape and robbery are banned because they cause social harm to a victim, other behaviors, such as prostitution and pornography, are outlawed because they conflict with social policy, prevailing moral rules, and current public opinion.

Statutes designed to uphold public order usually prohibit the manufacture and distribution of morally tinged goods and services such as erotic material, commercial sex, and mood-altering drugs. Prohibition of these acts can be controversial because they selectively criminalize desired goods or services. By outlawing sin and vice, they turn millions of otherwise law-abiding citizens into law violators. On the other hand, as the Beckman case shows, these acts may bring terrible harm and victimize people who are forced to participate without consent or free will.

This chapter covers these public order crimes. It first briefly discusses the relationship between law and morality. Next, it addresses public order crimes of a sexual nature: prostitution, pornography, and deviant sex acts called paraphilias. The chapter concludes by focusing on the abuse of drugs and alcohol.

## Law and Morality

In 2011, rising political star Anthony Weiner was forced to resign from office after compromising photos he "tweeted" to young women were posted online. At first, Weiner denied responsibility, telling the media that his account had been hacked and/or that the picture had possibly been altered. On June 6, 2011, Weiner admitted that he had sent sexually explicit text messages and photographs to several women, both before and after he had gotten married.[3] When Weiner tried a political comeback in 2013, his campaign for mayor of New York City came to an abrupt halt when the media found out that he had sent other women even more explicit photos of himself using the alias "Carlos Danger."

Did Weiner's behavior actually cause public harm? After all, he never actually met any of the women with whom he carried on a cyber-relationship. All his victims had to do was disconnect or delete his texts, tweets, and emails. Unlike James Alfred Beckman, Weiner never hurt anyone, or did he? Were the women receiving his tweets harmed?

While some may view Weiner's behavior as odd yet essentially harmless, others considered his "sexting" as immoral and unworthy of a public figure. After all, it is a crime to expose oneself in public (indecent exposure), behavior that is punishable by a fine or jail term. If it is a crime in a public park, why not on the Internet? Was Weiner's sexting grossly immoral or merely an example of those harmless human quirks and eccentricities we all possess in some measure?

The debate over morality has existed for all of recorded history. The line between behavior considered merely immoral and that which is considered criminal is often a fine one, but the consequences of crossing that line can be significant. As the Bible (Genesis 18:20) tells us, despite Abraham's intervention, God destroyed the "Cities of the Plain" because, "The outcry against Sodom and Gomorrah is so great and their sin so grievous."[4] What was the sin that God felt deserved such drastic punishment? According to modern Bible scholars, despite having exhibited pride, excess of food, and prosperous ease, their citizens did not aid the poor and needy.[5]

Today, acts that most of us deem highly immoral are not necessarily criminal. There are no laws banning *superbia* (hubris/pride), *avaritia* (avarice/greed), *luxuria* (extravagance or lust), *invidia* (envy), *gula* (gluttony), *ira* (wrath), and *acedia* (sloth), even though they are considered the "seven deadly sins." Nor is it a crime for a private citizen to ignore the pleas of a drowning child, even though to do so might be considered callous, coldhearted, and unfeeling.

Conversely, some acts that seem both well intentioned and moral are nonetheless considered criminal:

- It is a crime (euthanasia) to kill a loved one who is suffering from an incurable disease to spare him or her further pain; attempting to take your own life (attempted suicide) is also a crime.
- Stealing a rich person's money in order to feed a poor family is still considered larceny.
- Marrying more than one woman is considered a crime (bigamy), even though multiple marriages may conform to some groups' religious beliefs.[6]

As legal experts Wayne LaFave and Austin Scott Jr., put it, "A good motive will not normally prevent what is otherwise criminal from being a crime."[7]

## Are Victimless Crimes Victimless?

To answer this question, we might first consider whether there is actually a victim in so-called **victimless crimes**. Some participants may have been coerced into their acts, such as the children abused by James Alfred Beckman; if so, then they are victims. Opponents of pornography, such as Andrea Dworkin, charge that women involved in adult films, far from being highly paid stars, are "dehumanized—turned into objects and commodities."[8] Although taking drugs may be a matter of personal choice, it too has serious consequences. One study of crack cocaine–using women found that more than half had suffered a physical attack, one-third had been raped, and more than half had had to seek medical care for their injuries.[9] It has been estimated that women involved in street prostitution are 60 to 100 times more likely to be murdered than the average woman and that most of these murders result from a dispute over money rather than being sexually motivated.[10]

Some scholars argue that pornography, prostitution, and drug use erode the moral fabric of society and therefore should be prohibited and punished. They are crimes, according to the great legal scholar Morris Cohen, because "it is one of the functions of the criminal law to give expression to the collective feeling of revulsion toward certain acts, even when they are not very dangerous."[11]

According to this view, so-called victimless crimes are prohibited because one of the functions of criminal law is to express a shared sense of public morality.[12] However, basing criminal definitions on moral beliefs is often an impossible task. Who defines morality? Are we not punishing mere differences rather than social harm? As Supreme Court Justice William O. Douglas so succinctly put it, "What may be trash to me may be prized by others."[13] Would not any attempt to control or limit "objectionable" material eventually lead to the suppression of free speech and political dissent? Is this not a veiled form of censorship?

Research indicates that people who define themselves as liberals are also the most tolerant of sexually explicit material. Demographic attributes such as age, educational attainment, and occupational status may also influence views of pornography: the young and better educated tend to be more tolerant than older, less-educated people.[14] Whose views should prevail? If a majority of the population chooses to engage in what might objectively be considered immoral or deviant behavior, would it be fair or just to prohibit or control such behavior or render it criminal? While it's difficult to measure or calculate the visits to porn sites on the Internet, according to Google's DoubleClick Ad Planner, which uses cookies to track users across the Web, dozens of adult destinations populate the top 500 websites; the largest gets 4.4 billion page views per month, three times the size of CNN or ESPN.[15] However, the true extent of Internet porn is still a mystery, with guesstimates ranging from 3 to 30 percent of all Internet traffic. Even if the lowest estimates are correct it still means an awful lot of people are using Internet porn on a regular basis.[16]

**victimless crime**
Public order crime that violates the moral order but has no specific victim other than society as a whole.

## FACT OR FICTION?

Prostitution should be legalized because it is a victimless crime and many prostitutes make a substantial amount of money.

**FICTION** Although they may be glamorized in films like *Pretty Woman*, most prostitutes can be viewed as victims likely to suffer coercion, rape, and physical attacks.

Considering its popularity, should all obscenity and pornography be legalized, no matter the content and participants? And if a small segment of society tried to define or limit objectionable material, might it not eventually inhibit free speech and political dissent? Not so, according to social commentator Irving Kristol:

> If we start censoring pornography and obscenity, shall we not inevitably end up censoring political opinion? A lot of people seem to think this would be the case—which only shows the power of doctrinaire thinking over reality. We had censorship of pornography and obscenity for 150 years, until almost yesterday, and I am not aware that freedom of opinion in this country was in any way diminished as a consequence of this fact.[17]

Cultural clashes may ensue when behavior that is considered normative in one society is deplored by those living in another. Take for instance the practice of female genital mutilation, which has been performed on more than 100 million of the world's females; there are millions of girls who still suffer the procedure each year.[18] Custom and tradition are by far the most frequently cited reasons for mutilation, and it is often carried out in a ritual during which the young woman is initiated into adulthood. The surgery is done to ensure virginity, remove sexual sensation, and render the females suitable for marriage; a girl in these societies cannot be considered an adult unless she has undergone genital mutilation. Critics of this practice, led by American author Alice Walker (*The Color Purple*), consider the procedure mutilation and torture; others argue that this ancient custom should be left to the discretion of the indigenous people who consider it part of their culture. "Torture," counters Walker, "is not culture." Can an outsider define the morality of another culture?[19] Amnesty International and the United Nations have worked to end the practice. Because of outside pressure, the procedure is now forbidden in Senegal, Egypt, Guinea, and Togo, among other countries. However, it is growing in Western nations because immigrants continue the practice.

## The Theory of Social Harm

**LO1** Interpret what is meant by the term *social harm*.

There is little disagreement that the purpose of criminal law is to protect society and reduce social harm. When a store is robbed or a child assaulted, it is relatively easy to see and condemn the harm done to the victim. It is, however, more difficult to identify the victims of immoral acts, such as pornography or prostitution, where the parties involved may be willing participants. Some men and women who work for high-paid adult escort services earn more in a few days than a waitress or kindergarten teacher earns in a year. Can we consider high-paid escorts who dispense sexual favors "crime victims"? People who employ sex workers may be wealthy and powerful people who freely and voluntarily spend their money for sexual services; certainly they are not victims either. If there is no victim, can there be a crime? Should acts be made illegal merely because they violate prevailing moral standards? And if so, who defines morality?

**social harm**
The injury caused to others by willful wrongful conduct

According to the theory of **social harm**, immoral acts can be distinguished from crimes on the basis of the injury they cause. Acts that cause harm or injury are outlawed and punished as crimes; acts, even those that are vulgar, offensive, and depraved, are not outlawed or punished if they harm no one.

The theory of social harm can explain most criminal acts, but not all of them. Some acts that cause enormous amounts of social harm are perfectly legal, whereas others that many people consider virtually harmless are outlawed and severely punished. It is now estimated that more than 500,000 deaths in the United States each year can be linked to the consumption of tobacco and alcohol, yet these "deadly substances" remain legal to produce and sell. Similarly, sports cars and motorcycles that can accelerate to more than 150 miles per hour are perfectly legal to sell and possess, even though more than 30,000 people die each year in car accidents. On the other hand, using marijuana is not only nonfatal but is sold for medical purposes in some states and has been decriminalized in others such as Colorado. Yet the sale of marijuana is still banned both by the federal government and most state jurisdictions and punished with a prison sentence.[20] According to the theory of social harm, if more people die each year from alcohol, tobacco, and automobile-related causes, whereas smoking pot is relatively safe, then marijuana should be legalized and Corvettes, scotch, and Marlboros outlawed. But they are not.

## Moral Crusaders and Moral Crusades

Public order crimes often trace their origin to moral crusaders who seek to shape the law to reflect their own way of thinking; Howard Becker calls them **moral entrepreneurs**. These rule creators, argues Becker, operate with an absolute certainty that their way is right and that they are justified in employing any means to get their way: "The crusader is fervent and righteous, often self-righteous."[21] Today's moral crusaders take on such issues as prayer in school, gun ownership, same-sex marriage, abortion, and the distribution of sexually explicit books and magazines.

While some moral crusades are in fact aimed at curbing behavior that most of us find objectionable—for instance, animal cruelty or drunk driving—they can also create controversy when they are directed at behaviors engaged in by the majority of citizens. One popular focus for moral crusaders is anti-smut campaigns that target books considered too "racy" or controversial to be suitable for a public school library. According to the American Library Association, between 2000 and 2009, the *Harry Potter* series topped the yearly list of books challenged by critics who demanded their removal from school library shelves on charges they promoted Satanism and witchcraft. This past year, books such as *The Perks of Being a Wallflower*, by Stephen Chbosky, and *The Pillars of the Earth*, by Ken Follett, were pulled from libraries.[22] These are the top books banned or challenged in the last decade:

1. *Harry Potter* series, by J. K. Rowling
2. *Alice* series, by Phyllis Reynolds Naylor
3. *The Chocolate War*, by Robert Cormier
4. *And Tango Makes Three*, by Justin Richardson/Peter Parnell
5. *Of Mice and Men*, by John Steinbeck
6. *I Know Why the Caged Bird Sings*, by Maya Angelou

Should librarians accede to the demands of a vocal minority or to the will of the majority?

**THE SAME-SEX MARRIAGE CRUSADE** One of the most heated moral crusades of this century has focused on marriage equality. One group of crusaders was determined to prevent the legalization of same-sex marriage; its objective was passage of an amendment to the U.S. Constitution declaring that marriage is between one man and one woman. The Defense of Marriage Act, which was passed in 1996 and defined marriage, for the purposes of federal law, as a union of one man and one woman, was one of this group's legal achievements.[23]

Opposing them were activists who tirelessly campaigned for the civil rights of gay men and women. One of their most important victories occurred in 2003 when the Supreme Court delivered, in *Lawrence v. Texas*, a historic decision that made it impermissible for states to criminalize oral and anal sex (and all other forms of intercourse that are not conventionally heterosexual) under statutes prohibiting sodomy, deviant sexuality, or what used to be referred to as "buggery."[24] The *Lawrence* case involved two gay men who had been arrested in 1998 for having sex in the privacy of their Houston home. In overturning their convictions, the Court said this:

> Although the laws involved here do not more than prohibit a particular sexual act, their penalties and purposes have more far-reaching consequences, touching upon the most private human conduct, sexual behavior, and in the most private of places, the home. They seek to control a personal relationship that, whether or not entitled to formal recognition in the law, is within the liberty of persons to choose without being

**L02** Discuss the activities of moral crusaders.

**moral entrepreneur**
A person who creates moral rules, which thus reflect the values of those in power, rather than any objective, universal standards of right and wrong.

## CONNECTIONS

Moral entrepreneurs are likely to use the interactionist definition of crime discussed in Chapter 1: acts are illegal because they violate the moral standards of those in power and those who try to shape public opinion.

punished as criminals. The liberty protected by the Constitution allows homosexual persons the right to choose to enter upon relationships in the confines of their homes and their own private lives and still retain their dignity as free persons.

As a result of this decision, all sodomy laws in the United States were suddenly unconstitutional and unenforceable; acts that were once a crime were legalized. The *Lawrence* decision paved the way for states to rethink their marriage laws. In 2003, Massachusetts's highest court ruled that same-sex couples are legally entitled to wed under the state constitution and that the state may not "deny the protections, benefits, and obligations conferred by civil marriage to two individuals of the same sex who wish to marry."[25] After a long, drawn-out legal process, the issue of same-sex marriage was resolved in 2015, when the U.S. Supreme Court ruled in *Obergefell v. Hodges* that state-level bans on same-sex marriage are unconstitutional. The Court ruled that the denial of marriage licenses to same-sex couples and the refusal to recognize those marriages performed in other jurisdictions violates the due process and equal protection clauses of the Fourteenth Amendment of the U.S. Constitution.[26]

The same-sex marriage crusade raised a number of important issues: Is it fair to prevent one group of loyal tax-paying citizens from engaging in a behavior that is allowed others? Are there objective standards of morality or should society respect people's differences? After all, opponents of same-sex marriage claim, polygamy is banned, and there are age standards for marriage in every state. If same-sex marriage is legal, what about marriage to multiple partners or with underage minors? How far should the law go in curbing human behaviors that do not cause social harm? Who controls the law and should the law be applied to shape morality?

The public order crimes discussed in this chapter are divided into two broad areas. The first relates to what conventional society considers deviant sexual practices: paraphilias, prostitution, and pornography. The second area concerns the use of substances that have been outlawed or controlled because of the harm they are alleged to cause: drugs and alcohol.

## Sex-Related Offenses

**L03**  Describe the various forms of outlawed deviant sexuality.

On August 24, 2009, Phillip Garrido, a long-time sex offender, was placed under arrest for the kidnapping of Jaycee Lee Dugard, a California girl who had been abducted on June 10, 1991, when she was 11 years old. She had been held captive for 18 years and raped repeatedly, bearing him two children. In 2011, Garrido was sentenced to 431 years in prison; his wife received a sentence of 36 to life.

This case is not unique. On June 5, 2002, Elizabeth Smart was abducted from her bedroom in Salt Lake City, Utah, and held captive until found nine months later. Elizabeth had been kidnapped by Brian David Mitchell, who was indicted for her kidnapping and sent to a mental health facility after being ruled mentally unfit to stand trial.[27] And in a case that created a media sensation, three women missing at least a decade were freed from a home in downtown Cleveland. Amanda Berry, Gina DeJesus, and Michelle Knight were all held captive in a home owned by local musician and bus driver, Ariel Castro.[28] The three women had been chained up in the basement of Castro's home and repeatedly beaten and raped. Berry gave birth in captivity and her daughter was 6 years old at the time of the rescue.

Molly Shattuck (center) ex-wife of former Constellation Energy CEO Mayo A. Shattuck, leaves the Sussex County Courthouse, June 16, 2015, in Georgetown, Delaware, after pleading guilty to raping a 15-year-old boy at a vacation rental home. Shattuck, a former Baltimore Ravens cheerleader, must spend every other weekend in a Delaware work-release detention center for nearly two years and register as a sex offender.

AP Images/Algerina Perna

Although these sex-related kidnappings are stunning in their sordidness, they are not rare. Each year thousands of children are abducted by strangers, and hundreds of thousands are subjected to some form of sexual exploitation, including sexual abuse, prostitution, pornography, and molestation.[29]

# Paraphilias

In 2009, newspaper headlines around the world told the shocking story of actor David Carradine (*Kung Fu, Kill Bill*), who was found dead in a Thailand hotel. Authorities discovered the 72-year-old actor hanging in his closet, the victim of death resulting from engaging in an autoerotic practice known as asphyxiophilia, self-strangulation that restricts the supply of oxygen or blood to the brain in order to increase sexual intensity.[30]

Carradine's death was attributed to his involvement with a common **paraphilia**, a term derived from the Greek *para*, "to the side of," and *philos*, "loving." Paraphilias are bizarre or abnormal sexual practices that involve recurrent sexual urges focused on (a) nonhuman objects (such as underwear, shoes, or leather), (b) humiliation or the experience of receiving or giving pain (as in sadomasochism or bondage), or (c) children or others who cannot grant consent.[31] Paraphilias have existed and been recorded for thousands of years. Buddhist texts more than 2,000 years old contain references to sexually deviant behaviors among monastic communities, including sexual activity with animals and sexual interest in corpses. Richard von Krafft-Ebing's *Psychopathia Sexualis*, published in 1887, was the first text to discuss such paraphilias as sadism, bestiality, and incest.[32]

When paraphilias such as wearing clothes normally worn by the opposite sex (transvestite fetishism) are engaged in by adults in the privacy of their homes, they remain outside the law's reach. However, when paraphilias involve unwilling or underage victims, they are considered socially harmful and subject to criminal penalties. Outlawed paraphilias include:

**paraphilia**
Bizarre or abnormal sexual practices that may involve nonhuman objects, humiliation, or children.

- *Frotteurism.* Rubbing against or touching a nonconsenting person in a crowd, elevator, or other public area.
- *Voyeurism.* Obtaining sexual pleasure from spying on a stranger while he or she disrobes or engages in sexual behavior with another.
- *Exhibitionism.* Deriving sexual pleasure from exposing the genitals to surprise or shock a stranger.
- *Sadomasochism.* Deriving pleasure from receiving pain or inflicting pain on another.
- *Pedophilia.* Attaining sexual pleasure through sexual activity with prepubescent children.

## Pedophilia

Of all the commonly practiced paraphilias, pedophilia is the one that most concerns the general public. One focus of concern has been the ongoing scandals that have rocked the Catholic Church. Numerous priests have been accused of sexually molesting young children, among the most notorious being Father James Porter, convicted of molesting at least 200 children of both sexes over a 30-year period. Porter was sentenced to an 18- to 20-year prison term and died of cancer while incarcerated.

Men are not the only sexual predators; women are also involved. In one recent case that made national headlines, former Baltimore Ravens cheerleader Molly Shattuck was sentenced to two years of probation for engaging in a sex act with a 15-year-old boy.[33] At sentencing the prosecutor claimed, "This was not a momentary lapse in judgment. She groomed him, seduced him, supplied him with alcohol, then took advantage of him, all for her own gratification." Shattuck received a suspended 15-year prison sentence. She must report every other weekend to a probation center, register as a sex offender, and receive therapy. The Shattuck case is far from unique:

one study of more than 100 adult female sex offenders found that 77 percent of the cases involved sexual abuse of their own child and in about two-thirds of the cases the women had a male co-offender.[34]

The cause of pedophilia has not been determined, but suspected factors include abnormal brain structure, social maladaptation, and neurological dysfunction. Research using brain scans shows that the central processing of sexual stimuli in pedophiles may be controlled by a disturbance in the prefrontal networks of the brain.[35] Brain trauma has also been linked to child molesting. And although injury may occur before or at birth, it is also possible that the damage caused by injury and/or accident can produce the brain malfunctions linked to pedophilia.[36] There is also some evidence that pedophilia is heritable and that genetic factors are responsible for the development of pedophilia.[37] Other suspected connections range from cognitive distortions to exposure to pornography.[38]

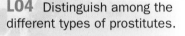

**L04** Distinguish among the different types of prostitutes.

**prostitution**
The granting of nonmarital sexual access for remuneration.

# Prostitution

Prostitution has been known of for thousands of years. The term derives from the Latin *prostituere*, which means "to cause to stand in front of." The prostitute is viewed as publicly offering his or her body for sale. The earliest record of prostitution appears in ancient Mesopotamia, where priests engaged in sex to promote fertility in the community. All women were required to do temple duty, and passing strangers were expected to make donations to the temple after enjoying their services.[39]

Modern commercial sex appears to have its roots in ancient Greece, where Solon established licensed brothels in 500 BCE. The earnings of Greek prostitutes helped pay for the temple of Aphrodite. Famous men openly went to prostitutes to enjoy intellectual, aesthetic, and sexual stimulation; prostitutes, however, were prohibited from marrying.[40]

Today, **prostitution** can be defined as granting nonmarital sexual access for remuneration, under terms established by mutual agreement of the prostitutes, their clients, and their employers. Included in this process are the following elements:

- *Activity that has sexual significance for the customer.* This includes the entire range of sexual behavior, from sexual intercourse to exhibitionism, sadomasochism, oral sex, and so on.
- *Economic transaction.* Something of economic value, not necessarily money, is exchanged for the activity.
- *Emotional indifference.* The sexual exchange is simply for economic consideration. Although the participants may know one another, their interaction has nothing to do with affection for one another.[41]

## Incidence of Prostitution

It is difficult to assess the number of prostitutes operating in the United States. According to the Uniform Crime Report (UCR), fewer than 50,000 prostitution arrests are now being made annually, a number that has been trending downward for some time; about 100,000 arrests were made in 1995.

How can these changes be accounted for? Changing sexual mores, brought about by the "sexual revolution," have liberalized sexuality. Men may be less likely to use prostitutes because legitimate alternatives for sexuality are more open to them. In addition, the prevalence of sexually transmitted diseases has caused many men to avoid visiting prostitutes for fear of irreversible health hazards.[42]

Prostitution remains a worldwide industry, and young women from poor nations are often forced to sell themselves in wealthier nations in order to survive. Here, Romanian prostitutes pose in the Pussy Club brothel in Schoenefeld, Germany, one of the few Western countries where prostitution is legal. But even in Germany prostitution has suffered during the recent economic downturn. The industry has responded with an economic stimulus package: modern marketing tools, rebates, and gimmicks to boost falling demand.

Hannibal Hanschke/Reuters/Landov

# Policies and Issues in Criminology

## SEX WORK IN CONTEMPORARY SOCIETY

Meredith Dank and her colleagues at the Urban Institute conducted a recent study of prostitution in contemporary society, focusing on eight U.S. cities: Atlanta, Dallas, Denver, Kansas City, Miami, Seattle, San Diego, and Washington, D.C. Contemporary prostitution runs the gamut from high-end escort services to high school "sneaker pimps." As a result, the sex trade leaves no demographic unrepresented and circuits almost every major U.S. city. The study found that the underground sex economy's worth to these cities was between $40 million and $290 million. Almost all types of commercial sex venues—massage parlors, brothels, escort services, and street- and Internet-based prostitution—existed in some degree.

### Pimps

Profiting from this vast enterprise were pimps and traffickers, who took home between $5,000 and $33,000 a week. Most pimps believed that the media portrayals exaggerated their violence; some even saw the term "pimp" as derogatory. They told the research team that they rarely used physical abuse for punishment, but instead relied on frequent use of psychological coercion to maintain control over their employees. Pimps used a variety of tactics to recruit and retain employees. Some even credited their entry into pimping with a natural capacity for manipulation. Rarely, however, were pimps the sole influence for an individual's entry into the sex trade.

Not all sex workers had pimps; some solicited protection from friends and acquaintances, some of whom had exposed them to the sex trade at a young age and influenced their decision to participate.

### The Internet Is Changing the Limitations of the Trade

Dank and her associates found that prostitution is decreasing on the street but thriving online. Pimps and sex workers advertise on social media and sites like Backpage .com to attract customers and new employees, and to gauge business opportunities in other cities. An increasing online presence makes it both easier for law enforcement to track activity in the underground sex economy and for an offender to promote and provide access to the trade.

The study also looked at the distribution of obscene material and found that explicit content involving younger victims is becoming increasingly available and graphic on the Internet. Online child pornography communities frequently trade content for free; offenders often consider their participation a "victimless crime."

### The Underground Sex Economy Is Perceived as Low Risk

Pimps, traffickers, and child pornography offenders said that their crimes were low risk despite some fears of prosecution. Those who got caught for child pornography generally had low technological know-how, and multiple pimp offenders expressed that "no one actually gets locked up for pimping," despite their own incarcerations.

What can be done to reduce or control the incidence of prostitution?

- Cross-train drug, sex, and weapons trade investigators to better understand circuits and overlaps
- Continue using federal and local partnerships to disrupt travel circuits and identify pimps
- Offer law enforcement trainings for both victim and offender interview techniques, including identifying signs of psychological manipulation
- Increase awareness among school officials and the general public about the realities of sex trafficking to deter victimization and entry into the trade
- Consistently enforce the laws for offenders to diminish low-risk perception
- Impose more fines for ad host websites

### Critical Thinking

Rather than control or eliminate prostitution, might we be better off to legalize and regulate it? After all, it's the world's oldest profession and it seems unlikely that it can be eliminated. What are the drawbacks to legalization?

**Source:** Meredith Dank, Bilal Khan, P. Mitchell Downey, Cybele Kotonias, Debbie Mayer, Colleen Owens, Laura Pacifici, and Lilly Yu, *Estimating the Size and Structure of the Underground Commercial Sex Economy in Eight Major US Cities* (Washington, DC: Urban Institute, 2014), www.urban.org/publications/413047.html (accessed 2015).

Of course, arrest trends must be interpreted with some caution. While it is possible that fewer people are seeking the services of prostitutes, the downward trend may also be explained by the fact that police are reluctant to make arrests in prostitution cases, or that more sophisticated prostitutes who use the Internet

# Policies and Issues in Criminology

## THE INTERNATIONAL SEX TRADE

In the popular 2008 film *Taken*, Bryan Mills, a former CIA agent played by Liam Neeson, must save his daughter Kim, who has been abducted while on a trip to Paris. Almost as soon as she arrives, Kim and a friend are kidnapped. As Bryan searches frantically for his beloved daughter, he uncovers an international scheme in which young women are taken, abused, forcibly addicted to drugs, and used as sex slaves. Luckily for Kim, Brian, who has a special set of skills, kills about 35 people and rescues her from her abductors. The film was so popular that a sequel, *Taken 2*, was released in 2012 and *Taken 3* in 2014. Can these dreadful scenarios be based on reality?

Unfortunately, they may be all too real. Every year, hundreds of thousands of women and children—primarily from Southeast Asia and Eastern Europe—are lured by the promise of good jobs and then end up in the sex trade in industrialized countries. The data are notoriously unreliable, but estimates of the number of people trafficked internationally each year range between 600,000 and one million men, women, and children from 124 different countries around the world, including the United States. Most victims are foreigners in the country where they have been abused and victimized, though most are from the region, often from neighboring countries (e.g., Eastern European women trafficked to Western Europe). Domestic trafficking is also widely practiced, and for one in three trafficking cases, the exploitation takes place in the victim's country of citizenship.

The majority of these victims are runaway or thrown-away youths who live on the streets and become victims of prostitution. These children generally come from homes where they have been abused or from families who have abandoned them. Often, they become involved in prostitution to support themselves financially or to get the things they feel they need or want (like drugs).

According to a report prepared by the United Nations, the most common form of human trafficking is sexual exploitation, and the victims are predominantly women and girls; about one-third of these victims are children. Others are taken for forced labor, to be used as combat troops, or forced to beg on the streets.

Even though films such as *Taken* depict human traffickers as almost entirely men, many sex traffickers are women. On average, some 10 to 15 percent of convicted offenders are women. For trafficking in persons, however, even though males still make up the vast majority, the share of women offenders is nearly 30 percent. Many were in the sex trade themselves and were encouraged by their recruiter/trafficker to return home and recruit other women, often under the scrutiny of people working for the trafficker to make sure they don't try to escape.

Because it is a global enterprise, there is a great deal of cooperation in human trafficking. A single gang in Eastern Europe may include Russians, Moldavians, Egyptians, and Syrians. Cooperation makes it possible to traffic sex slaves not only to neighboring countries but all around the globe. Victims from East Asia were detected in more than 20 countries in regions throughout the world, including Europe, the Americas, the Middle East, Central Asia, and Africa.

### Contributing Factors

Human trafficking is facilitated by social problems and disorder, such as disruptions in the global economy, war, and social unrest. Economic crisis hits young girls especially hard. Female victims are often poor and aspire to

---

or other forms of technology to "make dates" are better able to avoid detection by police. In fact e-hooking, in which prostitutes use the Internet to shield their identities and contact clients, may be responsible for a resurgence in sex for hire, especially in times of economic turmoil.[43] So despite this two-decade decline in the arrest rate, a recent survey by the Urban Institute shows that prostitution still flourishes in major cities; these findings are set out in the Policies and Issues in Criminology box.

**PROSTITUTION ABROAD** Prostitution flourishes abroad. In some nations it is legal and regulated by the government, whereas other nations punish prostitution with the death penalty. Germany, where the sex trade has been legalized, has at least 400,000 prostitutes—more than any other European nation per capita—serving 1.2 million men every day and bringing in more than $15 billion per year.[44] In contrast, many

a better life. They may be forced, coerced, deceived, and psychologically manipulated into industrial or agricultural work, marriage, domestic servitude, organ donation, or sexual exploitation. Some traffickers exploit victims' frustration with low salaries in their home countries, and others take advantage of a crisis in the victim's family that requires her to make money. The traffickers then promise the victim to take her abroad and find her a traditionally female service-sector job, such as waitress, salesperson, domestic worker, or au pair/babysitter.

Whereas victims often come from poorer countries, the market for labor and sex is found in wealthier countries or in countries that, though economically poor, cater to the needs of citizens from wealthy countries, of corporations, or of tourists.

### Combating Human Trafficking

Recently, the United States made stopping the trafficking of women a top priority. In 2000, Congress passed the Trafficking Victims Protection Act (TVPA), which created the first comprehensive federal law to address trafficking, with a significant focus on the international dimension of the problem. The law provides a three-pronged approach: *prevention* through public awareness programs overseas and a State Department–led monitoring and sanctions program; *protection* through a new visa and services for foreign national victims; and *prosecution* through new federal crimes and severe penalties.

As a result of the passing of the TVPA, the Office to Monitor and Combat Trafficking in Persons was established in October 2001. This enabling legislation led to the creation of a bureau within the State Department to specifically address human trafficking and exploitation on all levels and to take legal action against perpetrators. Along with the FBI, the U.S. Immigration and Customs Enforcement (ICE) is one of the lead federal agencies charged with enforcing the TVPA. Human trafficking represents significant risks to homeland security. Would-be terrorists and criminals often can access the same routes and use the same methods as human traffickers. ICE's Human Smuggling and Trafficking Unit works to identify criminals and organizations involved in these illicit activities.

A number of local law enforcement agencies have also created special branches to combat trafficking. The Massachusetts Human Trafficking Task Force uses a two-pronged approach, addressing investigations focusing on international victims and those focusing on the commercial sexual exploitation of children. The New Jersey Human Trafficking Task Force attacks the problem by training law enforcement in the methods of identifying victims and signs of trafficking, coordinating statewide efforts in the identification and provision of services to victims of human trafficking, and increasing the successful interdiction and prosecution of trafficking of human persons.

### Critical Thinking

1. If put in charge, what would you do to slow or end the international sex trade?

2. Should men who hire prostitutes be punished very severely in order to deter them from getting involved in the exploitation of these vulnerable young women?

**Sources:** Amanda Walker-Rodriguez and Rodney Hill, "Human Sex Trafficking," *FBI Law Enforcement Bulletin*, 2011," leb.fbi .gov/2011/march/leb-march-2011; United Nations Office on Drugs and Crime, "Global Reports on Trafficking in Persons, 2014," www .unodc.org/documents/data-and-analysis/glotip/GLOTIP_2014 _full_report.pdf (URLs accessed 2015).

Islamic countries punish prostitution with death, a punishment that is sometimes carried out by stoning in the public square.

There is also a troubling overseas trade in prostitution in which men from wealthy countries frequent marginally regulated sex areas in needy nations such as Thailand in order to procure young girls forced or sold into prostitution—a phenomenon known as *sex tourism*. In addition to sex tours, there has also been a soaring demand for pornography, strip clubs, lap dancing, escorts, and telephone sex in developing countries.[45] The outcry against human trafficking has resulted in laws and law enforcement efforts designed to stop it in its tracks. But these efforts have resulted in an ironic situation: if a 16-year-old girl is trafficked to the United States, she is considered a victim; if a 16-year-old girl who was born in the United States gets involved in the sex trade, she will be arrested for prostitution and considered a criminal.[46] The international trade in prostitution is the subject of the accompanying Policies and Issues in Criminology feature.

## Types of Prostitutes

Several different types of prostitutes operate in the United States.

Prostitution can take many forms and occur in a variety of venues. Here, Alexis Wright, 30, leaves the Cumberland County Courthouse in Maine. In 2013, Wright, a Zumba fitness instructor, pleaded guilty to prostitution and tax and welfare violations; she served six months in jail and must pay back more than $57,000 in fines and restitution. The case rocked the community when authorities revealed that 68 local people were her clients, the majority of whom pleaded guilty or no contest.

**STREETWALKERS** Prostitutes who work the streets in plain sight of police, citizens, and customers are referred to as hustlers, hookers, or streetwalkers. Although glamorized by the Julia Roberts character in the film *Pretty Woman* (who winds up with multimillionaire Richard Gere), streetwalkers are considered the least attractive, lowest paid, most vulnerable men and women in the profession. Streetwalkers wear bright clothing, makeup, and jewelry to attract customers; they take their customers to hotels. The term "hooker," however, is derived not from streetwalkers using their charms to "hook" clients, but from the popular name given women who followed Union General "Fighting Joe" Hooker's army and serviced the troops during the Civil War.[47]

Research shows that there are a variety of working styles among women involved in street-based prostitution. Some are controlled by pimps who demand and receive a major share of their earnings. Others are independent entrepreneurs interested in building a stable group of steady clients. Still others manipulate and exploit their customers and may engage in theft and blackmail.[48]

**BAR GIRLS** B-girls, as they are also called, spend their time in bars, drinking and waiting to be picked up by customers. Although alcoholism may be a problem, B-girls usually work out an arrangement with the bartender whereby they are served diluted drinks or water colored with dye or tea, for which the customer is charged an exorbitant price. In some bars, the B-girl is given a credit for each drink she gets the customer to buy. It is common to find B-girls in towns with military bases and large transient populations.[49]

**BROTHEL PROSTITUTES** Also called bordellos, cathouses, sporting houses, and houses of ill repute, brothels flourished in the nineteenth and early twentieth centuries. They were large establishments, usually run by madams, that housed several prostitutes. A madam is a woman who employs prostitutes, supervises their behavior, and receives a fee for her services; her cut is usually 40 to 60 percent of the prostitutes' earnings. The madam's role may include recruiting women into prostitution and socializing them in the trade.[50]

Brothels declined in importance following World War II. The closing of the last brothel in Texas is chronicled in the play and film *The Best Little Whorehouse in Texas*. Today the best-known brothels are in Nevada, where prostitution is legal outside large population centers.

**CALL GIRLS** The aristocrats of prostitution are call girls. They charge customers thousands of dollars per night and may net more than $200,000 per year. Some gain clients through employment in escort services; others develop independent customer lists. Many call girls come from middle-class backgrounds and serve upper-class customers. Attempting to dispel the notion that their service is simply sex for money, they concentrate on making their clients feel important and attractive. Working exclusively via telephone "dates," call girls get their clients by word of mouth or by making arrangements with bellhops, cab drivers, and so on. They either entertain clients in their own apartments or visit clients' hotels and apartments. When she retires, a call girl can sell her date book, listing client names and sexual preferences, for thousands of dollars. Despite the lucrative nature of their business, call girls run considerable risk by being alone and unprotected with strangers. They often request the business cards of their clients to make sure they are dealing with "upstanding citizens."

**ESCORT SERVICES/CALL HOUSES** Some escort services are fronts for prostitution rings. Both male and female sex workers can be sent out after the client calls a number published in an ad in the yellow pages. How common are adult escort services? In 2015, Las Vegas had 112 yellow page listings for escort services; New York City had 179.

AP Images/Robert F. Bukaty

A relatively new phenomenon, the call house combines elements of the brothel and of call girl rings. A madam receives a call from a prospective customer, and if she finds the client acceptable, she arranges a meeting between the caller and a prostitute in her service. The madam maintains a list of prostitutes, who are on call rather than living together in a house. The call house insulates the madam from arrest because she never meets the client or receives direct payment.[51]

**CIRCUIT TRAVELERS** Prostitutes known as circuit travelers move around in groups of two or three to lumber, labor, and agricultural camps. They ask the foreman for permission to ply their trade, service the whole crew in an evening, and then move on. Some circuit travelers seek clients at truck stops and rest areas.

Sometimes young girls are forced to become circuit travelers by unscrupulous pimps who make them work for months as prostitutes in agricultural migrant camps. The young women are lured from developing countries such as Mexico with offers of jobs in landscaping, health care, housecleaning, and restaurants. But when they arrive in the United States, they are told that they owe their captors thousands of dollars and must work as prostitutes to pay off this debt. The young women are raped and beaten if they complain or try to escape.[52]

**CYBERPROSTITUTES** The technological revolution has altered the world of prostitution. So-called cyberprostitutes set up personal websites or put listings on web boards, such as Adult FriendFinder or Craigslist, that carry personals. They may use loaded phrases such as "looking for generous older man" in their self-descriptions. When contacted, they ask to exchange emails, chat online, or make voice calls with prospective clients. They may even exchange pictures. This enables them to select clients they want to be with and to avoid clients who may be threatening or dangerous. Some cyberprostitution rings offer customers the opportunity to choose women from their Internet page and then have them flown in from around the country.

## Becoming a Prostitute

At 38, Lt. Cmdr. Rebecca Dickinson had risen from the enlisted ranks in the Navy to its officer corps. She had an assignment to the Naval Academy in Annapolis, Maryland, where she helped teach a leadership course. But faced with money and marital problems, Dickinson also worked as a prostitute for some of the richest and most powerful men in Washington, D.C. This desperate naval officer, whose career was destroyed in the scandal, was paid $130 for a 90-minute session.[53]

Why does someone turn to prostitution? Both male and female prostitutes often come from troubled homes marked by extreme conflict and hostility and from poor urban areas or rural communities. Divorce, separation, or death splits the family; most prostitutes grew up in homes without fathers.[54] Girls from the lower socioeconomic classes who get into "the life" report conflict with school authorities, poor grades, and an overly regimented school experience.[55] Young women involved in prostitution also have extensive histories of substance abuse, health problems, posttraumatic stress disorder (PTSD), social stigmatization, and isolation. Often having little family support, they turn to equally troubled peers for survival: self-medicating with drugs and alcohol and self-mutilation are the norm.[56] One survey of street-level sex workers in Phoenix, Arizona, found that women engaging in prostitution had limited educational backgrounds; most did not complete high school.[57]

Sexual abuse also plays a role in prostitution. Many prostitutes were initiated into sex by family members at ages as young as 10 to 12 years; they have long histories of sexual exploitation and abuse.[58] These early experiences with sex help teach them that their bodies have value and that sexual encounters can be used to obtain affection, power, or money.

Age may affect why girls become prostitutes. When Jennifer Cobbina and Sharon Oselin conducted 40 in-depth interviews with female street prostitutes they discovered that younger sex workers were more likely to come from homes that were physically and sexually abusive as an attempt to regain control of their lives. Another common theme among adolescent girls in the life is that prostitution is "normal" in the neighborhoods and environments in which they were raised. In contrast, older women are more likely to claim that supporting a drug habit and needing cash for survival were the reasons they became sex workers. Younger women tended to remain sex workers for longer periods and therefore faced the greater risk of violence, drug abuse, and other life-threatening events.[59]

**DANGERS OF SEX WORK** Once they get into the life, personal danger begins to escalate. Girls who may be directed toward prostitution because of childhood sexual abuse also are likely to be revictimized as adults.[60] When sociologist Jolanda Sallmann interviewed women in the Midwest with histories of prostitution, she discovered that they were hurt when people labeled and depersonalized them as "whores" or "hookers."[61] Despite their sensitivity, their lives were chaotic. The majority had suffered physical and/or sexual violence. One woman showed Sallman the scar across her neck where her pimp literally slit her throat years earlier. Another woman told how she was kidnapped and raped by a client at knifepoint while she was still a juvenile. Despite being told that she "was gonna die," she survived the incident. Considering these problems, why do women remain on the street? Even when street prostitutes try to go straight, they often return to prostitution because their limited education and lack of skills make finding employment very difficult. Without a means to support themselves and their children, they may think staying on the streets is less risky than leaving prostitution. Most self-identified as struggling with a substance use problem throughout most or all of their involvement in prostitution, typically involving crack cocaine, cocaine, and/or heroin.

## Controlling Prostitution

In the late nineteenth and early twentieth centuries, efforts were made to regulate prostitution in the United States through medical supervision and the licensing and zoning of brothels in districts outside residential neighborhoods.[62] After World War I, prostitution became associated with disease, and the desire to protect young servicemen from harm helped put an end to nearly all experiments with legalization in the United States.[63] Some reformers attempted to paint pimps and procurers as immigrants who used their foreign ways to snare unsuspecting American girls into prostitution. Such fears prompted passage of the federal Mann Act (1925), which prohibited bringing women into the country or transporting them across state lines for the purposes of prostitution. Often called the "white slave act," it carried penalties of a $5,000 fine, five years in prison, or both.[64]

Today, prostitution is considered a misdemeanor and is punishable by a fine or a short jail sentence. In practice, most law enforcement is uneven and aims at confining illegal activities to particular areas in the city.[65] Prostitution is illegal in all states except Nevada, where licensed and highly regulated brothels can operate as business enterprises in rural counties (population under 400,000; this leaves out the counties in which Las Vegas and Reno are located).

**L05** State the arguments for and against legalizing prostitution.

## Legalize Prostitution?

Should prostitution be legalized? Even though other countries such as England, France, Brazil, Mexico, and Germany have legalized and regulated prostitution, in most areas of the United States it remains a crime, most likely because it is considered a public safety and health concern.[66] Not surprisingly, there are strong feelings on both sides of this issue. One position is that women must become emancipated from male oppression and achieve sexual equality. The *sexual equality* view considers the prostitute a victim of male dominance. In patriarchal societies, male power is predicated on female subjugation, and prostitution is a clear example of this gender exploitation.[67] A similar view is that the fight for equality depends on controlling all attempts by men to impose their will on women. The *free choice* view is that prostitution, if freely chosen, expresses women's equality and is not a symptom of subjugation.[68] Advocates of both positions argue that the penalties for prostitution should be reduced (in other words, the activity should be decriminalized). Decriminalization would relieve already desperate women of the additional burden of severe legal punishment.

In her book *Brothel*, Alexa Albert makes a compelling case for legalization. A Harvard-trained physician who interviewed young women working at a legal brothel in Nevada, Albert found that the women remained HIV-free and felt safer working in a secure environment than alone on city streets. Despite long hours and rules that gave too much profit to the owners, the women actually took pride in their work. Besides benefiting from greater security, most were earning between $300 and $1,500 per day.[69] While persuasive, Albert's vision is countered by research conducted by psychologist Melissa Farley, who surveyed brothel girls in Nevada and found that many suffered abuse and long-lasting psychological damage. Farley found that numerous brothel prostitutes are coerced into prostitution and that brothel owners are not much different from pimps who control them with an iron fist. Subject to sexual harassment, sexual exploitation, and rape, many fear for their lives. Moreover, legal prostitution does not protect women from the violence, verbal abuse, physical injury, and exposure to diseases such as HIV that occur in illegal prostitution.[70]

Similarly, Roger Matthews studied prostitution for more than two decades and found that sex workers were extremely desperate, damaged, and disorganized. Many are involved in substance abuse and experience beatings, rape, and other forms of violence on a regular basis. Prostitution is, he concludes, the world's most dangerous occupation. His solution is to treat the women forced into prostitution as victims and the men who purchase their services as the criminals. He applauds Sweden's decision to make buying sexual services a crime, thus criminalizing the "johns" rather than the women in prostitution. When governments legalize prostitution, it leads to a massive expansion of the trade, both legal and illegal.[71]

As might be expected, this is not the final word on the matter. Some experts argue that while prostitution is an inherently dangerous profession, many other professions, such as all forms of law enforcement and security, are equally dangerous but legal. The danger of prostitution is outweighed by the need for women—the most poverty-stricken class in this country—to gain a source of income that can increase their chance for independence.[72]

# Pornography

The term **pornography** derives from the Greek *porne*, meaning "prostitute," and *graphein*, meaning "to write." In the heart of many major cities there are still adult stores that display and sell books, magazines, and films explicitly depicting every imaginable sex act; Miami, Florida, alone has ten adult stores. The Internet is now the main source of adult material. The purpose of this material is to provide sexual titillation and excitement for paying customers. Although material depicting nudity and sex is typically legal, protected by the First Amendment's provision limiting government control of speech, most criminal codes prohibit the production, display, and sale of obscene material.

**Obscenity**, derived from the Latin *caenum*, for "filth," is defined by Webster's dictionary as "deeply offensive to morality or decency, designed to incite to lust or depravity."[73] The problem of controlling pornography centers on this definition of obscenity. Police and law enforcement officials can legally seize only material that is judged obscene. "But who," critics ask, "is to judge what is obscene?" At one time, such novels as *Tropic of Cancer* by Henry Miller, *Ulysses* by James Joyce, and *Lady Chatterley's Lover* by D. H. Lawrence were prohibited because they were considered obscene; today they are considered works of great literary value. Thus, what is obscene today may be considered socially acceptable at a future time. After all, *Playboy* and other "men's magazines," which are sold openly in most bookstores, display

**pornography**
Sexually explicit books, magazines, films, and DVDs intended to provide sexual titillation and excitement for paying customers.

**obscenity**
Material that violates community standards of morality or decency and has no redeeming social value.

Here's a display at the Erotic Expo at the Penn Plaza Pavilion in New York City. The adult porn industry is a multibillion-dollar business reaching hundreds of millions of consumers annually. Worldwide pornography revenue is larger than the revenues of all professional football, baseball, and basketball franchises combined. In the United States, pornography revenue exceeds the combined revenues of ABC, CBS, and NBC.

nude models in all kinds of sexually explicit poses. The uncertainty surrounding this issue is illustrated by Supreme Court Justice Potter Stewart's famous 1964 statement on how he defined obscenity: "I know it when I see it." Because of this legal and moral ambiguity, violation of obscenity laws involving adults is rarely prosecuted in the United States.

## Is Pornography Harmful?

Opponents of pornography argue that it degrades both the people who are photographed and members of the public who are sometimes forced to see obscene material. Pornographers exploit their models, who often include underage children. Investigations have found that many performers and models are victims of physical and psychological coercion.[74]

One uncontested danger of pornography is "kiddie porn." Each year more than a million children are believed to be used in pornography or prostitution, many of them runaways whose plight is exploited by adults. Sexual exploitation by these rings can devastate the child victims. Exploited children are prone to such acting-out behavior as setting fires and becoming sexually focused in the use of language, dress, and mannerisms. They also may suffer physical problems ranging from headaches and loss of appetite to genital soreness, vomiting, and urinary tract infections, and psychological problems, including mood swings, withdrawal, edginess, and nervousness.[75]

## Does Viewing Pornography Cause Violence?

An issue critical to the debate over pornography is whether viewing it produces sexual violence or assaultive behavior. This debate reignited when serial killer Ted Bundy claimed his murderous rampage was fueled by reading pornography.

The scientific evidence linking sexually explicit material to violence is mixed.[76] Some research has found that viewing erotic material may act as a safety valve for those whose impulses might otherwise lead them to violence; in a sense, pornography reduces violence.[77] Viewing obscene material may have the unintended side effect of satisfying erotic impulses that otherwise might result in more sexually aggressive behavior. Thus, it is not surprising to some skeptics that convicted rapists and sex offenders report less exposure to pornography than control groups of nonoffenders.[78] The lack of a clear-cut connection between viewing pornography and violence is used to bolster the argument that all printed matter, no matter how sexually explicit, is protected by the First Amendment.

However, some research does find a link between consuming pornography and subsequent violent or controlling behavior.[79] Sex researcher Michael Flood reviewed the existing literature and concludes that exposure to pornography by young people leads to sexist and unhealthy notions of sex and relationships, as well as intensification of attitudes supportive of sexual coercion while increasing their likelihood of perpetrating assault.[80]

The evidence suggests that violence and sexual aggression are not linked to erotic or pornographic films per se but that erotic films depicting violence, rape, brutality, and aggression may evoke similar feelings in viewers. A leading critic of pornography, Diana Russell, contends that hatred of women is a principal theme in pornography and is often coupled with racism. Her research provides strong evidence linking pornography to misogyny (the hatred of women), an emotional response that often leads to rape.[81]

## Pornography and the Law

The First Amendment to the U.S. Constitution protects free speech and prohibits police agencies from limiting the public's right of free expression. However, the Supreme Court held, in the twin cases of *Roth v. United States* and *Alberts v. California*, that although the First Amendment protects all "ideas with even the slightest redeeming social importance—unorthodox ideas, controversial ideas, even ideas hateful to the prevailing climate of opinion, implicit in the history of the First Amendment is the rejection of obscenity as utterly without redeeming social importance."[82] These decisions left unclear how obscenity is defined. If a highly erotic movie tells a "moral tale," must it be judged legal even if 95 percent of its content is objectionable? A spate of movies made after the *Roth* decision claimed that they were educational or warned the viewer about sexual depravity, so they could not be said to lack redeeming social importance. Many state obscenity cases were appealed to federal courts so that judges could decide whether the films totally lacked redeeming social importance. To rectify the situation, the Supreme Court redefined its concept of obscenity in the case of *Miller v. California*:

> The basic guidelines for the trier of fact must be (a) whether the average person applying contemporary community standards would find that the work taken as a whole appeals to the prurient interest; (b) whether the work depicts or describes, in a patently offensive way, sexual conduct specifically defined by the applicable state law, and (c) whether the work, taken as a whole, lacks serious literary, artistic, political or scientific value.[83]

To convict a person of obscenity under the *Miller* doctrine, the state or local jurisdiction must specifically define obscene conduct in its statute, and the pornographer must engage in that behavior. The Court gave some examples of what is considered obscene: "patently offensive representations or descriptions of masturbation, excretory functions and lewd exhibition of the genitals."[84] Obviously, a plebiscite cannot be held to determine the community's attitude for every trial concerning the sale of pornography. Works that are considered obscene in Omaha might be considered routine in New York, but how can we be sure? To resolve this dilemma, the Supreme Court in *Pope v. Illinois* articulated a reasonableness doctrine: a work is obscene if a reasonable person applying objective (national) standards would find the material to lack any social value.[85]

These rulings are so elastic that cases involving adults are rarely if ever prosecuted and then under the most extreme circumstances—for example, sex with animals. During the first four years of the Obama administration federal authorities brought obscenity charges in only two cases.[86]

**THE LAW AND KIDDIE PORN** While obscenity involving adults is rarely prosecuted, the creation and distribution of obscene material involving children is the focus of vigilant legal action. After a number of initiatives failed to meet First Amendment standards because courts ruled that they violated free speech, being over-broad or vague, Congress passed the PROTECT Act of 2003 (Prosecutorial Remedies and Other Tools to end the Exploitation of Children Today), which provides prison sentences for anyone creating and selling sexual images involving children.[87] One part of the PROTECT Act prohibits computer-generated child pornography "when such visual depiction is a computer image or computer-generated image that is, or appears virtually indistinguishable from that of a minor engaging in sexually explicit conduct." In *United States v. Williams*, the Supreme Court ruled that statutes prohibiting the "pandering" of child pornography (offering or requesting to transfer, sell,

While few people are prosecuted for possessing pornography involving adults, buying or selling kiddie porn is frequently prosecuted. In a case that made national headlines in 2015, former Subway sandwich pitchman Jared Fogle agreed to plead guilty to allegations that he paid for sex acts with minors and received child pornography. The admission destroyed his career at the sandwich-shop chain and could send him to prison for more than a decade.

**LO6** Discuss the causes of substance abuse.

deliver, or trade the items) did not violate the First Amendment even if a person charged under the code did not in fact possess child pornography.[88] So it is a crime if someone offers to sell kiddie porn to another person even if they don't actually have any kiddie porn to sell or if they have virtual images they are claiming to be the real thing, as long as the purchaser *believes* they are buying kiddie porn using real children. The crime is the offer to sell and the agreement to buy, not the actual possession of the contraband.

Despite these legal changes, which make enforcement somewhat easier, the biggest challenge to those seeking to control the sale of obscene material involving children has been the shift to Internet sales. Today, the major initiative against Internet kiddie porn is the Innocent Images National Initiative (IINI) developed by the FBI, which coordinates multi-agency investigative operations worldwide. The focus is on the following:

- Online organizations, enterprises, and communities that exploit children for profit or personal gain
- Major distributors of child pornography, such as those who appear to have transmitted a large volume of child pornography via an online computer on several occasions to several other people
- Producers of child pornography
- Individuals who travel, or indicate a willingness to travel, for the purpose of engaging in sexual activity with a minor
- Possessors of child pornography

FBI and other law enforcement agents go online utilizing fictitious screen names and engaging in real-time chat or email conversations with subjects in order to obtain evidence of criminal activity involving exploitation of children.[89]

# Substance Abuse

On February 2, 2014, the Academy Award–winning actor Philip Seymour Hoffman was found dead in his Manhattan apartment of what the medical examiner's office ruled was an accidental "acute mixed drug intoxication," including heroin, cocaine, benzodiazepines, and amphetamine. His death followed that of other stars, including Heath Ledger, the great young actor (*The Patriot, Brokeback Mountain, The Dark Knight*) who at the age of 28 succumbed to an overdose of diazepam (Valium), temazepam (Restoril), alprazolam (Xanax), oxycodone (OxyContin), hydrocodone (Vicodin), and doxylamine (Unisom). In 2011, British singer Amy Winehouse was found dead in her home; her blood alcohol content at the time of her death was more than five times the legal drink–drive limit.[90]

The problem of substance abuse stretches all across the United States. Large urban areas are beset by drug-dealing gangs, drug users who engage in crime to support their habits, and alcohol-related violence. Rural areas are important staging centers for the shipment of drugs across the country and are often the production sites for synthetic drugs and marijuana farming.[91]

Another indication of why there is such concern about drugs has been the number of drug-related visits to hospital emergency rooms. According to the latest national data, between 2004 and 2011, the number of emergency room visits for drug abuse increased by 128 percent. In 2011, there were 5.1 million drug-related emergency room visits, of which 1,252,500 involved abuse of illicit drugs such as cocaine and heroin. The majority of visits involved illegally used or abused prescription drugs such as anti-anxiety and insomnia medications or narcotic pain relievers; oxycodone-related emergency room visits increased by 220 percent in the seven-year period.[92]

## When Did Drug Use Begin?

Chemical substances have been used to change reality and provide stimulation, relief, or relaxation for thousands of years. Mesopotamian writings indicate that opium was used 4,000 years ago—it was known as the "plant of joy."[93] The ancient Greeks knew and understood the problem of drug use. At the time of the Crusades, the Arabs were using marijuana. In the Western Hemisphere, natives of Mexico and South America chewed coca leaves and used "magic mushrooms" in their religious ceremonies.[94] Drug use was also accepted in Europe well into the twentieth century. Recently uncovered pharmacy records from 1900 to 1920 show sales of cocaine and heroin solutions to members of the British royal family; records from 1912 indicate that Winston Churchill, then a member of Parliament, was sold a cocaine solution while staying in Scotland.[95]

In the early years of the United States, opium and its derivatives were easily obtained. Opium-based drugs were used in various patent medicine cure-alls. Morphine was used extensively to relieve the pain of wounded soldiers in the Civil War. By the turn of the century, an estimated 1 million U.S. citizens were opiate users.[96]

## Alcohol and Its Prohibition

The history of alcohol and the law in the United States has also been controversial and dramatic. At the turn of the twentieth century, a drive was mustered to prohibit the sale of alcohol. This **temperance movement** was fueled by the belief that the purity of the U.S. agrarian culture was being destroyed by the growth of cities. Urbanism was viewed as a threat to the lifestyle of the majority of the nation's population, then living on farms and in villages. The forces behind the temperance movement were such lobbying groups as the Anti-Saloon League led by Carrie Nation, the Women's Temperance Union, and the Protestant clergy of the Baptist, Methodist, and Congregationalist faiths.[97] They viewed the growing cities, filled with newly arriving Irish, Italian, and Eastern European immigrants, as centers of degradation and wickedness. Ratification of the Eighteenth Amendment in 1919, prohibiting the sale of alcoholic beverages, was viewed as a triumph of the morality of middle- and upper-class Americans over the threat posed to their culture by the "new Americans."[98]

**Prohibition** failed. It was enforced by the Volstead Act, which defined intoxicating beverages as those containing one-half of 1 percent or more alcohol.[99] What doomed Prohibition? One factor was the use of organized crime to supply illicit liquor. Also, the law made it illegal only to sell alcohol, not to purchase it, which reduced the deterrent effect. Finally, despite the work of Elliot Ness and his "Untouchables," law enforcement agencies were inadequate, and officials were likely to be corrupted by wealthy bootleggers.[100] In 1933, the Twenty-First Amendment to the Constitution repealed Prohibition, signaling the end of the "noble experiment."

## Extent of Substance Abuse

Despite continuing efforts at control, the use of mood-altering substances persists in the United States. What is the extent of the substance abuse problem today?

A number of national surveys attempt to chart trends in drug abuse in the general population. One important source of information on drug use is the annual Monitoring the Future (MTF) self-report survey of drug abuse among high school students conducted by the Institute for Social Research (ISR) at the University of Michigan. This annual survey is based on the self-report responses of approximately 50,000 8th-, 10th-, and 12th-graders and is considered the most important source of data on adolescent drug abuse. MTF survey data indicate that drug use declined from a high point late in the 1970s until 1990, when it once again began to increase, finally stabilizing around 1996 and since then there has been a decline in both lifetime and current usage. In 2014, alcohol use by the nation's teens continued its long-term decline and students in all three grades showed a decline in the proportion reporting any alcohol use in the prior 12 months; the three grades combined dropped to 41 percent, down from more than 60 percent in 1997. Of perhaps greater importance, the proportion of teens who report **binge drinking**—consuming five or more drinks in a row at least once in the prior two weeks—fell to 12 percent, down from a high point of 22 percent in 1997. Still, one in five (19 percent) 12th graders report binge drinking at least once in the prior two weeks.

**temperance movement**
The drive to prohibit the sale of alcohol in the United States, culminating in ratification of the Eighteenth Amendment in 1919.

**Prohibition**
The period from 1919 until 1933 when the Eighteenth Amendment to the U.S. Constitution outlawed the sale of alcohol; also known as the "noble experiment."

**binge drinking**
Having five or more drinks on the same occasion (that is, at the same time or within a couple of hours of each other).

**FACT OR FICTION?**

Fewer kids are drinking today than 20 years ago.

**FACT** Alcohol consumption among youths is diminishing and is actually at a 20-year low.

**FIGURE 13.1**
**Past-Month Illicit Drug
Use Among Adolescents
Aged 12–17**

**Source:** U.S. Department of Health and
Human Services, Substance Abuse and
Mental Health Services Administration,
"Results from the 2013 National
Survey on Drug Use and Health," www
.samhsa.gov/data/sites/default/files
/NSDUHresultsPDFWHTML2013/Web
/NSDUHresults2013.pdf (accessed 2015).

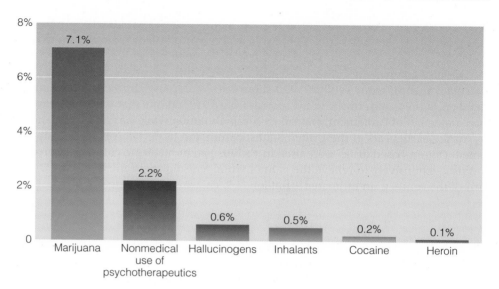

Drug use among teens has also declined significantly, and marijuana—which remains the most popular drug by far—declined in use in 2014 after rising for the past few years. Nonetheless, about 6 percent of all high school students claim to use marijuana every day and about 6 percent of 8th graders, 11 percent of 10th graders, and 16 percent of 12th graders used some other drug such as ecstasy, LSD, or cocaine in the prior 12 months.[101]

The National Household Survey on Drug Abuse and Health, sponsored by the federal government, also indicates the extent of drug use. The most recent data show similar patterns to the MTF. In the United States, the percentage of adolescents aged 12 to 17 who have used marijuana in the month prior to being surveyed increased from 2008 to 2011, then decreased in 2012 and 2013. As Figure 13.1 shows, about 9 percent (an estimated 2.2 million adolescents) reported using illicit drugs within the month prior to being surveyed.[102]

## Costs of Substance Abuse

Considering how many people indulge in illicit drug and alcohol abuse, it should not be surprising that the costs of this abuse are quite significant. The National Institute on Drug Abuse estimates that health and other costs directly related to substance abuse exceed $700 billion per year (see Table 13.1).[103]

In addition to these costs, enforcement efforts add additional billions. Recent research compiled by the Cato Institute, a Washington, D.C., think tank, estimates that legalizing drugs would save roughly $41 billion per year in government enforcement expenditure. State and local governments could save about $25 billion per year; while roughly $16 billion would accrue to the federal government.[104]

| TABLE 13.1  Costs of Drug and Alcohol Abuse | | |
|---|---|---|
| | **Health Care** | **Overall** |
| **Tobacco** | $130 billion | $295 billion |
| **Alcohol** | $25 billion | $224 billion |
| **Illicit Drugs** | $11 billion | $193 billion |

**Source:** National Institute on Drug Abuse, 2014, www.drugabuse.gov/related-topics/trends-statistics.

## Causes of Substance Abuse

What causes people to abuse substances? Although there are many different views on the causes of drug use, most can be characterized as seeing the onset of an addictive career either as an environmental matter or as a personal matter.

**SUBCULTURAL VIEW** Those who view drug abuse as having an environmental basis concentrate on lower-class addiction. Because a disproportionate number of drug abusers are poor, the onset of drug use can be tied to such factors as racial prejudice, devalued identities, low self-esteem, poor socioeconomic status, and the high level of mistrust, negativism, and defiance found in impoverished areas.

Residing in a deteriorated inner-city area is often correlated with entry into a drug subculture. Youths living in these depressed areas, where feelings of alienation and hopelessness run high, often meet established drug users who teach them that narcotics assuage their feelings of personal inadequacy and stress.[105] The youths may join peers to learn the techniques of drug use and receive social support for their habit. Research shows that peer influence is a significant predictor of drug careers that actually grows stronger as people mature.[106] Shared feelings and a sense of intimacy lead the youths to become fully enmeshed in the drug culture.[107] Some join gangs and enter into a career of using and distributing illegal substances, while also committing property and violent crimes.[108]

**PSYCHOLOGICAL VIEW** Some experts have linked substance abuse to psychological deficits such as impaired cognitive functioning, personality disturbance, and emotional problems that can strike people in any economic class.[109] These produce what is called a **drug-dependent personality**. Some teens may resort to drug abuse to reduce the emotional turmoil of adolescence or to cope with troubling impulses.[110]

Personality testing of known users suggests that a significant percentage suffer from psychotic disorders, including various levels of schizophrenia. Surveys show that youngsters with serious behavioral problems were more than seven times as likely as those with less serious problems to report that they were dependent on alcohol or illicit drugs. Youths with serious emotional problems were nearly four times more likely to report dependence on drugs than those without such issues.[111] The Policies and Issues in Criminology feature reviews research on this topic.

What is the connection between psychological disorders and drug abuse? Drugs may help people deal with unconscious needs and impulses and relieve dependence and depression. People may turn to drug abuse as a form of self-medication to reduce the emotional turmoil of adolescence, deal with troubling impulses, or cope with traumatic life experiences such as institutional child abuse (kids who were sexually or physically abused in foster care, mental institutions, juvenile detention centers, day care centers, etc.).[112] Survivors of sexual assault and physical abuse in the home also have been known to turn to drug and alcohol abuse as a coping mechanism.[113] Depressed people may use drugs as an alternative to more radical solutions to their pain, such as suicide.[114] Kids with low self-esteem, or those who are self-conscious about their body image or who have a poor self-image, may turn to drugs to ease psychological turmoil.[115] Unfortunately, while substance abuse may relieve psychological strain in the short term, this relief is later countered by feelings of depression and anxiety in the long term.[116]

**GENETIC FACTORS** Substance abuse may have a genetic basis. Evidence for this has been found in research showing that biological children of alcoholics reared by non-alcoholic adoptive parents develop alcohol problems more often than the biological children of the adoptive parents.[117] In a similar vein, a number of studies comparing alcoholism among identical twins and fraternal twins have found that the degree of concordance (both siblings behaving identically) is twice as high among the identical twin groups. Nonetheless, most children of abusing parents do not become drug dependent themselves, which suggests that even if drug abuse is heritable, environment and socialization must play some role in the onset of abuse.[118]

**drug-dependent personality**
A personal trait characterized by a pervasive psychological dependence on mood-altering substances.

# Policies and Issues in Criminology

## SUBSTANCE ABUSE AND PSYCHOSIS

Most estimates suggest that people diagnosed with mood or anxiety disorders are about twice as likely as the general population to also suffer from a substance use disorder. Studies exploring the link between substance use disorders and other mental illnesses have typically not included people with severe psychotic illnesses.

In a recent study, 9,142 people diagnosed with schizophrenia, schizoaffective disorder, or bipolar disorder with psychotic features were matched with 10,195 controls according to geographic region. Mental disorder diagnoses were confirmed using the Diagnostic Interview for Psychosis and Affective Disorder (DI-PAD), and the controls were screened to verify the absence of schizophrenia or bipolar disorder in themselves or close family members. The DI-PAD was also used for all participants to determine substance use rates.

Compared to the controls, people with severe mental illness were about four times more likely to be heavy alcohol users (four or more drinks per day), 3.5 times more likely to use marijuana regularly (21 times per year), and 4.6 times more likely to use other drugs at least 10 times in their lives. The greatest increases were seen with tobacco, with patients with severe mental illness five times more likely to be daily smokers.

This is of concern because smoking is the leading cause of preventable death in the United States. The association between mental issues and substance abuse was constant when controlling for gender, age, and race.

Previous research has shown that people with schizophrenia have a shorter life expectancy than the general population, and chronic cigarette smoking has been suggested as a major contributing factor to higher morbidity and mortality from malignancy as well as cardiovascular and respiratory diseases. These new findings indicate that the rates of substance use in people with severe psychosis may be underestimated, highlighting the need to improve the understanding of the association between substance use and psychotic disorders so that both conditions can be treated effectively.

### Critical Thinking

What is the connection between psychosis and substance abuse? Is it possible that people with severe mental disorders use drugs and alcohol to self-medicate and relieve their symptoms? What other reasons might there be for the connection?

**Source:** Sarah M. Hartz, Carlos N. Pato, Helena Medeiros, Patricia Cavazos-Rehg, Janet L. Sobell, James A. Knowles, Laura Bierut, and Michele T. Pato, "Comorbidity of Severe Psychotic Disorders with Measures of Substance Use," *JAMA Psychiatry* 71 (2014): 248–254.

**SOCIAL LEARNING** Social psychologists suggest that drug abuse may result from observing parental drug use. Parental drug abuse begins to have a damaging effect on children as young as 2 years old, especially when parents manifest drug-related personality problems such as depression or poor impulse control.[119] Children whose parents abuse drugs are more likely to have persistent abuse problems than the children of nonabusers.[120]

People who learn that drugs provide pleasurable sensations may be the most likely to experiment with illegal substances, and a habit may develop if the user experiences lower anxiety, fear, and tension levels.[121] Having a history of family drug and alcohol abuse has been found to be a characteristic of violent teenage sexual abusers.[122] Heroin abusers report an unhappy childhood that included harsh physical punishment and parental neglect and rejection.[123]

According to the social learning view, drug involvement begins with using tobacco and drinking alcohol at an early age, and this progresses to experimentation with marijuana and hashish and finally to cocaine and even heroin. Although most recreational users do not progress to "hard stuff," most but not all addicts begin their involvement with narcotics by first experimenting with recreational drugs. By implication, if teen smoking and drinking could be reduced, the gateway to hard drugs would be narrowed.

For example, a 2003 research study found that a 50 percent reduction in the number of teens who smoke cigarettes can cut marijuana use by 16 to 28 percent.[124]

**PROBLEM BEHAVIOR SYNDROME (PBS)** For many people, substance abuse is just one of many problem behaviors.[125] Longitudinal studies show that drug abusers are maladjusted, alienated, and emotionally distressed and that their drug use is one among many social problems.[126] Having a deviant lifestyle begins early in life and is punctuated with criminal relationships, a family history of substance abuse, educational failure, and alienation. Kids who abuse drugs lack commitment to religious values, disdain education, spend most of their time in peer activities, engage in precocious sexual behavior, and experience school failure, family conflict, and similar social problems.[127] In adulthood, people who manifest substance abuse problems also exhibit a garden variety of other social and legal problems.[128]

**RATIONAL CHOICE** Not all people who abuse drugs do so because of personal pathology. Some may use drugs and alcohol because they want to enjoy their effects: getting high, relaxation, improved creativity, escape from reality, and increased sexual responsiveness. Research indicates that adolescent alcohol abusers believe that getting high will make them powerful, increase their sexual performance, and facilitate their social behavior; they care little about negative future consequences.[129]

**IS THERE A SINGLE "CAUSE" OF DRUG ABUSE?** There are many different views of why people take drugs, and no theory has proved adequate to explain all forms of substance abuse. Recent research efforts show that drug users suffer a variety of family and socialization difficulties, have addiction-prone personalities, and are generally at risk for many other social problems.[130] One long-held assumption is that addicts progress along a continuum from using so-called gateway drugs such as alcohol and marijuana to using ever more potent substances, such as cocaine and heroin; this is known as the *gateway hypothesis*.[131] A great deal of research has attempted to find out whether there is truly a drug gateway, but results so far have been mixed. Some hard-core drug abusers have actually never smoked or used alcohol. And although many American youths have tried marijuana, few actually progress to crack or heroin abuse.[132] However, other research has found evidence that marijuana users are up to five times more likely than nonusers to escalate their drug abuse and try cocaine and heroin.[133] In sum, although most marijuana smokers do not become hard drug users, some do, and the risk of using dangerous substances may be increased by first engaging in recreational drug use.

## Drugs and Crime

One of the main reasons for the criminalization of particular substances is the significant association believed to exist between drug abuse and crime. Research suggests that many criminal offenders have extensive experience with alcohol and drug use and that abusers commit an enormous amount of crime.[134] Substance abuse appears to be an important precipitating factor in a variety of criminal acts, especially income-generating crimes such as burglary.[135]

New York City, along with other cities, is experiencing a deadly epidemic of synthetic marijuana usage, including varieties known as K2 or "spice," which can cause extreme reactions in some users. According to New York's health department, more than 120 K2 users visited an emergency room in the city in just one week. Although the state banned ingredients used to make K2, distributors have switched to other ingredients and product names in an attempt to circumvent the law. Here, an NYPD officer speaks with men who are high on K2, along a street in East Harlem.

Spencer Platt/Getty Images News/Getty Images

A number of data sources provide powerful evidence of a drug–crime linkage. Surveys conducted with adolescent drug users show that they are more likely to self-report delinquency than abstainers. For example, the latest national survey on drug use finds that youths aged 12 to 17 who had engaged in fighting or other delinquent behaviors were more likely than other youths to have used illicit drugs in the past month. Illicit drug use was reported by 18 percent of youths who had gotten into a serious fight at school or work in the past year, compared with 8 percent of those who had not engaged in fighting at school or work. Drug use was reported by 35 percent of those who had stolen or tried to steal something worth over $50 in the past year, compared with 8 percent of those who had not attempted or engaged in such theft.[136]

Known criminals have long histories with substance abuse. National studies of substance abuse among arrestees indicate that most were drug users when they were taken into custody—anywhere from 63 percent in Atlanta to 83 percent in Chicago and Sacramento.[137] Drug use is also substantial among people convicted of crime and in the correctional system. The most common substances of abuse reported by probation or parolees were alcohol (30 percent), marijuana (26 percent), and methamphetamines (15 percent); more than half (59 percent) reported more than one substance of abuse at admission to parole or probation.[138]

What causes this linkage? Drug use interferes with maturation and socialization. Drug abusers are more likely to drop out of school, to be underemployed, to engage in premarital sex, and to become unmarried parents. Even if drug use does not turn otherwise law-abiding citizens into criminals, it certainly amplifies the extent of their criminal activities. A recent analysis of the drug–crime association found distinct evidence that the relationship between drugs and crime is complex, and drug users are not a monolithic group that behaves in a uniform and predictable manner. Among the most important findings are the following:[139]

- There are different types of drug users; many do not commit crimes.
- There are differences among criminally active drug users: (a) one group gets involved with crime before or at the same time as they get involved with drugs; (b) another group gets involved with crime only after they get involved with drugs. The onset of addiction is a turning point and causes them to initiate a criminal career.
- Drug use and criminal activity feed off each other as a deviant lifestyle, and peer affiliations reinforce each other.
- Drug addiction does not turn nonviolent criminals into violent criminals, but active addiction increases the frequency of criminal activity.
- Drug use and criminal behavior share some common roots in psychological propensity for impulsive and deviant behavior.
- Drug use impacts criminal behavior by creating the need to finance a drug habit.
- Criminal deviance increases the probability of later drug use.

In sum, research examining both the criminality of known narcotics users and the narcotics use of known criminals reveals a very strong association between drug use and crime. Even if the crime rate of drug users were actually only half that reported in the research literature, users would be responsible for a significant portion of the total criminal activity in the United States.

## Drugs and the Law

The federal government first initiated legal action to curtail the use of some drugs early in the twentieth century.[140] In 1906, the Pure Food and Drug Act required manufacturers to list the amounts of habit-forming drugs on product labels but did not restrict their use. However, the act prohibited the importation and sale of opiates except for medicinal purposes. In 1914, the Harrison Narcotics Act restricted the importation, manufacture, sale, and dispensing of narcotics. It defined **narcotic** as any drug that produces sleep and relieves pain, such as heroin, morphine, and opium. The act was revised in 1922 to allow importation of opium and coca (cocaine) leaves for qualified medical

**CONNECTIONS**

Chapter 10 provides an analysis of the relationship between drugs and violence, which rests on three factors: (1) the psychopharmacological relationship, which is a direct consequence of ingesting mood-altering substances; (2) economic compulsive behavior, which occurs when drug users resort to violence to support their habit; and (3) a systemic link, which occurs when drug dealers battle for territories.

**narcotic**
A drug that produces sleep and relieves pain, such as heroin, morphine, and opium; a habit-forming drug.

practitioners. The Marijuana Tax Act of 1937 required registration and payment of a tax by all persons who imported, sold, or manufactured marijuana. Because marijuana was classified as a narcotic, those registering would also be subject to criminal penalty.

Subsequent federal laws were passed to clarify existing drug statutes and revise penalties. The Boggs Act of 1951 provided mandatory sentences for violating federal drug laws. The Durham-Humphrey Amendment of 1951 made it illegal to dispense barbiturates and amphetamines without a prescription. The Narcotic Control Act of 1956 increased penalties for drug offenders. In 1965, the Drug Abuse Control Act set up stringent guidelines for the legal use and sale of mood-modifying drugs, such as barbiturates, amphetamines, LSD, and any other "dangerous drugs," except narcotics prescribed by doctors and pharmacists. Illegal possession was punished as a misdemeanor and manufacture or sale as a felony. And in 1970, the Comprehensive Drug Abuse Prevention and Control Act set up unified categories of illegal drugs and attached specific penalties to their sale, manufacture, or possession. The law gave the U.S. attorney general discretion to decide in which category to place any new drug.

Since then, various federal laws have attempted to increase penalties imposed on drug smugglers and to limit the manufacture and sale of newly developed substances. The 1984 Controlled Substances Act set new, stringent penalties for drug dealers and created five categories of narcotic and nonnarcotic substances subject to federal laws.[141] The Anti-Drug Abuse Act of 1986 again set new standards for minimum and maximum sentences for drug offenders, increased penalties for most offenses, and created a new drug penalty classification for large-scale offenses (such as trafficking in more than one kilogram of heroin), for which the penalty for a first offense was 10 years to life in prison.[142] With then-President George H. W. Bush's endorsement, Congress passed the Anti-Drug Abuse Act of 1988, which created a coordinated national drug policy under a "drug czar," set treatment and prevention priorities, and, clearly reflecting the government's hard-line stance against drug dealing, instituted availability of the death penalty for drug-related killings.[143] For the most part, state laws mirror federal statutes. Some apply extremely heavy penalties for selling or distributing dangerous drugs, such as prison sentences of up to 25 years.

## Drug Control Strategies

Substance abuse remains a major social problem in the United States. Politicians looking for a safe campaign issue can take advantage of the public's fear of drug addiction by calling for a war on drugs. Such wars have been declared even when drug use was stable or in decline.[144] Can these efforts pay off? Can illegal drug use be eliminated or controlled?

A number of different drug control strategies have been tried, with varying degrees of success. Some aim to deter people from using drugs by stopping the flow of drugs into the country, apprehending and punishing dealers, and cracking down on street-level drug deals. Others focus on preventing drug use by educating potential users to the dangers of substance abuse (convincing them to "say no to drugs") and by organizing community groups to work with the at-risk population in their area. Still another approach is to treat known users so they can control their addictions. Some of these efforts are discussed next.

**SOURCE CONTROL** One approach to drug control is to deter the sale and importation of drugs through the systematic apprehension

Law enforcement agents leave a clothing store after a raid in the Los Angeles fashion district. Agents raided dozens of businesses in 2014 as part of an investigation into suspected money laundering for Mexican drug cartels.

of large-volume drug dealers, coupled with the enforcement of strict drug laws that carry heavy penalties. This approach is designed to capture and punish known international drug dealers and to deter others from entering the drug trade. A major effort has been made to cut off supplies of drugs by destroying overseas crops and arresting members of drug cartels in Central and South America, Asia, and the Middle East, where many drugs are grown and manufactured. The federal government has been in the vanguard of encouraging exporting nations to step up efforts to destroy drug crops and prosecute. The United States has contributed more than a billion dollars since 2009 to provide economic incentives and increased security to farmers in drug-producing regions in the Western Hemisphere.[145] However, translating words into deeds is a formidable task. Drug lords are willing and able to fight back through intimidation, violence, and corruption. The Colombian drug cartels do not hesitate to use violence and assassination to protect their interests. Mexico has been awash in blood as cartels compete for power and control of the drug trade.

The amount of narcotics grown each year is so vast that even if three-quarters of the opium crop were destroyed, the U.S. market would still require only 10 percent of the remainder to sustain its drug trade. The drug trade is an important source of foreign revenue for third-world nations, and destroying the drug trade undermines their economies. More than a million people in developing nations depend on the cultivating and processing of illegal substances. Adding to the problem of source control is the fact that the United States has little influence in some key drug-producing areas. War and terrorism also make source control strategies problematic. After the United States toppled Afghanistan's Taliban government, the remnants began to grow and sell poppy to support their insurgency. A 2014 World Drug Report by the U.N. Office on Drugs and Crime found that Afghanistan now leads the world in opium production and has continued to see more land being used for poppy farming—a record 520,000 acres.[146] And even though some guerillas may not be interested in joining or colluding with crime cartels, they finance their war against the government by aiding drug traffickers and "taxing" crops and sales.[147]

The federal government estimates that U.S. citizens spend more than $40 billion annually on illegal drugs, and much of this money is funneled overseas. Even if the government of one nation were willing to cooperate in vigorous drug suppression efforts, suppliers in other nations, eager to cash in on the "seller's market," would be encouraged to turn more acreage over to coca or poppy production.

**INTERDICTION STRATEGIES** Law enforcement efforts have also been directed at intercepting drug supplies as they enter the country. Border patrols and military personnel using sophisticated hardware have been involved in massive interdiction efforts; many impressive multimillion-dollar seizures have been made. Yet the U.S. borders are so vast and unprotected that meaningful interdiction is impossible. And even if all importation were shut down, home-grown marijuana and laboratory-made drugs, such as ecstasy, LSD, and PCP, could become the drugs of choice. Even now, their easy availability and relatively low cost are increasing their popularity among the at-risk population.

**LAW ENFORCEMENT STRATEGIES** Local, state, and federal law enforcement agencies have been actively fighting drugs. One approach is to direct efforts at large-scale drug

Erin Siegal/Redux

Border control is an established anti-drug policy, but one that is difficult to achieve. U.S. Customs and Border Patrol (CBP) agents work along the U.S.–Mexico border crossing joining Tijuana, Baja California, Mexico, to San Diego, California. Working dogs are used to track the scent of drugs and smuggled humans. Here, a woman suspected of smuggling is detained after a dog detected the scent of drugs in the vehicle she was driving. Do you believe such strategies can stem the flow of drugs or are they doomed to failure?

rings. The long-term consequence has been to decentralize drug dealing and encourage young independent dealers to become major suppliers. Ironically, it has proved easier for federal agents to infiltrate and prosecute traditional organized crime groups than to take on drug-dealing gangs. Consequently, some nontraditional groups have broken into the drug trade. Police can also target, intimidate, and arrest street-level dealers and users in an effort to make drug use so much of a hassle that consumption is cut back and the crime rate reduced. Approaches that have been tried include reverse stings, in which undercover agents pose as dealers to arrest users who approach them for a buy. Police have attacked fortified crack houses with heavy equipment to breach their defenses. They have used racketeering laws to seize the assets of known dealers. Special task forces of local and state police have conducted undercover operations and drug sweeps to discourage both dealers and users.

Although some street-level enforcement efforts have succeeded, others are considered failures. Drug sweeps have clogged courts and correctional facilities with petty offenders, while draining police resources. There are also suspicions that a displacement effect occurs; that is, stepped-up efforts to curb drug dealing in one area or city simply encourage dealers to seek friendlier territory.[148]

**PUNISHMENT STRATEGIES**   Even if law enforcement efforts cannot produce a general deterrent effect, the courts may achieve the required result by severely punishing known drug dealers and traffickers. A number of initiatives have made the prosecution and punishment of drug offenders a top priority. State prosecutors have expanded their investigations into drug importation and distribution and assigned special prosecutors to focus on drug dealers. The fact that drugs such as crack are considered a serious problem may have convinced judges and prosecutors to expedite substance abuse cases.

However, these efforts often have their downside. Defense attorneys consider delay tactics sound legal maneuvering in drug-related cases. Courts are so backlogged that prosecutors are eager to plea-bargain. The consequence of this legal maneuvering is that many people convicted on federal drug charges are granted probation or some other form of community release. Even so, prisons have become jammed with inmates, many of whom were involved in drug-related cases. Many drug offenders sent to prison do not serve their entire sentences because they are released in an effort to relieve prison overcrowding.[149]

**COMMUNITY STRATEGIES**   Another type of drug control effort relies on the involvement of local community groups to lead the fight against drugs. Representatives of various local government agencies, churches, civic organizations, and similar institutions are being brought together to create drug prevention and awareness programs.

Citizen-sponsored programs attempt to restore a sense of community in drug-infested areas, reduce fear, and promote conventional norms and values.[150] These efforts can be classified into one of four distinct categories.[151] The first involves efforts to aid law enforcement, which may include block watches, cooperative police–community efforts, and citizen patrols. These citizen groups are nonconfrontational: they simply observe or photograph dealers, write down their license plate numbers, and then notify police.

A second tactic is to use the civil justice system to harass offenders. Landlords have been sued for owning properties that house drug dealers; neighborhood groups have scrutinized drug houses for building code violations. Information acquired from these various sources is turned over to local authorities, such as police and housing agencies, for more formal action.

A third approach is through community-based treatment efforts in which citizen volunteers participate in self-help support programs, such as Narcotics Anonymous and Cocaine Anonymous, which have more than 1,000 chapters nationally. Other programs provide youths with martial arts training, dancing, and social events as alternatives to the drug life.

A fourth type of community-level drug prevention effort is designed to enhance the quality of life, improve interpersonal relationships, and upgrade the neighborhood's physical environment. Activities might include the creation of drug-free school zones (which encourage police to keep drug dealers away from the vicinity of schools). Consciousness-raising efforts include demonstrations and marches to publicize the drug problem and build solidarity among participants.

**DRUG EDUCATION AND PREVENTION STRATEGIES** According to this view, substance abuse would decline if kids could be taught about the dangers of drug use. The most widely known drug education program, Drug Abuse Resistance Education (D.A.R.E.), is an elementary school course designed to give students the skills for resisting peer pressure to experiment with tobacco, drugs, and alcohol. It is unique because it employs uniformed police officers to carry the antidrug message to the students before they enter junior high school. But even though more than 40 percent of all school districts incorporate assistance from local law enforcement agencies in their drug prevention programming, reviews of the program have not been encouraging, concluding that the program has only a marginal impact on student drug use and attitudes.[152] These negative evaluations caused D.A.R.E. to revise its curriculum. It is now aimed at older students and relies more on helping them question their assumptions about drug use than on having them listen to lectures on the subject.

**DRUG-TESTING PROGRAMS** Drug testing of private employees, government workers, and criminal offenders is believed to deter substance abuse. In the workplace, employees are tested to enhance on-the-job safety and productivity. In some industries, such as mining and transportation, drug testing is considered essential because abuse can pose a threat to the public.[153] Business leaders have been enlisted in the fight against drugs. Mandatory drug-testing programs in government and industry are common; more than 40 percent of the country's largest companies, including IBM and AT&T, have drug-testing programs. The federal government requires employee testing in regulated industries such as nuclear energy and defense contracting.

Criminal defendants are now routinely tested at all stages of the justice system, from arrest to parole. The goal is to reduce criminal behavior by detecting current users and curbing their abuse. Can such programs reduce criminal activity? Two evaluations of pretrial drug-testing programs found little evidence that monitoring defendants' drug use influenced their behavior.[154]

**TREATMENT STRATEGIES** Treatment strategies rely on helping substance abusers go straight rather than deterring their behavior through punishment. Specialized drug courts have been created whose magistrates are experts in dealing with substance abusers. There are now almost 3,000 drug courts across the nation and they handle more than 100,000 cases a year.[155]

A number of approaches are taken to treat known users, getting them clean of drugs and alcohol and thereby reducing the at-risk population (see Exhibit 13.1). One rests on the assumption that each user is an individual and successful treatment must be geared to the using patterns and personality of the individual offenders in order to build a sense of self.[156] Some programs have placed abusers in regimens of outdoor activities and wilderness training to create self-reliance and a sense of accomplishment.[157] Others focus on problem-solving skills, helping former and current addicts to deal with their real-world issues.[158] Providing supportive housing for formerly homeless drug addicts also may lead to better access to medical care, food, and job opportunities—all of which result in lower levels of addiction.[159] More intensive efforts use group therapy, relying on group leaders who have been substance abusers; through such sessions, users get the skills and support to help them reject social pressure to use drugs. These programs are based on the Alcoholics Anonymous

## Exhibit 13.1 Effective Treatment Approaches

- *Medications.* Medications can be used to help with different aspects of the treatment process.
- *Withdrawal.* Medications offer help in suppressing withdrawal symptoms during detoxification. Patients who go through medically assisted withdrawal but do not receive any further treatment show drug abuse patterns similar to those who were never treated.
- *Treatment.* Medications can be used to help reestablish normal brain function and to prevent relapse and to diminish cravings. Medications are now available for treating opioids (heroin, morphine), tobacco (nicotine), and alcohol addiction; others are being developed for treating stimulant (cocaine, methamphetamine) and cannabis (marijuana) addiction. A significant problem: many addicts are polydrug users, requiring multiple medications.
- *Behavioral treatments.* Behavioral treatments help patients engage in the treatment process, modify their attitudes and behaviors related to drug abuse, and increase healthy life skills. These treatments can enhance the effectiveness of medications and help people stay in treatment longer. Outpatient behavioral treatment encompasses a wide variety of programs for patients who visit a clinic at regular intervals. Most of the programs involve individual or group drug counseling. Some programs also offer other forms of behavioral treatment:
  - *Cognitive-behavioral therapy* seeks to help patients recognize, avoid, and cope with the situations in which they are most likely to abuse drugs.

- *Multidimensional family therapy* was developed for adolescents with drug abuse problems as well as their families. It addresses a range of influences on their drug abuse patterns and is designed to improve overall family functioning.
- *Motivational interviewing* capitalizes on the readiness of individuals to change their behavior and enter treatment.
- *Motivational incentives* (contingency management) use positive reinforcement to encourage abstinence from drugs.
- *Residential treatment* programs can be very effective, especially for those with more severe problems.
- *Therapeutic communities* (TCs) are highly structured programs in which patients remain at a residence, typically for 6 to 12 months. TCs differ from other treatment approaches principally in their use of the community—treatment staff and those in recovery—as a key agent of change to influence patient attitudes, perceptions, and behaviors associated with drug use. Patients in TCs may include those with relatively long histories of drug addiction, involvement in serious criminal activities, and seriously impaired social functioning. TCs are now also being designed to accommodate the needs of women who are pregnant or have children. The focus of the TC is on the resocialization of the patient to a drug-free, crime-free lifestyle.

**Source:** National Institute on Drug Abuse, "NIDA InfoFacts: Treatment Approaches for Drug Addiction," www.drugabuse.gov /publications/drugfacts/treatment-approaches-drug-addiction (accessed 2015).

approach, which holds that users must find within themselves the strength to stay clean and that peer support from those who understand their experiences can help them achieve a drug-free life.

There are also residential programs for the more heavily involved, and a large network of drug treatment centers has been developed. Some detoxification units use medical procedures to wean patients from the more addicting drugs to other drugs, such as methadone, that can be more easily regulated. Methadone is a drug similar to heroin, and addicts can be treated at clinics where they receive methadone under controlled conditions. However, methadone programs have been undermined because some users sell their methadone in the black market, and others supplement their dosages with illegally obtained heroin. Other programs use drugs such as Naxalone, which counters the effects of narcotics and eases the trauma of withdrawal, but results have not been conclusive.[160]

Other therapeutic programs attempt to deal with the psychological causes of drug use in "therapeutic communities." Hypnosis, aversion therapy (getting users to associate drugs with unpleasant sensations, such as nausea), counseling, biofeedback, and other techniques are often used. Some programs report significant success with clients who are able to complete the full course of the treatment.[161]

The long-term effects of treatment on drug abuse are still uncertain. Critics charge that a stay in a residential program can stigmatize people as addicts even if they never used hard drugs, and in treatment they may be introduced to hard-core users with whom they will associate after release. Users do not often enter these programs voluntarily and have little motivation to change. Supporters of treatment argue that many addicts are helped by intensive inpatient and outpatient treatment, and the cost saving is considerable. The biggest problem is availability: the federal government estimates that about 23 million people are in need of intense drug and alcohol treatment but only 2.5 million are in programs.[162]

**EMPLOYMENT PROGRAMS**  Research indicates that drug abusers who obtain and keep employment are likely to end or reduce the incidence of their substance abuse.[163] Not surprisingly, then, there have been a number of efforts to provide vocational rehabilitation for drug abusers. One approach is the supported work program, which typically involves jobsite training, ongoing assessment, and jobsite intervention. Rather than teaching work skills in a classroom, support programs rely on helping drug abusers deal with real work settings. Other programs provide training to overcome barriers to employment, including help with motivation, education, experience, the job market, job-seeking skills, and personal issues. For example, female abusers may be unaware of child care resources that would enable them to seek employment opportunities. Another approach is to help addicts improve their interviewing skills so that once job opportunities can be identified, they are equipped to convince potential employers of their commitment and reliability.

## Legalization of Drugs

"Like alcohol Prohibition in the 1920s, which was intended to banish certain substances from society, drug prohibition has not only failed its mission but has made its mission impossible. The failures of prohibition are painfully obvious: wasted money, wasted lives, and wasted opportunities. Determining what works best is less straightforward, but we have examples from all over the world and even our own states of policies that show progress and represent opportunities to improve."[164]

Amy Locane-Bovenizer cries as she is sentenced on February 14, 2013, in Somerville, New Jersey. Locane-Bovenizer, the former *Melrose Place* actress, was driving drunk when her SUV plowed into a car and killed a New Jersey woman. She faced up to 10 years in prison after a jury convicted her of vehicular homicide in the death of 60-year-old Helene Seeman. The judge shortened the sentence to three years, citing the hardship on Locane-Bovenizer's two children, one of whom has a medical and mental disability. Locane-Bovenizer's blood-alcohol level was nearly three times the legal limit when the crash occurred. One argument against the legalization of drugs is that it will result in many more deaths such as the one caused by Locane-Bovenizer, as people drive and take drugs. What do you think?

So claims the Drug Policy Alliance, a leading voice for reforming drug control laws and a group that believes the so-called "war on drugs" is both expensive and futile; it has cost more than $500 billion over the past 20 years. During the last three years alone, federal and local governments have spent $60 billion on drug control and treatment—money that could have been spent on education and economic development. The current budget is about $25 billion for drug treatment and control.[165]

Legalization is warranted, according to drug expert Ethan Nadelmann, because the use of mood-altering substances is customary in nearly all human societies;

people have always wanted—and will always find ways of obtaining—psychoactive drugs.[166] Banning drugs creates illicit networks of manufacturers and distributors, many of whom use violence as part of their standard operating procedures. Although some believe that drug use is immoral, Nadelmann questions whether it is any worse than the unrestricted use of alcohol and cigarettes, both of which are addicting and unhealthful. Far more people die each year because they abuse these legal substances than are killed in drug wars or die from abusing illegal substances.

Nadelmann also states that just as Prohibition failed to stop the flow of alcohol in the 1920s, while simultaneously increasing the power of organized crime, the policy of prohibiting drugs is similarly doomed to failure. When drugs were legal and freely available early in the twentieth century, the proportion of Americans who used drugs was not much greater than it is today. Most users led normal lives, largely because of the legal status of their drug use.

The futility of drug control efforts is illustrated by the fact that despite massive long-term efforts, the price of illegal narcotics such as crack cocaine and heroin has drifted downward as supplies have become more plentiful. In terms of weight and availability, there is still no commodity whose sale is more lucrative than illegal drugs. They cost relatively little to produce, and they provide dealers and traffickers with large profit margins. At the current average street price of $169 per gram in the United States, a metric ton of pure cocaine is worth more than $150 million; cutting it to reduce its purity can double or triple the value.[167] With that kind of profit to be made, can any strategy, whether treatment-oriented or punishment-oriented, reduce the lure of drug trafficking?

If drugs were legalized, the argument goes, price and distribution could be controlled by the government. This would reduce addicts' cash requirements, so crime rates would drop because users would no longer need the same cash flow to support their habits. Drug-related deaths would decline because government control would reduce needle sharing and the spread of AIDS. Legalization would also destroy the drug-importing cartels and gangs. Because drugs would be bought and sold openly, the government would reap a tax windfall both from taxes on the sale of drugs and from income taxes paid by drug dealers on profits that have been part of the hidden economy. Of course, as with alcohol, drug distribution would be regulated, keeping drugs away from adolescents, public servants such as police and airline pilots, and known felons. Those who favor legalization point to the Netherlands as a country that has legalized drugs and remains relatively free of crime.

Those who oppose drug legalization counter that this approach might indeed have the short-term effect of reducing the association between drug use and crime, but it might also have grave social consequences. Legalization might increase the nation's rate of drug usage, creating an even larger group of nonproductive, drug-dependent people who must be cared for by the rest of society. Also, while few people die from smoking marijuana, there are about 40,000 drug-related deaths each year in the United States.[168] In countries such as Thailand, where drugs are cheap and readily available, the rate of narcotics use is quite high. Historically, the availability of cheap narcotics has preceded drug use epidemics, as was the case when British and American merchants sold opium in nineteenth-century China.

AP Images/Brennan Linsley

While marijuana may be legally bought in Colorado by adults it is forbidden to underage minors. Here, young partygoers listen to music and smoke marijuana during the annual 4/20 marijuana festival in Denver's downtown Civic Center Park. Colorado schools are compiling data on the number of students who get busted for using marijuana, an idea aimed at gauging the impact of the drug's legalization and whether it affects usage among youth.

If juveniles, criminals, and members of other at-risk groups were forbidden to buy drugs, who would be the customers? Noncriminal, nonabusing, middle-aged adults? And would not those prohibited from legally buying drugs create an underground market almost as vast as the current one? If the government tried to raise money by taxing legal drugs, as it now does with liquor and cigarettes, that might encourage drug smuggling to avoid tax payments; these "illegal" drugs might then fall into the hands of adolescents.

Decriminalization or legalization of controlled substances is unlikely in the near term, but further study is warranted. What effect would a policy of partial decriminalization (for example, legalizing small amounts of marijuana as some states have done) have on drug use rates? Would a get-tough policy help to "widen the net" of the justice system and thus (through contact with users during incarceration) actually deepen some youths' involvement in substance abuse? Can society provide alternatives to drugs that will reduce teenage drug dependency? The answers to these questions have proved elusive. The different types of drug control strategies are summarized in Concept Summary 13.1.

## Concept Summary 13.1   Drug Control Strategies

| Control Strategy | Main Focus | Problems/Issues |
| --- | --- | --- |
| **Source control** | Destroy overseas crops and drug labs | Drug profits hard to resist; drug crops in hostile nations are off limits |
| **Interdiction** | Seal borders; arrest drug couriers | Extensive U.S. borders hard to control |
| **Law enforcement** | Police investigation and arrest of dealers | New dealers are recruited to replace those in prison |
| **Punishment** | Deter dealers with harsh punishments | Crowded prisons promote bargain justice |
| **Community programs** | Help community members deal with drug problems on the local level | Relies on community cohesion and efficacy |
| **Drug education** | Teach kids about the harm of taking drugs | Evaluations do not show programs are effective |
| **Drug testing** | Threaten employees with drug tests to deter use | Evaluations do not show drug testing is effective; people cheat on tests |
| **Treatment** | Use of therapy to get people off drugs | Expensive, requires motivation; clients associate with other users |
| **Employment** | Provide jobs as an alternative to drugs | Requires that former addicts become steady employees |
| **Legalization** | Decriminalize or legalize drugs | Political hot potato; danger of creating more users |

# Thinking Like a Criminologist

**Mental Illness and Crime** You have been called upon by the director of the Department of Health and Human Services to give your opinion on a recent national survey that found that serious mental illness (SMI) is highly correlated with illicit drug use. This research shows that adults who used an illicit drug in the past year were three times as likely to suffer mental illness than adults who did not use an illicit drug. One possible explanation of these data is that drugs cause people to become mentally ill while another is that mentally ill people use drugs to "self-medicate." Regardless of the cause we know that (a) people who use drugs commit more crime than nonabusers and (b) that the mentally ill commit more crime than the mentally sound.

## Writing Assignment

The director asks you to comment on the mental illness, substance abuse, and crime nexus. Write an essay spelling out the true association between these factors, how each may be an effect or cause, and how all three interact.

# SUMMARY

**L01** **Interpret what is meant by the term *social harm*.**

According to the theory of social harm, acts become crimes when they cause injury and produce harm to others. However, some dangerous activities are not considered crimes, and some activities that do not appear harmful are criminalized.

**L02** **Discuss the activities of moral crusaders.**

Moral crusaders seek to shape the law to reflect their own way of thinking. These moral entrepreneurs go on moral crusades to take on such issues as prayer in schools, gun ownership, same-sex marriage, abortion, and the distribution of sexually explicit books. One of the most visible crusades has been efforts to control the legality of same-sex marriage, which culminated in a 2015 Supreme Court ruling striking down laws banning the practice.

**L03** **Describe the various forms of outlawed deviant sexuality.**

The outlawed sexual behaviors known as paraphilias include frotteurism (rubbing against or touching a nonconsenting person), voyeurism (obtaining sexual pleasure from spying on a stranger while he or she disrobes or engages in sexual behavior with another), exhibitionism (deriving sexual pleasure from exposing the genitals to surprise or shock a stranger), sadomasochism (deriving pleasure from receiving pain or inflicting pain on another), and pedophilia (attaining sexual pleasure through sexual activity with prepubescent children).

**L04** **Distinguish among the different types of prostitutes.**

Prostitutes who work the streets in plain sight of police, citizens, and customers are referred to as hustlers, hookers, or streetwalkers. B-girls spend their time in bars, drinking and waiting to be picked up by customers. Brothel prostitutes live in a house with a madam who employs them, supervises their behavior, and receives a fee for her services. Call girls work via telephone "dates" and get their clients by word of mouth or by making arrangements with bellhops, cab drivers, and so on. Some escort services are fronts for prostitution rings. Prostitutes known as circuit travelers move around in groups of two or three to lumber, labor, and agricultural camps. Cyberprostitutes set up personal websites or put listings on Web boards such as Craigslist that carry personal ads.

**L05    State the arguments for and against legalizing prostitution.**

The sexual equality view considers the prostitute a victim of male dominance. The free choice view is that prostitution, if freely chosen, expresses women's equality and is not a symptom of subjugation. Advocates of both positions argue that prostitution should be decriminalized in order to relieve already desperate women from the additional burden of severe legal punishment. However, decriminalizing prostitution does not protect women from the violence, verbal abuse, physical injury, and diseases (such as HIV, AIDS) to which they are exposed in illegal prostitution.

**L06    Discuss the causes of substance abuse.**

The onset of drug use can be tied to such factors as racial prejudice, devalued identities, low self-esteem, poor socioeconomic status, and the high level of mistrust, negativism, and defiance typically found in impoverished areas. Some experts have linked substance abuse to psychological deficits such as impaired cognitive functioning, personality disturbance, and emotional problems. Substance abuse may have a genetic basis. Social psychologists suggest that drug abuse may also result from observing parental drug use. Substance abuse may be just one of many social problem behaviors. Some may use drugs and alcohol because they want to enjoy their effects: getting high, relaxation, improved creativity, escape from reality, and increased sexual responsiveness.

## Key Terms

| | | | |
|---|---|---|---|
| public order crime 414 | paraphilia 419 | temperance | drug-dependent |
| victimless crime 415 | prostitution 420 | movement 431 | personality 433 |
| social harm 416 | pornography 427 | Prohibition 431 | narcotic 436 |
| moral entrepreneur 417 | obscenity 427 | binge drinking 431 | |

## Critical Thinking Questions

1. Why do you think people take drugs? Do you know anyone with an addiction-prone personality, or do you believe that is a myth?

2. What might be the best strategy to reduce teenage drug use: source control, reliance on treatment, national education efforts, or community-level enforcement?

3. Under what circumstances, if any, might the legalization or decriminalization of sex-related material be beneficial to society?

4. Do you consider alcohol a drug? Should greater control be imposed on the sale of alcohol?

5. Is prostitution really a crime? Should men or women have the right to sell sexual favors if they so choose?

## Notes

*All URLs accessed in 2015.*

1. FBI, "Agencies Cooperate in Child Sexual Exploitation Case: Michigan Subject Gets 30 Years in Prison," October 23, 2014, www.fbi.gov/news/stories/2014/october/agency-cooperation-leads-to-30-year-sentence-in-child-exploitation-case/.

2. Edwin Schur, *Crimes Without Victims* (Englewood Cliffs, NJ: Prentice Hall, 1965).

3. Raymond Hernandez, "Weiner Resigns in Chaotic Final Scene" *New York Times*, June 16, 2011, www.nytimes.com/2011/06/17/nyregion/anthony-d-weiner-tells-friends-he-will-resign.html.

4. The Bible, New International Version, Genesis 18:20.

5. Bible Hub, Ezekiel 16:49, biblehub.com/ezekiel/16-49.htm.

6. Wayne LaFave and Austin Scott Jr., *Criminal Law* (St. Paul, MN: West, 1986), p. 12.

7. Ibid.

8. Andrea Dworkin, quoted in "Where Do We Stand on Pornography?" *Ms.* (January–February 1994): 34.

9. Russel Falck, Jichuan Wang, and Robert Carlson, "The Epidemiology of Physical Attack and Rape Among Crack-Using Women," *Violence and Victims* 16 (2001): 79–89.

10. C. Gabrielle Salfati, Alison James, and Lynn Ferguson, "Prostitute Homicides: A Descriptive Study," *Journal of Interpersonal Violence* 23 (2008): 505–543.

11. Morris Cohen, "Moral Aspects of the Criminal Law," *Yale Law Journal* 49 (1940): 1017.

12. See Joel Feinberg, *Social Philosophy* (Englewood Cliffs, NJ: Prentice Hall, 1973), Chapters 2, 3.

13. *United States v. 12 200-ft Reels of Super 8mm Film*, 413 U.S. 123 (1973), at p. 137.

14. John Franks, "The Evaluation of Community Standards," *Journal of Social Psychology* 139 (1999): 253–255.

15. Sebastian Anthony, "Just How Big Are Porn Sites?" ExtremeTech, April 4, 2012, www.extremetech.com/computing/123929-just-how-big-are-porn-sites.

16. Mark Ward, "Web Porn: Just How Much Is There?" BBC News, July 1, 2013, www.bbc.com/news/technology-23030090.

17. Irving Kristol, "Liberal Censorship and the Common Culture," *Society* 36 (September 1999): 5.

18. United Nations, World Health Organization, "Female Genital Mutilation, 2014," www.who.int/mediacentre/factsheets/fs241/en/.

19. David Kaplan, "Is It Torture or Tradition?" *Newsweek* (December 20, 1993): 124.

20. Ali Mokdad, James Marks, Donna F. Stroup, and Julie Gerberding, "Actual Causes of Death in the United States, 2000," *Journal of the American Medical Association* 291 (2004): 1238–1241.

21. Howard Becker, *Outsiders* (New York: Macmillan, 1963), pp. 13–14.

22. American Library Association, "Frequently Challenged Books," www.ala.org/bbooks/frequentlychallengedbooks.

23. U.S. Code, Title 1 § 7. Definition of "marriage" and "spouse."

24. *Lawrence et al. v. Texas*, No. 02-102, June 26, 2003.

25. *Hillary Goodridge et al. v. Department of Public Health and Another*, SJC-08860, November 18, 2003.

26. *Obergefell v. Hodges*, 576 U.S. ___ (2015),

27. David Gardner, "I Feel Guilty: Girl Held for 18 Years 'Bonded with Kidnapper,'" *London Evening Standard*, August 28, 2009, www.standard.co.uk/news/i-feel-guilty-girl-held-for-18-years-bonded-with-kidnapper-6745223.html.

28. Trip Gabriel and Steven Yaccino, "Officials, Citing Miscarriages, Weigh Death Penalty in Ohio Case," May 9, 2013, www.nytimes.com/2013/05/10/us/cleveland-kidnapping.html?_r=0; Eesha Pandit, "In the Cleveland Kidnapping Case, Bystander Intervention Worked. What Happens When It Doesn't?" *The Nation*, May 13, 2013, www.thenation.com/article/cleveland-kidnapping-case-bystander-intervention-worked-what-happens-when-it-doesnt/.

29. Richard Estes and Neil Alan Weiner, *The Commercial Sexual Exploitation of Children in the U.S., Canada, and Mexico* (Philadelphia: University of Pennsylvania Press, 2001).

30. Associated Press, "David Carradine Found Dead in Thailand Hotel," June 4, 2009.

31. See, generally, Spencer Rathus and Jeffery Nevid, *Abnormal Psychology* (Englewood Cliffs, NJ: Prentice Hall, 1991), pp. 373–411.

32. W. P. de Silva, "Sexual Variations," *British Medical Journal* 318 (1999): 654–655.

33. Associated Press, "Ex-Baltimore Ravens Cheerleader Molly Shattuck Gets Probation for Raping a 15-Year-Old Boy," *New York Daily News*, August 21, 2015.

34. Miriam Wijkman, Catrien Bijleveld, and Jan Hendriks, "Women Don't Do Such Things! Characteristics of Female Sex Offenders and Offender Types," *Sexual Abuse: A Journal of Research and Treatment* 22 (2010): 135–156.

35. Boris Schiffer, Thomas Paul, Elke Gizewski, Michael Forsting, Norbert Leygraf, Manfred Schedlowski, and Tillmann H. C. Kruger, "Functional Brain Correlates of Heterosexual Paedophilia," *Neuroimage* 41 (2008): 80–91.

36. Ray Blanchard, Bruce K. Christensen, Scott M. Strong, James M. Cantor, Michael E. Kuban, Philip Klassen, Robert Dickey, and Thomas Blak, "Retrospective Self-Reports of Childhood Accidents Causing Unconsciousness in Phallometrically Diagnosed Pedophiles," *Archives of Sexual Behavior* 31 (2002): 111–127.

37. Michael Allan and Randolph Grace, "Psychometric Assessment of Dynamic Risk Factors for Child Molesters," *Sexual Abuse: A Journal of Research* 19 (2007): 347–367.

38. For an analysis of this issue, see Theresa Gannon and Devon Polaschek, "Cognitive Distortions in Child Molesters: A Re-examination of Key Theories and Research," *Clinical Psychology Review* 26 (2006): 1000–1019.

39. See, generally, V. Bullogh, *Sexual Variance in Society and History* (Chicago: University of Chicago Press, 1958), pp. 143–144.

40. Spencer Rathus, *Human Sexuality* (New York: Holt, Rinehart and Winston, 1983), p. 463.

41. Charles McCaghy, *Deviant Behavior* (New York: Macmillan, 1976), pp. 348–349.

42. Michael Waldholz, "HTLV–I Virus Found in Blood of Prostitutes," *Wall Street Journal*, January 5, 1990, p. B2.

43. Scott Shuger, "Hookers.com: How E-commerce Is Transforming the Oldest Profession," *Slate Magazine*, www.slate.com/articles/briefing/articles/2000/01/hookerscom.html.

44. Nisha Lilia Diu, "Welcome to Paradise," *The Telegraph*, 2013, s.telegraph.co.uk/graphics/projects/welcome-to-paradise/.

45. Elizabeth Bernstein, "The Meaning of the Purchase: Desire, Demand, and the Commerce of Sex," *Ethnography* 2 (2001): 389–420.

46. Megan Annitto, "Consent, Coercion, and Compassion: Emerging Legal Responses to the Commercial Sexual Exploitation of Minors," *Yale Law and Policy Review* 30 (2011): 1–70.

47. Charles Winick and Paul Kinsie, *The Lively Commerce* (Chicago: Quadrangle, 1971), p. 58.

48. Celia Williamson and Lynda Baker, "Women in Street-Based Prostitution: A Typology of Their Work Styles," *Qualitative Social Work* 8 (2009): 27–44.

49. Winick and Kinsie, *The Lively Commerce*, pp. 172–173.

50. Paul Goldstein, "Occupational Mobility in the World of Prostitution: Becoming a Madam," *Deviant Behavior* 4 (1983): 267–279.

51. Yellow Pages, www.yellowpages.com/new-york-ny/escort-service; www.yellowpages.com/las-vegas-nv/escort-service.

52. Mireya Navarro, "Group Forced Illegal Aliens into Prostitution, U.S. Says," *New York Times*, April 24, 1998, p. A10.

53. Ginger Thompson and Philip Shenon, "Navy Officer Describes Working as a Prostitute," *New York Times*, April 12, 2008, www.nytimes.com/2008/04/12/us/12officer.html.

54. D. Kelly Weisberg, *Children of the Night: A Study of Adolescent Prostitution* (Lexington, MA: Lexington Books, 1985), pp. 44–55.

55. N. Jackman, Richard O'Toole, and Gilbert Geis, "The Self-Image of the Prostitute," in *Sexual Deviance*, ed. J. Gagnon and W. Simon (New York: Harper & Row, 1967), pp. 152–153.

56. Tammy Heilemann and Janaki Santhiveeran, "How Do Female Adolescents Cope and Survive the Hardships of Prostitution? A Content Analysis of Existing Literature," *Journal of Ethnic and Cultural Diversity in Social Work* 20 (2011): 57–76.

57. Lisa Kramer and Ellen Berg, "A Survival Analysis of Timing of Entry into Prostitution: The Differential Impact of Race, Educational Level, and Childhood/Adolescent Risk Factors," *Sociological Inquiry* 73 (2003): 511–529.

58. Gerald Hotaling and David Finkelhor, *The Sexual Exploitation of Missing Children* (Washington, DC: U.S. Department of Justice, 1988).

59. Jennifer Cobbina and Sharon Oselin, "It's Not Only for the Money: An Analysis of Adolescent versus Adult Entry into Street Prostitution," *Sociological Inquiry* 81 (2011): 310–332.

60. Michael Miner, Jill Flitter, and Beatrice Robinson, "Association of Sexual Revictimization with Sexuality and Psychological Function," *Journal of Interpersonal Violence* 21 (2006): 503–524.

61. Jolanda Sallmann, "Living with Stigma: Women's Experiences of Prostitution and Substance Use," *Afillia Journal of Women and Social Work* 25 (2010): 146–159.

62. Barbara G. Brents and Kathryn Hausbeck, "State-Sanctioned Sex: Negotiating Formal and Informal Regulatory Practices in Nevada Brothels," *Sociological Perspectives* 44 (2001): 307–335.

63. Ibid.

64. Mara Keire, "The Vice Trust: A Reinterpretation of the White Slavery Scare in the United States, 1907–1917," *Journal of Social History* 35 (2001): 5–42.

65. Ronald Weitzer, "The Politics of Prostitution in America," in *Sex for Sale*, ed. R. Weitzer (New York: Routledge, 2000), pp. 159–180.

66. Rebecca Hayes-Smitha and Zahra Shekarkharb, "Why Is Prostitution Criminalized? An Alternative Viewpoint on the Construction of Sex Work," *Contemporary Justice Review* 13 (2010): 43–55.

67. Andrea Dworkin, *Pornography* (New York: Dutton, 1989).

68. Annette Jolin, "On the Backs of Working Prostitutes: Feminist Theory and Prostitution Policy," *Crime and Delinquency* 40 (1994): 60–83, at 76–77.

69. Alexa Albert, *Brothel: Mustang Ranch and Its Women* (New York: Random House, 2001).

70. Melissa Farley, *Prostitution and Trafficking in Nevada: Making the Connections* (San Francisco: Prostitution Research & Education, 2007).

71. Roger Matthews, *Prostitution, Politics and Policy* (London: Routledge-Cavendish, 2008).

72. Hayes-Smitha and Shekarkharb, "Why Is Prostitution Criminalized? An Alternative Viewpoint on the Construction of Sex Work," p. 54.

73. *Merriam-Webster Dictionary* (New York: Pocket Books, 1974), p. 484.

74. Attorney General's Commission, *Report on Pornography, Final Report* (Washington, DC: U.S. Government Printing Office, 1986), pp. 837–901.

75. Michael Bourke and Andres Hernandez, "The 'Butner Study' Redux: A Report of the Incidence of Hands-on Child Victimization by Child Pornography Offenders," *Journal of Family Violence* 24 (2009): 183–191.

76. *Report of the Commission on Obscenity and Pornography* (Washington, DC: U.S. Government Printing Office, 1970).

77. Berl Kutchinsky, "The Effect of Easy Availability of Pornography on the Incidence of Sex Crimes," *Journal of Social Issues* 29 (1973): 95–112.

78. Michael Goldstein, "Exposure to Erotic Stimuli and Sexual Deviance," *Journal of Social Issues* 29 (1973): 197–219.

79. Catherine Simmons, Peter Lehmann, and Shannon Collier-Tenison, "Linking Male Use of the Sex Industry to Controlling Behaviors in Violent Relationships: An Exploratory Analysis," *Violence Against Women* 14 (2008): 406–417.

80. Michael Flood, "The Harms of Pornography Exposure Among Children and Young People," *Child Abuse Review* 18 (2009): 384–400.

81. Diana Russell, *Dangerous Relationships: Pornography, Misogyny, and Rape* (Thousand Oaks, CA: Sage, 1998).

82. *Roth v. United States*, 354 U.S. 476; 77 S.Ct. 1304 (1957).

83. *Miller v. California*, 413 U.S. 15 (1973).

84. R. George Wright, "Defining Obscenity: The Criterion of Value," *New England Law Review* 22 (1987): 315–341.

85. *Pope v. Illinois*, 107 S.Ct. 1918 (1987).

86. George Weaver, "Obama Administration Fails Obscenity Test," *World*, April 24, 2013, www.worldmag.com/2013/04/obama_administration_fails_obscenity_test.

87. Pub. L. 108-21, 117 Stat. 650, S. 151, enacted April 30, 2003.

88. *United States v. Williams*, 553 U.S. 285 (2008).

89. FBI, "Innocent Images National Initiative," www2.fbi.gov/publications/innocent.htm.

90. Matilda Battersby, "'I Don't Want to Die': Amy Winehouse's Words Just Hours Before Her Death," *The Independent*, January 8, 2013, www.independent.co.uk/arts-entertainment/music/news/i-dont-want-to-die-amy-winehouses-words-just-hours-before-her-death-8442698.html.

91. Ralph Weisheit, "Studying Drugs in Rural Areas: Notes from the Field," *Journal of Research in Crime and Delinquency* 30 (1993): 213–232.

92. U.S. Department of Health and Human Services, Substance Abuse and Mental Health Services Administration, Drug Abuse Warning Network, "Findings on Drug-Related Emergency Department Visits 2011," www.samhsa.gov/data/emergency-department-data-dawn; Drug Abuse Warning Network, "Highlights of the 2010 Drug Abuse Warning Network (DAWN) Findings on Drug-Related Emergency Department Visits," *The DAWN Report*, July 2, 2012, www.samhsa.gov/data/2k12/DAWN096/SR096EDHighlights2010.pdf.

93. James Inciardi, *The War on Drugs* (Palo Alto, CA: Mayfield, 1986), p. 2.

94. See, generally, David Pittman, "Drug Addiction and Crime," in *Handbook of Criminology*, ed. D. Glazer (Chicago: Rand McNally, 1974), pp. 209–232; Board of Directors, National Council on Crime and Delinquency, "Drug Addiction: A Medical, Not a Law Enforcement, Problem," *Crime and Delinquency* 20 (1974): 4–9.

95. Associated Press, "Records Detail Royals' Turn-of-Century Drug Use," *Boston Globe*, August 29, 1993, p. 13.

96. See Edward Brecher, *Licit and Illicit Drugs* (Boston: Little, Brown, 1972).

97. James Inciardi, *Reflections on Crime* (New York: Holt, Rinehart and Winston, 1978), pp. 8–10; see also A. Greeley, William McCready, and Gary Theisen, *Ethnic Drinking Subcultures* (New York: Praeger, 1980).

98. Joseph Gusfield, *Symbolic Crusade* (Urbana: University of Illinois Press, 1963), Ch. 3.

99. McCaghy, *Deviant Behavior*, p. 280.

100. Ibid.

101. Lloyd Johnston, Patrick O'Malley, Richard Miech, Jerald Bachman, and John Schulenberg, *Monitoring the Future, 2014*, www.monitoringthefuture.org/pubs/monographs/mtf-overview2014.pdf.

102. National Survey on Drug Use and Health (NSDUH), "Alcohol, Tobacco, and Other Drugs, 2013," www.samhsa.gov/atod.

103. National Institute on Alcohol Abuse and Alcoholism (NIAAA), "Alcohol Facts and Statistics, 2014," www.niaaa.nih.gov/alcohol-health/overview-alcohol-consumption/alcohol-facts-and-statistics.

104. Jeffrey Miron and Katherine Waldock, "The Budgetary Impact of Ending Drug Prohibition," Cato Institute, 2010, www.cato.org/sites/cato.org/files/pubs/pdf/DrugProhibitionWP.pdf.

105. C. Bowden, "Determinants of Initial Use of Opioids," *Comprehensive Psychiatry* 12 (1971): 136–140.

106. Marvin Krohn, Alan Lizotte, Terence Thornberry, Carolyn Smith, and David McDowall, "Reciprocal Causal Relationships Among Drug Use, Peers, and Beliefs: A Five-Wave Panel Model," *Journal of Drug Issues* 26 (1996): 205–228.

107. R. Cloward and L. Ohlin, *Delinquency and Opportunity: A Theory of Delinquent Gangs* (Glencoe, IL: Free Press, 1960).

108. Lening Zhang, John Welte, and William Wieczorek, "Youth Gangs, Drug Use and Delinquency," *Journal of Criminal Justice* 27 (1999): 101–109.

109. Peter Giancola, "Constructive Thinking, Antisocial Behavior, and Drug Use in Adolescent Boys With and Without a Family History of a Substance Use Disorder," *Personality and Individual Differences* 35 (2003): 1315–1331.

110. Amy Young, Carol Boyd, and Amy Hubbell, "Social Isolation and Sexual Abuse Among Women Who Smoke Crack," *Journal of Psychosocial Nursing* 39 (2001): 16–19.

111. Substance Abuse and Mental Health Services Administration, Office of Applied Studies, "The Relationship Between Mental Health and Substance Abuse Among Adolescents," Analytic Series: A-9, 1999.

112. Alan Carr, Barbara Dooley, Mark Fitzpatrick, Edel Flanagan, Roisin Flanagan-Howard, Kevin Tierney, Megan White, Margaret Daly, and Jonathan Egan, "Adult Adjustment of Survivors of Institutional Child Abuse in Ireland," *Child Abuse and Neglect* 34 (2010): 477–489.

113. Daniel Smith, Joanne Davis, and Adrienne Fricker-Elhai, "How Does Trauma Beget Trauma? Cognitions

About Risk in Women with Abuse Histories," *Child Maltreatment* 9 (2004): 292–302.

114. Sean Kidd, "The Walls Were Closing in, and We Were Trapped," *Youth and Society* 36 (2004): 30–55.

115. David Black, Steve Sussman, Jennifer Unger, Pallay Pokhrel, and Ping Sun, "Gender Differences in Body Consciousness and Substance Use Among High-Risk Adolescents," *Substance Use and Misuse* 45 (2010): 1623–1635.

116. Sung Joon Jang, Todd Ferguson, and Jeremy R. Rhodes, "Does Alcohol or Delinquency Help Adolescents Feel Better over Time? A Study on the Influence of Heavy Drinking and Violent/Property Offending on Negative Emotions," *International Journal of Offender Therapy and Comparative Criminology*, first published online December 2014.

117. D. W. Goodwin, "Alcoholism and Genetics," *Archives of General Psychiatry* 42 (1985): 171–174.

118. For a thorough review of this issue, see John Petraitis, Brian Flay, and Todd Miller, "Reviewing Theories of Adolescent Substance Use: Organizing Pieces in the Puzzle," *Psychological Bulletin* 117 (1995): 67–86.

119. Judith Brook and Li-Jung Tseng, "Influences of Parental Drug Use, Personality, and Child Rearing on the Toddler's Anger and Negativity," *Genetic, Social and General Psychology Monographs* 122 (1996): 107–128.

120. Thomas Ashby Wills, Donato Vaccaro, Grace McNamara, and A. Elizabeth Hirky, "Escalated Substance Use: A Longitudinal Grouping Analysis from Early to Middle Adolescence," *Journal of Abnormal Psychology* 105 (1996): 166–180.

121. Denise Kandel and Mark Davies, "Friendship Networks, Intimacy, and Illicit Drug Use in Young Adulthood: A Comparison of Two Competing Theories," *Criminology* 29 (1991): 441–471.

122. J. S. Mio, G. Nanjundappa, D. E. Verlur, and M. D. DeRios, "Drug Abuse and the Adolescent Sex Offender: A Preliminary Analysis," *Journal of Psychoactive Drugs* 18 (1986): 65–72.

123. D. Baer and J. Corrado, "Heroin Addict Relationships with Parents During Childhood and Early Adolescent Years," *Journal of Genetic Psychology* 124 (1974): 99–103.

124. The National Center on Addiction and Substance Abuse, "Reducing Teen Smoking Can Cut Marijuana Use Significantly," September 16, 2003.

125. Chie Noyori-Corbett and Sung Seek Moon, "Multifaceted Reality of Juvenile Delinquency: An Empirical Analysis of Structural Theories and Literature," *Child and Adolescent Social Work Journal* 27 (2010): 245–268.

126. John Wallace and Jerald Bachman, "Explaining Racial/Ethnic Differences in Adolescent Drug Use: The Impact of Background and Lifestyle," *Social Problems* 38 (1991): 333–357.

127. John Donovan, "Problem-Behavior Theory and the Explanation of Adolescent Marijuana Use," *Journal of Drug Issues* 26 (1996): 379–404.

128. Michael Hallstone, "Types of Crimes Committed by Repeat DUI Offenders," *Criminal Justice Studies* 27 (2014): 159–171.

129. A. Christiansen, G. T. Smith, P. V. Roehling, and M. S. Goldman, "Using Alcohol Expectancies to Predict Adolescent Drinking Behavior After One Year," *Journal of Counseling and Clinical Psychology* 57 (1989): 93–99.

130. Judith Brook, Martin Whiteman, Elinor Balka, and Beatrix Hamburg, "African-American and Puerto Rican Drug Use: Personality, Familial, and Other Environmental Risk Factors," *Genetic, Social, and General Psychology Monographs* 118 (1992): 419–438.

131. Bu Huang, Helene Raskin White, Rick Kosterman, Richard Catalano, and J. David Hawkins, "Developmental Associations Between Alcohol and Interpersonal Aggression During Adolescence," *Journal of Research in Crime and Delinquency* 38 (2001): 64–83.

132. Andrew Golub and Bruce D. Johnson, *The Rise of Marijuana as the Drug of Choice Among Youthful Adult Arrestees* (Washington, DC: National Institute of Justice, 2001).

133. Cesar Rebellon and Karen Van Gundy, "Can Social Psychological Delinquency Theory Explain the Link Between Marijuana and Other Illicit Drug Use? A Longitudinal Analysis of the Gateway Hypothesis," *Journal of Drug Issues* 36 (2006): 515–540.

134. Marvin Dawkins, "Drug Use and Violent Crime Among Adolescents," *Adolescence* 32 (1997): 395–406.

135. Denise Gottfredson, Brook Kearley, and Shawn Bushway, "Substance Use, Drug Treatment, and Crime: An Examination of Intra-Individual Variation in a Drug Court Population," *Journal of Drug Issues* 38 (2008): 601–630.

136. Substance Abuse and Mental Health Services Administration, *Results from the 2013 National Survey on Drug Use and Health: Summary of National Findings*, www.samhsa.gov/data/sites/default/files/NSDUHresults PDFWHTML2013/Web/NSDUHresults2013.pdf.

137. Office of National Drug Control Policy, *Adam II: 2010 Annual Report Arrestee Drug Abuse Monitoring Program II, May 2011*, www.whitehouse.gov/sites/default/files/ondcp/policy-and-research/adam2010.pdf.

138. Substance Abuse and Mental Health Services Administration, Center for Behavioral Health Statistics and Quality, March 3, 2011, *The TEDS Report: Characteristics of Probation and Parole Admissions Aged 18 or Older*, www.samhsa.gov/data/2k10/231Parole2k11Web/231Parole2k11.htm.

139. Benjamin R. Nordstrom and Charles A. Dackis, "Drugs and Crime," *Journal of Psychiatry and Law* 39 (2011): 663–668.

140. See Kenneth Jones, Louis Shainberg, and Carter Byer, *Drugs and Alcohol* (New York: Harper & Row, 1979), pp. 137–146.

141. Controlled Substance Act, 21 U.S.C. 848 (1984).

142. Anti-Drug Abuse Act of 1986, Pub. L. No. 99-570, U.S.C. 841 (1986).

143. Anti-Drug Abuse Act of 1988, Pub. L. No. 100-690; 21 U.S.C. 1501; Subtitle A–Death Penalty, Sec. 7001, Amending the Controlled Substances Abuse Act, 21 U.S.C. 848.

144. Eric Jensen, Jurg Gerber, and Ginna Babcock, "The New War on Drugs: Grass Roots Movement or Political Construction?" *Journal of Drug Issues* 21 (1991): 651–667.

145. "The 2012 National Drug Control Strategy: Building on a Record of Reform," www.whitehouse.gov/sites/default/files/ondcp/2012_national_drug_control_strategy_executive_summary.pdf.

146. United Nations Office on Drugs and Crime, *World Drug Report, 2014*, www.unodc.org/documents/wdr2014/World_Drug_Report_2014_exsum.pdf.

147. Francisco Gutierrez, "Institutionalizing Global Wars: State Transformations in Colombia, 1978–2002: Colombian Policy Directed at Its Wars, Paradoxically, Narrows the Government's Margin of Maneuver Even as It Tries to Expand It," *Journal of International Affairs* 57 (2003): 135–152.

148. Mark Moore, *Drug Trafficking* (Washington, DC: National Institute of Justice, 1988).

149. Peter Rossi, Richard Berk, and Alec Campbell, "Just Punishments: Guideline Sentences and Normative Consensus," *Journal of Quantitative Criminology* 13 (1997): 267–283.

150. Robert Davis, Arthur Lurigio, and Dennis Rosenbaum, eds., *Drugs and the Community* (Springfield, IL: Charles C Thomas, 1993), pp. xii–xv.

151. Saul Weingart, "A Typology of Community Responses to Drugs," in *Drugs and the Community*, ed. Davis, Lurigio, and Rosenbaum, pp. 85–105.

152. Dennis Rosenbaum, Robert Flewelling, Susan Bailey, Chris Ringwalt, and Deanna Wilkinson, "Cops in the Classroom: A Longitudinal Evaluation of Drug Abuse Resistance Education (D.A.R.E.)," *Journal of Research in Crime and Delinquency* 31 (1994): 3–31. Donald R. Lynam, Rich Milich, Rick Zimmerman, Scott Novak, T. K. Logan, Catherine Martin, Carl Leukefeld, and Richard Clayton, "Project D.A.R.E.: No Effects at 10-Year Follow-Up," *Journal of Consulting and Clinical Psychology* 67 (1999): 590–593.

153. Mareanne Zawitz, *Drugs, Crime, and the Justice System* (Washington, DC: U.S. Government Printing Office, 1992), pp. 115–122.

154. John Goldkamp and Peter Jones, "Pretrial Drug-Testing Experiments in Milwaukee and Prince George's County: The Context of Implementation," *Journal of Research in Crime and Delinquency* 29 (1992): 430–465; Chester Britt, Michael Gottfredson, and John Goldkamp, "Drug Testing and Pretrial Misconduct: An Experiment on the Specific Deterrent Effects of Drug Monitoring Defendants on Pretrial Release," *Journal of Research in Crime and Delinquency* 29 (1992): 62–78. See, generally, Peter Greenwood and Franklin Zimring, *One More Chance* (Santa Monica, CA: Rand Corporation, 1985).

155. National Drug Court Resource Center, "Drug Courts Today," www.ndcrc.org/content/how-many-drug-courts-are-there.

156. Katherine Theall, Kirk Elifson, Claire Sterk, and Eric Stewart, "Criminality Among Female Drug Users Following an HIV Risk-Reduction Intervention," *Journal of Interpersonal Violence* 22 (2007): 85–107.

157. See, generally, Peter Greenwood and Franklin Zimring, *One More Chance* (Santa Monica, CA: Rand Corporation, 1985).

158. Daniel Rosen, Jennifer Q. Morse, and Charles F. Reynolds, "Adapting Problem-Solving Therapy for Depressed Older Adults in Methadone Maintenance Treatment," *Journal of Substance Abuse Treatment* 40 (2011): 132–141.

159. Audrey Hickert and Mary Jane Taylor, "Supportive Housing for Addicted, Incarcerated Homeless Adults," *Journal of Social Service Research* 37 (2011): 136–151.

160. Tracy Beswick, David Best, Jenny Bearn, Michael Gossop, Sian Rees, and John Strang, "The Effectiveness of Combined Naloxone/Lofexidine in Opiate Detoxification: Results from a Double-Blind Randomized and Placebo-Controlled Trial," *American Journal on Addictions* 12 (2003): 295–306.

161. George De Leon, Stanley Sacks, Graham Staines, and Karen McKendrick, "Modified Therapeutic Community for Homeless Mentally Ill Chemical Abusers: Treatment Outcomes," *American Journal of Drug and Alcohol Abuse* 26 (2000): 461–480.

162. Office of Drug Control Strategy, "The National Drug Control Strategy: A 21st Century Approach to Drug Policy," July 2014, www.whitehouse.gov/sites/default/files/ondcp/policy-and-research/2014_strategy_fact_sheet.pdf.

163. The following section is based on material found in Jerome Platt, "Vocational Rehabilitation of Drug Abusers," *Psychological Bulletin* 117 (1995): 416–433.

164. Policy Statement, Drug Policy Alliance, 2015, www.drugpolicy.org/new-solutions-drug-policy.

165. Office of National Drug Control Policy, www.whitehouse.gov/ondcp.

166. Ethan Nadelmann, "The U.S. Is Addicted to War on Drugs," *Globe and Mail*, May 20, 2003, p. 1.

167. United Nations Office on Drugs and Crime, *World Drug Report, 2014*.

168. Karin A. Mack, "Drug-Induced Deaths, United States, 1999–2010," National Center for Injury Prevention and Control, CDC, November 22, 2013, www.cdc.gov/mmwr/preview/mmwrhtml/su6203a27.htm.

# 14 Crimes of the New Millennium: Cybercrime and Transnational Organized Crime

## Learning Objectives

**LO1** Discuss the concept of cybercrime and why it has become important.

**LO2** Distinguish among cybertheft, cybervandalism, and cyberterrorism.

**LO3** Describe the various types of cybercrimes, such as computer frauds, illegal copyright infringement, and identity theft.

**LO4** Discuss efforts to control cybercrime.

**LO5** Trace the evolution of organized crime.

**LO6** Discuss the activities of transnational organized crime.

Supporters of Army PFC Bradley Manning protest his imprisonment.

# Chapter Outline

## FACT OR FICTION?

▶ The next war may be conducted in cyberspace.

▶ Organized crime in the United States is still a local commodity, controlled by five Mafia families in New York City and a few other allied groups in Chicago, Los Angeles, and Miami.

Americans have become very familiar with a previously unknown website called WikiLeaks, an international organization that publishes classified and secret documents that are submitted by unnamed and anonymous sources. Launched in 2006 and run by Julian Assange, an Australian who emigrated to Sweden, WikiLeaks has supporters around the globe. A few years ago, the site began to post videos and documents that had been illegally appropriated from U.S. diplomatic and military computers by unknown hackers. One video showed a 2007 incident in which Iraqi civilians and journalists were killed by U.S. forces. WikiLeaks also leaked more than 76,000 classified war documents from Afghanistan, including U.S. State Department cables. In the aftermath of the leaks, Army Specialist Bradley Manning, 22, was arrested after an informant told federal authorities that he had overheard him bragging about giving WikiLeaks a video of a helicopter assault in Iraq plus more than 260,000 classified U.S. diplomatic cables taken from government computers. Both the U.S. and foreign governments were embarrassed when the confidential cables hit the Net.[1] Bradley Manning (now Chelsea Elizabeth Manning) was convicted under the espionage act and sentenced to up to 35 years in prison.

Wanted on a series of charges stemming from an alleged sexual assault in Sweden and threatened with extradition to the United States to face charges of espionage, Assange was granted asylum by the government of Ecuador and is currently residing in the Ecuadorian embassy in London (his status can change any day and he may be extradited). Despite Assange's physical ▶

restriction, WikiLeaks continues to publish secret documents. It made headlines in April 2015 when it published 30,287 documents and 173,132 emails misappropriated from Sony Pictures Entertainment, which allegedly had been stolen by North Korea's intelligence service in revenge for Sony's producing the comedy film *The Interview*, depicting a future overthrow of the North Korean government and the assassination of its leader, Kim Jong-un. Many of the hacked emails proved embarrassing to the studio, including ones mentioning actors' pay and others joking about President Obama and race. ■

**CONNECTIONS**

Chapter 12 reviewed the concept of enterprise crime and its motivations. Cybercrime can be viewed as a type of enterprise crime employing sophisticated technology to achieve illegal profits. It can also enable criminal gangs to engage in global conspiracies involving co-conspirators from around the world.

**LO1** Discuss the concept of cybercrime and why it has become important.

**cybercrime**
The theft and/or destruction of information, resources, or funds via computers, computer networks, or the Internet.

**transnational organized crime**
Criminal conspiracies that cross national and international borders and involve the planning and execution of illicit ventures by groups or networks of individuals working in more than one country.

Just a few years ago, complex, global incidents involving leaking classified documents could not have been contemplated, let alone transacted. Innovation brings change and with it new opportunities to commit crime. The technological revolution has provided new tools to misappropriate funds, damage property, and sell illicit material. It has created **cybercrime**, a new breed of offenses that can be singular or ongoing but typically involves the theft and/or destruction of information, resources, or funds utilizing computers, computer networks, and the Internet. The Internet age has also provided new tools and opportunities for criminals to create transnational criminal organizations whose illegal activities span not only national borders but continents. The Internet allows drug traffickers to communicate instantly with buyers around the world, move their product from one nation to another, and ply their trade across continents.

## Crime in the Cyber Age

Criminals have become more technologically sophisticated, routinely using the Internet to carry out their criminal conspiracies. The widespread use of computers and the Internet ushered in the age of information technology (IT) and made it an integral part of daily life in industrialized societies. IT involves computer networking, the Internet, and advanced communications. It is the key to the economic system, becoming ever more important as major industries shift their manufacturing plants to areas of the world where production is much cheaper. IT is responsible for the globalization phenomenon, creating transnational markets, politics, and legal systems—in other words, creating a global economy.

The cyber age has also generated an enormous amount of revenue. Worldwide enterprise IT is now more than $2.5 trillion per year.[2] More than 3.9 billion individuals and businesses use email, sending more than 190 billion messages per day. Social media sites like Facebook and Twitter are expanding exponentially. Facebook has more than 1.4 billion users; people tweet more than 500 million times a day.[3] Magnifying the importance of the Internet is the fact that many critical infrastructure functions are conducted online, ranging from banking to control of shipping on the Mississippi River.[4] Because of its scope, depth, and usage, the Internet opened up a broad avenue for illegal activity; cybercrime has become a feature of the new millennium.

In addition to cybercrime, the IT revolution has increased the scope of organized criminal enterprises. Criminal organizations that were originally local in scope and activity can now extend their operations from coast to coast and across international borders, hence the term **transnational organized crime**. Integrating IT into their plans, they are able to carry out criminal schemes on a global basis.

This new array of crimes presents a compelling challenge because (a) it is rapidly evolving, with new schemes being created daily, (b) it is difficult to detect through traditional law enforcement channels, and (c) its control demands that agents of the justice system develop technical skills that match those of the perpetrators. These crimes are vast in scope and place a heavy burden on society. It may even be possible that the recent crime drop is a result of cybercrime replacing traditional street crime. Instead of robbing a bank at gunpoint, contemporary thieves find it easier to hack into accounts and transfer funds to offshore banks. Instead of shoplifting from a brick and mortar store, the contemporary cyberthief joins an international enterprise group that devises clever schemes to steal from etailers. And instead of limiting their criminal escapades to the local population, these transnational gang members now find a whole world of opportunity.[5]

There are actually three general forms of cybercrime. Some cybercriminals use modern technology to accumulate goods and services. **Cybertheft** schemes range from illegally copying material under copyright protection to using technology to commit traditional theft-based offenses such as larceny and fraud.

Other cybercriminals are motivated less by profit and more by the urge to commit **cybervandalism**, or technological destruction. They aim their malicious attacks at disrupting, defacing, and destroying online reources they find offensive.

A third type of cybercrime is **cyberwar** or **cyberterrorism**, which consists of acts aimed at undermining the social, economic, and political system of an enemy nation by destroying its electronic infrastructure and disrupting its economy. This can range from stealing secrets from foreign nations to destroying an enemy's Web-based infrastructure.

# Cybertheft: Cybercrime for Profit

In 2014, a Russian national named Aleksandr Andreevich Panin pleaded guilty to a conspiracy charge associated with his role as the primary developer and distributor of SpyEye software. This software was designed specifically to facilitate online theft from financial institutions and enable users to transfer money out of victims' bank accounts and into accounts controlled by criminals. What makes this case unusual was that rather than using SpyEye himself, Panin sold the "product" online. He actually advertised the features of the program, extolling its criminal value. His 150 customers each paid him up to $8,500 for SpyEye, which they then used to hack into bank accounts and withdraw funds, create bogus credit cards, and engage in other criminal enterprise schemes.[6]

Cyberthieves now have the luxury of remaining anonymous, living in any part of the world, conducting their business during the day or in the evening, working alone or in a group, while at the same time reaching a much wider number of potential victims than ever before. No longer is the con artist or criminal entrepreneur limited to fleecing victims in a particular geographic locale; the whole world can be their target. The technology revolution opened novel methods for cybertheft, ranging from the unlawful distribution of computer software to Internet securities fraud.

Cyberthieves conspire to use cyberspace to distribute illegal goods and services or to defraud people for quick profits. Some of the most common methods are discussed here.

## Illegal Copyright Infringement

Ripping off software has become a billion-dollar computer crime because the comparative ease of making copies of computer software has led to a huge illegal market, depriving authors of very significant revenues. Because cyberspace has no borders, software pirates can ply their trade from anywhere in the world and the effects can be devastating to developers. Companies such as Microsoft, Adobe, and Oracle lose billions in yearly revenue from illegal copies of software pirated in and sold abroad.[7]

Groups of individuals work together to illegally obtain software and then "crack" or "rip" its copyright protections before posting it on the Internet for other members

**LO2** Distinguish among cybertheft, cybervandalism, and cyberterrorism.

**cybertheft**
The use of computer networks for criminal profits. Copyright infringement, identity theft, and Internet securities fraud are examples of cybertheft.

**cybervandalism**
Malicious attacks aimed at disrupting, defacing, and destroying technology.

**cyberwar/cyberterrorism**
Politically motivated attacks designed to compromise the electronic infrastructure of an enemy nation and disrupt its economy.

**CHECKPOINTS**

▶ Cybercrime is a relatively new breed of offenses that involves the theft and/or destruction of information, resources, or funds utilizing computers, computer networks, and the Internet.

▶ Criminals have become more technologically sophisticated, routinely using the Internet to carry out their criminal conspiracies.

▶ The cyber age has generated an enormous amount of revenue.

▶ The IT revolution has increased the scope of organized criminal enterprises.

▶ Criminal organizations that were originally local in scope and activity can now extend their operations from coast to coast and across international borders.

▶ This new array of crimes presents a compelling challenge to law enforcement.

▶ Cybercrimes are vast in scope and place a heavy burden on society.

**LO3** Describe the various types of cybercrimes, such as computer frauds, illegal copyright infringement, and identity theft.

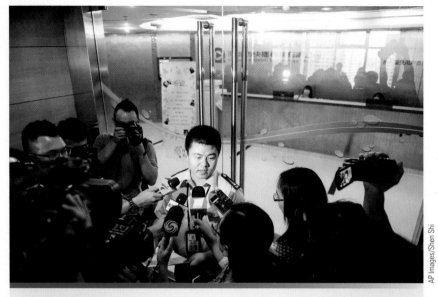

AP Images/Shen Shi

Illegal copyright infringement is now a transnational crime. Here, a Chinese officer from the Shenzhen Market Supervision Administration is interviewed outside the office of Shenzhen QVOD Technology after delivering a written decision of administrative penalty to the company. China is slapping the major online provider of pirated videos in the country with a 260 million yuan (US$42 million) fine. The Shenzhen Market Supervision Administration said that QVOD Technology had distributed a local movie and TV series online without the publishers' permission. The piracy amounted to 86 million yuan in illegal revenue. QVOD had not only repeatedly pirated the content but refused to stop its distribution after being caught. As a result, Chinese authorities levied a fine that was triple the amount of revenue QVOD made from the piracy. QVOD has been facing growing scrutiny from Chinese authorities. The company was found guilty of distributing pornography online and is facing a related police investigation. QVOD rose to notoriety after the company developed peer-to-peer video sharing software called Kuaibo. The software became a popular way for bootleggers to distribute pirated movies and TV shows without paying expensive video bandwidth costs.

of the group to use; this is called **warez**. Frequently, these pirated copies reach the Internet days or weeks before the legitimate product is commercially available. Even when warez members do not profit from their efforts, they deprive software companies of legitimate revenue.

The government has actively pursued members of the warez community, and some have been charged and convicted under the Computer Fraud and Abuse Act (CFAA), which criminalizes accessing computer systems without authorization to obtain information,[8] and the Digital Millennium Copyright Act (DMCA), which makes it a crime to circumvent antipiracy measures built into most commercial software and also outlaws the manufacture, sale, or distribution of code-cracking devices used to illegally copy software.[9]

**FILE SHARING** Another form of illegal copyright infringement involves file-sharing programs that allow Internet users to download music and other copyrighted material without paying the artists and record producers their rightful royalties. Although some students routinely share files and download music, criminal copyright infringement represents a serious economic threat. The United States Criminal Code provides penalties for a first-time offender of five years incarceration and a fine of $250,000.[10] Other provisions provide for the forfeiture and destruction of infringing copies and all equipment used to make the copies.[11]

On June 27, 2005, copyright protection of music and other types of entertainment distributed via the Internet was upheld by the Supreme Court in the case of *MGM Studios, Inc. v. Grokster, Ltd.* Grokster was a privately owned software company that created peer-to-peer file-sharing protocols. The Court unanimously held that software distributors such as Grokster could be sued for inducing copyright infringement if they market file-sharing software that might induce people to illegally copy protected material even if that software could also be used for legitimate purposes. Justice David Souter wrote:

> We hold that one who distributes a device with the object of promoting its use to infringe copyright, as shown by the clear expression or other affirmative steps taken to foster infringement, is liable for the resulting acts of infringement by third parties.

As a result, Grokster was forced to pay $50 million to the music and recording industries, which of course ended its operations.[12]

## Computer Fraud

There are many schemes that fall under this category of crime. The **salami slice fraud** involves loading programs that skim small sums from each transaction on the computers of financial organizations such as banks. The "slices" that are then deposited into the conspirators' account are so small that they bypass bank scrutiny. Typically an inside job, the salami slice relies on the fact that depositors will not notice if a few pennies are missing from their account each month, or if they do, they won't bother to report it to bank managers.

Other type of computer crimes include:

- *Theft of information.* The unauthorized obtaining of information from a computer (hacking), including software that is copied for profit.
- *Manipulation of accounts/banking systems.* Similar to a salami slice but on a much larger and usually more complex scale. Sometimes perpetrated as a "one-off kamikaze" fraud.
- *Corporate espionage.* Trade secrets are stolen by a company's competitors, which can be either domestic or foreign. The goal is to increase the rival companies (or nation's) competitive edge in the global marketplace.[13]

Internal attacks are now outgrowing external attacks at the world's largest financial institutions. According to one global security survey, about 60 percent of U.S. companies report being hit by computer network attacks each year.[14]

**THEFT FROM AUTOMATIC TELLER MACHINES** Automatic teller machines (ATMs) attract the attention of cybercriminals looking for easy profits. Rather than robbing an ATM user at gunpoint, the cybercriminal relies on stealth and technological skill to commit the crime. **ATM skimming** involves placing an electronic device on an ATM that scoops information from a bank card's magnetic strip whenever a customer uses the machine; skimmers can then create their own bank cards and steal from customer accounts.[15] ATM skimming now costs U.S. banks hundreds of millions of dollars annually.

The devices planted on ATMs are usually undetectable because they blend right into the ATM's physical structure. Some cybercriminals attach a phony keypad on top of the real keypad which records every keystroke as customers punch in their PINs. These skimming devices are installed for short periods of time—usually just a few hours—so they're often attached to an ATM by nothing more than double-sided tape. They are then removed by the criminals, who download the stolen account information and encode it onto blank cards. The cards are used to make withdrawals from victims' accounts at other ATMs. Skimmers can also make use of a hidden camera, installed on or near an ATM, to record customers' entry of their PINs into the ATM's keypad.

**ATM skimming**
Using an electronic device or camera on an ATM that copies information from a bank card's magnetic strip whenever a customer uses the machine or photographs their key strokes.

## Distributing Illegal or Dangerous Services and Materials

The Internet has become a prime source for the delivery of illicit or legally prohibited material. Included within this market is distribution of pornography and obscene material, including kiddie porn, and the distribution of dangerous drugs.

**DISTRIBUTING OBSCENITY** The IT revolution has revitalized the porn industry. The Internet is an ideal venue for selling and distributing obscene material; the computer is an ideal device for storage and viewing. It is difficult to estimate the vast number of websites featuring sexual content, including nude photos, videos, live sex acts, and webcam strip sessions among other forms of "adult entertainment."[16] While it is difficult to estimate the extent of the industry, it is estimated that the revenue generated from adult sites each year is greater than all movie box office sales and the combined income of ABC, NBC, and CBS.[17]

While there are no conclusive data on the extent of Internet porn sites, some experts claim that out of the million most popular websites in the world, about 5 percent, more than 42,000, are sex related; about 15 percent of all searches are for "adult" content.[18] That would mean that adult sites get more than 10 billion hits each year. The single most popular adult site in the world is LiveJasmin.com, a webcam site which gets around 32 million visitors a month, or almost 2.5 percent of all Internet

**CONNECTIONS**

Chapter 13 dealt with public order crimes, including illegal acts that are now being facilitated by the Internet. Cyberspace is being used to illegally distribute prescription drugs, advertise prostitution, and disseminate pornography.

users.[19] But these data may undercount the actual number of adult sites: a search in Google on the word "porn" returned over 418 million pages. People are often directed to these sites through "porn-napping" and "typosquatted" websites. Porn-nappers buy expired domain names of existing sites and then try to sell adult material to people who stumble on them while surfing. Typosquat websites are those where a pornographer has deliberately registered names with typos so that people surfing the Net are directed to pornography sites if they misspell a word or put in the wrong keystroke.[20]

How do adult sites operate today? There are a number of different schemes in operation:[21]

**CONNECTIONS**

As you may recall, Chapter 13 covered the law of obscenity and noted that few if any cases involve adults. Considering this, do you believe that all pornographic material involving adults should be legalized, no matter how outrageous the subject?

- A large firm sells annual subscriptions in exchange for unlimited access to content.
- Password services charge an annual fee to deliver access to hundreds of small sites, which share the subscription revenues.
- Large firms provide free content to smaller affiliate sites. The affiliates post the free content and then try to channel visitors to the large sites, which give the smaller sites a percentage of the fees paid by those who sign up.
- Webmasters forward traffic to another porn site in return for a small per-consumer fee. In many cases, the consumer is sent to the other sites involuntarily, which is known in the industry as *mousetrapping*. Web surfers who try to close out a window after visiting an adult site are sent to another web page automatically. This can repeat dozens of times, causing users to panic and restart their computers in order to escape.
- Adult sites cater to niche audiences looking for specific kinds of adult content.

The current legal status of Internet porn is still underdetermined, but images involving adults are typically unregulated. Child pornography is another matter, and violations are prosecuted whenever possible. Nonetheless, there are at least 100,000 sites worldwide that still offer kiddie porn. Section 18 U.S.C. 2257 of the United States Criminal Code requires that porn distributors maintain records showing that all performers were over the age of 18 at the time of the production. In addition, it is illegal to peddle virtual kiddie porn if the seller advertises the images as real or promises to deliver images of children even if they do not really exist.[22] Despite some successful prosecutions, it has been difficult to control Internet child pornography simply because offenders are scattered around the world, making identification and arrest difficult. There needs to be significant law enforcement agency cooperation to gather evidence and locate suspects. The difficulty of prosecution and the need for cooperation is illustrated in the Lost Boy case, discussed in the Profiles in Crime feature.

**DISTRIBUTING DANGEROUS DRUGS** In addition to sexual material, the Internet has become a prime purveyor of prescription drugs, some of which can be quite dangerous when they are used to excess or fall into the hands of minors. While federal law prohibits buying controlled substances such as narcotic pain relievers (e.g., OxyContin), sedatives (e.g., Valium), stimulants (e.g., Ritalin), and anabolic steroids (e.g., Equipoise) without a valid prescription and in many cases a physical examination, there are numerous websites that provide prescriptions written by "cyber doctors" relying on online questionnaires located on rogue websites housed in foreign countries. Drugs delivered by such websites may be the wrong drugs, adulterated or expired, the wrong dosage strength, or have no dosage directions or warnings.[23]

How big is the problem? The 2013 prosecution of a single online pharmacy, Pitcairn Internet pharmacy, revealed that it sold more than 14 million doses of Schedule III and IV controlled substances, earning over $69 million, in the four-year period it operated.[24] One study of 159 sites offering drugs for sale found that only two were certified by the National Association of Boards of Pharmacy as legitimate Internet pharmacy practice sites; the other 157 were rogue sites.[25] Another problem: there are no controls preventing children from ordering drugs. With access to a credit card, which many kids have, ordering controlled substances online can be rather easy.[26]

# PROFILES IN CRIME

## THE LOST BOY CASE

The Lost Boy online bulletin board was established to provide a forum for men who had a sexual interest in young boys to trade child pornography. Law enforcement authorities in the United States and abroad first became aware of the network when Norwegian and Italian authorities discovered that a North Hollywood, California, man was communicating via an Internet site with an Italian national about child pornography and how to engage in child sex tourism in Romania. Further investigation revealed that Lost Boy had 35 members; more than half were U.S. nationals. Other members of the network were located in countries around the world, including Belgium, Brazil, Canada, France, Germany, New Zealand, and the United Kingdom.

To shield themselves from prosecution, the Lost Boy network had developed a thorough vetting process for new members to weed out law enforcement agents. Members were required to post child pornography in order to join the organization and to continue posting child pornography to remain in good standing. Lost Boy members advised each other on techniques to evade detection by law enforcement, which included using screen names to mask identities and encrypting computer data.

As the investigation unfolded, law enforcement agencies identified child molestation suspects in South America, Europe, and New Zealand. Suspects in Romania, France, Brazil, Norway, and the United Kingdom were charged and convicted, receiving long prison sentences. In the United States, offenders were prosecuted under the Adam Walsh Child Protection and Safety Act, a 2006 law with a three-tier system of categorizing sex offenders, mandated lifetime sex offender registration for tier one offenders and increased penalties. It also allows judges to levy heavier sentences on child molesters who are engaged in cooperative, sustained criminal efforts with others, such as running the Lost Boy network. Fifteen U.S. Lost Boy defendants have been convicted, one died in custody, and three remain at large. All told, the authorities identified 200 victims as a result of the investigation.

At the time, the Lost Boy indictment was the largest-ever child exploitation enterprise investigation since the signing of the Walsh Act. Because of the sentencing enhancements, some of those prosecuted in the Lost Boy case received sentences of between 20 and 35 years in prison. One man, Jeffrey Greenwell, who produced pornographic images and videos that appeared on the Lost Boy online bulletin board, pleaded guilty to five counts of production of child pornography and was sentenced to a total of 100 years in prison. Since the Lost Boy case was prosecuted, Operation Delego, conducted by the Justice Department and the Department of Homeland Security, resulted in the indictment of 72 defendants for their participation in Dreamboard—a private, members-only, online bulletin board created to promote pedophilia.

The Lost boy case illustrates the difficulty of controlling Internet pornography. Getting evidence sufficient for prosecution involved the cooperation of law enforcement agencies around the world and the arrests of people in multiple countries, a very expensive and time-consuming activity.

Steven Martinez, Assistant Director of the FBI in Los Angeles, speaks to reporters after the Lost Boy international child pornography ring was dismantled.

Gabriel Bouys/Getty Images

**Sources:** Text of the Adam Walsh Child Protection and Safety Act of 2006, www.govtrack.us/congress/bills/109/hr4472/text; U.S. Department of Justice, "Ohio Man Sentenced to 35 Years in Prison for His Participation in an Online Child Pornography Bulletin Board," www.fbi.gov/losangeles/press-releases/2012/ohio-man-sentenced-to-35-years-in-prison-for-his-participation-in-an-online-child-pornography-bulletin-board (URLs accessed 2015).

# Denial-of-Service Attack

Used to harass or extort money from owners of an Internet site, a **denial-of-service attack (DoS)** involves threats or attacks designed to prevent the legitimate operation of the site. In some cases, there is no monetary objective and the attack is a type of cybervandalism. In 2015, an attack against Rutgers University interrupted Internet service for students, faculty, and staff; another attack knocked out New York City's email accounts.[27] However, some DoS attackers are seeking to extort money from site operators. Unless the site operator pays, the attackers threaten to keep up the interference until real consumers become frustrated and abandon the site. Even so-called respectable businesspeople have been accused of launching denial-of-service attacks against rival business interests.[28] Examples of DoS attacks include:

- Attempts to flood a computer network, thereby preventing legitimate network traffic
- Attempts to disrupt connections within a computer network, thereby preventing access to a service
- Attempts to prevent a particular individual from accessing a service
- Attempts to disrupt service to a specific system or person

Online gambling casinos—a $20 billion a year international industry—have proven particularly vulnerable to attack. Hundreds of attacks have been launched against online casinos located in Costa Rica, the Caribbean, and Great Britain. If the attack coincides with a big sporting event such as the Super Bowl, the casinos may give in and make payments rather than lose revenue and fray customer relations. Another vulnerable target is online gaming sites. In 2014, massive attacks disrupted service on games such as Blizzard's Battle.net, Riot Games' League of Legends, and the Origin service run by Electronic Arts.[29]

# Internet Extortion

Internet extortion schemes involve uploading malware, attached to an email or compromised website, that freezes a computer and fixes the screen with a pop-up message—supposedly from the FBI or another federal agency—saying that the user has violated some sort of federal law and the computer will remain locked until the victim pays a fine. There may also be a pop-up message saying that personal files have been encrypted and demanding payment to release the decryption codes. The extortionists demand anywhere from hundreds to thousands of dollars to release their hold on the computer. Not only have individuals been the victim of ransomware attacks, so have businesses, financial institutions, government agencies, and academic institutions.

While some of the earlier ransomware scams involved having victims pay the ransom with prepaid credit cards, victims are now increasingly asked to pay with Bitcoin, a decentralized virtual currency network that attracts criminals because of the anonymity the system offers. A fairly new ransomware variant called CryptoWall (and CryptoWall 2.0, its newer version), encrypts files on a computer's hard drive and any external or shared drives to which the computer has access. It directs the user to a personalized victim ransom page that contains the initial ransom amount (anywhere from $200 to $5,000), detailed instructions about how to purchase Bitcoins, and typically a countdown clock to notify victims how much time they have before the ransom doubles. Victims are infected with CryptoWall by clicking on links in emails that appear to be from legitimate businesses and through compromised advertisements on popular websites. Recovery can be a difficult process that may require the services of a specialist.[30]

# Internet Securities Fraud

Internet securities fraud involves intentionally manipulating the securities marketplace for profit. There are three major types of Internet securities fraud today:

- *Market manipulation.* Stock market manipulation occurs when an individual tries to control the price of stock by interfering with the natural forces of supply and demand. There are two principal forms of this crime: the **pump and dump** and the **cyber smear**. In a pump and dump scheme, erroneous and deceptive information is posted online to get unsuspecting investors interested in a stock while those spreading the information sell previously purchased stock at an inflated price. The cyber smear is a reverse pump and dump: negative information is spread online about a stock, driving down its price and enabling people to buy it at an artificially low price before rebuttals by the company's officers reinflate the price.[31]

- *Fraudulent offerings of securities.* Some cybercriminals create websites specifically designed to fraudulently sell securities. To make the offerings look more attractive than they are, assets may be inflated, expected returns overstated, and risks understated. In these schemes, investors are promised abnormally high profits on their investments. No investment is actually made. Early investors are paid returns with the investment money received from the later investors. The system usually collapses, and the later investors do not receive dividends and lose their initial investment.

- *Illegal touting.* Individuals make securities recommendations and fail to disclose that they are being paid to disseminate their favorable opinions. Section 17(b) of the Securities Act of 1933 requires that paid touters disclose the nature, source, and amount of their compensation. If those who tout stocks fail to disclose their relationship with the company, information misleads investors into believing that the speaker is objective and credible rather than bought and paid for.

## Phishing and Identity Theft

**Identity theft** occurs when a person uses the Internet to steal someone's identity and/or impersonate the victim to open a new credit card account or conduct some other financial transaction. It is a type of cybercrime that has grown at surprising rates over the past few years.[32] In fact, the threat is so real that a recent survey found that the general public would be willing to have their taxes increased in order to fund a program that reduced identity theft.[33]

Identity theft can destroy a person's life by manipulating credit records or stealing from bank accounts. Identity thieves use a variety of techniques to steal information. They may fill out change-of-address cards at the post office and obtain people's credit card bills and bank statements. They may then call the credit card issuer and, pretending to be the victim, ask for a change in address on the account. They can then charge numerous items over the Internet and have the merchandise sent to the new address. It may take months for the victim to realize the fraud because the victim is not getting bills from the credit card company.[34]

Some identity thieves create false emails or websites that look legitimate but are designed to gain illegal access to a victim's personal information; this is known as **phishing** (also known as *carding* and *spoofing*). Some phishers send out emails that look like they come from a credit card company or online store telling the victim there is a problem with their account credit or balance. To fix the problem and update their account they are asked to submit their name, address, phone numbers, personal information, credit card account numbers, and Social Security number (SSN). Once phishers have a victim's personal information, they can gain access to preexisting bank accounts or credit cards and buy things using those accounts or they can use the information to open brand new bank accounts and credit cards without the victim's knowledge. Another variation of this crime is **spear-phishing**, where cybercriminals target specific victims, sending them emails that contain accurate information about their lives, friends, and activities obtained from social networking sites, blogs, or other websites. Personal information makes the message seem legitimate, increasing the chances the victims will open the email or go to a tainted website.[35]

The cost of phishing and identity theft now runs in the billions. One example of the breadth of the loss can be found in a recent audit of the Internal Revenue Service

**pump and dump**
Placing deceptive information online to get unsuspecting investors interested in a stock while those spreading the information sell previously purchased stock at an inflated price.

**cyber smear**
Negative information is spread online about a stock, driving down its price and enabling people to buy it at an artificially low price.

**identity theft**
Using the Internet to steal someone's identity and/or impersonate the victim in order to conduct illicit transactions such as committing fraud using the victim's name and identity.

**phishing**
The creation of false emails or websites that look legitimate but are designed to gain illegal access to a victim's personal information.

**spear-phishing**
Targeting specific victims by using personal information gleaned from social media and then sending them messages that convince them to open tainted emails or go to a tainted website.

(IRS) that found the agency paid refunds to criminals who filed false tax returns, in some cases on behalf of people who had died. In all, the IRS is expected to lose as much as $21 billion in revenue between 2012 and 2017 due to identity theft.[36]

To meet the threat of phishing and identity theft, Congress passed the Identity Theft and Assumption Deterrence Act of 1998 (Identity Theft Act) to make it a federal crime when anyone:

> Knowingly transfers or uses, without lawful authority, a means of identification of another person with the intent to commit, or to aid or abet, any unlawful activity that constitutes a violation of Federal law, or that constitutes a felony under any applicable State or local law.[37]

### Etailing Fraud

**etailing fraud**
Illegally buying and/or selling merchandise on the Internet.

New fraud schemes are evolving to reflect the fact that billions of dollars in goods are sold on the Internet each year. **Etailing fraud** involves illegally buying and/or selling merchandise on the Net. One scam involves purchasing top of the line electronic equipment online and then purchasing a second, similar looking but cheaper model of the same brand. The cheaper item is then returned to the etailer after switching bar codes and boxes with the more expensive unit. Because etail return processing centers don't always check returned goods closely, they may send a refund for the value of the higher priced model.

In another tactic, called *shoplisting*, a person obtains a legitimate receipt from a store either by buying it from a customer or finding it in the trash and then returns to the store and casually shops, picking up identical products. He then takes the products and receipt to the returns departments and attempts to return them for cash, store credit, or a gift card. The thief can sell the gift card on the Internet at a discount for quick cash.

Reshipping frauds are a particularly clever form of etailing crime. Reshippers are recruited in various ways, commonly through employment offers and Internet chat rooms. One scheme involves the posting of help-wanted advertisements at Internet job search sites. The prospective employee is required to complete an employment application that asks for sensitive personal information, such as date of birth and Social Security number, which is then used to obtain credit in his or her name. The applicant is informed he or she has been hired and will be responsible for forwarding, or reshipping, merchandise purchased in the United States to the company's overseas home office. The packages quickly begin to arrive and, as instructed, the employee dutifully forwards the packages to their overseas destination. Unbeknownst to the victim, the recently received merchandise was purchased with fraudulent credit cards obtained using the victim's personal information. Weeks after shipping the merchandise abroad, the victim receives the credit card bill in the mail.[38]

### Mass Marketing Fraud

Mass marketing fraudsters use the Internet to deliver false or deceptive representations to induce potential victims to make advance fee–type payments for services that are never delivered. Exhibit 14.1 sets out some of the more common schemes.

# Cybervandalism: Cybercrime with Malicious Intent

In 2015, the online hookup site Ashley Madison was hacked, and stolen information from 32 million of the site's members, such as email addresses, was posted on the Net. The hackers claimed two motivations: they objected to Ashley Madison's intent of arranging affairs between

Cybervandalism can involve extortion schemes, encouraging people to create counter-extortion programs. Craig Petronella has a company in Raleigh, North Carolina, that helps when people or businesses are hit with a computer virus. There is a ransom virus called CryptoLocker going around that locks a computer unless money is paid electronically to the hackers.

Chris Seward/MCT/Landov

## Exhibit 14.1  Common Mass Marketing Schemes

### Advance Fee Fraud

This category of fraud induces victims into remitting upfront payments in exchange for the promise of goods, services, and/or prizes. For example:

- In Nigerian letter schemes (also known as "419 scams" because that's the number of the article in the Nigerian criminal code that deals with these types of frauds), victims are contacted by letter or email with a variety of scenarios that purport to involve the movement of substantial sums of money held in foreign bank accounts. The victims are requested to pay fees to secure the transfer of funds to the United States and in return are promised a large percentage of the transferred funds. Of course, there are no funds and the victims will even be asked to pay additional funds to cover "unanticipated" costs.

- In a foreign lottery/sweepstakes fraud, victims receive emails informing them they have won a substantial prize in a foreign drawing but must remit payment for various taxes/fees to receive their winnings. Alternatively, victims are provided with a counterfeit instrument (such as a cashier's check) that purports to represent a portion of the winnings. Similar to an overpayment fraud (see below), the victim is told to deposit the check, forward the required payments for taxes/fees,

and the victim can keep the balance. The check is ultimately returned as a counterfeit item and the victim is indebted to their financial institution for the withdrawn funds.

### Overpayment Fraud

Victims who have advertised some item for sale via the Internet are contacted by "buyers" who remit counterfeit instruments in excess of the purchase price as payment. The victims are told to cash the instruments, deduct any expenses, and return or forward the excess funds to the "buyer," but later discover the check was counterfeit. Victims in this fraud not only lose the value of the property sold, but they are also indebted to their financial institutions for the funds withdrawn on the counterfeit check.

### Recovery/Impersonation Schemes

Victims are contacted by perpetrators posing as law enforcement officers, government employees, or lawyers who reference the victim's losses in a prior fraud scheme. Victims are led to believe that the perpetrators have been arrested and funds have been seized to pay back their losses, but of course they must first pay fees for processing and administrative services before the seized funds can be released.

**Source:** FBI, "Mass Marketing Schemes," www.fbi.gov/about-us/investigate/white_collar/mass-marketing-fraud (accessed 2015).

married individuals, and they objected to its requirement that users pay $19 for the privilege of deleting all their data from the site.[39] The company issued a $500,000 reward for the identity of the hackers.

Not all cybercriminals are motivated by greed or profit. Some are motivated by the desire for revenge and destruction or—like the Ashley Madison hackers—some other malicious intent. These are the modern cybervandals. Cybervandalism ranges from sending destructive viruses and worms to stalking or bullying people using cyberspace as a medium:

- Some cybervandals target computers and networks seeking revenge for some perceived wrong.
- Some desire to exhibit their technical prowess and superiority.
- Some wish to highlight the vulnerability of computer security systems.
- Some desire to spy on other people's private financial and personal information (computer voyeurism).
- Some want to destroy computer security because they believe in a philosophy of open access to all systems and programs.

What forms does cybervandalism take?

## Worms, Viruses, Trojan Horses, Logic Bombs, and Spam

The most typical use of cyberspace for destructive intent comes in the sending or implanting of disruptive programs, called viruses, worms, Trojan horses, logic bombs, or spam.

**VIRUSES AND WORMS**  A **computer virus** is one type of malicious software program (also called **malware**) that disrupts or destroys existing programs and networks, causing them to perform the task for which the virus was designed.[40] The virus is then spread from one computer to another when a user sends out an infected file through email, a network, or portable media. **Computer worms** are similar to viruses but use computer networks or the Internet to self-replicate and send themselves to other users, generally via email, without the aid of the operator.

The damage caused by viruses and worms can be considerable. More than a decade ago, the Melissa virus disrupted email service around the world when it was posted to an Internet newsgroup, causing more than $80 million in damage. Its creator, David Smith, pleaded guilty to state and federal charges and was later sentenced to 20 months in prison (leniency was granted because he cooperated with authorities in thwarting other hackers).[41] Another damaging piece of malware was the MS Blaster worm—also known as W32.Blaster and W32/Lovsan—which took advantage of a vulnerability in a widely used feature of Microsoft Windows and infected more than 120,000 computers worldwide.[42]

**TROJAN HORSES**  Some hackers introduce a **Trojan horse** program into a computer system. The Trojan horse looks like a benign application but contains illicit codes that can damage the system operations. Sometimes hackers with a sense of irony will install a Trojan horse and claim that it is an antivirus program. When it is opened it spreads viruses in the computer system. Though Trojan horses do not replicate themselves like viruses, they can be just as destructive.

**LOGIC BOMBS**  A fourth type of destructive attack that can be launched on a computer system is the **logic bomb**, a program that is secretly attached to a computer system, monitors the network's work output, and waits for a particular signal such as a date to appear. Also called a *slag code*, it is a type of delayed-action virus that is set off when a program user makes certain input that sets it in motion. A logic bomb can cause a variety of problems ranging from displaying or printing a spurious message to deleting or corrupting data.

**SPAM**  An unsolicited advertisement or promotional material, **spam** typically comes in the form of an unwanted email message; spammers use electronic communications to send unsolicited messages in bulk. While email is the most common form of spam, it can also be sent via instant messaging, online forum, and mobile phone messaging, among other media.

Spam can simply be in the form of an unwanted and unwelcome advertisement. For example, it may advertise sexually explicit websites and get into the hands of minors. A more dangerous and malicious form of spam contains a Trojan horse disguised as an email attachment advertising some commodity such as free software or an electronic game. If the recipient downloads or opens the attachment, a virus may be launched that corrupts the victim's computer; the Trojan horse may also be designed to capture important data from the victim's hard drive and send it back to the hacker's email address. Sending spam can become a crime and even lead to a prison sentence when it causes serious harm to a computer or network.

## Website Defacement

Cybervandals may aim their attention at the websites of their victims. **Website defacement** is a type of cybervandalism that occurs when a computer hacker intrudes on another person's website by inserting or substituting codes that expose visitors to the site to misleading or provocative information. Defacement can range from installing humorous graffiti to sabotaging or corrupting the site. In some instances, defacement efforts are not easily apparent or noticeable—for example, when they are designed to give misinformation by substituting or replacing authorized text on a company's web page. The false information may mislead customers and frustrate

**computer virus**
A program that disrupts or destroys existing programs and networks, causing them to perform the task for which the virus was designed.

**malware**
A malicious software program.

**computer worms**
Programs that attack computer networks (or the Internet) by self-replicating and sending themselves to other users, generally via email without the aid of the operator.

**Trojan horse**
A computer program that looks like a benign application but contains illicit codes that can damage the system operations. Though Trojan horses do not replicate themselves like viruses, they can be just as destructive.

**logic bomb**
A program that is secretly attached to a computer system, monitors the network's work output, and waits for a particular signal such as a date to appear. Also called a slag code, it is a type of delayed action virus that is set off when a program user makes certain input that sets it in motion. A logic bomb can cause a variety of problems ranging from displaying or printing a spurious message to deleting or corrupting data.

**spam**
An unsolicited advertisement or promotional material, typically in the form of an unwanted email message. While email is the most common form of spam, it can also be sent via instant messaging, online forum, and mobile phone messaging, among other media.

**website defacement**
A type of cybervandalism that occurs when a computer hacker intrudes on another person's website by inserting or substituting codes that expose visitors to the site to misleading or provocative information. Defacement can range from installing humorous graffiti to sabotaging or corrupting the site.

their efforts to utilize the site or make it difficult for people using search engines to find the site as they surf the Web.

Almost all defacement attacks are designed to vandalize web pages rather than bring profit or gain to the intruders (though some defacers may eventually extort money from their targets). Some defacers are simply trying to impress the hacking community with their skills. Others may target a corporation when they oppose its business practices and policies (such as oil companies, tobacco companies, or defense contractors). Some defacement has political goals such as disrupting the website of a rival political party or fund-raising group.

Defacers are typically members of an extensive social network who are eager to demonstrate their reasons for hacking and often leave calling cards, greetings, and taunts on web pages.[43] It is a worldwide phenomenon. A few years ago, hackers from an organized group called Anonymous defaced hundreds of websites belonging to the Australian government, saying the action was in response to reports of spying by Australia. The websites were defaced with a message reading "Stop Spying on Indonesia." The Anonymous group has also targeted Singapore, Mexico, the Philippines, Australia, Egypt, the United States, Syria, and many more countries.[44]

Website defacement is a significant and major threat to online businesses and government agencies. It can harm the credibility and reputation of the organization and demonstrate that its security measures are inadequate. As a result, clients lose trust and may be reluctant to share information such as credit card numbers and personal information. An etailer may lose business if potential clients believe the site is not secure. Financial institutions, such as Web-based banks and brokerage houses, are particularly vulnerable because they rely on security and credibility to protect their clients' accounts.[45]

**cyberstalking**
Use of the Internet, email, or other electronic communications devices to stalk another person. Some cyberstalkers pursue minors through online chat rooms; others harass their victims electronically.

## Cyberstalking

**Cyberstalking** refers to the use of the Internet, email, or other electronic communication devices to stalk another person. Traditional stalking may include following a person, appearing at a person's home or place of business, making harassing phone calls, leaving written messages or objects, or vandalizing a person's property. In the Internet age, stalkers can pursue victims through online chat rooms. Pedophiles can use the Internet to establish a relationship with the child and later make contact for the purpose of engaging in criminal sexual activities. Today, Internet predators are more likely to develop relationships with at-risk adolescents and beguile underage teenagers than use coercion and violence.[46]

Not all cyberstalkers are sexual predators. Some send repeated threatening or harassing messages via email or text and use programs to send messages at regular or random intervals. A cyberstalker may trick other people into harassing or threatening a victim by impersonating their victim on social media sites, posting messages that are provocative, such as "I want to have sex." The stalker then posts the victim's name, phone number, or email address hoping that other site participants will stalk or hassle the victim without the stalker's personal involvement.

Pictured here are Rebecca Caine, 24, and ex-boyfriend Peter Atkinson, 21, who went on to stalk her for five months after their breakup. Atkinson terrorized Caine, bombarding her with hundreds of texts and calls a day and posting nude pictures of her online. He served just four months in prison for his crimes. Terrified when he was released, Caine was forced to change her job well as her name. She said: "Peter's sentence wasn't long enough. I couldn't be more disappointed. The time he spent in jail is less than the time he spent harassing me. I'm furious."

## Cyberbullying

On May 15, 2008, a federal grand jury in Los Angeles indicted Lori Drew, a Missouri woman, for her alleged role in a MySpace hoax played on Megan Meier, a teenage neighbor. Drew, along with her daughter and another teenage girl, created a fake online boy named Josh Evans, who established a cyber romance with 13-year-old Megan. Later, after being spurned and attacked by "Josh" on MySpace, Megan took her own life. She had received several messages from "Josh" suggesting that she kill herself and that the "world would be better off without her." Drew was found guilty on three lesser charges (reduced from felonies to misdemeanors by the jury); her conviction was later overturned on appeal.[47]

Megan Meier is one of a number of teens who have taken their lives after being victimized by cyberbullies. While school yard bullying is a well-known problem that remains to be solved, it has now morphed from the physical to the virtual. **Cyberbullying** is defined as the willful and repeated harm inflicted through the medium of electronic text. Like their real-world counterparts, cyberbullies are malicious aggressors who seek implicit or explicit pleasure or profit through the mistreatment of other individuals.

Cyberbullying has become common in the United States and has taken its toll on adolescent victims. Here, Alex Boston, 14, poses with her parents, Amy and Chris. In front of them is a screen shot of the phony Facebook account that was set up in Alex's name by two classmates. Alex was humiliated when they stacked the page with phony comments claiming she was sexually active, racist, and involved in drugs.

**cyberbullying**
Willful and repeated harm inflicted through the medium of electronic text.

**cyberspying**
Illegally using the Internet to gather information that is considered private and confidential.

Because of the creation of cyberspace, physical distance is no longer a barrier to the frequency and depth of harm doled out by a bully to his or her victim.[48] Although power in traditional bullying might be physical (stature) or social (competency or popularity), online power may simply stem from Net proficiency. Cyberbullies are able to navigate the Net and utilize technology in a way that puts them in a position of power relative to their victim. There are two major formats that bullies can employ to harass their victims: (1) a cyberbully can use a computer and send harassing emails or instant messages, post obscene, insulting, and slanderous messages to social media sites, or develop websites to promote and disseminate defamatory content; (2) a cyberbully can use a cell phone to send harassing text messages to the victim.[49]

How common is cyberbullying? Drs. Sameer Hinduja and Justin Patchin, leading experts on cyberbullying, have conducted yearly surveys using large samples of high school youth. Their most recent effort finds that about 24 percent of the more than 14,000 high school and middle school students they surveyed report having been the target of some form of Internet harassment; similarly, about 17 percent of the students said they have harassed someone via the Internet. Adolescent girls are significantly more likely to have experienced cyberbullying in their lifetimes. The type of cyberbullying tends to differ by gender; girls are more likely to spread rumors while boys are more likely to post hurtful pictures or videos.[50]

## Cyberspying

**Cyberspying** is illegally using the Internet to gather information that is considered private and confidential. Cyberspies have a variety of motivations. Some are people involved in marital disputes who may want to seize the emails of their estranged spouse. Business rivals might hire disgruntled former employees, consultants, or outside contractors to steal information from their competitors. These commercial cyberspies target upcoming bids, customer lists, product designs, software source code, voice mail messages, and confidential email messages.[51] Some of the commercial spying is conducted by foreign competitors who seek to appropriate trade secrets in order to gain a business advantage.[52]

## Cyberwarfare: Cybercrime with Political Motives

Will future warfare be conducted in cyberspace as well as on the ground? Destroying an enemy's computer network, incapacitating their defense systems, may soon become the opening salvo of hostilities. Sounds fanciful, but there have already been efforts to compromise an enemy's defense industry and military establishment. The most celebrated incident occurred in 2010 when it was widely reported that Iran's efforts to process nuclear material were compromised by a computer worm that infected Iranian nuclear computers and sabotaged the uranium enrichment facility at Natanz—where centrifuge operational capacity suddenly dropped by 30 percent. An attack by the Stuxnet worm was confirmed by the director of the Bushehr facility, whose computers were infected by the virus.[53]

Iran's military capability is not the only one subject to cyberattack. In 2011, Lockheed Martin, the world's largest aerospace company, announced that it detected and thwarted "a significant and tenacious attack" on its information systems.[54] Not to worry this time, a company spokesman claimed, because swift action protected the company's secrets. While this attempt at **cyberespionage** did not damage America's military capability, there have been other incidents in which agents have been able to steal top-secret government information.

The Chinese espionage ring known as Titan Rain was able to penetrate the Redstone Arsenal military base and NASA; the U.S. Army's flight-planning software was electronically stolen. Titan Rain agents entered hidden sections of hard drives, zipped up as many files as possible, and transmitted the data to way stations in South Korea, Hong Kong, and Taiwan before sending them to mainland China.[55] The Pentagon issued a report on China's cyberwarfare capabilities, acknowledging that hackers in China had penetrated the Pentagon's computer system.[56]

Responding to these threats, in 2009 the Secretary of Defense directed the Commander of U.S. Strategic Command to establish the United States Cyber Command (USCYBERCOM), whose duties are stated as:

> USCYBERCOM will fuse the Department's full spectrum of cyberspace operations and will plan, coordinate, integrate, synchronize, and conduct activities to: lead day-to-day defense and protection of DoD information networks; coordinate DoD operations providing support to military missions; direct the operations and defense of specified DoD information networks and; prepare to, and when directed, conduct full spectrum military cyberspace operations. The command is charged with pulling together existing cyberspace resources, creating synergy that does not currently exist and synchronizing war-fighting effects to defend the information security environment.[57]

U.S. Cyber Command went operational on May 21, 2010. In 2011, the U.S. government announced that computer sabotage by another country could constitute an act of war. However, not every attack would lead to retaliation, only those so serious that it would threaten American lives, commerce, infrastructure, or worse, and there would have to be indisputable evidence leading to the nation-state involved.[58]

**cyberespionage**
Efforts by intelligence agencies to penetrate computer networks of an enemy nation in order to steal important data.

Cyberwarfare can be aimed at an enemy nation's infrastructure. Here, an Iranian security guard stands at the Maroun Petrochemical plant at the Imam Khomeini port, in southwestern Iran. Technicians battling a complex computer virus took the ultimate firewall measures, shutting off all Internet links to Iran's oil ministry and the terminal that carries nearly all the country's crude exports.

## Cyberterrorism

Cyberspace may also serve as a venue for terrorism. While the term may be difficult to define, cyberterrorism can be seen as an effort by covert forces to disrupt the intersection where the virtual electronic reality of computers meets the physical world.[59] FBI expert Mark Pollitt defines cyberterrorism as "the premeditated, politically motivated attack against information, computer systems, computer programs, and data which results in violence against noncombatant targets by subnational groups or clandestine agents."[60]

Terrorist organizations now understand the power that disruption of cyberspace can inflict on their enemies even though, ironically, they may come from a region where computer databases and the Internet are not widely used. Terrorist organizations are adapting IT into their arsenal of terror, and agencies of the justice system have to be ready for a sustained attack on the nation's electronic infrastructure.

**WHY TERRORISM IN CYBERSPACE?** Cyberspace is a handy battlefield for the terrorist because an attack can strike directly at a target that bombs won't affect: the economy. Because technological change plays a significant role in the development of critical infrastructures, they are particularly vulnerable to attack. And because of rapid technological change, and the interdependence of systems, it is difficult to defend against efforts to disrupt services.[61]

Cyberterrorists have many advantages. There are no borders of legal control, making it difficult for prosecutors to apply laws to some crimes. Criminals can operate from countries where laws pertaining to cybercrime barely exist, making them almost untouchable. Cyberterrorists can also use the Internet and hacking tools to gather information on targets.[62] There is no loss of life and no need to infiltrate "enemy" territory. Terrorists can commit crimes from anyplace in the world and the costs are minimal. Nor do terror organizations lack for skilled labor to mount cyberattacks. There are highly skilled computer experts available at reasonable costs in most developing countries.

**CYBERATTACKS** Has the United States already been the target of cyberterrorism? While it may be difficult to separate the damage caused by hackers from deliberate attacks by terrorists, the Center for Strategic and International Studies has uncovered attacks on the National Security Agency, the Pentagon, and a nuclear weapons laboratory; operations were disrupted at all of these sites.[63] There have been numerous attacks and serious breaches in recent years. In addition to the Sony breach mentioned in the opening vignette, such companies as Anthem Health Care, Primera Blue Cross, Staples, and Home Depot have had their computer systems hacked and the names, Social Security numbers, birthdays, addresses, email, and employment information, and income data of current and former customers and employees stolen.[64] The financial service sector is a prime target and has been victimized by information warfare. In 2013, a massive cyberattack was directed at some of the nation's largest banks, including JPMorgan Chase, Bank of America, and Citigroup, by a hacker group calling itself Izz ad-Din al-Qassam Cyber Fighters. What made this attack different was that the traffic was coming from data centers around the world that had been infected with a sophisticated form of malware designed to evade detection by antivirus solutions. The bank attackers used those infected servers to simultaneously fire traffic at each banking site until it slowed or collapsed. The purpose of the attack: to punish the American financial system in retaliation for a film insulting to Moslems.[65]

Here are some possible scenarios:

- Logic bombs are implanted in an enemy's computer. They can go undetected for years until they are instructed through the Internet to overwhelm a computer system.
- Programs are used to allow terrorists to enter "secure" systems and disrupt or destroy the network.
- Using conventional weapons, terrorists overload a network's electrical system, thereby threatening computer security.[66]

- The computer system of a corporation whose welfare is vital to national security—such as Boeing or Raytheon—is breached and disrupted.
- Internet-based systems used to manage basic infrastructure needs—such as an oil pipeline's flow or water levels in dams—are attacked and disrupted, posing a danger of loss of life and interruption of services.

Terrorists use the Internet to recruit new members and disseminate information. For example, Islamic militant organizations use the Internet to broadcast anti-Western slogans and information. An organization's charter and political philosophy can be displayed on its website, which can also be used to solicit funds. ISIL has recruited young women from Western nations by posting videos on social media sites in which jihadists are introduced as potential husbands. The videos show burka-clad jihadi brides carrying Kalashnikovs and promote the virtues of fighting for the caliphate, telling the women they will receive a "guaranteed ticket to paradise."[67]

## Funding Terrorist Activities

Obtaining operational funds is a key to terrorist activity. Terrorist groups use the Internet to raise funds to buy arms and carry out operations.[68] One method of funding is through fraudulent charitable organizations claiming to support a particular cause such as disaster relief or food services. Using bogus charities to raise money is particularly attractive to cyberterrorists because they face far less scrutiny from the government than for-profit corporations and individuals. They may also qualify for financial assistance from government-sponsored grant programs. One such bogus group, Holy Land Foundation for Relief and Development (HLFRD), provided more than $12 million to the terrorist group Hamas; in total, HLFRD raised more than $57 million but only reported $36.2 million to the IRS.[69]

Bogus companies have also been used by terrorist groups to receive and distribute money. These shell companies may engage in legitimate activities to establish a positive reputation in the business community but produce bills for nonexistent products that are "paid" by another party with profits from illegal activities, such as insurance fraud or identity theft.[70] If a shell company generates revenues, funds can be distributed by altering financial statements to hide profits and then depositing the profits in accounts that are used directly or indirectly to support terrorist activities.

Another source of terrorist funding, which is discussed less often in the literature, is intellectual property (IP) crime. The illegal sale of counterfeited goods and illegal use of IP to commit other crimes, such as stock manipulation, have been used to support terrorist activities.[71]

The various branches of cybercrime are set out in Concept Summary 14.1.

## Concept Summary 14.1   Types of Cybercrime

| Crime | Definition | Examples |
|---|---|---|
| **Cybertheft** | Use of cyberspace to distribute illegal goods and services or to defraud people for quick profits | Illegal copyright infringement, identity theft, Internet securities fraud, warez |
| **Cybervandalism** | Use of cyberspace for revenge, destruction, and to achieve a malicious intent | Website defacement, worms, viruses, cyberstalking, cyberbullying |
| **Cyberwarfare** | An effort by enemy forces to disrupt the intersection where the virtual electronic reality of computers meets the physical world | Logic bombs used to disrupt or destroy "secure" systems or networks, Internet used to communicate covertly with agents around the world. Recruiting for terror groups. |

## The Extent and Costs of Cybercrime

How common are cybercrimes, and how costly are cybercrimes to American businesses and the general public? The Internet has become a vast engine for illegal profits and criminal entrepreneurs. An accurate accounting of cybercrime will probably never be made because so many offenses go unreported, but there is little doubt that its incidence is growing rapidly.

Though global business enterprises are subjected to millions of cybercrimes each year, most are not reported to local, state, or federal authorities. Some cybercrime goes unreported because it involves low-visibility acts—such as copying computer software in violation of copyright laws—that simply never get detected.[72] Some businesses choose not to report cybercrime because they fear revealing the weaknesses in their network security systems.

Despite this reluctance to report cyberattacks, there are growing indications that the cost of cybercrime already outstrips the losses attributed to common-law crimes such as burglary and robbery and is growing at a faster pace. It is now estimated that the cost of cybercrime will reach at least $2 trillion per year by 2019.[73]

A significant portion of cybercrime costs are borne by business enterprise. File sharing and the illegal reproduction and distribution of movies, software, games, and music now cost U.S. businesses an estimated $58 billion in annual economic output and more than 300,000 jobs each year.[74] One reason is the increased computer and Internet usage in emerging economies such as China, Eastern Europe, and Brazil, where piracy rates are highest.[75]

Not only are business enterprises the target of cybertheft, but they also lose billions each year to cybervandalism.[76] Symantec Corporation (publisher of Norton Antivirus) conducts an annual Internet security threat report that makes use of data from more than 24,000 security devices deployed in more than 180 countries.[77] According to Symantec, attackers trick companies into infecting themselves with Trojan horse software updates to common programs and patiently wait for their targets to download the malware. Once a victim has downloaded the software update, attackers are given unfettered access to the corporate network. Highly targeted spear-phishing attacks are a favorite tactic for infiltrating networks, as the total number of attacks rose 8 percent between 2013 and 2014. Attackers use stolen email accounts from one corporate victim to attack other victims higher up the food chain. They are learning to take advantage of companies' management tools and procedures to move stolen intellectual property around the corporate network before exfiltration.

The Symantec survey confirmed the prevalence and continued growth of malware, which increased 26 percent in 2014. In fact, there were more than 317 million new pieces of malware created in that year alone—that's nearly one million per day. A sizable portion of all software is now being installed without proper licensing, especially in emerging economies, where unlicensed software use is widespread.

Business enterprise is not the only target that bears the cost of cybercrime. Individuals are also targets, and the costs are high. Take for instance identity theft or phishing. The Internal Revenue Service (IRS) found that the agency paid refunds to criminals who filed false tax returns, in some cases on behalf of people who had died. In all, the IRS is expected to lose as much as $21 billion in revenue between 2012 and 2017 due to identity theft.[78]

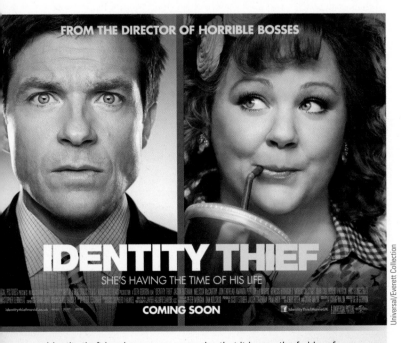

Universal/Everett Collection

Identity theft has become so pervasive that it is now the fodder of films and books, including the hit 2013 movie *Identity Thief* with Jason Bateman and Melissa McCarthy.

# Controlling Cybercrime

The proliferation of cybercrime and its cost to the economy have created the need for laws and enforcement processes specifically aimed at controlling its emerging formulations. Because technology evolves so rapidly, the enforcement challenges are particularly vexing. There are numerous organizations set up to provide training and support for law enforcement agents. In addition, new federal and state laws have been aimed at particular areas of high-tech crimes.

L04 Discuss efforts to control cybercrime.

Congress has treated computer-related crime as a distinct federal offense since the passage of the Counterfeit Access Device and Computer Fraud and Abuse Law in 1984.[79] The act protected classified U.S. defense and foreign relations information, financial institution and consumer reporting agency files, and access to computers operated for the government. The act was supplemented in 1996 by the National Information Infrastructure Protection Act (NIIPA), which significantly broadened the scope of the law.[80]

Existing laws are sometimes inadequate to address the problem of cybercrime. Therefore new legislation has been drafted to protect the public from this new breed of criminal. Before October 30, 1998, when the Identity Theft and Assumption Deterrence Act of 1998 became law, there was no federal statute that made identity theft a crime. The Identity Theft and Assumption Deterrence Act accomplished four things:

- It made identity theft a separate crime against the individual whose identity was stolen and credit destroyed. Previously, victims had been defined solely by financial loss and often the emphasis was on banks and other financial institutions, rather than on individuals.
- It established the Federal Trade Commission (FTC) as the federal government's one central point of contact for reporting instances of identity theft by creating the Identity Theft Data Clearinghouse.
- It increased criminal penalties for identity theft and fraud. Specifically, the crime now carries a maximum penalty of 15 years imprisonment and substantial fines.
- It closed legal loopholes, which previously had made it a crime to produce or possess false identity documents, but *not* to steal another person's personal identifying information.[81]

Today, federal prosecutors are making substantial use of the statute and are actively prosecuting cases of identity theft. In addition, almost all states have by now passed laws related to identity theft.

In the wake of the 9/11 attacks, the NIIPA was amended by sections of the USA Patriot Act to make it easier to prosecute crimes by terrorists and other organized enemies against the nation's computer systems. Subsection 1030(a)(5)(A)(i) of the act criminalizes knowingly causing the transmission of a program, code, or command, and as a result, intentionally causing damage to a protected computer. This section applies regardless of whether the user had authorization to access the protected computer; company insiders and authorized users can be culpable for intentional damage to a protected computer. The act also prohibits intentional access without authorization that results in damage but does not require intent to damage; the attacker can merely be negligent or reckless.

## International Treaties

Because cybercrime is essentially global, international cooperation is required for its control. The Convention on Cybercrime, ratified by the U.S. Senate in August 2006, was the first international treaty to address the definition and enforcement of cybercrime. Now signed by 46 nations, it focuses on improving investigative techniques and increasing cooperation among nations. The Convention includes a list of crimes that each signatory state must incorporate into their own law, including such cyber offenses as hacking, distribution of child pornography, and protection of intellectual property rights. It also allows law enforcement agencies new powers, including the ability to require that an Internet service provider monitor a person's online viewing and search choices in real time. The Convention also requires signatory states to cooperate whenever possible in the investigations and prosecution of cybercriminals. The vision is that a common legal framework will eliminate jurisdictional hurdles to facilitate the law enforcement of borderless cybercrimes.[82]

## Cybercrime Enforcement Agencies

To enforce these laws, federal, state, and local law enforcement agencies have put together a number of unified efforts to identify, control, and prosecute cybercrime. One approach is to create working groups that coordinate the activities of numerous agencies involved in investigating cybercrime. The International Mass-Marketing Fraud Working Group brings together representatives of numerous U.S. attorneys' offices, the FBI, the Secret Service, the Postal Inspection Service, the Federal Trade Commission, the Securities and Exchange Commission, Immigration and Customs Enforcement, and other law enforcement and regulatory agencies to share information about trends and patterns in Internet fraud schemes.[83]

The New York/New Jersey Electronic Crimes Task Force (NYECTF) is a partnership between the U.S. Secret Service and a host of other public safety agencies and private corporations. The task force consists of more than 250 individual members representing federal, state, and local law enforcement, the private sector, and computer science specialists from 18 universities. Since 1995, the NYECTF has charged more than 1,000 individuals with electronic crime losses exceeding $1 billion. It has trained more than 60,000 law enforcement personnel, prosecutors, and private industry representatives in cybercrime prevention. Its success has prompted similar electronic crime task forces to be set up in Boston, Miami, Charlotte, Chicago, Las Vegas, San Francisco, Los Angeles, and Washington, D.C.[84]

On a broader scale, the National Cyber Investigative Joint Task Force (NCIJTF) consists of nearly two dozen federal intelligence, military, and law enforcement agencies that work along with local law enforcement agencies and international and private industry partners. The NCIJTF serves as the government's central hub for coordinating, integrating, and sharing information related to cyber threat investigations. It is tasked with identifying hackers and understanding their motivations and capabilities, disrupting criminal operations, and minimizing the consequences of intrusions. Rather than focusing on narrow or localized cybercrimes, the NCIJTF looks at the overall cyber landscape, attempting to counteract broad strategic shifts in cybercriminals' tactics and movements. It helps train local operatives, coordinate the sharing of intelligence across government agencies, and integrate the response to intrusions and investigations.[85]

Another specialized agency that works with citizens who have been cybercrime victims, the Internet Crime Complaint Center, based in Fairmont, West Virginia, is run by the FBI and the National White Collar Crime Center. It brings together about 1,000 state and local law enforcement officials and regulators. Its goal is to analyze fraud-related complaints in order to find distinct patterns, develop information on particular cases, and send investigative packages to law enforcement authorities in the jurisdiction that appears likely to have the greatest investigative interest in the matter. The Internet Crime Complaint Center (IC³) receives nearly 300,000 complaints per year, which represent losses of close to $800 million. They investigate auction fraud, nondelivery, and credit/debit card fraud, as well as nonfraudulent complaints, such as computer intrusions, spam/unsolicited email, and child pornography.[86] Law enforcement has made remarkable strides in dealing with identity theft as a crime problem over the last several years.

**L05** Trace the evolution of organized crime.

# Transnational Organized Crime

Transnational organized crime (TOC or transnational crime) is a form of organized crime operating across national borders. (See the accompanying Policies and Issues in Criminology feature for the history of organized crime.) It involves groups or networks of individuals working in more than one country to plan and execute illegal business ventures. These criminal conspiracies involve ongoing criminal enterprise groups whose ultimate purpose is personal economic gain through illegitimate means. These groups do not hesitate to utilize systematic violence and corruption to get what they want and achieve their criminal goals: prostitution, pornography, gambling, and narcotics. The system may resemble a legitimate business run by an ambitious chief executive officer, his or her assistants, staff attorneys, and accountants, with thorough, efficient accounts receivable and complaint departments.[87] Cross-national gangs are often large criminal organizations, some with more than 20,000 members whose activities are bicoastal; the criminal activities of transnational gangs are global and have no borders.

This section briefly defines transnational organized crime, reviews its history, and discusses its economic effect and control.

Trafficking in humans can have deadly results. Here, on August 27, 2015, forensic experts investigate a truck in which 71 refugees were found dead on the autobahn A4 between Parndorf and Neusiedl, Austria. Europe is suffering a massive influx of refugees from the Middle East as fighting continues, and traffickers are looking to cash in on their desperation to emigrate to the West.

## Characteristics of Transnational Organized Crime

A precise description of the characteristics of transnational organized crime is difficult to formulate, but here are some of its general traits:[88]

- Transnational organized crime is a conspiratorial activity, involving the coordination of numerous people in the planning and execution of illegal acts or in the pursuit of a legitimate objective by unlawful means (e.g., threatening a legitimate business to get a stake in it).
- An offense is transnational if:
  - It is committed in more than one state or nation.
  - It is committed in one state or nation but a substantial part of its preparation, planning, direction, or control takes place in another state or nation.
  - It is committed in one state or nation but involves an organized criminal group that engages in criminal activities in more than one state or nation.
  - It is committed in one state or nation but has substantial effects in another state or nation.[89]
- Transnational organized crime involves continuous commitment by primary members, although individuals with specialized skills may be brought in as needed.
- Transnational organized crime is usually structured along hierarchical lines—a chieftain supported by close advisers, lower subordinates, and so on.
- Transnational organized crime has economic gain as its primary goal, although power and status may also be motivating factors. Economic gain is achieved through global supply of illegal goods and services, including drugs, sex slaves, arms, and pornography.
- In addition to providing illegal material such as narcotics, contemporary global syndicates engage in business crimes such as laundering illegal money through legitimate businesses, land fraud, and computer crime.
- Transnational criminal syndicates employ predatory tactics, such as intimidation, violence, and corruption.
- Transnational organized crime groups are quick and effective in controlling and disciplining their members, associates, and victims and will not hesitate to use lethal violence against those who flaunt organizational rules.

**FACT OR FICTION?**

Organized crime in the United States is a local commodity, controlled by five Mafia families in New York City and a few other allied groups in Chicago, Los Angeles, and Miami.

**FICTION** Traditional organized crime families are in decline, being replaced by transnational crime groups originating in Europe, Asia, and Latin and South America.

# Policies and Issues
# in Criminology

## ORIGINS OF ORGANIZED CRIME

While transnational gangs are a product of the IT age, organized crime has existed for more than 400 years. In the 1600s, London was terrorized by organized gangs that called themselves Hectors, Bugles, Dead Boys, and other colorful names. In the seventeenth and eighteenth centuries, English gang members wore distinctive belts and pins marked with serpents, animals, stars, and the like. The first mention of youth gangs in America occurred in the late 1780s, when prison reformers noted the presence of gangs of young people hanging out on Philadelphia's street corners. By the 1820s, New York's Bowery and Five Points districts, Boston's North End and Fort Hill, and the outlying Southwark and Moyamensing sections of Philadelphia were the locales of youth gangs with names like the Roach Guards, Chichesters, Plug Uglies, and Dead Rabbits.

At the turn of the twentieth century, La Mano Nera (the Black Hand), an offshoot of Sicilian criminal groups, established itself in northeastern urban centers. Gangsters demanded payments from local businessmen in return for "protection"; those who would not pay were beaten and their shops vandalized. Eventually the Black Hand merged with gangs of Italian heritage to form larger urban-based gangs and groups.

A turning point in the development of organized gangs occurred on January 16, 1919, when the Eighteenth Amendment to the U.S. Constitution was ratified. The new amendment prohibited the sale, manufacture, and transportation of intoxicating liquors. Until then gangs had remained relatively small and local, but now the national market for controlled substances opened the door to riches. What emerged was a national syndicate, referred to as La Cosa Nostra or the Mafia, that was centrally coordinated and whose various component gangs worked cooperatively to settle disputes, dictate policy, and assign territory. Despite efforts at cooperation and control, numerous and bloody gang wars and individual vendettas were common.

The Mafia remains the largest organized crime group in the United States. Major families have a total membership of about 1,000 to 2,000 "made men," who have been inducted into organized crime families, and another 17,000 "associates," who are criminally involved with syndicate members. The families control crime in distinct geographic areas. New York City, the most important organized crime area, alone contains five families—the Gambino, Columbo (formerly Profaci), Lucchese, Bonanno, and Genovese families—named after their founding "godfathers." In contrast, Chicago contains a single mob organization called the "outfit," which also influences racketeering in such cities as Milwaukee, Kansas City, and Phoenix. The families are believed to be ruled by a "commission" made up of the heads of the five New York families and bosses from Detroit, Buffalo, Chicago, and Philadelphia, which settles personal problems and jurisdictional conflicts and

- Transnational crime depends heavily on the instruments of the IT age: the Internet, global communications, rapid global transportation systems, universal banking system, and global credit card and payment systems.
- Transnational organized crime groups do not include terror organizations, though there may be overlap. Some terror groups are involved in criminality to fund their political objectives, and some have morphed from politically motivated organizations to ones solely involved in for-profit criminal activity. Transnational criminal organizations may aid terror groups with transportation and communication.

**L06** Discuss the activities of transnational organized crime.

## Activities of Transnational Organized Crime

What are the main activities of transnational organized crime? The traditional sources of income are derived from providing illicit materials and using force to enter into and maximize profits in legitimate businesses. Most organized crime income comes from such activities as human trafficking, narcotics distribution, smuggling, and illegal gambling. Theft rings, Internet pornography, and cargo theft are other sources of income.

enforces rules that allow members to gain huge profits through the manufacture and sale of illegal goods and services.

## Mafia in Decline

The American Mafia has been in decline. One reason: high-profile criminal prosecutions using up-to-date IT methods for surveillance and evidence collection. Chicago mob boss Frank Calabrese, Sr., was sentenced to life in prison in 2009 for his role in 18 gangland slayings dating back to 1970. His arrest—along with 13 others—meant that the Chicago mob does not have the power and influence it once had in the city. In another high-profile case, James "Whitey" Bulger was arrested after having been on the run for 16 years. Bulger, who once ran Boston's feared Winter Hill Gang, was wanted for his role in 19 murders.

The Mafia leadership is aging. A number of the reigning family heads are quite old, in their 80s and older. A younger generation of mob leaders have stepped in to take control of the families, and they seem to lack the skill and leadership of the older bosses. The code of silence that protected Mafia leaders is now broken regularly by younger members who turn informer rather than face prison terms. When Joe Calabrese was on trial, his own son testified against him in court. In addition, active government enforcement policies have halved what the estimated mob membership was 25 years ago, and a number of the highest-ranking leaders have been imprisoned.

Traditional organized crime has also been hurt by changing values in U.S. society. European American neighborhoods, which were the locus of Mafia power, have been shrinking as families move to the suburbs. Organized crime groups lost their urban-centered political and social base of operations. In addition, success has hurt organized crime families: younger family members are better educated than their forebears and are equipped to seek their fortunes through legitimate enterprise. So while the traditional Mafia is still in business, its power is being replaced by transnational crime cartels. Traditional organized families had well-defined turf; transnational gangs respect no boundaries.

## Critical Thinking

Can you think of parallels to the erosion of local crime families and their replacement by transnational groups? In other words, do changes in organized crime reflect changes in other social institutions?

**Sources:** Howard Abadinsky, *Organized Crime* (Belmont, CA: Wadsworth, 2012); FBI, "The Chicago Mafia: Down but Not Out," June 27, 2011, www.fbi.gov/news/stories/2011/june/the-chicago-mafia/the-chicago-mafia (accessed 2015); Christopher Adamson, "Defensive Localism in White and Black: A Comparative History of European-American and African American Youth Gangs," *Ethnic and Racial Studies* 23 (2000): 272–298; Donald Cressey, *Theft of the Nation* (New York: Harper & Row, 1969).

Because cross-national and transnational gangs are a product of the cyber age, members use cyberspace to communicate and promote their illicit activities. Gangs typically use the voice and text messaging capabilities of cell phones to conduct drug transactions and prearrange meetings with customers. Prepaid cell phones are used when conducting drug trafficking operations. Social networking sites, encrypted email, and instant messaging are commonly used by gang members to communicate with one another and with drug customers. Gang members use social networking sites such as YouTube and Facebook as well as personal web pages to communicate and boast about their gang membership and related activities. Some use the Internet to intimidate rival gang members and maintain websites to recruit new members. Gang members flash gang signs and wear gang colors in videos and photos posted on the Web. Sometimes, rivals "spar" on Internet message boards.[90]

## The Rise of Transnational Gangs

Traditional Eurocentric gangs are being replaced by transnational mega-gangs. Some, such as the Crips, Bloods, and MS-13, have expanded from local street gangs to national mega-gangs with thousands of members. For example, the Sureños is an alliance of hundreds of individual Mexican American street gangs that originated in Southern California. Sureños gang members' main sources of income are retail-level distribution of cocaine, heroin, marijuana, and methamphetamine within prison systems and in the community as well as extortion of drug distributors on the streets. Some members have direct links to Mexican drug traffickers, brokering large drug transactions; they are also involved in other criminal activities such as assault, carjacking, home invasion, homicide, and robbery. While most members remain in Southern California cities, the gang has spread significantly and can be found throughout much of the United States.[91]

In addition to these homegrown gangs, international gangs based in Asia, Eastern Europe, North, South, and Latin America use the Internet and other IT devices to facilitate their operations across nations and continents. Emerging transnational crime syndicates are primarily located in nations whose governments are too weak to present effective opposition. If they believe that the government is poised to interfere with their illegal activities, they will carry out a terror campaign, killing police and other government officials to achieve their goals. Easier international travel, expanded world trade, and financial transactions that cross national borders have enabled them to branch out of local and regional crime to target international victims and develop criminal networks within more prosperous countries and regions.[92] For example, Africa, a continent that has experienced political turmoil, has also seen the rise of transnational gangs. African criminal enterprises in Nigeria, Ghana, and Liberia have developed quickly since the 1980s due to the globalization of the world's economies and the great advances in communications technology. Nigerian criminal enterprises, primarily engaged in drug trafficking and financial frauds, are the most significant of these groups and operate in more than 80 countries. They are infamous for their email-based financial frauds, which cost the United States alone an estimated $1 billion to $2 billion each year.

Some of the most prominent transnational gang clusters are described here in some detail.

**EASTERN EUROPEAN GANGS** Eastern European gangs trace their origins to countries spanning the Baltics, the Balkans, Central/Eastern Europe, Russia, the Caucasus, and Central Asia. For example, Albanian organized crime activities in the United States include gambling, money laundering, drug trafficking, human smuggling, extortion, violent witness intimidation, robbery, attempted murder, and murder.[93] Organized groups prey upon women in the poorest areas of Europe—Romania, the Ukraine, Bosnia—and sell them into virtual sexual slavery. Many of these women are transported as prostitutes around the world, some finding themselves in the United States.

Balkan organized crime groups have recently expanded into more sophisticated crimes, including real estate fraud and cybercrimes. Take for instance Armenian Power (AP), an international organized crime group formed in the East Hollywood district of Los Angeles in the 1980s. In its heyday, the gang's 250-person membership consisted not only of those of Armenian descent but members from other countries within the former Soviet Union. Its members and associates carry out violent criminal acts, including murders, attempted murders, kidnappings, robberies, extortions, and witness intimidation and kidnapping. The government began to crack down on this group and eventually indicted 90 Armenian Power leaders, members, and associates, including the head man, Mher Darbinyan, aka "Hollywood Mike" and "Capone." Darbinyan was indicted for a bank fraud scheme that used middlemen and runners to deposit and cash hundreds of thousands of dollars in fraudulent checks drawn on the accounts of elderly bank customers and businesses. He also organized and operated a sophisticated debit card skimming scheme that involved the installation and use of skimmers to steal thousands of customers' debit card numbers and PIN codes. He was eventually sentenced to 32 years in prison; 87 other members have been convicted. The AP case shows how today's transnational crime groups rely more on sophisticated cybercrime conspiracies than they do on the brute force of yesterday's organized criminals.[94]

**RUSSIAN TRANSNATIONAL CRIME GROUPS** Since the collapse of the Soviet Union in 1991, criminal organizations in Russia and other former Soviet republics such as Ukraine have engaged in a variety of crimes: drugs and arms trafficking, stolen automobiles, trafficking in women and children, and money laundering.[95] No area of the world seems immune, especially not the United States. America is the land of opportunity for unloading criminal goods and laundering dirty money.

Russian criminals make extensive use of the state governmental apparatus to protect and promote their criminal activities. Most businesses in Russia—legal, quasi-legal, and illegal—must operate with the protection of a *krysha* (roof). The protection is often provided by police or security officials employed outside their "official" capacities for this purpose. In other cases, officials are "silent partners" in criminal enterprises that they, in turn, protect. Valuable properties are purchased through insider deals for much less than their true value and then resold for lucrative profits.

Criminals have been able to directly influence the state's domestic and foreign policy to promote the interests of organized crime, either by attaining public office themselves or by buying public officials. As a result of these activities, corruption and organized crime are globalized. Russian organized crime is active in Europe, Africa, Asia, and North and South America. Massive money laundering is now common, which allows Russian and foreign organized crime to flourish. In some cases, it is tied to terrorist funding. Russian criminals have become involved in killings for hire in Central and Western Europe, Israel, Canada, and the United States.

In the United States, with the exception of extortion and money laundering, Russians have had little or no involvement in some of the more traditional types of organized crime, such as drug trafficking, gambling, and loan sharking. However, thousands of Russian immigrants are believed to be involved in criminal activity, primarily in Russian enclaves in New York City.[96] Russian criminal groups are extensively engaged in a broad array of frauds and scams, including health care fraud, insurance scams, stock frauds, antiquities swindles, forgery, and fuel tax evasion schemes. Russians are believed to be the main purveyors of credit card fraud in the United States. Legitimate businesses, such as the movie business and the textile industry, have become targets of criminals from the former Soviet Union, and they are often used for money laundering and extortion.

**LATIN AMERICAN AND MEXICAN DRUG CARTELS** Transnational crime cartels operate freely in South American nations such as Peru and Colombia. Caribbean nations such as Jamaica, the Dominican Republic, and Haiti are home to drug and gun smuggling gangs. The money from illicit trade strengthens and enlarges the gangs, enabling them to increase their involvement in intraregional and transnational dealing in order to gain more money. Furthermore, drug trafficking has contributed to a sharp increase in the availability and usage of firearms.[97]

However, while island groups flourish, it is the Mexican drug cartels that are now of greatest concern. These transnational gangs have become large-scale suppliers of narcotics, marijuana, and methamphetamine to the United States, and Mexico has become a drug-producing and transit country. In addition, an estimated 90 percent of cocaine entering the United States transits Mexico. Mexican drug gangs routinely use violence, and fighting for control of the border regions has affected U.S. citizens. Americans have been kidnapped, and Mexican drug cartel members have threatened to kill U.S. journalists covering drug violence in the border region. Although Mexican drug cartels, or drug trafficking organizations, have existed for quite some time, they have become more powerful since Colombia was able to crack down on the Cali and Medellín cartels in the 1990s. Mexican drug cartels now dominate the wholesale illicit drug market in the United States. As a result, Mexican cartels are the leading wholesale launderers of drug money from the United States. Mexican and Colombian trafficking organizations annually smuggle an estimated $25 billion in drug proceeds into Mexico for laundering.

At one time numerous drug cartels operated in Mexico, including the Gulf, Tijuana, Los Zetas, Sinaloa, Juárez, Millennium, Oaxaca, and Colima cartels. In recent years, new cartels have formed, some have become allies, and others were decimated by government crackdowns and rival gangs, Today the dominant gangs seem to be the Sinaloa, Jalisco New Generation, La Resistencia, and Knights Templar cartels. However, in a constantly shifting landscape of drug activity, this lineup could change instantly.

**ASIAN TRANSNATIONAL CRIME GROUPS** Asian-based transnational crime groups are also quite active in such areas as human trafficking, narcotics, and money laundering.[98] Chinese gangs are involved in importing heroin from the neighboring Golden Triangle area and distributing it throughout the country. They are also involved in gambling and prostitution, activities that had all but disappeared under Mao Zedong's Communist regime. The two leading organized crime problems in Cambodia are drug production/trafficking and human trafficking. Drug traffickers also use Cambodia as a transit country and traffic Cambodian women into Thailand for sexual activities. In Taiwan, the number one organized crime problem is *heijin*, the penetration of mobsters into the legitimate business sector and the political arena. Gangs are now heavily involved in the businesses of bid-rigging, waste disposal, construction, cable television networks, telecommunications, stock trading, and entertainment. Further, starting in the mid-1980s, many criminals have successfully run for public office in order to protect themselves from police crackdowns. Taiwan's gangs are involved in gambling, prostitution, loan sharking, debt collection, extortion, and gang violence; kidnapping for ransom is also a serious concern.

Among the best-known Asian crime groups are:

- *Yakuza.* Japanese criminal group. Often involved in multinational criminal activities, including human trafficking, gambling, prostitution, and undermining licit businesses.
- *Fuk Ching.* Chinese organized criminal group in the United States. They have been involved in smuggling, street violence, and human trafficking.
- *Triads.* Underground criminal societies based in Hong Kong. They control secret markets and bus routes and are often involved in money laundering and drug trafficking.
- *Heijin.* Taiwanese gangsters who are often executives in large corporations. They are often involved in white-collar crimes, such as illegal stock trading and bribery, and sometimes run for public office.
- *Jao Pho.* Organized crime group in Thailand. They are often involved in illegal political and business activity.
- *Red Wa.* Gangsters from Thailand. They are involved in manufacturing and trafficking methamphetamine.[99]

## Controlling Transnational Crime

Efforts to combat transnational organized crime are typically in the hands of federal agencies. One approach is to form international working groups to collect intelligence, share information, and plot unified strategies among member nations. The FBI belongs to several international working groups aimed at combating transnational gangs in various parts of the world. For example, to combat the influence and reach of Eurasian organized crime the FBI is involved in the following groups and activities:

- *Eurasian Organized Crime Working Group.* Established in 1994, it meets to discuss and jointly address the transnational aspects of Eurasian organized crime that impact member countries and the international community in general. The member countries are Canada, Great Britain, Germany, France, Italy, Japan, the United States, and Russia.

- *Central European Working Group.* This group is part of a project that brings together the FBI and Central European law enforcement agencies to discuss cooperative investigative matters covering the broad spectrum of Eurasian organized crime. A principal concern is the growing presence of Russian and other Eurasian organized criminals in Central Europe and the United States. The initiative works on practical interaction between the participating agencies to establish lines of communication and working relationships, to develop strategies and tactics to address transnational organized crime matters impacting the region, and to identify potential common targets.

- *Southeast European Cooperative Initiative.* This is an international organization intended to coordinate police and customs regional actions for preventing and combating transborder crime. It is headquartered in Bucharest, Romania, and has 12 fully participating member countries. The United States has been 1 of 14 countries with observer status since 1998. The initiative's center serves as a clearinghouse for information and intelligence sharing, allowing the quick exchange of information in a professional and trustworthy environment. The initiative also supports specialized task forces for countering transborder crime such as the trafficking of people, drugs, and cars; smuggling; financial crimes; terrorism; and other serious transborder crimes.

**ANTI–ORGANIZED CRIME LAWS** Congress has passed a number of laws that have made it easier for agencies to bring transnational gangs to justice. One of the first measures aimed directly at organized crime was the Interstate and Foreign Travel or Transportation in Aid of Racketeering Enterprises Act (Travel Act).[100] The Travel Act prohibits travel in interstate commerce or use of interstate facilities with the intent to promote, manage, establish, carry on, or facilitate an unlawful activity; it also prohibits the actual or attempted engagement in these activities.

In 1970, Congress passed the Organized Crime Control Act. Title IX of the act, probably its most effective measure, is the **Racketeer Influenced and Corrupt Organizations Act (RICO)**.[101] RICO did not create new categories of crimes but rather new categories of offenses in racketeering activity, which it defined as involvement in two or more acts prohibited by 24 existing federal and 8 state statutes. The offenses listed in RICO include state-defined crimes (such as murder, kidnapping, gambling, arson, robbery, bribery, extortion, and narcotics violations) and federally defined crimes (such as bribery, counterfeiting, transmission of gambling information, prostitution, and mail fraud). RICO is designed to limit patterns of organized criminal activity by prohibiting involvement in acts intended to do the following:

> **Racketeer Influenced and Corrupt Organizations Act (RICO)**
> Federal legislation that enables prosecutors to bring additional criminal or civil charges against people whose multiple criminal acts constitute a conspiracy. RICO features monetary penalties that allow the government to confiscate all profits derived from criminal activities. Originally intended to be used against organized criminals, RICO has also been used against white-collar criminals.

- Derive income from racketeering or the unlawful collection of debts and use or investment of such income
- Acquire through racketeering an interest in or control over any enterprise engaged in interstate or foreign commerce
- Conduct business through a pattern of racketeering
- Conspire to use racketeering as a means of making income, collecting loans, or conducting business

An individual convicted under RICO is subject to 20 years in prison and a $25,000 fine. Additionally, the accused must forfeit to the U.S. government any interest in a business in violation of RICO. These penalties are much more potent than simple conviction and imprisonment.

## Why Is It So Difficult to Eradicate Transnational Gangs?

While international cooperation is now common and law enforcement agencies are willing to work together to fight transnational gangs, these criminal organizations

Transnational crime is extremely difficult to control. Here, an Afghan man harvests a poppy field in the Khogyani district of Jalalabad, east of Kabul. When foreign troops arrived in Afghanistan in 2001, one of their goals was to stem drug production. Instead, they have concentrated on fighting insurgents and have often been accused of turning a blind eye to the poppy fields. Afghanistan is now the leading provider of poppy, the basic ingredient for heroin. Controlling transnational crimes in places such as Afghanistan is all but impossible.

Rahmat Gul/AP Images

## CHECKPOINTS

▶ Transnational organized crime (TOC or transnational crime) is a form of organized crime operating across national borders.

▶ Cross-national and transnational gang members use cell phones and the Internet to communicate and promote their illicit activities.

▶ Transnational organized crime is a conspiratorial activity, involving the coordination of numerous people in the planning and execution of illegal acts or in the pursuit of a legitimate objective by unlawful means.

▶ Most organized crime income comes from such activities as human trafficking, narcotics distribution, smuggling, illegal gambling, theft rings, Internet pornography, and cargo theft.

▶ Efforts to combat transnational organized crime are typically in the hands of federal agencies.

▶ One approach is to form international working groups to collect intelligence, share information, and plot unified strategies among member nations.

▶ While international cooperation is now common and law enforcement agencies are willing to work together to fight transnational gangs, even when a gang can be taken out it is soon replaced as long as money can be made.

▶ Adding to control problems is the fact that the drug trade is an important source of foreign revenue.

are extremely hard to eradicate. The gangs are ready to use violence and well equipped to carry out threats. Take for instance Los Zetas, whose core members are former members of the Mexican military's elite Special Air Mobile Force Group (Grupo Aeromovil de Fuerzas Especiales, or GAFES). Military trained, Los Zetas members are able to carry out complex operations and use sophisticated weaponry.[102] Los Zetas began as enforcers for the Gulf cartel's regional domination but are now their rivals and considered the most powerful Mexican transnational gang. Their base is Nuevo Laredo, but the criminal organization's sphere of influence extends across Mexico and deep into Central America. Unlike most gangs, which obtain most of their income from narcotics, the Los Zetas cartel earns about half its income trafficking in arms, kidnapping, and competing for control of trafficking routes along the eastern half of the U.S.–Mexico border. The cartel is considered Mexico's most brutal.

Adding to control problems is the fact that the drug trade is an important source of foreign revenue, and destroying the drug trade undermines the economies of third-world nations. Even if the government of one nation were willing to cooperate in vigorous drug suppression efforts, suppliers in other nations, eager to cash in on the sellers' market, would be encouraged to turn more acreage over to coca or poppy production. Today, almost every Caribbean country is involved with narco-trafficking, and illicit drug shipments in the region are worth more money than the top five legitimate exports combined. Drug gangs are able to corrupt the political structure and destabilize countries. Drug addiction and violent crime are now common in Jamaica, Puerto Rico, and even small islands like St. Kitts. The corruption of the police and other security forces has reached a crisis point, where an officer can earn the equivalent of half a year's salary by simply looking the other way on a drug deal.[103] There are also indications that the drug syndicates may be planting a higher yield variety of coca and improving refining techniques to replace crops lost to government crackdowns.

The United States has little influence in some key drug-producing areas such as Taliban-held Afghanistan and Myanmar (formerly Burma). War and terrorism also may make gang control strategies problematic. After the United States toppled Afghanistan's Taliban government, the remnants began to grow and sell poppy to support their insurgency; Afghanistan now supplies 90 percent of the world's opium.[104] And while the Colombian guerrillas may not be interested in joining or colluding with crime cartels, they finance their war against the government by aiding drug traffickers and "taxing" crops and sales. Considering these problems, it is not surprising that transnational gangs continue to flourish.

# Thinking Like a Criminologist

## The Ethics of Monitoring Suspects

The president's national security advisor approaches you with a problem. It seems that a tracking device has been developed that can be implanted under the skin that will allow people to be constantly monitored. Implanted at birth, the data surveillance device could potentially cover *everyone*, with a record of every transaction and activity they engage in entered into databases monitored by powerful search engines that would keep them under constant surveillance. The surveillance device would enable the government to keep tabs on their whereabouts as well as monitoring biological activities such as brain waves, heart rate, and so on. The benefits are immense. Once a person becomes suspect in a crime or is believed to be part of a terrorist cell, they can be easily monitored from a distance without danger to any government agent. They cannot hide or escape detection. Physical readings could be made to determine if they are under stress, using banned substances, and so on.

To research the issue, you begin by reading what the American Civil Liberties Union has to say: "The United States is at risk of turning into a full-fledged surveillance society. The tremendous explosion in surveillance-enabling technologies, combined with the ongoing weakening in legal restraints that protect our privacy mean that we are drifting toward a surveillance society. The good news is that it can be stopped. Unfortunately, right now the big picture is grim."

### Writing Assignment

The director wants you to write a paper for the NSA expressing your opinion on this device. Address whether it is worthwhile, considering the threats faced by America from terrorists and criminals. Or, as the ACLU suggests, would it be unethical because it violates the personal privacy and freedom of people before they have broken any law?

# SUMMARY

**LO1** **Discuss the concept of cybercrime and why it has become important.**

Cybercrime is a relatively new breed of offenses that involves the theft and/or destruction of information, resources, or funds utilizing computers, computer networks, and the Internet. Cybercrime presents a challenge for the justice system because it is rapidly evolving, it is difficult to detect through traditional law enforcement channels, and its control demands that agents of the justice system develop technical skills that match those of the perpetrators. Cybercrime has grown because information technology (IT) has become part of daily life in industrialized societies.

**LO2** **Distinguish among cybertheft, cybervandalism, and cyberterrorism.**

Some cybercrimes use modern technology to accumulate goods and services (cybertheft). Cybervandalism involves malicious attacks aimed at disrupting, defacing, and destroying technology that the attackers find offensive. Cyberterrorism is aimed at undermining the social, economic, and political system of an enemy nation by destroying its electronic infrastructure and disrupting its economy.

**LO3** **Describe the various types of cybercrimes, such as computer frauds, illegal copyright infringement, and identity theft.**

There are a number of methods that hackers use to commit cybercrimes. *Warez* refers to groups of individuals who work together to illegally obtain software and then "crack" or "rip" its copyright protections before posting it on the Internet for other members of the group to use. Another type of illegal copyright infringement involves file-sharing programs that allow Internet users to download music and other copyrighted material without paying the artists and record producers their rightful royalties. Identity theft occurs when a person uses the Internet to steal someone's identity and/or impersonate the victim to open a new credit card account or conduct some other financial transaction. Phishing involves the creation of false emails and websites that look legitimate but are designed to gain illegal access to a victim's personal information.

**LO4    Discuss efforts to control cybercrime.**

The growth of cybercrime and its cost to the economy has created the need for new laws and enforcement processes specifically aimed at controlling its emerging formulations. Congress has treated computer-related crime as a distinct federal offense since passage of the Counterfeit Access Device and Computer Fraud and Abuse Law in 1984. Existing laws sometimes are inadequate to address the problem of cybercrime. Therefore new legislation has been drafted to protect the public from this new breed of criminal. Specialized enforcement agencies have been created to crack down on cybercriminals.

**LO5    Trace the evolution of organized crime.**

Organized criminals were traditionally white ethnics, but today other groups have become involved in organized crime activities. The old-line "families" are now more likely to use their criminal wealth and power to buy into legitimate businesses. The most common view of organized crime today is an ethnically diverse group of competing gangs dedicated to extortion or to providing illegal goods and services. Efforts to control organized crime have been stepped up by the federal government, which has used antiracketeering statutes to arrest syndicate leaders.

**LO6    Discuss the activities of transnational organized crime.**

With the aid of the Internet and instant communications, transnational groups are operating on a global scale to traffic drugs and people, launder money, and sell arms. Eastern European crime families are active abroad and in the United States. Russian organized crime has become a major problem for law enforcement agencies. Mexican and Latin American groups are quite active in the drug trade. Asian crime families are involved in smuggling and other illegal activities.

## Key Terms

cybercrime  454
transnational organized
   crime  454
cybertheft  455
cybervandalism  455
cyberwar/cyberterrorism
   455
warez  456

salami slice fraud  456
ATM skimming  457
denial-of-service attack
   (DoS)  460
pump and dump  461
cyber smear  461
identity theft  461
phishing  461

spear-phishing  461
etailing fraud  462
computer virus  464
malware  464
computer worms  464
Trojan horse  464
logic bomb  464
spam  464

website defacement  464
cyberstalking  465
cyberbullying  466
cyberspying  466
cyberespionage  467
Racketeer Influenced and
   Corrupt Organization
   Act (RICO)  479

## Critical Thinking Questions

**1.**  Which theories of criminal behavior best explain the actions of cybercriminals, and which ones do you believe fail to explain cybercrime?

**2.**  How would you punish a web page defacer who placed an antiwar message on a government site? Prison? Fine?

**3.**  What guidelines would you recommend for the use of IT in law enforcement?

**4.**  Are we creating a "Big Brother" society and is the loss of personal privacy worth the price of safety?

**5.**  What can be done to reduce the threat of transnational organized crime?

# Notes

*All URLs accessed in 2015.*

1. John F. Burns and Ravi Somaiya, "WikiLeaks Founder on the Run, Trailed by Notoriety," *New York Times*, October 23, 2010, www.nytimes.com/2010/10/24/world/24assange.html.

2. Gartner, Inc. "Forecast Alert: IT Spending, Worldwide, 2008–2015, 4Q11 Update," www.gartner.com/id=1886414.

3. Internet World Stats, www.internetworldstats.com/stats.htm; Radicati Group, "Email Statistics Report 2013–2017," www.radicati.com/wp/wp-content/uploads/2013/04/Email-Statistics-Report-2013-2017-Executive-Summary.pdf; Statista: The Statistics Portal, www.statista.com/statistics/264810/number-of-monthly-active-facebook-users-worldwide/.

4. Giles Trendle, "An E-Jihad Against Government?" *EGOV Monitor*, September 2002.

5. Majid Yar, *Cybercrime and Society* (Thousand Oaks, CA: Sage Publications, 2006), p. 19.

6. FBI, "Botnet Bust: SpyEye Malware Mastermind Pleads Guilty," January 28, 2014, www.fbi.gov/news/stories/2014/january/spyeye-malware-mastermind-pleads-guilty/.

7. Douglas A. McIntyre, "How Much Are China Sales Worth to Microsoft?" 24/7 Wall Street, May 27, 2011, 247wallst.com/2011/05/27/how-much-are-china-sales-worth-to-microsoft/.

8. Computer Fraud and Abuse Act (CFAA), 18 U.S.C. §1030 (1998).

9. Digital Millennium Copyright Act, Public Law 105-304 (1998).

10. Title 18, United States Code, Section 2319.

11. Title 17, United States Code, Section 506.

12. *MGM Studios, Inc. v. Grokster*, 125 S. Ct. 2764 (2005).

13. Australian Institute of Criminology, "Nine Types of Cyber Crime, 2014, www.crime.hku.hk/cybercrime.htm; Cross Domain Solutions, "Cyber Crime," www.crossdomainsolutions.com/cyber-crime/.

14. Pricewaterhouse Coopers, 2015 Global Survey, www.pwc.com/gx/en/consulting-services/information-security-survey/key-findings.jhtml.

15. FBI, "Taking a Trip to the ATM? Beware of 'Skimmers,'" July 14, 2011, www.fbi.gov/news/stories/2011/july/atm_071411.

16. Andreas Philaretou, "Sexuality and the Internet," *Journal of Sex Research* 42 (2005): 180–181.

17. Michael Arrington, "Internet Pornography Stats," techcrunch.com/2007/05/12/internet-pornography-stats/.

18. Julie Ruvolo, "How Much of the Internet Is Actually for Porn," *Forbes*, September 7, 2011, www.forbes.com/sites/julieruvolo/2011/09/07/how-much-of-the-internet-is-actually-for-porn/; Top Ten Reviews, "Internet Pornography Statistics," internet-filter-review.toptenreviews.com/internet-pornography-statistics.html.

19. Top Ten Reviews, "Internet Pornography Statistics."

20. Information Security, Nick Nikiforakis, Marco Balduzzi, Lieven Desmet, Frank Piessens, and Wouter Joosen, "Soundsquatting: Uncovering the Use of Homophones in Domain Squatting" in *Lecture Notes in Computer Science*, Vol. 8783 (Heidelberg: Springer, 2014), pp. 291–308.

21. Jeordan Legon, "Sex Sells, Especially to Web Surfers: Internet Porn a Booming, Billion-Dollar Industry," CNN, December 11, 2003, www.cnn.com/2003/TECH/internet/12/10/porn.business/.

22. *United States v. Williams*, 553 U.S. 285 (2008).

23. Drug Enforcement Administration, Office of Diversion Control, "Prescription Drugs," www.deadiversion.usdoj.gov/consumer_alert.htm.

24. U.S. Attorney's Office, Northern District of California, "Nine Sentenced for Illegally Distributing Controlled Substances over the Internet," March 27, 2013, www.justice.gov/usao-ndca/pr/nine-sentenced-illegally-distributing-controlled-substances-over-internet.

25. National Center on Addiction and Substance Abuse at Columbia University, "'You've Got Drugs!' V: Prescription Drug Pushers on the Internet 2008," www.casacolumbia.org/addiction-research/reports/youve-got-drugs-perscription-drug-pushers-internet-2008.

26. Ibid.

27. Top Tech News, "Rutgers Suffers Foreign DDoS Attack," March 30, 2015, www.toptechnews.com/article/index.php?story_id=1320044NONV0.

28. Saul Hansell, "U.S. Tally in Online-Crime Sweep: 150 Charged," *New York Times*, August 27, 2004, p. C1.

29. John Callaham, "Steam and Other Online Gaming Services Hit by DDoS Attacks," Neowin, January 3, 2014, www.neowin.net/news/steam-and-other-online-gaming-services-hit-by-ddos-attacks.

30. FBI, "Ransomware on the Rise," January 2015, www.fbi.gov/news/stories/2015/january/ransomware-on-the-rise/ransomware-on-the-rise.

31. Jim Wolf, "Internet Scams Targeted in Sweep: A 10-Day Crackdown Leads to 62 Arrests and 88 Indictments," *Boston Globe*, May 22, 2001, p. A2.

32. These sections rely on "Phishing Activity Trends Report," June 2014, docs.apwg.org/reports/apwg_trends_report_q2_2014.pdf; Anti-Phishing Working Group, www.antiphishing.org; U.S. Department of Justice Criminal Division, "Special Report on 'Phishing'" (2006), www.justice.gov/sites/default/files/opa/legacy/2006/11/21/report_on_phishing.pdf.

33. Nicole Leeper Piquero, Mark A. Cohen, and Alex R. Piquero, "How Much Is the Public Willing to Pay to Be Protected from Identity Theft?" *Justice Quarterly* 28 (2011): 437–459.

34. Linda Foley, Karen Barney, and Jay Foley, *Identity Theft: The Aftermath 2009*, Identity Theft Resource Center (ITRC), allclearid.com/themes/allclearid/docs /Aftermath_2009_20100520.pdf.

35. FBI, "Cyber Criminals Continue to Use Spear-Phishing Attacks to Compromise Computer Networks," June 25, 2013, www.ic3.gov/media/2013/130625.aspx.

36. Jeremy Kirk, "Identity Theft May Cost IRS $21 Billion over Next Five Years," *PC World*, August 3, 2012, www .pcworld.idg.com.au/article/432584/identity_theft_may _cost_irs_21_billion_over_next_five_years/.

37. Identity Theft and Assumption Deterrence Act, as amended by Public Law 105-318, 112 Stat. 3007 (October 30, 1998).

38. Internet Crime Schemes, Internet Crime Complaint Center, www.ic3.gov/crimeschemes.aspx.

39. Robert Hackett, "What to Know About the Ashley Madison Hack," *Fortune*, August 26, 2015, fortune .com/2015/08/26/ashley-madison-hack/.

40. Heather Jacobson and Rebecca Green, "Computer Crimes," *American Criminal Law Review* 39 (2002): 272–326.

41. U.S. Department of Justice, "Creator of Melissa Computer Virus Sentenced to 20 Months in Federal Prison," May 1, 2002, www.justice.gov/archive /criminal/cybercrime/press-releases/2002/melissaSent .htm; see also Jacobson and Green, "Computer Crimes," pp. 273–275.

42. Robert Lemos, "'MSBlast' Worm Widespread but Slowing," CNET News, August 12, 2003, news.cnet .com/2100-1002-5062655.html.

43. Trend Micro, "Website Defacement," www.trendmicro .com/vinfo/us/security/definition/website-defacement.

44. Wang Wei, "Rise in Website Defacement Attacks by Hackers Around the World," *Hacker News*, November 5, 2013, thehackernews.com/2013/11/rise-in-website -defacement-attacks-by.html.

45. Yona Hollander, "Prevent Web Page Defacement," *Internet Security Advisor* 2 (2000): 1–4.

46. Janis Wolak, David Finkelhor, Kimberly Mitchell, and Michele Ybarra, "Online 'Predators' and Their Victims: Myths, Realities, and Implications for Prevention and Treatment," *American Psychologist* 63 (2008): 111–128.

47. Fox News, "Missouri Woman Indicted in MySpace Cyber-Bullying Case that Ended in Teen's Suicide," May 15, 2008, www.foxnews.com/printer_friendly _story/0,3566,356056,00.html.

48. This section leans heavily on Justin Patchin and Sameer Hinduja, "Bullies Move Beyond the Schoolyard: A Preliminary Look at Cyberbullying," *Youth Violence and Juvenile Justice* 4 (2006): 148–169.

49. Sameer Hinduja and Justin Patchin, "Cyberbullying: An Exploratory Analysis of Factors Related to Offending and Victimization," *Deviant Behavior* 29 (2008): 129–156.

50. Data from Cyberbullying Research Center, www .cyberbullying.us.

51. Tom Yager, "Cyberspying: No Longer a Crime for Geeks Only," *InfoWorld* 22 (2000): 62.

52. Nathan Vardi, "Chinese Take Out," *Forbes* 176 (2005).

53. Kim Zetter, *Countdown to Zero Day: Stuxnet and the Launch of the World's First Digital Weapon* (New York: Broadway Books, 2015); William J. Broad, John Markoff, and David E. Sanger, "Israeli Test on Worm Called Crucial in Iran Nuclear Delay," *New York Times*, January 15, 2011, www.nytimes.com/2011/01/16 /world/middleeast/16stuxnet.html.

54. Reuters, "Lockheed Martin Hit by Computer Attack," *Los Angeles Times*, May 29, 2011, articles.latimes.com /2011/may/29/nation/la-na-lockheed-martin -20110529.

55. Nathan Thornburgh, Matthew Forney, Brian Bennett, Timothy Burger, and Elaine Shannon, "The Invasion of the Chinese Cyberspies (and the Man Who Tried to Stop Them)," *Time*, September 5, 2005, p. 10.

56. Andrew Gray "Chinese Hackers Worry Pentagon: A Recent Report Expresses Concerns About Technologi-cal Advances in Both Cyberspace and Space," *PC World*, March 9, 2008.

57. U.S. Department of Defense, "Cyber Strategy," www .defense.gov/home/features/2015/0415_cyber -strategy/.

58. NBC News, "Sources: U.S. Decides Cyber Attack Can Be 'Act of War,'" May 29, 2011, www.nbcnews.com /id/43224451/ns/us_news-security/t/sources-us -decides-cyber-attack-can-be-act-war/.

59. Barry Collin, "The Future of CyberTerrorism: Where the Physical and Virtual Worlds Converge," www .crime-research.org/library/Cyberter.htm.

60. Mark Pollitt, "Cyberterrorism—Fact or Fancy?" *Computer Fraud and Security* 2 (1998): 8–10.

61. Tomas Hellström, "Critical Infrastructure and Systemic Vulnerability: Towards a Planning Framework," *Safety Science* 45 (2007): 415–430.

62. Mathieu Gorge, "Cyberterrorism: Hype or Reality?" *Computer Fraud and Security* 2 (2007): 9–12.

63. Daniel Benjamin, *America and the World in the Age of Terrorism* (Washington, DC: CSIS Press, 2005), pp. 1–216.

64. Kevin Granville, "9 Recent Cyberattacks Against Big Businesses," *New York Times*, February 5, 2015, www .nytimes.com/interactive/2015/02/05/technology /recent-cyberattacks.html.

65. Nicole Perlroth, "U.S. Banks Again Hit by Wave of Cyberattacks," *New York Times*, January 4, 2013, bits .blogs.nytimes.com/2013/01/04/u-s-banks-again-hit -by-wave-of-cyberattacks/.

66. Yael Shahar, "Information Warfare," IWS: The Information Warfare Site, www.iwar.org.uk/cyberterror /resources/CIT.htm.

67. Aamer Anwar, "How ISIS's $2B Budget Helps It Recruit Western Teenagers to Terrorism," CNN, March 27, 2015, www.cnn.com/2015/03/27/opinions/aamer-isis -recruiting-western-teenagers/.

68. Nathan E. Busch and Austen D. Givens, *The Business of Counterterrorism: Public-Private Partnerships in Homeland Security* (New York: Peter Lang, 2014); Walter Enders and Todd Sandler, *The Political Economy of Terrorism*, 2nd ed. (London: Cambridge University Press, 2011).

69. *United States of America v. Holy Land Foundation for Relief and Development*, caselaw.findlaw.com/us-5th-circuit /1541982.html.

70. John Kane and April Wall, "Identifying the Links Between White-Collar Crime and Terrorism," paper presented at the annual meeting of the American Society of Criminology (ASC), Los Angeles, November 2006.

71. Loretta Napoleoni, *Modern Jihad: Tracing the Dollars Behind the Terror Networks* (Sterling, VA: Pluto Press, 2003).

72. Nicolas Dias Gomes, Pedro André Cerqueira, and Luís Alçada Almeida, "A Survey on Software Piracy Empirical Literature: Stylized Facts and Theory," *Information Economics and Policy*, published online August 5, 2015.

73. Juniper Research, "Cybercrime and the Internet of Threats," www.juniperresearch.com/document-library /white-papers/cybercrime-the-internet-of-threats.

74. Stephen Siwek, "The True Cost of Copyright Industry Piracy to the U.S. Economy," Institute for Policy Innovation, 2007.

75. Jodie Kelley, "BSA Global Survey Reveals Security Concerns with Unlicensed Software—and Points to the Solution," BSA TechPost, techpost.bsa.org/2014 /06/24/bsa-global-survey-reveals-security-concerns -with-unlicensed-software-and-points-to-the-solution/; Business Software Alliance, "Shadow Market: 2011 BSA Global Software Piracy Study," 9th ed., May 2012, portal.bsa.org/globalpiracy2011/downloads/study _pdf/2011_BSA_Piracy_Study-InBrief.pdf.

76. Lorine Hughes and Gregory DeLone, "Viruses, Worms, and Trojan Horses: Serious Crimes, Nuisance, or Both?" *Social Science Computer Review* 25 (2007): 78–98.

77. Symantec, "Highlights of the Internet Security Threat Report, 2015," www.symantec.com/security_response /publications/threatreport.jsp.

78. Jeremy Kirk, "Identity Theft May Cost IRS $21 Billion over Next Five Years," *PC World*, August 3, 2012, www .pcworld.idg.com.au/article/432584/identity_theft _may_cost_irs_21_billion_over_next_five_years/.

79. Public Law 98-473, Title H, Chapter XXI, [sections] 2102(a), 98 Stat. 1837, 2190 (1984).

80. Public Law 104-294, Title II, [sections] 201, 110 Stat. 3488, 3491-94 (1996).

81. Office of Victims of Crime, "Identity Theft and Financial Fraud: Federal Identity Theft Laws," ojp.gov/ovc/pubs /ID_theft/idtheftlaws.html.

82. U.S. State Department Fact Sheet, September 29, 2006, Council of Europe Convention on Cybercrime, www.cs.brown.edu/courses/csci1950-p/sources/lec16 /Vatis.pdf; Council of Europe Convention on Cybercrime, CETS No. 185, conventions.coe.int/Treaty/en /Treaties/Html/185.htm.

83. Bruce Swartz, Deputy Assistant General, Criminal Division, U.S. Justice Department, "Internet Fraud Testimony Before the House Energy and Commerce Committee," May 23, 2001.

84. U.S. Secret Service, "New York/New Jersey Electronic Crimes Task Force," www.secretservice.gov/ectf _newyork.shtml.

85. FBI, "Cyber Security: Task Force Takes 'Whole Government' Approach," October 20, 2014, www.fbi.gov /news/stories/2014/october/cyber-security-task-force -takes-whole-government-approach/.

86. FBI, Internet Crime Complaint Center, "2013 Internet Crime Report," www.ic3.gov/media/annualreport /2013_IC3Report.pdf.

87. See, generally, President's Commission on Organized Crime, *Report to the President and the Attorney General, The Impact: Organized Crime Today* (Washington, DC: U.S. Government Printing Office, 1986). Herein cited as *Organized Crime Today*.

88. Ibid., pp. 7–8.

89. James O. Finckenauer and Ko-lin Chin, *Asian Transnational Organized Crime and Its Impact on the United States* (Washington, DC: National Institute of Justice, 2007), www.ncjrs.gov/pdffiles1/nij/214186.pdf.

90. FBI, National Gang Intelligence Center, *National Gang Report, 2013*, www.fbi.gov/stats-services/publications /national-gang-report-2013.

91. Ibid.

92. FBI, "African Criminal Enterprises," www.fbi.gov /about-us/investigate/organizedcrime/african.

93. FBI, "Balkan Criminal Enterprises," www.fbi.gov /about-us/investigate/organizedcrime/balkan.

94. FBI, "Armenian Power Leader Sentenced to 32 Years in Prison for Racketeering, Extortion, and Fraud Offenses," November 10, 2014, www.fbi.gov/losangeles /press-releases/2014/armenian-power-leader -sentenced-to-32-years-in-prison-for-racketeering -extortion-and-fraud-offenses.

95. Louise I. Shelley, "Crime and Corruption: Enduring Problems of Post-Soviet Development," *Demokratizatsiya* 11 (2003): 110–114; James O. Finckenauer and Yuri A. Voronin, *The Threat of Russian Organized Crime* (Washington, DC: National Institute of Justice, 2001).

96. Omar Bartos, "Growth of Russian Organized Crime Poses Serious Threat," *CJ International* 11 (1995): 8–9.

97. Bilyana Tsvetkova, "Gangs in the Caribbean," *Harvard International Review*, June 2009, hir.harvard.edu /archives/1863.

98. This section leans heavily on Finckenauer and Chin, *Asian Transnational Organized Crime and Its Impact on the United States*.

99. National Institute of Justice, "Transnational Organized Crime," www.nij.gov/topics/crime/organized-crime /pages/welcome.aspx.

100. 18 U.S.C. 1952 (1976).

101. Public Law 91-452, Title IX, 84 Stat. 922 (1970) (codified at 18 U.S.C. 1961–68, 1976).

102. William Booth, "Mexican Azteca Gang Leader Arrested in Killings of 3 Tied to U.S.," *Washington Post*, March 30, 2010, www.washingtonpost.com/wp-dyn /content/article/2010/03/29/AR2010032903373.html.

103. Orlando Patterson, "The Other Losing War," *New York Times*, January 13, 2007.

104. Office of National Drug Control Policy, 2014 National Drug Control Strategy, www.whitehouse.gov/sites /default/files/ondcp/policy-and-research/ndcs_2014.pdf.

# Glossary

**abstainers** Adolescents who do not engage in any deviant behavior, a path that places them outside the norm for their age group.

**acquaintance robbery** Robbery in which the victim or victims are people the robber knows.

**active precipitation** Aggressive or provocative behavior of victims that results in their victimization.

**adolescent-limited offenders** Kids who get into minor scrapes as youth but whose misbehavior ends when they enter adulthood.

**age-graded theory** A state dependence theory formulated by Sampson and Laub that assumes that the causal association between early delinquent offending and later adult deviant behavior involves the quality of relationships encountered at different times in human development.

**aggravated assault** An unlawful attack by one person upon another, accompanied by the use of a weapon, for the purpose of inflicting severe or aggravated bodily injury.

**aggravated rape** Rape involving multiple offenders, weapons, and victim injuries.

**aging out** Phrase used to express the fact that people commit less crime as they mature.

**American Dream** The goal of accumulating material goods and wealth through individual competition; the process of being socialized to pursue material success and to believe it is achievable.

**androgens** Male sex hormones.

**anomie** A lack of norms or clear social standards. Because of rapidly shifting moral values, the individual has few guides to what is socially acceptable.

**anomie theory** The view that anomie results when socially defined goals (such as wealth and power) are universally mandated but access to legitimate means (such as education and job opportunities) is stratified by class and status.

**antisocial personality** Combination of traits, such as hyperactivity, impulsivity, hedonism, and inability to empathize with others, that make a person prone to deviant behavior and violence; also referred to as sociopathic or psychopathic personality.

**appeal** Taking a criminal case to a higher court on the grounds that the defendant was found guilty because of legal error or violation of his or her constitutional rights.

**arousal theory** The view that people seek to maintain a preferred level of arousal but vary in how they process sensory input. A need for high levels of environmental stimulation may lead to aggressive, violent behavior patterns.

**arraignment** The step in the criminal justice process in which the accused is brought before the trial judge, formal charges are read, defendants are informed of their rights, a plea is entered, bail is considered, and a trial date is set.

**arrest** The taking into police custody of an individual suspected of a crime.

**arson** The willful or malicious burning of a dwelling house, public building, motor vehicle, aircraft, personal property of another, or the like.

**assault** Either attempted battery or intentionally frightening the victim by word or deed (actual touching is not involved).

**ATM skimming** Using an electronic device or camera on an ATM that copies information from a bank card's magnetic strip whenever a customer uses the machine or photographs their key strokes.

**attachment theory** Bowlby's theory that being able to form an emotional bond to another person is an important aspect of mental health throughout the life span.

**attention deficit hyperactivity disorder (ADHD)** A developmentally inappropriate lack of attention, along with impulsivity and hyperactivity.

**authority conflict pathway** Pathway to deviance that begins at an early age with stubborn behavior and leads to defiance and then to authority avoidance.

**bail** A money bond intended to ensure that the accused will return for trial.

**battery** Offensive touching, such as slapping, hitting, or punching a victim.

**behavior modeling** The process of learning behavior (notably, aggression) by observing others. Aggressive models may be parents, criminals in the neighborhood, or characters on television or in movies.

**behavior theory** The view that all human behavior is learned through a process of social reinforcement (rewards and punishment).

**binge drinking** Having five or more drinks on the same occasion (that is, at the same time or within a couple of hours of each other).

**bipolar disorder** An emotional disturbance in which moods alternate between periods of wild elation and deep depression.

**blue-collar crimes** Traditional common-law theft crimes such as larceny, burglary, and arson.

**booking** Fingerprinting, photographing, and recording personal information of a suspect in police custody.

**booster (heel)** Professional shoplifter who steals with the intention of reselling stolen merchandise.

**burglary** Entering a home by force, threat, or deception with intent to commit a crime.

**capable guardians** Effective deterrents to crime, such as police or watchful neighbors.

**capital punishment** The execution of criminal offenders; the death penalty.

**Chicago School** Group of urban sociologists who studied the relationship between environmental conditions and crime.

**child abuse** Any physical or emotional trauma to a child for which no reasonable explanation, such as an accident or ordinary disciplinary practices, can be found.

**child sexual abuse** The exploitation of children through rape, incest, and molestation by parents or other adults.

**chiseling** Using illegal means to cheat an organization, its consumers, or both, on a regular basis.

**chronic offenders (career criminals)** The small group of persistent offenders who account for a majority of all criminal offenses.

**classical criminology** Theoretical perspective suggesting that people choose to commit crime and that crime can be controlled if potential criminals fear punishment.

**Code of Hammurabi** The first written criminal code, developed in Babylonia about 1750 BCE.

**cognitive theory** Psychological perspective that focuses on the mental processes by which people perceive and represent the world around them and solve problems.

**collective efficacy** Social control exerted by cohesive communities and based on mutual trust, including intervention in the supervision of children and maintenance of public order.

**commitment to conformity** Obedience to the rules of society and the avoidance of nonconforming behavior that may jeopardize an individual's reputation and achievement.

**common law** Early English law, developed by judges, which became the standardized law of the land in England and eventually formed the basis of the criminal law in the United States.

**compliance strategies** Methods of controlling white-collar crime that rely on the threat of economic sanctions or civil penalties to control potential violators, creating a marketplace incentive to obey the law.

**computer virus** A program that disrupts or destroys existing programs and networks, causing them to perform the task for which the virus was designed.

**computer worms** Programs that attack computer networks (or the Internet) by self-replicating and sending themselves to other users, generally via email without the aid of the operator.

**concentration effect** As working-class and middle-class families flee inner-city poverty-ridden areas, the most disadvantaged population is consolidated in urban ghettos.

**conduct disorder (CD)** A pattern of repetitive behavior in which the rights of others or social norms are violated.

**conflict view** The belief that criminal behavior is defined by those in power in such a way as to protect and advance their own self-interest.

**consensus view** The belief that the majority of citizens in a society share common values and agree on what behaviors should be defined as criminal.

**consent** The victim of rape must prove that she in no way encouraged, enticed, or misled the accused rapist.

**constructive possession** A legal fiction that applies to situations in which persons voluntarily give up physical custody of their property but still retain legal ownership.

**corporate (organizational) crime** Powerful institutions or their representatives willfully violate the laws that restrain these institutions from doing social harm or require them to do social good.

**covert pathway** Pathway to a criminal career that begins with minor underhanded behavior, leads to property damage, and eventually escalates to more serious forms of theft and fraud.

**crime** An act, deemed socially harmful or dangerous, that is specifically defined, prohibited, and punished under the criminal law.

**crime discouragers** People who serve as guardians of property or people.

**criminal career** Engaging in antisocial acts early in adolescence and continuing illegal behaviors into adulthood. A pattern of persistent offending across the life course.

**criminal environmental pollution** A crime involving the intentional or negligent discharge into the biosystem of a toxic waste that destroys plant or animal life.

**criminal justice system** The agencies of government—police, courts, and corrections—that are responsible for apprehending, adjudicating, sanctioning, and treating criminal offenders.

**criminal law** The written code that defines crimes and their punishments.

**criminogenic knowledge structure (CKS)** The view that negative life events are connected and produce a hostile view of people and relationships, preference for immediate rewards, and a cynical view of conventional norms.

**criminology** The scientific study of the nature, extent, cause, and control of criminal behavior.

**crisis intervention** Emergency counseling for crime victims.

**critical criminologists** Criminologists who believe that the cause of crime can be linked to economic, social, and political disparity.

**critical criminology** The view that crime is a product of the capitalist system.

**critical feminism** The view that gender inequality is a result of the exploitation of women in a male-dominated society.

**cultural deviance theory** Branch of social structure theory that sees strain and social disorganization together resulting in a unique lower-class culture that conflicts with conventional social norms.

**cultural transmission** Process whereby values, beliefs, and traditions are handed down from one generation to the next.

**culture conflict** Result of exposure to opposing norms, attitudes, and definitions of right and wrong, moral and immoral.

**culture of poverty** A separate lower-class culture, characterized by apathy, cynicism, helplessness, and mistrust of social institutions such as schools, government agencies, and the police, that is passed from one generation to the next.

**cumulative disadvantage** The tendency of prior social problems to produce future ones that accumulate and undermine success.

**cyberbullying** Willful and repeated harm inflicted through the medium of electronic text.

**cybercrime** The theft and/or destruction of information, resources, or funds via computers, computer networks, or the Internet.

**cyberespionage** Efforts by intelligence agencies to penetrate computer networks of an enemy nation in order to steal important data.

**cyber smear** Negative information is spread online about a stock, driving down its price and enabling people to buy it at an artificially low price.

**cyberspying** Illegally using the Internet to gather information that is considered private and confidential.

**cyberstalking** Use of the Internet, email, or other electronic communications devices to stalk another person. Some cyberstalkers pursue minors through online chat rooms; others harass their victims electronically.

**cybertheft** The use of computer networks for criminal profits. Copyright infringement, identity theft, and Internet securities fraud are examples of cybertheft.

**cybervandalism** Malicious attacks aimed at disrupting, defacing, and destroying technology.

**cyberwar/cyberterrorism** Politically motivated attacks designed to compromise the electronic infrastructure of an enemy nation and disrupt its economy.

**cycle of violence** The phenomenon in which abused children grow up to be abusers themselves.

**date rape** A rape that involves people who are in some form of courting relationship.

**decriminalized** Having criminal penalties reduced rather than eliminated.

**defensible space** The principle that crime can be prevented or displaced by modifying the physical environment to reduce the opportunity that individuals have to commit crime.

**deliberation** Planning a criminal act after careful thought, rather than carrying it out on impulse.

**delinquent subculture** A value system adopted by lower-class youths that is directly opposed to that of the larger society.

**denial-of-service attack (DoS)** Extorting money from an Internet service user by threatening to prevent the user from having access to the service.

**Department of Homeland Security (DHS)** An agency of the federal government charged with preventing terrorist attacks within the United States, reducing America's vulnerability to terrorism, and minimizing the damage and aiding recovery from attacks that do occur.

**deterrence strategies** Methods of controlling white-collar crime that rely on the punishment of individual offenders to deter other would-be violators.

**developmental theories** The view that criminality is a dynamic process, influenced by social experiences as well as individual characteristics.

**deviance amplification** Process whereby secondary deviance pushes offenders out of mainstream society and locks them into an escalating cycle of deviance, apprehension, labeling, and criminal self-identity.

**deviant behavior** Actions that depart from the social norm. Some are considered criminal, others merely harmless aberrations.

**deviant place theory** The view that victimization is primarily a function of where people live.

**differential association theory** The view that people commit crime when their social learning leads them to perceive more definitions favoring crime than favoring conventional behavior.

**differential opportunity** The view that lower-class youths, whose legitimate opportunities are limited, join gangs and pursue criminal careers as alternative means to achieve universal success goals.

**differential reinforcement** Behavior is reinforced by being either rewarded or punished while interacting with others; also called direct conditioning.

**differential susceptibility model** The belief that there is an indirect association between traits and crime.

**diffusion** An effect that occurs when efforts to prevent one crime unintentionally prevent another.

**Director of National Intelligence (DNI)** Government official charged with coordinating data from the nation's primary intelligence-gathering agencies.

**discouragement** An effect that occurs when crime control efforts targeting a particular locale help reduce crime in surrounding areas and populations.

**displacement** An effect that occurs when crime control efforts simply move, or redirect, offenders to less heavily guarded alternative targets.

**diversion programs** Programs of rehabilitation that remove offenders from the normal channels of the criminal justice process, thus enabling them to avoid the stigma of a criminal label.

**dizygotic (DZ) twins** Fraternal (nonidentical) twins.

**drift** Movement in and out of delinquency, shifting between conventional and deviant values.

**dropout factories** High schools in which the completion rate is consistently 40 percent or less.

**drug-dependent personality** A personal trait characterized by a pervasive psychological dependence on mood-altering substances.

**early onset** The view that kids who begin engaging in antisocial behaviors at a very early age are the ones most at risk for a criminal career.

**economic compulsive behavior** Violence committed by drug users to support their habit.

**economic crime** An act committed in violation of the criminal law for the purpose of monetary gain and financial benefits.

**egalitarian families** Families in which couples share similar positions of power at home and in the workplace.

**ego** The part of the personality developed in early childhood that helps control the id and keep people's actions within the boundaries of social convention.

**eldercide** Murder of a senior citizen.

**election fraud** Illegal interference with the process of an election. Acts of fraud tend to involve affecting vote counts to bring about a desired election outcome, whether by increasing the vote share of the favored candidate, depressing the vote share of the rival candidates, or both. Varieties of election fraud include intimidation, disruption of polling places, distribution of misinformation such as the wrong election date, registration fraud, and vote buying.

**embezzlement** A type of larceny in which someone who is trusted with someone else's personal property fraudulently converts it to his or her own use or for the use of others.

**eros** The life instinct, which drives people toward self-fulfillment and enjoyment.

**espionage** The practice of obtaining information about a government, organization, or society that is considered secret or confidential without the permission of the holder of the information. Commonly called spying.

**etailing fraud** Illegally buying and/or selling merchandise on the Internet.

**exploitation** Forcing victims to pay for services or contracts to which they have a clear right.

**expressive crimes** Offenses committed not for profit or gain but to vent rage, anger, or frustration.

**expressive violence** Violence that is designed not for profit or gain but to vent rage, anger, or frustration.

**extinction** An effect that occurs when crime reduction programs produce a short-term positive effect, but benefits dissipate as criminals adjust to new conditions.

**extraordinary rendition** The practice of sending suspected terrorists to foreign prisons that permit torture in the interrogation of suspects.

**failed state** A nation whose government has lost control of its own territory, is unable to provide public services and protection, and lacks the ability to interact with other states as a full member of the international community.

**felony** A serious offense that carries a penalty of imprisonment, usually for one year or more, and may entail loss of political rights.

**felony murder** A killing that accompanies a felony, such as robbery or rape.

**fence** A buyer and seller of stolen merchandise.

**feticide** Intentional or negligent killing of a human fetus.

**filicide** Murder of an older child.

**first-degree murder** Killing a person after premeditation and deliberation.

**focal concerns** Values, such as toughness and street smarts, that have evolved specifically to fit conditions in lower-class environments.

**forcible rape** Under common law, the carnal knowledge of a female forcibly and against her will. In 2012, a new broader definition of rape was implemented: "The penetration, no matter how slight, of the vagina or anus with any body part or object, or oral penetration by a sex organ of another person, without the consent of the victim."

**general deterrence** A crime control policy that depends on the fear of criminal penalties convincing the potential law violator that the pains associated with crime outweigh its benefits.

**general strain theory (GST)** The view that multiple sources of strain interact with an individual's emotional traits and responses to produce criminality.

**general theory of crime (GTC)** Gottfredson and Hirschi's developmental theory that links crime to impulsivity and a lack of self-control.

**globalization** The creation and maintenance of transnational markets.

**grand jury** A group of citizens chosen to hear testimony in secret and to issue formal criminal accusations (indictments).

**grand larceny** Theft of money or property of substantial value, punished as a felony.

**green-collar crimes** Crimes that affect the environment.

**guerilla** Armed military bands, typically located in rural areas, that use hit-and-run terror tactics to destabilize the existing government.

**hate crimes (bias crimes)** Violent acts directed toward a particular person or members of a group merely because the targets share a discernible racial, ethnic, religious, or gender characteristic.

**hegemonic masculinity** The belief in the existence of a culturally normative ideal of male behavior.

**hung jury** A jury that is unable to agree on a decision, thus leaving the case unresolved and open for a possible retrial.

**hypoglycemia** A condition that occurs when glucose (sugar) in the blood falls below levels necessary for normal and efficient brain functioning.

**id** The primitive part of people's mental makeup, present at birth, that represents unconscious biological drives for food, sex, and other life-sustaining necessities. The id seeks instant gratification without concern for the rights of others.

**identity theft** Using the Internet to steal someone's identity and/or impersonate the victim in order to conduct illicit transactions such as committing fraud using the victim's name and identity.

**impulsive** Lacking in thought or deliberation in decision making. An impulsive person lacks close attention to details, has organizational problems, and is distracted and forgetful. Criminals are impulsive risk takers.

**incapacitation effect** The idea that keeping offenders in confinement will eliminate the risk of their committing further offenses.

**indictment** A written accusation returned by a grand jury charging an individual with a specified crime, based on the prosecutor's demonstration of probable cause.

**individual vulnerability model** Assumes there is a direct link between traits and crime; some people are vulnerable to crime from birth.

**infanticide** Murder of a very young child.

**influence peddling** Using one's institutional position to grant favors and sell information to which one's co-conspirators are not entitled.

**information** A filing before an impartial lower-court judge who decides whether the case should go forward (this filing is an alternative to the use of a grand jury).

**information-processing theory** Theory that focuses on how people process, store, encode, retrieve, and manipulate information to make decisions and solve problems.

**insider trading** Illegal buying of stock in a company on the basis of information provided by someone who has a fiduciary interest in the company.

**institutional anomie theory** The view that anomie pervades U.S. culture because the drive for material wealth dominates and undermines social and community values.

**instrumental crimes** Offenses designed to improve the financial or social position of the criminal.

**instrumental theorists** Critical criminologists who view the law and justice system as serving the interests of the upper classes.

**instrumental violence** Violence used in a rational, controlled, and purposeful fashion; for example, an attempt to improve the financial or social position of the criminal.

**insurgent** The typical goal of an insurgency is to confront the existing government for control of all or a portion of its territory, or force political concessions in sharing political power. While terrorists may operate in small bands with a narrow focus, insurgents represent a popular movement and may also seek external support from other nations to bring pressure on the government.

**interactionist view** The belief that those with social power are able to impose their values on society as a whole, and these values then define criminal behavior.

**interrogation** The questioning of a suspect in police custody.

**involuntary or negligent manslaughter** A killing that occurs when a person's acts are negligent and without regard for the harm they may cause others.

**johns** Men who solicit sex workers.

**larceny** Taking for one's own use the property of another, by means other than force or threats on the victim or forcibly breaking into a person's home or workplace; simple theft.

**latent trait** A stable feature, characteristic, property, or condition, such as defective intelligence or impulsive personality, that makes some people crime prone over the life course.

**left realism** An approach that is left-leaning but realistic in its appraisal of crime and its causes. Crime is seen as class conflict in an advanced industrial society.

**liberal feminist theory** A view of crime that suggests that the social and economic role of women in society controls their crime rates.

**life course persisters** Delinquents who begin their offending career at a very early age and continue to offend well into adulthood.

**life course theory** Theory that focuses on changes in criminality over the life course brought about by shifts in experience and life events.

**lifestyle theories** Views on how people become crime victims because of lifestyles that increase their exposure to criminal offenders.

**logic bomb** A program that is secretly attached to a computer system, monitors the network's work output, and waits for a particular signal such as a date to appear. Also called a slag code, it is a type of delayed action virus that is set off when a program user makes certain input that sets it in motion. A logic bomb can cause a variety of problems ranging from displaying or printing a spurious message to deleting or corrupting data.

**malware** A malicious software program.

**mandatory sentences** A statutory requirement that a certain penalty shall be carried out in all cases of conviction for a specified offense or series of offenses.

**manslaughter** Homicide without malice.

**marginal deterrence** Occurs when a relatively more severe penalty will produce *some* reduction in crime.

**marginalization** Displacement of workers, pushing them outside the economic and social mainstream.

**marital exemption** The formerly accepted tradition that a legally married husband could not be charged with raping his wife.

**masculinity hypothesis** The view that women who commit crimes have biological and psychological traits similar to those of men.

**mass murder** The killing of four or more victims by one or a few assailants within a single event.

**merchant privilege laws** Legislation that protects retailers and their employees from lawsuits if they arrest and detain a suspected shoplifter on reasonable grounds.

**middle-class measuring rods** The standards by which authority figures, such as teachers and employers, evaluate lower-class youngsters and often prejudge them negatively.

**misdemeanor** A minor crime usually punished by a short jail term and/or a fine.

**monozygotic (MZ) twins** Identical twins.

**mood disorder** A condition in which the prevailing emotional mood is distorted or inappropriate to the circumstances.

**moral entrepreneur** A person who creates moral rules that reflect the values of those in power rather than any objective, universal standards of right and wrong.

**Mosaic Code** The laws of the ancient Israelites, found in the Old Testament of the Judeo-Christian Bible.

**motivated offenders** People willing and able to commit crimes.

**motor vehicle theft** The theft of a motor vehicle.

**murder** The unlawful killing of a human being with malice aforethought.

**murder and nonnegligent manslaughter** The willful (nonnegligent) killing of one human being by another.

**naive check forgers** Amateurs who cash bad checks because of some financial crisis but have little identification with a criminal subculture.

**narcissistic personality disorder** A pattern of traits and behaviors indicating infatuation and fixation with one's self to the exclusion of all others, along with the egotistic and ruthless pursuit of one's own gratification, dominance, and ambition.

**narcotic** A drug that produces sleep and relieves pain, such as heroin, morphine, and opium; a habit-forming drug.

**National Crime Victimization Survey (NCVS)** The ongoing victimization study conducted jointly by the Justice Department and the U.S. Census Bureau that surveys victims about their experiences with law violation.

**National Incident-Based Reporting System (NIBRS)** Program that requires local police agencies to provide a brief account of each incident and arrest within 22 crime patterns, including incident, victim, and offender information.

**nature theory** The view that intelligence is largely determined genetically and that low intelligence is linked to criminal behavior.

**negative affective states** Anger, frustration, and adverse emotions produced by a variety of sources of strain.

**negative reinforcement** Using either negative stimuli (punishment) or loss of reward (negative punishment) to curtail unwanted behaviors.

**neglect** Not providing a child with the care and shelter to which he or she is entitled.

**neurophysiology** The study of brain activity.

**neurotransmitters** Chemical compounds that influence or activate brain functions.

**neutralization techniques** Methods of rationalizing deviant behavior, such as denying responsibility or blaming the victim.

**neutralization theory** The view that law violators learn to neutralize conventional values and attitudes, enabling them to drift back and forth between criminal and conventional behavior.

*nolle prosequi* A declaration that expresses the prosecutor's decision to drop a case from further prosecution.

**nurture theory** The view that intelligence is not inherited but is largely a product of environment. Low IQ scores do not cause crime but may result from the same environmental factors.

**obscenity** Material that violates community standards of morality or decency and has no redeeming social value.

**occasional criminals** Offenders who do not define themselves by a criminal role or view themselves as committed career criminals.

**offender-specific crime** The view that offenders evaluate their skills, motives, needs, and fears before deciding to commit the criminal act.

**oppositional defiant disorder (ODD)** A pattern of negativistic, hostile, and defiant behavior, during which a child often loses her or his temper, often argues with adults, and often actively defies or refuses to comply with adults' requests or rules.

**overt pathway** Pathway to a criminal career that begins with minor aggression, leads to physical fighting, and eventually escalates to violent crime.

**paraphilia** Bizarre or abnormal sexual practices that may involve nonhuman objects, humiliation, or children.

**parental efficacy** The ability of parents to be supportive of their children and effectively control them in noncoercive ways.

**Part I crimes** The eight most serious offenses included in the UCR: murder, rape, assault, robbery, burglary, arson, larceny, and motor vehicle theft.

**Part II crimes** All other crimes, aside from the eight Part I crimes, included in the UCR arrest data. Part II crimes include drug offenses, sex crimes, and vandalism, among others.

**passive precipitation** Personal or social characteristics of victims that make them attractive targets for criminals; such victims may unknowingly either threaten or encourage their attackers.

**paternalistic families** Families in which fathers assume the traditional role of breadwinners, while mothers tend to have menial jobs or remain at home to supervise domestic matters.

**patriarchal** A social structure in which males hold primary power and enjoy social, political, economic, and social privilege.

**peacemaking** An approach that considers punitive crime control strategies to be counterproductive and favors the use of humanistic conflict resolution to prevent and control crime.

**penology** Subarea of criminology that focuses on the correction and control of criminal offenders.

**personality** The reasonably stable patterns of behavior, including thoughts and emotions, that distinguish one person from another.

**petit (petty) larceny** Theft of a small amount of money or property, punished as a misdemeanor.

**phishing** The creation of false emails or websites that look legitimate but are designed to gain illegal access to a victim's personal information.

**plea bargain** Agreement between prosecution and defense in which the accused pleads guilty in return for a reduction of charges, a more lenient sentence, or some other consideration.

**political crime** Illegal acts that are designed to undermine an existing government and threaten its survival. Political crimes can include both violent and nonviolent acts and range in seriousness from dissent, treason, and espionage to violent acts such as terrorism or assassination.

**population** All people who share a particular characteristic, such as all high school students or all police officers.

**population heterogeneity** The propensity to commit crime is stable; those who have it continue to commit crime over their life course.

**pornography** Sexually explicit books, magazines, films, and DVDs intended to provide sexual titillation and excitement for paying customers.

**positivism** The branch of social science that uses the scientific method of the natural sciences and suggests that human behavior is a product of social, biological, psychological, or economic forces that can be empirically measured.

**posttraumatic stress disorder (PTSD)** Psychological reaction to a highly stressful event; symptoms may include depression, anxiety, flashbacks, and recurring nightmares.

**power** The ability of persons and groups to control the behavior of others, to shape public opinion, and to define deviance.

**power–control theory** A criminological theory that maintains that the structure of gender relations within the family explains gender differences in the crime rate.

**precedent** A rule derived from previous judicial decisions and applied to future cases; the basis of common law.

**preemptive deterrence** Efforts to prevent crime through community organization and youth involvement.

**preliminary hearing** Alternative to a grand jury, in which an impartial lower-court judge decides whether there is probable cause sufficient for a trial.

**premeditation** Considering the criminal act beforehand, which suggests that it was motivated by more than a simple desire to engage in an act of violence.

**premenstrual syndrome (PMS)** Condition, postulated by some theorists, wherein several days before and during menstruation excessive amounts of female sex hormones stimulate antisocial, aggressive behavior.

**price fixing** The illegal control by agreement among producers or manufacturers of the price of a commodity to avoid price competition and deprive the consumer of reasonable prices.

**primary deviance** A norm violation or crime that has little or no long-term influence on the violator.

**primary prevention programs** Programs, such as substance abuse clinics and mental health associations, that seek to treat personal problems before they manifest themselves as crime.

**probable cause** A set of facts, information, circumstances, or conditions that would lead a reasonable person to believe that an offense was committed and that the accused committed that offense. It is the level of proof needed to make a legal arrest.

**problem behavior syndrome (PBS)** Antisocial behaviors that cluster together, including family dysfunction, substance abuse, smoking, precocious sexuality and early pregnancy, educational underachievement, suicide attempts, sensation seeking, and unemployment, as well as criminality.

**professional criminals** Offenders who make a significant portion of their income from crime.

**Prohibition** The period from 1919 until 1933 when the Eighteenth Amendment to the U.S. Constitution outlawed the sale of alcohol; also known as the "noble experiment."

**propensity theory** The view that a stable unchanging feature, characteristic, property, or condition, such as defective intelligence or impulsive personality, makes some people crime prone.

**prostitution** The granting of nonmarital sexual access for remuneration.

**psychodynamic (psychoanalytic) psychology** Theory, originated by Freud, that the human personality is controlled by unconscious mental processes that develop early in childhood and involve the interaction of id, ego, and superego.

**psychopharmacological relationship** In such a relationship, violence is the direct consequence of ingesting mood-altering substances.

**public order crime** Behavior that is outlawed because it threatens the general well-being of society and challenges its accepted moral principles.

**pump and dump** Placing deceptive information online to get unsuspecting investors interested in a stock while those spreading the information sell previously purchased stock at an inflated price.

**racial profiling** Police-initiated action directed at a suspect or group of suspects based solely on race.

**racial threat hypothesis** As the size of the black population increases, the perceived threat to the white population increases, resulting in a greater amount of social control imposed on blacks.

**Racketeer Influenced and Corrupt Organizations Act (RICO)** Federal legislation that enables prosecutors to bring additional criminal or civil charges against people whose multiple criminal acts constitute a conspiracy. RICO features monetary penalties that allow the government to confiscate all profits derived from criminal activities. Originally intended to be used against organized criminals, RICO has also been used against white-collar criminals.

**rape** Under common law, the carnal knowledge of a female forcibly and against her will. Contemporary statues are gender neutral ("a person") and can include various acts of sexual penetration.

**rational choice theory** The view that crime is a function of a decision-making process in which the would-be offender weighs the potential costs and benefits of an illegal act.

**reaction formation** Irrational hostility evidenced by young delinquents, who adopt norms directly opposed to middle-class goals and standards that seem impossible to achieve.

**recidivism** Relapse into criminal behavior after apprehension, conviction, and correction for a previous crime.

**recognizance** Pledge by the accused to return for trial, which may be accepted in lieu of bail.

**reflected appraisal** When parents are alienated from their children, their negative labeling reduces their children's self-image and increases delinquency.

**rehabilitation** Treatment of criminal offenders that is aimed at preventing future criminal behavior.

**Reign of Terror** The origin of the term *terrorism*, the French Revolution's Reign of Terror began in 1795 and was initiated by the revolutionary government during which agents of the Committee of Public Safety and the National Convention were referred to as terrorists.

**reintegrative shaming** The concept that people can be reformed if they understand the harm they have caused and are brought back into the social mainstream.

**relational aggression** Psychological and emotional abuse that involves the spreading of smears, rumors, and private information in order to harm his or her partner.

**relative deprivation** Envy, mistrust, and aggression resulting from perceptions of economic and social inequality.

**reliable measure** A measure that produces consistent results from one measurement to another.

**replacement** An effect that occurs when criminals try new offenses they had previously avoided because situational crime prevention programs neutralized their crime of choice.

**resource deprivation** The consequence of a lack of income and other resources, which cumulatively, leads to poverty.

**restitution** Permitting an offender to repay the victim or do useful work in the community rather than facing the stigma of a formal trial and a court-ordered sentence.

**restorative justice** A view of justice that focuses on the needs of victims, the community, and offenders, and focuses on nonpunitive strategies to heal the wounds caused by crime.

**restrictive (partial) deterrence** Refers to situations in which the threat of punishment can reduce but not eliminate crime.

**retributive terrorists** Terror groups who refrain from tying specific acts to direct demands for change. They want to instead redirect the balance between what they believe is good and evil. They see their revolution as existing on a spiritual plane; their mission is to exact retribution against sinners.

**retrospective reading** The reassessment of a person's past to fit a current generalized label.

**road rage** Violent assault by a motorist who loses control of his or her emotions while driving.

**robbery** The taking or attempting to take anything of value from the care, custody, or control of a person or persons by force or threat of force or violence and/or by putting the victim in fear.

**role exit behaviors** The process of disengagement from a role that is central to one's self-identity in order to establish a new identity.

**routine activities theory** The view that victimization results from the interaction of three everyday factors: the availability of suitable targets, the absence of capable guardians, and the presence of motivated offenders.

**salami slice fraud** Illegally removing small sums from the balances of a large number of accounts and converting them for personal use.

**sampling** Selecting a limited number of people for study as representative of a larger group.

**schemas** Cognitive frameworks that help people quickly process and sort through information.

**schizophrenia** A severe disorder marked by hearing nonexistent voices, seeing hallucinations, and exhibiting inappropriate responses.

**scientific method** The use of verifiable principles and procedures for the systematic acquisition of knowledge. Typically involves formulating a problem, creating hypotheses, and collecting data, through observation and experiment, to verify the hypotheses.

**secondary deviance** A norm violation or crime that comes to the attention of significant others or social control agents, who apply a negative label that has long-term consequences for the violator's self-identity and social interactions.

**secondary prevention programs** Programs that provide treatment, such as psychological counseling, to youths and adults after they have violated the law.

**second-degree murder** A person's wanton disregard for the victim's life and his or her desire to inflict serious bodily harm on the victim, which results in the victim's death.

**self-control** Refers to a person's ability to exercise restraint and control over his or her feelings, emotions, reactions, and behaviors.

**self-report survey** A research approach that requires subjects to reveal their own participation in delinquent or criminal acts.

**sentencing circle** A method of dispensing justice involving discussion between offenders, victims, and members of the community.

**serial killer** A person who kills three or more persons in three or more separate events.

**Sherman Antitrust Act** Federal law that subjects to criminal or civil sanctions any person "who shall make any contract or engage in any combination or conspiracy" in restraint of interstate commerce.

**shield laws** Laws that protect women from being questioned about their sexual history unless such questioning directly bears on the case.

**shoplifting** The taking of goods from retail stores.

**situational crime prevention** A method of crime prevention that seeks to eliminate or reduce particular crimes in specific settings.

**situational inducement** Short-term influence on a person's behavior, such as financial problems or peer pressure, which increases risk taking.

**snitch** Amateur shoplifter who does not self-identify as a thief but who systematically steals merchandise for personal use.

**social capital** Positive, life-sustaining relations with individuals and institutions.

**social class** Segment of the population whose members are at a relatively similar economic level and who share attitudes, values, norms, and an identifiable lifestyle.

**social conflict** The struggle for power in society. Human behavior in social contexts results from conflicts between competing groups.

**social control theory** The view that everyone has the potential to become a criminal, but most people are controlled by their bonds to society. Crime occurs when the forces that bind people to society are weakened or broken.

**social disorganization theory** Branch of social structure theory that focuses on the breakdown in inner-city neighborhoods of institutions such as the family, school, and employment.

**social ecology school** An interdisciplinary approach to the study of interdependent social and environmental problems that cause crime.

**social harm** The injury caused to others by willful wrongful conduct.

**socialization** Process of human development and enculturation. Socialization is influenced by key social processes and institutions.

**socialized** The process of acquiring social norms, values, behavior, and skills through interaction with significant others such as parents, peers, and teachers.

**social learning theory** The view that people learn the techniques and attitudes of crime from close relationships with criminal peers; crime is a learned behavior.

**social process theory** The view that criminality is a function of people's interactions with various organizations, institutions, and processes in society.

**social reaction (labeling) theory** The view that people become criminals when significant members of society label them as such and they accept those labels as a personal identity.

**social structure theory** The view that disadvantaged economic class position is a primary cause of crime.

**sociobiology** The view that human behavior is motivated by inborn biological urges to survive and preserve the species.

**sociological criminology** Approach to criminology, based on the work of Émile Durkheim, that focuses on the relationship between social factors and crime.

**spam** An unsolicited advertisement or promotional material, typically in the form of an unwanted email message. While email is the most common form of spam, it can also be sent via instant messaging, online forum, and mobile phone messaging, among other media.

**spear-phishing** Targeting specific victims by using personal information gleaned from social media and then sending them messages that convince them to open tainted emails or go to a tainted website.

**specific deterrence** The view that criminal sanctions should be so powerful that offenders will never repeat their criminal acts.

**spree killer** A killer of multiple victims whose murders occur over a relatively short span of time and often follow no discernible pattern.

**stalking** A course of conduct that is directed at a specific person and involves repeated physical or visual proximity, nonconsensual communication, or verbal, written, or implied threats sufficient to cause fear in a reasonable person.

**state dependence** The propensity to commit crime is constantly changing, affected by environmental influences and changing life events.

**state (organized) crime** Criminal acts committed by government officials.

**state political crime** Political crime that arises from the efforts of the state to either maintain governmental power or to uphold the race, class, and gender advantages of those who support the government. It is possible to divide state political crimes into five varieties: (1) political corruption, (2) illegal domestic surveillance, (3) human rights violations, (4) state violence such as torture, illegal imprisonment, police violence and use of deadly force, and (5) state corporate crime committed by individuals who abuse their state authority or who fail to exercise it when working with people and organizations in the private sector.

**state-sponsored terrorism** Terrorism that occurs when a repressive government regime forces its citizens into obedience, oppresses minorities, and stifles political dissent.

**status frustration** A form of culture conflict experienced by lower-class youths because social conditions prevent them from achieving success as defined by the larger society.

**statutory crimes** Crimes defined by legislative bodies in response to changing social conditions, public opinion, and custom.

**statutory rape** Sexual relations between an underage minor female and an adult male.

**stigmatize** To apply negative labeling with enduring effects on a person's self-image and social interactions.

**strain** The anger, frustration, and resentment experienced by people who believe they cannot achieve their goals through legitimate means.

**strain theory** Branch of social structure theory that sees crime as a function of the conflict between people's goals and the means available to obtain them.

**stratified society** People grouped according to economic or social class; characterized by the unequal distribution of wealth, power, and prestige.

**street efficacy** A concept in which more cohesive communities with high levels of social control and social integration foster the ability for kids to use their wits to avoid violent confrontations and to feel safe in their own neighborhood. Adolescents with high levels of street efficacy are less likely to resort to violence themselves or to associate with delinquent peers.

**structural theorists** Critical criminologists who believe the law is designed to keep the capitalist system operating in an efficient manner.

**subculture** A set of values, beliefs, and traditions unique to a particular social class or group within a larger society.

**subculture of violence** A segment of society in which violence has become legitimized by the custom and norms of that group.

**successful degradation ceremony** A course of action or ritual in which someone's identity is publicly redefined and destroyed and he or she is thereafter viewed as socially unacceptable.

**suitable targets** Objects of crime (persons or property) that are attractive and readily available.

**superego** The part of the personality representing the conscience, formed in early life by internalization of the standards of parents and other models of behavior.

**supranational criminology** Comprising the study of war crimes, crimes against humanity, and the penal system in which such crimes are prosecuted and tried.

**surplus value** The excess profits that are produced by the laboring classes and accrued by business owners.

**systematic forgers** Professionals who make a living by passing bad checks.

**systemic link** A link between drugs and violence that occurs when drug dealers turn violent in their competition with rival gangs.

**temperance movement** The drive to prohibit the sale of alcohol in the United States, culminating in ratification of the Eighteenth Amendment in 1919.

**terrorism** The illegal use of force against innocent people to achieve a political objective.

**testosterone** The principal male hormone.

**thanatos** The death instinct, which impels people toward self-destruction.

**theft** The intentional taking, keeping, or using of another's property without authorization or permission.

**three-strikes policies** Laws that require offenders to serve life in prison after they are convicted of a third felony.

**ticking bomb scenario** A scenario where some experts argue that torture can perhaps be justified if the government discovers that a captured terrorist knows the whereabouts of a dangerous explosive device that is set to go off and kill thousands of innocent people.

**torture** An act that causes severe pain or suffering, whether physical or mental, that is intentionally inflicted on a person for such purposes as obtaining a confession, punishing them for a crime they may have committed, or intimidating or coercing them into a desired action.

**trait theory** The view that criminality is a product of abnormal biological or psychological traits.

**trajectory theory** The view that there are multiple independent paths to a criminal career and that there are different types and classes of offenders.

**transitional neighborhood** An area undergoing a shift in population and structure, usually from middle-class residential to lower-class mixed-use.

**transnational organized crime** Criminal conspiracies that cross national and international borders and involve the planning and execution of illicit ventures by groups or networks of individuals working in more than one country.

**treason** An act of disloyalty to one's nation or state.

**Trojan horse** A computer program that looks like a benign application but contains illicit codes that can damage the system operations. Though Trojan horses do not replicate themselves like viruses, they can be just as destructive.

**turning points** According to Laub and Sampson, the life events that alter the development of a criminal career.

**underclass** The lowest social stratum in any country, whose members lack the education and skills needed to function successfully in modern society.

**Uniform Crime Report (UCR)** Large database, compiled by the FBI, of crimes reported and arrests made each year throughout the United States.

**USA Patriot Act (USAPA)** Legislation giving U.S. law enforcement agencies a freer hand to investigate and apprehend suspected terrorists.

**valid measure** A measure that actually measures what it purports to measure; a measure that is factual.

**victim compensation programs** Financial aid awarded to crime victims to repay them for their loss and injuries; may cover medical bills, loss of wages, loss of future earnings, and/or counseling.

**victimless crime** Public order crime that violates the moral order but has no specific victim other than society as a whole.

**victim–offender reconciliation programs (VORPs)** Mediated face-to-face encounters between victims and their attackers, designed to produce restitution agreements and, if possible, reconciliation.

**victimologists** Criminologists who focus on the victims of crime.

**victimology** The study of the victim's role in criminal events.

**victim precipitated homicide** Refers to those killings in which the victim is a direct, positive precipitator of the incident.

**victim precipitation theory** The view that victims may initiate, either actively or passively, the confrontation that leads to their victimization.

**victim–witness assistance programs** Government programs that help crime victims and witnesses; may include compensation, court services, and/or crisis intervention.

**virility mystique** The belief that males must separate their sexual feelings from their need for love, respect, and affection.

**voluntary or nonnegligent manslaughter** A killing committed in the heat of passion or during a sudden quarrel that provoked violence.

**warez** A term computer hackers and software pirates use to describe a game or application that is made available for use on the Internet in violation of its copyright protection.

**website defacement** A type of cybervandalism that occurs when a computer hacker intrudes on another person's website by inserting or substituting codes that expose visitors to the site to misleading or provocative information. Defacement can range from installing humorous graffiti to sabotaging or corrupting the site.

**white-collar crime** Illegal acts that capitalize on a person's status in the marketplace. White-collar crimes may include theft, embezzlement, fraud, market manipulation, restraint of trade, and false advertising.

**workplace violence** Violence such as assault, rape, or murder committed at the workplace.

# Name Index

# Subject Index

**Page numbers in italics refer to images.**